CW01667178

The complete Aquarium Encyclopedia

of tropical freshwater fish

The complete Aquarium Encyclopedia

of tropical freshwater fish

Managing editor:
Dr. J. D. VAN RAMSHORST
Photos by:
A. VAN DEN NIEUWENHUIZEN

OMEGA BOOKS

Contributors

W. VAN BERKOM

DR. R. BOOTSMA

H. VAN BRUGGEN

M. GEERTS

F. INGEN HOUSZ

A. VAN DEN NIEUWENHUIZEN

DR. J. D. VAN RAMSHORST

CHR. VISSER

Controlling editor

R. E. MADDISON

This edition published 1985 by Omega Books Ltd,
1 West Street, Ware, Hertfordshire, under licence
from the proprietor.

Copyright © 1978 Elsevier Publishing Projects, SA, Lausanne.

All rights reserved. No part of this publication may
be reproduced, stored in a retrieval system,
or transmitted, in any form or by any means, electronic,
mechanical, photocopying, recording or otherwise,
without the prior permission of the publishers.

ISBN 1 85007 031 8

Printed and bound in Italy by G. Canale, Turin

Contents

Introduction

THE CUSTOM OF KEEPING FISH in captivity is very old. The Romans maintained vivaria where fish were kept although their primary if not sole purpose was the practical one of providing fresh food: that was doubtless also the intention of those of whom the prophet Isaiah spoke when he referred to 'all that make sluices and ponds for fish' [Is. 19.10]. That tradition has continued and aquariums with edible fish, for example trout, are still to be found in or attached to restaurants today. The Aztecs kept fish and goldfish were fashionable among the Chinese over a thousand years ago and were bred solely for ornamental purposes. Goldfish were probably introduced into Europe and kept as ornamental fish sometime during the seventeenth century: before then anything like a modern aquarium was quite unknown. The earliest ornamental fish were however kept in dishes or opaque tanks or ponds and were therefore viewed from above: this may explain some of the early interest in bizarre specimens that were most striking when viewed from that angle.

The modern interest in aquariums began in the nineteenth century in England, Germany and other countries: it was then that the first public aquariums were established, including the very popular ones in London and Paris. During the second half of that century tropical fish began to be imported on a large scale and rapidly overtook in popularity the cold water species with which hitherto aquariums had been mainly stocked. The tropical fish were on the whole more attractive, more varied in color and shape and were usually easier to keep. Maintenance was not of course simple before the development of such modern devices as thermostatically controlled electric heaters, but the old aquarists persevered despite the hazards of kerosene heaters and related difficulties, of which some amateurs still living can tell harrowing tales. Prices for fish in those days were also relatively high because of the difficulties of transporting delicate fish over long distances with slow moving transport, and in some cases it would seem that what would today be regarded as astronomical prices were paid for specimens that now can be bought for no more than a few coppers.

The first aquarist journal seems to have been established in Germany in 1880: others arose in Great Britain and Europe during the early decades of the present century and some clubs for amateurs were founded about the same time and are still flourishing today. The leading clubs in both West Germany and the Netherlands have each a long history: both still flourish today and both publish leading journals, *Die Aquarien und Terrarien Zeitschrift* and *Het Aquarium*: details of these and other important journals will be found in the bibliography. This then briefly is the development of what is now one of the most popular as well as satisfying hobbies, with devotees in almost every country in the world.

As it has grown in popularity, the hobby has become more varied. There is for example a growing interest these days, in marine aquariums, both for tropical marine fish and those from temperate climates. Such salt water aquariums are however much more expensive to equip and maintain than are aquariums for fresh water fish: they are not therefore of interest to the majority of amateur aquarists. Likewise, there is a growing interest in keeping cold water fish, particularly European and North American species in the controlled conditions of the aquarium. Nevertheless, for the majority of enthusiasts, the aquarium is still the aquarium for tropical fresh water fish and it is to that popular aspect of the hobby that this encyclopaedia is confined.

Of course, it must be remembered that there is not always in practice a sharp and clear distinction between tropical fresh water fish and cold water fish because a number of the so-called tropical fish are really no more than sub-tropical in the wild and being highly adaptable can tolerate relatively low temperatures, so that they can in certain circumstances be treated as cold water fish. Thus the Chinese danio can be kept out of doors during the summer in temperate climates and so can a number of other species of non-European origin, as well as some species that come from the southern states of the USA. Likewise, there are other tropical freshwater fish that are found in the wild in the brackish waters of river estuaries and in the aquarium need salt to be added to the tank water: some species like this, for example the Argus fish are included in this encyclopaedia because customarily they are regarded as tropical fresh water fish, but in general the fish dealt with in this book are those suitable for the conventional tropical freshwater aquarium.

No book of this nature can be fully comprehensive. In addition to those species that are commonly kept there are a large number of unusual fish which are only imported occasionally: of these only a selection of those deemed to be of particular interest to amateurs, has been included. Moreover a number of novel species seem to be imported every year: sometimes these are very successful and ultimately become part of the stock in trade of most dealers, but others (particularly if attempts to breed them in captivity are unsuccessful) disappear as suddenly as they arrived. A number of fairly recently identified species, which in the opinion of the authors are of importance have been included but novelties of dubious worth have been omitted.

One of the most interesting aspects of keeping a tropical freshwater aquarium is the breeding of fish. Care has been taken to include in this encyclopaedia both general information on this matter as well as more detailed information on the breeding of particular species where reliable reports exist. It is however unfortunately true that many species have not as yet been bred successfully in captivity: in those cases, where possible, helpful advice has been given to those who might be prepared by patient experiment to achieve what others have hitherto failed to achieve. It is indeed important that progress should be made towards breeding successfully all the species favored by aquarists, otherwise the continuing export of specimens from their natural habitat will ultimately in all probability lead to the extermination of the species – or at least, severe controls on their export in the interest of conservation as had already happened for example in the case of *Hypostomus plecostomus*. In short, breeding fish can be an important contribution by the amateur to the preservation of the species as well as being in itself an exciting and satisfying task.

Modern aquarium technology has greatly simplified many aspects of caring for fish in captivity. This encyclopaedia includes notes on some basic matters in this field but it is important for the reader who is about to set up his first aquarium to realize that in fact very little equipment is essential for a well balanced aquarium. Accurate temperature control is of course vital but otherwise no great financial outlay is necessary although much useful equipment can be bought to make life easier for the aquarist. The beginner should not be put off by thinking that it need be either expensive or complicated to put himself in the position of deriving unlimited pleasure from an aquarium. One unusual feature of this hobby is that it can be pursued at a variety of different levels to suit every purse.

Finally, it is necessary unfortunately to say something about fish diseases for this is a problem which inevitably will face every aquarist sooner or later. The encyclopaedia includes a section on fish diseases which seeks to identify for the amateur the more common ailments but in some cases it is very difficult for the expert, let alone the amateur, to make an accurate diagnosis, let alone prescribe an effective remedy. This is one reason why so many aquarists will assert that the essence of this hobby is perseverance and a determination not to be downcast by the occasional failure or calamity. There is still much that is not fully understood or known about fish and thus all aquarists will come up against difficult and sometimes disheartening problems, but therein of course lies one of the main attractions of the hobby for each dedicated amateur who wrestles with those difficulties and, as he will, overcomes them has the chance, by carefully recording and reporting what he achieves, to add to the ever growing corpus of scientific knowledge and in that exchange of knowledge lies one of the supreme satisfactions of the aquarist.

How to use this Encyclopedia

To give the most assistance both to the experienced amateur and to the aquarist about to embark on the construction or purchase of his first aquarium, this encyclopaedia has been carefully arranged to give quick and easy access to the various sections into which it is divided.

It will be seen that these sections are:

- A series of articles on the principal aspects of the care of aquariums and tropical fish.
- A list of plants suitable for the aquarium.
- A list of fish that may be kept in an aquarium.
- A guide to the literature in the principal European languages.
- An index guide.

It may be helpful to comment briefly on each of these sections.

The guide to the care of aquariums and aquarium fish

In a series of short but authoritative articles, every important aspect of the construction and maintenance of an aquarium is treated in a practical way. Further articles give the basic information on the feeding and breeding of fish and the treatment of fish diseases. These articles also contain a great deal of background information which will allow the reader to understand more fully the information given on particular plants and fish in the later systematic lists.

The novice, who carefully studies these articles should thereby acquire all that basic knowledge he will need before embarking on a practical adventure in this fascinating hobby. It is hoped that the more experienced aquarist will also find in these articles something to interest him and perhaps, stimulate a new interest in some novel aspect of the hobby which has not hitherto concerned him. There can of course be no substitute for practical experience and the wise novice, once he has absorbed what he can from these articles will seek the company of experienced enthusiasts through whose practical experience he will be able to refine the basic knowledge he has gained from these introductory reviews. In time he should begin to keep his own records and will then, like all the best practitioners, draw increasingly on his own practical experience. These short review articles will nevertheless, it is hoped, remain for him a valuable quick reference review of the salient points of the practical basis of the hobby.

The list of Aquarium plants

A detailed list of the most suitable plants for the aquarium follows. This section has its own introduction which explains the basis on which the list has been drawn up. A short note on each of the families of plants involved is followed by an alphabetical list of species, in which advice is given on their cultivation and propagation. Many of these plants are known by a variety of different names and an index is provided of cross-references to the various names noted in the text. By studying this section and by referring to it as occasion arises, the amateur will be able to ensure that his aquarium is at all times appropriately planted.

The Systematic list of fish

No work on aquarium fish can claim to be comprehensive for not only are new species and varieties introduced as time goes by, but as fashions and interests change, other species and varieties not hitherto considered to be aquarium fish, gain a place in that class. Nevertheless it can with confidence be asserted that more species of likely interest to amateurs are included in this section than will be generally found in guides for aquarists. Each species is classified in its appropriate genus and family, the pattern of which arrangement is explained in the introductory article on the classification of fish, to be found in the first section of the encyclopaedia. A brief introductory article on each family and genus is included and there an attempt has been made to give some general background information. In the severely practical species entries as much information as is known about the care and breeding of the fish is given, after a description of its shape, coloring and markings designed to inform the aquarist about the decorative role the fish may play in the aquarium. It has been made clear that these descriptions are not scientific descriptions such as would satisfy a taxonomist, but nevertheless, within the limitations of the everyday language that has been deliberately employed, it is hoped that these descriptions will give the amateur an accurate and clear idea of the species he can select for his aquarium. Those who seek a more scientific treatment of particular fish will find the relevant literature recorded in the bibliography that follows.

A guide to the literature

If, as is hoped, this encyclopaedia, as well as being the handmaiden to many amateurs also inspires some to go further into the hobby, then those who seek more knowledge will inevitably have to turn to the specialist literature. Again, to give a comprehensive bibliography of works of possible interest, would be unwieldy and, in the end, unhelpful because bewildering. Instead, a careful selection has been made of the most immediately useful books in English, French, Dutch and German, classified broadly into the subjects into which this encyclopaedia is itself divided. Most of these books themselves have bibliographies, and accordingly the aquarist who seeks more detailed knowledge has only to use these as a starting point and he will soon find all the material he might need.

The index guide

The encyclopaedia concludes with an index guide designed to facilitate the location of each individual species of fish treated in the systematic list. The aquarium plants are themselves listed alphabetically and no difficulty therefore arises in finding a particular species. The fish however, for various practical reasons, and not least the similarity of care that related species often demand, are listed in genera within families and consequently to one not immediately familiar with the classification of fish, there will be some difficulty in locating an individual species. The reader should study the introductory note to the index and should thereafter have no difficulty in finding any species of which he knows the English or scientific name.

COMPENDIUM

1. THE AQUARIUM

Establishment and Maintenance

Before the amateur can begin to keep fish, he must build or buy an aquarium tank, and provide himself with the necessary basic equipment to maintain it in good order. This primary task involves questions relating to plants for the aquarium and the layout of the tank: these two major issues are dealt with separately in succeeding sections. This section is restricted to dealing with the construction of the tank, the problems relating to water, and the general care of the established aquarium, together with notes on the equipment most useful for doing that efficiently.

The Tank

The two basic alternatives facing the aquarist are to buy or build a tank. This is a choice that only the individual can make. To build a tank does not require enormous skill nor does it involve using very complicated equipment: it does however demand great accuracy, patience and care. To the practical man who is experienced in making things there is no problem, but the novice must be warned that he will more likely than not be disappointed if one of his first efforts in do-it-yourself is the building of an aquarium. If he does build, then obviously he must begin by planning his tank in the light of the general considerations set out below as guidance to those about to purchase a tank.

Buying a Tank

Before buying a tank the aquarist must decide the size of tank he needs, and as a corollary to that, where it is going to be kept. The answer to the latter question depends of course on individual circumstances, but it must not be forgotten that electric current will be needed – for lighting, pumps and so on, and therefore the tank must either be near a power point, or at least leads must be able to be brought to it, without making the room unsightly or creating a safety hazard. A tank can either be fixed to a wall or freestanding, on a base or within a cabinet, either specially made or serving some other purpose as well. Wall aquariums are more economic of space, but the weight that the wall must support should not be forgotten. A liter of water weighs a kilo, so a 200 liter tank will, when full, weigh 200 kilos, plus the weight of the tank itself, plus that of any rocks and sand in it.
When the aquarist has determined what he can accommodate, he must then decide what tank he needs to house the kind of aquarium he wishes to establish. Tanks can be obtained or built in almost any size or shape. However, the kind of tank to be purchased may be determined by the species of fish to be kept. Henceforth in this section the assumption will be made that the amateur is intending to set

1. A tank with non-standard measurements sometimes looks more effective than one of standard proportions. In particular, an increase in height often makes the tank more attractive.

2. A tank should never be overcrowded; this is very important especially with regard to the plants.
Symmetry should be avoided; never put together two or more objects or plants of identical size and shape.

up the conventional medium sized *community tank*, but that is not of course suitable for all aquarium fish. In the detailed descriptions of individual species given in the systematic list of fishes, notes are given on those species that are suitable only for large or small tanks, and those that in some other way need a special tank: the inexperienced amateur should consult those notes before deciding on the tank that he needs.

For the conventional one community tank aquarium, the best tank for the amateur to acquire is probably one with a capacity of 125–250 liters. A good size would be an 80 cm tank (80 × 40 × 40 cm) or a meter tank (100 × 50 × 50 cm): tanks are usually described in this way, by quoting their length (that is, the measurement from left to right along the front of the tank). An aquarium of such a standard size is designed to be in length twice as long as its depth and height. These proportions sometimes look inelegant. An aquarium of 250 liters capacity will blend more easily with a modern interior if the measurements are, length 125 cm, depth 50 cm and height 40 cm. However, the depth (the distance from front to back) should certainly be greater than the height. Walls and terraces will make the overall depth appear smaller, and in any case visual distortion caused by water will make everything inside look smaller than it really is.

Aquarium tanks can be made of *glass* or *perspex*. Perspex or plastic tanks are not to be recommended because inevitably – and fairly quickly – the front becomes scratched when (as it must be) it is scraped regularly, or by the effect of sand and rocks.

Equally strong objections are made by many against tanks moulded from one piece of glass. It is unusual to find these without unsightly air bubbles somewhere in the walls, and the pressure on the glass is such that this kind of tank is often liable to shatter. Both one piece glass and perspex tanks also distort the fish from some angles, more than other types of tanks.

By far the most practical kind of tank is one made of sheets of glass, joined in such a way as to make a watertight tank: that is, either joined by angle frames, or by being glued with special modern adhesives. Most conventional, traditional tanks have *angle frames*, but the all glass tank is becoming more and more popular. It has the great advantage that it is less likely to spring a leak than the tank with an angle frame, where the seal is made with putty which, as time passes becomes hard and brittle. This is incidentally a point that the aquarist must bear in mind if he is buying a second hand tank, particularly if it is not from a dealer. Many old angle frame tanks are perfectly watertight until they are drained and moved: it is then that leaks develop.

Making an Aquarium Tank

Assuming that the aquarist feels sufficiently confident to make the tank himself, he must first of all decide on its dimensions. The general principles must be observed – that the length is at least twice the depth, and that the height is at most the same as the depth, but within those principles (which are important because of the way the water pressure is spread against the bottom and sides) he can more exactly tailor the size to his requirements.
The sides and bottom can be of either glass or metal. Either way, it is important that the glass or metal is of the appropriate strength, which means, of the appropriate thickness. Table A gives the minimum safe measurements.

Table A
MINIMUM SAFE THICKNESSES OF METAL/GLASS FOR AQUARIUM TANKS

Measurement of Aquarium			*Thickness of Corner Profile*		*Thickness of Metal for Bottom and Sides*	*Thickness of Glass* mm
L cm	D cm	H cm	Width mm	Metal mm	mm	
60	30	30	20	1.5	2	3
70	30	30	20	1.5	2	3.5
80	30	30	20	1.5	2.2	3.5
80	40	40	25	1.5	2.3	5
90	45	45	25	1.5	2.5	6
100	45	45	30	2	2.5	6
100	50	50	30	2	3	7
130	50	50	30	2	3.5	7
130/200	50	50	40	2.5	4	7
130/200	50	55	40	2.5	4	8

The metal angle strips must be welded together to form a perfectly rectangular frame, and the inside surfaces of the metal must be absolutely smooth. The frame should be given a liberal undercoat of metal primer before being painted whatever color the aquarist chooses. A prime coat of epoxy resin can also be given, and this, when dry, will be a very good protection against rust. It is however important if possible, to complete the painting of the frame before beginning to put in the glass.
The front panel of the tank must obviously be of glass: the sides, back and bottom can, depending on choice, be either glass or metal. The metal inside the aquarium must be protected against rust, and metal should not be used if the amateur intends to keep any of those fish for whom rock salt should be added to the water. Indeed, with the increasing number of chemicals used by aquarists, the choice of metal sides and bottom may be a hazardous one, because it is not possible to predict what the effect on metal may be of a chemical that may be in use a few years hence. For the base, as an alternative, a 2 cm thick sheet of slate can be used.
The size of the panels must then be carefully calculated. The easiest way is to measure the *outside* dimensions of the frame, and deduct the space needed for the putty and the thickness of the adjoining pieces of glass or metal.
There are five pieces to be put in, and they may be inserted in the following order: the base, the back, the front, side one and side two.
Frame aquariums of this kind have two possibly serious disadvantages: they are

3. Frame aquariums are made in different sizes, depending on the purposes.
Shown are sketches of:
A: 'normal' community tank
B: special tank for bigger fishes
C: a breeding tank

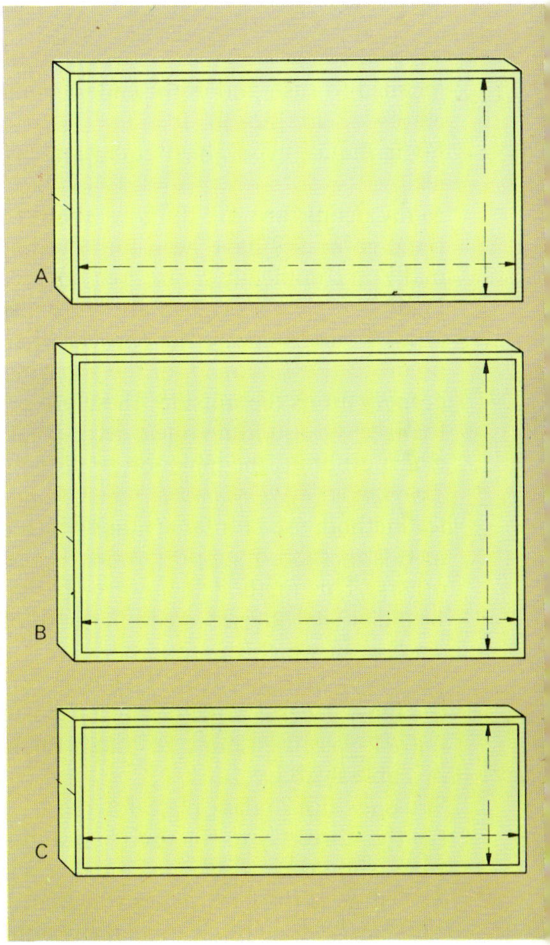

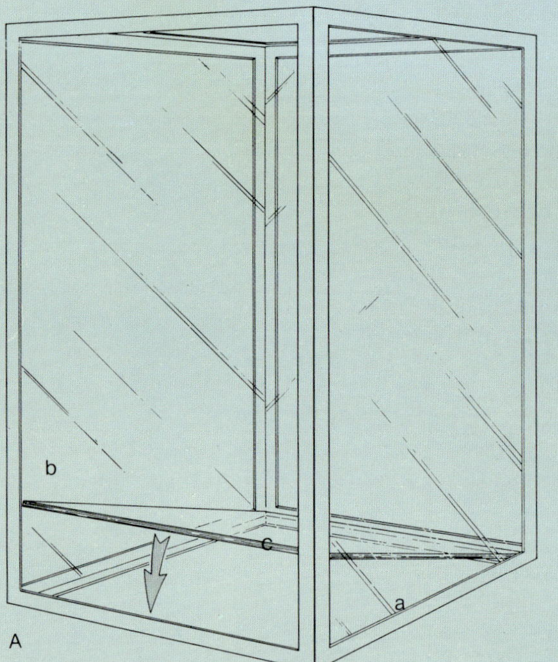

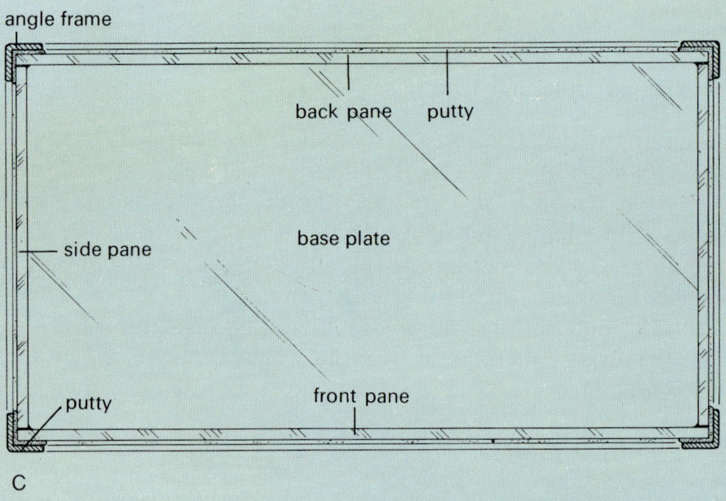

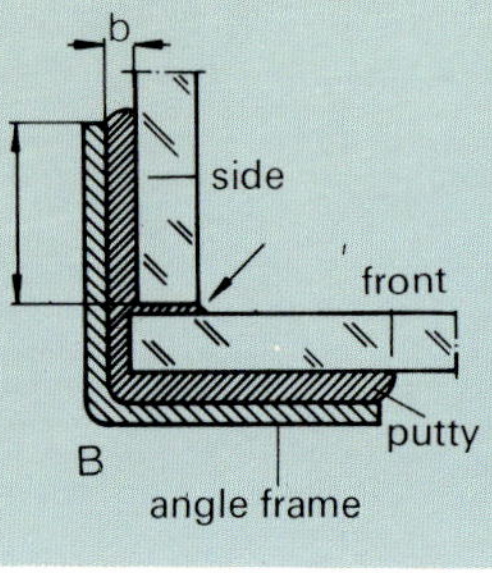

4. A. Making an angle frame tank.
a and b: back and front pane, already inserted
c: glass for side, fitted against the front, then pushed down at back.
B. Cross section of angle frame
C. Bottom of the tank with different widths of front and back, sides and base

inclined to rust, and in the end they may well leak, particularly if they have stood empty or are moved. It is for this reason that many experienced aquarists now favor the all glass glued aquarium, which will not rust and is far less likely to leak.

Many people are still dubious about the bonding power of *silicone adhesives*, but these adhesives have been improved so much in recent years that the joins they make on completely grease-free surfaces cannot be bettered. This is why aquariums made completely of glass are becoming so popular. The only weak points in this type of aquarium are the corners where three glass panes meet. If there is to be no protective surround for the aquarium, it is possible to glue plastic or aluminum corners on to the outside: these are available in various sizes. It is also essential to place the aquarium on an even surface on top of a layer of extruded *polystyrene*, which cushions the tank and protects it from undue stress from vibration.

Two kinds of *glass aquarium* can be made with these adhesives. There is a sophisticated method, used for large tanks which may have to be on a slightly uneven surface: in this method a support frame is used and none of the glass panes meets the others. This method is however perhaps difficult for the average amateur, who would be well advised to confine his efforts to what is known as the *rigid construction method*, in which the four sides are glued to the base, and to each other. Tanks up to 500 liters capacity have been built in this way. When making such a tank, the same general principles of proportion should be observed as for frame tanks, but all glass used must be 2 mm thicker than that recommended for such tanks in Table A above.

Starting with a glass plate for the bottom of length (l), width (w) and thickness (t), the correct size for the front and back panes can be determined. The sharp edges should be filed with wet, fine sandpaper, always rubbing in one direction. The edges of the glass plates which are to be glued must be completely grease-free. This can be done by cleaning them with alcohol. When the tank is being assembled,

4. There is another manner of building a tank, inserting first the back, then the front, then the sides and finally the base. This second method is perhaps preferable because then all four sides are locked in by the base plate. This system involves different measurements because glass cannot be cut with an edge angled at 45°: where the side joins the front glass, or the bottom meets the front, there must be a join of two straight edges, and the measurements must be made accordingly.

To glaze the frame, fill the whole of the angle iron frame with a good quality putty, in the same way as when glazing a window. The back panel should be put in first. The glass is allowed to gently fall on to the putty, and is then gently pressed down, to embed it in the putty, some of which will be forced out, outside the tank. This should be trimmed off with a sharp knife, and the glass pressed from the inside again, the process being repeated until about 3 mm of putty is left evenly all round the frame between it and the glass.

The front panel should then be put in. The sides should then be inserted in the same manner and if a good fit, may need to be eased into position: put them in at a slight angle, fitting them close to the front first of all, so that any scratches that are made by their sliding against a panel are on the back, not the front.

The base may then be put in, again taking care not to scratch the front panel. To put the base in last of all gives the amateur the chance to reach the other panels all the way round while inserting them and pressing them into position: if the base is put in first of all, much subsequent work has to be done from the top only.

Provided that the putty is of the right consistency, there should be a perfect seal immediately: the tank can be filled with water and left in a safe place for two or three days, to check for slow leaks, and to allow the glass panels to settle: a little more excess putty may be squeezed out as this happens, and this should be trimmed off.

the grease-free surfaces must on no account be touched because the slightest trace of sweat from the hands will reduce the strength of the bond and may eventually cause a leak.
The plastic nozzle of the tube of glue should be cut off at an angle so that the opening is 4–5 mm wide and a line of glue the same thickness of the glass squeezed along the edge of the bottom glass plate where the back pane is to be placed.
The back pane should be pressed on to the glue immediately and the two pieces should be set against a vertical wall or support so that the back plate stays upright. The support should be covered with polythene to prevent any surplus glue attaching the glass to the support. The join on the inside should be wiped immediately with a finger dipped in water containing washing-up liquid. Remember that a thin skin forms on the surface of these adhesives in 5 minutes, and after that it is no longer possible to clean off the excess glue.
When the aquarium is finished it should be placed on a horizontal base and left to set for about 24 hours. When it is set the excess glue which has been squeezed out should be removed with a sharp knife. Two glass strips can be fixed on the inside of the aquarium about 1 cm from the top so that a glass cover can rest on them.
Before plants and fish are put in, a finished aquarium should be left to allow the bonds to develop maximum strength, and to air: at least six days should be allowed for this. The tank can then be filled with water which should be left for 24 hours. This process should be repeated three times with fresh tap water. After this, the silicone glue will not be harmful to the fish or plants. If a sharp object is ever used for the maintenance of the tank, e.g. for scraping algae off the panes of glass, care should be taken to see that the silicone glue is not damaged.
Once the aquarium tank has been allowed to settle and checked for leaks, it can be set up. The aquarist must then design and install the bed, decide on ornaments and plants and fill the tank in anticipation of the arrival of the fish.

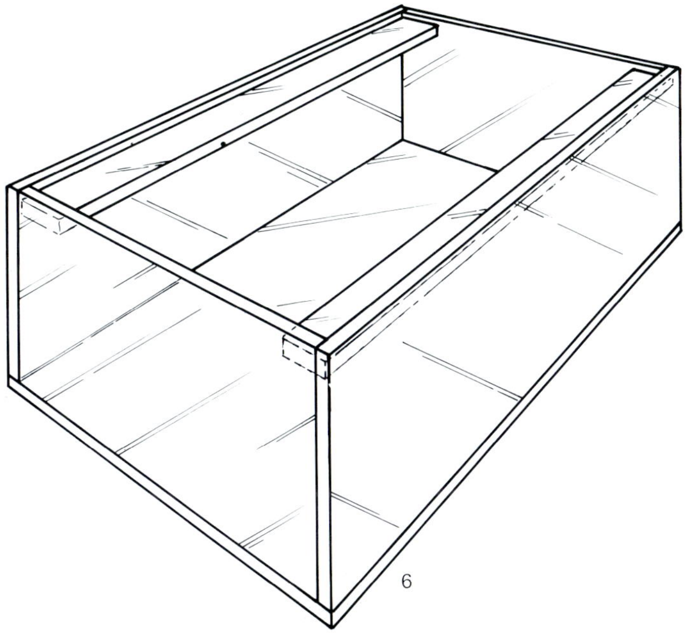

6

Two quite separate considerations now apply to all these matters, which might be called the technical and the aesthetic. A well ordered aquarium can be a truly beautiful and very satisfying sight: if it achieves that level much care will have had to be devoted to its arrangement, but equally, if it is to be attractive and function efficiently, just as much care will have to have been given to certain basic questions, such as the quality of the water, means of heating, methods of cleaning. The more aesthetic considerations are discussed below in the section on the layout of aquariums. The rest of this section is devoted to considering the more mundane but equally important questions which dictate the health and balance of the small, largely self-sustaining world the aquarist is to create.

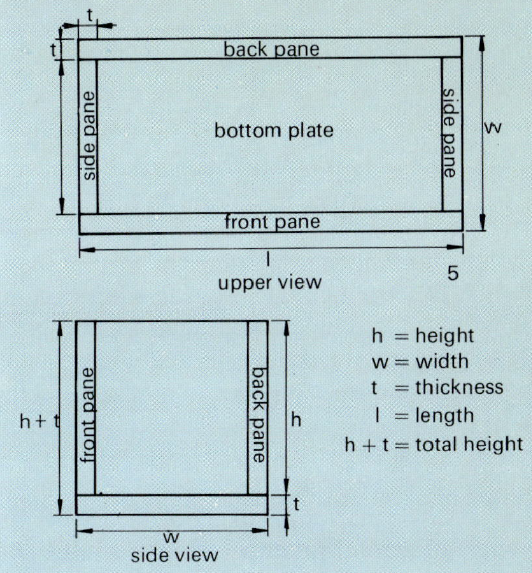

5. Determining the proportion of glass aquarium using the rigid construction method.

6. For a larger aquarium supports can be glued on the inside of the front and back panes to strengthen them. These supports should be between 4–10 cm wide and have the same length as the inside of the tank. The supports should be attached at least 5 mm below the top edges of the front and back plates. A temporary support frame of the right height should be placed in the tank so that the glue can be correctly applied and the supports themselves supported in position until they are set. Depending on the length of the aquarium, one or more supports can be fitted across the width of the tank (the length of these of course should be the same as the inside width of the aquarium).

7. Glue is applied along the bottom plate and up the edge of the back pane so that a side pane can be fitted in. This is then secured with adhesive tape and the glued edges should be smoothed on the inside with a wet finger. The other side pane and the front pane should be fitted in immediately in the same way.

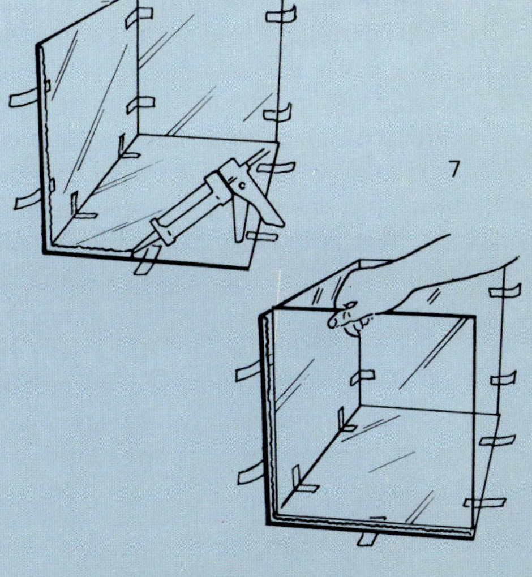

7

Various particular species of fish have special requirements: some need a dark, almost muddy bottom, others need salt added to the water, yet others require an aquarium with rocks and sand but no plants. These particular requirements are described in detail with the descriptions of those particular fish in the systematic section, and for them, special arrangements have to be made by the aquarist. In the following we describe merely the basic general rules that should be followed in setting up the less specialized community tank – that is, one in which a variety of different species, requiring more or less the same conditions can live peacefully together. Such a tank requires attention to heating, lighting and aeration as well as its physical make up and its stocking with suitable aquatic plants.

Walls

No aquarium is likely to be aesthetically pleasing if the back and sides are made of glass through which irrelevant external objects as well as aquarium apparatus can be seen: neither are sheer walls of glass or metal the best way of showing off the denizens of the tank against an attractive background. To the sides and back, walls of some material or other should be attached: various attractive designs are noted below in the section on layout, but here the technical aspects are discussed.
The walls can be made of various materials: cement, stone (slate or lava), peat, cork bark or polystyrene. Walls and terraces which contain cement should be thoroughly leached, that is to say, the mineral salts that could be harmful to plants and fish should be removed. This can be done by filling with water the aquarium containing the cement constructions and adding one cup of vinegar for every 100 liters of water. After 24 hours the water should be removed, the grey deposits which have appeared siphoned off, and fresh water and vinegar added. When the water has been changed like this three times, no more sediment will come from the cement and the constructions are then perfectly safe.
The fastest results are obtained with quick drying cements to which appropriate colors can be added if the cement will be seen when the aquarium is complete: for example, red should be added if the cement is used with lava stone. Slate, lava rock, peat and cork bark walls are most easily made by sticking the material to a pane of glass or sheet of thin asbestos building sheeting: in a large tank the back wall may be divided up into several sections. Walls made of peat have the disadvantage of crumbling easily so that the water becomes very acid, which leads to further problems. This can be avoided if just a thin layer of peat is stuck to the glass or asbestos and then impregnated with epoxy resin, which will waterproof it and prevent decay. If cork bark is used it should first be boiled, then carefully scrubbed and finally soaked in water until it is waterlogged.
Nowadays walls of extruded polystyrene are very popular and are available in aquarium shops in a variety of different styles. Unusual and irregular structures can be created by carefully burning holes in the material with a petrol or gas burner: the material should then be painted with black or green paint or with red/brown paint, or a combination of these colors: it may then be covered with *epoxy resin* to prevent it from crumbling.
The long back wall runs the length of the aquarium and is kept in place by the side walls. Polystyrene is very light and buoyant and must be fixed so that the walls cannot tip up and float when the aquarium is full of water. The supports in an all glass aquarium can also be used to keep the walls under water.
Once the walls are in place, the bed may be prepared. This may well be banked into terraces: some aesthetic aspects of terracing are considered in the section on lay-out, and the technical problems of constructing terraces are considered below. Before laying the bed the aquarist must consider if he is going to install one of the modern under gravel filters or heaters (described below), but if not, he can proceed immediately with laying the bed.
The bed has two basic purposes: to make the fish feel more at home, and to provide a growing medium for aquatic plants. Unless a particular species of fish has special requirements, the composition of the bed is mostly dictated by the needs of the plants.

8. Example of an aquarium, built as a piece of furniture.

9. Cork not only serves as an excellent material for the construction of walls, but also for the construction of terraces.

The Bed

Many aquarists believe that water plants draw their nourishment from the water and therefore that the composition of the bed of the aquarium is of secondary importance. This belief is true for free floating water plants but it is not true for the many varieties that are anchored in the bed: the latter most certainly do derive nourishment from it, although they also absorb dissolved mineral salts from the water. Many water plants, for example the various species of *Cryptocoryne,* are bog plants in the wild and for these it is essential to have a bed rich in nutritional elements.
The bed should have a basis of fairly dark, coarse river sand or of fine gravel with grains about 3 mm in diameter. Fine sand should not be used, for that tends to pack itself together too much. By using a bottom layer of coarse sand or fine gravel many open channels are formed in the bed, through which the water can run and circulate round the roots of the plants. Coarse river sand contains a lot of loamy substances which also contribute to making the bed as nutritious as it should be for the plants. Thus all but the top 3 cm of the bed should be made up of unwashed river sand: unwashed sand is in fact sand that has been rinsed only a few times, to remove scum and dirt. The top 3 cm should then be made up of absolutely clean sand. A more complicated bed, but one which is even better for the plants, can be made by putting a layer below the layer of coarse sand, about 2 cm deep of a mixture of 25 per cent clay or loam and 75 per cent peat. Some writer's suggest that leaf mould should be included in this bottom layer but that is not to be recommended because when it rots it can cause the tank to become very dirty and encourage the growth of blue-green algae.
The bed can be made much more attractive it is built up into irregular terraces so that the whole aquarium is not on one level: there are certain species, for example some seasonal fish, that need a tank arranged with terraces, if only to provide room at the front for a bowl of peat as a spawning medium.

Terraces

In making a terrace, banks of sand are built up and kept in place with barriers of some more stable material, Many different materials may be used for these barriers, but the most natural effect is achieved by using pieces of bogwood, natural rock or larva stone.
Bogwood is the name given to pieces of trunk or root which have been preserved

10. The use of bogwood in the build-up of terraces.

by organic acids in peat bogs: this makes bogwood very different from drift wood, or dead wood found in a forest. Bogwood can be bought in aquarium shops or sometimes obtained from people who have found it themselves in its natural environment. Before any piece of bogwood is used in a tank it should be thoroughly soaked so that it becomes completely waterlogged: this prevents its rising or floating in the aquarium. The soft parts of the wood should be removed and the hard core thoroughly scrubbed and cleaned before being put in the aquarium. If terraces are made of cork bark, the cork should be treated as it is suggested cork be treated when used for walls.

Stones are usually used for the walls and terraces of a species tank for Cichlids (a species tank, as opposed to a community tank is one specially designed for a particular species or group of species which for one reason or another should not be kept with other kinds of fish in the conventional community tank). Walls and terraces of stones should be built with extra care and on the floor of the tank and not on sand, otherwise they may be undermined by the fish and collapse.

The accompanying illustrations show how it is possible to build high terraces and create the hiding places or retreats so beloved by many species.

The aquarist must decide for himself the position and height of the terraces but should always remember that terraces which run parallel to the front of the tank give no illusion of depth. That can be achieved far more effectively by placing them at an angle, of say, 45°. In addition, the terraces should be at different levels and built up in steps, beginning at the bottom and working up, starting at the front of the tank and working backwards. A symmetrical arrangement should be avoided: terraces on the left and right of the tank should not be of the same height and shape. There should also be a clear view through to the back of the tank somewhere, though not in dead center and at that point the terraces should be kept very low. These matters are further discussed in the section on layout.

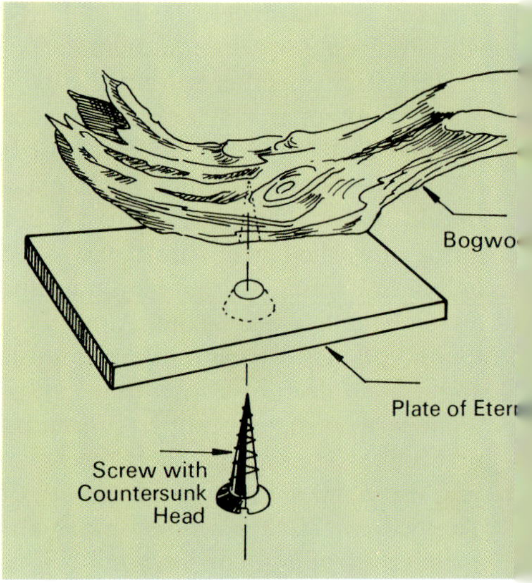

11. If the bogwood reaches down to the floor of the tank it can be secured on an eternit plate with a screw. If this is placed in the aquarium, the sand resting on it will keep the whole structure in place.

Once the terraces, bed and walls have been constructed the aquarist can introduce water into the tank, unless he chooses immediately before doing that, to plant the aquatic plants. If that is done however, the water must be put in immediately afterwards.

Filling the Tank

The overall importance of the quality of the water is discussed below, but it may be helpful here to give a hint on how to fill the tank. If water is simply poured into it, the careful arrangement of sand and terraces will be destroyed. The best way to fill it without this disaster occurring is to put a saucer with a good upward curving lip on the sand in the front of the tank and place in that a jar – something like a jam jar. A jug, of manageable size (one that can be lowered into the tank) filled with water at about 26°C should then be used very gently to fill the jar. When the jar is full and gentle pouring continues, the saucer will slowly fill as the jar overflows and then as the saucer overflows the water will gently trickle over the lip and start to be absorbed by the bed. The pouring should continue very slowly until the tank is full to a level above the level of the saucer: the speed of filling can then be increased and the curve of the saucer's lip will direct the flow upwards so that the bed will not be disturbed by the current. The tank should be filled to about 5 cm of the top.

The water that is put in the tank is the true focus of all life in the aquarium: it gives life to both the fish and the plants and allows a healthy ecological interaction between the two: if it is infected or unsuitable the same water will become the most likely source of trouble in the aquarium. It is therefore worth studying in some detail the composition of water and its effect on life, as that affects the aquarium.

Water is made up primarily of *oxygen* and *hydrogen*, although many other chemicals may also be present. Fish, like all animals, need oxygen to sustain life and they breathe (that is, draw oxygen into their bodies) through their gills. The gills are thin-skinned leaf-like structures which have a large number of small blood vessels, themselves so thin walled that the blood within these vessels comes into very close contact with the water as it passes through the gills. As the water passes through, the fish extract oxygen from it and get rid of carbon dioxide from the blood. The blood enriched with the oxygen is then distributed by the bloodstream throughout the body and feeds and fuels the muscles which allow all the fish's natural functions to operate. Without oxygen a fish dies: with insufficient oxygen it is sluggish and soon in ill-health. In short, oxygen is as vital to a fish as to a human being.

Plants behave in virtually a diametrically opposite way: they tend to give off oxygen and to absorb *carbon dioxide*. Some plants (known as oxygenaters) give off more oxygen, and are vital in an aquarium, but as a rule the oxygen derived from plants will not itself be sufficient to provide enough for the fish, nor will the amount of carbon dioxide absorbed by the fish be enough to clear from the water all that the fish exhale. The water needs to be able to receive additional oxygen from the air at the surface, and to give off carbon dioxide at the surface.

A very deep tank with a very small surface area at the surface will not provide enough room for this interaction between the water and the air.

The expulsion of carbon dioxide and the reception of oxygen by the water is much enhanced if the water in the aquarium is in motion: a pump will, by making the water circulate, allow up to 50 per cent more fish to be kept in any given tank. The circulation of water and its cleanliness are also much assisted by *filtration*. To ensure that the water is clean and adequately oxygenated is not however enough. It must be maintained at the right temperature, but that is relatively easy: the appropriate equipment is discussed below.

In addition, two other characteristics of water must concern the aquarist: its *hardness* and its *acidity*. Unless the amateur has a particular scientific interest in the technicalities of the subject, it is no longer, fortunately, necessary for him to become involved in the chemistry of water to determine its hardness or acidity. The growth of the hobby of aquarium keeping has been such in recent years that

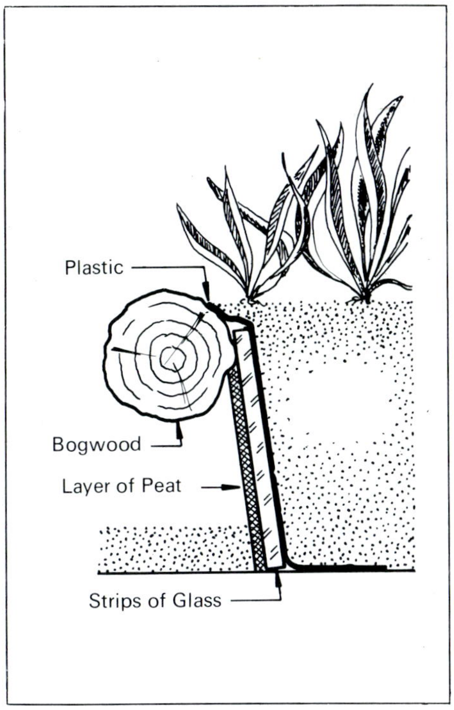

12. Cross section of a raised bogwood terrace. Strips of glass about 2 cm thick are placed at an angle, following the shape of the bogwood and covered with a sheet of plastic to prevent the sand from running away. The strips of glass are hidden from view by a layer of peat which is held in place between the bed and the glass bogwood structure. This provides the sort of hiding places that many fish require.

13. Bogwood, used for the construction of terraces.

there are now almost everywhere on sale in aquarist shops, both a wide range of kits for determining hardness and acidity and also many preparations for adjusting the water to make it of the required composition. The only cautions that must be given is to follow the instructions of the manufacturer exactly, never mix two proprietary remedies unless their compositions are known to be compatible, and never to be impatient: no radical or sudden changes in the water composition will be appreciated by the fish, even if the water does need adjusting.

Acidity is universally measured by the pH factor. Distilled water (neutral water) which is neither acid nor alkaline is given the value pH 7.0. The strongest acid solution has the value pH 0.0: the strongest alkaline solution the value pH 14.0. Degrees of acidity or *alkalinity* are measured within this range. In the systematic list of fishes, where a special degree of acidity or alkalinity is needed by a particular species, the requisite pH value is given. Slightly acid water, it is worth remembering has a pH of 6.5–6.8.

There is unfortunately no universally used scale of degrees of hardness or softness of water comparable to the pH scale. In this encyclopaedia one of the most commonly used scales is employed, that of °DH (standing for German degrees of hardness). Another scale often used is the Clark scale. Each °DH is 0.56 of a degree on the Clark scale, and so, to convert from °DH to degree on the Clark scale, multiply the °DH by 56/100.

Thus 6°DH = 6 × 56/100 = 3.36° Clark scale.

and as a rough guide it can be remembered that

1–5°DH = very soft water	10–20°DH = medium hard water
5–10°DH = soft water	20–30°DH = hard water
	30 plus °DH = very hard water

The amateur must be on his guard against the introduction of dangerous chemicals or salts into the water: copper salts from household copper pipes are, for example, a dangerous menace. There are further notes on this matter in the section on fish diseases.

The amateur preparing his first tank may be alarmed to find that after a few days the crystal clear water he introduced so carefully by the filling method described above has become very cloudy. This is quite natural, as the life within the tank begins to adjust: only if the cloudiness continues and increases is there any cause for alarm. If the cloudiness turns ultimately into green water, then a surfeit of algae, probably caused by too much light is the reason: if the water turns brown then bacteria are responsible and the water will have to be cleaned.

In the systematic section on fishes, peaty water is recommended particularly for the breeding of certain species. Full details of how this may be prepared are given in those species descriptions. It is as well to mention that there are however special peat filters on the market which make the preparation of such water very easy.

Except where it is specifically recommended that fresh tap water should not be used, most household water supplies are suitable for use in aquariums, but if the water is supplied through copper pipes then care must be taken to run off water before using any for the tank, so that the water that has been standing in the pipes is not used. Distilled water should not normally be used, for it is too pure and lacks essential trace elements. Well water, if not polluted is usually excellent. Rain water, provided it is clean and not collected off galvanised iron roofs is very good: in country districts it will be almost neutral, in built-up areas it will probably be slightly acid. Water from natural ponds, if carefully filtered can also be very good.

The requirements of the fish must, except in some specialised plant tanks, naturally be considered as paramount. There is not as a rule much of a conflict between the water requirements of plants and those of the fish, although some plants are

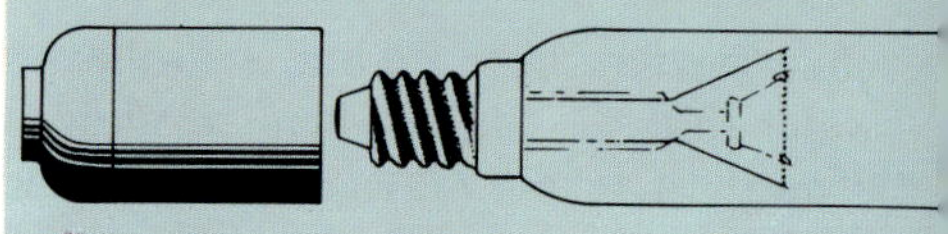

14. There will without doubt be sufficient light available if as many tubes are installed as the width of the tank allows. It is better if each light source has a separate switch for then the amount of light needed at any time can be provided without difficulty. It is useful to insta a few electric light bulbs as well as the fluorescent tubes: perhaps four in a 80 × 40 × 40 cm tank.
These can be switched on and off individually and allow particular areas to be highlighted. In this way a romantic underwater atmosphere can be created with subdued lighting in the evening and will allow the transition from day to night to be simulated gradually and naturally.
So that the lighting fixtures can be kept as compact as possible, small bulbs of 15–25 watts that can be mounted in miniature fitting should be used.
To avoid high temperatures near the water, the control apparatus for the lighting should be installed behind or underneath the aquarium. I put underneath then the considerable heat generated by this equipment can assist the heating of the tank. A warning must be given: do not amount the control apparatus directly on a wooden base: put it on an asbestos sheet The cheaper installations especially become so hot that there is a very real fire risk if they are mounted on wood.
The lighting cover should be neatly wired and certainly not contain a tangle of loose wires: every wire should be carefully insulated and clipped in place. Proper waterproofed cable with good insulation must be used: never use ordinary lighting flex. In a complicated set of lights, different colored cables will be very useful.

sensitive to different kinds of water and these peculiarities are noted in the species descriptions in the systematic section on plants. Nevertheless it is as well to remember that the quality of the water will affect the condition of the plants as well as that of the fish.

The plants grown in aquariums are often found in the wild in water that contains virtually no minerals or other nutrients. It is impossible to recreate these conditions in the aquarium and it is best on the whole to use ordinary tap water provided that is acceptable to the fish: nearly all aquatic plants will grow successfully in it. For the best development of plants it is however of crucial importance that about a fifth of the water be changed each week, and this is usually of course beneficial to the fish as well. Certainly regular changes of water seem to be the best way of inhibiting the growth of blue-green algae. It is important to remember that for plants it is not enough merely to filter the water in a tank: plants need regular supplies of fresh water that contains those trace elements that no amount of filtering will replace.

Plants of course are also affected by the quality and quantity of light in the aquarium, and this, as noted below, is another matter to which the aquarist must direct his attention.

15. The wiring has been worked off in the cover itself, the fittings are countersunk. Shown here is a combination of fluorescent tubes and ordinary bulbs.

Lighting

Lighting may be artificial, with either electric light bulbs or fluorescent tubes, or natural daylight. Daylight lighting is usually impractical: light should come into an aquarium from above and this makes it very difficult to exploit natural light. One or two species of fish, as noted in the systematic list do need natural sunlight but, with those exceptions, most aquarium fish are perfectly happy in controlled artificial light.

Various factors determine the amount of light required above the aquarium: the kinds of plants (quick growing plants need more light than slow growing plants): the height of the aquarium: the composition of the water: the reflecting properties of the lighting cover: the condition and age of the lamps: the thickness of the glass cover. For an average aquarium (40–50 cm high) with a conventional selection of plants, the general rule is 2–3 watts for every dm^2 of bed in the tank.

In practice the power of every fluorescent tube used is usually determined by the length of the aquarium or of the lighting attachment. Thus 20 watt tubes are suitable for an aquarium 80cm long, 25 watt tubes for a tank 1m long.

Table B
FLUORESCENT TUBES FOR AQUARIUMS

Watts	*Diameter mm*	*Length mm (Excluding the Ends (Mounting Points))*	*Watts*	*Diameter mm*	*Length mm (Excluding the End (Mounting Points))*
8	16	288	25	38	970
13	16	517	40	38	1200
20	38	590	65	38	1500

Depending on the width of the tank, three or four tubes can be placed side by side, and if the length of the tank is not almost the same as the length of the tubes, they can be staggered. There are many different shades of lighting available but those usually described as 'warm de luxe' or 'softone' (sometimes called 'comfort de luxe') have usually proved the most acceptable. Not only do these give an attrac-

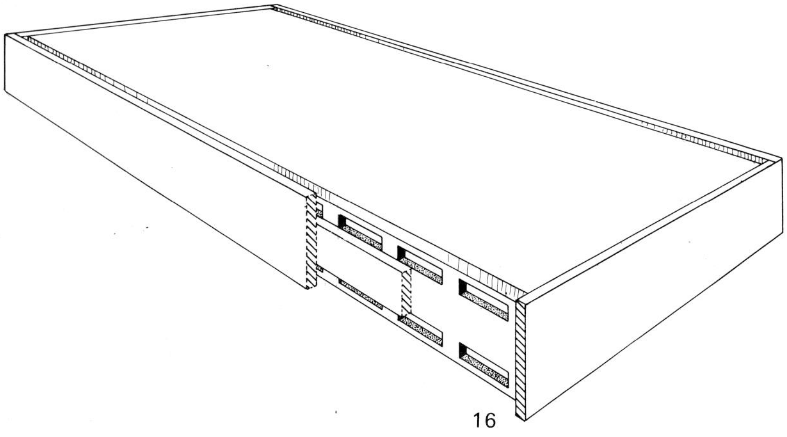

16

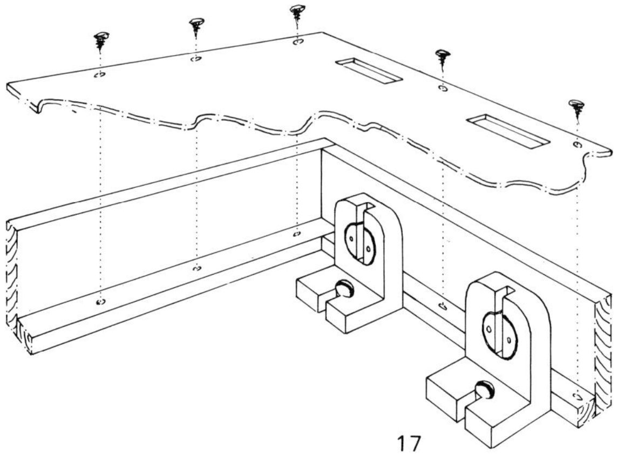

17

16. An efficient system of ventilation must be incorporated to remove the heat produced by the bulbs and tubes.
For safety's sake dampness in the lighting cover should be minimised by using cover panes. These can be fitted to the lighting cover itself although this means that the lamps are more difficult to reach and cleaning the glass from above is very difficult. It is better to have detachable cover panes (the number depends on the size of the aquarium) supported by strips mounted in the sides, or to purchase them complete with special plastic mountings which allow the panes to slide in and out at the side of the tank.

17. The interior of a lighting cover.
The material is white in order to ensure optimal lighting (reflection). The wiring has been made practically invisible.

tive illumination which flatters the plants and fish but also they provide a good balance between infra red and ultra violet light. The ultra violet provides energy for the plants to produce chlorophyll and influences the shape of the plant: the infra red is particularly important in the plant's assimilation of carbon dioxide.
It is advisable to make a circuit diagram before beginning: if the amateur is uncertain about the circuit diagram he should give it to an expert to check. The totally inexperienced aquarist would be well advised to seek professional assistance over the lighting for nothing is more dangerous than poorly arranged electrical equipment in contact with water. For this reason a metal lighting cover should never be used. It is simpler and much safer to buy or make a wooden cover which can then be varnished or painted to match the rest of the surround and harmonise with the interior of the aquarium.
The lighting cover should reflect well so as to fully exploit the light from the lamps. It should therefore be painted white on the inside or covered with foil or a sheet of white formica cut to size. Such a sheet can be mounted on batons about 1.5 cm thick and the wiring then hidden behind it and holes cut in it with a fret saw for the lighting units to come through. The formica should not be nailed down but screwed to the support batons with copper screws.
The strength of the lighting used in the aquarium will vary according to the number of hours for which it is used: this may vary between 12 and 16 hours. Regular periods of light and dark are essential for the well-being of both fish and plants and a time switch is very useful. This is one way of ensuring that the transition from light to dark and vice versa is gradual. Of course in the tropics night falls quickly but even there the light does not disappear at a stroke as it does in so many aquariums.

Heating

Keeping tropical fish and plants in a temperate climate inevitably involves artificially heating the water in the aquarium: keeping the tank in a heated room is not enough. The best temperature at which to keep any particular species is noted in the systematic list of fishes: in so far as these differ, an average temperature must be chosen for the community tank: in general a temperature of 23°–25°C is best.
To calculate the amount of heating (P) needed, the following formula is used:

$P = f \times A \times \Delta T$, where P = the power needed in watts; f = a factor, dependent on the degree of thermal insulation, to represent heat loss. In an insulated tank it is taken as 0.03: in an uninsulated tank it is taken as 0.06.

18. Immersion heaters with built-in thermostats can be purchased, and the thermostat can be set at a variety of temperatures. Other heating units available are designed to be used outside the tank in conjunction with filters and pumps, so that the water is filtered and heated in one process.
These units although more expensive have a number of distinct advantages: there is no electrical apparatus actually in the tank: there is no difficult problem of camouflaging an unsightly heating element in the aquarium: the water is more evenly heated, being in constant circulation.

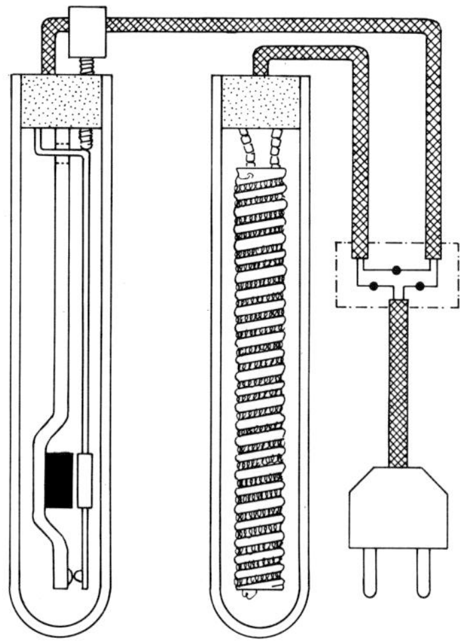

A = the total surface area in dm^2 of the heat losing panes; ΔT = the difference in degrees between the lowest temperature expected if the tank is not heated, and the temperature desired.
For a meter long tank ($100 \times 50 \times 50$ cm), A will be $2 \times 5 \times 15 = 150\ dm^2$: This assumes that with a lighting cover the heat loss from the top and bottom will be negligible.
If the minimum anticipated temperature without heating were, say, 15°C and the water in the aquarium was required at 25°C, then $T = 25 - 15 = 10$.
If the tank were insulated, then $f = 0.03$. Then using the formula above, $P = f \times A \times \Delta T$; thus, $P = 0.03 \times 150 \times 10 = 45$, and therefore 45 watts should be fed continuously.
Roughly twice the power, shown by this formula as necessary, should be installed so as to have some in reserve and to be able to compensate for emergencies, for example the result of a badly handled partial change of the tank water where the temperature drops more than anticipated.
Thus in the tank described above as an example, instead of the minimum 45 watts, 90 or 100 watts should be installed.
As will be seen from the two values given to f in the formula, the quantity needed for an uninsulated tank is twice that needed for an insulated tank.
It is advisable to install two heating elements, each of half the total required capacity so that not all heat is lost if one element breaks down. Two elements will also distribute the heat more evenly, especially in a large aquarium.
To provide the best circulation of heat the elements should be hidden as low as possible in the tank, but not on or in the bed (unless a special under bed heater is being used) because if it is, then its efficiency is reduced by the sand baking and the element will have a very short life. Special under bed heaters may be purchased which are run through step-down transformers, or, less acceptably, directly

19/20. There should be a separate switch for each lamp either in the lighting cover or in a separate switch box, behind or underneath the aquarium. Small tumble switches are very good, provided they can cope with the power involved. All leads, from the step-down transformer and other apparatus must be protected from sharp edges: they should be flexible and put through grummets so that they are not weakened when the hinged lighting cover is repeatedly opened and shut.
The switch-panel can be removed so that defects can easily be remedied.

off the mains. They are relatively expensive but being made of a long length of cable which is placed regularly over the floor of the bed in gravel before the proper bed is laid, do heat the tank efficiently without the sand being baked.
The heating element must of course be linked to a *thermostat*. Very often the leads are too short but as much care must be taken over lengthening these cables as is taken over the insulating of the lighting equipment. After some time an ordinary thermostat may stick and if that happens and goes unnoticed, the result is boiled fish and plants. To avoid this disaster, a second thermostat can be connected into the circuit in series with the first and set to a degree or two higher than the first thermostat. Then, if the first fails, the second will cut out the heat before a dangerous temperature is reached.

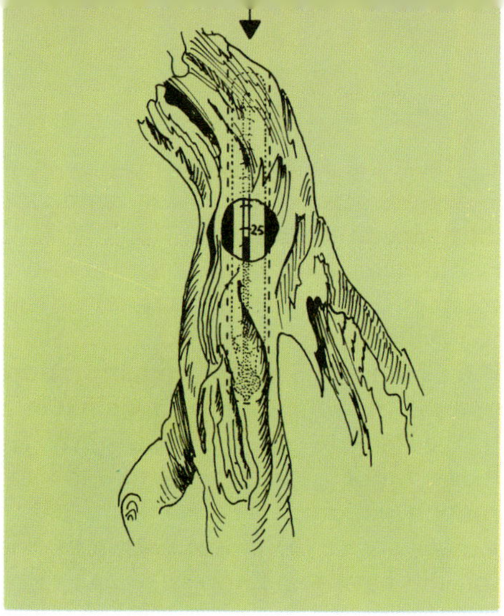

21. It is essential always to be able to tell at a glance what the temperature is of the water in the aquarium. A thermometer must be put in and kept in the tank. Alcohol thermometers are cheap, but mercury thermometers are more accurate. Whatever type is chosen it should be unobtrusive but nevertheless easy to see: it can often be fitted into bogwood or lava stone.

Filters and Pumps

Reference has already been made to the need to have a filter that will clean the water and an aerator that by circulating the water increases the amount of oxygen it absorbs. Once the principles involved are understood, little more practical advice can be given. A wide variety of filters, some put under the bed, others put in a corner of the tank, are on the market and the aquarist's preferences, the size of his pocket and the advice of his dealer must guide his choice. Filters and aerators are certainly equipment to purchase and not to attempt to make.

Miscellaneous Equipment

The items discussed above are all the pieces of equipment that the ordinary aquarist requires. All, that is, except for a few small items that may be needed in an emergency and must therefore be kept in stock. This is a short checklist:

- Glass jars of various sizes (to keep individual fish taken from the tank).
- One or two enamel buckets kept solely for aquarium use.
- Nets of various sizes, coarse and fine meshed.
- A pair of forceps or tongs to reach to the bottom of the tank.
- A siphon tube to siphon off water.
- A dip tube to pick unwanted food and rubbish off the bed.
- Scrapers to clean off algae.

All these items are self-explanatory except for the siphon and the dip tube.

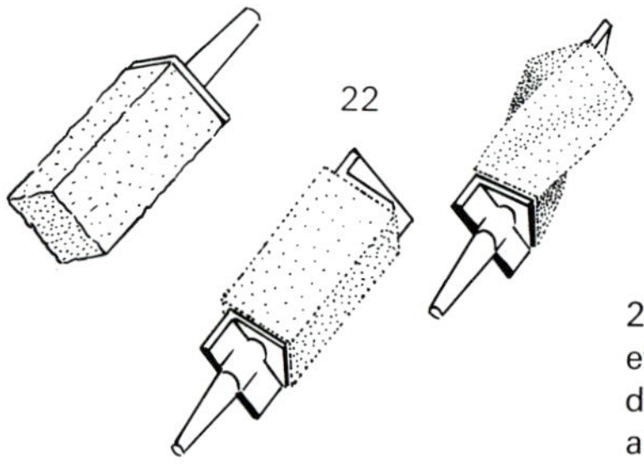

22. If a simple aerator is used, then its efficiency is much improved if the bubbles are diffused into a large number of smaller bubbles, and this is done by fitting a simple cheap accessory called an air stone.

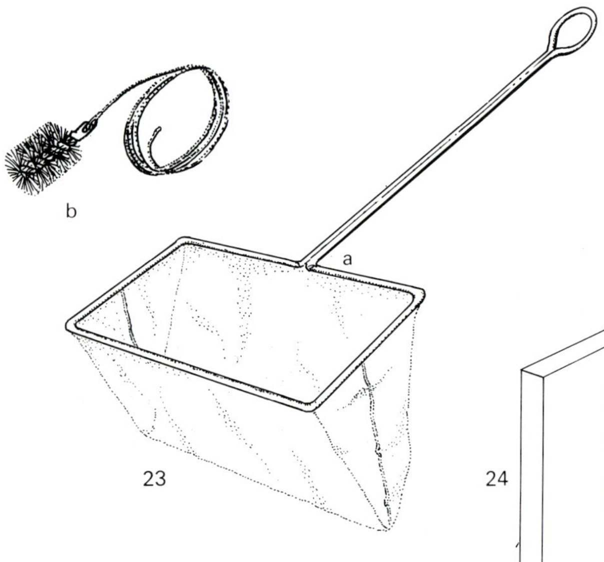

23. To the standard equipment of every aquarist belong nets of various sizes (a) and a tube cleaner (b).

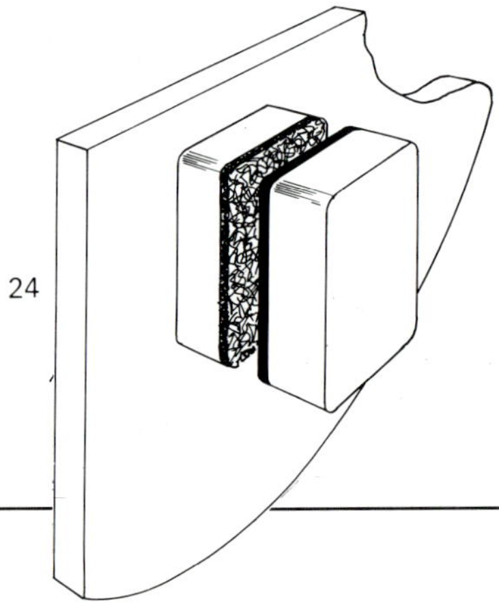

24. Algae can be cleaned off with scrapers; magnetic scrapers as shown here are widely used.

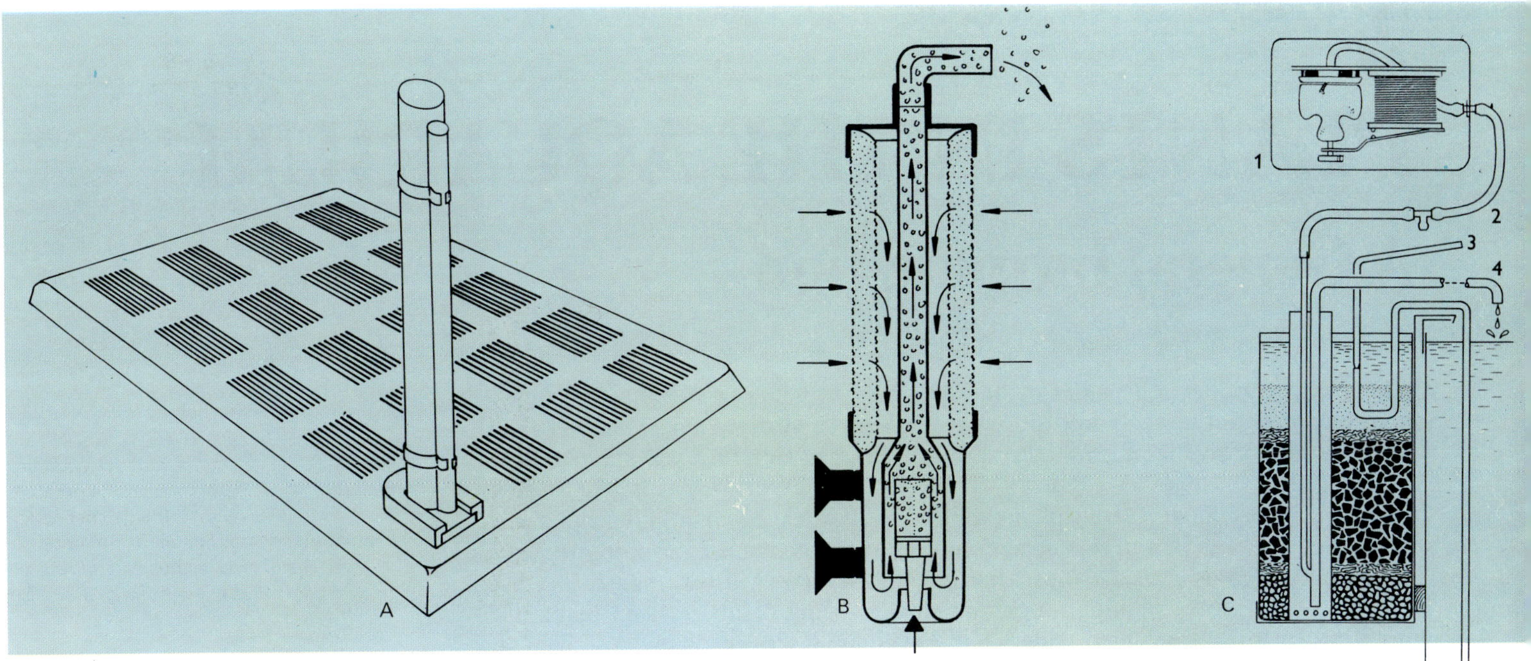

A siphon may either be purchased or improvised from about two meters of rubber tubing of inside diameter about 1 cm: it should be long enough to run from the bottom of the tank, up, over the rim, down to the floor and up to the aquarist's waist. With a tube of this length the flow can be started without the aquarist having a mouthful of aquarium water and the flow will be quite rapid: it can be regulated by pinching the tube.
A dip tube can be a simple length of glass tubing long enough to reach the bottom of the tank. It is inserted with the finger over the top end: when the other end has been placed over the rubbish to be removed, the finger is taken away from the top end: the water, and rubbish, will rush in: the finger is then replaced on the top end and the tube gently lifted up: the water and rubbish will remain in the tube, but another finger should be put over the bottom end as soon as it comes within reach. More sophisticated dip tubes can be purchased but are not necessary.
The golden rules of aquarium keeping may be summed up as follows:

1. Know the special needs of the species involved and ensure they are met.
2. As suggested in the section on fish diseases, always be alert for the first signs of trouble.
3. Always ensure that by aeration and a proper balance of life in the tank, the water is sufficiently oxygenated.
4. Ensure, by keeping the heating and thermostats in good order that the right temperature is maintained and the fish not subject to sudden fluctuations.
5. Check regularly that the aquarium plants are healthy and trim them if growth is excessive.
6. Feed the fish as advised in the section on feeding and ensure that various species receive the most appropriate diet, remembering that fish, like human beings enjoy variety.
7. Keep the tank as clean as possible, remembering that more fish die and more aquariums fail because of conditions brought about by neglecting this rule, than from any other cause.

As the aquarist grows in experience he will of course develop his own rules and routines but it is doubtful if anyone who ignored these elementary rules has ever been a successful aquarist.
The reward of the discipline inherent in the hobby is the visual satisfaction of a beautiful aquarium, the aesthetic satisfaction of maintaining a well-ordered world in miniature and not least the sense of discharging a duty and an obligation to perhaps humble but by no means unappreciative creatures.

25. In even the smallest and simplest of home aquariums, a filter is essential, if the water is to be kept clean, the tank well aerated and the bed maintained in proper condition.
Filters incorporate nylon filters which eliminate coarse particles and charcoal filters which remove various chemical impurities from the water. Peat filters are employed in special circumstances where peaty water is needed.
There are three basic kinds of filters. The under-gravel or biological filter (A): a false bottom, or series of perforated tubes is put on the bottom of the tank underneath the bed; the water is drawn, by a current of air, through the bed and filtered by it. The inside filter (B) is put in one corner of the tank and when connected to an air pump will draw the water through the cleansing filters. The outside filter (C) works on the same principle as the inside filter, but is placed outside the tank and water is siphoned off from the tank, cleaned by the filter and then returned to the tank.

2.
PLANTS IN THE AQUARIUM
A General Introduction

When setting up the aquarium for the first time it is better to put in some quick growing plants, rather than only those that grow more slowly. Tanks planted solely with such slow growing plants as the various species of *Cryptocoryne* are of course very beautiful but it takes a great deal of skill and experience to make such a tank look its best. Slow growing plants will not really settle down until the aquarium itself is mature, and in a new aquarium, unless adequate plant life is fairly quickly established, there is a great danger that blue-green algae will take control. A list of some of the more common quick and slow growing plants is given here, and more information is included under the individual species of plants described in the systematic section below.

Some important aquarium plants are of the floating variety: others are rooted in the bed. For those of course, the composition and arrangement of the bed is of importance, and that is dealt with above, in the section on techniques.

Plants that root in the bed can be divided for practical purposes into two quite different kinds: those that are stemmed varieties with leaves along the vertical stems, and whorled varieties where the leaves are arranged in whorls on the creeping stalk or rhizome. Both types of plants should be included in the tank to give variety.

Some plants such as *Microsorium pteropus* (Java fern) or *Bolbitis heudelotti* can be planted on the rocks or pieces of wood and in a very short time will be found to have anchored themselves securely to their host. In a similar way if *Vesicularia dubyana* (Java moss) is attached to the back wall of the tank, it will very soon cover it. The whorled varieties should be planted by pressing the roots carefully into the bed but making sure that the place where the whorls of leaves join the rhizome are free of the bed, otherwise the leaves will rot away. When planting varieties with stems, the lower leaves should be removed and the stem alone pressed

26. *Egeria densa*

27. *Lagarosiphon muscoides*

28. *Echinodorus amazonicus*

29. *Echinodorus latifolius*

26

27

28

29

into the sand: these types of plants will very rarely have any roots when planted, but they develop quickly. If young small pieces of stemmed plants are planted, it is preferable to put two or three pieces of stem together.

General Care of Plants

It is almost impossible for the plants not to thrive if they are given reasonable conditions and in the end the aquarium will become over-crowded. The plants with stems grow too tall and protrude above the surface or float on it: when this happens the stems can be topped and the cuttings replanted in the bed and the old stems, once the top cuttings have taken, can be removed. Very often, once they have been topped in this way, the old stems will throw out side shoots at the top and these can either be left or removed depending on how much vegetation is thought desirable.

The whorled varieties of plants need as a rule less trimming back. They grow somewhat more slowly but if any of the runners become unmanageable, they can be cut back. If the whorls of leaves that grow from the rhizome are themselves tall, as they are for example in *Vallisneria,* there is no point in trying to take cuttings from them, for they very rarely take root. The way to propagate the whorled varieties is by taking the runners that form naturally and transplanting them. In some cases, as with the species of *Cryptocoryne,* if a substantial portion of the rhizome is cut off and left to float free, a number of young plants will in time develop along the rhizome and these, when they have developed roots, can be planted as explained above.

Some water plants, in particular *Echinodorus* and *Aponogeton undulatus*, develop young plants on the flower stalks after flowering, and sometimes even develop them without flowering. When these young plants do develop they can be removed and planted separately without difficulty.

Only a few water plants reproduce by means of seeds in aquariums. Some however, such as *Barclaya* and *Ottelia* do produce seeds and these may be grown in a soft bed of a mixture of fine sand, fine peat and a little clay in very shallow water. As soon as the growth of the seedlings slows down they should be transplanted to another bed and great care must be taken not to damage the leaves while doing this. The seeds of *Barclaya* can be sown as soon as they are ripe, but seeds of *Ottelia* when ripe should be kept in water at 18°– 20°C for some months before being planted.

A few varieties of water plants, such as *Hygrophila* can be propagated by taking broken parts of the leaves: young plants will develop where the leaves have been broken. Other plants, such as *Microsorium pteropus* and *Bolbitis heudelotti,* which have creeping rhizomes are propagated by cutting the rhizome into pieces making sure that each piece has at least one leaf on it.

30. *Aponogeton crispus*

Composts

An aquarium that is properly designed and in which the fish are fed the correct varied diet will not as a rule be deficient in nitrogen, phosphorus or potassium, the normal constituents of artificial fertilisers: consequently it is not as a rule necessary to use any artificial fertilisers for aquatic plants, as it normally is for pot plants.

It is possible that an iron deficiency will arise in an aquarium, because iron, which is essential for the formation of chlorophyll, can easily form an insoluble compound with phosphorus. If that compound is present in the aquarium the plants will be unable to absorb iron and will suffer from the condition known as iron chlorosis. Not all aquatic plants are equally susceptible: the *Cryptocoryne* species are hardly ever affected to any extent but *Elodea, Vallisneria, Echinodorus* and other quick growing plants can be severely affected. The plants turn yellow and the leaves and stems both become very brittle. Fortunately very good antidotes can be purchased from aquarium shops which deal quickly and effectively with this condition. Unfortunately the more hygienic the aquarium, the more efficient the filter, the

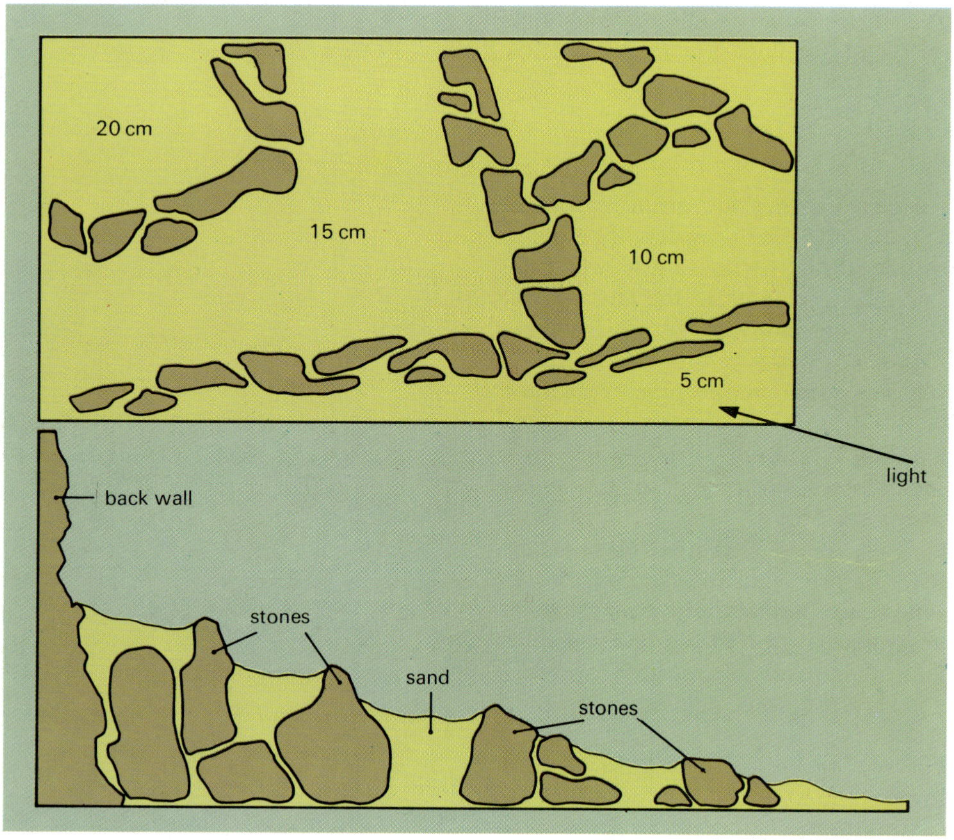

31. In order to get a good layout of plants in the aquarium, it is advisable to construct the terraces in such a way that the best illumination is reached; this is done by building the terraces in such a way that they slope upward and away from the direction of the incoming light. In this way, it is easier and more advantageous to arrange the various kinds of plants according to their habitus. Deep water plants should be placed in front and marsh-plants, growing in shallow waters on the higher terraces. Other plants may be set out on the remaining terraces so as to give a balanced picture, but not so as to impede the view or reduce the free swimming space.

32. Plants, carefully arranged in the tank, make an important contribution to the layout and general sight of an aquarium.

more likely this condition is to develop because it is under those circumstances that the insoluble compound is most likely to be formed. Another problem is however that when an aquarium tank is treated to deal with iron chlorosis, some plants such as duckweed, if present, may burgeon with quite extraordinary growth and unless effectively checked will soon choke the surface.

In any aquarium there must be an adequate supply of carbon dioxide: if there is insufficient the plants will be unable to play their full and necessary part in keeping, in turn, the right balance of oxygen. Some very good equipment is now available which will gradually diffuse carbon dioxide throughout a tank, using the cartridges sold for soda siphons. Adequate carbon dioxide in the water will prevent the growth of an unsightly white powdery deposit on the leaves of aquatic plants, which may otherwise occur if the water is hard. A pump of the right kind will ensure the proper circulation of the water.

Plant Diseases and Parasites

Very little is known about the diseases that affect plants in aquariums. Few specific diseases or deficiency conditions, which must occur, are identified. Except for iron chlorosis, described above, little is known about symptoms. Plants often suffer from incorrect lighting and it is sometimes obvious that they are not growing well in particular tanks, but there is little that can be put down that is specific or helpful. For example, the condition which causes the leaves of the *Cryptocoryne* to become completely covered with an unpleasant slime is well-known, but no cure is available.

Of course many species of aquarium fish are inimical to plants. Some are notorious as plant eaters. If such species are to be kept, the tank cannot be planted with beautiful and delicate plants: at most a few robust coarse bog plants can be put in, and these are best planted in individual pots which in turn can be concealed by rocks in the tank. In this way the fish cannot root up the plants so easily and any specimens that are damaged can be replaced without too much disturbance of the bed.

33. Contrasts in coloration of plants.

34. Contrasts between leaves.

35. *Microsorium pteropus* growing on bogwood.

Some species of snails are also a serious menace to plants, in particular *Ampullaria cuprina* (the apple snail) and *Planorbis corneus* (the ramshorn snail): *Melania tuberculata* (the Malayan snail) which lives on the bed usually leaves plants alone. It is advisable to feed apple snails adequate quantities of lettuce to distract them from the plants. If the snails become unmanageable, then blow fish, or puffers (of the genus *Tetraodon*) will, if introduced into the tank, eat up all the snails in no time, but then, if there are inadequate supplies of snails, they may attack other fish.

If there are too many floating leaves on the surface of the tank, there may be a plague of greenfly. These however can usually be dealt with effectively by using any of the sprays sold for that purpose: most are quite harmless to fish, but if in any doubt, a small quantity of the spray should be tried out on a small tank with one or two fish and some freshwater shrimps, for the latter are often seriously affected by such sprays.

Algae

There is probably no aquarium in existence that is completely free of algae. A little is of no consequence, but the problem is to maintain the right balance between algae and higher froms of plant life.

The most serious form of algae is the blue-green variety, the presence of which invariably means that the water is seriously polluted. It will cover the plants, bed and sides of the tank with loose blue-green films. There is an offensive smell. Blue-green algae occurs when there is a surplus of food in the tank which cannot be absorbed by the higher forms of plant life present.

The best remedy for blue-green algae is a clean tank. If it takes a hold then ten per cent of the water should be changed every day and all surplus food siphoned off: the fish should be fed sparingly and the water filtered continuously with the gauze filter itself being cleaned every few days. If this treatment is followed, the blue-green algae should disappear within a few weeks.

Another form of algae that has become much more common recently is that which covers plants, filters, pumps, rocks and even the sides of the tank with an unsightly

36. Some plants bloom on the surface of the water, e.g. *Barclaya longifolia*

growth of bluish grey fluff about 0.5–1 cm thick. There is no effective treatment known: it can sometimes be dealt with by adding tannic acid to the water but this is not always effective. Fish and snails will not eat this algae, although *Epalzeorhynchus siamensis* is alleged by some to eat it.

Other varieties of algae that may appear in the tank are the brown, green and thread algae. If green algae and thread algae develop it usually indicates that there is too much light: brown algae usually indicates that there is insufficient water and that what water there is is polluted. Thread algae is best removed by twirling it round a stick. Green and brown algae can be removed from the sides of the tank with an algae scraper: they can usually be removed from the leaves of plants by gently rubbing them with the thumb and index finger. The tank should be kept clean and the lighting reduced until the algae disappears. Whenever algae is present it becomes doubly important to have an efficient filter, otherwise dirt and food will accumulate where it can become a source of food for the algae.

Some common quick-growing Aquarium Plants

Egeria densa	*Najas guadalupensis*	*Riccia fluitans*
Hygrophila polysperma	*Pistia stratiotes*	*Sagittaria sublata*
		Vallisneria spiralis

37. A well-planted aquarium: in the foreground *Sagittaria* species.

38. *Vallisneria spiralis*

39. *Najas guadalupensis*

40. *Hygrophila polysperma*

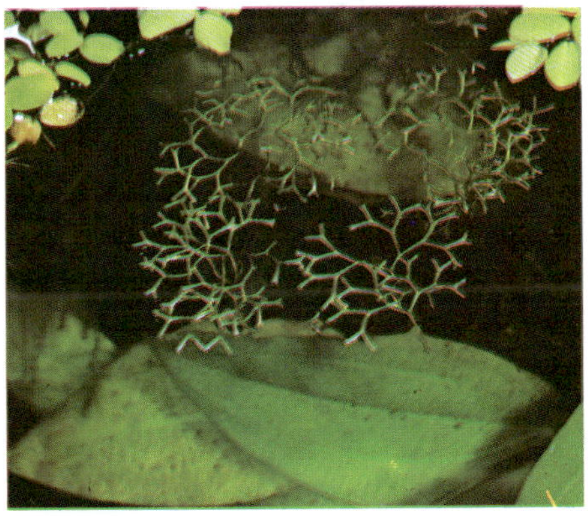

41. *Riccia fluitans*

42. *Pistia stratiotes*

3.

FISHES IN THE AQUARIUM

A General Introduction

Fishes as a whole form an important and numerically very large part of the animal kingdom. Their body structure, behavior patterns and appearance are of interest to both amateur aquarists and scientific workers, although the emphasis of that interest is different. The two different areas of concern meet on common ground when the biological features of a fish become the basis of its classification, for although most amateurs as aquarists have only a very limited interest in the scientific biological details, they are inevitably involved in questions pertaining to the classification and identification of species they may come across in the world of the aquarium. Because the whole basis of modern classification, or taxonomy, is the biological character of a fish, some knowledge of a fish's anatomy is therefore helpful to the amateur aquarist.

In this section a general review will be made of the main physical characteristics of fish, and the particular attributes and senses that determine in general, observable patterns of behavior. Some reference is also made to more technical matters which the amateur may encounter in the literature, but no attempt is made to deal in exact scientific terms, with those more complex questions which are of concern really only to the specialist or amateur with a particular scientific interest: they will already know the authorities that should be consulted for a more detailed review. The respiratory system of fish is treated above, in the section on water in the aquarium, and the digestive system is considered below in the section on feeding.

The Fins

The most obvious feature of most fish, which distinguishes them from other animals is the fins. To the fish these are most important organs, which with the swim bladder allow it to control movement. The fins are named after the parts of the body on or nearest to which they lie. Two of the fins are present in pairs, one on each side of the body: these are described as the paired fins. The other fins, if present, are solitary, and are described collectively as the unpaired fins.

The paired fins are:

The two pectoral fins which lie, one each side of the body, behind the gills; and

The two ventral fins, which lie, one each side of the body, below and to the back of the pectoral fins. The ventral fins are sometimes called the pelvic fins.

The unpaired fins are:

The anal fin, which lies below the body, behind the ventral fin, and the anus.

The caudal fin, or tail fin.

The adipose fin, which not all fish have, and which if present lies on the back, towards the rear of the body.

The dorsal fin which also lies on the back, but nearer to the head than the adipose fin.

The color and shape of the fins is of course one of the principal ways in which the amateur, who does not have a fish on the dissecting table, and cannot subject it to close scientific examination, identifies a particular species. Moreover from the point of view of the aquarist, the fin color pattern of some species is their most attractive feature. In this encyclopaedia, in the systematic section, a description

43. A school of Cardinal tetras *(Cheirodon axelrodi)*

44. Anatomy of the Fish

The principal external features of a fish

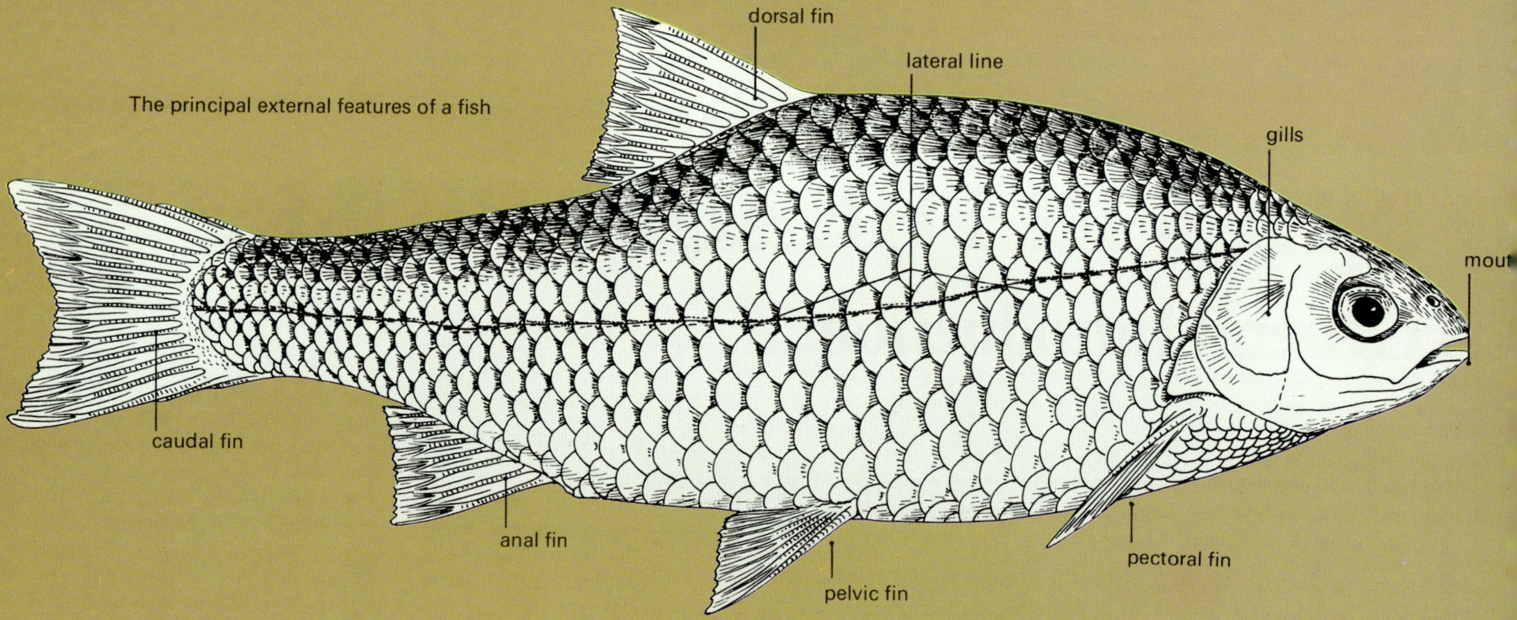

The internal organs of a fish

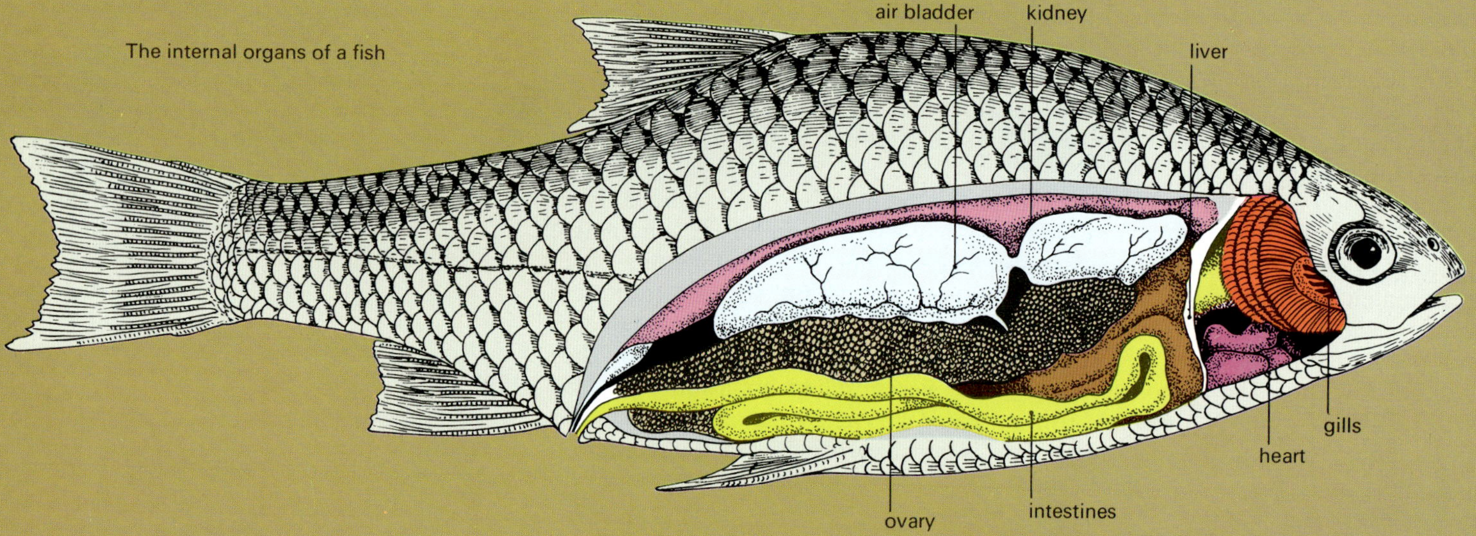

The skeleton of a fish

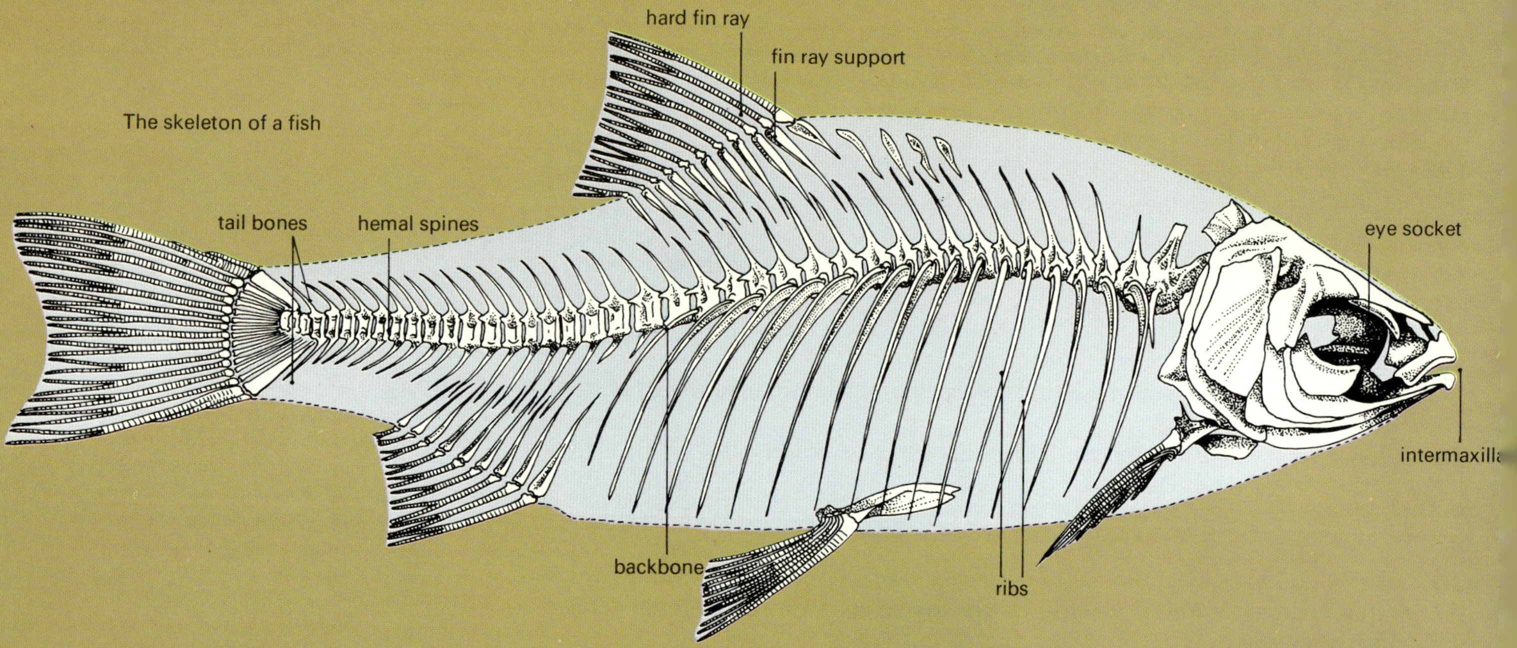

is always given of the color pattern of the fins and of their shape if that is in any way unusual. By no means all species have an adipose fin: in others the anal and dorsal fins are very large, in some the anal fin has so long a base as to be almost joined to the caudal fin. The caudal fin itself can be one of a wide variety of shapes: in some fish it is rounded at the end: in some deeply forked: in others it is concave, because the outer rays are elongated.

The fins are made up basically of rays, with membranes over and between them. The rays can be hard or soft: in some species the hard rays have developed into spines, and in some cases replace a fin, in the normal sense, entirely. Taxonomists are careful to distinguish the exact number of hard and soft rays in each fin: there is a special form of shorthand used by scientists to record these details. Each fin is described by a capital letter (D = Dorsal, or, if two, D_1 D_2, A = Anal, P = Pectoral, V = Ventral, C = Caudal), and the letter is followed by a number in Roman numerals, that represents the number of hard rays, and a number in Arabic numerals that represents the number of soft rays. Thus for example, in a scientific description of one of the Naked Catfish, *Mystus tengera*, the description of the fins begins D I/7, indicating that the dorsal fin has one hard ray and seven soft rays.

The Body Shape

The general body shape of the fish however is something which does concern all amateurs. Not only is it, like the fin pattern, an obvious guide to identification, but it is also significantly related to the life style of species in the wild and consequently, gives clues to the right conditions under which it should be kept in the aquarium.

Once again, in the description of body shapes, the scientist's approach is somewhat different from that of the aquarist. The scientist is concerned with exact measurements, and has the opportunity to carry these out: from a series of such exact measurements he can build up a very exact picture of the body profile or outline. Body Depth (abbreviated to BD), Length of Caudal Peduncle (abbreviated to LCP), and so on, taken together, give a very accurate picture. They are not however in themselves of great help to amateur aquarists, among whom has grown up the convention of describing the more common outlines by reference to well-known, everyday shapes which give immediately a good mental picture of the kind of fish in question. Thus worm-like, or eel-like, in the description of a species in the genus

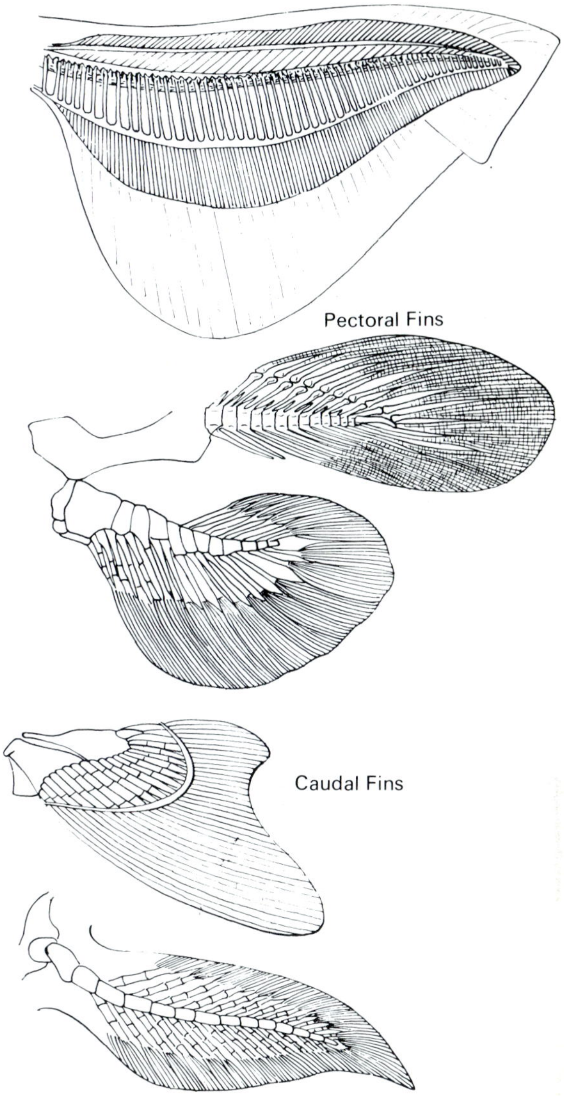

45. Pectoral Fins and Caudal Fins

46. The anal and caudal fin are almost grown together, as in Cichlids. *(Monodactylus argenteus)*

47. Clearly separated fins with the short anal fin bare, as in loaches. *(Botia macracantha)*

46

47

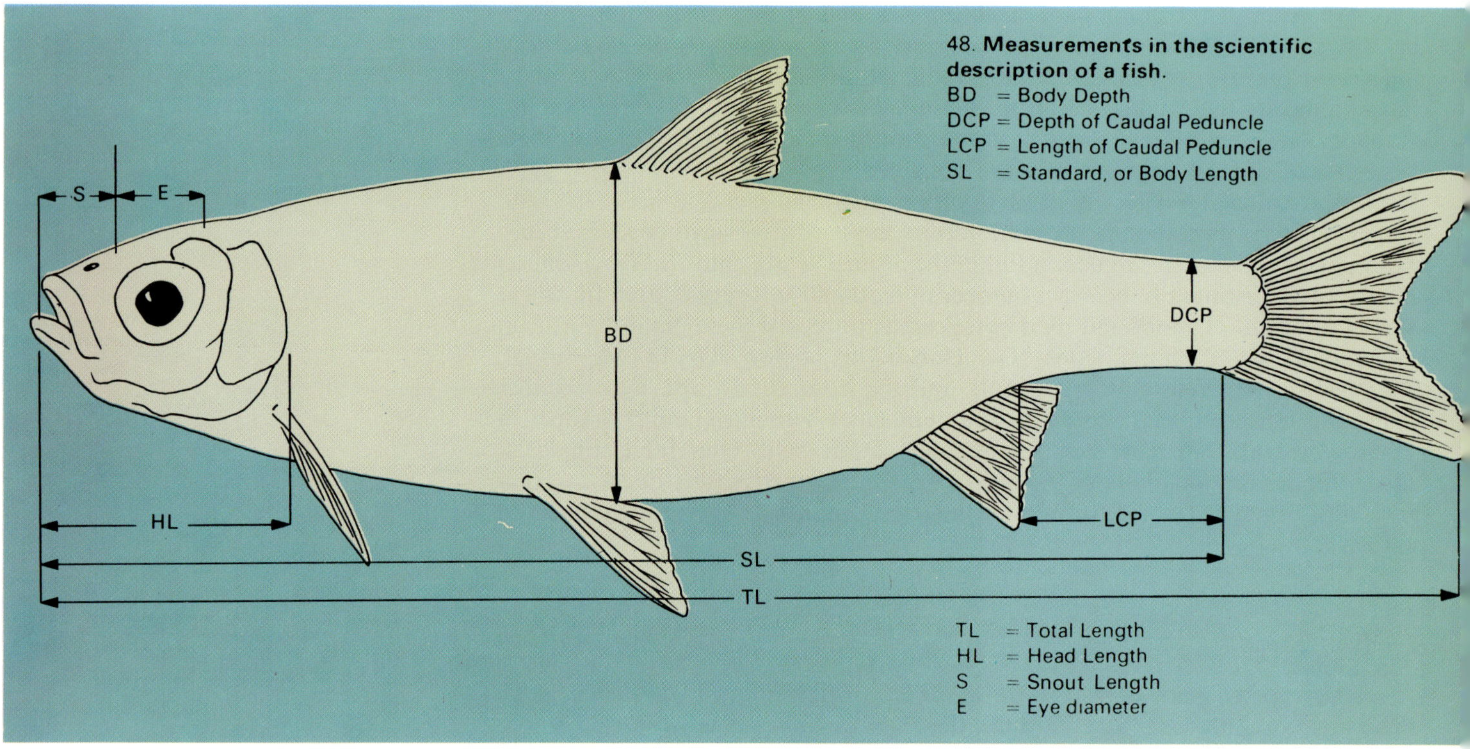

48. **Measurements in the scientific description of a fish.**
BD = Body Depth
DCP = Depth of Caudal Peduncle
LCP = Length of Caudal Peduncle
SL = Standard, or Body Length
TL = Total Length
HL = Head Length
S = Snout Length
E = Eye diameter

Acanthopthalmus, or disc-shaped for *Melynnis maculatus,* or boat-shaped for the Butterfly Fish, *Pantodon buchholzi,* gives immediately a vivid and visually accurate picture, as the reader will see from the systematic section. Most of these terms are, intentionally, self-explanatory.

The fin pattern and the body profile are the two most important obvious physical characteristics of a fish. There are however other important physical characteristics which determine not only the biological make up of the fish but also directly concern the amateur aquarist. These are the head, eyes, snout, mouth, and barbels.

The head will vary in shape as much as the body, not only because in nature (save in a few grotesque cases), there is always a fine and true balance between the parts of the body, but also because the shape of the head, like that of the body, is always that most appropriate to the creature's survival in the wild. Just as the body shape of a mud burrowing fish is worm-like, not hatchet-shaped, so the head of a surface loving fish will tend to be flat on the top, rather than high, to allow the fish to swim close to the surface without, as a rule, exposing its head to predators.

For although fish, like other animals, can receive sensory impressions through nerves situated elsewhere on the body, the head, for a fish as for a human being, is perhaps the most vital part: it not only contains the brain, but also other vital organs.

Both the snout and the mouth, like the head and body shape, are finely adjusted to suit the behavior of a species in its natural environment. Fish like *Mormyrus kannumae,* which live principally on worms they root out of the bed, have for example a long snout: predatory fish like the notorious Piranhas (*Pygocentris piraya* and related species) have large mouths with prominent teeth: fish that live off surface insects or insects that fall on to the surface as the *Epiplatys* species, have mouths that are upward pointing: on the other hand bottom loving catfish, like the *Corydoras* species, have a mouth which is if anything, downward pointing. The way in which both body shape and mouth are adjusted to the fish's environment is seen clearly in contrasting the profiles of for example *Corydoras julii,* the Leopard Corydoras, an active bottom loving fish, and *Epiplatys chaperi,* an active fish of the upper water levels and surface Not only is the position of the mouth quite different, but the whole bias of the body has altered: the bottom loving fish has

49. **Snout forms of fishes.**

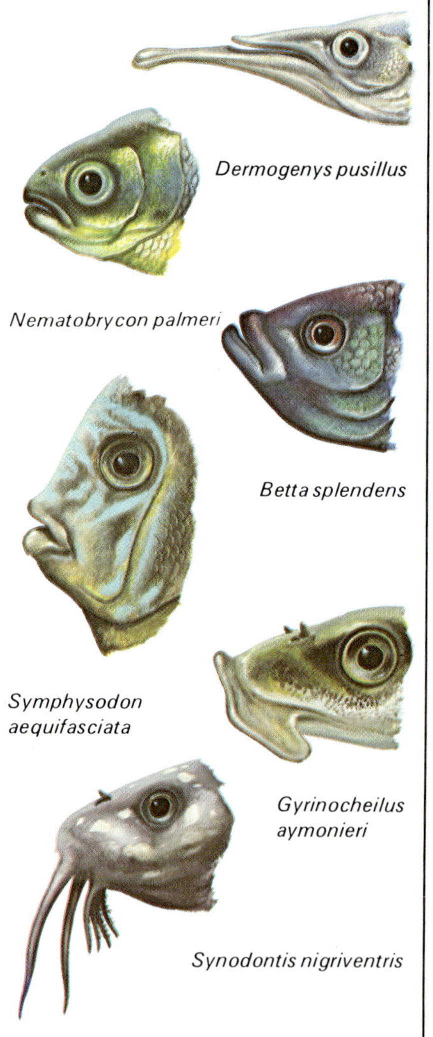

a high back for example, whereas the fish of the upper reaches has an almost flat back, and a deeper belly.

Bottom loving fish like the *Corydoras*, and other similar species have, in addition, the distinctive feature of barbels, which indeed for some give rise to the popular name of Catfish. These are extra sensory organs, and may be attached to either the lower or upper jaw, or indeed both: the particular position of the barbels is noted in the species descriptions in the systematic section.

Dentition

It is perhaps appropriate here to mention the matter of a fish's teeth. This is not something that is normally of great concern to amateurs, although in some fish, particularly the predators, the teeth are quite apparent even to a casual observer. It is interesting to note however that the form of the teeth, or pattern of dentition as the taxonomists describe it, does vary significantly from species to species, and once again is well adapted to the life style of the particular fish. For example, fish like those in the genus *Labeo* that live principally off algae that they find on stones and other impedimenta in a stream, have teeth that have developed into very effective rasping organs. It is as well also for amateurs to realise the very great importance now attached by taxonomists to the patterns of dentition: much of the modern revision of the classification of fishes within genera depends on

51. The lateral line
The lateral line runs along each side of the fish and can be seen by the naked eye. This line is made up of canals, or furrows, in which sense organs are found. These organs pick up sound waves from which the fish derives information about its immediate environment.

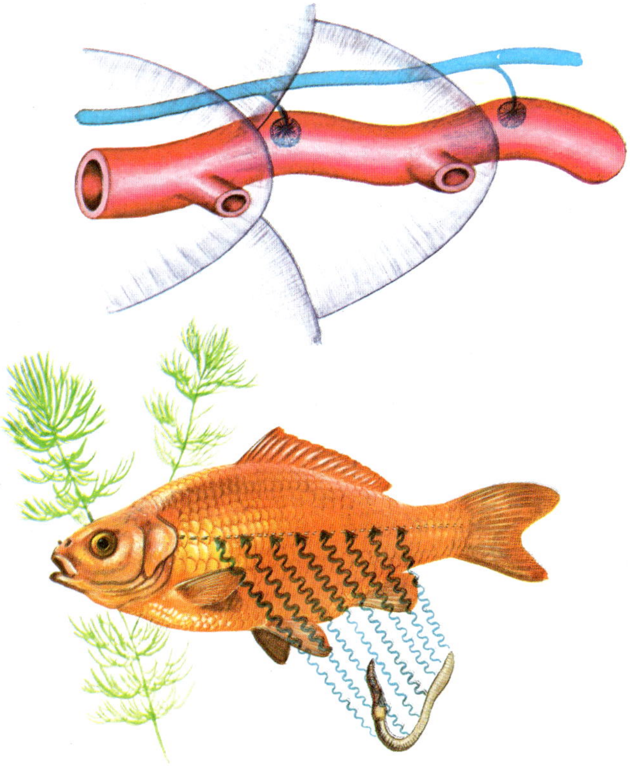

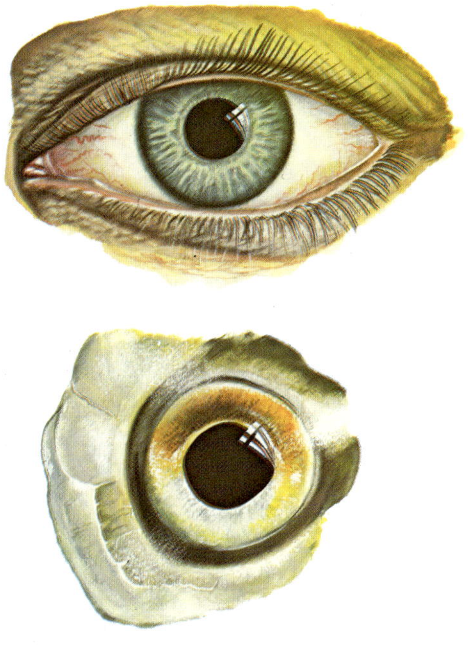

50. The eye
Most fish have good eyesight. Usually the eyes are set on either side of the head and each eye receives a separate different image.
The eyes of fish do not move, have no eyelids or tear ducts, for there is no need for the surface to be kept moist.
The lens is rigid, hard and spherical, which is ideal for seeing objects at short distances. Fish focus by drawing the lens closer to the retina by muscular action.

52

similarities or differences in dentition. The pattern of dentition for example is one of the distinctions made between Hatchetfish in the genus *Gasteropeleceus*, such as *G.maculatus*, the Spotted Hatchetfish, and those in the genus *Thoracocharax*.

The Eyes

Finally, a word should be said about the eyes. In most fish sight is well developed, although as a whole fish in one species or another demonstrate all stages of the natural phenomenon of the degeneration of a sense when it is not greatly used: that is to say there are blind fish, fish with poor sight, fish with acute sight (the majority) and even one fish with what are virtually four eyes!

There are only one or two true blind fish: *Anoptichthys jordani*, the Blind Cave Fish, which comes from subterranean streams in Mexico, and *Caeobarbus geertsi* which is found in subterranean waters in the lower Congo region. (The first of these is fully described in this encyclopaedia, the second is not, being a protected fish whose export is prohibited.) Some bottom living fish, such as some species of the Mormyridae, which have weak electrical impulse systems, although normally sighted, probably have less than average vision, and certainly rely on it less than other species. Some other fish that live in the lower reaches of the water have very sharp eyes, but situated almost on the top of the head, to give them an all round view, even when resting on the bed: such a fish is *Acanthopsis choiorhynchus*, a member of the Cobotidae family and an excellent aquarium scavenger from South-east Asia. The majority of fish however have the eyes placed on either side of the head and of course, unlike human beings, receive thus two separate views of the world about them, not one composite picture.

The eyes of most fish do not move although there are exceptions, notably among the catfish. The Mottled Catfish, *Corydoras paleatus*, has for example the endearing habit well-known to aquarists of sitting in the front of the aquarium, regularly winking at those observing it. However, fish have no eyelids, nor of course tear ducts, for there is no need for the surface to be kept moist, as is the case with other creatures. The lens in the eye of a fish is also radically different from that of, for example, a human being: it is rigid, hard and spherical, which is ideal for seeing objects at relatively short distances, but in a very wide field of vision. In so far as fish can focus, they do so by the whole lens being drawn closer to the retina by muscular action: they do not focus, as humans do, by changing the shape and thickness of the lens. The eye is also so built as to give sharpest vision when the fish is at rest, and then (when the fish is most at risk from predators) the reaction to changes in light (for example a shadow cast by an enemy) is extraordinarily quick. It seems also, from scientific experiments, that fish are well equipped with a visual sense of color – as indeed one would expect, from the beautiful colors of many species, for if female fish were unable to distinguish colors, there would be little point in the male displays.

53. **The profiles of fish**

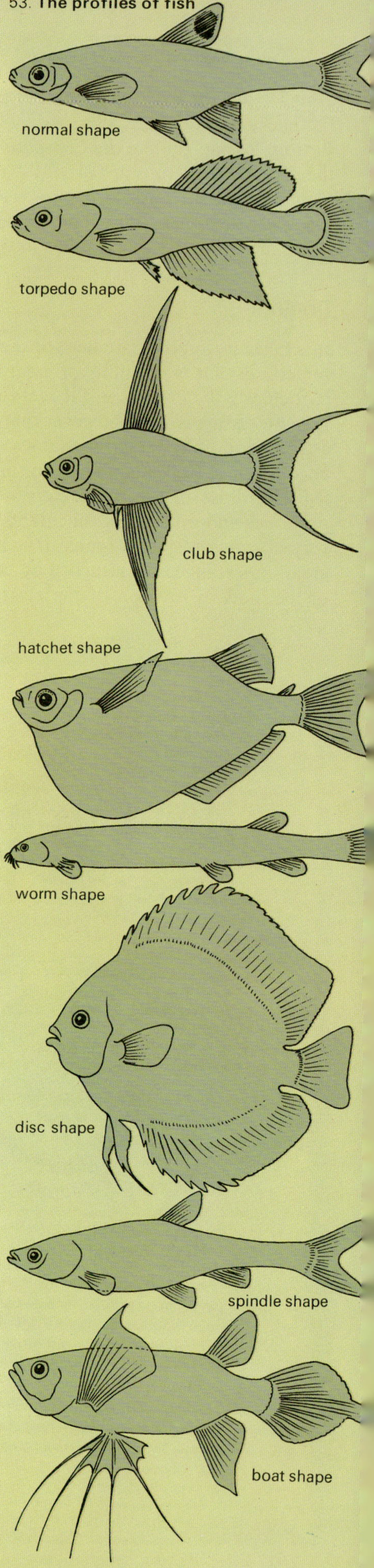

One unusual fish, which the more experienced amateur may at some time keep is distinctive in having virtually four eyes. This is *Anableps anableps,* a livebearer from Central America that swims as a rule very near to the surface. Its eyes are divided by a horny ridge so that while one set is focused under water, watching for predators, the other set is focused above water, on the look out for the surface insects it is hunting.

The Sense of Smell

Strange though it may seem, most fish have, for all practical purposes, a very acute sense of smell, although this statement may seem misleading, for, in relation to fish, it is virtually impossible to distinguish between smell and taste. The two senses are really inextricably linked. Fish have nostrils – one pair or two – lying above the snout, but the sensitive organs lie at the exterior end, where they are in contact with the water. Moreover, it seems clear that both taste buds and areas sensitive to smell are found on the lips, barbels and fin rays of various species. Where one sense ends and the other begins, is difficult to determine. Certainly, these organs play a great part in a fish's search for food, and it seems that shoaling fish use their olfactory organs to keep within the group.

Taste

The taste organs, so closely linked to the organs of smell, are found in the mouth, on the tongue, the lips, on the barbels and the snout, on the fins and sometimes scattered over the whole body. The Anabantidae family, for example, includes many species which have taste buds in the elongated thread-like rays of the ventral fins. *Helastoma temmincki,* the Kissing Gourami, has many taste buds on its thick and very sensitive lips.

Sensitivity, and the Organs of Touch

When considering the sense of touch, to obtain a complete picture it is necessary to also remember those ancillary sensory devices on which, to some extent all fish, and to a greater extent a few unusual species rely. Some fish, like the Mormorydae, emit weak electrical impulses, which act as a kind of sonar system: this is explained more fully below in the introductory note to that family in the systematic section on individual fish. All fish, in addition to what might be termed the conventional sense of touch, through barbels, fins and the impact of the body against obstacles, also have a very delicate pattern of sensitive cells located in the lateral line. This is an unusual feature present in all fish, that merits attention.

54

52. It is clear that the body shape and mouth are adjusted to the fish's environment. *Epiplatys sexfasciatus* is a fish of the upper water levels and surface.

54. The whole body shape of fish is adjusted to the behavior in its natural environment. *Corydoras julii* is an active bottom living fish.

The Lateral Line

The lateral line runs along each side of the fish. It is visible to the naked eye in most species, and looks like a scratch made along the length of the fish by a needle. In many species it is a straight line, following of course the line of the body, from the gill covers to the caudal peduncle. In some species however it turns up behind the gills and then down, to run horizontally through the caudal peduncle: in other species it curves down behind the gill covers and then rises to run along the caudal peduncle. The line itself is made up of canals, or furrows, in which sense organs are to be found. These organs pick up sound waves that travel through the water. Fish are, as a result, very sensitive to vibrations. It is also thought that through these sensory organs, a fish can distinguish others of its own species from those of alien species, through the variation in the frequency of the waves registered. This ability of fish to receive, and react, to sound waves in this way, gives a new dimension to their being, shared by very few other creatures.
The register of these sound waves is also sometimes transmitted to the swim bladder, which thus acts as an auxiliary hearing organ. The swim bladder itself is an internal organ of crucial importance to the fish, but before considering that, it is perhaps useful to say something of that other characteristic feature of most fish, the scales, and the related question of coloration.

The Scales

The amateur aquarist will not be much concerned with the technicalities of the scale pattern of fishes. For the fish itself, the scales form a protective barrier, not so much against predators, as against infections and foreign bodies. Over the scales there is usually a thin mucus-covered layer of skin. Very often, the coloration of the scales, or their dark edges, contributes significantly to the color pattern of the fish itself.
Some scales may well be lost by a fish that suffers rough treatment, or is attacked. The loss of the scales itself is of little consequence, because they grow again, but the aquarist will always, if careful, pay particular attention to a fish that has suffered a temporary loss of some scales, for it will be more at risk from infection while thus disabled.
To the taxonomist the scale pattern of a species is of considerable importance. Some fish are distinguished from others in the system of classification primarily, if not solely, on the basis of their scale pattern. Thus in the Characidae or Characin family, the only real difference between the genus *Hemigrammus* and the genus *Hyphessobrycon* is that the species in the genus *Hemigrammus* have scales at the base of the caudal fin, while scales are not present there in the *Hyphessobrycon* species.
In some fish, such as the armor-plated catfish in the Loricariidae family, the scales have been replaced by bony plates or scales, which provide much stouter protection: on the other hand, in some unusual species such as those in the family Bunocephalidae or Naked Catfish, the body carries no scales at all, nor any substitute plates.

Coloration

Apart from their technical interest and their functional protective value, the scales on a fish, as noted above, frequently contribute significantly to its color pattern. The scales may as in the case of *Epiplatys sexfasciatus*, the Six-Barred Epiplatys, each have a red mark, which show up quite vividly, or, as in the case of *Aplocheilus Panchax,* the Blue Panchax, each scale on the back carries a dark edge which shows up as a net-like pattern over the whole back.
The scales are not however themselves the prime source of the colors borne by a fish. These originate from special cells containing pigments and called chromatophores that are found in the skin of the fish. If a group of these cells, each containing the same color pigment, lie close together, they will show up as a patch of that color: if these cells lying next to each other contain different pigments, then the

55. The beautifully colored Firemouth Cichlid *(Cichlasoma meeki)*

resulting color will be a blend or shade. Sometimes these chromatophores are affected by light, which either causes them to expand, or to contract: these changes show up as a deepening or lightening of the patch of color. Some species are also distinctive by reason of the iridescence they show, particularly in certain lights. This iridescence is caused by deposits of guanin that by a natural process, are formed in the skin and muscle tissues.

The color pattern is thus the result of natural chemical processes that form part of the life cycle of the fish. It is not surprising therefore that color should be affected by, and be a valuable guide for the aquarist to, the state of health of the fish. The depth, prominence and sharpness of the color patterns is something that every aquarist should train himself to observe, so that, as recommended in the section on fish diseases, he is always alert to sudden changes that may indicate ill-health.

But color patterns change, or their intensity varies, not only according to the health of the fish, but according to mood – and in some cases, the environment. Fear usually leads to a shrinkage of the chromatophores, so that the fish then becomes paler: the advent of the mating season on the other hand usually brings an intensifying of the colors. Some species change color as the light changes: some species in the genera *Nannobrycon* and *Nannostomus,* the Pencilfish, have a quite different color pattern at night from that which they have during the day.

Apart from a few varieties produced by cross-breeding in captivity, all aquarium fish are still seen by their keepers bearing the natural colors of the wild. These patterns, attractive as they are, have of course a more utilitarian purpose for the fish: they are nature's device to attract friends and repel or deceive enemies.

Much of the gorgeous coloring of the males is designed to attract the females during courtship, and it is no accident that among the most beautiful – or if not that, at least the most vividly colored of aquarium fish are the seasonal fish, such as species in the genera *Roloffia* and *Aphyosemion:* for the survival of the species the males must be unusually active and successful during their brief life-spans. For other species, survival often depends on their ability to escape the attention of predators, or, if they do not escape it entirely, at least to avoid serious injury. Thus the color patterns will, in the wild, either allow the fish to blend with its surroundings or break up the true body shape so as to confuse an attacker. Thus a number of fish, for example *Cichlasoma festivum,* the Festivum, and *Rasbora maculata,* the Spotted Rasbora, have a very prominent spot on the caudal fin, or in that area, a spot which is almost invariably much more distinctive than the fish's eye. To the predator it looks like the eye (one of the most vulnerable parts of a fish), and an attack is more likely to be directed to the caudal fin than to the true eye: when attacked at the rear, the fish is also in any case most likely to be able to escape rapidly. Where the coloration has no such specific and positive purpose, it is nevertheless designed, by breaking up the shape, when seen among plants or against an irregular bed, through moving water, to make the fish less vulnerable.

56. *Melanochromis vermivorus* with the blue coloration, typical of many Cichlids.

The Swim Bladder

The fins allow the fish to control movement: the swim bladder allows it to control buoyancy, and to remain at rest in the water. The swim bladder, lying above the digestive tract, serves, by increasing or decreasing the amount of gas it contains, to make the fish, mass for mass, the same weight as that of the water it displaces, so that except in certain unusual species, the fish can float, without effort, at any level. As the fish moves from level to level, it experiences an increase or decrease in pressure from the water: by increasing or decreasing automatically the amount of gas in the swim bladder, a perfect balance between the fish and its element is achieved. In such a balance, in a wider sense, lies much of the satisfaction of the aquarist with his aquarium.

4.

LAYOUT OF THE AQUARIUM

Esthetics and Specialist Tanks

Laying out an aquarium is not just a matter of putting into a tank the few basic requirements of the fish that are to live in it. Their needs of course are paramount, and must never be ignored; they are the controlling factor in everything. However, without in any way ignoring what the fish need, the ingenious amateur can, with care and thought, create an aquarium which is also a thing of beauty and a satisfying recreation of the fishes' natural environment. This is an exercise in the artistic arrangement of sand and bogwood, stones and plants, and the judicious use of those other materials discussed above in the introductory section on the aquarium.

Experience of course is needed to do this job well: feeling for the materials, an awareness of their limitations, of what does and what does not in the end look effective, a knowledge of how water changes the appearance of a layout seen through glass – all these are skills that come only with practice. However, a great deal can be learnt from the work of others and the novice should always remember that really nothing he does in a layout is irrevocable: if, at the end of the day he is not satisfied with what he has created, he can always change it – with more work of course, but no artist has ever achieved perfection without a great deal of earlier experimentation and revision.

Before beginning to lay out a tank the amateur should carefully read the technical notes above on the construction of walls, beds and terraces, and the further notes on plants. These will give him the general principles on which the layout must be based and he should remember these golden rules:

(1) Never overcrowd a tank: it is easier to add to, than to remove from a display, without major upheavals.
(2) Always avoid symmetry: never put in anything dead center; avoid (except in rare cases) two or more objects or plants of identical size and shape.
(3) Attempt an asymmetrical layout that gives the impression of varying depth, with at least one off-center vista through to the back of the tank.

57/58. Symmetry or regimentation in a tank should always be avoided.

59. Bogwood can also be used as a decorative element.

60. Algae on bogwood

(4) Build up the bed in terraces of unequal height and size, left and right of the vista.
(5) Always leave, for hygienic as much as for artistic reasons, a low strip of bed in the front where rubbish may gather and be easily siphoned off.

The aquarist would be well advised then to study carefully the detailed suggestions below for the construction of species tanks for some particular and unusual fish. These suggested layouts will show him how experts can skilfully use materials to create special environments for those fish that need them, and should stimulate him to think of similar devices for his own tank.

Much can also be learnt from looking at tanks in public aquariums, in aquarist shops and public buildings where increasingly, aquariums, maintained by professionals, are part of the decor. Some, it must be confessed, will be found to be in execrable taste, but the discerning amateur can learn as much from the mistakes of others, as from their successes.

He should then carefully read the description, in the systematic section, of the species he intends to keep. This will give him some general information on the particular requirements of his pets: whether they need a lot of free swimming space, or many retreats among plants, or like to rest under broad leaved floating plants, or appreciate a dark well-planted corner. These features he must be sure to build into the layout. Where in a community tank different species tend to confine themselves to particular water levels, the amateur should adjust the layout to ensure that the right amount of swimming space and cover is provided at each level.

All this knowledge he can relate to the information on different plants and their growing habits, noted in the systematic section on plants. He must remember that plants do grow and that he is creating a layout which when established will be much fuller than when he first finishes the arrangement.

It is then advisable to spend a little while making a sketch, rather like those illustrated here, which, as in the design of a garden will probably not, in the end, be followed in every detail, but will crystallize the aquarist's thoughts, and give him some idea of the materials and plants he will need to acquire.

Such a sketch also gives the aquarist the opportunity to think of the ways in which the necessary equipment, heater, filters, thermometers, can best be concealed, and yet be easily reached and operated.

Thereafter only experience, patience and ingenuity will lead to sucess, but in creating his own personally satisfying layout the amateur will enjoy great satisfaction.

61. Bogwood as a decorative element.

Specialist Tanks

AN AQUARIUM FOR EGG-LAYING TOOTHCARPS, OR SEASONAL FISH

In the wild, seasonal fish have only a very short life: in favorable conditions they live for a year or eighteen months, but generally they live for only a few months. The pools and lakes where they live dry up during the dry season, and of course, all the fish die.

The unusual breeding habits of these fish, whereby the eggs buried in the mud can survive the dry season, are fully explained in the species descriptions in the systematic section, under the genera *Aphyosemion, Aplocheilus, Epiplatys, Nothobranchius* and *Roloffia,* in the family Cyprinodontidae.

These fish deserve a species tank not only because of their fascinating life cycle, but also because of the almost incredibly beautiful coloration of the males. In a species tank they sparkle like jewels. In a community tank, they are not shown off to advantage.

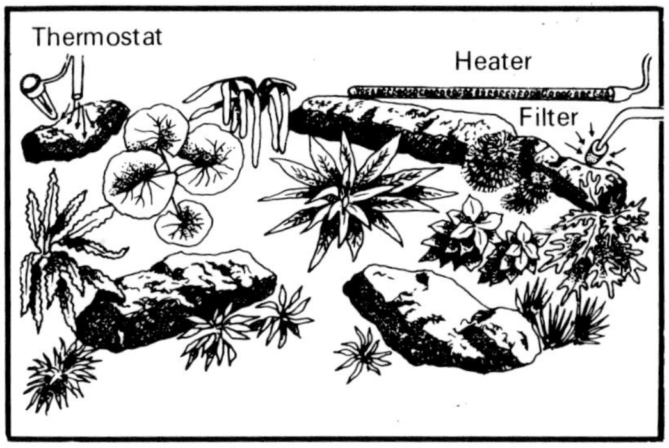

62. Hiding the heater, filter and thermostat behind rocks, giving an off center vista and a free swimming space area.

63. Good layouts of which an example is shown here. There are 2 vistas, neither in center.

64. In a center vista we find symmetry round the back and sides, but broken within; there is ample swimming space in the center.

This species tank is best put in a fairly dark corner, perhaps as part of a wall unit. These species do not require a great deal of space per fish. A tank 20 – 25 cm high is adequate: the width can be adapted to fit the space available, and so as to give as large a surface area as possible. The lighting cover should be a tight fit, and there should be a small light at the front, to highlight the iridescence of the fish.

The tank layout is simple. The bed should be a layer of fine-grained sand mixed with small pieces of boiled peat. This may be covered with some oak leaves or waterlogged peat fibre. The sides may be painted black or dark brown on the outside, or covered on the inside with cork bark. The tank should be decorated

with irregularly shaped pieces of bogwood positioned to give an impression of depth, by having low pieces at the front and larger pieces round the sides.
A single plant which does not require much light may be added. If there are more plants the desired effect, of a muddy pool with tree roots, is lost. Some moss should be encouraged to grow up the cork walls. The fish like to mate there, although small pieces of floating oak-leaf fern are just as suitable. These should be kept in place by nylon thread round the walls.
A small peat filter with a low flow-rate and an outlet at the water surface will prevent a skin forming. The temperature should be 22°–23° C. The water needs changing only every 4–6 weeks and even then only a third of it. The water should be just under 10° DH.
Fish can be put into an aquarium laid out in this way after two or three weeks. Adult egg-laying toothcarps are particularly sensitive to changes in their environment and it is preferable to select young specimens. For every male there should be at least two females. The different species tolerate each other well, and will leave the fry of other fish alone if they are properly and regularly fed with small live animal matter.

A SPECIES TANK FOR DISCUS FISH

The majestic and increasingly popular discus fish in the genus *Symphysodon* are another group that deserve a specially laid out species tank. Here the challenge is to recreate the calm waters along the shores of the shallow creeks, pools, lakes and network of small tributaries from the rain forest of the Amazon basin.
The discus lives peacefully among the dark shadows of the impenetrable off shore vegetation and where the gnarled roots of trees grow down into the soft, warm water, rich in humus, regularly replenished by the draining of the rain forest and providing a wide variety of animal food.
The virtual impossibility of recreating such an environment is probably why keeping and breeding discus fish has so often been disappointing. However, the disappointments of the past have provided the experience on which it is possible to attempt to layout a species tank which meets the requirements of these fish to some extent, and which may even encourage them to breed successfully.
The tank must be at least $100 \times 50 \times 50$ cm: ideally it should be $200 \times 60 \times 80$ cm. The sides may be covered with cork bark prepared as suggested in the introductory section on aquariums. The tank must not be dominated by a profusion of beautiful plants: they are not found in the natural environment of discus fish: they destroy

65. *Aplocheilus lineatus*
Example of egg-laying toothcarp

66. *Aplocheilus panchax*
Example of egg-laying toothcarp

◁ 67. A tank for egg-laying toothcarps must not have too many plants, because these fish like swimming space between clumps of vegetation.

69. Discus fish of the genus *Symphosidon* like ▷ to swim in calm waters, rich in humus; not too many plants; bogwood should be the dominant decoration.

68. *Nothobranchius rachovi*, egg-laying toothcarp.

the special character of the tank and provide unnecessary hiding places for the fish, which will thus be lost to view.

The dark bed of sand and peat has to be handled imaginatively, otherwise the largely unplanted tank will look too bare. The bed should rise steeply from the front to the back, supported by asymmetric terraces if necessary, built up with layers of peat, bogwood, or even cork bark. Flat stones can also be used, but they do not usually look quite natural.

The dominant decoration should be bogwood: a large number of big pieces of interesting shape should be piled up, from the front, where the pile will be fairly low, to the back where the pile should virtually reach the water surface. This will give the fish enough retreats. The bogwood and some of the cork wall can be overgrown with attractive moss: there may be the occasional plant, such as the Amazon swordplant, *Echinodorus horizontalis,* and here and there a clump of *Echinodorus tenellis*. However, discus like a large part of the sandy bed to remain bare. The overhead lighting can be filtered through a few floating plants and it should be limited to a few light bulbs, or if there is a lighting cover, some neon tubes with a very soft illumination. The fish will be regularly seen swimming about at the front of the tank if the lighting is subdued.

The composition of the water is extremely important: it must be very soft. The fish can be put in when the tank has stood for two weeks. The fish should preferably be half grown, and different color varieties can only really be kept together in a large aquarium: even then a vigilant watch has to be maintained to avoid cross-breeding, if indeed the fish mate.

The temperature should be kept constant at 28°–30°C: the soft water should be continuously filtered through an efficient biological filter which does not contain any materials that might increase the DH value.

A SPECIES TANK FOR ANGELFISH

The graceful angelfish (genus *Pterophyllum*), although now overshadowed by the discus fish, still have a large following among aquarists. In the wild they are found in calm waters in which a great deal of vegetation, reeds, grasses and other ribbon leaved plants are found. They hide amongst this vegetation and being predators hunt for young fish and other creatures.

70/71. Angelfish of the genus *Pterophyllum* feel at home in a calm environment, with predominantly reed and grass.

Angelfish on sale in aquarium shops have almost always been bred in captivity: these domesticated varieties have a fairly high resistance to disease and generally few special requirements in the aquarium. However, this in no way detracts from their beauty and in a properly laid out tank these graceful and dignified fish which can grow 20–25 cm high, are fascinating to watch.
The tank should be at least 100 × 50 × 50 cm. It can be placed in front of an illuminated shallow stand containing reeds and grasses to give the impression of a reedy shore, but the result is rather unnatural because of reflections in the glass. It is better to cover the back of the tank inside with a random arrangement of narrow pieces of flagstone: gaps left here and there should be filled in with peat and some low growing or hanging plants put in front of the walls. Bamboo canes can be stuck into the bed and interspersed with a few tall varieties of *Echinodorus*.
The plants should not however be allowed to dominate the tank. The bed, of coarse river sand mixed with dark gravel, should rise from the front to the back to give a suggestion of depth. A step-like arrangement of flagstones embedded in the bottom can be used to achieve this. The layout of the tank can be improved with a single piece of irregularly shaped bogwood and completed with the occasional attractive plant such as *Eichhornia azurea* or *Echinodorus horizontalis*. For variety, a beautiful clump of *Myriophyllum aquaticum* can be put in, floating its trailing leaves on the water surface.
The composition of the water is not critical, but a part should be changed regularly. The temperature should be 27°–30° C. Angelfish do not dislike light, but it should not be overdone. They are however very sensitive to sudden changes from light to dark and vice versa: they may indeed be literally frightened to death by such a sharp change, and the lighting should always be adjusted accordingly.

72. Simple construction of rocks with a hiding place in a specialist tank for Cichlids.

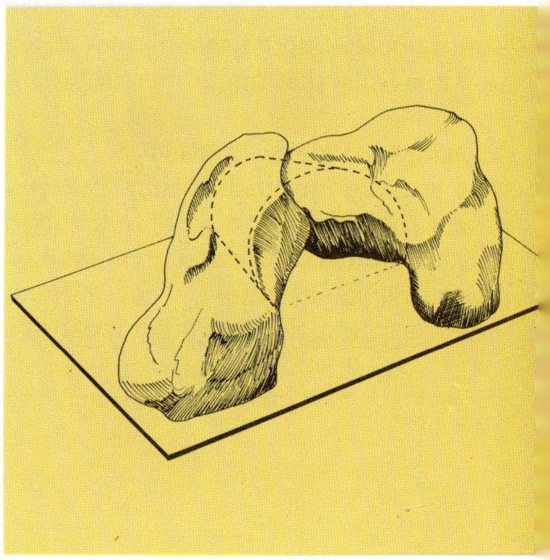

A SPECIES TANK FOR CICHLIDS

Details are given below of species tanks for dwarf cichlids and for Malawi and Tanganyika cichlids. This section deals with the tank for other varieties. Of course, if asked how to lay out a species tank for cichlids, many with experience of keeping them would assert there is no need to bother, because these fish arrange the lay out themselves! That is largely true.
Cichlids of one species or another are found in many different environments in Eurasia, Africa and South and Central America. They are intelligent fish, very adaptable but with an extremely individual lifestyle which can have great influence on the environment: in some places where cichlids have been introduced by man, for economic reasons, they have completely altered the balance of nature.
In the aquarium many species have their own ideas about where the plants should grow and will tear out of the bed or eat those whose position they dislike. They

73. *Cichlasoma festivum*.
Cichlids prefer rocky environments, with plenty of hiding places. Plants should be securely anchored among stones.

will undermine carefully laid out hiding places and move about heavy stones as if they were sponges. A sandy bed which rises attractively from the front to the back of the tank can be entirely upturned and redistributed within a few hours so that it is piled up against the front pane. The fish will not necessarily accept the companions chosen for them or the mates the aquarist thinks would be best. When the fish seem to have settled down well, there may be a sudden eruption and one specimen will be the victim of unexpected rivalry.

Even so, cichlids are fascinating fish, and it is worth laying out a special tank for them, provided the amateur is prepared to accept their moods and does not insist on having a beautifully planted aquarium: the latter is generally impossible with cichlids.

The tank should be at least 100 × 50 × 50 cm. Arrangements of rock should be stuck together with cement or silicone glue to prevent their destruction. There should be plenty of hiding places and a thick bed of smooth pebbles, possibly with some pieces of securely anchored bogwood. The sides of the aquarium can be covered on the inside with various materials: walls of pieces of lava cemented together are very effective.

Plants should be securely anchored amongst stones or rooted in plant pots which are covered with pieces of flagstone. Only sturdy plants with thick leaves are suitable as all others are usually eaten. Plants placed high up, against walls for example, are left alone. Alternatively some thick bamboo canes can also be put in the tank: if holes are drilled in them some way above the level of the bed, they can be filled with sand or peat and then plants put in.

Cichlids eat a lot and produce a great deal of waste matter. An efficient filter system with a substantial through-put is necessary. Good aeration is needed to provide sufficient oxygen but the position of the outlets should be chosen carefully to avoid too much turbulence: that will make the water cloudy and stimulate the growth of algae. The aquarium can be filled with tap water and the temperature should be between 23°–27°C, but the exact requirements in these respects should be checked against the notes on the particular species involved, in the systematic list.

74. *Aequidens pulcher*

75. *Apistogramma agassizi*
Members of the large family of Cichlids.

A SPECIES TANK FOR DWARF CICHLIDS

A number of very attractive dwarf cichlids come from South America, for example those in the genus *Apistogramma*. Their attractive lifestyle and reproductive behavior, which is usually accompanied by a touching degree of parental care, resembles that of larger cichlids., but they usually lack the uncertain temperament which makes their larger relatives such difficult fish to keep.

Many dwarf cichlids can easily be kept in community tanks. They are very tolerant, especially outside the spawning season: they do not have very many special requirements, and they do not interfere with the layout of an attractively arranged tank. They are indeed ideal aquarium fish, but the amateur who particularly wishes to study them will be well advised to construct a species tank for them.

The species in the genera *Apistogramma, Crenicara, Pelmatochromis,* among others, establish small territories in the wild, along the shores of lakes and slow moving waters. They have hiding places where they mate among stones, rotting wood, or in caves and crevasses. Their food consists mainly of aquatic insects and larvae. They are very rarely real predators and even more rarely feed on vegetable matter.

The species tank for dwarf cichlids can therefore be attractively planted if desired, though the vegetation should not be too dense because it will then obscure the fish from view. The most important thing is to provide plenty of hiding places in the form of caves, both in the walls of the tank and in the terraces, using a number of different materials. There should also be some areas of sand where a number of species like to dig 'sleeping holes' for their fry.

The size of the tank depends on the number of fish that are kept, taking into consideration their territorial instincts. As a basic rule, for four different pairs, the aquarium should be at least 80 cm long, and proportionately deep.

The aquarium can be filled with tap water as long as it is not too hard, and provided that some of the water is changed every week: it is not really necessary to install

76. Detail of a tank with mainly dwarf cichlids. The plants on the right are used as a protection for the territory with wood.

a filter system. Artificial aeration is not necessary if there are some water plants with a high rate of carbon dioxide assimilation. During the daytime the overhead lighting may be quite strong but in the evening it should be subdued. When the fish are breeding or looking after their young, there should be no sudden movements or disturbances near the tank.

A SPECIES TANK FOR MALAWI AND TANGANYIKA CICHLIDS

During the last few years various beautifully colored chichlids have been discovered throughout East Africa, particularly in Lakes Malawi and Tanganyika. The coloration of many of them is comparable to that of the most splendid coral fish.

These fish all live in very similar natural environments in the wild, although those environments themselves are quite varied. However, it is for other reasons inadvisable to mix, in one tank, specimens from both Malawi and Tanganyika. They should be kept separately, but the species tank for each group can be laid out in the same way.

Most of these imported cichlids come from areas around the rocky shores of these lakes, and in the wild live mainly off the algae, small shrimps and other small creatures found there in profusion.

The many different species and sub-species can be distinguished from each other by characteristic and specialised feeding habits: there is thus little aggression between them: those that show territorial instincts claim only very small territories, laying claim to only a few small caves and crevasses. When kept in captivity, nearly all the species adapt very easily, and provided that territorial instincts are respected, many different species can be kept together without difficulty.

The species tank for these beautiful fish should be very large: a minimum of 150 cm × 60 cm is needed. Many hiding places in cavities and crevasses must be provided: there must therefore be lots of arrangements of rock.

Some imagination is needed to plan this kind of lay out, preferably with no plants, and yet still make it look attractive. Big, rounded rocks should be used to build up the rock walls and other arrangements. Basalt blocks, marl stones or even lumps of lava can be used very effectively, but the lava will first have to be treated to remove any sharp edges.

The arrangements of rock can be brightened up by incorporating a few pieces of bogwood, but the contrast should not be too great: if it is, the overall effect is unnatural. For the same reason, bricks or other artificially regular stones should be avoided, unless they are used behind or underneath the pieces of natural rock to create extra hiding places. It is impossible to provide too many caves and crevasses.

77. *Pseudotropheus elongatus,* a Malawi Cichlid. Malawi Cichlids seek environments with big rounded rocks.

To simulate the natural environment as closely as possible, the arrangements of rock should really cover the whole of the bed right up to the front of the aquarium, but this is not possible because of the danger of the water spoiling as a result of the putrefaction of waste products amongst the stones. Even so, the strip of sand behind the front pane should be kept as narrow as practicable: just wide enough to make it possible for the dirt which collects there to be siphoned off.

It would be ideal if all the arrangements of rock were overgrown with algae and there were also some thick mosses on the bogwood, but the grazing instinct of the fish inhibits growth. If any plants are to be included they should be unusual ones not normally considered suitable for the conventional sized tanks, for example *Vallisneria gigantea,* a plant from New Guinea, related to *Vallisneria spiralis* (see systematic list of plants), but more delicate, as well as much larger than *V. spiralis.*

The aquarium should be filled with ordinary tap water, which is rarely too hard. The temperature should be 25°–27°C. The tank should be placed where it receives sunlight for a few hours a day: in the evening the overhead lighting should be subdued. A filter system with a large through-put should be installed to produce plenty of oxygen and ensure that the water is always crystal clear.

A SPECIES TANK FOR THE BLIND CAVE FISH

The Blind Cave Fish, *Anoptichthys jordani,* from Central America, is a very special fish. It does not have spectacular coloration or markings: it is colorless or a pale pink. It has however a unique evolutionary history and lifestyle. Some aquarists find it a particularly interesting fish to keep.

The Blind Cave Fish should not be kept in a community tank, because that environment is completely alien to it. It should be given a species tank which creates a miniature artificial cave. A small tank about 50 cm long is quite large enough for five or six specimens. A number of pieces of extruded polystyrene, in which large holes have been melted away with a soldering iron to leave fingers of polystyrene that look like stalagmites and stalactites, can be placed one behind the other to recreate a limestone cave, but plenty of swimming space should also be left.

Extruded polystyrene is extremely buoyant and should be clamped down under panes of glass. The bed should be covered with flat, chalky stones, marble chips, or even marble dust or coral sand. If the bed is completely flat it is easy to siphon off waste matter.

The aquarium should be filled with tap water: the temperature should be maintained at 18°–22°C. It is advisable to change the water regularly but not necessary to filter or aerate it. Obviously decorating the tank with plants, pieces of bogwood or stones, will detract from the special effect aimed for in this aquarium.

THE PALUDARIUM OR SHORE AQUARIUM

The sections above have shown that the natural environment of many fish is along the shores of lakes, rivers and creeks. These waters often run through the jungle – the rain forest – where the vegetation on the banks grows very tall with an almost unimaginable diversity and variety of beautiful colors. It is tempting to try to imitate this overwhelming work of nature in a home aquarium. This can be done in a paludarium or shore aquarium which is partly filled with water, water plants, bog plants and fish, and from which some dry land rises. This part can be built up using different materials including peat and bogwood, and it is also possible to incorporate many tropical plants: it is even possible to keep some small land creatures and amphibians in it. This is an extension of the aquarist's hobby on which it is not possible to dwell here, but an aspect which can be developed into an infinite variety of types by the interested amateur.

78. The Blind Cave Fish *(Anoptichthys jordani)* should be placed in a special tank with pieces of e.g. polystyrene, in which large holes have been melted away.

79. The Paludarium should be an imitation of the shores of tropical lakes, rivers and creeks. This implies very rich vegetation.

5.
DISEASES OF FISH
In Freshwater Aquaria

Discussions with aquarists show that a common problem is having to deal with the diseases of fish, without in the majority of cases, any professional assistance. The recognition and treatment of disease in aquarium fish should really be a matter for the veterinary surgeon, but in most countries a vet's training hardly touches on the subject. Thus the individual aquarist is forced to work on his own and to a large extent has to depend on remedies available in shops selling aquarium accessories and such places. Such remedies are usually unsatisfactory: in most cases the packet does not list all the ingredients in exact quantities and very often the remedy claims a quite impossible effectiveness against a multitude of diseases.

Aquarists who want something better will have to club together to obtain the basic equipment needed for the scientific examination of fish: this is the only way that the cause of the disease can be identified and the right treatment selected. Some scientific investigations will even then be beyond the resources of the amateur, but it is surprising how much can be done with a small amount of good but simple equipment. The cooperation of a practising veterinary surgeon will be essential: not only will he be able to help through his wide general knowledge of animal diseases and their treatments but there are some drugs that will only be obtainable through a vet.

1. How to Recognise a Diseased Fish

It is important that any disease in a fish be recognised as soon as possible: the longer a sick fish goes unnoticed, the less its chances of recovery. The aquarist should train himself to make regular and careful observations so that any change in behavior or appearance in the fish is immediately noted.

The first thing to consider is the behavior of the fish. If they are stationary, are they nevertheless, maintaining a proper balance in the water: on the other hand, are they sometimes tipping over, or floating or sinking to the bottom. Are the fins extended, or flattened against the body. Is the tail fin folded up. Are the swimming movements normal. Are some of the fish slower than the others of that species. Is any fish shying away from the rest. Of course, what is observed must then be related to the normal patterns of behavior for the species in question.

Respiration should be regular and gentle. When fish become anxious or unsettled, the movements of the gill covers (the *opercles*) become quicker and deeper. Such a change can have one of a variety of causes: it could be due to oxygen depletion, parasites on the gills or anaemia. If all the fish come to the surface then something very serious has happened and immediate action is needed: it will probably be because of severe oxygen depletion or poisoning.

Fish can sometimes be observed rubbing themselves against the sand lining the bottom of the tank, or against stones, plants or bogwood. That behavior may be because of some skin irritation caused, for example by parasites, though healthy fish may do this too. Attention should also be paid to feeding: never just place the food in the tank and walk away. The fish should always be watched to see if any are eating less than others or even nothing at all.

A watch should also be kept for possible physical changes in the body of the fish. Do they look well-fed, or have they become thinner? Are they excreting normally? Thinning fish often have a sunken belly (Fig. 89); a rounded belly may be an indication of proper feeding, but can also be due to ascites or peritonitis. Are the fish their normal color, or are they abnormally dark or pale? Are the fins in good condition or frayed? Is the epidermis colorless and transparent, or rather somewhat clouded and whitish? Some potential conditions may be subtle, but it is important to identify them in good time. Specks, dots or lumps can also signal certain diseases (Figs. 98 and 105). Deformations of the spinal column are sometimes caused by diseases such as tuberculosis and occasionally have other causes. Clouding of the outer tissue of the eye *(the cornea)*, often due to mechanical damage, must be distinguished from deeper clouding which is usually due to a lens condition. Generalised *oedema* produces a typical pathological picture in fish; a swollen abdomen *(ascites)*, bulging scales due to fluid accumulation in the skin and bilaterally bulging eyes caused by further fluid accumulations in the eye sockets.

2. The Examination of Diseased Tropical Fish

The symptoms, as they were described in the previous section, are seldom characteristic of a certain disease.

A whitish turbidity of the skin may have many causes, like *Costia necatrix*, *Ichthyophthirius multifiliis* (white spot), *Chilodonella cyprini*, *Trichodina* species, *Gyrodactylus* species and other parasites.

A white spot in the skin, often called 'fungus', is in fact almost never caused by fungi. This cannot be traced without closer investigation: drugs can only be applied on a guesswork basis.

Some basic equipment is needed for the scientific examination of fish: much of it can be obtained quite cheaply and most will be available from suppliers of medical and laboratory equipment. A few object glasses are needed (26 × 76mm), some cover slips (18 × 18 mm), a culture dish (6–8 cm in diameter depending on the size of the fish likely to be examined), and one or two watch glasses. A magnifying glass (×2 or ×3) is very useful. It is often necessary to anaesthetise fish and for that tricaine methane sulphonate (often referred to as MS 222) should be used: an acid solution of MS 222 should be neutralized by adding bicarbonate of soda in the proportion of two parts of bicarbonate of soda to one part of MS 222 (0.1 g MS 222: 0.2 g Bicarbonate of soda). Some dissecting instruments should also be obtained. Two lancet needles will be needed, a pair of fine scissors and two pairs of very fine tweezers. Those who can afford to do so would be well advised to buy also a pair of right-angled iris scissors and a pair of anatomical iris tweezers, but these are ophthalmic instruments and therefore of course relatively expensive.

Finally the most expensive but absolutely essential piece of equipment is the microscope. Many of the most important diseases cannot be diagnosed with any certainty without using a microscope because the pathogens cannot be seen without one. Unfortunately of course a good microscope is expensive and costs far too much for the ordinary amateur. It is so important for all amateur aquarists that every aquarist club should be encouraged to buy one which can then be used by its members: by that cooperative method the best equipment can be available to all serious aquarists.

When buying a microscope it is wisest to buy a basically simple model produced by a first class manufacturer with a reputation for the quality of his optical ware: any good optical dealer will be able to advise. The cheap microscopes that are sometimes offered to the public will be of little value. The microscope should have a lamp, a condenser (to concentrate the light brought to bear on the object), a mechanical stage (to focus the slide easily), objectives of magnification ×4, ×10 and ×40, and an eyepiece of magnification ×10. Those who feel they can spend more money will find a double eyepiece very useful but this is not essential.

The examination of live fish can be particularly important when the fish are expensive and kept in small numbers, such as discus fish, or where they are almost domestic pets. In such cases it is unacceptable to kill the fish for examination and accordingly microscopic examination will be limited to the investigation of the excreta and scrapings taken from the body surface and the gills. In the case

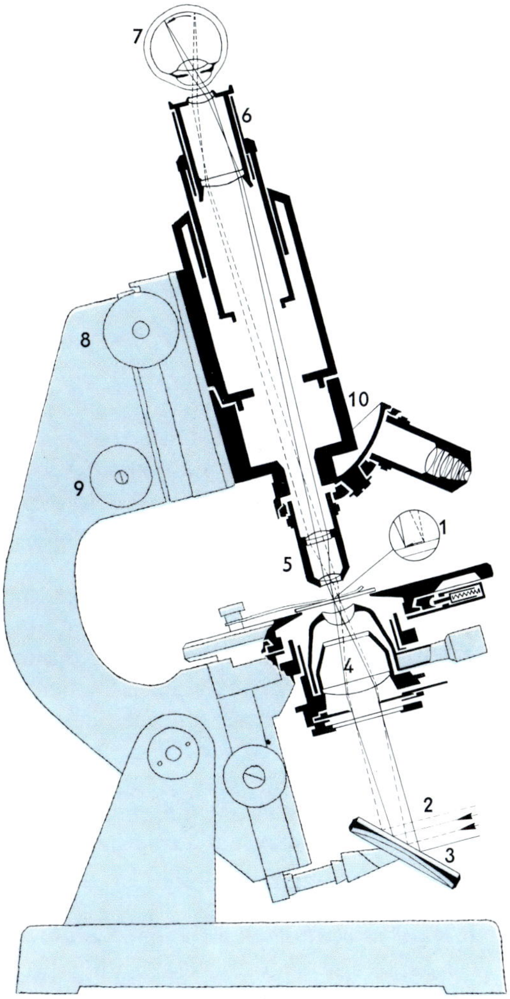

80. Only few diseases can be traced without a microscope. The working of a normal microscope is as follows: the specimen (1) is illuminated by a light source (2) with the aid of a mirror (3) and a condenser (4); the condenser system of lenses concentrates the light into a beam that illuminates the specimen. The objective lense (5) produces a magnified image of the specimen, which is viewed through the eyepiece lense (6) and is further magnified. On the retina (7) of the observer's eye the image of the object appears.
Many microscopes have three or four interchangeable objectives mounted side by side in a nosepiece (10) that can be rotated to bring each objective into service as required. The distance between the eyepiece and objective is varied by adjusting knobs to move the lenses together or apart. A microscope usually has a coarse adjustment knob (8) to produce an image that is almost in focus, and then the fine adjuster (9) is turned to give a sharp picture.

of obtaining fresh droppings of a diseased fish, the droppings are prepared as what is called a wet mount preparation: a small quantity of excreta is placed on an object glass, mixed with a very small drop of clean water, covered with a cover slip and then examined under the microscope at increasingly higher magnifications. Look out for worms, worm eggs (e.g. *Capillaria* eggs) and *Hexamita* or other flagellates.

To take skin or gill scrapings the fish must first be placed in a small separate tank. They are then examined under a strong light (such as a desk lamp) for symptoms such as fine brownish spots (Velvet disease), white patches (Fig. 98) or stained spots in the skin; the magnifying glass should be used. The fish is then anaesthetised by dissolving MS 222 (100 mg/l) and bicarbonate of soda (200 mg/l) in the tank at the same time. Wait until the fish has lost its balance and ceased to move, but is still breathing. It is then placed on an object glass as shown in Fig. 81. Larger fish are laid in a glass culture dish or on a damp cloth. With the fish held carefully behind the head, a cover glass is scraped over the skin towards the tail. From the material collected this way – skin cells, mucus and possibly parasites – a wet mount preparation is made up. If some peculiarity on the skin has already been observed scrapings of these particular areas should be taken.

In reasonably-sized fish the opercle can be lifted and a gill scraping taken using the point of a lancet needle. When doing this it is important to check the condition of the gills. Normal gills are a bright red; affected gills are faded and look rather frayed. Pale gills may indicate anaemia. The gill scrapings are also made into a wet mount preparation. Once the scrapings have been obtained the fish should be returned to a tank containing fresh water, kept in circulation with an air-pump.

These gill and skin-scrapings should then be examined under the microscope. The aquarist should look for fungus filaments (Fig. 112), Monogenea (Fig. 107), ciliates (Fig. 100, 101, 102), flagellates (Fig. 94, 95), gliding bacteria and *Pseudomonas* and *Aeromonas*. A surprising number of diseases can be definitively identified in this way.

When the investigation of the live diseased fish is not conclusive it may be best to kill the specimen to examine it further. This is usually necessary when the remaining fish are seriously threatened. There is rarely any point in examining fish found floating dead in the tank. Tissue breakdown after death is very rapid in fish: the gills become quite pale after 10–15 minutes and external parasites disappear very rapidly.

The fish to be dissected is first deeply anaesthetised by dissolving a double dose of MS 222 and bicarbonate of soda in its tank. When respiration has ceased it is transferred into a culture dish, together with an adequate amount of anaesthetic fluid. The left opercle can then be cut away and the skin and gills are studied using the same procedures as with a live fish. When the fish is very small a few gill clippings are used for the microscopic investigation rather than scrapings.

The fish is than laid on a piece of wet blotting paper and the left abdominal wall cut away. Starting at the anal orifice, the first cut is made forwards along the underside of the belly. Clear oedemic fluid may be discharged. Care should be taken not to damage the intestine during cutting or its contents may contaminate the abdominal cavity. The next cut is from the anus upwards and gradually left, following the edge of the abdominal cavity. Finally the abdominal wall behind the gills is removed, and the fish is replaced in the glass culture dish.

The organs and tissues can now be examined in detail with a magnifying glass. Sometimes large quantities of white spawn are found in the abdominal cavity (Fig. 82). If sexually mature females do not discharge their spawn, the cells die and become white.

Fish with tuberculosis sometimes have enlarged, pale organs with grey-white lumps up to the size of a pin-head.

The spleen should then be examined (Fig. 83): this is a small organ and is usually concealed between others. It can be recognised by its bright red color. The spleen (or part of it) is compressed between an object glass and a cover slip and the edges of the tissue are examined under the microscope. Under powerful magnification (× 400) flagellates or motile bacteria may be seen. The spleen must not be

81. Taking a skin scraping from a Cardinal Tetra *(Cheirodon axelrodi)*.

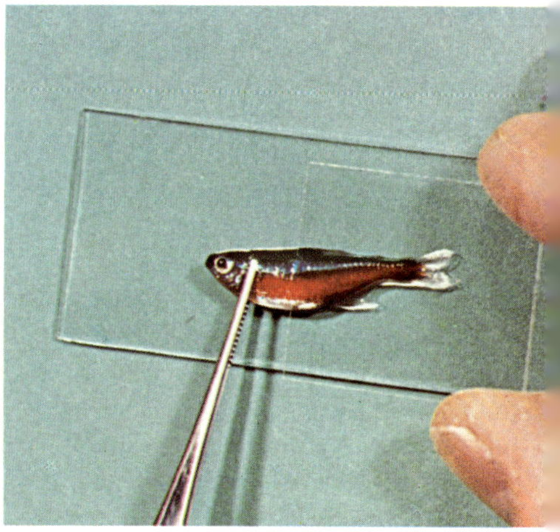

82. Necrotic ova in the abdominal cavity of a Cardinal Tetra *(Cheirodon axelrodi)*.

contaminated with feces when the abdomen is being cut open; if it is, it may be found to 'contain' bacteria when a bacterial infection is actually out of the question. Fattening or degeneration of the liver changes the color of the organ from red-brown to a pale-brown or yellow. A squash preparation of fatty liver reveals masses of fat seen as translucent fat globules. This fattening can occur either as a result of damage to the liver or because of mistakes in feeding. Parasites may also be found in squash preparations (Fig. 109).

The intestine is cut open longitudinally. It should be scrutinized under the microscope for worms, worm eggs (e.g. *Capillaria* eggs), and *Hexamita* (Fig. 96) or other flagellates.

If a fish is to be killed without further examination, it can simply be transferred to a vessel containing aquarium water at normal temperature, which is then placed in the freezing compartment of a refrigerator. The fish will be frozen stiff and die painlessly.

83. The position of some organs and tissues in a Sumatra Barb, *Barbus tetrazona*. The opercle and the abdominal wall have been removed. To expose the spleen, a small part of the liver has been cut away.

3. Virus Diseases

Very little is known about virus diseases in ornamental tropical fish. Only one virus disease is definitely known to occur in fresh-water aquariums.

3a. LYMPHOCYSTIS DISEASE

This disease is caused by a large virus which penetrates the cytoplasm of the body cells of the fish, usually interstitial cells. The infected cells start to grow, often to quite gigantic proportions (Fig. 84). Accumulation of these giant cells produces the typical pathological picture of lumpy growths, mostly on the fins in aquarium fish (Fig. 85). These growths or tumors are due to the expansion of individual cells and not to cell replication: this is a unique feature of lymphocystis disease. It does not occur very often in fresh-water aquariums and then in only a small percentage of fish. No effective treatment is known. It is best to keep the infected fish away from the rest. Spontaneous remission sometimes occurs after several months of illness.

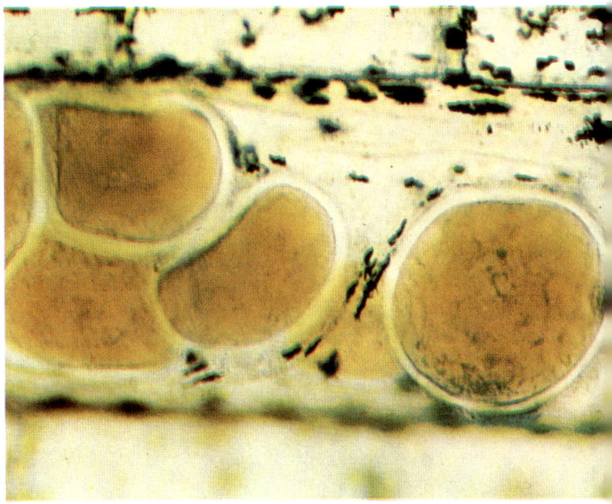

84. Lymphocystis cells in a fin, magnification × 120.

4. Bacterial Diseases

Bacterial diseases in tropical fish are still little understood. Three groups of bacteria however have been identified as giving rise to fish diseases: the rectilinear motile water bacteria (*Pseudomonas* and *Aeromonas*), the gliding bacteria (*Flexibacter*) and the acid-fast bacteria (*Mycobacterium* and *Nocardia*). These bacteria are explained more fully in the sections that follow.

4a. BACTERIAL INFECTIONS DUE TO MOTILE PSEUDOMONAS AND AEROMONAS SPECIES

Pseudomonas and *Aeromonas* species have frequently been described in cold water fish, but little is known about them in relation to tropical fish. They are generally rod-shaped and move in straight lines using one or more whip-like flagella present at the ends of the cell. They are pre-eminently water bacteria which can survive in the absence of fish, and are regarded as 'opportunistic pathogens', that is they can only cause external or internal infections in fish when certain particular conditions arise, although what these conditions are, is not yet fully understood. Even specialists in the field find it difficult to decide whether they are the primary cause of some conditions or whether they appear later, after some disease caused by something else, has already taken hold.

85. Crosby *(Trichogaster crosby)* with lymphocystis disease. Specimen fixed in 4% formalin.

The important point for the amateur to grasp is that under powerful magnification (at least ×400) the majority of these bacteria can be recognized by their type of movement. They always swim in a straight line, and usually shoot across the field of vision at speed. The genera *Pseudomonas* and *Aeromonas* cannot be distinguished by their movements. In cases of external infection these species may be found in scrapings from the skin or open wounds (ulcers). In cases of internal infection (septicaemia – blood poisoning) it is very important to make a squash preparation of the spleen and examine the edge of the tissue under the microscope. The bacteria will then be plainly visible.

Certain antibiotics are effective against *Pseudomonas* and *Aeromonas:* but these can only usually be obtained through a vet. *Pseudomonas* are unfortunately insensitive to some widely used antibiotics and there is little point in using special antibiotics until the role of the *Pseudomonas* is better understood. Antibiotics which are useful against *Aeromonas* include the tetracyclins such as tetracycline or oxytetracycline hydrochlorids and also chloramphenicol and neomycin sulphate. For external infections 20–30 mg/1 over 2 × 24 hours is sufficient. Internal infections are more difficult. If the fish will still take food, tetracyclin compounds can be given via the food: 100 mg/20g food over 5 days. For further details of this method see section 10. If the fish has stopped eating, chloramphenicol, 100 mg/1 over 2 × 24 hours can be tried; a sufficient amount may be picked up from the water.

4b. INFECTIONS CAUSED BY 'GLIDING' BACTERIA

Various species of 'gliding' bacteria of the order *Cytophagales* (Leadbetter, 1974) can cause disease in fish. These are long, thin, flexible bacteria which can glide over a surface without having flagella. They can usually be recognised in scrapings by their flexing movements. In general one end of the bacterial cell is attached to the tissue of the fish, and the free end sways backwards and forwards in the water. Sometimes several bacterial cells join together to form spherical mounds which resemble a ball of living tubifex in water.

Columnaris disease and mouth 'fungus' in aquarium fish are caused by these bacteria.

4c. COLUMNARIS DISEASE

Columnaris disease is caused by the bacterium *Flexibacter columnaris* (Leadbetter, 1974). It is one of the foremost infectious diseases of wild and domesticated cold-water fish in North America; in Europe it is still relatively unknown. The disease can cause heavy mortality amongst ornamental tropical fish.

The pathological picture is usually characterised by a localized or more general attack on the skin of the fish. In the later stages the subcutaneous muscle fibres may also be affected.

The disease can be recognised in the live bearing *Poeciliinae* by the pale areas of white to yellowish skin under the dorsal fin and on the caudal peduncle (Fig. 86). In these fish the disease takes an acute form, progresses quickly and there is significant mortality within a few days.

Columnaris disease sometimes occurs in goldfish. In this case the disease progresses more slowly (subacute to chronic); ulcers usually appear (Fig. 87). Mixed infections of *Flexibacter columnaris* and *Aeromonas salmonicida* may sometimes occur.

Is it possible to establish whether a fish is definitely suffering from columnaris disease or not? In principle this can only be done by making a culture of the pathogen and then studying it in more detail. For the amateur it is enough to take a scraping of the affected area and to examine the preparation under the microscope. This requires powerful magnification (about × 400) and strong contrast (achieved by turning the condenser down). The presence of a large number of bacteria, as described in section 4b indicates columnaris disease.

Various antibiotics and chemicals can be used for treating the condition: these are only obtainable through a vet.

Nifurpirinol is very effective against most strains of *F.columnaris* (Bootsma and Clerx, 1976). The fish may be bathed for a few hours in a solution of 1 mg per liter of water, or 0.25 mg/l solution can be added to the aquarium water. A southeast Asian strain of *F.columnaris* appeared to be resistant to this. (Bootsma and van Klingeren, unpublished results). The tetracyclin group of antibiotics, 25 mg/1 over 2 × 24 hours, has an inhibiting effect on *F.columnaris*. Benzylpenicillin sodium has been effective in resistant cases to date. 10,000–20,000 I.U. (International Units) per liter of water are given; the water should then be changed every 24 hours until a cure is achieved. In view of the risk to humans, penicillin should only be used as a last resort. Acriflavine hydrochloride, 5–10 mg/l over 2 × 24 hours (Fijan

86. Columnaris disease in a guppy *(Lebistes reticulatus)*. Yellowish discoloration of the peduncle.

87. Goldfish *(Carassius auratus auratus* L.*)* with columnaris disease.

and Voorhees, 1969) and 2-phenoxyethanol, 100 mg/l (van Duijn, 1973) can also be tried.

88. Mouth 'fungus' in a Firemouth *(Cichlasoma meeki)*.

4d. MOUTH 'FUNGUS'

Mouth infections may have many causes. One such infection, mistakenly labelled 'fungus' produces swollen and grey-white to yellowish lips. In serious cases the mouth cannot be closed; this interferes with respiration and prevents the fish from eating (Fig. 88). The condition is infectious and many fish may be affected in a single tank.

This 'fungus' is not caused by a real fungus but by the gliding bacterium *Flexibacter columnaris* (Davis, 1967). It can be countered using 2-phenoxyethanol: 100 mg/l over 2–3 days (van Duijn, 1973). Diseased cichlids (one is shown in Fig. 88) were cured by this. Nifurpirinol 1 mg/l applied for two hours can also be used. For further information see section 4c.

4e. FURUNCULOSIS

Furunculosis has been known since 1894 as a major disease of the salmon family Salmonidae. It also occurs in other types of cold-water fish, in the goldfish (Mawdesley-Thomas, 1969) and has also been described in ornamental tropical fish (Axelrod, 1962). The pathogen is the bacterium *Aeromonas salmonicida:* small, round to rod-shaped, and non-motile. The symptoms in affected goldfish are quite variable. Generally speaking superficial inflammatory processes are seen in various parts of the body: these gradually expand and lead to the formation of ulcers. Deeper-lying and generally red-colored foci of infection also occur. The disease usually lasts a few weeks (subacute to chronic). In order to arrive at the correct diagnosis the bacterium must be cultured and investigated in detail, but this is an operation beyond the resources of the amateur. The non-motile bacterium can not be recognized in tissue scrapings on account of its small size.

Furunculosis can be combated with certain antibiotics: these can only be obtained through a vet. The tetracycline group seems particularly valuable, though adding them to the water usually produces only temporary improvement: it is better to administer them in the food, at least while the fish is still eating. 0.2–0.5 gms. of tetracycline hydrochloride (depending on appetite) are given per 100 gms. of food: this is continued for many weeks. Large fish can be injected with tetracycline compounds: a fish weighing 10 gms. should receive 1/2 mg (50 mg/kg body weight) every other day. For details of administering drugs via the food and by injection see section 10.

4f. TUBERCULOSIS

Tuberculosis is one of the most important infectious diseases of ornamental tropical fish. Tuberculosis is typically a disease of the confined space of the aquarium. How tuberculosis bacteria first reach the aquarium and the fish is still unknown. Fish tuberculosis is caused by bacteria of the genus *Mycobacterium*. Especially *Mycobacterium marinum* and species of the *M.fortuitum* complex are very harmful to aquarium fishes. These bacteria are rod-shaped and non-motile. Some strains cannot reproduce at 37°C, so that only cold-blooded fish can become infected. *M.marinum* and the *M.fortuitum* complex can occasionally give rise to transitory, superficial infections of cuts on the hands or forearms of aquarists.

In principle there are various ways a fish may become infected: by contact with other fish with 'open' tuberculosis; by taking up bacteria from the water via the skin or gills; and by swallowing contaminated food and water or eating diseased or dead companions. The actual method is not known. Both the latter routes are probably involved, though tuberculosis of the gastrointestinal tract does not occur very often. In live-bearing species an infected female can pass the disease on before giving birth.

Once the bacteria have penetrated the body they can spread to any organ or tissue: they then reproduce locally. The body of the fish reacts by forming large, epithelium like cells, which absorb the bacteria (phagocytosis). These cells are mostly grouped together; they become more and more numerous, and form small nodules. In later stages these nodules become encapsulated in connective tissue, and necrosis (tissue breakdown) begins at their centre. Yellow-brown pigment may also accumulate in older nodules. These processes develop very slowly and can sometimes take weeks or months. In the end the original organs and tissues may be largely replaced by infected tubercular tissue.

The symptoms shown by sick fish may be quite varied. If the internal organs such as the liver, spleen and kidneys are affected these will include poor appetite, emaciation and a hollow belly (Fig. 89). The fish become slow, solitary and finally die. Generalised oedema expressed as abdominal dropsy, scale protrusion and bulging eyes (exophthalmus) on both sides (Fig. 115) may be seen occasionally. Peritonitis (inflammation of the abdominal lining) can occur as a complication and also causes a swollen abdomen. Occasionally there is distortion of the spinal column.

More localised disturbances also occur. A tuberculous process in or behind the eye often leads to the eye becoming swollen and starting to bulge outwards. Inflamed nodules in the muscles cause light brown patches which can break out at the surface: this is known as 'open' tuberculosis with mycobacteria continuously released into the water. An "open belly" may be left once a tuberculous process in the abdominal wall has broken open (Fig. 90). The inflammatory process may also penetrate the muscle tissues from outside the body (Fig. 91).

How can tuberculosis be diagnosed in fish with reasonable certainty? The symptoms of the sick fish may give a general indication. Dissection of a dead specimen may reveal pale, enlarged organs containing grey-white nodules the size of a pin-head or less. Only the older nodules will be clearly visible in a squash preparation of diseased tissue or organs. This will reveal a poorly delimited capsule of connective tissue sometimes surrounding accumulations of yellow-brown or darker pigments. All these details are indicative, but do not guarantee complete certainty. In order to reach a definitive diagnosis it is necessary to demonstrate the presence of *mycobacteria* in the tuberculous tissue. This can be done with the Ziehl-Neelsen stain. *Mycobacterium* species; to a lesser extent *Nocardia* species are stained red. (Fig. 92).

Control of tuberculosis is still a major problem. It is difficult to prevent the disease breaking out because it is not known how the aquarium becomes infected. Newly-purchased fish can introduce the disease, but a quarantine period of 2–3 weeks is too short to reveal a latent infection. Up to the present time treatment of diseased fish has proved very difficult. The *Mycobacterium* strains isolated from ornamental tropical fish are highly resistant to many antitubercular drugs (Engel et al. current research). When tuberculosis is definitely diagnosed in a fish it is best handled as follows. First, all diseased or weak fish should be killed and the density of fish in the aquarium reduced to a low level, say 1 g fish / 5–10 liters of water. The bottom should be carefully cleaned each day, and dead fish removed immediately. The resistance of the individual fish should be increased as far as possible by feeding them several times (3–5) a day with small quantities of varied high-quality food. These methods are sometimes successful in gradually forcing down the mortality rate. If they do not work it may be better to start afresh, killing all the fish and throwing the plants away. The sand, stones, wood and other aquarium objects should be decontaminated in boiling water: at least 15 minutes at 100°C. The tank itself and its various accessories should be washed with soap, rinsed with water and then disinfected with a solution of O-Benzyl-p-chlorophenol and O-Phenylphenol in water (1 : 100). Plastic or rubber gloves should be worn when handling this substance. The tank should be filled to the brim and left for a few hours while it takes effect. Finally all the items should be rinsed thoroughly under running water for several days.

A disease similar to tuberculosis was described by Conroy (1963) in neon tetra *(Hyphessobrycon innesi)* in Argentina. Diseased fish became highly emaciated. In some cases the colors in the dorsal fin region became paler; many fish developed ulcers. Later on it appeared that this disease was caused by *Nocardia asteroides*; this bacterium, like the tuberculosis pathogen, is acid-fast. It is therefore possible to confuse the two conditions, but nocardiosis probably occurs much less frequently than tuberculosis.

89. Variegated Platy *(Xiphophorus variatus)* extremely emaciated, with tuberculous inflammation in the muscles.

90. Perforation of the abdominal wall of a Variegated Platy *(Xiphophorus variatus)* caused by the eruption of a tuberculous process.

91. Purple-headed barb *(Barbus nigrofasciatus)* with superficial tuberculous inflammation.

92. Material scraped from a tuberculous skin ulcer, Ziehl-Neelsen stain. Magnification × 1200.

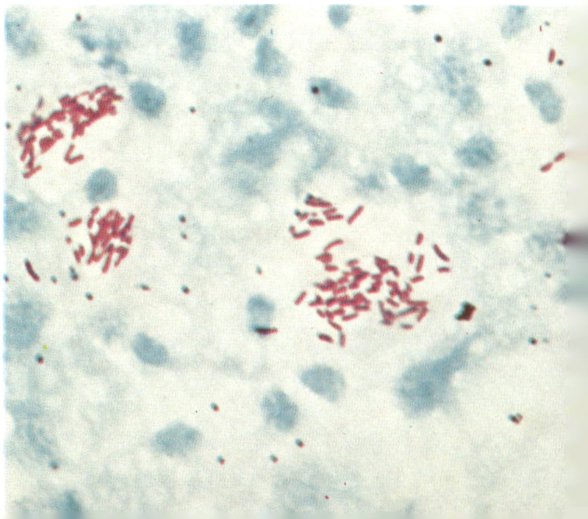

5. Diseases Caused by Unicellular Organisms (Protozoa)

5a. FLAGELLATES

Many flagellates cause diseases in fishes: these include those members of the order *Dinoflagellata* which are responsible for Velvet and coral fish disease. Other species are also parasitic on the skin and gills, or cause internal diseases.

5b. VELVET DISEASE: PLANT OR ANIMAL?

Velvet disease is caused by *Oödinium limneticum* (Jacobs, 1946) or *Oödinium pillularis* (Schäperclaus, 1951). Both species are members of the order Dinoflagellata. They are closely related to *Oödinium ocellatum* which is responsible for coral fish disease in marine aquaria.

Dinoflagellates are unicellular and move with the aid of two flagella. One flagellum lies in a transverse groove; the other is attached at the back of the cell and hangs free in the water. (Fig. 93, stage 8). Many species of Dinoflagellata also have chloroplasts and could be described as free-swimming unicellular plants. They live in the sunlight and are common amongst plankton.

One well-known Dinoflagellate is *Noctiluca scintillans:* it is this species which produces the light seen in the sea off Holland. Other species can reproduce on a massive scale in a short time and cause the so-called 'red tide'.

The pathogens of Velvet and Coralfish disease are different because the usual free-swimming shape (dinospore) attaches itself to the skin and gills of a fish and then changes shape. Both flagella disappear; newly formed root-like extensions (pseudopodia, rhizoids) penetrate the epidermis or the epithelial cells of the gill lamellae. The young parasite (trophont, Fig. 93 stage 9) feeds on the body of the fish and grows up into the adult stage. The fully developed parasite releases itself from its host and encysts; within this cyst further cell replication takes place (Fig. 93 stage 3 and 4). This gives rise to 32–64 *(O.pillularis)* or 256 *(O.limneticum)* young, free-swimming dinospores (Fig. 93, stage 8). In *O.pillularis* the dinospore has a red eye spot (ocellus); this is absent in *O.limneticum.*

How can a fish with Velvet disease be recognised? The spots on the body are much smaller than with White Spot disease, barely visible with the naked eye. A strong light is needed to show them up: at a certain angle of incidence the fish looks as though it has been powdered with brownish spots. A definitive diagnosis can only be achieved with the aid of a microscope. If a small section of affected fin is cut off and examined under magnification it can be seen that each 'spot' is in fact a small group of parasites (trophontes) (Fig. 94). A skin-scraping will reveal individual parasites: non-motile, pearshaped cells with yellowish-brown grains, maximum length 50–70 μm with a pale contrasting nucleus. The difference between *O.limneticum* and *O.pillularis* does not include the parasitic stage: it is not possible to decide from a microscopic investigation of the fish which of the two is responsible. Counter-measures are not simple. In recent years studies have shown that it is best to bathe affected fish in a solution of synthetic sea-salt (rock-salt) $^1/_2\%$ (5 g/l) for $1-2 \times 24$ hours. A certain amount of caution is necessary since some species tolerate a salt bath better than others. The fish should therefore be watched during this procedure; shorten it if it seems to be distressed.

5c. OÖDINIOIDES VASTATOR: A NEW PARASITIC DINOFLAGELLATE?

Research has been in progress on this unicellar organism since 1965. Up to now the results of this research have not yet been confirmed. For further information the reader is referred to a publication of Reichenbach-Klinke (1970).

5d. MOTILE FLAGELLATES ON THE SKIN AND GILLS

The most dangerous member of this group is *Costia necatrix:* in hatcheries this parasite can cause deaths amongst fry on a massive scale. It is by no means unknown in aquariums. Seen from above the body is oval or bean-shaped (Fig. 95); it is about 10 μm long and 5 μm across. The upper and lower sides are flattened, and there is an obliquely longitudinal groove on the underside. The species has two short and two long flagella.

93. Life-cycle of *Oodinium limneticum,* shortened, after Jacobs (1946). *1.* Young parasite or trophont, 60 hours after attaching itself to the skin of the fish.
3. *O.limneticum* after separating from the fish.
4. End of the first division.
6. Final division.
8. Free swimming dinospore.
9. Transition to the parasitic stage immediately after attaching to the skin of a fish.

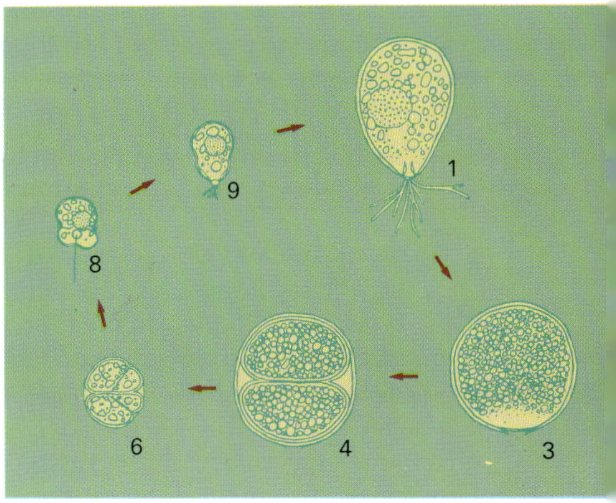

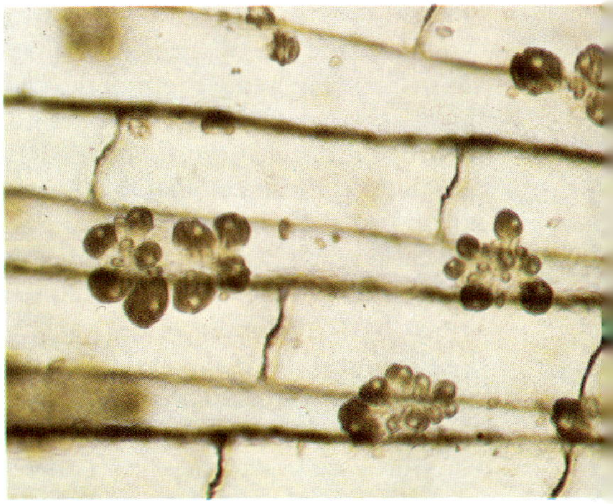

94. *Oodinium* species on the caudal fin of a young Sumatra Barb (Barbus tetrazona tetrazona), magnification × 120. Fish fixed in 4% formalin.

Costia necatrix moves freely over the surface of the skin and gills but can also attach itself firmly by means of a pseudo-sucker on the underside of the cell. There is no typical pathological picture: the changes are similar to those caused by other dangerous external parasites such as *Chilodonella cyprini*. Noticeable features in *Costia necatrix* infections are mainly the proliferation of skin cells and the increased secretion of mucus. The skin thickens and takes on a whitish tinge. Parasites can only be recognised in skin or gill scrapings under powerful magnification (at least ×400).

Other flagellates apart from *Costia necatrix* can also be parasitic on fish: in cold water fish these include *Cryptobia agitata* and *Cryptobia branchialis* (Bykhovskaya – Pavlovskaya, et al. 1964). These parasites are oblong in shape and have two flagella at the cell extremities. *Cryptobia agitata* is only 4.6–7.7 μm long and 3.2–4.6 μm across. Other unidentified flagellates can also occur as pathogens on ornamental tropical fish. It is not feasible to investigate them further in a skin scraping. Only very small and extremely mobile cellules are seen.

External flagellates in fishes can be countered by adding acriflavine hydrochloride (5–10 mg/l) or ethacridine lactate (2 mg/l) to the tank water. In view of the possibility of damage to aquatic plants it is best to apply this treatment in a separate tank. The fish should be left in the solution for two periods of twenty-four hours.

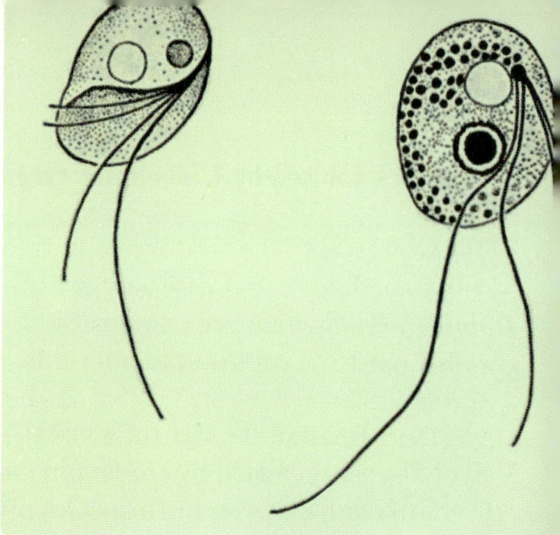

95. *Costia necatrix*, left, seen from below. There is a large clear vacuole next to the nucleus. After Davis (1967).

5e. INTERNAL DISEASES DUE TO HEXAMITA, OCTOMITUS AND SPIRONUCLEUS

The genera named above are all members of the Diplomonadina. They are bilaterally symmetrical organisms: important subsections (organelles) of the organism are duplicated. Those species described as pathogenic to ornamental tropical fishes include *Octomitus intestinalis truttae* (Schäperclaus, 1954), *Octomitus symphysodoni* (Amlacher, 1961), *Spironucleus elegans* (Kulda and Lom, 1964) and *Hexamita (Octomitus)* species (Herkner, 1969). The nomenclature of these species is rather confusing and sometimes based on incomplete data. The names *Hexamita* and *Octomitus* are sometimes interchanged.

A parasite can be recognised as belonging to the group by its general characteristics. The body of the cell is oval to pear-shaped or more elongate (Fig. 96). There are two nuclei and 2×3 flagella on the front of body. Two long fine fibres (axostyles) run back through the length of the cell to form two long flagella at the rear.

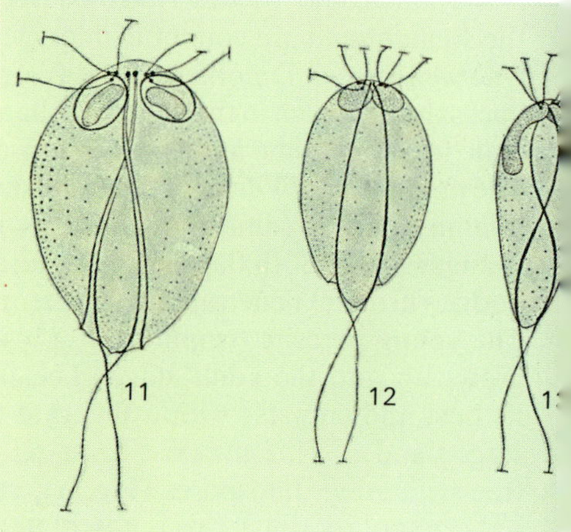

96. *Hexamita salmonis* (11), *Hexamita intestinalis* (12) and *Spironucleus elegans* (13). After Kulda & Lom (1964).

Hexamita species cause serious internal infections in ornamental tropical fish: Cichlidae are particularly sensitive to these. The parasites may be found in the intestine, gall-bladder, liver and blood of diseased specimens. The feces are generally mucus-like and pale in color. More generalised symptoms such as a lack of appetite and emaciation are also seen. In angelfish *(Pterophyllum scalare) Spironucleus elegans* is only found in the intestine (Kulda and Lom, 1964), and the fish did not become obviously ill. This parasite can pass on to fish from amphibians.

Herkner (1969, 1970) has associated *Hexamita* species with 'ulcer-disease' in discus fish (the *Symphysodon* species) and in the angelfish, *Pterophyllum scalare*. Accumulations of *Hexamita* build up under the skin and in the muscular tissues of infected fish. Localised tissue breakdown may occur. When the skin breaks open a whitish, worm-shaped plug of decayed tissue is discharged, creating a hole. In the later stages whole areas of skin may be undermined creating large open sores.

Hexamita, Octomitus or *Spironucleus* infections can be confirmed by microscopical examination of the feces, the contents of the intestine, gall-bladder or (if the parasite is in the blood) of a squash preparation of spleen. In ulcer disease the parasite can also be found in the subcutaneous decay zones. *Hexamita* remains detectable for a short period after the skin breaks open but then disappears (Herkner, 1970). Powerful magnification (×400) and strong contrast are required for these examinations: the microscope condenser should be turned down.

The treatments available for dealing with these parasites have improved substantially since the application of dimetridazole against *Hexamita* in trout (Ghittino, 1967). The drug was given in food: this route is at best difficult in aquarium fish, and obviously quite useless if they refuse to eat: dimetridazole is also effective when added to the tank water. The dose for 40% dimetridazole is 100 mg/l over 2×24 hours.

5f. CRYPTOBIA SPECIES AND OTHER BODONIDAE

Flagellates of the Bodonidae family are small, colorless, and oval to oblong in shape. They have two flagella, one pointing forwards and one backwards. The flagellum which points backwards may be attached to the surface of the cell for a certain part of its length. Fixed and stained preparations show in addition to the nucleus a superficial structure in the cell: this is the kinetoplast (Fig. 97).

The *Cryptobia* are known to be blood parasites of cold-water fish: they can also occur in ornamental tropical fish. Affected fish usually suffer from anaemia, associated with pale gills. They may become slow and anoxious, and succumb to the disease. The parasites can be located in a squash preparation of spleen under powerful magnification (× 400). Examination of the edges of such spleen tissue will show extremely small cells moving about very vigorously.

Other genera of the Bodonidae family may also occur in tropical fish: enormous numbers of a yet undetermined genus were found in the intestine of *Pelmatochromis subocellatus* (Fig. 97). The intestinal wall became highly inflamed and attached to organs nearby (peritonitis). The belly was swollen and there was considerable mortality.

These parasites can often be successfully combated using dimetridazole.

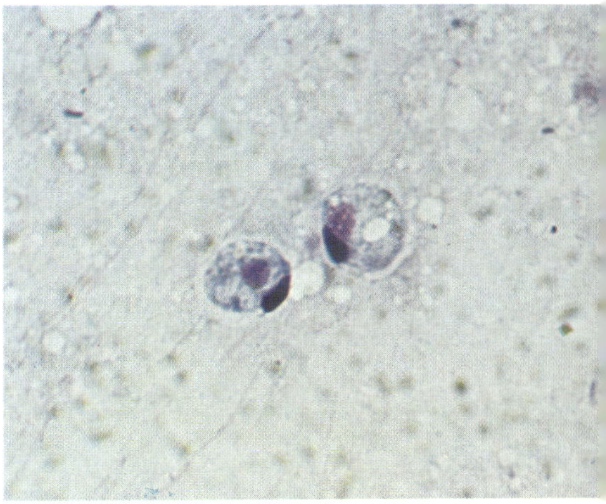

97. Undetermined flagellate from the intestine of a cichlid *(Pelmatochromis subocellatus)*. Preparation fixed and stained (Giemsa), magnification × 1200. Purple kinetoplast next to the red nucleus.

5g. CILIOPHORA

Ciliophora are unicellular organisms *(Protozoa)* possessing fine thread-like structures (cilia) for at least one phase of their life-cycle. These cilia enable the cell to move forward smoothly rather than with the jerky motions of flagellates.

Many fish pathogens are *Ciliophora:* almost all are parasitic on the skin or gills, with only the agent of white-spot disease parasitic in the skin.

98. Cardinal Tetra *(Cheirodon axelrodi)* with white spot disease.

5h. WHITE SPOT DISEASE

This is perhaps the best known disease of aquarium fish. It is caused by the ciliate *Ichthyophthirius multifiliis*. Literally translated, this name means 'the fish-destroyer with many sons': 'fish-destroyer' because of the damage it causes to the skin and gills, 'many sons' because of the large number of new parasites created by repeated cell-division during the reproductive stage (cyst).

To understand how a fish becomes infected and how the disease can be combated it is necessary to know something of various stages in the life of *I.multifiliis*. The mature parasite in the skin of the fish (Fig. 99, stage 1) is generally round, though the shape may alter since the cell body is easily deformed. It is 0.2 or 0.3–0.5 mm in size. The whole of the body is covered with longitudinal lines of fine hairs (cilia); at this stage these provide a continuous rotating movement. There is also a conspicuous horse-shoe shaped nucleus (macronucleus). In its younger stages in the skin of the fish the nucleus is oval or bean-shaped. In the cell body outside the nucleus (the cytoplasm) lie many small bubbles (vacuoles). These contain food-stuffs taken from the fish and make the parasite appear grainy and rather dark; the nucleus contrasts as a pale body.

The parasite is found in the epidermis of the infected fish in a cavity covered over with epidermal cells. Parasites and proliferated epidermal cells together form the white spot (Fig. 99, stage 1) which can be seen with the naked eye (Fig. 98). Diagnosis is simple at this stage. Rotating parasites are found in skin scrapings; larger specimens have a horse-shoe shaped nucleus (Fig. 100).

When *I. multifiliis* matures, it breaks out through the wall of the cavity, leaves the fish and swims about for a brief period. (Fig. 99, stage 2). Within an hour it settles, perhaps on a plant or stone, and then encysts (Fig. 99, stage 3). The cell then divides within the cyst. 11–12 divisions occur in tropical aquariums, generating 1000–2000 daughter cells (ciliospores) in the space of twenty-four hours. Each is 15–20 μm long (Wagner, 1960). The ciliospores break out through the cyst and swim about freely in the water. They have a rather extended shape with an elongated point (Fig. 99, stage 4). If they reach a fish they burrow into the epidermis and then assume the round shape. The reaction of the fish is to grow more epidermal cells. The parasite feeds on skin and at 25°C will attain the adult stage in about four days (Wagner, 1960).

In the gills *I. multifiliis* is not usually overgrown with fish cells (Hines and Spira, 1974), but immature and mature stages both create so much irritation that cell growth and overproduction of mucus result. Infected fish may therefore become anoxious and this is reflected by deeper and quicker movements of the gill-covers.

How can a fish with White spot disease be cured? Parasites in the skin (Fig. 99, stage 1) and the stage of cell division in the cyst are not directly vulnerable to drugs. Mature parasites, however, will always leave the fish, and the free swimming stages can be killed (Fig. 99, stages 2 and 4) by adding drugs to the water. Those parasites already present in the skin will gradually mature and leave, but the fish cannot become reinfected. It may take several days before any results are seen, and the drug may have to be added to the water every three to four days until a complete cure is achieved.

Which drugs are effective against the free-swimming stages of *I. multifiliis?* Quinine salts (quinine hydrochloride, quinine sulphate) are particularly efficacious: the dose level is 10 mg per liter of aquarium water. Quinine however has several disadvantages: it is expensive, and the aquarium plants may not be able to withstand it so well. Then there is malachite green oxalate. This is a highly poisonous stain, and 0.05 mg/l is the maximum dose. Such tiny quantities are very difficult to weigh, so it is better to start by dissolving 10 mg in 100 ml of distilled water (or 100 mg in 1 liter) and then use 0.5 ml of this solution per litre of aquarium water. Methylene blue, medicinal grade 2–4 mg/l is equally effective, and is very safe to use. Overdoses are not immediately dangerous, but the blue colour they produce may make the fish practically invisible in the water. Aquatic plants may not be so resistant to it.

Chloramine-T is sometimes used with good results. The presence of large amounts of organic matter (fish droppings, food remains, dead plants) in the tank soon

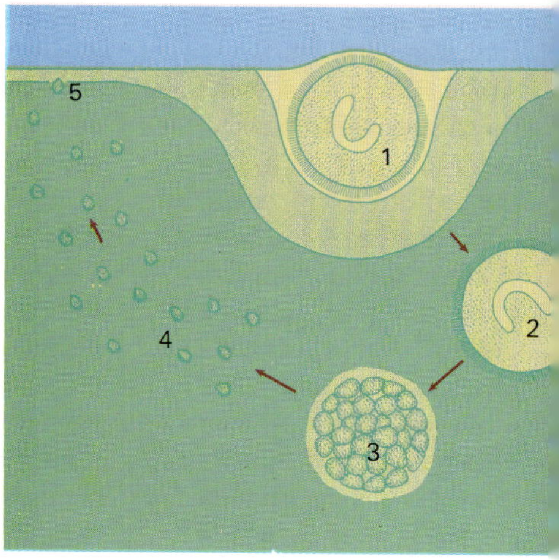

99. Life-cycle of *Ichthyophthirius multifiliis*, schematic representation.
1. Adult stage in the skin.
2. Free swimming unicellular adult after breaking through the skin.
3. Division stage (cyst).
4. Free swimming ciliospores.
5. Ciliospore penetrating the skin of a fish.

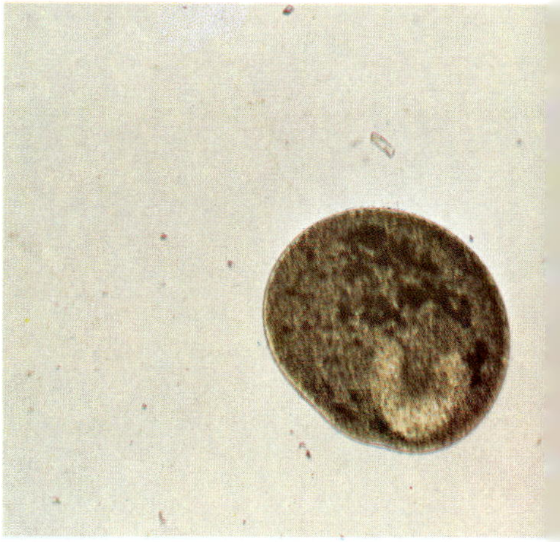

100. *Ichthyophthirius multifiliis:* full-grown. Live, magnification × 50.

makes it ineffective. Furthermore the action of Chloramine-T on both *I. multifiliis* and a fish depends very much upon the water constitution and temperature (Cross and Hursey, 1973).

The dose level for chloramine should therefore be adapted to the water constitution. 10 mg/l can be taken as an average; in hard water at pH 8.0, 20 mg/l; in soft water at pH 6.0, 2.5–5 mg/l.

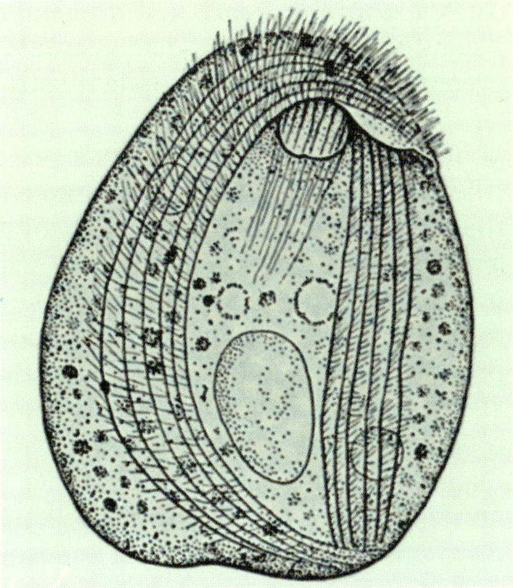

101. *Chilodonella cyprini,* seen from below. After Davis (1967).

5i. OTHER CILIATES: CHILODONELLA CYPRINI AND TRICHODINA SPECIES

Chilodonella cyprini is the most dangerous of this group: it has a round-oval and somewhat asymmetrically-shaped cell-body (Fig. 101), 33–70 μm in length. There are narrow parallel longitudinal grooves on the underside in which the cilia are rooted. Under the microscope these grooves are visible as fine stripes, and the objective should be adjusted until these appear in the field.

Trichodina species are bowl-shaped cells. Their size varies with the species; many are 30–80 μm across. On the top is the cytostome and two parallel spiralling lines of cilia. There is a ring of long cilia at the edge of the cell to provide forward movement; the disc-shaped adhesive mechanism with its pointed projections is located in the concave underside (Fig. 102).

Trichodina infections are generally mild, with few marked changes in skin and gills. Only massive infections are fatal. *Chilodonella cyprini* brings about changes in the skin (epidermis) cells, and the skin itself reacts with cell growth (proliferation) and increased mucus formation. In serious infections a whitish turbidity of the skin is visible with the naked eye. Essentially the same process can be observed in gill infections, and these changes can lead to anoxia and asphyxia.

The diagnosis can be confirmed by taking scrapings from the skin and/or gills and examining these under the microscope. Other parasitic ciliates apart from *Chilodonella cyprini* and *Trichodina* may also be found in the preparation, though less commonly.

Ciliates on the skin and/or gills can be dealt with in the same way as white spot disease. *Trichodina* species sometimes react better to formalin treatment, using 2–3 ml of filtered commercial formalin/10 l for half an hour, or alternatively ½ ml/10 l water for 2 × 24 hours.

102. *Trichodina* species, photographed live. Magnification × 110.

5j. UNICELLULAR ORGANISMS FORMING SPORES WITH THREADLIKE CNIDIAL (POLAR) FILAMENTS (CNIDOSPORA)

This group is distinguished by forming spores with one or more polar capsules. Each capsule contains a spiral polar filament. The spores are non-motile and lie on the bottom to be taken up by the fish when feeding. The filaments are projected in the gastrointestinal tract. Once the spore has opened, the embryo (sporoplasma) within is released and passes through the intestinal wall into the tissues of the fish. It is then thought to be distributed throughout the body in the blood.

Neon fish disease (Fig. 103) and white lumps in the skin (Fig. 105) or other tissues are caused by unicellular organisms from this group.

5k. NEON FISH DISEASE

Neon fish disease occurs in the neon tetra *(Hyphessobrycon innesi)* and other species of ornamental tropical fish: its victims develop whitish patches in the muscle which are swollen and sometimes rather smooth (Fig. 103). The blue-green longitudinal band sometimes breaks up in neon and cardinal tetra. Often only a few fish are affected.

103. *Petitella georgiae,* suffering from neon fish disease.

The disease is caused by the unicellular organism *Plistophora hyphessobryconis* (Schäperclaus). The infection is transmitted as described in section 5j. The sporoplasmata hatching from the spores are thought (Lom and Corliss, 1967) to multiply in the body in a series of asexual cell divisions (schizogony). Spore formation occurs because the cells develop from the stage of having one nucleus to that of having many and a thick capsule. Within this capsule a new cell forms around each nucleus. These newly-formed cells develop into immature spores (sporoblasts). Immature spores grouped together within a capsule are known as pansporoblasts (Fig. 104), which may be 26–33 μm in diameter. The spores continue to develop within the

capsule until they reach maturity and can infect further fish when released.
Neon fish disease can be demonstrated by the microscopic examination of a squash preparation of affected muscle tissue (Fig. 104). No treatment is known.

5l. LUMPS CAUSED BY MYXOBOLUS

Infection is as described in section 5j. The embryos (sporoplasmata) released from the spores develop within the body of the fish to form large and complex multinuclear stages (plasmodia). These are usually encapsulated in connective tissue and it is this which produces the lumps (Fig. 105). A complicated process of spore formation takes place within these bodies. The walls of *Myxobolus* spores consist of two dish-shaped halves joined at the rim. There are usually two polar capsules at the front (Fig. 106); behind them lies the embryo (sporoplasma). The spores of a common species such as *M.dispar* are 9–14 μm in length.
Diagnosis is straightforward: under the microscope (×400) a small sample of material from one of these lumps shows large numbers of spores (Fig. 106). The disease is not very common in aquariums and drugs are no help.

6. Worm Infections

6a. MONOGENEA AS SKIN AND GILL PARASITES

Monogenea are members of the class *Trematoda* (flukes). *Gyrodactylus* and *Dactylogyrus* are the most important as fish parasites; other representatives of this group will not be considered here. These worms have oblong bodies of variable size: many species are 0.3–0.5 mm long. The rear of the body is equipped with a few big hooks and a large number of small ones; there is a sucker at the front. A single worm contains both female and male sexual apparatus (hermaphroditism).
The *Gyrodactylus* are viviparous – they bear live young. These can attach themselves to fish at birth. They are mostly located on the skin but may also be found on the gills (Fig. 107). The species has two lobes at the front and no patches of pigmentation. The *Dactylogyrus* is an oviparous or egg-laying genus, producing larvae with cilia. Once a larva (oncomiracidium) has attached itself to a fish it loses its cilia and develops into an adult worm. *Dactylogyrus* species are usually parasitic on gills, though they can also affect the skin. There are four lobes on the front of the body with four visible spots of pigment ('eyes'). In all *Monogenea* development from egg to young parasite takes place without any intermediate host; *Digenea* require one or two transitional hosts.
Both *Gyrodactylus* and *Dactylogyrus* can kill fish. The epidermis and the gill epithelium are damaged by the action of the hooks, resulting both in breakdown and proliferation of tissue. Skin ulcers may be produced, and the gill damage may lead to anoxia. The diagnosis can only be confirmed by examining a scraping from the gills or skin under the microscope.
These worms are difficult to deal with. Adding trichlorphon to the aquarium water will kill them in time, and if necessary this substance can be reapplied after two weeks. The dose level for trichlorphon depends upon the species of fish and on the water temperature: the correct dose levels for ornamental tropical fish are not precisely known, but a dose of 1 mg/l can usually be given without injury to fish.
Brief dips in cooking salt (10 g/l for about half an hour) will reduce the number of parasites on the fish but cannot produce a complete cure. The same is true of formalin: 2–3 ml of filtered commercial formalin in 10 l of water, applied for half an hour, or 0.5 mg/10 l water for 2 × 24 hours.

6b. DISEASES DUE TO TREMATODA METACERCARIA

Monogenea and *Digenea* are two subdivisions within the class of *Trematoda* (flukes). Adult *Digenea* are generally flat and leaf-like: *Digenea* are only important in the aquarium context at one stage of their development, the metacercarian stage.
What are metacercaria, and how do they reach the fish? A certain familiarity with the life-cycle of particular *Digenea* species is necessary to answer this question. Adult worms are present in the gastrointestinal tract of predator fish or fish-eating birds. Fertilized worm-eggs then pass into the water in droppings. Larvae (mira-

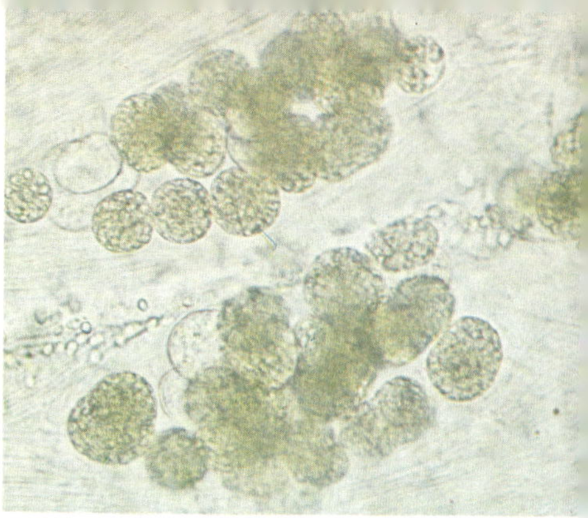

104. Pansporoblasts of *Plistophora hyphessobryconis* in the muscular tissue of *Petitella georgiae*. (ill. 103). Magnification × 280

105. Lumps in the skin of a Nile Mouth-Brooder *(Tilapia nilotica)* caused by a *Myxobolus* species.

106. *Myxobolus* spores from the skin of a Nile Mouth-Brooder, *Tilapia nilotica (ill. 105). Formalin fixation, magnification* × 420.

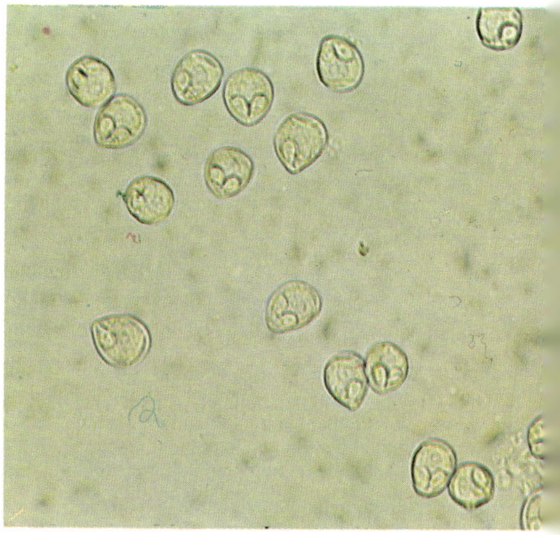

107. *Gyrodactylus* species from the gills of a goldfish *Carassius auratus auratus*. Preparation fixed in 4% formalin.

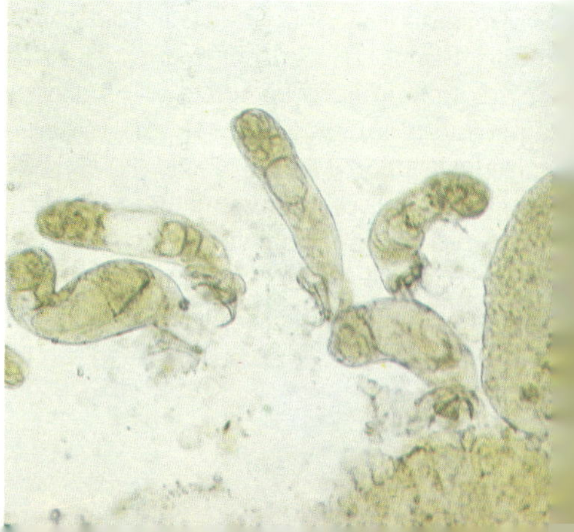

cidia) equipped with cilia emerge from these eggs, and bore into water snails. Cercaria are then formed inside the body of the snail; they are provided with a tail which is used when the organism leaves the snail (first intermediate host) and swims to a fish (second intermediate host). They penetrate the epidermis or are taken up in the food, lose the tail, and encyst; they then develop into metacercaria, which are similar in form to the adult. Hence fish can only be infected by cercaria leaving water snails. Metacercaria cannot transfer from fish to fish. If an infected fish is eaten by a predator the metacercaria are released in the gastrointestinal tract. The worm then develops into its adult form, and thus the life-cycle is completed.

Tropical fish can act as the second intermediate host and therefore as metacercaria carriers. Fish can only be infected regularly under natural conditions where the parasite can follow through the whole life-cycle, and so metacercaria are mostly found amongst fish newly imported from their natural habitat. Such fish may show a variety of symptoms. Sometimes lumps can be seen in the muscles (Fig. 108) but these do not seem to cause the fish too much discomfort. The situation is more serious when the metacercaria lodge in the liver or abdominal cavity (Fig. 109). Exhaustion, anaemia (associated with pale gills) and ultimately death may result. Diagnosis is not particularly difficult: microscopic examination reveals encapsulated, moving parasites a few millimeters long at most.

Little or nothing is known about the treatment of metacercaria in ornamental tropical fish. The parasite has a limited life-span; spontaneous recovery has been observed on various occasions, although it may take a few months.

108. Kissing Gourami *(Helostoma temmincki)* with parasitic cysts in the dorsal muscles due to *Digenea metacercaria*.

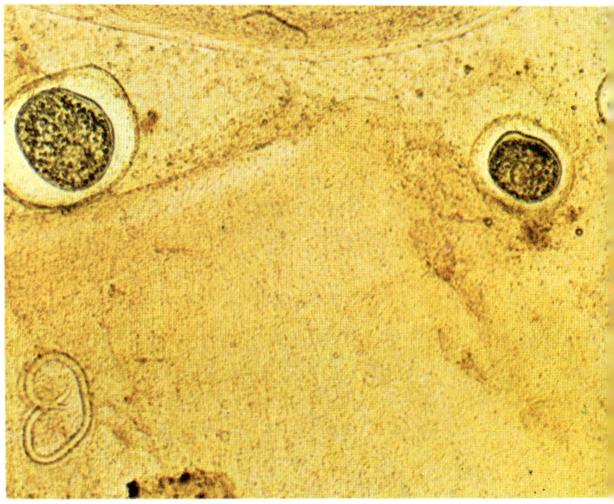

109. *Digenea metacercaria* and a threadworm larva in the abdominal cavity of *Corydoras punctatus*. The *metacercaria* are dark and surrounded by a capsule. Squash preparation magnification × 40.

6c. THREADWORMS (NEMATODA)

These worms have a fibre- or thread-like body, round in cross-section. There are two sexes: adult worms may possess either female or male sexual organs. Female worms may be either oviparous (egg-laying) or viviparous (bearing live young).

The genus *Capillaria* is the most important in the aquarium context. These worms vary in length: the smallest species are only a few millimetres long. Their life-cycle is still largely unknown. Water lice *(Copepods)* and water fleas *(Gammaridae)* would be capable of acting as intermediate hosts for immature worms (larvae). When adult worms are found in tropical fish it is usually in the intestine and the fish is the final host. In severe cases practically the whole intestinal content consists of worms, and one or more may be seen hanging from the anal orifice. Amlacher (1961) once counted thirty-two worms in the intestine of a guppy *(Lebistes reticulatus)*. In such cases the fish becomes very weak. *Capillaria* species in the intestine of discus fish (*Symphysodon* species) should be dealt with separately. The fish eat poorly and become emaciated; the feces are often colourless and translucent. Because discus fish are very expensive and usually only kept in small numbers most aquarians prefer to make their diagnosis with a live fish if at all possible: this means scrutinizing the feces for worm eggs. *Capillaria* eggs are elliptical, yellowish and have two polar plugs at their pointed ends. In the case of discus fish, and possibly other species too, treatment may be successful by adding trichlorphon (1 mg/l) to the aquarium water (Krause, 1973).

Apart from adult threadworms, which are generally found in the intestine of tropical fish, threadworm larvae can also be found in the fish. As with metacercaria infections the fish is the second intermediate host, and the life cycle of the fish-parasitic larva is similar to that described in 6b. Infestation takes place by feeding infested water lice and water fleas (first intermediate hosts).

Threadworm larvae can be found in practically all the organs and tissues of fish and particularly in the muscle, abdominal cavity and liver. Microscopic examination of a squash preparation reveals a mobile parasite which may be extremely small (Fig. 109). The symptoms shown by affected fish are as described in section 6b. No treatment is available at the moment.

6d. TAPEWORMS (CESTODA)

In tropical fishes particularly the larvae of tape worms are of some significance. Usually they are not found in the intestines, but in several internal organs and tissues.

The fish (second intermediate host) becomes infected by eating water-lice (first intermediate host).
The encysted larva (plerocercoid) is found in the body of the fish, for example in the liver (Fig. 110). When the fish is eaten by a predator (final host) the lifecycle has turned full circle. There is no treatment available for encysted tapeworm larvae.

7. Parasitic Crustaceae

This class includes some fish parasites which can occur in tropical species.

7a. ARGULUS FOLIACEUS

This is the most familiar of the fish lice (Argulidae family), often occurring in summer in freshwater plankton. The body is oval, extremely flat, transparent and about five mm long. Two large suckers on the abdominal side enable the parasite to attach itself to fish. The mouth organs have been partly adapted to form a long proboscis which can be moved up and down: poisonous glands discharge via this tube.
A.foliaceus can be introduced into the aquarium when feeding plankton: it then attaches itself to a fish and penetrates the skin with its proboscis. The poison it discharges is often fatal to young fish. The parasite is easy to spot with the naked eye, but may sometimes be missed because of its transparent body. Other species of *Argulus* many also occur, though these are less common.

7b. LERNAEA SPECIES

The species are members of the *Copepoda* family of Crustaceae, and are known as anchor worms. Adult females (Fig. 111) have oblong, unsegmented bodies. The chitinous adhesive apparatus is located on the head around the mouth. There are two egg-sacs on the rear of the body.
Only females are parasitic on fish. The front of the parasite pushes between the scales and attaches to the muscle tissue, creating a red-colored spot. The worms are rare in all tropical fish except goldfish: here *L. cyprinacea* and *L. carassii* occur regularly.
Parasitic crustaceae can be controlled by adding trichlorphon (1 mg/l) to the aquarium water; the preparation is particularly effective against fish-lice, but anchor worms are more resistant. If there are only a few it is best to remove them with tweezers.

110. Liver of an Argus fish *(Scatophagus argus)* infested with tape worm larvae: plerocercoids of a *Triaenophorus* species.

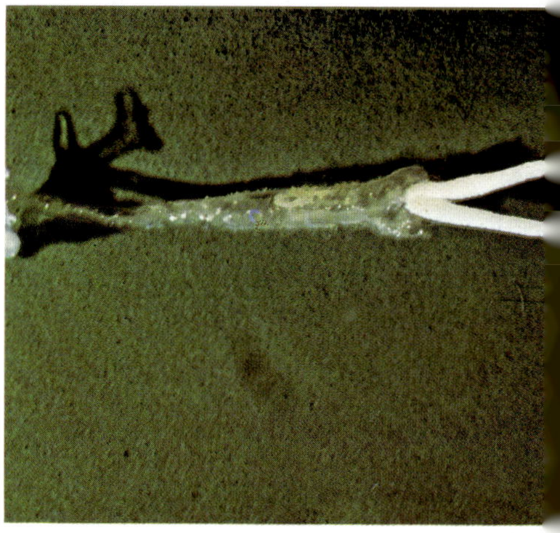

111. *Lernaea cyprinacea* fixed in glycerine/alcohol. On the right two two egg-sacs; left, the chitinous adhesive apparatus. Magnification approx. × 6.5.

8. Fungal Diseases

8a. WATER MOULD INFECTIONS: SAPROLEGNIA AND ACHLYA

Contrary to what many aquarists believe, these fungi are relatively uncommon in tropical fish. The inclination to call any white spot on the skin a fungus is very strong, but experience shows that such marks can have a variety of causes. Hence it is always important to prepare a scraping for examination under the microscope (Fig. 112). *Saprolegnia* and *Achlya* are members of the family Saprolegniaceae. Asexual reproduction takes place by the formation of sporangia at the ends of the filaments. These produce asexual spores (zoöspores) which can move about with the aid of 2 flagella. Sexual reproduction is rather more complicated: in this case immobile sexual spores are formed.
Saprolegnia and *Achlya* usually live as saphrophytes on vegetable and animal decaying matter. Fungus on dead fish-eggs is well-known in aquaria. However, live fish and fish eggs can also be affected. Such fungus occurs on live fish after damage to the epidermis or a reduction in its resistance. Fish become infected when mobile asexual fungal spores (zoöspores) settle in damaged tissue and germinate. Fungal threads then grow out into the water and the body of the fish: those in the water assume a radial pattern and give the affected area a fluffy appearance (Fig. 113). The filaments which penetrate the fish itself form a network (mycelium) and cause necrosis (tissue death). If vital organs or tissues such as the liver and the spinal cord are affected the fish will die.

Fungal infections can be controlled by adding malachite green oxalate (0.05 mg/l) or medicinal methylene blue (up to 10 mg/l, in a separate tank with no plants) to the water. See section 5h for further details of this method of treatment, which should be continued until the fungus disappears.

8b. ICHTHYOSPORIDIUM (= ICHTHYOPHONUS) DISEASE

Hofer described this disease in 1893 under the title 'Taumelkrankheit' ('the staggers'). He found a pathogen in trout which his successors later named *Ichthyophonus hoferi* or *Ichthyosporidium hoferi*. Most investigators regard *I.hoferi* as one of the fungi; a related species, however, belongs to the protozoans (Sprague, 1966). For a detailed description of *I.hoferi* see Dorier and Degrange (1960, 1961).
Ichthyosporidium disease is characterised by the appearance of small, whitish lumps in the various organs and tissues of the fish. These lumps contain the pathogen, which may be surrounded by granulocytes and epitheloid cells, encapsuled in connective tissue. The condition is particularly familiar in marine fish, where massive outbreaks may occur. The disease is seen in Europe in trout hatcheries where the offal of marine fish is used for feed.
Schäperclaus' publications in particular have drawn attention to the occurrence of Ichthyosporidium disease in aquarium fish. He did note (Schäperclaus, 1953) the differences between '*Salmonidae Ichthyophonus*' (in trout) and 'aquarium fish *Ichthyophonus*', but despite these differences he considered 'aquarium fish *Ichthyophonus*' the biggest problem in freshwater aquaria. This view was challenged by Amlacher (1965, 1968). After studying 'true' Ichthyosporidium disease in rainbow trout, and aquarium fish suspected of suffering from the same disease, he concluded that Ichthyosporidium disease is very unusual, if not unknown in aquarium fish. He believes that the confusion arises because fish tuberculosis is often taken for Ichthyosporidium disease.
How do these contradictory findings affect the aquarium keeper? It is very important to choose a method of examination which allows the disease to be recognized with reasonable certainty. This requires the study of stained tissue sections (histopathological examination, Fig. 114). This in turn means that the amateur aquarist will not be able to arrive at a diagnosis on his own. Secondly, it should be remembered that Ichthyosporidium disease is very unlikely to occur in fresh-water aquariums. Histopathological examinations carried out by the author so far yielded only negative results. There is no need for the aquarist to worry about this disease. No treatment for Ichthyosporidium disease is known.

9. Some Common Syndromes Which May Have Multiple Causes

9a. GENERALIZED OEDEMA

This produces a typical pathological picture (Fig. 115): a swollen belly due to fluid in the abdominal cavity, scale protrusion because of accumulation of fluid in the skin, and exophthalmos (bulging eyes) resulting from a build-up of liquid in the eye-sockets. The gills are pale. The blood plasma protein level is lowered and the blood is watery (hydraemia).
This condition is probably not caused by any single pathogen, as was formerly assumed. In aquariums it is often seen in fish with tuberculosis, though it may also occur in conjunction with other diseases. In a few cases no pathogen can be found. The protein levels of the blood plasma are almost always reduced (Riedmüller, 1965), reducing the colloidal-osmotic value of the blood so that the fish is literally 'flooded'. No recovery is possible, and fish suffering from this condition should be removed from the tank.

9b. FIN ROT

This is another condition on which little advice can be given at present. The condition starts at the rear edge of the fins (including the caudal fin) with a loss of color followed by breakdown of the tissue between the rays. The process advances gradually towards the base of the fin, producing a frayed appearance and making it shorter and shorter.

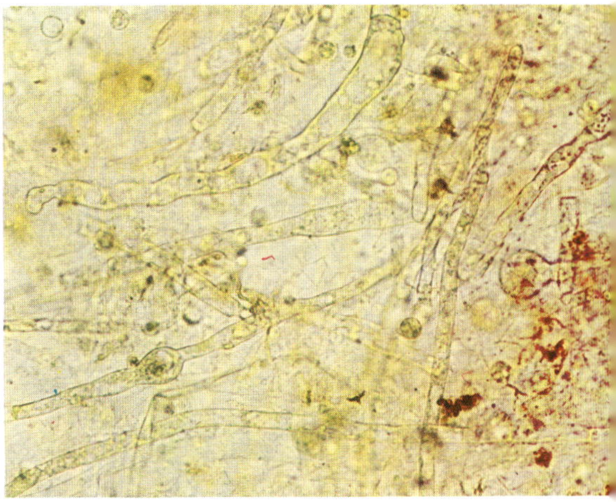

112. Fungus threads in a skin scraping, magnification × 260.

113. Young Pike Perch *(Lucioperca lucioperca)* with a fungal infection of the peduncle.

114. Cardiac muscle of a rainbow trout *(Salmo gairdneri)* with *Ichthyophonus hoferi* cysts. The cysts have a well-defined wall containing a multinuclear plasmodium. Histological section, PAS stain, magnification × 125.

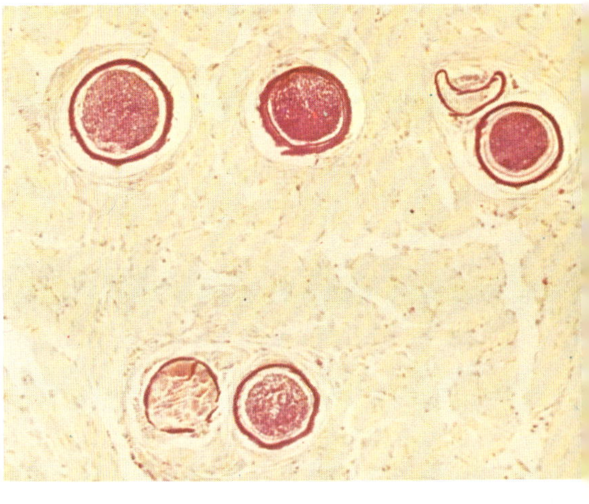

Fin rot can occur as an independent disease which is thought to be caused by bacteria. If this is so it can be successfully treated with broad-spectrum antibiotics such as tetracycline, chloramphenicol or neomycin sulphate, added to the water at 20–30 mg/l. Fin rot also appears as a secondary symptom in parasitic skin infestations and in some internal diseases such as tuberculosis. A few scrapings should always be taken from the skin and affected fins and examined under the microscope in order to check for the presence of ciliates, flagellates and *Monogenea*.

10. Applying Drugs to Tropical Fish

A comparatively large number of fish diseases is caused by pathogens located on the skin or on the gills (ectoparasites). In such cases it is sufficient to dissolve a drug in the water of either the aquarium itself or a separate tank and then leave the fish to swim about in it for a while. This will inhibit or kill external parasites. The method offers various obvious advantages including simplicity and ease of application. All fish are treated alike regardless of size or the fact that some may have stopped eating.

Some drugs are hardly taken up (resorbed) from the water at all, and hence can only be effective against external pathogens. Others are resorbed and so can also act against internal pathogens: an example of this is dimetridazole, which is effective against internal infections due to *Hexamita* species when applied via the water. Resorbtion probably operates via the gills rather than by 'drinking'. However, of many chemicals it is not known for certain whether they are resorbed, and if so to which degree.

Drugs can be dissolved in the aquarium water itself, or a separate container may be used. Both methods have advantages and disadvantages. The separate container should always be used for short treatments of 1/2–1 hour; at the end of this period the fish should be replaced in the aquarium. Treatment in a separate container may also be cheaper when using expensive drugs because of the smaller volume. The use of a separate container of fresh water also reduces the risk of unpredictable chemical reactions (turbidity, precipitation) between the drug and certain chemicals dissolved in the water. There is more danger of this in the aquarium itself and fish have been known to die unexpectedly.

If long term treatment (i.e. over several days) is required it is better still to dissolve the drug in the water of the aquarium itself. The most important advantage of this is that the fish do not need to be captured first, an operation that may be difficult and sometimes even impossible. Another advantage is that the pathogens in the aquarium itself are inhibited or killed with the result that the risk of the fish becoming reinfected when treatment is stopped is reduced. One point should be kept in mind: certain drugs such as methylene blue, quinine salts and acriflavine hydrochloride can have a very disadvantageous effect on aquatic plants.

Attention should be paid to the following points when adding a drug to water:

1. Drug dosages are usually expressed in milligrams per liter of aquarium water (mg/l). It is therefore necessary to calculate or measure the capacity of the aquarium in order to administer the correct quantity. The capacity of the tank is calculated by multiplying the three external dimensions together, i.e. length × breadth, × height (in decimetres). The actual water content of a frame aquarium in litres will then be about 60% (small tanks) to 80% (large tanks) of this figure.
2. It is important to mix the substance well with a small quantity of water, for example by shaking it up in a sealed vessel. This mixture is then spread evenly over the water surface. This method produces a quicker and more even distribution of the drug in the water.
3. Aerating the water also helps distribute the drug and guarantees an adequate oxygen level.
4. The filter should be turned off, because some drugs are taken up from the water by the carbon (adsorption) or by organic waste (oxidation). Bacteria in biological filters may be inhibited or killed though some antibiotics seem not to influence the nitrification. (Collins et al., 1976). In all cases the filter must be cleaned before being used again.

115. Black Molly (*Mollienesia sphenops*, black variety) with symptoms of generalized oedema.

Whenever a drug has been dissolved in the water of the aquarium itself it will gradually disappear due to chemical breakdown, the formation of chemical complexes, adsorption or precipitation. Some drugs such as trichlorphon act over a long period: these should be administered and then left. The same applies to drugs which are effective in very low concentrations, for example malachite green oxalate and substances which are definitely inactivated, such as Chloramine T. In other cases the water should be cleared of the substance after a certain period, for example 2×24 hours, since it is not known whether the breakdown products can be harmful or not. The water should be changed gradually. When half the water has been changed twice only a quarter of the original water will be left. In addition, many drugs are adsorbed by active charcoal: the filter can be used to remove the remains from the water (first clean the filter and change the charcoal).

Drugs can also be administered in the food; this method is used on a large scale in fish hatcheries. Some drugs are taken up (resorbed) into the body via the intestinal wall. The substance is then distributed throughout the body in the bloodstream. In general drugs are taken up better via the intestinal wall than from the water via the gills, and hence administration via the food is sometimes preferable for internal diseases. Some of the antibiotics such as chloramphenicol and the tetracyclines illustrate this well: they are only taken up from the water in small amounts, but after administration in food appear in high concentrations in the blood serum (Buza and Szakolczai, 1968). For 'bath' treatment antibiotics and chemotherapeutics should always be administered as pure substances; the use of 'soluble powders' for this purpose is not recommended. Drugs which cannot pass across the intestinal wall are only effective against pathogens in the tract itself, e.g. worms.

Unfortunately administering drugs to tropical fish in their food is not a very practical method and has a variety of disadvantages. The fish which need the drugs most are often too ill to eat, while those which are eating need them the least. Furthermore it is not easy to mix a drug with food. Powdered drugs can be mixed with semi-solid, kneadable, home-made food in the correct proportions. Drugs in solution can be sprayed over a finely grained fish food available in aquarium shops if this is spread out flat. The fine droplets are absorbed by the grains and these are then left to dry. This method makes it difficult to say how much of the drug finally reaches the fish. Furthermore, not all foods absorb fluids equally. In view of these practical difficulties the administration of drugs in food should be limited to cases where there is no alternative.

Injections may also be given. The injection fluid is usually injected into the abdominal cavity (intraperitoneal): the needle is inserted, pointing obliquely forwards, between the scales at a point on the side of the body closely above the pelvic fin. This is not too difficult in larger fish, but in small specimens it may be a rather precarious business bordering on cruelty. When injecting a reasonably sized fish it is best to use what is known as a tuberculin syringe, which has a 0.4 mm diameter needle with a plastic connection. The volume of the syringe is 1 ml; the distance between two of the calibration marks on it is equivalent to 1/100 ml. It may also be necessary to dilute the injection fluid before use in order to measure the quantity required. The choice of liquid to use as a dilutant depends upon the solvent used in the injection fluid. It is usually necessary to anaesthetise the fish since trying to holding down and inject a small squirming fish is a hopeless task.

11. How to Obtain Drugs

The remedies which are available in aquarium shops usually have a 'secret' constitution. As long as the manufacturers do not give a list of constituents on the packet the use of such preparations cannot be recommended.

The drugs and other chemicals have to be ordered through a veterinary surgeon, or pharmacist.

For many of them the prescription of a veterinary surgeon is needed. As was mentioned in the introduction, the cooperation of a practising veterinary surgeon will be essential.

12. Poisonous Substances in Aquarium Water

12a. NITROGEN GAS BUBBLE DISEASE

Though not a true 'poison', atmospheric nitrogen (N_2) can be lethal to fish when the water is oversaturated (over 100% saturation) with this gas.
Research with trout has shown that nitrogen embolism can occur with 103–118% nitrogen saturation and cause large-scale mortality (Rucker, 1972). The condition can be created in aquarium fish by replacing old tank water with recently-warmed fresh water. It is characterised by the presence of small bubbles of nitrogen beneath the skin, in the fins, tail or mouth, behind the eyes, and in the blood vessels (Fig. 116). Oversaturation with oxygen may not present immediate problems: these only occur when it reaches 350%; this percentage hardly ever occurs in an aquarium. Affected fish should be placed in well-aerated water and left until they possibly recover spontaneously. Water which has been warmed quickly should be well aerated for a while to clear the excess nitrogen.

12b. AMMONIA, NITRITE, NITRATE

These are nitrogen compounds, formed by the breakdown of proteins. They are produced in the aquarium itself and a small quantity is present in the water under normal conditions. Ammonia (NH_3) is the most important end product in the protein-metabolism of freshwater aquarium fishes. It is given off via the gills in the form of ammonium (NH_4^+); ammonia is also produced by the breakdown of proteins present in urine and feces of fish and in food fragments.
The ammonia and ammonium in the water are in balance according to the following chemical equation:

$$NH_3 + H_2O \rightleftharpoons NH_4^+ + OH^-.$$

This balance depends upon the acidity (pH) of the water and its temperature. When the pH is low the NH_3 levels are low and NH_4^+ high; when the pH is high the situation is reversed, as shown in the figures below (Trussel, 1972).

pH	6.5	7.0	7.5	8.0	8.5	9.0
% NH_3, 25°C	0.18	0.55	1.73	5.28	14.97	35.76

116. Goldfish *(Carassius auratus auratus)* with tiny bubbles of nitrogen in the blood vessels of the caudal fin causing bleeding.

It has been demonstrated that NH_3 is very poisonous for fish, while NH_4^+ is not (Wuhrmann and Woker, 1949).
An acute ammonia-poisoning will practically always occur in alkaline water, from 0,2 mg NH_3/l. However, only values of less than 0.025 mg/l are considered harmless (EIFAC, 1973).
Ammonia can be oxidized by bacteria in the aquarium itself or more effectively in a biological filter (slow sand filter):

$$\text{Ammonium } (NH_4^+) \rightarrow \text{Nitrite } (NO_2^-) \rightarrow \text{Nitrate } (NO_3^-).$$

This process is called nitrification. The interproduct, nitrite, is also very poisonous to fish; a dose as small as 0.5 mg NO_2^-/l caused heavy casualties among young rainbow trout (Russo, 1974).
Nitrite oxidizes the red blood pigment (haemoglobin to methaemoglobin); this compound can not transport oxygen (Smith and Russo, 1975).
The end product of nitrification, nitrate, is 2000 times less poisonous than nitrite, and relatively harmless to fish (Westin, 1974). Poisoning by ammonia or nitrite can be avoided by permanent care of the quality of aquarium water.

12c. ANAEROBIC DECAY

Anaerobic decay (decay in the absence of oxygen) can also produce substances

which are poisonous to fish. In the aquarium such anaerobic conditions are only found in the bottom, so that it is not entirely safe for fish to root too deeply. Similar conditions arise in the filter if the water ceases to circulate. Every filter contains bacteria which break down organic waste in the presence of oxygen. Once filtration ceases the oxygen present in the filter is quickly used up and anaerobic decay begins. If the filter is then restarted after a period its foul and poisonous contents pass out into the aquarium and produce large-scale mortality.
Apart from poisons which are produced in the aquarium itself and which are present in small quantities in all tanks, there are also poisonous substances which should have no place there.

12d. CHLORINE
Chlorine (Cl_2) is a powerful disinfectant which some water authorities add to the supply. Most of this chlorine is removed from drinking water, but chlorine levels which are too high for fish can still occur locally. As little as 0.1 mg/l is dangerous. Chlorine can be removed from water by filtration through activated charcoal or by vigorous aeration for several days.
The chlorine molecule (Cl_2) should not be confused with the chlorine ion (Cl^-) which occurs together with the sodium ion Na^+ in cooking salt solutions. The chlorine ion is not harmful to fish.

12e. CEMENT
Cement is used in the construction of rockwork; some aquariums use asbestos cement. One of the constituents of cement is calcium hydroxide ($Ca(OH)_2$). However, for a certain period after hardening cement gives off OH^- ions into the water, and this can gradually raise the pH to an unacceptably high level. Cemented rockwork and aquariums constructed with asbestos cement should therefore be rinsed under running water for 2–3 weeks to remove this risk.

12f. PLASTICS AND PLASTIC CEMENTS
These contain all kinds of substances such as softeners, anti-oxidants and stabilizers, and sometimes these can be released into the water and have a deleterious effect on fish. The plastics used in aquariums should therefore have to meet the same high standards required of those used for human foodstuffs.

12g. COPPER
Heavy metals such as copper are toxic to fish. The acute toxic effect is due to changes in the gills, which asphyxiate the fish. Tapwater may contain small quantities of copper, particularly when the water has been left standing in a copper pipe for some time. The tap should be left running for a while before the tank is filled. The toxicity of copper and other heavy metals depends very much upon the hardness of the water. In water of about 0.7 °DH copper sulphate ($CuSO_4 \cdot 5H_2O$) appears to be fatal to rainbow trout above 0.24 mg/l within 4×24 hours; in water of 18 °DH, from 2.4 mg/l (Erichsen Jones, 1964). The use of copper sulphate as a drug in fresh water aquaria would therefore seem fairly risky.

13. Can Fish Diseases be Prevented?

A detailed description of ways in which the best possible living conditions for fish can be provided is given elsewhere in this book. Food and the composition of the water are critical factors here.

13a. FOOD
A balanced diet is essential. The commercially available dry fish foods are almost always unbalanced. Furthermore the vitamin content gradually declines at room temperature. A dry food which is commonly used for trout will only keep about three months, and there is no reason to suppose that dry foods for tropical fish will last any longer. They should preferably be kept absolutely dry in a refrigerator. This diet should be supplemented with live food; and this means dealing with

Tubifex. These worms often live in contaminated water. They contain certain bacteria in their gastrointestinal tracts which can produce large quantities of gas in the intestine of the fish. Cases are known in which fish have died 4 hours after eating Tubifex. Only commercially obtained Tubifex which have been placed under running tapwater for at least 3 × 24 hours should be used; most of the contamination will clear in this time.

When feeding with plankton it should be remembered that they contain fish lice in summer (Redeke, 1948). This parasite is often fatal to smaller fish. In addition. certain plankton organisms can act as intermediate hosts for fish pathogenic thread-worms and tape worms.

It is also important to feed small amounts many times a day. *Cyprinidae* (which include goldfish) have no true stomachs and can only consume about 1% of their body weight at each feeding. At room temperature they need to eat 2–3% of their body weight per day, and so a single daily feeding is not sufficient.

13b. WATER CONSTITUTION

This is by far the most important environmental factor. The fish is in intimate contact with the water and any contamination will affect it. The fish itself discharges many substances into the water, for example, feces, urine and (via the gills) ammonium, so that it is in fact swimming about in a dilute solution of its own waste products. Under natural conditions this dilution is enormous, but in aquariums it can become very much reduced so that certain substances may start to accumulate. In order to avoid severe water pollution the following measures should be taken.

1. The population density should not exceed 1 g fish/3–4 l water (Smies and Murris, 1962). The goldfish in its bowl does badly according to this formula since its ratio is only about 1:0.5, 6–8 times less. The bowl should be fitted with an aerator and the water changed regularly.

Remains of food can contribute significantly to water pollution. Again, no more food should be given than the fish can eat at once, with the daily ration divided into several portions. Clear away any excess.

Dead fish will also pollute the aquarium. Cannibalization by other fish is common but serious, since it can spread certain diseases such as tuberculosis. Dead fish should be removed as quickly as possible.

13c. QUARANTINE

When new fish are purchased a quarantine period of 2–3 weeks is absolutely essential. A separate tank which is easy to handle and disinfect should be used for this. The new fish should only be introduced into the aquarium when it has been eating well for several weeks and shown no signs of illness.

6.
FEEDING
The Diet of Fish

The digestive processes of fishes are very similar to those of human beings. A fish must eat to live, and eat the right quantities of the appropriate food, if it is to remain in good health.

A fish takes in food through its mouth, digests it, in so doing absorbing from it the chemical and natural constituents it needs, and then expels the waste products through the anus.

From the food it eats the fish must be able to obtain *proteins,* which are body building foods used to replace the body cells as they wear out, *carbohydrates,* energy giving foods, fats, also used to provide energy and warmth, and minerals and vitamins, which are needed to help various organs to function properly, and are also an aid against disease.

Like human beings, to obtain these constituents, a fish needs a varied but balanced diet: like human beings, it also enjoys variety for its own sake.

In the wild a particular species naturally lives in an environment where it will find in generally abundant quantities the food which suits it best: indeed, it is as a rule the availability of suitable food that dictates a creature's habitat. Moreover, in the wild, a fish will spend the majority of its life hunting for food. The obtaining of food is probably, except in the spawning season, the over-riding factor determining what a fish does: it has been pointed out above in the general section on the biology of fishes, that a species' very shape, like that of *Corydoras julii* and *Epiplatys chaperi,* is determined by the methods it has developed for seeking food.

It is well to stress this dominant role that feeding plays in the lives of fishes as of other creatures, because it emphasizes the vital importance of ensuring that the fish in the aquarium are properly fed. Aquarium fish, although they may occasionally find some tasty morsel in the tank by accident, an insect, a crumb or something that has fallen into the tank, will be, in general, entirely dependent on their keeper for the provision of an appropriate well-balanced diet. Unlike fish in the wild, they cannot swim up or down stream if food in one particular area is scarce or unattractive.

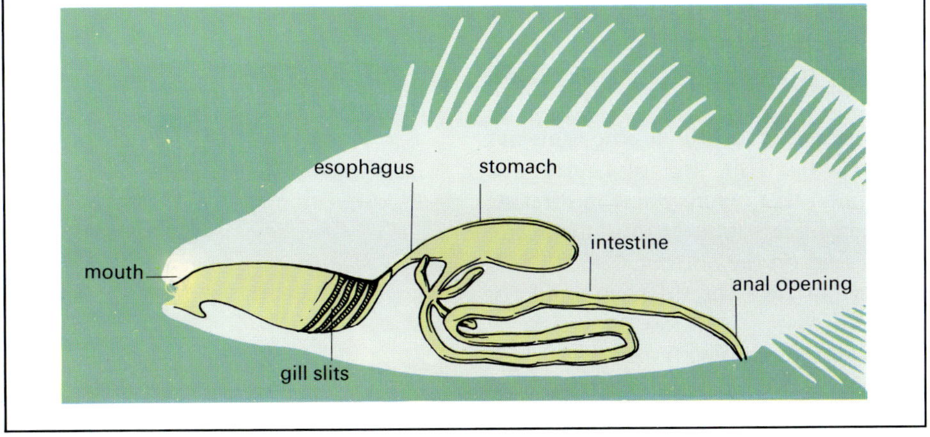

117. The digestive system of a fish is in principle the same as in other vertebrates.
Food enters the stomach and is broken down to a near liquid mass by the stomach juices.
The digestive process takes a long or short time depending on such factors as temperature and the kind of food taken.
The proteins, fat and other elements of the food are then broken down in such a way that they can be absorbed through the intestinal wall into the bloodstream.
The digestive track of a particular species varies according to its natural diet, the intestinal canal of flesh-eaters is short, that of plant-eaters very long. The mid-gut ends in the straight hind-gut, opening through the anal opening just in front of the anal fin.

There is another equally important related issue: most fish will not know when to stop eating. Of course most aquarists feed their fish regularly, but the fish will not appreciate that that is what will always happen. In the wild an animal eats as much as it can when it can, for there is no guarantee that the next meal will be successfully hunted in the near future, so that most wild animals spend their lives fluctuating between being gorged and being very hungry. Of course, after a very long time in a tank, with regular feeding, some intelligent fish will fall into a somewhat unnatural habit of eating in moderation because they know they will never go hungry. However, most aquarium fish will not do this – or at least they will be suffering from over-feeding and in poor health, long before their instincts are conditioned in this way.

Over-feeding on a large scale also contributes to the fouling of the tank. Most food is in very small granules, and most dried food disintegrates in the water after a little while so that it falls as microscopic particles onto the bed and works its way unnoticed into the sand where it rots, becoming a perfect medium for bacteria, and ultimately causes indirectly the destruction of the balance in the tank. Of course, all old food seen lying in the tank should be collected with the dip stick if it is not caught by the filter, but there is still a danger from old food which cannot be seen, and that danger is avoided by moderate feeding.

Under the descriptions of individual fish, in the systematic section, a note is always given of the most appropriate diet for that particular fish, and of course, the amateur must be careful to follow those instructions: there is no point in offering the best dried food to a fish that will only eat surface insects, nor the most attractive surface insects to a fish that only eats food it can find on the bottom.

Within that rule however, it is useful to examine in turn the different kinds of food the aquarist can buy, or prepare for his pets.

There are four basic different kinds of food: fresh food (including tinned and frozen food), dried food, cultured food and natural pond food. They will each be considered in turn.

118. The Fire Eel, *(Mastocembalus erythrotaenia),* burrows in the sand during the day. In spite of its protruding snout, the Fire eel feeds successfully with an otherwise unmodified mouth.

119. A naked catfish *(Synodontis flavitaeniatus)* with its four whisker-like barbels, which serve a sensory function in detecting food.

Fresh Food

Certain species need a vegetable supplement to their diet. These are usually species that in the wild derive the greater part of their nourishment from algae or other small plant life. For such species it is usually necessary, as noted in the systematic section, to ensure that there is plenty of algae in the tank, but because it is difficult to maintain an adequate level of algae when the fish are continuously feeding off it, limp lettuce leaves or boiled spinach are suggested as a supplement.
Some species are described as being omnivorous and eating almost anything they are offered: other species are recorded as eating lean meat. For such fish finely grated or chopped liver, heart or kidney, either raw or cooked is admirable food: many will also accept small quantities of lobster, prawn or white fish meat prepared in the same way, and very finely chopped hard boiled egg yolk will also be considered a delicacy. Even finely chopped firm cheese will be eaten for a change.
Most of these foods will be available at some time in the household and thus all can be used to introduce that much needed element of variety into the diet. Except for the very unusual species, none of these foods will provide the staple diet. That must either be live animal matter or dried food.

120. The Archer fish *(Toxotes jaculator)* is one of those species whose feeding is very unusual. It shoots droplets of water at insects above the surface. The fish pushes its snout out of the water and squirts a fine jet at the prey.

Dried Food

There are now a large number of excellent prepared dried foods on the market which the manufacturers claim, generally with justification, provide a well-balanced nutritious diet. Certainly they often give good roughage to the fish, and where fish are fed twice daily, it is a good idea to give an appropriate dried food as one of the two meals – but not of course to those species noted as never eating dried food. Equally, no aquarium fish should as a rule, be fed only on dried proprietary food. Uneaten dried food is more likely than other kinds of uneaten food, to decay in the tank and cause pollution, so it should always be given sparingly.
It would be invidious for any particular dried food to be recommended: the amateur should rely on the advice of his dealer and of course should pay close attention to what the manufacturer says about the food's appropriateness for different kinds of fish.
By far the majority of aquarium fish, whatever else they are fed, need at least some live animal matter in their diet. These kinds of food are generally cultured, in that they are produced under controlled conditions, and are then sold in aquarium shops. The amateur can of course, if so inclined, make his own cultures, and for some foods, such as infusoria, this is usually necessary. Sometimes these foods can be found in natural ponds, and can be collected by the amateur, although if using natural pond foods he must be careful in so doing never to introduce dangerous bacteria and other unwelcome guests into the aquarium.

121. Fresh food, e.g. lettuce, is a very important element in the diet of many fish in captivity *(Pterygoplichthys gibbiceps)*.

Cultured Foods

INFUSORIA

Infusoria is a general term used to describe various minute organisms, like *Paramecium*, which under certain conditions live and multiply in water – and, in lay terms, become a kind of fresh water plankton. These minute organisms are an excellent food for most fry. Various proprietary preparations are now available to form the basis of a culture of infusoria, and the amateur's task is made much easier. However, infusoria can be home made by boiling chopped hay for twenty minutes and then straining the liquid into jam jars then left exposed to the air until (very soon) they will become cloudy and infected with these micro-organisms. Alternatively, banana peel, hay and a few drops of milk are put in a jar of water which is left for a week, a few drops of milk being added each day. At the end of the week the banana and hay are removed, and the culture will continue to produce the micro-organisms, which can be drawn off and the culture topped up with tap water.
Infusoria when added to the aquarium tank is of course a liquid, and should be

at the same temperature as the tank water. This is best achieved by keeping the cultures at about 25° C, at which temperature in any case, they develop more quickly and efficiently.
Those inexperienced in these matters should however be warned that these preparations have a powerful and unpleasant smell: they should not be developed in a domestic kitchen near food for human consumption.

ARTEMIA NAUPLII: THE BRINE SHRIMP
Another excellent food for young fish are the freshly hatched eggs of the brine shrimp *(Artemia salina)*. These can be purchased as dried eggs in aquarium shops. In their dried state they will keep for years and years. To hatch them they should be put in a jar of salt water (20 grams of rock salt per liter) and after one to two days the tiny hatched shrimps (nauplii) will collect on the side of the jar receiving most light. They can be removed from the jar with a pipette and fed immediately to the fish.

MICROWORMS (MICROEELS, EELWORMS)
Larger than *Artemia nauplii,* but still very small and an admirable food for young fish, or fully grown small species, and also for fish that like to take their food from the bottom, are the tiny nematode worms *Anguillula silusiae*. These worms cannot swim, and those not eaten by fish in the middle reaches of the aquarium, as the worms slowly drop down the tank, rest on the bottom, where they will be snapped up.
Microworms are best cultivated in shallow dishes about 10 cm in diameter and 2½ cm deep, with a rough surface. Into each dish should be put a tablespoonful of cold cooked porridge, mixed with a little milk to a creamy consistency. About a third of a teaspoonful of microworms should be put on the porridge, and the dish, covered with a glass, put in the dark at about 23° C for seven to ten days. As the worms multiply they climb up the rough edges of the dish where they may be scooped up and fed to the fish. Each culture will produce ample supplies of worms for about a week, after which a new culture should be prepared by tranferring some microworms to newly prepared porridge and milk. Three cultures each staggered to come to maximum production as another declines, will ensure a regular supply of worms.

GRINDAL WORMS
Grindal worms are closely related to microworms, but larger. They are cultured in small wooden boxes, 12 × 17 cm and 4 cm deep, which are filled almost to the top with a well moistened mixture of peat, soil and leafmould. A small culture of the worms is put in the middle of the box, and a small amount of cooked cereal (porridge, bread or boiled potato) also added before the boxes are covered with glass and kept in a dark place at 24° C. After a few days worms will be found at the surface and can be removed for feeding: provided the box is kept warm and moist and further cereal added regularly, the culture will continue almost indefinitely as the worms breed and multiply.

ENCHYTRAE
Enchytraeus albidus, closely related to microworms and Grindal worms are even larger, but if cultured in the same way as Grindal worms (but kept at 10°–14° C), they will be available in different stages of growth and so will be taken by both small and large fish. They are a very good food in moderation, but being fatty, should not as a rule, be given in excess.

EARTHWORMS
Garden earthworms are an excellent food for aquarium fish but have to be washed and then chopped up before being fed to them. Many aquarists find this distasteful, and those who are also interested in the quality of their garden soil may be justifiably reluctant thus to destroy one of the most valuable creatures in their gardens. Suffice it to say that while there may be occasions when the odd worm should be sacrificed,

122/123. Many young fish may be fed with Artemia nauplii (brine shrimp eggs), as shown above with young specimens of *Julidochromis ornatus*.

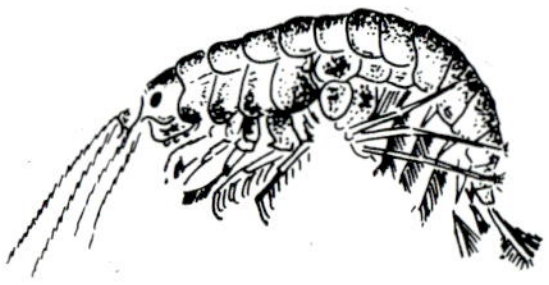

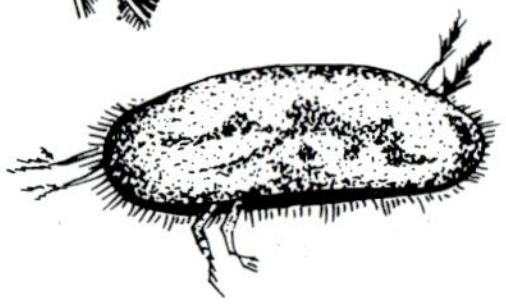

123. ARTEMIA

NATURAL POND FOOD

Rotifers
Rotifers are a group of very small creatures found in ponds, the most common being *Brachionus rubens* and *Hydatina senta*. They are best collected by using, in shallow waters, a fine nylon tapering net, 60 cm long, and of maximum diameter 15 cm, with the mouth covered with fine nylon to prevent larger creatures being taken up. The rotifers may later be strained off the water in which they have been taken home by the aquarist, and fed to the fish.

Daphnia
Daphnia, commonly called waterfleas, are a group of small creatures of which the most common species is *Daphnia pulex*. They will be found in ponds, in the filter beds of sewage works and in the filtration beds linked with

there is no need regularly to do this to keep the majority of aquarium fish in good condition.

All these foods (except the earthworms noted above to complete the consideration of worms as a type of food) are controlled in cultures by the aquarist himself. Other foods, naturally provided in ponds, have generally to be collected by the aquarist when he needs them, although they are now available in some aquarium shops prepackaged. These natural foods are of course in many ways the best for fish, provided that no dangerous parasites or enemies of fish are introduced with them into the aquarium.

How and When to Feed

Fish, as recommended above, should be fed regularly and in moderation. For most species it is sufficient to distribute the food gently on the surface of the water: those that feed from the surface will come for it, and those that only feed from the bottom will accept the food when it has sunk through the water. It is only necessary to ensure that bottom feeders are not given food of such buoyancy that it does not sink and, in a community tank, that bottom feeders are not left without food because other species have eaten it all before it has a chance to sink.

Feeding their fish is, for most aquarists, a significant part of the enjoyment of the hobby, and automatic feeding equipment is therefore as a rule neither necessary nor welcome. It is however possible to purchase equipment, electrically operated, in some cases, with which fish can be fed regularly without the aquarist being too bound to a feeding timetable. While not to be recommended for everyday use – if only because they deny the aquarist the opportunity, when feeding the fish, to check on their condition, such equipment can be very useful if the aquarist has to leave the tank unattended for a few days.

---

domestic water supply plants. They have to be caught by plunging a fine net into the water and catching them before they dart to the bottom. They are a good food for most fish, and attractive because they hop on the water and give the fish something to pursue. They can be purchased live in many aquarist shops, but it is difficult for the amateur to breed them himself. Dried Daphnia, although often offered for sale, are not very nutritious food for most fish.

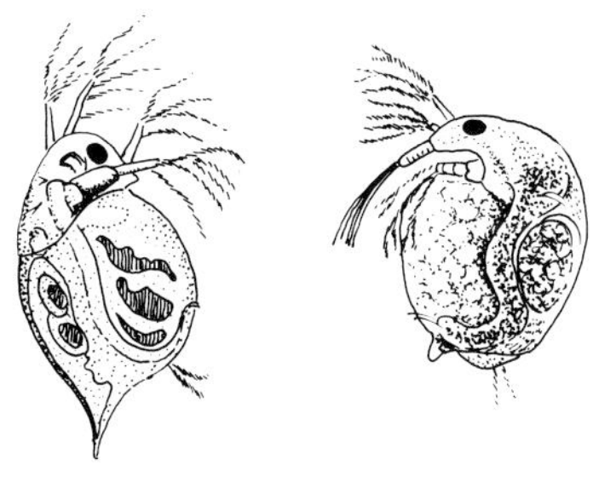

124. DAPHNIA

Cyclops

Cyclops, a one-eyed crustacea of the class Copepoda, is a creature found in the same environment as waterfleas, but usually slightly smaller than the Daphnia and greenish grey: in the colder months they are more common than Daphnia. They have to be caught like waterfleas. They are a good food for fish agile enough to catch them, but, as the amateur is warned in the systematic section under various species, they must not be introduced into breeding tanks where they will prey on the eggs or fry.

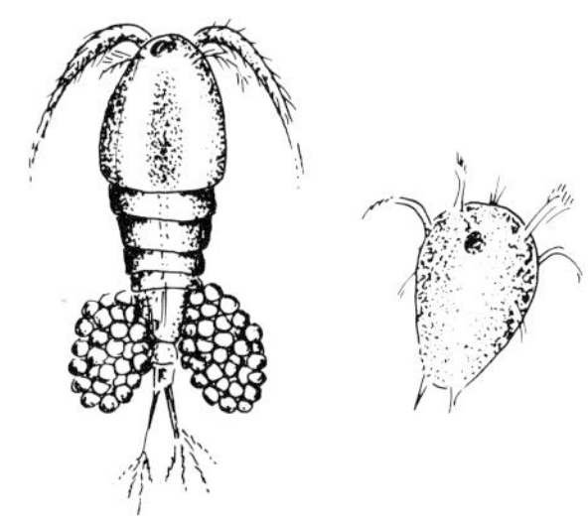

125. CYCLOPS

Tubifex worms

Tubifex (in the family Tubificidae) are thin dull reddish worms usually 1–5 cm long that live and breed in the filthiest of ponds, and in sewage outlets. Fortunately they are usually available at aquarium shops and the amateur is spared the disagreeable task of catching them from the sludge in which they live. When purchased they should be washed and fed to the fish straight away: they can be kept alive in running water. Tubifex should be kept in a shallow dish, preferably under running water. The dish should be filled in such a way that the tubifex is just submerged.

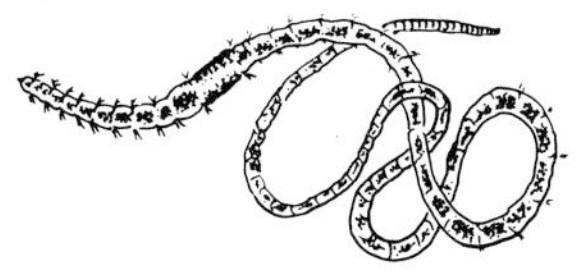

126. TUBIFEX

Although they are a valuable food for some species, Tubifex worms, living in unhygienic water, are suspected by some aquarists of being the cause of bacteria entering the aquarium. Other aquarists suspect them of remaining alive inside some fish. Whether these suspicions are justified is uncertain, but what is certain is that if these worms are not eaten by the fish, and begin to decay in the bed, they very soon pollute the tank. Perhaps, this is a food to avoid. In any event long worms must be chopped up before being fed to the fish.

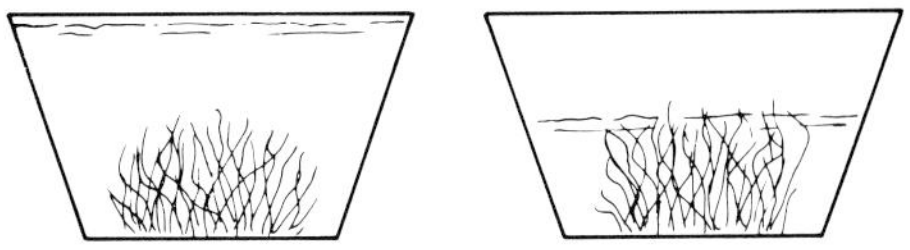

127. PRESERVATION OF TUBIFEX

Bloodworms

Bloodworms, the larvae of *Chironomus* midges are rather thick blood red worms whose bodies do in fact contain a large quantity of haemoglobin (the red pigment of blood) and for fish large enough to eat them, are a very good food. They are found in old water butts and similar places where there is rotting vegetation, but hardly ever in large numbers. If the water is clear there is no danger in using these worms as food, if they can be found.

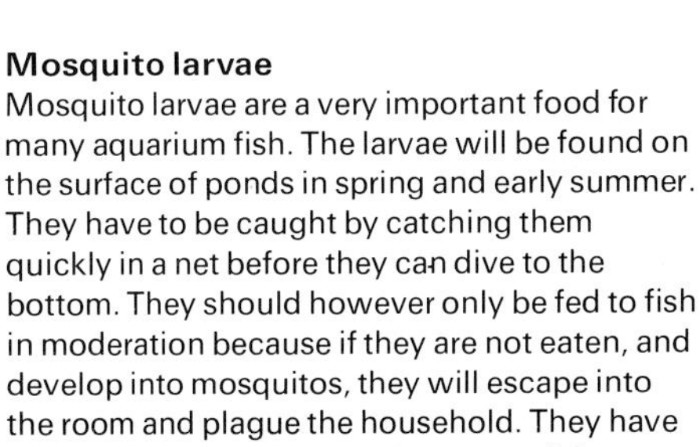

128. MOSQUITO LARVAE

Mosquito larvae

Mosquito larvae are a very important food for many aquarium fish. The larvae will be found on the surface of ponds in spring and early summer. They have to be caught by catching them quickly in a net before they can dive to the bottom. They should however only be fed to fish in moderation because if they are not eaten, and develop into mosquitos, they will escape into the room and plague the household. They have sharp pincers and can attack very small fry, so they should not be fed to fish in a breeding tank.

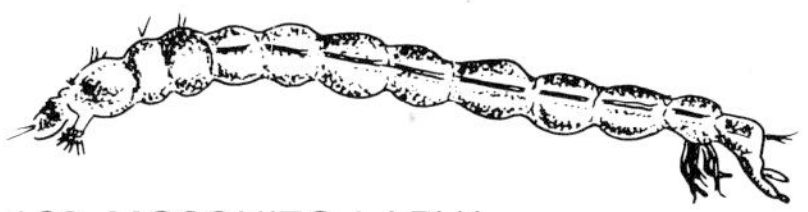

129. MOSQUITO LARVA

7.
BREEDING
The Development of Fish

The scientific details of the reproductive biology of fishes will not be of great concern to the majority of amateurs: those particularly interested in it will find full studies in the scientific literature. Only the briefest reference to this need be made here. Fish, like human beings reproduce through a sexual act during which the eggs of the female are fertilized by the sperm (called milt in fishes) of the male. Except in very rare cases, the sex of a fish is determined for all time by the fertilization of the egg: it will either produce a male or female fish which throughout its life will retain that sex. There are one or two very unusual species in which a sex change can occur during the life of an individual species, but these are not the rule.

The female has internal organs, the ovaries, in which the eggs are produced: the males have internal organs which produce the milt. All aquarium fish however fall into one or two categories: those which expel the eggs which only develop into fry outside the body of the female (egg-layer or oviparous fish) and those in which the embryonic fish develop within the body of the female and are expelled as very small but perfectly formed young (the livebearers, either viviparous where the young have been nourished in the mother's body or ovoviviparous, where they form in eggs which hatch in the mother's body).

Not only is this a basic difference which naturally radically affects the breeding

130. The mating game of *Trichogaster leeri*; the female reacts the male's advances by pushing the beak in the side of her partner.

habits of the species in question, but it is also one that, in general terms, leads to a physical difference in the males. Males of livebearing species must impregnate the female with the milt: males of egg-laying species need only to be able to fertilize the eggs themselves after they have left the body of the female. Both kinds of male fish discharge the milt from their bodies through an opening near the anus, but in the livebearers part of the anal fin has developed into a specific external sexual organ, the gonopodium, by which the female is impregnated. This interesting question is further examined in the descriptive articles in the systematic section on the livebearers in the families Anablepidae, Goodeidae, Hemirhamphidae, Jenynsiidae and Poeciliidae.

In those fish the gonopodium is an obvious external sexual characteristic which serves to distinguish the males from the females. Sexing fish is important for the aquarist, even if he is not intending to breed them, but it is not always easy.

131. A pair of *Brachydanio frankei* in a breeding tank. It is evident that the female in the foreground is swollen with eggs. In the background the bed is covered with vegetation in which the eggs will settle, thus discouraging egg-eating.

Selecting Breeding Pairs

It is not usually possible to buy adult pairs of breeders in aquarium shops. The aquarist has to select a pair himself from his tank. He should choose fish which show a positive interest in each other and a female if possible, already producing eggs although this is not absolutely essential.

Spawning females can often be identified by their more rounded bellies: the distended belly is usually particularly noticeable when the spawning female is viewed from above. However it is not always necessary for females to be visibly spawning before they are segregated for breeding. It is more important that they seem eager to mate: this is equally true for males. The fish may already hopefully have shown signs of this in their ordinary community tank.

Some fish are not very fussy about choosing a mate: this is so usually with species which live in shoals. Others choose their mates very carefully and only after a complicated introductory mating ritual. These individual traits are noted in the species descriptions below.

It is essential to match fish which are compatible. This is not always just a question of selecting one male and one female. Successful breeding is largely dependent on the skill born of experience, in identifying the chance of compatibility. The fish should also be extremely healthy and attractively colored specimens. It is advisable in most species to keep the selected breeders separate from each other for a while before transferring them to a breeding tank.

The fish should be brought to optimum condition on a very varied diet for a period of one or more weeks depending on the species. The food should preferably consist of live animal matter such as fruit flies, Enchytrae, various sorts of mosquito larvae, all kinds of small insects as well as larger animal matter such as meal-worms supplemented with minced beef heart and liver for larger species. Only then, when in tip-top condition should they be put in the specially prepared breeding tank.

132. Some species, like the albino *Barbus tetrazona tetrazona* are the result of selective breeding.

133. Mating display of the *Nannostomus bifasciatus*.

Spawning Media

Some species are called 'free layers' because they are happy merely to deposit their eggs in the water to be fertilized as they float about. Most species however like to lay their eggs on, in, or under, something in the tank. What that is varies enormously from species to species, and the best material for each species is noted in the systematic section. It may be that the spawning fish will seek out a broad or fine leaved plant, preferring perhaps those in a clump or one growing alone, or it may seek a collection of stones, lying flat, diagonally or standing upright, or grouped in irregular arrangements so that there are cracks and cavities; or sand, fine or coarse, or gravel, or a mixture of sand and gravel, or peat, in small or large pieces; or pieces of bogwood, or flower pots, or coconut shells, or pieces of bamboo.

If possible the most natural spawning medium should be put in the tank, but anything put in the breeding tank must be disinfected or at least thoroughly cleaned first. Plants can be disinfected by immersing them in slaked lime solution for a

maximum of two hours at 25°C. Care should be taken to remove all snails and snails' eggs which are often found on the underside of leaves or on the stems of plants as inconspicuous blobs of jelly. Snails are a danger to both eggs and fry.
Stones should be scrubbed clean with a hard scrubbing brush in running water, and boiling water should then be poured over them. Sand and gravel should be rinsed in plenty of water until no impurities are left and the water, as it rinses off, is crystal clear. If peat is used as a spawning medium, it should simply be rinsed gently in warm water to remove all the fine particles: if it is boiled or rinsed too thoroughly, it will lose those constituents that are important for the eggs and the water balance. Bogwood not used before should be scrubbed clean with a hard brush in plenty of water: it should be boiled until it no longer floats, and then rinsed again. All other equipment, including the thermometer, thermostat and heating elements should be thoroughly cleaned or rinsed in lukewarm water without soap or detergent.
The need to have all items in a very clean breeding tank encourages aquarists to keep the contents of the tank to the minimum, and where possible to use materials that can be sterilized. This has encouraged many to use as a spawning medium what is called a nylon breeding mop, made of strands of nylon wool run through a hole in a small round disc of cork. When these float in the tank they simulate both floating plants and the submerged roots of shore vegetation, and are thus an acceptable medium to many species. They are easy to make, can be thoroughly washed in very hot water, can be used again and again, and are easy to handle.

134. Breeding dwarf cichlids can be done with the aid of a flowerpot in which the eggs are laid.

The Water in the Breeding Tank

It will come as no surprise to the aquarist who has studied the earlier sections to learn that the quality and composition of the water in the breeding tank is of crucial importance. In the systematic section, in discussing the breeding of individual species, a careful note is made of the particular kind of water required for the different species. In the wild, it is a change in the composition of the water, brought about for example by the beginning of the rainy season, that stimulates the fish and heralds the beginning of the spawning season: the virtually immediate effect of appropriately soft water on the resting eggs of seasonal fish is to make them hatch. In addition, the eggs and fry are usually even more sensitive than mature fish to fluctuations in water temperature, or the harmful effects of unsuitable water. Great care must therefore be taken to ensure that the water is of the right kind, and probably more failures in breeding are due to not doing that, than to any other cause.
To ensure success in breeding it is often worthwhile spending more time to achieve the exact kind of water needed, than can reasonably be spent making exactly right the much larger quantities used in the community tank.
Fresh tap water is as a rule not suitable for breeding tanks: even if it is not too hard, it is likely to contain unacceptably high levels of chemicals, even if, for human beings, these levels are quite harmless. If matured however, it is usually a good basis from which to start, and it is best matured by being left exposed to the sunlight for a week of two, with a good number of oxygenating plants in it.
If this matured water has then to be made harder (which is very unlikely but occasionally necessary), then it should be filtered through a chalky substance, such as ground-up egg shells. This filtration will not alter the acidity of the water. If the water has to be made more soft, then the addition of distilled water will be effective, and should be done gradually, with the mixture tested from time to time, before the addition of further quantities of distilled water, to check on progress.
Rain water collected by spreading a large sheet of polythene sheeting between washing lines (thus avoiding the impurities in rain water that has run off roofs) is usually very soft and almost as neutral (i.e. neither acid nor alkaline) as distilled water, and may be used instead of distilled water to adjust tap water.
Some aquarists may have a domestic water softener in their homes. This device will produce soft water but the water is unstable and should be left to stand for twenty-four hours before being tested for hardness.

135. In a breeding tank with the right environment, i.e. with sufficient planting, the eggs are often laid against the pane *(Apistogramma ortmanni)*.

136. A specialist tank for bigger Cichlids can be ▷ decorated with rocks and with plants of the *Echinodorus* family or *Vallisneria gigantea*. The bottom around the plants is covered with smaller stones in order to avoid excavating by the fishes. Some places are left open so that the fishes can dig. Breeding will take place in these places and will be easily observable.

Finally, all these soft waters should be filtered for twenty-four hours through an active charcoal filter, and then once again tested for °DH. They are then suitable for adding to the hard, matured tap water. It will of course be virtually impossible to obtain soft water with a nil registration of °DH: the most soft achieved will probably be about 0.2°DH: at that kind of level however the effect is to reduce the hardness of the original water to half its former reading, thus: taking 10 liters (hard) water of 18°DH; adding 10 liters (very soft) water of 0.2°DH will give 20 liters of water of 9°DH.
To adjust the pH value of water for the breeding tank, either peat or oak leaves may be used. Water should be filtered through rinsed (not boiled) peat, and filtration continued until, after a series of checks, the right pH value has been achieved. The water will have become amber, and should be allowed to stand for twenty-four hours, which will give the suspended particles time to settle. That water must then be aerated before plants are put in the tank. Oak leaves that fall in autumn can be used to acidify water by being laid as a bed in a tank and the water then poured over them: they cannot be used as a filter.
Water that has had its hardness and acidity adjusted artificially will not be stable: the hardness and acidity vary after a time, and such water must be regularly tested.

The Layout of the Breeding Tank

The ideal layout for the breeding tank is, as a rule, a compromise between the hygienic desirability of having as little in the tank as possible that may encourage harmful bacteria, and providing the breeding fish with as natural an environment as possible, this being especially important with those species that are not so easy to stimulate to breed. Thus those species that breed in cavities, will not be satisfied with one coconut shell or flower pot in the middle of the tank: some active swimmers accustomed to darting about in a well-planted environment may be disconcerted if there is only one breeding mop in the tank. In the systematic section directions that take into account the particular requirements of individual species are noted, and these should be strictly followed. Only in this way will natural, and therefore most likely successful breeding be achieved.
It is advisable to take some precautionary measures against the possibility of the fish eating their eggs, a habit particularly common among freelayers. One possibility is to have some thick vegetation around the sides: fine-leaved plants where the eggs can gather and be sheltered. Alternatively, a lot of thick, low growing plants may be put on the bed or it can be covered with long pieces of peat fibre so that the eggs are largely out of the parent fishes' reach. If the species in question does not normally take food from the bed, then the fish will not look for the eggs there, so there will be no need to cover the bed. This can be advantageous, especially if the eggs have to be stored in sterile conditions, as with some species of seasonal

137. The breeding tank should be stable, easy to move, and clean. A tank 40 × 25 × 25 cm is ideal for most species. It should be possible to modify the interior by using movable partition panes, should this be necessary, as it will be for certain fish. However, smaller breeding tanks of 6–10 liters capacity can often be used and are helpful if very soft water is needed, which may be expensive to obtain and prepare. On the other hand a 40 cm tank will not be large enough for some species which need a lot of swimming space when mating.
If the amateur is going to make his own breeding tank with glass and silicone adhesives, as described in the introductory section above on Aquariums, then thicker glass than usual (at least 6 mm) should be used because the breeding tank must be more than usually robust to withstand frequent moving. Likewise if the old-fashioned all-glass moulded tanks are used, care must be taken to see that they do not shatter. Small perspex tanks can be used, but are also easy to damage when moving them.
With the exception of one long pane, all the sides and the bottom of the breeding tank can be painted dark brown or black on the outside. This gives the prospective breeders the peaceful environment they require. It is then not necessary to cover the walls inside the tank, or to lay a dark bed for fish that do not actually need a bed for breeding. The tank should be covered with a glass pane: it is rarely necessary to provide a lighting cover.
Before using the breeding tank, it should always be washed out thoroughly with clean, tepid tap water without soap or detergents. Only when all the dirt has been rinsed away or scrubbed off, can the tank be filled with a solution of slaked lime. Slaked lime should be stirred into water until no more lime is absorbed, and then this saturated solution should be diluted with six parts of pure water to one of the solution. The tank should then be left to stand for about twenty-four hours. When it has been disinfected in this way, the breeding tank is ready to be used, after all traces of the lime solution have been removed by repeated rinsing of the tank with clean water.

fish. If there is no bed then plants can be held in place with glass rods or pieces of lead: this has to be done if the bed is of peat, because it is not possible to root plants in such loose material. Unless it is essential to have a sandy bed for breeding, it is generally better to use peat. This makes an attractive dark bed and the fish feel more secure: moreover, many young fish seek protection at first, in or just above the bed, and peat fibre is an excellent refuge for them, but it should of course be washed before being put in the tank.

Arrangements of rock providing the cavities and hiding places for cave breeders should always be built on the floor of the aquarium: they should be put in sturdily and in such a way that the fish cannot undermine them. A shaky construction can easily lead to one of the glass sides of the tank being shattered. It may be very tempting to spy on the fish in their hiding place, but the entrance to it should always be screened off with plants or other obstacles in such a way that the fish do not feel they are being observed. The parent fish will often eat the eggs because they feel disturbed by an overinquisitive keeper.

For the Anabantidae or Labyrinth fish which build bubble nests and use the foliage of plants to strengthen their nests, there should always be an adequate number of floating plants. There should also be some thick clumps of plants where the female can seek refuge if pursued too much by an over-aggressive or over-zealous mate.

Breeding tanks should always be covered with a glass plate: for Labyrinth fish they should fit closely to exclude all draughts above the surface of the water, and the temperature of the air below the glass should preferably be the same as the temperature of the water.

The breeding of Labyrinth fish is perhaps one of the most interesting things that the amateur can do, for all these fish are bubble nest builders, and it is a fascinating process to watch. The fact that these fish, such as the Siamese Fighting Fish *(Betta splendens)* and the Dwarf Gourami *(Colisa lalia)*, both in the Anabantidae family, have this unusual supplementary respiratory organ, the labyrinth, which allows them to inhale air at the surface, is not of course unconnected with their reproductive behaviour of building bubble nests at the surface.

The breeding of Siamese Fighting Fish illustrates however the need, in some cases, to adapt the breeding tanks to the particular requirements of the species. A tank 60 × 30 × 15 cm is ideal and should have wooden slats or grooved rubber fitted down the middle to allow a glass partition to be inserted, so that the two breeders will be separated but each will have half the tank to itself.

As described in the sectional list below, the females can be identified as approaching the spawning period by the end of the ovipositor being visible at the vent. The selected pair are then put in the tank and only after two or so days, when the male has built the bubble nest among floating plants and is continually swimming to the glass partition to entice the female to the nest, should the partition be removed and the pair allowed to mate. When the mating is over (or even before) the female must be removed. If she is allowed to join the male too soon, or left with him too long, she will be killed.

After the male has tended the nest for about a week after the fry have hatched, he must be removed, or else he may eat the offspring. The fry have to be kept in well-covered tanks so that, as their labyrinths develop and they begin to breathe at the surface the air they breathe is moist and warm. Finally, as soon as the males can be sexed they must be transferred to special small tanks to avoid their fighting and damaging each other.

This example, although it has admittedly one or two unusual features, has been explained in some detail to illustrate the need for care and attention in breeding, the need to adjust equipment and, indeed, to have the necessary equipment available well before the event. It is not possible to prepare the breeding tank conveniently only when the female is identified as ready to spawn: the various small tanks for the male fry cannot be set up only when fighting between them is imminent, and it is clear from what has been said that over a period of two or three weeks, from the time the breeders are selected, the aquarist must closely observe and control the situation in the tank.

138. The male *Monocirrhus polycanthus*, the Leaf Fish, guards eggs spawned on the leaf of an Amazoneplant.

In general the water in the breeding tank should not be filtered: it is also rarely necessary to aerate it, and the turbulence that this would cause would only disturb the fish. It is only when breeding fish which normally live in waters where there is a strong current that such turbulence may be desirable. The breeding tank for such species will have to be laid out in a special way, with stones and sand or gravel – materials which can withstand a strong current and will not float up to the surface or turn the water cloudy.
Some fish prefer to lay their eggs in the early morning when the first rays of sun strike the tank: for those species the breeding tank should be suitably sited. Other species will be content with the limited daylight which comes in through the front

139. *Tilapia tholloni* male in breeding dress – the red on throat and belly.

pane of the tank. It is hardly ever necessary to provide overhead lighting: too much light is more likely to be harmful than too little. In the natural state, most fish seek out a very shaded spot for mating. For this reason it may even be desirable to screen off most of the breeding tank: this may also be necessary to protect the eggs which are often very sensitive to light, and are adversely affected by it.

Mating

The reproductive behavior of fish varies enormously from species to species. Information is given in the descriptions of the individual species in the systematic section. Either the male or the female may take the initiative in mating. The actual mating may be preceded by a long or short courtship, sometimes involving a number of mock matings in which neither eggs nor milt are produced. The courtship behavior and these mock matings may suddenly stop without leading to any proper mating. On the other hand, fish sometimes mate without any preliminary courtship.
Mating may be either boisterous or peaceful. They may, depending on the species, be spread over a period of hours, days, or in some cases weeks, with the sexual act occurring once or more frequently each day. In general it is not difficult to select pairs which will mate, but sometimes the prospective partners are not responsive: it may take a fairly long time for them to accept each other and in some cases they never do. In some species males will mate with a number of females: in others, a female will mate with more than one male: it is not unusual for both sexes to change partners frequently in the case of species that live in shoals.

The Care of the Eggs

The care which the amateur must give to the eggs varies from species to species: there are important notes on this in the species descriptions in the systematic list. Generally the aquarist does not have to take any special care of the eggs of those species of fish which themselves look after their young. Indeed, the less obtrusive attention they receive the better. However if those fish have bred in a tank which is really too small, then it may be wise to change some of the water, to prevent pollution through the action of excess milt. This is something which it is often good to do when other kinds of fish have spawned in a breeding tank.
When this is done, the temperature of the fresh water should be carefully adjusted so that it is exactly the same as that of the water already in the breeding tank.

140. In a community tank it is often not difficult to discern the existence of pairs. Pairs will separate from the others and will court, as here *Cichlasoma nigrofasciatum*.

141. The kissing gourami, *Helastoma temmincki*. This apparent sign of affection is in fact a ritual in asserting territorial rights.

In most cases the fresh water can, without danger, be slightly harder, but the pH value should be the same as that of the water already in the tank. About one third and no more of the total volume of water in the tank can be changed each day, for the first few days, so that the balance in the breeding tank is never disturbed too abruptly. Thus after three days or so all the water will have been changed and without damage to the eggs or any fry that have by then hatched.

It is usually desirable to remove parent fish of those species which do not care for their young, from the breeding tank as soon as spawning has ceased, to stop them eating the eggs or the fry. This should be done very carefully because too much disturbance of the water can damage the eggs.

Of course, alternatively, for some species it is possible to use breeding traps which are plastic containers inserted into the breeding tank and so designed that they confine the parent fish to a particular part of the tank while allowing the eggs to fall through holes or grilles to a part of the bed of the tank the parents cannot reach. These traps are particularly useful for livebearers, and allow many of the young to escape the predatory forays of the parents. However many traps on the market are too small to give the parent fish adequate freedom, and they must be used with care.

Many eggs are sensitive to light. If the breeding tank was not screened off from incoming light while the fish were mating, it should certainly be screened when the eggs are being hatched, whatever species is involved. Twilight or almost complete darkness will certainly never harm the eggs and is helpful for the newly hatched fry which naturally seek out shaded spots. After a few days the screens can be carefully and gradually removed, piece by piece, so that the tank is finally wholly exposed to ordinary daylight after about a week. Even then, direct sunlight should be avoided.

The eggs are usually clear and transparent: they can be seen most easily if the spawning medium is dark. Unfertilized eggs can be recognized immediately because they turn a yellowish-white after a short time. Unfertilized eggs should be removed from the breeding tank with a pipette or dip tube. If they are not removed they will encourage the growth of mould which will in turn spread to the fertilized eggs, particularly where the eggs are heaped together. Generally it is not advisable to use anti-mould preparations in the breeding tank. The eggs of the seasonal fish like the species in the genera *Aphyosemion, Epiplatys* and *Roloffia,* and those of other species where the incubation period is anything from fourteen days to several

142. *Notopterus notopterus* with eggs.

143. *Cichlasoma biocellatum* (female) with eggs.

months should be treated in a special way, details of which are given in the systematic list under the species in question.

Raising the Fry

Once again the degree of care that the aquarist has to devote to the raising of the fry depends on the extent of parental concern by the fish. The fry of those which take care of their young require the least attention from the aquarist. When those young are not raised apart from the parents, it is rarely necessary to feed them with the special foods for fry. The parents often chew up food and then spew it out amongst the young, making sure that each young fish feeds plentifully. As soon as the young of these species of fish are left to their own devices by the parents, they are in general big enough to be able to be fed with the normal sorts of food.

The young of all other fish should be very carefully raised from the moment the eggs hatch. The eggs of most fish develop a yolk sac which contains some reserves of food for the newly born fry: the size of the sac and therefore the reserve of food varies enormously from species to species. Sometimes it is even absent from the egg, as for example in the case of most egg-laying tooth-carps and livebearers. The young of the livebearers are of course well advanced as soon as they are born and immediately start to hunt for food. For those then, special small sized foods should be available immediately. These young, active fish can be fed very often with freshly hatched Artemia nauplii from the first day, as well as with finely sieved pond infusoria supplemented with finely ground dried food of a brand suitable for live bearing fish. The same sort of food can also be fed as a special treat to fish which take care of their young. Such foods cannot however be fed for the first few days to the fry of fish whose eggs develop a yolk sac, but it cannot at the same time be assumed that the yolk sacs will contain sufficient food to meet all the requirements of the fry for the first few days, until they are able to feed on the fry foods described above.

A supplement must be given if the fry are to be raised successfully, but many of these very young fish are so small that they can be fed at first only with the very finest infusoria. Moreover, the fry of some species have to be almost up to their necks in food before they are able to eat it. Even then it may happen that they will accept only a special diet. These matters are dealt with in further detail, where pertinent, in the individual species descriptions in the systematic list below.

It is important to make sure that there will be enough suitable food for the fry before starting the breeding. Adequate food is of paramount importance, especially during the first few weeks of the life of the young fish. If they do not get enough during this crucial period because available food is either unsuitable or insufficient, their development is inevitably impaired and they do not subsequently recover. If it is not possible to obtain the special foods that will be needed, it is better not to start breeding at all.

It is usually possible to collect pond infusoria suitable for most species. When infusoria is collected from a pond with a fine meshed net, it can be turned into very fine infusoria, as needed for some species, by sieving it through a succession of finer and finer sieves. Alternatively it is possible (and sometimes safer) for the aquarist to culture his own infusoria, as explained in the section above on Feeding.

Infusoria has an unpleasant smell, and not too much should be put into the breeding tank, because there is the slight possibility that the water might become polluted. It is also necessary of course to check regularly that the fry are accepting the infusoria and are eating enough of it. With a good magnifying glass, this can be determined from the shape of the belly; fry which are getting enough food in their early stages of development have a pointed belly.

With a magnifying glass it is also possible to determine when the young fish, which initially are quite colorless, are starting to develop coloration and markings. As soon as this happens, it is possible to change to slightly larger forms of food, for the beginning of pigmentation heralds the end of the critical first stage of development. As a general rule, from that moment, the size of the eyes gives a

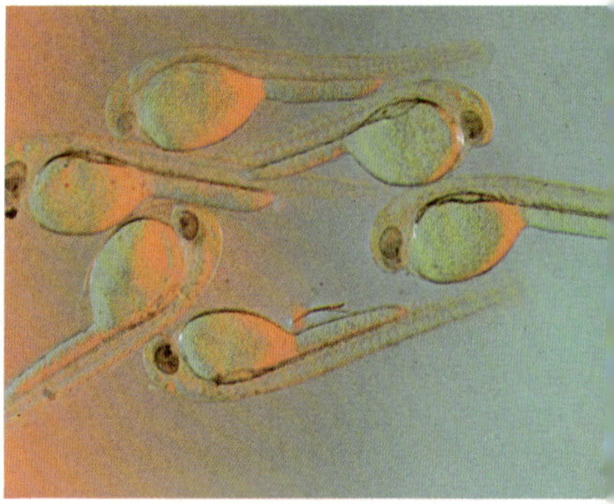

144a. Freshly hatched young of the *Barbus tetrazona tetrazona*; the body is totally transparent and still carries the yolk-sac.

144b. The same young at the final stage of their embryonic development; they swim around freely and hunt for food. The silver spot is the swimming bladder.

144c. A group of young *Rasbora daniconius*. After feeding, young fish fed correctly should have well-filled bellies like these specimens.

rough indication of the size of the animal matter which the fish are able to eat. By no means all young fish however bother to hunt actively for food. In many cases they will snap food up only if it happens to float past their noses. This must always be borne in mind, as well as the normal feeding habits of the particular species concerned.

In general the fry will take food from the same level as do the mature fish in that species – perhaps only from the bottom, or only from the surface, although as noted in the species description below, in the systematic list, some fry have individual inclinations of their own. In any case these are only general rules and the careful breeder will at all times closely observe the feeding of his fry to ensure that they are feeding properly, and if necessary, adjust the food, and the way it is fed to them, accordingly.

It is possible to bring Cyclops nauplii as well as other infusoria and the large number of fry together by putting a small source of light in a corner of the tank – in most cases a small torch connected to a transformer or a battery is quite sufficient. In this way the fish are surrounded by food. A similar arrangement can be installed near the surface for fish which look for their food there. However, if the food is to be spread more evenly through the tank, this can be achieved with very gentle aeration. If the fish have a preference for taking their food from the bed a small source of light can be installed there.

Larger types of food can be used for fry when the pigmentation starts to develop. Cyclops nauplii and sieved Daphnia are very suitable. This diet can be supplemented with small quantities of dried food to provide some variation, although this depends to a large extent on the species being bred. There are now on the market and obtainable at good aquarist shops some excellent prepared foods for fry. In general no fry should be fed solely on dried food, but these preparations can be a very good supplement.

The consequence of feeding fry liberally and the degree of experimentation frequently involved in choosing one food or another to see if it is welcomed by the fry, inevitably mean that some food will remain uneaten. In the breeding tank even more than in the community tank uneaten food is a dangerous source of pollution and the amateur must always ensure that the tank is kept as clean as possible and all uneaten food removed with a dip stick.

The Tank for Raising the Fry

In general the fry should not be kept in the limited confines of the breeding tank any longer than strictly necessary. They should remain in it only while they are too young and vulnerable to be transferred to a larger aquarium. It is however a help to the aquarist to have them in the breeding tank for two or so weeks because he can keep a very close eye on them in that small space, and it is easier also to ensure that such a small tank is kept scrupulously clean.

From the moment however that the fish start to hunt for their own food, pigmentation has fully developed and the fry are about 1 cm long, they can be carefully transferred to a tank for raising fry. A tank 1 m × 30 × 30 cm is best: a generous length and width are important to allow for the water to be well oxygenated, and to give the fry adequate swimming space. The opportunity to swim freely is important at this stage: it helps their physical development and stimulates their appetite, which in turn encourages their general development.

Moreover, in such a tank it is possible to have a lay out similar to that in a full sized aquarium. A sandy bed can be provided, possibly some hiding places amongst stones or pieces of bogwood and plants. Good oxygenating plants are the most suitable to include in the tank: these plants help to purify the water while at the same time enriching it with oxygen, which is very important for the healthy development of the fry. Various different species can be raised together in such a tank which should be sited where it will get plenty of light to stimulate plant growth. It can also be fitted with a lighting cover but the lighting must be turned off at night.

In most cases this tank can be filled with ordinary tap water, but before the young fish are transferred to the tank it should be allowed to mature for a week or two after being laid out. This means in fact that it will have to be prepared about the time that the eggs hatch in the breeding tank. When there are fish in the tank a third of the water should be changed once a week, a small amount each day. Tap water at the right temperature may generally be used unless it is very hard, that is above 20°DH.

If it is too hard, or if it is necessary to keep the composition of the water in the tank consistent at all times for some other reason, then the water must be filtered continuously through a charcoal filter and the filter mesh changed regularly. If it is necessary to maintain a constant level of acidity (though this is rarely the case in a tank for raising fry), either a peat filter or a combined peat/charcoal filter must be used. If a combined peat/charcoal filter is used, then the water should first pass through the charcoal and then the peat, for otherwise the charcoal will destroy the effect of the peat. If the composition of the water allows it, it is cheaper and simpler to change the water once a week with tap water than to filter it. Moreover, there is then no risk of a filter clogging up, which if it occurs can have disastrous consequences for the fry.

Whichever method is chosen, however, it is absolutely essential to change the water regularly. If this is not done, then elements which inhibit growth and slow down the development of the fry begin to develop in the water as a result of the decomposition of food and the excreta of the fish. There is also a very real danger of poisoning the water as the fry are fed considerably greater quantities of food than fish in a normal aquarium.

It is only necessary to aerate the tank for raising the fry if it is necessary to spread the food more evenly throughout the water. At any time when the fish gasp for oxygen at the surface, the reason probably is that the water is polluted or the tank is too crowded. Aerating the tank in these circumstances may seem to improve matters slightly but does not in fact remove the source of the problem. The number of fish must be reduced.

145. Tanks for the fry can be placed above the main tank. Individual breeding tanks should have different water levels, appropriate to the particular stage of development of the fry being reared in them. This facilitates feeding.

The Golden Rules

These notes on breeding will serve as a general introduction to the subject for the interested amateur, and the more detailed description given above of the special problems of breeding Siamese Fighting Fish will put him on his guard that before any breeding is undertaken, a careful study must be made of that species' particular requirements.

Perhaps this summary of the rules to be observed for successful breeding will be of some help:

(1) Decide, in the light of your stock of fish and *your future requirements*, what fish you want to breed.
(2) Make a careful study of the habits of that species, and read carefully the notes on the family, genus and species in the systematic list.
(3) Buy a notebook, which will become your permanent breeding record.
(4) List in that notebook all the equipment you will need, and check that you have it.
(5) Draw up a timetable in the book, listing when the various tanks must be ready, and when they must be set up to mature. Do this also for whatever additional supplies of water or food will be needed.
(6) Make a note of any special requirements and hazards to be avoided.
(7) Prepare your equipment.
(8) Begin the breeding, making a careful note (for future use), of what happens when: your experience will be more valuable to you than anything you can read in a book however helpful that is.
(9) When the breeding is completed, clean and store all equipment so that it is in good condition for the next operation.

PLANTS

FLORA OF THE AQUARIUM

A Selective Systematic List

THERE ARE many different species of plants that can, in certain conditions, be grown in an aquarium proper or in a shore aquarium. It would be impossible to try to make a complete list, but for this encyclopaedia about a hundred have been selected, the selection being drawn from both those that are well-known to most aquarists and others not as yet so popular but which, on account of their beauty or utility, deserve to be more widely cultivated by amateurs.

The list is arranged in alphabetical order, according to the latin names of the plants.

From the systematic descriptions will appear that plants, like fishes, have as a rule two latin names, the *generic*, which gives the *genus*, and the specific, which gives the *species* name. Unfortunately, there are very many more synonyms for plants than there are, for example, for fish, and although the most common synonyms have been indexed at the beginning of this section, the amateur should not be too surprised if at some time, he comes across one of these plants under yet another name.

The individual entries in this list give the family name, the English name where one exists, and the common synonyms. That is followed by information on the origin and natural habitat of the plant. A description of it follows. Where possible these descriptions are written in straightforward lay language even if this results in a slight scientific inaccuracy. However, some botanical terms are included, not only because they are the only way accurately to describe particular features of the plants, but also because the aquarist will almost inevitably come across them in other books, and it is well to understand what they mean. A short glossary of the terms will be found at the end of the alphabetical list.

Notes are also given on the propagation and cultivation of the plants, and additional comments on any other matter of particular interest. Some related species of which for one reason or another a full description is not given, are mentioned in the body of the text under the species described. These related species are listed in the table below with synonyms.

To most aquarists, quite rightly, the plants in the aquarium are only of secondary interest: it is the fish that are the amateur's primary concern. Nevertheless, very many aquarists become almost as attached to their plants as to their fish, and are as concerned about their welfare. It should be remembered that most aquatic plants are, in the wild, really bog plants, and to some extent most, in the aquarium are growing under slightly artificial conditions. There are very few families of plants, all the members of which are true water plants. It is for that reason that it is not helpful (as it is in the case of fish) to list the plants under their families, but rather under their generic and specific names.

Twenty-nine families of plants are however mentioned in this list, and for the interest of readers, these are listed below alphabetically, with short notes.

THE FAMILIES MENTIONED IN THE ALPHABETICAL LIST

Acanthaceae (the Acanthus family)
This is a very large family with 180 genera and some 2000 species, most of which grow in the tropics, and many of which are grown as ornamental plants in greenhouses. Of all these, only about three species are aquarium plants, including the species of *Hygrophila*.

Alismataceae (the water plantain family)
There are some 12 genera and some 50 species in this family, all of which are bog or true aquatic plants: it includes two genera well-known to aquarists, *Echinodorus* and *Sagittaria*.

Amaranthaceae (the Amaranth family)
This family contains about 500 species in 40 genera. Some are popular garden plants, but only one, *Alternanthera reineckii,* is usually grown in the aquarium: another species, *Alternanthera philoreroides,* Alligator weed, is sometimes mentioned in the literature.

Aponogetonaceae (the Aponogeton family)
One of the families of true aquatic plants, with only one genus, and some 25 species, nine of which are described below, and others of which the aquarist may well encounter from time to time. It contains the extraordinary and beautiful lace leaf plants (*Aponogeton madagascariensis* and its varieties).

Araceae (the Arum family)
This is a large family of more than 100 genera and more than 1500 species, one or another of which is found almost all over the world. It is of particular interest to aquarists because it contains the very beautiful but slow growing Cryptocoryne species, originally bog plants from Southeast Asia.

Azollaceae (the Azolla family)
This is a small family, which includes various species of *Azolla*, including *Azolla caroliniana*, the fairy moss. The genus *Azolla* is put by some authorities in the family Marsiliaceae.

Ceratophyllaceae (the Hornworts)
This is a very small family, with only one genus, *Ceratophyllum*, which contains the Hornworts, known to aquarists but not among the most popular of aquarium plants, because they are more suitable for outdoor ponds.

Cruciferae (the Crucifer family)
This is a very large family with over 200 genera and some 2000 species, including vegetables such as cabbages, garden flowers like wallflowers, and the cresses. It is one of these, *Cardamine lyrata*, that is known to aquarists. Another species, *Cardamine rotundiflora*, is sometimes put in cold water aquariums, but is unsuitable for heated tanks.

Cyperaceae (the Sedge family)
This is one of the largest of the plant families, with many thousands of species throughout the world. Very few of these plants can grow under water, but a submersed variety of *Eleocharis acicularis* is used in aquariums.

Haloragidaceae or **Haloragaceae** (the Water Milfoil family)
This is a relatively small family of both aquatic and terrestial plants, with eight genera and about 100 species. It is important for the aquarist because it contains the popular and useful *Myriophyllum* species.

Hydrocharitaceae (the Frog-bit family)
Although there are some 14 genera, there are in this family of aquatic floating plants only 40 species. It includes two well-known aquarium plants, *Egeria densa* (or *Elodea densa*) and *Elodea canadensis*, as well as species in the genus *Hydrilla*.

Hypnaceae
This is one of the families of mosses and contains within it *Vesicularia dubyana*, one of the most popular decorative plants for the aquarium.

Lobeliaceae (the Lobelia family)
Most of the 600 species in the 20 or so genera in this family are herbs, but some are also grown terrestrially for ornament. Only one aquatic species, *Lobelia cardinalis*, is well-known to aquarists, although another species, *Lobelia dortmanna* (synonym *Lobelia lacustris*), which produces pale blue flowers above the surface, is sometimes encountered.

Lomariospidaceae
A very small family of ferns, the principal species of which for aquarists is the unusual *Bolbitis heudelotii*, which was formerly placed in the family *Polypodiaceae*.

Lythraceae (the Loosestrife family)
There are some 12 genera and 400 species in this family whose members come principally from the tropics. Four aquarium plants, in the genera *Ammannia*, *Peplis* and *Rotala* are known to aquarists.

Marsileaceae (the Quatrefoils)
This is a large family of water ferns, which closely resemble in shape the four-leafed clovers, which have given them some of their popular names. Some of the better known species are described in the alphabetical list.

Najadaceae (the Najas family)
This is a very small family with only one genus, Najas, containing a number of species of very fine leaved plants popular with aquarists.

Nymphaeaceae (the Water Lily family)
There are eight genera, with some 60 species, in this family of well-known beautiful aquatic plants. The majority of course are more suitable for ponds than the aquarium, but some, notably the *Cabomba* species and *Barclaya longifolia* are well-known to aquarists.

Onagraceae (the Evening Primrose)
This is a large family with 35 genera and some 470 species, It includes a large number of ornamental garden plants and shrubs, including the Fuchsias. It is of interest to aquarists because it includes the *Ludwigia* species, of which *Ludwigia palustris* is the most popular.

Parkeriaceae (the Watersprite family)
This is a family of water ferns that include the very popular *Ceratopteris* species, of which there are both submersed and floating varieties.

Polypediceae (the Common Fern family)
There are over 5000 species in this enormous family of ferns. Of all these true ferns very few are properly to be considered aquatic plants, but one that is, is the popular *Microsorium pteropus* described below.

Pontederiaceae (the Pickerel weed family)
This is a small family of aquatic herbs all of which come from tropical or sub-tropical climes. To aquarists, the species in the genera *Eichhornia* and *Heteranthera* are of interest, particularly *Heteranthera zosteraefolia* which is the only species that can be grown submersed continuously.

Potamogetonaceae (the Pond weed family)
There are over 120 species in the genus *Potamogeton*, some of which are submersed and others are floating plants. The most popular with aquarists is *Potamogeton gayi*, an undemanding plant very suitable for a wide variety of aquariums.

146. *Alternanthera reineckii*

147. *Aponogeton madagascariensis*

148. *Aponogeton ulvaceus*

Primulaceae (the Primrose family)
The *Primulaceae* family is very large, with some 30 genera and over 700 species, many of which are popular garden plants. Both the *Hottonia* and the *Samolus* genera contain plants of interest to the aquarist.

Ricciaceae (the Crystalwort family)
This is a small family of floating plants of which *Riccia fluitans*, the Crystalwort, is much favored by aquarists as an oxygenating plant and a refuge for fry in a breeding tank.

Salviniaceae (the Salvinia family)
This is a small family of aquatic ferns, with only about 20 species in two genera. These floating plants are however of great interest to aquarists, and are often a valuable addition to a tank as a refuge for fry.

Sauvuraceae (the Sauvuras family)
A very small family in which only one species *Sauvurus cernuus* is of interest to aquarists. It has somewhat declined in popularity.

Scrophulariaceae (the Figwort family)
There are over 180 genera in this large family containing over 300 species, including such popular garden plants as the Veronicas and Antirrhinums. To aquarists, various species in the genera *Bacopa*, *Limnophila* and *Micracanthemum*, described below, are of interest.

Umbelliferae (the Parsley family)
This is another very large family with over 2000 species in some 250 genera, and it contains a number of very important herbs. Only the genus *Hydrocotyle* is of interest.

SYNONYMS AND RELATED SPECIES MENTIONED IN THE ALPHABETICAL LIST

Synonym (syn) or related species (sp):	To be found under:
Acorus calamus (sp)	*Acorus gramineus*
Acorus gramineus foliis variegatis (sp)	*Acorus gramineus*
Acorus humilis (syn)	*Acorus gramineus*
Acrostichum thalictroides (syn)	*Ceratopteris cornuta*
Alisma rostratum (syn)	*Echinodorus berteroi*
Alisma tenellum (syn)	*Echinodorus tenellus*
Alternanthera sessilis (sp)	*Alternanthera reineckii*
Alternanthera variegata (sp)	*Alternanthera reineckii*
Ambrosinia ciliata (syn)	*Cryptocoryne ciliata*
'Ammania, Red'	*Ammania senegalensis*
Ammania rotundifolia (syn)	*Rotala rotundifolia*
Anacharis densa (syn)	*Egeria densa*
Anubis barteri (syn)	*Anubis lanceolata*
Aponogeton boivinianus (syn)	*Aponogeton boivinanus*

Synonym (syn) or related species (sp):	To be found under:
Aponogeton fenestralis (syn)	*Aponogeton madagascariensis*
Aponogeton henkelianus (syn)	*Aponogeton madagascariensis*
Aponogeton monostachyos (syn)	*Aponogeton undulatus*
Aponogeton natans (syn)	*Aponogeton echinatus*
Aponogeton stachyosporus (syn)	*Aponogeton undulatus*
Aponogeton undulatus (syn)	*Aponogeton crispus*
Azolla densa (syn)	*Azolla caroliniana*
Azolla mexicanus (syn)	*Azolla caroliniana*
Azolla microphylla (syn)	*Azolla caroliniana*
Bacopa caroliniana (syn)	*Bacopa amplexicaulis*
Barclaya motleyi (sp)	*Barclaya longifolia*
Cambomba peltata (syn)	*Cabomba caroliniana*
Cabomba pinnata (syn)	*Cabomba caroliniana*
Cabomba pubescens (syn)	*Cabomba piauhyensis*

Synonym (syn) or related species (sp):	To be found under:
Ceratophyllum aspersum (syn)	*Ceratophyllum demersum*
Ceratophyllum cornutum (syn)	*Ceratophyllum demersum*
Ceratophyllum cristatum (syn)	*Ceratophyllum demersum*
Ceratophyllum submersum (sp)	*Ceratophyllum demersum*
Ceratopteris thalictroides forma cornuta (syn)	*Ceratopteris cornuta*
Cryptocoryne aponogetifolia (syn)	*Cryptocoryne usteriana*
Cryptocoryne cordata (syn)	*Cryptocoryne becketti*
Cryptocoryne cordata (syn)	*Cryptocoryne purpurea*
Cryptocoryne elata (syn)	*Cryptocoryne ciliata*
Cryptocoryne griffithii (syn)	*Cryptocoryne purpurea*
Cryptocoryne haerteliana (syn)	*Cryptocoryne affinis*
Cryptocoryne lingua (sp)	*Cryptocoryne versteegii*
Cryptocoryne lucens (sp)	*Cryptocoryne nevillii*
Cryptocoryne parva (sp)	*Cryptocoryne nevillii*
Cryptocoryne siamensis	*Cryptocoryne blassii*
Cryptocoryne somphongsii (syn)	*Cryptocoryne balansae*
Cryptocoryne undulata (syn)	*Cryptocoryne willisii*
Damasonium indicum (syn)	*Ottelia alismoides*
Didiplis diandra (syn)	*Peplis diandra*
Echinodorus brevipedicellatus (syn)	*Echinodorus amazonicus*
Echinodorus cordifolius (syn)	*Echinodorus berteroi*
Echinodorus grandiflorus (sp)	*Echinodorus horizontalis*
Echinodorus intermedius (syn)	*Echinodorus latifolius*
Echinodorus leopoldina (syn)	*Echinodorus maior*
Echinodorus macrophyllus (sp)	*Echinodorus horizontalis*
Echinodorus magdalenensis (syn)	*Echinodorus latifolius*
Echinodorus martii (syn)	*Echinodorus maior*
Echinodorus muricatus (sp)	*Echinodorus horizontalis*
Echinodorus nymphaefolius (sp)	*Echinodorus berteroi*
Echinodorus paniculatus (syn)	*Echinodorus bleheri*
Echinodorus parvulus (syn)	*Echinodorus tenellus*
Echinodorus peruensis (syn)	*Echinodorus parviflorus*
Echinodorus quadricostatus (sp)	*Echinodorus latifolius*
Echinodorus rostratus (syn)	*Echinodorus berteroi*
Echinodorus subulatus (syn)	*Echinodorus tenellus*
Eichhornia crassipes (sp)	*Eichhornia azurea*
Eleocharis vivipara (sp)	*Eleocharis acicularis*
Elodea densa (sp)	*Egeria densa*
Elodea latifolia (syn)	*Elodea canadensis*
Elodea nuttallii (sp)	*Elodea canadensis*
Glossadelphus zollingeri (sp)	*Vesicularia dubyana*
Gymnopteris heudelotti (syn)	*Bolbitis heudelotti*
Heleocharis acicularis (syn)	*Eleocharis acicularis*
Hemiadelphis polysperma (syn)	*Hygrophila polysperma*
Herpestes caroliniana (syn)	*Bacopa amplexicaulis*
Herpestes monnieria (syn)	*Bacopa monnieri*
Hottonia inflata (syn)	*Hottonia species*
Hottonia palustris (sp)	*Hottonia species*
Hydrilla alternifolia (syn)	*Hydrilla verticillata*
Hydrilla dentata (syn)	*Hydrilla verticillata*

149. *Cryptocoryne becketti*

Synonym (syn) or related species (sp):	To be found under:
Hydromystria stolinfera (syn)	*Limnobium laevigatum*
Hygrophila angustifolia (sp)	*Hygrophila polysperma*
Hygrophila stricta (syn)	*Nomaphila stricta*
Hypnum dubyanum (syn)	*Vesicularia dubyana*
Justica polysperma (syn)	*Hygrophila polysperma*
Justica stricta (syn)	*Nomaphila stricta*
Leptochilus decurrens (syn)	*Microsorium pteropus*
Limnobium stoloniferum (syn)	*Limnobium laevigatum*
Limnophila heterophylla (sp)	*Limnophila aquatica*
Limnophila indica (sp)	*Limnophila aquatica*
Limnophila sessiflora (sp)	*Limnophila aquatica*
Ludwigia arcuata (sp)	*Ludwigia palustris*
Ludwigia mullertii (syn)	*Ludwigia palustris*
Ludwigia natana (syn)	*Ludwigia palustris*
Ludwigia repens (syn)	*Ludwigia palustris*
Lysimachia monnieri (syn)	*Bacopa monnieri*
Micranthemum orbiculatum (sp)	*Micranthemum micranthemoides*
Myriophyllum aquaticum (sp)	*Myriophyllum species*
Myriophyllum brasiliense (syn)	*Myriophyllum species*
Myriophyllum hippuroides (sp)	*Myriophyllum species*
Myriophyllum serpinacoides (syn)	*Myriophyllum species*
Najas guadelupensis (sp)	*Najas species*
Najas indica (sp)	*Najas species*
Najas kingii (syn)	*Najas species*
Najas microdon (syn)	*Najas species*
(the) Narrow leaved blassii (sp)	*Cryptocoryne blassii*
Nectris aquatica (syn)	*Cabomba aquatica*
Nectris peltata (syn)	*Cabomba caroliniana*
Nomaphila corymbosa (syn)	*Nomaphila stricta*
Nuphar rivulare (syn)	*Nuphar luteum*

Synonym (syn) or related species (sp):	To be found under:
Nuphar sagittifolium (sp)	*Nuphar luteum*
Nymphaea dentata	*Nymphaca lotus*
Nymphaea lutea (syn)	*Nuphar luteum*
Obolaria caroliniana (syn)	*Bacopa amplexicaulis*
Ottelia indica (syn)	*Ottelia alismoides*
Ottelia ulvaefolia (sp)	*Ottelia alismoides*
Ouvirandra undulata (syn)	*Aponogeton crispus*
Parkeria pteridoides (syn)	*Ceratopteris cornuta*
Polypodium pteropus (syn)	*Microsorum pteropus*
Pontederia aquatica (syn)	*Eichhornia azurea*
Pontederia azurea (syn)	*Eichhornia azurea*
Rapuntium cardinale (syn)	*Lobelia cardinalis*
'Red Ammania' (sp)	*Ammania senegalensis*
Ricciella fluitans (syn)	*Riccia fluitans*
Rotala indica (sp)	*Rotala rotundifolia*
Sagittaria natans (syn)	*Sagittaria sublata*
Sagittaria platyphylla (sp)	*Sagittaria sublata*
Sagittaria teres (sp)	*Sagittaria sublata*

Synonym (syn) or related species (sp):	Te be found under:
Samolus americanus (syn)	*Samolus parviflorus*
Samolus aquaticus (syn)	*Samolus parviflorus*
Samolus floribundus (syn)	*Samolus parviflorus*
Saururus lucidus (syn)	*Saururus cernuus*
Scirpus radicans (syn)	*Eleocharis acicularis*
Serpentaria repens (syn)	*Saururus cernuus*
Serpicula verticillata (syn)	*Hydrilla verticillata*
Stratiotes alismoides (syn)	*Ottelia alismoides*
Synnema triflorum (syn)	*Hygrophila difformis*
Telanthera lilacina (sp)	*Alternanthera reineckii*
Telanthera osiris (syn)	*Alternanthera reineckii*
Trianea bogotenses (syn)	*Limnobium laevigatum*
Udora canadensis (syn)	*Elodea canadensis*
Vallisneria americana (sp)	*Vallisneria spiralis*
'Vallisneria contortionist' (sp)	*Vallisneria spiralus*
Vallisneria gigantea (sp)	*Vallisneria spiralis*
Vallisneria neotropicalis (sp)	*Vallisneria spiralis*
Villarsia aquatica (syn)	*Cabomba aquatica*

ALPHABETICAL LIST

150. *Acorus gramineus*

151. *Ammania senegalensis*

152. *Aponogeton boivinanus*

ACORUS GRAMINEUS Solander var.

Family: *Araceae*

English names: Japanese rush, Dwarf Calamus

Synonym: *Acorus humilis*

Origin: Eastern temperate Asia

Natural habitat: The shores of lakes and marshes: also found in dry areas among grass

DESCRIPTION: Grass green, hard, flat leaves grow from a prolifically branching rhizome: they are pointed, about 10 cm long and 0.3 cm wide, arranged in fan shaped rosettes. The flowers blossom along the side, below the tip of an almost triangular flowering stalk. The blossom is small, rod-shaped and set closely with small green flowers.

CULTIVATION: The Calamus would be an ideal plant along the sides of the tank were it not so difficult to cultivate. It is not really a water plant, as its natural habitat suggests, and it is unnatural for it to grow completely submersed: it does not usually survive long. Nevertheless occasionally a specimen takes root and slowly establishes itself. No particular soil, water composition or lighting will significantly affect growth. The temperature however must not be too high: maximum 22°C. *A.gramineus* does not usually survive transplanting. It is also a difficult plant to cultivate in marshy ground.

NOTE: Aquarium shops often offer for sale large numbers of these plants, and of *Acorus calamus*, the Sweet Flag, whose leaves are up to 50 cm long and 1 cm wide. There is also a variety *Acorus gramineus foliis variegatis*, with green and white variegated leaves. Both these plants are totally unsuited to the aquarium, although they can be cultivated in gardens where the winters are not too severe. The rhizome of *Acorus gramineus* and of *Acorus calamus* is used widely in pharmacy and the plants are cultivated for that reason. Surplus plants are then sold off to aquarium shops and it is this surplus production rather than their suitability for the aquarium that accounts for their being so generally available.

ALTERNANTHERA REINECKII
Family: *Amaranthaceae*
English name: none
Synonym: *Telanthera osiris*
Origin: Brazil, Paraguay
Natural habitat: Marshes and bogs

DESCRIPTION: The stems are up to 35 cm long with eliptical leaves up to 4 cm long and 1.5 cm wide. Depending on the age of the plant and the lighting, the upper surfaces of the leaves are a pale green or yellowish red, deepening to a purplish red: the lower surfaces vary from deep pink to purplish red. The insignificant little white flowers grow in small clusters in the leaf axils.

CULTIVATION: *A.reineckii* is sometimes difficult to cultivate. It is slow to take root and slow thereafter to grow. Strong lighting is needed if the plant is to develop its full color. The temperature should be about 25°C. Neither the composition of the water nor of the soil is important. Propagation is easy, by topping the plant, which itself is beneficial to the plant, or by rooting broken bits of the stem, or even broken bits of leaf from which young plants will develop. Above water the plant grows easily and flowers profusely.

NOTE: A related, more beautiful species, *Telanthera lilacina* is described below. Two other species, *A.sessilis* and *A.variegata* are sometimes offered for sale but are unsuitable for aquariums and die very quickly although both are easy to grow immersed. *A.sessilis* has dark red leaves about 4 cm long and 1 cm wide. *A.variegata* has broader, oval leaves with edges that usually curl up somewhat. When young the leaves are a carmine red, when mature they are red only at the tip and base. *A.variegata* is grown as a border plant in southern Europe and has even been grown as a hedge in Singapore where the most beautiful branches have been pruned and sent for sale to unsuspecting aquarists.

AMMANIA SENEGALENSIS Lamarck
Family: *Lythraceae*
English name: none
Synonym: none
Origin: Tropical Africa
Natural habitat: Marshy, sometimes brackish areas

DESCRIPTION: The stems are up to 40 cm long with leaves growing opposite each other at short intervals. The leaves are up to 6 cm long and 1.5 cm wide and in shape may be oval, wedge-shaped or strap-like and blunt at the ends. Depending on the lighting, the leaves will appear brownish-green to pink or an orange-red. The unobtrusive little flowers lie in the leaf axils but only develop when the plant grows in marshlands.

CULTIVATION: *A.senegalensis* is one of the few African plants suitable for the aquarium. It needs plenty of light preferably from the special fluorescent lamps used in horticulture. It dislikes fresh water and needs a bed with some clay and peat. It should never be overshadowed by other plants because of its need for light. Propagation is by cutting off and then planting the tops of branches that need to be trimmed back. It is very easy to grow out of water and is ideal for a paludarium.

NOTE: The older leaves of the plant often bend over in a strange and unusual way: this does not mean that the plant is unhealthy. A new variety has recently appeared, the Red Ammania, with splendid dark-red long and relatively narrow leaves. This variety, which has not as yet been identified botanically, needs a great deal of light and is very sensitive to being transplanted.

ANUBIUS LANCEOLATA N E Brown
Family: *Araceae*
Synonym: *Anubius barteri* var *glabra*
Origin: Tropical Africa
Natural habitat: Marshes and bogs

DESCRIPTION: The tough dark green waxlike leaves 20 cm long and 10 cm wide grow on leaf stalks up to 20 cm long, out of a stout horizontal trailing rootstock. The flowers are tiny blossoms set in spirals on the flower stalk which grows as high as the leaves. In the aquarium these beautiful but slow growing plants rarely reach the size they attain in the wild.

CULTIVATION: *A.lanceolata* likes warmth but should be protected from strong sunlight. The water should be soft and acid: the bed should contain some peat. The plants, when well established are propagated by root division.

NOTE: There are a number of other species of *Anubius* that the aquarist may encounter: they all require the same care and conditions.

APONOGETON

The Aponogeton species are among the most attractive and valuable aquarium plants. They have very attractive leaves and flowers. They are unusual in that they propagate only by seed and it is sometimes difficult to ensure that these are fertilised. They are however true aquatic plants and do not develop terrestrial forms.

These plants die down after a time and when that happens the rootstock must be carefully looked after to prevent it rotting: if that is done then new leaves will develop later. In the wild, the cycle of growth, flowering and rest which these plants observe is related to climatic conditions and the incidence of the rainy season. They all come from tropical or sub-tropical areas in Africa, Asia or Australia. A number of species are only found in Malagasy (Madagascar), including the well-known Lace Leaf plant. The species that come from Africa always have a flower stem which ends in two spikes or ears on which the flowers appear: species that come from other continents always have only one spike or ear of flowers on the flower stalk.

APONOGETON BOIVINANUS Baillon ex Jumelle
Family: *Aponogetonaceae*
Synonym: none but the plant is often incorrectly called *A.boivinianus*
Origin: Northwest Malagasy
Natural habitat: Found on volcanic rocks in slow and fast running waters, in both sunny and shady positions

DESCRIPTION: An extremely beautiful species with a round flattened light brown bulb up to 3 cm in diameter. The leaves are 30 cm long and 5 cm wide, growing on stalks 6–10 cm long. The leaf is sturdy and puckered: the base and top are round to wedge-shaped.

153. *Aponogeton crispus* (inflorescence)

There are 7–9 parallel veins. The flower stalk is up to 55 cm long with a marked thickening at the flowering end. The inflorescence consists of two spikes up to 20 cm, closely set with white or light pink flowers.

CULTIVATION: *A.boivinanus* is easy to cultivate and has few special requirements of soil or light: it does however need a lot of space to grow well and will stop growing if cramped. It is very absorbent and in hard water the leaves will become covered with a white deposit. However, it dislikes very soft water. When the plant begins to rest the bulb should be pulled above ground level, otherwise it will rot. The flowers do not effectively pollinate themselves: they have to be pollinated by the aquarist and this can be done by transferring pollen from one plant to another when two flower at the same time, with a fine brush.

NOTE: *A.boivinanus resembles Cryptocoryne usteriana* when growing in the aquarium, although the former can easily be distinguished by its bulb when examined. *A.boivinanus* is more suitable for the aquarium than *C.usteriana* because its growth is more compact and it is not prone to *Cryptocoryne* diseases.

APONOGETON CRISPUS Thunberg

Family: *Aponogetonaceae*

English name: Ruffled Sword Plant

Synonyms: *Anaponogeton undulatus, Ouvirandra undulata*

Origin: Found in the central mountainous regions of Sri Lanka

Natural habitat: Grows in clear, still or running waters, 20–100 cm deep, and in ponds and lakes unaffected by regular droughts

DESCRIPTION: *A.crispus* has an elongated rhizome up to 20 cm in diameter. The long and relatively narrow leaves vary in color from green to reddish-brown and can grow up to 30 cm long but are, at most, 4 cm wide. The leaf edge is wavy and usually finely curled. There are 7–9 main veins. The leaf stalk can be up to 45 cm long but is usually shorter. Floating leaves are not formed. The flowering stalk can be up to 80 cm long with hardly any thickening under the inflorescence, which consists of one spike up to 20 cm long, covered with small white or pink flowers.

CULTIVATION: An easy plant to keep in tropical aquariums. It has few special requirements and grows almost continuously, without the rest periods that characterise the growth of most other species. It may stop growing from time to time but will recommence of its own accord. Propagation is usually easy. Many seeds develop and may well be fertilised even without intervention by the aquarist.

NOTE: The above description is that of a plant commonly sold to aquarists as *A.crispus* but there is some doubt as to whether it really is a species of *Aponogeton*.

APONOGETON DISTACHYOS Linnaeus fils

Family: *Aponogetonaceae*

Synonym: none

English name: none

Origin: South Africa

Natural habitat: Found growing prolifically in clear waters, shallow pools and slow flowing rivers

DESCRIPTION: The bulb is up to 6 cm in diameter. All the leaves float and are 6–20 cm long and 1.5–7.5 cm broad, with 7–9 parallel veins and a leaf stalk up to 100 cm long. The flower stalk grows up to 80 cm. The very fragrant inflorescence consists of two spikes up to 4.5 cm long each with two rows of flowers.

CULTIVATION: *A.distachyos* is unsuitable for the aquarium but is excellent for a pond. In the aquarium it not only needs a lot of sunlight and cool water but is somewhat unattractive because of its floating leaves. Put in a basket with good soil it will however flower profusely in a pond and the bulb can be safely stored through the winter.

NOTE: When there were far fewer aquarium plants available than there are now, *A.distachyos* was often put in an aquarium but now there is little reason for that. It can sometimes be grown successfully as a pot plant out of water.

APONOGETON ECHINATUS Roxburgh

Family: *Aponogetonaceae*

English name: none

Synonym (incorrect): *A.natans*

Origin: Central and Southern India

Natural habit: Found in seasonal lakes and flooded grasslands

DESCRIPTION: The bulb is up to 5 cm in diameter. Submersed leaves are wavy, membraneous, up to 25 cm long and 4.5 cm wide, with a wedge-shaped or truncated base and a rounded top. There are 9 parallel veins. The leaf stalk is up to 25 cm long. Floating leaves are up to 20 cm long and 5 cm wide (but usually somewhat smaller) with a rounded base and top and 9–11 parallel veins. The flower stalk grows to 75 cm and thickens below the inflorescence. The inflorescence is one spike up to 15 cm long set with very fragrant white, pink or pale lilac flowers. The

154. *Aponogeton distachyos* (inflorescence)

155. *Aponogeton elongatus* (inflorescence)

fruits often have thorny irregular protuberances.

CULTIVATION: *A.echinatus* is an extremely easy plant to keep in the aquarium and has few special requirements. Bulbs recently imported grow especially well and can blossom abundantly. There is usually a wealth of fruits after self pollination so that it is easy to obtain a large number of young plants which can be raised without difficulty. Growth of this species is sometimes interrupted but the plant will begin to grow again after this rest period without special attention.

NOTE: *A.echinatus* is often called *A.natans*, the name of another species not now usually grown in aquariums. *A.echinatus* is also often imported under the name *A.crispus*. See also below under *Aponogeton ulvaceus*.

APONOGETON ELONGATUS
F. V. Mueller ex Bentham

Family: *Aponogetonaceae*

English name: Elongated Sword plant

Synonym: none

Origin: Eastern and Northern Australia

Natural habitat: Found growing in sunny and shady spots in still or flowing waters with a muddy bottom

DESCRIPTION: The size of the bulb, like many other characteristics of this species may vary. The leaves which always grow submersed are a bright green, but may become reddish brown under strong lighting: they are flat or wavy and 15–55 cm long and 1–5 cm wide. The flower stalk may be over 100 cm long, visibly thickening below the inflorescence, which appears on one spike which can be up to 20 cm long, covered with yellow flowers.

CULTIVATION: *A.elongatus* has few special requirements in the aquarium and is easy to cultivate. It grows all through the year without a rest period. It is however difficult to propagate because self pollination is rarely successful and even cross pollination may not succeed.

NOTE: Unfortunately *A.elongatus* is rarely imported. It is however the only species of *Aponogeton* at present cultivated which has a yellow flower. Various varieties of this species have been identified some of which being smaller would be suitable for the smallest aquarium.

APONOGETON MADAGASCARIENSIS

Family: *Aponogetonaceae*

English name: Lace Leaf plant, Madagascar lace plant

Synonyms: *Aponogeton fenestralis, Aponogeton henkelianus*

Origin: Malagasy, Mauritius

Natural habitat: Found in a variety of environments: still and flowing waters, rapids, waterfalls, both in the sun and in the shade

DESCRIPTION: A singularly lovely plant which always grows under water, with a bulb-shaped rhizome from the top of which grow beautiful leaves. They are unique: there is virtually no membrane between the veins, so that the leaves have a lace- or gauze-like structure: the exact pattern varies from specimen to specimen. The leaves can grow 55 cm long and 16 cm wide but in aquariums they usually remain much smaller. There are 7–21 veins lying the length of the leaf with others linking them across the leaf blade. The leaf stalk will be 3–35 cm long. The flowering stalk may be longer than 100 cm although it is usually much shorter in the aquarium. The inflorescence consists of two or four spikes about 10 cm long closely set with white or violet flowers.

CULTIVATION: *A.madagascariensis* is very difficult to cultivate: most newly imported plants die off within a year. No reliable rules for successful cultivation have yet been established. The plant seems to need very soft water with about 20% volume being changed each week. It must be grown in muted light to inhibit the growth of the algae which will otherwise choke it. The temperature should be higher than 24°C. The bulb must not be pressed into the bed: it should be anchored to the bed and the roots which then slowly develop will gradually pull the bulb into the bottom. When growth comes to a standstill, the root has to be pulled out of the bed again: if it is not, there is a great danger that it will rot. Many seeds develop on the inflorescence but although these germinate easily, they are virtually impossible to bring to maturity.

APONOGETON RIGIDIFOLIUS

Family: *Aponogetonaceae*

English name: none

Synonym: none

Origin: Southwest Sri Lanka

Natural habitat: Still and flowing waters, both in the shade and in the sun

DESCRIPTION: The creeping rhizome is cylindrical, long and thin like that of a wood anemone, up to 15 cm long and 1 cm in diameter. All the leaves are submersed, tough and strap-like, up to 60 cm long and 3 cm wide. They are dark green but young leaves are a reddish brown: the edges are smooth (in varieties that grow in swiftly running waters) or gently wavy (in varieties found in still waters). The base and tip of the leaf taper gently and there are 7–9 veins. The leaf stalk is up to 55 cm long. The flower stalk can be 90 cm long and is no thicker immediately below the inflorescence than lower down. There is only one flower spike, up to 15 cm long covered with small white flowers.

CULTIVATION: An easy species to cultivate. It is however not very prolific. It flowers fairly frequently but self pollination does not produce fertile seeds. Sometimes the creeping rhizome divides spontaneously and new plants are formed in that way.

NOTE: *A.rigidifolius* is not particularly suitable for the aquarium. It is however fairly frequently imported and because of the creeping rhizome is often mistaken for a *Cryptocoryne* and sold as such. In the aquarium the leaves often curl under and this detracts from the plant's appearance. The leaves are also prone to a black spot disease which gradually kills them.

APONOGETON ULVACEUS

Family: *Aponogetonaceae*

English name: none

Synonym: none

Origin: Central, West and Northwest Malagasy

Natural habitat: Found in still and flowing waters and swamps, in sunny and shady positions

DESCRIPTION: *A.ulvaceus* has an oval bulb up to 3 cm in diameter. The leaves are all submersed, 12–35 cm long and 2–8 cm wide. These bright green, very thin translucent leaves are wavy at the edges and sometimes spiralled like a corkscrew. The leaf stalk is 7–25 cm long. The flower stalk is up to 80 cm long, thickening below the inflorescence. The very sweet-smelling flowers on two spikes up to 15 cm long are white.

CULTIVATION: *A.ulvaceus* is easy to grow but needs a lot of light. It can only be put in a large tank because a healthy plant spreads very quickly. Propagation is more difficult: most plants do not self pollinate: they may be cross pollinated but then only when two plants flower at the same time. They are then very prolific and produce seeds which should be sown immediately on soft ground in shallow water.

NOTE: *A.ulvaceus* can easily be confused with *A.echinatus*, because the submersed leaves are very similar. However, the bulb of *A.ulvaceus* has a spiky top, while that of *A.echinatus* does not: *A.echinatus* develops floating leaves, *A.ulvaceus* never does: *A.ulvaceus* has two flower spikes, *A.echinatus* has only one.

156. *Barclaya longifolia* (cross – section of the frui

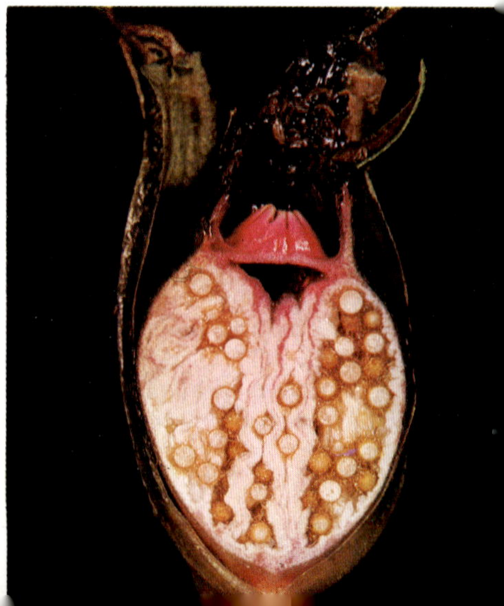

but the overall effect of its dense growth is green to red.

CULTIVATION: This dainty plant is tolerant of water composition but does need a winter temperature of about 19°C and a summer temperature of at least 22°C. It is best to propagate it through cultures grown in the open.

NOTE: An excellent plant for the paludarium and very useful, in the right conditions to give a blanket cover on the surface of an aquarium, where too much light is causing green water: however, if allowed to grow unchecked, it will cut off too much light from submersed plants.

157. *Bacopa amplexiicaulis*

158. *Bacopa amplexiicaulis* (leaf)

APONOGETON UNDULATUS Roxburgh

Family: *Aponogetonaceae*

English name: none

Synonyms: *Aponogeton monostachyos, Aponogeton stachyosporus*

Origin: Burma, Northeast India, Thailand

Natural habitat: Found in still waters, pools and lakes

DESCRIPTION: The bulb is often ball-shaped, very light in color and 0.6–2.5 cm in diameter. The submersed leaves are 10–25 cm long and 0.8–4.2 cm wide, irregularly dark and light green in color. The leaf edge is wavy and there are 5, 7 or 9 parallel veins. The leaf stalk is 10–35 cm long. Floating leaves are rare but when present may be 20 cm long and 3.5 cm wide with a rounded or heart-shaped base, 5–7 veins, and a stalk up to 70 cm long. The flower stalk may reach 55 cm, gradually thickening up the stem, but thinner just below the inflorescence. The white or pale pink flowers appear on a single spike up to 10 cm long.

CULTIVATION: *A.undulatus* is one of the easiest of aquarium plants to grow. It is very tolerant of the variable compostion of the soil or the water but it does need a lot of light. Propagation is easy from the young plants that are produced on runners. It rarely flowers and is therefore almost impossible to propagate from seed.

NOTE: *A.undulatus* cannot be mistaken for any other species because of the unique way in which young plants develop from runners. It is not however the most attractive species because the leaf stalks often look disproportionately long and the leaves tend to grow horizontally.

AZOLLA CAROLINIANA Wildenow

Family: *Azollaceae*

English name: Fairy moss

Synonyms: *Azolla microphylla, Azolla densa, Azolla mexicana*

Origin: Southern and Eastern North America, Central and South America

Natural habitat: Found as a floating plant on ponds, and also occasionally growing in mud

DESCRIPTION: The leaves of this small floating fern are 0.5–0.7 cm long and lie in two rows on a thallus usually no longer than 0.15 cm. The leaves are translucent and greyish-white,

BACOPA AMPLEXIICAULIS (Pursh) Wettstein

Family: *Scrophulariaceae*

English name: none

Synonyms: *Bacopa caroliniana, Obolaria caroliniana, Herpestes caroliniana*

Origin: USA, from Virginia to Florida and Texas

Natural habitat: Marshes

DESCRIPTION: The leaves are up to 3 cm long and 1.5 cm wide growing opposite each other on stalks up to 60 cm long. When the leaves are submersed, they are thin and wavy with, under strong lighting, beautiful reddish-brown veins. Leaves above the water are green, fleshy and shiny with hairy stalks. The blue flowers only develop out of the water on stalks, in the leaf axils.

CULTIVATION: *B.amplexiicaulis* is a fairly easy plant to grow: it requires good lighting and then the tops of the stalks turn a beautiful reddish-brown. It is easy to propagate by top cuttings. It has no special requirements of water or soil.

NOTE: This is a very attractive plant which

ought be more widely cultivated. It does not share the tendency of *Bacopa monnieri* to become covered with algae and is therefore a much more suitable species for the aquarium.

BACOPA MONNIERI (L) Wettstein

Family: *Scrophulariaceae*

English name: none

Synonyms: *Herpestes monnieria, Lysimachia monnieri*

Origin: All tropical and sub-tropical areas of the world except for Australia.

Natural habitat: Marshes

DESCRIPTION: The fleshy leaves grow opposite each other at short intervals along the vertical stalks. They grow up to 2 cm long and 1 cm wide and are always green, being in shape between an inverted oval and spatulate. The leaves are curly but never entwine themselves round the stalks as sometimes in the case of *B.amplexiicaulis*. The stalks above water have no hairs. The pink to pale lilac flowers grow on stalks in the axils and only out of water, as with *B.amplexiicaulis*.

CULTIVATION: *B.monnieri* has few special requirements but great care must be taken to ensure that the lighting is not too strong because if it is, the plant will soon be covered in algae. Growth is noticeably slower than in the case of *B.amplexiicaulis*. It is easy to propagate by topping.

BARCLAYA LONGIFOLIA Wallich

Family: *Nymphafaceae*

English name: none

Synonym: none

Origin: Burma, Thailand

Natural habitat: Found in shady spots in the jungle

DESCRIPTION: An extremely beautiful and unusual water-lily that always grows submersed. It has a short rhizome from which the leaves grow in a rosette. The blades can be up to 30 cm long and 3–5 cm wide and vary in color from olive green to violet red. The edges are wavy and the bases rounded or heart-shaped. The plant flowers fairly frequently in an aquarium although the flowers often grow on such short stems that they do not reach the surface. Five sepals up to 3 cm long grow under the flower which itself is 2 cm long, with 8–10 linked petals, greenish on the outside and reddish-purple on the inside. These petals form a tube or trumpet within which hang a few anthers on very short filaments. These anthers are however infertile, they do not carry any pollen. The style is unusual: it is like a cone divided into some ten separate lobes which form the stigma, so that a star-shaped opening is formed. A hollow space lies under the stigma, and the ovaries are below that. The sepals lie below the ovaries. The ripe fruit is a berry 1.5–1.8 cm in diameter. The seeds are only a few millimeters across and are closely covered with fine prickles.

CULTIVATION: *B.longifolia* is not difficult to grow but requires a temperature of at least 25°C if growth is not to be retarded. The flowers rarely reach the surface and do not open if they remain submersed but ripe fruits still often develop on the submersed flower stalks after self-pollination: this is an unusual but not unique botanical phenomenon known as hydrocleistogamy. The flowers which do reach the surface open but rarely seed. Fertile seeds can be cultivated by being put in a separate tray with a soft bed so that the roots can easily penetrate the soil. In some specimens daughter bulbs are regularly produced and quite often these small plants float to the surface: they can then be planted where they are wanted. *B.longifolia* sometimes stops growing for a time and during this period of rest most of the submersed leaves die: if the plant is left alone it will however start once again to grow.

NOTE: Another species, *B.motleyi* Hook f, is sometimes imported: this species with almost round fleshy hairy leaves of a beautiful red color, is not suitable for the aquarium.

BOLBITIS HEUDELOTII (Bory ex Fée) Alston

Family: *Lomariopsidaceae*

English name: none

Synonym: *Gymnopteris heudelotii*

Origin: Almost all of tropical Africa

Natural habitat: Found growing prolifically in or near running water, rapids and waterfalls, where there is a sandy or stony bed

---

DESCRIPTION: The deeply forked fern leaves grow at short intervals out of the creeping rhi-

159. *Barclaya longifolia*

160. *Cabomba aquatica*

161. *Cabomba aquatica* (inflorescence)

zome, which is attached to the bed with brownish-black roots. In the aquarium the leaves do not usually grow more than 50 cm long and are a translucent green. The leaf stalk is about half the length of the leaf itself, which consists of a central axis with 7–15 segments on either side, with irregular indentations or lobes.

CULTIVATION: One of the essential requirements of this very beautiful fern is that the rhizome never be embedded in the sand: this invariably causes it to rot. The rhizome should be anchored either on the sand or preferably on a piece of bogwood or stone which will then gradually be covered by it. *B.heudelotii* likes clear water but the lighting and soil composition seem to be of little importance. It can easily be propagated by dividing the rhizome: it very rarely propagates by forming young plants on the leaves like, for example, *Microsorium pteropus*. It can be grown out of water but only in a very humid atmosphere.

CABOMBA AQUATICA Aublet

Family: *Nymphaeaceae*

English name: none

Synonyms: *Nectris aquatica, Villarsia aquatica*

Origin: North Brazil, the Guianas, Surinam

Natural habitat: Found in rivers, streams and lakes: around Paramaribo (Surinam) it grows in a heavy clay soil

---

DESCRIPTION: This extremely beautiful submersed plant has stems up to 200 cm long, on which finely divided fan-shaped leaves 4 cm long and 7 cm wide grow opposite each other at regular intervals. The leaves are made up of 150–200 segments only some 0.4 mm wide, with no veins or other markings. The leaves are a beautiful light green. Floating leaves sometimes develop when the plant flowers: those are shield-shaped and 1–2 cm in diameter. The flowers are yellow.

CULTIVATION: *C.aquatica* is the most difficult of all the *Cabomba* species to cultivate. It requires soft water, a high temperature – 25°C, a great deal of light and protection against the algae that develop in strong light. It also dislikes being disturbed so that a plant that is growing well should not be topped. The very long stems that develop have to be accepted. Young plants develop from shoots at the base of the plant.

NOTE: *C.aquatica* has been used in aquariums for a very long time but has now lost some of its former popularity.

CABOMBA CAROLINIANA Gray

Family: *Nymphaeaceae*

English name: Carolinian Fanwort

Synonyms: *Cabomba peltata, Cabomba pinnata, Nectris peltata*

Origin: USA, from Southern Texas, to Missouri and Michigan, and from Florida to Massachusetts

Natural habitat: Found in shallow waterways and lakes

163. *Cabomba caroliniana*

DESCRIPTION: A submersed plant with a stem up to 150 cm long, on which the finely forked fan-shaped leaves 3–4 cm long and up to 6 cm wide grow opposite each other at regular intervals. There are both delicate and coarse leaved varieties. The delicate leaved variety has leaves of 80–150 leaflets 0.4–1 mm wide: the coarse leaved variety has leaves made up of 20–60 leaflets 1–1.8 mm wide. The leaflets are wider at the tip than at the bottom, have no distinctive veins and often bear some reddish spots or lines. The spiky floating leaves are 2 cm long and 0.3 cm wide. The flowers are white with a yellow center.

CULTIVATION: An easy plant to grow. It has no special requirements except good light. It is easy to propagate by top cuttings.

NOTE: A few years ago a new variety was developed in the German Democratic Republic in which the leaves wound round their axis so that the green upper side and the silvery under side of each leaf showed alternately, giving the plant a very attractive appearance: this variety is now increasingly seen.

162. *Cabomba piauhyensis*

CABOMBA PIAUHYENSIS Gardner

Family: *Nymphaeaceae*

English name: none

Synonym: *Cabomba pubescens*

Origin: North Brazil, Bolivia, Cuba, El Salvador

Natural habitat: Found in shallow lakes and pools with a muddy bottom

---

DESCRIPTION: An extremely beautiful reddish-brown plant with long stems on

164. *Cabomba piauhyensis* (inflorescence)

which grow finely divided leaves usually in whorls of three, but sometimes opposite each other. The leaves are made up of 75–200 leaflets 0.3 mm wide with a central vein and many short red lines so fine as sometimes to be visible only with a magnifying glass. Floating leaves though rarely formed are very narrow, about 3 mm wide. The violet purple flowers have a yellow center.

CULTIVATION: As for *C.aquatica* but *C.piauhyensis* seems to be a little easier to cultivate. Some aquarists have grown it successfully in an ordinary community tank filled with tap water. This species develops young shoots from the base but can also be propagated by top cuttings.

NOTE: Although a relatively new plant for the aquarium, *C.piauhyensis* has become popular because of its unusual and attractive color.

CARDAMINE LYRATA Bunge

Family: *Cruciferae*

English name: Chinese Ivy

Synonym: none

Origin: Northeast Asia, Japan

Natural habitat: Marshes and the banks of rivers

DESCRIPTION: Very thin light green leaves, egg-shaped or somewhat pointed, 3 cm wide grow on thin submersed branching stems. Usually the leaves are alternate but occasionally lie opposite each other. Above the water the shape of the leaves can change completely: they lie in whorls and are unevenly distributed, that is the leaves are made up of an uneven number of small leaflets, one of which lies at the tip. The white flowers only develop out of the water and lie in clusters.

CULTIVATION: *C.lyrata* is not easy to grow in an aquarium because it needs a great deal of light and dislikes high temperatures for it is not a tropical plant. When the temperature is high it grows too rapidly, becomes spiky, yellows and is finally covered with slime. Healthy plants are easy to propagate by top cuttings. It is much easier to grow out of water and is ideal for a paludarium: it creeps as it grows and can cover a wide area. It can also be grown out of doors in damp places during the summer. It is a very delicate plant and is likely to be damaged by snails or eaten by aquarium fish with a fondness for plants.

165. *Cabomba piauhyensis* (detail)

166. *Ceratophyllum demersum*

NOTE: *C.lyrata* is closely related to the European wild flower *C.pratensis*, Lady's smock, found in moist meadows.

CERATOPHYLLUM DEMERSUM (L)

Family: *Ceratophyllaceae*

English name: Hornwort

Synonyms: *Ceratophyllum aspersum, Ceratophyllum cornutum, Ceratophyllum cristatum*

Origin: worldwide

Natural habitat: Found in still or slow flowing fresh and brackish waters

DESCRIPTION: Naked stems up to 200 cm long bear whorls of at most 10 leaves, growing at a slight upward angle, each with 2–4 usually rigid leaflets, forked and spiky, reminiscent of a pair of horns. Male and female flowers develop on one plant: the fruits are tiny black nutlets.

CULTIVATION: *C.demersum* should be grown in good light, and needs nutritious water. The plants do not have to be anchored: they can be left to float freely. Each piece which breaks off will develop into a new plant. Hornwort is a very unusual plant. It is one of the very few more developed plants that never grow roots. The method of propagation is also unusual. When the pollen is ripe the stamens detach themselves from the plant and rise to the surface where they float. The pollen sacs then break open so that pollen is released into the water where it remains until it comes into contact with the stigma of a female flower, which is then fertilised by it. Hornwort will flower in the aquarium where it can be a valuable plant because of its water purifying properties. The plants grow very rapidly, using up a lot of the organic content of the water and can be very useful in combating the growth of blue algae. Given free rein however *C.demersum* will soon cover the surface completely and has to be thinned regularly. In the aquarium the plant grows all the year round although in the wild it is seasonal and in autumn 'winter buds' are formed – very closely set whorls of leaves at the tops of the stems, which when the rest of the plant dies off sink to the bottom and form the base for new growth in the spring.

NOTE: There is another less common species *Ceratophyllum submersum* which has less spiky leaves.

CERATOPTERIS CORNUTA Le Prieur

Family: *Parkeriaceae*

English name: Floating Fern

Synonyms: *Acrostichum thalictroides, Parkeria pteridoides*

Origin: Africa and possibly Southeast Asia

Natural habitat: Still and slow running waters

DESCRIPTION: A floating plant with whorls of large angular oval and sometimes three-lobed fleshy leaves. The whorls may be 50 cm in diameter, or sometimes even larger under very favorable conditions. The upper side of the leaves is a light to grassy green, with a rather oily sheen. Out of the water finely branched leaves, like antlers, develop.

CULTIVATION: As for *Ceratopteris thalictroides* (see below) but *C. cornuta* is a floating plant and cannot be cultivated under water. It can, if growth is uncontrolled, cut off all light from plants growing below it even more effectively than Water Sprite or Indian Fern. Superfluous growth must be ruthlessly removed.

NOTE: Many botanists consider *C.cornuta* to be no more than a variety of *C.thalictroides* but even is this is so, it is quite wrong to believe that if cuttings of the former are put under water they will develop into the latter.

CERATOPTERIS THALICTROIDES (L) Brongniart

Family: *Parkeriaceae*

English name: Water Sprite, Indian Fern

Synonyms: none

Origin: Found in almost all tropical areas

Natural habitat: Found growing on the banks, or floating on the surface of still or slow running waters

DESCRIPTION: There is a coarse leaved variety (Indian Fern) and a fine leaved variety (Water Sprite). The beautiful light green leaves grow in rosettes from thick bunched roots. Each main stem, which can be 100 cm long, has two or three branches whose stems may be long or short. The leaves out of water are more delicate than those submersed and branch like antlers.

CULTIVATION: *C.thalictroides* is not difficult to grow but does require good lighting and warmth. It propagates very easily: numerous young plants develop on the margins of the leaves which then break off and float to the surface. If the water is sufficiently nutritious they develop into splendid large floating whorls with finely branching roots about 30 cm long which hang down into the water and are popular as hiding places with fish. This floating variety can be used to create shaded areas in the tank but must be kept in check because it tends to block out a lot of light very quickly. If necessary these floating plants can be planted on the bed without difficulty.

167. *Ceratopteris cornuta*

CRYPTOCORYNE

The many *Cryptocoryne* species make up the most popular group of aquarium plants because of their abundant growth, attractive color and unusual flowers. They usually have a creeping rhizome from which rises the whorl of leaves. They are usually propagated from shoots, and it is impossible to take top cuttings. These plants have many attractive leaves but their most unusual feature is their inflorescence which looks like a long trumpet with, near the bottom, a prominent swelling. This is in fact an unusual but very effective device for ensuring that these plants, although principally underwater, are pollinated by insects. The female flowers and ovaries lie in the swelling at the bottom of the tube or trumpet: above lie male stamens. The top of the trumpet-like tube, called the spathe, is above the water surface although the greater part of the tube, including the swelling with the ovaries, is below the surface. Insects are attracted to the top of the tube by the flower there – which is both flamboyant and strong smelling (although to human beings the odor is unpleasant). The flower itself consists of a rod (the spadix) which lies in the spathe, and this is surrounded by a part of the spathe which has opened up, referred to here as the collar. The insects creep down the tube past the male flowers, where they are covered in pollen, to the female flowers where they are then trapped by a membrane which closes the tube above them until all the female flowers have been pollinated whereupon the membrane retracts to allow the insect to depart. In this way the female flower although under water and completely contained within the tube, hidden from view, is effectively pollinated.

It is the shape, color and structure of this long tube or spathe by which one species of Cryptocoryne is principally distinguished from another. Indeed most species cannot be conclusively identified until they flower: many are deceptively similar, especially when they are grown out of water.

One disadvantage of these plants is that some species are very prone to what is often called Cryptocoryne disease, a severe sliming of the leaves in which, after a few days the plant is choked and dies.

168. *Ceratopteris thalictroides*

169. *Cryptocoryne affinis*

CRYPTOCORYNE AFFINIS
N E Brown ex Hooker fils

Family: *Araceae*

English name: none

Synonym: *Cryptocoryne haerteliana*

Origin: Malaya

Natural habitat: Found in slow or swift running but shallow waters with sandy or gravelly beds

DESCRIPTION: A beautiful species with leaves up to 15 cm long and 3 cm wide, growing on leaf stalks up to 20 cm long. The leaf blade is rounded at the base and gradually tapers at the top. The leaf veins are a much lighter color than the dark velvety green of the upper sides of the leaves and form a fine contrast. The underside of the leaf is wine red. The inflorescence is up to 40 cm long of which 10 cm is the dark purple velvety collar above the white or greenish spathe.

CULTIVATION. *C.affinis* is one of the best species for an aquarium. It has no special requirements as to water or soil but it cannot tolerate direct sunlight, and even unscreened daylight is harmful. Artificial lighting is best and if this is not too weak, the undersides of the leaves will turn a beautiful red. Propagation is easy because a healthy plant produces many runners under the soil. It is difficult to grow out of water and rarely flowers when not submersed.

CRYPTOCORYNE BALANSAE
Gagnepain

Family: *Araceae*

English name: none

Synonym: *Cryptocoryne somphongsii*

Origin: Thailand, Vietnam

Natural habitat: Found in sluggish waters or on flooded land, in both shady and sunny spots, where there are gravelly beds

---

DESCRIPTION: The leaves are narrow, strap-shaped, 5–50 cm long, 1–2 cm wide and green but reddish-brown under strong light. Young leaves are blistered but become smoother as they mature. The leaf stalk may be 20 cm long but is usually shorter. The inflorescence may be 15 cm high. The spathe is 5–9 cm long and the collar which spirals is 3–5 cm long, smooth and pale brown with purple streaks and spots.

CULTIVATION. This beautiful and popular plant grows well in almost any lighting and soil conditions although it flourishes best with good light and a nutritious bed. 10–15% of the water in its tank should be changed each week. It is propagated like all *Cryptocorynes* from shoots, but this species does not produce very many. It seldom flowers but will do so if cultivated in very shallow water (less than 10 cm): it is difficult to grow out of water and will flourish only if the humidity is almost 100%.

NOTE. *C.balansae* looks like a diminutive version of *Cryptocoryne usteriana* and it easy to confuse the two species. However the leaves of *C.usteriana* when growing well are always wider than 2 cm while those of *C.balansae* are always considerably narrower than 2 cm.

CRYPTOCORYNE BECKETTII
Thwaites ex Trimen

Family: *Araceae*

English name: none

Synonym: No true synonym but sometimes incorrectly called *Cryptocoryne cordata*

Origin: Sri Lanka

Natural habitat: Found in rocky crevasses

DESCRIPTION: The leaves are submersed and elongated, 8–15 cm long and 3–4 cm wide, olive green on the upper side, often with reddish-brown marks and usually a dark or light reddish-brown on the underside. The leaf edges are wavy and often curled backwards. The leaf stalk is 10–20 cm long. Leaves which have grown above the water are wider but shorter and a dark brownish-green. The inflorescence is about 10 cm long, the spathe is 5 cm long and the spiralling collar about 3–5 cm long, smooth and brownish-yellow.

CULTIVATION: *C.beckettii* has few special requirements in the aquarium and has become, as a result, one of the most popular species with aquarists. If grown in no more than clean sand it often becomes a light green, small leaved plant suitable for use in the foreground of the tank. However it grows much more beautifully if some clay is added to the bed and it is given good lighting. Then the plants become sturdy and a beautiful dark green. Propagation is easy by means of runners. The plant rarely flowers under water. It will often flower profusely if grown out of water, which is not difficult to do.

NOTE: *C.beckettii* can easily be confused with *Cryptocoryne petchii*: the distinctions are described below under the latter species.

170. *Cryptocoryne beckettii* (inflorescence)

171. *Cryptocoryne ciliata*

172. *Cryptocoryne ciliata* (inflorescence)

CRYPTOCORYNE BLASSII de Wit

Family: *Araceae*

English name: none

Synonym: none

Origin: Thailand

Natural habitat: Found growing prolifically in the shade in slow running shallow waters where the leaves grow as large as the human hand and lie on the surface

---

DESCRIPTION: The oval, rather fleshy, blistered leaves are 12 cm long and 6 cm wide with a heart-shaped base. The upper surface varies from a bronze-green to a reddish-brown: the underside is reddish-brown to wine red. The leaf stalk grows up to 20 cm. The inflorescence can be 7 cm long, at least 3 cm being taken up by the collar which is a shiny yellow with transverse corrugations.

CULTIVATION: *C.blassii* is very easy to grow: it has no special requirements as to water, soil or lighting, although only in strong lighting will the plant become vividly colored. It cannot however tolerate direct sunlight. Plants which grow well propagate quickly by long runners. The size of the leaves can vary a great deal depending on the lighting and soil. Sturdy specimens with large leaves are very decorative. The plant rarely flowers except when grown above water.

NOTE: There is a variety very much like *C.blassii* but with narrower leaves and usually called the 'narrow leaved Blassii': this may be another species, *Cryptocoryne siamensis*, though this is uncertain.

CRYPTOCORYNE CILIATA

Fischer ex Schott

Family: *Araceae*

English name: none

Synonyms: *Ambrosinia ciliata, Cryptocoryne elata*

Origin: Southeast Asia from India to New Guinea

Natural habitat: Found growing above the water level in salt water creeks, brackish river estuaries and in mangrove swamps

DESCRIPTION: The leaves are lance-shaped, narrower and more pointed at the tip than in related species. They are 15–40 cm long and 5–8 cm wide, light green on both sides with a very broad mid-rib. The leaf stalk is 20–40 cm long. The inflorescence grows up to 30 cm: the collar is purple, pink or greenish, frayed around the outside and with a yellow center.

CULTIVATION: *C.ciliata* is suitable only for very deep tanks. The leaves always try to reach the surface even when the tank is 50 cm deep. This species will remain slightly smaller if grown in just clean sand. Growth can also be inhibited by occasionally cutting through the roots so that its food supply is hindered. There are some varieties that are naturally smaller but these seem to be imported rarely. Otherwise *C.ciliata* has few special requirements in the aquarium and grows well in any kind of soil. The water can be brackish but it also grows well in fresh water. Fairly strong lighting is desirable. Propagation is easy but two different varieties of *C.ciliata* propagate in different ways. In some plants young plants develop in the leaf axils: in others they develop at the end of long runners. If the young plants develop in the leaf axils then when the leaf dies off the young plant may be removed from the axil and planted: if they develop at the end of runners they may be detached from the runner in the usual way. Submersed plants rarely flower. This species is easy to grow out of water if the atmosphere is very humid.

NOTE: If an inflorescence does develop in the aquarium it may well have ripe fertile seeds and sometimes newly imported specimens bear them, round fruits 2–3 cm in diameter, growing on a short stem at the base of the plant. If the opportunity arises to buy such a specimen it should not be missed: propagation by seed occurs in a remarkable way. When the seed is ripe the pod opens and the seeds, lighter than water are ejected and rise to the surface where they float for some time. The seeds then open and a perfectly formed miniature plant, with a crest of leaves like a wig appears, and then sinks to the bottom to take root.

CRYPTOCORYNE NEVILLII

Trimen ex Hooker fil.

Family: *Araceae*

English name: none

Synonym: none

Origin: Sri Lanka

Natural habitat: Shady and sunny positions in damp grasslands: rarely in water

DESCRIPTION: The leaves are oblong, 3–7 cm long and 1–1.5 cm wide, green on both sides and sometimes slightly tinged reddish-brown, especially when grown in strong light. The leaf stalk grows up to 7 cm. The inflorescence is 5–8 cm long, the collar being 2 cm long, purple, covered with blisters and having a yellow center.

CULTIVATION: *C.nevillii* grows close to the ground and propagates rapidly with runners so that in the wild whole fields of it can develop in a short space of time. This species is very suitable for use as a foreground plant in the aquarium. It has few special requirements as to water or soil but reasonably strong lighting is necessary for compact growth. It is very easy to grow out of water in damp earth and in those conditions it will flower regularly but does so rarely when grown submersed.

NOTE: A closely related species is *Cryptocoryne lucens* de Wit but this plant, with its longer, thinner and very shiny leaves is rarely grown in aquariums. Another species, *Cryptocoryne parva* de Wit looks like a dwarf *C.nevillii* but is unfortunately almost impossible to grow under water.

173. *Cryptocoryne nevillii*

174. *Micranthemum micranthemoides*

CRYPTOCORYNE PETCHII Alston
Family: *Araceae*
English name: none
Synonym: none
Origin: Sri Lanka
Natural habitat: Found growing in sandy soil in marshy areas beside all kinds of waters both in the shade and the sun.

DESCRIPTION: The leaves are 10–20 cm long and 1–2 cm wide and depending on the lighting are olive to brownish-green. The leaf edge may be smooth or wavy and the leaf stalk is slightly shorter than the leaf. The inflorescence is about 7 cm long: the collar, 2–3 cm long has fine wrinkles and is an olive green to light brown: it does not spiral and has a deep purple-brown center.

CULTIVATION: *C.petchii* has few special requirements of water soil or lighting and will thrive in almost any conditions. However fairly strong lighting is needed to produce beautifully colored specimens. It grows compactly and may therefore be used as a border plant in the aquarium, but compact growth will only develop under strong lighting: in weak lighting the plants become straggly. *C.petchii* will only flower when grown emersed.

NOTE: *C.petchii* closely resembles *C.beckettii* and the two can only be easily distinguished when they flower, but whereas the leaves of *C.beckettii* often curl at the edges, this never happens with *C.petchii.*

CRYPTOCORYNE PURPUREA Ridley
Family: *Araceae*
English name: none
Synonyms: *Cryptocoryne cordata, Cryptocoryne griffithii*
Origin: Malaya
Natural habitat: Found in very shady places in small jungle streams

DESCRIPTION: The leaves are oval, about 10 cm long and 5 cm wide with a rounded or slightly heart-shaped base. The upper side is a deep green, the underside a lighter green with reddish-brown veins, sometimes even with red patches. The leaf stalk is 20–30 cm long. The inflorescence grows up to 20 cm. The lower part of the spathe resembles an ordinary stalk: the swelling is quite round: the collar about 3 cm long is warty and purple, the flowers yellow, orange or pale purple.

CULTIVATION: For no obvious reason this is a difficult species to grow. It used to be widely grown but was very prone to Cryptocoryne disease. The soil must be fairly rich and the light fairly strong if the plant is to become a good color. The composition of the water does not seem to be important. *C.purpurea* propagates fairly rapidly by means of runners. It flowers fairly frequently in the aquarium, and will open out as a flower if the water is too deep for the collar to reach the surface. *C.purpurea* cannot be grown emersed.

NOTE: *C.purpurea* is often called *C.griffithii* though that is a different although closely related species that is almost never imported and is almost impossible to grow in an aquarium.

CRYPTOCORYNE USTERIANA Engler
Family: *Araceae*
English name: none
Synonym: *Cryptocoryne aponogetifolia*
Origin: The Philippines, the islands of Panay and Guimaras
Natural habitat: Found growing in shallow waters

DESCRIPTION: A very large species with dark green leaves, 25–40 cm long and 2–5 cm wide, growing on leaf stalks 30 cm long. The leaves have pronounced blisters and are markedly narrower at the base and tip. The inflorescence is up to 45 cm long, sometimes with a long stem. The collar is 5 cm long, a dark blood-red and smooth, with a slightly lighter colored flower with fine red spots.

CULTIVATION: *C.usteriana* is a true water plant almost impossible to grow emersed. It has few special requirements as to soil, water or lighting. It propagates easily by means of runners. Because of its size it is only suitable for large aquariums. It very rarely flowers in the aquarium but might be encouraged to do so if given a short day, that is, less than twelve hours of light per day.

176. *Cryptocoryne purpurea*

◁177. *Cryptocoryne purpurea* (inflorescence)

NOTE: The name *C.usteriana* may not be correct: *C.aponogetifolia* may one day be adopted. Some authorities suggest that the latter name should be adopted for the emersed form of *C.usteriana,* but the matter is at present confused. When growing in the aquarium *C.usteriana* closely resembles *Aponogeton boivinanus.*

CRYPTOCORYNE VERSTEEGII Engler
Family: *Araceae*
English name: none
Synonym: none
Origin: New Guinea
Natural habitat: No information is available

DESCRIPTION: The leaves are thick and fleshy, oval or almost triangular with a truncated or nearly heart-shaped base. They are bright green, 3–7 cm long and 2–4 cm wide on a leaf stalk 5–10 cm long. The inflorescence is about 8 cm: the collar is 2–3 cm long, narrow, dark purple and warty: the flower is yellow.

CULTIVATION: In the wild *C.versteegii* probably grows emersed for it only grows very slowly in the aquarium under water. It is thus difficult to propagate it by means of runners, although occasionally for no apparent reason the plant flourishes in the aquarium and produces a large number of runners. To grow well, emersed, *C.versteegii* should be treated as a marsh plant and grown in a very humid atmosphere.

NOTE: Another species *Cryptocoryne lingua* which closely resembles *C.versteegii* has been imported in recent years from Borneo. The leaves of *C.lingua* are however more spoon-shaped and it is very difficult to grow in the aquarium.

CRYPTOCORYNE WENDTII de Wit

Family: *Araceae*

English name: none

Synonym: none

Origin: Southeast Asia, Thailand

Natural habitat: No information is available

DESCRIPTION: The size and color of the leaves can vary a great deal: they are either olive green with leaden-grey veins or blotches on the upper side and light green, often tinged with red on the underside or purplish-brown both above and below. They are usually 10 cm long and 3 cm wide, on a leaf stalk up to 15 cm long. The inflorescence is about 10 cm long, the collar is a brownish-purple and almost smooth but with a warty edge: the flowers are a deep violet with fine white spots. A dwarf variety of *C.wendtii* exists which does not grow higher than 8 cm.

CULTIVATION: *C.wendtii* is easy to grow and has few special requirements as to water, soil or light. It will tolerate a lot of light and propagates easily by runners. The plant rarely flowers under water but is very suitable for growing as a bog plant when it will flower profusely. The dwarf variety which is not yet common makes an excellent border plant.

178. *Cryptocoryne wendtii* ▷

179. *Cryptocoryne versteegii* (inflorescence)

180. *Cryptocoryne versteegii*

CRYPTOCORYNE WILLISII
Engler ex Baum
Family: *Araceae*
English name: none
Synonym: *Cryptocoryne undulata*
Origin: Sri Lanka
Natural habitat: Marshes

Description: The leaves are 10–15 cm long and 1–2 cm wide, green or olive, with characteristic reddish-brown veins branching from the midrib. The undersides of the leaves are lighter, often tinged with reddish-brown: the leaf edge is slightly wavy. The inflorescence is about 10 cm long: the collar is 3 cm, greenish-yellow or a matt ochre, serrated along the edge. The flower is pale green.

Cultivation: *C.willisii* is fairly easy to cultivate: it has no special requirements as to water, soil or light. It used to be common in aquariums but declined in popularity because it was prone to Cryptocoryne disease. Runners develop regularly on plants that grow well. The rather large rhizome often grows straight up from the bed in an unusual way, so that the plants appear to be growing on stilts. The plants can be topped when this occurs and many young plants will then sprout from the cut-off rhizome. *C.willisii* will not flower when grown under water but will do so if grown as a bog plant in a humid atmosphere.

ECHINODORUS

There are many species in the genus *Echinodorus* but by no means all are suitable for the aquarium and moreover, it is by no means certain that all the newer kinds, imported in recent years, are true species: it is possible that some are merely local varieties. Nevertheless the genus is one with an unusually large number of popular aquatic plants.

All the species share a number of common characteristics. The leaves are arranged in a rosette growing out of a rhizome, and there may be more than one plant along the length of this rootstock. The leaves vary in shape: they are elongated, lance-shaped, oval or heart-shaped. The flower stalks may grow vertically or they may lie along the bottom, or even float on the surface. The inflorescence is either a spike of flowers or a cluster in an umbel.

The flowers are hermaphrodite: that is they contain both male and female elements, both stamens and ovaries: they are usually white, but sometimes yellow or pink; they usually have three petals and 6, 9, 12, 18, 24 or even more stamens and anything between 6 and 20 ovaries. Very often the flowers do not develop fully in the aquarium but the flower stalk bends over into the water and young plants then develop on it: these young plants can be put into soil and will flourish. This is the most common way of propagating these species.

Some species are very sensitive to the number of daylight hours to which they are exposed. For this reason aquarists talk of 'short day' and 'long day' species, distinguishing between those that should have no more than 12 hours daylight at the most and those that flourish best if they have somewhat more daylight than that. In other ways most of these plants are not fussy, although most enjoy having a fairly nutritious bed but in the species descriptions that follow, a note is given on any particular requirements of soil and water.

ECHINODORUS AMAZONICUS Rataj
Family: *Alismataceae*
English name: Small (or narrow) leaved Amazonian Sword Plant
Synonym: *Echinodorus brevipedicellatus*
Origin: Brazil, the Amazon basin
Natural habitat: No information available

Description: The leaves are narrow and lance-shaped, pointed at both the base and the tip: frequently they are curved like a scimitar. They are 20–40 cm long and 2–4 cm wide, light green in color. The leaf stalk is 5–15 cm long. The flower stalk grows up to 100 cm and has 4–6 small whorls, each with 4–9 white flowers about 1 cm across.

Cultivation: *E.amazonicus* needs a lot of light and a nutritious bed: it should also be given a lot of space to allow for its ample growth. The flower stalk usually remains submersed in the aquarium and many small plants develop on it. This species seems not to be affected by the number of daylight hours it is given.

Note: *E.amazonicus* is difficult to distinguish from *Echinodorus bleheri*.

ECHINODORUS ASCHERSONIANUS
Graebner
Family: *Alismataceae*
English name: none
Synonym: none
Origin: Argentina, Brazil, Paraguay, Uruguay
Natural habitat: Found in a variety of shallow still and slow flowing waters

Description: The leaves are oval to broad, lance-like in shape, with a wedge or heart-shaped base. They grow up to 15 cm long and 8 cm wide on a leaf stalk 10–30 cm long and vary from a very light to a slightly dark green, in contrast to their very dark green veins. The flower stalk is 20–40 cm long with two or four groups of rather large white flowers.

Cultivation: *E.aschersonianus* needs a nutritious bed and a lot of light. It is ideal for an aquarium because it does not grow above the water surface. The flower stalks only grow up a short way and then creep along the bottom.

181. *Echinodorus amazonicus*

This is a species in which the flowers usually remain closed and the young plants develop from the buds.

Note: When given at least 12 hours of daylight the leaves become broader and more obviously heart-shaped at the base. More than 14 hours daylight is needed to ensure that the flower heads open.

ECHINODORUS BERTEROI (Sprengel) Fassett

Family: *Alismataceae*

English names: Amazonian Sword Plant, Cellophane Plant

Synonyms: *Alisma rostratum, Echinodorus cordifolius, Echinodorus rostratus*

Origin: Southern USA, Central America, the West Indies

Natural habitat: Found in a variety of still and slow running seasonal waters

DESCRIPTION: The shape of the leaves varies. Those of submersed plants are always dark green, thin and transparent (which accounts for the name 'cellophane plant'). The young leaves are strap-like or lance-shaped, and narrow at the base: when mature they have a well-defined leaf stalk (20–80 cm long) and are oval or heart-shaped. Floating and aerial leaves are light green, with heart-shaped blades. Each leaf has 3–7 prominent veins. The flower stalk may be 100–150 cm long with up to eight groups of flowers, each with three to six flowers, 1–1.5 cm across.

CULTIVATION: The plant needs a lot of light but is otherwise undemanding. It thrives if given a long day but when there are more than 12 hours of daylight floating and aerial leaves inevitably form and the submersed leaves then die off. It is therefore best to give it a short day. It is difficult to propagate. This can only be done with seeds. A flowering plant will produce a lot of seed which, stored in a dry place for 2–3 months can then be sown in damp earth at 23°–25°C. Usually most of the seeds germinate after a week but they may germinate irregularly and germination can take two years: the experiment should not therefore be hastily abandoned even if no results are seen after a few weeks. The ripe seeds do not fall off the flower stalk but remain attached to it after it has dried out. *E.berteroi* can be grown in ponds during the summer.

NOTE: A very similar species, *Echinodorus nymphaefolius* but with a more plumelike inflorescence is sometimes mentioned but it seems not to have been imported as yet.

ECHINODORUS BLEHERI Rataj

Family: *Alismataceae*

English name: none

Synonym: *Echinodorus paniculatus*

Origin: Northern South America

Natural habitat: No details are available

DESCRIPTION: The leaves are usually 20–30 cm long but occasionally even 50 cm in length and 2–6 cm wide. They are lance-shaped and taper to a point at both the base and the tip. They have five veins and a leaf stalk up to 30 cm long. The flower stalk may be 100 cm long and has five to eight clusters of white flowers 2 cm across.

CULTIVATION: *E.bleheri* requires the same care and conditions as *E.amazonicus*. Propagation is identical but difficult because the flower stalk rarely develops in the aquarium: it must be grown as a bog plant with a lot of light if it is to flower.

NOTE: *E.bleheri* is easy to confuse with *E.amazonicus*, although it has broader leaves if the two species are cultivated under the same conditions.

ECHINODORUS HORIZONTALIS Rataj

Family: *Alismataceae*

English name: none

Synonym: none

Origin: The Amazon basin

Natural habitat: Found principally in marshes and bogs

DESCRIPTION: A beautiful species: the leaves grow up to 15 cm long and 8 cm wide horizontally on leaf stalks from 10 to 25 cm long. The leaves are heart-shaped and green but in strong lighting young leaves are initially often a reddish-brown. The flower stalk is 25–60 cm long with usually three groups of flowers, about 1.5 cm across.

CULTIVATION: *E.horizontalis* is very easy to grow. It propagates by means of young plants developing on the inflorescance as well as from seeds fertilised by artificial pollination. The plant grows better if given a long day.

NOTE: The best small-leaved species of Echinodorus for the aquarium. There are other species with smaller leaves, *Echinodorus macrophyllus* (synonym *Echinodorus grandiflorus*) and *Echinodorus muricatus* but these are larger plants and they will only grow submersed when given a short day: if given a long day they invariably form large floating leaves and aerial leaves.

ECHINODORUS LATIFOLIUS (Seubert) Rataj

Family: *Alismataceae*

English name: Dwarf Amazon Sword Plant

Synonyms: *Echinodorus intermedius, Echinodorus magdalenensis*

Origin: Northwestern South America

Natural habitat: Found in very marshy areas

DESCRIPTION: A very beautiful species which develops many runners. The light green lance-shaped leaves, 10–25 cm long and 1 cm broad are often slightly curved like a scimitar. The flower stalk is 10–20 cm long, growing vertically at first but then lying along the bottom, usually with 4–7 groups of white flowers, 1.5 cm in diameter.

CULTIVATION: *E.latifolius* is a very easy plant to grow. It has no special requirements in the aquarium. The many runners form a thick mat of vegetation which makes it a very good plant for the front of a large tank. It is also a very good bog plant.

NOTE: Submersed, and given a long day *E.latifolius* has lance-shaped leaves without stalks. If given a short day the leaves are shorter and grow on long stalks: that is how it usually grows as a bog plant and only emersed plants will flower in short days. A related species found in the aquarium is *Echinodorus quadricostatus* var. *xinguensis*: this species needs more light and remains smaller than *E.latifolius* but is otherwise almost indistinguishable from it.

ECHINODORUS OSIRIS Rataj

Family: *Alismataceae*

English name: none

Synonym: none

Origin: Southern Brazil

Natural habitat: Grows profusely on the rather cool beds (18°–24°C) of rivers fed by mountain streams

DESCRIPTION: An extremely beautiful species with submerged leaves, lance-shaped, up to 30–40 cm long and 8 cm wide, tapering to a point at the tip and the base, which grow on leaf stalks 8–15 cm long. The fully grown leaves are dark green: young leaves are a vivid reddish-brown. There are 3–5 prominent veins. The flower stalks may be 150 cm long and grow vertically, although they may subsequently lie along the bottom: it bears a number of widely spaced clusters, each with 6–9 flowers, although these do not open.

CULTIVATION: *E.osiris* is a large plant and must therefore be grown in a large tank. It requires a lot of light, which accentuates the colors and shades of the leaves. The best temperature for this species is 20°C but fluctuations in temperature will not harm it and lower temperatures may improve the color even if they inhibit growth. Propagation is easy from the many young plants that develop on the flower stalk.

NOTE: *E.osiris* will only flower if given a long day: given a short day the leaves will grow longer.

182. *Echinodorus bleheri*

183. *Echinodorus horizontalis*

184. *Echinodorus latifolius*

185. *Echinodorus osiris*

ECHINODORUS MAIOR (Micheli) Rataj

Family: *Alismataceae*

English name: Ruffled leaf Sword Plant

Synonym: *Echinodorus Leopoldina, Echinodorus martii*

Origin: Western South America

Natural habitat: No details are available

Description: The dark green prominently veined leaves are usually narrow and lance-shaped, 30–50 cm long and 2–7 cm wide. The base is wedge-shaped, round or almost heart-shaped, on a 10 cm long leaf stalk. Many clusters of white flowers about 1 cm across grow on the flower stalk which may be 100 cm long.

Cultivation: *E.maior* is a large plant which requires a lot of space, a nutritious bed and a great deal of light. It is not easy to propagate because the inflorescence rarely develops. When it does, if it is pressed underwater, then young plants will develop. Alternatively if the plant is left to flower naturally, many fertile seeds will be produced if it is pollinated artificially. Young plants sometimes develop in the rhizomes of mature plants.

Note: *E.maior* is not significantly affected by the number of daylight hours it is given but the leaves become broader as the amount of light is increased.

ECHINODORUS PARVIFLORUS

Family: *Alismataceae*

English name: none

Synonym: *Echinodorus peruensis*

Origin: Probably Peru and possibly Bolivia

Natural habitat: No details are available

Description: The leaves, in shape broad, lance-like and pointed at the base and tip, or oval with a truncated base, are 25 cm long and 5 cm wide, initially light green with a striking dark reddish-brown pattern in the veins and later become dark green. The leaf stalk is 5–10 cm long. The flower stalk is 30–40 cm long with 2–5 clusters of white flowers about 0.6 cm across.

Cultivation: An easy species to grow, even in poor light although under those conditions it remains small. In stronger light the colors of the young leaves become more vivid. *E.parviflorus* usually propagates by the formation of young plants on the flower stalks but robust plants also sometimes can be divided.

Note: *E.parviflorus* is very sensitive to the length of day. It flowers almost exclusively when given a short day and then produces broader oval leaves. Flowering is restricted and the leaves are narrower when it is given a long day. Each well-developed plant may have as many as forty leaves and it is a very good plant to put on its own in a large aquarium.

ECHINODORUS TENELLUS (Martius) Buchenau

Family: *Alismataceae*

English name: Junior Amazon Sword Plant

Synonyms: *Alisma tenellum, Echinodorus parvulus, Echinodorus subulatus*

Origin: Central America, Southern Brazil

Natural habitat: Usually found growing in wet sand near the banks of rivers that periodically flood

Description: A very attractive species which grows many runners and produces light green leaves, 2–7 cm long and 0.1–0.3 cm wide under water. Aerial leaves are lance-shaped, 1–4 cm long and 0.25–1 cm wide, with a leaf stalk 3–6 cm long. The vertical flower stalk is thin, 3–20 cm long with 1–2 clusters of white flowers.

Cultivation: *E.tenellus* is very suitable for the front of even the smallest aquarium: it soon forms a close grassy patch with its numerous runners. However, it needs a long day and does not thrive if mud collects around its roots: this should be siphoned off regularly. Otherwise the species has few special requirements and is also a good bog plant, when, grown above water, it flowers profusely.

EGERIA DENSA Planchon

Family: *Hydrocharitaceae*

English name: Argentinian Acharis

Synonyms: *Anacharis densa, Elodea densa*

Origin: Argentina, Brazil, Uruguay

Natural habitat: Found in freshwater rivers, lakes and ponds

Description: A submersed plant with stalks 0.1–0.4 cm in diameter and up to 400 cm long. The lower leaves are generally gathered into whorls of three, and those above in whorls of four or five. The upper whorls are very closely set together but lower down the distance between the whorls may be as much as 1 cm. The leaves are bright green, without stalks, 1.5–3 cm long and 2–5 cm broad: they have a single midrib. *E.densa* is unisexual, that is male and female flowers grow on separate plants. The flowers appear in the axils. Male flowers start as clusters of 2–4 in a spathe, developing a long stem up to the surface where they open out. Female flowers grow singly in a spathe. Both male and female flowers are white, the male flowers 2 cm across, the female 1 cm.

Cultivation: *E.densa* requires a great deal of light but is indifferent to the composition

186. *Echinodoris tenellus*

◁187. *Echinodorus tenellus* (inflorescence)

of the water or soil. Propagation is by topping and this must be carried out regularly to keep this pretty but quick growing plant in check. It can be cultivated in either a rooted or free-floating form.

NOTE: It seems that only the male plant grows when it is cultivated: even in the wild, female plants are rare. *E. densa* has become naturalised in many parts of the world.

EICHHORNIA AZUREA (Swartz) Kunth

Family: *Pontederiaceae*

English name: Blue Water Hyacinth

Synonyms: *Pontederia aquatica, Pontederia azurea*

Origin: Tropical South America

Natural habitat: Found in marshy ground

DESCRIPTION: A perennial plant with submersed erect stalks bearing narrow light green alternate leaves, 10–20 cm long and about 5 cm wide. These leaves lie on the stalk in two opposite rows, giving the plant the appearance of a feather or palm leaf. When the stalks reach the surface, leaves of quite a different shape grow out of the water, being rather flat and round, some 12 cm in diameter. The plant may flower and the large blue flowers flecked with yellow are arranged in a spike.

CULTIVATION: *E. azurea* makes a splendid display on its own in a middle to large sized aquarium. It requires a great deal of light and must be handled with care to avoid damage to the delicate leaves: if bruised they will drop off. It is important to prevent the plant reaching the surface: if it does, the emersed form will develop. The plant must be topped to prevent this. If the old stalk is allowed to stand after topping then one or more shoots may appear on it. If the emersed form is held underwater (with weights for example), submersed shoots may appear after a time.

NOTE: Another species, *Eichhornia crassipes*, the Water Hyacinth, is sometimes offered for sale. This is a floating plant with a rosette of large round leaves and swollen stalks that give the plants its buoyancy. *E.crassipes* has become a notorious weed in many parts of the world and is not suitable for the aquarium although some aquarists regard its hanging roots as a useful cover for fry.

ELEOCHARIS ACICULARIS
(L) Römer et Schultes

Family: *Cyperaceae*

English name: Slender Spike Rush

Synonyms: (among many) *Heleocharis acicularis, Scirpus radicans*

Origin: Europe, North America, Northeast and Southeast Asia

Natural habitat: Found in sandy, loamy or clay soil subject to occasional flooding

DESCRIPTION: A thin creeping rhizome bears rosettes of very slender long stems, without leaves, 10–30 cm long and about 0.05 cm thick. Emersed plants are much smaller, reaching a height of no more than 2–10 cm: these form spikelets 0.2–0.7 cm long with flowers at the tip.

◁188. *Eichhornia azurea*
189. *Eichhornia azurea* (inflorescence)

CULTIVATION: The slender spike rush is very suitable for the background of small aquariums or the middle ground of larger tanks. It requires a sandy soil and quite a lot of light. Under favorable conditions numerous runners are formed and a thick mat of vegetation quickly develops.

NOTE: Many different species, including some dwarf varieties, are sold to aquarists under the one name. One fine species now not often seen is *Eleocharis vivipara* which has stems identical to those of *E.acicularis* up to 60 cm long but new rosettes with shorter stems grow near their tops and can themselves be removed from the parent plant and grown on the bed. *E.vivipara* makes a fine display when set alone in the tank: it needs a lot of light.

ELODEA CANADENSIS Michaux

Family: *Hydrocharitaceae*

English names: Canadian pondweed, Water Pest, Ditchmoss, Babington's Curse

Synonyms (among many): *Elodea latifolia, Udora canadensis*

Origin: North America, from Quebec and Saskatchewan to Alabama and California

Natural habitat: Found growing in a variety of waters

190. *Eleocharis acicularis*

DESCRIPTION: A submersed plant with thickly leaved branched stems up to 50 cm in length and 0.1 cm thick. The leaves are dark green, generally arranged in whorls of three and often curled down: they are elliptical or oblong, 0.5–1 cm long and 0.1–0.3 cm wide. The upper leaves tend to partially overlap each other rather like the tiles on a roof. The flowers lie in the leaf axils and develop very long stalks so as to reach the surface.

CULTIVATION: Canadian pondweed needs a lot of light but is otherwise undemanding. It has been naturalized throughout Europe for a century and its initial spread was so explosive that it even impeded fishing and navigation in some places: hence it got the name 'water pest'. Despite its exhuberant growth it is a very good water purifier and therefore an excellent plant for the aquarium. Propagation is easy: new shoots will sprout from every severed section of the stem and the plant grows well either rooted or free floating.

NOTE: *E.canadensis* is no longer considered a noxious weed. It is now, in the wild threatened itself by another North American species, *Elodea nuttalii* (Planchon) St. John This species has narrower leaves, only 0.05–0.15 cm across and the upper leaves do not overlap as do those of *E.canadensis*. *E.nuttallii* is also suitable for the aquarium and is slightly more decorative. The male flowers break away form the stalks and float freely on the surface.

HETERANTHERA ZOSTERAEFOLIA
Martius

Family: *Pontederiaceae*

English name: none

Synonym: none

Origin: Bolivia, Brazil

Natural habitat: Found in very wet marshes and bogs

DESCRIPTION: The many branched stalks up to 100 cm long bear alternate light green leaves up to 5 cm long and about 0.5 cm broad. Immediately below the growth tip, the leaves are bunched tightly in a star pattern. If the plant reaches the surface it first develops a few floating leaves and subsequently flowers: the flowers are in groups of two or three and open one after the other: they are 0.5 cm tall, light blue and sometimes mottled with yellow.

CULTIVATION: *H.zosteraefolia* requires a great deal of light and dislikes fresh water: it should never be planted in a freshly set up tank. To see the plant at its best, with its beautiful flowers it must be allowed to grow up to the surface, but then, unfortunately it looks untidy

in the tank, and so *H.zosteraefolia* is often grown at the front of the tank and regularly trimmed so that it does not exceed 7 cm in height. This form of cultivation although unnatural is generally well tolerated.

HOTTONIA

Family: *Primulaceae*

English name: Featherfoil

Synonym: (but probably incorrectly) *Hottonia inflata*

Origin: Venezuela

Natural habitat: No details are available

DESCRIPTION: The stalks are branched and bear alternate or irregularly whorled leaves, elliptical to oval, 3–5 cm long and 2–3 cm across, bright green on the upper side and silvery green on the underside.

CULTIVATION: This plant grows quickly if given sufficient light. It prefers a light soil and moderate temperature. In most cases the plant is topped frequently and used at the front of the tank: the old stalks should not

191. *Heteranthera zosteraefolia*
◁ 192. *Heteranthera zosteraefolia* (inflorescence)

be allowed to remain or they will begin to sprout again.

NOTE: It is not absolutely certain that this plant is a species of *Hottonia. Hottonia palustris*, the Water Violet, is found in the wild and although very similar to this plant, is unsuitable for the aquarium.

193. *Hydrocotyle leucocephala* ▷
194. *Hottonia*

HYDRILLA VERTICILLATA (L.fils) Presl

Family: *Hydrocharitaceae*

English name: Bottom nettle

Synonyms: *Hydrilla alternifolia, Hydrilla dentata, Serpicula verticillata*

Origin: Europe (except in the northwest), Africa, Asia, Australia

Natural habitat: Found in still or slow running waters

DESCRIPTION: The stalks up to 300 cm long, bear at short intervals whorls of 2–9 straight, dark green leaves about 2 cm long and 0.3 cm wide. The leaves have a light- to brownish-red midrib and toothed margins. The plant is hermaphrodite: the female flowers appear in the upper leaf axils and reach the surface: the male flowers are grouped in the lower axils and float to the surface after detaching themselves from their stalks.

CULTIVATION: *H.verticillata* is very easy to grow either in its rooted or free floating form provided it is given a good deal of light. Planting calls for care because the very fragile stalks must not be damaged.

NOTE: *H.verticillata* and *Elodea canadensis* are sometimes confused. *H.verticillata* has leaves with a red midrib and finely toothed margins visible to the naked eye: the leaves of *E.canadensis* have a green midrib and are smooth at the edge.

HYDROCOTYLE LEUCOCEPHALA

Family: *Umbelliferae*

English name: none

Synonym: none

Origin: Tropical South America

Natural habitat: Marshes and bogs

DESCRIPTION: Kidney shaped leaves 3–8 cm in diameter with a regularly serrated edge lie on the leaf stalk which grows vertically under water but creeps along the ground if the plant is emersed. Only the terrestial stalks will bear flowers which will develop where it takes root. The flowers are so small that the white clusters can only be seen clearly with a magnifying glass.

CULTIVATION: *H.leucocephala* needs a great deal of light but is otherwise undemanding, though a deep tank is desirable because of its rapid growth. When the plant reaches the surface the stalks continue to grow along the surface and the leaves start to float. They can become very large and will then block off all light from the plants below. The plants can be kept submersed by regular topping and then the leaves remain much smaller. If as a result of this the plant begins at any time to look weak, it can be revived quickly by allowing a few tendrils to grow up to the surface.

NOTE: *H.leucocephala* closely resembles *Cardamine lyrata* but is more robust.

HYGROPHILA DIFFORMIS (L.fils) Blume

Family: *Acanthaceae*

English name: none

Synonym: *Synnema triflorum*

Origin: Tropical Asia

Natural habitat: Found growing in a variety of waters

195. *Hygrophila difformis*

DESCRIPTION: The stems, 30–40 cm high have light green finely divided submersed leaves 12 cm long and 5 cm wide which lie opposite in pairs: emersed leaves and those near the surface are elliptical with tooth-like margins, 5 cm long and 3 cm wide: emersed leaves are very hairy. The pale violet flowers, which only grow above water are 1–1.5 cm tall.

CULTIVATION: *H.difformis* is an easy plant to grow: all it requires is plenty of light. Propagation by cuttings is simple: even severed leaves will produce young plants where they have been cut. Runners are also produced at the foot of the plant. Emersed sections can be planted underwater without risk although they should be rinsed well in water. The sap of the highly aromatic emersed plant seems to be mildly poisonous.

NOTE: *H.difformis* is a particularly pretty plant suitable for larger aquariums: it contrasts well with darker plants, stones and wood.

HYGROPHILA POLYSPERMA
(Roxburgh) T. Anderson

Family: *Acanthaceae*

English name: Indian Water Star

Synonyms: *Hemiadelphis polysperma, Justica polysperma*

Origin: Tropical Asia

Natural habitat: Found in marshes and bogs

DESCRIPTION: The many branched stalks, about 50 cm long bear leaves without leaf stalks, arranged in opposite pairs. They are 3–4 cm long, about 1.5 cm broad and 1–1.5 cm apart. Emersed leaves are fleshier, smaller and darker. No inflorescence is known.

CULTIVATION: *H.polysperma* is a very suitable plant for the aquarium where it grows well provided it is given enough light. Propagation is as for *H.difformis*.

NOTE: The exact classification of this plant is uncertain, and will remain so until it flowers in cultivation. Another species, *Hygrophila angustifolia* is sometimes offered for sale: the stalks of this species have no branches and narrower but much longer leaves: it grows more slowly and is less decorative than *H.polysperma.*

196. *Hygrophila polysperma*

LAGENANDRA THWAITESII Engler

Family: *Araceae*

English name: none

Synonym: none

Origin: Sri Lanka

Natural habitat: Found in marshy ground in low-lying tropical forests

DESCRIPTION: Dark green leaves are arranged in a whorl on a tough rootstock: they are 8–25 cm long, 2–6 cm broad, somewhat oval and gently tapering at the tip, with a wavy silvery edge. The leaf stalk is 5–20 cm long, dark green to purple. The inflorescence is 5–10 cm long, resembling that of a *Cryptocoryne,* brownish-red on the outside and a dark purple within.

CULTIVATION: *L.thwaitesii* is no more satisfactory an aquarium plant than any other species of *Lagenandra.* It can survive for a long time under water but it neither grows nor propagates well in those conditions. If grown emersed, in a humid atmosphere, it grows vigorously and flowers regularly, and is therefore an ideal plant for a paludarium.

LIMNOBIUM LAEVIGATUM
(Humboldt et Bonpland ex Willdenow) Heine

Family: *Hydrocharitaceae*

English name: South American Frogbit

Synonyms: *Limnobium stoloniferum, Hydromystria stolonifera, Trianea bogotensis*

Origin: Mexico, Paraguay, Southern Brazil

Natural habitat: Found growing in shallow still waters

DESCRIPTION: A floating plant with whorls of short stemmed broadly oval to almost round but often slightly pointed leaves, 2–3.5 cm long and 1.5–3 cm broad with a spongy thickening below that gives buoyancy. The leaves are often so closely set together that they overlap. The roots hang free in the water or may be attached to the earth below: they are white, with fine hairs. The plants are usually unisexual but occasionally bisexual. Male flowers are rare and have two circles of petals and six stamens: the female flowers have only one circle of petals and six to twelve pistils.

CULTIVATION: This is an easy plant to grow but it requires a good deal of light. It is very prolific and can quickly cover the surface of the tank. It must be thinned regularly if the plants below are not to be deprived of light. In hot summers it can be grown out of doors in a vivarium: it does not often flower in the aquarium.

197. *Lagenandra thwaitesii*

LIMNOPHILA AQUATICA
(Roxburgh) Alston

Family: *Scrophulariaceae*

English name: none

Synonym: none

Origin: Southeast Asia

Natural habitat: Found in marshes, watercourses and rice paddies.

DESCRIPTION: The submersed stalks up to 60 cm long bear many whorls of finely divided leaves each up to 6 cm long with threadlike lobes. The leaves on emersed stalks are placed opposite each other or in groups of three or four, grow 3.5–6.5 cm long and 0.6–1.5 cm across: they are lance-shaped to elliptical with finely serrated edges and feathering at the base, tending to clasp the stem. The flowers are violet to white, with purple marks, located either singly in the axils or in groups on the side or on the terminal spikes.

198. *Limnophila aquatica*

CULTIVATION: *L.aquatica* becomes one of the most attractive of aquarium plants if carefully nurtured. It needs plenty of light, a fairly high temperature and a rich soil. It will then grow very quickly – a whorl a day. Propagation by cuttings is straightforward.

NOTE: *L.aquatica* is sensitive to the amount of daylight it is given. Given long days it will try and grow up out of the water and will then bloom. Given a short day it generally remains submersed and does not flower. A more common species *L.sessiliflora* is not so attractive as *L.aquatica* and usually has smaller leaf whorls with coarser leaf lobes. It is often difficult to distinguish *L.aquatica* grown under poor conditions from *L.sessiliflora* grown under optimum conditions. It is impossible to confuse them however when both are grown together in the same tank: the whorls of *L.aquatica* are then much larger and the leaves more finely divided. Other species of *Limnophila* (*L.indica* and *L.heterophylla*) used to be grown but now seem to be out of favor with aquarists.

LOBELIA CARDINALIS (L)

Family: *Lobeliaceae*

English name: Cardinal Flower, Cardinal Lobelia

Synonym: *Rapuntium cardinale*

Origin: North America, from southern California to the Gulf of Mexico

Natural habitat: Marshes and river banks

DESCRIPTION: The submersed plant has short stemmed oval leaves placed alternately, 2–6 cm long and 1–1.5 cm broad. Emersed, the plant can grow to a height of 200 cm and the stem, then visibly hairy, can reach a thickness of 3 cm. The leaves are grass green, lance-shaped, with a saw edge. The scarlet flowers lie in clusters on the sides of the main stems.

CULTIVATION: A plant very suitable for the heated aquarium because it demands only adequate light and clean water. It grows to the height of a man out of water but is generally used as a foreground plant in the aquarium, being kept low by regular topping: its slow rate of growth helps it to tolerate this treatment. Cardinal flowers provide a good contrast to darker plants such as species of *Cryptocoryne*. They can also be effective if cultivated emersed as a garden plant in a damp place. Flowers will then form from July to September and the ripe seed can be sown the following spring in wet ground. The submersed form of the plant suitable for the aquarium can then be developed by constantly raising the water level.

LUDWIGIA PALUSTRIS (L) Elliot × **LUDWIGIA REPENS** Forster

Family: *Onagraceae*

English name: none

Synonyms: (among others) *Ludwigia mullertii, Ludwigia natans, Ludwigia repens*

Origin: Unknown but both *L.palustris* and *L.repens* are found in North America

Natural habitat: No information is available

DESCRIPTION: The leaves lie opposite in pairs, alternately at right angles, at 4 cm intervals: they grow up to 3 cm long and 1.5 cm wide with a leaf stalk of 1 cm: elliptical to oval in shape they are olive-green to reddish-brown above and red to light violet below. Flowers only form above the water surface and are always infertile.

CULTIVATION: This plant is easy to grow. If the lighting is too weak however, the lower leaves will be shed and the remaining leaves will all be green. If that happens then it must be topped. Propagation is easy by top cuttings, which can be planted in groups to decorate the aquarium.

NOTE: This plant used to be known as *L.mullertii* and today it is often called *L.natans* but these names are incorrect: it is a cross between *L.palustris* and *L.repens* but it is not known when this crossing took place. Another

199. *Lobelia cardinalis*

200. *Ludwigia repens* ▷

201. *Ludwigia repens* (inflorescence)

species sometimes offered for sale is *L.arcuata*, a pretty plant with submersed leaves about 3.5 cm long and only 2 cm wide, with often somewhat curved and emersed leaves broadly lance-shaped, up to 2 cm long and 0.5 cm wide. Unfortunately this species is very difficult to grow under water.

LYSIMACHIA NUMMULARIA (L)

Family: *Primulaceae*

English names: Creeping Jenny, Creeping Charlie, Moneywort, Herb Twopence

Synonym: none

Origin: Europe, naturalized in USA and Japan

Natural habitat: Along river banks, in ditches, wet pastures and woods, on clay, sandy or loamy soil

DESCRIPTION: A submersed erect stem bears opposite well-spaced leaves, light green, almost oval but wider at the top than at the bottom, 0.8–1 cm long and 0.5–0.7 cm broad with no (or very short) leaf stalks. Emersed, the plant is a creeper with stems 10–60 cm long and with almost circular leaves 1–3 cm broad. The flowers are yellow with five petals: they are 1.5–3 cm across and are usually found in the leaf axils.

CULTIVATION: Creeping Jenny does particularly well in cold water aquariums. Emersed specimens collected in the wild can be put in the tank without difficulty. The plant needs very strong lighting if it is to survive in a tropical aquarium: if the light is insufficient, *L.nummularia* will grow too much and then die. It can be grown successfully in damp positions in a garden provided the winters are not too severe.

MARSILEA

Family: *Marsileaceae*

English name: Four-leaved Water Clover, Clover Fern

Origin: Temperate and sub-tropical areas of the world

Natural habitat: Found on muddy river banks and in very marshy ground

DESCRIPTION: Four-lobed leaves closely resembling those of clover grow on short clover-like stalks from a creeping stem. The separate leaf segments may be triangular, wedge-shaped or rounded on the outside edge. If grown underwater these leaves will have less than four segments and indeed sometimes no separate segments at all. When the plant grows out of water sporocarps form at the base of the leaf stalks.

CULTIVATION: There are many different species of *Marsilea* and these can only be distinguished by an expert. It is unsatisfactory as an aquarium plant because the leaf stalks tend to become disproportionately long and untidy. No doubt subtle differences in care are needed for the various species but the impossibility for the amateur to identify the particular species he has in the tank makes it difficult to give good advice for its cultivation. If given a good deal of light it will tend to remain shorter but then it will grow so abundantly that other plants may be choked.

202. *Marsilea quadrifolia*

MICRANTHEMUM MICRANTHEMOIDES (Nuttall) Wettstein

Family: *Scrophlulariaceae*

English name: none

Synonym: none

Origin: Cuba, Southeast USA

Natural habitat: Found in shallow waters and on waterlogged banks

DESCRIPTION: A graceful and very delicate plant with thin stems which may be either erect or creeping, with whorls of three leaves at 0.5–1 cm intervals. The delicate leaves are lance-shaped or oval, 7.5 cm long and 2.5 cm wide. Plants grown out of the water are more compact with relatively broader leaves set more closely together. The small white flowers are inconspicuous and only develop out of the water, in the axils, on stalks 2.5–5 cm long.

CULTIVATION: *M.micranthemoides* needs a lot of light but is otherwise undemanding. It is very fragile and can be damaged easily by snails or fish. It is very decorative when planted in the foreground of the tank and can be propagated by topping. It sends out creepers and these produce branches and roots, so that a whole field of these plants may be created.

NOTE: Another species, *Micranthemum orbiculatum* Michaux is very occasionally cultivated in aquariums. It is very decorative but more difficult to grow.

MICROSORIUM PTEROPUS

Family: *Polypodiaceae*

English name: none

Synonymes: *Leptochilus decurrens, polypodium pteropus*

Origin: South China, India, the Philippines

Natural habitat: Found on rocks and tree roots standing in water and during the monsoons it grows completely submersed

DESCRIPTION: The thick green rhizome is closely set with short brown hairs and has many almost black hair-like roots with which this fern clings to the rock or soil. The dark green leaves, 30 cm long and 5 cm wide appear at short intervals along the rhizome: they are hard but brittle, wavy and may be pointed or rounded at the tip. Emersed leaves are longer.

CULTIVATION: *M.pteropus* is a very easy plant to grow and one to be highly recommended for the aquarium. It may be grown in sand but it is better to attach the rhizome to bogwood or stone, which will then gradually become overgrown with the fern. It has no particular requirements as to water or light. Propagation is simple by dividing the rhizome: however young plants often appear at the roots or even form on the underside of the leaves, from small dark swellings that appear about 1 cm from the leaf edge. These young plants can be detached and transplanted.

NOTES: There are a number of varieties of this fern in the wild, including some with very narrow or segmented leaves but these do not seem to be imported.

MYRIOPHYLLUM

Family: *Halorrhagaceae*

English name: Milfoil

Synonym: See below

Origin: Worldwide, except for the Arctic

Natural habitat: Found in a variety of fresh waters

DESCRIPTION: Whorls of three to six leaves appear irregularly on long garland-like stems.

203. *Microsorium pteropus*

204. *Nomaphila stricta*

The leaves are feathery and thread-like. Emersed leaves are less feathery, oblong to oval with toothed edges. The flowers are inconspicuous and lie either in the axils or on short spikes at the end of the main stems.

CULTIVATION: *Myriophyllum* species generally need a good deal of light and clear water. They must be protected against the attacks of algae, particularly thread algae, which can ruin a thriving plant. Otherwise these species make few demands and are easy to propagate by topping.

NOTE: *Myriophyllum* is a very popular plant with aquarists and a variety of species are available. Unfortunately nomenclature is at present confused and names change with disconcerting frequency. *Myriophyllum aquaticum* (also known as *Myriophyllum brasiliense* and *Myriophyllum serpinacoides*) is the only species with a universally recognised name. It has very striking emersed blue-grey leaves and can be found in almost all botanical gardens. Another species, *Myriophyllum hippuroides*, is brownish-red when submersed: the thick top of the stalk looks like a foxtail.

NAJAS

Family: *Najadaceae*

English name: none

Synonyms: See below

Origin: All temperate and tropical zones

Natural habitat: Found in both fresh and brackish waters

DESCRIPTION: A submersed plant with many branched often brittle stems with groups of three or more strap-like curved leaves without leaf stalks but with sheaths which gradually blend into the blades of the leaves. Both the leaves and the sheaths are toothed or prickly. The leaves are usually an attractive dark green, up to 4 cm long and 0.3 cm broad, but often narrower and shorter. Their size varies from species to species. The flowers are inconspicuous, located either singly or in groups of two to four in the axils: they are unisexual.

CULTIVATION: The Najas species are not difficult to grow but do need good light and clear water: some species will thrive when free floating provided the water is nutritious. Propagation is by means of topping.

NOTE: Various species will be found in aquariums but they can only be distinguished by experts. One of the most common is *Najas guadelupensis* (synonym *Najas microdon*) with leaves 1–1.5 cm long and 0.1 cm broad which may occasionally be as long as 2.5 cm. Another, coarser species is *Najas indica* (synonym *Najas kingii*) with leaves 2–4 cm long and 0.1 cm across.

NOMAPHILA STRICTA (Vahl) Nees

Family: *Acanthaceae*

English name: Giant Indian Water Star

Synonyms (among many): *Hygrophila stricta, Justica stricta, Nomaphila corymbosa*

Origin: Southeast Asia, India

Natural habitat: Found on the banks of all kinds of watercourses, especially where it is submersed when the waters are in flood.

DESCRIPTION: Oval or elliptical light green leaves up to 12 cm long and 4 cm broad lie in opposite pairs on erect, angular stems. The leaf stalks are short and the leaf margins serrated. Emersed leaves are the same shape and size but noticeably darker. The light blue flowers are grouped in loose bunches of 2–15 in the axiis.

CULTIVATION: *N.stricta* is an easy plant to grow but does require a great deal of light. It should be topped before it reaches the surface of the water because if it is allowed to grow out of the water the submersed leaves will drop off. It can be grown successfully out of water and even in well-watered window boxes or in the open in summer. The leaves will then have a reddish-brown tint. Cuttings taken from plants cultivated like this can be put in the aquarium without difficulties.

NUPHAR LUTEUM (L) Smith

Family: *Nymphaeaceae*

English name: Yellow water lily, Spatterdock

Synonyms: *Nuphar rivulare, Nymphaea lutea*

Origin: Europe, Northern Asia

Natural habitat: Freshwater lakes, ponds and ditches

DESCRIPTION: A rosette of extremely thin heart-shaped light green leaves, almost transparent and nearly circular but with wavy edges, 10–30 cm in diameter grows out of a thick fleshy rootstock. Floating leaves are oval, 12–40 cm long and 8–30 cm across, thick and a glistening green. The yellow flowers may be 3–5 cm across and have an unpleasant smell.

CULTIVATION: Despite the unpleasant smell of its flowers, the yellow water lily is a good plant for the tropical aquarium in which it remains fairly small and does not develop floating leaves: if such a leaf does develop it should be removed immediately and the plant will thus be encouraged to revert to its submersed form. If possible, a seed lily which has not yet developed a rootstock should be selected for the tank. If no seed lily is available from the dealers, they can be cultivated by the aquarist. Seeds should be planted in soft soil in shallow water and kept in the dark because it seems likely that the seeds will only germinate in the dark. *N.luteum* needs a great deal of light, but the soil should be too rich if the plant is to remain fairly small.

NOTE: Other species of *Nuphar* are sometimes available, including *Nuphar sagittifolium* with rounded leaves shaped like arrow-heads, but it is a difficult plant to keep healthy.

NYMPHAEA LOTUS L.

Family: *Nymphaeaceae*

English name: none

Synonym: *Nymphaea dentata*

Origin: Tropical Africa

Natural habitat: Sluggish or fast flowing clear waters

DESCRIPTION: A rosette of long-stemmed leaves (up to 40 cm long) sprouts from a small rootstock. The leaves are almost circular, with a deeply incised base and a toothed edge: they may be up to 20 cm in diameter and are either green with small red specks or red with small green specks. The flower is white, 7 cm in diameter and only opens at night.

CULTIVATION: *N.lotus* is a striking plant on its own in the larger aquarium and demands little of its environment. Good lighting is important however for a compact plant and it needs ample space. The floating leaves so typical of water lilies are rarely formed, those that do form tend to grow too large and hang just below the surface, cutting off a great deal of light and exposing to view the underside of the leaf and the stalk. The plant can be encouraged to return to its smaller submersed form by these leaves being removed immediately. It may flower in the aquarium but of course the flowers will be open only at night. Young plants are sometimes formed on the rootstock or on short runners.

NOTE: Many other species of water lily are available commercially but are less suitable

205. *Peplis diandra* (foreground)

for the aquarium: *N.lotus* is easy to identify because of its spotted leaves with their toothed edges.

OTTELIA ALISMOIDES (L) Persoon

Family: *Hydrocharitaceae*

English name: none

Synonyms: (among many) *Damasonium indicum, Ottelia indica, Stratiotes alismoides*

Origin: Tropical and sub-tropical zones of Asia, Australia and Northeast Africa: naturalised in the rice fields of North Italy

Natural habitat: Found on muddy soils in still or slow moving waters

DESCRIPTION: A submersed plant with broad oval or almost round leaves which may grow up to 22 cm long, pale green, on very brittle leaf stalks up to 25 cm long. The flowers are white, about 2 cm across and project above the surface. Young plants first develop strap-like leaves resembling those of *Vallisneria spiralis*: later leaves are broader and gradually develop the shape described above.

CULTIVATION: *O.alismoides* is sometimes difficult to grow. It needs a great deal of space, good light and warmth. It is prone to be eaten by fish that have a liking for vegetable matter. Propagation is by seed, for no shoots are formed. The plants do not have to be artificially pollinated and will produce a lot of seeds. After flowering, the flower stem contracts rather like a spiral and the seed head is drawn below the surface: it ripens in 10–14 days and then opens. To collect the seed, the seed heads should be enveloped in fine nylon net as soon as they are drawn below the surface: in this way the seed will be prevented from floating about the tank. Once collected they should be kept in water at the same temperature as the aquarium until they germinate: this may be anything from two weeks to a year. Once the seedlings have developed roots they may be planted out with care in trays.

NOTE: Although *O.alismoides* is one of the prettiest of aquarium plants it is not always easy to obtain. Another species *Ottelia ulvaefolia* with yellow flowers and reddish-brown oblong leaves is sometimes imported but no reliable method of caring for this species is yet known.

PEPLIS DIANDRA Nuttall ex DC

Family: *Lythraceae*

English name: none

Synonym: *Didiplis diandra* (Nuttall ex DC) Wood

Origin: Southeastern USA, principally in the catchment area of the Mississippi

Natural habitat: Found in and around the banks of shallow ponds and in marshes

DESCRIPTION: An erect plant 20–40 cm high with thin stalks with only a few branches. The leaves are set close together, opposite each other, and bright green, strap-like when submersed and lance-shaped when emersed: they are 1–2 cm long. The flowers are a striking shade of brown and develop in the axils both above and below the surface.

CULTIVATION: *P.diandra* needs a great deal of light but will tolerate a wide variety of soils and waters. Propagation is by topping: the old stalks soon grow again and a dense plant is soon produced. It looks particularly effective when set in front of darker stones, plants or bogwood.

PISTIA STRATIOTES L.

Family: *Araceae*

English name: Water lettuce

Synonym: none

Origin: All tropical and some sub-tropical zones

Natural habitat: Found in still waters in rivers, lakes and marshy grounds

DESCRIPTION: A floating plant with shell-like rosettes of thick broadly tongue-shaped velvety blue-green leaves 10–20 cm long and 7 cm wide. The undersides are pale green and spongy. The roots hang freely in the water as a fine cluster initially whitish and later darker. The yellowish-white flowers are about 1 cm high and stand singly in the axils. In the aquarium *P.stratiotes* remains smaller than in the wild and the leaves lie more or less flat on the water.

CULTIVATION: The normal form of *P.stratiotes* needs a lot of light, sunlight if possible. Only an open tank without a glass cover will give it adequate ventilation. In covered aquariums an inhibited growth form of the plant almost always develops. This plant propagates profusely by means of underground stems.

NOTE: In the wild *P.stratiotes* is an aggressive and unwelcome weed but it can be useful in the aquarium where good cover is needed.

POTAMOGETON GAYI A Bennett

Family: *Potamogetonaceae*

English name: none

Synonym: none

Origin: South America

Natural habitat: Found in a variety of small watercourses

DESCRIPTION: Stalks sprout from a thin underground rootstock at regular intervals and grow 30–100 cm. They bear alternate thin strap-like leaves about 0.3 cm wide and up to 6 cm long, light brown to olive green, with a clear midrib. The flowers stand above the water on spikes 1–1.5 cm long but are somewhat unimpressive.

CULTIVATION: A very easy plant to grow in the aquarium, requiring little more than good light. Propagation is by cuttings but new branches sprout from runners at regular intervals and these come up from the bed some way from the mother plant: if the aquarium is not to be full of *P.gayi* these must be

206. *Pistia stratiotes*

207. *Potamogeton gayi*

208. *Rotala macrandra*

209. *Rotala rotundifolia* ▷

removed. Sometimes the stalks only branch when they reach the surface and this growth can in time cover the whole of the top of the tank.

RICCIA FLUITANS L.
Family: *Ricciaceae*
English name: Crystalwort
Synonym: *Ricciella fluitans*
Origin: Worldwide
Natural habitat: Found in still waters and also in marshes

DESCRIPTION: This plant consists of a thallus (that is a body without true roots, stems or leaves), light green, narrow 0.5–1 mm broad, forking regularly and broadening out somewhat towards the tips.

CULTIVATION: *R.fluitans* can be found in almost all aquariums. It provides excellent cover for fry and if the water is nutritious will spread very quickly. It will mesh together to form a mat of floating vegetation, but it can be destroyed by blue-green algae.

ROTALA MACRANDRA Koehne
Family: *Lythraceae*
English name: none
Synonym: none
Origin: Western India
Natural habitat: Found in small watercourses

DESCRIPTION: The stalks 30–50 cm high bear opposite leaves in pairs, at short intervals of about 2 cm. The oval leaves are 3 cm long and 2 cm wide, green to blood red on the upperside with lighter contrasting ribs and purple red on the underside. The flowers are red and lie in branching spikes at the tips of the stalks.

CULTIVATION: Given good light *R.macrandra* is one of the most rewarding aquarium plants. In sunlight the leaves turn a deep red: the weaker the light the paler the plant and it may even turn green. Specimens of *R.macrandra* should therefore be given ample room so that they receive ample light and should not be planted close together nor too near other plants. The soil should contain as little lime as possible and peat dust should be added. A temperature of 25° C is needed and the plant is very sensitive to sudden changes in temperature. Propagation is easy: cuttings may be taken from both the tops and from lateral branches, but should be planted as soon as possible. The plant will not flower underwater. *R.macrandra* is an annual and usually starts to die after it has flowered, so it is essential to keep a stock of submersed plants.

NOTE: *R.macrandra* is now often offered in aquarium shops and these specimens are usually more robust than the wild plants described above. Their leaves are about 5 cm long and 3 cm broad and a very deep shade. However, once planted in the aquarium these specimens revert to their natural delicate form. *R.macrandra* when cultivated emersed is virtually indistinguishable from *Rotala rotundifolia* described below.

ROTALA ROTUNDIFOLIA
(Roxburgh) Koehne
Family: *Lythraceae*
English name: none
Synonym: *Ammania rotundifolia*
Origin: Southeast Asia
Natural habitat: Found in small waterways and marshes

DESCRIPTION: The stalks are up to 50 cm long and bear opposite leaves in pairs at very short intervals of less than 1 cm. The leaves are of various shapes, oblong, elliptical, strap-like or almost needle-like: they are up to 1.5 cm long and 0.4 cm broad, a pale green to reddish underneath and a pale green to dark red on the upper side. The emersed form of the plant has leaves which are more or less oval and may be up to 1.2 cm in diameter. The small pink flowers are found at the tips of the branches.

CULTIVATION: *R.rotundifolia* is an easy plant to grow which makes few demands. It does need strong lighting however if it is to develop a good color. Propagation is by topping and is not difficult. If topped regularly it is suitable for the front of the tank where it forms a good contrast to darker plants. It will only flower if grown emersed.

NOTE: *R.rotundifolia* is indistinguishable from another species *Rotala indica* except when it flowers: it is then seen that whereas the flowers of *R.rotundifolia* lie on branched spikes, those of *R.indica* appear as solitary flowers in the axils. If grown emersed *R.rotundifolia* is also indistinguishable from *R.macrandra* but there is no possibility of confusion when the two species are grown under water.

210. *Salvisia auriculata*

211. *Samolus parviflorus*

SAGITTARIA SUBLATA (L) Buchenau

Family: *Alismataceae*

English name: Arrowhead, Arrow wort

Synonym: *Sagittaria natans*

Origin: USA, from Massachusetts to Alabama and Florida

Natural habitat: The shallow parts of rivers, lakes and ponds

DESCRIPTION: A submersed plant with rosettes of strap-like green leaves up to 40 cm long and 0.8 cm wide with three ribs, the two outermost of which do not extend to the tip of the leaf but run into the edges. In shallow waters floating leaves are often formed: these are elliptical, 2–6 cm long and 1–1.5 cm wide with a thin stalk. The flower stalk floats on the surface and bears 1–6 whorls, each with three white flowers up to 1 cm across.

CULTIVATION: This is very easy. *S.sublata* has no special requirements. Propagation is by the many runners which develop.

NOTE: *S.sublata* can be confused with *Vallisneria spiralis* but the two can be distinguished by the ribs of the leaves: in *S.sublata* only one runs the length of the leaf, in *V.spiralis* all three run the whole length of the leaf. Other species of *Sagittaria* are sometimes found but they are not definitively named. One species sometimes found is *Sagittaria teres*: this is a short plant with leaves up to 15 cm long and 0.9 cm wide: it is very suitable for the front of a tank. Another species is known (probably incorrectly) as *Sagittaria platyphylla*: this has a tuberous rootstock and leaves up to 30 cm long and 2 cm wide.

SALVINIA AURICULATA Aublet

Family: *Salviniaceae*

English name: Small-leaved Salvinia

Synonym: none

Origin: South America from Cuba to Paraguay

Natural habitat: Found in still or slow running but not very clear waters

DESCRIPTION: A floating plant whose stalk lies horizontally just below the surface and bears whorls of three leaves, two of which float on the surface. They have short stalks, are circular or elliptical, light green and grow up to 1 cm in the aquarium. The surface of the leaf is rough, with short stiff bristles. In hothouses or in sunny garden ponds the floating leaves, which turn up at the edges, can reach a length of 1.5–1.8 cm. The third leaf in the whorl hangs down freely in the water: it is 2–5 cm long and very finely dissected.

CULTIVATION: This is comparatively simple provided *S.auriculata* is given adequate light and nutritious water. The plant grows very quickly throwing out lateral branches which are then cast free. Superfluous growth must therefore be cleared away at regular intervals. It is a very appropriate plant for the tropical aquarium and provides good cover for fry.

NOTE: *Salvinia* does not have a true root: the root function is carried out by the floating leaves.

SAMOLUS PARVIFLORUS Rafinesque

Family: *Primulaceae*

English name: Green Water Rose

Synonyms: *Samolus americanus*, *Samolus aquaticus*, *Samolus floribundus*

Origin: Tropical and temperate zones of America

Natural habitat: Found in shallow fresh and brackish waters

DESCRIPTION: When cultivated submersed this is an attractive plant with rosettes of light green, oblong to spatulate-shaped leaves up to 10 cm long and 4.5 cm across. The ribs are much lighter than the body of the leaf and form a marked contrast. When cultivated emersed the plant develops a flower stalk up to 50 cm tall which bears a cluster of white flowers.

CULTIVATION: *S.parviflorus* needs good light and a moderate temperature: it is otherwise undemanding. Its green leaves contrast well with stones and darker plants. It can be propagated by topping: when the plant is about 15 cm tall the upper half can be trimmed off and replanted. *S.parviflorus* will not flower underwater and when grown submersed sometimes develops instead of a flower stalk, a stem which will simply produce a number of small plants. Such plants may also develop from severed leaves laid on wet earth. Plants cultivated emersed on marshy ground will flower profusely: ripe seeds will then be produced and which may be left, when they fall off the plant, to germinate naturally at its foot. When these seedlings have grown a little they can then be transferred to the aquarium.

212. *Lysimachia nummularia*

213. *Saururus cernus*

214. *Teleanthera lilacina*

SAURURUS CERNUS L.

Family: *Saururaceae*

English name: none

Synonyms: *Saururus lucidus*, *Serpantaria repens*

Origin: North America, especially along the east coast of Florida but also as far north as Canada

Natural habitat: Marshes, waterlogged meadows, and woods bordering on streams

DESCRIPTION: Emersed it has stems up to 150 cm and a thick rampant rootstock from which new stalks sprout at regular intervals. The alternate heart-shaped leaves, pointed at the tips are 10–15 cm long and 6–8 cm wide, on leaf stalks 8–12 cm long. The spiky flowers stand in the axils or at the tips of the stalks. When submersed, the plant grows in a very much more compact way so that the leaves look as though they are arranged in a rosette: then the plant grows up to 10 cm with leaves 7 cm long and 4 cm broad, with leaf stalks 3–6 cm long. *S.cernus* will not flower underwater.

CULTIVATION: *S.cernus* is easy to grow: it has no special requirements as to soil, water or light. If the plant is topped regularly but the old stalks allowed to stand, a large spread of vegetation will develop. It forms a good contrast to darker plants. It is easy to grow emersed provided it is given a lot of water. If the stalk of an emersed plant is cut and laid on wet ground, side shoots will develop in the axils and these can then be transplanted to the aquarium.

'TELANTHERA LILACINA'

This is the name, certainly botanically incorrect, under which the plant described below is commercially sold. It may be a species of the genus *Alternanthera* (Family: *Amaranthaceae)*

Origin: Brazil, Goiás.

Natural habitat: Marshes

DESCRIPTION: Stalks up to 40 cm bear at regular intervals, opposite pairs of lance-shaped leaves up to 8 cm long and 2 cm wide, ranging from a deep red, when grown in strong light, to a yellow green in poor light. The ribs are darker than the rest of the leaves. The inflorescence is unknown.

CULTIVATION: As for *Alteranthera reineckii* although its reaction to aquarium conditions varies from specimen to specimen: some flourish and others do not. Certainly they should be topped regularly. The plant is easy to grow as a marsh plant.

VALLISNERIA SPIRALIS L.

Family: *Hydrocharitaceae*

English name: Common Eel Grass

Synonyms: This well-known aquarium plant has at least 12 synonyms in the literature but is almost universally known as *V.spiralis*

Origin: Almost all tropical and sub-tropical zones of the world

Natural habitat: Rivers and lakes with clear waters

DESCRIPTION: A creeping rootstock bears rosettes of transparent green leaves 30–80 cm long and 0.4–0.8 cm broad which are sometimes twisted several times around their axes. Three to five parallel veins run the length of the leaf. There are both male and female plants: the male plants are smaller. In the male plants the flowers stand in a spathe at the base of the stem and later break loose and float to the surface. Female flowers are attached to long stems and when the female flower has been pollinated by a free floating male flower the flower stem contracts spirally and the fruit matures at the base of the plant.

CULTIVATION: *V.spiralis* is easy to grow but it must be given a great deal of light and it likes a lot of iron in the soil. Propagation is easy because of the many runners that are produced.

NOTE: *V.spiralis* is often confused with *Sagittaria sublata* but the distinctions are noted above under the description of the latter species. Some other species of *Vallisneria* are sometimes found in aquariums. *Vallisneria gigantea* the Giant Eel Grass has green leaves up to 150 cm long and 1–2 cm broad. *Vallisneria neotropicalis* has even broader leaves. *Vallisneria americana* has leaves 10–40 cm long and 0.4–0.8 cm wide, which are visibly serrated towards the tip. Varieties with twisted leaves are often sought after: one, called *'Vallisneria contortionist'* is probably a variety of *V.spiralis*. There is also a dwarf variety of *Vallisneria* which grows no more than 20 cm high, but this is rarely seen.

VESICULARIA DUBYANA

(C. Muller) Brotherus

Family: *Hypnaceae*

English name: Java Moss

Synonym: *Hypnum dubyanum*

Origin: Southeast Asia

Natural habitat: Usually found above water, growing up tree trunks, around stones or on the ground

DESCRIPTION: The many branched stalks bear two lines of lance-shaped, light green leaves up to 1.5 cm long and 0.5–0.7 cm wide. The plant is attached to the ground below by means of a large number of red-brown root-like threads. Red-brown sporocarps are formed both above and below the water.

CULTIVATION: *V.dubyana* is a very undemanding plant. It looks very attractive when it forms a carpet of green over bogwood, stones or the back of the tank. It grows well either anchored to the bed or to bogwood or stones, or when floating free. The free floating form can however cause problems as it is inclined to envelop other plants. Egg-laying fish like it as a spawning medium. It grows well out of water and is suitable for a paludarium.

NOTE: A similar but more ornamental plant is *Glossadelphus zollingeri* which closely resembles *V.dubyana* but which has longer stalks and fewer branches. *G.zollingeri* can be distinguished also by the fact that unlike *V.dubyana* it never forms sporocarps underwater.

215. *Vesicularia dubyana*

FISHES

Classification and Nomenclature

SCIENTISTS have found it helpful to divide both the animal and plant kingdoms into groups and this has always been done, since the days of the earliest scientific classifiers in the seventeenth and eighteenth centuries, on the basis of various identified characteristics in individual animals or plants, which could be linked with the same characteristics in other animals or plants to indicate a connection between the two species involved: in the same way, basic differences in characteristics have been used to distinguish one animal or plant from another. The earliest classifications were made along what seem now to be very artificial lines: their basis was laid by Linnaeus (Carl von Linné) who published his *Systema naturae* or system of nature, in 1735.

These early classifiers or taxonomists had to rely on what they could see with the naked eye or by using relatively low-powered microscopes. Moreover both they and their successors sometimes adopted a classification that owed as much to their own preconceived ideas on the development of the animal and plant kingdom, as it did on their observations of characteristics. As science developed, and new instruments afforded scientists the opportunity of making more detailed studies, so many changes were made in the orginal system of classification. Changes still occur today as a result of new or more detailed studies (for example on the teeth patterns of various tropical fish which have led to a number of species being re-classified) so that the classification – and hence the Latin names by which animals and plants are known to science – are continually changing.

The names change as species are re-classified because in fact those names are themselves the record of the place occupied in the classification system by the particular species. The basic unit of classification is the species: a species may be broken down into sub-species or varieties, but the species remains the fundamental unit. Closely related species are grouped together in a genus (plural genera): it may be that a genus will contain only one species. The Latin name of an animal or plant is in fact its genus, or generic name (spelt with an initial capital letter) followed by its species or specific name (spelt with no initial capital). Thus in the case for example of the Zebra Danio, *Brachydanio rerio, Brachydanio* is the generic name and *rerio* the specific name: in the case of the Pearl Danio, *Brachydanio albolineatus, Brachydanio* is once again the generic name and *albolineatus* the specific name. Thus seeing the two names together, the scientist immediately knows that they are closely related (in the same genus and thus with many characteristics in common) but different in some respects and accordingly different species. Where a sub-species is identified and accepted, then the Latin name will be in three parts, not two: the first is still the generic name, the second is the specific name – the species to which both sub-species belong and the third name will be the one by which the two or more sub species are distinguished. Often one sub-species will have the second name repeated as the third: this means as a rule that it was the first to be recognised and was once the only species, and that subsequently another sub-species has been recognised. Thus in the genus *Rasbora* will be found *Rasbora lateristriata lateristriata* and *Rasbora lateristriata elegans. Rasbora lateristriata lateristriata* was first described in 1854 and was than simply called *Rasbora lateristriata:* when a sub-species was discovered in 1903 with a difference in the lateral line, that new subspecies became *Rasbora lateristriata elegans* and the original species was given the extended name *Rasbora lateristriata lateristriata.*

In zoology it is still customary in scientific circles, to append to the name of the species the name of the person who first described it and the year in which that description was published and accepted. Thus the Sailfin Molly when first described and identified in 1914 was given the name *Molliensia velifera:* it was described by Charles Tate Regan and so its full name in scientific circles was then *Molliensia velifera* Regan 1914. If subsequently there is a change in classification, then the name of the original discoverer with the original date, will be retained in the new name but put in brackets. This happened with the Sailfin Molly. Sometime after Regan had described it and placed it in the genus *Molliensia,* it was agreed that it should really be classified as a species in the genus *Poecilia:* its name was accordingly changed to *Poecilia velifera:* its full scientific name then became, and has remained *Poecilia velifera* (Regan 1914): every research worker immediately knows, because of the brackets, that there has been a change in nomenclature since the fish was first described. This is of course very useful for scientific workers, but it is not often of much interest to the amateur aquarist: it is certainly not necessary to use the full scientific name except when writing a scientific paper. It is explained here in case the aquarist is confused when looking up particular species in reference books, but as a rule, in this encyclopaedia, fish are referred to solely by their generic and specific Latin names.

Indeed, many of the intricate details of nomenclature need not concern the amateur at all, but in addition to knowing sufficient to allow him to look up the species in the literature, it is useful to realise the relationships implied by the system

216. *Pterophyllum altum*

of classification and the names given to species for, when faced with an unfamiliar species, the amateur who can identify its genus and family can often deduce, from that relationship, useful guidelines on care and maintenance, by recalling the requirements of species in the same family with which he is familiar.

So far the relationship of species and genus has been explained. Genera are themselves grouped together in families. The family names invariably end in -idae, as for example, *Anostomidae,* the family of headstanders. Families in turn are grouped together in sub-orders and orders. The sub-orders have the ending -oidea: for example, the family *Anastomidae* and the family *Characidae* both belong (with other families) to the sub-order *Cyprinoidea.* Sub-orders are grouped together in orders (but some orders have no sub-orders and are merely groups of families). There is no invariable ending for the names of orders, but as an example, both the sub-order *Cyprinoidee* mentioned above and the sub-order *Siluroidea* make up the order *Ostariophysi.* Orders themselves are grouped together in classes, superclasses, sub-phyla, phyla or divisions: again the subject becomes complex and as a rule the amateur is not concerned with any level of classification wider than that of the family.

Suffice to say that all fish, together with a variety of other animals are put in the superclass *Gnathostomata.* Within that superclass, there are two separate classes of fish, but of those, only one class, the *Osteichthyes* is of concern to aquarists, for practically all aquarium fish are within this class.

The class *Osteichthyes* contains several sub-classes, including the *Paleopterygii,* the *Crossopterygii* and the *Neopterygii.* The first two of these sub-classes are again of little interest to aquarists: virtually all tropical aquarium fish are found in the sub-class *Neopterygii.*

Class:	OSTEICHTHYES		
Subclass:	NEOPTERGII		
Order	*Suborder*	*Family*	*Subfamily*
ISOSPONDYLI	—	*Mormyridae*	
	—	*Notopteridae*	
	—	*Pantodontidae*	
OSTARIOPHYSI	CYPRINOIDEA	*Anostomidae*	
		Characidae	
		Citharinidae	
		Cobitidae	
		Curimatidae	
		Cyprinidae	
		Gasteropelecidae	
		Gyrinocheilidae	
		Hemiodontidae	
	SILUROIDEA	*Bagridae*	
		Bunocephalidae	
		Callichthyidae	*Callichthyinae* *Corydoradinae*
		Clariidae	
		Loricariidae	
		Mochokidae	
		Siluridae	
MICROCYPRINI		*Cyprinodontidae*	*Cyprinodontinae*
		Poeciliidae	
		Goodeidae	
SYNENTHOGNATI	—	*Hemirhamphidae*	
PERCOMORPHI	PERCOIDEA	*Centrarchidae*	
		Centropomidae	
		Cichlidae	
		Monodactylidae	
		Nandidae	
		Scatophagidae	
		Toxotidae	
	GOBIOIDEA	*Gobiidae*	
		Eleotridae	
	OPHICEPHALOIDEA	*Ophicephalidae*	
	ANABANTOIDEA	*Anabantidae*	
	MUGILOIDEA	*Atherinidae*	
PLECTOGNATHI	—	*Tetraodontidae*	
OPHISTHOMI	—	*Mastocembelidae*	

THE FAMILY MORMYRIDAE

An introductory description

THE extensive Mormyridae family is only found in Africa where there are more than 100 species, divided into 11 genera. They are all freshwater fish, but particular species are restricted to specific environments, although as a whole the family is found in a wide variety of natural habitats. They are adaptable fish with the result that within the one family there is an unusually wide variation in body shapes, each reflecting the particular conditions under which the species live in the wild. In particular there are significant differences in the shape and development of the snout and the mouth.

Most species in the Mormyridae family have poor eyesight. This is particularly so among those species that live naturally in very muddy waters: in some species the eyes have a transparent protective covering which though it impedes vision, protects the eyes while the fish are searching on the bottom. All species have narrow tails, and the caudal fin is deeply forked and has a fleshy base. The dorsal and anal fins generally lie far back along the body, usually opposite each other: in many species the ventral fins are very poorly, but the pectoral fins very strongly developed.

The most remarkable feature of the Mormyridae is the natural in-built radar system which allows the fish to find their way about in their twilight natural environments. An organ in the tail generates weak electric impulses of a few microvolts. As a result an electric field is set up around the fish, and the field alters according to whatever objects (such as prey, rocks, plants) lie in the fish's immediate vicinity. These changes in the field are sensed by the fish through various nerve centres on its body: as a result, and after the pattern of the field has been analysed by the brain, the fish is able to navigate and find its prey in the half-light. These fish can for example be seen in the aquarium investigating pieces of metal to which their attention has been drawn by the messages brought to them by these impulses.

This unusual system allows members of the Mormyridae family to orientate themselves faultlessly even in complete darkness, tracking down edible food and distinguishing it from other objects. The majority of species live in muddy or marshy waters and have to cope with life in semi-darkness: this electrical sounding system is obviously a very useful mechanism and no less remarkable because many other types of fish living in similar waters have adapted to their surroundings in a completely different way. This system works so well however that it is probably the reason why these fish now have such poor eyes.

Clearly these are fascinating fish for the aquarist. Some species are imported regularly and others can be seen in large public aquariums. The amateur aquarist should only keep those species that do not demand too specialised a diet. In general those will be the species in which the snout is either not elongated at all or is only slightly elongated. Such species can, in the right conditions, be kept for a long time in an aquarium without any special problems arising, provided adequate supplies of worm-like food can be obtained: the fish will also catch Daphnia, Cyclops and all varieties of mosquito larvae, but the unusual shape of the mouth means that in general swimming prey can only be caught with difficulty. On the other hand, creatures like worms in the bed are adroitly pulled out from the mud by these fish, after they have tracked them down relentlessly. Tubifex, if strewn on the surface through a sieve, will also soon be discovered and greedily consumed. The Mormyridae, despite their small cylindrical mouths can consume vast quantities of food and indeed must eat voraciously if they are to remain healthy. Many of these fish kept in captivity suffer from chronic malnutrition because so many aquarists do not understand their dietary needs. Only if a fish has a really spherical belly after feeding at least once a fortnight can the aquarist be sure it has had enough to eat. If the fish do not have these distended stomachs, even though apparently ample live animal food has been offered, another diet must be tried. Live red mosquito larvae in particular are an excellent food for these fish.

As much as possible should be done to recreate the natural environment of these fish in the aquarium, if their natural behavior is to be observed. The Mormyridae are accustomed to a perpetual half-light and are not of course therefore really suitable for the conventional brightly-lit home aquarium. For them, the ideal tank is one that is dimly lit, provided with lots of hiding places among irregularly shaped pieces of wood and rock and with dense leafy plants. The composition of the water is not critical. The temperature should be between 20°C and 30°C, but fluctuations within this range will not harm the fish.

Contrary to popular belief, the Mormyridae are not only active in the evening and at night. They are of course twilight fish but in their natural habitat it is twilight all the time and if their tank is appropriately furnished and lit they will be seen to be active during the day as well.

Mormyridae can usually be kept together with all other kinds of fish without difficulty. The degree of mutual tolerance however varies from species to species. *Marcusenius isidori* and *Petrocephalus bovei* for example, live in shoals in the wild and consequently can, indeed should be kept together in groups in captivity. Other species, such as *Gnathonemus macrolepidotus*, *Mormyrops nigricans* and *Mormyrus kannume* are solitary fish in the wild. They are among those that are also less tolerant of other species, but this intolerance only extends to other fish with electrical properties. These particular species are among the larger varieties and are in any case consequently of less interest to amateur aquarists: they are nevertheless, extremely interesting fish to study in public aquariums.

Very little is known about the reproductive behavior of the Mormyridae. It is believed that a number of species build bubble nests at the surface, but no species seems as yet to have been bred successfully in captivity. There are no reliable notes of external sexual characteristics.

GNATHONEMUS ELEPHAS

Family: *Mormyridae*
Genus: *Gnathonemus*
English name: none
Origin: The Congo and Cameroun
Size: Approximately 20 cm
Habitat: Found in marshes and fresh waters with muddy bottoms

Shape, coloring and markings: The body is elongated and laterally very compressed: the tail is slender. *G.elephas* closely resembles *G.petersi*, but has an elongated and cylindrical snout, with a protruding lower lip. The basic coloration is a dark blue-black or brownish-violet: the belly is lighter. There is a deep black more or less triangular patch with a light border at both front and back, between the dorsal and anal fins, which lie opposite each other. The fleshy base of the caudal fin is dark or deep black. The unpaired fins are the same color at the front: for the rest, the fins are a dark grey.

217. *Gnathonemus schilthuisiae.*

The pectoral fins are well developed. There are no known external sexual characteristics.

General care: This species is not suitable for the ordinary community tank. It requires many hiding places to be provided between rocks and pieces of wood, or under thick clumps of broad leaved plants. If the tank is too brightly lit, *G.elephas* will be active only at night. It keeps mainly to the bottom of the tank, but after becoming acclimatised will take food from the surface. It prefers worm-like food such as Tubifex, enchitrae and red mosquito larvae but will also catch other small aquatic insects and larvae. It is very intolerant of members of its own species.
The composition of the water is not critical. Temperature 20°–28° C.

Breeding: Nothing is known about the reproductive behavior of this species.

Additional information: *G.elephas* emits a relatively strong electrical impulse. Although unsuitable for the home aquarium, this species is particularly interesting to study in public aquariums.

GNATHONEMUS MACROLEPIDOTUS

Family: *Mormyridae*
Genus: *Gnathonemus*
English name: none
Origin: East Africa
Size: Approximately 30 cm
Habitat: Found only in fresh waters, where it is common

Shape, coloring and markings: The body is elongated and laterally slightly compressed: the tail is slender. The mouth is small with a protruding lower lip. The basic coloration is a greyish-brown: the back is darker, the belly usually silvery or off-white. There are irregular dark patches over the whole of the body. The fins are grey, with some patches, and transparent. The pectoral fins are large. The front dorsal fin rays extend further back than the front rays of the anal fin.
There are no known external sexual characteristics.

General care: Only young specimens, are suitable for the home aquarium. The tank should be furnished as for *G.elephas*, although *G.macrolepidotus* is in fact somewhat less shy of the light. It will keep to the bottom and middle reaches of the tank, but will take food from the surface. The preferred diet is worm-like animal matter, but *G.macolepidotus* will also hunt aquatic insects, larvae and small fish: dried food will not be taken. It is intolerant of its own species but can be kept with other fish provided they are not too small. The composition of the water is not critical but the fish greatly benefit from a regular change of part of the water in the tank. Temperature 20°–28° C.

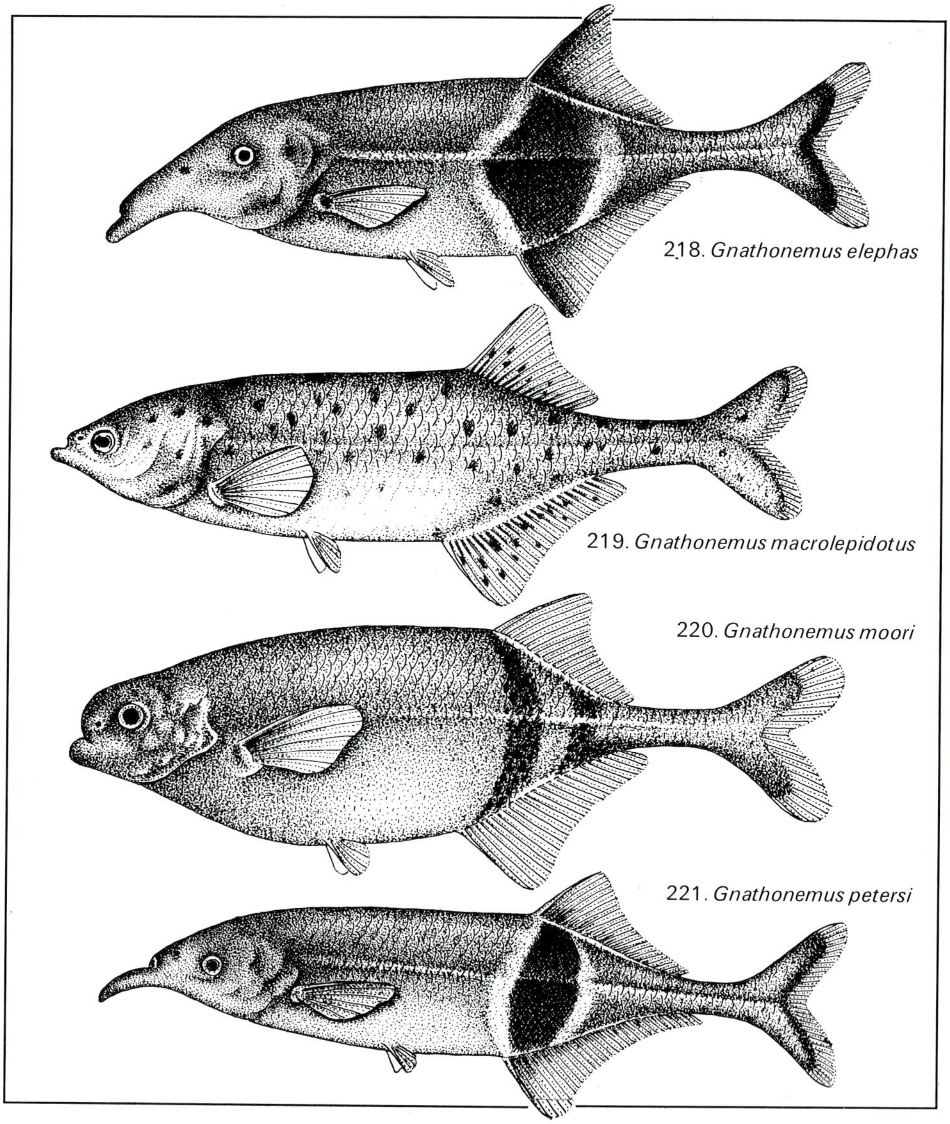

218. *Gnathonemus elephas*
219. *Gnathonemus macrolepidotus*
220. *Gnathonemus moori*
221. *Gnathonemus petersi*

222. *Gnathonemus petersi*

Breeding: Nothing is known of the reproductive behavior of this species.

Additional information: *G.macrolepidotus* emits a fairly strong electrical impulse. This is another species well worth observing in public aquariums.

GNATHONEMUS MOORI

Family: *Mormyridae*

Genus: *Gnathonemus*

English name: none

Origin: The Congo, Zaire, Cameroun, Gabon

Size: Approximately 30 cm

Habitat: Found only in fresh waters where it is common

Shape, coloring and markings: The body is elongated and laterally very compressed: the tail is slender. The mouth is small with a protuberant lower lip. The basic coloration is a dark brown, tinged with violet: the belly is considerably lighter or off-white. There is a deep black stripe from the dorsal to the anal fin and in many specimens a second and identical stripe lies adjacent to it. All the fins are grey and transparent. The pectoral fins are large: the dorsal and anal fins lie opposite each other.
There are no known external sexual characteristics.

General care: As for *G.elephas*.

Breeding: Nothing appears to be known about the reproductive behavior of this species.

Additional information: This is a species that is very rarely imported.

GNATHONEMUS PETERSI

Family: *Mormyridae*

Genus: *Gnathonemus*

English name: none

Origin: Cameroun, the Congo, Zaire

Size: Approximately 23 cm

Habitat: Found in very shady marshes and fresh waters with muddy bottoms

---

Shape, coloring and markings: The body is elongated and laterally very compressed: the tail is slender. The mouth is small and cylindrical: the lower lip is so extended as to resemble a finger. The basic coloration is an anthracite blue-black or brownish violet: the belly is lighter. A deep black oval patch with a lighter border at the back and front is to be found between the dorsal and anal fins, which lie opposite each other. The fleshy base of the caudal fin is dark: otherwise all the fins are grey or black. The pectoral fin is well developed.
There are no known external sexual characteristics.

General care: As for *G.elephas*.

Breeding: Nothing is known about the reproductive behavior of this species.

Additional information: *G.petersi* is fairly well known among aquarists but few seem fully to appreciate the special needs of all species in this family, and accordingly specimens rarely survive for long in aquariums.

GNATHONEMUS SCHILTHUISIAE

Family: *Mormyridae*

Genus: *Gnathonemus*

English name: none

Origin: The Congo

Size: Approximately 10 cm

Habitat: Found in fresh waters with gravelly bottoms

Shape, coloring and markings: *G.schilthuisiae* closely resembles *G.moori* in body shape, although it is a little more slender and altogether a smaller fish. The basic coloration is brownish, with a violet or violet blue tinge: the head and caudal peduncle are darker. A black transverse band runs across the body from the dorsal to the anal fin. The fins are greyish and transparent.
There are no known external sexual characteristics.

General care: This species is not suitable for the ordinary community tank. It requires many hiding places to be provided between rocks and pieces of wood, or under thick clumps of broad leaved plants. If the tank is too brightly lit, *G.schilthuisiae* will be active only

at night. It keeps mainly to the bottom of the tank, but after becoming acclimatised will take food from the surface. It prefers worm-like food such as Tubifex, enchitrea and red mosquito larvae but will also catch other small aquatic insects and larvae. It is less tolerant of members of its own species.
The composition of the water is not critical. Temperature 20°–28° C.

BREEDING: Nothing is known about the reproductive behavior of this species.

MARCUSENIUS ISIDORI

Family: *Mormyridae*

Genus: *Marcusenius*

English name: none

Origin: The lower reaches of the Nile and the upper reaches of the Zambezi

Size: Approximately 10 cm

Habitat: Found only in fresh waters

SHAPE, COLORING AND MARKINGS: The body is fairly deep and laterally very compressed: the tail is slender. The snout is oval: the mouth small and underpositioned. The basic coloration is a brownish-grey: the back is darker or reddish brown, the flanks lighter and the belly silvery or off-white. A violet tinge is evident in bright light. Some specimens bear dark lines along the body from the back edge of the gill covers to the tail. The fins are grey and transparent. The pectoral fins are well developed. The dorsal and anal fins lie far back on the body, the latter slightly further back than the former.
There are no known external sexual characteristics.

GENERAL CARE: As for *Gnathonemus elephas*, but temperature about 28° C. *M.isidori* is tolerant of other members of its own species

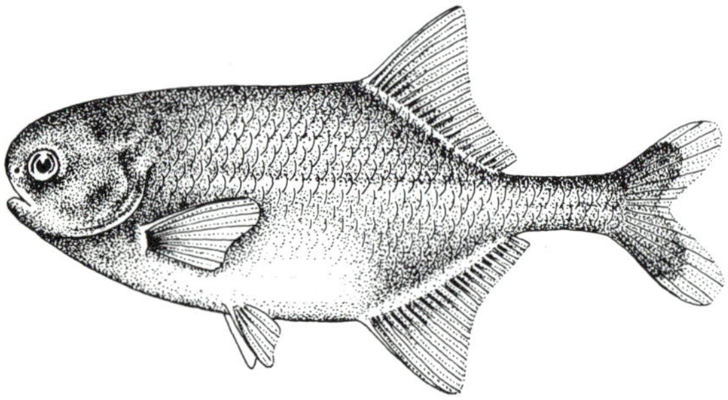

223. *Marcusenius isidori*

but aggressive towards other species with electrical properties.

BREEDING: Nothing is known of the reproductive behavior of this species.

ADDITIONAL INFORMATION: *M.isidori* is a very social fish and should always be kept in a large group of its own kind.

MARCUSENIUS LONGIANALIS

Family: *Mormyridae*

Genus: *Marcusenius*

English name: none

Origin: The lower reaches of the Niger and some areas of Cameroun

Size: Approximately 15 cm

Habitat: Found only in fresh waters

SHAPE, COLORING AND MARKINGS: The body is very slender and laterally only slightly compressed. The mouth is small and under-positioned. The basic coloration is brownish: the back is brownish-black or dark brown, the belly ochre or off-white. There are dark patches over the whole body. The fins are dark grey or black. The pectoral fins are well developed. The dorsal fin lies far back and the anal fin, which is relatively very long, lies half-way along the body.
There are no known external sexual characteristics.

GENERAL CARE: As for *Gnathonemus elephas*.

BREEDING: Nothing is known about the reproductive habits of this species.

ADDITIONAL INFORMATION: *M.longianalis* appears to be unusually intolerant of other members of its own species as well as other species with electrical properties. According

224. *Marcusenius longianalis*

to some authorities it will eat algae in addition to its normal diet.

MORMYROPS BOULENGERI

Family: *Mormyridae*

Genus: *Mormyrops*

English name: none

Origin: Probably the basin of the Congo, but reliable information is not available

Size: The size of mature fish is unknown

Habitat: No details are available of its natural habitat, but presumably it is found in fresh waters

SHAPE, COLORING AND MARKINGS: The body is elongated: very slender in young fish and laterally very compressed. The trunk-like snout is distinctive. The basic coloration of young fish is a bluish-black or dark brown, with a violet tinge: the body is lighter towards the belly. The fins are grey and transparent. The pectoral fins are well developed: the anal fin is considerably longer than the dorsal fin. There are no known external sexual characteristics.

GENERAL CARE: As for *Gnathonemus elephas*. It is very important to regularly change part of the water in the tank.

BREEDING: Nothing is known about the reproductive behavior of this species.

ADDITIONAL INFORMATION: *M.boulengeri* has only been kept in large public aquariums.

MORMYROPS NIGRICANS

Family: *Mormyridae*
Genus: *Mormyrops*
English name: none
Origin: The lower reaches of the Congo
Size: Approximately 35 cm
Habitat: Found only in fresh waters

SHAPE, COLORING AND MARKINGS: The body is very slender, elongated and laterally only slightly compressed. In young fish the mouth is end-positioned but in mature specimens it becomes spoon-shaped and under-positioned. The basic coloration of young fish is a uniform dark brown tinged with violet or blue-black: older fish often have dark bands lying across the body but the patches or thread-like lines characteristic of related species are absent. The fins are grey and transparent. The pectoral fins are well developed: the anal fin is noticeably larger than the dorsal fin.
There are no known external sexual characteristics.

GENERAL CARE: As for *Gnathonemus elephas* but *M.nigricans* will never take food from the surface. It will also hunt smaller fish and should therefore only be kept with other large fish. It is very intolerant of other fish with electrical properties, including other members of its own species.

BREEDING: Nothing is known about the reproductive behavior of this species.

ADDITIONAL INFORMATION: *M.nigricans* is one of the true Nile pike. It is known to aquarists only through large public aquariums.

MORMYRUS KANNUME

Family: *Mormyridae*
Genus: *Mormyrus*
English name: none
Origin: The basin of the Nile
Size: Approximately 50 cm
Habitat: Found only in fresh waters

SHAPE, COLORING AND MARKINGS: The body is elongated and laterally very compressed. It has a small elongated cylindrical mouth. The basic coloration is greyish-brown: the flanks are reddish brown, becoming lighter towards the ochre or dull orange-yellow belly. The fins are grey and transparent, and slightly darker at the base. The ventral fins are well developed: the anal fin is small and the dorsal fin is very wide, running from the extreme end of the pectoral fins to halfway along the tail. There are no known external sexual characteristics.

GENERAL CARE: As for *Gnathonemus elephas*.

225. *Mormyrus kannume* ▷

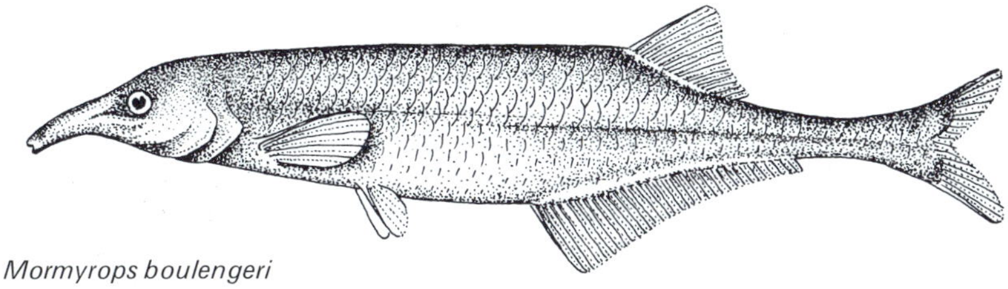

226. *Mormyrops boulengeri*

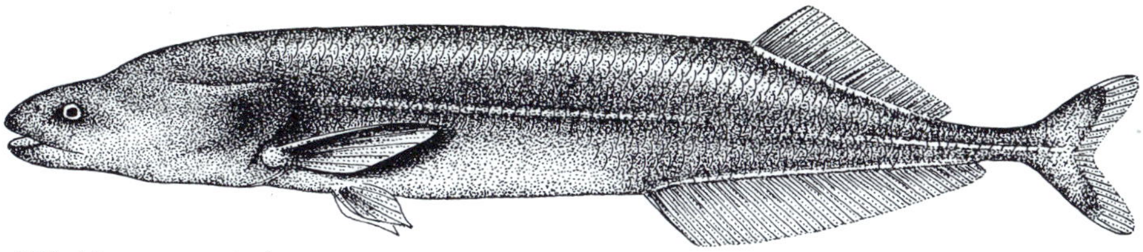

227. *Mormyrops nigricans*

M.Kannume will swim in the middle reaches of the tank but lives mainly on the bottom: only after a long time in the tank will it take food from the surface. The spoon-shaped mouth is singularly unsuited to catching swimming prey. It is very intolerant both of its own species and other fish with electrical properties.

BREEDING: Nothing is known about the reproductive behavior of this species.

ADDITIONAL INFORMATION: A species unknown among aquarists but one that it is extremely interesting to study in large public aquariums.

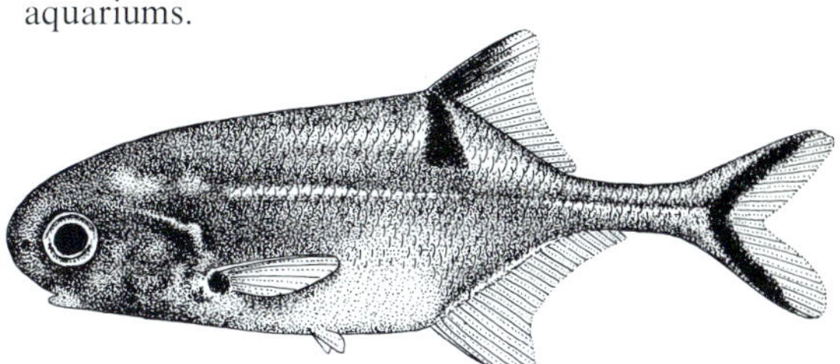

228. *Petrocephalus bovei*

PETROCEPHALUS BOVEI

Family: *Mormyridae*
Genus: *Petrocephalus*
English name: none
Origin: The lower reaches of the Nile
Size: Approximately 12 cm
Habitat: Found only in fresh waters

SHAPE, COLORING AND MARKINGS: The body is deep, stocky and laterally very compressed. The snout is oval and the mouth small and under-positioned. The eyes are remarkably large for a member of the Mormyridae family: it is probable that this species orientates itself visually rather than by means of the electrical sounding system so well developed in other species. The basic coloration is a silvery grey with a reddish brown tinge: the back is noticeably darker than the belly. Young specimens have a dark stripe across the body at the level of the first dorsal fin ray: in older fish this becomes a roughly cone shaped pattern. The front dorsal fin rays and the fleshy base of the caudal fin are dark: otherwise the fins are grey and transparent.
There are no known external sexual characteristics.

GENERAL CARE: As for *Gnathonemus elephas*.

BREEDING: Nothing is known about the reproductive habits of this species.

ADDITIONAL INFORMATION: The members of this genus closely resemble in appearance the species in the genus *Marcusenius* described above.

THE FAMILY NOTOPTERIDAE

An introductory description

The fish in this family have elongated bodies which are laterally very compressed. On account of this unusual shape they are often popularly known as knife fish. Their scientific name alludes to the relatively small dorsal fin which looks very much like a small pennant or flag above the body. The ventral fins, if present at all, are only rudimentary. The pectoral fins however are very well developed and so is the anal fin which runs along a large part of the lower edge of the body like a long narrow ribbon and merges with the small caudal fin. The anus lies towards the front of the body below the pectoral fins.

The anal fin is the most important organ of propulsion: the body is moved forwards or backwards by means of the waving motion of this fin. The fish can swim backwards or forwards with equal ease and in this way can escape easily from enemies without making any movement of the body.

The jaw is relatively, very large with many small teeth. The scales are very small, barely visible with the naked eye. The lateral line is complete and clearly visible in adult fish. The tentacles on the nostrils are prominent. The Notopteridae use their very well developed swim bladders as an ancillary respiratory system and in the aquarium the fish will swim to the surface from time to time to obtain air.

There are two genera and four species in this family. Although they bear a close resemblance to the South American knife fish they are in no way related to them. The Notopteridae are found throughout West and Central Africa and Southeast Asia, but only in fresh waters. They are prized as food by the indigenous population, even though these fish have a very large number of very fine bones.

The largest species is *Notopterus chitala* which grows to a length of 90 cm.

In view of the size to which these fish grow, it is obvious that only young fish can be considered for the home aquarium: they are in fact far more attractive than the mature fish. However, if the fish are well fed they grow steadily and then will have to be moved to a special tank: otherwise they will rapidly eat any other fish to be found in the tank.

Young fish should be provided with a tank furnished with irregularly shaped pieces of wood and dense vegetation, to provide shelter for the fish during the day. These fish are only active towards evening and hunt for food as night falls. They like a diet of large insect larvae, Daphnia and red mosquito larvae, but they will also prey on smaller fish. They are tolerant of larger fish of other species but will savagely attack their own kind. In their native habitats they live in shoals but seem very rarely to accept a group in an aquarium. The species that come from Africa prefer slightly acid water, preferably filtered over peat but otherwise the composition of the water is not critical. A fairly high temperature, 24°–28° C is required, although temporary drops in temperature do not appear to harm the fish.

It must be emphasised that with the exception of the smallest African species, *Xenomystus nigri* which does not grow to more than 20 cm these fish are too large to be kept in the home aquarium although it is always a temptation to try and keep young specimens of the other kinds because they are so beautiful.

229. *Notopterus chitala*

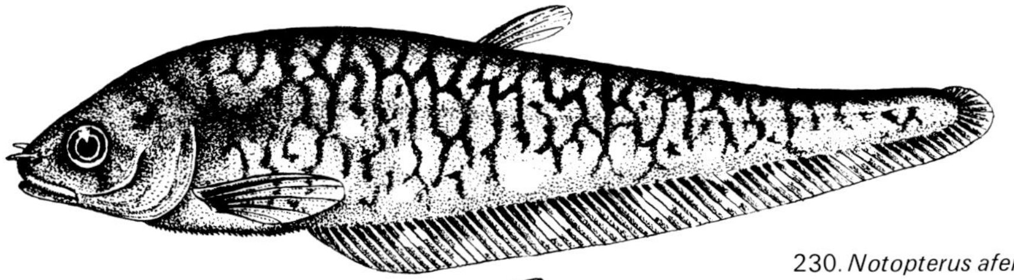

230. *Notopterus afer*

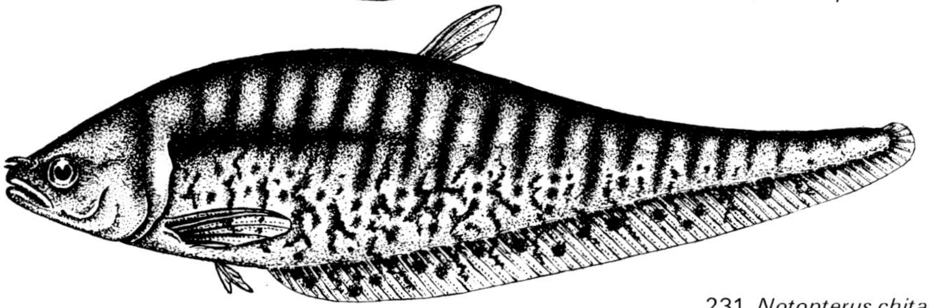

231. *Notopterus chitala*

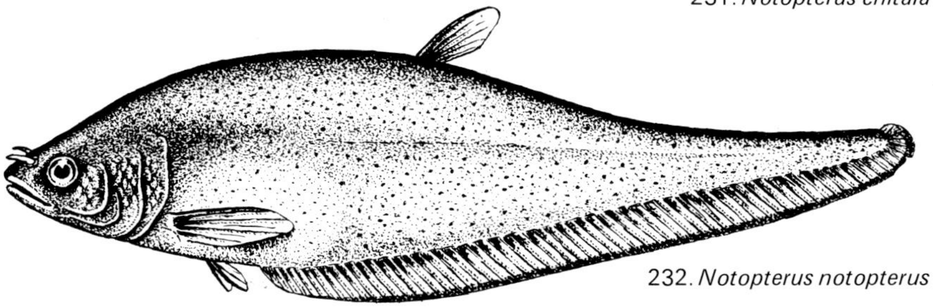

232. *Notopterus notopterus*

NOTOPTERUS AFER

Family: *Notopteridae*

Genus: *Notopterus*

English name: none

Origin: West Africa, from Cameroun to Zaire

Size: Maximum 60 cm

Habitat: Found in calm waters with dense vegetation, and the backwaters of rivers

SHAPE, COLORING AND MARKINGS: The body is elongated and laterally very compressed. In older specimens the back is noticeably arched. The mouth is large, the eyes expressive and the tentacles on the nostrils are clearly visible. The keel of the belly has a serrated edge. The basic coloration of adult fish is a dark to purplish brown with no markings. The coloring of young fish varies a great deal and is usually remarkably attractive. A wide variety of dark marks, stripes, patches and thread-like lines appear on a salmon or ochre background and combine to give the fish a beautiful marbled appearance. The dorsal fin is small and like a pennant. The pectoral fins are very well developed: there are no ventral fins. The anal fin runs along the entire lower side of the body and merges into the small caudal fin.
There are no known external sexual characteristics.

GENERAL CARE: Only young specimens are suitable for even large home aquariums. They should be kept singly for *N.afer* is generally very intolerant of other members of its own species. It is predatory and therefore should not be kept with any small fish. It needs a tank with a lot of hiding places among pieces of wood: the vegetation should also be fairly dense. The water should be slightly acid and not too hard: if possible it should be filtered over peat. Temperature 24°–28°C. *N.afer* lives mainly in the lower and middle reaches of the tank and remains rather shy even after being kept in captivity for some time. It will eat large quantities of any sort of live animal matter, and larger specimens should have a regular supplement of lean beef or raw fish.

BREEDING: This species has not as yet it seems been bred successfully in captivity.

ADDITIONAL INFORMATION: *N.afer* is a twilight fish active only at night. It was first imported in 1912.

NOTOPTERUS CHITALA

Family: *Notopteridae*

Genus: *Notopterus*

English name: Indian Knife fish

Origin: Burma, India, Thailand

Size: Maximum 90 cm

Habitat: Found in calm waters with dense vegetation, such as the backwaters of rivers

SHAPE, COLORING AND MARKINGS: The body is elongated and laterally very compressed: the belly and the back are both noticeably arched. The mouth is large, the eyes expressive and the tentacles on the nostrils very pronounced. Adult fish are basically a silvery-grey with a large number of transverse bands that run across the body at a slight forward angle. Fish that are halfgrown are considerably darker. Young fish have, as a rule, very attractive markings. The upper half of the body bears transverse bands similar to those of adult fish while the lower half of the body is salmon or yellow-gold with a variety of dark marks, patches, irregular thread-like lines and stripes which combine to give a marbled effect. The dorsal fin is small and pennant-like. The pectoral fins are well developed: the ventral fins are very small. The anal fin runs along the entire length of the lower body like a ribbon and merges with the poorly developed caudal fin: depending on age, there may be some dark patches on the anal fin.
There are no known external sexual characteristics.

GENERAL CARE: As for *N.afer*, but the use of fresh water in the tank should be avoided.

BREEDING: This species has not yet been bred succesfully by amateurs.

ADDITIONAL INFORMATION: *N.chitala* is a twilight fish that is really only active at night. Although it will remain considerably smaller in captivity than in the wild, it is still not really suitable for the normal home aquarium.

NOTOPTERUS NOTOPTERUS

Family: *Notopteridae*

Genus: *Notopterus*

English name: none

Origin: Indonesia, Java and Sumatra, India, Thailand

Size: Maximum 35 cm

Habitat: Found in calm waters with dense vegetation, such as the backwaters of rivers

SHAPE, COLORING AND MARKINGS: The body is elongated and laterally very compressed: the back and belly are markedly arched, especially in older specimens. The mouth is large, the eyes expressive and the tentacles on the nostrils prominent. *N.notopterus* can easily be distinguished from related species by the unusual scales on the cheeks and gill covers which are considerably larger than the scales on the rest of the body: no other species has scales of this kind. The basic coloration is a silvery-grey: the back is noticeably darker. The dorsal fin has a white dot and the anal

fin usually has a dark edge. The pectoral fins are well developed: the ventral fins are only rudimentary.
There are no known external sexual characteristics.

GENERAL CARE: As for *N.afer*, but the use of fresh water in the tank is to be avoided.

BREEDING: Little is known about the reproductive habits of this species; it has not yet been bred successfully.

ADDITIONAL INFORMATION: Like related species, *N.notopterus* is a twilight fish which will only hunt for food at night. It was first described in 1933.

XENOMYSTUS NIGRI

Family: *Notopteridae*

Genus: *Xenomystus*

English name: African Knife fish

Origin: The entire West coast of Africa and central Africa around the sources of the Nile

Size: Approximately 20 cm

Habitat: Found in calm waters with dense vegetation, such as the backwaters of rivers

SHAPE, COLORING AND MARKINGS: The body is elongated and laterally very compressed: it is less deep than in related species. *X.nigri* is easily distinguished from other knife fish because in this species the dorsal fin is completely absent. The basic coloration is a mousey-grey to brown: the head is darker and the belly lighter or dull yellow. There are usually a number of dark stripes running the length of the body. The pectoral fins are well developed, the ventral fins are rudimentary. The anal fin has a cream-colored edge and during the mating season it becomes more or less purple.
The are no known external sexual characteristics.

GENERAL CARE: As for *Notopterus afer*.

BREEDING: It does not appear that this species has as yet been bred in captivity.

ADDITIONAL INFORMATION: As in the case of related species, this fish is a twilight fish that only hunts by night. It has however adapted itself well to aquarium life and often lives to a great age in captivity.

233. *Xenomystus nigri*

THE FAMILY PANTODONTIDAE

An introductory description

This family is somewhat isolated. Only one genus, and only one species within it have as yet been identified.
That species is found solely in West Africa and there, only in fresh waters. It belongs to the group of flying fish although in practice of course this fish never actually flies. The pectoral fins however are extremely well developed so that these fish are capable of jumping out of the water with some force. It is not unusual for these fish to skim over the water for some two meters or so, but the the pectoral fins are not then used like wings as they are for example by members of the Gasteropelecidae family. These fish are popularly known as Butterfly fish partly because of their unusual pectoral fins and partly because of their equally unusual ventral fins which have degenerated into four completely independent and greatly elongated fin rays.
The Butterfly fish, *Pantodon buchholzi* is a twilight fish that only becomes active at night. During the day it can spend hours without moving, resting under large leaves floating on the surface: of course in the wild, these fish are very conspicuous and it is natural for them to seek shelter from predators in this way. No such threats exist in the aquarium and after some time the fish adapt to their new conditions: they will even hunt for food by day but will even then retire, after a successful sortie, to some safe hiding place. Some broad leaved plants should therefore always be put in their tank. While they are not true shoaling fish, they live together in large colonies in the wild and in the aquarium are very tolerant both of their own kind and other species.

PANTODON BUCHHOLZI

Family: *Pantodontidae*

Genus: *Pantodon*

English name: Butterfly fish

Origin: Tropical West Africa, Cameroun, the Congo basin, the Niger

Size: Approximately 10 cm

Habitat: Found in still waters and pools and in the backwaters of rivers where the vegetation is dense

234. *Pantodon buchholzi*

SHAPE, COLORING AND MARKINGS: The body is more or less boat-shaped: the head and back are flattened above, the belly is rounded. The basic coloration is brown, with irregular patches and stripes: the back is a shiny green, the belly an iridescent yellowish brown. The scales are large, with dark edges. The mouth lies towards the top of the head: the nostrils are elongated and rather tube-like. The well developed pectoral fins are shaped like wings: the ventral fins are rudimentary with four fin rays that are so extended as to have become tentacles: the rays of the anal and caudal fins are also elongated. All the fin rays are banded alternately with light and dark rings.
Females have blunt anal fins.
Males have deeply forked anal fins and the rays in the centre form a tube.

GENERAL CARE: *P.buchholzi* is only suitable for the larger aquarium well stocked with plants with broad leaves floating on the surface. The water should be old and preferably filtered over peat. Temperature 25°–30°C. It keeps to the surface of the tank. Predatory by nature it should not be kept with smaller species. All kinds of live animal matter will be eaten especially if they can be snapped up from the surface: even meal worms and maggots will be devoured with relish.

BREEDING: This is not easy but has been done successfully and is extremely interesting. The actual mating is preceded by a long courting session during which the male embraces the female with his pectoral fins. It is presumed that the eggs are fertilized before they are released by the female. The eggs are laid on the surface of the water and float until they hatch after about 48 hours. It is very difficult to raise the fry as they will only accept the smallest of food from the surface.

ADDITIONAL INFORMATION: These fish can jump very considerable distances and appropriate precautions must always be taken, especially when the tank is being cleaned.

THE FAMILY ANOSTOMIDAE

An introductory description

The Anostomidae are found over the whole of South America except in the far south of the continent: some species are also found in Central America and in the West Indies. Generally these fish live in small shoals in sluggish or still waters, the composition and level of which may vary a great deal in the course of the changing seasons. The fish are accordingly very adaptable and will accommodate themselves happily to different kinds of water and different diets. They are thus excellent aquarium fish, robust and making few special demands on the aquarist.

In the wild all these fish live in waters that lie in thickly wooded areas, so the habits of members of the Anostomidae family may be regarded as typical of forest fish. They are for example rather shy and dislike bright light: when they are found outside forest areas in more open waters, these are still waters that have dense vegetation around them.
They are omnivorous. They will hunt for worms and other aquatic animals with the same determination that they will seek out rocks and plants from which they can obtain algae. If food becomes scarce the plants themselves will be eaten. Such a lack of dietary discrimination is further evidence of the singular ability of these fish to adapt to their surroundings.
Most species are among the so-called headstanders. They are often to be seen, with their heads inclined downwards searching the bottom for worms: when seeking algae among plants they can however turn their bodies into whatever posture is most convenient. When avoiding enemies they swim horizontally and can achieve remarkably high speed in a short time.

Most species have small mouths, but the shape varies a great deal from species to species and generally the shape relates to whatever special circumstances in the wild, determine the diet. Some species have thick swollen lips, others have lips that are shaped so as to be a very effective sucking device. The genus *Anostomus* is characterised by the small upper-positioned mouth which forces the fish to make all kinds of strange contortions of the body when searching for food: on the other hand these fish are very free in their movements because of their slender bodies and can glide very easily through dense vegetation and similar obstacles. At one time it was thought that this upper-positioned mouth indicated that the *Anostomus* species preferred surface food but it is clear now that this is not the case.

Most species of Anostomidae remain fairly small and this is another reason why over the years they have proved to be ideal fish for the aquarium. Some of the larger species are splendid exhibits in public aquariums: others are important sources of food in their native habitats.
The genus *Leporinus* in the Anostomidae family which has the largest number of species. Ten are described here and all may be of considerable interest to amateur aquarists: there are other species known to science but infortunately full and reliable descriptions of them are not available. As a genus they are distinguished by their unusually pointed heads and by the way that whereas young specimens are very attractively colored, as the fish mature, so the color pattern becomes less vivid. All are fish that need substantial vegetable diets.

235. *Anostomus anostomus*

ANOSTOMUS ANOSTOMUS

Family: *Anostomidae*

Genus: *Anostomus*

English name: Striped Anostomus

Origin: Western Guyana and the upper reaches of the Amazon

Size: Approximately 14 cm

Habitat: Mainly found in still or sluggish waters surrounded by dense vegetation

SHAPE, COLORING AND MARKINGS: The body is extremely slender and only slightly laterally compressed. The mouth is upper-positioned. The basic coloration is a bright ochre often tinged with red. Three prominent dark bands run the length of the body: their color can vary from a brownish-green to a red or blackish-brown depending on the age and mood of the fish. The upper band runs from the upper side of the head to the adipose fin, the second from the snout to the base of the caudal fin and the third from the throat to the outer extremity of the anal fin. The unpaired fins are reddish-violet or dark red at the base becoming yellowish, and colorless at the edges. The anal fin may have dark or black pigmentation at the front.
There are no known external sexual characteristics.

GENERAL CARE: This fish is only suitable for larger aquariums and should be kept with a large number of its own species. The composition of the water is not critical but medium hard slightly acidic water, preferably filtered over peat, is best. Although this fish likes a well planted aquarium, there should also be plenty of open swimming space immediately above the bed. *A.anostomus* likes to hide among plants and to feed off the algae to be found on them, and this should be taken into account when furnishing the tank. This species will keep mainly to the lower and middle reaches of the tank, swimming with its head inclined towards the bottom. It will be seen that when taking worms from the bed the fish will turn itself on its back so that its upper-positioned mouth can reach the food. If kept alone without the company of others of its species it will be very shy and hostile to other fish. Temperature 25°–27° C. Almost any food will be accepted but worms and lettuce are essential.

BREEDING: This species does not seem to have been bred successfully in captivity as yet.

ANOSTOMUS FASCIATUS

Family: *Anostomidae*

Genus: *Anostomus*

English name: none

Origin: Northern South America

Size: Approximately 40 cm

Habitat: Found over a wide area in many different kinds of waters

SHAPE, COLORING AND MARKINGS: The body is very slender and laterally only slightly compressed. The mouth is upper-positioned. The basic coloration is silvery: the back is greenish-brown. The flanks are tinged with green and have six brown transverse stripes which stop just short of the belly and the back. The third and fifth bands bear prominent marks. All the fins are more or less yellowish at the base and are otherwise colorless and transparent. The marking of young fish is less striking.

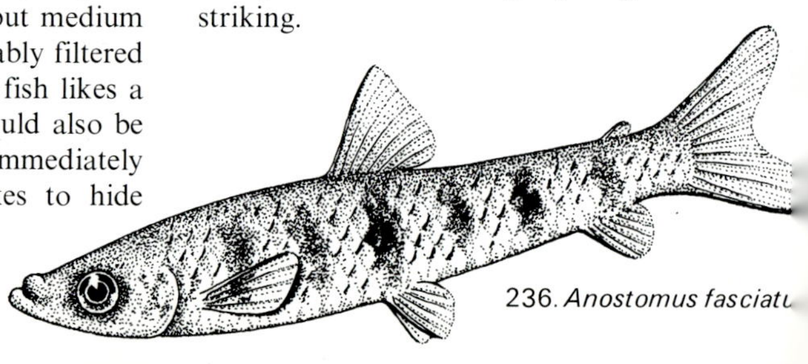

236. *Anostomus fasciatu*

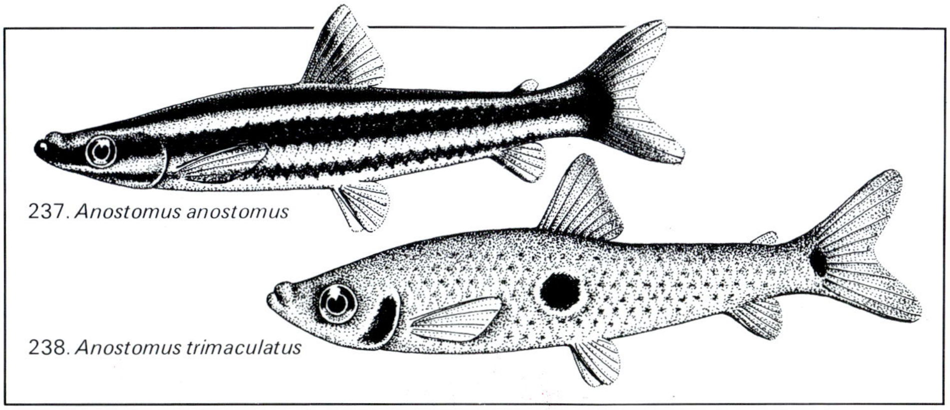

237. *Anostomus anostomus*

238. *Anostomus trimaculatus*

There are no known external sexual characteristics.

GENERAL CARE: As for *A.anostomus* but temperature 23°–26°C. Almost any food will be accepted.

BREEDING: This species has not as yet been bred successfully in captivity.

ADDITIONAL INFORMATION: In its natural habitat this species is much valued as food.

ANOSTOMUS TRIMACULATUS

Family: *Anostomidae*

Genus: *Anostomus*

English name: Three-spot Anostomus

Origin: The Guianas and the lower reaches of the Amazon

Size: Approximately 20 cm

Habitat: Found in still or very sluggish waters, with dense vegetation

SHAPE, COLORING AND MARKINGS: The body is extremely slender and laterally only slightly compressed. The mouth is small and upper-positioned: the head is slightly more blunt than that of *A.anostomus*. The upper half of the body is olive brown: the flanks are ochre or brownish-yellow. The lower half of the body is a soft yellow, with a dark pigmentation at the base of each scale, that shows up as lines of dots along the body. A crescent-shaped mark on the gill covers is surrounded by a gleaming golden patch. A deep black mark with a golden edge lies below the dorsal fin and a similar but less striking mark lies at the base of the caudal fin. The unpaired fins are yellowish at the base and otherwise reddish with a striking red edge. The pectoral and ventral fins are colorless and transparent.
There are no known external sexual characteristics.

GENERAL CARE: As for *A.anostomus*. Almost any food will be accepted.

BREEDING: This species has not as yet been bred successfully in captivity.

ANOSTOMUS TERNETZI

Family: *Anostomidae*

Genus: *Anostomus*

English name: none

Origin: Venezuela, the basin of the Orinoco river

Size: Approximately 8 cm

Habitat: Found in still and sluggish waters with dense vegetation

SHAPE, COLORING AND MARKINGS: The body is extremely slender and laterally only very slightly compressed. The mouth is upper-positioned. *A.ternetzi* lacks the red coloration present in the fins of *A.anostomus* but otherwise closely resembles that species. Like *A.anostomus* it has three deep blackish-brown bands running the length of the body. The upper band runs from the top of the head to the adipose fin: the second from the snout to the base of the caudal fin: the third from the throat to the back edge of the anal fin. The areas between the bands are a plain dull yellow. All the fins are colorless and transparent and devoid of all marks.
There are no known external sexual characteristics.

GENERAL CARE: As for *A.anostomus* though temperature should be 23°–27°C.

BREEDING: No information is available on the reproductive habits of this species, which has only recently been identified.

LEPORINUS FASCIATUS AFFINIS

Family: *Anostomidae*

Genus: *Leporinus*

English name: Striped Leporinus

Origin: South America, from the Guianas to the area of the Paraguay river

Size: Maximum 25 cm

Habitat: Found in sluggish waters with gravelly bottoms

SHAPE, COLORING AND MARKINGS: The body is elongated and laterally only slightly compressed. The snout is pointed, the mouth small and somewhat like a hare-lip, whence the genus derives its name, 'young hare'. The basic coloration is a mid- to bright yellow. Nine wide dark bands run across the body: the first lies on the shoulder, the last on the base of the caudal peduncle. An additional dark band crosses the lower jaw. The fins are grey or colorless.
There are no known external sexual characteristics.

239. *Anostomus ternetzi*

240. *Leporinus frederici*

GENERAL CARE: *L.fasciatus affinis* is only suitable for larger aquariums. The water quality is not critical but medium-hard water, of low acidity and preferably filtered through peat is best. Temperature 22°–28°C. The tank should have dense vegetation round the sides, although it must be remembered that adult specimens can inflict serious injury to soft leaved plants. There should be bogwood or rocks to provide enough hiding places. The bottom should be of coarse river sand or fine gravel. The fish usually keep to the lower reaches of the tank but they are good jumpers and appropriate precautions must be taken. The diet for *L.fasciatus affinis* should be primarily vegetable, and should be supplemented with lettuce, deep-frozen spinach and chopped oats. A very tolerant fish, both towards its own and other species.

BREEDING: Nothing is known about the reproductive behavior of this species.

LEPORINUS FASCIATUS FASCIATUS

Family: *Anostomidae*

Genus: *Leporinus*

English name: none

Origin: South America from the Guianas to the river Plate

Size: Maximum 30 cm

Habitat: Found in sluggish waters with gravelly bottoms

SHAPE, COLORING AND MARKINGS: This species is identical in body shape and coloring to *Leporinus fasciatus affinis* but instead of nine wide bands across the body, *L.fasciatus fasciatus* has ten somewhat narrower bands. Females are somewhat more slender and have a deeper orange tint to the snout and throat. Males are as described above.

GENERAL CARE: As for *L.fasciatus affinis*.

BREEDING: There are no records of this species having been as yet bred in captivity.

LEPORINUS FREDERICI

Family: *Anostomidae*

Genus: *Leporinus*

English name: none

Origin: South America, from the Guianas to the Amazon

Size: Maximum 35 cm

Habitat: Found in sluggish waters with gravelly bottoms

SHAPE, COLORING AND MARKINGS: The body shape is identical to that of *L.fasciatus affinis*. The basic coloration is grey: the flanks are yellow-grey, with a tinge of silver. The belly is yellowish and the caudal peduncle a bright yellow. The whole body except for the head is covered with irregular dark patches which increase in intensity towards the tail. The anal fin is dark, the adipose fin has a dark border: otherwise the fins are colorless.
There are no known external sexual characteristics.

GENERAL CARE: As for *L.fasciatus affinis*.

BREEDING: This species does not seem as yet to have been bred successfully in captivity.

LEPORINUS MACULATUS

Family: *Anostomidae*

Venus: *Leporinus*

English name: none

Origin: South America from the Guianas to the Amazon

Size: Maximum 15 cm

Habitat: Found in sluggish waters with gravelly bottoms

SHAPE, COLORING AND MARKINGS: The body shape is identical to that of *L.fasciatus affinis*. The basic coloration is grey. Nine short dark bands run across the back. There is a large oval black spot on the flanks at the back of the dorsal fin, another smaller mark mid-way between that fin and the caudal peduncle, and a third, smaller still, at the base of the caudal fin. The snout is crossed by a black streak that goes as far as the eyes. There are rows of dark spots on the flanks, which vary in number and intensity from one specimen to another.
There are no known external sexual characteristics.

GENERAL CARE: As for *L.fasciatus affinis*.

BREEDING: This species has not as yet been bred successfully in captivity.

LEPORINUS MELANOPLEURA

Family: *Anostomidae*

Genus: *Leporinus*

English name: none

Origin: Western Brazil between the Amazon and Rio de Janeiro

Size: Maximum 20 cm

Habitat: Found in sluggish waters with gravelly bottoms

SHAPE, COLORING AND MARKINGS: The body is somewhat less elongated than that of related species, but otherwise the body shape is similar to that of *L.fasciatus affinis*. The basic coloration is an olive brown: the flanks are a lighter brown becoming yellowish-brown towards the belly. The caudal peduncle is tinged with red and bears a number of small brown flecks. There is a prominent greenish longitudinal line from the gill covers to the root of the caudal fin. The fins are colorless or tinged with yellow.
Females are as described above.
Males have often a dark edge to the anal and dorsal fins.

GENERAL CARE: As for *L.fasciatus affinis*.

BREEDING: This species has not as yet been bred in captivity.

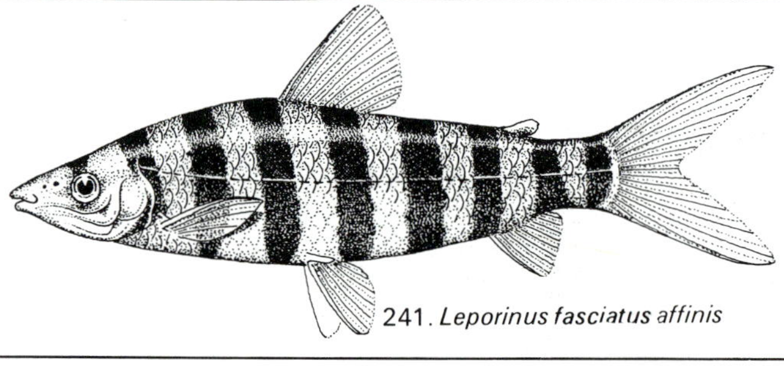

241. *Leporinus fasciatus affinis*

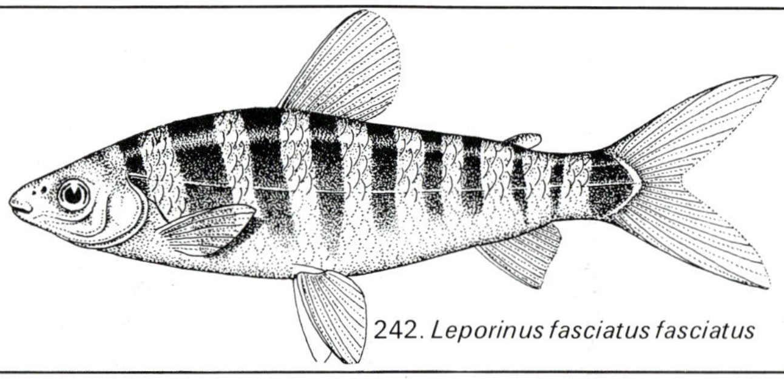

242. *Leporinus fasciatus fasciatus*

THE FAMILY CHARACIDAE

An introductory description

The Characidae family, the Characins, is one of the largest of the freshwater fish families. In all, there are more than 1300 species in this family, but of those no more than some thirty or forty are of interest to amateur aquarists. The various species are found mainly in South and Central America, while a few are also found in North America and some in Central Africa. The family includes some unique species such as the Blind Cave-Fish *(Anoptichthys jordani)* and the many varieties of Tetras, so well-known to aquarists.

The family is too large for much helpful information to be given in a general introduction: the species are so varied in their requirements and come from such different natural habitats that details of breeding and care can only usefully be given under the various genera and species. It is however true that with the exception of the notorious piranhas (in the genera *Serrasalmus, Rooseveltiella* and *Pygocentrus*), the characins are peaceful fish. Most are vividly colored, which together with their peaceful and often undemanding character, has justifiably made them popular aquarium fish. In size, they vary considerably, in shape most are the classic fish shape. None has barbels, but most species have a small adipose fin.

THE FAMILY CHARACIDAE

The genus Acestrorhamphus

Acestrorhamphus hepsetus is the only species in this genus of large predatory fish that is likely to be of any interest to aquarists although, as is noted in the description of the species that follows, the size to which it grows and its demanding diet make even this species one that is unlikely to become popular or common. Although not rare in its natural habitat, it is not surprising that it is in fact only infrequently handled by dealers.

ACESTRORHAMPHUS HEPSETUS

Family: *Characidae*
Genus: *Acestrorhamphus*
English name: none
Origin: Southeast Brazil
Size: Approximately 20 cm
Habitat: Found over a wide area in many different kinds of waters

SHAPE, COLORING AND MARKINGS: The body is almost oval, elongated and laterally somewhat compressed. The dorsal fin is set forward, where the body is approximately half its full depth. The anal fin is wide: the adipose fin small. The lateral line is complete and slightly turned down as it approaches the caudal peduncle. The fish has a large mouth and very strong teeth. The basic coloration is silvery with a light blue tinge: the back is darker or a brownish-olive green. There is a deep black mark on the shoulder and a very thin horizontal line runs from there to the base of the caudal fin where it ends in a diamond-shaped dark mark with a light edge. The fins are colorless and transparent.
These are no known external sexual characteristics.

GENERAL CARE: *A.hepsetus* is a predatory fish. This and its large size makes it unsuitable for a conventional community tank. It is however a very attractive fish and therefore popular in large public aquariums, where it is successfully kept in shoals of its own kind and with other sturdy fish. If it is to be kept by the amateur, then the tank must be furnished with irregular arrangements of wood to afford the fish sufficient hiding places, where it likes to wait for its prey. The composition of the water is not critical, but fresh tap water should be avoided. Temperature 24°–25°C. The diet should preferably be of live fish supplemented with a variety of large live insect larvae. If this diet cannot be obtained, then *A.hepsetus* can be fairly easily accustomed to veal and horsemeat. It will also eat lettuce and porridge oats soaked in water for variety.

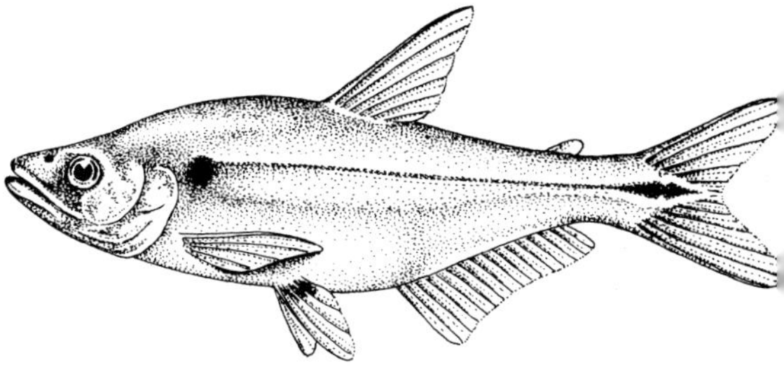
243. *Acestrorhamphus hepsetus*

BREEDING: There are no reliable reports to date of this species having been bred successfully in captivity.

THE FAMILY CHARACIDAE

The genus Alestes

The genus *Alestes* is one whose members, unlike the majority of Characins, come from Africa. Several species are imported and the ones described in this encyclopaedia all make suitable fish for a larger aquarium.
They are hardy and lively fish but on the whole are not vividly colored and thus have not as yet secured the popularity their disposition merits.
The members of the genus *Alestes* are in general difficult to keep in an average community aquarium because of their length; some species can grow to 50 cm. The only species suitable for the aquarist are *Alestes longipinnis* and *Alestes chaperi* which are both described below.
Until recently the members of this genus were grouped under the genus *Bryconalestes*.

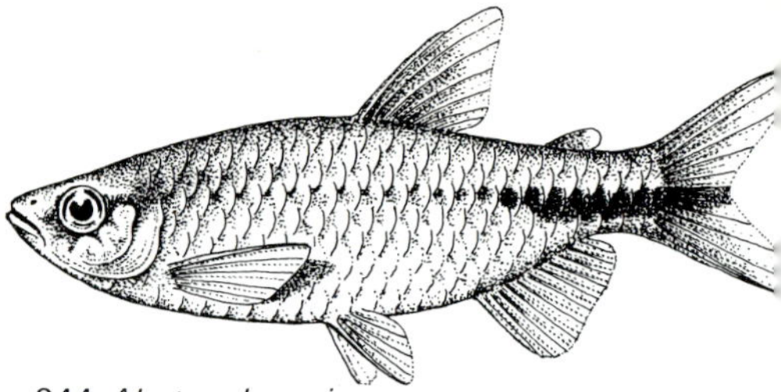

244. *Alestes chaperi*

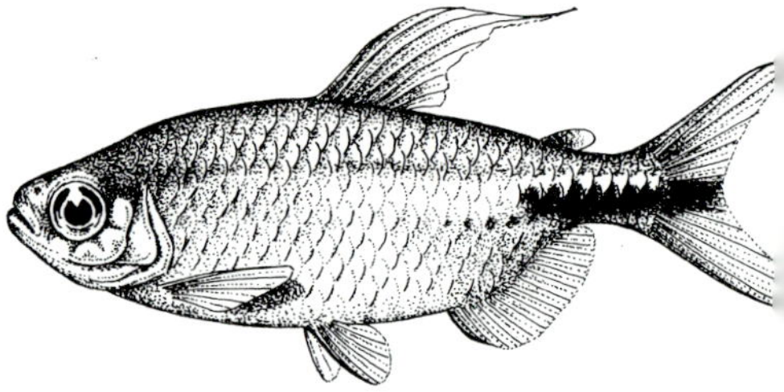

245. *Alestes longipinnis*

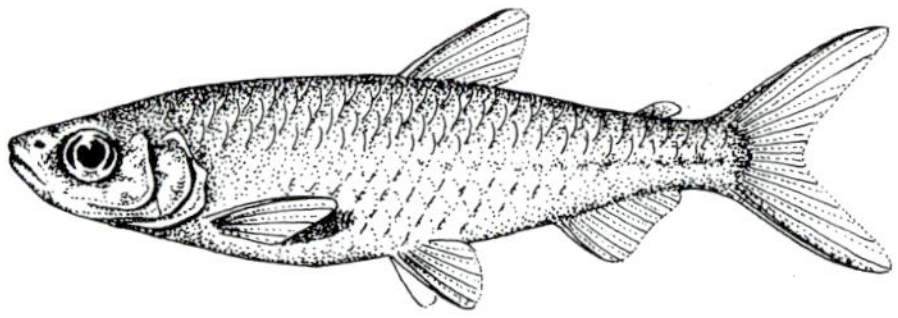

246. *Alestes macrophthalmus*

ALESTES CHAPERI

Family: *Characidae*

Genus: *Alestes*

English name: Chaper's Characin

Origin: Tropical West Africa, Ghana

Size: Approximately 9 cm

Habitat: No details are available of its natural habitat

SHAPE, COLORING AND MARKINGS: The body is slender, fairly deep and laterally compressed: the typical body shape, in fact, of a fast swimming fish. The basic coloration is silver. The upper half of the body is a clear olive green; the flanks are a beautiful grass green. There is a very dark wide black band running the length of the caudal peduncle and the dark color extends into the central rays of the caudal fin. In young fish this dark band can run from the back edge of the gill covers or alternatively from a distinct mark on the shoulders. The dorsal and caudal fins are a brick red and transparent, with a wide yellow border. The other fins are yellowish and transparent. The eyes are large, a beautiful red in the upper half and yellow below.
There are no known external sexual characteristics.

GENERAL CARE: *A.chaperi* is only suitable for very large aquariums and should always be kept in a large group of its own kind. It is also very tolerant towards other species and is therefore suitable for a community tank. Various different plants can be put in the tank but there must be adequate free swimming space, for this species is a very active swimmer. It prefers a dark bed, of for example, peat. Irregular arrangements of wood are a suitable decoration and make a good contrast to the silvery gleam of the fish. The water should be filtered over peat to make it slightly acid: fresh tap water should not be used. Temperature 23°–25° C. *A.chaperi* will stay mainly in the middle reaches of the tank. The diet should consist of the usual animal feeding matters and *A.chaperi* also likes to eat surface insects. These should certainly be included in the diet if the fish are being prepared for breeding (but see below).

BREEDING: There are no records of this species having as yet been bred successfully in captivity.

ADDITIONAL INFORMATION: According to some authorities this species belongs to the genus *Brycon*.

ALESTES LONGIPINNIS

Family: *Characidae*

Genus: *Alestes*

English name: Long-finned Characin

Origin: Tropical West Africa, Sierra Leone

Size: Approximately 13 cm

Habitat: Found in many different kinds of waters but principally fairly large fast flowing streams

SHAPE, COLORING AND MARKINGS: The body is slender, fairly deep and laterally very compressed. The basic coloration is silvery: the back is an olive green. The flanks are almost ochre: the lower half of the body is silvery-white. Below a golden gleaming patch there are dark marks running the length of the caudal peduncle, extending into the central rays of the caudal fin. All the fins are transparent: the dorsal and caudal fins are yellowish: the other fins are colorless. The eyes are large and a beautiful red.
Females are as described above.
Males have an elongated dorsal fin, like a pennant. The dorsal and caudal fine are often tinged with red and the anal fin is yellowish.

GENERAL CARE: As for *A.chaperi* but *A.longipinnis* prefers old aquarium water, filtered over peat. Fresh tap water can however be used for a partial change of the tank water. Temperature and diet as for *A.chaperi.*

BREEDING: This species has not as yet been bred successfully in captivity.

ADDITIONAL INFORMATION: A species well known to aquarists and first described in 1864 by Albert Carl Guenther.

ALESTES MACROPHTHALMUS

Family: *Characidae*

Genus: *Alestes*

English name: none

Origin: The Congo, Zaire, Lake Tanganyika

Size: Approximately 45 cm

Habitat: Very common in rivers and streams

SHAPE, COLORING AND MARKINGS: The body is very slender and laterally compressed. The basic coloration is silvery: the back is

247. *Alestes longipinnis*

greenish. All the fins are colorless and transparent except for the caudal fin which is a soft red.
There are no known external sexual characteristics.

GENERAL CARE: This species is not suitable for the home aquarium because of the size to which it grows.

BREEDING: There is no record of this species having as yet been bred successfully in captivity.

248. *Alestes chaperi*

THE FAMILY CHARACIDAE

The genus Alestopetersius

This genus is closely related to the genus *Micralestes* (see below). Only one species, *Alestopetersius caudalis*, is generally included in this genus, although another species, *Micralestes hilgendorfi*, is sometimes known as *Alestopetersius hilgendorfi*. *M. hilgendorfi* indeed does closely resemble *A.caudalis*, although it is somewhat darker, and has a more pronounced lateral line.
A.caudalis is one of the few characins found in Africa, and in many ways is one of the most interesting African Characins, for it is possible to breed this species in the aquarium, although to do that is no easy task: the fry are very delicate and can be extremely difficult to raise.
This is not a species that is very well-known amongst aquarists, but it deserves to be more widely kept: it is, in many respects, a more attractively colored fish than the species in the genus *Alestes* described above.

ALESTOPETERSIUS CAUDALIS
Family: *Characidae*
Genus: *Alestopetersius*
English name: Yellow Congo Characin
Origin: The Congo basin
Size: Maximum 7 cm
Habitat: Found in still and sluggish waters with dense vegetation on the banks

SHAPE, COLORING AND MARKINGS: The body is slightly elongated and laterally very compressed. The basic coloration is yellowish, becoming off-white towards the belly. Under spotlights however this somewhat plain shade will be seen to contain all the colors of the spectrum except red and orange. The outer fin rays of the elongated dorsal fin are black. The middle rays of the caudal fin are also a deep black and are edged with white. The anal fin has a narrow milky white edge.
Females are slightly smaller than the males. The fin rays of the dorsal and anal fins are not elongated.
Males are as described above.

GENERAL CARE: *A.caudalis* is of an extremely peaceful nature, but it is also somewhat timid and needs a large tank with dense vegetation round the sides but also plenty of open swimming space in the middle. There should be plants with surface floating leaves and the bed should be dark. The water should not be too hard. Temperature about 24°C. The diet should consist of the normal small animal matter such as Daphnia and Cyclops, but black mosquito larvae, the eggs of flies and small aquatic insects should also be given. There should be a vegetable supplement and the fish like to take duckweed from the surface.

BREEDING: This is difficult. The breeding fish will only spawn after they have been fed for a considerable time on black mosquito larvae. It is best to put a number of breeding pairs in the tank at the same time. As soon as the eggs have been laid they swell up to a diameter of about 2 mm. They are completely transparent. The eggs hatch after about six days and the fry swim about freely immediately. They should be fed with the *nauplii* of *Artemia* and finely powdered dried food: on no account should they be fed *Cyclops nauplii*, for these are too swift for the fry to catch and if they develop, they may attack the fry. The fry are very sensitive to the composition of the water and a proportion should be changed regularly.

THE FAMILY CHARACIDAE

The genus Anoptichthys

Anoptichthys jordani is the only known species in the genus *Anoptichthys* (eyeless fish) and it is also the only species in the family Characidae which is really blind. It is only found in some subterranean lakes and rivers in Central Mexico. It has now been discovered in five separate places: the furthest north is Cueva del Pachon, the furthest south is La Cueva Chica: the three other places are Sótano de la Arroya, Cueva de los Sabinos and Sótano de la Tinajo, all within some 10 kilometers north of La Cueva Chica.
La Cueva Chica is the best known of these caves: it is a limestone cave that runs some 200 meters into the mountain and is part of the drainage system of the Rio Tampaan. In fact this cave is no more than a winding subterranean corridor with a dead end, which drops gradually about 15 meters by way of a series of terraces, the deepest point being the last terrace. Originally the cave was connected directly with the

249. *Anoptichthys jordani*

Rio Tampaan or one of its tributaries, so that the fish could swim in or out of this subterranean branch at will. At some time, earth tremors probably caused what had hitherto been a branch of the river to be cut off, isolating what wild life was then present in it. It seems likely that the other subterranean habitats of *A.jordani* were formed in the same way. Whatever the cause, all the subterranean lakes that lie on these terraces are now completely cut off from the outside world. Water only reaches the lakes when there are serious floods, and even then only in very small quantities, because the entrances to the caves lie above the normal level of the river. Because of the 15 meter incline it is impossible for the fish to swim out of the caves, so the fish in the lakes have had to adapt considerably to survive in their isolated environment. These caves are also famous for their bats but they of course have no difficulty in flying in and out at will, and find the high domed cavities perfect places in which to roost.

In general *A.jordani* needs a spacious breeding tank with clean, not too hard, bacteria-free water with a bed of clean sand and stones. The best temperature for breeding seems to be 18°–23°C, although good results have also been obtained at lower temperatures. It may be of course that the temperature of the water, conditions the pattern of reproductive behavior. The eggs hatch after three or four days and on the sixth day the fry swim freely around and hunt for food. From the start the fry can be fed with the newly hatched *nauplii* of *Artemia* and afterwards they are not difficult to raise with the normal food for fry. The young fish have small eyes, but these have no function and disappear after a while.

Despite the absence of eyes, the adult fish are quite free in their movements through the water, although they tend to be more restless than sighted fish. They will move restlessly over the bottom, searching for food and apparently relying on a sense of touch. They will swim in the body of the tank and successfully avoid all obstacles in their path. It is believed that *A.jordani* guides itself by what is really a technique of echo-sounding: the tail moves all the time the fish is swimming and this sets up currents which, when reflected back off obstacles, are picked up by sensitive nerve ends on the fish's skin, thus giving the fish an awareness of anything in its path.

There is no reason why *A.jordani* should not be kept in the conventional brightly lit tank, but it should not be kept in a community tank with other fish. It is very disturbed by the presence of other fish and then does not behave normally so that its unique life style cannot be observed. It should be kept in a special small tank with a sandy bed and some stones: subdued lighting though not essential is to be preferred. If the room is centrally heated, no additional heating for the tank is needed.

ANOPTICHTHYS JORDANI

Family: *Characidae*

Genus: *Anoptichthys*

English name: Blind Cave-Fish

Origin: Central Mexico: see Introductory note for details

Size: Approximately 8 cm

Habitat: Found only in the subterranean lakes and streams noted in the Introduction

SHAPE, COLORING AND MARKINGS: The body is fairly deep, almost cone-shaped and laterally very compressed: it greatly resembles *Astyanax mexicanus*, from which it probably derives. The basic coloration is a soft shade of pink, tinged with a very shiny silvery sheen. The fins are colorless and transparent. It has no eyes. Young fish have rudimentary eyes but these have no function: young fish also have a reddish diamond shaped mark on the caudal peduncle.

Females are more robust and less vividly colored.

Males are more slender.

GENERAL CARE: See Introductory note for details of the most appropriate aquarium. The composition of the water is not critical but it should be free of harmful bacteria. Temperature 18°–23°C. An unheated tank is acceptable if the room in which it is kept is centrally heated. All normal animal matter is acceptable as food: the fish, which keep to the bottom of the tank, will search the bed almost constantly for food.

BREEDING: See Introductory note.

ADDITIONAL INFORMATION: There seem to be a number of different varieties of *A.jordani*, but there is only this one species in the genus *Anoptichthys*.

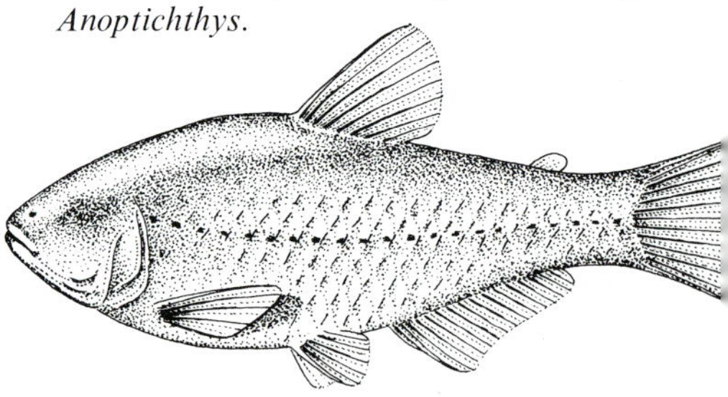

250. *Anoptichthys jordani*

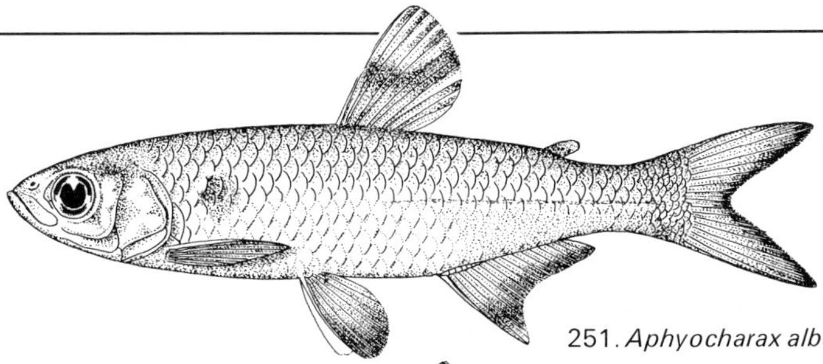

251. *Aphyocharax alburnus*

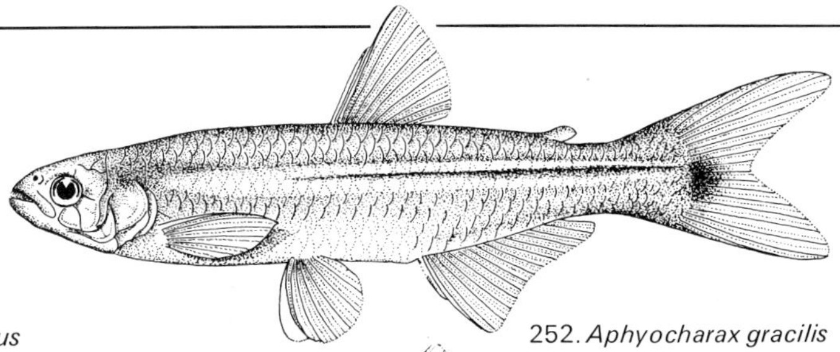

252. *Aphyocharax gracilis*

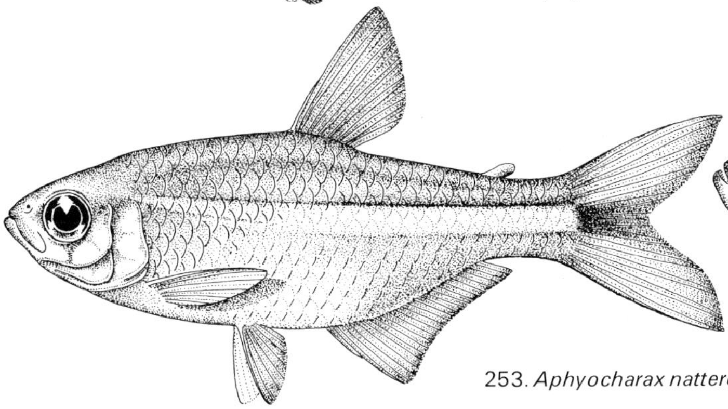

253. *Aphyocharax nattereri*

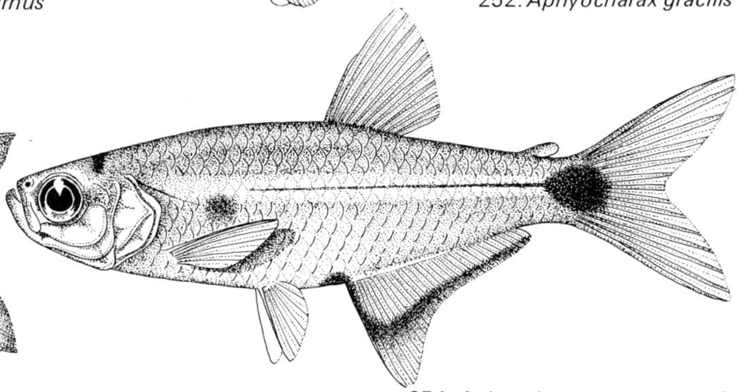

254. *Aphyocharax paraguayensis*

THE FAMILY CHARACIDAE

The genus Aphyocharax

All species in the genus *Aphyocharax* are found in fresh waters in South America. There are now some twenty different species known of these attractive small shoaling fish, but only six species are of general interest to aquarists, and these are described below. All these fish are suitable for community tanks. They can be kept in all sizes of tanks but prefer relatively large ones with ample free swimming space.

Two species at least are not difficult to breed, but these fish are notorious egg-eaters, and the eggs should be removed from the tank immediately after the fish have spawned.

The *Aphyocharax* species have become popular with many aquarists, and they can be recommended unreservedly as aquarium fish for the amateur.

APHYOCHARAX ALBURNUS

Family: *Characidae*
Genus: *Aphyocharax*
English name: none
Origin: Brazil, Peru, Bolivia
Size: Approximately 5 cm
Habitat: Fairly common in many different kinds of streams

SHAPE, COLORING AND MARKINGS: The body is slender, elongated and laterally slightly compressed. The basic coloration is between a grey and blue, which under strong light becomes an iridescent green. The back is olive, the belly silvery. There is a mark on the shoulders above the pectoral fins: this is either round or oblong. The fins are reddish with dark edges, and may have irregular patches. There are no known external sexual characteristics.

GENERAL CARE: This fish is suitable for both large and small aquariums but should always be kept in a small group of its own species. The composition of the water is not critical but fresh tap water should be avoided. The colors show up best over a dark bed and in water given a yellow tinge by being filtered over peat. All kinds of plants can be used but they must include clumps of those with fine leaves. *A.alburnus* keeps mainly to the middle and upper reaches of the tank. Temperature 22°–25° C. It can be kept in a community tank with other small species. It will accept almost any sort of food, though it has a preference for surface insects, such as fruitflies. Larger animal matter and Tubifex are less suitable.

BREEDING: This species can be bred without too much difficulty. The guidance given for *Aphyocharax rubripinnis* should be followed.

APHYOCHARAX GRACILIS

Family: *Characidae*
Genus: *Aphyocharax*
English name: none
Origin: Brazil, Bolivia
Size: Approximately 4 cm
Habitat: Fairly common in a variety of streams and rivulets

SHAPE, COLORING AND MARKINGS: The body is slender, elongated and laterally slightly compressed. The basic coloration is grey to blue. A light band with fine dark stripes runs from the back edge of the gill covers to the base of the caudal fin. The fins are reddish: the caudal fin has a dark patch at its base. There are no known external sexual characteristics.

GENERAL CARE: As for *A.alburnus*.

BREEDING: There are no records to date of successful breeding in captivity, but there is no reason to believe that its reproductive habits are different from those of *A.rubripinnis*.

APHYOCHARAX NATTERERI

Family: *Characidae*
Genus: *Aphyocharax*
English name: none
Origin: Brazil, Peru
Size: Approximately 4 cm
Habitat: Found in a variety of different kinds of streams

SHAPE, COLORING AND MARKINGS: The body is deep, and laterally only very slightly com-

pressed. The basic coloration is a grey-blue: the back is slightly darker. A progressively wider, light band runs from the back edge of the gill covers to the base of the caudal fin: above it lies a pattern of fine dark lines. The fins are reddish with a dark edge: the caudal fin is darker in the center.
There are no known external sexual characteristics.

General care: As for *A.alburnus.*

Breeding: No information is available on the reproductive habits of this species.

255. *Aphyocharax rubripinnis*

APHYOCHARAX PARAGUAYENSIS

Family: *Characidae*
Genus: *Aphyocharax*
English name: none
Origin: Brazil, the Paraguay river
Size: Approximately 4 cm
Habitat: No details are available of its natural habitat

Shape, coloring and markings: The body is fairly deep and laterally only slightly compressed. The basic coloration is greyish-blue: the back is darker. A light band running from the back edge of the gill covers to the base of the caudal fin is made up of a pattern of fine dark lines which terminates in a large dark patch on the caudal peduncle. There is also an inconspicuous dark mark on the shoulders above the pectoral fin. The fins are reddish: the anal fin has a darker edge.
There are no known external sexual characteristics.

General care: As for *A.alburnus.*

Breeding: This species has not yet been successfully bred in captivity.

APHYOCHARAX PUSILLUS

Family: *Characidae*
Genus: *Aphyocharax*
English name: none
Origin: Brazil, Peru, Bolivia
Size: Approximately 5 cm
Habitat: No further details of its natural habitat are available

Shape, coloring and markings: The body is fairly deep and laterally only slightly compressed. The unusual line of the neck is a distinctive feature of this species. The basic coloration is greyish-blue: the back is darker. Below an area of dark pigmentation, a light band runs from the back of the gill covers to the base of the caudal fin. The fins are reddish with a dark edge: the caudal fin has a dark center.

General care: As for *A.alburnus* but although *A.pusillus* can be kept together with other fish in a community tank, its companions should not be selected from among very active species. It will accept any small animal matter as food and this should be balanced with vegetable matter and vitamin enriched dried food.

Breeding: *A.pusillus* has not as yet been bred successfully in captivity.

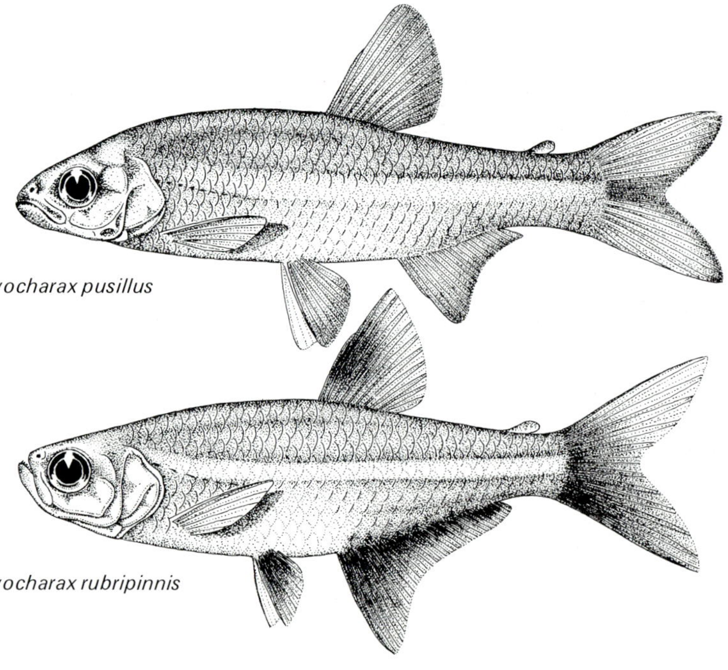

256. *Aphyocharax pusillus*

257. *Aphyocharax rubripinnis*

APHYOCHARAX RUBRIPINNIS

Family: *Characidae*
Genus: *Aphyocharax*
English name: Bloodfin
Origin: Argentina, Paraná
Size: Approximately 5 cm
Habitat: Found in a variety of different kinds of streams

Shape, coloring and markings: The body is fairly deep and laterally slightly compressed. The basic coloration is greyish-blue: the back is darker. A light band, most evident under bright light, runs from the back edge of the gill covers to the base of the caudal fin. The fins are blood red with a darker base, except for the upper lobe of the caudal fin and the pectoral fin which are colorless and transparent.

General care: As for *A.alburnus.*

Breeding: *A.rubripinnis* can be bred fairly easily in a spacious breeding tank about 40 cm long. The water should be soft and slightly acid, the temperature 26°–27°C. During a vigorous mating session the eggs are laid amongst fine leaved plants or at random in the open water. Mating takes place usually in the early morning, and for preference, in direct sunlight. The eggs are crystal clear and at the above temperature hatch after about 30 hours. The fry then hang among the plants or on the aquarium glass for two or three days before hunting for food. For the first week they should be fed on infusoria and thereafter on the usual fry foods.

THE FAMILY CHARACIDAE

The genus Arnoldichthys

The genus *Arnoldichthys* in which there is only one species, is found only in the area of Lagos and the delta of the Niger, in West Africa. Here, *A.spilopterus* is found in the larger streams. It is always found in shoals. A truly social fish, it should always be kept in larger aquariums, particularly because it is a very active swimmer and needs plenty of free swimming space.
This beautiful fish was first imported in 1907 and in 1911, but it then almost completely lost favor with aquarists, partly because all attempts to breed it failed. In recent years however it has been imported regularly and it is now becoming a well-known species.
There have been a number of chance breedings, but there are still no detailed reports available on the breeding habits of this species and thus no further information can be given. This is strange for the fish has been the subject of study for some years and it has obvious external sexual characteristics. The males are easily recognized by the pattern of nearly horizontal black stripes on the anal fin, a pattern never present on females: it may also be absent in some males but even those males without that pattern still show a striking orangey-yellow or orangey-red pigmentation in the anal fins, which unmistakably distinguishes them from the females.
Recently imported fish should be kept in quarantine for a time. They need an aquarium that is not too brightly lit and in which thick vegetation and lumps of wood will provide sufficient places of concealment. The fish are very good jumpers and will try and escape if there are any sudden changes in the light or water: the tank should therefore be kept well-covered. In all other respects, *A.spilopterus*, when it has become acclimatised, makes a very suitable fish for the larger aquarium.

ARNOLDICHTHYS SPILOPTERUS

Family: *Characidae*

Genus: *Arnoldichthys*

English name: none

Origin: West Africa, Lagos the delta of the Niger

Size: Approximately 12 cm

Habitat: Found in large streams and possibly also in brackish water

SHAPE, COLORING AND MARKINGS: The body is slender, cylindrical and laterally slightly compressed. The upper half of the body is brownish, with a green iridescent sheen. A dark band runs from the back edge of the gill covers to the middle rays of the caudal fin. Above there is an equally wide band which, depending on the way the light shines on it, will show all the different colors of the spectrum. The lower half of the body is a golden yellow with a red iridescent sheen. The iridescent flanks are a grass to bluish-green. The dorsal fin is greyish and transparent, with a large black mark. The irises are a beautiful iridescent red.
Females are slightly smaller than the males with less vivid coloring. The anal fin is greyish, transparent and with a dark mark.

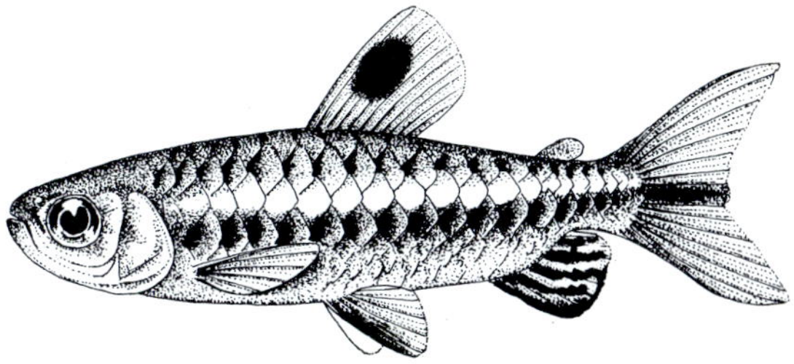

259. *Arnoldichthys spilopterus*

Males are slightly larger than the females. They also usually have the black stripes, and always the pigmentation in the anal fins described in the Introductory note.

GENERAL CARE: *A.spilopterus* is only suitable for larger aquariums. It should be kept in a large group of its own species: it is a very tolerant fish, even of other species smaller than itself. The aquarium should have a dark bed, a number of widely spaced but thick plants and appropriate arrangements of wood or rocks. The composition of the water is not critical but fresh water should not be used and it is advisable to change part of the water regularly. Temperature 24°–27° C. *A.spilopterus* will keep to the upper and middle reaches of the tank: its prowess as a jumper, noted in the Introduction should not be forgotten. All the larger kinds of aquatic insects and larvae can be given as food, but the fish have a preference for land insects which can be taken from the surface, such as mosquitoes, flies, spiders and fruitflies. Dried food will also be eaten for a change. *A.spilopterus* will not however take food that has sunk to the bottom and it does not interfere with the plants in the aquarium.

BREEDING: Nothing is known about the breeding habits of this species. It does not seem to have been bred in captivity although occasional chance breedings have been reported.

258. *Arnoldichthys spilopterus*

THE FAMILY CHARACIDAE

The genus Astyanax

This genus includes about 75 species which are, on the whole, quite difficult to tell apart purely on the basis of their appearance. They all closely resemble the smaller and more familiar members of the genera *Hyphessobrycon, Cheirodon* and *Hemigrammus:* they are distinguished from those by their complete lateral lines, for the latter species all have lateral lines which are incomplete. In the members of the genus *Astyanax* the lateral line runs without interruption from the back edge of the gill covers to the base of the caudal fin.

Adult fish in this genus are usually over 10 cm long, and *Astyanax maximus* from Peru, the largest known species, reaches a length of about 20 cm.

The distribution area of these species stretches from Arizona, through Mexico and the whole of Central America down to the northern parts of South America. Within this extensive area, various species are found in very different kinds of waters. Depending on their origin, the individual species need quite different conditions in the aquarium: these special requirements are noted under the descriptions of the individual species. These fish are however on the whole very adaptable: few are unable to survive outside their particular natural environment, even though these vary from more or less brackish water in river estuaries to pure mountain streams.

In captivity these lively darting fish usually have the same basic requirements. They should be kept in fairly large tanks because of the size to which they grow and because they are essentially social fish which should be kept in a group. The tank should be at least a meter long and there should not be too many plants, particularly in the middle of the tank, so as to allow plenty of swimming space. The fish feel happiest and their colors are shown off to best advantage with subdued lighting and a dark bed in the tank. Rocks can be put into the tank but it is more natural to use pieces of wood: these can be arranged to simulate the roots of shore vegetation which, in their natural habitats, penetrate the waters in which these species live. Floating plants can be a very useful way of shielding the fish from too much overhead light, and they like to lay their eggs among the thick roots that such plants develop. *Pistia stratiotes* is one floating plant that is appropriate, for example, and it will grow steadily in the tank provided there is not too much overhead light and there are not too many mineral salts in the water.

A number of species have already been bred successfully in captivity. The mating is vigorous. The eggs are not very adhesive: they are laid in dense clumps of plants or merely at random in the open water. They hatch after about 24–36 hours at a temperature of about 24°C. The fry hang among fine leaved plants for about five days, during which time they digest the yolk of the egg. They then begin to seek food. It is not difficult to raise the fry with the usual foods. However, these very prolific fish become a great deal less attractive after the first generation bred in captivity: successive generations are usually predominantly silvery, and lack the pearly colors of newly imported specimens: the same drawback applies to the breeding of those species that, in the wild, have a basically bronze color.

260. *Astyanax bimaculatus*

ASTYANAX BIMACULATUS

Family: *Characidae*

Genus: *Astyanax*

English name: Two-spot Astyanax

Origin: Columbia, Venezuela, the Guianas

Size: Approximately 15 cm

Habitat: Found in large numbers in various kinds of waters

SHAPE, COLORING AND MARKINGS: The body is roughly lozenge-shaped and laterally very compressed. The markings vary significantly according to the place of origin. The basic coloration is silvery, tinged with a gold sheen. The back is olive green. A black elongated mark lies on the shoulders above the pectoral fins, level with the eyes. Another long dark mark on the base of the caudal fin may extend into the caudal peduncle or into the middle fin rays. The fins are usually without any markings. In older fish the body is considerably deeper than in younger fish.

Females, when sexually mature have deeper bodies.

Males when sexually mature have caudal and anal fins that are yellowish or pale red.

GENERAL CARE: *A.bimaculatus* is only suitable for larger aquariums and should be kept in a large group of its own species. It feels happiest and the colors show up best over a dark bed and in subdued lighting. It is particularly important for there to be adequate free swimming space between widely spaced plants, in the middle of the tank: there should be some thick clumps of plants around the edges to provide hiding places. The composition of the water is not critical but fresh tap water should not be used: part of the tank water should be changed regularly. Temperature 16°–24°C. *A.bimaculatus* keeps mainly to the middle and upper reaches of the tank: it is tolerant of other species provided it is kept in a small shoal. In addition to the usual animal matter, algae and lettuce should be included in the diet.

BREEDING: This species has not as yet been bred successfully in captivity.

ASTYANAX FASCIATUS FASCIATUS

Family: *Characidae*

Genus: *Astyanax*

English name: Banded Astyanax

Origin: Arizona through Mexico and Central America to the north of South America.

Size: Approximately 17 cm

Habitat: Very common in a variety of different waters

SHAPE, COLORING AND MARKINGS: The body is roughly lozenge-shaped and laterally very compressed. The markings can vary significantly according to the place of origin. The basic coloration is silvery, tinged with a

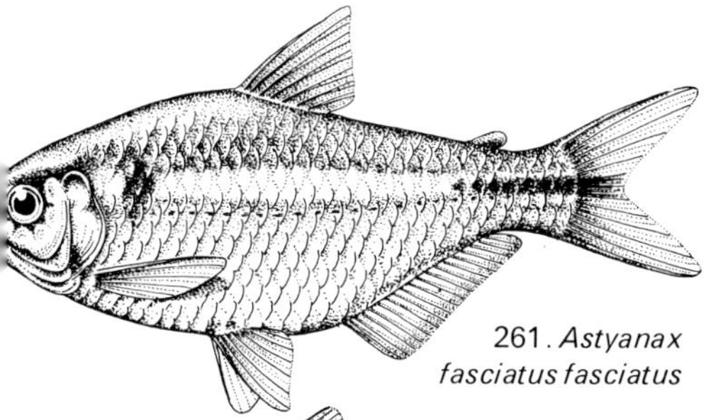

261. *Astyanax fasciatus fasciatus*

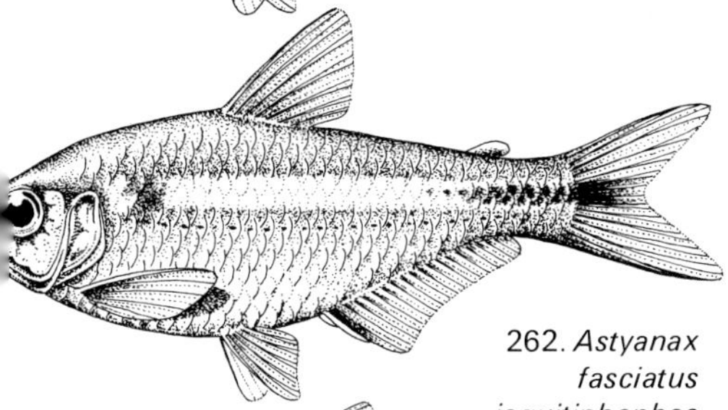

262. *Astyanax fasciatus jequitinhonhae*

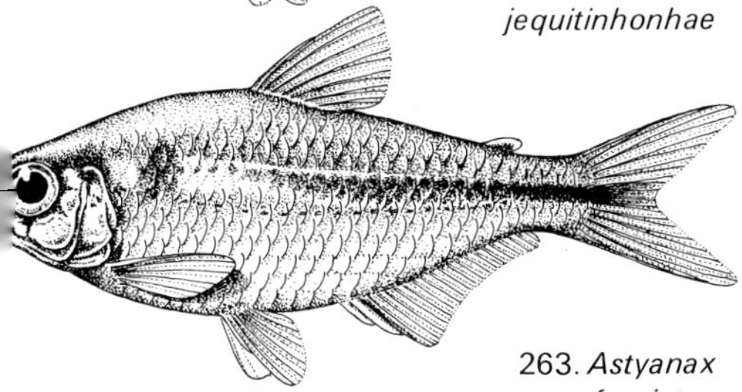

263. *Astyanax fasciatus macrophthalmus*

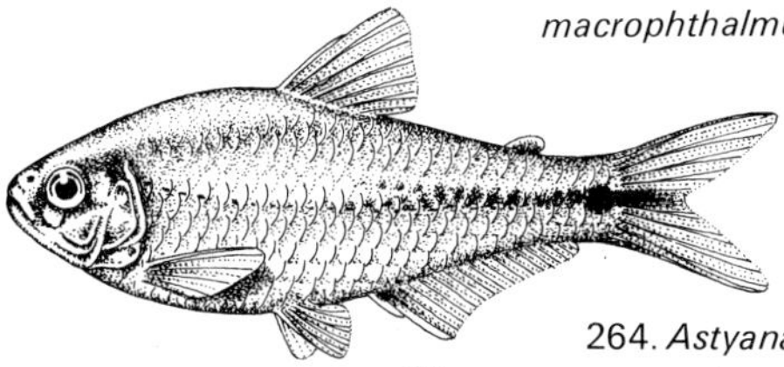

264. *Astyanax mexicanus*

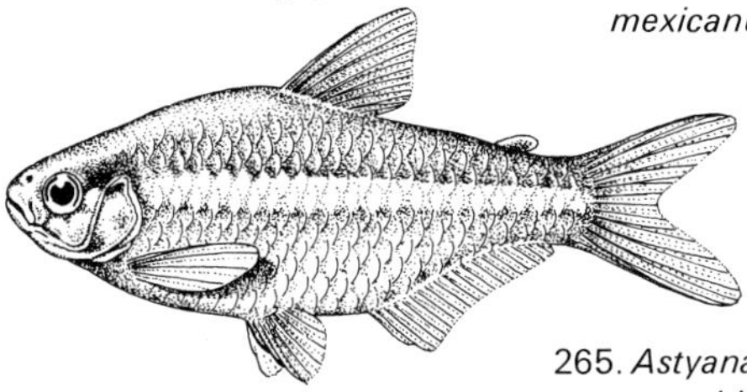

265. *Astyanax poetzschkei*

golden sheen. The back is greenish brown. A wide shiny silvery band runs from the back edge of the gill covers to the base of the caudal fin: in the caudal peduncle it mingles with a dark patterning that extends into the middle caudal fin rays. There is usually an inconspicuous mark on the shoulders behind the edge of the gill covers, but this is sometimes absent. The fins are yellowish and transparent: the anal fin has a greyish black edge. Some specimens have soft reddish fins and speckled dorsal fins.
There are no known external sexual characteristics.

General care: As for *A.bimaculatus*.

Breeding: This species does not seem to have been bred successfully in captivity.

ASTYANAX FASCIATUS JEQUITINHONHAE

Family: *Characidae*

Genus: *Astyanax*

English name: none

Origin: Eastern Brazil

Size: The maximum size of adult specimens is not known, but it is probably similar to that of *A.fasciatus fasciatus*

Habitat: No details are available of its natural habitat

Shape, coloring and markings: The body is less deep than that of related species, but that apart, this species closely resembles *A.fasciatus fasciatus*. The basic coloration is silvery, tinged with a very shiny gold sheen. The back is greenish-brown. There is a silvery band on the body identical to that borne by *A.fasciatus fasciatus*, but in *A.fasciatus jequitinhonhae*, the mark on the shoulders is always distinct. The fins are colorless and transparent: the front anal fin rays are milky white. There are no known external sexual characteristics.

General care: As for *A.bimaculatus*, but temperature 19°–24°C.

Breeding: This species has not as yet been bred successfully in captivity.

ASTYANAX FASCIATUS MACROPHTHALMUS

Family: *Characidae*

Genus: *Astyanax*

English name: none

Origin: Southern Mexico

Size: The maximum size of adult specimens is uncertain but it is probably akin to that of *A.fasciatus fasciatus*

Habitat: No details are available of its natural habitat

Shape, coloring and markings: The body is less deep than that of related species and the eyes somewhat larger. Older specimens have deeper bodies. The basic coloration is silvery, tinged with a golden or pearly sheen. The back is greenish-brown: a silvery band identical to that borne by *A.fasciatus fasciatus* runs along the body. The shoulder marks are always distinct. The fins are pale yellow or colorless and transparent.
Females, when sexually mature are clearly larger and sturdier.
Males when sexually mature have soft red caudal and anal fins.

General care: As for *A.bimaculatus* but temperature 16°–23°C.

Breeding: This is not difficult. See Introductory note.

Additional information: Many other subspecies of *A.fasciatus fasciatus* have been discovered over the years and many color variants as well: very few of these seem to have been imported however.

ASTYANAX MEXICANUS

Family: *Characidae*

Genus: *Astyanax*

Origin: From Texas to Panama

Size: Approximately 9 cm

Habitat: Found in a variety of different kinds of waters

Shape, coloring and markings: The body is fairly deep, more or less club-shaped, and laterally very compressed. The basic coloration is silvery, tinged with a golden sheen. The upper half of the body is greyish-green. This species bears a silvery band across the body identical to that borne by *A.fasciatus fasciatus*. There is a round dark mark on the base of the caudal fin. The fins are yellowish or a soft red: the front anal fin rays are milky white.
Females when sexually mature are clearly sturdier and larger.

General care: As for *A.bimaculatus* but temperature 16°–22°C. *A.mexicanus* will swim in all levels of the tank. It is tolerant of other species provided it is kept in a group of at least six of its own kind. The usual animal feeding matter, as well as dried food will be accepted.

Breeding: This is not difficult. See Introductory note.

Additional information: *A.mexicanus* is thought to be the ancestor of *Anoptochthys Jordani*, the Blind cave fish, with which it can be cross-bred.

ASTYANAX POETZSCHKEI

Family: *Characidae*

Genus: *Astyanax*

English name: none

Origin: The Amazon basin and Eastern Brazil

Size: Approximately 10 cm

Habitat: Fairly common in certain localities which together constitute a wide variety of different waters

Shape, coloring and markings: The body is more or less lozenge-shaped and laterally very compressed. It closely resembles its near relative *A.bimaculatus*. The basic coloration

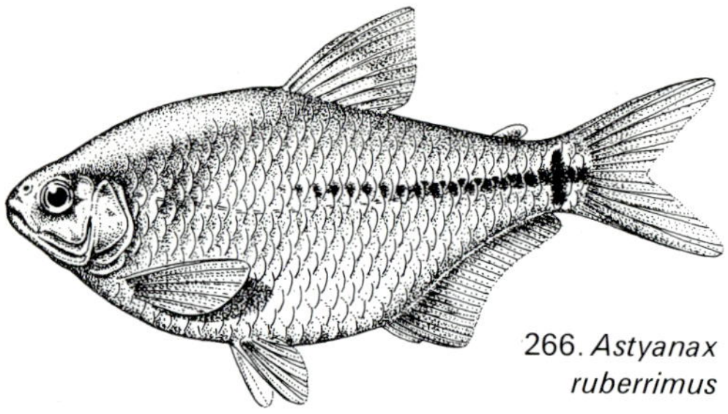

266. *Astyanax ruberrimus*

is a very shiny silver: the upper half of the body is a yellowish-brown. There are no shoulder marks or any dark patterning on the caudal peduncle, but a wide light iridescent band runs from the back edge of the gill covers into the base of the caudal fin. The fins are colorless and transparent.
There are no known external sexual characteristics.

GENERAL CARE: As for *A.bimaculatus* but temperature 20°–24°C.

BREEDING: This species has not as yet been bred successfully in captivity.

ADDITIONAL INFORMATION: This species is fond of nibbling at plants and seems to be particularly partial to *Vallisneria*. It would thus seem advisable to supplement the diet with some vegetable matter such as lettuce.

ASTYANAX RUBERRIMUS
Family: *Characidae*
Genus: *Astyanax*
English name: none
Origin: Panama and Colombia
Size: Approximately 12 cm
Habitat: Found in a variety of different waters

SHAPE, COLORING AND MARKINGS: The body is roughly lozenge-shaped and laterally very compressed. The basic coloration is silvery with a greenish-yellow or slightly reddish tinge. The back is fawn. A dark line runs along the body from the level of the dorsal fin to the caudal peduncle, where a similar dark line crosses it, forming a dark cross with a bright yellow background. The fins are red, and the center of the anal fin and the base of the dorsal fin are yellow.
Females are more sturdy and the fins are more yellow.
Males are as described above.

GENERAL CARE: As for *A.bimaculatus* but temperature 20°–24°C.

BREEDING: This is not difficult. See Introductory note.

THE FAMILY CHARACIDAE

The genus Chalceus

Only two species of interest to aquarists are found in this genus. Both require large tanks and are by nature aggressive towards other fish smaller than themselves. They are however hardly and undemanding fish and for that reason can be an attractive proposition for amateurs unwilling to assume the responsibility for more delicate or demanding kinds.
Chalceus macrolepidotus is the better known and more widely kept species: it is decribed in detail below. A somewhat less common species is *Chalceus erythurus*. *C.erythurus* is somewhat larger than *C.macrolepidotus*, with a darkish grey back, red belly and red dorsal, anal, adipose and caudal fins. Its disposition is similar to that of *C.macrolepidotus*, but it tends to keep more to the lower and middle reaches of the tank.

CHALCEUS MACROLEPIDOTUS
Family: *Characidae*
Genus: *Chalceus*
English name: Pink-tailed Characin
Origin: The Guianas
Size: Approximately 25 cm
Habitat: Found in a variety of waters

SHAPE, COLORING AND MARKINGS: The body is elongated and laterally somewhat compressed. The basic coloration is silvery-grey: the upper half of the body is a dark bluish-grey: the belly silvery to white. The scales on the upper half of the body are unusually large. There is a dark, usually prominent patch on the shoulders. The caudal fin is red: the other fins a yellowish-grey or yellowish-red.
There are no known external sexual characteristics.

GENERAL CARE: These fish are only suitable for larger aquariums, with ample free swimming space and adequate surface plants. They are tolerant of other fish of their own size and are best kept in a small group of their own kind. Temperature 24°–26°C. *C.macrolepidotus* is not particular about its diet: larger specimens will eat earthworms and raw meat as well as the usual foods.

267. *Chalceus macrolepidotus*

BREEDING: This species has not as yet been successfully bred in captivity, but it is a species that merits more attention from aquarists.

ADDITIONAL INFORMATION: *C.macrolepidotus* is a good jumper and adequate precautions must be taken.
Older specimens of this genus should be given substantial food, because they can be extremely voracious.

THE FAMILY CHARACIDAE

The genus Charax

The only species in this genus here described is unusual in that it is one of the headstanders that is fairly easy to breed in captivity – unlike many other fish of that kind which have not as yet been bred in the aquarium.

Charax gibbosus is closely related to the species in the genus Roeboides, the Glass-characins. Neither *Roeboides guatemalensis,* the Guatemala Glass-characin, nor *Roeboides microlepis,* the Small-scaled Glass-characin has become as popular an aquarium fish as *Charax gibbosus*. These fish however can also be bred in the aquarium and if kept by the amateur, require much the same care as suggested below for *Charax gibbosus*. Headstanders are interesting and unusual that well merit being kept in aquariums.

268. *Charax gibbosus*

CHARAX GIBBOSUS

Family: *Characidae*
Genus: *Charax*
English name: Humpbacked Headstander
Origin: The Guianas, the Amazon and Paraguay rivers
Size: Maximum 15 cm
Habitat: Found in fairly fast-flowing waters

SHAPE, COLORING AND MARKINGS: The body is elongated and laterally very compressed: as the English name suggests, the back is very arched. The basic coloration is a light yellow-brown with a silvery sheen: the back is somewhat darker with a green tinge: the belly is lighter. On the upper half of the body there are a number of silver or golden spots: there is a large dark mark lying below the gill covers. All the fins are colorless and transparent.
Females are more robust.
Males are as described above and have a more pronounced yellow color during the mating season.

GENERAL CARE: *C.gibbosus* needs a large aquarium with plenty of free swimming space. The tank should be furnished with some large plants to give the fish adequate shade when they need it, although as a rule they like the sun. The composition of the water is not critical. Temperature 23°–25°C.
All kinds of animal matter are acceptable as food.

BREEDING: This is not difficult. The fish will be more inclined to spawn in clear water of medium hardness. The eggs are laid among plants and hatch after about 30 hours. The fry can be raised with the usual fry foods.

THE FAMILY CHARACIDAE

The genus Cheirodon

The genus *Cheirodon* is distributed throughout Central and South America: The genus closely resembles the genera within the sub-family Tetragonopterinae (represented in this work by the genera *Hemigrammus* and *Hyphessobrycon*). Those fish are spread over the whole continent, but the *Cheirodon* are found only in some particular localities, which are noted under the descriptions of individual species. These localities represent a wide variety of natural habitats, the differences between which have led to widely different life-styles for individual species.
Most *Cheirodons* however live in shoals, sometimes with other small fish. They are usually to be found in still or sluggish waters such as swamps connected to rivers or jungle streams. Their main source of food is the mass of land insects which accidentally fall onto the surface of the water. This diet is supplemented with vegetable matter and the larvae of all kinds of small water creatures.
Characteristic features of the *Cheirodon* species include the presence of only one row of teeth in the upper and lower jaws, an incomplete lateral line, the siting of the anterior rays of the dorsal fin about half way down the body, the presence of adipose fins, barbs on the anterior rays of the anal fin and on the ventral fin in the male and small spikes on the underside of the caudal fin.
The external sexual characteristics are usually difficult for the amateur aquarist to identify. Both males and females have virtually the same color patterns and the fins are not always distinctive. In some species the males have a rather slimmer body than the females, or they are smaller, but of course these differences are only apparent in mature fish. Generally speaking, sex can be established with reasonable certainty from the shape of the swim bladder and its position within the body cavity. The swim bladder can usually be seen easily if the fish is examined against a strong light. In the male the rear part of the swim bladder is rather pointed and curves down sharply towards the anus. In the female it is more evenly shaped and the space between the swim bladder and the internal organs is occupied by the ovary, which shows up as a darker shadow.
Only a few species of *Cheirodon* are known, and of these only two, *C.axelrodi* and *C.innesi* are familiar to most aquarists. *C.innesi* has only recently been placed in this genus: it was previously classified as one of the species in the genus

Hyphessobrycon. C.axelrodi was also at one time regarded as being within the genus *Hyphessobrycon*, and was known as *Hyphessobrycon cardinalis*.
Both these species come from areas south of the Equator in the upper Amazon. Their remarkable color patterns have made them both extremely popular as aquarium fish. They are also both very undemanding and suitable for all sizes of aquariums. They should be kept in well-maintained tanks preferably together with other small fish and in large groups of their own kind. Soft, mildy acid water filtered through peat is best. The temperature should be about 21°–24° C. A wide range of small living creatures will serve for food and dried food of good quality will also be greedily eaten. Breeding is complicated. It is clear that the composition of the water is highly critical. Suitable water can be prepared from distilled water. For *C.innesi* a hardness of 1°–2° DH is required: the acidity should be pH 5.5–6. For *C.axelrodi* the water should be 3.5°–4° DH and of acidity pH 6–6.5. The water can be matured artificially by filling a breeding tank with about five liters of water, putting in some assimilating plants such as *Myrophyllum* and then leaving it in a sunny place for one or two weeks. The water can be artificially acidified either by filtering it through peat or by adding a number of oak leaves to it. It is important to clean thoroughly all materials to be used, especially when dealing with *C.innesi*. The breeding tank containing the parent fish should be placed so that it catches the morning sun. Once the eggs have been laid the parent fish should be removed from the tank and the tank then shaded from the light. The eggs hatch after 24 or 36 hours at 24° C. The fry then hang between the plants or on the sides of the tank. The tank should still be shaded from the light and the shading removed gradually over about a week. Feeding should commence as soon as the fish start to swim freely. Infusorians should be used for the first two or three days. After the third day freshly hatched brine shrimps may be given. As long as the water is changed regularly, the newly-hatched fry will grow very quickly during the first few weeks. Fresh tap water can be used for these changes of water provided it is of a hardness less than 12° DH. The changes should not of course be made too abruptly: the fry must be given a chance to acclimatise themselves to the water as it changes. The fry can be transferred into larger tanks after four to six weeks and will continue to grow vigorously as long as the water in the tank is regularly changed.

CHEIRODON ARNOLDI

Family: *Characidae*
Genus: *Cheirodon*
English name: none
Origin: Mexico and central America
Size: Approximately 9 cm
Habitat: No details are available of its natural habitat

Shape, coloring and markings: The body is rather deep and laterally very compressed. The basic coloration is silvery: the back is a faded green. The flanks and belly are silvery to clear white. In young specimens there is a blue-black spot, edged by an iridescent zone on the base of the caudal fin. In some lighting a narrow, rather dark longitudinal stripe is visible. The unpaired fins are an orange red. The anal and ventral fins have cream specks. The iris is a clear red.
Females have yellow fins and rather thick-set bodies.
Males are slimmer and as described above.

General care: *C.arnoldi* is only suitable for larger aquariums with plenty of free swimming space, but with clumps of dense vegetation round the sides. The bed should be dark: either covered with peat matting or a growth of short plants. Bogwood makes excellent decoration, and scattered rocks can be made to look interesting. The composition of the water is not critical, but fresh tap water should not be used. Temperature 20°–25° C. *C.arnoldi* will be found in all levels of the tank. It is not always tolerant of other species and will only associate with other large fish. All types of food, including dried food will be accepted. It is a very greedy species.

Breeding: This is not difficult in tanks in sunny positions. See Introductory note.

CHEIRODON AXELRODI

Family: *Characidae*
Genus: *Cheirodon*
English name: Cardinal Tetra
Origin: The Amazon, the basin of the Negro river
Size: Approximately 5 cm
Habitat: Found in small rivulets and pools in the jungle, most of which are characterised by soft water

Shape, coloring and markings: The body is fairly deep and laterally slightly compressed. At first sight this species closely resembles *Cheirodon innesi*, but *C.axelrodi* is less robust and has a more striking color pattern. The back is brownish or red: the lower part of the body is a deep red, except for a small area round the belly. There is an attractive blue-green iridescent stripe running from the eye as far back as, or beyond the adipose fin. The fins are colorless and transparent: the dorsal and anal fins have a narrow white border along the front. The iris has an impressive blue iridescence.
Females, when adult, are rather more robust.
Males are slimmer and usually smaller.

General care: *C.axelrodi* is suitable for all sizes of aquariums provided a group of six or more is kept. The composition of the water is not critical but fresh tap water should be avoided. The body colors will show up best in yellow tinted water against a dark bed. The tint can be obtained by filtering the water through peat. A wide range of plants can be used but some fine leaved varieties should always be included. This species will occupy all levels of the tank. Temperature 22°–25° C. A tolerant species that will associate with other small fish. All kinds of food, including dried food will be accepted. The smaller flying insects will be eaten with relish: Tubifex is less suitable and will only be accepted with some reluctance.

Breeding: Not too difficult for the experienced amateur. See Introductory note.

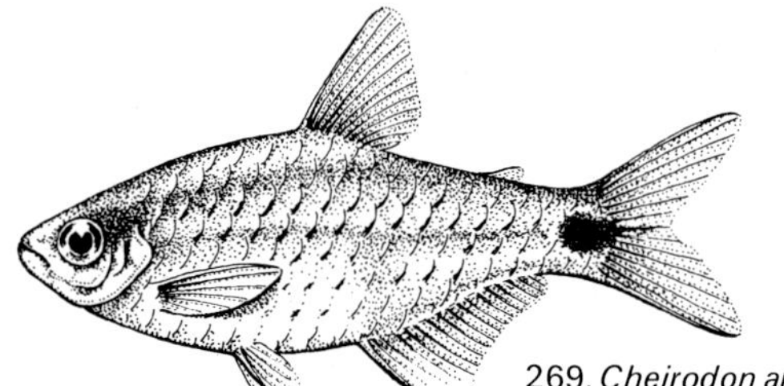
269. *Cheirodon arnoldi*

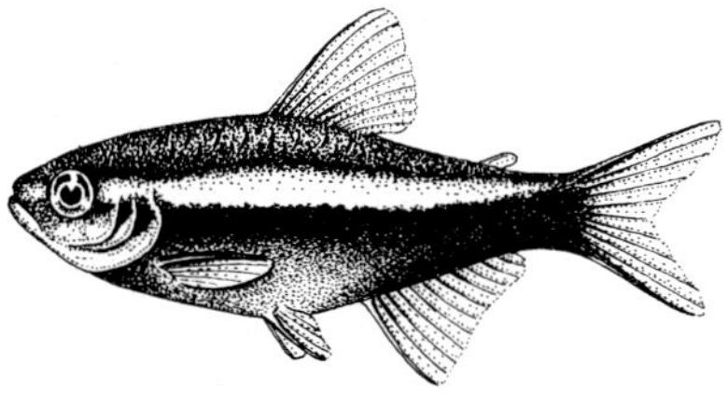
270. *Cheirodon axelrodi*

271. *Cheirodon axelrodi.* The Cardinal Tetra is easily distinguished from other related species, by its more vivid color pattern. ▷

272. *Cheirodon innesi*

273. *Cheirodon interruptus*

CHEIRODON INNESI

Family: *Characidae*

Genus: *Cheirodon*

English name: Neon Tetra

Origin: The Amazon and the basin of the Negro river

Size: Approximately 4.5 cm

Habitat: Found in small jungle rivulets and pools, with soft water

SHAPE, COLORING AND MARKINGS: The body is fairly deep and laterally slightly compressed. *C.innesi* at first sight closely resembles *C.axelrodi*. The back is brownish-yellow: the belly yellow-white. An attractive blue-green iridescent stripe runs back from the top of the eye up to or beyond the adipose fin: below this stripe lies an attractive area of red, starting at the level of the middle rays of the dorsal fin. The fins are colorless and transparent. The anterior rays of the dorsal and anal fins are milk white. The iris has an iridescent blue-green shade, with a number of glistening spots in the upper half.
Females are rather more robust than males with more rounded bellies.
Males are slimmer with flattened bellies.

GENERAL CARE: The tank should be furnished as for *C.axelrodi*. This species stays mainly in the lower and middle reaches of the tank. Temperature 21°–23°C. *C.innesi* is tolerant and will associate with other small fish. Diet as for *C.axelrodi*.

BREEDING: This is not too difficult. The breeding tank should stand in a sunny position. See Introductory note.

CHEIRODON INTERRUPTUS

Family: *Characidae*

Genus: *Cheirodon*

English name: none

Origin: The Rio Grande do Sul and the basin of the river Uruguay

Size: Approximately 6 cm

Habitat: Found in small jungle pools and rivulets with soft water

SHAPE, COLORING AND MARKINGS: The body is quite deep and laterally very compressed. The upper half of the body is a light brown with a green tinge: the flanks are silvery with a dark blue tinge: the belly is off-white, A dark grey longitudinal stripe, which gradually becomes broader, runs back from the edge of the gill covers to the caudal fin where it becomes a lozenge-shaped mark: the color may extend into the central rays of the caudal fin. The fins are colorless or pale yellow. In particularly well-marked specimens the dorsal and caudal fins may be rather red. There are no known external sexual characteristics but some authorities believe that the anal fin is more curved in front, in males.

GENERAL CARE: As for *C.innesi* but temperature 22°–25°C. Males may be rather intolerant of smaller species.

BREEDING: Not difficult in moderately hard water (5°–7°DH: pH 6.5–7). This species needs a rather large breeding tank and shallow water. See Introductory note.

ADDITIONAL INFORMATION: *C.interruptus* is often confused with other related species.

CHEIRODON LEUCISCUS

Family: *Characidae*

Genus: *Cheirodon*

English name: none

Origin: The basin of the Paraná river

Size: Approximately 8 cm

Habitat: No further details are available of its natural habitat

SHAPE, COLORING AND MARKINGS: The body is fairly deep and laterally very compressed. The basic coloration is a light brown, tinged

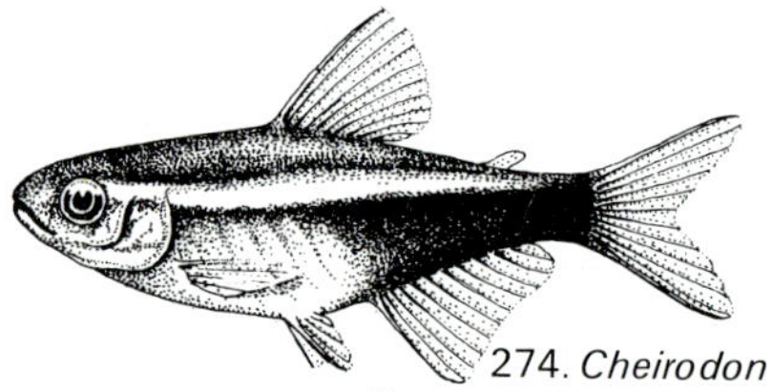

274. *Cheirodon innesi*

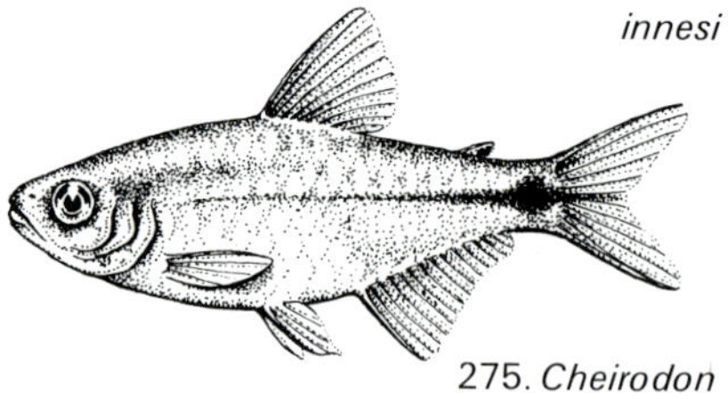

275. *Cheirodon interruptus*

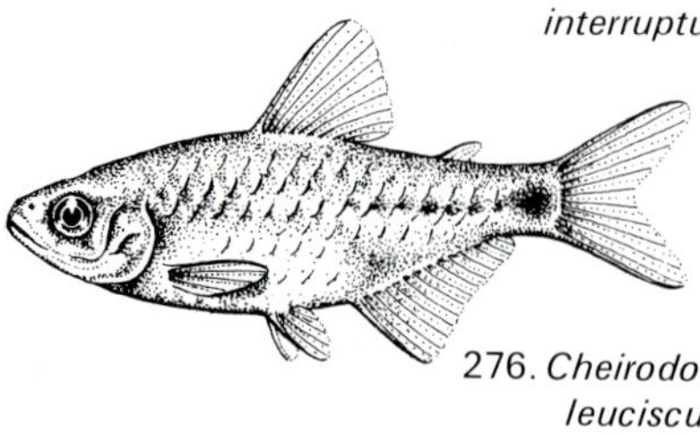

276. *Cheirodon leuciscus*

with green: the head is darker and sometimes even a dark brown. The flanks are greyish-green with a bluish tinge, especially on the caudal peduncle. The belly is a silvery white. A dark but not always very distinct mark lies on the caudal peduncle. The fins are colorless and transparent.
There are no known external sexual characteristics.

GENERAL CARE: Tank as for *C.innesi* but temperature 22°–25°C. This species is suitable only for larger aquariums: it should be kept in a group of at least six of its own kind and also only with other large fish, for it is sometimes intolerant of smaller fish. The males may sometimes fight among themselves. Diet as for *C.axelrodi* but *C.leuciscus* has a preference for winged surface insects and mosquito larvae.

BREEDING: This species has not as yet been bred successfully in captivity.

CHEIRODON MEINKENI

Family: *Characidae*
Genus: *Cheirodon*
English name: none
Origin: The coastal areas of East Brazil
Size: Approximately 5 cm
Habitat: No further details are available of its natural habitat

---

SHAPE, COLORING AND MARKINGS: The body is fairly deep and laterally very compressed. The upper half of the body is between an olive and brownish-green: the flanks are silvery with a violet tinge. Under bright light, a thin horizontal stripe can be seen, running along the body becoming wider towards the base of the caudal fin, where it turns into a dark patch. The fins are a soft yellow and transparent. The iris is yellowish.
There are no known external sexual characteristics but it may be that the anal fin of the male is more rounded at the front.

GENERAL CARE: As for *C.innesi* but temperature 22°–25°C. Males can be somewhat intolerant of smaller fish. Diet as for *C.leuciscus*.

BREEDING: This species does not yet seem to have been bred successfully in captivity.

ADDITIONAL INFORMATION: This species, although first described in 1936, is still almost unknown among aquarists.

CHEIRODON PIABA

Family: *Characidae*
Genus: *Cheirodon*
English name: none
Origin: Eastern Brazil
Size: Approximately 5 cm
Habitat: No further details are available of its natural habitat

---

SHAPE, COLORING AND MARKINGS: The body is quite deep and laterally very compressed. *C.piaba* closely resembles *C.interruptus* and is often confused with it. The basic coloration can vary according to the place of origin. The

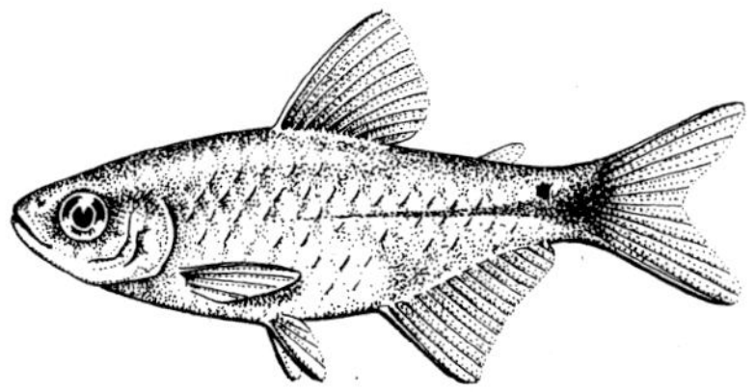

277. *Cheirodon meinkeni*

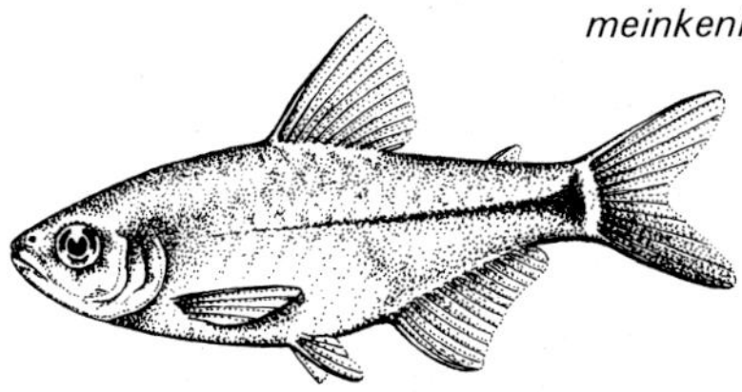

278. *Cheirodon piaba*

upper half of the body is brown to olive green. The flanks are greenish with a bright silvery gleam. A narrow dark stripe runs along the centre of the body, broadening towards the tail and forming a large blue-black patch at the base of the caudal fin. In some specimens this line runs on into the central rays of the caudal fin. The fins are transparent and either colorless or light yellow.
Females are as described above.
Males have a very rounded edge to the anterior of the caudal fin and the lower lobe of that fin is particularly reddish.

GENERAL CARE: As for *C.meinkeni.*

BREEDING: Not too difficult. As for *C.interruptus.*

ADDITIONAL INFORMATION: This is still a fairly unfamiliar species despite having been described as early as 1874 by Christian Frederik Lütken.

THE FAMILY CHARACIDAE

The genus Copeina

The members of the two very closely related genera *Pyrrhulina* and *Copeina* are found over a wide area of South America. They are usually very small and live in the upper levels of small sluggish or still waters in the jungles: they are usually found together with other fish such as *Cheirodon, Hyphessobrycon* and *Hemigrammus*. In appearance the *Pyrrhulina* and *Copeina* have many features in common with some of the genera of the Cyprinodontidae family, for example, the genera *Fundulus* and *Rivulus*. In all these genera the dorsal fin is set well down the back, the head is somewhat flattened and the line of the mouth turned up: all these features are characteristic of fish that live near the surface. All the species in these two genera have a rather large upper lobe in the caudal fin, and this may be particularly well developed in males. The fold of skin which passes for an adipose fin, is only present, and then only in a rudimentary way, in young specimens: it is totally absent in mature fish.
According to many authorities these species do not belong to the Characidae family at all but should be classed in another family that has developed along very similar lines. This view is based on a wide range of characteristics, but is perhaps too technical a matter to pursue here. Nevertheless it is advisable for amateur aquarists to bear in mind the possibility that there may one day be a radical change in the nomenclature of these fish.
Many species in the family Characidae are difficult to distinguish and to classify. Recent work on classification has tended to concentrate on the question of dentition: that is to say, only by a careful analysis of the pattern of the teeth in the various species, it is believed, will a true and authentic classification be established. As a very simple example, whereas fish in the genus *Pyrrhulina* have two rows of teeth in the upper jaw, those in the genus *Copeina* have only one row.
These fish are rather nervous and are best kept in large tanks together with smaller and more placid species. They will be shown off to their best advantage if provided with a special tank containing as many broad leaved plants as possible, such as *Nymphaea, Echinodorus* and *Barclaya.* The males usually establish themselves in a fairly fixed fixed position underneath a leaf growing one or two centimeters below the surface. This

leaf is then regarded as marking the center of a territory and no other member of the same species, except a mate, will be allowed close to it.

These rather delicate fish require water which is fairly soft, between 6° and 10° DH, and which is mildly acid. The required degree of acidity will be achieved by filtering it through peat or by adding some oak leaves. The ideal temperature is just over 25° C: at lower temperatures the fish become sluggish and lose some of the intensity in their colors. The tank should be shaded from bright overhead light, but some sunshine entering the tank is very desirable. A dark base will overcome much of the species' natural shyness and allow the coloration to be shown off to greater advantage. All kinds of living matter may serve for food, including Daphnia, Cyclops and black and white mosquito larvae. Small winged insects such as might in the wild fall accidentally onto the surface are relished: dried food will also be taken.

These species will usually mate spontaneously, whether they are kept in a large community tank with other fish or separately in a species tank. The matings often bring disappointment to the aquarist for the eggs and fry are often eaten by other members of the tank community. Successful breeding demands a special tank at least 40 cm long: a broad leaved plant with a number of leaves floating just below the surface should be put in the center. A handful of fine leaved plants can also be put in a rear corner to afford some protective hiding places for females if they are pursued by too aggressive a male. A sandy bottom is not necessary, but if provided, the sand should be boiled after being rinsed. If no soil bottom is available, the plants in the tank can be held down with string or stones.

The best breeding results are obtained using soft water (2°–6° DH) with an acidity of Ph 5.4–6.7. The males are most active when the temperature is 26°–27° C. Breeding will commence after a very short time. A few days may elapse before the male begins to look for a suitable spawning spot, but when that has happened the male will lurk about in the selected spot defiantly fanning its fins until a female swims close by. It then swims up to her and tries to shepherd her towards the chosen spot by swimming round and round her and nudging her forward with small bites. If the first attempts fail, the male becomes rougher and the female is more or less driven to the spot. However as soon as the male's intentions become clear to the female she seems to swim to the place with less hesitation. She then swims with her belly skimming the leaf surface, the male moving round her: the eggs are not released immediately. No eggs will be released until the female is in the exact and correct position. Depending on whether the opening on the female's genitalia is on the left or the right, she must align herself on the right or left of the male. When that position has been achieved, the male twists the side of his belly towards the genital area of the female and pushes his anal fin under her body. There is a brief moment of stillness during which a number of eggs are discharged and fertilized. The process will be repeated until about 200 eggs or more are attached to the leaf. The female then leaves the mating site but the male remains over the cluster of eggs, fanning it with powerful movements of the fins. This may loosen a few eggs which will sink to the bottom. All the eggs hatch in 24–28 hours. For the first two or three days the fry hang between the plants and on the sides of the aquarium. By the fifth or sixth day they are swimming freely and they acquire pigmentation.

Correct feeding during the first few days is vital. The fry generally move about just below the surface so care must be taken to see that the food lies on the surface. Rotifers are very good as they are held there by the surface tension. After about a week the fry will move down into the other levels of the tank and can be fed successively with *Artemia nauplii*, filtered Daphnia and Cyclops. After the first two critical weeks, normal fry foods can be used. Well fed specimens will be sexually mature in six months. *Copeina arnoldi* however has a completely different pattern of mating behavior: it is the only species in this sub-family which lays its eggs above the water level on the underside of leaves which stick out of the water. The eggs may also be deposited on the glass sides of the tank.

The breeding site is selected by the male. He rushes against the underside of the selected leaf several times. Some observers see this as practice for the actual mating: others believe that the male is cleaning the leaf surface. Whatever the reason, similar behavior is observed among other species that also lay their eggs in this way, for example, the cichlids. The male and females then both test the underside of the leaf several times before mating begins. The eggs are then laid and fertilized. Both fish lift themselves out of the water at the same time and are held against the leaf for a moment by the movement of their fins.

After mating, the male remains under the egg cluster, splashing water over it with vigorous movements of his tail: this may cause some of the eggs to fall to the bottom. Both those that adhere to the leaf and those that fall away, normally hatch in a day or two. The procedure for raising the fry is the same as for the fry of other species, as noted above.

279. *Copeina guttata*

280. *Copeina callolepis*

281. *Copeina arnoldi*

COPEINA ARNOLDI

Family: *Characidae*

Genus: *Copeina*

English name: The Spraying Characin

Origin: The lower reaches of the Amazon, the Para river

Size: Approximately 7 cm

Habitat: Found in sluggish and still jungle streams and swamps

SHAPE, COLORING AND MARKINGS: The body is very slender and laterally only slightly compressed. The back is dark brown to fawn: the flanks yellowish-green with a rusty overtone, becoming a clear yellow towards the belly. The scales of the upper half of the body have a dark edge producing something of the effect of a net. There is a dark stripe running back from the snout to the eye and a prominent iridescent green spot on the gill covers. The caudal fin is mainly yellow, with a red border and very often, black spots: the upper lobe is lengthened substantially. The ventral and anal fins are a similar yellow with red spots. Females are smaller with less strongly developed fins.
Males are more brightly colored and with tapered fins: otherwise as described above.

GENERAL CARE: *C.arnoldi* is suitable for larger aquariums and should be kept with other placid, reasonably-sized fish. An ordinary well-planted aquarium, preferably with a dark base and with decorative arrangements of bogwood will be admirable: a number of broad leaved plants should be included. Ideally, a few leaves of these plants should project out of the water. The water should be hard and slightly acid, the temperature 24°–26° C. *C.arnoldi* is a very tolerant fish that stays in the lower and middle reaches of the tank. All kinds of small live creatures can be used for feeding, and small winged insects are particularly good: dried food can also be given for variety.

BREEDING: See Introductory note.

COPEINA CALLOLEPIS

Family: *Characidae*

Genus: *Copeina*

English name: Beautiful-scaled Characin

Origin: The lower reaches of the Amazon

Size: Maximum 6 cm

Habitat: Found in sluggish and still jungle creeks, especially those with dense vegetation on the shores

SHAPE, COLORING AND MARKINGS: The body is extremely slender and laterally only slightly compressed. It somewhat resembles the closely related species *Pyrrhulina nattereri*. The back is a dark yellowish brown: the flanks fawn or yellowish with a greenish tinge becoming yellowish-white towards the belly. The scales have dark edges, creating a net-like pattern, especially on the upper half of the body. Nearly all the scales have also a decorative bright red or rust colored dot which show up as lines on the body. A thin horizontal line runs from the snout across the eye to above the pectoral fin. The fins are yellowish-brown. The dorsal fin has a dark mark bordered by a bright white area at the base of the fin. The upper lobe of the caudal fin is greatly elongated.
Females are smaller with less well developed fins and no pigmentation.
Males are more colorful and have tapered fins, otherwise as described above.

GENERAL CARE: As for *C.arnoldi*.

BREEDING: There are no records of this species having been successfully bred in captivity: accordingly it is not possible to say whether its habits are those of *C.arnoldi* or those of the related species of *Pyrrhulina*.

COPEINA GUTTATA

Family: *Characidae*

Genus: *Copeina*

English name: Red-spotted Copeina

Origin: The middle reaches of the Amazon

Size: Approximately 15 cm in the wild, remains considerably smaller in captivity

Habitat: Very widely distributed in different kinds of waters

SHAPE, COLORING AND MARKINGS: The body is thick-set and laterally slightly compressed. *C.guttata* is quite obviously more robustly built than related species. The back is olive green: the flanks an iridescent light blue, paling to white towards the belly. All the

282. *Copeina guttata*

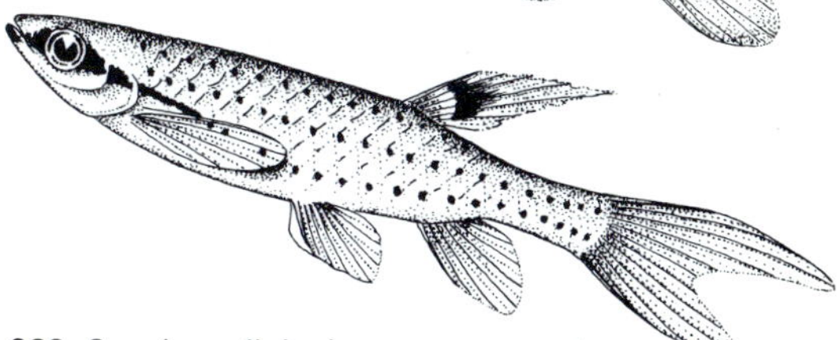

283. *Copeina callolepis*

scales are adorned with blue to violet iridescent spots which show up as lines across the body. The dorsal fin is a transparent yellow with a darker spot. The remaining fins are bright yellow with an orange or red border.
Females are rather smaller and less richly colored: the dark spot on the dorsal fin is more pronounced.
Males have a more strongly developed upper lobe to the caudal fin: otherwise as described above.

GENERAL CARE: As for *C.arnoldi*.

BREEDING: A very prolific species which is not difficult to breed. *C.guttata* prefers to lay its eggs on the bed, in a depression it forms by circular movements of the body during mating. The composition of the breeding water is not critical.

ADDITIONAL INFORMATION: In size, shape and breeding habits, *C.guttata* is most unusual.

THE FAMILY CHARACIDAE

The genus Creagrutus

Although not found very often in aquariums, *Creagrutus beni* the only fish in this genus that is of interest to aquarists, is very common indeed in the wild. It is closely related to the better known species in the genus *Hemigrammus* and to the species in the genus *Astyanax:* from the latter it is distinguished by its shorter anal fin and the structure of the jaws.

It is strange that *C.beni* has not become more popular among aquarists. It is an attractively colored species, and one that is not difficult to keep, provided it is given the kind of environment described below. It is indeed a species that can be very interesting for the amateur to keep, for its reproductive behaviour is quite unusual. Nevertheless, it is not difficult to breed in the aquarium.

CREAGRUTUS BENI

Family: *Characidae*

Genus: *Creagrutus*

English name: Gold-striped Characin

Origin: The upper reaches of the Amazon basin, Venezuela, Columbia, Bolivia

Size: Maximum 7 cm

Habitat: Found in many different kinds of waters

SHAPE, COLORING AND MARKINGS: This fish is found over a very wide area and consequently the appearance and maximum length of individual specimens can vary significantly. The body is elongated and laterally very compressed towards the tail. The basic coloration is between a yellowish and greenish-brown, becoming silvery towards the belly. A brownish-black shoulder mark lies behind the gill covers. A golden line runs across the body from the dorsal fin to the caudal peduncle: this is divided into two parallel narrow lines by an intervening band of brownish-black. The dorsal and anal fins are a soft red: on the former appears a triangular mark: the caudal fin varies from reddish to pale yellow.
Females are slightly larger than the males and have more vivid colors, their bellies are more rounded especially during the mating season.
Males are as described above.

GENERAL CARE: *C.beni* is very peaceful but needs a large aquarium with dense vegetation round the sides and plenty of open swimming space. The water should not be harder than 6°DH with a pH 6.8–7. Temperature 24°–26°C. *C.beni* is essentially a shoal fish that keeps mainly to the bottom of the tank. It is not particular about food and will accept both live animal matter and dried food.

BREEDING: An unusual feature of this species is that the eggs are fertilised while inside the female and are not laid until some time afterwards. They are deposited among fine leaved plants and hatch after about 24 hours at a temperature of about 25°C. The fry hang among the plants for about three days and then begin to swim freely: at that time they should be fed with ditch infusoria and as they grow can be fed with the usual foods.

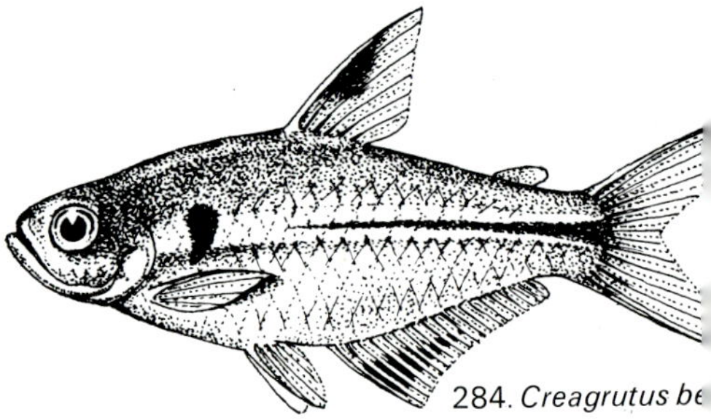

284. *Creagrutus be*

THE FAMILY CHARACIDAE

The genus Crenuchus

It is not surprising that so large a family as the Characidae should contain within it some species with very unusual profiles: among these must be numbered the Sailfin Characin described below.
Although a somewhat delicate species and, when mature, a possible danger to smaller fish, *Crenuchus spilurus* is a very attractive addition to the aquarium, in the right conditions.
In the wild it lives only in waters with dense vegetation along the banks, which overhanging the banks, thus provides *C.spilurus* with good cover.
If denied adequate cover in an aquarium, *C.spilurus* will become very nervous and unsettled. A very graceful fish, *C.spilurus* deserves to receive the careful attention to its needs. It requires if it is to become an ornament to the aquarium.

285. *Crenuchus spilurus* (female) — 286. *Crenuchus spilurus* (male)

CRENUCHUS SPILURUS

Family: *Characidae*

Genus: *Crenuchus*

English name: Sailfin Characin

Origin: Guyana and the middle Amazon region

Size: Maximum 6 cm

Habitat: Found usually in waters that have dense vegetation on the banks

SHAPE, COLORING AND MARKINGS: The body is elongated and laterally very compressed. The basic coloration is a bright brownish-red: the belly is a yellowish-white. The scales have a dark edge, most prominent on the back. A dark band bordered above by a yellow line, runs from the gill covers to the caudal peduncle. There is a large dark mark at the base of the caudal fin. The dorsal, anal and caudal fins are vividly patterned in orange and brown: the ventral fins are orange: the pectoral fins colorless.
Females have less vivid colors and shorter anal and dorsal fins.
Males are as described above.

GENERAL CARE: This peaceful and beautiful species should be kept in a tank furnished with thick clumps of vegetation and given plenty of shade. The water should be fairly soft, preferably filtered over peat. Temperature 25°C. All kinds of live animal matter will be accepted as food: mature fish may prey on smaller species.

BREEDING: This species has not as yet been bred successfully in captivity.

THE FAMILY CHARACIDAE

The genus Exodon

It is unfortunate that one of the most beautiful and active of the smaller characins should also be one of the most agressive species.

Found in the wild in larger waters than many related species, *Exodon paradoxus* likes subdued sunlight and can only be kept in good condition if the tank is so arranged as to provide *E.paradoxus* with all its rather exacting requirements. The beauty and remarkable activity of a shoal of these fish when healthy however more than repays the demands they make on their keeper.

This is one of the more unusual South American characins. It is not as vividly colored as many related species and its attraction for the amateur aquarist lies rather in its vivacity than in its coloring. It is not a species suitable for the conventional small community tank, but it is an admirable fish for the rather more advanced amateur, who is interested in creating a special species tank or who is setting up a large community tank which will be stocked with a variety of larger fishes.

EXODON PARADOXUS

Family: *Characidae*

Genus: *Exodon*

English name: none

Origin: Guyana, the waters of the Branco and Rupununi rivers

Size: Maximum 15 cm

Habitat: Found in waters with dense vegetation on the banks

SHAPE, COLORING AND MARKINGS: The body is elongated and laterally very compressed. The basic coloration of mature fish is a dull yellowish-grey: there are few distinctive marks. Young fish are a light yellow with large areas of iridescent silver. Two large dark patches, one in the center of the body in front of the line of the dorsal fin and the other at the root of the caudal fin are particularly distinctive. The fins are yellowish, with varying areas of vivid red.
Females are more robust.
Males are as described above.

287. *Exodon paradoxus*

GENERAL CARE: Only suitable for larger aquariums with plenty of free swimming space and sufficient dense vegetation to shade the fish from the light and provide hiding places. *E.paradoxus* is an aggressive and very active fish and should either be kept in a species tank or in a community tank with other robust fish. The water should be soft and peaty: temperature 23°–28°C. All kinds of live animal food will be accepted and dried food and lettuce should be given for variety.

BREEDING: Breeding so far has not been successful in captivity; spawning has been observed incidentally. The process of breeding takes place probably in the same way as with other characins; relatively large eggs are spawned in rather small quantities. The eggs are laid among the plants. The fry hatch after 24–30 hours but are difficult to raise.

THE FAMILY CHARACIDAE

The genus Gephyrocharax

Two species in this genus are to be found in aquariums, *Gephyrocharax atracaudatus* and *Gephyrocharax valencia.* Both are South American fish and each comes from a fairly restricted area. *G.atracaudatus,* the more popular species, described in detail below, is found in Panama; *G.valencia,* a less common species, is found only in Venezuela, in Lake Valencia. *G.valencia* is generally slightly smaller than *G.atracaudatus,* and in color darker, more bluish green, with a strong silvery sheen: the mouth is edged with black, the dorsal fin with white.

Both *G.atracaudatus* and *G.valencia* are attractive additions to the aquarium: neither is difficult to keep or to breed, but both the same unusual pattern of reproductive behavior as *Creagrutus beni.*

GEPHYROCHARAX ATRACAUDATUS

Family: *Characidae*

Genus: *Gephyrocharax*

English name: Platinum Tetra

Origin: Central America, Panama

Size: Maximum 6 cm

Habitat: No details of its natural habitat are available

SHAPE, COLORING AND MARKINGS: The body is very elongated and laterally very compressed. The basic coloration is silvery: the back is darker and olive green. There is a horizontal line edged with light blue running across the body and ending on the caudal peduncle as a deep black mark which runs into the caudal fin as a dark mark the shape of a swallow's tail. Two luminescent golden dots lie within this mark. There is a short spine below the caudal fin.
Females have no spine below the caudal fin. The underside of the anal fin is straight.
Males are less sturdy than the females. The underside of the anal fin is slightly curved.

GENERAL CARE: A very lively fish which should be kept in a small group of its own kind in a fairly large tank. Plenty of open swimming space should be provided with dense vegetation round the sides. The tank must be securely covered for this species is capable of jumping considerable distances. The composition of the water is not critical: temperature 20°–24°C. Any sort of live animal matter provided it is not too large, as well as dried food will be accepted.

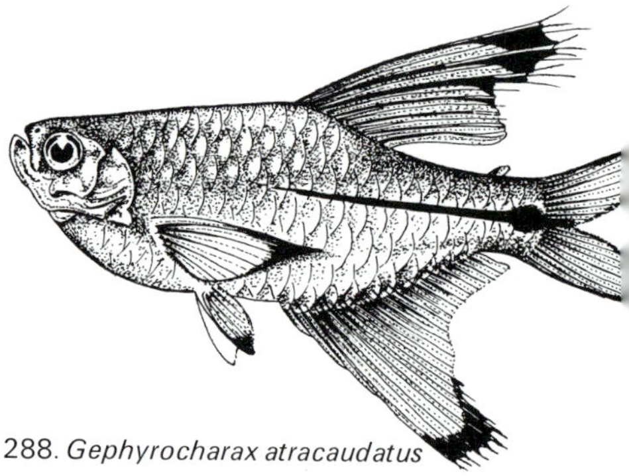

288. *Gephyrocharax atracaudatus*

BREEDING: This species breeds in the same unusual way as *Creagrutus beni.* The fry should be reared in the same way.

THE FAMILY CHARACIDAE

The genus Gymnocorymbus

The genus *Gymnocorymbus* is very widely distributed over a broad zone of central South America. These fish are found in many different kinds of waters but they avoid open water and areas which are unshaded by vegetation on the banks. They seem to prefer the smaller tributaries of jungle rivers, where the flow is very sluggish.

The only species well-known among amateur aquarists is *Gymnocorymbus ternetzi,* which has been known in Europe since 1934. Another species, *Gymnocorymbus thayeria* was described by Carl Eigenmann in 1908 but has proved difficult to keep in captivity. *G.ternetzi* on the other hand makes an ideal aquarium fish and will also breed very easily under normal conditions.

It may be assumed with some certainty that any fish offered for sale in this genus will be *G.ternetzi* and even specimens recently or newly imported are very unlikely to have come from their natural habitat. Almost certainly they will have been bred by local breeders who breed large numbers each year for the aquarium trade.

289. *Gymnocorymbus ternetzi*

GYMNOCORYMBUS TERNETZI

Family: *Characidae*

Genus: *Gymnocorymbus*

English names: Black Tetra, Petticoat fish, Blackamoor

Origin: Virtually the whole of Central America

Size: Approximately 5 cm

Habitat: Found in a wide variety of shaded waters

SHAPE, COLORING AND MARKINGS: The body is deep and laterally very compressed. The back is olive green, the belly white with a marked silvery tinge. Vertical black bands appear on the snout and cross the eye: wider bands are found behind the gill covers and under the dorsal fin. The whole of the posterior half of the body is black: so are the dorsal, adipose and anal fins. The other fins are transparent and almost colorless: the caudal fin has white flecks. Young fish are very attractive but older fish are less so.
Females are usually rather bigger than the males: they have no white flecks on the caudal fin.
Males are as described above.

GENERAL CARE: *G.ternetzi* is suitable for both large and small aquariums provided that a group of at least six is kept. The composition of the water is not critical but fresh tap water should be avoided. A dark or dense background of plants will show up the colors of this species very effectively. A wide range of plants can be used as well as rocks and bogwood. The fish usually keep to the upper and middle reaches of the tank. *G.ternetzi* is very tolerant of other species in the aquarium. Temperature 24°–28°C. Most foods will be accepted though the fish prefer small winged insects such as fruitflies.

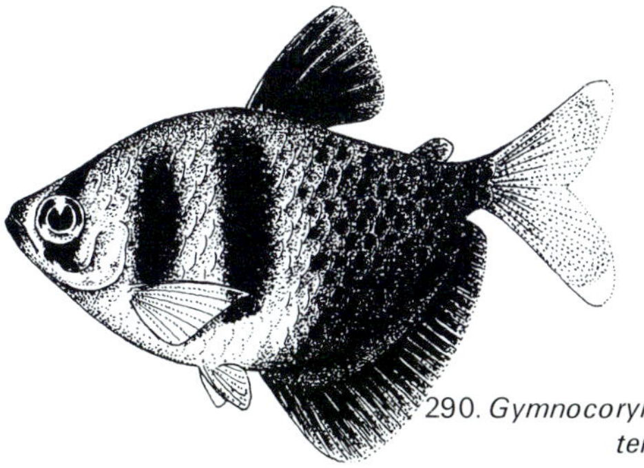
290. *Gymnocorymbus ternetzi*

BREEDING: This is not difficult in a fair-sized breeding tank using moderately hard water. The temperature should be about 30°C. The species is very prolific. The eggs hatch after about 50 hours and then the fry can be raised on the usual foods.

THE FAMILY CHARACIDAE

The genus Hasemania

All known members of the genus *Hasemania* come from southeast Brazil, from the upper reaches of the Rio San Francisco. These tiny fish are usually found in small forest streams heavily shaded by dense vegetation on their banks. The nature of the water in these streams varies greatly according to the season: during the rainy season it becomes very soft, with a DH value of between 0.1° and 1.6° and an acidity of pH 4–4.7. The heavy rainfall washes large quantities of soil into the streams so that the river water, like that of the Amazon basin, becomes dark with humus, as well as rather acid. Outside the rainy season the DH value can rise to 4 or to as much as 6 and the pH value to over 6.5.
These fish therefore live in an environment which is very similar to that of the familiar species *Hyphessobrycon* and *Hemigrammus*, to which in fact they are closely related, and which they closely resemble, except that the *Hasemania* species have no adipose fin.
The guidelines suggested for the care of the *Hyphessobrycon* and *Hemigrammus* species are broadly applicable to these fish. Over the years, only one species *Hasemania marginata*, has become widely known among amateur aquarists. There has been some confusion over the naming of this species. It was defined by Meinken in 1938 but according to Hoedeman, the fish generally known to aquarists as *H.marginata* is in fact identical to the species defined as *H.melanura* in 1911.

HASEMANIA MARGINATA

Family: *Characidae*

Genus: *Hasemania*

English name: none

Origin: Southeast Brazil, the lower reaches of the Rio San Francisco

Size: Approximately 4 cm

Habitat: Found in shallow flooded forest streams

SHAPE, COLORING AND MARKINGS: The body is quite deep, elongated and laterally very compressed. See introductory note for similarities between this species and the *Hyphessobrycon*. The basic coloration is a yellowish-green. There is a silvery overtone to the gill covers and the flanks. The iris is usually blue with a silvery glint. The scales have a fairly dark edge. There is a silvery longitudinal

291. *Hasemania marginata*

stripe starting on the body at the level of the pectoral fin which narrows towards the caudal peduncle. At the root of the caudal fin there is a darker stripe which runs into the central rays. The unpaired fins are a rusty brown with gold-cream borders: the other fins are a pale yellow.

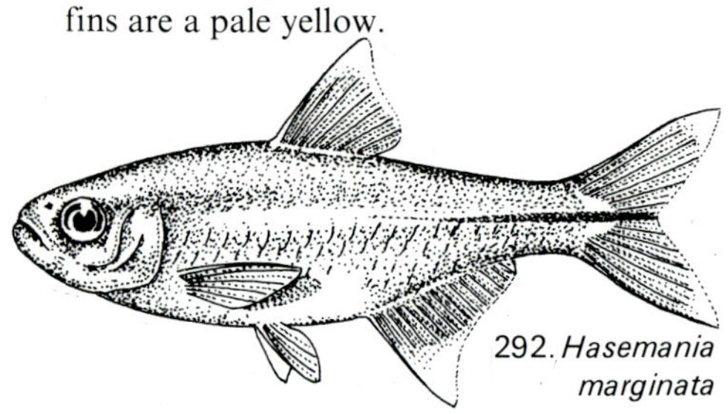

292. *Hasemania marginata*

Females have more thick set bodies and are less vividly colored.
Males are slimmer and have an attractive copper color during the spawning season.

GENERAL CARE: Suitable for both large and small aquariums, provided a group of at least six is kept. The composition of the water is not critical but fresh tap water should not be used. The colors show up best in a tank with a dark bed and yellow tinted water: the tint can be produced by filtering the water through peat. All kinds of plants can be used for the tank, but there should be some with fine leaves. Bogwood can be used for decorating the tank. *H.marginata* will usually remain in the middle and upper reaches of the tank and will associate with other small species. Temperature 22°–25°C. Most food will be accepted, including dried food but surface insects such as small flies, fruitflies and mosquitoes are preferred: Tubifex is less suitable and is usually only accepted with reluctance.

BREEDING: Not too difficult. The fish should be put in a small breeding tank with water of hardness DH 3°–4° and a pH of 6–6.5 at a temperature of 24°–25°C. They will usually breed in the early morning a few days after being put in the tank. The brownish eggs are usually deposited among *Myriophyllum* plants.

THE FAMILY CHARACIDAE

The genus Hemigrammus

The *Hemigrammus* are distributed over the whole of the South American continent with the exception of its southern tip. Most species live in shoals in the sluggish or still waters of jungle streams or swamps. They do not usually occupy waters devoid of vegetation, for many of the species derive a significant proportion of their nourishment from vegetable matter. No external sexual characteristics are usually present. Males and females are identical in color and have identically shaped fins. In some species the males are smaller than the females, but of course this is only apparent in mature fish. The only reliable way of determining sex is to examine the position of the swim bladder.
Almost all species in the *Hemigrammus* genus are suitable fish for the aquarium. The composition of the water is not usually critical. Most species are tolerant of other fish, although there are a few species that are aggressive. Most are small fish that do not require a great deal of food and are not very particular about what they eat: some of the larger species however do have a tendency to eat soft-leaved plants and their diet should be supplemented with lettuce: it is a fallacy to assume that the presence of plenty of algae in the tank will discourage this habit. Algae is very uncommon in their shaded natural habitats and does not appeal to them, moreover the algae to be found in aquariums is usually far less tasty than natural algae and it will be found that even those species of fish that are known algae-eaters will be of little use if put in a tank to clear excessive growth.
The natural vivacity of these fish and their beautiful colors are best displayed in tanks with dark bottoms, or bottoms covered with dense growths of plants. Fresh water should not be used: water filtered through peat can be used. The temperature should be 22°–25°C. It does not matter if the night temperature is slightly lower than the day temperature, provided it does not fall below 22°C. No special plants need be put in the tank but some bunches of fine leaved plants in the corners are advisable. Some species like to hide among such plants from time to time and spawning may well take place above them.
Because these fish are relatively undemanding they have acquired the reputation of being particularly suitable for beginners: as a result many have the misfortune to be kept under the most unsuitable conditions. It should always be remembered that the less delicate fish are as entitled to a reasonable life style as are their more sensitive cousins.
For the smaller species a tank of 30–40 liters capacity is needed. The larger species need a great deal more free swimming space and therefore a tank of 100–150 liters capacity. Care must always be taken to see that the tank does not become too crowded. Because some species live in large shoals in the wild it must not be assumed that they will enjoy living in grossly overcrowded aquarium tanks.
The *Hemigrammus* will feed on practically any small land insect such as may be found in their natural habitat: they will eat in the aquarium Daphnia, Cyclops, mosquito larvae and Grindal worms. Tubifex will be accepted with less enthusiasm. Good dry foods will be eaten but cannot of course be made their staple diet. Vegetable matter such as lettuce should always be included: purée of spinach is often recommended but is in fact to be avoided: it breaks up in the water and will cloud the tank or create more serious troubles as it decays.
Smaller tanks are best used for breeding. The eggs are usually discharged above or among fine leaved plants or between the roots of floating plants. Tank ornaments such as whorled or knotted bogwood, ferns or even long fibres of peat matting lining the bottom are also good spawning media – the last is particularly good. It is easy to sterilise by boiling and rinsing and can then be used again: in soft water it improves the acidity and eggs laid over it sink down out of the reach of the mature fish. In itself it also provides a good dark bottom.

293. *Hemigrammus armstrongi*

Breeding tanks should be placed so that the morning sun shines into them: on the other hand they should be shaded from the sun as soon as spawning has occurred.
The mating pair should be introduced into the tank during an afternoon: spawning will then usually occur the next morning. The mating behavior is vigorous and both male and female may take the initiative in turn. Some species produce adhesive eggs, in other cases the eggs fall immediately to the bottom of the tank. Most species are notorious egg-eaters and the breeding pair should be removed from the tank as soon as the eggs have been laid. Most but not all light should also then be excluded from the tank by putting newspaper or a similar protection round it: if all light is excluded the young fish will subsequently be very shy for a long time, and this in turn may affect their breeding potential.
The eggs hatch after 24 to 36 hours at 24°C. The fry will hang from the plants or on the sides of the tank like fine splinters of glass. The tank should still be shaded from the light and the shading only removed gradually over the course of a week. Feeding should begin as soon as the fry begin to swim freely. At first they should be fed on infusoria: after two or three days they can be given newly hatched brine shrimps. Provided the water is regularly changed the fry will grow rapidly during the first few weeks. Fresh tap water can be used provided it is not harder than 12° DH. The changes of water must not be too abrupt: the fry must have a chance to acclimatise themselves. After four to six weeks the fry can be transferred to larger tanks.

HEMIGRAMMUS ARMSTRONGI

Family: *Characidae*

Genus: *Hemigrammus*

English name: Golden Tetra

Origin: Guyana

Size: Approximately 4.5 cm

Habitat: Found in overgrown or very shady jungle rivulets, and swamps linked with running waters

SHAPE, COLORING AND MARKINGS: The body is fairly deep and elongated: laterally it is very compressed. Imported specimens have an attractive golden sheen over the whole body and there are some particularly attractive specimens with iridescent areas on the head and at the base of the caudal fin. A dark longitudinal line runs along the body from roughly the level of the first dorsal fin ray into the base of the caudal fin where it becomes a lozenge-shaped patch. The caudal fin is usually tinted with red. The other fins are transparent and colorless.
Females are rather more robust and have a less intense golden sheen.
Males are as described above but slimmer.

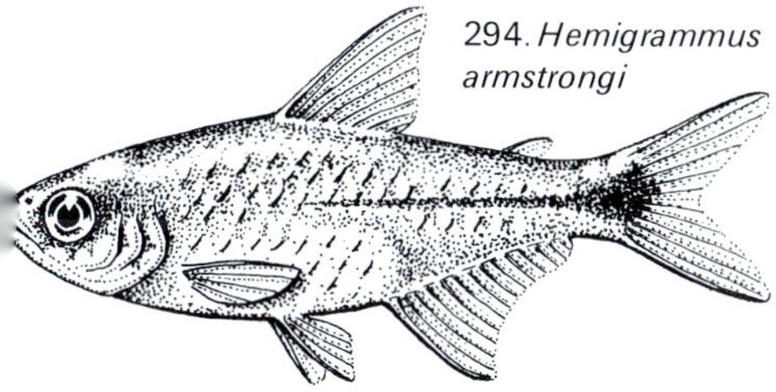

294. *Hemigrammus armstrongi*

295. *Hemigrammus caudovittatus*

GENERAL CARE: *H.armstrongi* is suitable for all sizes of aquarium provided a group of six or more is kept. The composition of the water is not critical but fresh tap water should be avoided. A dark background and yellow-tinted water will show off to best advantage the colors of these fish and the water may be filtered through peat to achieve the required shade. All kinds of plants may be used, but they should certainly include some with fine leaves. Bogwood will make attractive tank decoration. *H.armstrongi* will usually remain in the lower and middle reaches of the tank. Temperature 22°–25°C. It is a tolerant fish that will associate with other small species. Almost all food will be accepted: winged surface insects will be much appreciated, Tubifex will only be eaten with some reluctance.

BREEDING: This is not difficult. The water should be soft and a little acid. (4°–6° DH, pH 6–6.5). Unfortunately the golden sheen found on imported specimens generally disappears after the first generation bred in captivity: the dominant color then becomes silvery and the red tints to the fins are stronger.

ADDITIONAL INFORMATION: This species is often confused with *Hyphessobrycon eos*.

HEMIGRAMMUS CAUDOVITTATUS

Family: *Characidae*

Genus: *Hemigrammus*

English name: Buenos Aires Tetra

Origin: The basin of the river Plate

Size: Approximately 7 cm

Habitat: Found in many different kinds of waters

SHAPE, COLORING AND MARKINGS: The body is fairly deep, elongated and laterally very compressed. The basic coloration is a brownish-yellow. The back is a pale green or brown: The flanks have a metallic iridescence. A narrow silvery blue-black stripe runs along the body from the level of the first dorsal fin rays: it broadens out considerably before the base of the caudal fin and then narrows again to form a lozenge-shaped pattern, bordered above and below by a paler area. Under certain lighting an ill-defined patch may be seen on the shoulders. The upper half of the iris is an attractive shade of red. The dorsal and caudal fins are yellowish with red overtones at the base. The anal fin is a bright terracotta.
Females when seen from above have more rounded and fuller bodies: the fins are rather colorless and if they have any tint at all it is red.
Males are slimmer and otherwise as described above.

GENERAL CARE: *H.caudovittatus* is only suitable for larger aquariums, furnished as for *H.armstrongi.* Temperature 22°–26°C. *H.caudovittatus* has a tendency to nibble at plants and lettuce should be included in its diet.

BREEDING: Not difficult: see Introductory note. A very prolific species.

ADDITIONAL INFORMATION: A widely domesticated species. Its tolerance of low temperatures makes it possible to keep this species in unheated aquariums in the home.

HEMIGRAMMUS ERYTHROZONUS

Family: *Characidae*
Genus: *Hemigrammus*
English name: Glowlight Tetra
Origin: Guyana
Size: Approximately 4.5 cm
Habitat: Found in shady jungle rivulets and swamps

SHAPE, COLORING AND MARKINGS: The body is fairly deep, elongated and laterally very compressed. In shape *H.erythrozonus* closely resembles *Cheirodon innesi.* The basic coloration is a grey-green. A wide pale red longitudinal stripe runs back from the margin of the gill covers to the base of the caudal fin, where it merges with a patch of the same color. When this red iridescent stripe is viewed under bright light it can be seen to be bordered above by a line of gleaming gold. The anterior rays of the dorsal and anal fins, and sometimes of the ventral fins as well, are an attractive shade of red. The tips of the dorsal and anal fins are yellowish-white. The remaining fins are transparent. The upper part of the iris is red.
Females are a little larger and rather more laterally compressed.
Males are much slimmer, the belly is flatter.

GENERAL CARE: As for *H.armstrongi.*

BREEDING: Not too difficult for the experienced amateur. A small nursery tank of about five liters capacity is needed. The water should be soft and mildly acid (2°–3° DH, pH 6.5). Temperature 28°C. Spawning will occur after about 24 hours. The fry should be well fed on *Cyclops nauplii.* The water must be changed regularly.

ADDITIONAL INFORMATION: For years this species was second only to the Neon Tetra *(Cheirodon innesi)* in popularity among fish of this kind: now both species are seen much less frequently.

HEMIGRAMMUS HYANUARI

Family: *Characidae*
Genus: *Hemigrammus*
English name: none
Origin: Lake Hyanuary in the Amazon basin
Size: Maximum 5 cm
Habitat: Found only in this particular locality

SHAPE, COLORING AND MARKINGS: The body is fairly deep, elongated and laterally very compressed. The basic coloration is a dark golden brown, with darker areas on the back and the flanks. A distinct golden line runs from the back of the gill covers to the caudal peduncle. All the fins have a distinct and sometimes deep blue tinge, and the base of the caudal fin is very dark.
Females are noticeably larger, with deeper and fuller bodies.
Males are as described above.

296. *Hemigrammus erythrozonus*

297. *Hemigrammus marginatus*

GENERAL CARE: Suitable for all sizes of aquariums provided a group of at least six are kept together. Tank as for *H.armstrongi,* although *H.hyanuari* will normally keep to the upper and middle reaches of the tank. Temperature

298. *Hemigrammus caudovittatus*

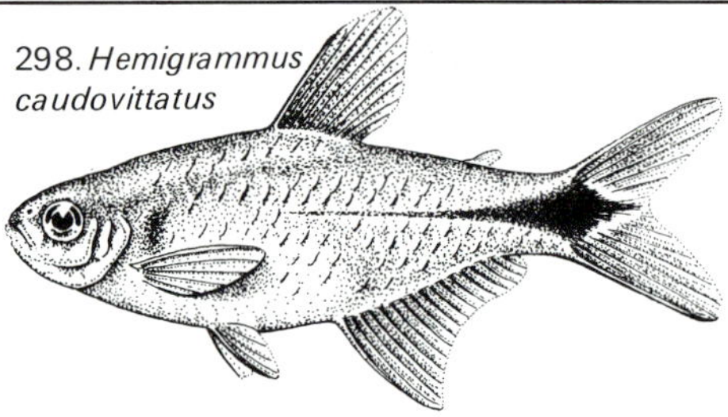

299. *Hemigrammus erythrozonus*

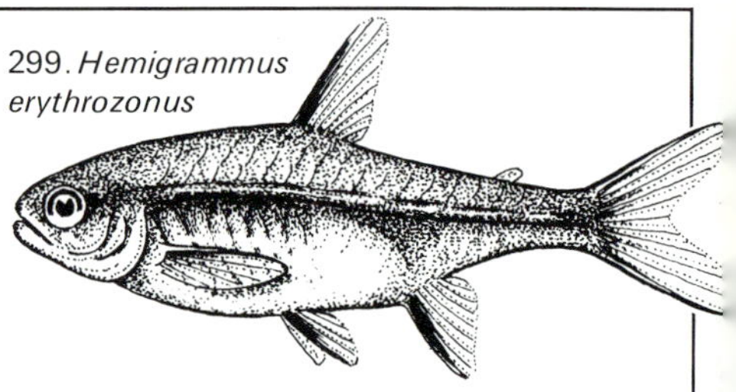

300. *Hemigrammus marginatus*

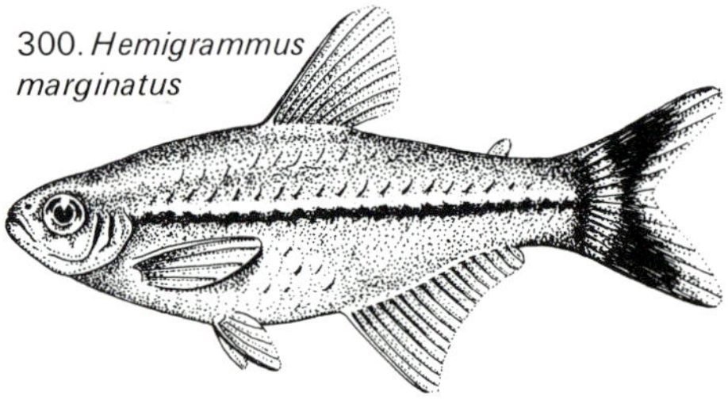

301. *Hemigrammus ocellifer falsus*

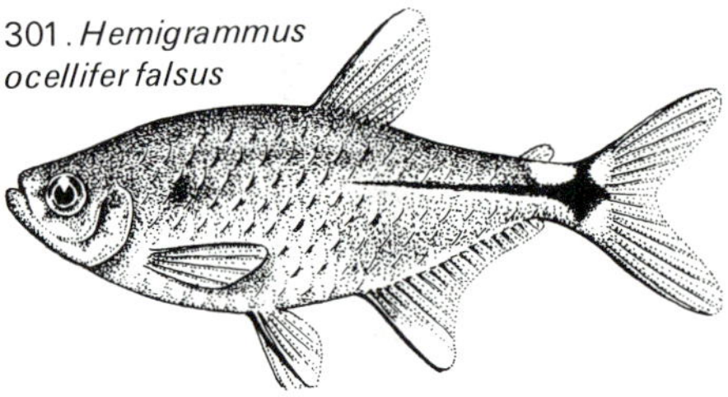

24°C. This species requires medium hard water and much appreciates the regular change of part of it. Lettuce should form part of the diet, as well as the normal foods for this genus.

BREEDING: Not too difficult: see Introductory note.

HEMIGRAMMUS MARGINATUS

Family: *Characidae*

Genus: *Hemigrammus*

English name: none

Origin: Brazil and Venezuela

Size: Approximately 8 cm

Habitat: Found in many different kinds of waters

SHAPE, COLORING AND MARKINGS: The body is fairly deep, elongated and laterally very compressed. The basic coloration is a greyish-green with violet overtones. The back is olive-green: the belly whitish. A very dark, almost black longitudinal line runs from the edge of the gill covers to the base of the caudal fin: it is bordered by a zone of white above. The dorsal and anal fins are yellow-green with cream spots. The base of the caudal fin is marked with a crescent-shaped area of black: the fin itself is a lemon yellow, with a wide dark transverse band. The upper part of the iris is a golden yellow.

Females have yellow anal fins and the same color at the base of the dorsal fin.

Males are as described above.

GENERAL CARE: As for *H.caudovittatus* but temperature 25°–27°C.

BREEDING: Very little information is available. Only a few chance matings in very large aquariums are recorded.

ADDITIONAL INFORMATION: A species that does not seem to have been imported since 1939: previously it was imported from Lake Valencia and the immediate vicinity, in Venezuela.

HEMIGRAMMUS OCELLIFER FALSUS

Family: *Characidae*

Genus: *Hemigrammus*

English name: Beacon fish

Origin: The basin of the Amazon

Size: Approximately 4 cm

Habitat: Very widely distributed in many different kinds of waters

SHAPE, COLORING AND MARKINGS: The body is quite deep and laterally very compressed. The basic coloration is brownish to yellowish-green: the back is a little darker. The belly is yellow to white. A thin dark longitudinal stripe starts at the level of the posterior rays of the dorsal fin: it broadens out at the caudal peduncle to form a lozenge-shaped patch on the tail. There are also iridescent gold patches in the area beneath the adipose fin and at the base of the caudal fin. A indistinct spot may be visible on the shoulders under certain lights. The fins are transparent and colorless: some ice-blue spots lie on the dorsal and anal fins. The upper half of the iris is red, the lower half gold.

Females have rather deeper and larger bodies.

Males are thinner and otherwise as described above.

GENERAL CARE: As for *H.armstrongi*.

BREEDING: Not too difficult. See Introductory note. This species is very prolific.

ADDITIONAL INFORMATION: This species was first described in 1911 and named as *H.ocellifer*. Another closely related species was found in 1958, the most striking feature of which is the very prominent shoulder patch. This has now been adopted as the genuine *H.ocellifer* and this present species renamed *H.ocellifer falsus*.

303. *Hemigrammus ocellifer ocellifer*

HEMIGRAMMUS OCELLIFER OCELLIFER

Family: *Characidae*

Genus: *Hemigrammus*

English name: Beacon fish

Origin: Northern South America, including the lower reaches of the Amazon

Size: Approximately 4 cm

Habitat: Found in a wide variety of waters

SHAPE, COLORING AND MARKINGS: The body is fairly deep and laterally very compressed. The basic coloration is brown or yellow-green. The back is a good deal darker and the belly yellow. A narrow and not particularly prominent longitudinal stripe starts at the level of the pectoral fin and ends in a lozenge-shaped blue black patch. Another very distinct blue-black patch lies behind the gill covers enclosed within a golden border: this is most prominent towards the rear. The outer sections of both caudal fins are an attractive wine-red color with cream spots. The dorsal and anal fins have white spots. The upper part of the iris is red: the lower part gold.

Females have rather deeper and sometimes larger bodies.

Males are slimmer and otherwise as described above.

GENERAL CARE: As for *H.armstrongi*.

BREEDING: Not difficult. See Introductory note. This is a very prolific species.

ADDITIONAL INFORMATION: See under *H. ocellifer falsus* for the relationship between that species and *H.ocellifer ocellifer*.

304. *Hemigrammus pulcher*

HEMIGRAMMUS PULCHER

Family: *Characidae*

Genus: *Hemigrammus*

English name: Pretty Tetra, Black Wedge Tetra

Origin: The lower reaches of the Amazon

Size: Approximately 6 cm

Habitat: No further details are available of its natural habitat

SHAPE, COLORING AND MARKINGS: The body is deep, almost elliptical and laterally very compressed. The basic coloration varies significantly according to the lighting in the aquarium. The back is brown or light green, the posterior fins bright green to grey. The belly is yellow or white: the head is a deeper green, which becomes even deeper towards the snout. The upper iris is purple to red: the lower iris blue-green. There is a golden iridescence on the throat and gill covers: an additional golden-red iridescent patch lies behind. Another very prominent zone of the same color surrounds a cone-shaped blue black patch on the base of the caudal fin. The unpaired fins are a beautiful copper color: the other fins are colorless and transparent.
Females are deeper and larger in the body.
Males are slimmer and otherwise as described above.

GENERAL CARE: As for *H.armstrongi* but temperature 24°–25° C.

BREEDING: Not too difficult. See Introductory note. It is sometimes difficult to establish a breeding pair, but once the two fish are used to each other they usually stay together.

ADDITIONAL INFORMATION: First described in 1938, this species first became known to aquarists in 1945.

305. *Hemigrammus rhodostomus*

HEMIGRAMMUS RHODOSTOMUS

Family: *Characidae*

Genus: *Hemigrammus*

English name: Red-nosed Tetra

Origin: The lower reaches of the Amazon and the area around Para.

Size: Approximately 4 cm

Habitat: No further details are available of its natural habitat

SHAPE, COLORING AND MARKINGS: The body is very slim and laterally somewhat compressed. The basic coloration varies according to the lighting in the aquarium. The back is brown to olive green: the flanks are off-white to pale green: the belly paler. A thin dark longitudinal line starts at the anterior rays of the dorsal fin, broadens out at the root of the tail and then runs on into the central rays of the caudal fin. Above this lies a narrow border of green iridescence which becomes a patch of gold at the caudal fin. The snout and eyes are a very attractive shade of red and sometimes the whole head is this color. The fins are colorless or pale green. The lobes of the caudal fin bear large patches of black: the base of the fin is yellow.
Females are more robust.
Males are very much slimmer.

GENERAL CARE: As for *H.armstrongi* but temperature 23°–25° C.

BREEDING: As for *H.pulcher*.

ADDITIONAL INFORMATION: This is an unusually shy species and sensitive to changes in the composition of the water.

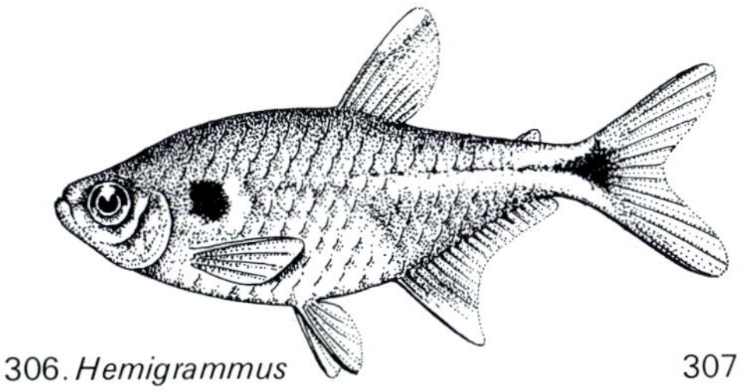

306. *Hemigrammus ocellifer ocellifer*

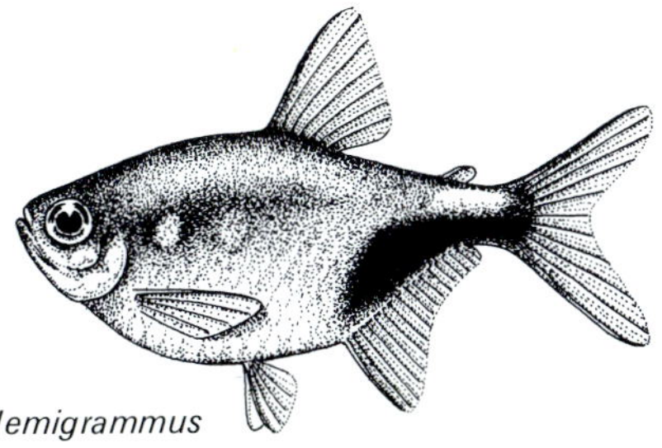

307. *Hemigrammus pulcher*

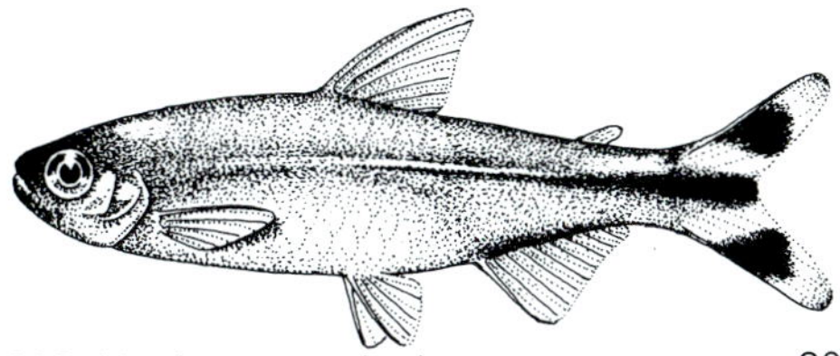

308. *Hemigrammus rhodostomus*

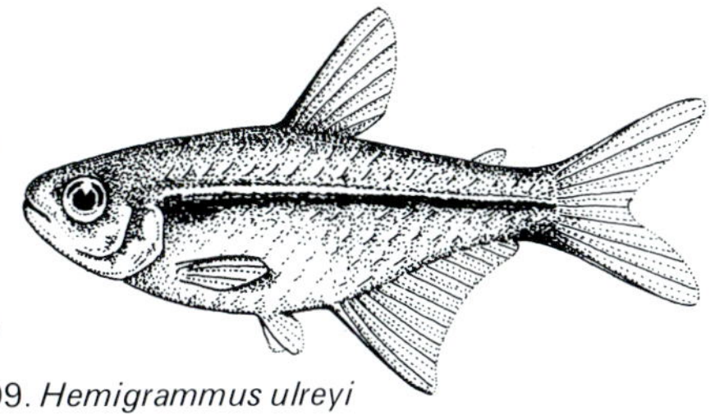

309. *Hemigrammus ulreyi*

HEMIGRAMMUS ULREYI

Family: *Characidae*

Genus: *Hemigrammus*

English name: Ulrey's Tetra

Origin: The Mato Grosso and the basin of the Paraguay river

Size: Approximately 5 cm

Habitat: No further details are available of its natural habitat

Shape, coloring and markings: The body is fairly deep and laterally very compressed. The basic coloration is between a greyish and brownish-green: the back is hardly any darker. The flanks and belly are colorless, or silvery and iridescent under bright lighting. The whole fish is more or less transparent. There is an indistinct shoulder mark behind the gill covers which may be almost invisible in some specimens. A tricolored horizontal line runs from this mark to the base of the caudal fin. The bottom is black, above there is a narrower whitish-green iridescent line, above that is a line of luminescent red.
The dorsal fin is yellowish, with a dark edge at the front. All the other fins are more or less yellowish.
Females have a stockier body. The adipose fin is a light orange.
Males are clearly more slender and often slightly smaller. The adipose fin is a striking red.

General care: As for *H.armstrongi.*

Breeding: Nothing seems to be known about the reproductive behavior of this species.

Additional information: *H.ulreyi* is very rarely imported and largely unknown among aquarists. At first sight it closely resembles the darker and more slender *Hyphessobrycon heterorhabdus.*
It should be noted that the *Hemigrammus ulreyi* is sensitive to changes in the water. The greatest care should be taken when transferring it from one tank to another.
Specimens obtained commercially should be kept in quarantine for a few weeks, as they usually have been imported.

310. *Hemigrammus ulreyi*

THE FAMILY CHARACIDAE

The genus Hydrocinus

There are only two species in this genus, *Hydrocinus cuvieri* and *Hydrocinus maculatus.* Very little is known about the life of these fish in the wild, but they are certainly closely related to species in the genus Luciocharax.
They are very shy fish but nevertheless, predatory and most be kept under rather special conditions.

The species in both genera share the characteristically elongated snout which is so delicate that it is difficult for these fish to be imported without suffering mortal injury to that sensitive organ. They are accordingly rare in captivity: in any case their behaviour patterns make them unsuitable for the domestic aquarium, but they are nonetheless interesting fish to study under the right conditions.

HYDROCINUS CUVIERI

Family: *Characidae*

Genus: *Hydrocinus*

English name: none

Origin: South America, probably the Amazon basin

Size: Approximately 60 cm

Habitat: No details are available of its natural habitat

Shape, coloring and markings: The body is very slender and only slightly compressed laterally. The head is long, the jaws like a beak and the mouth spoon-shaped. *H.cuvieri* closely resembles *Luciocharax insculptus* but it can be distinguished from that related species by its unbroken lateral line, its button-ended snout and by the position of the dorsal fin, which in *H.cuvieri* lies slightly nearer to the front of the body. The basic coloration is a pale green or white. The back is noticeably darker, greenish-yellow with a black tinge. A dark, wide stripe runs below the lateral line from the back edge of the gill covers to the lower half of the base of the caudal fin. This stripe is often broken, and is not always distinct. There is a dark round patch with a lighter edge in the center of the base of the caudal fin: the gill covers also have a triangular dark patch. The upper jaw is completely black: the lower jaw is dark at the point and along the line of the mouth. The caudal fin is predominantly black, the lobes are fawn. The other fins, except for the pectoral fins,

are colorless, transparent and have dark stripes.
There are no known external sexual characteristics.

GENERAL CARE: This species is a predator: that and its large size make it unsuitable for an aquarium in the home. These are however interesting fish to study in large public aquariums, where they can be kept with other large fish. A timid fish, the tank must have adequate hiding places where *H.cuvieri* can lie in wait for its prey. The composition of the water is not critical but fresh tap water should not be used. Temperature 22°–24°C. Its diet should really be live fish and this very greedy species can devour other fish of its own length.

BREEDING: This species has not as yet been bred successfully in captivity.

ADDITIONAL INFORMATION: This species, so much like a pike, is rarely imported and almost unknown among aquarists even though it was first described by Jean Louis Agassiz in 1829.

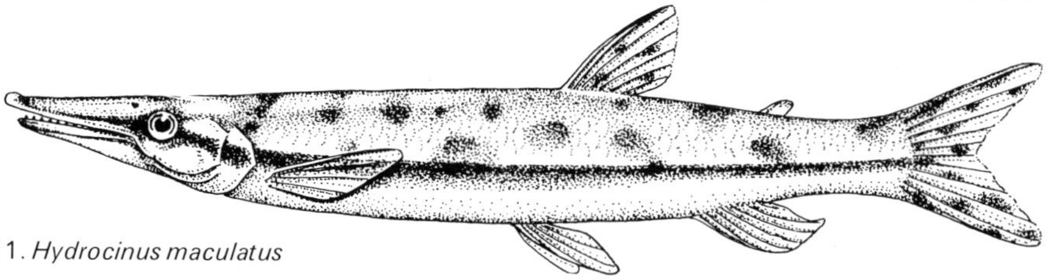
311. *Hydrocinus maculatus*

HYDROCINUS MACULATUS

Family: *Characidae*

Genus: *Hydrocinus*

English name: none

Origin: South America, probably the area around the Amazon

Size: Approximately 35 cm

Habitat: No details are available of its natural habitat

SHAPE, COLORING AND MARKINGS: The body is very slender and laterally only slightly compressed. The head is long, the jaws beak-shaped and the mouth spoon-shaped. *H.maculatus* closely resembles *H.cuvieri* although the markings are quite different and the former is much smaller than the latter. The basic coloration is a pale yellow-brown: the back is noticeably darker: the lower half of the body is yellow to white. A very dark unbroken horizontal line runs from the eye to the base of the caudal fin, and shows up strongly against the almost white background. There are many irregular dark marks, of different sizes, lying on the body above this line. The caudal peduncle is tinged with red. The unpaired fins are yellowish with a dark base and brown flecks.
There are no known external sexual characteristics.

GENERAL CARE: As for *H.cuvieri*. The diet should consist of live fish and the larger aquatic insects: if this diet is unobtainable, *H.maculatus* can be persuaded to eat lean horsemeat. Occasionally it will eat dried food and porridge oats soaked in water.

BREEDING: This species has not as yet been bred in captivity.

312. *Hydrocinus cuvieri*
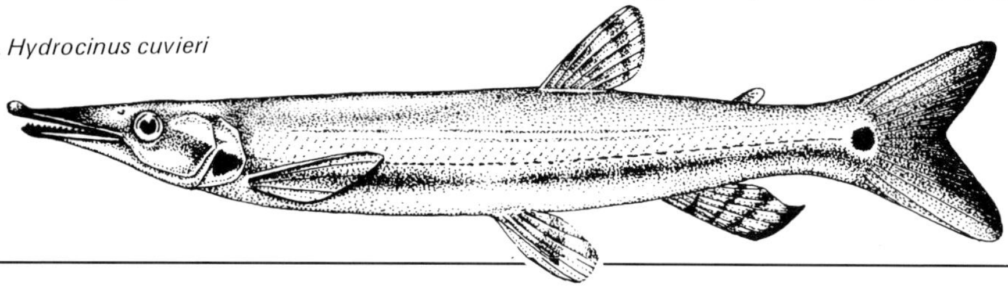

THE FAMILY CHARACIDAE

The genus Hyphessobrycon

The genus *Hyphessobrycon* is distributed over the whole of the South American continent except in the far south: several species are also found in Central America and as far north as Texas. Most species are very active and live in large shoals in the same waters as other species of fish. They are to be found in both still and flowing waters, in swamps and in sluggish jungle streams. They prefer peaty water, low in calcium and will certainly seek out this kind of water during the mating season. That season tends to coincide with the annual rainy season in their natural surroundings, when the rains wash a great deal of soil into the streams. Their food consists mainly of small water insects, although land insects that fall onto the water surface will also be eaten.
Fish in this genus have as a rule fairly slim bodies which are quite deep and laterally somewhat compressed. There is a general impression given of squareness, which is emphasised by the erect dorsal fin and well-developed anal fins. It is this square shape that gives rise to the name of the sub-family *Tetragonopterinae,* in which these species are placed, with other genera such as *Astyanax, Gymnocorymbus* and *Hemigrammus.*
It is not always possible to distinguish the sexes by their external characteristics. Generally adult males are slimmer than adult females but of course this test cannot be applied to young specimens. In some species, such as *H.erythrostigma H.ornatus* and *H.rosaceus,* the males have rather longer dorsal fins than the females. The only sure test is to examine the shape and position of the swim bladder, in the way described in the Introductory note for the genus *Cheirodon.*
The majority of *Hyphessobrycon* species are undemanding and accordingly, like their near relatives in the genus *Hemigrammus,* they often suffer from being kept in totally unsuitable conditions. That they are less delicate than some aquarium fish is no reason for their being kept in unsatisfactory conditions and of course they lose much of their natural vivacity and do not show off their beautiful colors to advantage unless they are looked after properly.
The smaller species need tanks with a minimum capacity of 30–40 liters: the larger ones need more space, and tanks of 100–150 liters capacity. All kinds of different plants may be put in the aquarium, provided adequate free swimming space is left between the thick clumps of vegetation. This is particularly important for those species, such as *H.ornatus* and *H.rosaceus* that have well-developed fin structures. A dark base should be provided in the tank: this makes the fish feel more at home in their surroundings and also serves to show off their extremely attractive colors. The composition of the water is less critical than used to be believed, particularly if the aquarist

is not concerned with breeding these fish. Old aquarium water, perhaps filtered through peat will normally be satisfactory. Fresh tap water should however never be used. These species should never be subjected to abrupt changes of water. Many species are very susceptible to shock which can lead to disease and thus great care must be taken to ensure that the fish are gradually acclimatised to changes, as for example when they are moved from one tank to another. It is not enough merely to ensure that the temperature of the new water is the same as that in which the fish have hitherto been kept.

Most species need a day temperature of 22°–25°C. At night most will accept a drop to 20°C: for some species such a drop is even to be recommended. It should be remembered that similar significant changes in temperature occur in the natural habitats of these fish.

The diet can be almost all kinds of small animal matter: mosquito larvae, Cyclops, Daphnia and surface insects such as fruitflies: Tubifex is not so suitable. Most species will accept dried food and dried mosquito larvae and Artemia are particularly good if fresh insect food is not available. Only a few of these species have the reputation of nibbling at the plants in the aquarium.

The smaller species can be bred in plastic trays with a capacity of about 6 liters: for the larger species breeding tanks with a capacity of 20–30 liters will be needed. The eggs will be laid in clumps of thick vegetation, such as *Myriophyllum, Fontinalis* or *Nitella* and such plants ought be put in the breeding tanks: alternatively, a peat bottom, as described in the Introductory note on the *Hemigrammus* can be used and will give excellent results.

313. *Hyphessobrycon callistus callistus*

HYPHESSOBRYCON BENTOSI

Family: *Characidae*

Genus: *Hyphessobrycon*

English name: Bentos Tetra

Origin: The lower reaches of the Amazon, in the neighborhood of Bentos

Size: Maximum 6 cm

Habitat: Found in marshes, still and sluggish jungle creeks and larger streams

SHAPE, COLORING AND MARKINGS: The body is fairly deep and laterally very compressed. The basic coloration is pale ochre. Characteristic features of this species are a barely visible brownish-black shoulder mark, and an equally indistinct narrow horizontal line. The dorsal fin has a large black mark: its first fin rays and points are white.

There are no known external sexual characteristics.

GENERAL CARE: *H.bentosi* is only suitable for larger aquariums. A social fish, it should be kept in a fairly large group of its own kind. The tank should have a dark bed, slightly acid water, dense vegetation round the sides and plenty of free swimming space in the center. This species will stay in the lower and middle reaches of the tank. Temperature 22°–26°C. All kinds of live animal matter will be acceptable as food: *H.bentosi* likes to snap up mosquito larves, fruitflies and other winged insects from the surface.

BREEDING: Nothing is known about the reproductive behavior of this fish, but it is likely to be similar to that of related species.

ADDITIONAL INFORMATION: Although this species was first described in 1908, there do not appear to have been any later definitive descriptions of it derived from living specimens. Accordingly, the color patterns now accepted may not be correct. One authority believes this alleged species to be merely a transitional stage in the development of *Hyphessobrycon rosaceus*.

314. *Hyphessobrycon bentosi*

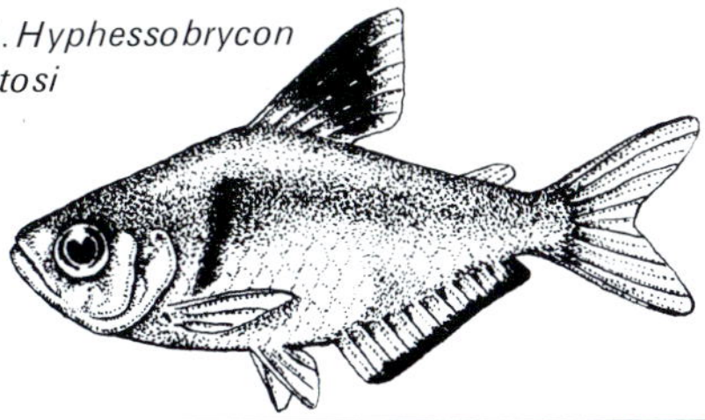

HYPHESSOBRYCON CALLISTUS CALLISTUS

Family: *Characidae*

Genus: *Hyphessobrycon*

English name: none

Origin: Paraguay and the area around the Mato Grosso

Size: Maximum 4 cm

Habitat: Found in streams, jungle rivulets and the less turbulent waters of larger rivers

SHAPE, COLORING AND MARKINGS: The body is rather deep and laterally very compressed. The basic coloration is a light red, becoming more yellow or orange towards the belly. The head and gill covers are bright red: the back is darker. The eyes are an iridescent red. There is a very striking semicircular or sickle-shaped patch on the shoulders behind the gill covers: this may lose some of its intensity when the fish matures. The colors are much more vivid when this fish is kept in the right kind of tank. The dorsal fin is generally a deep black, and white at its base and tips. The anal fin is blood red with a black border which becomes wider at the back: The ventral and caudal fins are bright red: the pectoral fin has a pale red gleam.

Females when sexually mature have more rounded bellies.

Males may have elongated dorsal fins.

GENERAL CARE: *H.callistus callistus* is suitable for all sizes of aquariums, provided a group of at least six is kept. A very social fish. The tank should furnished as for *H.bentosi*: the water should be slightly acid. Temperature 22°–24°C. *H.callistus callistus* will remain mainly in the middle and upper reaches of the tank. Diet as for *H.bentosi*.

BREEDING: This is not easy. The water must be mildly acid (pH 6–6.8) and no harder than 4°–6° DH. Temperature 24°–26° C.

ADDITIONAL INFORMATION: Some authorities maintain that *H.callistus callistus, H.bentosi, H.minor* and *H.rosaceus* should not be regarded as separate species but that the last three should be regarded as sub-species of the first: this proposed re-classification has not however as yet been adopted.

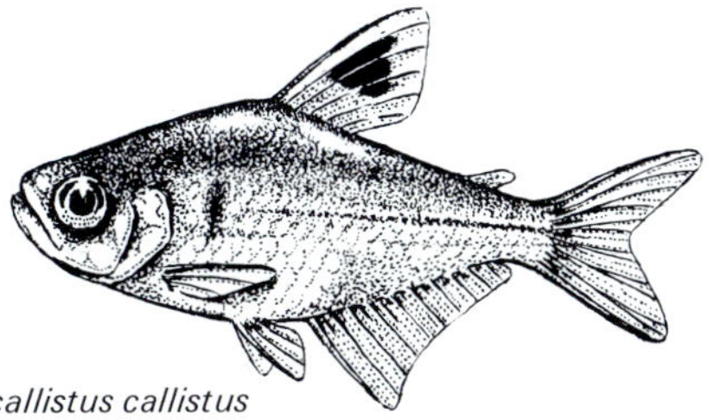

315. *Hyphessobrycon callistus callistus*

HYPHESSOBRYCON EOS

Family: *Characidae*
Genus: *Hyphessobrycon*
English name: Dawn Tetra
Origin: Guyana
Size: Approximately 4.5 cm
Habitat: Found in still and sluggish waters

SHAPE, COLORING AND MARKINGS: The body is fairly deep and laterally very compressed. The basic coloration is a brown to olive green: the back is darker, with black-edged scales. There is a scarcely perceptible patch on the shoulders behind the gill covers, and a narrow, practically invisible longitudinal stripe along the body. Darker spots are scattered over the whole body and are particularly dense on the cheeks. The area of the throat is orange to yellow. The base of the dorsal fin is yellowish: the caudal fin is a bright yellow with an orange-red gleam, particularly prominent on the lower lobe. The base of the anal fin is reddish. The remaining fins are colorless and transparent.
There are no known external sexual characteristics.

GENERAL CARE: As for *H.callistus callistus* but the plants in the tank should include *Myriophyllum*. The composition of the water is not critical.

BREEDING: This species has not as yet been bred in captivity.

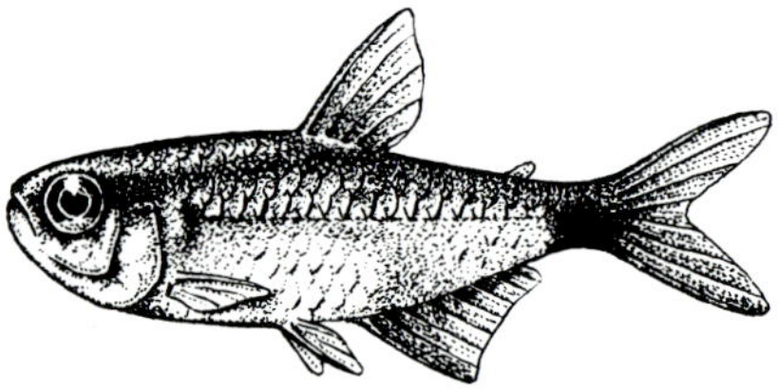

316. *Hyphessobrycon eos*

HYPHESSOBRYCON ERYTHROSTIGMA

Family: *Characidae*
Genus: *Hyphessobrycon*
English name: Bleeding Heart Tetra
Origin: Colombia
Size: Maximum 8 cm
Habitat: No further details are available of its natural habitat

SHAPE, COLORING AND MARKINGS: The body is rather deep and laterally very compressed. The basic coloration is a light yellow: the back is olive-green to brown, with pale red overtones. The lower part of the body is red with a silvery gleam: the throat and belly have a

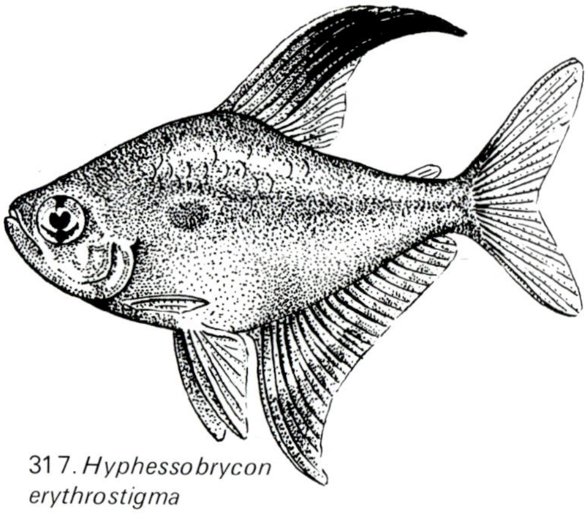

317. *Hyphessobrycon erythrostigma*

more orangey or yellowish tint. Above the ventral fin, level with the eye, there is a very prominent red spot, bordered by an iridescent area of white. The dorsal fin is well-developed, with a black patch behind a white ray. The base of the anal fin is white, becoming dark grey or black towards the front, and more reddish towards the tail. The other fins are colorless and transparent.
Females are smaller with less vivid colors.
Males are as described above and have a crescent-shaped elongation of the dorsal and anal fins.

GENERAL CARE: As for *H.bentosi* but temperature 23°–27°C.

BREEDING: This is difficult and few successful attempts are recorded.

HYPHESSOBRYCON FLAMMEUS

Family: *Characidae*
Genus: *Hyphessobrycon*
English name: Flame Tetra
Origin: Brazil, around Rio de Janeiro
Size: Approximately 4.5 cm
Habitat: Found in still and sluggish waters and swamps

SHAPE, COLORING AND MARKINGS: The body is rather deep and laterally very compressed. The basic coloration is a brassy yellow: the back is olive-green: the belly paler. The back half of the body is an iridescent red. There are tapering marks on the shoulders and a narrow longitudinal stripe which may only be visible in good light. All the fins, except for the pectoral fin, are an attractive red. The leading edge of the dorsal fin is cream, and the anal fin has a black border.

318. *Hyphessobrycon flammeus*

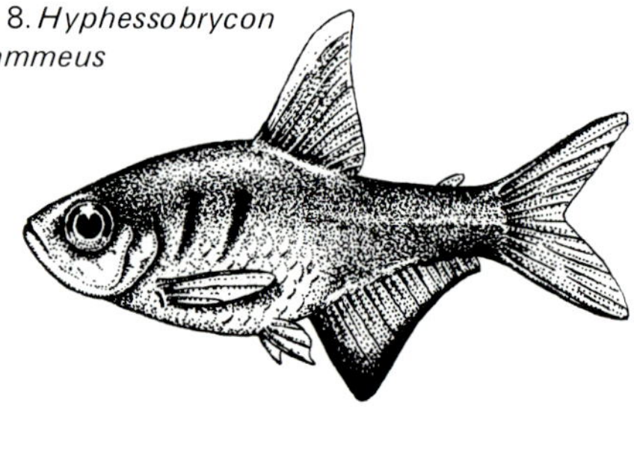

Females have no black border to the anal fin and the ventral and anal fins are a pale red. Males are as described above and the ventral and anal fins are scarlet.

GENERAL CARE: As for *H.eos* but temperature 22°–26°C.

BREEDING: This is not difficult. *H.flammeus* is a very prolific species. Moderately hard water should be used.

ADDITIONAL INFORMATION: A very easy species to keep, and one which continues to look interesting after many years. A very social fish, particularly when young. Older specimens may become somewhat intolerant and the females can become particularly pugnacious. The bigger the group, the less likely is this to happen.

319. *Hyphessobrycon flammeus*

320. *Hyphessobrycon griemi*

HYPHESSOBRYCON GRIEMI

Family: *Characidae*
Genus: *Hyphessobrycon*
English name: Griem's Tetra
Origin: Brazil, around Goiás
Size: Approximately 3 cm
Habitat: Found in still and sluggish jungle waters and swamps

SHAPE, COLORING AND MARKINGS: The body is quite deep and laterally very compressed. The basic coloration is a translucent fawn with a hint of dull green: the back is a matt green and the belly off-white to yellow. There are two patches on the shoulders, the first is

321. *Hyphessobrycon erythrostigma*

often broken up and the second contains a splash of gold. The dorsal fin is reddish, with cream anterior rays backed by others that are darker. The anal fin is also reddish, with the tip and anterior rays cream, in contrast to a much darker zone above. The caudal fin is also red: the remaining fins are transparent and colorless. A copper glow suffuses the whole body when the fish is excited.
Females have a less pronounced dark area on the anal fin.
Males have a very pronounced dark area on the anal fin.

General care: As for *H.eos*.

Breeding: This is not difficult. See Introductory note for guidance.

Additional information: *H.griemi* is closely related to *H.flammeus*: it has only been imported since 1956.

HYPHESSOBRYCON HETERORHABDUS

Family: *Characidae*
Genus: *Hyphessobrycon*
English name: Flag Tetra
Origin: The lower reaches of the Amazon, the Tocantine river
Size: Approximately 5 cm
Habitat: No details are available of its natural habitat

Shape, coloring and markings: The body is quite deep and laterally very compressed. The basic coloration is a yellow-brown: the back is reddish-brown, the belly yellow to off-white. A rather broad longitudinal stripe runs back from the gill covers into the base of the caudal fin: it consists of three parallel lines: the uppermost is an iridescent red, the central is golden or silvery and the lowest deep blue to black. The upper part of the eye is an attractive shade of scarlet. The fins are pale yellow or colorless and transparent.
While mature females may well seem more sturdy in the body, sex is best determined by examining the position of the swim bladder: see Introductory note on the genus.

General care: Suitable for all sizes of aquariums provided a group of at least six is kept. A rather shy species, *H.heterorhabdus* needs dense plant cover and there should not be too many other fish in the tank. If the group is to thrive, the acidity of the water must be low: it should also preferably be filtered through peat. Temperature should be maintained at 24°C. *H.heterorhabdus* usually remains in the middle reaches of the tank where it seeks out areas of shade. Preferred diet, Daphnia and Cyclops, but white mosquito larvee will also be enjoyed: dried food can be given for variety.

324. *Hyphessobrycon griemi*

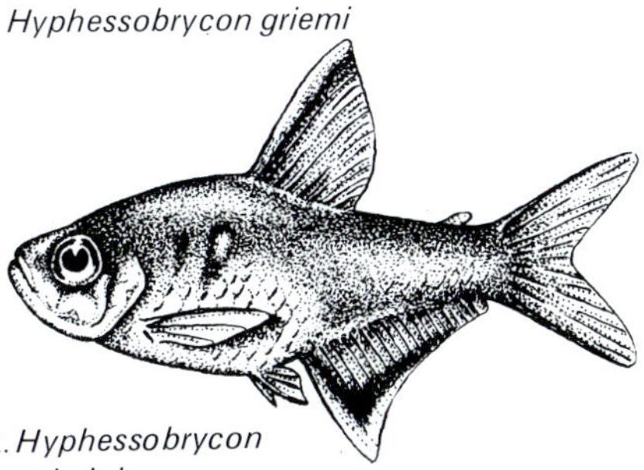

322. *Hyphessobrycon heterorhabdus*

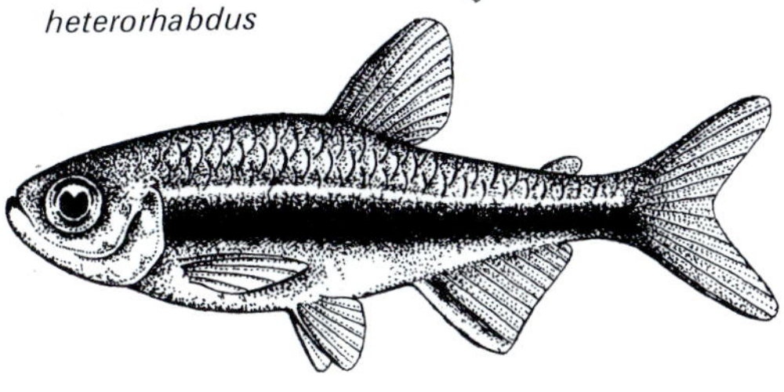

Breeding: This is not easy. Extremely soft water, of 1.2°–1.4° DH with an acidity of pH 6.4–6.8 is needed. Temperature 24°C. Smaller specimens make the best breeders and nests of about 100 fry are most likely to be raised successfully.

Additional information: *H.heterohabdus* is less resilient and more susceptible to disease than related species: this ought be borne in mind when transferring the fish from one environment to another.

HYPHESSOBRYCON LORETOENSIS

Family: *Characidae*
Genus: *Hyphessobrycon*
English name: none
Origin: Peru, the upper reaches of the Amazon around Iquitos
Size: Maximum 4 cm
Habitat: No details are available of its natural habitat

323. *Hyphessobrycon loretoensis*

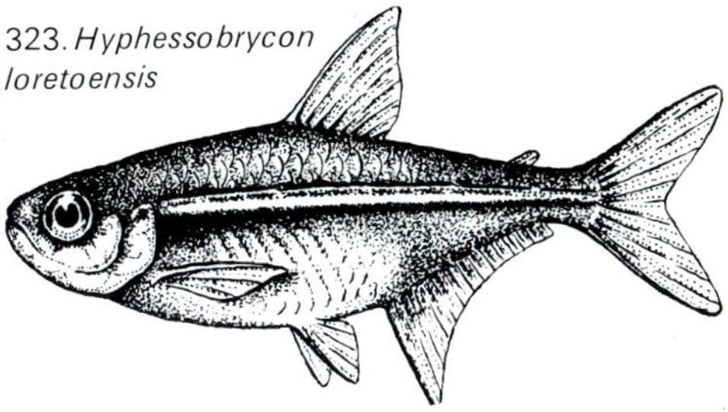

Shape, coloring and markings: The body is quite deep and laterally compressed. In build *H.loretoensis* closely resembles *H.heterorhabdus*. The basic coloration is a greenish-grey: the back is somewhat darker or brownish, with green overtones. The scales on the upper half of the body have a dark margin. A broad blue-black, greenly iridescent stripe runs from the edge of the gill covers to the base of the caudal fin where it may fragment and run out into the rays. Above lies a very narrow zone of greenish-yellow to golden-red which may only be visible in certain lights. The belly, where it is not crossed by the broad stripe, is a greenish-grey or yellow, and paler lower down. The caudal fin is an attractive terra-cotta. The base and leading edge of the dorsal fin are dull red: the back part is a greenish-yellow or brownish-green. The anal fin is a pale translucent red: the adipose fin yellow. The upper part of the iris is yellow or orange and the lower section a yellowish-green or green. There are iridescent green flecks on the gill covers.

325. *Hyphessobrycon loretoensis*

326. *Hyphessobrycon heterorhabdus*

327. *Hyphessobrycon minor*

Females are somewhat larger and when sexually mature have much darker bellies. Males are slimmer and as described above.

General care: As for *H.heterorhabadus* but temperature 24°–26° C.

Breeding: Not easy: as for *H.heterorhabdus.*

HYPHESSOBRYCON LUETKENI

Family: *Characidae*

Genus: *Hyphessobrycon*

English name: Lütken's Tetra

Origin: Paraguay, the Paraguay river

Size: Maximum 6.5 cm

Habitat: No further details are available of its natural habitat

Shape, coloring and markings: The body is fairly deep and laterally very compressed. The basic coloration is greyish-green with a beautiful silvery sheen when seen in bright light. There is a shoulder mark behind the gill covers, but this is not always very distinct: immediately behind lies a dark brown mark surrounded by a shiny pearly patch. A luminescent horizontal line runs from the gill covers to the dark caudal peduncle. The fins are a dull white and transparent: the caudal fin has a dark brown or black base.
Females when sexually mature have a distinctly more rounded shape.
Males are as described above.

General care: As for *H.bentosi* but the composition of the water is not critical, provided that fresh tap water is not used.

Breeding: This species has not as yet been bred successfully in captivity.

Additional information: *H.luetkeni* is a little known species that is unlikely to be imported. It was first mentioned by George Albert Boulenger in 1887.

HYPHESSOBRYCON MINOR

Family: *Characidae*

Genus: *Hyphessobrycon*

English name: none

Origin: Guyana

Size: Maximum 2.5 cm

Habitat: No further details are available of its natural habitat but it is likely that it inhabits waters similar to those frequented by related species

Shape, coloring and marking: The body is quite deep and laterally very compressed. Distinctive features of this species are the almost invisible shoulder patch and the very fine longitudinal line. The dorsal fin has a large black patch and only the extreme tip and base are white.

General care: As for *H.callistus callistus.*

Breeding: No information is available on the reproductive behavior of this species.

Additional information: *H.minor* was first described in 1909 but it never seems to have been imported. The *'H.minor'* known to amateur aquarists is probably either *H.callistus callistus* or a cross-breed of that species with another. It is however important to be aware of the existence and characteristics of the true *H.minor* in view of the suggestions by some authorities that it is no more than a sub-species of *H.callistus callistus* (see under which species for details of this viewpoint). The differences in dentition between the species make it unlikely that this hypothesis is correct.

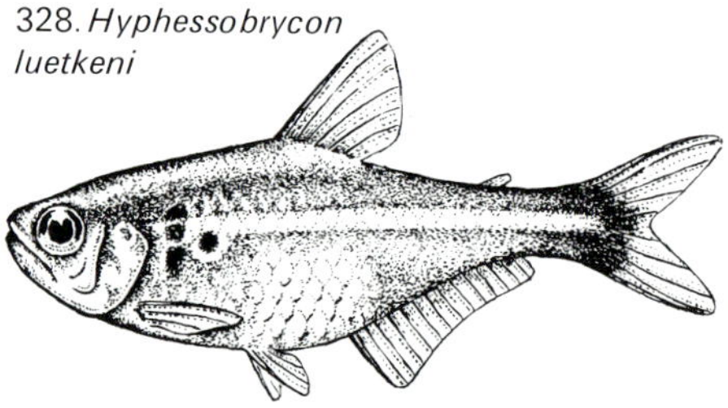

328. *Hyphessobrycon luetkeni*

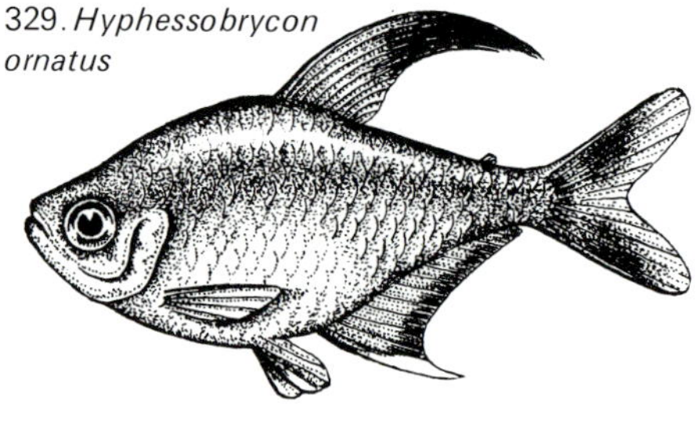

329. *Hyphessobrycon ornatus*

HYPHESSOBRYCON ORNATUS

Family: *Characidae*

Genus: *Hyphessobrycon*

English name: none

Origin: The Guianas and the lower reaches of the Amazon

Size: Maximum 4 cm

Habitat: No further information is available on its natural habitat

Shape, coloring and markings: The body is deep and laterally very compressed. The basic coloration is yellow with crimson overtones: the back is a little darker, the underside a little paler. There is no mark on the shoulders. The dorsal fin has a large irregularly-shaped black patch, dark flecks and a white anterior. The caudal fin is yellow or pink with a splash of bright red in each lobe. The anal fin is yellowish-red with a white anterior.
Females are more thick-set and lack the elongated rays on the dorsal fin.
Males are as described above with elongated dorsal fin rays.

General care: As for *H.callistus callistus.*

Breeding: This is not easy but not beyond the capability of the experienced amateur. Water of low acidity ought be used. Not every female seems to be fertile, so different pairs should be tried. The eggs are brown or red.

Additional information: *H.ornatus* is often confused with *H.rosaceus*: it may be that the infertile females referred to above are in fact members of the latter species, unable to interbreed with *H.ornatus.* There is no difficulty in distinguishing the males of the two species: those of *H.ornatus* have elongated dorsal fin rays, which are never present in the males of *H.rosaceus.*

HYPHESSOBRYCON PERUVIANUS

Family: *Characidae*

Genus: *Hyphessobrycon*

English name: none

Origin: Peru, the upper reaches of the Amazon around Iquitos

Size: Maximum 4 cm

Habitat: No details are available of its natural habitat

SHAPE, COLORING AND MARKINGS: The body is quite deep and laterally compressed. In body shape it closely resembles *H.heterorhabdus:* in other respects it is very similar to *H.loretoensis* which comes from the same region. The basic coloration is grey-green: the back is darker or brown, with green overtones. The scales on the upper half of the body have a dark edge. A broad greenly iridescent, blue-black band runs from the snout across the eye into the base of the lower half of the caudal fin. Under good light another very fine green-yellow to golden-red iridescent line may be visible above this, running from the gill covers to the tail. That part of the belly which is not covered by the broad band is a greenish-grey or yellow, and silvery-white underneath. The caudal fin is an attractive shade of terracotta: all the other fins are pale red. The anal fin has a white spot bordered above by a narrow dark band. The upper iris is orange, the lower part darker.

Females are very similarly colored to males, but are more robust: the swim bladder is only partially visible when illuminated from behind.

Males are slimmer and the swim bladder is fully visible when illuminated from behind.

330. *Hyphessobrycon peruvianus*

GENERAL CARE: As for *H.loretoensis.*

BREEDING: This is not easy: see *H.heterorhabdus.*

ADDITIONAL INFORMATION: *H.peruvianus* is easily distinguished from *H.loretoensis* by the longitudinal stripe that runs across the eye and which is not present in the latter species.

HYPHESSOBRYCON PULCHRIPINNIS

Family: *Characidae*

Genus: *Hyphessobrycon*

English name: Lemon Tetra

Origin: The Amazon basin

Size: Maximum 5 cm

Habitat: No further details are available of its natural habitat

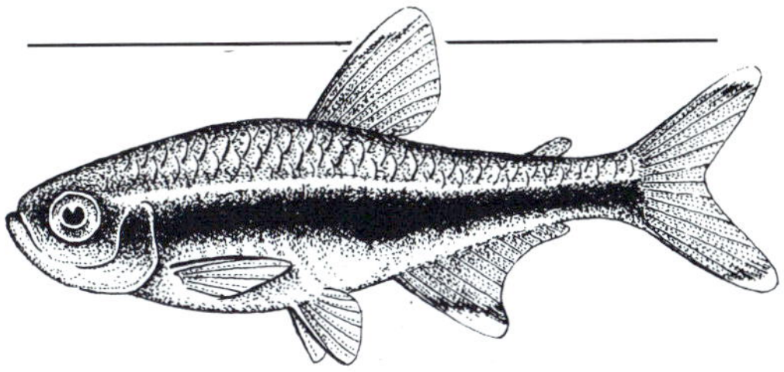

331. *Hyphessobrycon peruvianus*

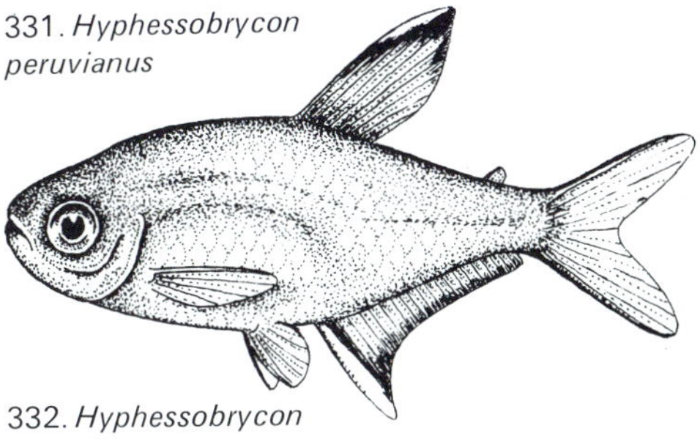

332. *Hyphessobrycon pulchripinnis*

SHAPE, COLORING AND MARKINGS: The body is quite deep and laterally very compressed. The basic coloration is a translucent yellow: the back is a pale brown to green: the flanks silvery with yellow overtones. There is an almost invisible longitudinal line. The dorsal fin is a translucent yellow, sometimes with dark overtones: it usually has a black border with a creamy patch at the tip. The anal fin is yellow with black edging: the anterior rays are bright yellow with a deep black band behind. The remaining fins are colorless and transparent. The upper part of the iris is a delightful shade of red.

Females may lack the black border to the anal fin, or it may be merely a little darker than the fin itself.

Males are clearly distinguished by the pattern on the anal fin.

GENERAL CARE: As for *H.flammeus.*

BREEDING: It is not difficult to encourage the fish to spawn: water of acidity pH 6–6.8, hardness 4°–6° DH and temperature 24°–

333. *Hyphessobrycon pulchripinnis*

26°C is required. The parent fish however are notorious egg eaters. Furthermore the fry are difficult to raise because they tend to crawl away into the material lining the tank during the first few weeks, where food cannot reach them. They grow extremely slowly: it may be four to five weeks before they are swimming freely. A great deal of care and patience is needed for successful breeding.

ADDITIONAL INFORMATION: *H.pulchripinnis* looks a very delicate fish but in fact is not very susceptible to disease and makes an excellent aquarium subject. They are tolerant of other species and not aggressive towards their own during the mating season.

HYPHESSOBRYCON ROBERTI

Family: *Characidae*

Genus: *Hyphessobrycon*

English name: none

Origin: No information is available on the origin or natural habitat of this species (see below under additional information)

Size: Maximum 5 cm

SHAPE, COLORING AND MARKINGS: The body is rather deep and laterally very compressed.

334. *Hyphessobrycon roberti*

The basic coloration is a yellow-red with a violet-blue tinge. The back and top half of the head are darker or greenish-brown. A strong red overtone suffuses the body when the fish is in good condition. The fins are pale or bright red. The dorsal fin is well-developed and has a broad black zone bordered by an area of white. The anal fin is also well-developed, with a black patch on the anterior rays and a black band below.
Females are smaller and less strikingly colored.

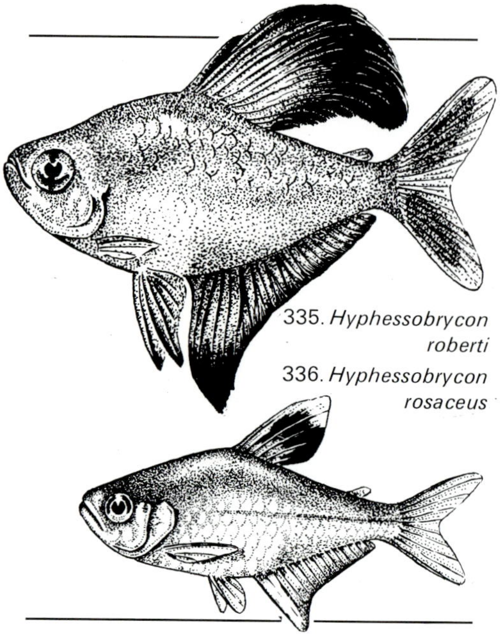

335. *Hyphessobrycon roberti*
336. *Hyphessobrycon rosaceus*

Males are easily recognised by the crescent-shaped elongations of the dorsal and anal fins.

GENERAL CARE: As for *H.bentosi* but temperature 23°–27°C.

BREEDING: There are no reports of this species having as yet been bred successfully in captivity.

ADDITIONAL INFORMATION: This attractive species, very similar in behavior to *H.erythrostigma* is a very recent import. Little is known about it: the name *roberti* may well be incorrect: it may indeed not be a species of *Hyphessobrycon* at all. It is only used here as a provisional name.

HYPHESSOBRYCON ROSACEUS

Family: *Characidae*

Genus: *Hyphessobrycon*

English name: Rosy Tetra

Origin: British Guyana, the Essequibo river and the area around Rockstone

Size: Maximum 4 cm

Habitat: Found in jungle streams and the less turbulent waters of larger rivers

SHAPE, COLORING AND MARKINGS: The body is rather deep and laterally very compressed. The basic coloration is a pale red becoming yellowish-orange towards the belly. When in good condition the whole body is suffused with red. This species has no mark on the shoulders. There is no longitudinal line visible. The dorsal fin has a red base: the anterior rays and the extreme tip are white and it has a large black patch. The caudal fin is yellow-white with a black border: the anterior rays are white. The rest of the fins are transparent and colorless.
Females when sexually mature have more rounded bellies.
Males are slimmer and have no elongated dorsal fin.

GENERAL CARE: As for *H.bentosi.*

BREEDING: Not difficult. Water of acidity pH 6–6.8, hardness 4°–6° DH and temperature 24°–26°C is needed.

ADDITIONAL INFORMATION: Very few fish have given rise to so much confusion as *H.rosaceus.* Many other related species, such as *H.callistus callistus* and *H.serpae* have been labelled *rosaceus.* The true *H.rosaceus* is distinguished by the absence of any patch on the shoulders and in males, any elongation of the dorsal fin.

HYPHESSOBRYCON SERPAE

Family: *Characidae*

Genus: *Hyphessobrycon*

English name: none

Origin: The middle reaches of the Amazon river and southwards to Paraguay

Size: Maximum 4.5 cm

Habitat: Found in jungle streams and rivulets and the less turbulent waters of larger rivers

SHAPE, COLORING AND MARKINGS: The body is rather deep and laterally very compressed. The basic coloration and patterning can vary a great deal from one specimen to another. In general the back tends to be olive green, the flanks a more greyish-green and the belly an iridescent yellow-green or yellow-white. The posterior half of the body takes on a bright red color during courting display. The shoulder mark is present only in outline and even that is difficult sometimes to discern. The base of the dorsal fin is a translucent grey to white, with, in the center, a black patch that extends over the anterior rays: the top and rear of the fins are white. The caudal fin is red, the anal fin is red with an irregularly shaped black band. The dorsal and ventral fins are pale red.
Females are less brightly colored.
Males have strong red overtones.

GENERAL CARE: As for *H.eos* but temperature 22°–26°C.

BREEDING: This is not difficult. The same conditions are required as for *H.rosaceus.*

ADDITIONAL INFORMATION: This is another species known to aquarists under a variety of different names. This is not surprising when a whole range of different color patterns occur naturally and the matter is further complicated by interbreeding. Thoroughbred specimens are only very rarely imported.

THE FAMILY CHARACIDAE

The genus Luciocharax

The fish in this genus are closely related to those in the genus *Hydrocinus* with which they share the characteristic of a very elongated snout and with which they share the same behavior pattern. Like those fish they are difficult to transport without suffering injury and are in consequence rare in captivity. The species described below, although not suitable for most domestic aquariums, has aroused considerable interest among aquarists and will repay study.

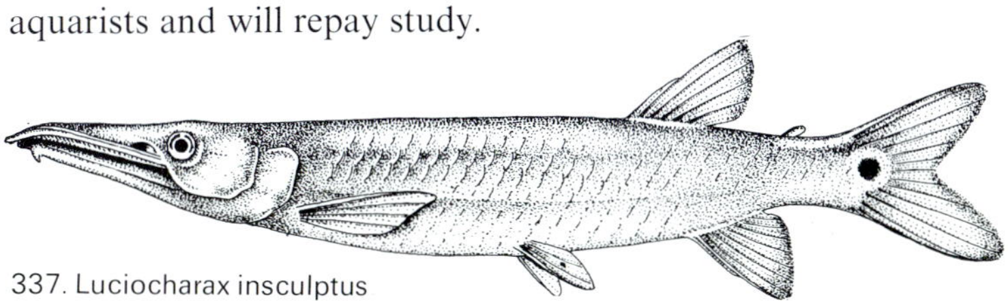

337. Luciocharax insculptus

LUCIOCHARAX INSCULPTUS

Family: *Characidae*

Genus: *Luciocharax*

English name: none

Origin: Colombia, the basin of the Magdalena river

Size: Approximately 70 cm

Habitat: No further details are available of its natural habitat

SHAPE, COLORING AND MARKINGS: The body is very slender and laterally only very slightly compressed. The head is long, the jaws shaped like a beak and the mouth spoon-shaped and down pointing. The dorsal fin lies far back on the body. The lower lobe of the caudal fin is slightly larger than the upper lobe. The lateral line is incomplete. The basic coloration is ochre: the back is olive or brown: the belly a silvery-white. A round dark patch with a yellow border lies at the base of the caudal fin: the fin itself is brick red at the base, becoming violet, with a dark edge. The dorsal and anal fins are yellow with a black border. There are no known external sexual characteristics.

GENERAL CARE: *L.insculptus* is a predator: that and its large size make it unsuitable for the ordinary aquarium in the home, but these fish are fascinating to study and watch in large public aquariums, when kept with other large fish. Large irregular pieces of wood must be provided in the tank for this is a shy species and needs adequate retreats, where it can also lurk for prey. The composition of the water is not critical but fresh tap water should not be used. Temperature 22°–24° C. Live fish are the only really suitable diet: this is a voracious species that can devour fish its own length.

BREEDING: This species does not appear to have been bred in captivity.

ADDITIONAL INFORMATION: This species that resembles a pike is very rarely imported and is almost unknown to aquarists. It was first described by the distinguished naturalist Franz Steindachner in 1878.

THE FAMILY CHARACIDAE

The genus Megalamphodus

Not a great deal is known about the species in this genus and they are one group that would repay careful observation by keen amateurs. At first sight they look very much like fish in the genus *Hyphessobrycon:* although the body is less deep, the fin pattern is remarkably similar.

These are delightful small fish, but not as yet very common in aquariums. They are social and peaceful by nature. The males may often be seen threatening each other with outspread fins, but such aggressive displays never lead to anything serious.

338. *Megalamphodus megalopterus*

MEGALAMPHODUS MEGALOPTERUS

Family: *Characidae*

Genus: *Megalamphodus*

English name: none

Origin: Brazil, the Matto Grosso

Size: Approximately 4 cm

Habitat: No details are available of its natural habitat

SHAPE, COLORING AND MARKINGS: The body is rather deep and laterally very compressed. The basic coloration is a transparent dark grey to black with strong blue-black iridescence and a pale patch near the shoulders. The unpaired fins are a transparent grey with darker patches and darker borders.

Females are smaller than the males: the body is deeper. The dorsal fin has no extended rays: the anal fin is bright red. The background tint is reddish.

Males are noticeably slimmer. The dorsal and anal fins are highly developed, with elongated rays: the adipose fin is colorless or grey.

GENERAL CARE: Suitable for both large and small aquariums, but must be kept in a group of at least six specimens: a social fish which will hide itself if not provided with enough companions. The tank should have a dark base, and be planted with dense vegetation, including some plants with fine leaves, round the sides. *M.megalopterus* usually stays in the middle and upper reaches of the tank: it will seek out the more shaded areas in brightly lit aquariums. The composition of the water is not critical, provided it is mildly acid, but fresh tap water should not be used: the fish best like mature water filtered through peat. Temperature 22°–26° C. The main diet should be small living creatures, Daphnia, Cyclops and black mosquito larvae: winged insects will be eagerly snapped up from the surface. Dried food can be given for a change.

BREEDING: Not easy. Fairly soft (5° DH) and mildly acid (pH 5–6) water at a temperature of 24°–26° C is needed. The breeding tank should be small, with a capacity of 6–10 liters: it should contain some fine-leaved plants into which the eggs can be deposited. The females spawn easily but not all males make suitable mates. Young females will pair with older males. The fry hatch after 24 hours and swim about in five days. They should be fed at first on rotifers, and after two days on the nauplii of Artemia and Cyclops. Growth during the first few weeks is rapid, but slower thereafter. The water must be changed regularly. The young fish show female characteristics for a long time: sexual maturity is indicated by the appearance of the dark patterning and the fin structure noted above.

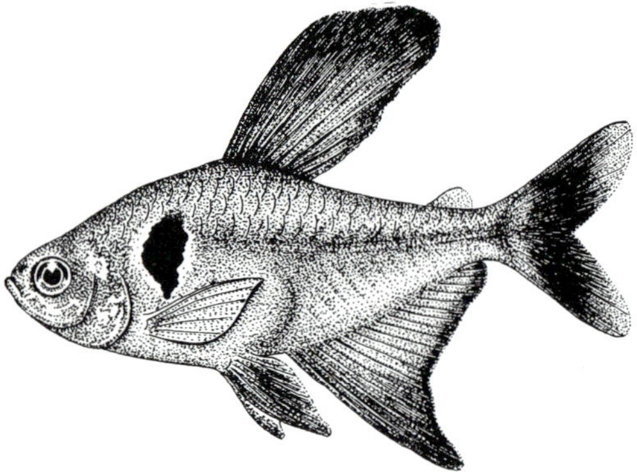

339. *Megalamphodus megalopterus*

340. *Megalamphodus sweglesi*

MEGALAMPHODUS SWEGLESI

Family: *Characidae*

Genus: *Megalamphodus*

English name: none

Origin: Brazil: the tributaries of the Solimoes

Size: Approximately 4 cm

Habitat: No details are available of its natural habitat

SHAPE, COLORING AND MARKINGS: The body is rather deep and laterally very compressed. The basic coloration is a transparent reddish, with a blue-black patch on the shoulders. The unpaired fins are a transparent grey: the ventral fins a darker or reddish-grey: the dorsal fin is predominantly black.
Females are rather smaller than males: the body is deeper: the dorsal fin is less developed and less rounded but has a white border.
Males are noticeably slimmer. The dorsal fin is well-developed with extended rays and has no white border. Young fish of both sexes however have this white border for the male characteristics only appear on mature male specimens.

GENERAL CARE: As for *M.megalopterus*.

BREEDING: Not easy but certainly possible for the more experienced amateur. The same kind of breeding tank is needed as for *M.Megalopterus*. The first mating will take place three to five days after the fish have been introduced into the tank and have become acclimatized. It may be difficult to establish a breeding pair. The females produce generally a large number of eggs, but few hatch out. Both the eggs and the young fry are very prone to attack by bacteria. The fry hatch after about two and a quarter hours and swim about freely after five days. They may be fed on the usual breeding foods, but development is slow.

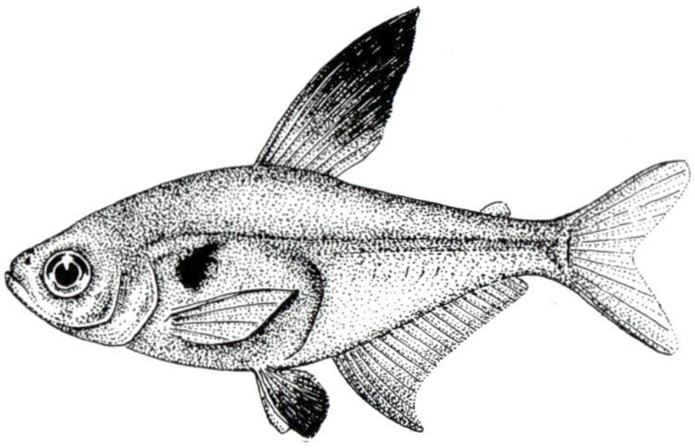

341. *Megalamphodus sweglesi*

THE FAMILY CHARACIDAE

The genus Metynnis

Fish of this genus are found over the whole of South America. They live in large shoals in all kinds of waters, particularly where vegetation is sufficiently prolific to satisfy their need for vegetable food.
They have deep, very compressed, disc-shaped bodies, a spine in front of the dorsal fin, a serrated abdominal keel, and a remarkably elongated adipose fin. They are distinguished from similar genera by peculiarities of dentition. Although because of their serrated bellies these fish might seem akin to the saw-bellied *Characins* such as the Piranha fish, they are in both general shape and life-style, quite different. The saw-bellied *Characins* are predators: the *Metynnis* are essentially vegetarians, although they will eat aquatic insects and larvae when these are available.
They are social fish and only thrive in captivity if kept in a large group of their own kind. They need an aquarium at least 1.5 m long to provide adequate swimming space. In a smaller

tank they will be very shy, hiding wherever they can and losing their natural vivacity. They are therefore hardly suitable fish for the ordinary aquarium in the home.
The composition of the water in the tank is not critical but fresh tap water should not be used. The most appropriate temperature varies from species to species and is noted in the descriptions that follow. Obviously these fish, living as they do primarily on vegetable matter cannot be kept in a tank full of decorative plants. At most, some sturdy bog plants can be included: these will usually be left alone as long as enough lettuce or other soft-leaved vegetable matter is provided in the diet. These fish are not fussy about their food, but it is advisable to feed them with some aquatic insects as well as vegetable matter and some species are fond of porridge oats soaked in water.
As well as adequate free swimming space the fish must be provided with sufficient hiding places in the tank: irregular-shaped pieces of wood are best. Reflecting glass should not be used for the tank and the colors show up best against a dark bottom.
It seems that only one or two species have been bred successfully in captivity: details are given under *M.schreitmuelleri*.

METYNNIS ANISURUS

Family: *Characidae*
Genus: *Metynnis*
English name: none
Origin: Brazil, the Tapajos river
Size: Approximately 12 cm
Habitat: No further details are available of its natural habitat

SHAPE, COLORING AND MARKINGS: The body is very deep, disc-shaped and laterally very compressed. The body of older specimens is less deep. The back is a soft olive green: the flanks silvery, tinged with a striking iridescent blue. A dark mark, sometimes indistinct, lies on the shoulders. The fins are greyish and transparent, with narrow dark edges. The adipose fin is reddish.
There are no known external sexual characteristics but it is likely that the males have a more pronounced sickle shape to the anal fin – a sexual characteristic of many related species.

GENERAL CARE: *M.anisurus* is hardly suitable for the ordinary aquarium in the home. A social fish it should be kept together with a large number of its own kind and also needs a large amount of free swimming space. The aquarium must also have plenty of retreats among irregularly-shaped pieces of wood. The only vegetation possible is sturdy bog plants: soft-leaved plants will be eaten. The fish feels most at home over a dark bed. The composition of the water is not critical but fresh tap water should not be used. Temperature 24°–27°C. *M.anisurus* keeps mainly to the middle reaches of the tank. It is a very tolerant fish, even towards much smaller species. It will greedily eat aquatic insects and larvae but the diet should consist principally of vegetable matter such as lettuce and other soft-leaved plants.

BREEDING: No information is available on the reproductive behavior of this species.

342. *Metynnis anisurus*

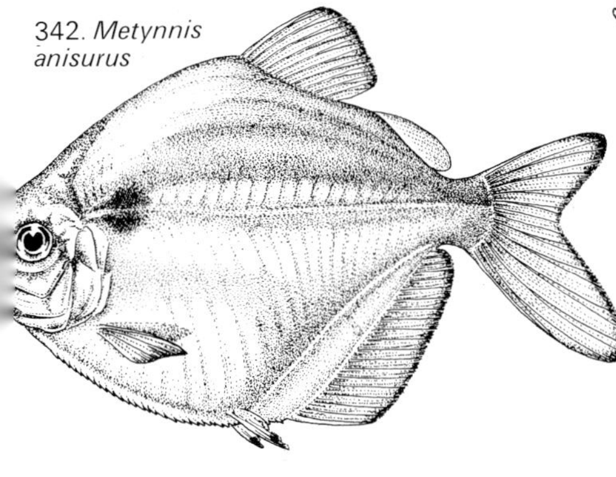

METYNNIS CALICHROMIS

Family: *Characidae*
Genus: *Metynnis*
English name: none
Origin: Brazil, the Jamundá river
Size: Approximately 15 cm
Habitat: Found in waters with dense vegetation

SHAPE, COLORING AND MARKINGS: The body is very deep, disc-shaped and laterally very compressed. The back is greyish or brown: the flanks silvery, tinged with a striking iridescent blue or green. Many specimens have dark transverse bands on the upper part of the body which become narrower towards the belly and break up into a series of marks. There is hardly ever a distinct shoulder mark. The dorsal fin has a dark edge and dark marks along the fin rays. The anal fin is sickle shaped, ochre, with a red area at the front and a dark edge. The caudal fin is colorless and transparent, but with a wide reddish border. In some specimens the fins have dark edges.
Females are as described above.
Males have a more powerfully developed anal fin.

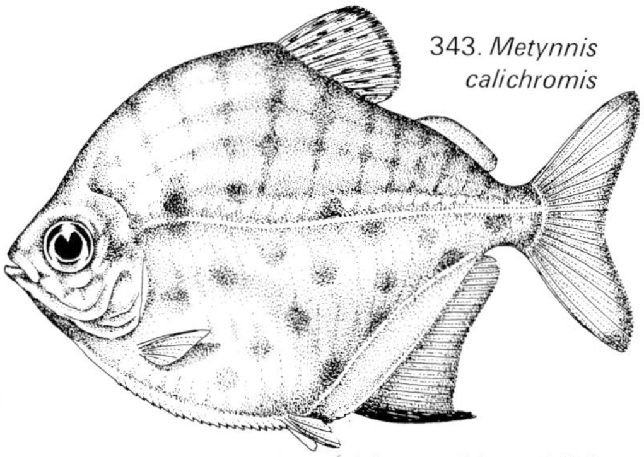

343. *Metynnis calichromis*

GENERAL CARE: As for *M.anisurus*.

BREEDING: This species has not as yet been bred in captivity.

METYNNIS DUNGERNI

Family: *Characidae*
Genus: *Metynnis*
English name: none
Origin: The Amazon basin
Size: Approximately 12 cm
Habitat: Very common in waters with dense vegetation

SHAPE, COLORING AND MARKINGS: The body is very deep, disc-shaped and laterally very compressed. The back is greyish-green, paler towards the belly, which is silvery tinged with an iridescent blue. Some specimens have dark marks on the body which lie in rows to form fairly distinct transverse bands, but these marks are never wider than the diameter of the eye. Most specimens have small dark marks forming decorative clusters on the scales. The pectoral region has a reddish or golden sheen. The dorsal fin is black: the anal fin wine red and transparent. The irises are red to orange.
There are no known external sexual characteristics but see under *M.anisurus*.

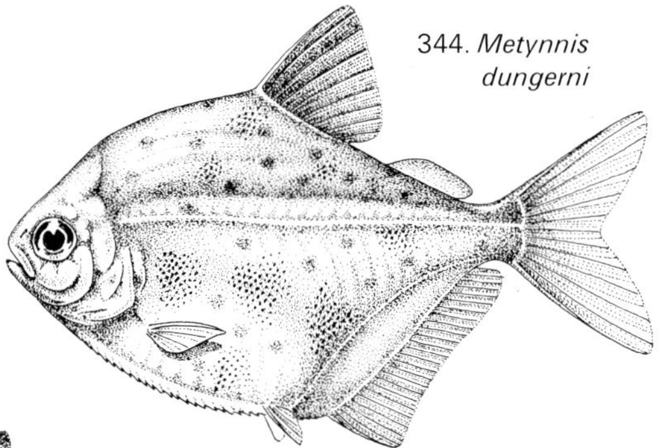

344. *Metynnis dungerni*

GENERAL CARE: As for *M.anisurus*.

BREEDING: This species does not seem to have been bred as yet in captivity.

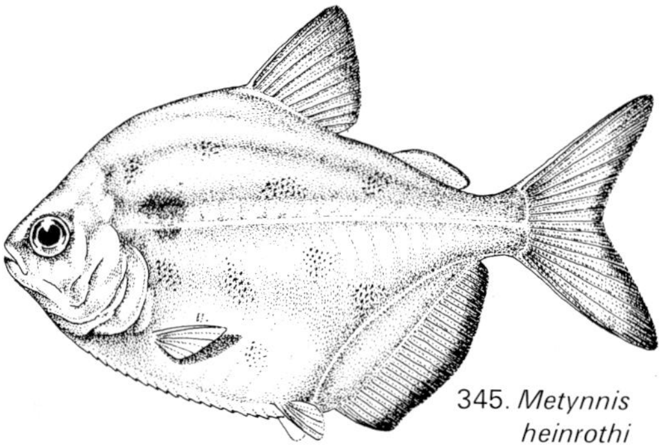

345. *Metynnis heinrothi*

METYNNIS HEINROTHI

Family: *Characidae*

Genus: *Metynnis*

English name: none

Origin: Brazil, the Amazon basin

Size: Approximately 10 cm

Habitat: No further details are available of its natural habitat, but it is likely to be as for related species

SHAPE, COLORING AND MARKINGS: The body is very deep, disc-shaped and laterally very compressed. *M.heinrothi* closely resembles *M.dungerni* in coloring but there is always a prominent dark mark on the shoulders. The dorsal fin is black, lighter at the base: the anal fin has a deep black edge: the caudal and adipose fins have dark borders.
There are no known external sexual characteristics but see under *M.anisurus*.

GENERAL CARE: As for *M.anisurus*.

BREEDING: This species has not as yet been bred in captivity.

METYNNIS HYPSAUCHEN

Family: *Characidae*

Genus: *Metynnis*

English name: none

Origin: The Guianas, the Amazon basin

Size: Approximately 14 cm

Habitat: Very common in still and sluggish waters

SHAPE, COLORING AND MARKINGS: The body is very deep, disc-shaped and laterally very compressed. The back is a soft greyish-green, becoming lighter or silvery towards the flanks, which are tinged with pale blue. Older specimens often have dark marks on the body which lie in rows, to show up as transverse bands. *M.hypsauchen* bears one or sometimes two distinct shoulder marks. All the fins are bright yellow: the front of the anal fin is reddish.
There are no known external sexual characteristics but see under *M.anisurus*.

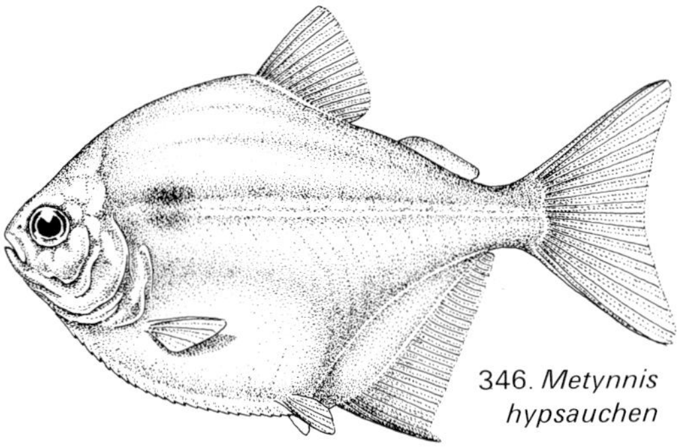

346. *Metynnis hypsauchen*

GENERAL CARE: As for *M.anisurus*.

BREEDING: This species has not as yet been bred in captivity.

METYNNIS MACULATUS

Family: *Characidae*

Genus: *Metynnis*

English name: none

Origin: The Guianas, the Amazon and Paraguay rivers

Size: Approximately 18 cm

Habitat: Found in sluggish and still waters with dense vegetation

SHAPE, COLORING AND MARKINGS: The body is very deep, disc-shaped and laterally very compressed. In older specimens the body is less deep. The back is fawn, often tinged with an iridescent greyish-blue sheen. The flanks are greyish, light brown or an earthy color, often with a large number of brown, roughly oval, marks which frequently lie in rows to form transverse bands on the upper half of the body. The belly is silvery. An iridescent orange mark lies on the gill covers in front of one or two prominent marks on the shoulders. All the fins except the colorless pectoral fin have a dark edge. The caudal fin is orangey: the anal fin is rust brown to brick red towards the front.
Females have a straight anal fin.
Males have a sickle shaped anal fin.

GENERAL CARE: As for *M.anisurus*.

BREEDING: This species has not as yet been bred in captivity.

METYNNIS SCHREITMUELLERI

Family: *Characidae*

Genus: *Metynnis*

English name: none

Origin: The Amazon basin

Size: Approximately 15 cm

Habitat: No details are available of its natural habitat but that is likely to be similar to that of related species

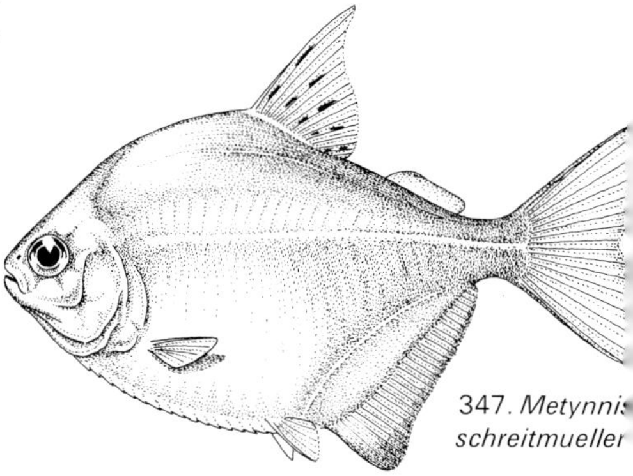

347. *Metynnis schreitmuelleri*

SHAPE, COLORING AND MARKINGS: The body is very deep, disc-shaped and laterally very compressed. The back is a deep olive: the flanks and belly have a beautiful silver sheen, often tinged with blue or green. The dorsal fin has dark stripes along the rays: the caudal fin often has a dark edge. The anal fin is a clear orange or brick red at the front.
Females have a striking red edge to the anal fin during the mating season.
Males have a dark edge to the anal fin during the mating season.

GENERAL CARE: As for *M.anisurus*.

BREEDING: *M.schreitmuelleri* has been bred successfully a number of times. The water should be fairly hard of pH 6.8. Temperature 26° C. Up to 2000 eggs are laid. Each is about 2 mm. The fry hatch after about 70 hours at a temperature of 28° C. For the first three or four days they keep to the bottom of the tank: after four or five days they will begin to hunt for food. They should be fed on *nauplii*.

THE FAMILY CHARACIDAE

The genus Micralestes

The fish in the genus *Micralestes* are very closely related to those in the genus *Alestes*, although as their name would suggest, they are much smaller. Three species, *Micralestes acutidens, Micralestes hilgendorfi* and *Micralestes interruptus* have been kept from time to time in aquariums, but of these only *Micralestes acutidens* is likely to be of general interest to amateurs. *M.hilgendorfi*, a somewhat larger fish than *M.acutidens* and of a more yellow hue, but otherwise almost identical to it, is rarely if ever imported from its home in the Congo river basin and *M.interruptus*, the Congo Tetra has proved extremely difficult to keep in good condition in captivity. *M.acutidens*, described below, is a much easier fish to keep.

MICRALESTES ACUTIDENS

Family: *Characidae*

Genus: *Micralestes*

English name: none

Origin: Tropical central Africa, the upper reaches of the Nile, the basin of the Congo, the Zambesi, the Niger

Size: Maximum 6.4 cm

Habitat: Found in waters with dense vegetation on the banks

348. *Micralestes acutidens*

SHAPE, COLORING AND MARKINGS: The body is elongated and laterally somewhat compressed. The snout is rather pointed and the mouth set at an upward angle. The basic coloration is silvery, which when the light catches it at certain angles becomes a shiny metallic blue. A dark but not always distinct horizontal line lies across the body. The dorsal fin is pointed and bears a dark mark at the top of the front fin rays: the caudal fin is deeply forked.

Females are more sturdy than the males, with less pointed fins and more rounded bellies.

Males are as described above, with anal fins considerably larger than those of females.

GENERAL CARE: *M.acutidens* is a shoal fish and should be kept in a large aquarium with dense vegetation round the sides and plenty of free swimming space in the center. The overhead lighting should be filtered through floating plants. The water should be no more than 6° DH with a pH of 7. The temperature must on no account be too low: preferably it should be 25°–28° C and certainly no lower than 24° C. All kinds of aquatic insects will be eaten as well as dried food.

BREEDING: Success depends on the condition of the parent fish. It is essential to feed them with black mosquito larvae and flies' eggs. The eggs when laid are about 2 mm in diameter. They are not adhesive and will sink to the bottom. The fry swim freely after about six days, when they can be fed with *Artemia nauplii* and other food provided it is very fine. On no account should they be fed with Cyclops for they are too fast for the fry to catch.

THE FAMILY CHARACIDAE

The genus Moenkhausia

The genus *Moenkhausia* is distributed over a wide area of northern South America, from the Guianas through the upper Amazon basin and Bolivia down to Paraguay and Uraguay. About 40 species have been identified, of which only a small number are of concern to the amateur aquarist. This genus however, named after William Moenkhaus who identified it, is one that has become particularly important for the scientific study of the extensive *Characidae* family of which it forms part. Physically, one of the main distinguishing characteristics of the diverse species found within the genus, is the straight lateral line.

In many respects these fish are similar in behavior to those in the genus *Hemigrammus*. Those species which are imported have proved ideal for the aquarium. They tend however to eat quite substantial amounts of vegetable matter and one or two species have earned themselves the reputation of being formidable plant eaters.

Breeding will generally occur spontaneously in reasonably soft water (5°–7° DH), which has been filtered though peat. Breeding tanks should be quite large, of about 5–6 liters capacity and contain scattered clumps of fine leaved plants. The temperature should be about 25° C. If the breeding pair' are introduced into the tank in the morning and exposed to the afternoon sun, spawning will generally have begun by the next morning. The mating is very energetic. The eggs are laid over the plants but are not adhesive. The fry hatch after some 24 hours, and will be swimming freely a day or so later. Rearing is straightforward.

MOENKHAUSIA OLIGOLEPIS

Family: *Characidae*

Genus: *Moenkhausia*

English name: none

Origin: Guyana and the upper Amazon

Size: Maximum 12 cm

Habitat: Very widely distributed in swamps, rivulets and other shallow waters

SHAPE, COLORING AND MARKINGS: The body is elongated, deep and laterally very compressed. The basic coloration is a gleaming silvery-white with a green iridescence. The back is olive to yellow green: the belly silvery-white. The scales have usually a dark margin. One or two rather prominent shoulder patches lie behind the gill covers. The root and base of the caudal fin are black and generally there are two glistening gold spots in front. A rather indistinct longitudinal line runs from the gill covers back to the caudal fin. The upper half of the eye is an attractive red. The dorsal caudal and anal fins are a pale yellow or red.

Females are as described above.

Males have more powerful fins and the rays of the anal fin are elongated.

GENERAL CARE: *M.oligolepis* is only suitable for larger aquariums. An exceptionally social fish it should be kept in a group of at least five of its own kind. The tank should have a dark base, old rather than fresh water and be so arranged that in addition to clumps of dense vegetation, adequate free swimming space is provided. The species will live in the middle and upper reaches. Bogwood is a very suitable decoration. Temperature 20°–25° C. *M.oligolepis* is a very tolerant fish and will associate with both larger and smaller species. Live food of all kinds will be eaten but dried food accepted only with reluctance. Lettuce should also be offered.

BREEDING: Not difficult: a very prolific species.

ADDITIONAL INFORMATION: Young specimens are particularly attractive in the aquarium: they are constantly on the move without being too active.

MOENKHAUSIA PITTIERI

Family: *Characidae*
Genus: *Moenkhausia*
English name: none
Origin: Venezuela
Size: Maximum 7 cm
Habitat: Found in lake Valencia and the surrounding region

SHAPE, COLORING AND MARKINGS: The body is rather deep and laterally very compressed. The basic coloration is a light brassy-yellow: the back is darker and the underside pale yellow to white. In young fish the lateral line is very distinct. Under bright light the upper half of the body has a very attractive golden gleam and the underside acquires a more metallic iridescence. The whole body is covered with a stippling of green to blue. The dorsal, caudal and anal fins are pale violet with white tips.
Females are less vividly colored.
Males have very extended rays on the dorsal fin.

GENERAL CARE: As for *M.oligolepsis* but temperature 22°–26° C. A very peaceful fish, *M.pittieri* does not care for the company of other very active species. Diet as for *M.oligolepis* but dried food is more acceptable.

BREEDING: Not difficult but not a very prolific species.

ADDITIONAL INFORMATION: A very attractive fish, very similar in behavior to *Hyphessobrycon erythrostigma*. Like those long-finned fish it glides through the aquarium sparkling like a diamond and shows up particularly well in sunlight. Although as a rule very tolerant, adults can become aggressive during the mating season.

349. *Moenkhausia oligolepis*

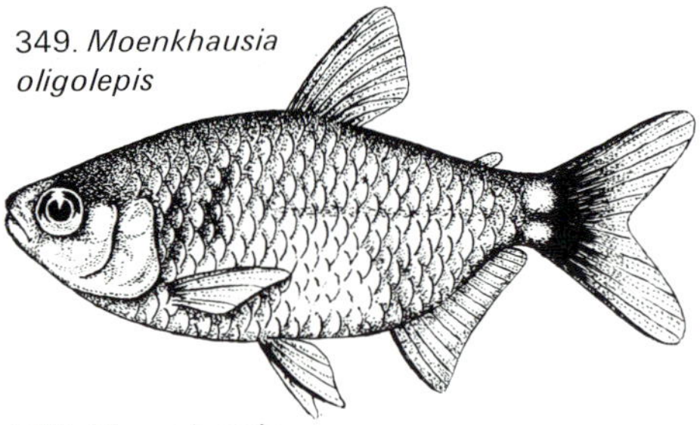

350. *Moenkhausia pittieri*

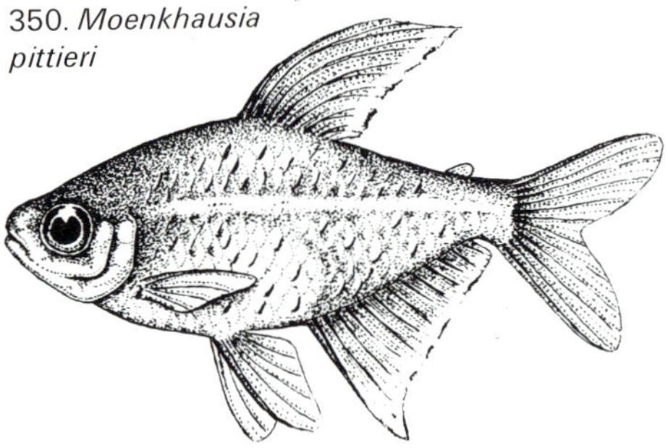

351. *Moenkhausia sanctae filomenae*

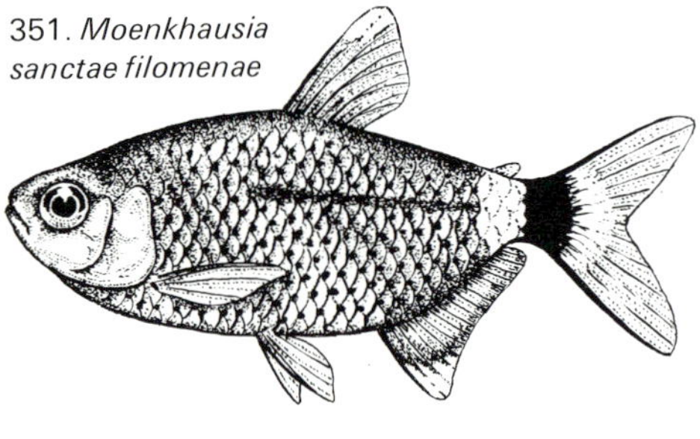

352. *Moenkhausia pittieri*

353. *Moenkhausia sanctae filomenae*

MOENKHAUSIA SANCTAE FILOMENAE

Family: *Characidae*

Genus: *Moenkhausia*

English name: none

Origin: The basins of the Paraguay and Paranaiba rivers

Size: Maximum 7 cm

Habitat: Found in swamps, marshes and other small waters

SHAPE, COLORING AND MARKINGS: The body is elongated, deep and laterally very compressed. *M.sanctae filomenae* closely resembles *M.oligolepis* although the body is somewhat less deep and it has fewer scales, but those are more darkly marked at the edges. There is a very prominent golden-yellow area in front of a dark band on the caudal fin. The basic coloration is silvery-white with a green iridescence. The back is brownish to green: the belly yellow-white to pure white. The quite prominent lateral line runs from the first ray of the dorsal fin to the root of the caudal fin. The upper half of the eye is scarlet. Areas of the fins are a yellowish-grey and the anal and dorsal fins have white spots.

Females when sexually mature have more rounded bellies.

Males are as described above.

GENERAL CARE: Suitable for both large and small aquariums: otherwise, as for *M.oligolepis*.

BREEDING: Not difficult: see Introductory note on the genus. A prolific species.

ADDITIONAL INFORMATION: Its small size makes *M.sanctae filomenae* a more attractive aquarium fish than the closely related *M.oligolepis*.

THE FAMILY CHARACIDAE

The genus Nematobrycon

This small genus which includes the increasingly popular Emperor Tetra, *Nematobrycon palmeri* has only become familiar to most aquarists in recent years. Not a great deal is known about these fish in their natural habitat, but in the aquarium they have shown themselves to be peaceful shoaling fish that are both attractive and relatively undemanding. Only the Emperor Tetra has it seems to date been bred in captivity but it is to be hoped that some aquarists will persevere with efforts to breed the other species that are now imported from time to time from the wild: their reproductive behavior is unlikely to be significantly different from that of the Emperor Tetra, for all the species have the same provenance.

NEMATOBRYCON AMPHILOXUS

Family: *Characidae*

Genus: *Nematobrycon*

English name: none

Origin: Colombia

Size: Approximately 6 cm

Habitat: No details are available concerning its natural habitat

SHAPE, COLORING AND MARKINGS: The body is fairly deep and laterally compressed. *N.amphiloxus* closely resembles both in shape and patterning, the more well-known *Nematobrycon palmeri*, the Emperor Tetra, but is distinguished from it by its rather deeper body and somewhat darker patterning: it has also, technically, a different fin structure, differences in dentition and a different number of scales. The basic coloration is brown with a bluish-black tinge. An iridescent blue stripe runs from the back edge of the gill covers to the caudal fin and above lies a broad area of dark blue or bluish black. The belly is pink or yellowish-white with an iridescent blue tinge. The fins are grey and transparent. The front fin ray of the dorsal fin and the middle fin rays of the caudal fin are black: the anal fin has a black border: the ventral fins have black tips.

Females are slightly smaller and less deeply colored.

Males are as described above.

GENERAL CARE: *N.amphiloxus* is suitable for all but the smallest aquariums. Vegetation, of alternately broad and fine leaved plants should be put round the edges. Irregular pieces of wood not only provide attractive decoration but also give the fish the chance to mark out territories. *N.amphiloxus* is not a particularly social fish but it is still advisable to keep a group of three to five together. The composition of the water is not critical but fresh tap water should not be used: sudden changes in water temperature should be carefully avoided. Old aquarium water is best. Temperature about 24° C. All kinds of aquatic insects and larvae will be suitable food, provided they are not too large, but surface insects such as fruitflies are best.

BREEDING: Nothing is known about the reproductive behavior of this species.

NEMATOBRYCON LACORTEI

Family: *Characidae*

Genus: *Nematobrycon*

English name: none

Origin: Colombia

Size: Approximately 6 cm

Habitat: No details are available of its natural habitat

SHAPE, COLORING AND MARKINGS: The body is fairly deep and laterally compressed. In shape this species closely resembles *Nematobrycon palmeri*. The back is olive-brown becoming a reddish or yellowish-brown tinged with red on the flanks. Beneath the flanks lies a dark area marbled in brown and salmon with patches of iridescent green and blue particularly above the anal fin. A broad deep black stripe lies below the lateral line: along the caudal peduncle this line is unbroken, but towards the front of the body it is patterned with iridescent blue and green patches. The area between the stripe and the anal fin is almost transparent and salmon: the belly and lower half of the head are silvery-white. The snout and top half of the head are dark brown: the jaws chestnut. The irises are pale green, iridescent with red specks. The dorsal fin is colorless and transparent, but the front rays are black. The caudal fin is grey and transparent: both the upper and lower lobes have a narrow white border and ice blue tips. The anal fin is grey and transparent with a black stripe and a light blue border. The other fins are colorless.

Females are slightly smaller and less strikingly patterned.

Males are as described above.

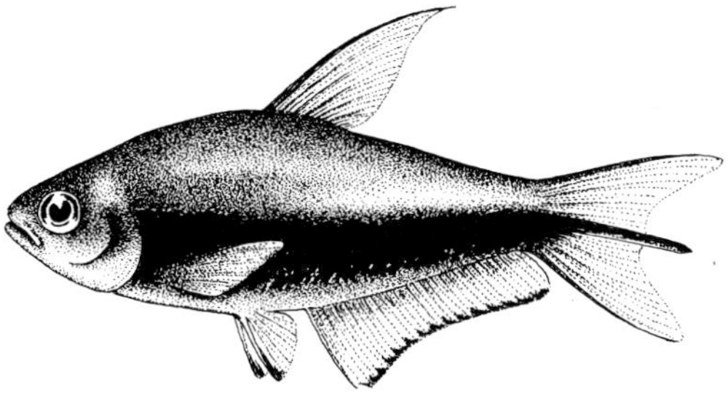

354. *Nematobrycon amphiloxus*

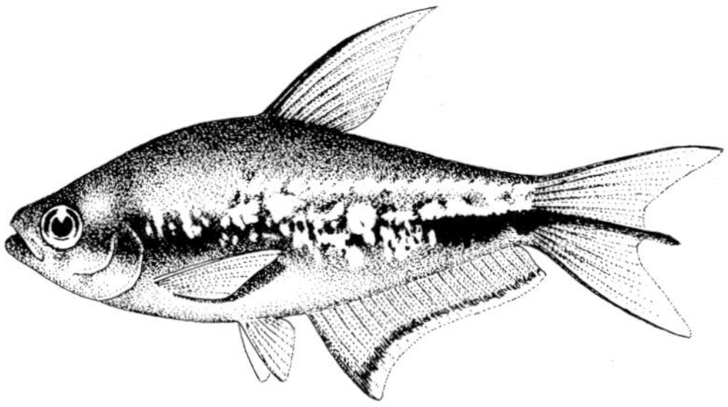

355. *Nematobrycon lacortei*

356. *Nematobrycon lacortei*

357. *Nematobrycon palmeri*

General care: As for *N.amphiloxus*.

Breeding: Nothing is known about the reproductive behavior of this species.

NEMATOBRYCON PALMERI

Family: *Characidae*

Genus: *Nematobrycon*

English name: Emperor Tetra

Origin: Colombia

Size: Approximately 6 cm

Habitat: No details are available of its natural habitat

Shape, coloring and markings: The body is quite deep and laterally compressed. The basic coloration is brownish or salmon which in bright light becomes an iridescent green or bluish-purple. The back is darker, tinged with purple. A beautiful iridescent blue stripe runs from the back edge of the gill covers to the base of the caudal fin: beneath lies a large area of dark blue or bluish-black which extends across the gill covers, below the eyes to the snout. The belly is a pink or yellowish-white. The fins are yellow and transparent. The front dorsal fin ray is purplish-brown. Both lobes of the caudal fin have a purplish-brown border and the middle rays are elongated and bluish. The anal fin has a lemon yellow border edged with red. The irises are a striking iridescent blue.

Females are smaller, with less vivid patterning. The middle caudal fin rays are only slightly elongated. The irises are more green. Males are as described above with strikingly elongated central caudal fin rays.

General care: As for *N.amphiloxus*. The males may be aggressive towards each other, but otherwise *N.palmeri* is a tolerant fish.

Breeding: Not difficult in fairly soft water. Temperature 26°C. The eggs will be laid among plants and are semi-adhesive. The parent fish should be removed after spawning. Some 50–100 eggs will be laid and the fry hatch after about 48 hours. They will swim freely after three or four days and grow quickly. The first week they should be fed on infusoria, the second week on *Artemia nauplii*. It must be noted that this is not a very productive fish.

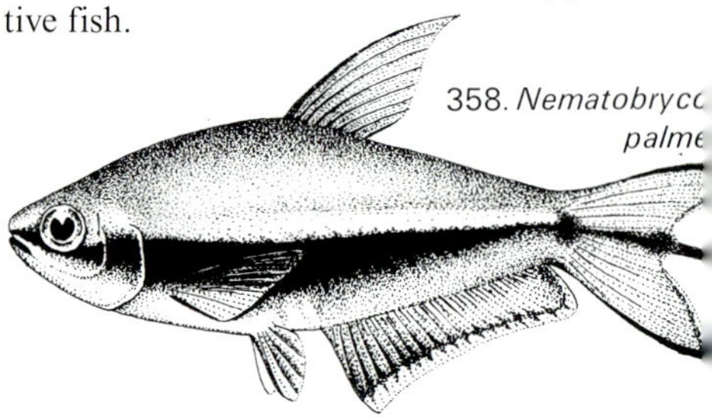

358. *Nematobrycon palmeri*

359. *Petitella georgiae*

THE FAMILY CHARACIDAE

The genus Petitella

There is only one species in the genus *Petitella* that is of likely interest to amateur aquarists, and even that species, *Petitella georgiae* described below, is not as yet very well known. It is very closely related to the *Hemigrammus* species and at first sight can easily be mistaken for *Hemigrammus rhodostomus*. Although it needs a relatively large tank if it is to feel at home and is somewhat particular about the composition of the water, *P.georgiae* is not too difficult to keep and is an attractive fish that is likely to increase in popularity.

PETITELLA GEORGIAE

Family: *Characidae*

Genus: *Petitella*

English name: none

Origin: Peru, Venezuela, the lower reaches of the Hualaga river and the upper reaches of the Amazon around Iquitos: the Carrao region in southeast Venezuela. It is possible that this species may also be found in the basins of the rivers Negro and Branco in northeast Brazil

Size: Maximum 6 cm

Habitat: Found in small streams with dense vegetation on the banks

SHAPE, COLORING AND MARKINGS: The body is extremely elongated and laterally only slightly compressed. The basic coloration is silvery with a metallic blue sheen which becomes greenish towards the back. The whole head, including the gill covers and the neck is blood red. The fins are colorless except for the deeply forked caudal fin, the two lobes of which are divided by a deep black line which begins at the base: a deep black oval mark surrounded by an area of creamy white lies on each lobe and the two outer fin rays are dark.

Females are more sturdily built and have fuller bellies.

Males are as described above: they are more slender and have a shiny golden green mark on the forehead.

GENERAL CARE: A shoal fish, *P.georgiae* should be kept in a fairly large aquarium with vegetation round the sides and plenty of free swimming space in the center. This species keeps to the middle and upper reaches of the tank. The composition of the water is important: it should be soft, under 6° DH and fairly acid, pH 6–6.8. Temperature 24°C and slightly higher for breeding. All small live animal matter will be eaten and dried food also accepted.

BREEDING: This is not easy but has been done successfully. The eggs can be laid either by a single pair or while the fish are in a group. The parent fish must have been very well fed. The water must be very soft, 3° DH and acid, pH 6. The lighting must be subdued, and all must be very quiet in and around the tank. The eggs are laid among fine leaved plants and the parent fish should be removed as soon as they have spawned for they have a tendency to eat the eggs. When the fry begin to swim freely they should be fed with ditch infusoria. At first they grow slowly but after three weeks grow much more quickly. The fry are very sensitive to polluted water. Waste matter must continually be siphoned off and the water changed regularly: that which is added must be the same temperature as that in the tank.

THE FAMILY CHARACIDAE

The genus Phenacogrammus

There is only one species in this genus of interest to aquarists. *Phenacogrammus interruptus*, described below, is by some authorities known as *Micralestes interruptus* and certainly the two genera are very closely related. An appealing fish in the aquarium, it is also one of the small group of African Tetras that can be bred with some success in captivity: it is interesting that all breeders to date report that its eggs take very much longer to hatch than those of its cousins, the South American Tetras.

360. *Phenacogrammus interruptus*

PHENACOGRAMMUS INTERRUPTUS

Family: *Characidae*

Genus: *Phenacogrammus*

English name: none

Origin: Central Africa, the Congo basin

Size: Maximum 8 cm

Habitat: No details are available of its natural habitat

SHAPE, COLORING AND MARKINGS: The body is fairly elongated and only slightly laterally compressed. In some lights the fish shows off all the colors of the spectrum. The back is brownish with an iridescent metallic blue tinge: the flanks vary from a dark iridescent yellow to olive-green or bluish-green: the belly is a silvery-violet. The head is relatively small: the eyes very large: the mouth points upwards. The fins are distinctive. The large dorsal fin and the caudal fin have elongated rays that look like a fringe. The fins are grey, tinged with violet: the caudal and anal fins have a narrow white edge. The caudal fin also bears a pattern of irregular black stripy marks.

Females are smaller with less vivid colors: the fins are smaller and have no fringe of elongated rays.

Males are as described above.

GENERAL CARE: *P.interruptus* needs a large aquarium with dense vegetation round the sides, plenty of free swimming space and a dark bed. Its colors show up best under very bright light from the front of the tank. Some floating plants should be included, preferably duckweed, which the fish like to eat. The water should be slightly acid and not too hard. Temperature 24°C. Fairly large aquatic insects, mosquito larvae and flies' eggs are the staple diet but dried food will also be accepted from time to time.

BREEDING: To be successful attention must be paid to both the rearing of the parent fish and the composition of the water. The breeding pair should have been kept in an aquarium as described above, and their diet must have been of black mosquito larvae and flies' eggs. The best results will be obtained from having two males and four females all about a year old, breeding in a group. The eggs are amber and about 2 mm in diameter. They are not adhesive and the bed to which they sink should if possible be covered with *Vesicularia dubyana*, Java moss. If a little Trypaflavine is added to the water it will prevent the unfertilised eggs from becoming mouldy. The eggs may be laid over three or four days and the breeding fish should be kept in the tank for four days from when the first eggs are laid. The parents do not seem to eat the eggs. As soon as the fry hatch and swim freely they should be fed with *Artemia nauplii* and very finely powdered food.

On no account should Cyclops be given to them.

THE FAMILY CHARACIDAE

The genus Prionobrama

Only one species, the Glass Bloodfin, *Prionobrama filigera* is found in the genus *Prionobrama* and it is very closely related to *Aphyocharax rubripinnis*. Not a great deal is known about the behavior of this species in its natural habitat, which is a somewhat restricted locality, but as will be seen from the description below, its requirements in the aquarium are well-established and it is not difficult for the aquarist either to keep or breed.

PRIONOBRAMA FILIGERA

Family: *Characidae*

Genus: *Prionobrama*

English names: Glass Bloodfish, Translucent Bloodfin, Glass Bloodfin.

Origin: Central Brazil, the basin of the river Madiera

Size: Maximum 6 cm

Habitat: No further details are available of its natural habitat

SHAPE, COLORING AND MARKINGS: The body is very elongated and laterally very compressed. It is more or less translucent but in some lights it looks green. The back is darker: the belly silvery. The front fin rays of the anal fin are elongated, giving the lower side of the fin an unusual hooked edge. The caudal peduncle is slightly reddish, this pigmentation often extending into the caudal fin. The front edge of the anal fin is creamy with behind, a black stripe.
Females have more rounded bellies and no black stripe on the anal fin.
Males are as described above.

GENERAL CARE: A typical shoal fish, *P.filigera* should be kept in a group in a fairly large aquarium with vegetation round the sides and plenty of free swimming space in the center. The water should be no more than 6° DH and of pH 6.5–6.8. Temperature 24°–26° C. All kinds of small live animal matter will be eaten and dried food also accepted.

BREEDING: Fairly easy if one pair are put in a spacious breeding tank, at least 40 cm long. The water should be very soft, slightly acid and filtered through peat. Some fine leaved plants should be put in, and moss provided on the bed.
Sunlight will encourage the fish to spawn. After the eggs have been laid the parent fish should be removed from the tank. The eggs, which are very small, hatch after about three days. For two days the fry will hang from the plants. As soon as they begin to swim freely, they should be fed on infusoria and subsequently on the usual fry foods.

THE FAMILY CHARACIDAE

The genus Pristella

There are at present only two species known in the genus *Pristella: Pristella riddlei,* described below and *Pristella aubynei* concerning which no reliable information is at present available. The genus is closely related to the genus *Hemigrammus:* indeed biologically it differs only in the pattern of dentition. It is not surprising therefore that *P.riddlei* was at one time considered merely to be a variety of the uncommon species of *Hemigrammus unilineatus*. It is now clearly established as a separate species. A very lively and active fish. *P.riddlei* is now deservedly popular among aquarists.

PRISTELLA RIDDLEI

Family: *Characidae*

Genus: *Pristella*

English name: X-ray fish

Origin: North South America, from the Guianas down to the lower reaches of the Amazon

Size: Maximum 5 cm

Habitat: No further details are avaiable of its natural habitat

SHAPE, COLORING AND MARKINGS: The body is slightly elongated and laterally somewhat compressed. The head is comparatively small: the mouth points upwards: the eyes are relatively large. The body is almost translucent and silvery. A dark horizontal line runs from a dark mark on the shoulders to the caudal peduncle. The caudal fin is red: the dorsal and anal fins are yellow with white points and a large deep black mark. There is a smaller black mark on the otherwise colorless ventral fin.
Females are somewhat larger than the males. Males are slightly smaller and more slender but in color identical to the females.

GENERAL CARE: As large a group as possible of these exceptionally beautiful fish should be kept in a large aquarium with plenty of plants round the edges and adequate free swimming space in the center. The fish show up to best advantage when the overhead light is filtered through floating plants and the bed is dark. The composition of the water is not critical but it should not be too hard. Temperature 20°–26° C. Both live and dried food will be accepted but some lettuce should always be included in the diet.

BREEDING: Not every pair makes a successful breeding pair: only by trial and error can a good breeding pair be established. Otherwise as for *Prionobrama filigera*.

361. *Pristella riddlei*

362. *Prionobrama filigera*

THE FAMILY CHARACIDAE

The genus Pseudocorynopoma

There are only two species in the genus *Pseudocorynopoma* of possible interest to aquarists. One, *Pseudocorynopoma heterandia* from the vicinity of São Paulo does not seem to have been imported to date, save for the very occasional male. The other species is however well-known being the popular and attractive Dragon-finned Characin, *Pseudocorynopoma doriae,* described below. It is closely related to the Swordtail Characin, *Stevardia riisei* (sometimes named *Corynopoma riisei*). However the male Dragon-finned Characins lack the appendage to the gill covers borne by male Swordtail Characins (hence the name *Pseudocorynopoma*) but as their name suggests, they have extremely beautiful, elongated fins. The Dragon-finned Characin is well worth the attention of the amateur aquarist.

364. *Pseudocorynopoma doriae*

PSEUDOCORYNOPOMA DORIAE

Family: *Characidae*

Genus: *Pseudocorynopoma*

English name: Dragon-finned Characin

Origin: Southern Brazil, northwest Argentina and Uruguay

Size: Maximum 8 cm

Habitat: No details are available of its natural habitat

SHAPE, COLORING AND MARKINGS: The body is elongated and laterally very compressed. The belly is very rounded: the mouth is large and directed upwards. The body is deepest at the level of the base of the front rays of the dorsal and anal fins, which lie opposite each other. The dorsal fin is greatly elongated: the middle fin rays are so long that they stretch half way along the caudal fin, which itself is deeply forked. The anal fin has a very long base: its front rays are also very long. The pectoral fins are large and taper to a point. The basic coloration is silvery and in certain lights has an iridescent greenish-blue tinge. An attractive dark band lies across the dorsal fin: the caudal and anal fins end in dark points.

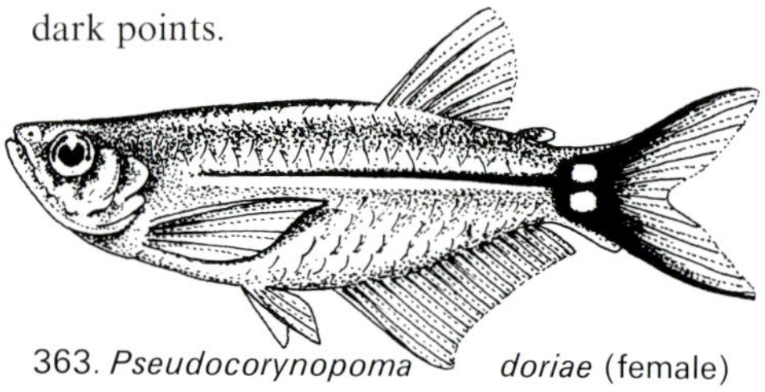

363. *Pseudocorynopoma doriae* (female)

Females are slightly smaller than the males, with less well developed dorsal and anal fins but more rounded bellies.
Males are as described above.

GENERAL CARE: *P.doriae* is a very fast swimmer and lives in shoals. It should therefore be kept in a large tank in a group of its own kind. The colors show up best with a dark bed and some floating plants: there should also be adequate free swimming space. The composition of the water is not critical. Temperature 22°C, *P.doriae* can jump quite large distances and the tank must be securely covered. All normal small live animal matter will be accepted as food.

BREEDING: A spacious breeding tank with a low water level is needed: the bed should be of coarse gravel to prevent the parent fish eating the eggs: they will try to eat them even as they are being laid. The fry will swim freely after about two days and should be fed with infusoria. Sexual characteristics will become apparent after three months. A good pair of breeders will produce very large nests.

THE FAMILY CHARACIDAE

The genus Pyrrhulina

The general characteristics of this genus have already been noted in the Introduction to the very closely related genus *Copeina*. It was noted there that for practical purposes, as far as the amateur aquarist is concerned, these two genera are virtually identical, although there are some technical distinctions of concern to taxonomists. Readers should consult the Introduction to the *Copeina* for general comments on the behavior, care and breeding of the *Pyrrhulina*.

365. *Pyrrhulina filamentosa*

PYRRHULINA BENI

Family: *Characidae*

Genus: *Pyrrhulina*

English name: none

Origin: Bolivia, the basin of the Beni river

Size: Approximately 7 cm

Habitat: Found in sluggish and still jungle creeks with dense vegetation on the banks, and in marshes

SHAPE, COLORING AND MARKINGS: The body is very slender and laterally only slightly compressed. The basic coloration is salmon: the back is darker or fawn: the flanks are yellowish, becoming silvery-white towards the belly. A very prominent almost black horizontal zig-zag line runs from the snout, through the eye to the base of the caudal peduncle. The fins are greyish and transparent. The dorsal fin bears a large dark mark and the base is bordered by an area of yellow.

Females are slightly smaller and less vividly colored. Both lobes of the caudal fin are of equal size.
Males are as described above. The upper lobe of the caudal fin is noticeably larger than the lower lobe.

GENERAL CARE: *P.beni* is only suitable for large aquariums and should be kept with other small peaceful fish. An ordinary well planted aquarium is suitable: it should preferably have a dark bed and irregular arrangements of wood. A number of broad-leaved plants preferably with some leaves above the water surface, should be included. The water should be medium-hard and slightly acid. Temperature 24°–26°C. *P.beni* is a very tolerant but rather shy species: it keeps to the middle and upper reaches of the tank. All sorts of live animal matter can be given as food but this species has a preference for winged land insects such as fruitflies: it will accept dried food for a change.

BREEDING: This species does not yet seem to have been bred in captivity but its reproductive behavior is likely to be similar to that of related species.

PYRRHULINA BREVIS

Family: *Characidae*
Genus: *Pyrrhulina*
English name: Short Pyrrhulina
Origin: The basins of the Amazon and Negro rivers
Size: Approximately 8 cm
Habitat: Found in sluggish and still jungle creeks, especially where the banks are heavily overgrown with vegetation

---

SHAPE, COLORING AND MARKINGS: The body is very slender and laterally only slightly compressed. The back is an iridescent brown or bronze: the flanks have a blue iridescent tinge and become silvery with a red tinge towards the belly. A dark band runs from the snout, through the eye to the dorsal fin. The scales on the flanks bear red dots which show up as horizontal lines. The fins are a striking red with broken black edges. The front fin rays of the dorsal fin have a prominent dark patch. The caudal fin is only slightly forked.
Females are slightly smaller. The fins are yellowish and without a dark edge. Both lobes of the caudal fin are the same size.
Males are as described above, with the upper lobe of the caudal fin larger than the lower.

GENERAL CARE: As for *P.beni.*

BREEDING: This species does not appear to have been bred as yet in captivity.

PYRRHULINA FILAMENTOSA

Family: *Characidae*
Genus: *Pyrrhulina*
English name: none
Origin: Surinam
Size: Approximately 6 cm
Habitat: Found in sluggish and still jungle streams with dense vegetation on the banks

---

SHAPE, COLORING AND MARKINGS: The body is slender and laterally only slightly compressed. The basic coloration is brownish: the back is darker or fawn. The flanks are salmon, becoming off-white tinged with greenish-yellow towards the belly. A dark pattern of lines runs from the snout, through the eye to above the gill covers. On the lower half of the body the scales carry red dots which show up as two horizontal lines. There is a red patterning below the base of the caudal fin, and three red dots immediately above the anal fin. The fins are almost transparent, with a reddish tinge. The dorsal fin is bright red at the front and lighter behind. The caudal fin has a light blue edge: the anal fin is red at the front.
Females are smaller and less vividly colored.
Males are as described above. The upper lobe of the caudal fin is larger than the lower lobe.

366. *Pyrrhulina beni*

GENERAL CARE: As for *P.beni.*

BREEDING: This species does not seem as yet to have been bred in captivity.

PYRRHULINA LAETA

Family: *Characidae*
Genus: *Pyrrhulina*
English name: none
Origin: The central region of the Amazon and the Guianas
Size: Approximately 8 cm
Habitat: Found in still and sluggish jungle streams with dense vegetation on the banks, and in marshy areas

---

SHAPE, COLORING AND MARKINGS: The body is very slender and laterally slightly compressed. The basic coloration is brownish: the back is darker, usually with two fairly prominent black marks between the head and the dorsal fin. The flanks are a dull brown, with a blue sheen: the belly is ochre to off-white. The scales on the upper half of the body have dark edges creating a net-like pattern. A dark pattern of stripes runs diagonally from the snout, through the eye towards the anal fin: in many specimens these are broken up into irregular patches. The fins are yellowish, tinged with red. The dorsal fin has a large dark mark bordered by a paler area.
Females are slightly smaller and less vividly colored.
Males are as described above, with a very large upper lobe to the caudal fin.

GENERAL CARE: As for *P.beni.*

BREEDING: This species has not as yet been bred successfully in captivity.

PYRRHULINA NATTERERI

Family: *Characidae*
Genus: *Pyrrhulina*
English name: Natterer's Pyrrhulina
Origin: The central Amazon region and possibly also the Negro river basin.
Size: Approximately 5 cm
Habitat: Found in sluggish and still jungle creeks with dense vegetation on the banks and in marshy areas

---

SHAPE, COLORING AND MARKINGS: The body is very slender and hardly if at all laterally compressed. The caudal peduncle is very long and thin. The back is a dark bronze: the flanks are a pale olive green to yellow, becoming

---

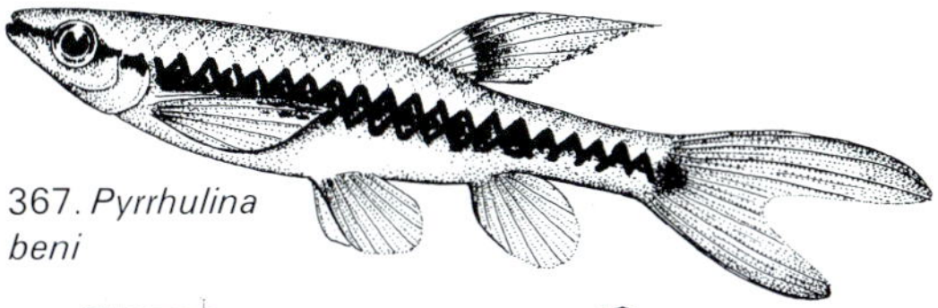

367. *Pyrrhulina beni*

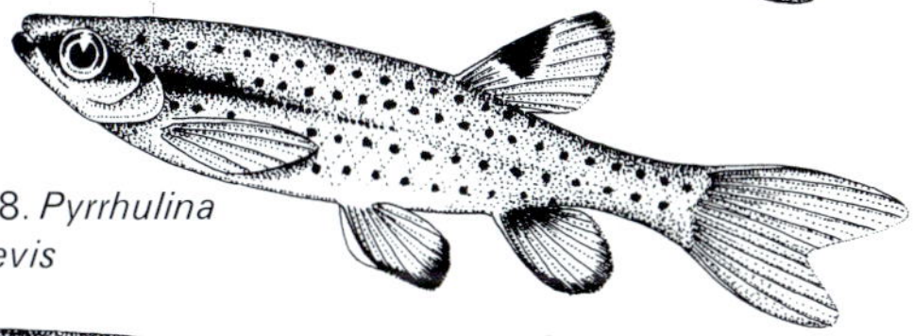

368. *Pyrrhulina brevis*

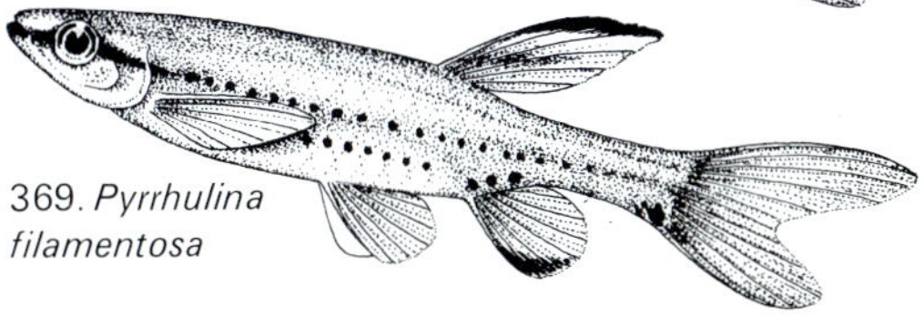

369. *Pyrrhulina filamentosa*

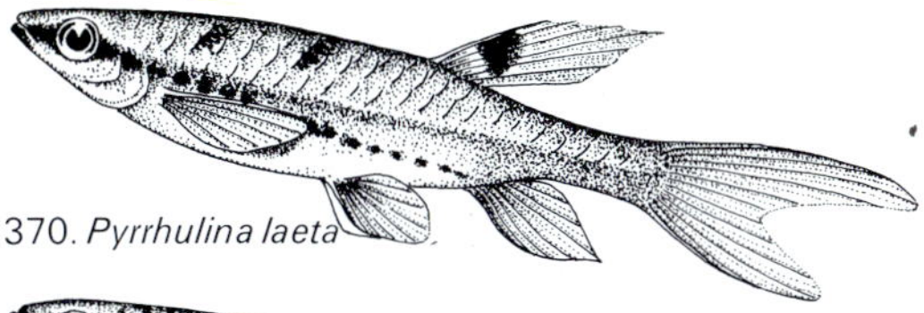

370. *Pyrrhulina laeta*

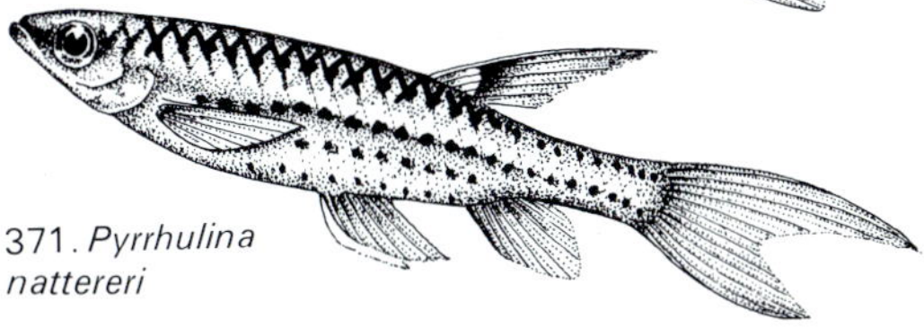

371. *Pyrrhulina nattereri*

372. *Pyrrhulina nattereri*

yellowish-white towards the belly. On the upper half of the body the scales have a dark edge, creating a net-like pattern and rust-brown dots which show up as lines. A dark horizontal line, sometimes indistinct, runs from the snout, through the eye to the base of the caudal fin. The fins are pale yellow: the dorsal fin has a reddish or bright red base and a large dark mark. The caudal fin is deeply forked.
Females are slightly smaller. The upper and lower lobes of the caudal fin are of equal size. Males are as described above. The upper lobe of the caudal fin is noticeably larger than the lower lobe.

GENERAL CARE: As for *P.beni*

BREEDING: This species does not seem as yet to have been bred in captivity.

ADDITIONAL INFORMATION: *P.nattereri* is rarely imported and is little known among aquarists.

373. *Pyrrhulina nigrofasciata*

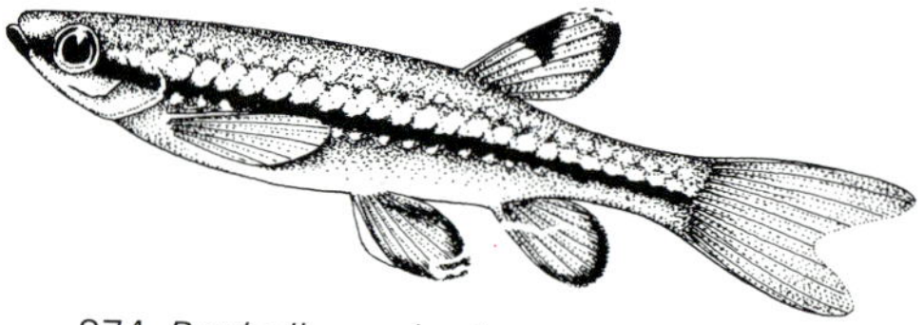

374. *Pyrrhulina rachoviana*

375. *Pyrrhulina vittata*

PYRRHULINA NIGROFASCIATA

Family: *Characidae*

Genus: *Pyrrhulina*

English name: Black-banded Pyrrhulina

Origin: Probably the central Amazon region but no precise information is available.

Size. Approximately 6 cm

Habitat: Probably found in small still and sluggish streams

SHAPE, COLORING AND MARKINGS: The body is very slim and laterally only slightly compressed: it greatly resembles *Copeina arnoldi.* The basic coloration is brown: the back is darker: the underside is a yellowish-brown. A broad dark brown longitudinal stripe runs from the snout over the eye and then along the body as a zig-zag, to the base of the caudal fin. Each scale has a blood red dot and these are aligned to each other. The red marks are most intense on the head and above the pectoral fins: the fins are yellow to rusty brown. The base of the dorsal fin is white and above lies a dark or black patch.
Females are smaller and less brightly colored. Males have fins that are more powerfully developed, particularly the upper lobe of the caudal fin: the anal fin has a dark or black border.

GENERAL CARE: As for *P.beni*. *P.nigrofasciata* is a very timid species which is particularly partial to fruitflies as diet.

BREEDING: This species has not as yet been bred successfully in captivity, but it is likely that its reproductive habits are similar to those of related species.

PYRRHULINA RACHOVIANA

Family: *Characidae*

Genus: *Pyrrhulina*

English name: Fanning Characin

Origin: The basins of the rivers Paraná and Plate.

Size: Approximately 5 cm

Habitat: Found in still and sluggish jungle streams with dense vegetation on the banks, and in marshy areas

SHAPE, COLORING AND MARKINGS: The body is very slender and laterally slightly compressed. The basic coloration is brownish: the back is considerably darker and shiny: the lower half of the body is ochre or yellowish-white. A shiny golden horizontal line runs from the snout to the base of the caudal fin, bordered below by a band of brown. The fins are yellowish-green: the dorsal fin has a large dark mark at the front.
Females are less vividly colored and smaller. Males have a brick-red edge to the ventral and anal fins, and the upper lobe of the caudal fin is very large.

GENERAL CARE: As for *P.beni.*

BREEDING: This species is easy to breed: for general instructions see the Introductory article for the genus *Copeina.*

ADDITIONAL INFORMATION: *P.rachoviana* is imported fairly regularly. If only males are kept they become very hostile to each other.

PYRRHULINA VITTATA

Family: *Characidae*

Genus: *Pyrrhulina*

English name: Striped Pyrrhulina

Origin: The Amazon basin around Santarem and the Tapajós river

Size: Approximately 7 cm

Habitat: In sluggish and still waters, especially those with dense vegetation on the banks

SHAPE, COLORING AND MARKINGS: The body is quite thick-set, and laterally only slightly compressed. *P.vittata* is noticeably less slim than related species. The basic coloration is greenish. The back is darker or olive green: the flanks silvery with a blue overtone. The underside is whitish with a pale red sheen. Practically every scale has a dark edge, creating a criss-cross pattern over the body. There are up to three dark marks on the body which can vary from narrow transverse bands to large blotches: the first lies on a level with the pectoral fin, the second roughly above the anal fin and the third at the base of the caudal fin. A darker stripe runs back over the eye to just beyond it. The fins are transparent to reddish, with a blue-white border. The dorsal fin has a prominent black patch at the front.
Females are rather larger, with entirely colorless fins, or fins only edged with blue.
Males are as described above: the upper lobe of the caudal fin is noticeably larger.

GENERAL CARE: As for *P.beni.*

BREEDING: This species is easy to breed in captivity: see Introductory note on the genus *Copeina.*

376. *Pyrrhulina nigrofasciata*

THE FAMILY CHARACIDAE

The genera Pygocentrus, Rooseveltiella and Serrasalmo

These genera are found over almost the whole of South America, in many different kinds of waters. They have a sharply serrated keel to the belly, which accounts for their popular name of Saw-toothed Characins. The species in these genera are also known as Piraya or Piranha fish. They are extremely voracious, although popular literature somewhat exaggerates their bloodthirsty nature. Their natural food is fish: animals and human beings are rarely attacked. The local population often quite happily bathes in waters that are infested with piranhas, although they naturally know from experience which stretches of water are dangerous and which are not. The real danger arises if an animal or human being goes into the water with an open bleeding wound. As soon as the piranhas scent the blood mingled with the water they attack: why they should be thus provoked by blood is not known. From some accounts it seems that the behavior of the fish varies from locality to locality: in some places even wounded animals that fall into the water are not attacked, whereas one or two miles up or down stream in the same waters, such animals are immediately and viciously attacked. Even those who fish for them have to be very careful, for the piranha's razor sharp teeth can inflict severe wounds on the angler as the fish is taken off the hook.
In the wild these fish live in large shoals. They should be kept in large groups in captivity and that, together with their predatory nature makes them unsuitable for the ordinary home aquarium. When kept in large species tanks however, or with other large fish (and this is not always successful), a shoal of piranhas can be a very impressive sight.
They look best against a dark background, which if made of irregularly-shaped lumps of wood will very nearly approximate to their natural habitat. Neither the composition of the water nor the temperature is critical. To create a shoal it is necessary to start off with a large number of very young fish: they will then grow to accept each other while attacking the weaker members so that a natural shoal will emerge through selection.
The diet is basically fish, although from what has been said above it is clear that meat will also be eaten. There are no records of piranha fish in captivity attacking their keeper but it would obviously be wise to avoid putting the hand in the tank if it has an open wound.
In this encyclopaedia the following species are described in alphabetical order: *Pygocentrus piraya, Rooseveltiella nattereri, Serrasalmo rhombeus, Serrasalmo spilopleura.*

377. *Rooseveltiella nattereri*

PYGOCENTRUS PIRAYA

Family: *Characidae*

Genus: *Pygocentrus*

English name: Piranha

Origin: The lower reaches of the Amazon, and its tributaries.

Size: Approximately 35 cm in the wild: remains considerably smaller in captivity.

Habitat: Very common in many different kinds of waters.

SHAPE, COLORING AND MARKINGS: The body is deep, stocky and laterally very compressed. The head is large, the forehead high. The keel of the belly is serrated from the pectoral fin. The caudal fin is slightly forked: the anal fin is long and sickle-shaped in adults. An adult specimen is difficult to distinguish from *Rooseveltiella nattereri,* but *P.piraya* has a tufted adipose fin. The coloring and markings depend largely on the exact locality from which the fish comes and also on the age of the specimen. Healthy half-grown specimens have a bluish or greenish grey back, which becomes more green or pale brown on the flanks: the whole of this part of the body is deeply tinged with silver and bears a large number of iridescent specks. The belly is vermilion or dark red. The dorsal and caudal fins are dark, the latter having a lighter patch in the middle. The anal fin is red with a wide black edge. The pectoral and ventral fins are vermilion.
There are no known external sexual characteristics.

GENERAL CARE: Only young specimens if any are suitable for large aquariums in the home. They cannot usually be kept with other fish. They can also be extremely intolerant of one another and it is only possible to build up a group from specimens kept together almost since they were fry. *P.piraya* is a nervous fish and needs plenty of hiding places in the tank and fairly subdued lighting. Arrangements of wood and leafy plants should be provided for this purpose.
The composition of the water is not critical, but fresh tap water should be avoided. Temperature 24°–27°C. *P.piraya* is not fussy about food, but has a preference for fish: it will also eat lean meat. Young fish are happy with a diet of large aquatic insects and larvae. A very voracious fish.

BREEDING: This species does not appear to have been bred as yet in captivity: nothing is known about its reproductive behavior.

ROOSEVELTIELLA NATTERERI

Family: *Characidae*

Genus: *Rooseveltiella*

English name: Red Piranha

Origin: The Amazon: this species is very widely distributed.

Size: Approximately 30 cm in the wild but remains considerably smaller in captivity

Habitat: Found in a very wide variety of waters

SHAPE, COLORING AND MARKINGS: The body is deep, stocky and laterally very compressed. The keel of the belly is serrated from the pectoral fins. The caudal fin is slightly forked: the anal fin is long and sickle-shaped in adults. The colors and markings, as well as the depth of the body vary according to the age of the fish. Half-grown well-cared for specimens have a bluish or brownish-grey back: the flanks are paler or a greenish-brown with a strong silvery sheen and innumerable iridescent metallic specks and small dots. The belly and the area to the throat are vermilion or dark blood red. The dorsal and caudal fins are blackish, the latter with a lighter patch in the middle. The anal fin is red with a broad black edge. The pectoral and ventral fins are a dark vermilion.
There are no known external sexual characteristics.

378. *Pygocentrus piraya*

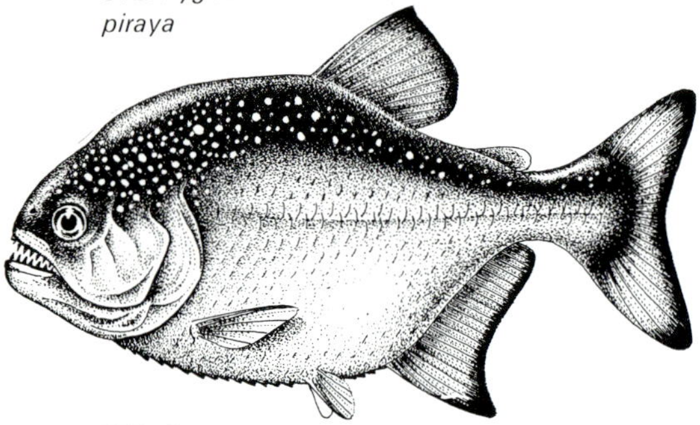

379. *Roseveltiella nattereri*

GENERAL CARE: As for *Pygocentrus piraya.*

BREEDING: This species has not as yet been bred in captivity.

ADDITIONAL INFORMATION: Members of the genus *Rooseveltiella* are distinguished from members of the genus *Serrasalmo* by the absence of teeth at the back of the upper palate.

SERRASALMO RHOMBEUS

Family: *Characidae*

Genus: *Serrasalmo*

English name: Spotted Piranha

Origin: The basin of the Amazon and a large area to the north of it.

Size: Approximately 35 cm in the wild but remains considerably smaller in captivity.

Habitat: Found in a wide variety of waters

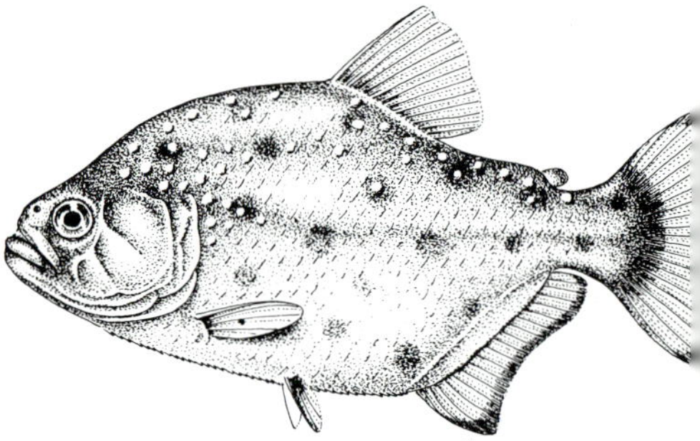

382. *Serrasalmo rhombeus*

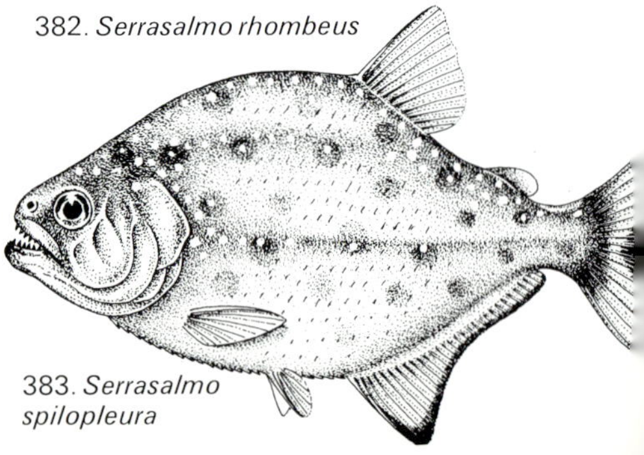

383. *Serrasalmo spilopleura*

◁ 380. *Pygocentrus piraya*

△ 381. *Serrasalmo rhombeus*

SHAPE, COLORING AND MARKINGS: The body is deep, stocky and laterally very compressed. The keel of the belly is serrated from the pectoral fins. The head and upper part of the body are a dark grey to olive green: the bottom half is off-white or silvery. A large number of dark patches lie irregularly over the body surface: in many specimens there is a distinct mark on the shoulders. The fins are grey and transparent. The caudal fin is black at the base and also edged with black: the central area is reddish. The fins of young fish are quite colorless and transparent with no markings at all. Adult fish have a very high forehead and are often almost completely black.
There are no known external sexual characteristics.

GENERAL CARE: As for *Pygocentrus piraya.*

BREEDING: This species has not as yet been bred in captivity.

SERRASALMO SPILOPLEURA

Family: *Characidae*
Genus: *Serrasalmo*
English name: none
Origin: The Amazon basin
Size: Approximately 24 cm
Habitat: Found in many different kinds of waters

SHAPE, COLORING AND MARKINGS: The body is very deep, stocky and laterally very compressed. The keel of the belly is serrated from the pectoral fins. The body is deeper and more stocky than that of *S.rhombeus,* and adult specimens closely resemble *Rooseveltiella nattereri.* The basic coloration of young fish is a greyish-green with a strong silvery sheen and many dark or light round patches on the flanks: many specimens have a distinct shoulder mark, which disappears when the fish grows older. The anal fin is completely black or has a black edge.
There are no known external sexual characteristics.

GENERAL CARE: *S.spilopleura* has not as yet been imported, but it is likely that it will require similar care to *Pygocentrus piraya.*

BREEDING: No information is available on the reproductive behavior of this species.

ADDITIONAL INFORMATION: *P.spilopleura* is still quite unknown to amateur aquarists. It may be that the color patterns given above are not entirely accurate as to date only preserved specimens have been described.

THE FAMILY CHARACIDAE

The genus Stevardia

This genus is closely related to the genus *Pseudocorynopoma* whose species exhibit the same unusual courting display. Despite its unusual and extremely interesting patterns of behavior, *Stevardia riisei* is not often seen in aquariums.

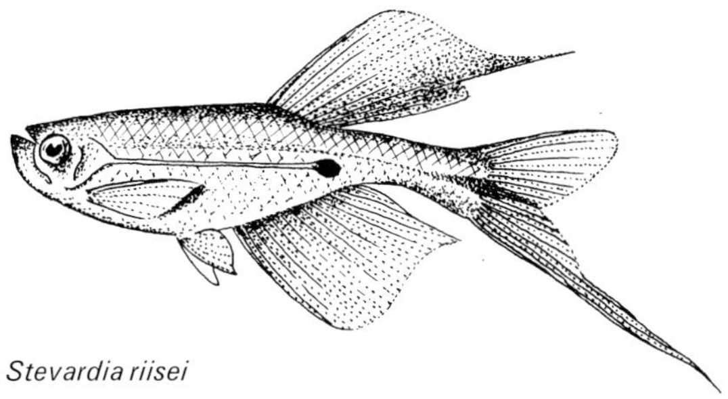

384. *Stevardia riisei*

STEVARDIA RIISEI

Family: *Characidae*
Genus: *Stevardia*
English name: Swordtail Characin
Origin: Trinidad and Venezuela
Size: Maximum 7 cm
Habitat: No further details are available of its natural habitat

SHAPE, COLORING AND MARKINGS: The body is very elongated and laterally slightly compressed. The head is relatively small and the mouth upward-pointing. The belly has a strong downward curve. The narrow-based, greatly elongated dorsal fin is positioned slightly further back than the middle of the body. The elongated broad-based anal fin is positioned slightly to the fore of the middle of the body. The caudal fin is deeply forked and the outer rays of the lower lobe are very elongated. The gill covers terminate in long feelers which have a small spoon-shaped organ at the tip. The coloration of *S.riisei* is subdued: it is a shiny silver with a narrow dark horizontal line along the body. The lower edge of the caudal fin has a yellowish-white border.
Females are not as large as the males. The fins are less well-developed and the gill covers terminate in a short spine.
Males as described above.

GENERAL CARE: An extremely lively but peaceful fish that requires a large tank with plenty of free swimming space. The composition of the water is not critical. Temperature 22°–24° C. All kinds of live animal matter will be accepted.

BREEDING: The eggs are fertilised in the oviduct of the female. The organs on the gill covers clearly play a part in mating: it is almost certain that they serve to bring the female into close enough contact with the male for the milt to be transferred. A male ready to mate will swim up to the female, move alongside her and extend the feelers on his gill covers. The spoon-shaped tip turns very dark and vibrates, so that it resembles prey. The female is thus attracted and swims alongside the male for a few moments: this is when the milt is implanted in her. The female is impregnated only once in her life. The eggs are laid among fine-leaved plants: the fry will be free swimming a few days after they hatch and should be fed on infusoria.

ADDITIONAL INFORMATION: The synonym for this species is *Corynopoma riisei.*

THE FAMILY CHARACIDAE

The genus Thayeria

The fish in the genus *Thayeria* are closely related to species in the genera *Hemigrammus, Nannobrycon* and *Nannostomus:* they are distinguished from all these species however by a more robust lower caudal fin lobe and the shape of the swim bladder. It is the unusual shape of the latter, that causes the fish in this genus to swim in the aquarium, at an oblique angle. This is one aspect of their behavior which makes them attractive and unusual fish to keep.

These fish are however, in the wild found almost exclusively in densely overgrown streams, with a great deal of vegetation not only on the banks but in the streams themselves as well. Accordingly, to simulate their natural environment it is necessary, as noted below, to keep them in very well-planted, shady tanks. When provided with a tank furnished in this way, the species in this genus become very pleasing fish. They are not, in other respects, very demanding fish and can accordingly be strongly recommended for amateurs looking for species that are unusual but not too difficult to keep. Four species are found in this genus of interest to amateur aquarists and are described below: one, *T.boehlkei* is not too difficult to breed.

385. *Thayeria obliqua*

THAYERIA BOEHLKEI

Family: *Characidae*

Genus: *Thayeria*

English name: none

Origin: Peru and the basin of the Marañón river

Size: Maximum 8 cm

Habitat: Found in small jungle streams and in the shallower waters of larger rivers, where overhanging vegetation provides shade and the water is rich in humus

386. *Thayeria boehlkei*

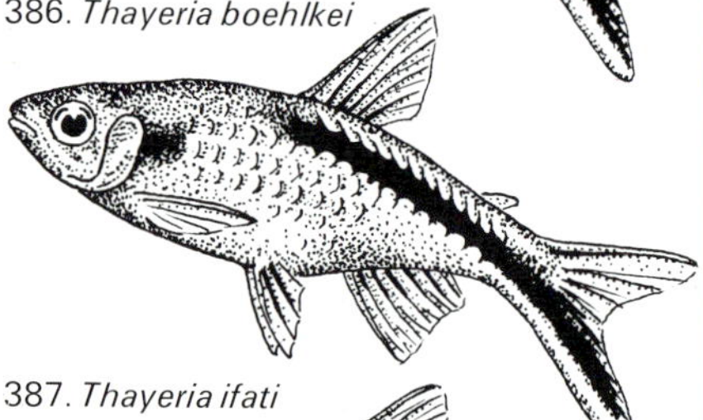

387. *Thayeria ifati*

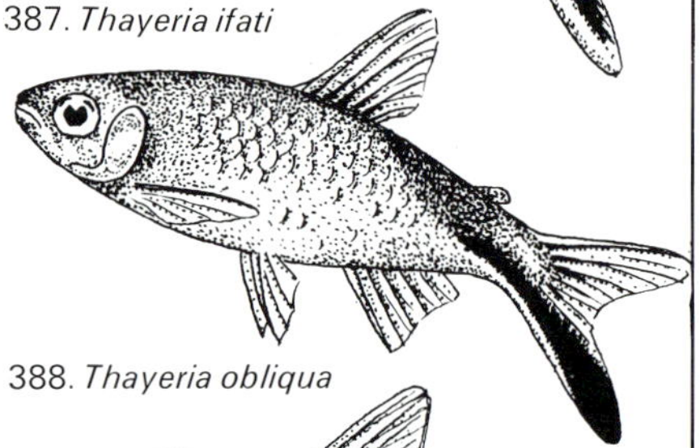

388. *Thayeria obliqua*

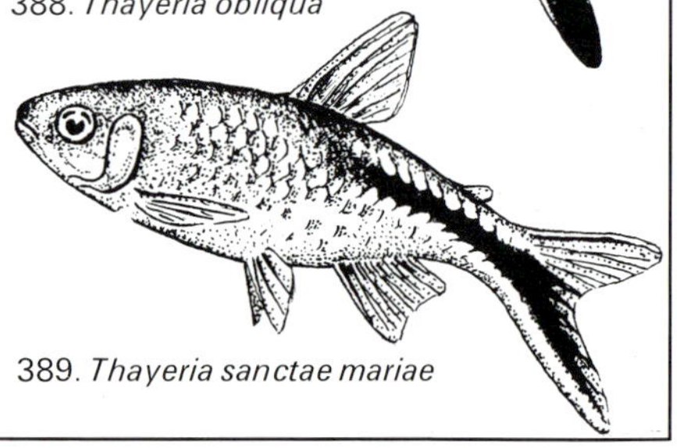

389. *Thayeria sanctae mariae*

Shape, coloring and markings: The body is slender and laterally somewhat compressed. The basic coloration is a silvery-white: the back is dark green with glistening patches of gold: the belly is a muddy yellow to light green. A deep black longitudinal stripe runs from the gill covers to the lower lobe of the caudal fin, bordered below by an area of gold. This line is much longer than in the related species described below. The front edge of the anal fin has a white border. The other fins are transparent and colorless.

Females, when sexually mature have much more rounded bellies.

Males are as described above.

General care: *T.boehlkei* is suitable for large aquariums and should be kept in a small group of its own kind. A dark bed and dense clumps of vegetation should be provided but there should also be adequate free swimming space in the upper reaches of the tank, where these fish are usually to be found. The water should be slightly peaty. Temperature 23°–28°C. All live animal matter such as mosquito larvae, fruitflies, Daphnia and Cyclops will be accepted and dried food may also be given for variety.

Breeding: This is not difficult. The eggs are laid in dense clumps of *Myriophyllum*. The breeding water should be soft and slightly acid. *T.boehlkei* is a very prolific species frequently with nests of over 1000 fry. The parent fish should be removed from the tank immediately after spawning and some of the water changed.

Additional information: When stationary *T.boehlkei* hangs in the water at an oblique angle with its head up: until recently it was frequently known as *Thayeria obliquus* or *obliqua*. It is the most common species of this genus, but still a beautiful and elegant fish. It has been known since 1908 and for many years has been a well established aquarium fish.

Some amateurs wrongly believe it to be a delicate species.

THAYERIA IFATI

Family: *Characidae*

Genus: *Thayeria*

English name: none

Origin: The lower reaches of the Amazon

Size: Maximum 8 cm

Habitat: Widely distributed in jungle swamps and streams where dense vegetation gives shade and the water is rich in humus

Shape, coloring and markings: The body is slender and laterally somewhat compressed. The basic coloration is a pale yellow or silvery-white: the back is brown to dark green with an attractive golden sheen: the belly is white or a rather muddy yellow. A deep black longitudinal strips runs from the front of the dorsal fin to the lower lobe of the caudal fin with, below, an area of attractive gold. A black spot lies behind the gill covers level with the eye. The base of the caudal fin is a yellowish-brown: the rest of the fins are colorless. There are no known external sexual characteristics.

General care: As for *T.boehlkei.*

Breeding: No information is available but it is likely that the reproductive behavior of this species is similar to that of related species.

Additional information: *T.ifati* is closely related to *T.boehlkei.*

THAYERIA OBLIQUA

Family: *Characidae*

Genus: *Thayeria*

English name: Penguin Fish

Origin: The lower reaches of the Amazon basin

Size: Maximum 8 cm

Habitat: Found in jungle streams with dense vegetation on the banks and water rich in humus

SHAPE, COLORING AND MARKINGS: The body is slender and laterally somewhat compressed. The basic coloration is a light yellow or silvery-white. The back is dark green or brown, with an attractive golden sheen: the belly is white or a muddy yellow. A zone of dark pigmentation bordered below by gold, begins at the back of the dorsal fin, grows much darker at the level of the adipose fin and extends back to the lower lobe of the caudal fin, where it meets a green or gold spot. The base of the dorsal fin is yellow to brown: otherwise the fins are colorless and transparent.
There are no known external sexual characteristics.

GENERAL CARE: As for *T.boehlkei.*

BREEDING: No information is available on the reproductive behavior of this species, but it is likely to be similar to that of related species.

ADDITIONAL INFORMATION: The name *T.obliqua* is often mistakenly applied to *T.boehlkei.*

390. *Thayeria boehlkei*

THAYERIA SANCTAE-MARIAE
Family: *Characidae*
Genus: *Thayeria*
English name: none
Origin: The lower reaches of the Amazon basin
Size: Maximum 8 cm
Habitat: Found in innumerable jungle streams where dense vegetation grows along the banks and the water is rich in humus

SHAPE, COLORING AND MARKINGS: The body is slender and laterally somewhat compressed. The basic coloration is a light yellow or silvery-white: the back is brown to dark green with an attractive golden sheen: the belly is white or muddy yellow. A dark zone bordered below by a line of gold begins below the dorsal fin, becomes a deep black at the level of the adipose fin and extends back to the lower lobe of the caudal fin, where it meets a green or gold spot. The base of the caudal fin is yellow to brown: otherwise all the fins are colorless and transparent.
There are no known external sexual characteristics.

GENERAL CARE: As for *T.boehlkei.*

BREEDING: This species does not appear to have been bred in captivity.

ADDITIONAL INFORMATION: *T.sanctae-mariae* is distinguished from the identically marked *T.obliqua* by its much shorter lateral line.

THE FAMILY CITHARINIDAE

An introductory description

The *Citharinidae* species make up a small family of African fish closely related to the *Characidae* family of Characins. In behavior the *Citharinidae* greatly resemble the Pencilfish, the *Nannostomi.* They are not very well known among aquarists but there is no reason why they should not be more generally kept in aquariums, for they present few unusual problems to the amateur. Six genera are known: *Distichodus, Nannaethiops, Neoborus, Neolebias, Phago* and *Citharinus.*
The species in the genus *Citharinus* are only suitable for the largest public aquariums. They, and the *Distochodus* (which also require very large tanks) and the *Neoborus* species are very rarely if ever imported: consequently they are not dealt with further in this encyclopaedia, for it is very unlikely that the amateur aquarist will either come across them or be concerned with their care. The three remaining species are all more suitable for conventional aquariums. The *Nannaethiops* and *Neolebias* species are small and rather timid fish: they must be kept in groups of their own kind, sharing the tank only with other smaller peaceful species. On the other hand the *Phago* species are much larger fish, predatory by nature and accordingly require quite different conditions and companions.

The genus Nannaethiops

Two species of these peaceful attractive shoaling fish form a welcome addition to the aquarium. They are particularly attractive because they are suitable for any size of community tank. A third species. *Nannaethiops geisleri* (only some 2.5 cm long) which unlike the species here described has no adipose fin, has not as yet, it seems, been imported.

NANNAETHIOPS TRITAENIATUS

Family: *Citharinidae*

Genus: *Nannaethiops*

English name: none

Origin: The upper reaches of the Congo river and its tributaries

Size: Approximately 4 cm

Habitat: No further details are available of tis natural habitat

391. *Nannaethiops tritaeniatus*

392. *Nannaethiops unitaeniatus*

Shape, coloring and markings: The body is elongated and laterally very slightly compressed. The back is brownish to fawn, with dark edged scales. The belly is silvery-white with a soft red lustre. An almost straight longitudinal line runs from the snout across the eye to the caudal peduncle, where it terminates in a round golden-edged patch: both above and below are narrower, less prominent stripes and in between them, vivid areas of gold. The dorsal fin is orange-red: the caudal and anal fins red to rust-brown: the ventral fins are reddish with a blue front edge.

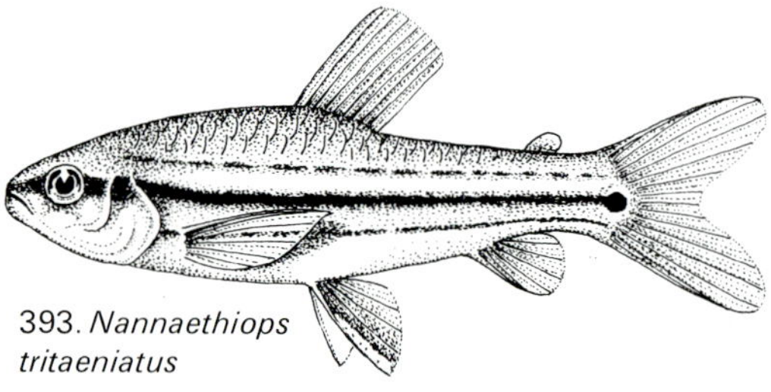

393. *Nannaethiops tritaeniatus*

Females are a little larger: in the mating season the whole body is suffused with gold. Males are as described above: the dorsal fin is deeper than in females: during the mating season the fins and the longitudinal stripe become bright red.

General care: Suitable for both large and small aquariums provided the community tank is shared with only smaller quiet species. *N.tritaeniatus* is rather timid and the tank must have an adequate number of hiding places: arrangements of bogwood are very good. The fish are best kept in a large group of their own kind. They usually keep to the lower reaches of the tank, remaining just above the bed, which should preferably be of fine river sand. The tank vegetation should not be too dense. The composition of the water is not critical but fresh tap water should be avoided. Temperature 23°–26° C. All small live animal matter will be accepted as food: dried food may be given for a change.

Breeding: *N.tritaeniatus* is a prolific species not difficult to breed. The breeding tank should be at least 40 cm long. The water should be rich in oxygen and not too hard: mature aquarium water is ideal. The tank should be placed to catch the evening sun. The eggs will be laid between the plants or over the sandy bottom. At 25° C the eggs hatch after 24–36 hours: the fry swim free some four or five days later. The usual fry foods will be appropriate.

395. *Neolebias ansorgei*

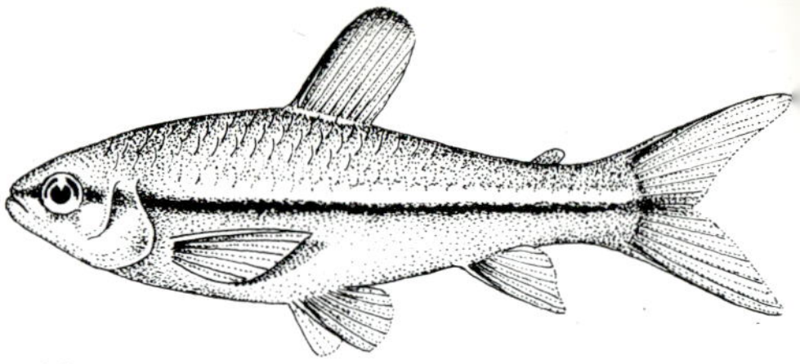

394. *Nannaethiops unitaeniatus*

NANNAETHIOPS UNITAENIATUS

Family: *Citharinidae*

Genus: *Nannaethiops*

English name: One-striped African Characin

Origin: Almost the whole of equatorial Africa

Size: Approximately 6.5 cm

Origin: Found in many different waters

Shape, coloring and markings: The body is elongated and laterally very slightly compressed. The back is dark brown to greenish-brown: the lower part of the body and the throat are yellowish to white with a marked silvery gleam. A thin dark brown to blue-black longitudinal stripe runs back from the snout across the eye to the base of the caudal fin: above and below lie golden or red iridescent zones. The fins are yellowish to grey-white with a greenish sheen.

Females are less vividly colored.

Males are as described above: during the mating season the dorsal fin and the lobes of the caudal fin are a brilliant red.

General care: As for *N.tritaeniatus*.

Breeding: As for *N.tritaeniatus*.

THE FAMILY CITHARINIDAE

The genus Neolebias

There three species at present in this genus. The two of interest to aquarists are described below: the third, *Neolebias landgrafi* which is found in the Cameroons, is very similar to *Neolebias ansorgei* but has not as yet, it seems been imported. Smaller than the fish in the genus *Nannaethiops*, the *Neolebias* species are very like them in behavior: physically they are different in that usually they have no adipose fin.

Although in general these fish require the same kind of care as the species in the genus *Nannaethiops*, some authorities suggest that they can be very sensitive and react adversely to hard water. Accordingly the composition of the water in the tank should be carefully monitored. They also sometimes tend not to flourish in a community tank and it may be necessary to isolate them as a pair in a separate species tank.

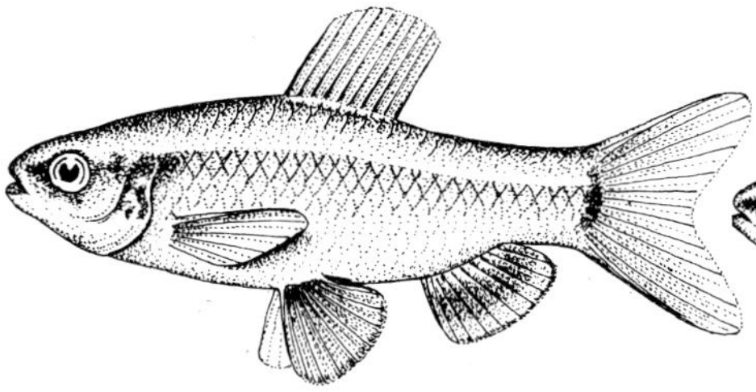

396. *Neolebias ansorgei*

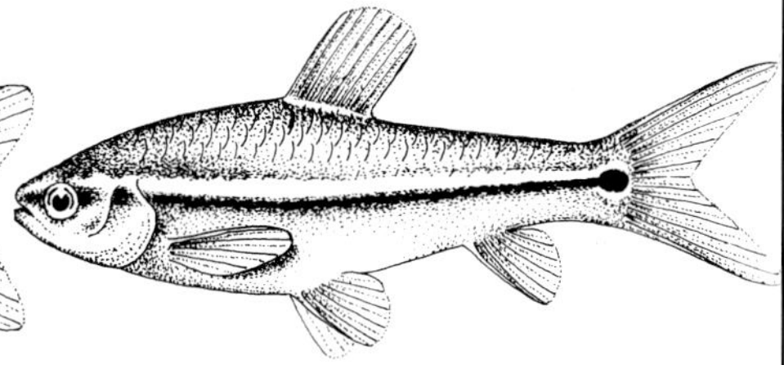

397. *Neolebias unifasciatus*

NEOLEBIAS ANSORGEI

Family: *Citharinidae*

Genus: *Neolebias*

English name: none

Origin: West central Africa

Size: Approximately 4.5 cm

Habitat: Found in a wide variety of different waters

SHAPE, COLORING AND MARKINGS: The body is fairly deep, somewhat thick-set and laterally slightly compressed. The back is brownish with green overtones: the flanks are pale green to iridescent greenish-blue, with violet overtones: the lower part of the body is yellowish. Some specimens have a network pattern on the flanks produced by the dark edgings of the scales. The shoulders carry pale bordered patches. A crescent-shaped dark green patch lies on the base of the caudal fin. The unpaired fins are yellow with a red overtone and black borders: the ventral fins are reddish.

Females are more robust and with more rounded bellies. The eggs in the oviduct of females ready to spawn are clearly visible if the fish is examined against the light.

Males are as described above.

GENERAL CARE: As for *Nannaethiops tritaeniatus*.

BREEDING: An all-glass or plastic breeding tank of six liters capacity should be filled with well oxygenated mature water. Temperature 30°C. Part of the tank should have dense vegetation. The eggs are laid between the plants: ten eggs are laid each time, 300 in all. The fry hatch after 20–24 hours. Only the finest foods will be accepted and the fry are difficult to raise during the first three to four weeks: thereafter normal fry foods may be given. The fry reach sexual maturity after about six months.

NEOLEBIAS UNIFASCIATUS

Family: *Citharinidae*

Genus: *Neolebias*

English name: none

Origin: Tropical West Africa

Size: Approximately 4.5 cm

Habitat: No details are available of its natural habitat

SHAPE, COLORING AND MARKINGS: The body is deep, somewhat thick-set and laterally slightly compressed. The basic coloration is reddish: the back is a red-brown. A dark brown to black longitudinal stripe runs back from the snout across the eye to the base of the caudal fin where it becomes a round patch, bordered above by a zone of gleaming gold. The unpaired fins are reddish, usually with a darker border.

Females are more robust and have very rounded bellies.

Males are as described above.

GENERAL CARE: As for *Nannaethiops tritaeniatus*, but temperature 24°–28°C.

BREEDING: As for *Neolebias ansorgei*.

ADDITIONAL INFORMATION: *N.unifasciatus* was first described by Frans Steindachner in 1894, although it has only become known to aquarists in recent years.

THE FAMILY CITHARINIDAE

The genus Phago

These very slender fish with very elongated snouts are predatory by nature and *Phago maculatus*, described below, is well named the Pike Characin: it is odd that at the same time they have the reputation in the aquarium of being exceptionally shy and timid fish, so much so that if alarmed they will refuse to eat. Indeed, they have the reputation of being at all times difficult feeders and they are unlikely to appeal as much to amateurs as the species described in the two other genera in this family, although in other respects they are interesting fish.

These species will not only eat smaller fish but are also notoriously prone to biting the fins, and otherwise harassing, larger fish that they do not actually kill. Unlike some predators however, the *Phago* species are not restricted in diet to live fish and can be fed principally on other live animal matter. They are still however fish for the specialist.

398. *Phago loricatus*

PHAGO LORICATUS

Family: *Citharinidae*

Genus: *Phago*

English name: none

Origin: West Africa, the Niger basin

Size: Maximum 15 cm

Habitat: No details are available of its natural habitat

SHAPE, COLORING AND MARKINGS: The body is very elongated and cylindrical: the mouth is pointed and beak-like, with an upper jaw that can be moved upwards. The body is covered with tough scales that have spines and a comb-like edge. The basic coloration is light brown: the back is dark brown: the belly a muddy yellow to white. There are usually three longitudinal stripes on the body, the second being the most prominent: between the stripes are patches of lustrous gold. The fins are a soft yellow or colorless. The dorsal and caudal fins carry dark brown to black bands.

GENERAL CARE: *P.loricatus* is only suitable for large community tanks containing other large fish. It is not a social fish and one or two specimens suffice. There must be plenty of free swimming space and also adequate dense vegetation to provide hiding places: bogwood arrangements are also appreciated. *P.loricatus* will stay in the upper and middle reaches of the tank and seek out shady areas. The composition of the water is not critical. Temperature 26°–28°C.
This species is predatory and must not be kept with smaller fish. The diet consists mainly of small fish but it will also eat the larvae of larger insects.

BREEDING: This species has not as yet been bred successfully in captivity.

ADDITIONAL INFORMATION: *P.loricatus* is only really at home in large specialised aquariums. If it lacks adequate space and quiet it will start to refuse food and soon deteriorate. It is rarely kept by aquarists although it has been known since it was first imported in 1912.

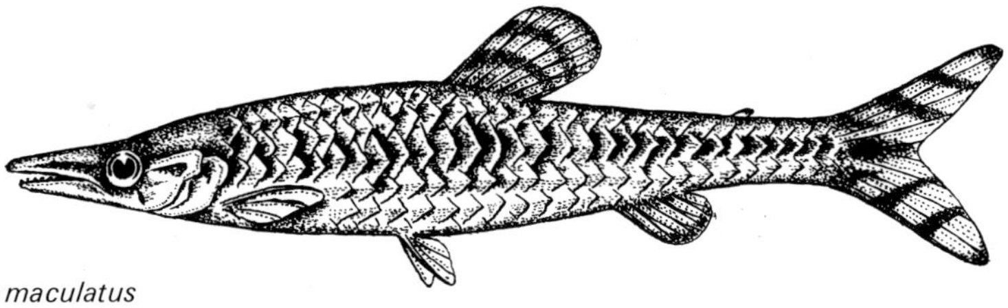

399. *Phago maculatus*

PHAGO MACULATUS

Family: *Citharinidae*

Genus: *Phago*

English name: Pike Characin

Origin: West Africa, the Niger basin

Size: Maximum 14 cm

Habitat: No further details are available of its natural habitat

SHAPE, COLORING AND MARKINGS: The body is very elongated and in all respects closely resembles that of *P.loricatus* except that it is less slender. The basic coloration is light brown: the back is dark brown or black with a marbled gleam: the belly is a muddy yellow to silvery-white. A large number of diagonal lines appear on the body. The upper jaw is brown or black. The dorsal and caudal fins are dark brown to black with black banding. There are no known external sexual characteristics.

GENERAL CARE: As for *P.loricatus*.

BREEDING: This species has not yet been bred in captivity.

ADDITIONAL INFORMATION: Like *P.loricatus*, *P.maculatus* if kept in inappropriate conditions, will refuse to eat.

THE FAMILY COBITIDAE

An introductory description

The Cobotidae or Spine Loaches are a relatively small family and these fish are found only in the Old World: none is native to the Americas. There are seven genera, *Acanthophthalmus, Acanthopsis, Botia, Cobatis, Lepidocephalus, Misgurnus* and *Noemacheilus*. Of these, only four, *Acanthophthalmus, Acanthopsis, Botia* and *Lepidocephalus* are tropical genera and of interest to amateur aquarists in general, although the genus *Misgurnus,* in which are placed the charming Japanese Weather-fish *Misgurnus anquillicaudatus* and the Weather-fish *Misgurnus fossilis fossilis* is a genus of interest to some aquarists with more specialist tastes.
All the tropical genera are made up of shy, bottom-loving fish, with a protective spine below the eye which, when erected, is an effective defence against many predators and can even inflict a sharp wound on the unwary aquarist, but the spine is not poisonous and the amateur will suffer no permanent harm. Worm-like in shape, these fish are very adept hunters of food on the bottom and are aided by their well-developed and acutely sensitive barbels. Some species have a secondary respiratory system which ensures their survival in muddy, poorly oxygenated waters.
While they are neither the most vividly colored nor most active of fish, the *Cobotidae* are very interesting and rewarding species to keep, but although they can be kept in a community tank, they will only be seen to best advantage by the amateur willing to devote his full attention to them and provide a group of them with a properly ordered species tank.

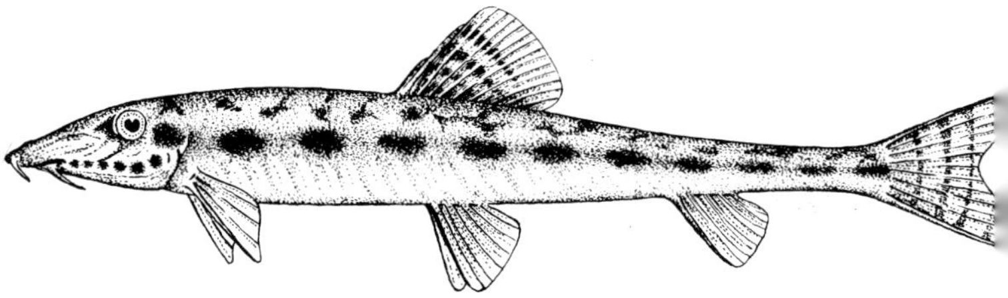

400. *Acanthopsis choiorhynchus*

The genus Acanthopsis

Only the one species, *Acanthopsis choiorhynchus* described fully below, is to be found in this genus. It is quite unlike any other species in the family *Cobotidae:* it is considerably larger than species in the genus *Acanthopthalmus* for example, and its very long head and snout give it a most unusual appearance. It is still a somewhat unusual fish to come across in an aquarium.

ACANTHOPSIS CHOIORHYNCHUS

Family: *Cobitidae*

Genus: *Acanthopsis*

English name: none

Origin: Southeast Asia, Sumatra, Borneo and Java

Size: 18 cm

Habitat: Found in both still and fairly fast-flowing waters, with a sandy bed

SHAPE, COLORING AND MARKINGS: The body is long, slender and laterally slightly compressed. It has a fairly large head with a pointed snout, the upper half of which is elongated to form a kind of trunk. The mouth is small, under-positioned and with three pairs of barbels: the thorns below the eyes have two points. The basic coloration varies from a dull ochre to rust-brown. There are usually a number of dark marks which merge to form an irregular stripe running the length of the body. Above this line and on the back more irregular marks and stripy patterns appear, varying in color from a luminescent yellow to brown or deep black. The fins are yellowish and transparent: the dorsal and caudal fins carry rows of dark spots and flecks.
There are no known external sexual characteristics.

GENERAL CARE: *A.choiorhynchus* is only suitable for larger aquariums, provided with sandy beds preferably covered with a layer of peat dust. There should be plenty of hiding places afforded by irregular arrangements of stones or wood. These fish always keep to the bottom of the tank and are fond of wallowing about in the bed: the water must therefore always be efficiently filtered. It is also unwise to plant fine-leaved, low-growing plants in the tank. These are tolerant fish and their behavior is similar to that of the *Acanthophthalmus* species. Temperature 25°–28°C. Any kind of worm-like food will be greedily accepted: Tubifex, red mosquito larvae, Enchytraeus and small earthworms are all suitable. Dried food will also be eaten.

BREEDING: No information is available on the breeding habits of this species.

ADDITIONAL INFORMATION: This species is a decidedly twilight fish which likes to spend the day burrowing into the bed. It was first imported in 1929.

THE FAMILY COBITIDAE

The genus Acanthophthalmus

The members of this genus are found over a fairly large area of Southeast Asia. They live in shallow waters with sandy beds, such as are found along the shores of many different kinds of waters. They are particularly fond of spots sheltered from the currents where sediment collects to provide them with an ideal habitat. They like to swim along the bed, seeking the worms that live in it and which are their main diet. They will also eat insect larvae living on the bed and vegetable matter they can find there.
This fish has a worm-like, cylindrical shape and is covered with extremely small scales hardly visible to the naked eye. Its eyes are small and covered by a transparent membrane which protects them from damage when the fish is twisting and turning on the bed. There is a spine below the eyes which can be erected and becomes a formidable weapon of defence. This thorn-like spine has given rise to the scientific name for the genus, *Acanthophthalmus*, Thorn-eye.
The genus includes a number of distinct species although exactly how many should be classified as separate species is debatable, which is not surprising for the coloring and markings of the fish can vary significantly not only between specimens from different localities but also between specimens from the same area. It is particularly difficult for amateur aquarists who usually have no other specimens for comparison, to be absolutely sure of the species to which a particular fish belongs.
Many books advise that there should be no sharp sand in the tank in which these fish are to be kept because they might injure themselves. In fact the sharp sand used by aquarists, which is natural river sand is not at all sharp in the ordinary sense of the word. Neither that sand nor silver sand will injure these fish in any way: to make the bed of the aquarium with it will in fact simulate the natural habitat. There should be adequate hiding places in the tank, for these fish are shy: bogwood, piles of stones and even plastic tubes of 1 cm diameter embedded in terraces will all be appropriate. The *Acanthophthalmus* will be happy in community tanks where indeed they

401. *Acanthophthalmus kuhli*

fulfill a useful role. They should be kept in a group of their own kind and then they lose some of their timidity. Unlike many fish that live on the bottom, they do not stir up the sediment very much: in fact they have never actually been observed burrowing into the bed.
Like many other fish of the *Cobitidae* family, these species are very sensitive to changes in atmospheric pressure. This may be due to their unusual swim bladders, which have a front section enclosed in a bony case and a rear section that is, at best rudimentary. The intestines function as a secondary respiratory system, and the fish can often be seen swimming to the surface to take in air: this happens particularly in the early hours of the morning when the oxygen content of the water is at its lowest.
Very little is known about the reproductive behavior of these species. There have been reports of occasional spawnings in aquariums where these fish have been kept for a long time but the mating cycle has never been observed in detail. It seems that the pair mate near the surface.
In the large storage tanks of exporters where many of these fish are kept for a long time small specimens are regularly discovered that must have been born in the tank. It should therefore be possible for them to be bred in captivity and to do so would be an interesting challenge for the amateur.
It is suggested that if this is to be attempted a fairly large breeding tank should be used and some eight to ten fish introduced into it. A small amount of peat dust should be spread

thinly over a sandy bed and a number of retreats created as suggested for the normal tank above. A water level of 10 cm should be adequate. The water should be about pH 6.5. The temperature should be 22°–24°C, but an increase to 26°C might stimulate mating if the fish seem to have paired off. Probably this tank should be removed from direct sunlight but allowed some daylight. A few *Cryptocoryne* varieties should be put in the tank as well as some floating plants such as *Pistia stratiotes*. No doubt the water would benefit from being circulated through a peat filter but undue disturbance of the surface should be avoided. Perhaps the fish should be fed sparingly with dried food that sinks to the bottom as well as with Tubifex. Daphnia and Cyclops. It may be that such a tank would have to stand for a long time before anything occurred but it would be rewarding and well worth-while if at the end, this mystery of the mating behavior of the *Acanthophthalmus* species were solved. It should be remembered that the spine below the eyes can inflict nasty wounds. Great care must be taken when handling these fish. Moreover, when catching them a fine net in which the spine could be caught and damaged should never be used: either a very coarse meshed net or a suitable trap should be employed.

402. *Acanthophthalmus cuneovirgatus*

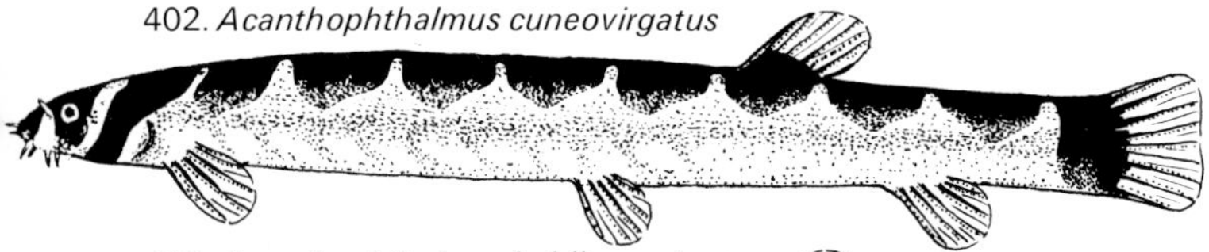

403. *Acanthophthalmus kuhli sumatranus*

404. *Acanthopthalmus kuhli kuhli*

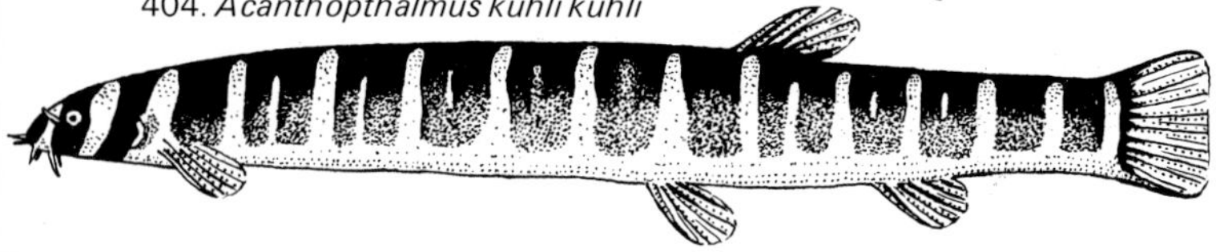

405. *Acanthophthalmus robiginosus*

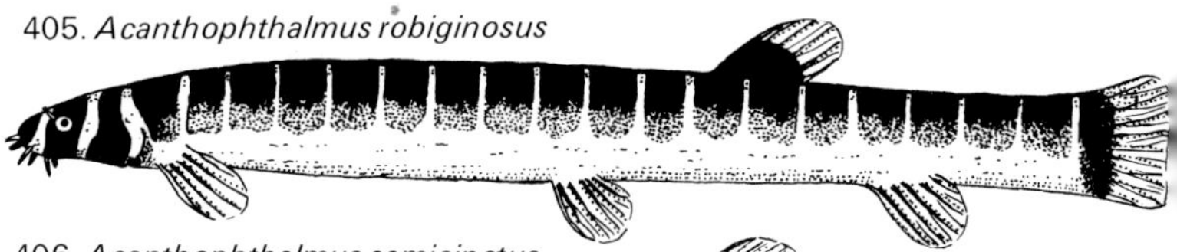

406. *Acanthophthalmus semicinctus*

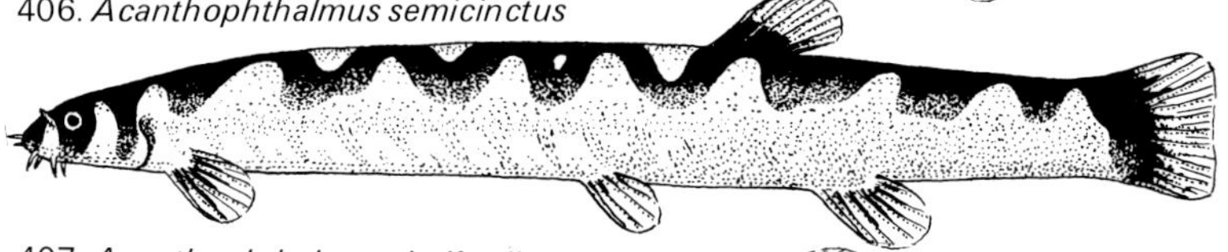

407. *Acanthophthalmus shelfordi*

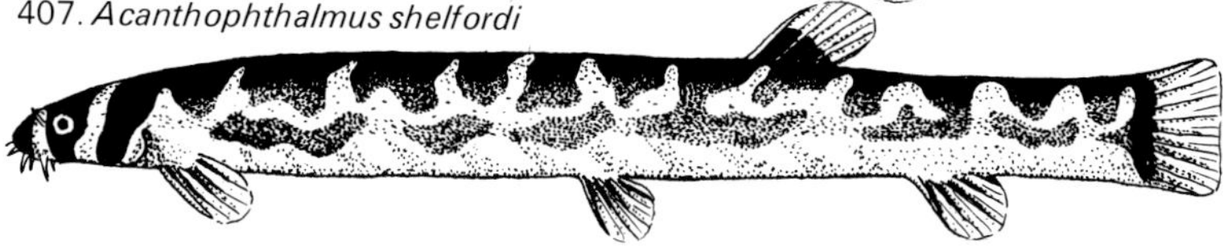

ACANTHOPHTHALMUS CUNEOVIRGATUS

Family: *Cobitidae*

Genus: *Acanthophthalmus*

English name: none

Origin: Malaya, Johore

Size: Maximum 6 cm

Habitat: Found in shallow waters with sandy beds, such as mountain streams and meandering rivers

SHAPE, COLORING AND MARKINGS: The body is elongated, worm-shaped and laterally compressed towards the tail. The mouth is underpositioned with three pairs of barbels. The basic coloration is bright yellow, becoming pale yellow to off-white towards the belly. There are three unbroken bands across the head and a large dark mark on the caudal peduncle. A number of deep black more or less cone-shaped marks run from the back halfway down the body. The fins are colorless and transparent.
Females have smaller pectoral fins.
Males have more well developed pectoral fins and, in sexually mature specimens, a pearly sheen over the belly.

GENERAL CARE: *A.cuneovirgatus* is suitable for both large and small aquariums with a sandy bed and adequate hiding places. The composition of the water is not critical but should be changed regularly. Temperature 22°–24°C. These fish keep to the bottom of the tank. The preferred diet is worm-like food, such as Tubifex and red mosquito larvae.

BREEDING: This should be possible: see Introductory note.

ADDITIONAL INFORMATION: Although *A.cuneovirgatus* will rarely be seen swimming about the aquarium it will swim restlessly to and fro along the glass when the water has been changed or the fish has been put in a different tank.

ACANTHOPHTHALMUS KUHLI KUHLI

Family: *Cobitidae*

Genus: *Acanthophthalmus*

English name: Coolie Loach

Origin: Indonesia, Sumatra and Java

Size: Maximum 8 cm

Habitat: Found in shallow waters with sandy beds such as mountain streams and meandering rivers

SHAPE, COLORING AND MARKINGS: The body is elongated, worm-like and laterally compressed towards the tail. The mouth is underpositioned, with three pairs of barbels. The basic coloration is pale yellow to salmon: the belly is off-white or pale yellow. Three deep black unbroken transverse bands run across the head. A large number of dark brown or black bands, often broken halfway along by thin light stripes or marks run across the body but do not quite reach the underside. The fins are colorless.
There are no known external sexual characteristics.

GENERAL CARE: As for *A.cuneovirgatus* but *A.kuhli kuhli* will be much less timid if there is some dense vegetation in the tank as well as other hiding places.

BREEDING: This species has not as yet been bred in captivity: see Introductory note for further details.

ACANTHOPHTHALMUS KUHLI SUMATRANUS

Family: *Cobitidae*

Genus: *Acanthophthalmus*

English name: none

Origin: Indonesia, Sumatra

Size: Maximum 8 cm

Habitat: Found in shallow waters with sandy beds such as mountain streams and meandering rivers

SHAPE, COLORING AND MARKINGS: The body is elongated, cylindrical and laterally compressed towards the tail. The mouth is underpositioned with three pairs of barbels. The basic coloration is bright yellow, becoming paler or off-white towards the belly. Three striking deep black transverse bands cross the head. On the body some 12–15 black cone-shaped marks (some of which have a light patch in the center) run halfway down the body, but never as far as the belly: on the back the marks are interspersed with patches of dark red or reddish-brown. The belly is salmon. The fins are grey to off-white, and transparent.
Females are fuller in the body with more rounded bellies.
Males have more powerfully developed rays to the pectoral fins.

GENERAL CARE: As for *A.cuneovirgatus*.

BREEDING: This should be possible: see Introductory note.

ADDITIONAL INFORMATION: It is possible that *A.kuhli sumatranus* is no more than a subspecies of *A.Kuhli kuhli*.

ACANTHOPHTHALMUS MYERSI

Family: *Cobitidae*
Genus: *Acanthophthalmus*
English name: none
Origin: Thailand
Size: Maximum 8 cm
Habitat: Found in shallow waters with sandy beds, such as mountain streams and meandering rivers.

SHAPE, COLORING AND MARKINGS: The body is elongated, cylindrical and laterally compressed towards the tail. The mouth is underpositioned with three pairs of barbels. The basic coloration is bright yellow to salmon. On the body 10–14 wide, dark brown transverse bands run into the belly where they merge: these bands are all identical in color and have no light patches. The fins are grey to off-white and transparent.

Females have paler bellies.
Males have more powerfully developed pectoral fins.

GENERAL CARE: As for *A.cuneovirgatus*.

BREEDING: This should be possible: see Introductory note.

ADDITIONAL INFORMATION: Is is possible that *A.myersi* is no more than a sub-species of *A.kuhli kuhli*.

ACANTHOPHTHALMUS ROBIGINOSUS

Family: *Cobitidae*
Genus: *Acanthophthalmus*
English name: none
Origin: Indonesia, Java, around Rangkasbitung
Size: Maximum 5 cm
Habitat: Found in shallow waters with sandy beds such as mountain streams and meandering rivers

SHAPE, COLORING AND MARKINGS: The body is elongated, cylindrical and laterally compressed towards the tail. The mouth is underpositioned with three pairs of barbels. The basic coloration is a dull yellowish-brown to rust-brown: the belly is lighter, but never white. In bright light the flanks are iridescent and almost steel blue. Three unbroken dark

408. *Botia hymenophysa*

transverse bands lie on the head and a fourth at the base of the caudal fin. Some 15–17 dark brown bands lie across the body, extending just over halfway down. None of the bands has a light patch. The fins are colorless and transparent.
Females are as described above.
Males have more powerfully developed fins: the second ray of the pectoral fin is a little more elongated.

General care: As for *A.cuneovirgatus*, but *A.robiginosus* is also very partial to dried food.

Breeding: No information is available on the reproductive behavior of this species, but see Introductory note.

Additional information: *A.robiginosus* is a fairly recently identified species, first described in 1957.

ACANTHOPHTHALMUS SEMICINCTUS

Family: *Cobitidae*

Genus: *Acanthophthalmus*

English name: Half-banded Coolie Loach

Origin: Indonesia

Size: Maximum 8 cm

Habitat: Found in shallow waters with sandy beds, such as mountain streams and meandering rivers

---

Shape, coloring and markings: The body is elongated, cylindrical and laterally compressed towards the tail. The mouth is under-positioned with three pairs of barbels. The basic coloration is a coppery red, becoming salmon towards the belly: the underside is white. *A.semicinctus* can be distinguished from related species by the dark brown or black, cone-shaped or zig-zag pattern on the back: this is sometimes flecked with gold. An unbroken transverse band runs across the snout, through the eye: a similar band lies on the caudal peduncle. The fins are colorless and transparent.
Females are as described above.
Males have more powerfully developed fins.

General care: As for *A.cuneovirgatus* but temperature 24°–30°C.

Breeding: No information is available on the reproductive behavior of this species but see Introductory note.

Additional information: *A.semicinctus* was first described in 1940 but the date of its introduction into Europe is unknown.

ACANTHOPHTHALMUS SHELFORDI

Family: *Cobitidae*

Genus: *Acanthophthalmus*

English name: none

Origin: Borneo, Sarawak

Size: Maximum 8 cm

Habitat: Found in shallow waters with sandy beds such as mountain streams and meandering rivers

---

Shape, coloring and markings: The body is elongated, cylindrical and laterally compressed towards the tail. The mouth is under-positioned with three pairs of barbels. The basic coloration is salmon to yellowish-orange: the underside is white. Three unbroken transverse bands lie on the head. A very large number of irregular cone-shaped dark marks appear on the upper part of the body, above similar marks underneath which may mingle with them. The pattern thus created, which varies from specimen to specimen, somewhat resembles the camouflage pattern of a tiger. The caudal fin has dark bands: the other fins are colorless and transparent.
There are no known external sexual characteristics.

General care: As for *A.cuneovirgatus* but temperature 24°–30°C.

Breeding: Little is known about the reproductive behavior of this fish, but see the Introductory note.

Additional information: *A.shelfordi* is still uncommon in aquariums.

THE FAMILY COBITIDAE

The genus Botia

The genus *Botia* is distributed over a wide area, the whole of Indonesia and the Far East, including India and Malaya. These fish live mainly in still or sluggish waters, usually in those with sandy beds or beds with deposits of organic waste matter, such as are found in backwaters and the bends of rivers. Their diet consists of worm-like creatures they dig up from the bed and in their natural state they supplement this diet with organic waste matter such as rotting vegetation.
They have under-positioned mouths and more or less flattened lower halves to their bodies, typical features of fish that live largely on the bed and in the lower water levels. They also have the barbels that are characteristic of fish that grub about on the bottom for food. Many aquarists call these fish 'mud creepers', an unattractive name that puts some people off these extremely interesting species which in fact, in captivity have never been seen to creep into the mud at all, even when threatened by enemies. In fact they are not even fish that confine themselves to the bottom of the tank: most species will swim freely from time to time at all water levels. In this respect they are similar to Barbs, another group of fish very fond of grubbing about on the bottom in search of food, but also quite happy to swim about the tank.

409. *Botia lucas bahi*

These fish are often alleged to twist and turn a great deal on the bottom, but this is a habit less common than usually supposed. Well-known species such as *B.macracantha* and *B.sidthimunki* very rarely twist and turn about in this way when kept in a small group of their own species: it is a habit they seem to acquire when kept alone. It is then probably the result of restlessness and boredom. It is of course true of all fish that the behavior of a single specimen can never be taken as typical of the species if, in its natural state, the fish is accustomed to living in a shoal.
These fish are sometimes called 'Thorn eyes', a good name, referring as it does to a characteristic feature of this group, a movable spine or thorn below each eye, which can become a formidable weapon. These razor sharp spines should be treated with respect, especially when catching the fish: they can cause a painful injury and moreover, if the spines become entangled in a net, the fish can be injured.
Double plastic bags should always be used to carry the fish, otherwise a lot of trouble will be caused if the spine punctures the bag.
Some species are twilight and night fish: others are active in the day and retreat to their hiding places when it grows dark. It is the species that like to be kept in a small group, such as *B.macracantha* and *B.sidthimunki,* that are most active during the day. Another species which has recently become popular, *B.striata,* is also active during the day when it has become accustomed to the tank. However, all species are very shy and easily frightened, particularly by sudden movements outside the aquarium: the surroundings of the tank must therefore be quiet if these fish are to be seen.
Those species that are really twilight fish establish their own territory in the tank, which they then defend fiercely against undesirable intruders: these are usually other members of their own species, for members of other species are not, as a rule, molested. Fish of quite different species and genera are also usually left alone. All species of *Botias* however defend their own chosen hiding places, and when doing this the knocking sounds they make can quite often be heard outside the tank.
Nothing definite is known about the reproductive behavior of these species and no external sexual characteristics have been identified. In fact there is still a great deal of uncertainty about the habits of these fish, and this uncertainty extends even to those species such as *B.macracantha* that have been popular for many years. That species will grow up to about 18 cm in captivity under very favorable conditions, but in the wild adult specimens can reach 30 cm. It is possible that fish kept in captivity never reach full sexual maturity. If this is really so, there are important opportunities for the dedicated aquarist to cast light on the behavior of this genus, by studying closely the behavior of some of the species that are mature when much smaller than *B.macracantha.*
It is however difficult to know how to encourage growth and maturity in these species. It is clear that the regular changing of the water in the tank encourage growth, but of course this is true of many fish. It is possible that the amount of swimming space made available (that is, the quantity of free water in the tank for each fish) is also important. Although most species of Botia can be kept in community tanks, it may be that the presence of other kinds of fish discourages growth – or at least inhibits their keeping to their natural life style. Diet could also be a significant factor, but unfortunately very little is known about the natural diet of these fish and so only by trial and error can an appropriate diet for them in captivity be established: in that way however, it is never possible to be certain that some essential ingredient is not missing from the diet. Any one, or all these factors might be significant in determining whether members of these species will reproduce in captivity.

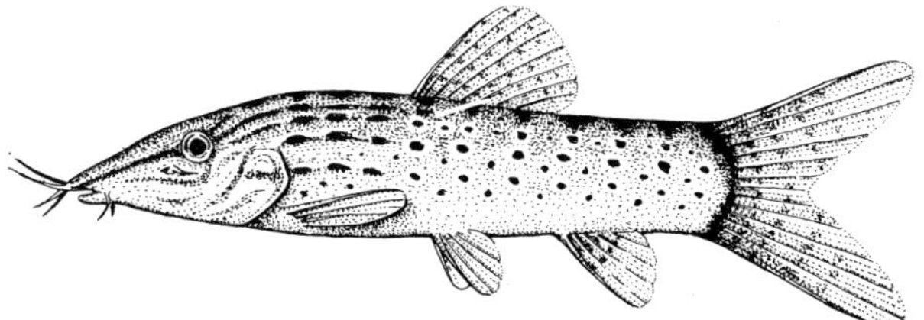

410. *Botia beauforti*

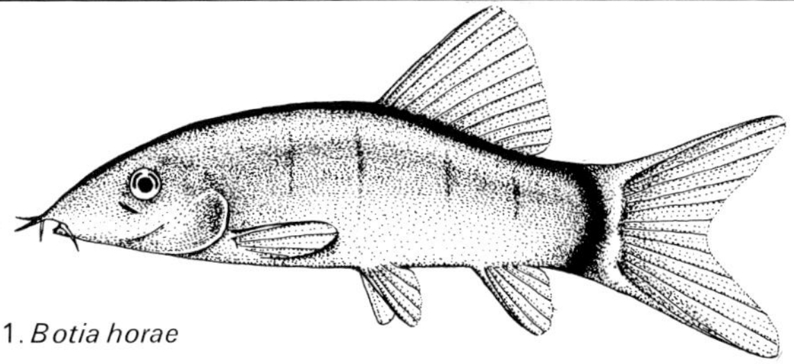

411. *Botia horae*

BOTIA BEAUFORTI
Family: *Cobitidae*
Genus: *Botia*
English name: none
Origin: Thailand
Size: Approximately 20 cm
Habitat: Found in still and sluggish waters

SHAPE, COLORING AND MARKINGS: The body is elongated and laterally very compressed, except for the head. The upper part of the body is almost completely straight and the snout pointed. The basic coloration is grey or greyish-green, with little variation in shade. A number of dark stripy markings start behind the eyes and turn into a pattern of dots which stretch roughly to the first dorsal fin rays. There are about four rows of dark dots on the flanks, the bands which these form becoming lighter at the edges. The unpaired fins are transparent, orange with rows of dark dots.
There are no known external sexual characteristics.

GENERAL CARE: *B.beauforti* is only suitable for larger aquariums providing plenty of hiding places for the fish among thick clumps of plants or in arrangements of wood or rock. The composition of the water is not critical, but fresh tap water should be avoided, although it may be used subsequently for partial changes of the water: there should be a partial change in the water after some weeks. Temperature 23°–26°C. Not a social fish, *B.beauforti* should be kept alone or with other species of fish. It establishes its own territory in the tank and will defend that fiercely against other members of its own species and less fiercely against members of other species of *Botia. B.beauforti* stays mainly at the bottom of the tank but does not restrict itself to the bed. It is fond of resting just above the bed on low growing plants or other objects. Its favorite food is Tubifex, red mosquito larvae and Enchitraeus: it probably also

412. Botia horae

413. Botia striata

414. Botia modesta

eats some vegetable matter such as algae and the soft parts of plants.

ADDITIONAL INFORMATION: This species was first described by Hugh McCormick Smith in 1931. It does not seem yet to be imported. According to the authorities it is closely related to the species *B.lucas-bahi,* and *B.hymenophysa.*

BOTIA HORAE

Family: *Cobitidae*

Genus: *Botia*

English name: none

Origin: Thailand

Size: Approximately 10 cm

Habitat: Found in large numbers, over a wide area, in sluggish waters

SHAPE, COLORING AND MARKINGS: The body is stocky, the back arched and the belly straight: laterally the body is very compressed. The basic coloration is greenish-yellow with a soft metallic sheen. The upper half of the body is slightly darker, or greyish: the underside is lighter, or a soft yellowish-white. From the snout, over the back there runs a line of black dots, set very closely together: just before the base of the caudal fin this dorsal line becomes a deep black transverse stripe. There are four narrow transverse bands with dark pigmentation on the flanks, but these are not always well-defined. The fins are colorless, transparent or of varying shades of greyish-green. The caudal fin is yellowish, with often a number of dark spots.
There are no known external sexual characteristics.

GENERAL CARE: As for *B.beauforti.* It is however a social fish which should be kept in a small group of its own species: it will defend its own hiding place against intruders but will not establish a territory like *B.beauforti.* It is an energetic swimmer and will be very active as one of the shoal. It keeps mainly to the bottom of the tank but will swim in all reaches. Diet as for *B.beauforti.*

BOTIA HYMENOPHYSA

Family: *Cobitidae*

Genus: *Botia*

English name: none

Origin: Thailand, Malaya, Singapore and the larger islands in the Sunda Strait

Size: Approximately 20 cm

Habitat: Found in sluggish waters

SHAPE, COLORING AND MARKINGS: The body is elongated, very slender and laterally very compressed. Very similar to *B.lucas-bahi,* to which it is closely related. The basic coloration is ochre or yellowish-green: the back is brown or brownish-yellow, and the lower half of the body is yellowish. There are a number of transverse bands which run back along the body obliquely and vary in color from a greyish-blue to brown, with dark edges. The spaces between these bands are narrower than the bands themselves. The fins are yellow or greenish and the caudal and dorsal fins carry bands of dark spots and flecks. The dorsal fin has often a dark pigmentation round its edges.
There are no known external sexual characteristics.

GENERAL CARE: As for *B.beauforti.*

BOTIA LECONTEI

Family: *Cobitidae*

Genus: *Botia*

English name: none

Origin: Thailand

Size: Approximately 7 cm

Habitat: Found in still and slow running waters.

SHAPE, COLORING AND MARKINGS: The body is elongated, very thin and laterally very compressed: it closely resembles *B.hymenophysa,* but the snout is less pointed. The basic coloration is something between a greenish and pale greyish-blue, with a soft satin sheen. The back is hardly any darker and the underside is off-white. There is a dark round mark, not always well-defined, on the base of the caudal fin. Some specimens also have a narrow and somewhat indistinct series of transverse bands on the upper half of the body. The fins vary from yellow to orangey-red.
There are no known external sexual characteristics.

GENERAL CARE: The behavior of this fish is identical to that of *B.horae* and it should be given the same care as *B.beauforti.*

BOTIA LOHACHATA

Family: *Cobitidae*

Genus: *Botia*

English name: none

Origin: India and Pakistan

Size: Approximately 7 cm

Habitat: Found in still and slow running waters

SHAPE, COLORING AND MARKINGS: The body is elongated, very slender and laterally very compressed. The basic coloration is a silvery-grey or pale gold. On the upper part of the body there is a coarse net-like pattern of dark pigmentation and this turns into a number of transverse bands across the flanks, extending almost but not quite to the underside of the body. Dark but not well-defined marks are found between these bands. The fins are transparent and greyish: the unpaired fins carry a pattern of dark marks that usually make up transverse bands.
There are no known external sexual characteristics.

GENERAL CARE: As for *B.beauforti. B.lohachata* is similar in habits to *B.horae* although it tends to keep to the bottom of the tank and has a tendency to burrow under plants or other obstacles it encounters. Once it has grown used to its regular feeding times it is possible to see it regularly during the day, although it is really a twilight fish.

ADDITIONAL INFORMATION: An extremely

beautiful species, but, curiously, little known to aquarists even though it was first described as long ago as 1912 by the Indian scientist B. L. Chaudhuri. It was not however imported until 1956.

415. *Botia lohachata*

BOTIA LUCAS-BAHI

Family: *Cobitidae*

Genus: *Botia*

English name: none

Origin: Thailand, Malaya, Singapore and the larger islands of the Sunda Strait

Size: Approximately 20 cm

Habitat: Found in still and sluggish waters

Shape, coloring and markings: The body is elongated, very slender and laterally very compressed: it closely resembles the related species *B.beauforti* and *B.hymenophysa*. The caudal peduncle is like that of *B.hymenophysa* and much thinner than in *B.beauforti*. The basic coloration is grey or greyish-blue, varying according to the environment of the fish. There are a number of dark stripy markings which begin behind the eyes and develop into series of dots that extend roughly to the first dorsal fin rays. There are three or four rows of dark spots on the flanks, and the bands which these form are lighter at the edges. There are also a number of transverse bands which, dark in color, can best be seen on the caudal peduncle but are also sometimes present on the front part of the body. There is a dark line across the snout which runs up to the eyes and there may also be some less well-defined lines below this line. All the fins are a greyish-blue, with transverse bands of dark spots and flecks on the dorsal and caudal fins.

There are no known external sexual characteristics.

General care: As for *B.beauforti*.

BOTIA MACRACANTHA

Family: *Cobitidae*

Genus: *Botia*

English name: Clown Loach

Origin: Indonesia, Sumatra, Borneo

Size: Approximately 30 cm in the wild, but remains considerably smaller in captivity, up to about 12 cm

Origin: Found in still and sluggish waters

Shape, coloring and markings: The body is stocky, laterally compressed, with a rounded back and straight belly. The basic coloration is a splendid orangey-red. There are three deep black, cone-shaped transverse bands across the body. The first runs across the head over the eyes, the second lies in front of the dorsal fin and the third runs below the dorsal fin and on the caudal peduncle. The dark pigmentation of this third transverse band is carried through into the dorsal and anal fins. All the other fins are reddish or a dark red, and the ventral fins also often have some black pigmentation.

There are no known external sexual characteristics.

General care: As for *B.beauforti*. *B.macracantha* however is not a twilight fish like so many related species and it is less timid. It must however be kept in a small group: it will happily associate with other fish of a similar color, such as a group of Sumatra Barbs (*Barbus tetrazona*). It is a social fish that will be found swimming about at all levels of the tank: it does not claim its own territory but will of course defend its chosen hiding spot.

Additional information: The best known of all the species of *Botias*. In recent years this beautiful fish has been imported in ever-increasing numbers so that its price has dropped considerably.

BOTIA MODESTA

Family: *Cobitidae*

Genus: *Botia*

English name: none

Origin: Malaya, Thailand and Vietnam

Size: Approximately 10 cm

Habitat: Found in still and sluggish waters

Shape, coloring and markings: The body is rather stocky, laterally compressed and with a rounded back and straight belly. The basic coloration is greyish, with a soft silky

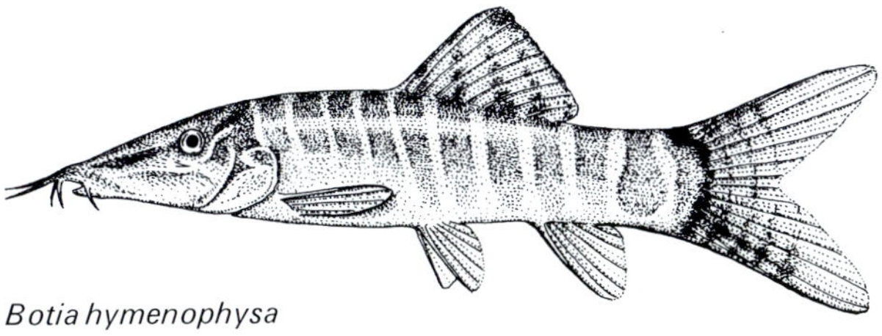
416. *Botia hymenophysa*

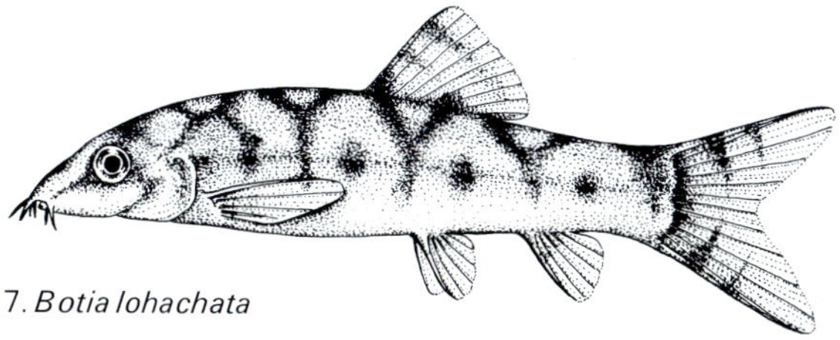
417. *Botia lohachata*

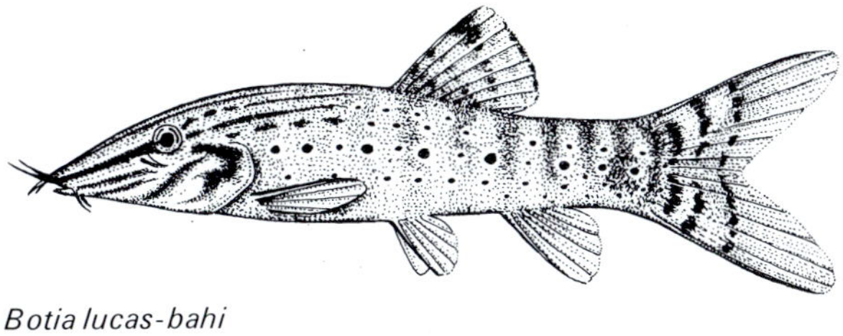
418. *Botia lucas-bahi*

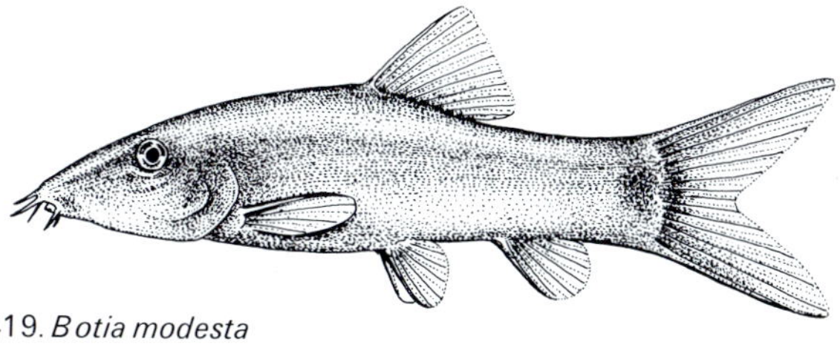
419. *Botia modesta*

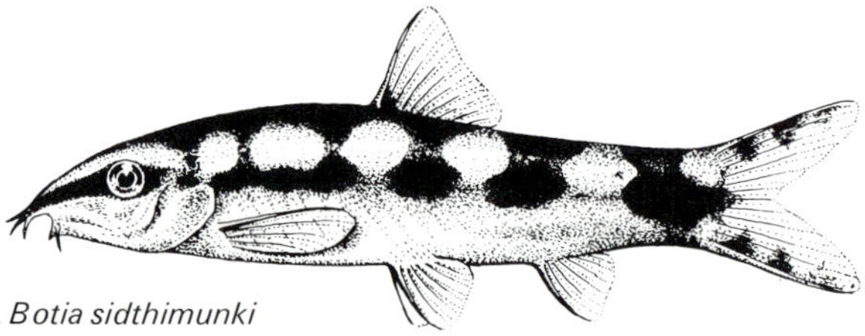
420. *Botia sidthimunki*

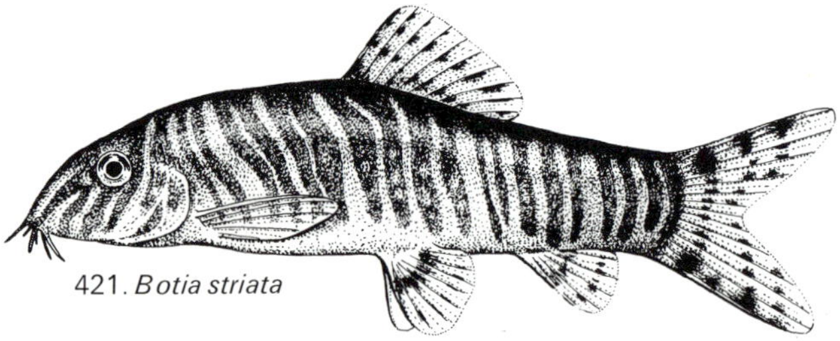
421. *Botia striata*

green sheen. There is often but not always an inconspicuous dark mark at the base of the caudal fin. The fins are a dull yellow except for the caudal fin, which is a clear yellow. The coloring somewhat resembles that of *B.lecontei*, but *B.modesta* can be easily distinguished from that species by its stockier body.
There are no known external sexual characteristics.

General care: As for *B.beauforti*. The habits of *B.modesta* much resemble those of *B.horae*, but *B.modesta*, after swimming about the tank in a group will then often rest in the upper reaches.

Additional information: Not a species that is often imported. It has the reputation of being particularly fond of burrowing in the bottom, but like other species of *Botias* is much less likely to do that if kept in a small group.

BOTIA SIDTHIMUNKI

Family: *Cobitidae*

Genus: *Botia*

English name: none

Origin: The Far East, the northern provinces of Thailand

Size: Approximately 5 cm

Habitat: Found in still and sluggish waters

Shape, coloring and markings: The body is very slender and laterally slightly compressed. The basic coloration is silvery tinged with yellow. The back is darker or golden-brown and the underside silvery-white. There is a pattern of deep black marks on the body which often merge together leaving only round patches of the basic color visible. This dark pigmentation may be restricted to the back and upper half of the body or it may also extend to the lower half. There is always a distinct stripe on the head which runs from the snout through the eyes. The dark pigmentation becomes brown as the fish grows older. The fins are colorless and transparent. Dark patches develop in both lobes of the caudal fin in older fish and the number of patches (up to a maximum of three) increases as the fish grows older.

There are no known external sexual characteristics.

General care: As for *B.beauforti*. *B.sidthimunki* is a social fish akin in habits to *B.horae* but it is less timid than most species of *Botias*. It will eat almost any kind of food.

Additional information: A very recent addition to the aquarium. It was first described by Klausewitz in 1959 and is the smallest known species of *Botias*.

BOTIA STRIATA

Family: *Cobitidae*

Genus: *Botia*

English name: none

Origin: India

Size: Approximately 7 cm

Habitat: Found in still and slow running waters

Shape, coloring and markings: The body is elongated, slender and laterally greatly compressed. *B.striata* greatly resembles *B.lohachata*, but has a less pointed snout. The basic coloration is golden. There are a number of dark green transverse bands across the whole body, which can vary considerably in number and shape. There is another group of bands on the flanks and these too vary in number. The fins are greyish and transparent: the unpaired fins have dark marks which are arranged more or less in rows: there are sometimes dark markings on the ventral fins as well.

There are no known external sexual characteristics.

General care: As for *B.beauforti:* in its habits *B.striata* resembles *B.horae*.

Additional information: This exceptionally beautiful species was first described by Yelseti Ramachandra Rao in 1920. It is only in recent years however that it became known to aquarists, but it has is certainly a species that will become popular.

422. *Botia sidthimunki*

THE FAMILY COBITIDAE

The genus Lepidocephalus

There are only three species at present classed in this genus and they are all native to India. The species described below, *Lepidocephalus guntea* is found throughout the sub-continent. Another species, *Lepidocephalus thermalis*, a smaller fish, is found principally around Malabar as well as in Sri Lanka *L. thermalis*, however, is not usually considered to be of interest to many aquarists; neither is L. *octocirrhus*, a species which is found mainly in Indonesia and Thailand. *L. guntea* is a more attractive fish and better suited to life in an aquarium, given the right kind of tank.

LEPIDOCEPHALUS GUNTEA

Family: *Cobitidae*

Genus: *Lepidocephalus*

English name: none

Origin: Southeast Asia

Size: Maximum 15 cm

Habitat: Found in shallow sluggish or very clear still waters

SHAPE, COLORING AND MARKINGS: The body is very elongated and torpedo-shaped: the mouth is under-positioned with four pairs of barbels and a spine like that borne by the genus *Acanthophthalmus*. The basic coloration is yellowish. A pale horizontal line runs from the mouth to the caudal peduncle: above and below lies a pattern of irregular dark marks. A small deep black mark surrounded by a lighter ring appears on the caudal peduncle. The dorsal and caudal fins have rows of dark spots: otherwise the fins are colorless. There are no known external sexual characteristics.

GENERAL CARE: *L.guntea* should be kept in a group of its own kind in a fairly large aquarium: it needs clean clear water and a soft bed into which it can dig from time to time. Hiding places must be provided and the lighting should be subdued. The composition of the water is not critical but it should not be too hard: *L.guntea* needs a lot of oxygen and the tank should be aerated. Dried food will be accepted as well as the usual live animal matter: the fish can often be seen searching the bed for food. Only coarse broad-leaved plants are suitable for the tank and there must be an efficient filtering system working all the time: if the water is not kept clean the fish will suffer.

BREEDING: There are no records of this species having as yet been bred in captivity.

THE FAMILY CURIMATIDAE

An introductory description

The Curimatidae family consists of a number of different fish which are found on the South American continent.
It contains some genera of Headstanders, *Chilodus* and *Caenotropus*. The characteristics of this family are quite similar to those of the Anostomidae family, described earlier.

The genus Chilodus

Until recently, the genus *Chilodus* was classified under the Anostomidae family, with which it in fact shares many characteristic features.
This genus consists of only one species, *Chilodus punctatus*, wellknown under the name of Spotted Headstander.

423. *Chilodus punctatus*

CHILODUS PUNCTATUS

Family: *Curimatidae*

Genus: *Chilodus*

English name: Spotted Headstander

Origin: Northeastern South America, the Guianas

Size: Maximum 9 cm

Habitat: Found in still and sluggish waters with dense vegetation

SHAPE, COLORING AND MARKINGS: The body is almost kite-shaped, the back being deepest at the line of the dorsal fin which itself is positioned quite far forward. The basic coloration is brownish-yellow: the back is darker, the belly silvery. The scales on the back and flanks bear a dark dot and a dark horizontal line runs from the mouth to the caudal peduncle. The fins are colorless, except for the dorsal fin which bears dark marks at the front. The fish almost always swims with its head inclined downwards, and only assumes a horizontal posture when anxious to move very quickly. It is unusual in that it makes a metallic clicking noise especially when looking for food or during courtship: this noise is clearly audible outside the tank.
There are no known external sexual characteristics.

GENERAL CARE: The tank should be furnished as for *Anostomus anostomus*. The water should be not more than 6° DH and slightly acid. *C.punctatus* will eat dried food as well as Daphnia, Cyclops and Enchytraeus. It should also receive some vegetable matter such as lettuce regularly.

BREEDING: As soon as they have been laid, the eggs swell up to a diameter of 2–2.5 mm. The eggs hatch after four days at a temperature of about 26° C. The fry hang among the plants for two or three days and then begin to swim freely: they should be fed on *Artemia nauplii* and finely powdered dried food which will sink to the bottom, for even as fry this species swims with its head inclined downwards.

THE FAMILY CYPRINIDAE

Distribution of the Cyprinidae

The Cyprinidae family (the carps and carp-like fish) is very large: one species or another is found somewhere in the world except for Australia, Madagascar, New Zealand, South America, northern Canada, Iceland and Greenland. Some 1500 species have been identified to date.
They inhabit the most diverse environments. Various species of Cyprinidae have also been introduced to alien waters for commercial purposes and have generally successfully adapted themselves to their new environments.
The majority of carps have the classic fish outline. The body is usually only moderately compressed laterally and the upper and lower body lines are equally curved: only a few unusual species have a different shape. The caudal fin is usually fairly deeply forked and there is no adipose fin. The mouth, which is toothless is protractile, that is, so structured that it is flexible and can be protruded at will. The well developed pharyngeal bone in the throat bears multiple rows of teeth: the pattern and arrangement of the teeth vary from species to species and is a very important factor in the classification of these fish into genera and species.
In almost all species the body is evenly covered with relatively large scales. The head is always without scales. The *Cyprinidae* may have up to two pairs of barbels but they are no help to identification and classification for individual specimens within a particular species may develop with or without barbels. However, in general most of the *Cyprinidae* will be found to have barbels.
These fish tend to occupy the lower water levels and obtain a large proportion of their food from the bottom. Species from waters richer in animal life spend less of their time grubbing about on the bottom and in consequence usually have less well-developed barbels. The problems to which the presence or absence of barbels has given rise, in the field of classification, are well illustrated by the history of the genus *Barbus* (or *Puntius*) as noted in the Introduction to that genus.
Many members of the carp family are very attractively colored. By far the majority of species are also very small, although the largest known, *Barbus tor* which comes from India can grow to a length of 2.5 m. Most of the *Cyprinidae* are undemanding fish and a large number of the species are very suitable for the aquarium. Most of those commonly kept are of tropical or subtropical origin, but many European carps, particularly when young, can also be kept successfully in large aquariums. Many species are also suitable for unheated home aquariums. Such an unheated aquarium should be sited so that the water temperature does not rise too high during the summer. Although these fish can withstand temperatures of up to 28°C if they are in well aerated tanks and not subjected to such a temperature for too long, they should really be kept at 20°–22°C. During the winter the temperature can drop to 5°C without any damage being done; indeed so low a temperature is even recommended for one or two species.
Many of these species grub about on the bottom and the tank should have a bed of fine river sand. The natural environment can be well simulated by using stones and pieces of bogwood and adding some European water plants. The water should preferably be of natural origin: it can be topped up with mature aquarium water or otherwise with well aerated tap water. Constant aeration is necessary in the tank, especially during the summer: a good sized filter is also needed to keep the water clear, especially if active grubbers are in the tank.
Most European Cyprinidae are easy to feed: insect larvae, Daphnia, mosquito larvae, Tubifex, Enchytrae, maggots and earthworms are all acceptable food: bread, lettuce and spinach will also be eaten.
Most species from hotter climates are small and are suitable for small community tanks: they are usually easy to keep in captivity. They are very social fish that enjoy being in a group of their own kind and with other related species. On the whole they are very tolerant although occasionally some will bite the fins of other fish. In general they are very active swimmers and should be kept with other fish of a similar disposition.

FAMILY CYPRINIDAE

The genus Aphyocypris

The genus *Aphyocypris* has at present only one species in it, the delightful undemanding and hardy fish *Aphyocypris pooni* described below. Coming as it does from a more temperate climate than many aquarium fish, *A.pooni* is one of the few species that can be kept successfully in an unheated tank. As noted in the description below, there was for long, confusion between this fish and *Tanichthys albonubes*. *A.pooni* has been much cross-bred in captivity and there are now very few pure strains.

424. *Barbus bariloides*

APHYOCYPRIS POONI

Family: *Cyprinidae*
Genus: *Aphyocypris*
English name: Venus Fish
Origin: China, around Hong Kong
Size: Approximately 4 cm
Habitat: No details are available of its natural habitat

SHAPE, COLORING AND MARKINGS: The body is very slender and only slightly laterally compressed. This fish greatly resembles *Tanichthys albonubes,* with which, as noted below, it has often been confused. The back is a brownish-green or yellowish-brown: the flanks are considerably lighter: the belly is whitish. A prominent stripe runs across the body from the snout to the base of the caudal fin where it becomes a more or less sickle-shaped mark. This stripe is green or golden and shiny, depending on how the light strikes it: in young fish the stripe is a beautiful iridescent bluish-green. The yellow dorsal fin is red at the base and edged with blue. The anal fin is yellowish and green.
Females are more sturdy and usually larger than the males.
Males are noticeably slimmer.

GENERAL CARE: *A.pooni* is suitable for smaller aquariums, but it should be kept in a large group. The tank need not be arranged in any particular way. The composition of the water is not critical but fresh water is better than mature water. The fish like a tank rich in oxygen and it is advisable to stock it with vegetation which will assist: *Myriophyllum* and other similar plants are good. Temperature 16°–24°C. *A.pooni* can be kept in either a heated or an unheated tank: it is advisable in any case to keep the temperature low during the winter for those fish selected for breeding in the spring. Almost any food will be accepted, including dried food. *A.pooni* is a tolerant fish and can be kept in a community tank with other smaller species.

BREEDING: Not difficult. Fresh water is needed. Temperature 20°–22°C. The eggs are scattered among fine-leaved plants. Some females are much more prolific than others. Very good results have sometimes been obtained from breeding in groups, when a number of breeding pairs have been put together in the one breeding tank. The parent fish do not usually eat the eggs nor do they molest the fry. However the fish must be fed regularly with a varied diet. The fry can be raised easily with the normal food for fry, and finely ground dried food can also be given.

ADDITIONAL INFORMATION: This species so greatly resembles *Tanichthys albonubes,* the White Cloud Mountain Minnow that many authorities used to think that the two species were no more than local varieties of the same species.

THE FAMILY CYPRINIDAE

The genus Barbus

Members of the genus *Barbus* are found only in the eastern hemisphere. Various species are found throughout nearly the whole of Africa, India, Ceylon, southeast Asia, Indonesia and China. They are found in many different environments and often in very large shoals. They are all egg layers (ovipars) except for *Barbus viviparus,* which comes from southeast Africa and is apparently a live bearer.
There is still much debate about the classification of members of this large genus, which includes both small and very large species. Initially the river barbel, *Ciprinus barbus,* was adopted as the prototype and gave its name to the genus *Barbus*. However, because of a flood of discoveries of new species, many of which deviated from that prototype in various ways, it became increasingly difficult to define the genus and a new system of classification was needed.
The new genus *Puntius* was instigated by Buchanan in 1822, with *Puntius puntio* as the prototype. *Puntius puntio* is a species notable for having no barbels and barbels had originally been considered to be one of the essential characteristics of species of the genus *Barbus*. It became apparent later however that within the new genus *Puntius* there were indeed some species with barbels and so new attempts were made to revise the whole classification.
Schultz then tried to devise a better system of classification, suggesting that three separate genera should be recognized:

Puntius species with no barbels
Capoëta species with two barbels
Barbodes species with four barbels

Problems however remain for the number of barbels is not in itself solely a reliable guide to the identification of a particular species. A great deal of uncertainty remains and *Barbus* and *Puntius* are both used as names for this genus: authors vary and are not even always consistent in their use of these names. In some quarters the name *Barbus* has become generally accepted, but the name *Puntius* also occurs in some reference books and some scientific reports. The name *Barbus* is used in this encyclopaedia as a help to the use of works of reference in which it is also used, but the reader must remember that in some books he may consult the same species will be found under the genus *Puntius.*
Most fish of this genus are very active swimmers. They need a lot of swimming space in the aquarium. For the smaller species the tank must be at the very least 50 cm long: larger fish obviously need considerably more space. Almost all species prefer a dark bed, preferably covered with a thin layer of peat dust: in this they can root about. Most species prefer slightly subdued lighting: floating plants on the surface of the water, such as *Pistia, Riccia, Salvinia* and floating oak leaf fern can be used as a very effective way of filtering overhead light. All species like water rich in oxygen and thus plants that encourage this are an essential part of the vegetation in the aquarium itself. In the aquarium, the plants should be fairly widely spaced so that the fish have ample opportunity to dart about and indulge in the very active play which is characteristic of them. Many species like to keep to the bottom of the tank although others distribute themselves evenly throughout it. Nearly all species are of a peaceful disposition and tolerant of other fish. Generally the composition of the water is not critical, but fresh tap water should be avoided. Some of the water should be changed from time to time, especially in those aquariums which are not equipped with efficient carbon filters. The tropical species require a fairly high temperature, but in general are not harmed by occasional drops in temperature to about 18°C.
Few of the species are fussy about food. They will hunt and then greedily devour all live animal feeding matter. but they

will also accept dried food: a few species also like the occasional lettuce leaf. Many species like to chew their way through the layer of peat dust on the bed, searching for something edible. For this reason, it is advisable to equip a tank for barbs with an efficient filtering device.

On the whole these fish are fairly easy to breed. A number of species even readily reproduce in simply furnished breeding tanks with just a few floating plants on the surface or breeding mops made artificially of nylon wool. Some species however need carefully furnished breeding tanks and are quite particular in the choice of a mate. For these species any fine-leaved plants can be used as a spawning medium and there should be a layer of well boiled and rinsed peat fibre on the bed. For breeding nearly all the species have a preference for old soft water with a neutral degree of acidity, approximately 7 pH. In some cases the reproductive urge can be stimulated by adding some fresh water to the tank. Breeding tanks should be positioned so that they catch the morning sun. When the breeding fish have been segregated one evening they usually start mating at dawn the next morning. The female takes the initiative and the mating is very tempestuous. The fish rub closely against each other between the plants or hanging roots, vibrating forcefully. The eggs are released and fertilized simultaneously. The fish mate repeatedly in quick succession, so that the whole process is usually over in a relatively short time. The eggs are generally quite adhesive and hang easily on the plants. The parent fish are rather partial to fresh eggs and so it is advisable to remove the parent fish immediately the mating is over. The superfluous male spawn can easily pollute the water so it is advisable to replace a large proportion of the water in the breeding tank with fresh water immediately but care must be taken to ensure that this fresh water is the same temperature as the water already in the breeding tank. The composition of the fresh water is not however critical. The eggs usually swell considerably and hatch after 24–36 hours. For the first two days the fry stay on the bed or hang on the glass or plants. In addition to the usual food for fry such as infusoria and the nauplii of the brine shrimp, it is also possible to give them very finely ground dried food and even better, stinging nettle leaves which have been dried in the sun and then ground to powder.

The fry usually prosper and provided they are raised in a larger tank they are sexually mature after 9–12 months. In general all these species are very productive and nests of many hundreds are not exceptional: moreover, healthy fish can be stimulated to reproduce a number of times each year.

BARBUS ARULIUS

Family: *Cyprinidae*

Genus: *Barbus*

English name: none

Origin: Southeast India, Travancore, Cauvrey

Size: Approximately 12 cm

Habitat: Found in both still and running waters

SHAPE, COLORING AND MARKINGS: The body is fairly deep and hardly at all laterally compressed. This is an exceptionally beautiful species but one whose coloring it is difficult to describe accurately. The upper half of the body is a soft fawn, the flanks are silvery, tinged with red and highlighted with a green fleck. The throat and belly are yellowish. The gill covers are flecked with green iridescent dots. A dark transverse stripe begins below the first dorsal fin rays and gradually becomes broader as it extends to the flanks. There is a prominent dark mark underneath the last dorsal fin rays and cone shaped transverse mark above the anal fin, which does not quite extend to the lower surface of the body: another dark mark appears on the caudal peduncle. A fairly wide band, of different color shades runs across the body from the gill covers. The ventral and pectoral fins are whitish, the caudal fin is yellowish-red with striking red tips and the anal fin has a beautiful carmine red edge.

Females have dorsal fins with no elongated fin rays.

Males have exceptionally beautiful fin rays: dark or red pigmentation on these elongated fin rays.

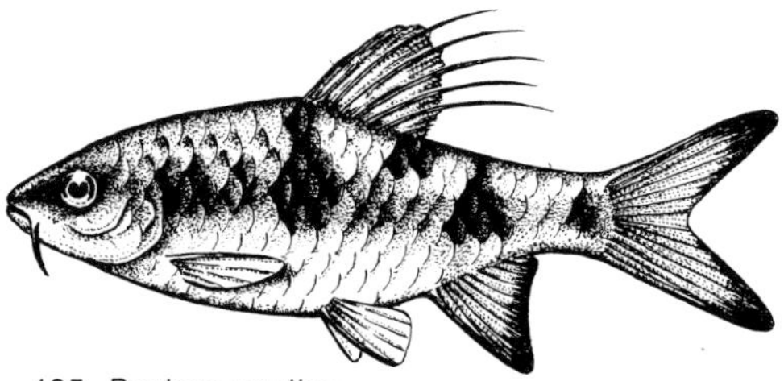

425. *Barbus arulius*

GENERAL CARE: *B.arulius* is only suitable for larger aquariums with a dark peaty bed and irregular arrangements of wood. Many different leafy plants should be put round the edges but there should be plenty of open swimming space in the middle of the tank. It is definitely a shoal fish and should be kept in a small group of about 6 specimens. The composition of the water is not critical, but fresh water should be avoided. *B.arulius* will be found distributed evenly throughout the tank and likes to roll about in the sediment on the bed. It is a very active swimmer. Temperature 23°–25°C. It will accept any sort of live animal food and, for a change, dried food.

BREEDING: Not difficult but not a very prolific breeder. Breeding temperature about 25°C. The water for breeding should be slightly acid.

ADDITIONAL INFORMATION: This exceptionally beautiful species is sold widely but its coloring is only really seen at its best in an adapted environment, so the fish does not look very remarkable when seen in aquarium shops.

BARBUS BARILOIDES

Family: *Cyprinidae*

Genus: *Barbus*

English name: none

Origin: Southwest Africa, Northern Rhodesia, Katanga and Angola

Size: 6 cm

Habitat: Found only in small colonies, in pools and jungle creeks with dense vegetation

SHAPE, COLORING AND MARKINGS: The body is elongated, slender and only slightly laterally compressed. *B.bariloides* somewhat resembles the better known species *B.semifasciolatus* but it has a noticeably more slender body. The basic coloration varies according to the place of origin from a rusty brown to a reddish-violet. The back is slightly darker and the belly is yellow or yellowish-brown. On the flanks and the slender caudal peduncle there are a number of well-defined transverse bands. The first band is immediately behind the gill cover and the last two run diagonally across the caudal peduncle. There is a small dark diamond-shaped mark at the base of the caudal fin. The fins are pale brown and trans-

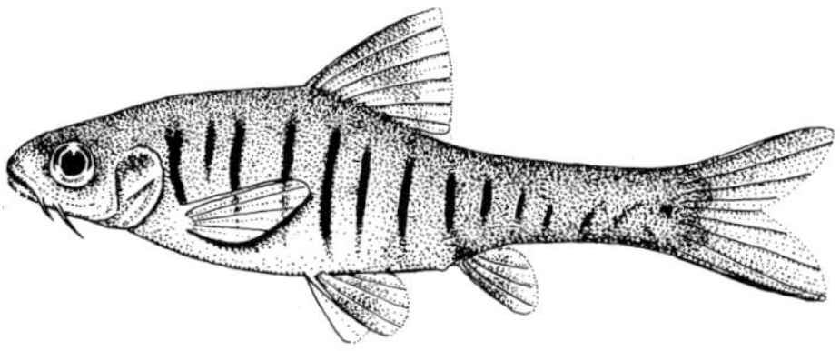

426. *Barbus bariloides*

parent: the unpaired fins have a rusty brown center.
Females when spawning can be easily identified by their more rounded bellies.
Males are more slender: their more vivid coloring is their particularly distinctive feature.

General care: Only suitable for larger aquariums, constructed as for *B.arulius*. Should be kept in a group of at least five. Composition of the water is not critical but old water is much better than fresh water. Temperature 22°–25°C: in the winter the temperature can be 20°–22°C. Diet as for *B.arulius*.

Breeding: Not too difficult. The breeding fish will usually mate the morning after being put in the breeding tank. Old water should be used: temperature 25°C. Fine leaved plants should be put in the breeding tank although *B.bariloides* will often spawn in a tank with no other spawning medium than some long peat fiber.

Additional information: This species is a particularly active swimmer. It has only become popular with aquarists in recent years but has been known for a long time. It was first described by George Albert Boulenger.

BARBUS BINOTATUS

Family: *Cyprinidae*
Genus: *Barbus*
English name: Spotted Barb
Origin: Indonesia, the large islands of the Sunda Strait, Bangka, Billiton, Bali.
Size: Maximum 18 cm
Habitat: Widely distributed in almost all still and running waters

Shape, coloring, markings: The body is fairly deep and laterally hardly at all compressed. The basic coloration is predominantly silver. The back is olive and the flanks are tinged with a shiny blue sheen. The dark markings characteristic of this species vary largely according to the place of origin and also according to the age of the fish. Young fish usually have a shoulder mark, two separate marks below the first dorsal fin rays, two separate marks above the front anal fin rays and a mark on the caudal fin ray. The mark above the anal fin generally disappears in sexually mature fish but a fairly distinct pattern of horizontal stripes may appear during the mating season. The marks disappear altogether in older specimens. The dorsal and caudal fins are salmon in color with a dark edge: the anal fin is white with reddish dots. Females have yellowish fins and when spawning they have fuller bodies.
Males are more slender.

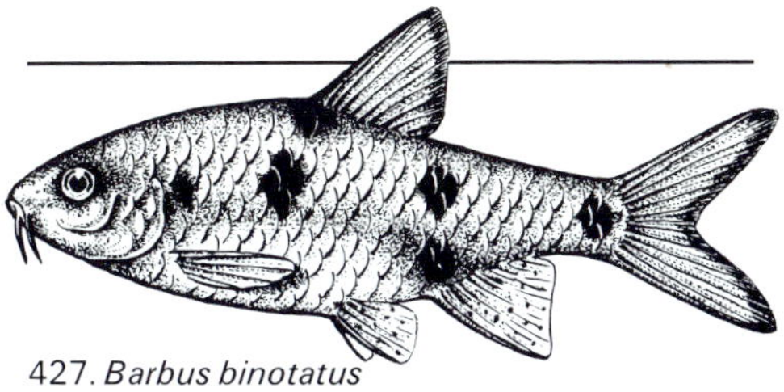

427. *Barbus binotatus*

General care: As for *B.arulius*. At least four *B.binotatus* should be kept together.

Breeding: Not difficult. A very prolific species. Breeding temperature 27°C: Breeding tank water as for *B.arulius*.

Additional information: This species was first imported in 1907 and then called *Barbus maculatus*.

BARBUS CALLIPTERUS

Family: *Cyprinidae*
Genus: *Barbus*
English name: none
Origin: Nigeria, the Cameroons and Lagos
Size: Approximately 9 cm in the wild: remains considerably smaller in captivity
Habitat: Found only in running waters

Shape, coloring and markings: The body is slender and laterally very compressed. The caudal fin is deeply forked. The basic coloration is yellowish: the back is ochre or brownish: the flanks silvery tinged with yellow or gold: the underside is silver or pure white. The scales have a dark edge, especially on the upper half of the body: those on the lateral line are darkly pigmented at the base, thus showing up as a dark horizontal line. The fins are yellowish at the base and in sexually mature females, often reddish in color: on the dorsal fin there is a large black cone-shaped band.
There are no known external sexual characteristics. However it is likely that, as in related species, the females are more powerfully developed than the males.

General care: As for *B.arulius* but temperature 22°–26°C. This species has a particular liking for water rich in oxygen, and benefits greatly from the regular changing of part of the tank water. Large live animal matter is particularly good for this species: it should also have a vegetable supplement in its diet.

Breeding: There is no record of this species having been as yet successfully bred in captivity.

Additional information: According to George Albert Boulenger, this species is also found in hot springs, but there is no evidence recorded to support this view, which may be based on a misunderstanding. Unfortunately, for some reason this beautiful species has now almost entirely disappeared from collectors' aquariums.

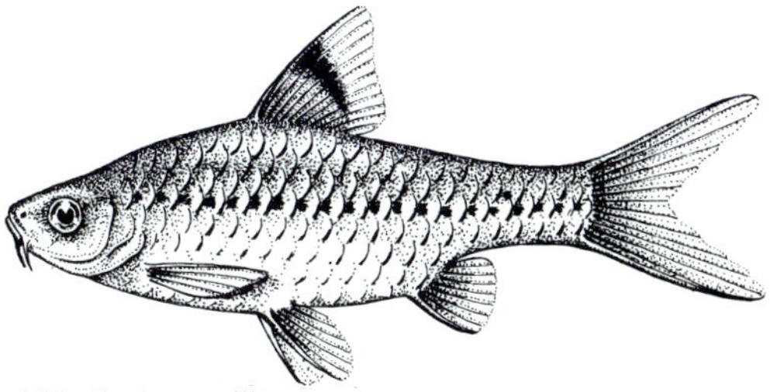

428. *Barbus callipterus*

BARBUS CHOLA

Family: *Cyprinidae*
Genus: *Barbus*
English name: Swamp Barb
Origin: A wide area of India
Size: Maximum 15 cm in the wild: remains considerably smaller in captivity
Habitat: Found in nearly all kinds of waters

Shape, coloring and markings: The body is fairly deep and hardly at all laterally compressed. On the whole it is slightly stockier than related species. The basic color is silvery, with a beautiful olive green back, pale yellow iridescent flanks and a white belly and underside. There is a prominent black mark on the caudal peduncle and this is often surrounded by a shining golden patch. The gill covers have yellow or gold iridescent patterns. The fins are all a soft yellow: older fish have brownish red flecks on the dorsal, caudal and anal fins.
Females are slightly larger and noticeably more rounded in shape when spawning.
Males have more reddish fins, especially during the mating season: the bodies are more slender.

General care: as for *B.arulius*. *B.chola* how-

429. *Barbus callipterus*

430. *Barbus chola*

ever keeps mainly to the bottom and middle reaches of the tank where it is an extremely active swimmer. Temperature 21°–23°C: this may be reduced to 17°–20°C during the winter. Diet as for *B.arulius*.

BREEDING: Not difficult but the best results will be obtained if the temperature during the winter months is kept low as suggested above. Mating takes place in early spring: the temperature should then be raised to about 24°C.

ADDITIONAL INFORMATION: Although this species is found over a wide area and is therefore fairly common it is seldom imported. If kept in an aquarium it should be remembered that *B.chola* can jump extremely well and suitable precautions ought be taken.

BARBUS CONCHONIUS

Family: *Cyprinidae*

Genus: *Barbus*

English name: Rosy Barb

Origin: North India, Bengal, Assam

Size: Maximum 14 cm in the wild: remains considerably smaller in captivity: the fish are sexually mature when they reach 6 cm

Habitat: Found in still and running waters, where it is common

SHAPE, COLORING AND MARKINGS: The body is fairly deep and somewhat laterally compressed. The coloring shows up best under bright lighting. The back is a beautiful shiny olive green: the rest of the body, including the belly, is mainly silvery, shiny and tinged with a soft red. During the mating season this red color predominates. There is a round deep black mark edged with gold on the flanks below the last dorsal fin rays. The fins are a soft red and transparent: the dorsal and anal fins have a dark pigmentation on their tips. Females are fuller in the body and have almost colorless fins.
Males are more slender and have more coloring on the fins.

GENERAL CARE: *B.conchonius* is suitable for both small and large aquariums. It is best kept in a group of at least six. There are no special requirements in the furnishing of the aquarium: arrangements of both rock and wood can be used as decoration. The composition of the water is not critical but fresh water should be avoided. The fish tend to keep to the bottom and middle reaches of the tank, although if there are plenty of floating plants on the surface, they will swim at all levels. Temperature about 22°C, and this may be reduced in winter to as low as 14°C. *B.conchonius* will eat almost anything digestible but some live animal matter is essential in the diet.

434. *Barbus conchonius*

BREEDING: Not difficult. Old soft water should be used. Temperature about 25°C. The fish will breed very easily in the early spring if kept during the winter at a lower temperature. The fry are fairly easy to raise.

ADDITIONAL INFORMATION: This is an easy species to keep and has been popular with aquarists for many years.

BARBUS CUMINGI

Family: *Cyprinidae*

Genus: *Barbus*

English name: Cuming's Barb

Origin: Ceylon

Size: Approximately 5 cm

Habitat: Found in mountain streams and jungle creeks

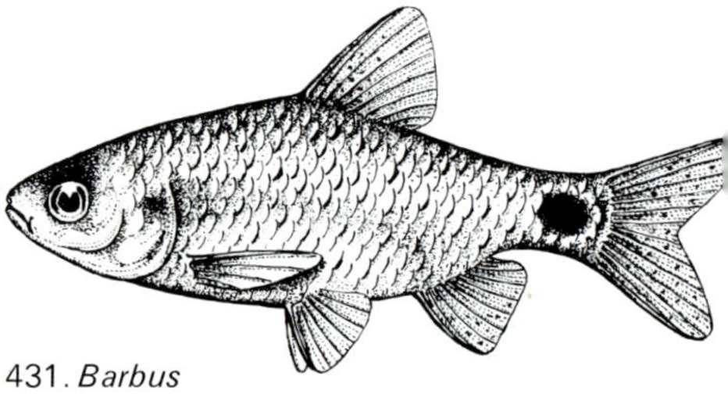

431. *Barbus chola*

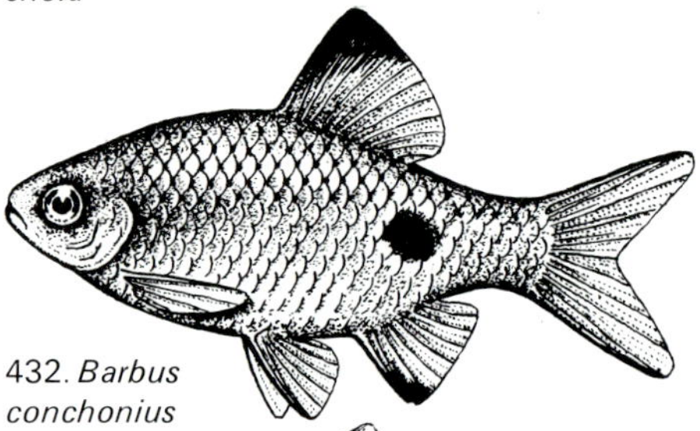

432. *Barbus conchonius*

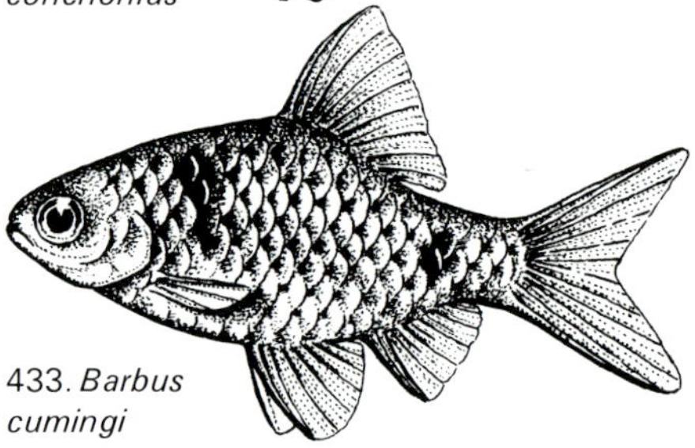

433. *Barbus cumingi*

435. *Barbus cumingi*

SHAPE, COLORING AND MARKINGS: The body is fairly deep and laterally somewhat compressed. The basic coloration is off-white with a brilliant silver sheen: the head and front parts of the body have a golden sheen: all the scales have a more or less dark edge. There are two irregular dark marks on the body: one begins above the pectoral fins and stretches cone-shaped to the neck: the other, smaller mark lies on the caudal peduncle, roughly at the level of the back anal fin rays. The anal and caudal fins are a matt yellow: the dorsal and ventral fins are orange-red: the pectoral fins are colorless and transparent.
Females when sexually mature have more rounded bellies.
Males are more slender and usually have more colorful fins.

GENERAL CARE: As for *B.conchonius*. The temperature should be 23°–27°C. This species will be found at all levels of the tank, but it also likes to search for food on the bed. Diet as for *B.conchonius*.

BREEDING: Not difficult. Old soft water should be used for the tank. Temperature about 28°C. The reproductive urge of these fish can be stimulated by changing some of the water. The fry are easy to raise with the usual fry foods.

ADDITIONAL INFORMATION: *B.cumingi* has never been a favorite with aquarists because of its rather plain coloring and markings. It is however often offered by dealers and provided it is kept in a small group it can, with its energetic movements, become a lively addition to the aquarium of every aquarist; it is fairly easy to keep.

BARBUS DORSIMACULATUS

Family: *Cyprinidae*
Genus: *Barbus*
English name: none
Origin: Indonesia, Sumatra
Size: Approximately 3.5 cm
Habitat: No details of its natural habitat are available

SHAPE, COLORING AND MARKINGS: The body is more slender than in related species and is only slightly laterally compressed. The basic coloration is silvery-white and the back has a light brown pigmentation. A very narrow line runs from the gill covers across the body to the base of the caudal fin. The fins are colorless and transparent: the dorsal fin bears a large black cone-shaped mark.
Females when sexually mature probably have more rounded bellies.
Males are more slender.

GENERAL CARE: There is little detailed information about this species available. In general it can be assumed that they require the same conditions and care as other small barbs. Treat as *B.arulius*, with a diet principally of small live animal matter.

436. *Barbus dorsimaculatus*

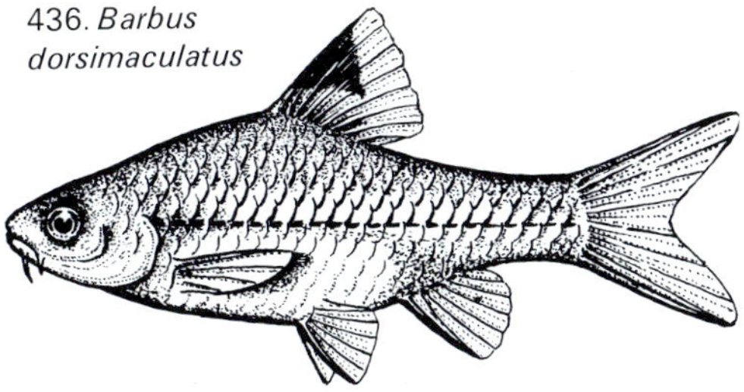

BREEDING: Nothing is recorded about the reproductive behavior of this fish, but it is likely to be similar to that of related species.

ADDITIONAL INFORMATION: *B.dorsimaculatus* was first imported in 1913 but has never become popular among aquarists. Now it is rarely if ever seen in aquariums, although a few specimens find their way to dealers when imported by accident with other fish.

BARBUS EVERETTI

Family: *Cyprinidae*
Genus: *Barbus*
English name: Clown Barb
Origin: Singapore, Sarawak, Borneo
Size: Maximum 13 cm
Habitat: Found in many different kinds of waters

SHAPE, COLORING AND MARKINGS: The body is fairly deep and only slightly compressed laterally. It is a very attractive species, closely resembling *B.dunckeri*, with which it is often confused. It has a brown or reddish-brown back, beautiful shiny yellowy-golden flanks with striking green-black marks. The first of these marks is cone-shaped and runs from the neck to the lateral line: a large oval mark lies above the ventral fins and another separate mark runs right into the dorsal fin from its base. Another cone-shaped mark stretches from behind the dorsal fin to the lateral line. A small round mark, surrounded by a shiny golden patch appears on the caudal peduncle. There is usually another dark patch over the anal fin which stretches along the lower side of the caudal peduncle. The lower part of the body is a striking orange, with a burnished sheen. All the fins are a soft red, translucent, with more or less violet tips.
Females are usually slightly larger and have less vivid coloring.
Males are more slender.

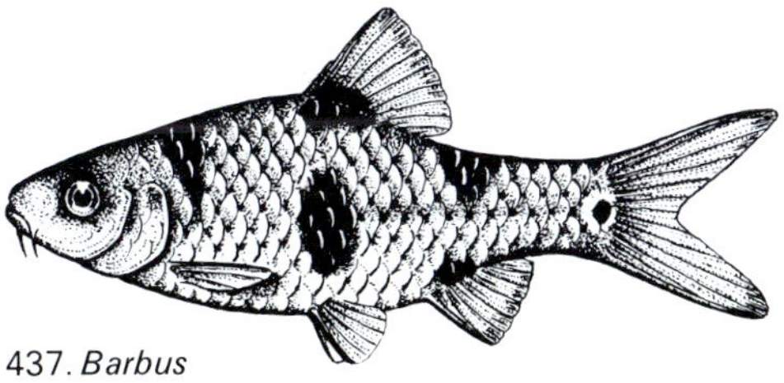

437. *Barbus everetti*

GENERAL CARE: As for *B.arulius* but the water should be old and soft, preferably filtered over peat.

BREEDING: Not easy, although it has been done successfully a number of times. The breeding fish should be kept apart for three or four weeks and be well provided with worms and mosquito larvae: it is very impor-

438. *Barbus everetti*

tant that there should also be some vegetable matter, such as algae or lettuce leaves, in the diet. The breeding tank should be quite large and placed where it will catch the morning sun. Thick clumps of *Myriophyllum* are the spawning medium. The water should be old and slightly acid. Temperature 25°–27°C.

BARBUS FASCIATUS

Family: *Cyprinidae*

Genus: *Barbus*

English name: Striped Barb

Origin: Malaya, Borneo, Indonesia, Sumatra and Bangka

Size: Maximum 12 cm

Habitat: Found in many different kinds of waters

SHAPE, COLORING AND MARKINGS: The body is less deep and the caudal peduncle more slender than in related species. The basic coloration is something between yellow and a silvery-brown, which in bright light appears to be tinged with violet. There are four to six clearly separated dark blue or blue-black lines running the length of the body. The dorsal and anal fins are rust-colored or yellow and transparent: the other fins are colorless.
Females have fuller bodies and less vividly colored stripes.
Males are as described above.

GENERAL CARE: As for *B.everetti* but the temperature should be 22°–25°C and the water slightly acid.

BREEDING: Difficult; no successful attempts are recorded. Another variety *B.lineatus,* found in Johore and distinguished from *B.fasciatus* only by the absence of barbels, breeds easily in captivity. If *B.lineatus* is no more than a variety of *B.fasciatus* (and not a distinct species) the difference in breeding habits is strange. It may be that experiments in the cross-breeding of the two fish will throw light on this matter.

BARBUS FASCIOLATUS

Family: *Cyprinidae*

Genus: *Barbus*

English name: none

Origin: The Congo, Angola

Size: Approximately 7 cm

Habitat: Found in nearly all still and sluggish waters

SHAPE, COLORING AND MARKINGS: The body is deep and laterally greatly compressed. The head is blunt and the throat noticeably curved. The basic coloration is silvery, with a bluish-green tinge. The back is greyish-green. There are 12 short narrow transverse bands running across the body: the second of these is always the most prominent. The unpaired fins are light brown at the base and otherwise colorless. The other fins are colorless and transparent.
Females when adult are more rounded than the males.
Males are noticeably more slender.

GENERAL CARE: As for *B.arulius* but the temperature should never be lower than 22°C and must be maintained between 22°C and 25°C. *B.fasciolatus* should be kept in a group of sturdy specimens. The males have a tendency to bite other males of the same species, expecially during the mating season. *B.fasciolatus* can also be somewhat intolerant of other species of fish: they sometimes even attack small fish. This species is a very voracious eater.

BREEDING: Nothing is known about the breeding habits of this species which does not yet seem to have been bred successfully in captivity.

ADDITIONAL INFORMATION: This fish was first imported in 1911 and was imported regularly until 1939. Since that date there seem to have been no references to this species which suggests that it is no longer of interest to aquarists.

BARBUS GELIUS

Family: *Cyprinidae*

Genus: *Barbus*

English name: none

Origin: India, Assam, Bengal, Orissa

Size: Approximately 4 cm

Habitat: Found in slow flowing waters, especially amongst the vegetation growing near the banks

SHAPE, COLORING AND MARKINGS: The body is fairly deep and laterally only slightly compressed. The coloration is difficult to describe precisely because it varies according to the direction of the light and the composition of the soil. *B.gelius* is more or less transparent with an olive green or brownish back and a silvery-white belly and throat. In bright lighting it has a beautiful golden sheen. There is a stripe running the length of the body, widening towards the tail, which is a beautiful golden-red or copper color and particularly striking in male fish. The flanks have irregular markings and stripes which can vary in color from dark blue to deep black. All the fins, except for the pectoral fins, are a soft yellow and the caudal fin is tinged with red.
Females are larger with more rounded bellies.
Males are more slender.

GENERAL CARE: This species is suitable for both large and small aquariums. The aquarium should be arranged as recommended for *B.arulius*. At least six of these fish should be kept in a group together. *B.gelius* does not necessarily have to be provided with a dark bed. Temperature about 20°C, reduced during the winter to 16°–18°C. *B.gelius* will be found at all levels of the tank and can be kept happily with other species of fish. It has a particular fondness for Daphnia, Cyclops and small mosquito larvae: dried food will also be accepted.

BREEDING: Not too difficult. Temperature not above 21°–22°C. The eggs are very adhesive and hatch after 24 hours. It is extremely difficult to see the fry when first hatched and when they hang on the plants or the sides of the tank. They should be raised with the smallest available food such as rotifers and nauplii: very finely powdered dried food can also be given.

439. *Barbus gelius*

440. *Barbus holotaenia*

BARBUS HOLOTAENIA

Family: *Cyprinidae*

Genus: *Barbus*

English name: none

Origin: Africa, an area from the central Congo region (Zaire) to the Cameroons

Size: Approximately 12 cm

Habitat: Found especially in the tributaries of the Congo river

SHAPE, COLORING AND MARKINGS: The body is elongated and laterally compressed. The back is slightly more rounded than the belly. The basic coloration is silvery-yellow: the back is greyish-brown or dull green: the belly is a silvery-white. A deep black stripe runs from the snout through the eyes and the gill covers into the base of the caudal fin and the middle fin rays. The scales above and below this stripe have a dark pigmentation at the base, forming sickle-shaped patterns, especially at the front of the body. All the fins are a beautiful red, with milk-white edges, except for the pectoral fin: on the dorsal fin there is also a black cone-shaped mark.
There are no known external sexual characteristics.

GENERAL CARE: As for *B.arulius*. At least four specimens should be kept in a group and all should be more or less the same size. Temperature 25°–27°C. The water should be soft and slightly acid, preferably filtered over peat. *B.holotaenia* keeps mainly to the bottom and middle reaches of the tank: it is tolerant of other fish. Diet as for *B.arulius*.

BREEDING: Nothing is recorded about the breeding habits of this species and it does not seem as yet to have been bred in captivity.

ADDITIONAL INFORMATION: This is a little known species although it was described by George Albert Boulenger as long ago as 1913.

BARBUS LATERISTRIGA

Family: *Cyprinidae*

Genus: *Barbus*

English name: Spanner Barb

Origin: Southeast Asia, Singapore, Moluccas, Thailand, Sumatra, Bangka, Java and Borneo

Size: Maximum 18 cm in the wild: remains considerably smaller in captivity

Habitat: Commonly found in clear streams, pools and jungle creeks

SHAPE, COLORING AND MARKINGS: The body is fairly deep and somewhat laterally compressed: young fish are considerably more

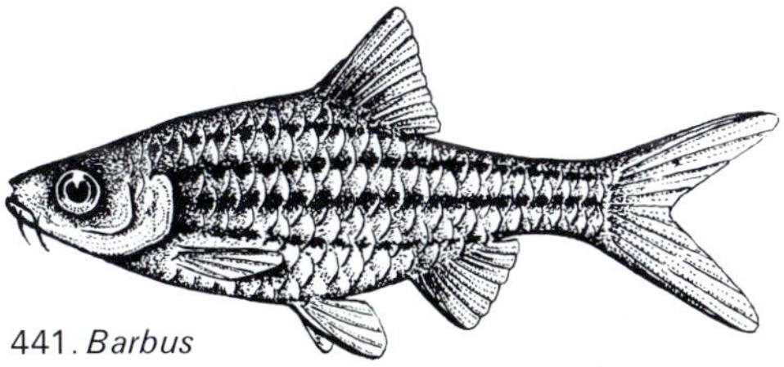

441. *Barbus fasciatus*

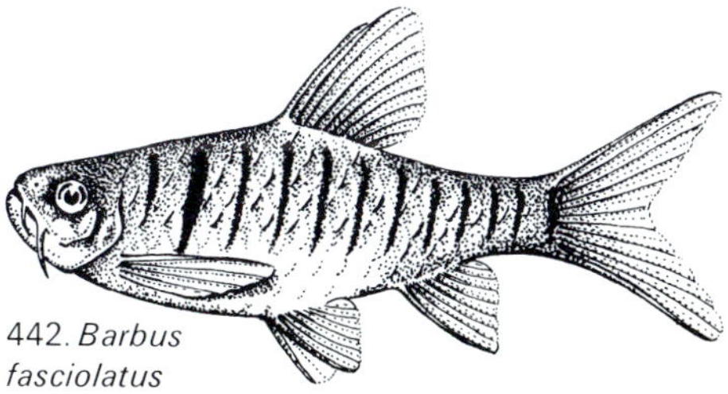

442. *Barbus fasciolatus*

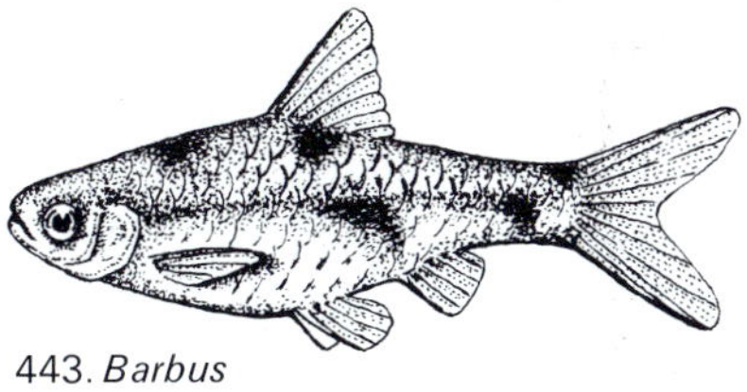

443. *Barbus gelius*

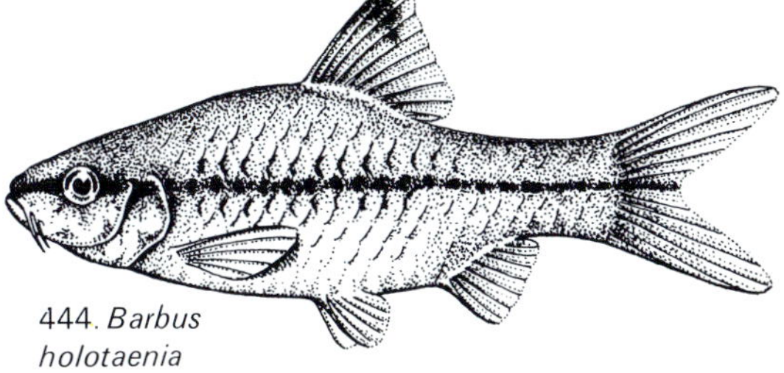

444. *Barbus holotaenia*

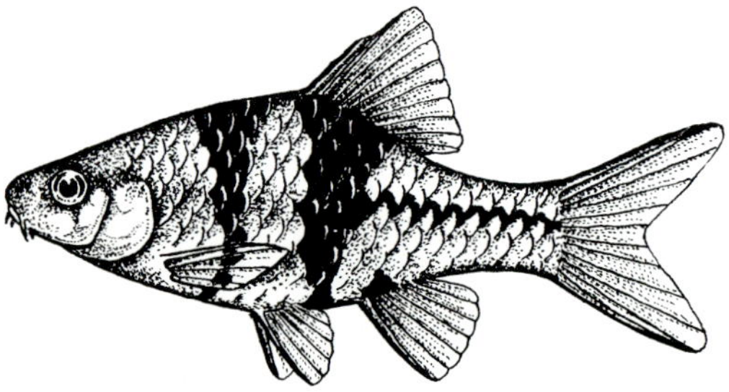

445. *Barbus lateristriga*

slender than adult specimens. There are a great number of local varieties of this species, because of the very wide area over which it is found: these varieties can differ greatly in shape, color and markings. The young fish are particularly beautiful, with greenish-orange backs, golden-yellow flanks and vivid orange bellies. Two cone-shaped transverse bands stretch across the whole width of the front part of the body and there is a dark mark above the anal fin that runs into the first anal fin rays. From the second transverse band, a dark bluish zigzag line runs along the length of the rest of the body into the caudal peduncle. The fins are reddish and transparent, frequently with a light blue edge.
Females have soft red and transparent dorsal fins.
Males are more vividly colored.

General care: As for *B.arulius*. *B.lateristriga* keeps mainly to the bottom and middle reaches of the tank. Temperature approximately 25°C: during the winter 22°–24°C. This species benefits from old and soft water, some of which should be changed regularly.

Breeding: Not difficult: this species is very prolific.

Additional information: This popular species has been imported since 1914 and has been a particular favorite with aquarists since then. When young the fish can very easily be confused with other species.

BARBUS NIGROFASCIATUS

Family: *Cyprinidae*
Genus: *Barbus*
English name: Black Ruby
Origin: Southern Ceylon
Size: Approximately 5 cm
Habitat: Found in slow running waters: the distribution area is restricted but the fish are found in large numbers within it

---

Shape, coloring and markings: The body is deep and laterally compressed. The coloring and markings vary a great deal according to the season and whether the fish reproduces or not. Except during the spawning season *B.nigrofasciatus* is basically a dull yellow, with three or four more or less cone-shaped, but rather ill-defined transverse bands. In females these transverse bands are often broken and reduced to irregular patches. The head of the fish is a beautiful red, and during the mating season it becomes a bright purplish-red. All the scales have decorative silver-white edges, making the fish, especially under bright light, look as though they have been sprinkled with sequins. The dorsal fin is deep black: the anal fin dark red or black: the ventral fins a soft red. During the mating season the fins become the same dark red as the front of the body, and the whole body in turn is covered with a beautiful green sheen.
Females usually have light pigmentation at the base of the fins.
Males have more vivid coloring.

General care: As for *B.arulius*. Its habits are similar although it will be found at all levels of the tank. The water and temperature should be as for *B.arulius*, and like that species it should be kept in a group of at least six. It is very fond of Daphnia, Cyclops and the *nauplii* of the brine shrimp.

Breeding: Not difficult. A very prolific species. Mating takes place in the early morning sun at a temperature of about 25°–28°C.

Additional information: A species very suitable for a community tank.

446. *Barbus nigrofasciatus*

BARBUS OLIGOLEPIS

Family: *Cyprinidae*
Genus: *Barbus*
English name: Island Barb
Origin: Indonesia, Sumatra
Size: Approximately 5 cm
Habitat: Found in nearly all still and running waters

Shape, coloring and markings: The body is fairly deep and laterally greatly compressed. The basic coloration is a reddish or yellowish-brown: the back is darker and the belly ochre. Under bright lighting the whole body is seen to be covered with a greenish pearly sheen, which is slightly more blue on the back. There is a beautiful net-like pattern covering the whole body, produced by the dark edges of the scales. In the middle part of the body each scale is adorned with a blue iridescent mark at its base. Young fish have a number of irregular dark marks which disappear in time and only the mark on the caudal peduncle remains in mature specimens.
Females have ochre colored, unpaired fins.
Males have reddish or brick-red, black edged unpaired fins.

General care: As for *B.arulius*. Temperature 22°–24°C. Diet as for *B.gelius*. This species particularly needs water rich in oxygen and the appropriate vegetation should be planted in the aquarium. Part of the water should be changed regularly.

BREEDING: Not difficult.

ADDITIONAL INFORMATION: Although *B.oligolepis* is a very tolerant fish and eminently suitable for a community tank, the males are sometimes rather aggressive to each other, particularly during the spawning season. Thus only one male should ever be put in a breeding tank with one or two females. *B.oligolepis* will occasionally eat a lettuce leaf as a delicacy and in the aquarium it is easy to see how fond these fish are of eating algae.

447. *Barbus oligolepis*

BARBUS PENTAZONA HEXAZONA

Family: *Cyprinidae*
Genus: *Barbus*
English name: none
Origin: Indonesia, central Sumatra
Size: Maximum 5.5 cm
Habitat: Found in nearly all kinds of still and running waters

SHAPE, COLORING AND MARKINGS: The body is deep and laterally very compressed. The basic color is reddish-brown: the back is darker and the underside is orangey-yellow. This species is in many ways very similar to *B.pentazona pentazona,* the only differences lying in the shape and direction of the transverse bands found on both species. In this species, *B.pentazona hexazona,* the bands are broader and lie within a light green iridescent area. The first band, on the head, is wide and incorporates the whole eye: the second runs right through to the underside of the body: the third runs from the front of the dorsal fin to just above the pectoral fins but does not quite reach to the underside of the body. The scales lying within the area of the bands

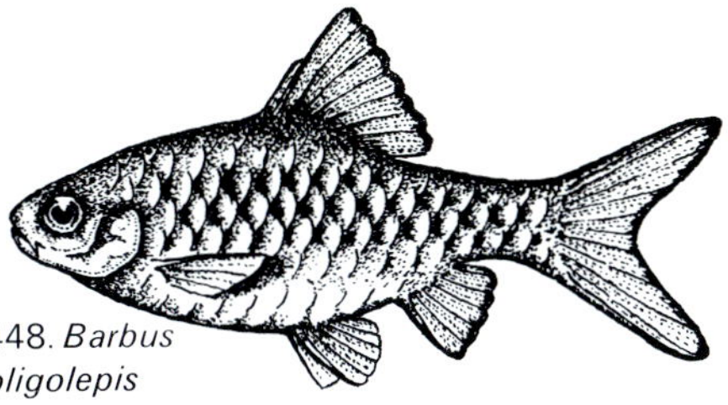

448. *Barbus oligolepis*

have green iridescent edges. All the fins are a dark red at the base, becoming lighter towards the edges which are themselves colorless. The ventral fins are colorless and transparent.
Females when spawning have more rounded bellies: they are less vividly colored.
Males are more slender: colored as described above.

GENERAL CARE: Suitable for large or small aquariums provided there is ample swimming space and also some thick vegetation. This species is somewhat timid: it prefers a dark bed, does not have to be kept in a group, and will remain at the bottom or in the middle reaches of the tank. Diet as for *B.gelius.*

BREEDING: Problematical. Temperature 27°–30°C.

ADDITIONAL INFORMATION: This species can be cross-bred easily with the related species *B.pentazona pentazona.*

BARBUS PENTAZONA PENTAZONA

Family: *Cyprinidae*
Genus: *Barbus*
English name: none
Origin: Malaya, Singapore, Borneo, Indonesia, Sumatra
Size: Approximately 5 cm
Habitat: Found in almost all still and running waters

SHAPE, COLORING AND MARKINGS: The body is deep and laterally very compressed. The basic color is reddish-brown: the back is darker and the underside is an orangey-yellow.

449. *Barbus pentazona hexazona*

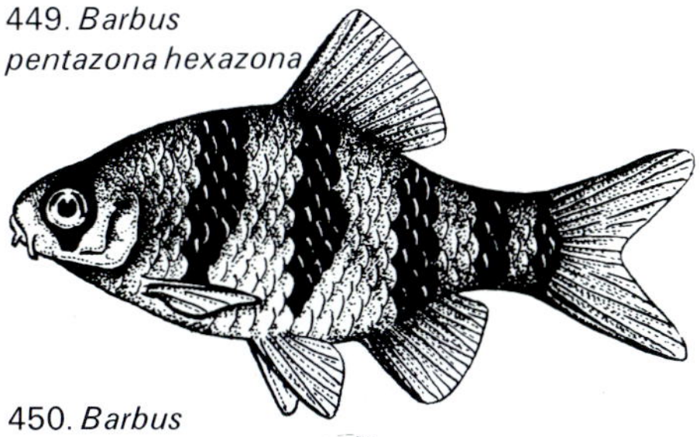

450. *Barbus pentazona pentazona*

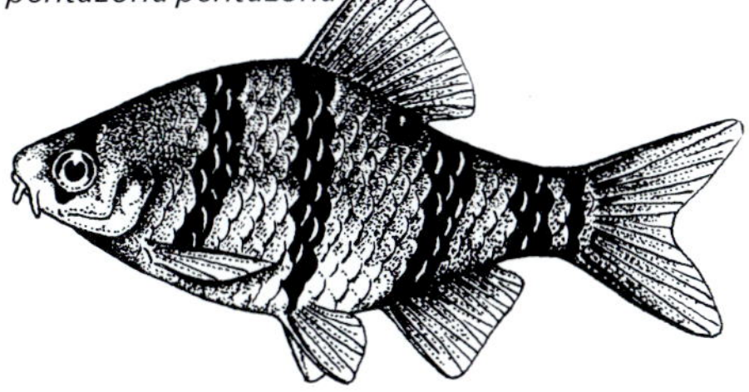

There are six bluish black transverse bands on the body. The first runs across the head through the eye, finishing just underneath it: the second runs from the back to the base of the pectoral fin: the third runs from the front of the dorsal fin to the front of the ventral fins: the fourth starts just behind the dorsal fin and extends to the anal fin: the fifth runs over the caudal peduncle to the back of the anal fin: the sixth lies across the base of the caudal fin. Some specimens have also a black mark in front of the fourth transverse band at the base of the dorsal fin. The scales between the bands have green iridescent edges. The transverse bands themselves often lie within a shiny yellow patch. All the fins have a dark red base which becomes lighter towards the edges which themselves are nearly colorless. The ventral fins are colorless and transparent.
Females are less vividly colored than the males and during the spawning season have much more rounded bellies.
Males are more slender.

GENERAL CARE: As for *B.pentazona hexazona.*

BREEDING: Problematical. Temperature 27°–30°C. See under *B.pentazona hexazona* for the possibility of cross-breeding.

451. *Barbus pentazona hexazona*

BARBUS PENTAZONA TETRAZONA

Family: *Cyprinidae*
Genus: *Barbus*
English name: none
Origin: Borneo, especially the basins of the Kahajan and Kapoeas rivers
Size: Approximately 6 cm
Habitat: Found in nearly all still and running waters

SHAPE, COLORING AND MARKINGS: The body is deep and laterally very compressed: it dif-

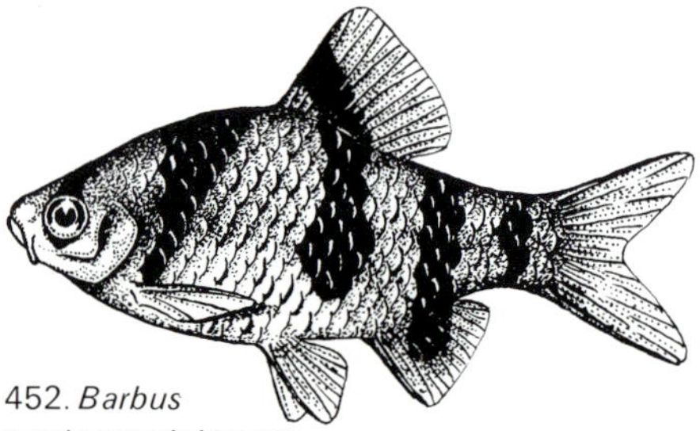

452. *Barbus pentazona tetrazona*

fers from closely related species in having a body slightly less deep, but a snout more pointed. The basic color is a silvery-white with a beautiful red iridescent sheen on the flanks: the back is a reddish-brown tinged with a shiny green sheen. There are five bluish-black transverse bands across the body. The first runs across the head, through the eye and finishes just below it: the second is cone-shaped, running from the dorsal fins to the base of the pectoral fins: the third is keyhole-shaped and, starting in the front dorsal fin rays, reaches almost to the belly: the fourth band lies behind the dorsal fin and stretches from the upper side of the caudal peduncle to the anal fin where it ends in a round mark: the fifth transverse band lies just in front of the base of the caudal fin. The scales lying within these bands have green iridescent edges. The dorsal and anal fins are brick red at the base and become lighter towards their edges which are themselves almost colorless. All the other fins are reddish and more or less transparent.
Females when spawning have heavier bellies.
Males are slightly more slender.

General care: As for *B.pentazona hexazona*. This species is however somewhat less timid than closely related species.

Breeding: Not difficult. Temperature 27°–30° C.

BARBUS PHUTUNIO

Family: *Cyprinidae*

Genus: *Barbus*

English name: Dwarf Barb

Origin: India and Ceylon

Size: Approximately 5 cm in captivity

Habitat: Found in small streams, rice paddies, pools and shallow lakes

---

Shape, coloring and markings: The body is deep and laterally compressed. Older specimens have a particularly deep body. The basic coloration is silvery, tinged with a soft violet: the back is brownish or greyish-green with a beautiful emerald sheen on the scales of the neck: the belly is silvery-white. All the scales are dark at the base and beautifully iridescent at the edges. When *B.phutonio* becomes excited, five steel-blue transverse bands become visible: these then subsequently pale into three more or less well-defined marks. All the fins are a soft red or orange except for the pectoral fins: the dorsal fin often has a dark edge.
Females frequently have no marks on the flanks.
Males are more slender than the females.

General care: While suitable for a small aquarium, *B.phutonio* does better in larger aquariums. Thick vegetation and a dark bed are needed. It is a social but timid species and should be kept with other tranquil fish. It usually keeps to the bottom and middle reaches of the tank. Old clear water is needed: temperature 20°–24° C. Diet as for *B.gelius*.

Breeding: Not too difficult but it is not a prolific species. Temperature about 25° C. The fry hatch after about 30 hours and are easy to raise with the usual foods.

Additional information: In the wild this species grows to about 8 cm: it always remains considerably smaller in captivity. During the winter *B.phutunio* can be kept at a minimum temperature of 16° C. If this is done, breeding, which occurs in the spring, will be encouraged. This species is more prone to disease than are related species.

453. *Barbus phutunio*

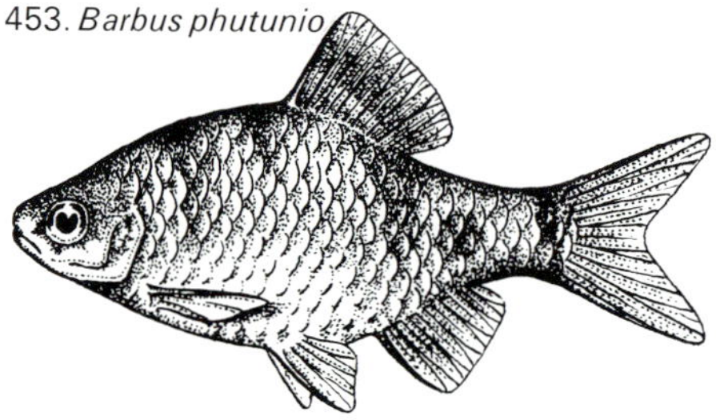

454. *Barbus schuberti*

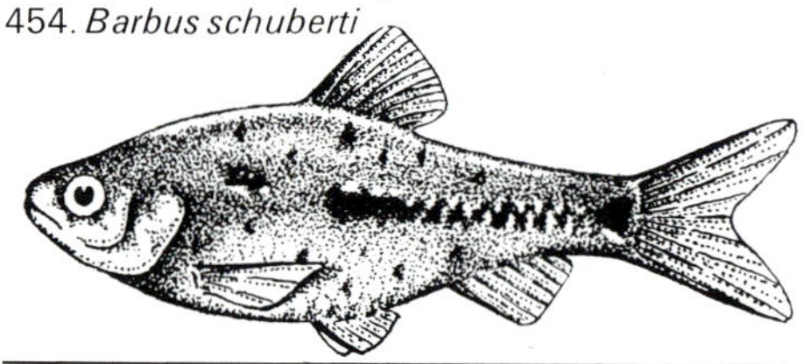

BARBUS SCHUBERTI

Family: *Cyprinidae*

Genus: *Barbus*

English name: Golden Barb

Origin: Nothing at all seems to be known about the origin or natural habitat of this species.

Size: Approximately 6 cm

Shape, coloring and markings: The body is fairly deep and laterally compressed. The basic coloration is golden-yellow tinged with a silvery sheen. There is a well-defined black

455. *Barbus schuberti*

mark on the caudal peduncle. Below the dorsal fin there are a few random marks and dots varying in color from bluish-green to black. On the middle of the bodies of older fish there are a number of marks which, especially in males, often merge together into an irregular stripe over the length of the body.
Females have larger and deeper bodies.
Males are more slender with a well-defined stripe running the length of the body.

General care: A species suitable for both small and large aquariums, provided there is ample and varied vegetation and a dark bed. Although not a social fish it is better to keep a small group rather than one pair in a tank. The composition of the water is not critical but fresh water should be avoided. Temperature 20°–24° C. An active swimmer and a voracious eater of both live and dried food: it is possible to hear these fish smacking their lips as they feed.

Breeding: Not difficult: a very prolific species. Temperature about 26° C. Slightly acid water is needed. The eggs are very adhesive and are scattered among the clumps of vegetation or simply on the peaty bed during the tempestuous mating session. Sexually mature fish often spawn spontaneously without any spawning medium being provided. The fry hatch after about 36 hours and swim freely after two days. They are easy to raise and reach sexual maturity after eight to twelve months.

Additional information: The first specimens of *B.schuberti* came from America and it is generally accepted that this species is a product of breeding. It is obviously closely related to *B.semifasciolatus* with which it can be crossbred. Some writers maintain that it is a variety of *B.sachsi*, the Gold-finned Barb, a golden yellow to yellowish green species from Southeast Asia, and a species rarely kept by aquarists, even though young specimens, with black green stripes on the flanks, can be quite attractive.

BARBUS SCHWANENFELDI

Family: *Cyprinidae*

Genus: *Barbus*

English name: Schwanenfeld's Barb

Origin: Indonesia, Sumatra, Borneo, Moluccas, Thailand

Size: Maximum 35 cm in the wild: remains considerably smaller in captivity

SHAPE, COLORING AND MARKINGS: The body is deep and laterally very compressed: younger specimens are considerably more slender. The basic coloration is silvery with a golden sheen: the back is no darker than the rest of the body. The dorsal and caudal fins are a beautiful carmine red: the former has a large black mark in its upper half and a white patch at the tip: the caudal fin is bordered by dark red or black rays at both the top and the bottom. The other fins are an orangey-yellow and usually darker at the base. There are no known external sexual differences, but no doubt when spawning the females will be recognisable by their more rounded bellies.

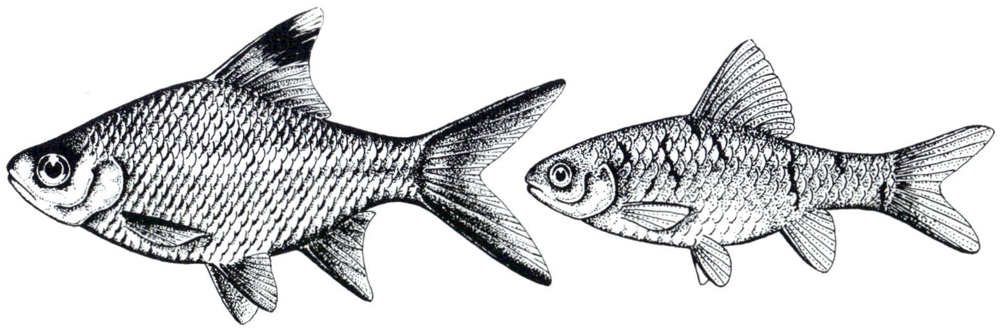

456. *Barbus schwanenfeldi* 457. *Barbus semifasciolatus*

458. *Barbus schwanenfeldi*

459. *Barbus semifasciolatus*

GENERAL CARE: *B.schwanenfeldi* needs a large aquarium with a dark peaty bed and arrangements of wood. Only sturdy plants can be included because this species will eat fine leaved varieties. The composition of the water is not critical but fresh water should be avoided. Temperature 22°–25°C. It will swim at all levels in the tank. A very voracious species: it will eat large quantities of live animal matter and dried food: some lettuce leaves must be included in the diet. It should not be kept with smaller fish.

BREEDING: Not too difficult. The breeding tank must be at least 1 m long. The water must be slightly acid: temperature about 27°C. The eggs are scattered over the peaty bed or among the plants during a tempestuous mating session. The fry hatch after about 24 hours. They are easy to raise and nests of over 500 young are quite common.

ADDITIONAL INFORMATION: This species is not suitable for the home aquarium.

BARBUS SEMIFASCIOLATUS

Family: *Cyprinidae*

Genus: *Barbus*

English name: Green Barb

Origin: Southeast China, from Hong Kong to Hainan

Size: Maximum 7 cm

Habitat: No details are known of its natural habitat

SHAPE, COLORING AND MARKINGS: The body is fairly deep and laterally slightly compressed: older specimens have a fairly deep back. The basic coloration is burnished yellow and the back is darker or reddish-brown: the upper half of the body has a green metallic sheen: the lower half of the body is a golden-yellow: the belly is whitish but becomes an orangey-red when the fish is mating. There are five to seven irregularly placed transverse bands across the body which are not all always well-defined, though there is usually a distinct mark at the base of the caudal fin. The unpaired fins vary from a soft reddish-brown to brick red: the ventral fins are brownish or yellow: the pectoral fins are colorless and transparent. All the scales have a dark edge.

Females are particularly heavy and somewhat colorless when spawning.
Males are more slender and somewhat smaller.

GENERAL CARE: *B.semifasciolatus* is only suitable for larger aquariums constructed as for *B.arulius*, and should be kept in a small group. The composition of the water is not critical but fresh water should be avoided. Temperature 22°–24° C but considerably lower temperatures will be tolerated during the winter. A strong swimmer *B.semifasciolatus* keeps to the bottom and middle reaches of the tank. Diet as for *B.arulius*.

BREEDING: Not difficult in tanks with a capacity of 40 litres. Temperature about 25° C. The fish mate very tempestuously and if the female is unwilling the male forces her into the plants with strong movements of his tail. Before this he will have tried to impress her by swimming towards her belly with his mouth wide open. The eggs are quite large and yellowish in colour. The fry hatch after about 24 hours and are not difficult to raise with the usual foods.

ADDITIONAL INFORMATION: Although this species has been imported since 1909 it has never gained much popularity among aquarists.

BARBUS STIGMA

Family: *Cyprinidae*

Genus: *Barbus*

English name: none

Origin: India, Bengal, Burma

Size: Approximately 15 cm in the wild: remains considerably smaller in captivity

Habitat: Found in may different kinds of waters, and a very common species

---

SHAPE, COLORING AND MARKINGS: The body is very deep and laterally very compressed: in adult males the back is very deep. The basic coloration is silvery-white: the back is darker, or brownish. The upper half of the body is greyish-green: the flanks are tinged with blue: the lower half of the body is a pure white. There is a striking round black mark on the base of the caudal fin, and another similar mark on, or just below the dorsal fin. The anal and ventral fins are brick red: the other fins are colorless and transparent.
Females are bigger and sturdier, especially during the spawning season.
Males when adult have brick red anal and ventral fins. During the spawning season a soft red horizontal line appears running from the back edge of the gill covers to the dark mark on the caudal peduncle.

GENERAL CARE: As for *B.arulius*. A voracious eater: diet as for *B.arulius*, but *B.stigma* also likes an occasional lettuce leaf.

ADDITIONAL INFORMATION: This species was first imported in 1927 and again in 1936: it has however never become very popular among aquarists.

BARBUS STOLICZKANUS

Family: *Cyprinidae*

Genus: *Barbus*

English name: Stoliczka's Barb

Origin: Eastern Burma, the lower reaches of the Irrawaddy

Size: Maximum 6 cm

Habitat: No details are available of its natural habitat

SHAPE, COLORING AND MARKINGS: The body is fairly deep and laterally very compressed. There are no barbels. The basic coloration is a very shiny silvery color: the back is darker or greenish: the flanks have a beautiful blue or yellow sheen. The scales have dark edges and the belly is white. Above the pectoral fins there is a pear-shaped mark on the shoulder and behind that a luminescent patch. A striking dark round mark the size of the eye appears on the caudal peduncle, roughly at the level of the back anal fin rays. The caudal fin is colorless and transparent except for its golden-yellow base. The ventral and anal fins are reddish: the pectoral fins colorless and transparent. The irises are golden and marked at the top with a beautiful red.
Females have light red dorsal fins, but all the other fins are colorless and transparent, quite unlike those of males.
Males can be easily identified by the beautiful coloration of the dorsal fin. The first fin rays are deep black and the whole fin is suffused with red. The base is reddish and its edges black. The central part of the fin bears a dark sickle-shaped mark and a few pear-shaped marks randomly arranged behind that.

GENERAL CARE: As for *B. semifasciolatus*, but some fine leaved plants may be included in the vegetation of the aquarium.

BREEDING: Not too difficult. The fry hatch after about 30 hours at a temperature of 24°–26° C.

BARBUS TERIO

Family: *Cyprinidae*

Genus: *Barbus*

English name: none

Origin India, Bengal

Size: Approximately 9 cm

Habitat: Very common in different waters

SHAPE, COLORING AND MARKINGS: The body is fairly deep and laterally very compressed. There are no barbels. The basic coloration is a silvery-white: the back is slightly darker or greenish: the flanks have a greenish tinge. The lower half of the body is silvery-white with a reddish or violet sheen. There is a large shiny bluish-black round mark surrounded by a patch of gold in the middle of the body, almost directly above the anal fin. There is also a sickle-shaped but not always distinct transverse band on the base of the caudal fin. The fins are a soft yellow at the base: otherwise they are colorless and transparent. The dorsal fin sometimes has a dark edge and a random pattern of dots and flecks.
Females during the spawning season have much heavier bellies.

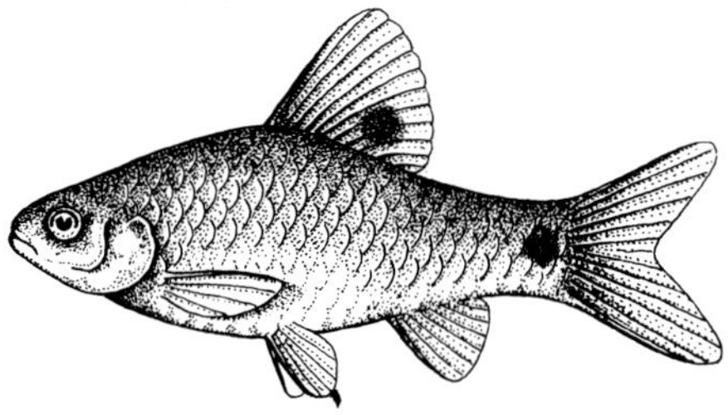

460. *Barbus stigma*

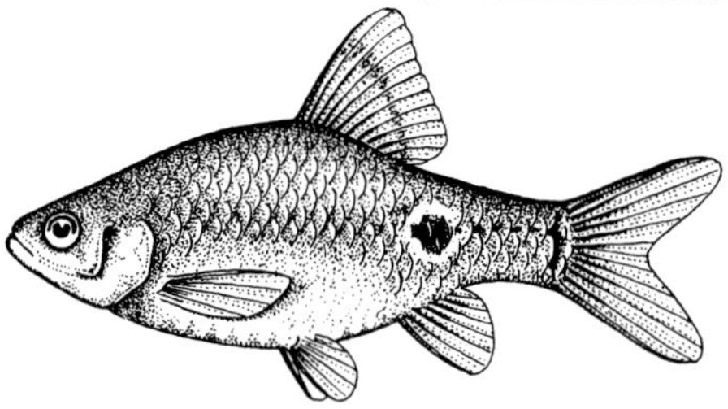

461. *Barbus terio*

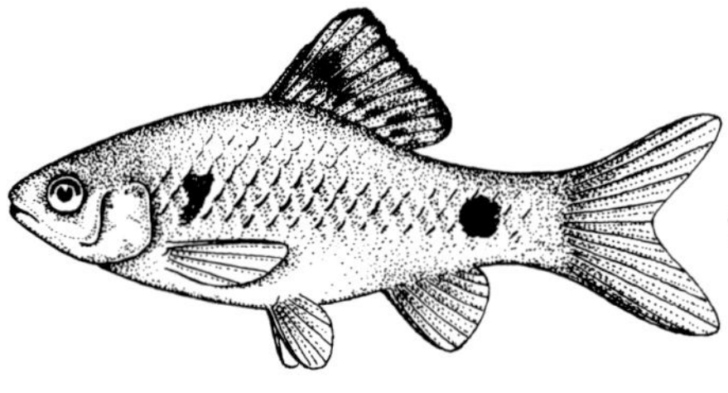

462. *Barbus stoliczkanus*

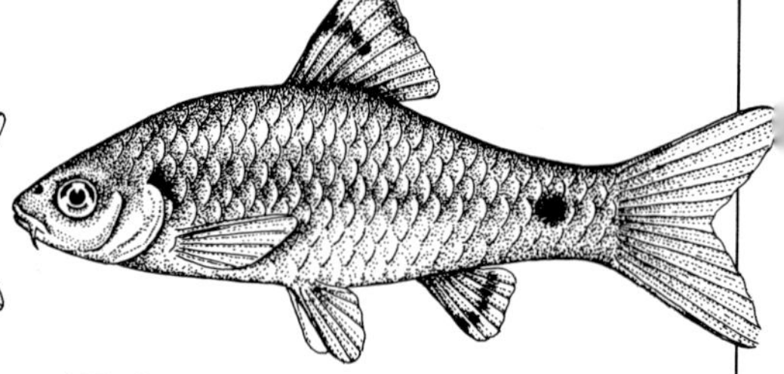

463. *Barbus tetrarupagus*

464. *Barbus tetrazona tetrazona*

Males are more slender and during the spawning season are reddish and iridescent.

General care: As for *B.arulius* but temperature 22°–24° C, and preferably no higher than 18°–20° C during the winter. Diet as for *B.arulius* but this should be supplemented with algae and lettuce leaves.

Breeding: Nothing is known about the breeding habits of this species, which does not yet seem to have been bred successfully in captivity.

Additional information: This species is only very infrequently mentioned in the literature. It was first described by Francis Hamilton Buchanan in 1822.

BARBUS TETRARUPAGUS

Family: *Cyprinidae*

Genus: *Barbus*

English name: none

Origin: India, Assam, Bengal

Size: Approximately 12 cm

Habitat: No details are available of its natural habitat

Shape, coloring and markings: The body is elongated and the upper half is considerably more rounded than the underside. It is laterally slightly compressed. The basic coloration is ochre: the back is a striking brownish-green: the flanks are brownish with a beautiful silvery sheen. The underside is off-white or yellowish. There is a dark mark immediately behind the gill covers, and another, as large as the eye, on the caudal peduncle, between the base of the caudal fin and the outer edge of the anal fin. There is a dark band on the dorsal fin which has also a dark edge: the ventral and anal fins are orangey, the latter with a dark band: the other fins are colorless and transparent.

There are no known external sexual characteristics.

General care: *B.tetrarupagus* requires an aquarium as suggested for *B.arulius*, but temperature 22° C and only 12°–16° C in the winter. It is thus suitable for unheated home aquariums. The composition of the water is not critical, but fresh water should be avoided. *B.tetrarupagus* is a tolerant fish suitable for a community tank, and should be kept in a group of at least four. Diet, any kind of live animal matter and dried food for a change.

BREEDING: Nothing is known about the breeding habits of this species which does not yet seem to have been bred successfully in captivity.

ADDITIONAL INFORMATION: This is a little known species and is rarely imported. It was first described by John McClelland in 1831.

BARBUS TETRAZONA PARTIPENTAZONA

Family: *Cyprinidae*

Genus: *Barbus*

English name: none

Origin: Southeast Thailand

Size: Approximately 6 cm

Habitat: Found in nearly all still and running waters and also in mountain streams

SHAPE, COLORING AND MARKINGS: The body is deep and laterally very compressed. The basic coloration is silvery-yellow often with a red iridescence. The back is brownish tinged with red and the belly is white. The scales on the upper half of the body have a dark edge. There are four deep black transverse bands running across the body. The first runs across the head past the eye, covering a large part of the cheek: the second is more or less cone-shaped and runs from the back to the lower half of the body down to the pectoral fins: the third band begins behind the dorsal fin and continues into the first anal fin rays: the fourth band crosses the base of the caudal fin.

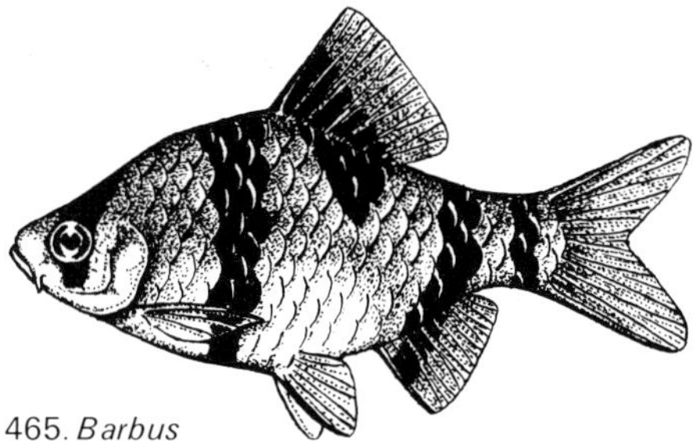

465. *Barbus tetrazona partipentazona*

466. *Barbus tetrazona tetrazona*

There is also a cone-shaped mark below the dorsal fin which reaches about half way down the body and extends upwards into the front dorsal fin rays. The scales which lie within the bands have beautiful golden-green iridescent edges. The dorsal fin is brick red and the other fins are a bright red, especially at the base.
Females have more rounded bellies when spawning: their dorsal and anal fin rays are less vividly pigmented.
Males are slightly more slender.

GENERAL CARE: As for *B.stoliczkanus*. The colors show off to their best advantage over a very dark bottom which also makes these fish less timid. A very strong swimmer that should not be kept together with quieter fish. Fond of gnawing at the fins of moonfish and similar species. Temperature 20°–26°C. Water should be old, clear and rich in oxygen. Its diet should consist of small live food such as Daphnia and Cyclops, alternated with the nauplii of the brine shrimp.

BREEDING: Not difficult. Temperature about 27°C.

BARBUS TETRAZONA TETRAZONA

Family: *Cyprinidae*

Genus: *Barbus*

English name: Sumatra Barb

Origin: Indonesia, Sumatra and Borneo

Size: Approximately 7 cm

Habitat: Found in nearly all still and running waters as well as in mountain streams.

SHAPE, COLORING AND MARKINGS: The body is deep and laterally very compressed. The basic coloration is silvery-white: the upper half of the body is brownish with a green tinge: the flanks have a reddish-brown iridescence. There are four bluish-black transverse bands running across the body. The first band runs across the head, past the eye and covers the greater part of the cheek below: the second band is more or less cone-shaped and runs from the back down to the lower half of the body to the level of the pectoral fin: the third band starts immediately behind the dorsal fin and continues into the first anal fin rays: the fourth band crosses the base of the caudal fin. The scales which lie within the bands have beautiful shiny golden-green edges. The dorsal fin has a black base and is otherwise the same blood red as the anal fin. The other fins are reddish and more or less transparent. Some specimens have a very dark or completely black central fin.
Females when spawning have more rounded bellies: the pigmentation of the dorsal and anal fin rays is less vivid.
Males are slightly more slender.

GENERAL CARE: As for *B.tetrazona pentazona*. But part of the water should be changed regularly.

BREEDING: Not difficult. Temperature 27°C.

BARBUS TICTO

Family: *Cyprinidae*

Genus: *Barbus*

English name: none

Origin: India and Ceylon

Size: Approximately 10 cm

Habitat: Found in nearly all still and running waters

SHAPE, COLORING AND MARKINGS: The body is deep and laterally very compressed. Older specimens have a particularly deep back. The basic coloration is silvery: the back is a dull grey or grass green: there is a beautiful silvery sheen on the flanks: the belly is whitish. There is a more or less dark comma-shaped mark above the pectoral fins. A dark round mark on the caudal peduncle at the level of the anal fin rays is surrounded by a shiny golden patch in particularly well-marked specimens. All the fins are a pale green and transparent except during the spawning season.
Females – when spawning have more rounded bellies and the pectoral and anal fins are then tinged with red.
Males – during the spawning season the lower part of the body becomes an attractive fawn color and a number of dark flecks and spots appear on the dorsal fin.

GENERAL CARE: As for *B.arulius*. *B.ticto* is a very active swimmer, swimming freely and very smoothly throughout the tank. Temperature during the winter about 14°–16°C: in summer 23°C. A very hardy species and one very tolerant towards other fish.

BREEDING: Easy, especially after a cold winter. A very prolific species.

ADDITIONAL INFORMATION: This species was fairly common in aquariums before 1939. but seems to have been rarely imported since then.

BARBUS TITTEYA

Family: *Cyprinidae*

Genus: *Barbus*

English name: Cherry Barb

Origin: Ceylon

Size: Approximately 5 cm

Habitat: Found in densely overgrown or very shady streams

SHAPE, COLORING AND MARKINGS: The body

Additional information: Although this species has now been bred for some years it is still very timid and if possible will retire to a shady spot. The males are sometimes quite aggressive to each other.

BARBUS VITTATUS

Family: *Cyprinidae*

Genus: *Barbus*

English name: none

Origin: India and Ceylon

Size: Approximately 6 cm

Habitat: Found in large numbers in nearly all still and running waters

Shape, coloring and markings: The body is fairly deep and laterally somewhat compressed. The basic coloration is silvery. The back is green or olive green: the flanks are a silvery-green: all the scales have a dark pigmentation at the base and shiny silvery edges. The belly is silvery-white. On the caudal peduncle there is a dark round or oval mark,

◁ 467. *Barbus ticto*

468. *Barbus titteya*

is fairly deep, elongated and laterally slightly compressed. The tail is slender. The back is fawn, with a green iridescent sheen: the flanks and belly are shiny, silvery and tinged with red. A brownish or bluish-black stripe runs across the body from the snout to the base of the caudal fin. The upper side of this stripe is bordered by a wider lightish area, shiny and golden at the front and a beautiful iridescent bluish-green towards the tail. Fish in good condition show a red edge to the lower side of this lightish area. Below the dark stripe there are usually a number of dark marks. The gill covers are reddish. All the fins are reddish with a fine black edge and the anal fin has particularly distinct colors.
Females are duller in color and have yellowish fins.
Males become a deep red during the mating season.

General care: A species suitable for both large and small aquariums with a great deal of vegetation: the fish like the shade. Although not a social fish a few specimens should be kept together. A dark bed will show the colors off to their best advantage. Temperature 22°–24°C. The water should be slightly acid: fresh water should be avoided but some of the water should be changed regularly. Diet as for *B.gelius*.

Breeding: Not too difficult. The fish should be prepared with *Enchytrae* and fruit flies. Temperature about 26°C. The breeding tank need have a capacity of only a few liters. The eggs are scattered on the bed, on fine leaved plants and in the peat fiber. One nest can contain up to 200 young. The fry hatch after about 24 hours: they are very timid and keep out of sight, for the first few weeks appearing only sporadically.

469. *Barbus titteya*

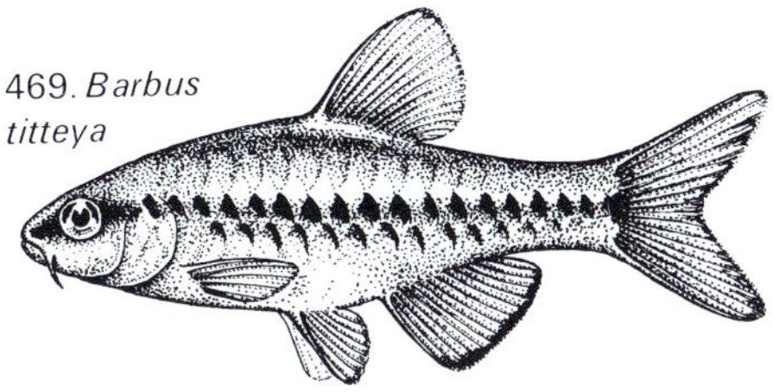

surrounded by a yellow iridescent patch. The dorsal fin has a yellow-golden base and above this there is a black band with an orange edge. All the other fins are clear or brownish-yellow, except for the pectoral fins.
Females – sexually mature specimens are clearly stronger and larger than the males.
Males are smaller and more slender.

General care: As for *B.arulius*, but temperature 22°–24°C.

Breeding: Not difficult.

THE FAMILY CYPRINIDAE

The genus Brachydanio

The fish in the genus *Brachydanio* are all found in India and neighboring areas of Southeast Asia. They are closely related to the genus *Danio,* being distinguished by taxonomists only by differences in the number of rays in the dorsal and anal fins and by differences in the lateral line. The fish in the *Brachydanio* species have an incomplete lateral line while the *Danio* species have the lateral line complete. So far as the amateur aquarist is concerened the two genera are virtually identical. All the species in both genera are small lively shoaling fish and require more or less the same conditions in the aquarium. They are not very demanding fish, neither fussy about food nor difficult to breed. In general they are fish that should appeal to every aquarist who has a tank large enough to provide them with the free swimming space they need to feel at home and thrive.

BRACHYDANIO ALBOLINEATUS

Family: *Cyprinidae*
Genus: *Brachydanio*
English name: Pearl Danio
Origin: Southeast Asia
Size: Approximately 5.5 cm
Habitat: Found in sluggish and still waters and in rice paddies

SHAPE, COLORING AND MARKINGS: The body is slender and laterally moderately compressed. The mouth is directed upwards. The lateral line is incomplete. The basic coloration changes with the light. When seen against the light the body is a grey-green: the back is rather darker: the belly a muddy white. A narrow flesh-colored stripe bordered above and below by blue to violet zones, runs from the level of the pectoral fins to the caudal peduncle. The dorsal fin and the tips of the caudal fin are yellow-green: the anal fin is yellowish with a darker band, or lines of spots. In reflected light the colors are quite different. The basic coloration is an iridescent blue or violet: the belly is a bluish-silver. The longitudinal stripe is red-brown with a blue to green border. The unpaired fins are grass green with a red overtone: the base of the anal fin is red-brown to orange-red: the central area of the caudal fin brown-red: the pectoral and ventral fins reddish.
Females are more thick-set in the body with less vivid colors.
Males are as described above.

GENERAL CARE: *B.albolineatus* is suitable for large aquariums and is best kept in a group of its own kind and related species. The composition of the water is not critical but fresh water is to be preferred. The water must be changed frequently to keep the fish in good condition. A wide variety of plants may be put round the sides of the tank and these should include some with fine leaves. Adequate free swimming space must be provided for these active fish. Stones and bogwood may be used for decoration. Temperature 22°–24°C.
B.albolineatus: will be found in all levels of the tank. A tolerant species happy with both larger and smaller fish. Most normal foods, including dried food will be eaten.

BREEDING: This is not difficult. The tank should be put in a sunny position. Temperature 26°–28°C. The best results are achieved when one female and two males are put in the tank.

ADDITIONAL INFORMATION: A very popular species of which many color variants are available.

BRACHYDANIO FRANKEI

Family: *Cyprinidae*
Genus: *Brachydanio*
English name: Leopard Danio
Origin: There is some uncertainty about the origin of this species, which only became known a few years ago. Some authorities assert it is a native of Thailand, other believe it to be a mutation bred from *Brachydanio rerio* in an aquarium in Czechoslovakia.
Size: Maximum 5 cm
Habitat: No details are available.

SHAPE, COLORATION AND MARKINGS: The body is slender and laterally fairly compressed. The basic coloration is a beautiful brassy gold flecked with a large number of small irregularly shaped dark blue marks. The back is darker: the belly yellowish-white. The anal and caudal fins are flecked with a pattern of light to dark blue dots: the dorsal fin has a very narrow white edge.
Females are slightly larger than the males with whitish rounded bellies.
Males are much more slender than females and usually slightly smaller.

GENERAL CARE: As for *B.albolineatus* but temperature 20°–24°C.

BREEDING: Not difficult. The tank should be placed in the sun. Only sturdy well grown and vividly colored specimens, preferably with different ancestries should be selected for breeding pairs. The composition of the water is not critical but it should be fresh. Temperature 24°–25°C. The breeding tank should be fairly large and given a bed of coarse gravel, for the fish are egg-eaters. Fine leaved plants make an excellent spawning medium. The parents should be removed after the eggs have been laid. The eggs hatch in three to four days and the fry will be free swimming after two days. They should be fed on infusoria. Nests of 500 are not uncommon.

BRACHYDANIO KERRI

Family: *Cyprinidae*
Genus: *Brachydanio*
English name: none
Origin: Thailand
Size: Approximately 4 cm
Habitat: In sluggish and still waters

SHAPE, COLORING AND MARKINGS: The body is slender and laterally moderately compressed. The mouth points upwards. The lateral line is incomplete. The basic coloration is a strong blue: the back is paler: the belly whitish. A striking golden longitudinal stripe runs from the edge of the gill covers to the base of the caudal fin, above a pattern of thin, twisting gold-tinted marks. The intense blue body color runs into the middle rays of the caudal fin: otherwise the fins are a transparent yellow.
Females are more robust and less vividly colored.
Males are slimmer and the intense blue tone suffuses the whole body including the caudal fin.

470. *Brachysanio frankei*

471. *Brachydanio albolineatus*

GENERAL CARE: As for *B.albolineatus* but temperature 22°–25° C.

BREEDING: Not difficult: as for *B.albolineatus*

ADDITIONAL INFORMATION: First described in 1931, *B.kerri* became familiar to amateur aquarists in 1956 and has remained popular.

BRACHYDANIO NIGROFASCIATUS

Family: *Cyprinidae*
Genus: *Brachydanio*
English name: Spotted Danio
Origin: Northern Burma
Size: Approximately 4 cm
Habitat: Found in sluggish streams and in lakes and pools which for part of the year are linked with moving waters

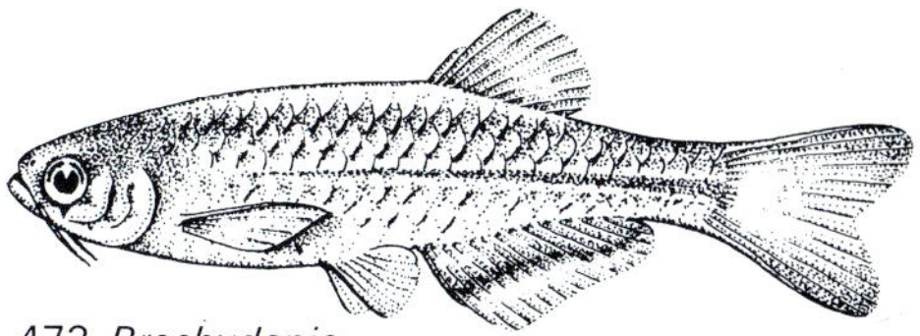

473. *Brachydanio albolineatus*

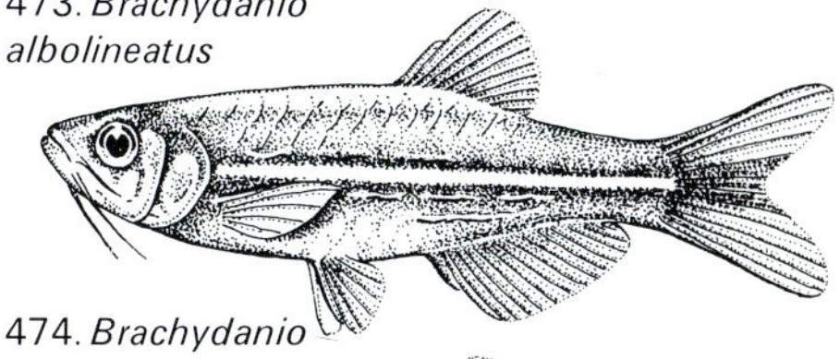

474. *Brachydanio kerri*

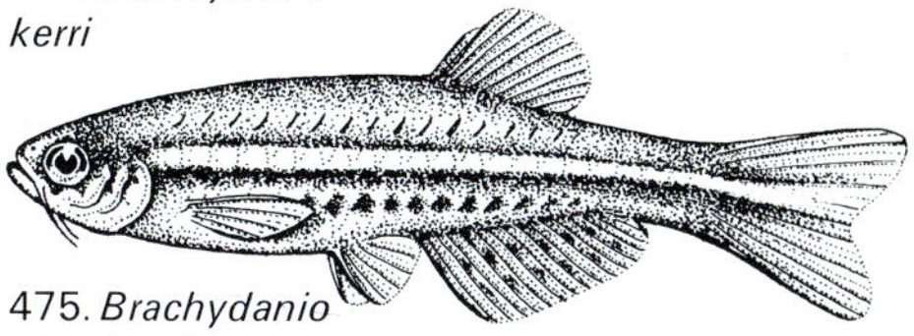

475. *Brachydanio nigrofasciatus*

SHAPE, COLORING AND MARKINGS: The body is slender and laterally slightly compressed. The mouth is pointed upwards. The lateral line is incomplete. The upper part of the head and the back are an olive brown: the flanks are an attractive iridescent blue: the belly is orange to off-white. An iridescent golden-brown longitudinal stripe runs from the edge of the gill covers to the central rays of the caudal fin and is bordered above and below by a blue-black zone, beneath which, on the lower half of the body are a number of darker patches which may also merge to form an irregular longitudinal line. The unpaired fins are yellow to brownish-yellow; the anal fin has a bluish dot and a pattern of stripes.
Females are more robust: the belly is yellowish-white.
Males are slimmer and the belly is orange.

GENERAL CARE: As for *B.albolineatus* but temperature 22°–25° C.

BREEDING: As for *B.albolineatus:* once the fish have paired the females remain very loyal to their mates.

ADDITIONAL INFORMATION: A well-known species that continues to be popular with aquarists.

BRACHYDANIO RERIO

Family: *Cyprinidae*
Genus: *Brachydanio*
English name: Zebra Danio
Origin: Eastern India
Size: Approximately 4.5 cm
Habitat: Found in sluggish and stationary waters and in rice paddies

SHAPE, COLORING AND MARKINGS: The body is very slender and laterally only moderately compressed. The back is a brown olive: the belly yellowish-white: the flanks are an attractive blue with four gleaming gold longitudinal stripes running from the edge of the gill covers to the caudal fin. The anal fin has a blue-gold pattern. The dorsal fin is yellow-green at the base, becoming blue, with a milky-white border. The remaining fins are colorless and transparent. The iris is red-gold.
Females are more robust: the longitudinal

472. *Brachydanio nigrofasciatus*

stripes are more yellow or silver.
Males are as described above and noticeably slimmer than females.

GENERAL CARE: As for *B.albolineatus* but temperature 20°–24° C. *B.rerio* is fond of seeking out the shady parts of the tank.

BREEDING: Straightforward in tanks placed in the sun. Only males with the most intense of gold stripes should be chosen for breeding. Temperature no higher than 24° C. The females are very loyal to their mates and the best results are achieved by keeping the same pair together.

ADDITIONAL INFORMATION: *B.rerio* is the most widely domesticated of species in this genus: it is however now very rarely imported from the wild and most specimens seen in aquariums are but a pale imitation of the vividly-colored wild specimens.

476. *Brachydanio rerio*

THE FAMILY CYPRINIDAE

The genus Chela

The fish in the genus *Chela* are closely related to those in the genera *Danio* and *Esomus:* they have however a shorter dorsal fin and a different shape to the belly. These fish are found over a wide area in Southeast Asia and most are shoaling fish. Although *Chela mouhoti,* a recently imported species from Thailand is very occasionally met with, the only species of general interest to aquarists is the Indian Glass Barb, *Chela laubaca,* described below. The name of this species has often led to confusion and discussions. It was sometimes called *Laubuca laubuca,* but is nowadays definitely labelled *Chela.* The species described below, *Chela laubuca,* is an undemanding fish; however, it should be watched carefully during the time of acclimatization, as it tends to be rather delicate in that period.

CHELA LAUBUCA

Family: *Cyprinidae*

Genus: *Chela*

English name: Indian Glass Barb

Origin: Burma, Indonesia, Malaya and Sri Lanka

Size: Maximum 6 cm

Habitat: Found in still and sluggish waters and especially common in flooded rice paddies

SHAPE, COLORING AND MARKINGS: The body is elongated, fairly deep and laterally very compressed. The basic coloration is silver to greyish-green, with a violet tinge on the caudal peduncle. The back is darker. A green to black longitudinal stripe runs from the level of the dorsal fin to the root of the caudal fin, where in some specimens it becomes a deep black mark encircled with gold. Another narrower gold stripe lies above and runs forward to the gill covers where it may also terminate in a black mark with a gold surround. The fins are colorless or light orange.
There are no known external sexual characteristics.

GENERAL CARE: As for *Brachydanio albolineatus,* but temperature 24° C.

BREEDING: As for *Brachydanio kerri,* but spawning takes place at twilight.

477. *Chela laubuca*

THE FAMILY CYPRINIDAE

The genus Danio

This genus is closely related to the genus *Brachydanio* from which it is distinguished, by taxonomists only by technical differences in the pattern of fin rays and the lateral line: these points are described in the Introductory note on the genus *Brachydanio* above. Details of the general character of these fish, indistinguishable in that respect from the *Brachydanio* species will also be found there.

478. *Danio aequipinnatus*

DANIO AEQUIPINNATUS

Family: *Cyprinidae*

Genus: *Danio*

English name: Giant Danio

Origin: Southwest India and Sri Lanka

Size: Maximum 15 cm in the wild, but remains considerably smaller in captivity

Habitat: Found in clear flowing waters

SHAPE, COLORING AND MARKINGS: The body is elongated, slender and laterally very compressed. The mouth is upper-positioned with two pairs of barbels, those on the upper jaw being not fully developed. The basic coloration is golden-yellow. The head is silvery: the back dark blue or bluish-green: the belly is white with a hint of pink. Four shiny steel blue horizontal lines lie along the body behind a series of vertical yellow and bluish-green stripes found behind the gill covers, on which lies a golden-green mark. The pectoral fins are colorless and transparent: the other fins are a delicate blue or pink.
Females are less vividly colored and have more rounded bellies.
Males are as described above and more slender than the females.

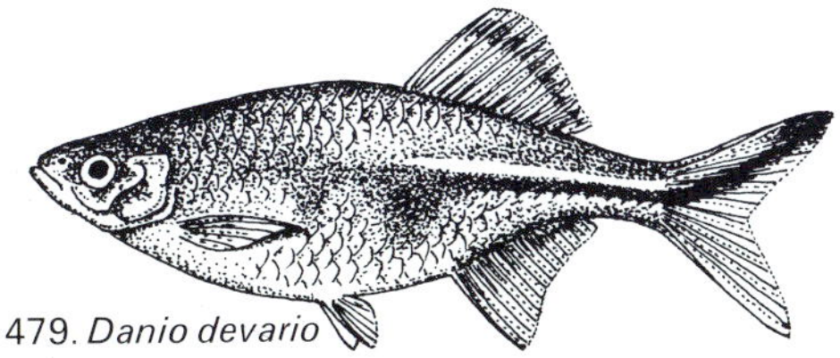

479. *Danio devario*

GENERAL CARE: As for *D.devario*.

BREEDING: As for *D.devario*.

DANIO DEVARIO

Family: *Cyprinidae*

Genus: *Danio*

English name: none

Origin: Northwest India, Pakistan and southeast Iran

Size: Maximum 8 cm

Habitat: Found in large numbers in a variety of shallow waters

SHAPE, COLORING AND MARKINGS: The body is elongated and laterally very compressed. The belly is remarkably deep. The basic coloration is silvery with a metallic blue or green sheen, according to the light. An irregular pattern of alternately blue and yellow, usually vertical, lines appears on the front half of the body. Further back there is a pattern of three shiny steel blue horizontal lines divided by bands of yellow. The blue lines merge together on the caudal peduncle to run halfway along the upper lobe of the fairly deeply forked caudal fin. The rest of the fins are light brown or greenish: the dorsal fin has an attractive narrow white edge.
Females are less vividly colored: the off-white belly is more rounded especially during the spawning season and females appear generally sturdier than males.
Males are as described above: they are visibly more slender than females.

GENERAL CARE: *D.devario* is a lively shoal fish best kept in a fairly large group of its own kind in a spacious tank with ample free swimming space. Its colors are best shown off when the tank is put in a sunny position and has a dark bed. The composition of the water is not critical: temperature about 24°C. Both live animal matter and dried food will be accepted but a varied diet is essential to keep the fish in good condition. A very tolerant fish, *D.devario* can be kept in a community tank with smaller species.

BREEDING: A fairly large rectangular tank with thick clumps of fine leaved plants is needed. The composition of the water is not critical: temperature about 26°C. The breeding pair should be generously fed with mosquito larvae and *Enchytrae* before being put into the tank: this will discourage egg eating. The parents should however always be removed form the tank immediately after spawning. The eggs hatch after about 24 hours. The fry hang, looking like commas, for three or four days. When they are free swimming they should be fed on the finest powdered dried food, and later with *Cyclops* and *Artemia nauplii*. The water must be changed regularly. The fry grow quickly and are not difficult to raise: the nests may be very large and adequate tank space must therefore be made ready for the young fry.

THE FAMILY CYPRINIDAE

The genus Epalzeorhynchus

Two species in the genus *Epalzeorhynchus*, both from Southeast Asia are of considerable interest to aquarists although neither is a common fish and indeed *E.siamensis* must by any standard be accounted rare. Both species are remarkable algae eaters and are even alleged to eat types of algae that other algae eating fish will avoid.

These fish, will also, it is claimed eat Planarians, or flatworms which can be introduced into an aquarium with live food, and although harmless to fish are not welcomed by the aquarists. For this reason these species have justly acquired the reputation of being useful scavengers.

EPALZEORHYNCHUS KALLOPTERUS

Family: *Cyprinidae*
Genus: *Epalzeorhynchus*
English name: Flying Fox
Origin: Indonesia, Sumatra, Borneo and Java
Size: Maximum 14 cm in the wild, remains considerably smaller in captivity
Habitat: Found in shallow waters with dense vegetation on the banks

SHAPE, COLORING AND MARKINGS: The body is slender, elongated but hardly at all laterally compressed. The head is pointed, with a protruding snout: the upper lip is fringed. The basic coloration is golden-brown to olive green: the belly is white. A broad yellow to gold longitudinal line runs from the snout to the base of the tail, and below it runs another wide but dark band. Below that is a zig-zag pattern formed by the dark edges that appear on some of the scales. The pectoral fins are reddish-brown: the same color appears at the base of the other fins.
There are no known external sexual characteristics.

480. *Epalzeorhynchus kallopterus*

◁481. *Epalzeorhynchus siamensis*

GENERAL CARE: *E.kallopterus* is suitable for larger aquariums, with a dark bed and ample vegetation including some broad leaved plants.
This species keeps mainly to the bottom of the tank and needs appropriate hiding places: hollow pieces of wood are ideal. The water should be soft: temperature 23°–26° C. Tolerant of other species. *E.kallopterus* can be aggressive towards its own kind. All sorts of live animal matter will be accepted and this species also eats algae.

BREEDING: This species has not as yet been bred in captivity.

ADDITIONAL INFORMATION: *E.kallopterus* has the unusual habit of remaining at rest in the tank by supporting itself on the bed or on the leaves of broad-leaved plants by means of its pectoral fins. This long-bodied fish is an elegant addition to the aquarium, provided the tank is big enough to accommodate so swift a swimmer. *E.kallopterus* can also be very useful in the aquarium to control algae.

EPALZEORHYNCHUS SIAMENSIS

Family: *Cyprinidae*
Genus: *Epalzeorhynchus*
English name: none
Origin: Thailand and Malaya
Size: Maximum 15 cm in the wild but remains considerably smaller in captivity

SHAPE, COLORING AND MARKINGS: The body shape is very similar to that of *E.kallopterus*, but somewhat fuller. The basic coloration is golden. There is a prominent black longitudinal line running from the lips to the fork of the tail. The large dorsal and caudal fins are red. The other fins are orangey.
Females have fuller bellies and paler fins. Males are as described above.

GENERAL CARE: As for *E.kallopterus* but *E.siamensis* should only be kept with other fairly large fish, of which it is tolerant.

BREEDING: This species has not as yet been bred successfully in captivity.

ADDITIONAL INFORMATION: A rare species which is seldom imported.

THE FAMILY CYPRINIDAE

The genus Esomus

The species in this genus are closely related to those in the genera *Chela* and *Danio*. They are all found in India and other parts of Southeast Asia. Four species are known to specialist aquarists: *E.danrica, E.goddardi, E.lineatus* and *E.malayensis*. *E.goddardi* is rarely if ever imported however and *E.lineatus* is almost as rare outside its place of origin.

The most attractive as well as the best known species is *E.danrica* described below: *E.malayensis* is not much favored by aquarists: it is almost exactly half the size of *E.danrica,* virtually identical in shape and coloring but, if anything, marginally less decorative: it requires the same care as its more attractive cousin.
All species in this genus are very delicate looking fish and their long barbels and large wing like pectoral fins give them an unusually graceful appearance. Although they appreciate warmth, they are not however unusually delicate fish.

ESOMUS DANRICA

Family: *Cyprinidae*

Genus: *Esomus*

English name: Flying Barb

Origin: India, Sri Lanka, Thailand

Size: Maximum 15 cm in the wild, but remains considerably smaller in captivity.

SHAPE, COLORING AND MARKINGS: The body is very slender, elongated and laterally very compressed towards the tail. The head is pointed and very long slender barbels curve back from the mouth almost to the middle of the belly. The lateral line is incomplete: the pectoral fins are wing-like and very large. The basic coloration is an olive to grey-green: the back is flecked with dark spots and has an iridescent sheen: the flanks are violet to red: the belly silver-white. A wide dark longitudinal band runs from the mouth to the root of the tail, becoming, in the caudal peduncle, a prominent dark triangular mark. The ventral fins are reddish: the other fins are brown to orange.

Females have more rounded bellies and the mark on the caudal peduncle is less prominent.

Males are smaller and the mark on the caudal peduncle is a brilliant rust red.

GENERAL CARE: Suitable for larger aquariums with plenty of broad-leaved plants, *E.danrica* likes light and warmth and will usually be found swimming just below the surface. The composition of the water is not critical: temperature 22°–24°C. All kinds of live animal matter will be accepted as food.

BREEDING: This is not too difficult. A fairly large breeding tank is required, with some clumps of dense vegetation. The water should be moderately soft: temperature 27°C. The yellow eggs will be laid among the plants. The fry will hang for two days and will be free swimming after five days. They should be fed on infusoria and then on *Artemia nauplii*.

482. *Esomus danrica*

483. *Labeo erythrurus*.

THE FAMILY CYPRINIDAE

The genus Labeo

The species of fish in the genus *Labeo* are all distinguished by their unusual lips which have developed into very effective sucking organs: internally they have sharp or horny ridges which assist the fish in grazing off algae they find on stones and rocks. Four species, all from Southeast Asia and of particular interest to aquarists are described below.

LABEO BICOLOR

Family: *Cyprinidae*

Genus: *Labeo*

English name: Red-tailed Black 'Shark'

Origin: Thailand, Menam Chao Phya, Bangkok, Silom canal and the Tachin river

Size: Approximately 12 cm

Habitat: Found in a variety of flowing waters

SHAPE, COLORING AND MARKINGS: The body is elongated, laterally very slightly compressed and the belly is almost flat. The basic coloration is a deep or blue black: in older specimens there is a greenish overtone. There are one or two dark patches above the pectoral fins: the larger specimens have one such patch, smaller fish have a number of these patches. The caudal fin is an attractive deep red. The pectoral fins are a darker red brown or black. In adults, all the other fins are black: in young fish the dorsal and anal fins have a white border which disappears after a few months.

There are no known external sexual characteristics, but it is likely that females will have more rounded bellies than males.

GENERAL CARE: *L.bicolor* is only suitable for larger aquariums. It establishes its own territory in the tank and there must be plenty of hiding places for it, provided for example by arrangements of bogwood. Generally speaking this species is tolerant towards other species but hostile to other members of the same species. It is very difficult to keep two specimens together but a larger number may settle down together as a group. Mature aquarium water, some of which is changed regularly is best. Temperature 24°–27°C. Most forms of live food will be gobbled up greedily: worms are particularly popular, and some vegetable matter, such as algae and lettuce leaves should be given for variety.

BREEDING: No information is available on the breeding habits of this species.

LABEO ERYTHRURUS

Family: *Cyprinidae*

Genus: *Labeo*

English name: none

Origin: Thailand, Mekong, Kemarat

Size: Approximately 12 cm

Habitat: Found in a variety of flowing waters

SHAPE, COLORING AND MARKINGS: The body is elongated and laterally only slightly compressed: the belly is remarkably flat. The basic coloration varies according to the mood of the fish and according to the place of origin: it can be light brown, a darker brown or even blue-black, with a paler area round the belly, and generally rather spotty. A darker patch stretches from the snout to the eyes. There may be one or two dark patches above the

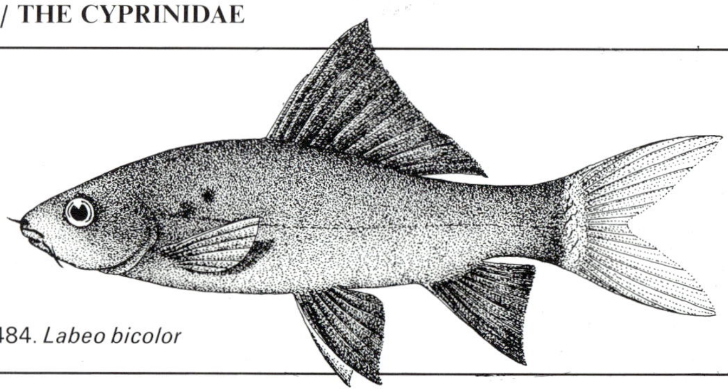

484. *Labeo bicolor*

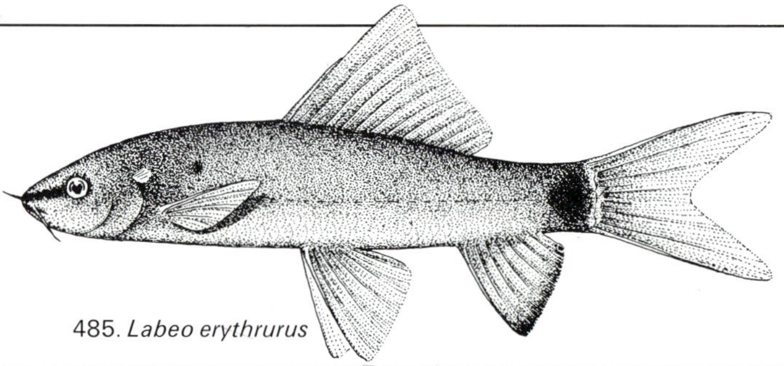

485. *Labeo erythrurus*

pectoral fin, but these are sometimes indistinct. The ventral fins are transparent and colorless or greyish: the remaining fins have dark membranes.
There are no known external sexual characteristics: the females can probably be recognised by their more rounded bellies and some authorities suggest that males can be recognised by a black edge along the anal fin.

General care: As for *L.bicolor*.

Breeding: No information is available on the breeding habits of this species.

Additional information: This species is very closely related to *L.frenatus*: it is sometimes thought that *L.frenatus* is either *L.erythrurus* when immature or merely a local variety of this species, but nothing can be said with certainty about this.

LABEO FRENATUS

Family: *Cyprinidae*

Genus: *Labeo*

English name: none

Origin: Thailand, Chiengmai, the Tachin river

Size: Approximately 8 cm

Habitat: Found in a large variety of flowing waters

Shape, coloring and markings: The body is elongated and laterally only slightly compressed. The basic coloration varies a great deal according to the mood of the fish and its condition: it can vary from a grey green to a brownish green, or be a darker mousy grey with brownish overtones: the color lightens towards the belly. There is a dark stripe running from the snout across the eye as far as the gill covers.
A patch roughly diamond shaped lies on the base of the caudal fin. All the fins are a brick to orange red: the anal fin has a dark or black border.
There are no known external sexual characteristics, but some authorities maintain that the same differences between the sexes exist.

General care: As for *L. bicolor*.

Breeding: No information is available about the breeding habits of this species.

Additional information: This species closely resembles *L.erythrurus*, under which the theories about the relationship of the two species are noted. *L.frenatus* however has a much slimmer body.

LABEO MUNENSIS

Family: *Cyprinidae*

Genus: *Labeo*

English name: none

Origin: Thailand, Menam Mum

Size: Approximately 12 cm

Habitat: Found in a large variety of flowing waters

Shape, coloring and markings: The body is elongated, laterally very slightly compressed and almost cylindrical. The basic coloration is a dark red-brown which becomes lighter towards the belly. There is a dark patch, more or less diamond shaped on the caudal fin and a darker mark at the back of the gill covers on a level with the eyes. A dark line runs back from the snout across the eye as far as the gill covers. The dorsal anal and ventral fins are a deep black with a white border: the caudal fin is white: the pectoral fins are translucent and greyish. There are no known external sexual characteristics.

General care: As for *L.bicolor*.

Breeding: No information is available on the breeding habits of this species.

Additional information: As far as is known, this species has never been imported. It was first described by Hugh McCormick Smith in 1934.

488. *Labeo bicolor*

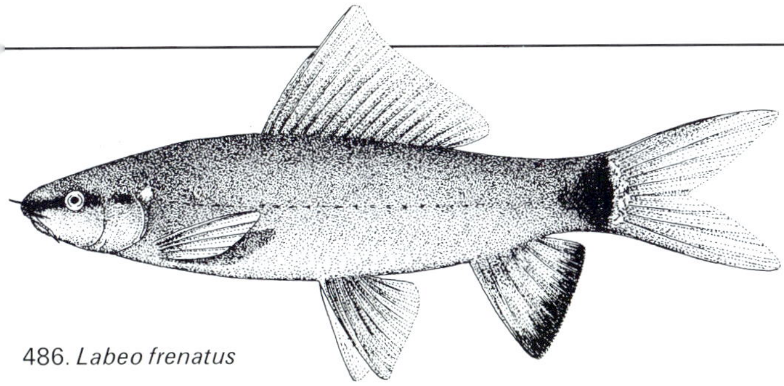
486. *Labeo frenatus*

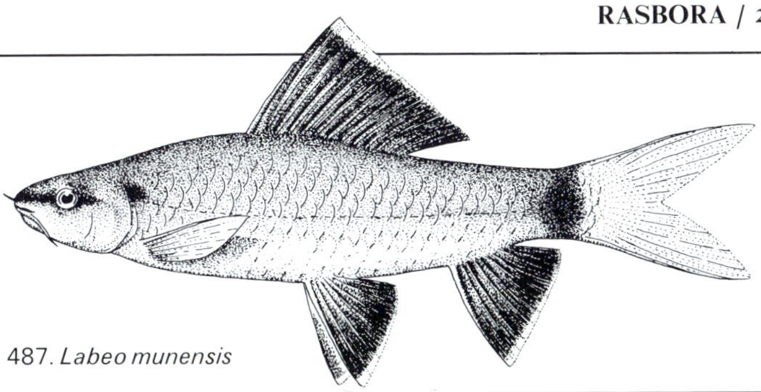
487. *Labeo munensis*

THE FAMILY CYPRINIDAE

The genus Luciosoma

Only one species in this genus, the large, predatory but very attractive *Luciosoma spilopleura* is of interest to aquarists. Not a very common fish and one that is rather particular about conditions in the aquarium, it is nevertheless a very lively and interesting species to keep if the opportunity arises.
It likes to swim near the surface of the water, living in shoals, and hunting for insects. It is however a delicate fish and difficult to keep in good condition.

489. *Luciosoma spilopleura*

LUCIOSOMA SPILOPLEURA

Family: *Cyprinidae*
Genus: *Luciosoma*
English name: none
Origin: Indonesia, Sumatra, Malaya, Thailand, Vietnam
Size: Maximum 25 cm
Habitat: Found in a variety of different waters

SHAPE, COLORING AND MARKINGS: The body is very elongated, slender but hardly at all laterally compressed: the back is almost straight. The head is pointed with a large upper-positioned mouth. The dorsal and anal fins lie far back on the body. The pectoral and ventral fins are pointed: the caudal fin is fairly deeply forked. There are two pairs of short barbels on the mouth. The back which is olive green, becomes yellowish and then white towards the belly. A dark horizontal line runs from the head through the eye to the base of the caudal fin where it divides to run into both lobes. The upper edge of this line zigzags and in every depression is a glittering golden mark. The outer rays of the caudal fin and the front rays of the anal, dorsal and ventral fins are milky-white. The dorsal and anal fins sometimes have dark marks on the points.
There are no known external sexual characteristics, but some specimens have larger anal and dorsal fins devoid of marks: this may indicate a sex difference.

GENERAL CARE: *L.spilopleura* is only suitable for very large aquariums. Soft slightly acid water is best: temperature about 25°C. This species needs a lot of free swimming space and likes sunshine or strong overhead lighting. It needs a great deal of food and aquatic insects and other live animal matter should be given alternately to dried food. *L.spilopleura* should not be kept with smaller fish, otherwise they will soon become part of its diet.

BREEDING: This species has not as yet been bred in captivity.

THE FAMILY CYPRINIDAE

The genus Rasbora

This genus was first described under the name *Leuciscus* in 1859–60 by the Dutch scientist Pieter Bleeker. The name *Rasbora* which Bleeker later adopted is nowhere explained: it is generally assumed to be derived from a native name.

The *Rasbora* species are slender fish with laterally compressed bodies, although there are a few exceptions, with deep, thickset bodies, including *R.heteromorpha* and *R.vaterifloris*. The mouth is oblique, pointing upwards with a projecting lower jaw. Barbs may be present or absent. There are large to medium-sized scales over the whole body. The lateral line first curves downwards and then turns up to run out into the lower part of the tail. In those species with an incomplete lateral line, such as *R.hengeli*, *R.heteromorpha*, *R.pauciperforata* and *R.vaterifloris*, it curves down sharply at the beginning.
Members of this genus are found over a wide area, from East Africa, across southern and eastern Asia to Canton and then on into Indonesia and the Philippines. These fish usually live in large schools in the upper water levels of both moving and still waters. A few species, including *R.heteromorpha* and *R.maculata* live exclusively in soft and peaty waters.
Practically all the species in this genus are excellent aquarium fish: they make no special demands, are very tolerant of other fish, and (because they are small) are suitable for all sizes of

490. *Rasbora hengeli*

tanks: in spite of these attractions few species have become popular with amateur aquarists. Of the 40 or so species imported to date, only the following are well-known: *R.heteromorpha, R.maculata, R.pauciperforata, R.trilineata, R.urophthalma* and *R.vaterifloris*. It is also surprising that no aquarist seems to take a special interest in this group of fish. They are easy to keep and those with an extended longitudinal stripe reproduce particularly well in captivity.

These fish are lively swimmers. They should be given a large tank with a variety of broad and fine leaved plants round the edges. Any quiet species of fish, large or small make suitable companions. A small group of these fish should always be kept together. The temperature should be 22°–26°C. A dark bottom is not essential but, as with many other small species a dark bed will make the fish feel much more relaxed and show off their colors to better effect. A dark bed is however essential for a few species, such as *R.hengeli, R.heteromorpha, R.maculata, R.urophthalma* and *R.vaterifloris*, and for these species the water should be filtered through peat. Most small or medium-sized animal matter will be accepted as food, for example mosquito larvae, fruitflies, ants, ants eggs and brineshrimps. Most species will accept dry food but that should not be allowed to dominate the diet.

Breeding *R.dorsiocellata dorsiocellata, R.dorsiocellata macrophthalma, R.lateristriata elegans, R.lateristriata lateristriata, R.taeniata* and *R.trilineata* is not very difficult. Breeding is encouraged in a medium-sized tank at about 25°C. It may be filled with matured aquarium water or fresh water which is not too hard and has been matured and somewhat acidified by filtration through peat. The eggs will be laid over the plants or above any artificial spawning material on the bed.

Breeding *R.heteromorpha, R.maculata, R.pauciperforata, R.urophthalma* and *R.vaterifloris* is less straightforward. Both the composition of the water and the selection of breeding pairs are important. Extremely soft and fairly acid water (1.5–2.5°DH: pH 5.3–5.7) should be matured by filtering through well-boiled and rinsed peat: good results can also be obtained by using water from fens and woodland springs. If a pair do not spawn after six or seven days in the tank, a new pair must be tried. The breeding fish should be well fed with live surface food such as fruitflies. Food, which if uneaten might sink to the bottom and foul the tank should be avoided. In some cases breeding has been induced by restricting feeding of the mating pair for a week or two and then feeding them up shortly before putting them in the breeding tank.

The parent fish should be removed from the tank after spawning. The eggs hatch after 25–30 hours. The fry will be free swimming in three to five days. They should be fed at first on infusoria: after three to five days they should be able to manage *Artemia nauplii* and then, when larger they can be fed on small Daphnia and Cyclops. The fry grow quickly and growth will be encouraged by regular changes of the water and the use of an efficient carbon filter.

RASBORA ARGYROTAENIA

Family: *Cyprinidae*

Genus: *Rasbora*

English name: Silver Rasbora

Origin: China, Japan, Malaya, Thailand

Size: Maximum 17 cm in the wild but remains considerably smaller in captivity

Habitat: Found in sluggish and still waters

SHAPE, COLORING AND MARKINGS: The body is slender and laterally somewhat compressed: the mouth is upward pointing. The basic coloration is gold and brown: the belly and flanks are a bright silver. A thin longitudinal cream line runs from below the gill covers to the root of the tail: beneath and parallel to it runs a narrow black stripe which becomes blue-green on the caudal peduncle. All the fins are light yellow: the caudal fin has a dark border. Females have more rounded bellies and colorless fins.

Males are slimmer and as described above.

GENERAL CARE: *R.argyrotaenia* is suitable for all community tanks that can allow these very active swimmers sufficient free swimming space. There should be fine and broad-leaved plants round the edges. The composition of the water is not critical but mature water filtered through peat is best: temperature 18°–25°C.

This species usually keeps to the upper and middle reaches of the tank. *R.argyrotaenia* is a tolerant fish but should be kept in a group of at least six of its own kind. Small surface insects such as fruitflies and mosquito larvae will be eaten greedily: dried food will also be accepted, and a varied diet is beneficial.

BREEDING: This species has not as yet been bred in captivity.

RASBORA BORAPETENSIS

Family: *Cyprinidae*

Genus: *Rasbora*

English name: none

Origin: Thailand, around Bung Boraphet

Size: Approximately 5 cm

Habitat: Found in sluggish and still waters, in large schools

SHAPE, COLORING AND MARKINGS: The body is elongated and laterally fairly compressed. The lateral line is incomplete. The basic coloration is pale yellow to green: the back is darker: the belly pale yellow to white. A deep black longitudinal stripe, broadening at the gill covers, runs from the snout over the eye to the base of the tail. Above, lies a narrow zone of green or gleaming gold. Above the anal fin to the caudal peduncle is an even darker stripe. The lower lobe of the caudal fin is

reddish: the remaining fins are colorless and transparent.
There are no known external sexual characteristics.

General care: As for *R.argyrotaenia,* but temperature 23°–26° C.

Breeding: *R.borapetensis* prefers to mate during the evening under dim light, or on an overcast day: a change of water will often stimulate mating. A few days of mutual appraisal usually pass before the pair will mate. Two to six eggs are laid each time: the whole process may take some days. The male is a confirmed egg-robber but once the eggs have sunk to the bottom they will not be touched. The breeding tank should have dense vegetation on the bottom.

Additional information: *R.borapetensis* is a species which has only been imported in the last few years.

RASBORA CEPHALOTAENIA

Family: *Cyprinidae*

Genus: *Rasbora*

English name: none

Origin: Indonesia, the east coast of Sumatra, West Borneo, Malaya

Size: Maximum 13 cm

Habitat: Found in fairly large numbers in both still and flowing waters

Shape, coloring and markings: The body is slender and laterally slightly compressed. The basic coloration is brownish: the back is greenish-brown with an attractive net-like pattern created by the black edges of the scales on the upper half of the body: The flanks are soft brown to yellow: the belly and underside are off-white to pure white. A deep black stripe runs from the snout through the eye and over the gill covers where it divides into two rows of black marks which cross over each other above a yellow or gold patch behind the pectoral fins. These marks, which form horizontal stripes, are widest apart at the level of the dorsal fin: further back they merge together as a zig-zag pattern on the caudal peduncle and end in a large deep black round mark on the base of the caudal fin. A prominent dark line appears on the lower part of the body and runs from the pectoral to the anal fin. The fins are colorless and transparent, except the pectoral fins which are a smokey grey to yellow, and the middle rays of the caudal fin which are dark. Well marked specimens sometimes have a pale yellow, transparent caudal fin with a fine dark edge. There are no known external sexual characteristics.

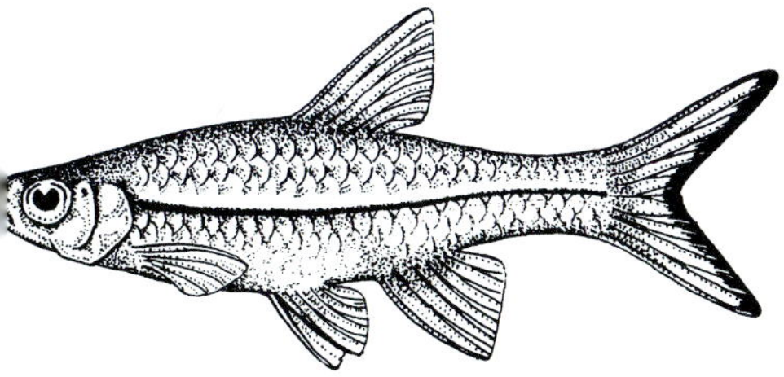

491. *Rasbora argyrotaenia*

492. *Rasbora borapetensis*

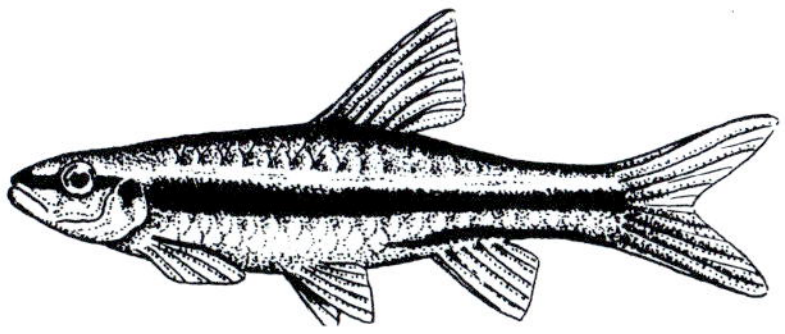

493. *Rasbora borapetensis*

494. *Rasbora cephalotaenia*

General care: As for *R.argyrotaenia* but temperature 20°–24° C, and during the winter 18–20° C. A group of at least four should be kept together.

Breeding: This species has not as yet been bred in captivity. One authority however suggests that it should be possible by providing a breeding tank with medium-hard water, a dark bed, fine leaved plants and algae, and a temperature of about 25° C. The females should be put in the tank two days before the males. Early morning sunlight will very likely stimulate mating.

RASBORA DORSIOCELLATA DORSIOCELLATA

Family: *Cyprinidae*

Genus: *Rasbora*

English name: Eye-spot Rasbora

Origin: Indonesia, Sumatra and Malaya

Size: Approximately 6.5 cm

Habitat: Found in calm streams and other small waterways

Shape, coloring and markings: The body is slender and laterally only moderately compressed. The basic coloration is silvery-yellow with a bluish to violet tinge on the flanks: the back is brownish to dark olive green: the belly silvery-white. Two black longitudinal lines which diverge at the center of the body, run from the back of the gill covers into the root of the tail: the lower line can often be seen clearly only when the fish is excited. *R.dorsiocellata dorsiocellata* has an unusual dorsal fin with a deep black patch with a milk-white rim. The remaining fins are a pale yellow and transparent. The eye is yellowish. Females have fuller bellies and a yellow caudal fin.
Males are slimmer and have a more reddish caudal fin.

General care: As for *R.borapetensis.*

BREEDING: Not difficult. See Introductory note.

ADDITIONAL INFORMATION: *R.dorsiocellata dorsiocellata* is a little-known species although imported since 1935. It is closely related to *R.trilineata*. As with most *Rasbora* species, the scales are, relatively, very large although many authors describe them as exceptionally small.

RASBORA HENGELI

Family: *Cyprinidae*

Genus: *Rasbora*

English name: none

Origin: Indonesia, Sumatra around Telanaipura

Size: Maximum 3 cm

Habitat: Found in small schools in shallow swamps as well as deeper waters

SHAPE, COLORING AND MARKINGS: The body is rather deep and laterally very compressed. The lateral line is incomplete. *R.hengeli* closely resembles *R.heteromorpha*. The basic coloration is silvery-grey with a soft red to violet

495. *Rasbora heteromorphia*

◁ 496. *Rasbora dorsiocellata*

overtone: the fish is almost transparent. A blue-violet cone-shaped patch, less prominent than the similar mark on *R.heteromorpha*, lies on the rear of the body. In many specimens only the outline of this mark is to be seen. Above the anal fin, lies an area of darker pigmentation which runs into the caudal peduncle. The fins are a soft yellow, transparent but with dark pigmentation on the anterior rays. Females are more powerful and generally less vividly colored. Males are slimmer.

GENERAL CARE: Suitable for all sizes of aquariums provided the size of the group is adjusted: four to six may be kept in a small tank, in a large tank, 10–12. The tank should be densely planted with *Cryptocoryne* or other broad-leaved vegetation over a bottom of peat matting with arrangements of bogwood. The water should be mature, preferably filtered over peat. Temperature 24°–27°C. *R.hengeli* only occupies the middle and upper reaches of the tank. They are playful swimmers: they may wait quietly for some time between plants and then suddenly become very active again. Peaceful fish, they prefer the company of other peaceful species. Diet as for *R.argyrotaenia*.

BREEDING: Mildly acid water perhaps filtered through peat is needed: fresh water from woodland springs has given good results. Temperature about 28°C. The eggs will be laid on the underside of *Cryptocoryne* leaves. Not a very prolific species.

ADDITIONAL INFORMATION: During the night the whole of the body becomes paler and the fish rests among the plants. A little-known species among aquarists.

497. *Rasbora hengeli*

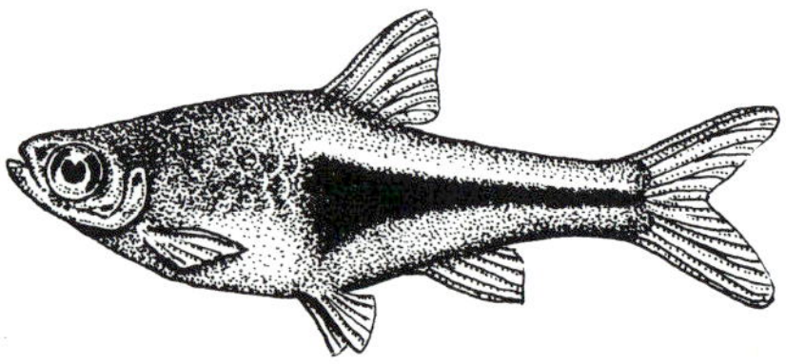

RASBORA HETEROMORPHA

Family: *Cyprinidae*

Genus: *Rasbora*

English names: Harlequin Fish, Red Rasbora

Origin: Indonesia, Sumatra, Thailand

Size: Approximately 4.5 cm

Habitat: Found in schools in marshy pools, mountain rivulets and densely shaded overgrown streams

SHAPE, COLORING AND MARKINGS: The body is deep, elongated and laterally very compressed. The lateral line is incomplete. The basic coloration is silvery-grey with pale red to iridescent violet overtones. A prominent blue-black cone-shaped patch lies on the rear half of the body: the area in front has an attractive golden glint. The fins are yellowish: the dorsal and anal fins have a red gleam at the base and the anterior rays are brown-red to black. See under *R.hengeli* for differences in the patterning.
Females have more rounded bellies and are more robust.
Males are much slimmer. The lowest point of the cone-shaped patch lies over the base of the ventral fin.

GENERAL CARE: As for *R.hengeli*.

BREEDING: As for *R.hengeli*. For a long time *R.heteromorpha* was considered to be an extremely difficult species to breed: this is no longer the case.

RASBORA KALOCHROMA

Family: *Cyprinidae*

Genus: *Rasbora*

English name: Clown Rasbora

Origin: Malaya, Johore, Malacca, Singapore

Size: Approximately 10 cm

Habitat: Found in sluggish and still waters of low acidity and rich in humus

SHAPE, COLORING AND MARKINGS: The body is fairly slender and laterally slightly compressed. The basic coloration is salmon: the back is orange-red with pale green overtones: the flanks are an iridescent pale green in some lights: the belly is yellowish to pink. An almost pure red patch lies above the pectoral fins and a more prominent egg-shaped patch lies above the anal fin. The anal fin is orange-red with a narrow black border: the other fins are a yellow-orange and transparent.
Females when adult are noticeably more robust.

498. *Rasbora kalochroma*

499. *Rasbora lateristriata elegans*

Males are slimmer and when sexually mature have more red on the anal fin.

GENERAL CARE: As for *R.borapetensis* but temperature 25°–28° C. *R.kalochroma* looks best in mature yellow-tinted water and is also least sensitive to skin parasites under such conditions.

BREEDING: This species has not as yet been bred in captivity.

ADDITIONAL INFORMATION: *R.kalochroma* is a very attractive species first described by Pieter Bleeker in 1850: it is closely related to the smaller *R.maculata*: both species come from the same area and for a long time it was thought that the one was only the immature form of the other. *R.kalochroma* is not often seen: it has a poor survival rate because it is often badly looked after and transferred too quickly to an aquarium without being given sufficient time in quarantine.

RASBORA LATERISTRIATA ELEGANS

Family: *Cyprinidae*

Genus: *Rasbora*

English names: Yellow Rasbora, Elegant Rasbora

Origin: Indonesia, Malaya

Size: Maximum 13 cm

Habitat: Found in large shoals in still and running waters

SHAPE, COLORING AND MARKINGS: The body is slender and laterally somewhat compressed. The basic coloration is brownish, which in certain lights has an iridescent green sheen: the back is darker: the flanks are ringed with red: the belly is ochre: the underside silvery-white. The scales have dark edges, especially on the upper half of the body. There are two bluish-black marks: one lies on the body roughly over the ventral fins, the other lies at the base of the caudal fin. In some specimens a narrow horizontal iridescent blue line is found between the two marks. A dark line runs from the first anal fin ray along the lower side of the caudal peduncle. The unpaired fins are pale yellow, especially at the base: the caudal fin has dark or black tips. All the other fins are colorless and transparent.
Females when adult are more robust in shape and less vividly colored.
Males are smaller and as described above.

GENERAL CARE: As for *R.argyrotaenia* but summer temperature 21°–23° C: winter 18°–20° C. At least four should be kept.

BREEDING: This is not difficult. See Introductory note.

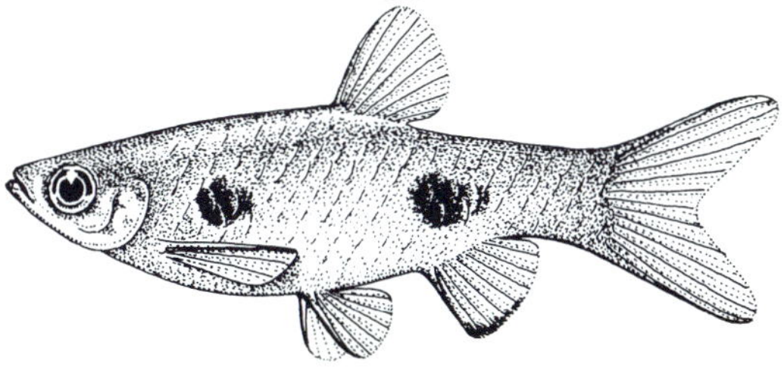

500. *Rasbora kalochroma*

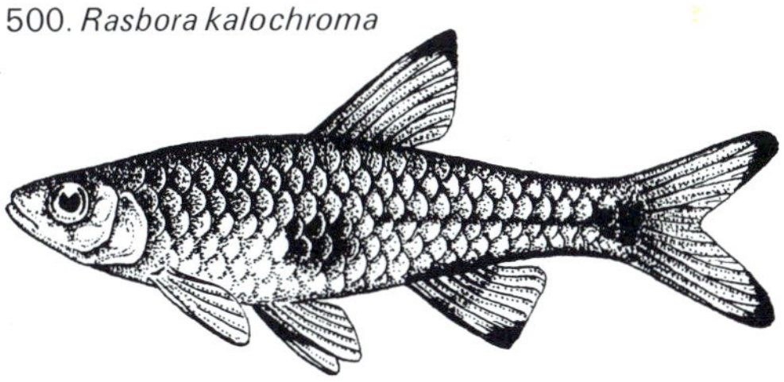

501. *Rasbora lateristriata elegans*

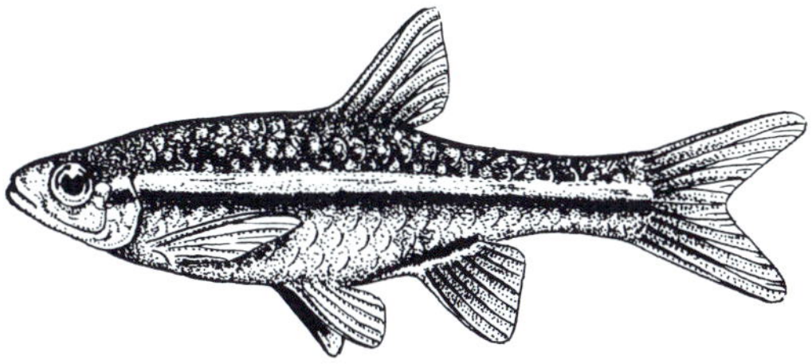

502. *Rasbora lateristriata*

ADDITIONAL INFORMATION: *R.lateristriata elegans* is sometimes found in mountain streams, and consequently it is better not to keep it at too high a temperature.

RASBORA LATERISTRIATA LATERISTRIATA

Family: *Cyprinidae*

Genus: *Rasbora*

English name: none

Origin: Thailand, the islands of the Sunda Strait

Size: Maximum 12 cm

Habitat: Found in large shoals in still and running water

SHAPE, COLORING AND MARKINGS: The basic coloration is brown with, in bright light, a striking green iridescent sheen: the back is darker: the flanks are pale brown with a shiny gold sheen: the underside is greenish-white. The scales have dark edges, and on the upper part of the body they have decorative, shiny silver flecks. A brownish-red horizontal line runs from the eye to the base of the caudal fin, and underneath, parallel to this, is a bluish or violet iridescent band. A dark line runs above the anal fin. The unpaired fins are rust brown to reddish: the other fins are colorless and transparent.
Females when adult are fuller in the body with more rounded bellies.
Males are more slender.

General care: As for *R.lateristriata elegans*, but at least six should be kept in the group.

Breeding: Not difficult with this very prolific species which may produce nests of up to 1,000 fry. See Introductory note.

RASBORA MACULATA

Family: *Cyprinidae*

Genus: *Rasbora*

English names: Spotted Rasbora, Dwarf Rasbora

Origin: Indonesia, Sumatra, Malaya, Malacca

Size: Approximately 2.5 cm

Habitat: In still and sluggish waters with dense vegetation

Shape, coloring and markings: The body is slender and laterally only moderately compressed. The basic coloration is a pale olive green: the back is brick red: the flanks orange-red: the belly yellowish. A round, blue-black spot lies in the center of the body at the level of the pectoral fin: similar patches lie above the anal fin and may merge to form a large irregular blotch: a further area of dark pigmentation is found on the base of the caudal fin. All the fins are yellow-red and darker at the base: the dorsal fin has a black front and tip: the anal fin has a black spot on the front.
Females have more rounded bellies and are less vividly colored.
Males are slimmer and have red overtones.

General care: Only suitable for small aquariums, *R.maculata* should be kept in a group of about ten. The sides of the tank should be lined with fine-leaved plants and mosses: there should be a bottom of turf and low terraces of peat, with small pieces of bogwood.

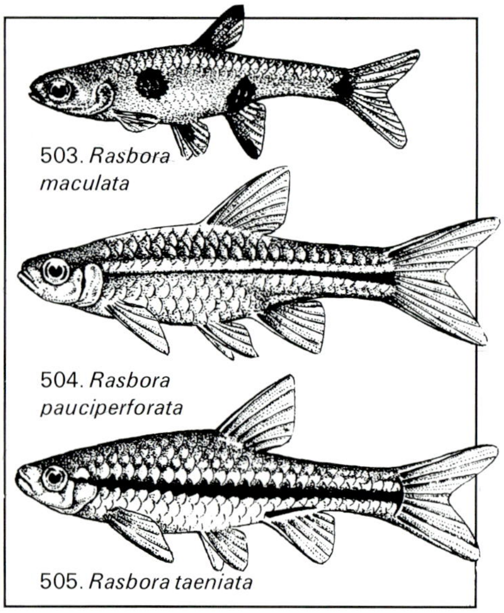

503. *Rasbora maculata*

504. *Rasbora pauciperforata*

505. *Rasbora taeniata*

Mature water of low acidity which has been filtered through peat is needed. Temperature 22°–26°C. *R.maculata* prefers to keep to the lower and middle reaches of the tank, where it will move about between the fine-leaved vegetation. It does not like the company of large fish. Small living creatures, Daphnia, Cyclops and *Artemia nauplii* are the best diet: dry food although accepted is best avoided.

Breeding: Not too difficult in water of low acidity, pH 6, 0.5–2.5° DH. Temperature about 26°C. The eggs will be released when the early morning sun shines into the tank. The breeding pair should be separated for about 14 days before being put in the tank, and in that time very well fed. Good specimens produce about 200 eggs which hatch after about 24 hours. For the first week the fry need the very finest foods.

Additional information: Although a very delicate species, *R.maculata* remains very popular among amateur aquarists.

RASBORA PAUCIPERFORATA

Family: *Cyprinidae*

Genus: *Rasbora*

English name: Red Striped Rasbora

Origin: Indonesia, eastern Sumatra

Size: Maximum 7 cm

Habitat: Found in streams and other small waterways

Shape, coloring and markings: The body is slender and laterally only moderately compressed. The basic coloration is yellow-white with a silver lustre: the back is yellow to brown and translucent: the head is yellow-orange on top: the belly silver-white. An iridescent copper or pale red longitudinal stripe runs from the fill covers back to the root of the rail: below, lies a narrow blue-black band which broadens towards the tail. The lower part of the caudal peduncle is dark to glistening gold. The fins are pale yellow and transparent.
Females have more rounded bellies and the fins are almost colorless.
Males are rather smaller and more slender.

General care: As for *R.borapetensis* but *R.pauciperforata* occupies the middle and lower reaches of the tank. Dry food will be accepted only reluctantly.

Breeding: This species has not as yet been bred in captivity.

Additional information: *R.pauciperforata* is rather shy and will favor shady parts of the tank. It prefers a winter temperature of 19°–21°C: when the temperature is raised in the

506. *Rasbora maculata*

507. *Rasbora pauciperforata*

508. *Rasbora sarawakensis*

509. *Rasbora taeniata*

spring the fish will show a tendency to mate. The breeding temperature, is 28° C it has been suggested, but when introduced into the breeding tank the fish often lose all inclination to mate: it may be that the change in temperature is too great.

RASBORA SARAWAKENSIS

Family: *Cyprinidae*

Genus: *Rasbora*

English name: none

Origin: Borneo, Sarawak, near Kuching

Size: Approximately 5 cm

Habitat: In swamps and streams with dense vegetation on the shores

SHAPE, COLORING AND MARKINGS: The body is slender and only slightly compressed laterally. The basic coloration is bronze, becoming lighter or yellowish-white towards the belly. A blue iridescent horizontal line broadens as it runs from the back edge of the gill covers to the caudal peduncle, and is bordered above by a line of shiny gold. A prominent orangey-red mark lies in the upper half of the base of the caudal fin: a fine black stripe lies above the anal fin. The dark edges on the scales on the upper part of the body, form a net-like pattern. In bright light a milky-white patch becomes visible on the upper side of the caudal peduncle: similar patterns appear immediately below the dorsal fin and on top of the head. The dorsal fin is rust brown to bronze, with white or ice-blue front fin rays. The caudal fin is bronze with white or ice-blue edges. The other fins are transparent and colorless or at most very slightly pigmented.
Females when spawning have a more rounded shape.
Males are more slender.

GENERAL CARE: As for *R.borapetensis.*

BREEDING: No information is available.

RASBORA SOMPHONGSI

Family: *Cyprinidae*

Genus: *Rasbora*

English name: none

Origin: Thailand

Size: Approximately 3 cm

Habitat: Found in quiet shallow waters.

SHAPE, COLORING AND MARKINGS: The body is slender and laterally only slightly compressed. The basic coloration is ochre: the back is fawn with a net-like pattern: the belly is whitish with a silvery sheen. A more or less cone-shaped horizontal line runs across the flanks at the level of the first dorsal fin rays: the front is a deep black: towards the tail the line becomes paler. Above and below, shiny golden bands run from the gill covers to the caudal peduncle. The scales on the belly have a beautiful bronze glow. A black stripe above the anal fin runs into the lower rays of the caudal fin. The dorsal, caudal and anal fins are pale yellow, brownish at the base and edges. The ventral fins are pale yellow: the pectoral fins are colorless and transparent.
Females have more rounded bellies.
Males are more slender, with a more vivid golden sheen: the upper lobe of the caudal fin is often more powerfully developed.

GENERAL CARE: As for *R.argyrotaenia* but really only suitable for small aquariums. Temperature 23°–25° C. It will not touch food that has fallen to the bottom.

BREEDING: As for *R.maculata* but few successes have been reported.

ADDITIONAL INFORMATION: *R.somphongsi* is closely related to *R.urophthalma,* but is easily distinguished by its different color pattern. At night the body becomes considerably paler and the fish rests among the vegetation.

RASBORA TAENIATA

Family: *Cyprinidae*

Genus: *Rasbora*

English name: Black-striped Rasbora

Origin: Indonesia, Sumatra

Size: Maximum 8 cm

Habitat: No details are available of its natural habitat

SHAPE, COLORING AND MARKINGS: The body is slender and laterally somewhat compressed. The basic coloration is greenish: the back is darker or olive green: the belly is silvery, tinged with a soft red. In bright light the fish is mainly grass green. A dark blue to black horizontal line runs from the gill covers to the caudal peduncle. A narrow sickle-shaped line divides the base of the caudal fin from the fin itself. The fins are colorless and transparent.
Females, when adult are fuller in the body with more rounded bellies.
Males are more slender: the caudal fin is reddish.

GENERAL CARE: As for *R.argyrotaenia* but temperature 22°–25° C.

BREEDING: This is not difficult: a prolific species: see Introductory note.

ADDITIONAL INFORMATION: *R.taeniata* is undemanding and has survived in aquariums for many years. It is however now but rarely imported and few aquarists seem interested in breeding this, or related, species.

RASBORA TORNIERI

Family: *Cyprinidae*

Genus: *Rasbora*

English name: none

Origin: Indonesia, central and west Sumatra

Size: Maximum 10 cm

Habitat: No further details are available of its natural habitat

SHAPE, COLORING AND MARKINGS: The body is slim and laterally moderately compressed. The basic coloration is yellow-brown to soft violet: the back is very slightly darker: the belly silvery. All the scales have a dark edge.

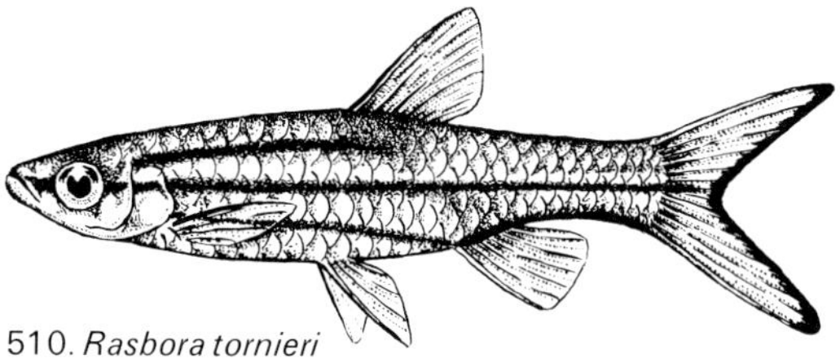

510. *Rasbora tornieri*

Three fairly prominent grey to blue-black longitudinal stripes lie on the body: the uppermost stretches from the edge of the gill covers to about halfway through the dorsal fin: the second extends from the snout to the base of the caudal fin, usually running on into its central rays: the third curves down from the gill covers to the base of the anal fin and then follows the line of the caudal peduncle. The areas between the stripes on the upper part of the body are filled with gleaming gold or iridescent red-yellow bands: on the lower half of the body these zones are more brassy. The unpaired fins are pale yellow, brown at the base: the anal fin has a delicate black band.
Females have more rounded bellies.
Males are slimmer and as described above.

GENERAL CARE: As for *R.argyrotaenia,* but temperature 18°–26° C.

BREEDING: No information is available on the reproductive behavior of this species.

RASBORA TRILINEATA

Family: *Cyprinidae*

Genus: *Rasbora*

English names: Scissors-tail Rasbora and Three-line Rasbora

Origin: Malaya

Size: Maximum 15 cm

Habitat: Found in sluggish and still waters

SHAPE, COLORING AND MARKINGS: The body is very slender and laterally only moderately compressed. The basic coloration is silvery: the back is ochre-yellow to green with rather dark overtones: the belly is white: young specimens are somewhat translucent. A very wide dark longitudinal stripe begins at about the level of the first rays of the dorsal fin and extends to the base of the tail, where it broadens out and passes into the rays of the caudal fin. The pectoral fins are colorless and transparent: the dorsal, ventral and anal fins are yellow-brown: the caudal fin white with a black bar in each lobe. Under reflected light *R.trilineata* has a multicolored sheen.
Females have more rounded bellies.
Males are as described above.

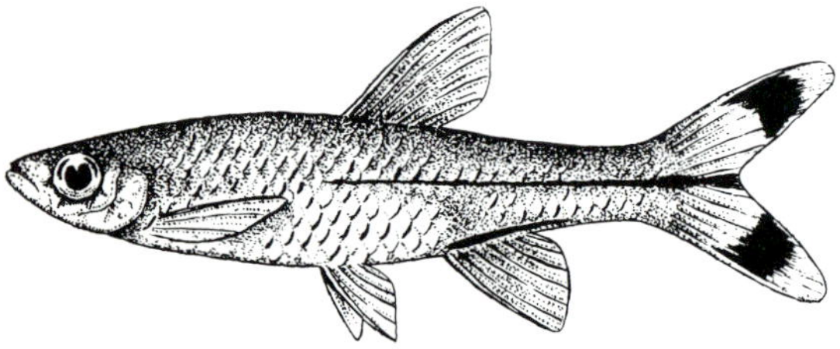

511. *Rasbora trilineata*

GENERAL CARE: As for *R.argyrotaenia.*

BREEDING: This is not difficult. See introductory note.

ADDITIONAL INFORMATION: This is a very popular species and new batches are imported regularly: it will however become scarcer unless more amateurs breed it.

RASBORA UROPHTHALMA

Family: *Cyprinidae*
Genus: *Rasbora*
English name: none
Origin: Indonesia
Size: Maximum 2.5 cm
Habitat: No further details are available of its natural habitat

SHAPE, COLORING AND MARKINGS: The body is slim and laterally only moderately compressed. The basic coloration is brownish: the neck and back are red-brown: the flanks lighter or yellowish: the belly a silvery-white. Below a narrow red stripe, a steely blue longitudinal line runs back from the edge of the gill covers and narrows, to end in a round spot set in a gleaming gold patch on the base of the tail. All but the pectoral fins are a translucent pale brown: the dorsal and anal fins are dark at the base. Particularly well-marked specimens have darker outermost rays to the caudal fin.
Females have no marks on the dorsal fin.
Males are slimmer: the dorsal fin usually has a milk-white spot as well as being darker.

GENERAL CARE: As for *R.somphongsi.*

BREEDING: Not difficult. Very small tanks are best. The fish prefer to lay the eggs on the undersides of fine-leaved plants and among algae. The process takes a few days. Well-fed breeding fish do not eat the eggs. Temperature 26°–28° C. The fry should be raised on the smallest of foods.

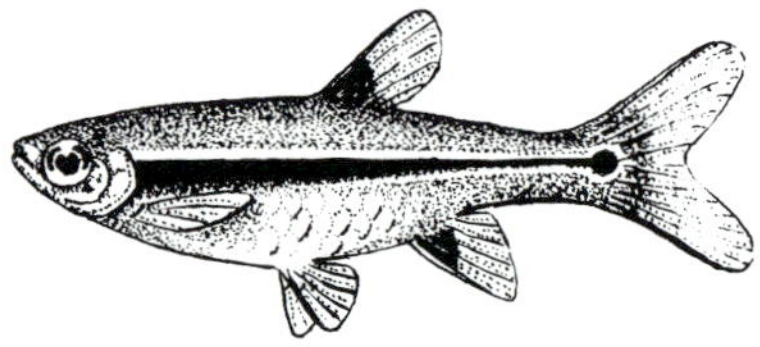

512. *Rasbora urophthalma*

ADDITIONAL INFORMATION: Various authorities believe that the specimens kept and bred by amateur aquarists are only a diminutive form of a species which in the wild would grow to a significantly larger size. However there is no evidence to support this for no specimen longer than 2.5 cm has ever been imported.

RASBORA VATERIFLORIS

Family: *Cyprinidae*
Genus: *Rasbora*
English name: Pearly Rasbora
Origin: Sri Lanka
Size: Approximately 4 cm
Habitat: Found in quiet mountain streams

SHAPE, COLORING AND MARKINGS: The body is less slender than in related species, but laterally somewhat compressed. The basic coloration is a greenish-brown: the back is olive green: the flanks a matt green: the belly whitish to muddy yellow. In bright light the body is suffused with a sheen of violet mother-of-pearl. Except for the upper lobe of the caudal fin, all unpaired fins are orange-yellow to to reddish: both dorsal and anal fins are well-developed.
Females are usually rather more robust than males, with yellowish fins.
Males have fins more orange to red.

GENERAL CARE: Suitable for larger aquariums with other quiet fish, in groups of at least six of their own kind. The bottom should be dark, with dense clumps of *Cryptocoryne* which may be broken up with arrangements of bogwood. Old, low-acid water, preferably filtered through peat is to be preferred. Temperature 22°–24° C. *R.vaterifloris* will live in all levels of the tank but will seek out shady spots. Diet as for *R.argyrotaenia.*

BREEDING: This is not easy. Mature water of low acidity should be used: temperature about 25° C. The mating is very energetic. The eggs are laid in thick clumps of vegetation but immediately sink to the bottom. The bed should therefore be of loose fibres of peat into which the eggs can sink. The breeding fish will eat the eggs and should therefore be removed as soon as possible from the tank. The fry hatch after about 40 hours and are free swimming after three to five days. The level of the water in the tank should be lowered to 10 cm after spawning and regular changes of water will encourage the growth of the fry. They should be fed on the normal fry foods.

513. *Rasbora urophthalma*

THE FAMILY GASTEROPELECIDAE

An introductory description

The *Gasteropelecidae* species or Hatchetfish make up a small family, whose members are found over a wide area of South America. All these fish, as their name suggests, are of the same unusual but characteristic shape: the back is almost straight, but the breast region protrudes like that of a bird, the belly is very deep, and then the line of the underside of the body rises more sharply towards the caudal peduncle so as to give the fish its unusual profile. The pectoral fins have very strong and large muscles, so that the fish can beat these fins very rapidly and use that facility to glide over the water for considerable distances: for this reason of course it is necessary to make sure that the aquarium is always well covered, and these species live more naturally in relatively long tanks. They are quite suitable for community tanks, but the other species selected as companions should preferably be peaceful fish that stay in the lower water levels.
There are three genera in the family, *Carnegiella, Gasteropelecus,* and *Thoracocharax,* the most important species of which are described below.

The genus Carnegiella

Two very attractive species *Carnegiella marthae* and *Carnegiella strigata* are of general interest to aquarists and are described below. Both are smaller than the species in the related genera and are also somewhat more delicate, but not so much so as to make them unsuitable for domestic aquariums. A third species, *Carnegiella myersi,* found in some areas of Peru, is also occasionally encountered: it is even smaller than *C.marthae,* and the underside of its body and flanks are lighter, but otherwise it is virtually identical to *C.marthae.*

CARNEGIELLA MARTHAE

Family: *Gasteropelecidae*
Genus: *Carnegiella*
English name: Black-winged Hatchetfish
Origin: The basins of the Amazon and Orinoco rivers, Peru, Venezuela
Size: Maximum 3.5 cm
Habitat: Found in sluggish shady jungle streams and in the quiet parts of pools and lakes rich in humus.

SHAPE, COLORING AND MARKINGS: The body is hatchet-shaped and laterally very compressed. The basic coloration is a light yellow-green. A darker longitudinal stripe runs from the gill covers to the caudal peduncle and is bordered above by a narrow glinting zone of silver or gold. Beneath are a number of narrow bands which run obliquely to the front of the body and consist of flecks and irregular patches. Dark spots lie behind the eyes and immediately in front of the roots of the pectoral fins. The throat and belly are edged with black. The central section of the wing-like pectoral fins is black: the remaining fins are colorless and transparent. There is no adipose fin.
There are no known external sexual characteristics.

GENERAL CARE: Suitable for both large and small aquariums but *C.marthae* should always be kept in a group of at least 10 of its own kind. The tank should have a dark bottom and plenty of free swimming space at the surface, but also a few large plants with floating leaves to provide shelter. This species keeps to the upper reaches of the tank. The water should be peaty: temperature 23°–30°C. Diet: ants, ants eggs, fruitflies, greenfly and similar small creatures.

BREEDING: It appears that this species has been bred in captivity but no reliable reports can be quoted for guidance.

ADDITIONAL INFORMATION: *C.marthae* is the smallest of all the known species of *Carnegiella*: its small size and subdued colors probably explain why it is so infrequently seen in aquariums. However if kept under the proper conditions and in a large group, *C.marthae* can prove as interesting as its bigger relations.

CARNEGIELLA STRIGATA

Family: *Gasteropelecidae*
Genus: *Carnegiella*
English name: Marbled Hatchetfish
Origin: The Guianas and the basin of the Amazon
Size: Maximum 4.5 cm
Habitat: Found in sluggish jungle streams, the still waters of lakes and pools and marshes

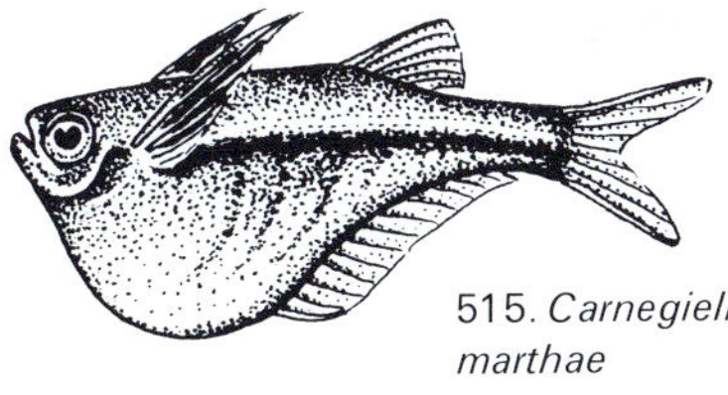

515. *Carnegiella marthae*

514. *Carnegiella marthae*

SHAPE, COLORING AND MARKINGS: The body is hatchet-shaped and laterally very compressed. The basic coloration is yellow to green or pale violet with areas of a silver luster. The back is a darker olive green with a very dark stripe and dark spotting. A longitudinal stripe running from the gill covers into the lower lobe of the caudal fin is bordered above by an area of gleaming silver. Below there are three bands that run obliquely towards the front of the body. The throat and belly are edged with yellow. All the fins are colorless and transparent. Particularly well marked specimens may have an area of light pigmentation on the base of the caudal fin with two white patches.

There are no known external sexual characteristics.

GENERAL CARE: As for *C.marthae* but the minimum size of the group for this species is six, and the tank should include a dense growth of fine-leaved plants as well as plants with large floating leaves.

BREEDING: See *C.marthae*.

ADDITIONAL INFORMATION: A very attractive species and one of the most popular with aquarists. Its colors are best shown off under lighting of medium intensity, when *C.strigata* loses much of its natural timidity. Like related species this fish is a very good jumper and appropriate precautions must be taken.

516. *Gasteropelecus levis*

THE FAMILY GASTEROPELECIDAE

The genus Gasteropelecus

This genus contains three species of interest to aquarists: *Gasteropelecus levis, Gasteropelecus maculatus* and *Gasteropelecus sternicla,* the Common Hatchetfish. They are larger than the *Carnegiella* species, but are still somewhat timid fish, and they should only be kept in community tanks if the other species are peaceful fish that will stay in the lower reaches of the tank. Another species, *Gasteropelecus species* is occasionally encountered in the literature: it has a more rounded profile than related species, and is almost entirely a yellowish bronze color. It is not very well-known among aquarists.

GASTEROPELECUS LEVIS

Family: *Gasteropelecidae*
Genus: *Gasteropelecus*
English name: Silver Hatchetfish
Origin: The lower reaches of the Amazon
Size: Maximum 6 cm
Habitat: Found in sluggish streams, the still waters of lakes and pools and marshes

SHAPE, COLORING AND MARKINGS: The body is hatchet-shaped and laterally very compressed. The basic coloration is yellowish to a dull silver, which gleams when illuminated. A dark longitudinal stripe runs from the gill covers to the root of the caudal peduncle and is bordered above and below by a lighter zone. A dark transverse band lies on the caudal peduncle: there is a prominent patch on the dorsal fin. The fins are colorless and transparent.
There are no known external sexual characteristics although males are often slightly smaller than females.

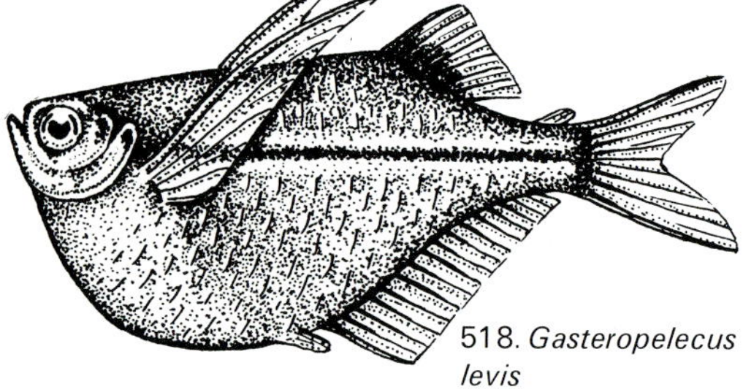

518. *Gasteropelecus levis*

GENERAL CARE: As for *C.marthae*.

BREEDING: This species does not seem as yet to have been bred in captivity.

ADDITIONAL INFORMATION: Together with related species *G.levis* shares a dislike of the disturbance of the water surface of the tank: it should therefore be kept with other quiet species that favor the lower water levels in the community tank.

GASTEROPELECUS MACULATUS

Family: *Gasteropelecidae*
Genus: *Gasteropelecus*
English name: Spotted Hatchetfish
Origin: West Colombia, Panama
Size: Maximum 9 cm
Habitat: Found in sluggish streams, in the still waters of lakes and pools and in marshes

SHAPE, COLORING AND MARKINGS: The body is hatchet-shaped and laterally very compressed. The basic coloration is yellowish to dull silver, which shines with a light blue gleam under illumination. A dark longitudinal stripe runs from the gill covers to the caudal peduncle, bordered above by a line of glittering silver. Innumerable light and dark spots lie in roughly transverse bands across the body. The fins are transparent and colorless: the dorsal fin has a darker border and the anal fin a touch of pigment at the base.
There are no known external sexual characteristics.

517. *Gasteropelecus maculatus*

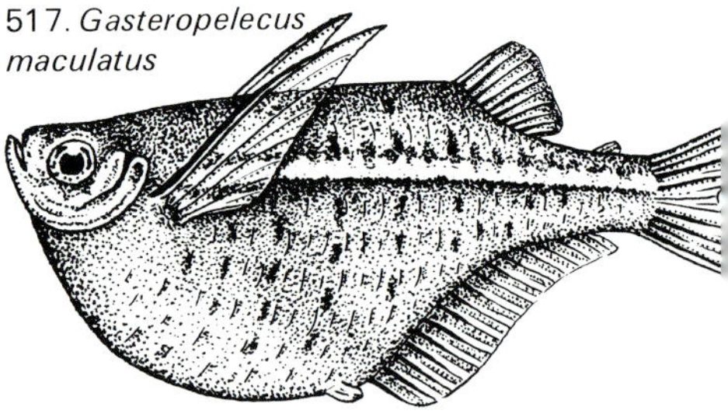

GENERAL CARE: As for *C.marthae,* but see below.

BREEDING: There is no information available on the reproductive behavior of this species.

ADDITIONAL INFORMATION: *G.maculatus* is far too robust for the small aquarium. Despite its size however, it is a very timid species: only quiet fish that live at the lower levels of the tank are suitable companions and *G.maculatus* is particularly prone to trying to jump out of the tank when frightened: great care must be taken when cleaning the tank.

GASTEROPELECUS STERNICLA

Family: *Gasteropelecidae*

Genus: *Gasteropelecus*

English name: The Common Hatchetfish

Origin: Brazil, in the area of the Amazon, British Guyana, Peru, Surinam.

Size: Maximum 7 cm

Habitat: Found in sluggish streams and the still waters of lakes and marshes.

SHAPE, COLORING AND MARKINGS: The body is hatchet-shaped and laterally very compressed. The basic coloration is a yellowish or greyish silver. A dark narrow line, bordered above and below by a paler stripe, runs from the back of the gill covers to the caudal peduncle. All the fins are colorless, but the dorsal fin has sometimes a dark front edge.
There are no known external sexual characteristics, although females are usually somewhat larger than males.

GENERAL CARE: As for *C.marthae*, but *G.sternicla* is a relatively hardy species. It has the same dislikes as *G.levis* and its companions should be selected with that in mind.

BREEDING: This species has not yet been bred in captivity.

THE FAMILY GASTEROPELECIDAE

The genus Thoracocharax

Taxonomists distinguish the species in the genus *Thoracocharax* from related species by rather technical differences – noted below under the description of *Thoracocharax securis*. However, so far as the amateur aquarist is concerned, these fish are virtually indistinguishable from the species in the genus *Gasteropelecus*. Certainly their behavior in the aquarium is identical, and the care they need is the same. They are rather less common than their cousins, and the only two species ever likely to be imported are *T.securis* and *T.stellatus* described below.

THORACOCHARAX SECURIS

Family: *Gasteropelecidae*

Genus: *Thoracocharax*

English name: none

Origin: The Amazon basin

Size: Maximum 9 cm

Habitat: Found in sluggish streams, the still waters of pools and lakes and marshy areas

SHAPE, COLORING AND MARKINGS: The body is hatchet-shaped and laterally very compressed. The basic coloration is a brownish-yellow to light violet, with a glittering silver gleam. A light blue to iridescent green line runs from the gill covers to the caudal peduncle, broadening as it progresses. The fins are colorless and transparent. The pectoral fins are well-developed.
There are no known external sexual characteristics.

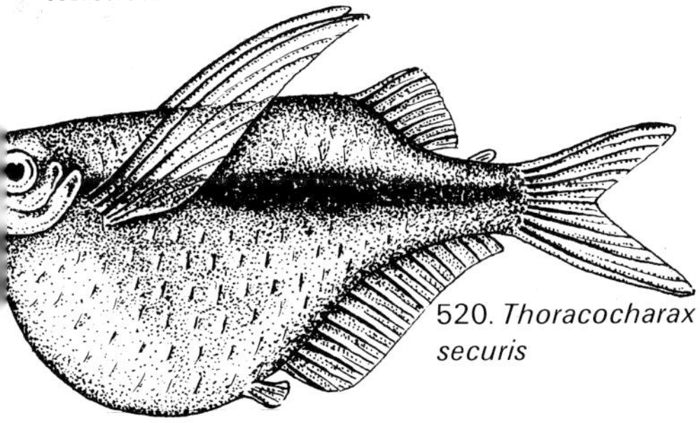

520. *Thoracocharax securis*

GENERAL CARE: As for *Carnegiella marthae* but temperature 22°–25°C.

BREEDING: This species has not as yet been bred in captivity.

ADDITIONAL INFORMATION: The genus *Thoracocharax* is distinguished from the genus *Carnegiella* by differences in dentition, larger scales and a different number of rays in the dorsal and anal fins. The species in the genus *Thoracocharax* also have very large pectoral fins and extremely deep bodies. They are very shy fish and should only be kept with other very quiet species.

THORACOCHARAX STELLATUS

Family: *Gasteropelecidae*

Genus: *Thoracocharax*

English name: none

Origin: The Amazon basin

Size: Maximum 7 cm

Habitat: Found in sluggish streams, the still waters of lakes and pools and marshy areas

SHAPE, COLORING AND MARKING: The body is hatchet-shaped and laterally very compressed. *T.stellatus* closely resembles *T.securis*, but the former has less well developed pectoral fins and displays a dark patch on the anterior rays of the dorsal fin which is not present in *T.securis*. The basic coloration is a light yellow to light blue or violet with a silvery tinge. A broadening longitudinal stripe runs from the gill covers to the base of the caudal fin. Under illumination this stripe has a light blue to green iridescence. The fins are colorless and transparent.
There are no known external sexual characteristics.

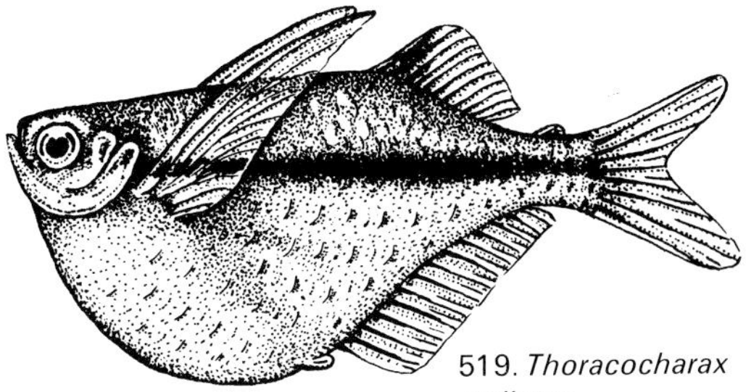

519. *Thoracocharax stellatus*

GENERAL CARE: As for *Carnegiella marthae* but temperature 22°–25°C.

BREEDING: No information is available on the reproductive habits of this species.

THE FAMILY GYRINOCHEILIDAE

An introductory description

This is a very small and unusual family of fish, found only in Southeast Asis, and in particular in Thailand. There is only one genus, in which there are but three species and of these in fact only one, *Gyrinocheilus aymonieri*, is of interest to aquarists. These fish were formerly classified in the family *Cobitidae*. They are great algae eaters, and their unusual body form is adapted solely to increase their efficiency in that respect. The mouth is a large downward directed sucking organ and so that their feeding should not be interrupted, these fish do not breathe by taking in water through the mouth. They have a special opening above the normal opening through which fish expel water, and this special opening is used for inhaling it. The swim-bladder is very small, and is indeed too small to be used as a movement control as it is by most other fish: these fish move entirely by the motion of the fins.

The genus Gyrinocheilus

This is the only genus in the family *Gyrinocheilidae,* and as noted above, of the three species in the genus, only *Gyrinocheilus aymonieri,* described below, is of interest to aquarists. An interesting and unusual fish, it is however, when full-grown rather aggressive towards other species, which somewhat detracts from its attraction as a most effective algae clearer. It is also a very quick fish, and one that will immediately disappear into the thickest vegetation when the aquarist attempts to catch it. If the fish really has to be caught, this very often involves emptying the tank. Only the very interested amateur will keep this fish.

GYRINOCHEILUS AYMONIERI

Family: *Gyrinocheilidae*

Genus: *Gyrinocheilus*

English name: none

Origin: Thailand

Size: Maximum 25 cm in the wild, but remains considerably smaller in captivity

Habitat: Found in a variety of waters, usually in large numbers

SHAPE, COLORING AND MARKINGS: The body is elongated and hardly at all compressed. The fins, particularly the dorsal fin, are relatively large. The mouth has developed into a large sucking organ. The basic coloration is a greyish brown. The back has dark irregular markings, and similar blotches appear on the sides. The belly is lighter. The fins are colorless or brownish.
Females are more robust when sexually mature.
Males are as described above.

GENERAL CARE: *G.aymonieri* requires a fairly large tank, well aerated or thickly planted, with a sandy bottom. The compostition of the water is not critical: temperature 21°–30°C. *G.aymonieri* will stay mainly on or near the bottom of the tank, and is incapable, because of its peculiar swim bladder, of floating in the water: it must either actually swim or rest on the bed. It should be fed on algae and limp lettuce; it will also eat dried food that falls to the bottom.

BREEDING: *G.aymonieri* has not as yet been bred in captivity.

ADDITIONAL INFORMATION: Young specimens are very peaceful and undemanding fish: mature specimens are somewhat aggressive towards other species.

521. *Gyrinocheilus aymonieri*

THE FAMILY HEMIODONTIDAE

An introductory description

This is a family of South American fish which although by no means large, has yet presented some very difficult problems for taxonomists. Originally the family was classed as a subfamily of the *Characidae,* but it is now generally agreed that they constitute a separate family.
There is however no agreement on the classification of the genera within the family. In this encyclopaedia the species are set out under five genera; *Characidium, Hemiodus, Nannobrycon, Nannostomus* and *Poecilobrycon:* some authorities however would put both the *Nannobrycon* and *Peocilobrycon* genera in the genus *Nannostomus.* This question is further explored below.
Of course, the technicalities of these questions of classification are of little concern to the amateur aquarist, but there is so much confusion in this particular family that it is well for aquarists to be on their guard, for otherwise occasionally it will be difficult to trace a particular species in the literature.
It is curious, in a way, that this family should have such a confused nomenclature, because it contains some fish that are much favored by aquarists and very often to be found enlivening aquariums: it is not a remote or unusual group of fish.

The genus Characidium

The genus *Characidium* derives its name from *Charax,* a pallisade, an allusion to the curious appearance of the rows of cone-shaped teeth of these fish. These species have many features commonly associated with fish that live on muddy beds: they also seem in some ways to resemble the carp family. It is an interesting genus but one about which comparatively little is known. Some 20 species have been identified to date but very few of these are usually found in aquariums: these fish are but rarely imported and this may be because, living as they do on the bottom, they are probably difficult to capture: moreover, on the whole they are not very brightly colored and professional collectors doubtless find it more profitable to collect for sale the many popular and brightly colored species that are found in South America. Most specimens that are imported arrive by accident in batches of other fish. One species however, *Characidium fasciatum,* has become quite popular and this may be because it is very easy to breed.

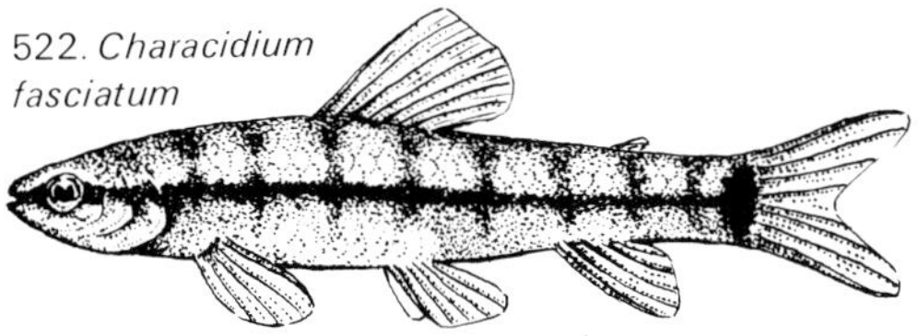

522. *Characidium fasciatum*

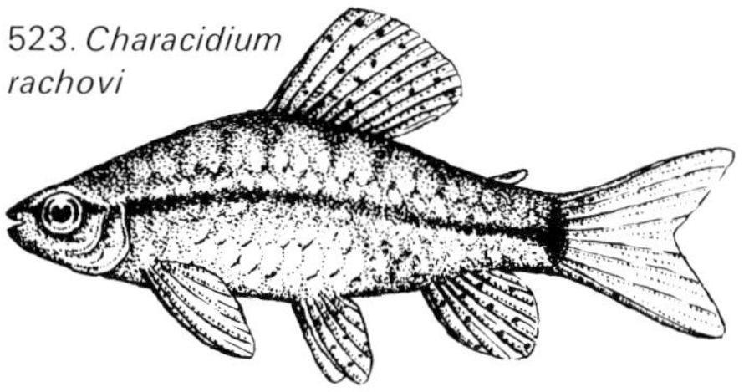

523. *Characidium rachovi*

CHARACIDIUM FASCIATUM

Family: *Hemiodontidae*

Genus: *Characidium*

English name: none

Origin: The basins of the Amazon and Orinoco rivers, and the river Plate.

Size: Maximum 10 cm

Habitat: Found in many different waters.

SHAPE, COLORING AND MARKINGS: The body is elongated and almost round. The basic coloration varies significantly according to the place of origin: it may be a muddy yellow to a brownish olive green: the belly is a clear white. A dark longitudinal stripe, sometimes broken up into irregular patches, runs from the snout, over the eyes to the caudal peduncle, on which there is usually a dark patch. Most specimens have a large number of transverse bands on the upper half of the body and these too may break up the lateral line into segments. The fins are colorless and transparent. The pectoral fins are well-developed. Females are usually more robust and never have any marks on the fins.
Males often have small brown flecks on the base of the dorsal and anal fins.

GENERAL CARE: Suitable for large and small aquariums with a sandy bed and arrangements of rock to provide hiding places. Not a very social fish, *C.fasciatum* stays in the lower reaches of the tank. The composition of the water is not critical: temperature 18°–22°C. This species will eat a wide variety of food but prefers worm-like matter such as Tubifex, red mosquito larvae and worms: *C.fasciatum* will eat soft-leaved plants and the diet should include lettuce.

BREEDING: Not difficult in a tank with very soft water at about 25°C. The eggs are small and are laid over plants, although most sink to the bottom. The eggs hatch after 30–40 hours and the fry are free swimming after about four days. They should be fed on *Artemia nauplii.*

CHARACIDIUM RACHOVI

Family: *Hemiodontidae*

Genus: *Characidium*

English name: none

Origin: Southern Brazil, Paraguay

Size: Approximately 7 cm

Habitat: Found in almost all kinds of waters

SHAPE, COLORING AND MARKINGS: The body is less elongated than that of related species. The basic coloration is a dull yellow: the back is brown to yellowish-brown: the belly a pale yellow. A dark but sometimes indistinct horizontal line runs from the snout to a dark mark lying on the caudal peduncle. Above this line are a number of indistinct transverse bands which are often no more than irregular marks. The dorsal, anal and ventral fins are decorated with rows of brownish-red flecks. The caudal fin is a pale yellow to light orange and the pectoral fins colorless and transparent.
Females have fuller bodies and a more rounded back. Males are more slender with dark edges to the dorsal and anal fins.

GENERAL CARE: As for *C.fasciatum.*

BREEDING: As for *C.fasciatum.*

ADDITIONAL INFORMATION: Some authorities do not recognise it as a member of this genus because it has an incomplete lateral line.

THE FAMILY HEMIODONTIDAE

The genus Hemiodus

There are only two species in this genus that are of interest to aquarists: *Hemiodus gracilis* and *Hemiodus semitaeniatus.* These fish are very much bigger than those in related genera and are therefore far less suitable for the average aquarium. *H.gracilis,* described below, can be kept in very large domestic tanks, but *H.semitaeniatus* which grows to 20cm. is too large even for these. Its care however is as for *H.gracilis,* but that can only be of interest to specialists: in appearance it is identical to *H.gracilis,* except that it lacks the blue-red band found in the lower lobe of the latter's caudal fin.

HEMIODUS GRACILIS

Family: *Hemiodontidae*

Genus: *Hemiodus*

English name: none

Origin: The Amazon, British Guyana

Size: Maximum 16 cm

Habitat: Found in a wide variety of waters

SHAPE, COLORING AND MARKINGS: The body is very slender and laterally compressed. The mouth is small and downward-pointing. The caudal fin is large and deeply forked with the lobes set at a wide angle to each other. The basic coloration is silver. The back is a green-brown to silver: the flanks are green to silver: the belly silver to white. A narrow but broadening band runs from a dark spot on the flanks through the caudal peduncle to the lower caudal lobe, where there lies also a blue-red band: the upper lobe of the caudal fin is tinged with orange. The other fins are colorless and transparent.
There are no known external sexual characteristics.

GENERAL CARE: A peaceful sociable fish suitable for larger aquariums with dense vegetation round the sides and plenty of free swimming space. *H.gracilis* will stay in the middle and upper reaches and will swim at an oblique angle with the head up. It likes sunshine or strong overhead lighting. The quality of the water is not critical: temperature 23°–28°C. All small live animal matter will be accepted.

BREEDING: This species has not as yet been bred in captivity.

THE FAMILY HEMIODONTIDAE

The genus Nannobrycon

Opinion differs on the correct classification of fish in the genera *Nannobrycon* ('small biter'), *Nannostomus* ('small mouthed') and *Poecilobrycon* ('spotted biter'). The three genera were formerly treated as one, called Nannostomus. It was then felt that this one genus should be divided into two, one for those fish with adipose fins and one for those without: about 1900 a new genus, Poecilobrycon was accordingly created for the species with adipose fins.

However it soon became clear that the distinctive genera could not be based solely on the presence or absence of that one external feature, because the adipose fin may be either present or absent in species both in the genus *Nannostomus* and in the genus *Poecilobrycon*. In 1950 Hoedeman, a Dutch expert, published a completely new analysis of these genera in *The Amsterdam Naturalist*. He looked at other distinctive characteristics of these fish and suggested a completely new genus, *Nannobrycon,* for those fish that swim at an oblique angle, and have a distinctive enlarged lower lobe to the caudal fin and a particular shape to the swim bladder.

Hoedman's classification has not been universally accepted, but many authors do recognise now the genus *Nannobrycon.* The non-specialist can easily identify fish in this genus by their curious oblique posture when swimming. In appearance there is less difference between the genera *Nannobrycon* and *Poecilobrycon,* but the latter are usually much slimmer in the body. These graceful fish come from the north of South America. They are found mostly in sluggish densely overgrown jungle streams where the water is soft and often dark with suspended soil particles. They are also found in the shallow swampy backwaters of the larger rivers, particularly where these also are overshadowed by jungle vegetation.

One remarkable feature of these fish is that they change color radically at night. In most cases the whole appearance of the fish is changed, and the position and direction of the markings alters: details of these changes are noted under the entries for particular species.

The majority of these fish live close to the surface, finding their food on the surface itself, or lying in wait until some prey passes close to it. The oblique swimming posture is well suited to this. In a tank the fish can be regularly observed hanging apparently motionless under the surface before leaping up to seize some prey on the surface. Creatures that live in the water are also eaten, but they of course are caught in a less unusual way.

Imported specimens should be carefully acclimatized to aquarium conditions: a quarantine tank should always be used for the first few weeks. This should be filled initially with mildy acid water, and then replaced gradually later with aquarium water. Once acclimatized, the fish present few problems, although care must be taken to ensure that they feed regularly on a varied diet. Fruitflies, greenfly, small insects, ants and ants eggs are all excellent foods. Most species can tolerate a varying temperature, in the range 23°–28°C. Provided they are kept in a small group, the fish will feel as much at home in a small tank as in a large one: in all cases however, it is best to provide a dark bottom and scatterings of dense vegetation. Except when dealing with specimens that have been newly imported, the composition of the water is not critical, although fresh water should never be used. These fish do not like any vigorous disturbance of the surface taking place.

For breeding, small tanks with a capacity of about five liters should be used. The composition of the water will depend on the species involved and also on whether newly imported specimens or aquarium bred fish are concerned. With imported specimens, extremely soft water must always be used initially: this should then be acidified by aerating it over 48 hours by using, for the base layer, well boiled moorland peat. The water thus artificially matured should then be allowed to settle for a few days until it becomes a clear amber. The tank can then be planted and after that, the pairs selected for breeding can be transferred carefully to it. The water should then be slowly raised to 26°–27°C.

The same procedure should be used for aquarium bred fish but for them, mature aquarium water can be used for the breeding tank: it should of course be free from harmful bacteria. The *Nannobrycon* species prefer to lay their eggs on the undersides of the leaves of *Hygrophila.* Well-fed breeding fish of thse species show absolutely no interest in their eggs, and only a few sections of these plants need be put into the tank. Members of both the *Nannostomus* and *Poecilobrycon* genera are however quite different in their habits: all indulge in egg eating. *N.marginatus* has acquired a particularly bad name for this over the years. When breeding this species the tank should be planted thickly with *Myriophyllum* and the fish removed immediately after spawning. *N.espei* and *N.trifasciatus* are somewhat different in their habits. *N.espei* prefers to lay eggs on the undersides of broad-leaved plants: *N.trifasciatus* prefers a large breeding tank with a low water level (about 10

524. *Nannobrycon eques*

cm) and a dense superficial growth of *Salvinia, Riccia* or *Pistia*. The eggs are discharged between vertical strands of peat or the dense roots of *Pistia*. Several fish should be put into the breeding tank at the same time. This species needs a comparatively long time to grow accustomed to the breeding tank and several weeks may pass before mating starts, although this is probably largely only true of recently imported specimens. Most species however are not difficult to breed. If introduced into the breeding tank one evening, they will usually have started to mate by the next morning: a true mating may be preceded by a large number of sham matings. The two fish press together with quivering flanks: one to three eggs are laid and fertilized at each mating. The process may be repeated dozens of times, though it is rare for more than 80 eggs to be produced. A new breeding cycle can begin after a break of three or four days, and the cycle may be repeated many times. The time between each cycle is spent mainly in eating.

When kept at a temperature of about 27° C the eggs will hatch after 20–25 hours. At first the fry sink to the bottom of the tank, but after 24 to 30 hours they can be seen hanging between the plants and on the sides of the tank. They are swimming about by the fifth day and from then on infusoria must be available. After three more days the *nauplii* of the brine shrimp will be accepted and the fry can be fed on those until they are big enough to eat sieved pond organisms. Growth is slow, but juvenile pigmentation is visible at a very early stage. The ribbon-like embryonic adipose fin is a distinctive characteristic: this once served as an embryonic organ of propulsion.

NANNOBRYCON EQUES

Family: *Hemiodontidae*

Genus: *Nannobrycon*

English name: Tube-mouthed Pencilfish

Origin: Guyana and the middle reaches of the Amazon

Size: 5 cm

Habitat: Found in shallow waters where the banks are overgrown with reeds and grasses

SHAPE, COLORING AND MARKINGS: The body is torpedo shaped and less slim than in related species. The basic coloration is muddy white to yellow brown. There are two brown to black longitudinal stripes made up of tiny dots on the upper part of the body, above a pale zone. A very dark patch on the underside of the body stretches to the lower lobe of the caudal fin, to fill the area below the white field. The scales are dark with a gleaming golden edge. The caudal and anal fins have a red base and the latter has also, as a rule, a dark border and some ice blue spots.

Females are more rounded in the body and less vividly colored.

Males are noticeably slimmer: the ventral fins have ice blue spots.

GENERAL CARE: Suitable for both large and small aquariums provided a small group is kept. A dark bed and peaty water are needed with an abundance of plants, including some with ribbon leaves. *N.eques* only occupies the upper reaches of the tank. Temperature 22°–28° C. The diet should consist of small living creatures such as fruitflies, greenfly and ants.

BREEDING: Not usually difficult. These fish prefer to lay their eggs on broad leaved plants.

ADDITIONAL INFORMATION: This is the best known of these species. It swims at a very oblique angle: it is often seen to be vertical. It grows much paler at night: the only part of the body that remains dark is the area behind the ventral fin: a dark band in front of the dorsal fin then appears and a spot on the gill covers.

525. *Nannobrycon unifasciatus*

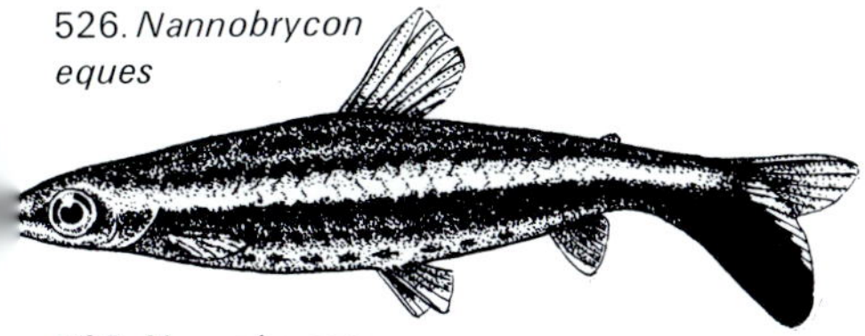

526. *Nannobrycon eques*

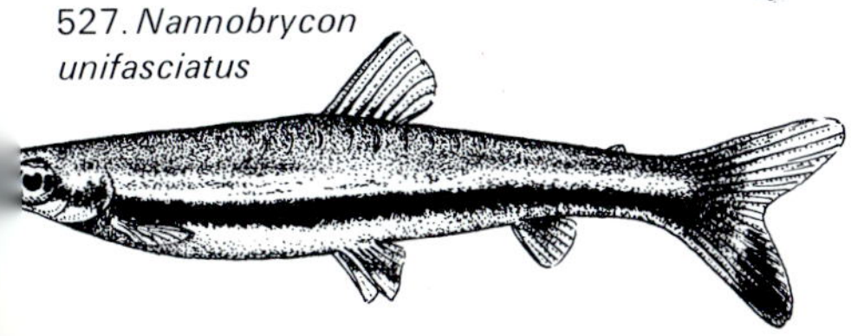

527. *Nannobrycon unifasciatus*

NANNOBRYCON UNIFASCIATUS

Family: *Hemiodontidae*

Genus: *Nannobrycon*

English name: One-lined Pencilfish

Origin: Guiana

Size: 6.5 cm

Habitat: Found along the banks of shallow waters overgrown with reeds and grasses

SHAPE, COLORING AND MARKINGS: The body is slim and torpedo shaped. The basic coloration is yellow to golden brown. A brown to black longitudinal line runs back from the snout across the eye into the caudal peduncle. Above this line there is a zone of yellow or gold. The scales on the upper half of the body have dark edges. The belly is a light yellow to silver white. The caudal fin is red at the base, and darker on the lower lobe. The dorsal fin is colorless and transparent: the anal fin has a red patch flecked with ice blue spots. There is a red gold patch on the head.

Females have angular anal fins and more rounded bodies.

Males have rounded anal fins and are a more brilliant red.

GENERAL CARE: As for *N.eques* but temperature 22°–26° C.

BREEDING: Little information is available, but this species has probably breeding habits similar to *Poecilobrycon harrisoni*.

ADDITIONAL INFORMATION: Like related species, *N.unifasciatus* swims at a very oblique angle. At night the fish has two dark transverse bands: one in front of the dorsal fin, the other above the anal fin.

THE FAMILY HEMIODONTIDAE

The genus Nannostomus

For details of the classification of fish in this genus, see above, in the introductory note to the *Nannobrycon*. In this encyclopaedia, seven species have been included in this genus: they include some of the most attractive and popular of aquarium fish. These attractive fish are on the whole peaceful species in the aquarium, but they do occasionally become aggressive and must accordingly be watched. Males often rigorously threaten their rivals.

528. *Nannostomus espei*

NANNOSTOMUS BECKFORDI ANOMULUS

Family: *Hemiodontidae*

Genus: *Nannostomus*

English name: Golden Pencilfish

Origin: Guiana, Rio Negro, the middle and lower reaches of the Amazon

Size: Approximately 4.5 cm

Habitat: Found in the many jungle rivulets and along the banks of larger streams where the shallow waters are shaded and contain a great deal of humus

SHAPE, COLORING AND MARKINGS: The body is slim and spindle-shaped: the snout tapered and the mouth small. The basic coloration is a pale yellow: the back is yellow brown to olive green: the belly pale yellow to white. A dark brown longitudinal stripe runs from the snout, over the eyes and back to the central rays of the caudal fin. Above this dark zone there is a lustrous golden patch which in males may have a red border.
Females are more compressed and duller in color: all the fins are colorless.
Males are slimmer with a more vivid color. The lower lobe of the caudal fin and the anal fin are brick red and become bright red during the mating season and when the fish is excited.

GENERAL CARE: Suitable for both small and large aquariums provided a group of six or more is kept. The tank should have a dark bottom, peaty water and dense fine-leaved vegetation. *N.beckfordi anomulus* keeps mainly to the upper and middle reaches of the tank. Temperature 24°–28°C. The main diet should be of small living creatures: fruitflies, ants and ants eggs will be snapped up eagerly from the surface of the water. Dried food will be accepted for a change.

BREEDING: This is straightforward.

ADDITIONAL INFORMATION: The nocturnal coloration of *N.beckfordi anomulus* is two dark transverse bands on a very pale body.

NANNOSTOMUS BECKFORDI BECKFORDI

Family: *Hemiodontidae*

Genus: *Nannostomus*

English name: Golden Pencilfish

Origin: Guiana

Size: Approximately 6.5 cm

Habitat: Found in sluggish, densely overgrown and shaded jungle rivulets and in the quiet backwaters of larger rivers where the water contains a good deal of humus

SHAPE, COLORING AND MARKINGS: The body is slim and spindle-shaped. The snout is tapered and the mouth small. The basic coloration is a pale yellow: the back is fawn, with a marked gold luster: the belly is silvery white. A longitudinal stripe, usually deep black, runs from the snout, across the eyes to the root of the tail. This stripe is edged above by a lustrous golden band, and this in turn is bordered by a zone of attractive iridescent green. The scales on the upper half of the body have a dark edge. The fins are pale yellow with an orange glow: the anal fin and the lower lobe of the caudal fin are brick red. There is no adipose fin.
Females are more compressed in the body and duller in color. The anal fin is angular and during the mating season the eggs in the oviduct are visible against the light.
Males are slimmer in the body and more vividly marked: the anal fin is rounded.

GENERAL CARE: As for *N.beckfordi anomulus*.

BREEDING: This is straightforward.

ADDITIONAL INFORMATION: The species has many features in common with *N.beckfordi anomulus*: individual specimens may however vary considerably in size and color and may demonstrate different mating behavior. The nocturnal coloration is two dark transverse bands on a very pale body.

529. *Nannostomus beckfordi beckfordi*

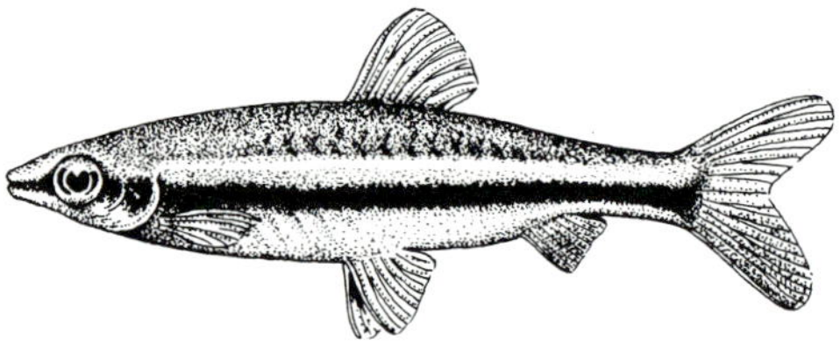

NANNOSTOMUS BIFASCIATUS

Family: *Hemiodontidae*

Genus: *Nannostomus*

English name: none

Origin: Surinam

Size: Approximately 6 cm

Habitat: Found in still and sluggish streams that are densely overgrown and shaded

SHAPE, COLORING AND MARKINGS: The body is slim and spindle-shaped. The snout is tapered and the mouth small. The basic coloration is white to bright silver: the back is yellow: the belly is white. A deep black longitudinal stripe runs from the lower jaw across the eyes and along the body to merge into the lower lobe of the caudal fin. A second and less prominent dark line consisting of a series of contiguous spots and patches, runs from the upper part of the eye into the upper part of the caudal peduncle. A bright golden zone lies between the two stripes. The lower lobes of the caudal and anal fins are brick red: the remaining fins are colorless except for some bluish white dots on the ventral fin. The adipose fin is either entirely absent or present only in a very rudimentary form.
Females have no dots on the ventral fins.
Males have a more lustrous zone of gold, and a gleaming green on the snout.

GENERAL CARE: As for *N.beckfordi anomulus*.

BREEDING: Not difficult: this is a very prolific species.

ADDITIONAL INFORMATION: *N.bifasciatus* is less common than related species: it is little known and rarely imported. Specimens that are imported seem to find it difficult to adjust to an aquarium environment.

NANNOSTOMUS ESPEI

Family: *Hemiodontidae*

Genus: *Nannostomus*

English name: none

Origin: British Guiana

Size: Approximately 4 cm

Habitat: Only found it seems, in the upper reaches of the Mazaruni and its tributaries.

SHAPE, COLORING AND MARKINGS: The body is very slim and spindle-shaped. The snout is tapered and the mouth small. The basic coloration is yellow to brown green, lightening to silvery white towards the belly. The scales on the upper half of the body have a dark edge. A golden longitudinal stripe extends from the snout through the upper half of the eye, to the caudal peduncle. On the head there is a deep black stripe which runs below the gold stripe, across the eye and ends behind the gill covers. There are four very striking bands which run obliquely across the lower half of the body. There is a dark patch on the lower half of the root of the caudal fin: otherwise the fins are colorless and translucent with a soft red gleam.
Females are sturdier and less rividly colored.
Males have a little pigmentation in the anterior rays of the anal fin.

GENERAL CARE: As for *N.beckfordi anomulus* but at least ten of this species should be kept together. Temperature 22°–25° C.

BREEDING: Little information is available but it would seem that breeding is possible. Unlike other related species, *N.espei* prefers to lay its eggs on the undersides of broad-leaved plants.

ADDITIONAL INFORMATION: The oblique bands on *N.espei* closely resemble the bands that appear at night on other related species. On *N.espei*, at night a fifth band appears between the first two always present, and this stretches from the dorsal fin to the belly, while the four other bands remain almost as prominent as they are during the day.

NANNOSTOMUS MARGINATUS

Family: *Hemiodontidae*

Genus: *Nannostomus*

English name: Dwarf Pencilfish

Origin: Guiana and the lower reaches of the Amazon

Size: Approximately 4 cm

Habitat: Found in sluggish densely overgrown jungle streams where the water contains a good deal of humus

SHAPE, COLORING AND MARKINGS: The body is more compressed than that of other related species. The basic coloration is a silvery to purple brown: the back is olive green to dark brown, with a black dorsal stripe: the belly is silver white. There are three dark brown to black longitudinal stripes: the second is the most prominent and above it lies a zone of bright gold edged with a vivid red. The anterior rays of the dorsal fin are a deep black with a lighter patch behind: the anal fins are brick red with black edges: the ventral fins

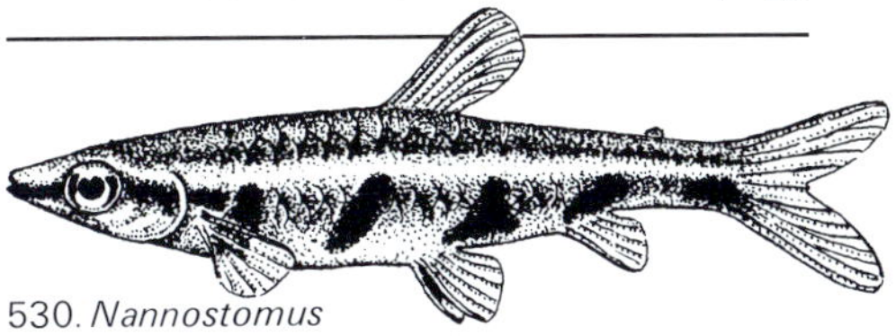

530. *Nannostomus espei*

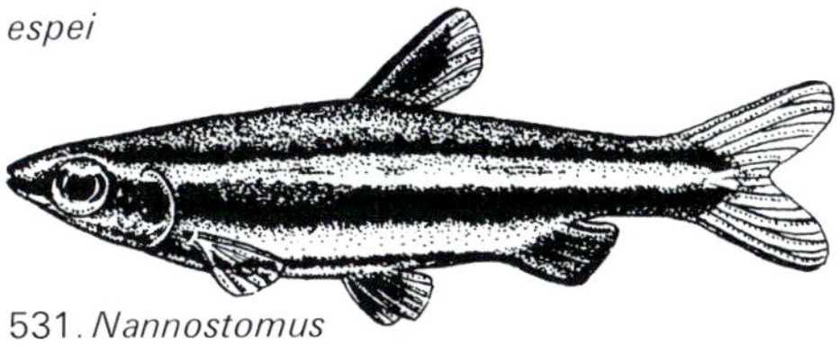

531. *Nannostomus marginatus*

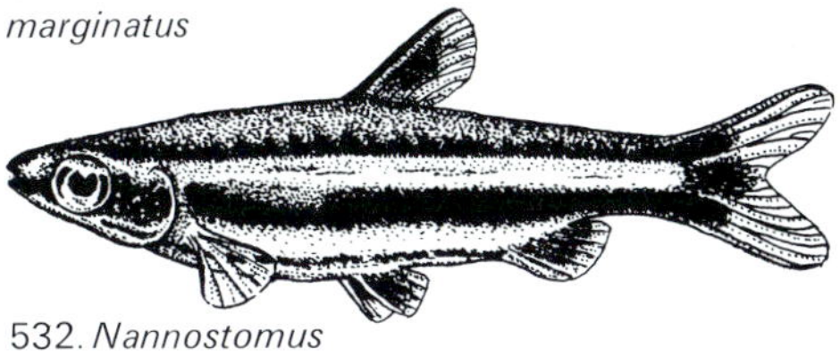

532. *Nannostomus picturatus*

have a red patch: the other fins are colorless. There is no adipose fin.
Females have angular anal fins: the eggs in the oviduct of sexually mature specimens can be seen against the light.
Males have more rounded anal fins with prominent black borders.

GENERAL CARE: As for *N.beckfordi anomulus.*

BREEDING: Not difficult although there is rarely a large brood. The breeding tank should be densely planted with fine-leaved vegetation. The parent fish should be removed from it immediately after spawning, because they have a marked propensity for eating the eggs. If given the right diet, the parent fish can be reintroduced into the breeding tank for mating every three days during the spawning season.

ADDITIONAL INFORMATION: The usual nocturnal coloration of *N.marginatus* consists of a large dark patch under the anal fin and stipples on the gill covers.

533. *Nannostomus marginatus*

NANNOSTOMUS PICTURATUS

Family: *Hemiodontidae*

Genus: *Nannostomus*

English name: none

Origin: Guiana and the lower reaches of the Amazon

Size: Approximately 4 cm

Habitat: Found in sluggish jungle streams and waters which contain a good deal of humus

SHAPE, COLORING AND MARKINGS: This species closely resembles in shape the related species *N.marginatus*. The basic coloration is silvery to purple brown: the back is olive green to dark brown and there is a dark dorsal stripe:

534. *Nannostomus picturatus*

the belly is silver white. There are three dark brown to black longitudinal stripes across the body: the second is the most prominent and above it lies a zone of bright gold edged with a vivid red. The anterior rays of the dorsal fins are a deep black with a red patch: the anal fin is a brick red with a yellow border: the ventral fins also bear a red mark: there is another red patch in the tail, which links with the longitudinal line. The other fins are colorless: there is no adipose fin.
Females have angular anal fins: the eggs in the oviducts of sexually mature females can be seen against the light.
Males have more rounded anal fins, edged with black.

General care: As for *N.beckfordi anomulus.*

Breeding: As for *N.marginatus.*

Additional information: This species is closely related to *N.trifasciatus* and *N.marginatus,* of which it may be a variety.

NANNOSTOMUS TRIFASCIATUS

Family: *Hemiodontidae*

Genus: *Nannostomus*

English name: Three Banded Pencilfish

Origin: Guyana

Size: Approximately 6 cm

Habitat: Found in sluggish and densely overgrown jungle rivulets, where the water contains a good deal of humus

---

Shape, coloring and markings: The body is slim and spindle-shaped. The snout is tapered and the mouth small. The basic coloration is silvery to purple brown: the back is olive green to dark brown: the belly is silvery white: there is a gold patch above the snout. One black longitudinal stripe runs from the snout to the lower part of the root of the caudal fin: another runs parallel to the first stripe from the upper part of the eye into the upper part of the root of the tail: a third less prominent stripe runs from the pectoral fin to the anal fin. There is a zone of gold above the second stripe and a red patch behind the gill covers. All the fins, except the ventral fin, have a bright red patch. The ventral and anal fins carry blue white dots.
Females have more rounded bellies and less vivid coloring.
Males are markedly slimmer.

General care: As for *N.beckfordi anomulus.*

Breeding: This is not easy. *N.trifasciatus*

535. *Nannostomus trifasciatus*

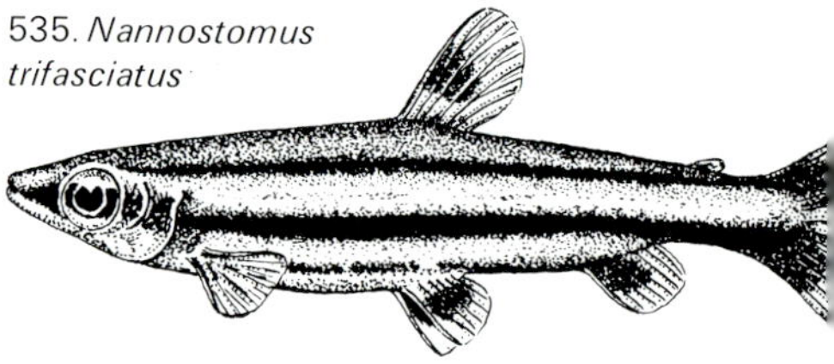

needs a large breeding tank with shallow water (about 20 cm): well shaded from the light (but not artificially dimmed). The water should be of low acidity. There must be a large group of the fish in the tank, which should have a peat bed, with a lot of loose strands sticking up into the water. The breeding fish should be well fed on fruitflies: care must be taken not to give any food that might sink to the bottom. Temperature about 20°C. Several weeks may pass before any of the fish spawn.

536. *Nannostomus trifasciatus*

537. *Nannostomus trifasciatus* (night coloration)

538. *Poecilobrycon harrisoni*

THE FAMILY HEMIODONTIDAE

The genus Poecilobrycon

See above, under the introductory note to the genus *Nannobrycon*, for details of the classification of these genera. In this encyclopaedia two species are described: the well-known *P.harrisoni*, and *P.diagrammus*, a less familiar fish which swims at an oblique angle, and may indeed be no more than a sub-species of *P.harrisoni*.

POECILOBRYCON DIAGRAMMUS

Family: *Hemiodontidae*

Genus: *Poecilobrycon*

English name: none

Origin: No information is available about the place of origin of this species, but it is likely that it comes from the same area as the closely related *P.harrisoni*

Size: Maximum 6 cm

SHAPE, COLORING AND MARKINGS: The body is very slender and torpedo-shaped. The back is fawn to olive green in vivid contrast to the straw-colored or shiny golden horizontal line that runs across the body from the snout to the tail. Below that line a brownish-black band runs from the snout, through the eye to the lower part of the caudal peduncle, but does not extend into the rays of the caudal fin as it does in the case of *P.harrisoni*. The belly is white to silvery, with light pigmentation between the ventral and anal fins. The dorsal and caudal fins are colorless and transparent: the anal fin is brick red with dark pigmentation at the base. The ventral fins have bluish-white points.
Females have more rounded bellies during the spawning season.
Males usually have bluish white points to the pectoral fins.

GENERAL CARE: *P.diagrammus* is suitable for large and small aquariums provided it is kept in a group of at least six of its own kind. The bed should be dark, the water peaty. Temperature 23°–26°C. Thick clumps of fine-leaved plants should be put into the tank. *P.diagrammus* keeps mainly to the upper and middle reaches of the tank. All small live animal matter will be eaten, and the fish has a particular fondness for mosquito larvae and fruitflies.

BREEDING: There are no reports of this species having been as yet bred in captivity, but it is likely that its reproductive behavior will be similar to that of *P.harrisoni.*

ADDITIONAL INFORMATION: This species swims in the tank with its head pointing upwards at an angle: it is likely that it is in fact a sub-species of *P.harrisoni.*

POECILOBRYCON HARRISONI

Family: *Hemiodontidae*

Genus: *Poecilobrycon*

English name: Harrison's Pencilfish

Origin: The western Guianas

Size: Maximum 6 cm

Habitat: Found in sluggish and still waters, jungle creeks and pools with dense vegetation on the banks and water rich in humus

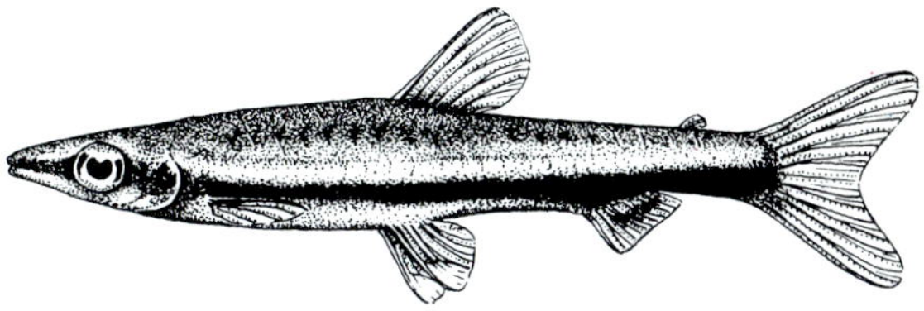

539. *Poecilobrycon diagrammus*

SHAPE, COLORING AND MARKINGS: The body is very slender and torpedo-shaped. The color pattern is identical to that of *P.diagrammus* except that the dark band running across the body extends, in *P.harrisoni* into the rays of the caudal fin. The species can also be distinguished by their swimming postures: *P.diagrammus* swims at an oblique angle, *P.harrisoni* swims on an even keel.
Females have more rounded bellies.
Males usually have brilliant white points to the pectoral fins.

GENERAL CARE: As for *P.diagrammus.*

BREEDING: This is not easy. Fairly soft water, pH 6.6–6.8 is needed in a breeding tank with dense clumps of fine-leaved plants, over which the eggs will be laid. The male fans the eggs, which will number 50–75. The eggs hatch in 48 hours and the fry are free swimming after four days. They should be fed at first on infusoria and then on *Artemia nauplii.*

THE FAMILY BAGRIDAE

An introductory description

The *Bagridae* family of naked catfish, without any armor-plating, is made up of a number of genera, found over a wide area of Africa, Asia Minor, southern and eastern Asia and Japan. All species have toothed jaws, three or four pairs of barbels, one pair of which is often very long, a dorsal fin with a well-developed spine and a large adipose fin. They are all twilight fish, and in captivity extremely timid and shy. Almost all species grow to a very large size and are consequently totally unsuitable for the domestic aquarium. Indeed many can hardly be considered to be aquarium fish at all, as that term is usually understood.

The genus Mystus

There are only two species in this genus: *Mystus tengera,* described below, and *Mystus vittatus,* a rather larger fish (and hence unsuitable for the domestic aquarium), but otherwise in many ways similar to *M.tengera,* found over a wide area of India, Burma and Southeast Asia.

MYSTUS TENGARA

Family: *Bagridae*

Genus: *Mystus*

English name: none

Origin: Northern India

Size: Maximum 18 cm in the wild but remains considerably smaller in captivity

Habitat: Found in sluggish and still waters

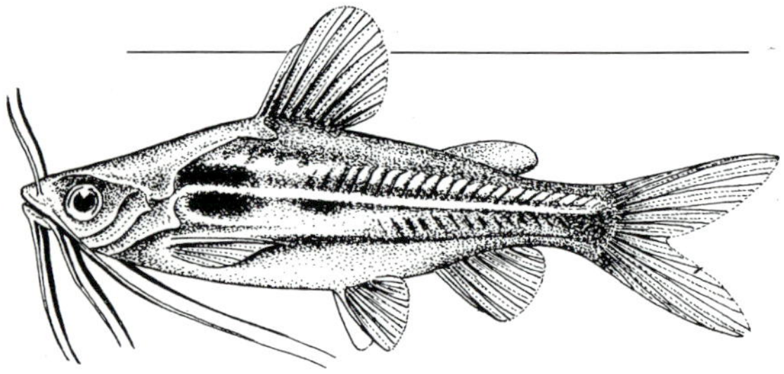

540. *Mystus tengara*

SHAPE, COLORING AND MARKINGS: The body is elongated and laterally slightly compressed. The mouth is wide, with four pairs of barbels, one pair being extremely long. The front rays of the dorsal and pectoral fins are hard and form a strong spine. The adipose fin is large: the caudal fin deeply forked. The basic coloration is yellowish.
Four or five dark brown bands run the length of the body: a mark, not always distinct, lies on the shoulders. The fins are grey and transparent.
There are no known external sexual characteristics.

GENERAL CARE: *M.tengera* like all catfish is only active at night. It needs a large aquarium with plenty of hiding places among rocks and wood and in thick clumps of vegetation. It will usually hide throughout the day and is therefore really only of interest to aquarists who specialise in this type of fish. The bed should be dark and the lighting fairly subdued. The composition of the water is not critical: temperature about 24°C. The diet should consist of larger animal matter such as the larvae of aquatic insects, earthworms and meal worms: flies' eggs are also relished. Small specimens can be kept with other small fish but larger specimens may prey on smaller fish.

BREEDING: There is no information about the reproductive behavior of this species, which has not as yet been bred in captivity.

THE FAMILY BUNOCEPHALIDAE

An introductory description

The *Bunocephalidae* is a small family of South American catfish, found in the western Amazon basin and of a most unusual and curious appearance. They are called colloquially both 'Frying pan' catfish and 'Banjo' catfish, which gives some idea of their strange shape, which is described more exactly in the note on *Bunocephalus bicolor* below. Some authorities do not recognize them as a separate family, but describe them as the *Bunocephalinae*, a sub-family, with the *Aspredininae*, of the family *Aspredinidae*.

The only genus of likely interest to aquarists is the *Bunocephalus*.

The genus Bunocephalus

As noted under the description of *Bunocephalus bicolor* below, there is much confusion over how many real species are to be found in this genus. These fish are very rarely imported, and insufficient study has been made of them for there to be any certainty about their status. *B.bicolor* can at the lowest however be taken as a typical species, and it is unlikely that related fish, either different species or sub-species, require radically different care. These fish are not uncommon in their native habitat, and if more interest in them were evinced by aquarists, there is no reason why more regular imports should not be made, which, in turn, would allow for more accurate study leading to the end of the present confusion.

BUNOCEPHALUS BICOLOR

Family: *Bunocephalidae*

Genus: *Bunocephalus*

English name: Frying-Pan Catfish

Origin: The western Amazon basin

Size: Maximum 15 cm

Habitat: No further details are available of its natural habitat

SHAPE, COLORING AND MARKINGS: The shape is unusual. The head, with its wide mouth, and the stocky body are both laterally very compressed: the tail becomes increasingly narrow and is somewhat compressed laterally. The fish is thus more or less shaped like a frying pan and is sometimes popularly known by that name. There are no scales but the skin is wrinkled and covered with warty protuberances. There are three pairs of bar-

541. *Bunocephalus bicolor*

bels, one of which is quite long. The front rays of the pectoral fin have developed into a pair of formidable serrated spines. The basic coloration is brown, with a patchy black marbled patterning. The fins are brown with dark marks at the tips.
There are no known external sexual characteristics.

GENERAL CARE: As for *Mystus tengra* but even less light should be provided. *B.bicolor* is omnivorous, but it is sometimes difficult to persuade newly-imported specimens to eat at all.

BREEDING: There have been reports of successful breedings in the USA. The nests are supposedly very large and may contain 4,000 or 5,000 eggs. The fry however will, it seems, only eat one species of rotifers and are accordingly very difficult to raise. *B.bicolor* has not as yet been bred in Europe.

ADDITIONAL INFORMATION: In many books on aquarium fish a number of species of the genus *Bunocephalus* are often listed: *B.amaurus, B.coracoides, B.kneri* among them, but it is doubtful how many of these are true species. *B.kneri* for example may be a sub-species of *B.bicolor* or even a synonym for it.

THE FAMILY CALLICHTHYIDAE

An introductory description

The *Callichthyidae* is a family of relatively small, heavily armored catfish which are found widely in inland waters in South America and Trinidad. All these fish have two rows of overlapping bony plates on the flanks, and in some the head and back are also protected by similar armor plates. The adipose fin has a strong movable spine, and the large dorsal fin also usually has a strong spine. One or two pairs of barbels are found on the upper jaw, but none on the lower jaw.
There are five genera in the family: *Callichthys, Brochis, Corydoras, Dianema* and *Hoplosternum;* of these by far the most populous is the genus Corydoras, of which no less than 26 species, described below, are of interest to aquarists. In contrast, the genera *Callichthys* and *Brochis* have only one species each, and *Dianema* and *Hoplosternum* two.
In many respects somewhat strange fish, they are nonetheless appealing, and keeping them can give great pleasure to the amateur aquarist.

542. *Callichthys callichthys*

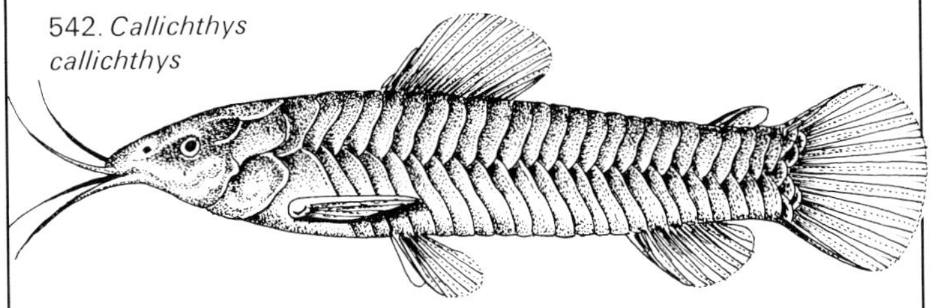

The genus Callichthys

Only one species (although there are a number of local varieties of it), *Callichthys callichthys,* is to be found in this genus, and is described in detail below. It is unusual among catfish in that it builds a foam nest, but like most related species, it is difficult to breed in the aquarium, and amateur aquarists who are willing to devote time to perfecting the techniques for successfully breeding these fish will do a great service to the hobby.

CALLICHTHYS CALLICHTHYS

Family: *Callichthyidae*
Genus: *Callichthys*
English name: Bubble-nest building Catfish
Origin: Almost the whole of tropical South America
Size: Maximum 18 cm
Habitat: Found in fairly shallow, still waters with dense vegetation along the banks

SHAPE, COLORING AND MARKINGS: The body is elongated, almost cylindrical and laterally slightly compressed. The head is wide, with two pairs of barbels. The flanks are armored with two rows of bony plates which overlap. The front rays of the dorsal, pectoral and fairly large adipose fin have developed into strong spines. The basic coloration is usually a plain brownish-grey: there are few if any markings but when the light catches the bony plates of the females they have a metallic sheen. The fins are greyish-brown with light or reddish edges.
Females are less vividly colored. The spines on the pectoral fin are slightly shorter than in the males.
Males are more vividly colored. The spines on the pectoral fin are longer.

GENERAL CARE: *C.callichthys* grows to a considerable size and should be kept in a large aquarium tank with fairly shallow water. The bed should be dark and of fine sand. The vegetation should not include too many fine leaved plants for *C.callichthys* can vigorously stir up the bed when looking for food. An efficient filtering system is also needed for this reason. The fish has a supplementary intestinal respiratory system and can take in air at the surface through its mouth: air, after passing through this supplementary system is expelled through the anus. The composition of the water is not critical. *C.callichthys* needs a temperature of 24°–26°C, although temperatures as low as 18°C will be tolerated for short periods. *C.callichthys* is practically omnivorous: it is no danger to smaller fish but its eating habits make it unsuitable for a well-planted community tank.

BREEDING: The male builds a bubble-nest between plants at the surface: in the wild the nest is often built among clumps of overhanging grass. When the female has laid the eggs, the male guards the nest for a few days until they hatch. When the eggs have hatched both parents ignore the nest and the fry will have to be raised by the breeder. Only the very finest powdered dried foods can be given a first. The best temperature for breeding is about 20°C but fluctuations in temperature may well stimulate the female to lay the eggs.

ADDITIONAL INFORMATION: These fish make good scavengers and although rather shy, are a welcome addition to the aquarium on account of their unusual behavior: when courting, for example, the male can be heard making quite loud grunts.

543. *Brochis splendens*

THE FAMILY CALLICHTHYDAE

The genus Brochis

The fish in this genus are closely related to the species in the genus *Corydoras*: indeed they are identical except for their somewhat deeper bodies, and the greater number of rays in the dorsal fin. In behavior they are no different at all.
Brochis splendens, described below, is the only species likely to be encountered by the amateur aquarist, but another species *Brochis multiradiatus* has very occasionally been imported.

BROCHIS SPLENDENS

Family: *Callichthyidae*

Genus: *Brochis*

English name: none

Origin: Brazil, the upper reaches of the Amazon: Peru, near Iquitos, in the river Ucayali

Size: Maximum 9 cm (females) 7.5 cm (males)

Habitat: Found in sluggish waters with dense vegetation on the banks

---

SHAPE, COLORING AND MARKINGS: The body is sturdy, elongated and laterally very compressed. The head, flanks and pectoral region are covered with bony plates: those on the flanks join at the back and the upper and lower rows overlap. Strong spines lie at the front of the dorsal, pectoral and adipose fins. The snout has two pairs of barbels. The basic coloration is a shiny metallic blue or emerald green, depending on the way the light catches it. *B.splendens* has a supplementary respiratory system similar to that of *Callichthys callichthys.* At first sight *B.splendens* looks like members of the genus *Corydoras* but is easily distinguished by its armored snout and large dorsal fin.
Females when adult have more rounded bellies and are larger than the males.
Males are more slender than females and smaller.

GENERAL CARE: *B.splendens* should be kept in a small group of its own kind in a fairly large tank with a dark soft bed and plenty of hiding places. The only suitable vegetation is clumps of coarse leaved plants. The composition of the water is not critical: temperature about 24°C. Small live animal matter and dried food will be accepted but this diet must be supplemented with some vegetable matter.

BREEDING: The first reports of successful breeding are as recent as 1972. The species tank contained two females and three males and was equipped and maintained as suggested above. Each female mated with one of the males near the bed. The eggs were laid in the folded pectoral fin of the female and fertilised about 10 at a time in the manner of the *Corydoras* species: the eggs were then taken one by one to different places in the tank and stuck there: floating plants on the surface *(Riccia fluitans)* were particularly favored. The eggs were gathered and placed in breeding tanks with different waters but it was later evident that the composition of the water had no effect on the time or likelihood of hatching. An adult female will lay 300 or more eggs. The eggs hatch after about four days at 24°C. The fry do not resemble the adult fish: they have an unusually high dorsal fin and bear a pattern of dark marks and stripes on a light background. The characteristic emerald green sheen only develops when the fry have grown to 35 mm. After two months they are some 40 mm and after six months about 50 mm. When the fry begin the swim freely they must be fed on the finest powdered dried food and freshly hatched *Artemia nauplii.* After about four days they can be fed on micro-eels and later with Grindal worms and finely chopped *Enchytrae.*

ADDITIONAL INFORMATION: *B.splendens* is also known as *B.corerulus.*

THE FAMILY CALLICHTHYIDAE

The genus Corydoras

The most populous genus in the family *Callichthyidae*. There are over 100 species of *Corydoras* that have been described by biologists, but of these, the 26 described below are alone of interest to aquarists, and it is very likely that many of the so-called species are in truth no more than local varieties.

Some authorities tend to class these fish in groups: those of *C.aeneus, C.barbartus, C.paleatus* and *C.punctatus,* based on common physical characteristics or provenance. However, these details of classification hardly concern the amateur.

Some species in this genus have acquired considerable popularity in recent years, and deservedly so, for they are on the whole hardy fish, some can be bred without too much difficulty, and some are extremely beautiful.

CORYDORAS AENEUS

Family: *Callichthyidae*

Genus: *Corydoras*

English name: Bronze Catfish

Origin: Venezuela, the Guianas, Brazil, to the basin of the river Plate

Size: Maximum 7 cm

Habitat: Found in sluggish creeks with clear water

SHAPE, COLORING AND MARKINGS: The body is stocky with a double row of bony plates which overlap. The mouth is small, upper-positioned and with three pairs of barbels. The basic coloration is yellowish or a soft reddish-brown with, on the head and flanks, a striking metallic sheen which, depending on how the light catches it is green or a shiny iridescent gold. A dark wedge-shaped patch lies on the shoulders. The fins are unmarked.
Females are sturdier and larger, with a more rounded dorsal fin.
Males are smaller with a more pointed dorsal fin.

GENERAL CARE: *C.aeneus* is suitable for large aquariums and should be kept in a small group of its own kind even though it is not really a shoal fish. It has few special requirements as to the furnishing of the tank: rocks and wood are both suitable decorations. Fine leaved plants should be avoided because of this species' habit of stirring up the bed. The composition of the water is not critical but

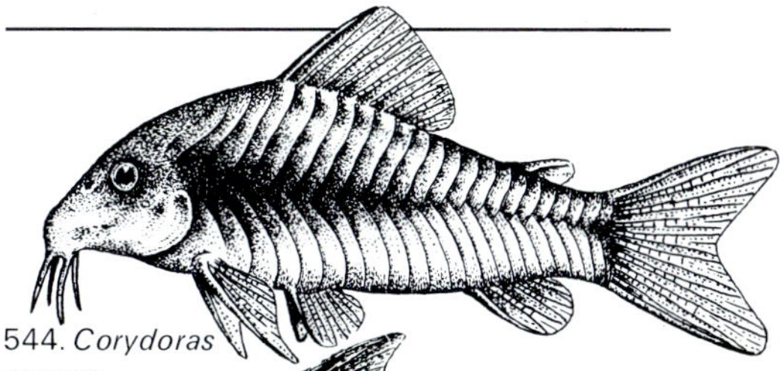

544. *Corydoras aeneus*

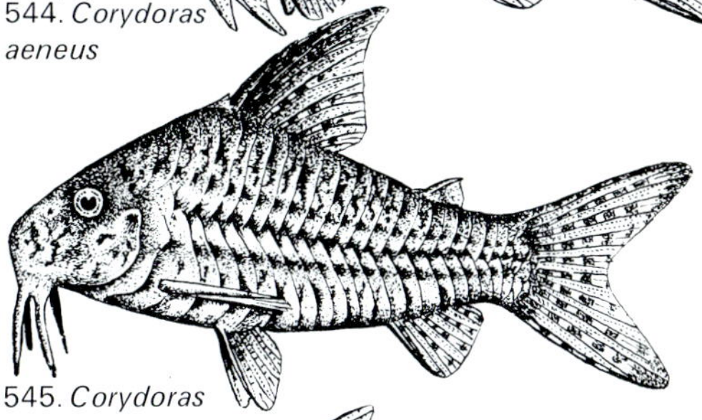

545. *Corydoras agassizi*

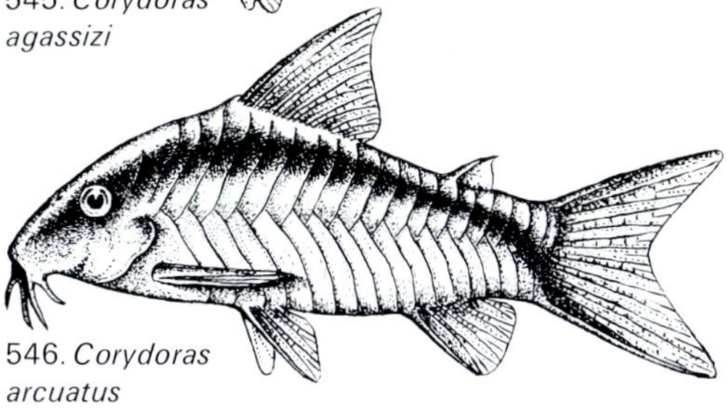

546. *Corydoras arcuatus*

it should not be acid. Temperature 18°–26° C. *C.aeneus* keeps to the bottom of the tank but occasionally will swim to the surface to take in air through its secondary intestinal respiratory system. It is a peaceful fish that can be kept with both smaller and larger species *C.aeneus* is omnivorous but has a preference for worm-like food such as Tubifex, Enchytrae and red mosquito larvae.

BREEDING: A fairly large breeding tank is required. The water should be about pH 7: temperature 24° C. The eggs will be laid on the leaves of plants and hatch in about six days. The fry are free swimming after about eight days and should be fed on *Artemia nauplii*.

ADDITIONAL INFORMATION: A popular species which was first imported in 1933.

CORYDORAS AGASSIZI

Family: *Callichthyidae*

Genus: *Corydoras*

English name: Agassiz's Corydoras

Origin: Western Brazil, the Amazon basin

Size: Maximum 5 cm

Habitat: Found in sluggish creeks with clear alkaline water

SHAPE, COLORING AND MARKINGS: The body is stocky with a double row of bony plates which overlap. The mouth is small, under-positioned with two pairs of barbels. The basic coloration is ochre with a silvery sheen: the back is fawn. Between the gill covers and the caudal peduncle are dark marks arranged in three bands separated from each other by distinctly paler areas. A large number of more or less semi-circular marks are scattered over the entire body. The fins are greyish and transparent. The dorsal, anal and caudal fins have brown dots: the first rays of the dorsal fin are dark brown or black.
There are no known external sexual characteristics.

GENERAL CARE: As for *C.aeneus*.

BREEDING: This species has not as yet been bred in captivity.

ADDITIONAL INFORMATION: A little-known species although first imported in 1936.

CORYDORAS ARCUATUS

Family: *Callichthyidae*

Genus: *Corydoras*

English name: Arched Corydoras

Origin: Brazil, the Amazon basin, in the neighborhood of Tefé

Size: Maximum 5 cm

Habitat: Found in sluggish creeks with clear alkaline water

SHAPE, COLORING AND MARKINGS: The body is stocky, with a double row of bony plates which overlap. The mouth is small, under-positioned and with two pairs of barbels. The basic coloration is a dull yellow to dull green: the underside is white. A wide but gradually narrowing dark band runs along the body from the snout: it goes through the eye, follows the contour of the back, turns down sharply on the caudal peduncle and continues into the lower rays of the caudal fin. The fins are colorless and transparent but in some specimens the upper edge of the caudal fin is dark.
There are no known external sexual characteristics.

GENERAL CARE: As for *C.aeneus* but temperature 22°–26° C.

BREEDING: This species has not as yet been bred in captivity.

ADDITIONAL INFORMATION: *C.arcuatus* is a very active fish in the aquarium. One of the more popular armored catfish, it was first imported in 1938.

CORYDORAS BARBATUS

Family: *Callichthyidae*

Genus: *Corydoras*

English name: Banded Corydoras

Origin: Brazil, between Santos and Rio de Janeiro

Size: Maximum 10 cm

Habitat: Found in sluggish and fairly fast flowing clear alkaline waters

---

547. *Corydoras aeneus*

548. *Corydoras barbatus*

SHAPE, COLORING AND MARKINGS: *C.barbatus* has a body that is more elongated than that of related species, but otherwise it is very similar to them. There is a double row of bony plates which overlap. The mouth is small, under-positioned with two pairs of barbels. The basic coloration is a shiny, yellow-brown, with a beautiful golden sheen on the lower half of the body. The underside is pale yellow to white: the flanks carry beautiful brownish-black or yellow-brown marks: two very decorative golden-yellow iridescent patches lie behind the dorsal fins. A large number of shiny bronze marks and flecks appear on the dark head and cheeks. The dorsal, caudal and anal fins have rows of brown dots.
Females have more rounded dorsal fins.
Males have cheeks covered with bristles: the dorsal fin is more pointed: the pectoral fins are more powerfully developed.

GENERAL CARE: As for *C.aeneus* but temperature 22°–26° C. In addition to arrangements of rock and wood, there should be a generous layer of fine river sand on the bed, for *C.barbatus* likes to burrow in the bed and sometimes digs itself in completely.

BREEDING: Nothing is known about the reproductive behavior of this species.

ADDITIONAL INFORMATION: This extremely beautiful species is still relatively unknown. It was first imported in 1932.

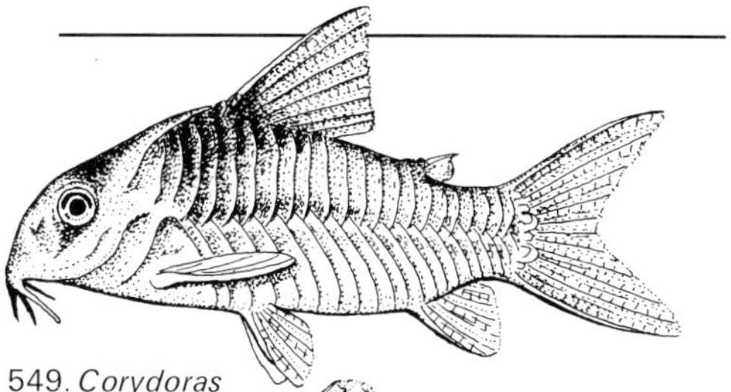

549. *Corydoras bicolor*

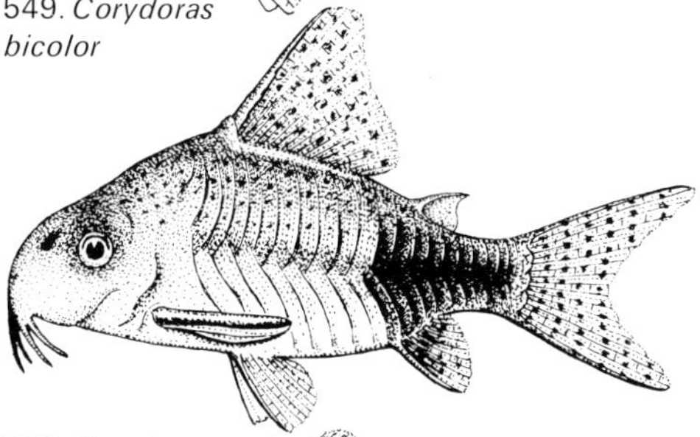

550. *Corydoras caudimaculatus*

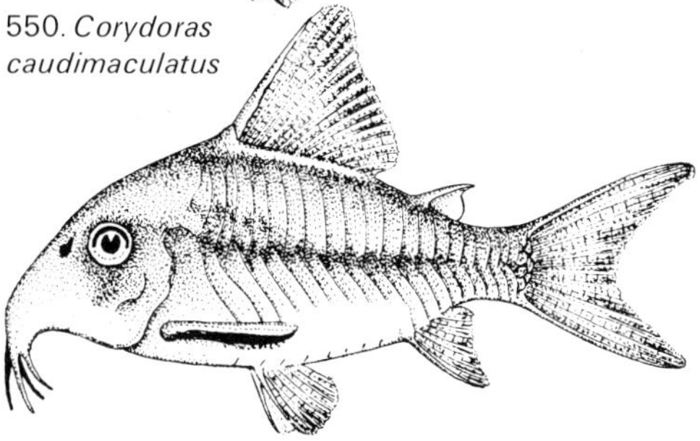

551. *Corydoras concolor*

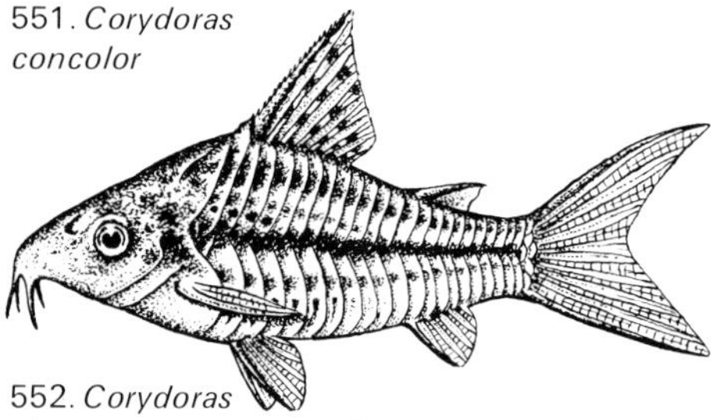

552. *Corydoras elegans*

553. *Corydoras funnelli*

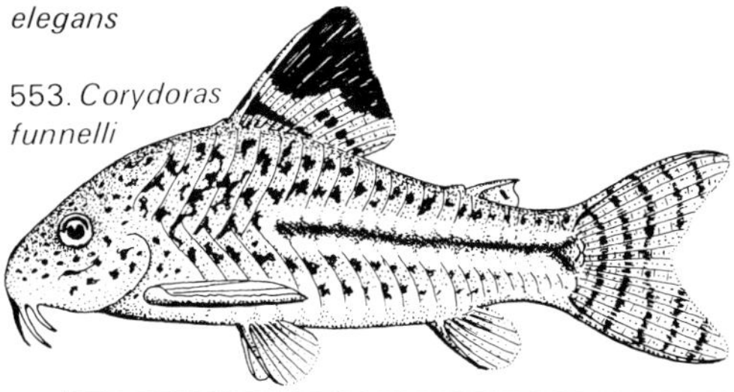

CORYDORAS BICOLOR

Family: *Callichthyidae*

Genus: *Corydoras*

English name: none

Origin: Surinam, in the basin of the river Corantijn, in the Sipaliwini river

Size: Approximately 3 cm

Habitat: Found in flowing waters

SHAPE, COLORING AND MARKINGS: The body is stocky with a double row of bony plates which overlap: there are 23 plates in the upper row and 20–21 in the lower. No descriptions are available of living specimens: those which have been preserved in alcohol have a basic coloration that is yellowish-brown: the underside and throat are off-white. A dark brown patch below the dorsal fin runs into the base of that fin. A dark brown cone-shaped mark surrounds the eyes. Where the rows of bony plates divide the upper plates are darkly pigmented. All the fins are greyish-white except for the dorsal fin which is dark at the base.
There are no known external sexual characteristics.

GENERAL CARE: Nothing is known of the lifestyle of *C.bicolor* but it is likely that it would require the same care as *C.aeneus* with a temperature probably of 22°–26° C.

BREEDING: Nothing is known of the reproductive behavior of this species.

ADDITIONAL INFORMATION: *C.bicolor* is closely related to the popular *C.melanistius* from British Guyana from which it can be distinguished by the absence of dots on the head and body. It was first described in 1967.

CORYDORAS CAUDIMACULATUS

Family: *Callichthyidae*

Genus: *Corydoras*

English name: none

Origin: Brazil, the Mato Grosso

Size: Approximately 6 cm

Habitat: Found in sluggish and still waters such as pools and lakes in the tropical rain forests

SHAPE, COLORING AND MARKINGS: The body is stocky and unusually deep. The mouth is under-positioned with two pairs of barbels. There are two rows of bony plates that overlap. The basic coloration is a greyish-brown: the lower half of the body is more yellowish. On the dark areas of the head and back brown dots are arranged in diagonal or horizontal lines. An ill-defined dark patch lies between the eyes: a large black mark, extending to the base of the dorsal fin, lies on the caudal peduncle, beginning a little to the fore of the spine on the adipose fin. Dark dots appear on the unpaired fins: on the caudal fin these form six transverse bands.
There are no known external sexual characteristics.

GENERAL CARE: As for *C.aeneus.*

BREEDING: This species has not as yet been bred in captivity.

CORYDORAS CONCOLOR

Family: *Callichthyidae*

Genus: *Corydoras*

English name: none

Origin: Southern Venezuela

Size: Approximately 4.5 cm

Habitat: Found in sluggish and still waters such as the lakes and pools of tropical rain forests

SHAPE, COLORING AND MARKINGS: The body is stocky and unusually deep. The eyes are very large. The mouth is under-positioned with two pairs of barbels. There are two rows of bony plates. There are no descriptions available of living specimens but those preserved in alcohol have a basic coloration that is mainly a clear brown, the upper part of the body and the head being a little darker. The lower part of the snout and the belly are white: some brownish pigmentation appears on the flanks, mainly where the two rows of bony plates divide. Some brown marks appear on the head and gill covers.

554. *Corydoras elegans*

There are no known external sexual characteristics.

General care: As for *C.bicolor*.

Breeding: Nothing is known about the reproductive behavior of this species.

CORYDORAS ELEGANS

Family: *Callichthyidae*
Genus: *Corydoras*
English name: none
Origin: Brazil, the middle Amazon region
Size: Maximum 6 cm
Habitat: Found in sluggish creeks with celar alkaline water

Shape, coloring and markings: The body is stocky with two rows of bony plates that overlap: there are 21–22 in the upper row, 20 in the lower. The small under-positioned mouth has two pairs of barbels. The basic coloration is yellowish: the back is darker or ochre: the underside is yellowish-white. The top of the head has greyish-brown marks which become a cone-shaped horizontal stripe of regular marks at the level of the first dorsal fin rays. Below lies a sharply contrasting light patch which, in turn, is bordered by a number of less prominent marks which merge into a dark horizontal stripe at the level of the spine on the dorsal fin and stretch across the flank into the base of the caudal fin: parallel to this stripe is a row of dark marks, below which on the first four to six bony plates are sharply contrasting cone-shaped marks. The lower half of the body is a light yellow becoming off-white towards the belly. The gill covers are an iridescent blue. The fins are grey and transparent: only the dorsal fin in some specimens carries any marks. The first spine of the dorsal fin has a row of very small teeth-like indentations along the front.
There are no known external sexual characteristics.

General care: As for *C.aeneus*.

Breeding: Nothing is known about the reproductive behavior of this species.

Additional information: *C.elegans* does not seem to have been imported since 1938. The color pattern noted above, drawn from a preserved specimen may not be accurate: a totally different color pattern has sometimes been given for *C.elegans*.

CORYDORAS FUNNELLI

Family: *Callichthyidae*
Genus: *Corydoras*
Origin: No information is available on the origin or natural habitat of this species
Size: Approximately 5.5 cm

Shape, coloring and markings: The body is stocky though less so than in related species. There are two rows of bony plates that overlap. The mouth is under-positioned with two pairs of barbels. The basic coloration is grey. A dark horizontal stripe runs from about the middle of the dorsal fin to the base of the caudal fin where it becomes cone-shaped. Above and below lie lighter patches of equal width. Dark irregular marks lie roughly in lines on the flanks, and similar but smaller marks appear on the head. The dorsal fin has a large prominent dark mark and a dark band running half way across it from the first fin ray: other dark patches lie to the back of the fin. A small diagonal mark appears on the adipose fin and five dark transverse bands lie on the caudal fin. The other fins are colorless. The iris is black.
There are no known external sexual characteristics.

General care: As for *C.aeneus* but *C.funnelli* is also suitable for smaller tanks.

Breeding: Nothing is known of the reproductive behavior of this species.

CORYDORAS GRISEUS

Family: *Callichthyidae*
Genus: *Corydoras*
English name: none
Origin: Brazil in the region of the Amazon
Size: Maximum 5 cm
Habitat: Found in small streams with clear alkaline water

Shape, coloring and markings: The body is stocky with a double row of bony plates which overlap. The small under-positioned mouth has two pairs of barbels. The basic coloration is a dull yellow. A dark transverse band across the head runs through the eyes and completely surrounds them. A dark herring-bone pattern is formed on the body by the dark edges of the bony plates: the junction of the plates shows up as a dark horizontal stripe running into the caudal peduncle. The fins are colorless, transparent and without any marks.
There are no known external sexual characteristics.

General care: As for *C.aeneus* but temperature 18°–22° C.

Breeding: Nothing is known about the reproductive behavior of this species.

ADDITIONAL INFORMATION: Descriptions of *C.griseus* vary considerably: it may be that there are a number of sub-species or the color patterns may change from locality to locality.

CORYDORAS GUIANENSIS

Family: *Callichthyidae*

Genus: *Corydoras*

English name: none

Origin: Surinam, around Brokopondo, in the basin of the river Saramacca

Size: Approximately 4 cm

Habitat: Found over a wide area in alkaline waters

SHAPE, COLORING AND MARKINGS: The body is stocky and unusually deep. There are two rows of bony plates that overlap: there are 23–24 plates in the upper row, 20–21 in the lower. No descriptions are available of living specimens but those preserved in alcohol have a basic coloration of yellowish-brown: the upper half of the head is brown: the deep back and upper part of the caudal peduncle are dark brown and this color becomes progressively lighter, or greyish-white, towards the underside of the body. The dorsal and pectoral fins are brownish, usually with a darker base. The other fins are grey.
There are no known external sexual characteristics.

GENERAL CARE: As for *C.aeneus.*

BREEDING: Nothing is known about the reproductive behavior of this species.

ADDITIONAL INFORMATION: A new species first described in 1970.

CORYDORAS HASTATUS

Family: *Callichthyidae*

Genus: *Corydoras*

English names: Dwarf Corydoras and Pigmy Corydoras

Origin: Bolivia, the Amazon basin around Villa Bella

Size: Maximum 3 cm

Habitat: Only found in freshwater areas

SHAPE, COLORING AND MARKINGS: The body is stocky with two rows of bony plates that overlap: there are 22 plates in the upper row, and 20 in the lower. The basic coloration is a greyish-green to golden-yellow: the back is slightly darker: the flanks are yellow: the belly whitish. The whole body, including the head and fins, is covered with small dark marks. A horizontal dark line runs from the snout through the eyes to the caudal peduncle where it becomes a roughly lozenge-shaped mark bordered above and below by a patch of gold. A second dark horizontal line runs above the anal fin: in well-marked specimens a number of dark marks appear above the pectoral fins. All the fins are greyish and transparent: the lower caudal fin rays have a dark pigmentation.
There are no known external sexual characteristics.

GENERAL CARE: As for *C.aeneus* but *C.hastatus* only really thrives when kept in a fairly large group of its own kind. Temperature 23°–26°C. *C.hastatus* is less inclined than related species to keep to the bottom of the tank and does not wallow in the bed.

BREEDING: As for *C.aeneus.*

563. *Corydoras hastatus*

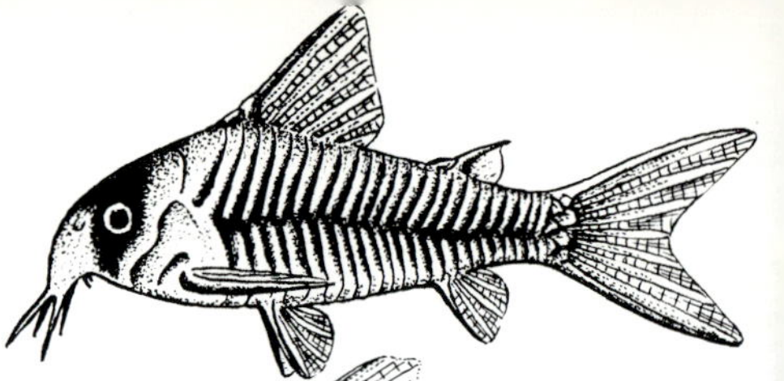

555. *Corydoras griseus*

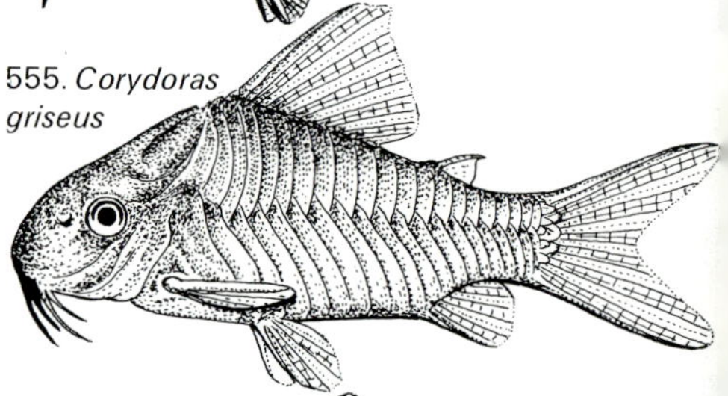

556. *Corydoras guianensis*

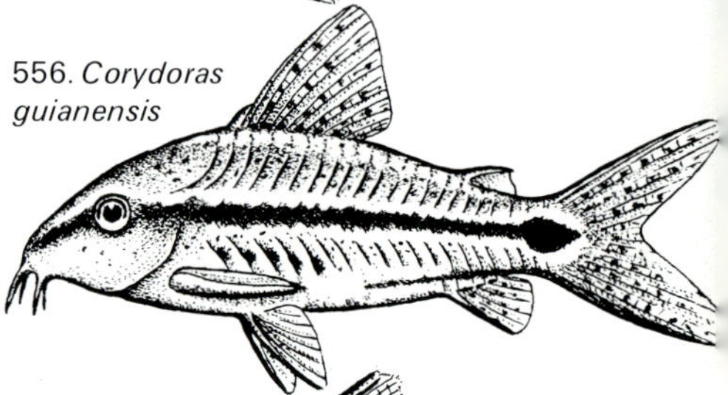

557. *Corydoras hastatus*

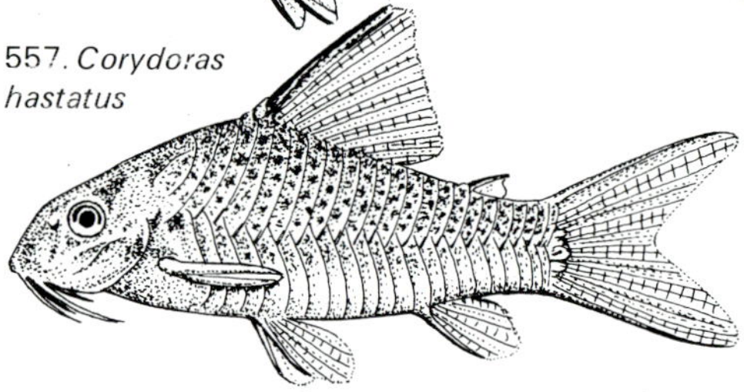

558. *Corydoras heteromorphis*

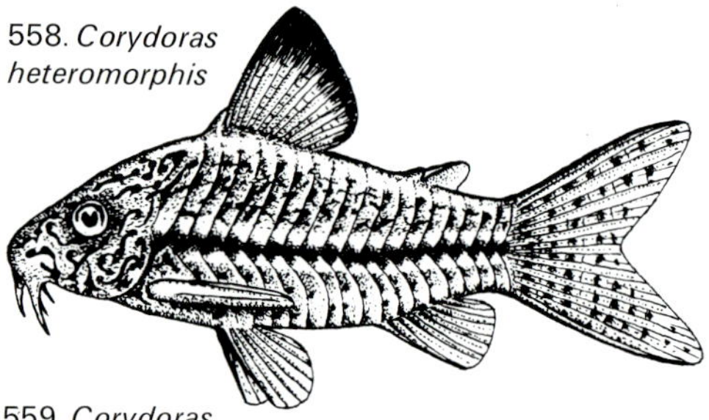

559. *Corydoras jullii*

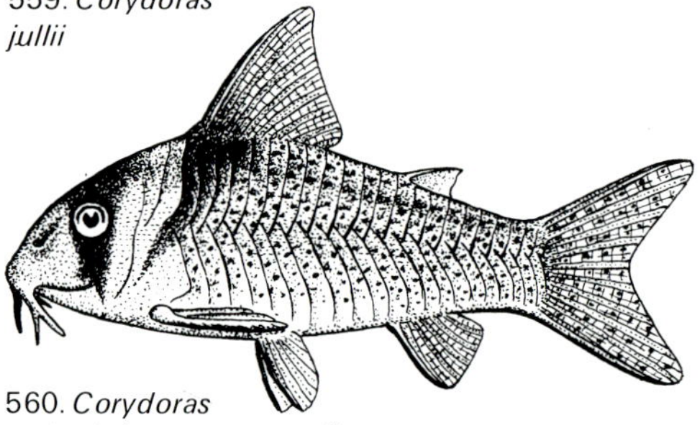

560. *Corydoras melanistius*

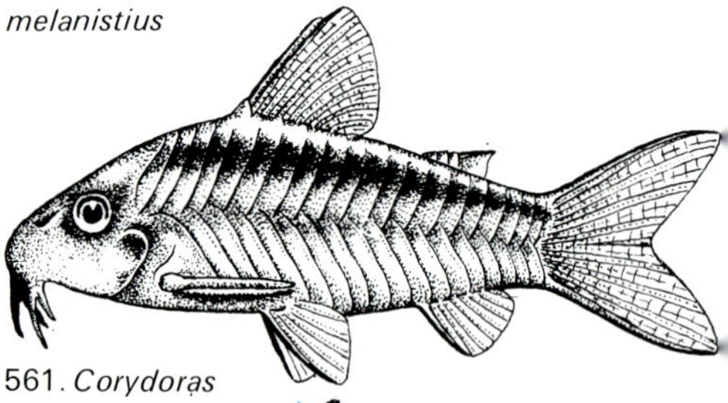

561. *Corydoras meyersi*

562. *Corydoras nanus*

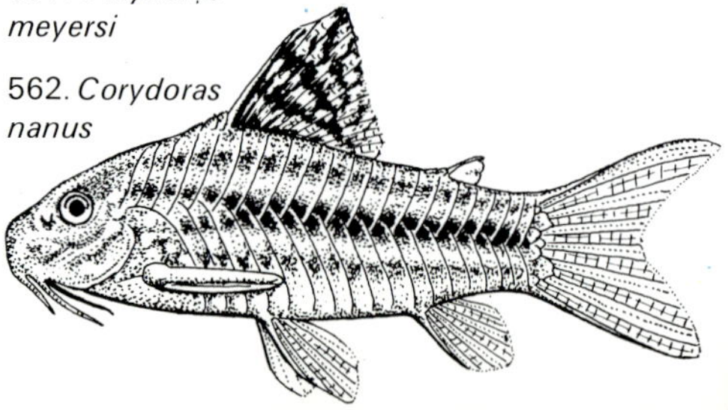

564. *Corydoras melanistius*

565. *Corydoras myersi*

ADDITIONAL INFORMATION: A well-known species first imported in 1912.

CORYDORAS HETEROMORPHUS

Family: *Callichthyidae*

Genus: *Corydoras*

English name: none

Origin: Surinam around Saramacca in the basin of the Coppename river

Size: Approximately 5 cm

Habitat: Found in sluggish alkaline waters

SHAPE, COLORING AND MARKINGS: The body is stocky and unusually deep. There are two rows of bony plates which overlap: in the upper row there are 24–25 plates, in the lower 21–22. No descriptions are available of living specimens but those preserved in alcohol have a basic coloration that is yellowish-brown. Small grey-brown flecks appear on the head and upper part of the body and these, lying regularly over the bony plates appear as diagonal stripes particularly under the dorsal fin. The spine and front rays of the otherwise colorless dorsal fin are greyish. There is some pigmentation in the outer rays of the caudal fin and sometimes marks on the center area as well. The anal and ventral fins are yellowish-brown.
There are no known external sexual characteristics.

GENERAL CARE: As for *C.aeneus*.

BREEDING: Nothing is known of the reproductive behavior of this species.

ADDITIONAL INFORMATION: A new species first described in 1970.

CORYDORAS JULLII

Family: *Callichthyidae*

Genus: *Corydoras*

English name: Leopard Corydoras

Origin: Eastern Brazil

Size: Maximum 6 cm

Habitat: Found exclusively in fresh waters

SHAPE, COLORING AND MARKINGS: The body is stocky with a double row of bony plates which overlap: there are 22 in the upper row and 21 in the lower. The basic coloration is silvery-grey. The whole body is flecked with small dark marks which run together to form zig-zag lines, especially on the head and upper half of the body. On the dividing line between the upper and lower bony plates there is a dark horizontal line which runs from the gill covers to the caudal peduncle, bordered above and below by a shiny silvery patch. In bright light the whole of the fish is covered with a soft greenish metallic sheen. The fins are silvery-grey and transparent: the dorsal fin has a wide black edge: the caudal fin has rows of small dark marks.
There are no known external sexual characteristics.

GENERAL CARE: As for *C.aeneus*, but temperature 20°–26°C.

BREEDING: *C.jullii* has been bred in captivity: see *C.aeneus*.

ADDITIONAL INFORMATION: The fish described in many books on aquariums as *C.leopardus* closely resembles *C.jullii* and is, probably a sub-species.

CORYDORAS MELANISTIUS

Family: *Callichthyidae*

Genus: *Corydoras*

English name: Black-Spotted Corydoras

Origin: Northern South America

Size: Maximum 6 cm

Habitat: Found only in fresh waters

SHAPE, COLORING AND MARKINGS: The body is stocky with a double row of bony plates that overlap: there are 21–23 in the upper row and 19–20 in the lower. The basic coloration is yellowish-white to grey with a soft reddish tinge. A large number of brown specks are scattered at random over the whole body. One very dark cone-shaped mark runs from the neck through the eye to the edge of the gill covers: a second mark runs from the front dorsal fin rays to the base of the pectoral fins. The fins are greyish and transparent: the caudal and anal fins have dark specks.
There no known external sexual characteristics.

GENERAL CARE: As for *C.aeneus* but temperature 22°–26°C.

BREEDING: *C.melanistius* has been bred in captivity: see *C.aeneus*.

ADDITIONAL INFORMATION: *C.melanistius* is very active at the bottom of the tank. Closely related to *C.bicolor* (under which species see for differences in the color pattern of the two species *C.melanistius* was first imported in 1934.
C.wotroi may be a sub-species of *C.melanistius*.

CORYDORAS MYERSI

Family: *Callichthyidae*

Genus: *Corydoras*

English name: Myer's Corydoras

Origin: The upper reaches of the Amazon

Size: Maximum 6 cm

Habitat: Found only in fresh waters

SHAPE, COLORING AND MARKINGS: The body is stocky with a double row of bony plates which overlap: there are 22–23 plates in the upper row and 20–21 in the lower. The basic coloration is a beautiful orange-red, tinged with black here and there. The throat and belly are lighter, or yellowish. A dark brown band stretches from the front dorsal fin rays into the upper part of the caudal peduncle. Attractive green iridescent patches lie on the gill covers: the eyes are surrounded by a dark brown patch. The fins are light grey, transparent and without marks.
There are no known external sexual characteristics.

GENERAL CARE: As for *C.aeneus* but temperature 24°–28°C. *C.myersi* is unusually sensitive to fluctuations in temperature and cannot tolerate low temperatures. The attractive colors are only shown to advantage when the fish feels at home in a fairly large shoal.

BREEDING: Nothing is known about the reproductive behavior of this species.

ADDITIONAL INFORMATION: A relatively new species, first imported in 1954. Often confused with *C.rabauti*.

CORYDORAS NANUS

Family: *Callichthyidae*

Genus: *Corydoras*

English name: none

Origin: Surinam, the basin of the Marowijne river

Size: Approximately 4 cm

Habitat: Found in fresh water streams

SHAPE, COLORING AND MARKINGS: The body is stocky with a double row of bony plates which overlap: there are 23–24 in the upper row and 20–21 in the lower. No descriptions are available of living specimens but preserved specimens have a basic coloration of yellowish-brown. A dark Y-shaped line lies across the body: one arm runs from the neck to the dorsal fin, the other arm begins at the base of the pectoral fin and joins the first arm at the dorsal fin to run, as a single line into the caudal peduncle. Two less prominent horizontal stripes follow the dividing line between the upper and lower rows of plates, but are separated from that line by paler zones. A dark patch lies above and around the eyes. The ventral and dorsal fins are reddish-brown: the caudal, anal and pectoral fins are greyish.
Females are as described above.
Males have irregular dark marks on the dorsal fin.

GENERAL CARE: As for *C.aeneus*.

BREEDING: Nothing is known of the reproductive behavior of this species.

ADDITIONAL INFORMATION: *C.nanus* is a recently identified species, first described in 1967.

566. *Corydoras paleatus*

CORYDORAS NATTERERI

Family: *Callichthyidae*

Genus: *Corydoras*

English name: none

Origin: Eastern Brazil from Rio de Janeiro to the river Doce

Size: Maximum 6.5 cm

Habitat: Found only in fresh waters

SHAPE, COLORING AND MARKINGS: The body is stocky with a double row of bony plates which overlap: there are 21–23 in the upper row and 20–21 in the lower. The basic coloration is brown: the back is darker, tinged with green: the flanks are a beautiful iridescent blue: the belly is yellow to soft orange. A more or less cone-shaped horizontal line runs from the gill covers to the caudal peduncle. A dark, ill-defined mark lies under the first dorsal fin rays. The fins are greyish and transparent: sometimes irregular dark marks appear on the dorsal fin.
There are no known external sexual characteristics.

GENERAL CARE: As for *C.aeneus* but temperature 18°–20°C. *C.nattereri* shows clear symptoms of distress at temperatures above 24°C but, because of its tolerance to low temperatures is an easy species to keep.

BREEDING: *C.nattereri* has been bred in captivity: see *C.aeneus*.

ADDITIONAL INFORMATION: A very active species in the aquarium. First imported in 1920.

CORYDORAS PALEATUS

Family: *Callichthyidae*

Genus: *Corydoras*

English name: Peppered Corydoras

Origin: Northern South America, especially the rivers Plate, Grande del Sol and Catarina

Size: Maximum 7 cm

Habitat: Found only in fresh waters

SHAPE, COLORING AND MARKINGS: The body is stocky, with a double row of bony plates which overlap: there are 22–24 in the upper row and 20–22 in the lower. The basic coloration is light brown: the back is darker, or greenish: the flanks are yellowish-green: tinged with a metallic sheen: the belly is yellowish or off-white. The whole body is covered with small dark flecks: on the back and flanks appear large irregular black marks which often merge to form irregular transverse bands. The fins are greyish: the unpaired fins have dark flecks.
Females are larger and sturdier than the males.

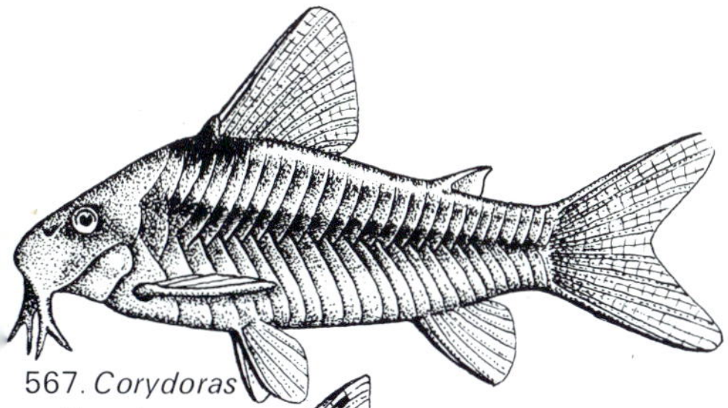

567. *Corydoras nattereri*

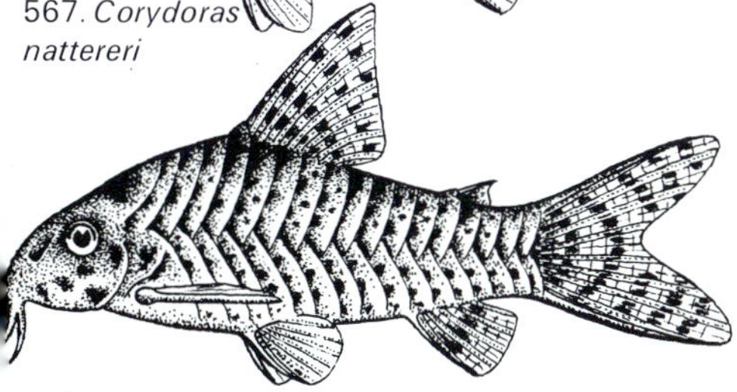

568. *Corydoras paleatus*

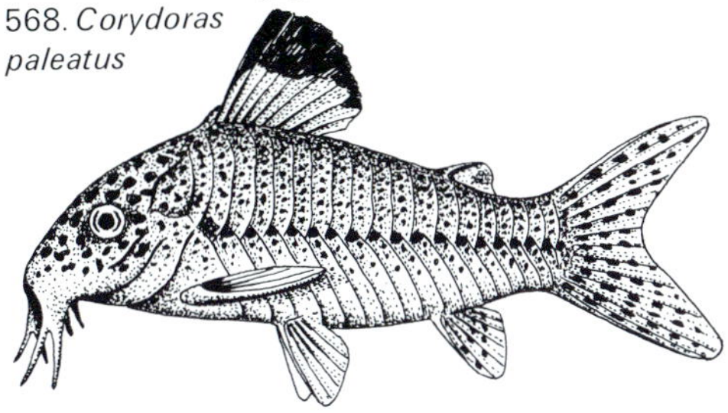

569. *Corydoras punctatus*

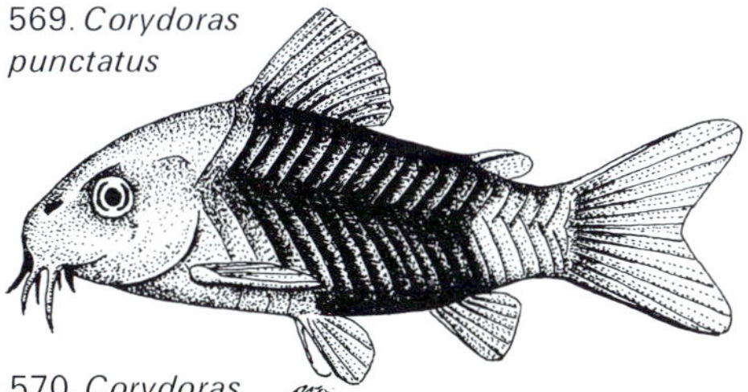

570. *Corydoras rabauti*

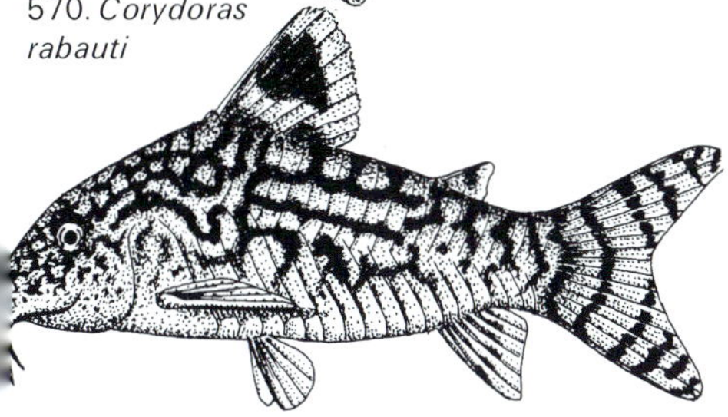

571. *Corydoras reticulatus*

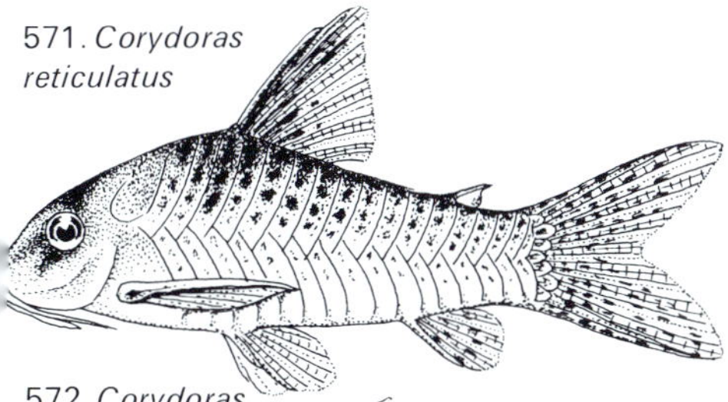

572. *Corydoras saramaccensis*

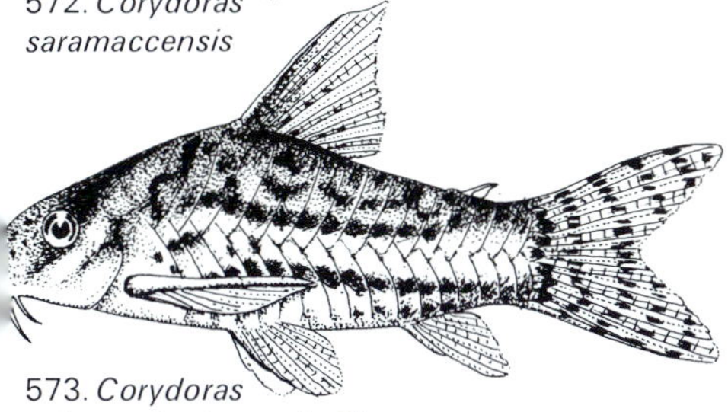

573. *Corydoras schwartzi schwartzi*

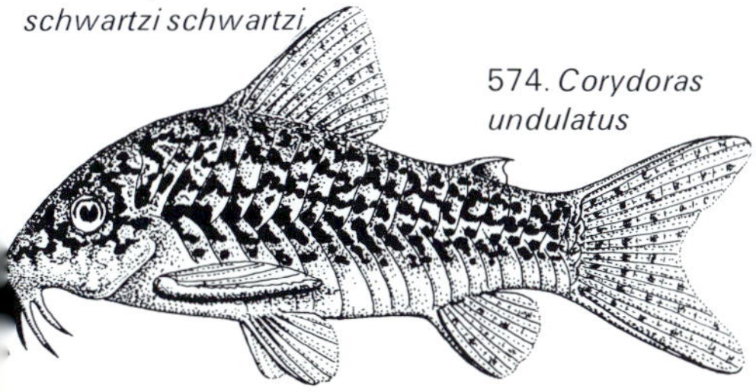

574. *Corydoras undulatus*

Males are more slender and smaller: the dorsal fin is more pointed, the pectoral fins are more strongly developed.

GENERAL CARE: As for *C.aeneus* but temperature 18°–20°C and certainly no higher than 23°C.

BREEDING: This is not difficult at 22°–26°C. See *C.aeneus*.

ADDITIONAL INFORMATION: A fairly well-known species that can live in the aquarium to a very advanced age: it has been bred in aquariums for nearly a century.

CORYDORAS PUNCTATUS

Family: *Callichthyidae*

Genus: *Corydoras*

English name: none

Origin: The basins of the Amazon, Essequibo and Orinoco rivers

Size: Maximum 6 cm

Habitat: No further details are available of its natural habitat

SHAPE, COLORING AND MARKINGS: The body is stocky with a double row of bony plates which overlap: there are 22–24 in the upper row and 20–21 in the lower. The basic coloration varies from grey to greyish-yellow. Countless small dark flecks lie close together over the whole body and are largest on the head. On the dividing line between the rows of plates a series of cone-shaped marks form a dark line across the body. The fins are grey and transparent: the dorsal fin has a dark edge, the adipose fin a dark mark and the caudal and anal fins, rows of dark flecks. *C.punctatus* closeley resembles *C.funnelli* but has no black iris.
There are no known external sexual characteristics.

GENERAL CARE: As for *C.aeneus* but temperature 20°–26°C.

BREEDING: This species has been bred successfully in captivity: see *C.aeneus*.

ADDITIONAL INFORMATION: A widely-known species first described in 1794.

CORYDORAS RABAUTI

Family: *Callichthyidae*

Genus: *Corydoras*

English names: Rabaut's Corydoras and Dwarf Corydoras

Origin: The Amazon, in the region of Manãos

Size: Approximately 3 cm

Habitat: No further details are available of its natural habitat

SHAPE, COLORING AND MARKINGS: The body is stocky with a double row of bony plates which overlap. The most distinctive feature

575. *Corydoras Schwartzi schwartzi*

of this very small species is the bluish-black band which runs round almost the whole body. The head and neck are orangey-yellow to the first dorsal fin rays: the same color is present between the upper edge of the gill covers and the front ventral fin rays. The dark band on the body ends in a wedge on the caudal peduncle where it is bordered by a yellowish-orange patch. All the fins, except for the caudal fin, are a soft orange: the dorsal and ventral fins are slightly darker than the others.
There are no known external sexual characteristics.

General care: *C.rabauti* is suitable for small tanks but should always be kept in a large group of its own kind. Conditions as for *C.aeneus* but temperature 20°–26° C. It is so small that other fish may well mistake it for prey and it should therefore not be kept with larger fish or less peaceful species.

Breeding: Nothing is known about the reproductive behavior of this species.

Additional information: *C.rabauti* is often mistakenly described as *C.myersi* and vice versa. First described in 1941, *C.rabauti* is still rarely imported.

CORYDORAS RETICULATUS

Family: *Callichthyidae*

Genus: *Corydoras*

English name: Reticulated Corydoras

Origin: The Amazon, in the neighborhood of Monte Alegre

Size: Maximum 7 cm

Habitat: Found only in fresh water

Shape, coloring and markings: The body is stocky with a double row of bony plates which overlap. There are 22 on the upper row and 21 on the lower. The basic coloration is reddish, tinged with a beautiful strong iridescent green. Curious dark brown or black marks, reminiscent of Arabic script lie on the back, the upper part of the body and on the flanks: they are less distinct on the underside. The belly is off-white or yellowish. Numerous small irregular marks and flecks are scattered over the snout and the front of the head. The fins are colorless and transparent. The dorsal fin has a dark area at the base and a large black mark, usually edged with white, in the center. In older specimens this mark is replaced by a group of random dots. The caudal fin has dark brown or black sickle-shaped marks: a few similar marks appear on the anal fin. Very young specimens of *C.reticulatus* are often very indistinctly marked and thus young fish are frequently incorrectly identified.
Females have less prominent dark marks on the fins and body.
Males are as described above.

General care: As for *C.aeneus* but temperature 20°–26° C. Both fresh tap water and acid water should be avoided.

Breeding: No information is available on the reproductive behavior of this species.

CORYDORAS SARAMACCENSIS

Family: *Callichthyidae*

Genus: *Corydoras*

English name: none

Origin: Surinam, in the Brokopondo district, in the basin of the Saramacca river

Size: Approximately 5 cm

Habitat: Found in clear fresh water streams

Shape, coloring and markings: The body is stocky: the snout almost pointed. There is a double row of bony plates which overlap: there are 25–26 plates in the upper row and 22–23 plates in the lower. No descriptions are available of living specimens but those preserved in alcohol have a basic coloration that is brownish-yellow: a brown mask covers the eyes. An area of brownish pigmentation lies under the dorsal fin, stretching on to the caudal peduncle, below which the patch becomes a series of brown lines. The base and front rays of the dorsal fin are dark: the caudal fin has eight or nine greyish transverse bands.
There are no known external sexual characteristics.

General care: Nothing is known of the life style of *C.saramaccensis* but it is likely to need care as for *C.aeneus*.

Breeding: Nothing is known of the reproductive behavior of this species.

Additional information: A new species first described in 1970.

CORYDORAS SCHWARTZI - SCHWARTZI

Family: *Callichthyidae*

Genus: *Corydoras*

English name: none

Origin: Brazil, in the basin of the river Purus

Size: Approximately 5 cm

Habitat: Found in fresh waters

Shape, coloring and markings: The body is stocky, rather deep and with two rows of bony plates that overlap: there are 22 plates in the upper row and 20 in the lower. The basic coloration is yellowish-brown. A black mask surrounds the eyes: the snout is grey with a few dark horizontal marks. The upper half of the body is brownish with many irregular black marks bordered by an unbroken black line just above the join in the rows of plates: a similar line runs across the lower half of the body. The base and front rays of the dorsal fin are dark. The caudal fin has five, or sometimes four, dark transverse bands: the first crosses the base of the fin, the last runs across the lobes. In some specimens dark marks also appear on the anal fin.
There are no known external sexual characteristics.

General care: As for *C.aeneus,* but temperature 22°–26° C.

Breeding: Nothing is known of the reproductive behavior of this species.

Additional information: First described in 1963: a sub-species, *C.schwartzi surinamensis,* was identified in 1970.

CORYDORAS UNDULATUS

Family: *Callichthyidae*

Genus: *Corydoras*

English name: none

Origin: Eastern South America, in the region of La Plata

Size: Approximately 5.5 cm

Habitat: Found in fresh water streams

Shape, coloring and markings: The body is stocky with two rows of bony plates which overlap: there are 21–23 plates in the upper row and 19–20 in the lower. The mouth is under-positioned with two pairs of barbels. The basic coloration is yellow: the back is yellowish-brown, tinged with green: the flanks are lighter: the underside ochre: the lower surfaces of the head and throat yellowish-white. On the head and back numerous dark marks and small flecks join together to form wavy lines across the body, especially on the flanks. Between these darks marks are green iridescent spots which, on the gill covers, themselves form wavy lines. The unpaired fins, and especially the caudal fin, have dark flecks arranged in regular rows. The other fins are colorless and transparent. There are no generally accepted external sexual characteristics but possibly in males the front tip of the dorsal fin is dark or black.

General care: As for *C.aeneus* but temperature 22°–26° C.

Breeding: Nothing is known about the reproductive behavior of this species.

576. *Corydoras wotroi*

CORYDORAS WOTROI

Family: *Callichthyidae*

Genus: *Corydoras*

English name: none

Origin: Surinam, in the Saramacca river

Size: Approximately 4 cm

Habitat: Found in clear fresh waters

SHAPE, COLORING AND MARKINGS: The body is stocky and deeper than in related species. It has a double row of bony plates which overlap: there are 23–24 in the upper row and 20–21 in the lower. The basic coloration is grey to ochre. A dark mask covers the eyes and stretches to the spine of the dorsal fin, under which lie dark cone-shaped patches. Countless irregular brownish-black marks are scattered over the body but become smaller and less distinct towards the belly. The dorsal fin has a light green or yellow spine and the rays behind that are usually darker, sometimes with irregular flecks. Six or seven irregular transverse bands lie on the caudal fin: the first appears at the base, the last is a broken line across the lobes.
There are no known external sexual characteristics.

GENERAL CARE: As for *C.aeneus*, but temperature 22°–26°C. The use of fresh tap water should be avoided.

BREEDING: Nothing is known of the reproductive behavior of this species.

ADDITIONAL INFORMATION: See *C.melanistus*.

THE FAMILY CALLICHTHYDAE

The genus Hoplosternum

There was a great deal of confusion at one time, over the species in this genus. Many local varieties were raised to the status of separate species, but following a revision of the classification, two certain species remain, *Hoplosternum littorale* and *Hoplosternum thoracatum* described below. Some authorities also still recognize a third species *Hoplosternum magdalenae*, from the region of the Magdalena river in Colombia, but others regard this as a local variety of the two species noted above.

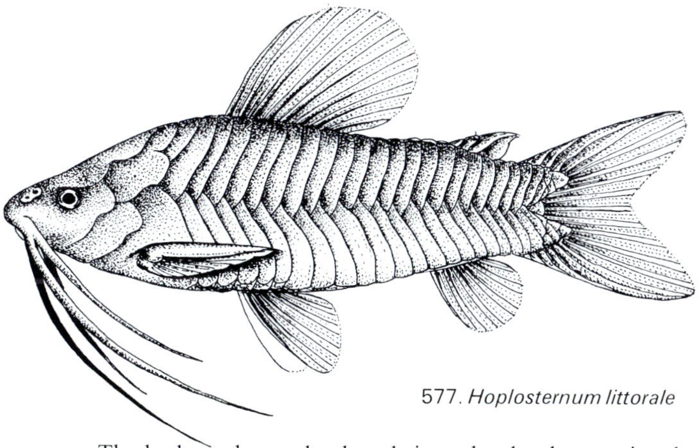

577. *Hoplosternum littorale*

HOPLOSTERNUM LITTORALE

Family: *Callichthyidae*

Genus: *Hoplosternum*

English name: none

Origin: North Brazil, the Guianas, Venezuela

Size: Maximum 20 cm

Habitat: No further details are available of its natural habitat

SHAPE, COLORING AND MARKINGS: The body is elongated and laterally slightly compressed. The line of the back arches upwards from the mouth as far as the base of the dorsal fin: thereafter the body remains the same depth. There are two pairs of barbels, both rather long. The back, flanks and pectoral regions carry bony plates: those on the back are fused with the upper row on the flanks, although the latter can move independently. The front rays of the dorsal, pectoral and adipose fins have developed into hard, sharp-pointed spines. The basic coloration is greenish-black: the flanks are grey or bluish-grey: the colors can vary significantly according to the conditions under which the fish is kept, and its place of origin. *H.littorale* is in consequence, often confused with other species.
Females have less powerfully developed spines on the pectoral fins, and the pectoral region is not entirely covered with armor plates.

Males have more powerfully developed pectoral fin spines and the pectoral region is wholly covered by the armor plates.

General care: As for *Callichthys callichthys* but temperature 24° C.

Breeding: A large breeding tank with shallow water, planted with coarse leaved plants, or plants with floating leaves is required. After a complicated courting ritual, the eggs are laid on the lower side of a large leaf where the male will have made a bubble nest. The large number of eggs are guarded by the male and will hatch after a few days at 28° C. Once the fry have hatched, the male ignores them completely. They fry are not difficult to raise with finely powdered dried food.

HOPLOSTERNUM THORACATUM

Family: *Callichthyidae*

Genus: *Hoplosternum*

English name: none

Origin: Tropical South America from Panama to Paraguay

Size: Maximum 18 cm

Habitat: Found in a variety of waters

Shape, coloring and markings: The body shape and appearance of *H.thoracatum* is virtually identical to that of *H.littorale* but in *H.thoracatum* both pairs of barbels are somewhat shorter. The basic coloration is a brown to greyish-brown, with dark flecks.

Females have a pectoral region which is not fully covered by the bony plates.

Males have a pectoral region wholly covered by the plates.

General care: As for *H.littorale*.

Breeding: As for *H.littorale*.

578. *Hoplosternum thoracatum*

THE FAMILY CLARIDAE

An introductory description

Members of the Clariidae family are found over the whole of Africa and much of Southeast Asia. Many are eel-like in appearance: the skin is quite naked, the head rather flat, the body elongated or torpedo-shaped. All species have an auxiliary breathing system, which not only allows them to survive in poorly oxygenated waters but also exist for some hours out of water. Thus, in their natural habitat these species often come on to dry land at night in search of food and others burrow in the mud during the dry season. They are long lived and robust fish: they are also however very voracious and often predatory.

There are five genera that are from time to time imported and species of which are kept in aquariums, that is, the genera *Channallabes, Clarias, Gymnallabes, Heterobranchus* and *Heteropneustes*. Many of these fish however are too large for the domestic aquarium and in recent years only a few species in the genus *Clarias* have retained their former popularity with amateur aquarists.

The genus Clarias

The species in this genus are torpedo-shaped fish with long-based dorsal and anal fins and well-developed pectoral and ventral fins: unlike species in some related genera however, they have no adipose fin. They are all endowed with the remarkable and unusual facility of moving across dry land, with the assistance of their fins, and sometimes cover quite considerable distances. There are seven species which the amateur may encounter from time to time, but the three most commonly imported are *Clarias batrachus* (by far the most common species in captivity) *Clarias dumerili* and *Clarias mossambicus*: these are described below. It is very unlikely that *Clarias angolensis, Clarias anguillaris, Clarias lazera* or *Clarias platycephalus* will come the way of the amateur.

CLARIAS BATRACHUS

Family: *Clariidae*

Genus: *Clarias*

English name: none

Origin: Eastern Asia, Malaya, Sri Lanka

Size: Approximately 55 cm

Habitat: Found in a wide variety of waters

Shape, coloring and markings: The body is torpedo-shaped: the head is low and broad with four pairs of barbels: one pair at the level of the nose, one on the upper lip and two on the lower jaw. The basic coloration is a brownish or bluish-green: the back is darker, with a striking green tinge: the underside is either light brown, soft red or bluish-white. Numerous irregular near or pure white marks lie on the flanks. The dorsal and anal fins are extremely long. The unpaired fins have a dark edge and are otherwise dull green and transparent. The dorsal fin is yellowish-green with an irregular arrangement of dark marks.

Females are less vividly colored and the dorsal fin is unmarked.

Males are as described above: a dark patch lies at the rear of the dorsal fin.

GENERAL CARE: Only young specimens are suitable for large specialised aquariums with a sandy or peaty bed. Plenty of retreats should be provided with irregular arrangements of wood, plant pots or coconut shells partly embedded. Only sturdy bog plants (potted if necessary) should be put in the tank. The composition of the water is not critical. Temperature 20°–25°C. A remarkably voracious species, *C.batrachus* should only be kept with larger fish. Although it has a preference for worm-like food, it will also greedily devour raw fish, lean beef, bread, potatoes, and steeped porridge oats. It is almost impossible to satisfy its appetite, even when its belly is distended like a balloon.

BREEDING: No information is available on the reproductive behavior of this species.

ADDITIONAL INFORMATION: *C.bactrachus* is decidedly a twilight fish. In the wild, it digs itself into mud pools during the dry season. It can spend hours or even days out of water and by using its supplementary respiratory system, travel long distances over land. It was first imported in 1899.

581. *Clarias batrachus*

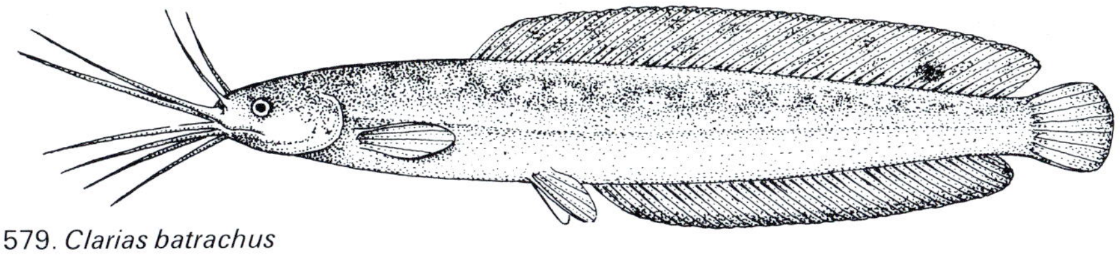

579. *Clarias batrachus*

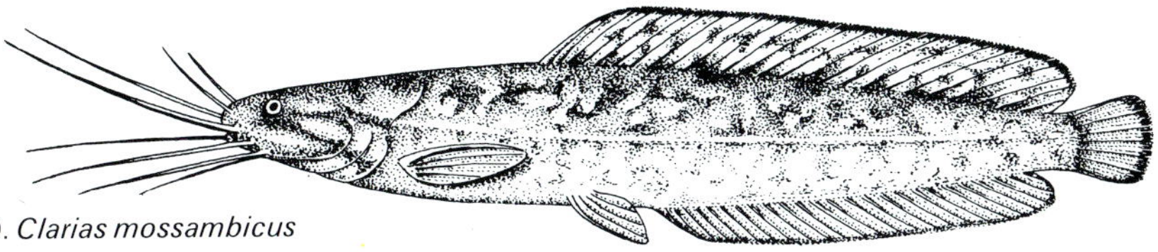

580. *Clarias mossambicus*

CLARIAS DUMERILI

Family: *Clariidae*
Genus: *Clarias*
English name: none
Origin: Angola
Size: Approximately 16 cm
Habitat: Found in still and sluggish fresh waters

SHAPE, COLORING AND MARKINGS: The body is torpedo-shaped: the head and barbels are identical to those of *C.batrachus*. The basic coloration is a striking chocolate brown: the back is slightly darker, tinged with green: the belly is light brown or whitish. The anal and dorsal fins are extremely long. All the fins are brownish and transparent.
There are no known external sexual characteristics.

GENERAL CARE: As for *C.batrachus*.

BREEDING: Nothing is known about the reproductive behavior of this species.

ADDITIONAL INFORMATION: *C.dumerili* has the same unusual habits and powers of locomotion as *C.batrachus*. It is much smaller, but also less attractively colored than the other species in the genus.

CLARIAS MOSSAMBICUS

Family: *Clariidae*
Genus: *Clarias*
English name: none
Origin: East Africa
Size: Approximately 70 cm
Habitat: Found in many different kinds of waters

SHAPE, COLORING AND MARKINGS: The body is torpedo-shaped: the head and barbels are identical to those of *C.batrachus*. The basic coloration is an olive brown with a dark or light brown and white marbling. The belly is greyish or white. The unpaired fins are dark brown, often with a dark edge: the dorsal fin has a pattern of marbling.
Females have a sexual organ without the cone-shaped tip present on the male organ.
Males have an elongated sexual organ with a cone-shaped tip.

GENERAL CARE: As for *C.batrachus*.

BREEDING: This species has not as yet been bred successfully in captivity.

ADDITIONAL INFORMATION: *C.mossambicus* has the same unusual habits and powers of locomotion as *C.batrachus*.

THE FAMILY LORICARIIDAE

An introductory description

Members of the Loricariidae family are found only in northern and central parts of South America. They are all freshwater fish except for some species in the genera *Ancistrus, Plecostomus* and *Xenocara* which are also found in the mildly brackish waters of river estuaries near coasts. The natural environments of these fish are very varied ranging from fast or slow flowing mountains streams with no vegetation in their rocky beds, to jungle creeks, some of which have a great deal of vegetation and all of which have waters rich in humus. In large streams the fish are found usually on the shelves lying along the banks, where the current is least strong. Very occasionally the Loricariidae are found in the still waters of marshes and pools with very soft acid water. A characteristic feature of all the members of this family is the armor plating over the body, giving rise to the popular name 'evenly armored catfish'. The Loricariidae are similar in many respects to the Callichthyidae, the armored catfish, found in many of the same areas although the Callichthyidae are usually confined to the more sluggish waters. The most obvious difference between the Loricariidae and the Callichthyidae lies in the pattern of armor plating. The Callichthyidae have two rows of bony plates which overlap: the Loricariidae have three to five rows of plates and the armor continues onto the head and completely covers it. In some species of Loricariidae the armor plating extends to the lower parts of the head and belly. The Loricariidae also have an adipose fin which is absent from the Callichthyidae.

The Loricariidae usually have extremely flat bodies, especially on the underside, and wide heads: the caudal peduncle is slightly elongated and laterally compressed. The front rays of all the fins, except for the caudal fin, have developed into very strong spines which aid the fish in 'walking' over the bed or indeed overland. The mouth is under-positioned, with fleshy lips that allow the fish to attach itself to rocks and stones by suction, which to such poor swimmers, is very important in strong currents. The mouth has an abrasive organ which the fish use to feed off algae to be found on rocks and stones.

A remarkable feature of these fish is the papillary growth in the upper part of the iris which covers the black pupil. When the light is strong this 'iris flap' expands to cover most of the pupil: when there is less light, it contracts leaving the pupil almost fully open. In this way, and lacking the eye muscles that animals use for the same purpose, the fish can enlarge or decrease the effective size of the pupil according to the intensity of the light. No other species of fish has this feature.

In the wild the Loricariidae live in waters with strong currents and rich in oxygen. Even so, most imported specimens have proved very adaptable to aquarium life and have lived to a great age. It is best to keep them in well-planted aquariums, with a bed of fine river sand or a layer of peat. Irregularly shaped pieces of bogwood make very effective decorations. The composition of the water is not critical, but fresh tap water should be avoided: part of the water should be changed regularly. The temperature should be 20°–26° C.

Some of the species look fierce at first sight but all are extremely tolerant and do not even attack the fry of other fish. Their diet in the wild is principally algae and vegetable waste matter, sometimes supplemented with worm-like creatures. In the aquarium they will eat algae and can also be fed with boiled lettuce, small worms of finely chopped Tubifex and Enchytrae: they will also accept dried food. They have a small appetite: in the ordinary community tank their diet does not usually have to be supplemented. Some species will dispose of all the algae in a tank in a very short time.

There are a number of reports of successful breeding of various species in this family. The mating season is from the end of December to June. Females can be encouraged to spawn by adding lettuce and other vegetable matter to the diet. The fish will select a suitable spot for the eggs on a piece of wood and then polish it until it is absolutely smooth. While the female lays the eggs, the male lies along side her facing the opposite direction. The female then pushes her head under his body, causing him to stretch convulsively: the male's ventral fins and back move upwards and the long caudal peduncle points straight up. The female then clamps herself onto the right ventral fin of the male. The female then lies on the eggs, alternately

582. *Ancistrus dolichopterus*

making flapping movements with the pectoral and anal fins and strong sweeping movements of the caudal peduncle. The eggs are probably fertilised by the milt being ejaculated when the male convulses, and then being carried to the eggs by the fin movements of the female. There are 100–200 eggs, 2 mm in diameter. They are first whitish and then yellowish and later brown. They hatch after 9–12 days at 20°–30° C. The male looks after the eggs and spends much time keeping them clean. The fry should be raised for the first week in a small tank with a filter but no bed. They will soon hunt for food on the bottom and should be fed on micro eels or *Artemia nauplii* which sink to the bottom very quickly in fresh water. The fry should not be overfed. During the first few weeks very small quantities of chopped up Tubifex and Grindal worms may be given, together with algae and lettuce: at all times it is essential to give a vegetable supplement.

The family Loricariidae contains some very interesting fish, but it is a family little known to most amateur aquarists. Indeed among biologists there is a great deal yet to be known about these fish. The literature is sparse and for a number of species no reliable description is available. There is a great deal of useful work that could be done by enthusiastic amateurs who might be fortunate to be able to secure specimens of these fish, some of which occasionally turn up by accident in batches of other imported fish.

The genus Ancistrus

The fish in the genus *Ancistrus* are among those in the *Loricariidae* family that are found in brackish as well as fresh water. They are also distinguished by having no armor plating on the underside of the body. Two species that are occasionally imported, *Ancistrus cirrhus* and *Ancistrus dolichopterus* are described below: a third species, *Ancistrus oligospilus*, a smaller fish (which never grows larger than 10 cm) from the tributaries of the middle Amazon, has also very occasionally turned up in batches of other imported species. It is unlikely however to be encountered by most amateurs.

ANCISTRUS CIRRHUS

Family: *Loricariidae*

Genus: *Ancistrus*

English name: none

Origin: The eastern Amazon basin, the Guianas, Paraguay, Trinidad

Size: Maximum 14 cm

Habitat: Found in running waters and sometimes in slightly brackish river estuaries

SHAPE, COLORING AND MARKINGS: The body is elongated: the belly almost flat. The head is vertically compressed and the back slopes upwards increasing the depth of the body from the wide snout to the base of the first ray of the large dorsal fin: thereafter the body depth decreases. A cross section through the tail would show it to be almost triangular. The back and flanks are covered with a large number of bony plates: the head is also armored, but the belly is naked. Below the gill covers are 9–13 spines with retractable hooks. On the snout are a large number of tentacles with forked ends. The upper-positioned mouth has fleshy lips that give great suction force allowing the fish to attach itself to rocks. The small teeth are peculiarly well suited for grazing off algae. The front rays of all the fins except the caudal fin have developed into hard spines. The basic coloration is dark or blackish-brown: the whole body is covered with light marks. The fins are brown but with dark marks. A large dark mark lies between the first and third dorsal fin rays.

Females have a slightly more pointed head, with fewer and smaller tentacles.

Males are as described above.

GENERAL CARE: *A.cirrhus* is best kept in a small group of four or five of its own kind in a community tank provided with a number of good retreats. *A.cirrhus* is very tolerant and its armor plating protects if from other potentially aggressive fish. The composition of the water is not critical but imported specimens will have been accustomed to running, usually clear, water in the wild and it is therefore advisable regularly to change the water and to install a filter to circulate the water. *A.cirrhus* will usually hide during the day and come out for food at night. Its diet is mainly algae but it will indeed eat any food, including dried food, left by other fish. Fresh, well-washed lettuce if attached to a pellet of lead or a pebble will sink to the bottom and will be greedily eaten: such vegetable matter is an essential part of the diet but *A.cirrhus* will not take it from the surface.

BREEDING: There are no reports of this species having as yet been bred successfully in captivity but it is likely that its reproductive behavior will be similar to that of *Ancistrus dolichopterus*.

ANCISTRUS DOLICHOPTERUS

Family: *Loricariidae*

Genus: *Ancistrus*

English name: none

Origin: The Guianas, the northern part of the Amazon basin

Size: Maximum 13 cm

Habitat: Found in running waters and sometimes in slightly brackish river estuaries

SHAPE, COLORING AND MARKINGS: The body shape is almost identical to that of *A.cirrhus*, but *A.dolichopterus* is a slightly smaller fish and has fewer hooked spines (no more than six to nine) under the gill covers. The basic coloration varies from dark brown to bluish-black: both the body and fins are covered with a pattern of off-white dots. The dorsal and caudal fins are edged with white.

Females have only one row of short thin tentacles on the snout, which is more pointed than in the males.

Males have many, often forked tentacles and are generally lighter in color.

GENERAL CARE: As for *A.cirrhus*.

BREEDING: Not every pair will make successful breeders: it is best to use a pair that has come together naturally and transfer them to a separate breeding tank where the problems that may arise in a community tank caused by the protective territorial instincts of spawning males will be avoided. Fights between males which result from this well-developed instinct can disrupt the whole breeding process. A breeding tank made completely of glass (about 50×30×30 cm) is required, with no bed, plants or overhead lighting. In the darkest corner of the tank rocks (for example pieces of flagstone) should be arranged so that there is an opening about 5 cm wide, 20 cm long and 2 cm high. Fresh tap water should be used: temperature about 28°C. The eggs are laid inside the hollow, against the roof, after both fish have examined it thoroughly and approved it. The male guards and cares for the eggs, removing any that have not been fertilised and fanning a constant flow of fresh water through the hollow.

The eggs hatch after about five days and the fry feed on the yolk for about three days. During that time the first food for the fry should be prepared by floating a few lettuce leaves in a separate brightly lit tank. The algae grows quickly if the water is kept at about 28°C. As soon as the fry are free swimming they should be fed this food. The breeding tank can then be lit properly and later well-washed lettuce leaves put straight in the tank. The parent fish will eat any leaves that go soft or rot and sink to the bottom: only excreted waste will remain and this should be removed daily. The water siphoned off when that is done should be replaced with fresh tap water. The diet should also regularly include dried food and animal matter such as chopped Tubifex and Enchytrae. Not a very productive species: 100 fry would be a large brood, but old well-cared for breeders may produce nests of 200 eggs.

THE FAMILY LORICARIIDAE

The genus Loricaria

Three of the better known species in this genus, *Loricaria filamentosa, Loricaria lanceolata* and *Loricaria parva* are described below. Other species, on which full and reliable information is not unfortunately available, include *L.apeltogaster, L.cariniale, L.claripinna, L. laticeps* and which are found principally in Brazil. Although not very much information is available, it is certainly true that these fish are very interesting for the aquarist, because they are not extremely difficult to keep, and even breeding them has proved to be succesful.

583. *Loricaria filamentosa*

LORICARIA FILAMENTOSA

Family: *Loricariidae*

Genus: *Loricaria*

English name: none

Origin: Colombia, the basin of the Magdalena river

Size: Approximately 25 cm in the wild: remains considerably smaller in captivity

Habitat: Found only in fresh waters

SHAPE, COLORING AND MARKINGS: There are 31–38 bony plates on the body. The upper ray of the caudal fin is extremely long. Two or three rows of irregularly-shaped bony plates lie over the belly, in between the plates on the sides: a large number of very small irregularly-shaped plates lie in front of these. The basic coloration varies from grey to yellowish-brown, with many irregular marks: the underside is pale yellow to white. All the fins carry dark flecks: the caudal fin has a dark edge.
Females are as described above.
Males when adult, have bristles on the cheeks.

GENERAL CARE: *L.filamentosa* is suitable for both large and small community tanks, well planted and with the overhead light filtered through floating plants: the bed should be soft or peaty. The tank should be furnished with pieces of wood or rock off which *L.filamentosa* will take algae. The water should be fairly acid and not too hard: fresh tap water should be avoided. Temperature 21°–28°C. The diet should be principally algae, vegetable waste matter and small worm-like creatures: *L.filamentosa* usually finds everything that it needs in an ordinary community tank, but if there is not much algae then lettuce should be given. *L.filamentosa* keeps to the bottom of the tank, resting on plants or other objects, or moves by 'walking' with its fins over the bed in search of food.

BREEDING: *L.filamentosa* has been bred successfully a number of times: see Introductory note on the family.

ADDITIONAL INFORMATION: *L.filamentosa* was first described in 1878: it is often confused with *L.parva*.

LORICARIA LANCEOLATA

Family: *Loricariidae*

Genus: *Loricaria*

English name: none

Origin: The upper reaches of the Amazon

Size: Approximately 13 cm

Habitat: Found only in frsh waters

SHAPE, COLORING AND MARKINGS: There are 29–30 bony plates on the body, and small plates lie over the belly as on *L.filamentosa.* Both the upper and lower caudal fin rays are elongated and appear as fine threads. The basic coloration is grey or greyish-yellow with numerous dark marks which often lie in transverse bands. A distinct pattern of dark stripes runs from the pectoral fins to the lower half of the caudal peduncle. The lower half of the body is light yellow. The dorsal fin is greyish and transparent with brown marks which also often become transverse bands. The base of the caudal fin is dark, bordered by a light area. The other fins are almost colorless but have as a rule a dark edge.
Females are as described above.
Males have, when adult, bristles on the cheeks.

GENERAL CARE: As for *L.filamentosa.*

BREEDING: *L.lanceolata* has not as yet been bred in captivity.

LORICARIA PARVA

Family: *Loricariidae*

Genus: *Loricaria*

English name: none

Origin: Paraguay

Size: Approximately 12 cm

Habitat: Found only in fresh waters

SHAPE, COLORING AND MARKINGS: *L.parva* closely resembles *L.lanceolata* in body but *L.parva* has 28 plates on the body and there are three or four rows of small plates on the belly. The basic coloration is greyish-green to greyish-yellow with numerous marks which often lie in transverse bands. The lower half of the body is whitish or ochre. A pattern of dak stripy marks runs from the eye to the snout: a dark line runs the length of the body from the back edge of the gill covers to the lower part of the caudal peduncle. The fins are greyish and transparent, with dark patches on the rays.
Females are as described above.
Males when adult have bristles on the cheeks.

GENERAL CARE: As for *L.filamentosa.*

BREEDING: *L.parva* has been bred in captivity: see Introductory note on the family.

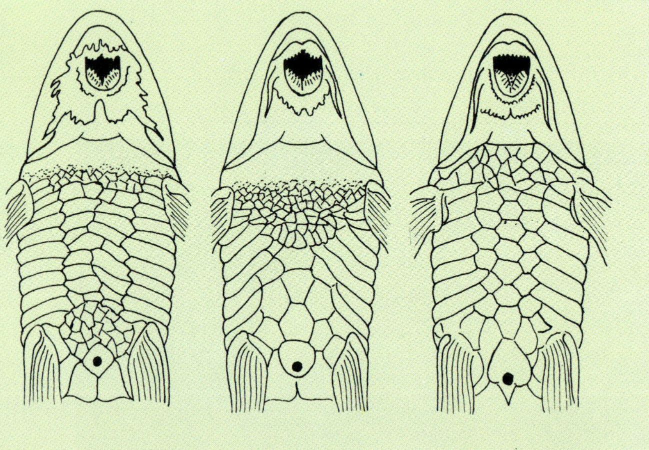

584. *Heads of L. filamentosa, lanceolata, parva*

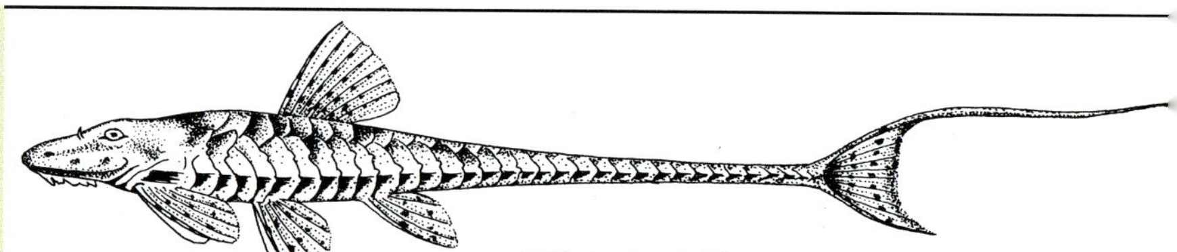

585. *Loricaria filamentosa*

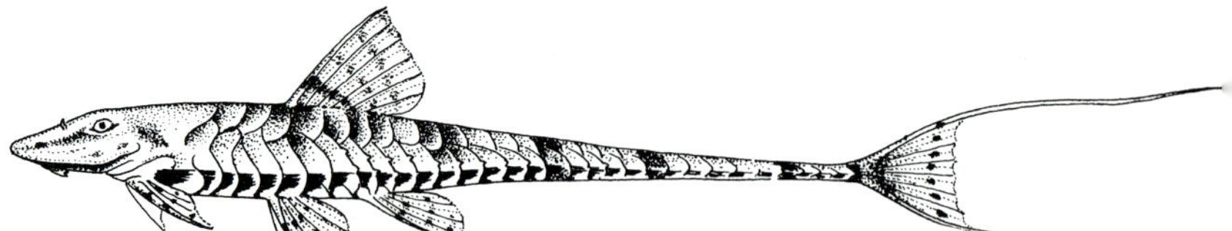

586. *Loricaria lanceolata*

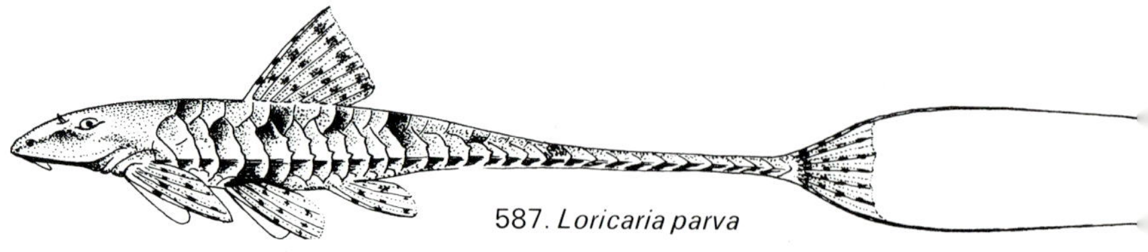

587. *Loricaria parva*

THE FAMILY LORICARIIDAE

The genus Hypostomus

As noted below under the description of *Hypostomus plecostomus*, there has been considerable confusion about the nomenclature of this and related species. *H.plecostomus* is a most interesting fish and so unusual as to appeal to many aquarists but if amateurs are to continue to be able to enjoy these remarkable species in their aquariums, very serious efforts must be made to breed them successfully in captivity.

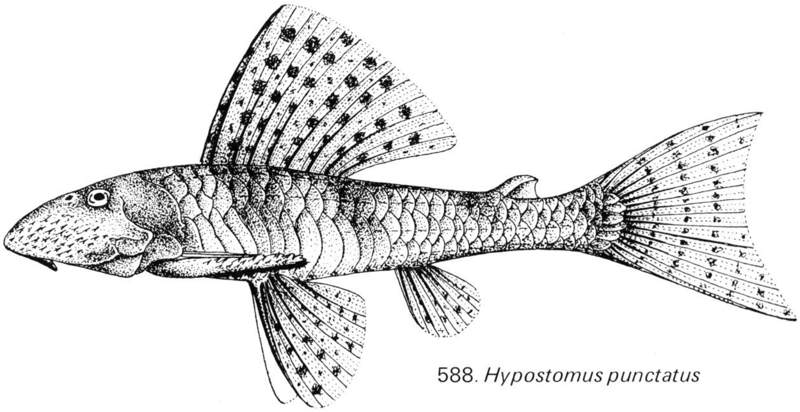

588. *Hypostomus punctatus*

HYPOSTOMUS PLECOSTOMUS

Family: *Loricariidae*
Genus: *Hypostomus*
English name: none
Origin: Venezuela, the Guianas
Size: Approximately 45 cm in the wild: rarely more than 25 cm in captivity
Habitat: Found in clear, swift flowing waters

SHAPE, COLORING AND MARKINGS: The body is elongated and club-shaped: the underside is flat, and the back rises sharply to the first front ray of the dorsal fin. The fins are all exceptionally large and the front rays are developed into hard sharp spines. The mouth is under-positioned with large lips that constitute an effective sucker: there are two barbels. The back is plated and a row of fine spines runs from below the eye to the adipose fin. The basic coloration is brownish-grey, with many darker specks. Four indistinct transverse bands lie across the body between the dorsal fin and the caudal peduncle. The fins are flecked with dark spots.
There are no know external sexual characteristics.

GENERAL CARE: *H.plecostomus* is suitable only for a very large community tank with a bed of subdued colored sand. There should be plenty of hiding places. *H.plecostomus* is really a twilight fish but will often appear during the day to look for food. Its diet is mainly vegetable matter but it will also accept small live animal matter. It is excellent for cleaning algae but will not always eat thread algae. Once the tank has been cleared of algae, care should be taken to ensure that *H.plecostomus* does not starve to death as a reward for its industry. Well-washed lettuce, weighted to ensure that it sinks to the bottom of the tank, is essential. The composition of the water is not critical: temperature 20°–25°C.

BREEDING: This species has not as yet been bred in captivity.

ADDITIONAL INFORMATION: There is a great deal of confusion about the classification of this and related species, such as *Hypostomus punctatus*. The genus itself is often called *Plecostomus* instead of *Hypostomus*. *H.plecostomus* became so popular with aquarists at one time because of its unusual appearance, that exports were restricted to preserve the species.

HYPOSTOMUS PUNCTATUS

Family: *Loricariidae*
Genus: *Hypostomus*
English name: none
Origin: The southern part of the Amazon basin
Size: Maximum 30 cm in the wild, but remains considerably smaller in captivity
Habitat: Found in clear swift flowing waters

SHAPE, COLORING AND MARKINGS: The body is elongated and club-shaped; the underside is flat and the body shape is identical to *H.plecostomus*. *H.punctatus* has the same kind of mouth and the same arrangement of the teeth. The basic coloration is yellowish-brown, with a pattern of dark brown dots: the fins also carry dark dots.
There are no known external sexual characteristics.

GENERAL CARE: As for *H.plecostomus*. The fish must be handled carefully to avoid damage to the large fins.

BREEDING: *H.punctatus* has not as yet been bred successfully in captivity.

THE FAMILY MOCHOKIDAE

An introductory description

The *Mochokidae* are found only in Africa. In this family of catfish, there are seven genera, *Acanthocleithron, Atopochilus, Chiloglanis, Euchilichthys, Microsynodontis, Mochokus* and *Synodontis*, but only some species in the genus *Synodontis* are normally considered to be aquarium fish.
The characteristics of the species in that genus are described below.

The genus Synodontis

Members of the genus *Synodontis* are found over the whole of Africa, except for the north, in many different environments and usually in large shoals. They have a stocky body, only slightly compressed towards the tail: the back is usually considerably more rounded than the belly. These fish have a formidable defensive weapon in the spines with sharp hooks that have developed in the rays of the dorsal and pectoral fins. Their skin is naked, with no scales. There are three pairs of barbels, those on the upper jaw usually being the most powerfully developed and serving as organs of touch. The barbels on the lower jaw and chin are often feathered and carry taste buds. The teeth are so arranged as to make it very easy for the fish to browse off algae, which is part of their staple diet although they will also eat the smaller aquatic insects and larvae and even take pieces of dead fish as bait.

Nearly all these species are twilight fish, most active at night. They can be observed during the day however if kept in a spacious well-planted tank with plenty of retreats and fairly subdued lighting. Once they have grown accustomed to a particular tank they will show themselves more often, despite their natural shyness. Some species, including the well known *Synodontis nigriventris* have acquired the habit of swimming on their backs: those species keep mainly to the upper levels of the tank and are less shy of the light than other species. All these species are very tolerant towards other fish, although other species may sometimes be frightened by the movement of the prominent barbels. Most species are quite large in the wild but remain considerably smaller in captivity. For that reason and also because of their peaceful and undemanding nature, they make admirable aquarium fish. The composition of the water is not critical: the temperature should be 21°–28°C.

If there is a lot of algae in the tank, the fish will often be seen swimming along the panes of the tank, grazing off it: they are very agile and twist and turn into the most extraordinary postures. Those that swim on their backs usually have dark bellies, in contrast to the lighter undersides of other species.

There is on the whole among aquarists very little interest in these catfish, which are erroneously thought to be fidgety fish which rarely show themselves during the day. The *Synodontis* however can be recommended without reservation: they rarely wallow in the bed, indeed, rarely go to the bottom of the tank. Many species are very useful in keeping down algae, and also clear away other waste matter, including dead fish. They are also a genus which can be fascinating for the aquarist who feels adventurous, for very little is known about them.

SYNODONTIS ACANTHOMIAS

Family: *Mochokidae*

Genus: *Synodontis*

English name: none

Origin: The Congo

Size: Maximum size unknown

Habitat: Found in sluggish streams and lagoons

SHAPE, COLORING AND MARKINGS: The body is stocky and laterally only slightly compressed. There are three pairs of barbels: those on the upper jaw are not feathered. The basic coloration is greyish-white with a light brown tinge. A number of large brownish-black marks lie on the body and are most prominent on the back, in front of and below the dorsal fin and on the caudal peduncle. A very distinct pattern of marks lies also above the ventral fins and a number of less prominent marks appear on the lower half of the body. Except for the snout, the head is covered with small brownish wavy stripes and dots. The fins are nearly white with a pale blue tinge. The dorsal and caudal fins have dark brown bands, the other fins patches of brown. The irises are a rust brown.

There are no known external sexual characteristics.

GENERAL CARE: *S.acanthomias* is suitable for large particularly well-planted community tanks provided with plenty of retreats in irregular arrangements of wood. A very tolerant species which may unintentionally frighten other fish with its barbels. *S.acanthomias* will swim freely through the tank but prefers to swim along pieces of wood or along the sides of the tank in search of algae. The composition of the water is not critical. Temperature 22°–26°C. All sorts of aquatic insects and larvae will be eaten: algae and a vegetable supplement such as lettuce must also be provided.

BREEDING: Nothing is known about the reproductive behavior of this species.

ADDITIONAL INFORMATION: A twilight fish that dislikes a brightly lit tank. First described by George Boulenger in 1899.

SYNODONTIS ALBERTI

Family: *Mochokidae*

Genus: *Synodontis*

English name: none

Origin: The Congo

Size: Approximately 16 cm in the wild: remains considerably smaller in captivity

Habitat: No details are available of its natural habitat.

SHAPE, COLORING AND MARKINGS: The body is stocky and laterally only slightly compressed. There are three pairs of barbels, those on the upper jaw being exceptionally long and unfeathered. The basic coloration is greyish-blue to greenish-brown, becoming lighter towards the belly. Over the whole body, particularly on the upper half (including the adipose fin) are scattered large but indistinct dark marks. The fins are greyish and transparent, with rows of dots or marks.

There are no known external sexual characteristics.

GENERAL CARE: As for *S.acanthomias* but *S.alberti* has a partiality for Tubifex and other worm-like food.

BREEDING: Nothing is known about the reproductive behavior of this species.

ADDITIONAL INFORMATION: *S.alberti* was first described in 1891.

SYNODONTIS ANGELICUS

Family: *Mochokidae*

Genus: *Synodontis*

English name: none

Origin: Tropical West Africa

Size: Approximately 20 cm in the wild but remains considerably smaller in captivity.

Habitat: No further details are available of its natural habitat

---

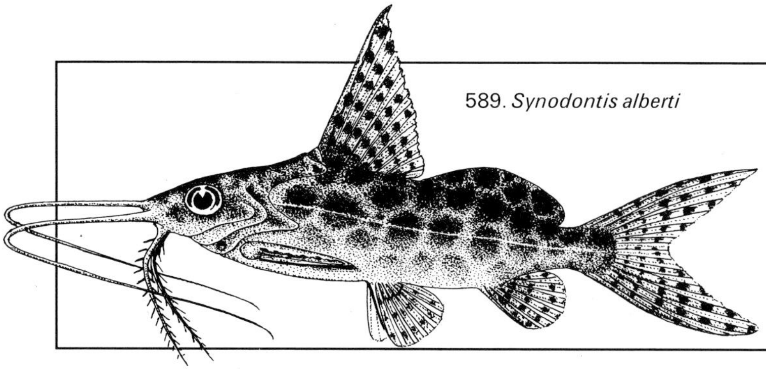

589. *Synodontis alberti*

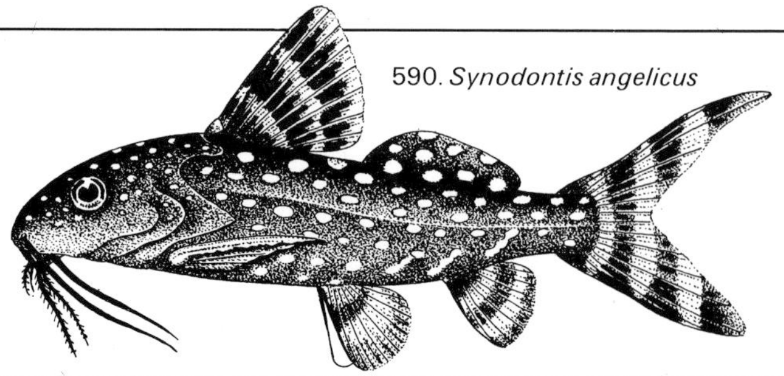

590. *Synodontis angelicus*

591. *Synodontis clarias*

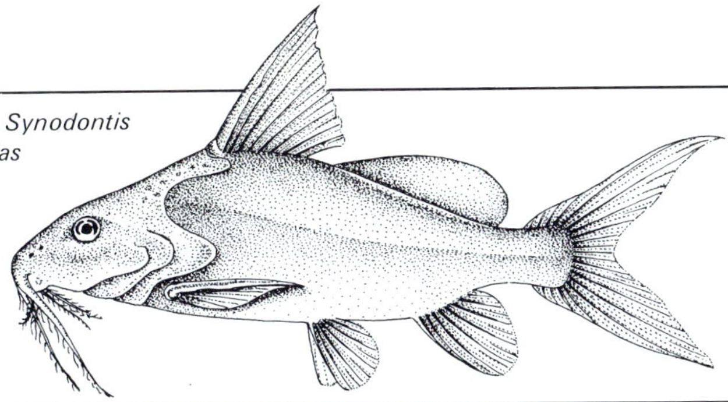

592. *Synodontis flavitaeniatus*

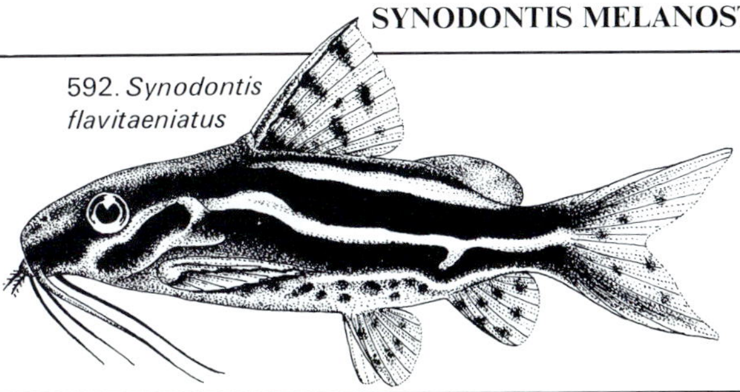

SHAPE, COLORING AND MARKINGS: The body is stocky and laterally slightly compressed towards the tail. There are three pairs of barbels, those on the upper jaw being feathered. The basic coloration varies according to the age of the specimen. Adults are mainly greyish or dark violet with numerous large rust brown or reddish-brown marks with dark edges on the head, body and large adipose fin. The other fins have wide dark bands. Young specimens are very beautiful, with a large number of luminescent pearl-shaped marks on a violet background.
There are no known external sexual characteristics.

GENERAL CARE: As for *S.acanthomias*. If the aquarium is not too brightly lit, *S.angelicus* will be active during the day. Diet as for *S.alberti*.

BREEDING: Nothing is known about the reproductive behavior of this species.

ADDITIONAL INFORMATION: *S.angelicus* is one of the most beautiful species: it was first described in 1891.

593. *Synodontis acanthomias*

SYNODONTIS CLARIAS

Family: *Mochokidae*

Genus: *Synodontis*

English name: none

Origin: The Nile basin, Lake Chad, Senegal, the Niger and Gambia rivers

Size: Approximately 27 cm

Habitat: Found in many different kinds of waters

SHAPE, COLORING AND MARKINGS: The body is stocky, rather deep and laterally only slightly compressed towards the tail. All the barbels are feathered but those on the upper jaw, only along the front. The upper lobe of the caudal fin is slightly longer than the lower lobe. The basic coloration is greyish-blue: the back is olive green: the belly lighter. Young specimens are covered with large very dark marks. The fins are greyish and transparent: the caudal fin is usually tinged with red.
There are no known external sexual characteristics.

GENERAL CARE: As for *S.acanthomias*.

BREEDING: Nothing is known about the reproductive behavior of this species.

ADDITIONAL INFORMATION: *S.clarias* is still unknown among aquarists even though it was first described by Linnaeus in 1762.

SYNODONTIS FLAVITAENIATUS

Family: *Mochokidae*

Genus: *Synodontis*

English name: none

Origin: The Congo

Size: Approximately 15 cm

Habitat: No further details are available of its natural habitat

SHAPE, COLORING AND MARKINGS: The body is stocky and laterally only slightly compressed. There are three pairs of barbels: only those on the chin are feathered. The basic coloration is a brownish-white. A broad irregular band runs across the upper part of the body to the caudal fin. Other irregular bands run across the head and lower part of th body, to disintegrate into an intricate pattern of marks and stripes before reaching the caudal fin. The otherwise colorless dorsal fin has dark brown patches and a yellowish-brown spine. The caudal fin has yellowish brown top and bottom edges, bordered by dark brown marks. The rest of the fins are colorless and transparent with dark brown patches.
There are no known external sexual characteristics.

GENERAL CARE: As for *S.acanthomias*.

BREEDING: Nothing is known about the reproductive behavior of this species.

SYNODONTIS MELANOSTICTUS

Family: *Mochokodae*

Genus: *Synodontis*

English name: none

Origin: The Zambezi river, Lake Tanganyika, Lake Bangweulo

Size: Approximately 32 cm

Habitat: No details are available of its natural habitat

SHAPE, COLORING AND MARKINGS: The body is stocky and laterally only slightly compressed. There are three pairs of barbels: only those on the upper jaw are feathered and have very thin membranes. The upper lobe of the caudal fin is slightly larger than the lower. The basic coloration is brownish and marbled, becoming considerably lighter towards the belly. A large number of dark patches and dots are spread over the body and head. The fins are greyish to soft brown, with dark spots.
There are no known external sexual characteristics.

GENERAL CARE: As for *S.acanthomias*.

BREEDING: Nothing is known of the reproductive behavior of this species.

594. *Synodontis nigriventris*

SYNODONTIS NIGRITA

Family: *Mochokidae*

Genus: *Synodontis*

English name: none

Origin: Bahr el Jebel (the White Nile), Senegal and the rivers Gambia and Niger

Size: Approximately 17 cm

Habitat: Found in large number in a variety of waters

SHAPE, COLORING AND MARKINGS: The body is stocky and laterally only slightly compressed. There are three pairs of barbels: those on the upper jaw are unfeathered and have a wide membrane at the base. The caudal fin is less deeply forked than in related species: the upper lobe is slightly more powerfully developed than the lower. Young specimens are more or less coffee-colored with numerous dark dots and flecks arranged in rows on the flanks: the lower half of the body is considerably lighter. Three narrow transverse dark bands lie on the caudal peduncle. A luminescent patch appears just above the eye. Adult specimens are predominantly brown, tinged with green, and with numerous dark marks. The fins are dark with rows of dots: the dorsal and caudal fins have dark transverse bands.
There are no known external sexual characteristics.

GENERAL CARE: As for *S.acnathomias*.

BREEDING: Nothing is known about the reproductive behavior of this species.

ADDITIONAL INFORMATION: *S.nigrita* was first described by Cuvier and Valenciennes in 1840.

SYNODONTIS NIGRIVENTRIS

Family: *Mochokidae*

Genus: *Synodontis*

English name: Upside-down Catfish

Origin: The Congo

Size: Approximately 6 cm

Habitat: Very common in many different kinds of waters

SHAPE, COLORING AND MARKINGS: The body is stocky and laterally slightly compressed. There are three pairs of barbels, of which only the outer pair on the lower jaw are feathered. The basic coloration is greyish to cream: the belly is very dark or black. The whole body is covered with irregular marks which can run together to form transverse bands. The fins are colorless and bear numerous dark flecks. Females have more rounded bellies.
Males are more slender.

GENERAL CARE: As for *S.acanthomias*. *S.nigriventris* always keeps to the top of the tank and seeks food on the surface while swimming on its back.

BREEDING: *S.nigriventris* has been bred: apparently the fish mate in holes, for example in inverted coconut shells, but unfortunately no further information is available.

ADDITIONAL INFORMATION: *S.nigriventria* is fairly familiar to aquarists. Most species of *Synodontis* are capable of swimming on their backs and do so from time to time, but *S.nigriventris* has adopted this curious stance as its normal posture when seeking food. It will also feed off the undersides of broad leaved water plants.

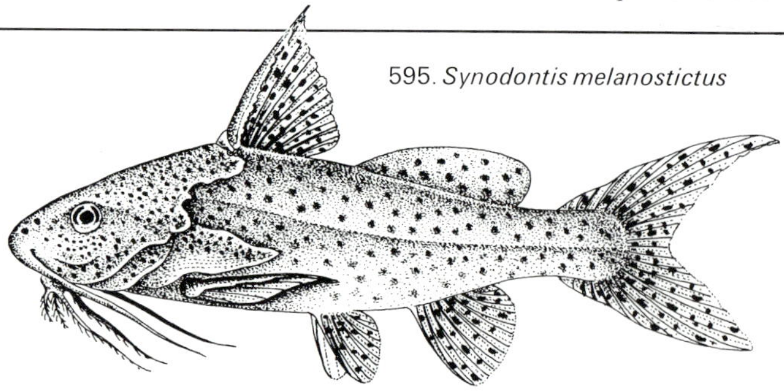

595. *Synodontis melanostictus*

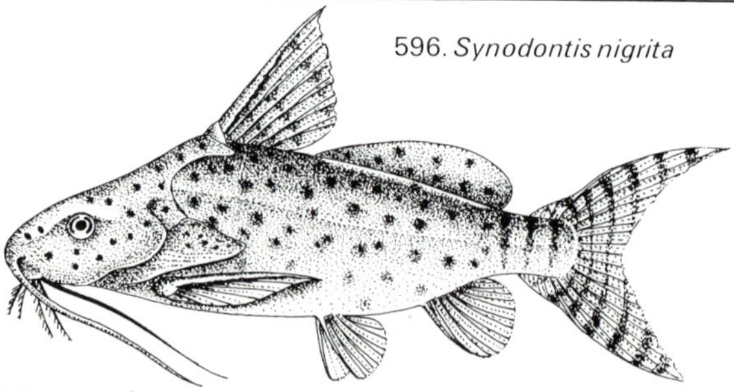

596. *Synodontis nigrita*

THE FAMILY SILURIDAE

An introductory description

The *Siluridae* family is a group of naked catfish that are only found in the Old World, but nevertheless have a wide distribution in both Europe and Asia. There are two sub-families, the *Silurinae* and the *Kryptopterinae* and a number of genera within those sub-families but very few indeed of the species in this family can be accounted aquarium fish. Among those obviously inappropriate, for example, is the European Catfish, *Silurus glanis* found in the Danube and Dutch polders, where it can attain a length of over three meters. Occasionally specimens of *Silurichthys phaiosoma*, a small brown fish that grows to only 12 cm, are brought from Malaya, but in general only species in the genus *Kryptopterus* are ever kept by amateur aquarists: two species are described below.

The genus Kryptopterus

The naked catfish in this genus are characterised by an extremely small dorsal fin and by the enlarged lower lobe of the deeply forked caudal fin, which gives that fin an unusual and rather unbalanced look.
Two species, *Kryptopterus bicirrhus* and *Kryptopterus macrocephalus*, of interest to aquarists are described below. A third species, *Kryptopterus species*, which although larger than *K.bicirrhus* is otherwise very similar to it except for a patch of bronze around the gill covers, is also occasionally encountered.

KRYPTOPTERUS BICIRRHUS

Family: *Siluridae*

Genus: *Kryptopterus*

English name: Ghost fish

Origin: Indonesia, Borneo, Sumatra, Thailand

Size: Maximum 15 cm in the wild, no more than 12 cm in captivity

Habitat: Found in shady spots in running waters

Shape, coloring and markings: The body is very elongated and laterally very compressed. The head and body cavity are no more than a fifth of the total length. There are two long hair-like barbels on the upper jaw which serve as a tactile organ as well as an organ of taste. The anal fin is very long and runs from the anal opening to the base of the caudal fin, although the two fins are clearly separated. The dorsal fin consists of a single hard ray. The caudal fin is deeply forked and the upper lobe is noticeably larger than the lower. The basic coloration is grey and *K.bicirrhus* is completely translucent except for the stomach cavity. Depending on the way the light catches it, the fish becomes iridescent and any color from a bright yellow to a dark purplish-violet, without losing its translucence. In semi-darkness the fish seems to be a fluorescent blue.
No external sexual characteristics have been identified with certainty but some authorities claim that the males are always smaller and more slender than the females.

General care: *K.bicirrhus* is a twilight fish but likes to keep in a small group during the day in a shady spot in the tank, where there is a slight current (produced for example by a pump circulating the water) and where it will remain at a slightly oblique angle, making undulating movements with its anal fin and the back part of its body: a group will remain like this for hours although within the group individual fish will change position. When transferred from one tank to another *K.bicirrhus* becomes very shy for some time. A very tolerant species, it is also no threat to plants and accordingly ideal for a community tank, preferably with other peaceful fish. The composition of the water is not critical: temperature about 26° C. Imported specimens are particularly prone to White Spot disease at lower temperatures. A diet of live animal matter, especially mosquito larvae should be given.

Breeding: This species does not seem to have been bred in captivity as yet.

597. *Kryptopterus bicirrhus*

KRYPTOPTERUS MACROCEPHALUS

Family: *Siluridae*

Genus: *Kryptopterus*

English name: none

Origin: Indonesia, the islands of the Sunda Strait

Size: Maximum 15 cm

Habitat: Found in shady spots in running waters

SHAPE, COLORING AND MARKINGS: *K.macrocephalus* is very similar to *K.bicirrhus* but is not as translucent and is somewhat yellowish. Two dark, not always distinct stripes run from the gill covers and end as a dark mark on the caudal peduncle. A pattern of fairly distinct, irregular marks appears on the back. The caudal and anal fins are linked, unlike in *K.bicirrhus* where the two fins are clearly separate. There are no known external sexual characteristics.

GENERAL CARE: As for *K.bicirrhus.*

BREEDING: *K.macrocephalus* has not as yet been bred in captivity.

598. *Kryptopterus macrocephalus*

THE FAMILY CYPRINODONTIDAE

An introductory description

One or other of the species of egg-laying toothcarps that make up the very large *Cyprinodontidae* family is to be found almost everywhere in the world except for Australia. Among the large number of genera are some of great interest to aquarists and within them are to be found some of the most beautiful of aquarium fish. Unfortunately many species are aggressive if not predatory and must therefore be kept in community tanks only after a very careful appraisal of their behavior patterns. As is not surprising in so large a family, there are many very different kinds of fish to be found among these toothcarps or killifish as they are often known. Indeed, so varied are their demands and requirements in the aquarium that more detailed information is best given under the various genera and species descriptions that follow.

The genus Aphanius

In recent years there has been much scientific interest in this genus and the small number of species recognised some years ago have now increased to several dozen. Nevertheless, few of these species are of interest to aquarists. The four most likely to be encountered, *Aphanius dispar, Aphanius ibericus, Aphanius cypris* and *Aphanius fasciatus* are described below. There has been some confusion also over nomenclature and this is noted under the species descriptions. It should be remembered that the *Aphanius* species can be particularly aggressive and suitable precautions must be taken.

APHANIUS CYPRIS

Family: *Cyprinodontidae*
Genus: *Aphanius*
English name: none
Origin: Asia Minor, Cyprus, Israel, Jordan, Syria
Size: Maximum 6.5 cm
Habitat: Found in fresh and brackish waters

SHAPE, COLORING AND MARKINGS: The body is elongated and laterally slightly compressed. The basic coloration is normally greenish-brown with a pattern of dull, silvery blue flecks. During the spawning season *A.cypris* becomes a bluish-black or jet black with glittering silver dots, a jewel among fish rivaling the Dwarf Sunfish *(Elassoma evergladei)*.
Females are yellowish-brown with blue dots, with colorless fins and generally more rounded bellies.
Males are as described above.

GENERAL CARE: *A.cypris* needs a fairly large aquarium with plenty of hiding places so that if conflicts arise between the fish, the loser has a place to which to retreat, even though most such conflicts are harmless quarrels. *A.cypris* is not really suitable for a community tank. Five grams of sea salt should be added for every liter of water in the tank, but otherwise the composition of the water is not critical: temperature 15°–25° C. The main diet should be aquatic insects, mosquito larvae and Cyclops, with a regular supplement of vegetable matter.

BREEDING: Most healthy females regularly lay large greyish-white eggs among floating plants and clumps of algae. These eggs may be collected and transferred to a breeding tank. The eggs will be at less risk however if the spawning female is put into a special tank with two males. A small glass tank should be used, with only a small clump of fine leaved plants or a nylon breeding mop in it. The eggs will hatch after about 14 days. The fry are free swimming about a day later and can be fed with *Artemia nauplii.*

ADDITIONAL INFORMATION: *A.cypris* is one of the most beautiful but also least tolerant of these species: the males may well be aggressive during the spawning season. *A.cypris* is often sold under its synonym *Aphanius mento* and is sometimes erroneously described as *Aphanius sophiae.*

APHANIUS DISPAR

Family: *Cyprinodontidae*
Genus: *Aphanius*
English name: none
Origin: The Persian Gulf, the Red Sea and generally, the Southeast Mediterranean
Size: Maximum 6 cm
Habitat: Found in fresh and brackish waters

SHAPE, COLORING AND MARKINGS: The body is elongated and laterally slightly compressed. The basic coloration is brown or blue, with a pattern of silvery specks on the front part of the body and light, vertical stripes on the back part and the caudal fin. During the spawning season *A.dispar* becomes a blackish-blue or black with bright luminescent silvery spots which extend to the fins and a pattern of silver and black stripes on the back part of the body. The anal, ventral and pectoral fins are lemon yellow.
Females are dull brown with a slight bluish sheen but no specks or stripes: they are more sturdily built than males.
Males are as described above but the color and markings of individual specimens may vary significantly according to the locality of origin.

GENERAL CARE: As for *A.cypris*.

BREEDING: As for *A.cypris*.

APHANIUS FASCIATUS
Family: *Cyprinodontidae*
Genus: *Aphanius*
English name: none
Origin: The North African and South European coastal areas of the Mediterranean
Size: Maximum 6 cm
Habitat: Found in fresh and brackish waters

599. *Aphanius iberus*

◁ 600. *Aphanius fasciatus*

SHAPE, COLORING AND MARKINGS: The body is elongated and laterally slightly compressed. The basic coloration is greyish-green with a large number of narrow dark transverse bands. The fins are pale to deep orangey-yellow: the dorsal fin has a dark edge and the caudal fin an indistinct pattern of stripes. Females are more robust and a plain greyish-brown with small, dark flecks and stripes over the whole body.
Males are as described above.

GENERAL CARE: As for *A.cypris*.

BREEDING: As for *A.cypris*.

APHANIUS IBERUS
Family: *Cyprinodontidae*
Genus: *Aphanius*
English name: none
Origin: Southern Spain, Algeria, Morocco
Size: Maximum 5 cm
Habitat: Found mainly in fresh waters

SHAPE, COLORING AND MARKINGS: The body is elongated, relatively low and laterally slightly compressed. The basic coloration is bluish-green with a large number of vertical light blue transverse bands. The caudal fin is blue with darker vertical stripes and a lighter edge; the dorsal and anal fins are dark, flecked with a pattern of light dots: the ventral fins are greenish-yellow with a dark marbling. Females are plain green with a pattern of brown dots and stripes: the fins are colorless. Males are as described above.

GENERAL CARE: As for *A.cypris* but for *A.iberus* no salt should be added to the water. *A.iberus* is intolerant of smaller species and thus unsuitable for the normal community tank.

BREEDING: As for *A.cypris*.

ADDITIONAL INFORMATION: Live-bearing tooth carps of the genus *Gambusia (G.patruelis)* were introduced into Spanish waters to combat malaria: since then *A.iberus* has become much less common, no doubt because its staple diet, mosquito larvae which are also the staple diet of *G.patruelis*, are less abundant.

THE FAMILY CYPRINODONTIDAE

The genus Aphyosemion

Members of the genus *Aphyosemion* are only found in an area of West Africa south of the Sahara and north of the equator. Within this comparatively small area however there are many different regional varieties of these fish and much confusion has arisen in the identification and correct classification of the various species.
Most species live naturally in the small pools and lakes that develop during floods and the monsoon rains, in the rain forests and open grasslands, called the savanna. These pools are all seasonal. There is of course no lasting vegetation in these waters: anything that manages to grow there during the rainy season disappears during the dry season, when most if not all of the water itself evaporates. The beds of these seasonal pools and lakes are made up of layers of organic waste matter and consequently the water is usually dark and quite acid. A lot of vegetation does however develop along the banks of these pools: thick roots and tendrils creep into the pools themselves and they are usually overshadowed by thick foliage. The pools become ideal breeding grounds for a large number of insects, including mosquitoes, whose larvae are an important part of the diet of these fish.
When the pools dry up, the fish die. They are often called 'seasonal fish' for this reason. Others survive in pools where only very small amounts of water remain. A number survive as species although their pools dry out completely and they themselves die, by laying their eggs in the mud, where the eggs lie dormant and only hatch when, once again after a long period of drought, the waters return to the pool during the next rainy season.
The composition of the water in these pools varies a great deal, according to the local environment: for example, near

the coast and in river estuaries the water may be brackish during the rains. However, despite these local variations in their natural habitat, virtually all species of *Aphyosemion* need the same conditions in aquariums. Like the other genera of egg-laying tooth carps, to which family these fish belong, the *Aphyosemions* will only thrive in special aquariums which largely if not entirely recreate their natural environment. If kept in community tanks most species show only a fraction of their beautiful color forms and natural vivacity. Indeed, they often pine away and soon die.

It may be necessary to keep only one pair of these fish because the males are extremely aggressive towards each other: it is preferable however to put one male with a few females for the fish have a sexual appetite that is sometimes insatiable and it is quite common for a single female to be pursued until she dies from exhaustion. Most species shun the light and will hide themselves away if the aquarium is too brightly lit. The water surface of the tank should therefore preferably be provided with an abundance of plants which will filter the overhead light: the natural liveliness and beautiful coloring of the fish will then be apparent. Such plants will also be attractive to those species that like to lay their eggs in roots trailing in the water.

Although there is no vegetation in the natural environment of these fish, it is possible to put a few plants in the tank, provided of course varieties are chosen that require little light: irregular arrangements of wood and some peat fiber with long tendrils can also be put in. The bed should be as dark as possible: it can be made up of dark river sand mixed with some lumps of peat, so that the peat lies in places on the top of the bed. The sides and back of the tank can be covered with cork and/or peat.

The water will become light yellow as a result of the action of the peat and wood in the tank: this effect can be enhanced by filtering the water permanently over peat. Depending on its degree of hardness, that will make the water more acid, an excellent thing for these fish, which thrive best when the water registers pH 6–6.5 and DH 5°–7°. Although the temperature in their natural pools is fairly high, particularly during the day, the fish can be kept at 22°–24°C in captivity: their life span is reduced by higher temperatures. In captivity most species live only up to eight months, but if they are kept under the right conditions, they will usually have no trouble in reproducing, and the species survives as in the wild.

The diet can include all sorts of aquatic insects and larvae, but they prefer the larvae of black and white mosquitoes.

For many years biologists and aquarists have been making extensive studies of the reproductive behavior of egg-laying tooth carps, and in particular of the developmental biology of the eggs. The most recent advances in research are fully documented by Jordan Scheel in *Rivulins of the old world.*

There are may interesting features about the reproductive behavior of these fish. It is clear that the genus can be divided into two groups: egg-hangers and egg-buriers. The egg-hangers, such as *A.striatum, A.australe* and *A.bivittatum* lay their eggs between the roots of plants growing on the surface of the water or overhanging it on the bank, whose roots trail into the water. The egg-buriers lay their eggs in the sand, mud or humus present in the pool. It is not always possible however to make a clear distinction between these two groups. Many species are very adaptable to circumstances: egg-buriers will often lay their eggs between submerged roots and some egg-hangers will lay their eggs in or just above the bed, if no suitable roots are present.

The breeding fish can be encouraged by putting them in small glass tanks or plastic breeding aquariums. The volume depends on the particular species: for the smaller species it should be about six liters, for the larger species it should be between 10 and 16 liters. The bed and sides of these tanks should be painted dark brown or black on the outside. The same kind of water should be used as is recommended above for the species tank: the temperature should also be the same. The best results are obtained with fish which have been kept apart for one or two weeks before being introduced as a breed-

601. *Aphyosemion bivittatum*

ing pair into the breeding tank: if the males and females have always been kept separate, results will be even better. Before being put into the breeding tank the fish should be fed liberally with mosquito larvae, fruitflies and Tubifex so that they are in first-class condition. These rules apply to all species: the behavior of the two groups is however different.

Egg-hangers

These species have few if any specials requirements over the furnishing of the tank. There need not as a rule be a bed at all: if there is one, it should consist of very thoroughly-boiled peat dust or charcoal granules. Nylon breeding mops have proved an excellent spawning medium. These can be made from a disc of cork and nylon wool. The threads of wool (10–15 per disc) should be about 10 cm long and made to hang down from the water surface into the tank. There should be

602. *Aphyosemion bualanum*

two or three such mops per tank. As a rule the fish begin to mate quite soon after the breeding pair have been put into the tank. Usually only one egg is laid and fertilized at each stage of the mating, but the whole mating cycle can go on for a number of weeks. During this time the fish mate almost daily. In the first few days 15–30 eggs are laid daily, depending on the species, but thereafter the numbers are fewer. Many more eggs may be produced if there is more than one female to each male, though this does not always happen: a second female in the tank may even inhibit breeding because of the limited space available in the breeding tank. Various factors can influence the sequence of events and the individual breeder must determine for himself by trial and error, what are, under the circumstances, the best policies to adopt. It is often advisable to separate the breeding pair after two or three days and keep them apart for four days or so, feeding them well while they are separated: they can be re-introduced into the breeding tank for another two or three days: the cycle can be repeated for a few weeks, The rather large glassy or yellowish eggs are clearly visible, particularly against a dark background. The casing of the shell is hard and so they can be picked off the breeding mops with tweezers or with the fingers either immediately after being laid or once a day: of course the mops have to be taken out of the tank before this is done. The eggs must be transferred to small breeding bowls with no more than 2 cm depth of water. The composition of this water is not critical, and does not even have to be the same as that in the breeding tank. A small amount of Trapaflavin should be added to this water to guard against bacteria (1 gm to 200–300 liters). The eggs will hatch in this solution, with no adverse effect on the fry, after 10 to 14 days, at a temperature of about 18° C. Higher temperatures should be avoided: lower temperatures do no harm but delay the development of the eggs. The breeding bowls should be covered to prevent the eggs being damaged by light. The eggs should be inspected regularly and any unfertilised eggs, which will be white, should be removed carefully with a pipette.
The eggs can be stored for a long time: they can even be transported provided they are kept cool and in thoroughly-boiled and washed damp peat dust. It is possible to hatch eggs simultaneously which were laid at different times, by changing the water and adding a large quantity of infusorians or a small quantity of micro-eels. Very often the same results can be achieved merely by thoroughly stirring the water.
As soon as the eggs have hatched the fry should be transferred to small tanks where they can be raised. At first the volume of water in the tanks need be no more than was to be found in the breeding bowls. The fry grow very quickly and greedily accept *Artemia nauplii* from the very first hour. They can also be fed with sieved Cyclops and Daphnia: Grindal norms and Enchytrae are also an excellent food. The fish are sexually mature after six to eight weeks.
If any species of *Aphyosemion* are bred for commercial purposes, it is advisable if possible to raise the fry in ordinary tap water.

Egg-buriers

The breeding habits of the egg-buriers are very similar to those of the species *Nothobranchius* from East Africa and the species *Cynolebias* and *Pterolebias* from South America. The eggs are deposited in the bed, although the fish do not themselves penetrate it. Mating takes place just above the bed and the newly-laid egg is pushed into the bed of sand, mud or humus with a sharp flick of the fish's tail. The best bed to provide in the breeding tank for these fish is one of sifted peat: this should be thoroughly washed and rinsed and then rubbed through the sieve to make it crumbly. Alternatively a layer of nylon wool will provide a good bed for some species, such as *A. sjoestedti*. It is of course much easier to find the eggs if nylon wool is used as a bed. The eggs of *A. sjoestedti* must be treated in the same way as the eggs of egg-hangers: it is therefore particularly important to be able to find them easily. The eggs of this species will hatch out after about 14 days if treated in this way: if kept dry for some time before being prepared for hatching, then the eggs take considerably longer to hatch: it is not yet certain whether this is also true for other species.

603. *Aphyosemion gulare*

Egg-buriers should be prepared as breeding fish in the same way as egg-hangers. When the eggs have been laid they do not, except as noted above in the case of *A.sjoestedte* need any further attention. They are more sensitive to light than the eggs of egg-hangers; they seem to develop more slowly and to require a period of rest before hatching. Traditionally one male is placed in the breeding tank with two females. During the fortnight over which the mating cycle is spread, the fish should be fed daily with the larvae of white or black mosquitoes: other food which could foul the bed should be avoided. The temperature of the breeding tank can fluctuate between 22°C and 24°C. When it is clear that mating has ceased, the breeding fish should be removed from the tank and the water carefully siphoned off. The tank should then be left to stand so that the peat bed dries out naturally as it would in the wild. Alternatively however, the water can be squeezed out carefully from the peat by using a net and the peat then stored in a plastic bag to give the eggs the chance to rest. No exact information can be given on how long the eggs should be allowed to rest for each species, but in general they should be left for at least six weeks. If slightly acid water and infusorians are then added, the first eggs will hatch out in a few hours, but it may be a fortnight – or as long as the original mating cycle, before all the eggs have hatched. The fry are very voracious so they should be separated as soon as possible, otherwise the smaller will be eaten by the larger.

The curious cycle of development of these eggs has been described by Foersch who believes that after the eggs have been laid and fertilised, they lie completely dormant for a while: then, there is a period of embryonic development: this is followed by another period of rest for the embryo, and when that ends, the egg hatches. It is clear however that very often there is no dormant stage after the eggs are laid: the embryonic development begins immediately: in some cases however this dormant period can be as long as some months. Experiments with the eggs of other fish that lay eggs in a similar way have shown that sometimes the eggs that are dried and stored immediately they have been laid, develop more quickly than those that have been allowed to remain submerged for a longer time. The eggs of yet other genera of fish have been shown to remain alive and capable of hatching even after being stored for some years. These extremely interesting phenomena, which must be related in some way to the peculiar conditions in which the fish live in the wild, have been fully detailed by Jordan Scheel in *Rivulins of the old world.*

In general changing the environment stimulates the eggs: changing the water and lowering the temperature to 15°C have made them hatch. It is noteworthy that the fish hatched from eggs kept at high temperatures are usually less vividly colored than those hatched from eggs kept at lower temperatures. There can be variations in the color of the fish due to many other factors and it is important that fish selected as breeding pairs should be very carefully chosen to preserve the purity and quality of the strains.

Many aquarists have little interest in these fish because of their short life-span: however, they reproduce fairly easily in captivity and because it is possible to recreate their entire life cycle in the aquarium they can be extremely interesting fish to keep. Some are of unparalleled beauty and it is to be hoped that these species will become increasingly popular among amateur aquarists. Even though they are somewhat demanding fish, unsuitable for a community tank.

604. *Aphyosemion cognatum*

605. *Aphyosemion ahli*

606. *Aphyosemion chrystyi*

607. *Aphyosemion australe*

APHOSEMION AHLI

Family: *Cyprinodontidae*

Genus: *Aphyosemion*

English name: none

Origin: The eastern part of Cameroon

Size: Approximately 6 cm

Habitat: Found in seasonal lakes and pools and marshy areas

SHAPE, COLORING AND MARKINGS: The body is elongated, fairly deep and only slightly laterally compressed. The basic coloration and markings vary significantly according to the place of origin. The specimen illustrated comes from the area of the Mboumboula river. It has a brownish-green back tinged with yellow or red. The front half of the body is silvery greyish-green and the back is more or less purple, tinged with red or blue. There are fantastic red stripes and dots on the head, the gill covers and on the area in front of the ventral fins: there are vertical red wavy lines running from the ventral fins to the caudal peduncle. The underside of the body is orangey-red. The dorsal fin is yellowish-red, liberally flecked with dark red: it has a cobalt blue edge, bordered by a narrow dark red band. The anal fin is a beautiful cobalt blue at the base and has a golden-yellow edge separated from a dark red band by a fine blue stripe. The caudal fin is predominantly cobalt blue with dark red marks in the central area. The lower lobe is elongated, has a broad golden-yellow edge and like the anal fin, a dark red band: the upper lobe is similar, but the yellow edge is narrower and less bright. The ventral fins resemble the anal fins though in many specimens the edge is white. The pectoral fins are reddish, tinged with yellow.
Females have more rounded fins which are less vividly colored: they are sometimes greenish-brown tinged with yellow. There are no bands on the fins and the body marks are less prominent.
Males are as described above.

GENERAL CARE: See Introductory note.

BREEDING: See Introductory note under egg-hangers.

ADDITIONAL INFORMATION: Synonyms: *A.calliurum ahli* and *A.pascheni*. This species has often been cross-bred and it is difficult to find a pure strain.

APHYOSEMION ARNOLDI

Family: *Cyprinodontidae*

Genus: *Aphyosemion*

English name: none

Origin: Nigeria, the delta of the Niger

Size: Approximately 5.5 cm

Habitat: Found in seasonal lakes and pools, and in both fresh and brackish waters

SHAPE, COLORING AND MARKINGS: The body is elongated, fairly deep and laterally slightly compressed. The basic coloration and markings vary significantly according to the locality of origin. The specimen illustrated comes from the area of the Wokocha river. The back is light brown tinged with red: the flanks are silvery-blue: the underside is yellowish-brown. There are distinctive deep red stripes and marks on the head, lower lip and gill covers. The pectoral fins vary in color from a light to a bluish-green and have a wide dark edge and a number of deep red marks which becoming more diffuse on the flanks merge together as diagonal wavy lines below the dorsal fin. The dorsal fin itself is a bluish-violet, with a greenish base and yellowish-green at the back: it is edged with red and carries numerous red marks and stripes. The light blue ventral and anal fins both have a greenish-brown base and are edged and flecked with red. The central part of the caudal fin is greenish-yellow with deep red marks and a red edge. The lower lobe is elongated and varies in color from light blue to yellow: it is separated from the central area by a deep red band. The upper lobe is also elongated and edged with a deep red band with a light blue border.
Females have more rounded fins which are less vividly colored: they are sometimes greyish-brown: the red flecks on the flanks are less vivid.
Males are as described above.

GENERAL CARE: See Introductory note.

BREEDING: See Introductory note under egg-buriers.

ADDITIONAL INFORMATION: The various local varieties are distinguished by differences in the basic coloration and the markings on the fins. They have been cross-bred to produce *A.arnoldi walkeri* and *A.arnoldi filamentosum*.

APHYOSEMION AUSTRALE

Family: *Cyprinodontidae*

Genus: *Aphyosemion*

English name: Lyretail

Origin: Gabon

Size: Approximately 6 cm

Habitat: No details are available of its natural habitat.

SHAPE, COLORING AND MARKINGS: The body is elongated, fairly deep and laterally slightly compressed. The basic coloration is greenish with a striking orange tinge: the back is light brown, the flanks light green and the head, belly and caudal peduncle predominantly orange-brown. There are prominent wavy lines on the lower jaw, the gill covers and

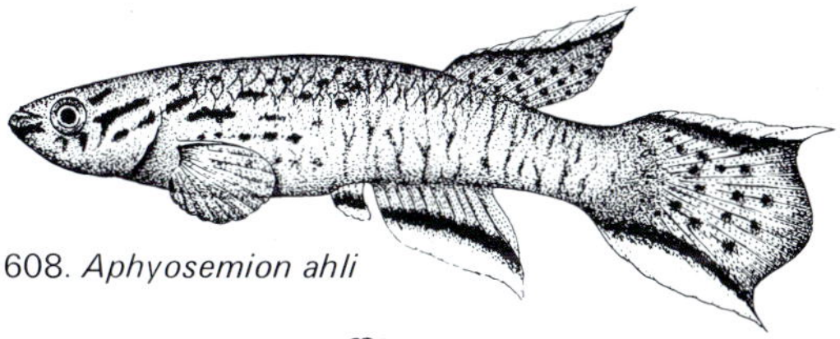
608. *Aphyosemion ahli*

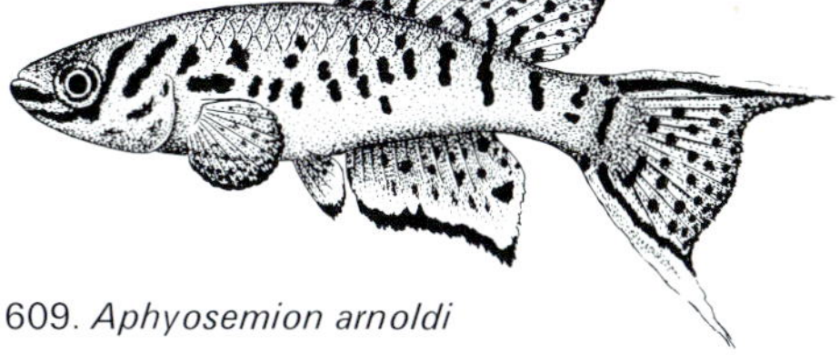
609. *Aphyosemion arnoldi*

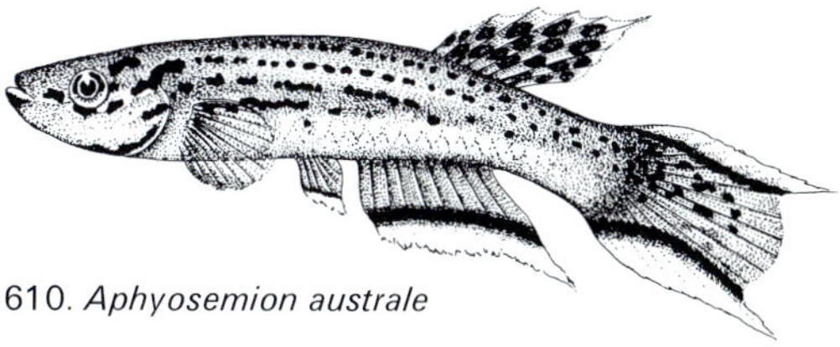
610. *Aphyosemion australe*

611. *Aphyosemion arnoldi*

above the pectoral fins, as well as numerous deep red flecks distributed randomly over the rest of the body. The dorsal fin is orangey-red, flecked with red: it has a milky-white or light blue edge bordered by a deep red band. The anal fin is orangey-yellow, edged with red and with a white tip. The centre part of the caudal fin, irregularly flecked with red, is bluish: the base and edge are orangey-brown: the upper and lower lobes, elongated and identical in shape, are yellowish-white and divided from the central part by a deep red band. The ventral and pectoral fins are yellowish-orange: the former is edged, the latter tinged, with red.
Females have more rounded fins, less vividly colored: sometimes they are greenish-brown: the red flecks on the flanks are less prominent. Males are as described above.

General care: See Introductory note.

Breeding: See Introductory note under egg-hangers.

Additional information: *A.polychromum* is a synonym. *A.australe* is one of the most popular species with aquarists, but curiously, little or nothing is known about its natural habitat. It does not seem to have been imported recently which suggests that nearly all specimens now found in aquariums have been bred or cross-bred in captivity. The most common cross-breed is the orange variety bred by Hjerresen in 1953. There have also been reports of cross-breeds with *A.ahli* and *A.gardneri*.

APHYOSEMION BATESII

Family: *Cyprinodontidae*
Genus: *Aphyosemion*
English name: none
Origin: Cameroon
Size: Approximately 7 cm
Habitat: Found in seasonal lakes and pools and marshy areas

Shape, coloring and markings: The body is elongated, fairly deep and laterally slightly compressed. In shape *A.batesii* closely resembles *A.ahli*. Its coloration is different but difficult to describe because no live specimens are available for study. In general its color form resembles that of *A.splendidum*, to which it is closely related. However *A.batesii* is more irregularly flecked with red. *A.batesii* also lacks the distinctively elongated caudal fin rays of *A.splendidum*: it does have the same golden-yellow border to the caudal fin.
No external sexual characteristics can be identified with certainty but it is reasonable to assume that as in related species, the female will have more rounded fins and less vivid colors than the male.

General care: This species should be treated in the same way as other species: see introductory note.

Breeding: Nothing is known about the breeding habits of this species.

Additional information: It seems unlikely that this species has ever been imported. It was first described by George Albert Boulenger in 1911.

APHYOSEMION BIVITTATUM

Family: *Cyprinodontidae*
Genus: *Aphyosemion*
English name: none
Origin: Togo, Equatorial Guinea
Size: Approximately 4 cm
Habitat: Found in seasonal pools and lakes as well as marshy areas

Shape, coloring and markings: The body is elongated, fairly deep and laterally slightly compressed. The basic coloration and markings vary significantly according to the place of origin. The specimen illustrated comes from Southwest Nigeria, from the area of Ljebu-Ode. The basic coloration is bluish-green: the back is darker: the belly an orange-brown tinged with yellow. There are extraordinary red stripes on the head and gill covers and a beautiful checkered pattern on the upper part of the body, of red and golden-yellow or light brown. All the scales have red or red-brown edges. The dorsal fin is very strongly developed and varies from orange red to rust brown, with dark patches and stripes on the membranes. The anal fin is orange-red with a light green base and a narrow blue edge bordered by a deep red band. The ventral fins are light bluish-green with blue and red bands round the edges. The red, blue edged pectoral fins have a yellow base.
Females have more rounded fins. The basic color is yellowish and there are two distinct dark horizontal lines on the body.
Males are as described above.

General care: See Introductory note.

Breeding: See Introductory note. *A.bivittatum* is an egg-hanger but unusually this species lays its eggs on plants just above the bed.

Additional information: *A.bivittatum* has been closely studied by scientists who have discovered that it is in fact really a whole group of sub-species: these sub-species cannot however be distinguished except by biochemical tests. Some sub-species can inter-breed without difficulty: others cannot. There are many synonyms: *A.bitaeniatum*, *A.bivittatum hollyi*, *A.loennbergii*, *A.multicolor*, *A.nigri*, *A.pappenheimi*, *A.riggenbachi*, *A.rubrostictum*, *A.splendopleuris*, *A.unicolor*.

APHYOSEMION BUALANUM

Family: *Cyprinodontidae*
Genus: *Aphyosemion*
English name: none
Origin: Cameroon
Size: Approximately 5 cm
Habitat: Found in seasonal lakes and pools and marshy areas

Shape, coloring and markings: The body is elongated, fairly deep and laterally slightly compressed. The basic coloration varies significantly according to the place of origin. The specimen illustrated here comes from the marshes in west Cameroon. The back is light grey tinged with brown: the flanks are cobalt blue: the lower jaw and belly are yellowish-white. There are irregular deep red wavy lines on the lower jaw and the gill covers. Vertical bands, made up of dark red spots, run down the body, particularly between the front anal fin rays and the caudal peduncle. The dorsal

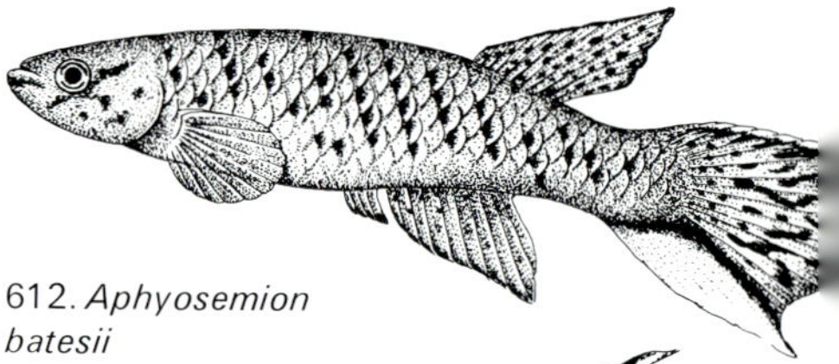

612. *Aphyosemion batesii*

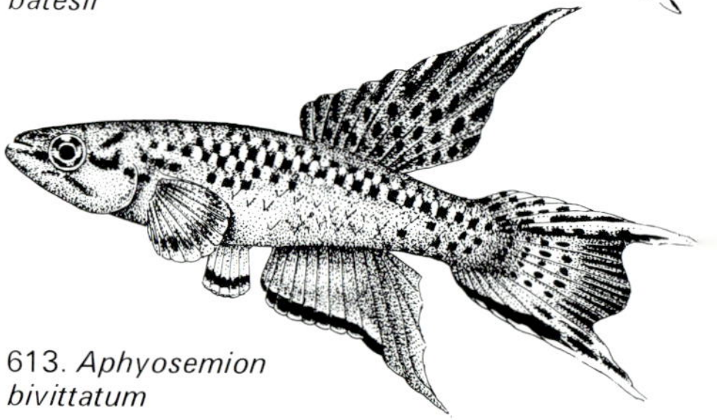

613. *Aphyosemion bivittatum*

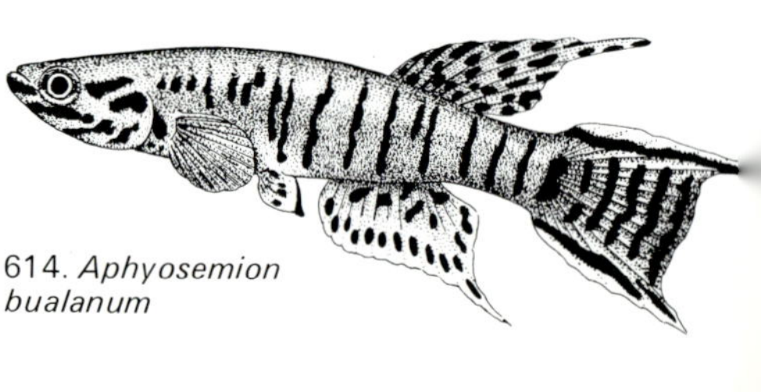

614. *Aphyosemion bualanum*

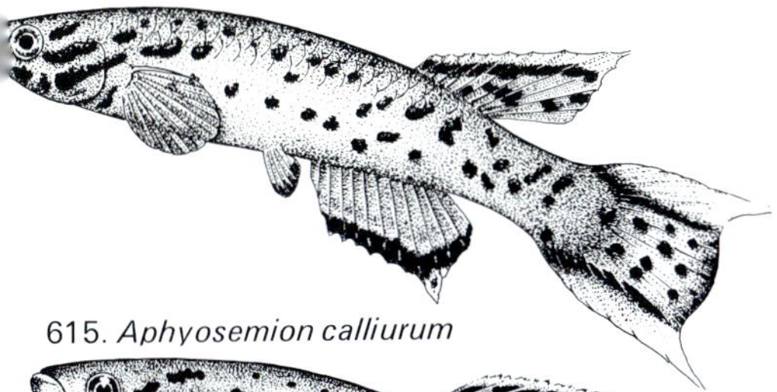

615. *Aphyosemion calliurum*

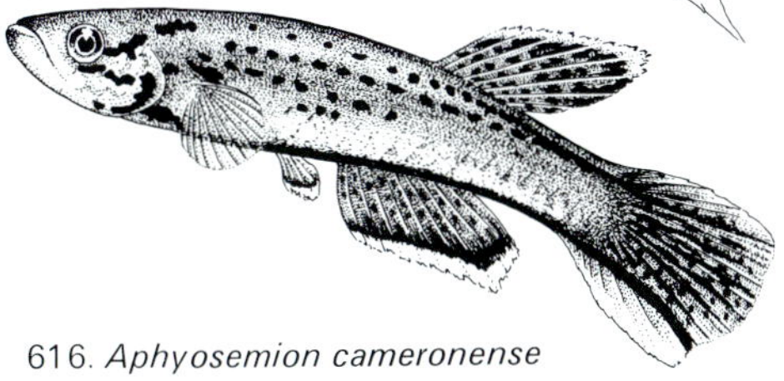

616. *Aphyosemion cameronense*

fin is light green tinged with brownish-red at the front, marked with red dots and rectangles running parallel to the fin rays. Similar marks appear on the anal fin, a beautiful cobalt blue, lightening at the edge. The caudal fin is a bluish-red, with two vivid dark red marks at the base, and five dark red transverse bands in the center. The lower fin ray is elongated and light blue, separated from the central part of the fin by a prominent horizontal red line: the upper fin ray is similar but more elongated. The ventral fins are cobalt blue flecked with red: the pectoral fins are orangey-red tinged with purple.
Females have more rounded fins, are less brightly colored and sometimes greenish-brown: there are no prominent marks on the fins but a number of reddish dots and transverse bands on the body.
Males are as described above.

General care: See Introductory note.

Breeding: See Introductory note under egg-hangers.

Additional information: Synonyms: *A.elberti, A.rubrofascium, A.tessmanni*. This is an exceptionally beautiful species but one still relatively unknown to aquarists. Various local varieties have very different basic color forms. This species has been cross-bred, for example with *A.exiguum*, to which it is very closely related. Both the fry and young specimens of these two species look very much alike, and the differences are noted under *A.exiguum*.

APHYOSEMION CALLIURUM

Family: *Cyprinodontidae*
Genus: *Aphyosemion*
English name: none
Origin: Nigeria
Size: Approximately 5 cm
Habitat: Found in seasonal lakes and pools and marshy areas

Shape, coloring and markings: The body is elongated, fairly deep and laterally slightly compressed. The basic coloration and markings vary significantly according to the place of origin. The variety which comes from the neighborhood of Ljebu-Ode, which is a fairly typical variety is mainly brownish-red in color. The yellowish head has extraordinary red patches and stripes. The back, as far as the dorsal fin, is bluish-violet: the belly is yellowish-white. On the back and flanks, especially on the upper half of the body, there are rows of red circles. The dorsal fin is a rust brown, with a narrow yellow edge and large red marks on the membranes. The anal fin is rust brown with a wide clear yellow edge and a red band: similar marks appear on the ventral fins. The caudal fin is also rust brown at the base, becoming predominantly red, with a central orange-yellow patch. The lower fin lobe has a very vivid yellow edge bordered by a red band: the upper lobe has a rather deeper yellow edge and a red band. The pectoral fins are colorless and transparent, edged with orange.
Females have less variation in the basic rust brown coloration and no striking marks. The fin rays of the caudal fin are not elongated and the other fins are less powerfully developed.
Males are as described above.

General care: See Introductory note.

Breeding: See Introductory note under egg-hangers.

Additional information: Synonym: *A.vexillifer*. *A.calliurum* is well-known among aquarists but it is unusual to come across a pure strain. This particular red-brown variety from the area of Ljebu-Ode is almost unknown to aquarists: the variety cross-bred with *A.ahli*, known as *A.calliurum ahli* is more common. There are now many other cross-breeds on the market which, although often very beautifully colored, seriously prejudice the attempts of conscientious breeders to maintain a pure strain.

617. *Aphyosemion batesii*

APHYOSEMION CAMERONENSE

Family: *Cyprinodontidae*
Genus: *Aphyosemion*
English name: none
Origin: Cameroon
Size: Approximately 6 cm
Habitat: Found in seasonal lakes and pools and marshy areas

Shape, coloring and markings: The body is elongated, fairly deep and laterally slightly compressed. It greatly resembles the related species *A.ridianum*. The basic coloration and markings vary significantly according to the place of origin. Nevertheless all varieties have a distinctive and characteristic pattern of red marks on the lower half of the body, from the pectoral fin to the lower lobe of the caudal fin, where the pattern is bordered by a yellowish-white area. The pattern may be either an unbroken red line, or a series of red flecks and stripes. A similar area of red marks stretches from below the dorsal fin to the upper lobe of the caudal fin, where it meets a patch of yellowish-white or greenish-yellow. The basic coloration is greenish or brilliant green and the back varies from a brown to a greenish-brown. There are prominent deep red marks and irregular stripes on the head

and gill covers. Similar marks on the flanks form irregular red lines. The dorsal fin is greenish with a yellowish-white edge and many flecks of red: the anal fin is greenish, flecked with red, with a more prominent yellowish-white edge, also bordered with red. The caudal fin is greenish with numerous red marks in the center.
Females are less brightly colored: sometimes merely a brownish-green with no red marks on the body or fins.
Males are as described above.

General care: See Introductory note.

Breeding: Nothing is recorded about the mating habits of this species.

Additional information: *A.cameronense* is still hardly known among aquarists, even though it was first imported into Europe as long ago as 1913. An unusual characteristic of *A.cameronense* is that it always swims near the surface. Like the *Epiplatys* and *Panchax* fish, it lies in wait for prey that may appear on the surface, and keeps absolutely still: when the prey comes within range it attacks suddenly.

APHYOSEMION CELIAE

Family: *Cyprinidontidae*
Genus: *Aphyosemion*
English name: none
Origin: South Cameroon, in the neighborhood of Kumba
Size: Approximately 5 cm
Habitat: Found in lakes and pools and small sluggish streams

Shape, coloring and markings: The body is elongated, fairly deep and laterally slightly compressed. Both in shape and color *A.celiae* greatly resembles *A.cinnamemeum*, but it has less prominent markings. The basic coloration is a beautiful reddish-brown with an iridescent blue tinge, particularly evident on the front half of the body. Irregular deep red stripes run from the eye, over the gill covers and the upper half of the head. The body is covered with a more regular pattern of red marks. The pectoral fins are colorless and transparent: the other fins have a light red base, a dark red band and a yellow border with a bluish-white edge.
Females have less variation in the rust brown coloring. The red marks on the body are not very prominent and there are very few if any on the fins.
Males are as described above.

618. *Aphyosemion celiae*

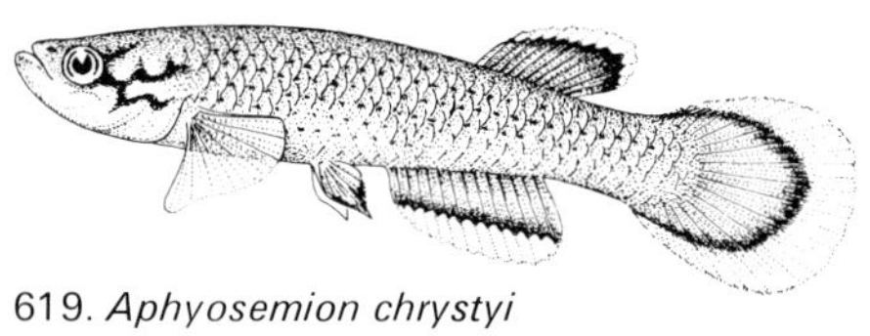

619. *Aphyosemion chrystyi*

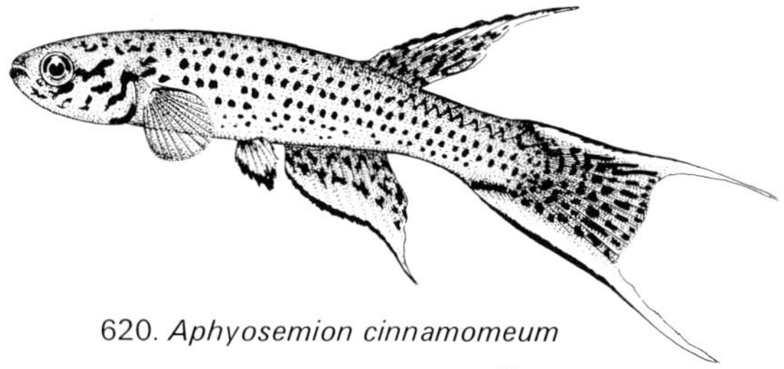

620. *Aphyosemion cinnamomeum*

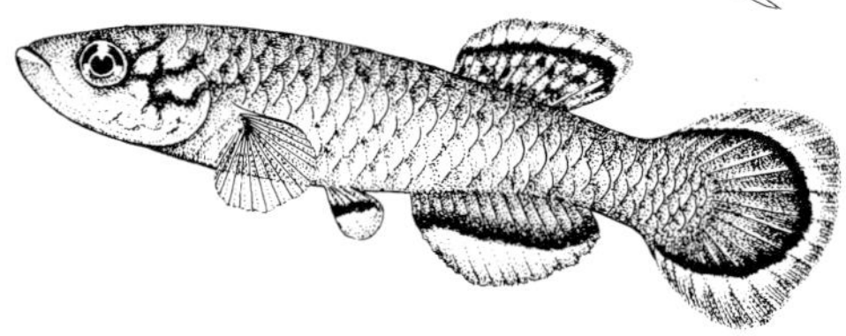

General care: See Introductory note.

Breeding: *A.celiae* prefers to lay its eggs in the bed but will also lay them just above the bed among fine leaved plants if no suitable bed is available. See Introductory note under egg-buriers.

Additional information: This species was first described by the well-known authority on the Cyprinodontidae, Jorgen Scheel in 1971. *A.celiae* has proved to be a hardy species which can be kept with other fish, preferably from similar natural environments, without difficulty.

APHYOSEMION CHRISTYI

Family: *Cyprinodontidae*
Genus: *Aphyosemion*
English name: none
Origin: Zaire
Size: Approximately 5 cm
Habitat: Found in the neighborhood of Stanleyville, in seasonal lakes and pools

Shape, coloring and markings: The body is elongated, fairly deep and laterally slightly compressed. The basic coloration is salmon with a greenish-blue tinge. The back varies from green to brown. The upper half of the head and snout are yellowish-orange, and there are prominent red flecks and irregular stripes on the gill covers. Nearly all the scales have a red mark, giving the whole body a regular patterning of red. The dorsal fin has a dark red base and edge, the latter bordered by an area of light green: the membranes are flecked with red. The caudal fin varies from bluish-green to a brownish-red: flecked and lined with bright red it has very elongated rays: both the upper and lower lobes are yellowish-green and edged with red. The anal fin is also yellowish-green, with a dark red edge and a bluish-green base with bright red patches. The ventral fin has similar marks. The pectoral fins are orangey-yellow flecked with red.
Females are yellowish-brown with less prominent marks on the body and fins: the fin rays are not elongated.
Males are as described above.

General care: See Introductory note.

Breeding: See Introductory note under egg-hangers.

Additional information: Synonym: *A.congicum*. This beautiful species was first described by George Albert Boulenger in 1915. It has only recently become well-known and a number of cross-breeds have now become available. It is unusual to find a pure strain. This species is often confused with *A.elegans*, which it closely resembles.

APHYOSEMION CINNAMOMEUM

Family: *Cyprinodontidae*
Genus: *Aphyosemion*
English name: none
Origin: Cameroon
Size: Approximately 4 cm
Habitat: Found north of Kumba in shallow streams in the mountainous district

Shape, coloring and markings: The body is elongated, fairly deep and laterally only slightly compressed. At first sight *A.cinnamomeum* closely resembles members of the genus *Nothobranchius* because of its rounded fins: it also closely resembles *A.celiae*, although it is more vividly colored than that related species. The basic coloration is mainly brownish: the back varies from fawn to dark brown: the flanks are an iridescent green: the underside of the head and the belly are greyish-green. There are prominent red patches and irregular stripes on the head and gill covers. The dorsal fin is rust brown, flecked with light blue and with a light blue iridescent edge and a brownish-red band. The anal fin has a greyish-green base and a wide, yellowish-white edge bordering on a brownish-red band. The caudal fin is greyish-green with a semi-circular brownish-red band bordered by an area of light green, which merges into the greenish-yellow or ochre edge of the fin. The pectoral fins are orangey-red: the ventral fins have a greyish-green base, a brownish-red band and a wide yellowish-white edge.
Females are mainly brownish in color: there are no prominent marks on the fins.
Males are as described above.

General care: See Introductory note. This species keeps to the bottom of the tank.

621. *Aphyosemion filamentosum*

BREEDING: See Introductory note under egg-buriers.

ADDITIONAL INFORMATION: This species was discovered only very recently and was first described by Clausen in 1963. Little is yet known about its habits. According to Jorgen Scheel, *A.cinnamomeum* is difficult to keep in hard alkaline water and it is very sensitive to bacteria and *Oodinium* present in soft and acid waters. It is interesting that members of the genus *Nothobranchius* to which this fish has so close a resemblance at first sight, are also very sensitive to bacteria and *Oodinium*.

APHYOSEMION COGNATUM

Family: *Cyprinodontidae*

Genus: *Aphyosemion*

English name: none

Origin: Central Congo

Size: Approximately 6 cm

Habitat: Found in seasonal lakes and pools and marshy areas

SHAPE, COLORING AND MARKINGS: The body is elongated, slender and laterally only slightly compressed. The back is a dark olive: the flanks are greenish-brown: the belly and underside of the head vary from white to cream. The whole body is covered with a pattern of red flecks, regular except above the pectoral fin where the marks are irregular and vary in size. Additional red patches and stripes appear on the gill covers and below the eyes. The upper half of the head is dark brown with further red marks. The dorsal fin is greenish, flecked with red and it has a grass green edge. The base of the anal fin is cream becoming grass green, heavily flecked with red and with a narrow red edge. The upper and lower lobes of the caudal fin are pale green: the lower lobe carries a band of red: the central area of the caudal fin is brownish-green, irregularly flecked with red. The ventral and pectoral fins are transparent: both are flecked with red and the pectoral fin has a yellow border.
Females are brownish-yellow with innumerable rust colored marks.
Males are as described above.

GENERAL CARE: See Introductory note.

BREEDING: See Introductory note under egg-buriers.

ADDITIONAL INFORMATION: This species was first described by Meinken in 1951 and since that date has become quite popular with aquarists.

APHYOSEMION ELEGANS

Family: *Cyprinodontidae*

Genus: *Aphyosemion*

English name: none

Origin: Central Congo, Bikore, Eala, Flandria, Kunumgu, Madja

Size: Approximately 4 cm

Habitat: Found in seasonal lakes and pools and marshy areas

SHAPE, COLORING AND MARKINGS: The body is elongated, slender and laterally slightly compressed. The basic coloration is salmon with a bluish-green tinge. The back varies from green to brown: the upper side of the head and snout are yellowish-orange. Beautiful red patches and dramatic stripes lie on the gill covers. Nearly all the scales have a red mark, giving a regular pattern over the whole body. The dorsal fin, flecked with bright red on the membranes has a dark red base and edge, the latter bordering on an area of pale green. The caudal fin can vary from bluish-green to brownish-red: it has bright red patches and stripes and the fin has very elongated rays. Both the upper and lower lobes have red edges which form a vivid contrast to the adjacent areas of yellowish-green. The anal fin has a bluish-green base, bright red patches and stripes: it has a dark red edge and is otherwise a striking yellowish-green. Similar marks appear on the ventral fin. The pectoral fins are orangey-yellow tinged with red.
Females are yellowish-brown, without elongated fin rays and with less prominent marks on the body and fins.
Males are as described above.

GENERAL CARE: See Introductory note.

BREEDING: See Introductory note under egg-hangers. The eggs are adhesive and are laid on underwater plants or other submerged articles.

ADDITIONAL INFORMATION: *A.elegans* was first described as *Haplochilus elegans* by George Albert Boulenger as long ago as 1889. Since then *A.elegans* has been known by a variety of names. *A.elegans* is now the generally accepted name but there is still a great deal of confusion between. *A.elegans* and *A.christy* which it closely resembles.

APHYOSEMION EXIGUUM

Family: *Cyprinodontidae*

Genus: *Aphyosemion*

English name: none

Origin: East Cameroon

Size: Approximately 4 cm

Habitat: Found in seasonal lakes and pools and in marshy areas

SHAPE, COLORING AND MARKINGS: The body is elongated, fairly deep and laterally slightly

622. *Aphyosemion cognatum*

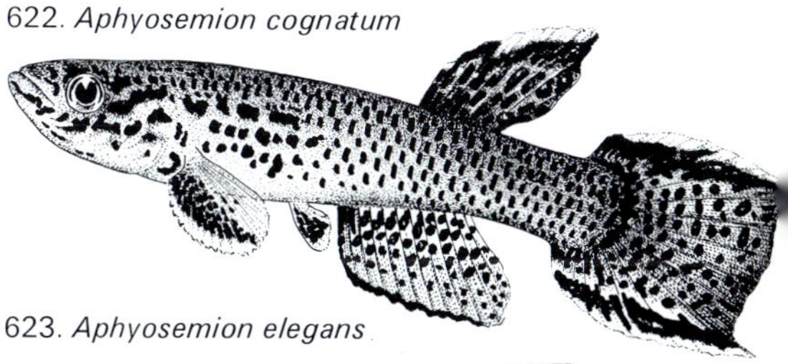

623. *Aphyosemion elegans*

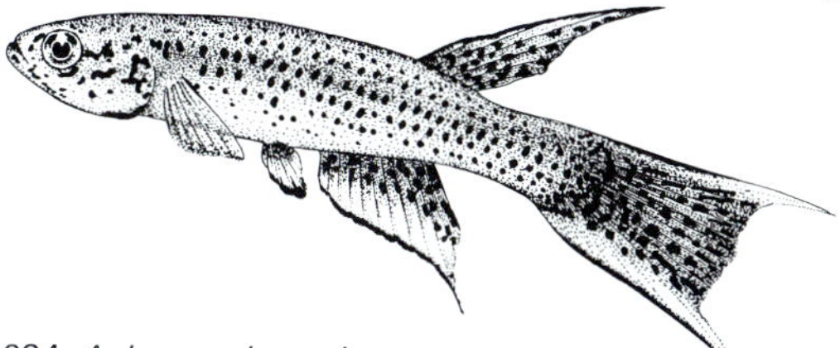

624. *Aphyosemion exiguum*

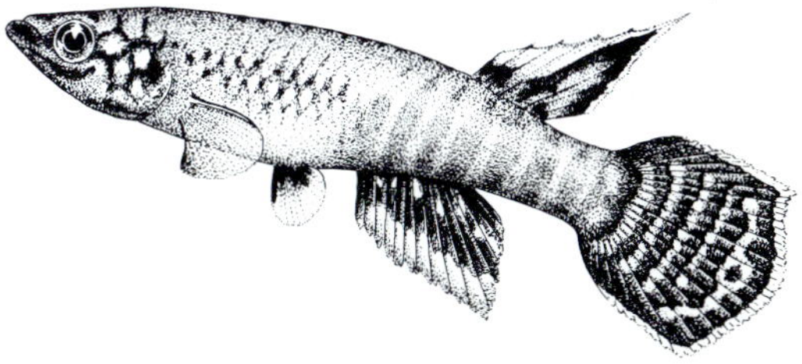

compressed. The basic coloration is golden-yellow, tinged with pale green. The back is olive green and the belly ochre. There are prominent red stripes on the head, cheeks and lower lip and iridescent emerald patches between the marks on the gill covers. An orangey-red net-like pattern is to be seen on the flanks above the belly: behind, beginning above the front anal fin rays, seven or eight orangey-red transverse bands run almost as far as the back. The dorsal fin is grass green with wide red bands and a yellow patch at the front. The anal fin is also grass green except for the base and central area which are both bright red. The caudal fin is bright red with a narrow light blue edge and four or five green bands in the center. The ventral fins are cobalt blue, with a red base: the pectoral fins are yellowish with a blue-red edge.
Females are mainly yellowish-green or brownish: the fin rays are not elongated and the fin markings are less striking.
Males are as described above.

General care: See Introductory note.

Breeding: See Introductory note under egg-hangers. The eggs are adhesive and laid on submerged plants.

Additional information: This extremely beautiful species as first described by George Albert Boulenger in 1911. He saw only one specimen. In 1966 Jorgen Scheel discovered fairly large numbers in the localities Boulenger had listed. Scheel noted that the hardness of the water in the natural environment is only 0.1–1.5 °DH and the acidity fluctuates between 4.2 pH and 6.8 pH. Scheel found this species with specimens of *A.bualanum:* the fry of the two species closely resemble each other. Young fish of these two species also look very similar: they both have the same predominantly blue color. However young specimens of *A.exiguum* have a red pigmentation which is never present in the young fish of *A.bualanum*. Nevertheless the two species are obviously very closely related.

APHYOSEMION FILAMENTOSUM

Family: *Cyprinodontidae*
Genus: *Aphyosemion*
English name: Plumed Lyretail
Origin: West Nigeria
Size: Approximately 6 cm
Habitat: Found in seasonal lakes and pools and in marshy areas

Shape, coloring and markings: The body is elongated, fairly deep and laterally slightly compressed. The basic coloration is brownish, with a steel blue tinge. There are dramatic reddish-brown stripes on the cheeks and lower lip. The upper half of the body and the caudal peduncle have a reddish tinge. The dorsal fin is steel blue with a brownish- red tinge and a light blue edge: a large number of irregular reddish-brown marks also appear on the dorsal fin and are largest at its base. The anal fin is the same steel blue with large irregular reddish-brown marks that form two bands. The caudal fin has a greenish-blue base and is otherwise steel blue with light blue lobes and numerous red patches and stripes. The pectoral and ventral fins are blue with red pigmentation.
Females are considerably smaller, up to about 4.5 cm. Females have less vivid coloring, and in particular lack the red pigmentation seen in males, and their elongated fin rays.
Males are as described above.

General care: See Introductory note.

Breeding: See Introductory note under egg-buriers. The eggs are not adhesive and are laid just above the bed or may be pushed into it.

Additional information: This exceptionally beautiful specimen was for many years thought to be no more than a blue variety of the more popular *A.arnoldi.* It was quite well-known under the name Fundulus of Togo and it was first described by Meinken in 1933 as *Fundulopanchax filamentosus*. It is a species closely related to *A.arnoldi* but easily distinguished from it by the different coloring of the fins. In older males red bands may appear in both the anal fin and the lower lobe of the caudal fin and the fish takes on a more greenish color generally.

APHYOSEMION GARDNERI

Family: *Cyprinodontidae*
Genus: *Aphyosemion*
English name: none
Origin: West Cameroon and East Nigeria
Size: Approximately 6 cm
Habitat: Found in seasonal lakes and pools

Shape, coloring and markings: The body is elongated, fairly deep and laterally only slightly compressed. The basic coloration and markings can vary significantly according to the place of origin. The specimen illustrated comes from the neighborhood of Port Harcourt in Eastern Nigeria. The neck and back are fawn, becoming bluish-green towards the tail. The flanks are a grass green with a number of red marks which towards the front of the body, before the dorsal fin and above the caudal peduncle, are arranged in regular rows. The lower lip has a red edge which runs into the prominent red stripes under the eye and on the gill covers. The dorsal fin is bluish-green with a wide orangey-red edge and red

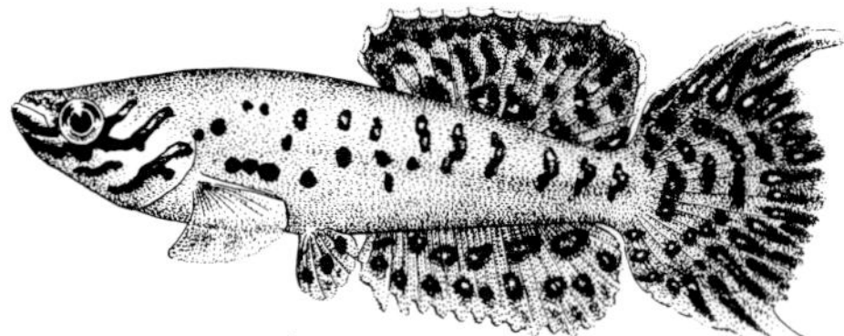
625. *Aphyosemion filamentosum*

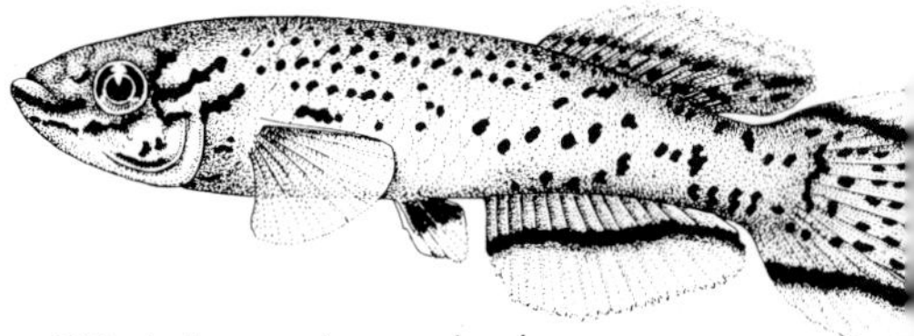
626. *Aphyosemion gardneri*

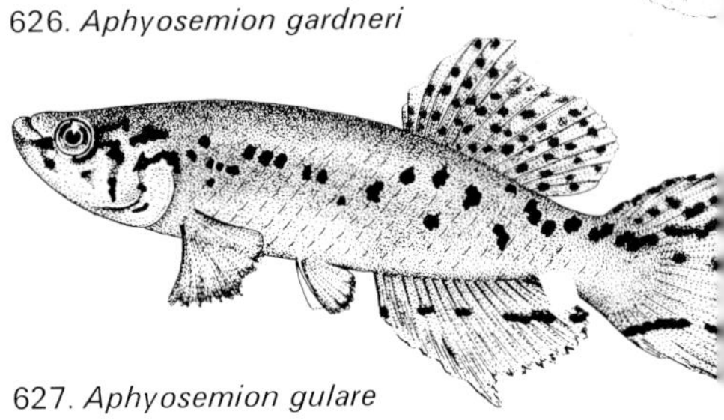
627. *Aphyosemion gulare*

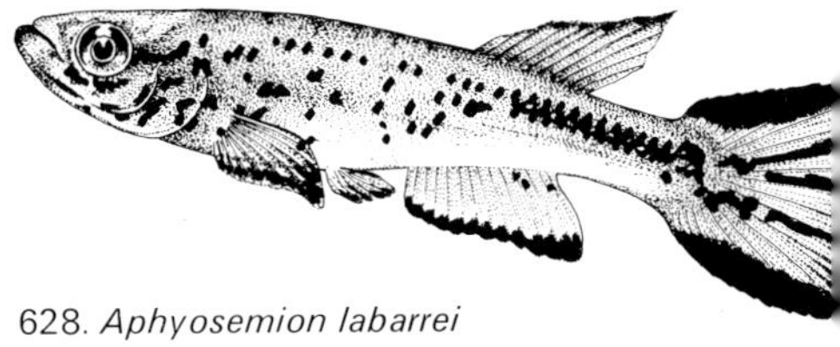
628. *Aphyosemion labarrei*

spots. The anal fin has a bluish-green base, a striking red band and a wide yellowish-orange edge. The caudal fin has bright yellow lobes which are separated from the bluish-green, red flecked central part by red bands. The ventral fins are dark red with a yellowish-green edge and the pectoral fins are pale green, translucent and with red marks.
Females have no elongated rays. The basic coloration is brownish-green with rust colored marks: there are no prominent marks on the body.
Males are as described above, but *A.gardneri* is an unusual species in that there are in fact two distinct color patterns shown by males. Some, as described above have the distinctive wide yellow orange bands on the caudal and anal fins. Others lack these bands entirely. This unusual feature – of two separate color patterns – is called polymorphism and is a particularly interesting feature of this species.

General care: See Introductory note.

Breeding: See Introductory note under egg-hangers. The eggs are adhesive and are usually laid on plants or floating roots.

Additional information: Synonyms: *A.brucei, A.nigerianum.* Many cross-breeds have been produced in aquariums and sometimes these are marketed as 'new' imports. This obviously seriously prejudices the maintenance of a pure strain, which is now difficult to find.

APHYOSEMION GULARE

Family: *Cyprinodontidae*

Genus: *Aphyosemion*

English name: none

Origin: Southwest Nigeria

Size: Approximately 6 cm

Habitat: Found in seasonal lakes and pools and marshy areas

SHAPE, COLORING AND MARKINGS: The body is elongated, fairly deep and laterally only slightly compressed. The basic coloration is a pale bluish-violet: the back varies from a fawn to an olive brown. The number of red marks on the flanks varies greatly according to the age of the fish and the locality from which it comes. These marks never from a cohesive pattern: at most they merge together as an irregular wavy line. There is a wide red edge along the lower lip and prominent red patches and stripes on the gill covers. The dorsal fin varies in color from bluish-violet to green, with numerous red flecks on the membranes. The anal fin is pale blue with a red band, which may or may not run the width of the fin. The caudal fin is between a violet and a cobalt blue, with pale blue or green lobes, red flecks and/or a red band in the lower lobe. The ventral and pectoral fins are a pale blue, edged with a brownish-violet.
Females are slightly smaller than males and less vividly colored. The fins are rounded and there are no elongated rays.
Males are as described above.

GENERAL CARE: See Introductory note.

BREEDING: See Introductory note under egg-buriers.

629. *Aphyosemion gardneri*

APHYOSEMION LABARREI

Family *Cyprinodontidae*

Genus: *Aphyosemion*

English name: none, but known in the USA as Blue Panchax

Origin: The lower reaches of the Congo river; Madimba, Kisantu, Thysville and Kigemba

Size: Approximately 5 cm

Habitat: Found in seasonal lakes and pools and in marshy areas

SHAPE, COLORING AND MARKINGS: The body is elongated, fairly deep and laterally only slightly compressed. The basic coloration is a grass green: the back has a light brown or ochre tinge, and the lower half of the body is silvery-white. The snout and upper half of the head are orangey-brown. There are prominent red patches and stripes on the gill covers and very irregular red marks on the flanks which join together below the dorsal fin as a wavy band stretching over the caudal peduncle. The dorsal fin is grass green, with a rust colored or reddish base, and a dark edge. The anal fin is pale green with a few widely dispersed dark marks, the number of which depends on the age of the fish. The caudal fin is grass green with wide rust colored edges along the upper and lower lobes and prominent reddish-brown patches and stripes in the central part. The ventral fins are pale green with a dark edge: the pectoral fins are translucent and pale green with a rust colored edge.
Females are mainly greenish-brown: the fins have less conspicuous marks and the fin rays are not elongated.
Males are as described above, with elongated fin rays and bodies tinged with an iridescent blue sheen.

GENERAL CARE: See Introductory note.

BREEDING: See Introductory note under egg-hangers. The eggs are adhesive and laid on the roots of floating plants or among vegetation growing on the banks.

ADDITIONAL INFORMATION: *A.labarrei* is one of the most beautiful of the species. Unfortunately most of the eggs of these fish produce males when bred in captivity and it is therefore difficult to maintain a line of this species.

630. *Aphyosemion labarrei*

631. *Aphyosemion louescense*

APHYOSEMION LOUESCENSE

Family: *Cyprinodontidae*

Genus: *Aphyosemion*

English name: none

Origin: Congo: the rivers Lousse and Kouilou, the area around Mindouli on the upper reaches of the river Niari

Size: Approximately 6 cm

Habitat: Found in seasonal lakes and pools and in marshy areas

SHAPE, COLORING AND MARKINGS: The body is elongated, fairly deep and laterally only slightly compressed. The basic coloration is pale green: the belly varies in color from yellowish-green to orangey-yellow. The back and upper half of the head vary from fawn

to dark greenish-brown: the lower half of the head varies from yellowish-green to off-white. Red marks are found on the gill covers and very irregular carmine red marks on the flanks may merge together to form a vivid pattern of stripes. The dorsal fin is rust colored tinged with green and with red stripes. The anal fin is light green with a narrow blue edge and numerous red flecks. The pale green caudal fin has narrow luminescent bluish-green edges and numerous red marks in lines parallel to the central fin membranes. The pectoral and ventral fins are translucent, orangey-yellow with bright yellow edges.
Females are mainly greenish-brown with only a small number of patches of red. The fin rays are not elongated and the fins have little prominent coloring.
Males are as described above and have elongated fin rays.

General care: See Introductory note.

Breeding: See Introductory note under egg-hangers. The eggs are adhesive and are laid on the roots of floating plants or of vegetation growing on the bank.

Additional information: *A.louescense* does not seem to be closely related to any other species in this genus: attempts to cross-breed it have not to date been successful. In captivity it is extremely sensitive to *Oodinium*.

APHYOSEMION MELANOPTERON

Family: *Cyprinodontidae*

Genus: *Aphyosemion*

English name: none

Origin: The central Congo

Size: Approximately 5 cm

Habitat: Found in lakes and pools and in slow running streams

---

Shape, coloring and markings: The body is elongated, fairly deep and laterally only slightly compressed. The basic coloration varies from brownish-yellow to brownish-orange, with a bright green tinge to the gill covers and the lower half of the body, most evident when the light catches it at an angle. There are small red dots scattered irregularly over the body and larger red marks on the gill covers which merge to form patches and stripes. The back is darker, or brownish-green. Both the dorsal and caudal fins are, for a species of *Aphyosemion*, unusual in their coloring. The dorsal fin has a brownish base, but otherwise it is a deep bluish-black. The central part of the caudal fin is brownish-orange with a random pattern of bluish-black flecks and stripes and a bluish-black edge. The ventral and anal fins are orangey-yellow, translucent, with narrow dark edges: the anal fin is also flecked with small dark spots. The pectoral fins are pale yellow, translucent, with a light blue edge.
Females are a dull brownish-yellow color with rounded, colorless fins.
Males are as described above. Older specimens often have elongated fin rays in the unpaired fins.

General care: See Introductory note.

Breeding: See Introductory note under egg-hangers. The eggs are laid among the roots of floating plants or in some artificial spawning medium. The fish are not very prolific but will apparently become more so if the composition of the water in which they are put is changed. The hardness of the water should fluctuate between 4° and 8° DH.

Additional information: *A.melanopteron* was discovered by Ricco in 1968 among a consignment of fish from the Congo. In 1970 it was named and described by Goldstein. It is largely unknown among aquarists.

APHYOSEMION MIRABILE MIRABILE

Family: *Cyprinodontidae*

Genus: *Aphyosemion*

English name: none

Origin: West Cameroon, Mbio

Size: Approximately 5 cm

Habitat: Found in seasonal lakes and pools and in small sluggish streams

---

Shape, coloring and markings: The body is elongated, fairly deep and laterally slightly compressed. The upper half of the front of the body is brownish. The flanks can vary from light to dark blue: they bear red marks which join together to form stripes on the front half of the body, and further back turn into larger more irregular patches with a purplish tint. The basic coloration of the unpaired fins and the ventral fins is purplish with iridescent light blue marks. The caudal fin has a light blue edge at top and bottom: the pectoral fins are mainly colorless, transparent and carry luminescent yellow spots.
Females are basically brownish with red marks that merge together. All the fins are colorless and transparent: the dorsal fin alone has a few red marks.
Males are as described above.

General care: See Introductory note.

Breeding: See Introductory note under egg-hangers. The eggs will be laid on the roots of floating plants and also on artificial spawning mediums. It is important that the water be soft and slightly acid if this beautiful species is to thrive.

Additional information: *A.mirabile mirabile* was named by Radda in 1970: in the same year he named the sub-species *A.mirabile moense* and in 1972 he described the sub-species *A.mirabile traudeae*.

APHYOSEMION MIRABILE MOENSE

Family: *Cyprinodontidae*

Genus: *Aphyosemion*

English name: none

Origin: West Cameroon, tributaries of the river Mo

Size: Approximately 5 cm

Habitat: Found in seasonal pools and lakes and in small sluggish streams

---

632. *Aphyosemion melanopteron*

Shape, coloring and markings: The body is elongated, fairly deep and laterally only slightly compressed. Its color form greatly resembles that of *A.mirabile mirabile*. The upper half of the front of the body is brownish. The flanks are mainly dark blue with purplish red marks at the front which further back turn into larger more irregular patches. The caudal fin has bright yellow edges at the top and bottom, which are bordered by a narrow bright blue stripe which in turn lies next to the red center of the fin, itself flecked with blue. The dorsal and anal fins are purplish, with light blue marks. The dorsal fin is edged with yellow at the back: the anal fin is edged with yellow at the front. The pectoral and ventral fins are a pale orangey-yellow.
Females are basically brownish with red marks that merge together. The unpaired fins have narrow yellow edges and the dorsal fin has small red marks.
Males are as described above.

General care: See Introductory note.

Breeding: See Introductory note and supplementary comments under *A.mirabile mirabile*.

633. *Aphyosemion mirabile mirabile*

ADDITIONAL INFORMATION: The origin of this sub-species is noted under *A.mirabile mirabile*.

APHYOSEMION MIRABILE - TRAUDEAE

Family: *Cyprinodontidae*
Genus: *Aphyosemion*
English name: none
Origin: West Cameroon, Manyemen
Size: Approximately 5 cm
Habitat: Found in seasonal lakes and pools and small sluggish streams

SHAPE, COLORING AND MARKINGS: The body is elongated, fairly deep and laterally only slightly compressed. The pattern of red marks on the body is very similar to that of *A.mirabile mirabile* but otherwise the color form is radically different. The front part of the body is bluish: the back, emerald green. The caudal fin has wide, bright yellow edges and the central part is a dark red, with irregular green marks. The dorsal fin is also edged with yellow and has a red base, patterned green. The anal and ventral fins are emerald green with red flecks and irregular stripes, and black edges bordered by very narrow violet fringes. The pectoral fin is a striking orangey-yellow. Females are basically brownish: the upper half of the body is darker than the underside and the scales bear small red dots. There are red marks on the dorsal fin: all the other unpaired fins have a dull yellow edge.
Males are as described above.

GENERAL CARE: See Introductory note.

BREEDING: As for *A.mirabile mirabile*.

ADDITIONAL INFORMATION: See under *A.mirabile mirabile* for the history of this sub-species.

APHYOSEMION NDIANUM

Family: *Cyprinodontidae*
Genus: *Aphyosemion*
English name: none
Origin: West Cameroon
Size: Approximately 6 cm
Habitat: Found in fairly large numbers in the basin of the river Ndian

SHAPE, COLORING AND MARKINGS: The body is elongated, fairly deep and laterally only slightly compressed. *A.ndianum* greatly resembles the closely related species *A.cameronense*. The basic coloration is a beautiful iridescent blue tinged with violet. The red marks on the flanks are more numerous and more extended than those of *A.cameronense* and they may merge together to form a pattern of stripes on the lower half of the body from the anal to the caudal fin: in *A.cameronense* this pattern is more regular and continues along the whole of the belly. A characteristic feature of this species is a number of bands on the chin: these are either absent completely or very broken up in *A.cameronense*. The unpaired fins are a beautiful blue and the dorsal fin has innumerable red flecks and stripes. The caudal fin is edged with light blue at the top and bottom and also bears a very irregular pattern of stripes running parallel to the fin rays. The anal fin is edged with red and may be irregularly marked. The pectoral and ventral fins are more or less transparent and carry red bands.
Females are basically brownish with a salmon colored belly: they have no prominent marks.
Males are as described above.

GENERAL CARE: See Introductory note.

BREEDING: See Introductory note under egg-buriers.

ADDITIONAL INFORMATION: *A.ndianum* was first described by Clausen in 1959. Jorgen Scheel managed to breed a number of specimens in captivity and cross-bred this species with *A.cinnamemeum*, *A.gardneri* and *A.cognatum*.

APHYOSEMION OESERI

Family: *Cyprinodontidae*
Genus: *Aphyosemion*
English name: none
Origin: The island of Fernando Póo (Gulf of Guinea) in the immediate vicinity of Santa Isabel
Size: Approximately 4.5 cm
Habitat: Found in seasonal lakes and pools and sluggish streams

634. *Aphyosemion louessense*

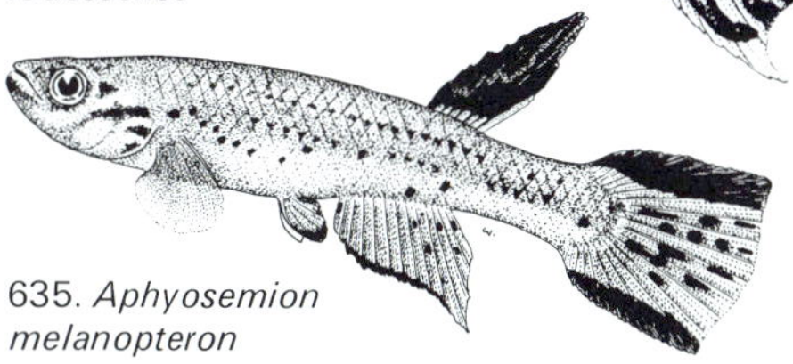

635. *Aphyosemion melanopteron*

636. *Aphyosemion mirabile mirabile*

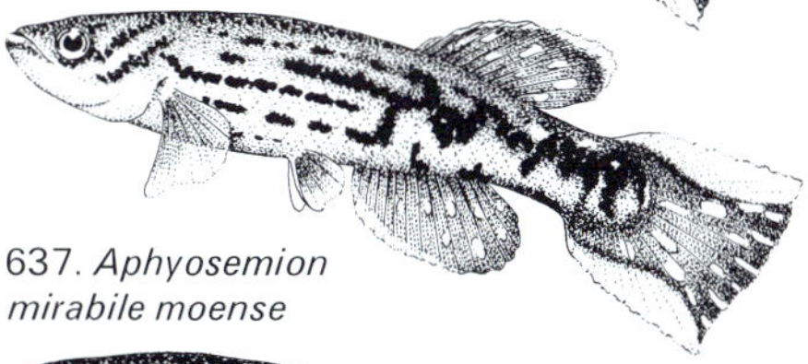

637. *Aphyosemion mirabile moense*

638. *Aphyosemion mirabile traudeae*

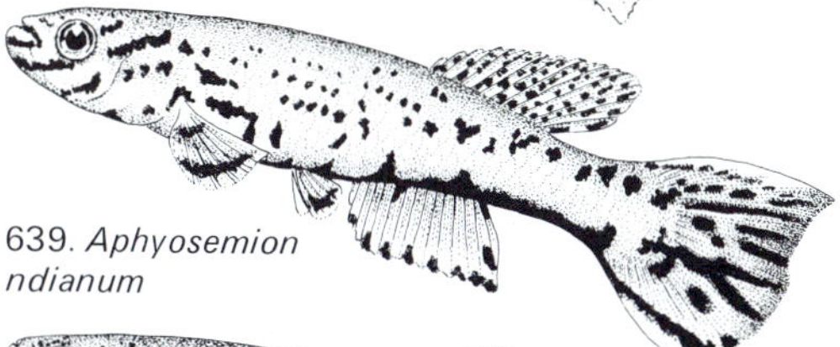

639. *Aphyosemion ndianum*

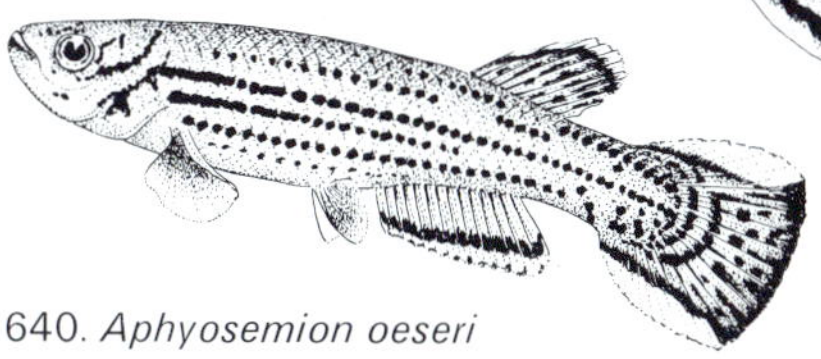

640. *Aphyosemion oeseri*

SHAPE, COLORING AND MARKINGS: The body is elongated, fairly deep and laterally only slightly compressed. The basic coloration is iridescent emerald green: both the front and lower parts of the body are tinged with yellow. The red marks on the body merge into lines, which are most distinct on the flanks. There is a brownish-green net-like pattern on the back: the red marks on the belly are small and irregular. There are dramatic red stripes on the gill covers but no red on the throat. The dorsal fin is emerald green with small red marks, an orangey-yellow edge and an irregular narrow red band. The anal fin is flecked with red at the base, is a striking orange color, with an iridescent green tinge, a bright yellow edge and a red band. The caudal fin is predominantly emerald green with red marks, most of which merge into a pattern of stripes. The color is darker towards the edge, becoming a dark reddish-violet or bluish-black. The caudal fin is edged with a pale green border along top and bottom, separated from the central part by red bands: that on the lower lobe is wider than that on the upper lobe. Both pectoral and ventral fins are a pale orange.
Females are basically brownish-yellow, with five lines of red dots. The unpaired fins and the ventral fins are yellowish-green and translucent: the anal fin and the ventral fin are often tinged with orange. The dorsal fin carries a large number of small red dots: the pectoral fins are often flecked with black.
Males are as described above.

GENERAL CARE: See Introductory note.

BREEDING: See Introductory note under egg-hangers. *A.oeseri* however always lays its eggs in plants near the bed, never near the surface. The eggs take about 14 days to develop at a temperature of 25° C.

ADDITIONAL INFORMATION: This species was known to aquarists for many years as *Panchax oeseri:* It was re-discovered by Jorgen Scheel in 1968, who called it *A.santaisabella,* which is currently a synonym. The species was first described by Schmidt in 1928.

APHYOSEMION SJOESTEDTI

Family: *Cyprinidontidae*
Genus: *Aphyosemion*
English name: none
Origin: Nigeria and Cameroon
Size: Approximately 10 cm
Habitat: Found in seasonal lakes and pools and marshy areas

SHAPE, COLORING AND MARKINGS: The body is elongated, slender and laterally only slightly compressed. There are a number of local varieties of *A.sjoestedti,* which differ principally in their basic coloration. The patterning on the head, body and fins is a characteristic common to all varieties. There are eight or nine reddish-brown transverse bands on the body which are particularly distinct in younger fish: the first of these bands is roughly above the ventral fins and the last is on the caudal peduncle. In older specimens these bands break up into purplish-brown marks of irregular size. There are vivid spots and stripes on the head and gill covers which form a striking contrast to the bluish-green iridescent background. A similar pattern continues behind the gill covers to the front of the anal fin. The dorsal fin is greenish with numerous reddish-brown dots and stripes running parallel to the fin rays: there is also a dark band along the base. The anal fin is greenish, tinged with orangey-red at the back: the front fin rays are elongated and have light blue tips, bordered by a brown band, and carry irregular red marks. The upper half of the caudal fin is greenish with dark stripes again running parallel to the fin rays: the lower half varies from an orangey-yellow to a pale brown, with pale green tips and dark bands. The pectoral fins are greenish and translucent, with a dark band.
Females are considerably smaller than males: they have no elongated fin rays and less vivid colors.
Males are as described above.

GENERAL CARE: See Introductory note.

BREEDING: See Introductory note under egg-buriers.

ADDITIONAL INFORMATION: Synonym: *A.coeruleum.* This species was originally described as *Fundulus sjoestedti* by Axel Johan Einar Lönnberg in 1895. George Albert Boulenger described it as *A.coeruleum* in 1915 and it is known to many aquarists still under that name.

641. *Aphyosemion oeseri*

642. *Aphyosemion sjoestedti*

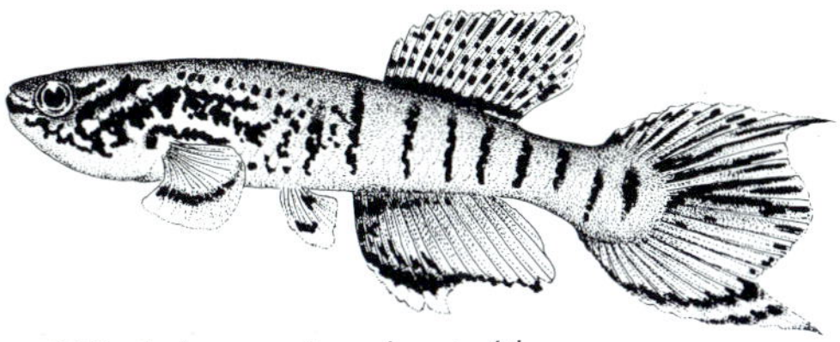

643. *Aphyosemion sjoestedti*

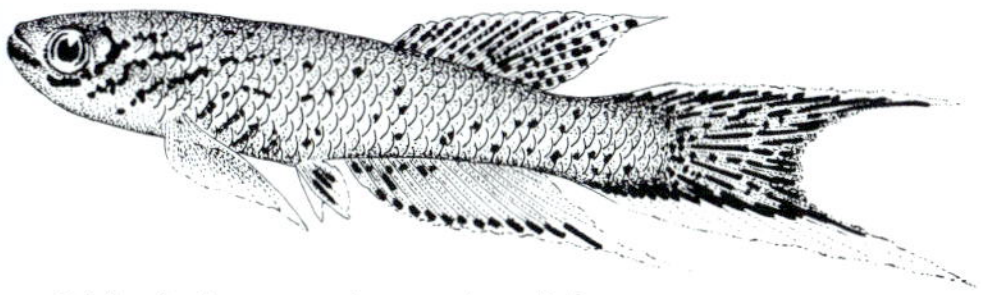

644. *Aphyosemion splendidum*

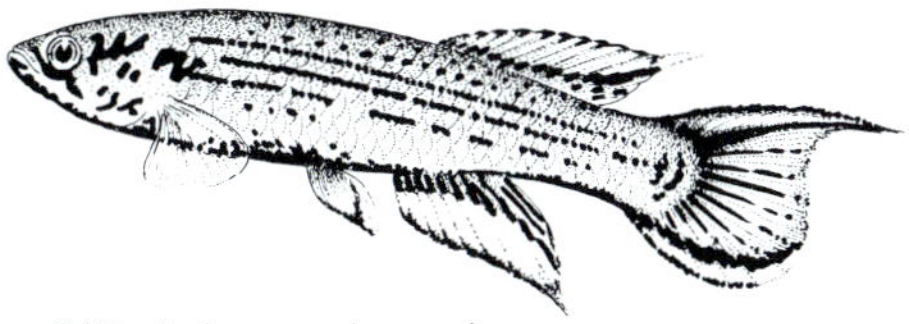

645. *Aphyosemion striatum*

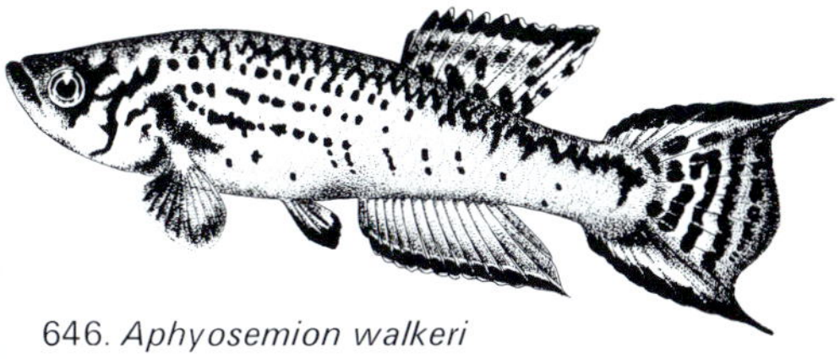

646. *Aphyosemion walkeri*

APHYOSEMION SPLENDIDUM

Family: *Cyprinodontidae*
Genus: *Aphyosemion*
English name: none
Origin: North Gabon
Size: Approximately 5 cm
Habitat: Found in seasonal lakes and pools and in marshy areas

SHAPE, COLORING AND MARKINGS: The body is elongated, slender and laterally only slightly compressed. The basic coloration varies from a yellowish- to an orangey-brown, and the body is completely covered with a net-like pattern produced by the dark edges to the scales. On the flanks there are a small number of random red marks. There are three distinct stripes on the gill covers and a wide red band along the lower lip. The fins are yellowish-green, and the dorsal fin has numerous red flecks and stripes running parallel to the fin rays. The anal fin is edged with red, with a number of marks at the base. There is a wide, bright yellow edge along the bottom of the caudal fin and a narrower border along the top: numerous flecks and stripes run in lines parallel to the fin rays. The ventral fin is also marked with red. The pectoral fins are colorless or greenish and translucent.
Females have more rounded fins and less vivid colors.
Males are as described above: the unpaired fins have very elongated rays.

GENERAL CARE: See Introductory note.

BREEDING: Nothing is known about the breeding habits of this species.

ADDITIONAL INFORMATION: Although described by Jacques Pellegrin in 1930, this species is still, rather curiously, largely unknown to aquarists.

APHYOSEMION STRIATUM

Family: *Cyprinodontidae*
Genus: *Aphyosemion*
English name: none
Origin: North Gabon
Size: Approximately 5 cm
Habitat: Found in seasonal lakes and pools and in marshy areas

SHAPE, COLORING AND MARKINGS: The body is elongated, slender and laterally only slightly compressed. It has an olive green back and yellowish flanks, becoming yellowish-white towards the belly. From the back edge of the gill covers there are three or four carmine red horizontal lines made up of individual marks: more vivid stripes lie on the gill covers and under the eyes. The dorsal fin has a red band, is edged with red and has a yellowish-white tip. The anal fin has a dark edge, with red marks on the base. The fin rays of the upper lobe of the caudal fin are elongated: whitish and carmine red bands appear at the top and bottom of the fin, and in the central area there are dark marks running parallel to the fin rays. The pectoral fins are colorless and transparent: the ventral fins have carmine red marks.
Females have rounded fins and less vivid colors.
Males are as described above.

GENERAL CARE: See Introductory note.

BREEDING: See Introductory note under egg-hangers.

ADDITIONAL INFORMATION: *A.striatum* was first described as *Haplochilus striatus* by George Albert Boulenger in 1911. It has become quite well known among aquarists in recent years and will probably become more common in the future.

APHYOSEMION WALKERI

Family: *Cyprinodontidae*
Genus: *Aphyosemion*
English name: none
Origin: Ghana, the Ivory Coast
Size: Approximately 6 cm
Habitat: Found in seasonal lakes and pools and in marshy areas

SHAPE, COLORING AND MARKINGS: The body is elongated, deeper than that of related species and laterally slightly compressed. The basic coloration is bluish-green: the back is yellowish-green: the belly is yellowish tinged with violet. On the back there is a regular pattern of reddish-brown marks which form a coarse net-like pattern. Behind the gill covers there are two lines made up of marks which are almost joined together. On the gill covers there are fairly large stripes on a metallic blue iridescent background. The snout and upper half of the body are a dark reddish-brown. The dorsal fin is greenish with a wide reddish-brown edge and oval marks: the back part of the fin is orangey-red. The anal fin has a greenish-blue base which gradually becomes an orangey-red, and a dark or purplish-red edge. The caudal fin has a sky blue base, gradually becoming bluish-red or brownish-red towards the back edge. The top and bottom are edged with reddish-brown, and there are irregular bands in the central area. The ventral and pectoral fins are ochre at the base, becoming reddish-brown.

647. *Aphyosemion walkeri*

Females are more or less brown and have less vivid colors.
Males are as described above.

GENERAL CARE: See Introductory note.

BREEDING: See Introductory note under egg-hangers.

ADDITIONAL INFORMATION: *A.walkeri* was first described by George Albert Boulenger in 1911 as *Fundulus walkeri*. This beautiful species has become fairly well known to aquarists in the last few years.

THE FAMILY CYPRINODONTIDAE

The genus Aplocheilichthys

The fish in the genus *Aplocheilichthys* are sometimes known by the generic name *Micropanchax*. They are all relatively small killifish from tropical Africa. As will be seen from the species descriptions below, they are not too difficult to breed and, if kept under the right conditions, make very attractive aquarium fish. Unfortunately they are not suitable for a community tank but well repay the extra trouble needed to create the species tank in which they will thrive.

648. *Aplocheilichthys flavipinnis*

APLOCHEILICHTHYS FLAVIPINNIS

Family: *Cyprinodontidae*
Genus: *Aplocheilichthys*
English name: Yellow-finned Panchax
Origin: Tropical West Africa, Lagos
Size: Maximum 3 cm
Habitat: Found in small sluggish streams

SHAPE, COLORING AND MARKINGS: The body is very elongated and slightly cylindrical. The caudal peduncle is laterally compressed. The dorsal, anal and pectoral fins taper to a point: the caudal fin is rounded. The eyes are large, bluish-green and remarkably iridescent. The basic coloration is a metallic greenish-blue or silver, more or less translucent. The fins, except for the pectoral, are orangey to light yellow.
Females are less vividly colored, especially on the fins. The body cavity at the back and the belly are more rounded than in males.
Males are as described above.

GENERAL CARE: *A.flavipinnis* is unsuitable for the normal community tank. It should be kept in a group of eight or ten in a small tank with a dark bed, plenty of fine leaved plants, pieces of bogwood and adequate hiding places but at the same time ample free swimming space just below the surface. The composition of the water is not critical but should not be too hard. *A.flavipinnis* is extremely sensitive to changes in environment and if it has to be moved from one tank to another this must be done with extreme care. Temperature 23°C. This fish prefers to take its food from the surface: fruitflies will be greedily accepted, as well as other small live animal matter and finely powdered dried food.

BREEDING: The relatively large eggs can be seen in the female oviduct against the light. The eggs are laid over a period of weeks among fine leaved plants. Java moss *(Vesicularia dubyana)* is a particularly good spawning medium. The eggs should be collected regularly and transferred to separate breeding tanks with shallow water. Temperature 23°–24°C. The fry keep mainly to the surface and should be fed with very fine pond infusoria or very finely powdered fry food as soon as they are free swimming. The breeding tank must be absolutely clean and the water changed regularly.

ADDITIONAL INFORMATION: *A.flavipinnis* is sometimes known by the name *Micropanchax flavipinnis*.

APLOCHEILICHTHYS KATANGAE

Family: *Cyprinodontidae*
Genus: *Aplocheilichthys*
English name: none
Origin: Zaire, around Katanga
Size: Maximum 4 cm
Habitat: Found in still and sluggish waters

SHAPE, COLORING AND MARKINGS: The body is elongated and laterally very slightly compressed. The mouth is small, the eyes large and the fins rounded. The basic coloration is dark ochre on the back, bluish-green on the flanks and silvery on the belly. A brownish-black line runs from the mouth to the base of the caudal fin, often with a narrower jet black zig-zag line superimposed on it. The eyes are bluish-green but less luminescent than in related species. The fins, except for the pectoral fins are yellow.
Females are less vividly colored than males: the fins are colorless and the belly more rounded.
Males are as described above.

649. *Aplocheilichthys katangae*

GENERAL CARE: *A.katangae* requires a tank like that suggested for *A.flavipinnis* and is equally sensitive to changes in environment. Unlike many related species it will swim freely throughout the tank. Temperature 24°C. Almost any food that can be accommodated in the small mouth will be accepted. *A.katangae* can be kept with other small peaceful species.

BREEDING: The relatively large clear eggs will be laid among fine leaved plants even in a community tank. Niether the eggs nor the fry are at risk from the parent fish. The eggs can be left to hatch in the community tank but the fry are best transferred to a small separate tank with water of the same composition as that in the community tank. Diet as for *A.flavipinnis*.

ADDITIONAL INFORMATION: *A.katangae* is sometimes described as *Micropanchax katangae*.

APLOCHEILICHTHYS MACROPHTHALMUS

Family: *Cyprinodontidae*
Genus: *Aplocheilichthys*
English name: Lamp-eyed Panchax
Origin: The southern parts of Dahomey and Nigeria
Size: Maximum 4 cm
Habitat: Usually found in small streams

SHAPE, COLORING AND MARKINGS: The body is very elongated, almost cylindrical, and laterally slightly compressed. The mouth is small and upward-directed: the eyes are large. The anterior rays of the dorsal and anal fins are elongated so that these fins taper to a point. The basic coloration, depending on the light, is greenish to a translucent bronze. A bluish-green iridescent stripe runs the length of the body. The fins are yellowish or blue, according to the locality of origin. The caudal fin usually has a delicate pattern of orangey-red dots and stripes.
Females have colorless fins which do not taper to a point.
Males are as described above.

GENERAL CARE: As for *A.flavipinnis,* but *A.macrophthalmus* is even more sensitive to environmental changes. Temperature 24°–26°C. This fish is very fond of snapping up fruitflies from the surface.

BREEDING: As for *A.flavipinnis.*

ADDITIONAL INFORMATION: Sometimes described as *Micropanchax macrophthalmus.*

APLOCHEILICHTHYS MEYBURGI

Family: *Cyprinodontidae*
Genus: *Aplocheilichthys*
English name: none
Origin: East Africa, the northern shores of Lake Victoria
Size: Maximum, less than 3 cm
Habitat: Found amongst water plants and reeds

SHAPE, COLORING AND MARKINGS: The body is elongated, laterally slightly compressed and more or less cylindrical. The mouth is upward-positioned: the eyes are relatively large, the fins rounded. The basic coloration is green to greenish-blue: the back is brownish: the throat and belly brown to yellow. Some specimens have a golden-yellow short horizontal line and others a number of extremely narrow black transverse stripes. All the fins, except the pectoral fin are brownish to green.
Females are less vividly colored and have more rounded bellies.
Males are as described above. Some have an attractive tomato-colored stripe on the caudal and anal fins.

GENERAL CARE: As for *A.katangae* but temperature 23°C.

BREEDING: As for *A.katangae.*

ADDITIONAL INFORMATION: *A.meyburgi* is sometimes described as *Micropanchax meyburgi.*

APLOCHEILICHTHYS SPILAUCHEN

Family: *Cyprinodontidae*
Genus: *Aplocheilichthys*
English name: none
Origin: The West coast of tropical Africa
Size: Maximum 7 cm
Habitat: Found mainly in brackish river estuaries

SHAPE, COLORING AND MARKINGS: The body is elongated, laterally slightly compressed and more or less cylindrical. The mouth is end-positioned: the eyes large. The dorsal fin is set far back and tapers to a point: the rounded anal fin is unusually large. The basic coloration is yellowish-green, in certain lights tinged with blue: the back bears a pattern of silvery transverse bands. The fins vary from yellow to green and are more or less translucent. The ventral fins have extremely decorative bluish-green iridescent flecks and marks.
Females are less vividly colored: the fins are almost colorless.
Males are as described above.

GENERAL CARE: *A.spilauchen* requires a tank sited in a sunny position and furnished as for *A.flavipinnis.* Five grams of sea salt should be added for each liter of water. Temperature 26°C. This species is omnivorous but has a preference for insects.

BREEDING: The all-glass breeding tank should be furnished with only a bundle of nylon or peat fibre. The eggs are laid over a period of a few weeks and the spawning medium should be taken out at least once a week and inspected: if it has eggs on it it should be transferred to a separate tank. The eggs hatch after some weeks. When the fry swim freely they should be fed on *Artemia nauplii* and finely powdered dried food. Even when well cared for they grow very slowly.

650. *Aplocheilichthys meyburgi*

651. *Aplocheilichthys macrophthalmus*

THE FAMILY CYPRINODONTIDAE

The genus Aplocheilus

There are a number of species in this genus, the members of which are found in India and Southeast Asia, but only the four species described below are usually imported as aquarium fish. *Aplocheilus panchax* has been found in aquariums for the last three quarters of a century and must be one of the oldest species regularly kept in captivity. These fish are very closely related to the species in the genera *Epiplatys* and *Pachypanchax.*

652. *Aplocheilus dayi*

APLOCHEILUS BLOCKI

Family: *Cyprinodontidae*

Genus: *Aplocheilus*

English names: Panchax and Green Panchax

Origin: Sri Lanka, India, Madras

Size: Approximately 5 cm

Habitat: Found in densely overgrown, shallow, sluggish or still waters

SHAPE, COLORING AND MARKINGS: The body is elongated and laterally slightly compressed. The basic coloration is an iridescent yellow-green: the belly is an iridescent blue-green: the flanks have many red or gleaming gold spots. The unpaired fins are a lemon yellow with red-brown spots and patches. The ventral fins are orange: the pectoral fins colorless and transparent.
Females are muddy yellow or green, with a dark longitudinal band and a number of narrow transverse stripes. The fins are colorless but a dark patch appears at the base of the dorsal fin.
Males are as described above.

GENERAL CARE: *A.blocki* is suitable for large and small aquariums with thick vegetation round the sides and a number of floating plants, a dark bottom and scattered pieces of bogwood. The composition of the water is not critical: temperature 22°–24°C. *A.blocki* swims in the upper and middle reaches of the tank. A predatory fish on related species but it can be kept with larger fish: *A.blocki* is best kept as a pair or in a group of one male and several females. The diet is almost exclusively live animal matter but dried food will be accepted occasionally.

BREEDING: This is not difficult. The fish will spawn even in community tanks. Temperature 28°C. The tough shells allow the eggs to be picked off the vegetation where they will be laid, and transferred to a special tank. The fry hatch after 12–14 days and can be fed on the usual fry foods.

ADDITIONAL INFORMATION: This well-known species, the smallest of its genus is the most suitable for a community tank.

APLOCHEILUS DAYI

Family: *Cyprinodontidae*

Genus: *Aplocheilus*

English name: Killifish

Origin: Sri Lanka

Size: Approximately 7 cm

Habitat: Found in shallow, densely overgrown, still and sluggish waters

SHAPE, COLORING AND MARKINGS: The body is elongated and laterally only slightly compressed. The basic coloration is greenish: the back has a strong golden gleam: the belly is pale blue to violet. Small red dots are distributed over the whole body. The dorsal fin is yellowish: the anal fin has a greenish base and a large number of spots and stripes.
Females are less vividly colored with a number of narrow transverse bands on the caudal peduncle.
Males are as described above.

GENERAL CARE: As for *A.blocki* but suitable only for larger aquariums for *A.dayi* is a larger species and more agressive and predatory by nature.

BREEDING: Not difficult. *A.dayi* lays its eggs near the bed, on low growing plants or on the roots of floating plants in shallow tanks. Breeding temperature 25°C. The fry hatch after about 12 days and can be raised on the usual fry foods.

APLOCHEILUS LINEATUS

Family: *Cyprinodontidae*

Genus: *Aplocheilus*

English name: Sparkling Panchax

Origin: India and Sri Lanka

Size: Maximum 10 cm

Habitat: Found shallow, densely overgrown, still and sluggish waters

SHAPE, COLORING AND MARKINGS: The body is elongated and torpedo-shaped. The basic coloration varies significantly according to the locality of origin. Males have a brown-green back: the flanks are lighter, the belly yellowish. Practically all the scales have a green to gleaming gold spot which make up longitudinal stripes. Iridescent red spots are scattered over the belly and above the anal fin. Six to eight darker transverse bands lie on the flanks and the base of the caudal fin. The gill covers have a yellow-green to blue-green gleam. The dorsal fin is yellow with red overtones: the base of the caudal fin is orange, the rest red with variable light and dark shades in the lobes. The base of the anal fin is yellowish-green to blue with bright light patches but otherwise red. The pectoral and ventral fins are yellowish, generally with red edges.
Females are darker and the transverse bands are broader and more numerous, hence they are more prominent: the dorsal fin has a darker patch at the base.

GENERAL CARE: As for *A.dayi.*

BREEDING: As for *A.blocki.*

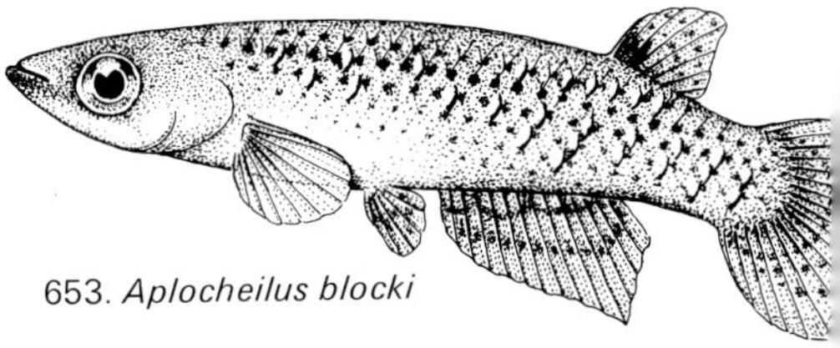

653. *Aplocheilus blocki*

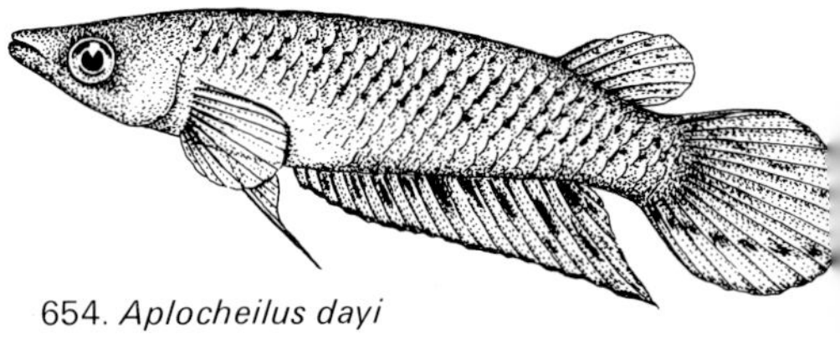

654. *Aplocheilus dayi*

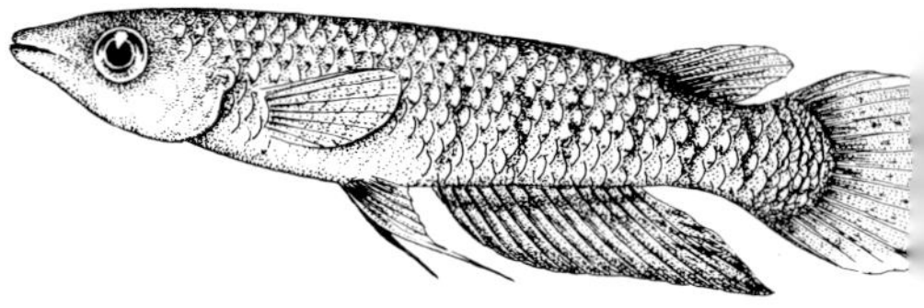

655. *Aplocheilus lineatus*

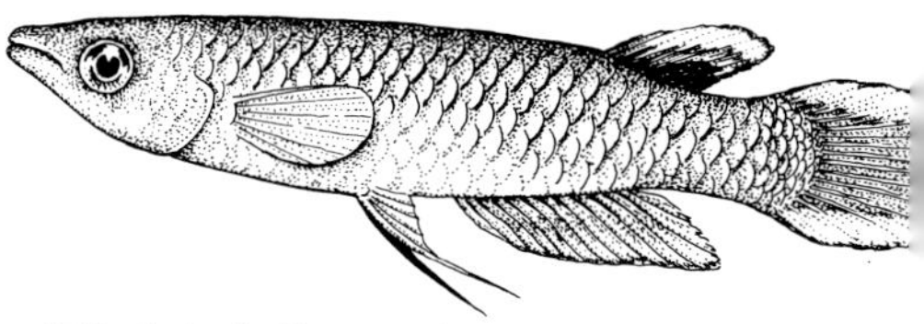

656. *Aplocheilus panchax*

APLOCHEILUS PANCHAX

Family: *Cyprinodontidae*

Genus: *Aplocheilus*

English name: Blue Panchax

Origin: India, Indonesia, Sri Lanka

Size: Maximum 8 cm

Habitat: Found in shallow, densely overgrown, still and sluggish waters

SHAPE, COLORING AND MARKINGS: The body is elongated and torpedo-shaped. The basic coloration varies significantly according to the locality of origin. Males are a pale yellow: the back is darker: the belly yellowish. There is an iridescent blue overtone in certain lights. The scales on the upper part of the body have a dark edge which shows up as a network pattern. The dorsal fin has a prominent black patch at the base and dark margins: the caudal fin has a white edge and a yellow center. Particularly well-marked young specimens have a black edge to the caudal fin. The anal fin is orange at the base, becoming reddish with a pattern of dark dots.
Females are less vividly colored: the dorsal and anal fins are rounded.

GENERAL CARE: As for *A.dayi.*

BREEDING: Not difficult. As for *A.blocki* but temperature 25°C. Best results are obtained however by transferring the breeding pair into a small breeding tank of about 10 liters capacity.

THE FAMILY CYPRINODONTIDAE

The genus Astrofundulus

Only the species described below, *Astrofundulus dolichopterus*, is, in the genus, of interest to aquarists. A small and rare killifish from Venezuela, it has only been imported in recent years: while it is not particularly colorful its unusual fin structure makes it very attractive. As noted below, it is however unsuitable for the ordinary domestic community tank. Nevertheless it is not difficult to keep, nor, indeed too difficult to breed, if the instructions given below are followed and is a fish that well merits the attention of aquarists.

657. *Austrofundulus dolichopterus*

AUSTROFUNDULUS DOLICHOPTERUS

Family: *Cyprinodontidae*
Genus: *Astrofundulus*
English name: Sabre fin
Origin: Northwest Venezuela
Size: Maximum 5 cm
Habitat: Found in seasonal lakes with muddy beds covered with rotting vegetation, dry from December to May.

SHAPE, COLORING AND MARKINGS: The body is elongated, almost club-shaped and laterally compressed. The mouth is upper-positioned: the eyes are large. The arrangement of the fins is unusual. The dorsal and anal fins are set opposite each other at the deepest point of the body, just forward of center. Both fins are sickle-shaped and are spread out when the fish is not swimming so that the distance between their tips is roughly equal to the fish's total body length. The outer rays of the caudal fin are very long and about twice the length of the middle rays, so that the fin ends in two tapering points. This remarkable arrangement of the fins gives rise to the popular English name Sabre fin and the German names Säbalflosser or Flügelflosser. The basic coloration is reddish-brown, with many dark spots: the throat and belly are golden-yellow: under some lighting there is a violet or bluish-green tinge. The dorsal and anal fins vary from green or bluish-green to pale violet with dark dots: the caudal fin is translucent, reddish-brown with bluish-green stripes and dark dots.
Females are considerably smaller than males: the fins are shorter.
Males are as described above.

GENERAL CARE: *A.dolichopterus* is not suitable for the ordinary community tank. One male should be kept with two females in a small aquarium, or a few males with a larger number of females in a larger tank. Ample hiding places must be provided. *A.dolichopterus* is shy, and the males may be aggressive towards each other. The bed should be dark, the lighting subdued. The water should be soft and slightly acid. Temperature 23°–24°C, certainly no higher if this seasonal fish is to live as long as possible. About one-third of the water in the tank should be changed regularly. The diet should be live animal matter, especially mosquito larvae.

BREEDING: In the wild *A.dolichopterus* lays its eggs in the bed and then dies when the water dries up. This life style will not alter in the aquarium and the fish will not live more than one year at the most. It must therefore be bred if it is to be a permanent feature of the aquarium. A small tank of 5–10 liters with a layer of boiled peat and a few pieces of wood is required. One male should be put in the tank with two females. The eggs are laid on or above the bed: the number depends on the condition of the breeding pair. After two or three weeks the bed should be removed and left to dry in in a nylon net until the peat is only slightly damp: it should then be stored in plastic boxes at 20°–23°C. It takes five to six months for the embryonic stage, which can be seen and followed with a good magnifying glass, to be completed. When the embryos are fully developed the peat should be transferred to a tank and soft water added to a depth of a few centimeters. The young will hatch within seven days and can be fed immediately with freshly hatched *Artemia nauplii*. The fish are sexually mature at about ten weeks. If the fish are kept in their ordinary tank and not transferred to a special tank for breeding, then, if during the spawning season a bowl of boiled peat is put in the tank, the fish will lay their eggs in it and the contents of the bowl should be treated as the peat bed of the breeding tank as described above.

THE FAMILY CYPRINODONTIDAE

The genus Cynolebias

The very beautiful small fish in this genus are never common, for as well as being seasonal fish that only appeal to a minority of aquarists, they are not easy to breed and are somewhat demanding in their requirements in the aquarium. They are however so attractive that most amateurs who have kept them are agreed that they more than repay the care and attention they require. There are a number of species in the genus but only the two described below, *Cynolebias belotti* and *Cynolebias nigripinnis* are usually kept by amateurs.
The other species, it would seem, are very rarely if ever imported. Of these however, it is worth noting *Cynolebias adloffi* and *Cynolebias schreitmuelleri*, both the same size as *C.belotti*, *Cynolebias wolterstorffi* which grows to 10 cm and *Cynolebias elongatus* from the basin of the river Plate, a predominantly brownish-yellow and olive brown fish which can attain the unusual size, for these species, of 15 cm.

CYNOLEBIAS BELOTTI

Family: *Cyprinodontidae*

Genus: *Cynolebias*

English name: Argentine Pearl

Origin: Argentina, in the basin of the river Plate

Size: Maximum 5 cm

Habitat: Found in seasonal pools and lakes

SHAPE, COLORING AND MARKINGS: The body of the male is slightly elongated, fairly deep and laterally compressed. The rounded dorsal and anal fins have a very long base: the dorsal fin runs from halfway along the body to the caudal peduncle: the front rays of the anal fin lie even further forward and the fin also extends to the caudal peduncle. The caudal fin is rounded but with a straight back. The body and fins are greyish to deep midnight blue, flecked with green and blue dots. The female is smaller than the male and the dorsal and anal fins are smaller with fewer rays. The female is brownish-yellow with a very irregular pattern of dark brown dots and stripes.

GENERAL CARE: This fairly sturdy fish can be kept in an ordinary community tank but is best kept in a special fairly small tank with plenty of hiding places among bogwood The males may be aggressive towards each other and to ensure generation there must be more males than females. The water should be fairly soft and a quarter of it should be changed each week. Temperature 15°–20°C. The diet should be Daphnia, Cyclops, and black and white mosquito larvae: Tubifex and red mosquito larvae are less suitable.

BREEDING: As for *Austrofundulus dolichopterus.*

CYNOLEBIAS NIGRIPINNIS

Family: *Cyprinodontidae*

Genus: *Cynolebias*

English name: none

Origin: Argentina, the basin of the Paraná river

Size: Maximum 5 cm

Habitat: Found in seasonal lakes and pools

SHAPE, COLORING AND MARKINGS: The body of the male is slightly elongated, fairly deep and laterally compressed. The rounded dorsal and anal fins are squared at the back: they have long bases as in *C.belotti.* The caudal fin is almost circular. The basic coloration varies from bluish-grey to a velvety black. The body is flecked with numerous silver and bluish-green iridescent dots: the caudal and anal fins have a beautiful bluish-green border. The female is smaller than the male: the dorsal and anal fins have fewer rays and thus much shorter bases. Females are brownish-yellow with a pattern of darker dots and stripes.

GENERAL CARE: *C.nigripinnis* even when carefully tended, declines in vitality when older than seven months. One male should be kept with two females in a small tank: in a larger tank adequate hiding places must be provided, and then more than one male can be kept. Soft slightly acid water is needed. Temperature 15°–20°C. Diet as for *C.belotti.*

BREEDING: As for *Austrofundulus dolichopterus.* The best results will be obtained if the breeding pair have been separated for a week before being put in the breeding tank. The eggs will have developed fully as embryos after about five weeks. When the eggs are transferred to a tank for hatching they should be covered by no more than 2 cm of soft water. The fry will hatch after about an hour. They can be fed from the beginning with Cyclops *nauplii.* The eggs can however be kept up to six months if it is not convenient to hatch them as soon as the embryos seem fully developed and any eggs that do not hatch when first covered with water may be put back in the tank again later. The fish will be sexually mature after about eight weeks. If more than 2 cm of water is poured over the eggs damage will be done to the development of the swim bladder in the young fish.

658. *Cynolebias belotti*

659. *Cynolebias nigripinnis*

THE FAMILY CYPRINODONTIDAE

The genus Epiplatys

The genus *Epiplatys* (the broad-backed fish) is restricted to tropical West Africa. The genus comprises many species and sub-species with innumerable regional variations. The definition of the genus is still tentative. As with the genus *Aphysemion,* whose species are distributed over very much the same area, much confusion long surrounded the identification and nomenclature of the *Epiplatys* and even today many problems remain.

The *Epiplatys* species are usually found in small still or sluggish waters, such as ponds, pools and ox-bow lakes: the majority of these waters are seasonal, formed during the rains or as a result of subsequent flooding. Such waters contain little or no true aquatic vegetation: any which does develop will perish during the next dry season: only swift growing plants that reproduce vegetatively can survive. A wide range of plants however develop along the banks of these waters and their runners and deep roots penetrate the boggy basal soil and the waters are shaded by their leaves. The bottom is a deep layer of humus which acidifies the water and makes it dark. These are ideal breeding conditions for all kinds of aquatic insects, for example mosquitoes, and their larvae are the staple diet of these seasonal fish. Such fish have to adapt to a wide range of bizarre environments. The bottom dwelling *Aphysemion, Cynolebias* and *Nothobranchius* species, for example lay eggs which can survive a prolonged period of drought and hatch out when the next rainy season fills the seasonal pools anew. The *Epiplatys* species are not as adaptable as that, but they do lay hard-shelled eggs that hatch out after a few weeks. It may be that these too can survive a prolonged period of drought: certainly aquarists now send *Epiplatys* eggs by post wrapped in damp peat in the same way as the eggs of the species mentioned above have been transported for many years. No doubt experience will in the next few years solve this riddle.

The *Epiplatys* species occupy the same habitats as the true seasonal fish, but they are not themselves truly seasonal fish for in captivity at least, their life span is considerably longer than a season or at most a year.

Most amateur aquarists are unfamiliar with these fish, probably because although a number of the species have been imported regularly they are all unsuitable for the normal community tank. The males are extremely intolerant of each other. Thus the fish are best kept as breeding pairs or, if in a group, several females to one male: the males pursue the females very hard and a single female may perish if left on her own. Contrary to popular accounts, these fish do not dislike the light, although the tank should have plenty of floating plants to provide suitable hiding places. The *Epiplatys* are very like the common pike in the way they like to lurk in vegetation waiting for unsuspecting prey. Most species are rather torpid and it is therefore a good idea to introduce other species into the lower water levels to make them more active. The *Aphysemion* species are ideal for this, and of course, in the wild share the same natural habitats. The *Epiplatys* are not primarily predators of smaller fish: they are essentially surface dwellers with upturned mouths designed for snapping up food from the surface, including a whole range of insect that pupate on the surface or fly on to it. Most species have an iridescent patch on the top of their heads, the purpose of which may well be to lure insects, although it could also be a light-sensitive third eye warning the fish of shadows that might indicate danger such as a predatory bird.

Even though very few plants are found in their natural habitat, varieties that do not need a great deal of light can be put into the tank, scattered among bogwood and strands of peat. The base of the tank should be covered with the darkest river sand obtainable and strewn with irregular heaps of peat. The sides and back of the tank should be lined with cork or sections of peat.

660. *Epiplatys annulatus*

The peat and bogwood in the tank will tint the water yellow and the water will become more acid, thus creating an ideal environment for these fish. The water should be fairly soft (pH 6–6.5; 5°–7° DH). Despite the high temperatures to which they are accustomed in their natural habitats, the best temperature for the aquarium is 23°–25°C. Higher temperatures usually shorten their lifespan.

Under these conditions the fish will reproduce spontaneously. The eggs are deposited on the roots of floating plants and hatch after about 14 days: the exact time varies from species to species and the temperature of the water. Unless they are underfed or lack variety in their diet, the parents will not eat the eggs. The diet for the adults should be mainly black and white mosquito larvae and winged insects such as fruitflies. If sufficient floating plants are in the tank, these too will afford useful retreats and protection for the fry.

Alternatively the adult fish can be transferred to special breeding tanks. Small all-glass tanks or plastic trays are best. The amount of water will vary from species to species: smaller species need about six liters, the larger species 10–15 liters. Breeding is more natural in the larger tanks for the fry can be reared with the parent fish.

The outsides of the bottom and sides of small breeding trays should be painted dark brown or black. The water composition and temperature should be the same as in the main tank where the fish are usually kept. The breeding pairs should be separated for a week or so before being put in the breeding tank: even better results will follow if the pair have been reared separately. The diet suggested above will put the fish in good breeding condition and may be suplemented with small amounts of *Enchytrae*.

The furnishing of the breeding tank is not important. No bottom is needed, but if one is provided it should be of well-boiled peat. Two or three nylon breeding mops should be put in the tank. Only a single egg is laid and fertilised at each mating and the cycle may extend over several weeks, with a mating each day and more than one in the early days when up to some 20 eggs may be laid. The number of eggs produced is of course greater when one male is put in the tank with a number of females, but in a small tank to have more than one female in the confined space may prove to be counterproductive. If the fish are separated periodically for two or three days and well-fed before being put back in the tank, then even better results will be achieved.

The eggs are glassy and rather large, quite easy to see against a dark background. They have a tough case and be removed from the tank with tweezers or even with the bare hands either after they have been laid or once a day. The breeding mops should be lifted out and the eggs transferred to small dishes containing water of no more than 2 cm depth. The quality of that water is not critical and need not be the same as in the breeding tank: the temperature should be 18°–21°C.

662. *Epiplatys barmoiensis*

A small amount of Trypaflavin (1 g to 200/300 liters of water) will inhibit bacterial activity and the eggs can hatch in this solution without problems. The eggs will hatch in about 14 days and the clutch of eggs should be regularly checked and any yellowish-white, opaque eggs which have not been fertilised should be removed. Those eggs will have a tendency to adhere to the bottom of the dish and can be taken out quite easily with a pipette.

The eggs can be transported in well-boiled peat. Eggs laid at different times can be induced to hatch simultaneously by adding a small amount of infusoria or a tiny quantity of micro eels to the water, or even by agitating the water gently.

The fry should be transferred to separate tanks similar in size to those in which the eggs have been hatched and containing only about the same amount of water. The fry grow quickly and greedily devour *Artemia nauplii* during the first hour: this diet should be varied with sieved Daphnia and Cyclops. They are sexually mature at eight to twelve weeks and if raised in ordinary tap water will be more resistant to disease.

The colors of fish raised at high temperatures are usually less intense than those bred at lower temperatures. In breeding these seasonal fish it is important to preserve the quality of the strains by only selecting the best adults for breeding and avoiding the temptation to preserve or encourage mutations.

661. *Epiplatys bifasciatus*

EPIPLATYS ANNULATUS

Family: *Cyprinodontidae*

Genus: *Epiplatys*

English name: Rocket Panchax

Origin: Guinea, Liberia

Size: Approximately 3 cm

Habitat: Found in sluggish and still waters with overhanging vegetation

SHAPE, COLORING AND MARKINGS: The body is elongated, fairly deep and laterally slightly compressed. The basic coloration and fin pattern vary according to the locality of origin. All varieties however have wide dark transverse bands, from muddy green to chocolate brown or dark brown to blue-black. The bands contrast sharply with a paler background that may be muddy yellow, pale brown or salmon. The anterior rays of the dorsal fin are generally pale blue, but sometimes are bright red, with an area behind, that is the same color as the transverse bands, as is the base of the anal fin, while the posterior rays of that fin are lighter yellow and light blue, with a broad red border which has usually a narrow light blue edge. The central rays of the caudal fin are generally very long and are orange-brown or red: the lobes are sky blue and separated from the center by a deep red zone. The pectoral fins are colorless and transparent but with a deep red border.

Females have a similar color pattern but rounded fins.

Males are as described above.

GENERAL CARE: Suitable for small community tanks with smaller species but preferably no other surface fish. There should be some floating plants but not so many as to deprive *E.annulatus* of the free swimming space it needs. The water, filtered through peat should be neither too fresh nor too hard. Temperature 23°–26°C. Violent agitation of the water surface should be avoided. All kinds of small surface insects will be eaten, including fruitflies, mosquitoes, ants and greenfly. Dried food can be given for variety and the fish will hunt Daphnia and mosquito larvae, but it is essential that they be given adequate supplies of surface insects.

BREEDING: This is not difficult: see Introductory note.

EPIPLATYS BARMOIENSIS

Family: *Cyprinodontidae*
Genus: *Epiplatys*
English name: none
Origin: Liberia, Sierra Leone
Size: Approximately 5 cm
Habitat: Found in sluggish and still waters with dense vegetation on the banks

SHAPE, COLORING AND MARKINGS: The body is very slender and laterally only moderately compressed. The basic coloration and fin pattern vary according to the locality of origin. *E.barmoiensis* is closely related to *Epiplatys bifasciatus* but the pectoral fins are very well developed in *E.barmoiensis,* while the patterning on the lower jaw and gill covers and the red network over the body, distinctive features of *E.bifasciatus,* are absent. The back is greenish, with red overtones: the flanks and belly are off-white. The fins are greenish with red specks and dots: the anal fin is reddish with a dark border and red stipples.
Females have rounded fins with no patterning: the body is a faded green, with a wide dark longitudinal band on the lower half.
Males are as described above.

GENERAL CARE: As for *E.annulatus,* but *E.barmoiensis* is suitable for both large and small aquariums.

663. *Epiplatys annulatus*

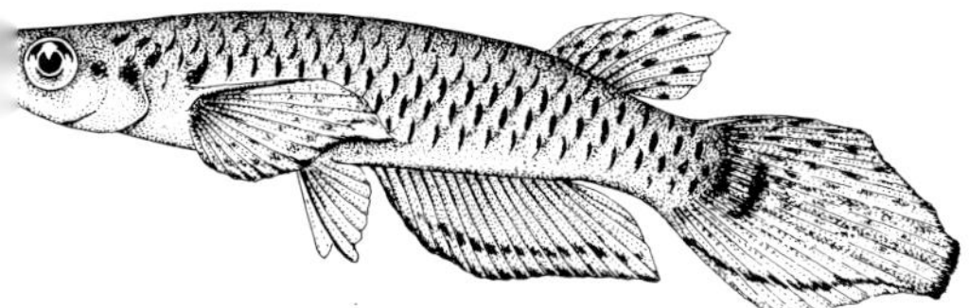

664. *Epiplatys barmoiensis*

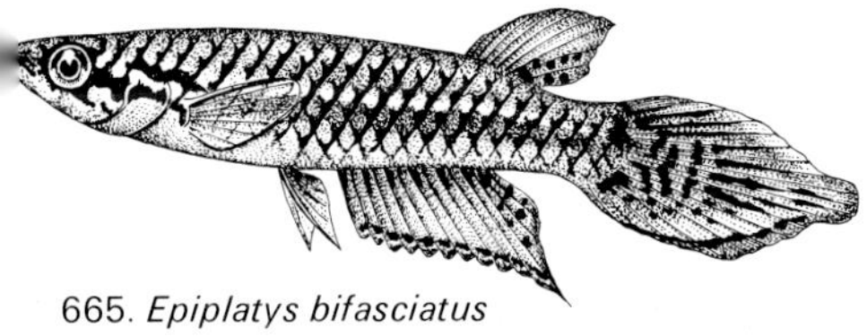

665. *Epiplatys bifasciatus*

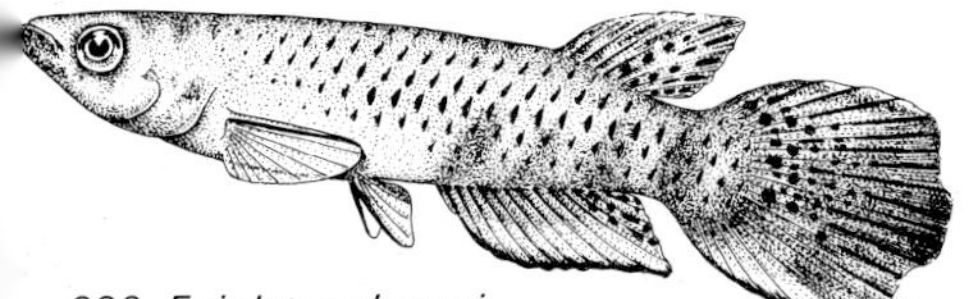

666. *Epiplatys chaperi*

667. *Epiplatys chevalieri*

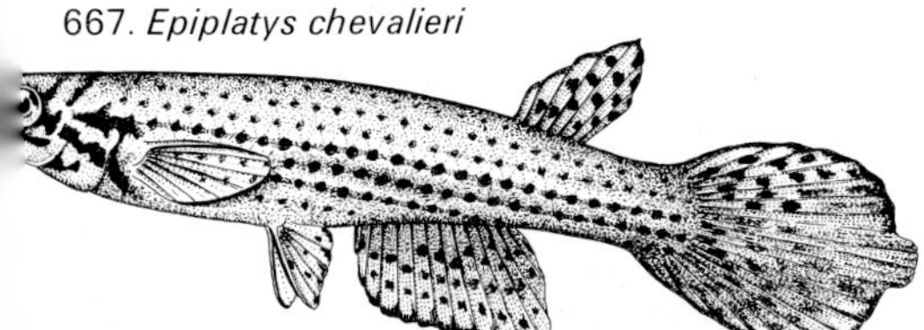

BREEDING: Not too difficult. See Introductory note.

ADDITIONAL INFORMATION: A very new species first described in 1968, and not very commonly imported as yet.

EPIPLATYS BIFASCIATUS

Family: *Cyprinodontidae*
Genus: *Epiplatys*
English name: none
Origin: West Africa
Size: Approximately 5 cm
Habitat: No details are available of its natural habitat

SHAPE, COLORING AND MARKINGS: The body is very slender and laterally only slightly compressed. The basic coloration and fin patterning vary significantly according to the locality of origin. The basic color can vary from off-white to greenish. The back is darker with a strong red gleam. A red-brown longitudinal band runs from the root of the pectoral fins to the caudal peduncle: a number of irregular red lines on the snout and gill covers merge into this stripe. An attractive red network pattern lies over the body and may become the dominant body color in some varieties. The fins are also often red, but in some specimens they are yellow-green with a large number of red spots, specks and patches: the base of the anal fin is red-brown: all the fins have a red or brown border and the pectoral fins are colorless and transparent.
Females have more rounded fins and less vivid colors.
Males are as described above.

GENERAL CARE: As for *E.barmoiensis.*

BREEDING: Nothing is known of the reproductive behavior of this species but it is likely to be similar to that of related species.

ADDITIONAL INFORMATION: Synonyms include *E.ndelensis, E.steindachneri, E.taeniatus.*

EPIPLATYS CHAPERI

Family: *Cyprinodontidae*
Genus: *Epiplatys*
English name: Fire-mouth Epiplatys
Origin: Ghana, Ivory Coast
Size: Approximately 7 cm
Habitat: Found in overgrown, sluggish and still waters

SHAPE, COLORING AND MARKINGS: The body is rather more compact than in related species and laterally only moderately compressed. The basic coloration and fin patterning vary significantly according to the locality of origin, but all varieties have transverse bands of varying intensity behind the first anal fin rays. Three very differently colored varieties have been reported from Ghana: one orange-red, one predominantly purple and one lemon-yellow with glittering patches on the fins. This last variety is predominantly a lemon yellow with orange-red bands and comma-shaped red marks on the scales on the flanks. The dorsal fin is yellow-green with dark red to green-red stripes and stipples. The base of the anal fin is emerald green with a yellow-red border and red specks. The base of the caudal fin is emerald green: the lower lobe has a red border with, above, a yellow zone which gradually becomes red, and many dark stripes and stipples. The ventral fins are yellow with a red border: the pectoral fins are lemon yellow.
Females have rounded fins and less vivid colors.
Males are as described above.

GENERAL CARE: As for *E.barmoiensis.*

BREEDING: Not too difficult: see Introductory note.

ADDITIONAL INFORMATION: This species is the true *E.chaperi,* first described in 1882: the name was for many years incorrectly applied to *E.dageti.*

EPIPLATYS CHEVALIERI

Family: *Cyprinodontidae*
Genus: *Epiplatys*
English name: Chevalier's Epiplatys
Origin: The central Congo
Size: Approximately 7 cm
Habitat: Found in overgrown, still and sluggish waters

SHAPE, COLORING AND MARKINGS: The body is very slender and laterally only moderately compressed. The basic coloration is a pale green to yellow, with a pale red overtone. A large number of small red spots lie on the body and merge together on the lower part as longitudinal lines. The head bears irregular red lines characteristic of so many of the *Epiplatys* species. The fins are pale green: the unpaired fins have a darker border and red stipples and patches: the ventral and pectoral fins are colorless and transparent.
Females have more rounded fins and less prominent red spots on the body.
Males are as described above.

GENERAL CARE: As for *E.barmoiensis.*

BREEDING: Not too difficult: see Introduction.

668. *Epiplatys dageti*

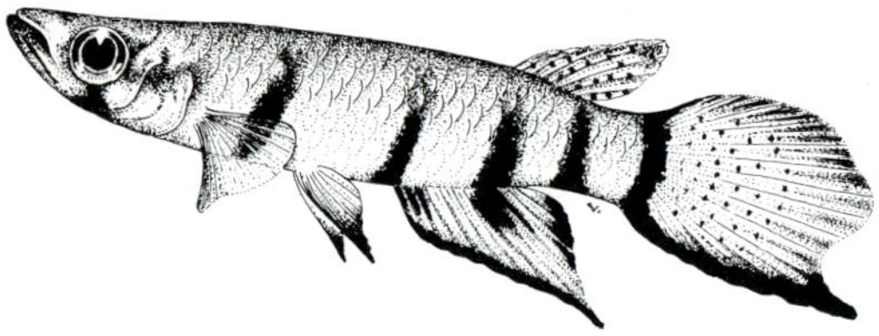

669. *Epiplatys dageti monroviae*

670. *Epiplatys esekanus*

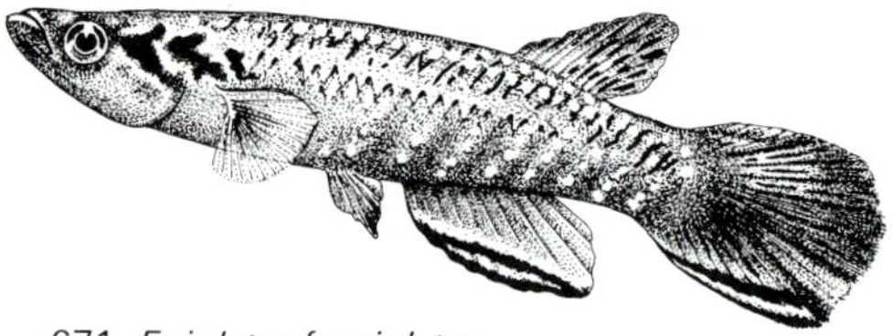

671. *Epiplatys fasciolatus*

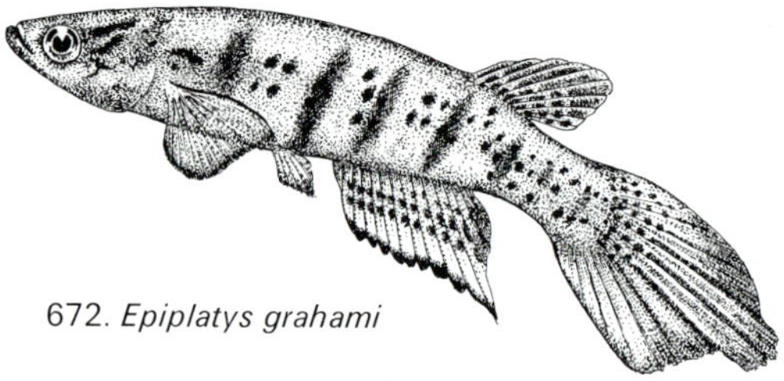

672. *Epiplatys grahami*

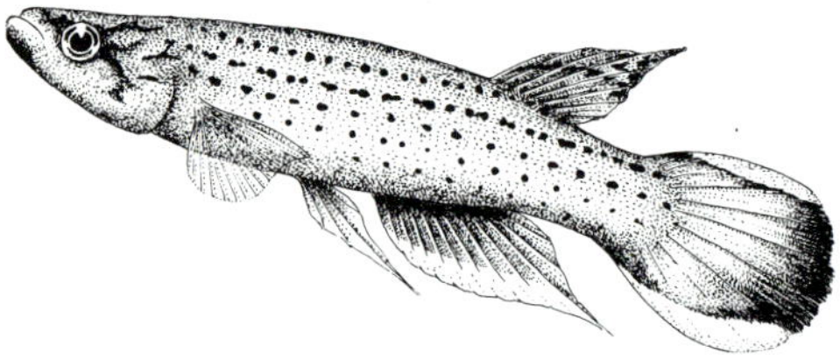

673. *Epiplatys lamottei*

EPIPLATYS DAGETI

Family: *Cyprinodontidae*
Genus: *Epiplatys*
English name: none
Origin: Ghana, Liberia
Size: Approximately 6 cm
Habitat: Found in sluggish and still waters with dense vegetation

SHAPE, COLORING AND MARKINGS: The body is elongated, fairly deep and laterally very compressed. The basic coloration is yellow-green: the back is olive green: the flanks yellow to blue-green: the belly off-white to ochre yellow. The scales on the back have a reddish tinge, those on the flanks a blue-black margin. Five or six transverse bands lie across the body, the last of which lies on the caudal peduncle and runs into the extended lower rays of the fin: this band and the preceding three are always the most prominent. The lower jaw and throat are orange-red with black edges. The unpaired fins are grey-green: the dorsal fin has dark stipples: the anal fin has a dark border and dark patches below the transverse bands: the caudal fin has a dark border and many dots and stripes. The other fins are colorless and transparent.
Females have more rounded fins and are less vividly colored being predominantly brown.
Males are as described above.

GENERAL CARE: As for *E.barmoiensis*.

BREEDING: Not difficult: see Introductory note.

ADDITIONAL INFORMATION: This is one of the most widely known of these species: for many years it was known as *E.chaperi*, a species of little interest to aquarists.

EPIPLATYS DAGETI MONROVIAE

Family: *Cyprinodontidae*
Genus: *Epiplatys*
Origin: Ghana, Ivory Coast
Size: Approximately 6 cm
Habitat: Found in overgrown still and sluggish waters

SHAPE, COLORING AND MARKINGS: *E.dageti monroviae* is a sub-species of *E.dageti* of identical body shape but with a different color pattern. The flanks of *E.dageti monroviae* have a dominant brassy overtone: the underside of the head is off-white to yellow ochre. Five well-defined transverse bands lie on the body: the first lies immediately behind the pectoral fin: the rest lie in front of the anal fin, above the center of the anal fin, on the caudal peduncle and on the base of the caudal fin. The unpaired fins are a grey-green: the dorsal fin has dark flecks: the anal fin is greyish to pale green with a dark border and large dark patches: the caudal fin has dark stipples and a broad dark border in the lower lobe: the ventral fins have dark borders: the pectoral fins are colorless and transparent.
Females have more rounded fins and lack the prominent marks of the males.
Males are as described above.

GENERAL CARE: As for *E.barmoiensis*.

BREEDING: No information is available on the reproductive behavior of this species but it is likely to be similar to that of related species.

EPIPLATYS ESEKANUS

Family: *Cyprinodontidae*
Genus: *Epiplatys*
English name: none
Origin: Cameroon
Size: Approximately 3 cm
Habitat: Found in still and sluggish overgrown waters

SHAPE, COLORING AND MARKINGS: The body is elongated, fairly deep and laterally slightly compressed. The basic coloration is yellowish: the back is a bright yellow with a pale brown network pattern: the belly and underside of the head are orangey-red: a pattern of deep red spots and stripes covers the head, gill covers and lower lip. The scales on the upper half of the body are brown to reddish at the base: on the lower half of the body each scale has a bright red spot, which appear as two, three or more red lines, between which are areas of pale blue most evident above the gill covers and pectoral fin. The dorsal fin is a grassy green, paler towards the tip, with dark brown spots becoming orangey-red: the anal fin is a deep brown at the base, becoming pale green, then orange-red and finally bright yellow at the front, with a dark brown border. The caudal fin is predominantly pale green, with brown rays and brown patches at the base: the lobes are orangey-red and light blue, the lower lobe being the more vividly colored. The ventral and pectoral fins are a pale yellow to orangey-red.
Females are yellowish-brown with no pronounced patterning: the fins are rounded.
Males are as described above.

GENERAL CARE: As for *E.barmoiensis*.

BREEDING: Not difficult: see Introductory note.

ADDITIONAL INFORMATION: A new species first described in 1968.

674. *Epiplatys dageti monroviae*

675. *Epiplatys fasciatus*

EPIPLATYS FASCIATUS

Family: *Cyprinodontidae*
Genus: *Epiplatys*
English name: Banded Epiplatys
Origin: Sierra Leone
Size: Approximately 7 cm
Habitat: Found in sluggish and still waters with dense vegetation on the banks

SHAPE, COLORING AND MARKINGS: The body is very slender and laterally only moderately compressed. The basic coloration and fin patterns vary significantly according to the locality of origin. An attractive sky-blue variety comes from west Sierra Leone but in general the basic color is a green or rusty brown: the back is a darker brown or olive green: the head is brown, with a pattern of red or blue iridescent spots and stripes. The upper half of the body has pale green iridescent marks and darker diagonal bands above the anal fin, separated by patches of pale green. The dorsal fin is pale green at the base, with rust marks in the center and a wide violet border. The anal fin is pale to rusty brown, with a red edge and pale green bands. The caudal fin is predominantly brown, with pale green membranes, a violet border to the upper lobe and a red band with a violet area and red-brown border in the lower lobe. The ventral and pectoral fins are rusty brown.
Females are a yellow-brown: the lower half of the body is darker: the fins are colorless and without marks.
Males are as described above.

GENERAL CARE: As for *E.barmoiensis* but one to two teaspoonfuls of salt should be added for each 10 liters of water in the tank.

BREEDING: See Introductory note.

ADDITIONAL INFORMATION: *E.fasciatus* has also been known as *E.dorsalis*, *E.sexifasciatus leonensis* and *E.matloki*.

EPIPLATYS GRAHAMI

Family: *Cyprinodontidae*
Genus: *Epiplatys*
English name: Graham's Epiplatys
Origin: Cameroon, Nigeria
Size: Approximately 4 cm
Habitat: Found in still and sluggish, densely overgrown waters

SHAPE, COLORING AND MARKINGS: The body is very slender and laterally only moderately compressed. The basic coloration is ochre: the back and top of the head are brownish with irregular red lines and spots on the head. Red marks are irregularly distributed over the flanks, mainly on the caudal peduncle. A number of brown transverse bands lie on the body: the three above the ventral and pectoral fins being the most pronounced. The dorsal fin is yellowish with a violet-brown border and an orange-red membrane. The anal fin is brownish-violet at the base and otherwise green with a brown border and orangey-red specks and stripes in the center. The base of the caudal fin is predominantly yellow: the rest of the fin is brownish-green with orangey-red rays and red spots: the lower lobe is pale green. The pectoral fins are pale green with an orangey-red or deep brown border.
Females are a bright yellow but otherwise less vividly colored: the fins are rounded.
Males are as described above.

GENERAL CARE: As for *E.barmoiensis*.

BREEDING: Not difficult although not a prolific species: see Introductory note.

ADDITIONAL INFORMATION: *E.grahami* is a tolerant species: it is still little known among aquarists even though it was first described by George Albert Boulenger in 1911 and small batches are regularly imported. It is a lively species that deserves to be better known.

EPIPLATYS LAMOTTEI

Family: *Cyprinodontidae*
Genus: *Epiplatys*
English name: none
Origin: Guinea
Size: Approximately 6 cm
Habitat: Found in still and sluggish waters with dense vegetation on the banks

SHAPE, COLORING AND MARKINGS: The body is very slender and laterally only slightly compressed. The basic coloration is a clear to ochre yellow with deep red patches and lines on the head and underside of the snout. The back and belly are orange. Almost pure red marks lie on the body in regular lines, most numerous on the back. The dorsal fin is bright yellow with green overtones and deep red specks at the tips. The anal fin is dark at the base and has a broad bright yellow border. The caudal fin is predominantly yellowish-brown, becoming brownish-red: the two lobes have wide bright yellow borders.
Females are bright yellow but otherwise less vividly colored: the fins are rounded.
Males are as described above.

GENERAL CARE: As for *E.barmoiensis* but temperature 22°–24° C.

BREEDING: No information is available on the reproductive behavior of this species but it is likely to be similar to that of related species: see Introductory note.

ADDITIONAL INFORMATION: A new species, only described in 1954, little if at all known among aquarists: it may not have yet even been imported.

EPIPLATYS LONGIVENTRALIS

Family: *Cyprinodontidae*
Genus: *Epiplatys*
English name: none
Origin: Nigeria, the delta of the Niger river
Size: Approximately 6 cm
Habitat: Found in still and sluggish waters with dense vegetation

SHAPE, COLORING AND MARKINGS: The body is very slender and laterally only slightly compressed. The basic coloration is yellowish-white: the back is pale brown: the lower part of the body salmon to light violet. The head is orangey-brown with a red overtone: golden yellow patches on the cheeks reach back to a point above the pectoral fins. The scales on the upper half of the body are brownish at the base and show up as a network pattern. Six to seven dark brown diagonal transverse bands lie on the lower half of the body: the

676. *Epiplatys lamottei*

first is above the pectoral, the second above the ventral and the third and fourth lie above the anal fin: the rest lie on the caudal peduncle with the last on the base of the fin. Four or five rows of red spots run along the body: the lowermost extends across the belly as far as the rear rays of the anal fin: the remainder usually stretch to the caudal peduncle. The dorsal and anal fins are brown with yellow and green marks: the caudal fin is brownish with parallel patterns of blue, yellow, green and violet marks. The pectoral and ventral fins are a translucent yellow brown.
Females are somewhat smaller, with rounded fins and less pronounced marks.
Males are as described above.

General care: As for *E.barmoiensis* but temperature 23°–26°C.

Breeding: This is not difficult: see Introductory note.

EPIPLATYS MULTIFASCIATUS

Family: *Cyprinodontidae*
Genus: *Epiplatys*
English name: none
Origin: Angola, in the district of Lunda
Size: Approximately 5 cm
Habitat: Found in still and sluggish waters with dense vegetation on the banks

Shape, coloring and markings: The body is very slender and laterally only slightly compressed. The basic coloration varies significantly according to the locality of origin. Specimens from Lake Tumba have six dark transverse bands: two above the base of the the anal fin and two which run into the fin itself. The dark pigmentation of the last band, on the caudal peduncle runs into the outer rays of the caudal fin. The back is yellowish-brown: the belly is yellowish-orange: the cheeks and the area immediately behind the pectoral fins have a bluish-green iridescence. The caudal peduncle is reddish-violet to purple. The dorsal fin is orange-red, with dark red marks: the caudal fin is orangey-red or salmon: occasionally it is olive green.
Females are somewhat smaller with less well developed fins.
Males are as described above.

General care: As for *E.barmoiensis*.

Breeding: This species does not seem as yet to have been bred in captivity.

Additional information: The species was first described in 1913 by George Albert Boulenger who named it *Haplochilus multifasciatus*. *E.boulengeri* is a synonym. *E.multifasciatus* is almost unknown among aquarists.

EPIPLATYS NIGRICANS

Family: *Cyprinodontidae*
Genus: *Epiplatys*
English name: Black-Edged Epiplatys
Origin: West Africa, the basin of the Congo river
Size: Approximately 5 cm
Habitat: Found in overgrown still and sluggish waters

Shape, coloring and markings: The body is very slender and laterally only slightly compressed. The basic coloration is olive green: the back is darker or brownish: the belly is yellowish-green or yellow. Almost all the scales carry a red mark which show up as a regular pattern over the body. A brownish-violet longitudinal stripe runs from the eye back to the base of the caudal fin. A reddish metallic glint is seen on the cheeks and the underside of the head which becomes a yellowish-orange. Two darker transverse bands are usually but not always found on the caudal peduncle. All the fins are yellowish: the unpaired fins usually have a reddish to brown stippling.
Females are somewhat smaller, with rounded fins: the marks on the scales are more of a rusty brown and the overall patterning is less intense.
Males are as described above, and usually have a bluish overtone.

General care: As for *E.barmoiensis*.

Breeding: Nothing is known about the reproductive behavior of this species.

Additional information: *E.nigricans* was named *Haplochilus nigricans* by George Albert Boulenger in 1913: it is still a species little known among aquarists.

EPIPLATYS SEXIFASCIATUS

Family: *Cyprinodontidae*
Genus: *Epiplatys*
English name: Six-Barred Epiplatys
Origin: Eastern Ghana
Size: Approximately 8 cm
Habitat: Found in still and sluggish waters with dense vegetation

Shape, coloring and markings: The body is very slender and laterally only slightly compressed. The basic coloration is yellow to yellowish-green: the back is very slightly darker or brownish the lower half of the body is yellow with bluish-violet overtones. Scattered red lines appear on the cheeks and in a zone above the pectoral fins: a dark brown band runs along the lower lip. All the scales have a red mark and in the lower part of the body these merge into diagonal stripes. Transverse bands varying in number and prominence are present and the color pattern may vary according to the locality of origin.
The dorsal fin is greenish to yellow, with brown-blue and red or orangey-red specks and stipples: the caudal fin is brownish to orangey-red with a number of dark red to brown spots at the base and violet, red, yellow and green marks running in parallel lines along the rays: the upper edge usually has a light green iridescent border. The anal fin is brown to orangey-red, with a broad dark brown to bright orange border next to an area of bright yellow or pale violet. The ventral fins are a transparent yellowish-orange: the pectoral fins are yellowish with a narrow darker border.
Females are somewhat smaller and less vividly colored.
Males are as described above.

General care: Only suitable for large aquariums and the company of even more robust fish. Otherwise as for *E.barmoiensis*.

Breeding: Not too difficult: see Introductory note.

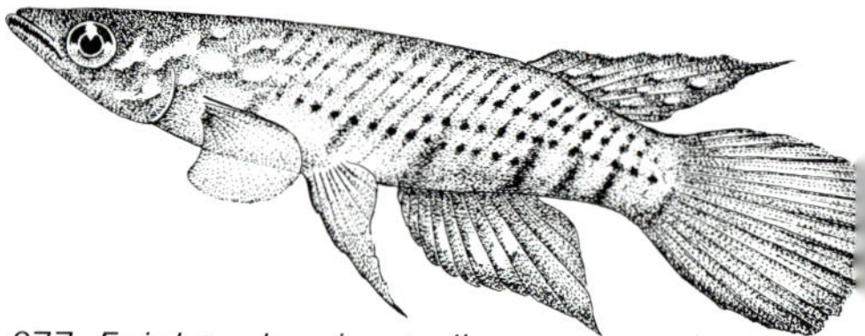

677. *Epiplatys longiventralis*

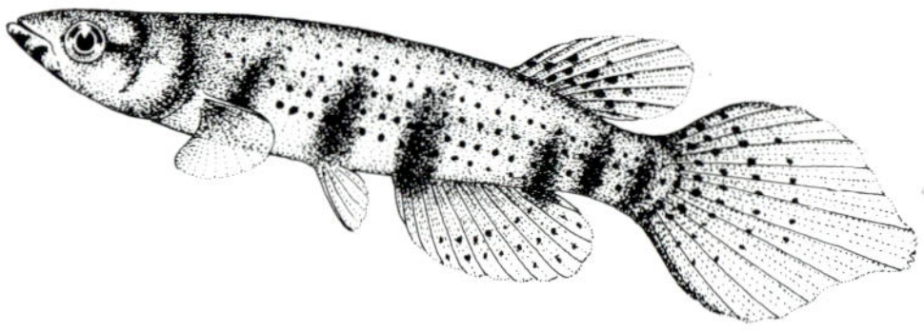

678. *Epiplatys multifasciatus*

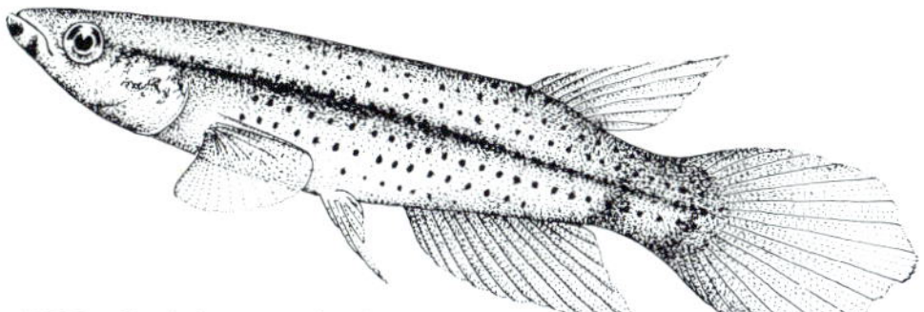

679. *Epiplatys nigricans*

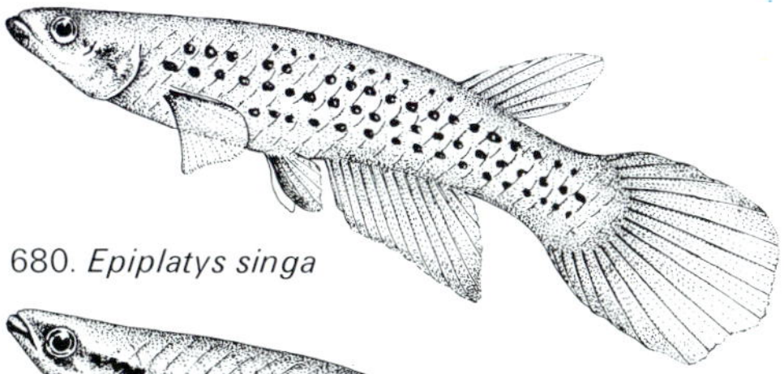

680. *Epiplatys singa*

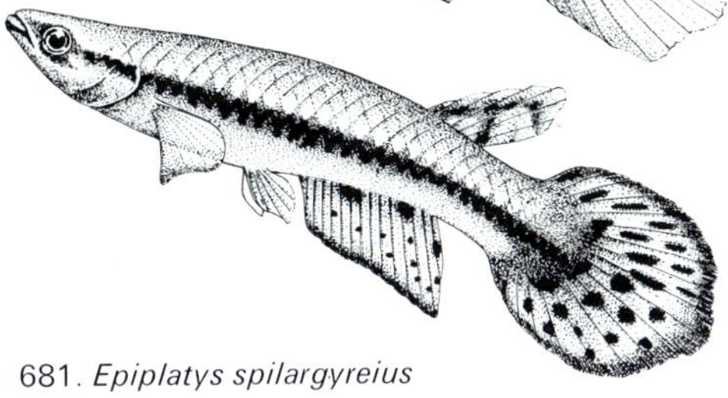

681. *Epiplatys spilargyreius*

SHAPE, COLORING AND MARKINGS: The body is elongated, fairly deep and laterally slightly compressed. The basic coloration is greenish to yellowish-white. A wide dark brown longitudinal line stretches back from the snout along the lower half of the body to the caudal peduncle: the area below is orangey-brown. The dorsal fin is greenish with brown marks. The anal fin is a grassy green with a broad brown border and dark brown patches. The caudal fin is predominantly grassy green, with a darker green or brown border and alternate brown and red patches. The ventral fins are pale green with a brownish base: the pectoral fins are yellowish to pale blue. Younger specimens have many reddish-brown diagonal stripes as well as the longitudinal stripe: the fins are mostly a rusty brown with narrow dark brown borders.
Females have a more rounded anal fin and the other fins are reddish-brown with darker transverse bands.
Males are as described above.

GENERAL CARE: As for *E.barmoiensis.*

BREEDING: Not difficult. See Introductory note.

ADDITIONAL INFORMATION: *E.spilargyreius* was first described by André Marie Constant Dumeril in 1861.

EPIPLATYS SINGA

Family: *Cyprinodontidae*
Genus: *Epiplatys*
English name: none
Origin: The lower reaches of the Congo river
Size: Approximately 4.5 cm
Habitat: No details are available of its natural habitat

SHAPE, COLORING AND MARKINGS: The body is very slender and laterally only slightly compressed. Curiously, no characteristic color pattern is recorded for this species, although from a drawing made by George Albert Boulenger in 1915 it seems to have a great deal of red over the body.
There are no known external sexual characteristics.

GENERAL CARE: No certain information is available but probably as for related species.

BREEDING: Nothing is known of the reproductive behavior of this species.

ADDITIONAL INFORMATION: First described in 1899: many writers consider that it should be placed in the genus *Aphyosemion.*

EPIPLATYS SPILARGYREIUS

Family: *Cyprinidontidae*
Genus: *Epiplatys*
English name: none
Origin: Northern Nigeria
Size: Approximately 4.5 cm
Habitat: Found in still and sluggish overgrown waters

EPIPLATYS CHAPERI SHELJUZHKOI

Family: *Cyprinodontidae*
Genus: *Epiplatys*
English name: none
Origin: Ghana, Ivory Coast
Size: Approximately 6 cm
Habitat: Found in sluggish and still waters with dense vegetation

SHAPE, COLORING AND MARKINGS: The body is elongated, fairly deep and laterally slightly compressed. *E.chaperi sheljuzhkoi* is a subspecies of *E.chaperi* but easily distinguished from the latter by its more slender body and the absence of any crossbars. The basic coloration is pale brown becoming pale blue towards the tail: the neck is a pale iridescent greenish-yellow: the back is orangey-brown: the belly orangey-red: the head predominantly a rusty brown or orangey-red. All the scales have a crimson mark at the base which merge to form lines in a very regular pattern. The dorsal fin is brownish, with a wide dark brown border and darker patches at the base and scattered red marks. The caudal fin is greenish with a brown overtone, dark stripes in the center and red marks at the base: the lower lobe has a dark brown border and a zone of pale green: the upper lobe and tip

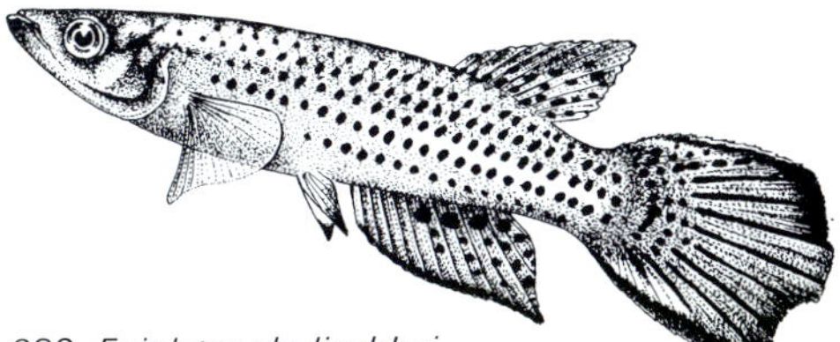

682. *Epiplatys sheljuzhkoi*

of the fin are edged with brown. The ventral fins are a transparent yellow-brown with dark spots: the pectoral fins are a transparent yellowish-orange.
Females have more rounded fins.
Males are as described above.

GENERAL CARE: As for *E.barmoiensis.*

BREEDING: Not difficult. See Introductory note.

683. *Epiplatys sheljuzhkoi*

THE FAMILY CYPRINODONTIDAE

The genus Fundulus

The three species in the genus *Fundulus* described below are unusual among aquarium fish in that they come not from tropical or semi-tropical climates but from more temperate zones in the USA. It is for this reason that they can be kept even as pond fish during the summer months in most countries. Not many amateurs pay much attention to these fish, but they are well worth keeping and are not at all difficult to breed.

685. *Fundulus dispar dispar*

FUNDULUS CHRYSOTUS

Family: *Cyprinodontidae*

Genus: *Fundulus*

English names: Golden Ear and Golden Eared Killifish

Origin: Southeast USA, from South Carolina to Florida

Size: Maximum 7 cm

Habitat: Found in fresh and brackish shallow waters

SHAPE, COLORING AND MARKINGS: The body is elongated, almost cylindrical and laterally compressed. The mouth is wide and upward-pointing. The dorsal and anal fins are set far back and slightly rounded. The caudal fin is rounded at the back. The back is a dark olive green, becoming greenish-white towards the belly. An iridescent bluish-green mark lies on the gill covers: the irises are golden. Rows of bright red dots cover the body. The pectoral and ventral fins are colorless: the other fins are canary yellow and flecked with red spots.

Females are brownish and less vividly colored: the body has a number of glistening dots and a marbled pattern.

Males are as described above.

GENERAL CARE: *F.chrysotus* needs a fairly large tank with floating plants and adequate free swimming space: bogwood may be used for decoration. The composition of the water is not critical: temperature 18°–20° C. It will tolerate temperature as low as 15° C and can be kept in an outdoor pond during the summer. Part of the pond should be marshy and there should be reeds in the deeper part. Fish put in the pond in May will have bred prolifically by September unless preyed on by birds. In the pond the fish need Daphnia and Cyclops.

BREEDING: The male and females should be segregated and well fed before being put in a breeding tank with fine leaved plants and clumps of algae, on which the eggs will be laid. Mating can be stimulated by putting the tank in the sun. The fish mate daily over a period: some 300 eggs will be laid in a week if one male is put in the tank with two females. The parent fish will not eat the eggs but may attack the fry and they should therefore be removed to a separate tank after laying the eggs. The fry are large and not difficult to raise on very fine pond infusoria. The breeding tank must be kept scrupulously clean and part of the water changed regularly.

684. *Fundulus chrysotus*

FUNDULUS DISPAR DISPAR

Family: *Cyprinodontidae*

Genus: *Fundulus*

English name: Star Head Top Minnow

Origin: Southeast USA

Size: Maximum 6 cm

Habitat: Found in shallow waters

SHAPE, COLORING AND MARKINGS: The body shape is very similar to that of *F.chrysotus*. The basic coloration is greenish; the back is olive brown to reddish-brown: the flanks, which carry red spots, and the belly are lighter. A wide dark band runs across the head and narrow transverse bands are sometimes found on the body. The pectoral and ventral fins are colorless: the rest of the fins are yellowish-green, tinged with red and with brown patches.

Females have more distinct red spots and more rounded dorsal and anal fins.

Males are as described above.

GENERAL CARE: As for *F.chrysotus*.

BREEDING: As for *F.chrysotus*.

FUNDULUS NOTTI NOTTI

Family: *Cyprinodontidae*
Genus: *Fundulus*
English name: none
Origin: Southeast USA
Size: Maximum 6 cm
Habitat: Found in shallow still waters in low lying areas

SHAPE, COLORING AND MARKINGS: The body is elongated, relatively low and laterally compressed. The mouth is wide and upward-pointing. The dorsal and anal fins, set far back, are almost diamond-shaped. The caudal fin is almost completely round. The basic coloration is olive brown: the flanks are lighter: the belly yellowish. A black vertical stripe runs through the eye and becomes narrower towards the throat. A large number of sometimes indistinct transverse bands lie on the body and many dark spots are found on the dorsal, caudal and anal fins.
Females are less vividly colored although the dots on the body may be more distinct. The only vertical band is the one that runs through the eye.
Males are as described above.

GENERAL CARE: As for *F.chrysotus*, but *F.notti notti* can tolerate even lower temperatures and accordingly is even more suitable for keeping in a pond in the summer.

BREEDING: As for *F.chrysotus*.

686. *Jordanella floridae*

THE FAMILY CYPRINODONTIDAE

The genus Jordanella

This is one of the genera in this family which is almost certainly restricted to the Americas. There have been some reports of specimens of *Jordanella floridae* being found in Borneo, but it is thought that these fish had originally been imported. *J.floridae* described below is quite popular with aquarists, who are attracted by its beauty, but unfortunately it is by no means always available from dealers.

JORDANELLA FLORIDAE

Family: *Cyprinodontidae*
Genus: *Jordanella*
English name: American Flag fish
Origin: Florida, Yucatán
Size: Approximately 6 cm
Habitat: Found in pools, lakes and swamps

SHAPE, COLORING AND MARKINGS: The body is stocky, quite deep and laterally rather compressed. The coloration is very variable.
Females are predominantly yellowish and always have a prominent dark patch below the front of the dorsal fin and a darker patch on the back of the fin. During the mating season there is a chequer-board pattern of dark patches over the body.
Males are an olive to brownish-green: the back is darker. The scales have a steel blue to yellow-green iridescent patch giving a glitter, under illumination, to the whole body. A dark but sometimes indistinct patch lies under the front of the dorsal fin, roughly in the center of the body. The dorsal and anal fins are yellowish to pale green with rust-brown patches or bands: a darker patch lies on the back part of the dorsal fin. The caudal fin is orange to blue, with red stipples.

GENERAL CARE: *J.floridae* is not really suitable for the ordinary community tank. The tank should only contain a few clumps of robust plants for this species will nibble at soft-leaved plants. The bed should be dark and plenty of floating leaves should be present to give overhead cover, for *J.floridae* is rather shy. The composition of the water is not critical: temperature 19°–22° C. All types of small live animal matter will be accepted but this diet should be regularly supplemented with algae or lettuce.

BREEDING: This is not difficult. The breeding tank need not be larger than 10 liters capacity. The temperature should be about 25° C. The composition of the water is not critical. The eggs are laid near the bottom: the mating cycle may be spread over several days with about 25 eggs being laid each day. The fry hatch after five or six days and should be transferred to a separate tank, containing plenty of algae after about two weeks: until then the male fish should be left to guard the brood but the female should be removed immediately after spawning. Algae is vital for rearing the fry.

687. *Jordanella floridae*
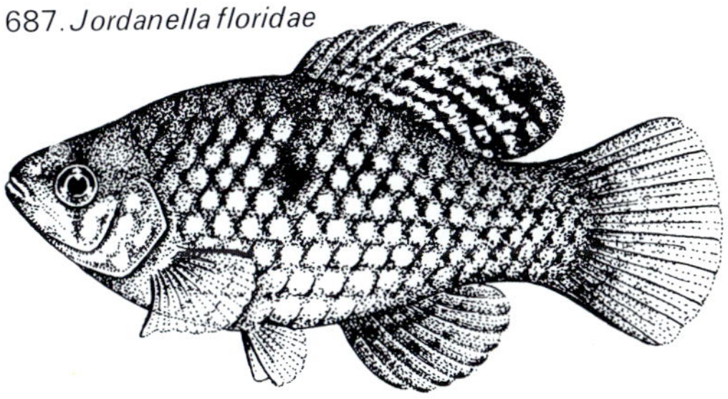

688. *Leptolucania ommata* (♂)
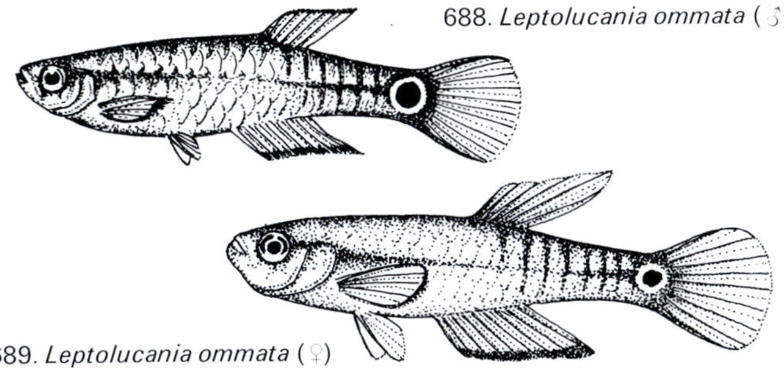
689. *Leptolucania ommata* (♀)

THE FAMILY CYPRINODONTIDAE

The genus Leptolucania

There is only one species, the Swamp Killie, *Leptolucania ommata*, in this genus, which, as noted below in the description of *L.ommata* is closely related to the species in the genus *Fundulus* described above. This is another genus of Cyprinodontidae that is found only in North America.

LEPTOLUCANIA OMMATA

Family: *Cyprinodontidae*
Genus: *Leptolucania*
English name: Swamp Killie
Origin: From South Georgia to Florida
Size: Approximately 3.5 cm
Habitat: Found in freshwater pools lakes and swamps

SHAPE, COLORING AND MARKINGS: The body is elongated and very similar to that of the closely related species in the genus *Fundulus*. *L.ommata* has however the dorsal fin set further back along the body and the females have no genital sac.
Females are a yellow to light brown and have a prominent dark longitudinal band on the body and two dark patches, one above the base of the caudal fin, another above the anal fin. The fins are predominantly yellowish.
Males are an ochre-yellow to light brown: the flanks and caudal peduncle have an overtone of iridescent blue. A brown, sometimes ill-defined longitudinal stripe runs from the eye to the base of the caudal fin, ending in a light-edged black patch. Six to eight black cross-bars may also appear. The dorsal and anal fins are yellowish or orange and generally have a blue border.

GENERAL CARE: *L.ommata* is best kept in a small aquarium without too much vegetation, a dark bottom and pieces of bogwood. The composition of the water is not critical: temperature 22°–24°C. The colors of this species are shown up best if the water has a yellowish tint, by being filtered through peat. *L.ommata* is a very peaceful fish which will live happily with other small species. All types of live animal matter will be accepted as food but dried food will not usually be eaten.

BREEDING: Not too difficult. The eggs are discharged immediately above the bed on to plants or between long strands of peat. The fry hatch out after ten or twelve days and will hunt for food almost immediately. The normal fry foods may be used but for swift growth it is very important to change the water regularly and to leave plenty of free swimming space between the plants in the tank.

THE FAMILY CYPRINODONTIDAE

The genus Lucania

The only species in this genus of interest to aquarists is the very attractive but not particularly well-known *Lucania goodei* described below. It is another of those species that benefits from being kept at not too high a temperature, and as noted below, can be an extremely decorative fish if kept in a small shoal, and in a community tank with related species.
The genus *Lucania* is very closely related to the genus *Fundulus*, but is distinguished by taxonomists, by differences in dentition. Whereas species in the genus *Fundulus* have two rows of teeth, those in the genus *Lucania* have the teeth set in one row. In all respects however that concern amateurs aquarists, the two genera can be regarded as identical. Species of both genera will live happily together.

690. *Lucania goodei*

LUCANIA GOODEI

Family: *Cyprinodontidae*
Genus: *Lucania*
English name: none
Origin: Florida
Size: Approximately 6 cm
Habitat: Found in shallow, still fresh waters with plenty of vegetation

SHAPE, COLORING AND MARKINGS: The body is elongated, cylindrical and hardly compressed. The mouth is end-positioned but set at an upward angle. The dorsal and anal fins are rounded and set far back. The back of the caudal fin is slightly rounded and set far back. The back of the caudal fin is slightly rounded. The back is olive brown: the flanks a shiny, yellowy bronze: the belly and throat a soft yellow. The scales on the back and flanks have a narrow dark edge which create a network pattern. A horizontal black wavy line runs from the snout, through the eye to the base of the caudal fin. The dorsal and anal fins are a brilliant blue with a dark edge and a pattern of orangey-red marks. The caudal fin is pale red at the base, becoming colorless. Females are less vividly colored: all the fins are colorless.
Males are as described above.

GENERAL CARE: This exceptionally beautiful species of the Cyprinodontidae should be kept in a group of about six of its own kind in a tank well-furnished with plants that do not require a high temperature. It will be content to share the tank with similar species, for example *Jordanella floridae*, *Elassoma evergladei* and *Fundulus notti*. The water should be slightly soft and the tank unheated, to simulate the variations in temperature experienced by *L.goodei* in its natural habitat. Part of the water should be changed each week. The diet should be Daphnia, Cyclops and the larvae of aquatic insects, particularly black and white mosquito larvae. Tubifex is less suitable and dried food will not normally be eaten, but it is important that the fish be given a varied diet.

BREEDING: *L.goodei* will breed spontaneously in a community tank but the best results will be achieved by using a special breeding tank 30 × 20 × 20 cm, with a bed of well-rinsed sand, some fine-leaved plants and some floating plants such as Crystalwort *(Riccia fluitans)* or the floating variety of *Ceratopteris thalictroides*. The water should be soft. The one selected male and two breeding females should be kept apart for a week or two before being put into the tank. The eggs are laid over a fairly long period and the fish should therefore be transferred to another similarly equipped tank after about a week. The large, light amber eggs hatch after a few days and the fry should be fed immediately with very fine pond infusoria. They are then fairly easy to raise.

THE FAMILY CYPRINODONTIDAE

The genus Nothobranchius

Members of the genus *Nothobranchius* are found only in East Africa. Like the *Aphyosemion* species, the *Nothobranchius* (literally, the false-gilled fish) are egg-laying toothcarps and seasonal fish.

In the wild, these fish are almost without exception only found in still waters such as pools and lakes which dry up either completely or partially each year during the dry season. The *Nothobranchius* survive in these extreme conditions because of their peculiar life style and in particular their strange reproductive habits.

Like nearly all seasonal fish the male *Nothobranchius* are exceptionally beautifully colored, rivalling even the most beautiful of the coral fish. The females however are quite plain and females of one species are so similar to those of another as to be easily confused: the males of the various species, despite local variations in color, are usually easily distinguishable.

The water in the natural habitats of these fish varies a great deal and changes its composition from season to season. During the rainy season the hardness of the water may be as low as 1°–2° DH: during the dry season it can rise to about 8° DH. The water is also likely to be acid. The temperature will fluctuate from 20° C in the mornings to 25° C at noon.

The *Nothobranchius* species are among the egg-burying fish. The eggs are laid just above the bed and the male then pushes them into it with a strong flick of the tail. The spawning season lasts some weeks, during which the males will mate with any willing female. When the pools and lakes dry up the parent fish die but the eggs remain safely embedded in the mud where they are protected from the sun. The eggs will stay thus at rest for a period of a few weeks or even up to six months depending on the local climate. When the bed in which the eggs are lying is flooded again, the eggs develop very quickly. These pools are of course also the breeding ground of many insects such as mosquitos: accordingly the fry are never short of food: they develop very rapidly and are often sexually mature after six to eight weeks.

A number of species have been bred successfully in captivity. Selected males and females should be kept separate for six to eight weeks before being put in the breeding tank. Small plastic tanks of about six liters capacity are best. The water should be slightly acid and the bottom covered with 2 cm of thoroughly boiled and well-washed fine peat. Two females and one male should be put in the tank which should be so positioned that it receives a few hours of sunlight each day. The mating cycle goes on for about two weeks. During this period the breeding fish should preferably be fed only on black and white mosquito larvae. The temperature should be 23°–24° C.

When the fish have stopped mating they should be removed from the tank and the water carefully removed. The peat bed should then be allowed to dry out naturally. Alternatively the peat may be drained in a net, placed in a plastic bag and stored away to give the eggs the necessary period of rest. The appropriate period of rest for the different species has not yet been determined with any degree of certainty, but it should normally be at least six weeks. Slightly acid water should then be added, and the first eggs will very soon hatch: it may however take up to two weeks (that is, the length of the mating season) for the last of the eggs to hatch. The fry grow rapidly and eat voraciously: they should therefore be sorted and separated from time to time.

There are about twenty species in the genus but it is not a genus to which taxonomists have as yet paid a great deal of attention and accordingly there is still some confusion over nomenclature. Five species, fairly well known to aquarists, are described below: of these, probably *N.guentheri* and *N.rachovi* are the best known. Some other species, notably *N.mayeri, N.neumanni* and *N.orthonotus* are sometimes mentioned in the literature but are hardly ever, if at all, imported. Other species sometimes encountered, including *N.kirki* and *N.tanzania* are probably not true species at all, but at best local varieties.

691. Nothobranchius brieni

NOTHOBRANCHIUS BRIENI

Family: *Cyprinodontidae*

Genus: *Nothobranchius*

English name: none

Origin: Zaire, from Likasi to Lubumbashi

Size: Approximately 7 cm

Habitat: Found in seasonal pools

SHAPE, COLORING AND MARKING: The body is stocky, laterally only slightly compressed. The dorsal and anal fins are powerfully developed. The basic coloration is a metallic blue: all the scales have a broad red edge, making the fish predominantly a dull red. Red marks and stripes lie on the cheeks and gill covers. The dorsal fin is wine red with an irregular pattern of yellow stripes and marks and a bluish-white band edged with a narrow black border. The anal fin has a dark red base with a light blue band and otherwise is an orangey-yellow with irregular dots and marks and a narrow black edge. The caudal fin has a wide bluish-white band edged with a narrow black border. The ventral fins have a pattern of red marks: the pectoral fins are colorless and transparent, but with a faint blue tinge.

Females are smaller, dull brown with colorless fins.

Males are as described above.

General care: *N.brieni* is suitable for both large and small aquariums, with a dark peaty bottom and arrangements of bogwood. Only one male however should be kept with two females: the males are very aggressive towards each other. No special plants are required in the tank. The water should be soft and slightly acid. Temperature 20°–24°C. *N.brieni* will keep mainly to the bottom of the tank. All live animal matter will be accepted, but not, as a rule, dried food.

Breeding: See Introductory note. The eggs need a rest period of at least six weeks. The breeding temperature should be about 27°C.

NOTHOBRANCHIUS GUENTHERI

Family: *Cyprinodontidae*

Genus: *Nothobranchius*

English name: none

Origin: East Africa, in the Pangani river and as far north as Mombasa

Size: Approximately 7 cm

Habitat: Found in seasonal pools

Shape, coloring and markings: The body is stocky and laterally only slightly compressed. The dorsal and anal fins are powerfully developed. The basic coloration is sky blue: the back is bluish-green: the flanks are iridescent yellowish or bluish-green: the belly a light yellow tinged with green. The scales are edged with red, and the scales on the back have a dark red mark. Irregular carmine red marks are sometimes found on the cheeks and gill covers. The dorsal fin is brownish-red with irregular carmine red marks and flecks: it has a dark red band edged with a bluish-white border. The caudal fin is brownish, with a carmine red base and edged with a dark brown or black border. The anal fin is reddish-brown with irregular red stripes and flecks. The pectoral and ventral fins vary from blue to white.

692. *Nothobranchius guentheri*

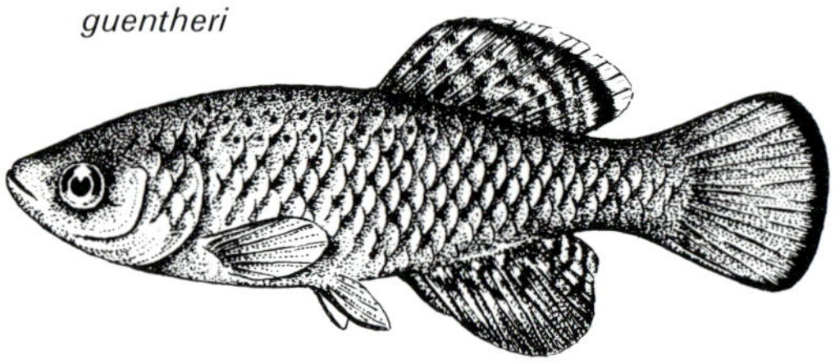

693. *Nothobranchius rachovi*

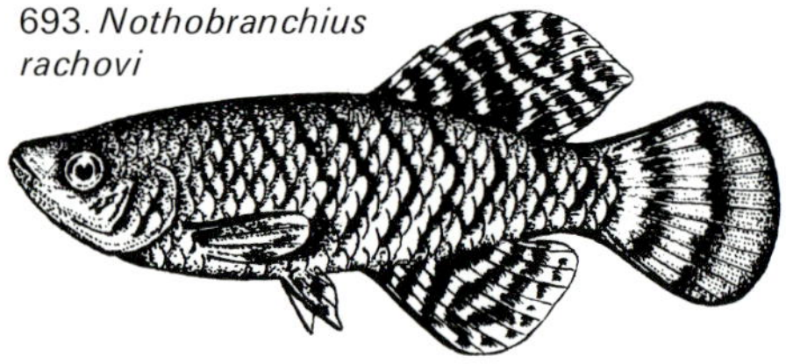

Females are a dull brown, yellowish-white towards the belly: the fins are colorless. Males are as described above.

General care: As for *N.brieni.*

Breeding: See Introductory note. The eggs need a period of rest of four to six weeks. The breeding temperature should be about 26°C.

NOTHOBRANCHIUS MELANOSPILUS

Family: *Cyprinodontidae*

Genus: *Nothobranchius*

English name: none

Origin: East Africa, Tanzania

Size: Approximately 7 cm

Habitat: Found in seasonal pools

Shape, coloring and markings: The body is elongated, cylindrical and laterally only slightly compressed. The mouth is set at an upward angle. The dorsal and anal fins are set far back, and like the back of the caudal fin, are rounded. Although at first sight the males give the impression of being a brilliant red, the basic coloration is really an iridescent blue: the snout is greenish: the gills and throat are blue, becoming yellowish towards the belly. All the scales have a blood red edge, creating a vivid net-like pattern over the whole body. The red dorsal fin has irregular golden stripes and a black border with a brilliant blue edge. The anal fin is similarly but slightly less brilliantly colored. The caudal fin is red, edged with black. The pectoral fins have a golden-yellow base, are lighter in the center and have light blue edges.
The female has a dark olive brown back: the flanks are lighter: the belly greyish. A pattern of black marks on the back extends to the bases of the fins. The head and gill covers are an iridescent greenish-blue.
Males are as described above.

General care: *N.melanospilus* can be kept in a community tank but its beauty is best displayed in a small species tank. If more than one male is kept then the tank must be large and with adequate retreats among bogwood. The males are very aggressive. Plenty of floating plants, such as the floating variety of *Ceratopteris thalictroides* should be included. The bed should be dark. The water should be fairly soft (8° DH) and slightly acid (pH 6.5–7). *N.melanospilus* is very sensitive to changes in water and temperature but one-third of the tank capacity should be changed each week. Temperature 22°C. Substantial quantities of varied live animal matter should be given as diet.

Breeding: *N.melanospilus* may be allowed to

694. *Nothobranchius melanospilus*

695. *Nothobranchius palmquisti*

spawn in the species tank, by placing a small bowl of peat in the tank. Alternatively breeding tanks as described in the Introductory note may be used. The selected male and two females should be left in the tank for a week and then a new group of breeders put in, in their place. The original group may then be put back subsequently after the second group have in turn been removed at the end of a week, but meanwhile should be kept apart and fed well. The water in the breeding tank should be changed regularly, even once a day. Breeding temperature about 23°C. The eggs need a period of rest of about four to five months at 20°–22°C. The eggs hatch after only about one hour after being covered with 2 mm of soft water. The fry should be fed on fine pond infusoria and *Artemia nauplii.*
After a few days the peat from which the young have hatched should be stored again in a dry place for about six weeks: soft water should then be added to it for a second time. Very often more eggs will then hatch out: sometimes even more than hatched when the peat was first immersed in water. This is a natural safety measure which ensures that the whole generation is not lost if the very first spell of rain, in the wild, is followed by a second period of drought. If properly cared for (liberally fed and given frequent changes of water in the tank) the fry grow quickly and will be sexually mature after a few months.

NOTHOBRANCHIUS PALMQUISTI

Family: *Cyprinodontidae*

Genus: *Nothobranchius*

English name: none

Origin: Tanzania, around Dar es Salaam, Tanga and Usambara

Size: Approximately 6 cm

Habitat: Found in seasonal pools

SHAPE, COLORING AND MARKINGS: The body is stocky and laterally only slightly compressed. The dorsal and anal fins are powerfully developed. The basic coloration is a luminescent steel blue: the belly and throat are yellow. The scales have a dark edge. The dorsal and anal fins are greenish-grey, flecked with yellow. The caudal fin is a dull red and the pigmentation extends into the caudal peduncle. The ventral and pectoral fins are a dull greyish-green. Generally, *N.palmquistii* is less vividly colored than related species.
Females are smaller and brownish, with a blue sheen: the fins are yellowish.
Males are as described above.

GENERAL CARE: As for *N.brieni*.

BREEDING: See Introductory note. The eggs require a period of rest of about eight weeks. Breeding temperature 26° C. Females bred in the aquarium are usually significantly smaller than imported specimens and are unsuitable for breeding after the third generation.

NOTHOBRANCHIUS RACHOVI

Family: *Cyprinodontidae*

Genus: *Nothobranchius*

English name: none

Origin: Mozambique, Beira

Size: Approximately 5 cm

Habitat: Found in seasonal pools

SHAPE, COLORING AND MARKINGS: The body is stocky and laterally only slightly compressed. The dorsal and anal fins are powerfully developed. The basic coloration is sky blue: the back is dark green: the flanks an iridescent blue with wedge-shaped orange, golden-yellow and red marks. Irregular marks of the same colors appear on the dorsal and anal fins. The caudal fin has two dark bands, a golden-yellow band and a reddish-brown edge. The ventral fins are dark red: the pectoral fins have a light blue base and are golden-yellow at the tips. In bright light *N.rachovi* displays a magnificent range of colors: the blue becomes azure, the yellow a liquid gold and the entire body has a bluish-green sheen.
Females are smaller and much less vividly colored.
Males are as described above.

GENERAL CARE: As for *N.brieni*.

BREEDING: See Introductory note. The eggs require a period of rest of six to twelve weeks. The breeding temperature should be about 27° C.

ADDITIONAL INFORMATION: *N.rachovi* is the most beautiful species of *Nothobranchius* yet discovered: it is quite rare in aquariums even though it was found in 1926.

THE FAMILY CYPRINODONTIDAE

The genus Oryzias

The *Oryzias* species are closely related to those in the genus *Aplocheilus*: both genera are found throughout Southern and Eastern Asia. Technically the *Oryzias* are distinguished by their pointed snouts, and the unusually short upper jaw. The *Oryzias* are found in a variety of waters, but most commonly in rice paddies, hence their common name of rice fish or rice paddy fish. They are all surface-loving fish, and some species are so useful in controlling mosquitoes that they are protected in some areas.
The *Oryzias* are unusual in that the eggs, after being fertilized, remain attached for some hours to the body of the female by fine filaments, and are only released when suitable plants are encountered. This is a characteristic these fish share with some species of the genus *Michropanchax*, and the Cuban Killie, *Cubanichthys cubensis*, (but these fish are not usually thought of as aquarium fish).
There are only four species known in this genus: *Oryzias melastigma* however very similair to *O.celebensis*, is not, it seems imported.

696. *Oryzias celebensis*

ORYZIAS CELEBENSIS

Family: *Cyprinodontidae*

Genus: *Oryzias*

English name: Celebes Medaka

Origin: Indonesia, southern Sulawesi (Celebes)

Size: Maximum 5 cm

Habitat: Found in small streams and particularly rice paddies

SHAPE, COLORING AND MARKINGS: The body is elongated and laterally compressed. The back is almost straight. The line of the belly descends fairly steeply from the pointed snout and then slopes gradually upwards as far as the beginning of the caudal fin: the fish has thus almost a triangular profile. The mouth is upward-pointing. The basic coloration is greyish-green: in some lights there is a bronze and blue sheen. The eyes are a beautiful iridescent greenish-blue. A narrow dark horizontal line runs across the body from behind the gill covers and forks on the base of the caudal fin, continuing as two distinct lines which end only at the extreme upper and lower edges of the caudal fin.
Females have a smooth edge to the dorsal and anal fins.
Males have elongated rays to the dorsal and anal fins that accordingly taper to a point, and the fins are larger than those of the females.

GENERAL CARE: *O.celebensis* is very rarely found in aquariums and nothing is known with certainty about its requirements: it is reasonable however to give it experimentally the same care as indicated for *O.javanicus*.

BREEDING: Nothing is known about the reproductive behavior of this species.

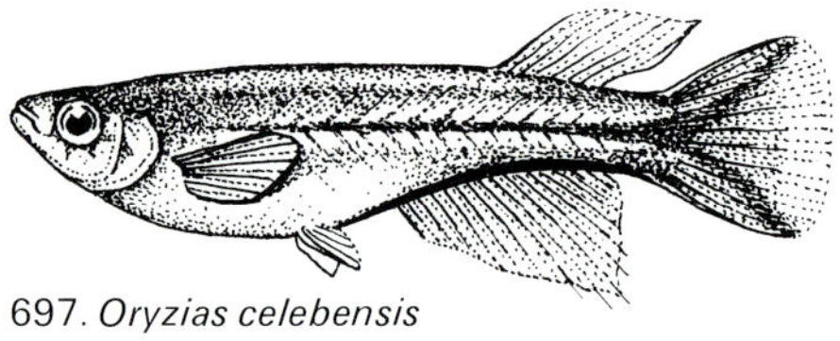

697. *Oryzias celebensis*

ORYZIAS JAVANICUS

Family: *Cyprinodontidae*

Genus: *Oryzias*

English name: Java Medaka

Origin: Indonesia, Java and Sumatra

Size: Maximum 4 cm

Habitat: Found in small streams and rice paddies

SHAPE, COLORING AND MARKINGS: The body is almost identical in shape to that of *O.celebensis* but *O.javanicus* has a somewhat deeper belly. The basic coloration is grey, sometimes with fine black vertical stripes, and slightly translucent. The fins are almost colorless but the small dorsal fin and the very large anal fin have a milky-white or light blue edge. In some lights the whole fish may have an iridescent blue tinge. The large eyes are an iridescent bluish-green.
Females have a short rounded dorsal fin: the edge of the anal fin is straight.
Males have some elongated rays in the in the dorsal and anal fins, giving them a frayed appearance.

GENERAL CARE: *O.javanicus* is suitable for an ordinary community tank with other peaceful species provided the tank is not overcrowded. The water should be slightly alkaline and not too soft. Temperature 24°–25°C, and no higher. Some floating plants should be included and adequate free swimming space also provided. Both dried food and live animal matter will be accepted.

BREEDING: A fairly large breeding tank, perhaps 60 × 30 × 30 cm with a bed of ordinary well-washed sand is required. Some floating plants, such as *Synnema triflorum* and the floating variety of *Ceratopteris thalictroides* should be included. The water should not be too hard (not more than 8° DH). A number of males and females may be put in one tank. The fish usually mate during the night or early morning: the male and female simultaneously eject the milt and the eggs. For a while the female continues to carry the eggs under her body in a bundle containing anything from five to fifty eggs. After some time she deposits the eggs on a plant as a bundle, although females have been sometimes observed placing the eggs on plants individually. The eggs should be removed from the breeding tank and put in a tank filled with very soft water, rich in oxygen. The eggs hatch in ten to twelve days. The fry swim about just below the surface and can be raised on the very finest pond infusoria and artificial fry foods. They grow extremely slowly. Many specimens raised in aquariums never grow larger than 1 or 2 cm, but stunted growth is less likely if the fry are hatched and raised in very soft water.

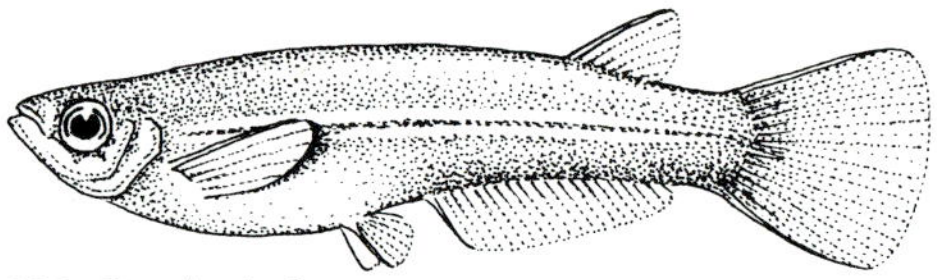

699. *Oryzias latipes*

698. *Oryzias javanicus*

ORYZIAS LATIPES

Family: *Cyprinodontidae*

Genus: *Oryzias*

English names: Geisha-girl Medaka, Japanese Medaka and Ricefish

Origin: Japan

Size: Maximum 4 cm

Habitat: Found in small streams and rice paddies

SHAPE, COLORING AND MARKING: *O.latipes* is smaller than *O.celebensis*, but is otherwise identical in shape. The basic coloration is the same but in certain lights *O.latipes* is greyish-green with a slight iridescent bluish tinge. *O.latipes* does not have the dark forked horizontal line present in *O.celebensis*.
The external sexual characteristics are as in *O.celebensis*.

GENERAL CARE: As for *O.javanicus*.

BREEDING: As for *O.javanicus*.

ADDITIONAL INFORMATION: Breeders in Japan have bred a red variety larger than the wild variety: the strain is unreliable; after two or three generations its characteristics disappear.

THE FAMILY CYPRINODONTIDAE

The genus Pachypanchax

Only four species of this small genus are known, all of which are native to Malagasy (Madagascar) and the Seychelles. They are closely related to the fish in the genera *Aplocheilus* and *Epiplatys*, but are somewhat larger than most of those species and have a fin that is covered with scales.
Of the four species *Pachypanchax homolonotus*, *Pachypanchax nuchimaculatus*, *Pachypanchax playfairi* and *Pachypanchax sakaramyi*, only two, *P.homolonotus* and *P.playfairi* are known to aquarists, and are described below.
P.homolonotus is not very frequently imported: *P.playfairi* is more commonly found in dealers' stock and is a most unusual fish in that according to some authorities specimens can undergo a sex change, in the same way as *Xiphophorus helleri*.

700. *Pachypanchax playfairi*

PACHYPANCHAX HOMALONOTUS

Family: *Cyprinodontidae*

Genus: *Pachypanchax*

English name: none

Origin: Malagasy

Size: Maximum 8 cm

Habitat: Found in brackish and fresh, still waters

SHAPE, COLORING AND MARKINGS: The body is elongated, cylindrical and laterally scarcely compressed. The small dorsal fin, with a base only half the length of that of the anal fin, is set very far back. The caudal fin is slightly rounded at the back. The basic coloration is a beautiful deep brown on the back, becoming pale yellow towards the belly. In some lights the flanks have an attractive iridescent bluish-green tinge. The dorsal, anal and caudal fins are usually transparent, brownish and bluish-green in color, edged with pale yellow: sometimes they are a pale yellow with a dark edge. Females have slightly fuller bellies and rounded dorsal and anal fins.
Males are as described above: the dorsal and anal fins taper to a point.

GENERAL CARE: *P.homalonotus* is eminently suitable for all sizes of community tank. It usually keeps to the top of the tank and often remains motionless, hiding among the roots of floating plants. Very tolerant, it should not however be kept with very small fish for it may prey on them from time to time. The composition of the water is not critical: temperature 24°C. *P.homalonotus* prefer to take food from the surface and should be fed live animal matter, especially mosquito larvae.

BREEDING: *P.homalonotus* will breed in a community tank if there is plenty of vegetation and particularly, adequate floating plants. If a supply of fine food is regularly put in the tank, young fish will suddenly appear as if by magic. Alternatively, a breeding tank, about 50 × 30 × 30 cm with floating plants or nylon breeding mops may be used. One gram of sea salt added for every liter of water may stimulate breeding. Two males and four females should be put in the tank. The floating plants or nylon mops should be removed from the tank every ten days and transferred to a separate breeding tank. The eggs hatch in 12–16 days. The fry can be fed immediately with fine pond infusoria and *Artemia nauplii*. The fry keep mainly to the surface and so it is necessary to aerate the water slightly, to keep the food on the surface. A fifth or a quarter of the water in all the breeding tanks must be changed daily.

PACHYPANCHAX PLAYFAIRI

Family: *Cyprinodontidae*

Genus: *Pachypanchax*

English name: none

Origin: East Africa, Malagasy, the Seychelles, Zanzibar

Size: Maximum 10 cm

Habitat: Found in brackish and fresh still waters

SHAPE, COLORING AND MARKINGS: The body is elongated, cylindrical and laterally hardly at all compressed. The fairly wide mouth is upward pointing. The dorsal and anal fins are set far back: the caudal fin is almost completely round. The back is a dark olive green,

701. *Pachypanchax homalonotus*

becoming paler towards the belly. A number of shiny red dots lie in rows on the flanks. Under bright lighting the whole fish shimmers with an iridescent green tinge, dominated by a brilliant bronze sheen on the flanks. The vertical yellow fins are speckled with red dots. The caudal fin is edged with black.
Females are rather less stocky than the males. They have no red dots on the flanks. The dorsal fin has a black mark but there is no black edge to the caudal fin. The fins are more rounded and transparent.
Males are as described above, but have no black mark on the dorsal fin. The dorsal and anal fins are longer.

GENERAL CARE: *P.playfairi* is neither predatory nor aggressive. In well-planted community tanks, it will swim in the upper and middle reaches. Fairly soft water is preferred: temperature about 25°C. Dried food will be accepted after a time but the main diet should be Daphnia, Cyclops, pond infusoria and insect larvae.

BREEDING: As for *P.homalonotus*.

THE FAMILY CYPRINODONTIDAE

The genus Pterolebias

The fish in the genus *Pterolebias* are closely related to those in the genus *Rivulus*, but are distinguished by their unusually long fins. Until fairly recently the only known species in the genus was *Pterolebias longipinnis*, the Longfin or Longfin Killie. *Pterolebias peruensis*, a relatively new species, has now occasionally been imported. Two other species, *Pterolebias bockermanni* and *Pterolebias zonatus* have also been identified in the genus, but neither to date has been imported, it seems, as an aquarium fish. The two species known to aquarists are singularly beautiful, but unfortunately they are seasonal fish and accordingly of interest at present only to a limited number of amateurs willing to take the trouble to breed them, although this is not too difficult.

PTEROLEBIAS LONGIPINNIS

Family: *Cyprinodontidae*

Genus: *Pterolebias*

English names: Longfin and Longfin Killie

Origin: The lower reaches of the Amazon: also reported around Santarem

Size: Maximum 10 cm, of which 3 cm is the length of the caudal fin

Habitat: Probably found in seasonal pools

702. *Pterolebias peruensis*

SHAPE, COLORING AND MARKINGS: The body is elongated, cylindrical and laterally hardly at all compressed. The mouth is upper-positioned. The line of the back is almost straight. The dorsal fin is set far back and tapers to a point: the elongated caudal fin is fan-shaped. The large anal fin tapers to a point: the ventral fins are very long and pointed, with elongated front rays. The basic coloration is brown: the back is reddish-brown: the belly yellowish-brown. Under bright light

the entire body has a metallic blue sheen: glistening dots, which according to the light are silvery-blue or green, lie over the body and fins and are interspersed with somewhat indistinct smaller reddish-brown or reddish specks. A number of irregular red and black dots lie on the shoulders. All the fins (except for the pectoral) are brown, becoming darker towards the edges, with a decorative pattern of brownish-red, or red dots and stripes.
Females have colorless fins: the caudal fin is rounded. They are smaller and less vividly colored than the males.
Males are as described above.

General care: *P.longipinnis* will live for only one year. It requires a species tank with soft acid water: temperature 24°–26° C. To allow the tank to serve also as a breeding tank, the back should be terraced with a sandy bed behind decorative plants: the rest of the tank should be filled with floating plants to filter the light and the front part of the bottom should be covered with a 3 cm deep layer of boiled peat. The diet should be the larger types of live animal matter, preferably black and white mosquito larvae: red mosquito larvae and Tubifex are less suitable.

Breeding: If the species tank is laid out as suggested above the fish will soon spawn. The eggs will be laid in the part of the tank with the peat bottom. When the eggs are laid both fish will disappear into the peat. The female will lay eggs at regular intervals for some time. The peat containing the eggs should be removed with a nylon net every three or four weeks, and then drained until it is only damp. It should then be stored in sealed plastic bags in a dark place for two or three months at 23° C. After that period of rest the peat should be returned to a tank and covered with a few centimeters of very soft, slightly acid water. The first eggs will hatch after a few hours and the fry will begin to swim almost immediately. They should be fed on *Cyclops nauplii* and other fine foods. Not all the eggs will hatch at the same time and the peat should be drained again and the whole process repeated after a second rest period of about six weeks. The eggs can be stored for a longer period than that suggested above if appropriate food for the fry is not available at the time, for the fry grow very quickly and will not survive unless large quantities of suitable food are available.

703. *Pterolebias longipinnis*

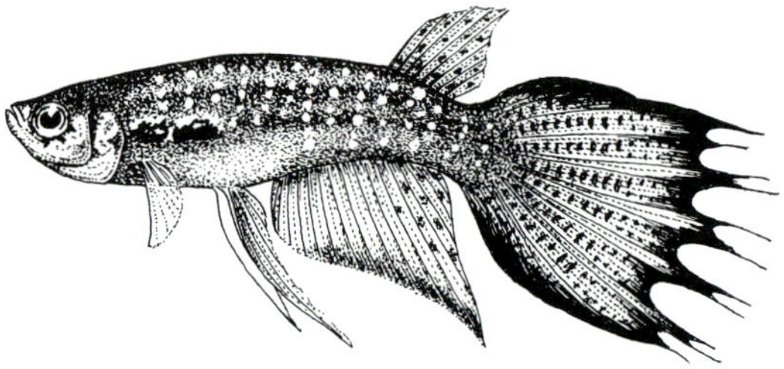

704. *Pterolebias longipinnis*

PTEROLEBIAS PERUENSIS

Family: *Cyprinodontidae*

Genus: *Pterolebias*

English name: none

Origin: The upper reaches of the Amazon, Peru

Size: Maximum 10 cm

Habitat: Found in seasonal pools

Shape, coloring and markings: The body shape is very similar to that of *P.longipinnis* but *P.peruensis* is more slender. The caudal fin is less fan-shaped, although the outer rays are very long and grow longer as the fish matures. The basic coloration is olive brown: the belly is ochre. In some lights the body has a bluish-green metallic sheen. A number of light vertical stripes run across the back: a similar pattern is found on the dorsal and caudal fins which, combined with the dark rays of that fin, give the caudal fin a checkered pattern.
Females are smaller, with more rounded fins and a less intricate color pattern.
Males are as described above.

General care: As for *P.longipinnis* but *P.peruensis* tends to stir up a lot of sediment when it digs into the bed, covering the plants in the tank with peat. Many breeders therefore separate the spawning fish for a few days so that the female is prevented from laying her eggs in the bed of the tank: a single pair of the fish is then placed for one day in a small tank with a bed of 4 cm of well-boiled peat. If the fish have been well fed they will then usually mate without interruption until the female has laid all her eggs. Those fish are then removed from that special tank and another pair put in, and so the process is repeated. The peat in that small tank should then be treated and stored as suggested in the instructions for breeding *P.longipinnis*.

THE FAMILY CYPRINODONTIDAE

The genus Rivulus

The genus *Rivulus* is found over a wide area: southern North America, Central America and much of South America. The natural habitats of these fish are extremely varied, although they prefer the smaller, richly vegetated and densely overgrown streams in which they are found in the middle layers or those immediately adjacent to the bottom. There are however a few species which enjoy spending brief periods on a floating leaf immediately below the water surface, or even above the surface in the sun.
The body of these species is approximately cylindrical and laterally slightly compressed towards the tail. The dorsal fin is set well back. The back itself, in front of the dorsal fin, and the top of the head, are flattened.
The males are similar in shape to the females but can usually be distinguished by their more brilliant coloring. All females have a distinct dark round patch or ocellus in the upper part of the caudal fin: this may also be present in the male, but if present is less prominent.

Although many species are as attractively colored as the *Aphysemions*, only a few are well-known in amateur circles, and only one or two species have become widely known. This is curious because the *Rivulus* species are undemanding and very tolerant fish, and hence suitable for an ordinary community tank. A clump of broad-leaved plants, with the leaves reaching to the surface, will usually provide adequate shelter. The composition of the water is not critical, although two species appreciate the addition of a little salt: details are given below in the species descriptions. Some latitude is also permitted as to temperature: 22°–27° C is acceptable, and temperatures as low as 18°–20° C are tolerated without harm to the fish.
When kept under these conditions in a community aquarium most species reproduce spontaneously. The eggs are usually laid among the roots of floating plants or among fine-leaved

705. *Rivulus agilae*

plants if no roots are available. They hatch after about 14 days, the exact time varying according to the species and the water temperature. The parents do not usually eat the eggs unless their diet is insufficiently varied: fruit-flies, ants, ant-eggs, greenfly and similar small flies should always therefore be fed to the breeding fish.
For productive breeding it is best to use a small tray of 10–15 liters capacity: modern plastic aquarium tanks are ideal. Larger shallow trays in which the young can be raised more 'naturally' with their parents are commonly recommended, but these are less productive because it is more difficult to keep the eggs and the fry under careful observation.
The bottom and sides of the tray should be painted dark brown or black on the outside. Old but bacteria-free aquarium water is best. Alternatively, fresh water can be artificially matured by filtering it through peat for several days, or by introducing a number of assimilating plants which will remove salts from the water and enrich it with oxygen. The temperature should be 25°–28° C. Before introducing the fish into the breeding tank, the males and females should be separated for about 14 days and well fed.
No bed is needed in the breeding tank, but if one is provided, it should be of peat cuttings or filter carbon, well-boiled and rinsed. Long fibres of peat should be removed, otherwise the eggs may be laid amongst these instead of in the breeding mops, of which two or three should be put in the tank.

706. *Rivulus milesi*

Mating behavior usually begins soon after the fish have been introduced into the tank. Only a single egg is laid and fertilized at a time. The entire mating cycle may extend over several weeks with couplings almost every day. At first about 20 eggs are laid daily, but the daily total then decreases. When breeding some species it is best to put one male with several females: if the fish are then separated after a day or two, kept apart for several days, and then brought together again, and this procedure repeated several times over a period of weeks, then even better results will be obtained.
The eggs are large, and transparent to pale yellow, plainly visible against a dark background: this is why any bed is the tank should be as dark as possible. The eggs have hard shells and can be removed with the fingers from the tank either once a day or immediately after being laid. The eggs should be put in small flat dishes with at least 2 cm of water. The composition of this water is not critical: the temperature should be 20°–22° C. A small amount of Trypaflavin (1 gram in 200–300 liters of water) should be added to inhibit bacteria. The young will hatch out in this solution without injury.
For the first few days the clutch should be checked regularly for unfertilized eggs, easily identified as yellowish-white and opaque, with a tendency to cling to the bottom of the dish. They are easily removed with a pipette.
Eggs laid at different times can be induced to hatch out simultaneously if a small quantity of infusoria or microworms is added. The same result can often be achieved by gently agitating the water.
The fry should be transferred into separate tanks similar in size to those in which they were hatched, with initially only about the same amount of water. The fry grow very quickly and will greedily eat *Artemia nauplii* within an hour of hatching. *Artemia nauplii* can be given alternately with sieved Cyclops and Daphnia. Grindal worms are also excellent for rearing fry. The young become sexually mature at 4–5 weeks, and will be more resistant to common aquarium maladies if they are raised in ordinary tapwater.
There are some forty species in the genera: twelve species, all of which are excellent aquarium fish, are described below. A few other species in particular *R.dorni*, *R.langesi* and *R.marmoratus*, are occasionally met with in the literature.

RIVULUS AGILAE

Family: *Cyprinodontidae*
Genus: *Rivulus*
English name: none
Origin: Surinam, around Agila
Size: Approximately 6 cm
Habitat: Found in mountain streams

SHAPE, COLORING AND MARKINGS: The body is slim, almost cylindrical, with only the caudal peduncle fairly compressed. The basic coloration is a pale bluish-green blending to yellow-white towards the belly. The back is a pale orange-brown, becoming a strong orange-red towards the tail. There are seven lines of orange-red spots on the tail, which merge into one, on the caudal peduncle. A bluish-violet patch runs from the eye to the gill-covers, behind which lies a blue iridescent shoulder mark. The dorsal fin is transparent, with orange-red to yellow spots and stripes: the anal fin is a pale orange-yellow, with an orange-yellow border. The upper lobe of the caudal fin is patterned in orange, green and yellow: the lower lobe is pale blue with a very dark border: the fin has also a yellow edge. The pectoral fins are pale blue and transparent.
Females are less intensely colored and have a dark patch on the caudal fin.
Males are as described above.

GENERAL CARE: *R.agilae* is suitable for both large and small community tanks containing other peaceful species. A male may associate with more than one female, and may be aggressive to other males: otherwise this species is very tolerant. A well-planted tank with a fairly dark bottom and attractive arrangements of stones is best. The composition of the water is not critical but fresh tapwater should be avoided. Temperature 24°–26°C. *R.agilae* occupies the middle and lower reaches of the tank. All kinds of small living creatures will serve for food but land insects which fall on the surface of the water, such as flies, ants and greenfly are preferred. Dry food may be given for variety.

707. *Rivulus cylindraceus*

BREEDING: *R.agilae* has not as yet been bred in captivity.

ADDITIONAL INFORMATION: *R.agilae* was first described by Hoedeman in 1954.

RIVULUS CYLINDRACEUS

Family: *Cyprinodontidae*
Genus: *Rivulus*
English names: Green, Brown or Cuban Rivulus
Origin: Cuba and Florida
Size: Approximately 5 cm
Habitat: Found particularly along densely overgrown banks of smaller streams

SHAPE, COLORING AND MARKINGS: The body is slim, almost cylindrical, with only the caudal peduncle somewhat laterally compressed. The basic coloration is brownish-green. The back is darker, or olive-brown: the throat and belly are orange to yellow. A dark but not always distinct longitudinal band runs back from the snout through the eye and the gill covers. Immediately behind the gill covers lies a cobalt blue to green iridescent patch. Red patches appear on the lower half of the body and the caudal peduncle. All the fins are ochre yellow to green: the unpaired fins have dark stipples and patches arranged in lines: the dorsal fin has a pale border.
Females have a prominent dark red patch on the upper lobe of the caudal fin. Their basic coloration is ochre yellow to rust-brown.
Males are as described above.

GENERAL CARE: As for *R.agilae* but temperature 23°–26°C. *R.cylindraceus* likes to spend quite a lot of time at the surface among floating leaves: the tank vegetation should therefore include a number of broad-leaved plants. *R.cylindraceus* should always be kept in a small group with two or three females to each male.

BREEDING: Not difficult. See Introductory note.

RIVULUS HARTI

Family: *Cyprinodontidae*
Genus: *Rivulus*
English name: Hart's Rivulus
Origin: Colombia, Venezuela and adjacent islands
Size: Approximately 10 cm
Habitat: Found particularly along the banks of smaller streams

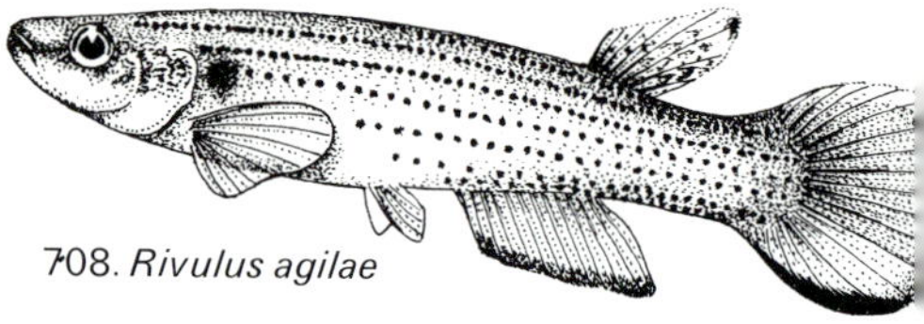

708. *Rivulus agilae*

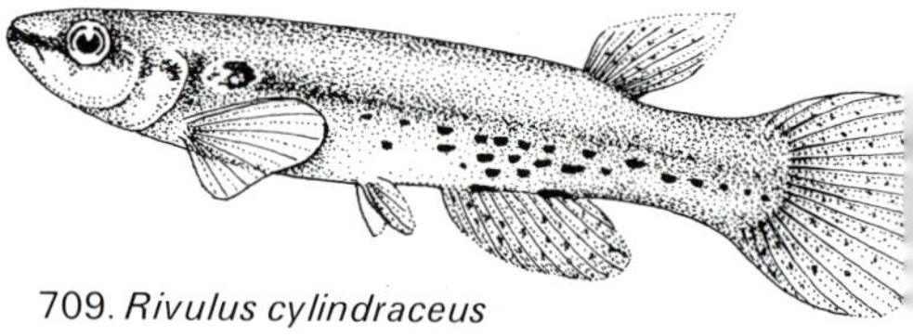

709. *Rivulus cylindraceus*

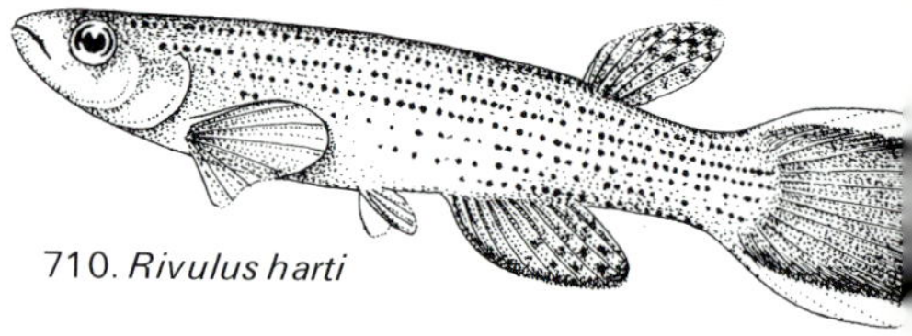

710. *Rivulus harti*

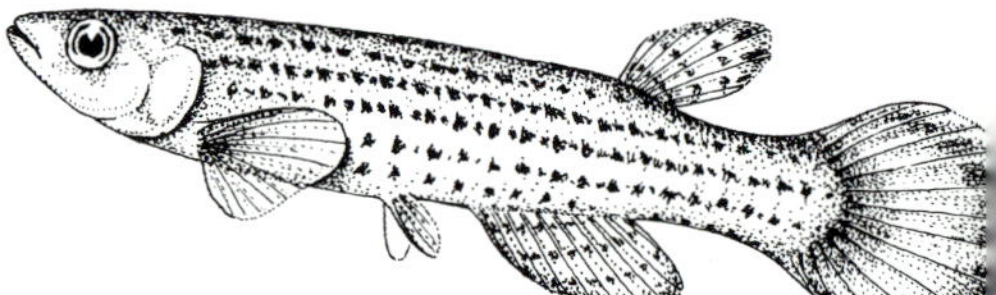

711. *Rivulus holmiae*

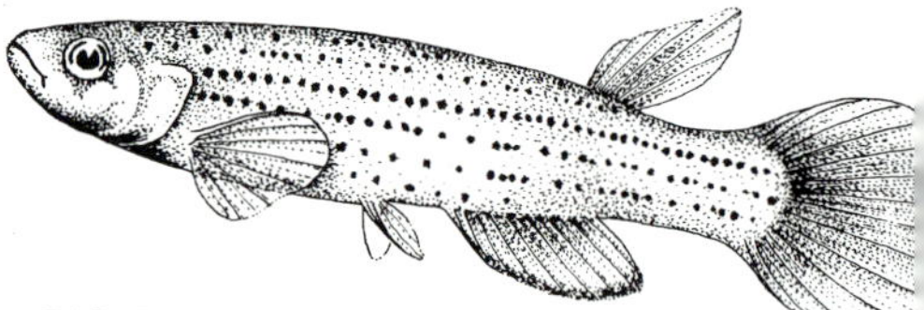

712. *Rivulus isthmensis*

SHAPE, COLORING AND MARKINGS: The body is slender and almost cylindrical, with only the caudal peduncle laterally compressed. The basic coloration varies according to the locality of origin. The back is usually chocolate to greenish-brown: the flanks are iridescent yellowish to grass-green. The belly is ochre yellow, yellow-green or off-white. The caudal peduncle has a bluish tinge. Each scale carries a red mark which together show up as lines. The dorsal and anal fins are green with clear red stipples and stripes: the caudal fin is predominantly black with green iridescent stripes and a salmon-colored border. The other fins are colorless and translucent.
Females are very vividly colored. The upper half of the body is a rusty brown becoming a canary yellow towards the belly. The scales have gleaming golden marks. The dorsal and anal fins are yellow with red overtones. The caudal fin is a bright orange-red with a black border and a black patch on the base.
Males are as described above.

GENERAL CARE: As for *R.cylindraceus*, but *R.harti* is only suitable for larger aquariums. Temperature 22°–26°C.

BREEDING: Not difficult: see Introductory note.

RIVULUS HOLMIAE

Family: *Cyprinodontidae*

Genus: *Rivulus*

English name: none

Origin: Colombia, Venezuela and adjacent islands

Size: Approximately 6 cm

Habitat: Found in a variety of waters and particularly along the banks of small streams

SHAPE, COLORING AND MARKINGS: The body is slender, almost cylindrical, except for the caudal peduncle which is laterally quite compressed. *R.holmiae* closely resembles *R.harti*, and some authorities consider *R.holmiae* to be only a variety of *R.harti*. The basic coloration varies significantly according to the locality of origin. The back is brownish with a green overtone: the flanks yellow-green with a bluish overtone, the lower part of the body ochre yellow to off-white. The scales are rather large and each bears a red spot which show up as a pattern of stripes. The caudal fin is dark red to black at the base and edges: the center is paler and the lower edge off-white.

Females are predominantly yellow-white: a conspicuous white patch lies on the caudal fin.

Males are as described above.

GENERAL CARE: As for *R.harti*.

BREEDING: *R.holmiae* has not yet been bred in captivity, but its reproductive behavior is likely to be broadly similar to that of related species.

RIVULUS ISTHMENSIS

Family: *Cyprinodontidae*

Genus: *Rivulus*

English name: none

Origin: Panama

Size: Approximately 7 cm

Habitat: No details are available of its natural habitat

SHAPE, COLORING AND MARKINGS: The body is slender and almost cylindrical: only the caudal peduncle is laterally compressed. The back is brownish with a green overtone: the flanks bluish with yellow-green overtones. The throat is red, the gill covers have a silver sheen. The belly is yellow to off-white. Most of the scales have a red mark, which show up as lines. The dorsal and anal fins are a transparent green, with darker patches. The anal fin has a dark border: the caudal fin is red, with a yellow-green border above and an orange-yellow edge below.

Females are ochre yellow to brown, with irregular dark patches, and a prominent dark patch on the caudal fin.

Males are as described above.

GENERAL CARE: As for *R.harti*, but temperature 23°–26°C. *R.isthmensis* keeps to the upper and middle reaches of the tank and is usually extremely tolerant even towards smaller species.

BREEDING: *R.isthmensis* has not as yet been bred in captivity.

RIVULUS MILESI

Family: *Cyprinodontidae*

Genus: *Rivulus*

English name: none

Origin: Venezuela

Size: Approximately 6 cm

Habitat: No details are available of its natural habitat

SHAPE, COLORING AND MARKINGS: The body is slender, almost cylindrical and only slightly compressed laterally, towards the tail. The back is a pale brown, with a greenish lustre. The flanks are blue-green, becoming a yellowish-red towards the belly. The lower half of the body and the caudal peduncle carry irregular red marks. The dorsal fin is bright red, brownish at the base and with a dark brown border. The anal fin is salmon-colored, with a black border. The caudal fin is predominantly brown, with a black border, top and bottom and a wide salmon to orange-yellow edge at the tip.

Females are less vividly colored but have a conspicuous dark patch on the caudal fin.

Males are as described above.

GENERAL CARE: As for *R.isthmensis*.

BREEDING: Not difficult: see Introductory note.

RIVULUS OCELLATUS

Family: *Cyprinodontidae*

Genus: *Rivulus*

English name: Ocellated Rivulus

Origin: Brazil, from Rio de Janeiro to Santos

Size: Approximately 7 cm

Habitat: Found in brackish waters

SHAPE, COLORING AND MARKINGS: The body is slender, almost cylindrical and only slightly compressed laterally towards the tail. The upper half of the body is a pale brown with a green sheen. The flanks are ochre yellow to bright green. The whole body has a pattern of dark marbling, which in detail will vary from specimen to specimen. The dorsal and anal fins are a strong yellowish-green: a dark patch and a very dark area surrounded by a zone of bright yellow lie in the upper lobe.

Females are darker, with colorless fins and a very conspicuous patch in the caudal fin.

Males are as described above.

GENERAL CARE: As for *R.isthmensis* but it is advisable to add a small quantity of rock or cooking salt to the water.

BREEDING: Not difficult: see Introductory note.

RIVULUS ROLOFFI

Family: *Cyprinodontidae*

Genus: *Rivulus*

English name: Roloff's Rivulus

Origin: Haiti, San Domingo

Size: Approximately 4 cm

Habitat: Found principally in small streams

SHAPE, COLORING AND MARKINGS: The body is slender, almost cylindrical and laterally slightly compressed towards the tail. The back is greenish-brown: the flanks are an iridescent blue, with a greenish gleam. All the scales have a brick red mark at the base, which show up as regular longitudinal lines. A prominent iridescent patch lies on the shoulder behind the gill covers. The dorsal fin is brownish-green, with a black patch: the caudal fin is yellowish at the base, but otherwise colorless. The anal fin and the pectoral fins are yellowish with a dark border.

Females are somewhat smaller and less vividly colored. Sometimes a number of indistinct transverse bands lie on the flanks.

Males are as described above.

GENERAL CARE: As for *R.cylindraceus* but temperature 22°–24°C.

BREEDING: *R.roloffi* has not as yet been bred in captivity, but its reproductive behavior is likely to be similar to that of related species.

713. Rivulus holmiae

714. *Rivulus xanthonotus*

715. *Rivulus urophthalmus*

RIVULUS SANTENSIS

Family: *Cyprinodontidae*

Genus: *Rivulus*

English name: Santos Rivulus

Origin: Brazil, from Rio de Janeiro to Santos

Size: Approximately 7 cm

Habitat: Found in a variety of waters but principally small streams

SHAPE, COLORING AND MARKINGS: The body is slender, almost cylindrical and slightly compressed laterally towards the tail. The basic coloration is pale green to yellowish. The back is darker or olive green: the belly is yellow-green to off-white. The scales are rather large and all bear a red mark at the base which show up as longitudinal stripes. The dorsal fin is dark green to black, with a pale border. The caudal fin has dark marks, a white border at the top and a black border at the bottom. The anal fin is dark, with a deep black border. Females are rather smaller, predominantly brown, with blue iridescent stipples and almost colorless fins.

GENERAL CARE: As for *R.ocellatus*.

BREEDING: Not difficult: see Introductory note.

RIVULUS STRIGATUS

Family: *Cyprinodontidae*

Genus: *Rivulus*

English name: Herringbone Rivulus

Origin: The Guianas

Size: Approximately 3.5 cm

Habitat: Found in small streams with dense vegetation on the banks

SHAPE, COLORING AND MARKINGS: The body is slender, almost cylindrical and only slightly compressed towards the tail. The back is a dark olive green, with brown overtones: the flanks are blue, the throat and belly orange. Bright red dots on a vivid green background lie on the body from the line of the ventral fins and form a herringbone pattern. The dorsal, anal and caudal fins are yellow-green, with red dots: the caudal fin has an orange border. The ventral fins are yellow-green, the pectoral fins bluish.
Females are less vividly colored with less prominent markings.
Males are as described above.

GENERAL CARE: As for *R.cylindraceus*, but temperature 26°–28° C.

BREEDING: This is not easy but see Introductory note.

ADDITIONAL INFORMATION: The most beautiful of the *Rivulus* species but one that can sometimes unfortunately be quarrelsome.

RIVULUS UROPHTHALMUS

Family: *Cyprinodontidae*

Genus: *Rivulus*

English names: Green Rivulus, Golden Rivulus

Origin: Almost the whole of South America

Size: Maximum 7 cm

Habitat: Found in a variety of waters but principally in small streams

SHAPE, COLORING AND MARKINGS: The body is slender, almost cylindrical and laterally slightly compressed towards the tail. The back is fawn to dark brown: the flanks are dark brown with green overtones. The lower half of the body is a pale greenish-yellow to off-white. Almost all the scales have a red mark at the base which show up as a pattern of lines. The unpaired fins are green to greenish-yellow, with rows of red stipples. The caudal fin has a coppery red border above and a black edge below. The pectoral and ventral fins are pale green.
Females are rusty brown, with marbled flanks. A very conspicuous pale-edged, dark round patch lies on the caudal fin.
Males are as described above. Young males have a caudal patch.

GENERAL CARE: As for *R.harti* but temperature 22°–27° C.

BREEDING: This is not difficult: see Introductory note. *R.urophthalmus* is a very prolific species.

ADDITIONAL INFORMATION: *R.urophthalmus* is well known to aquarists. Various differently colored varieties exist including green, blue and yellow-orange varieties, the last being particularly attractive.

RIVULUS XANTHONOTUS

Family: *Cyprinodontidae*

Genus: *Rivulus*

English name: none

Origin: Probably the area of the Amazon, but exact details are unavailable

Size: Approximately 7 cm

Habitat: Found almost certainly in the smaller streams

SHAPE, COLORING AND MARKINGS: The body is slender, almost cylindrical, but slightly compressed laterally towards the tail. The upper half of the body, except for the caudal peduncle is a bright orange-yellow. The flanks are dark brown, marbled with yellow. The throat and belly are whitish, with reddish overtones. A red mark lies at the base of each scale. The unpaired fins are yellow to grey, with red patches. The caudal fin is reddish, with a black border.
Females are principally ochre and the caudal fin has a round dark spot.
Males are as described above.

GENERAL CARE: As for *R.harti* but temperature 22°–27° C.

BREEDING: This species has not as yet been bred in captivity.

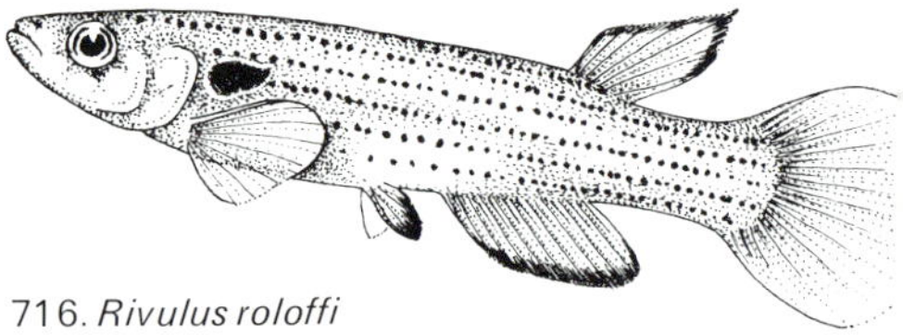

716. *Rivulus roloffi*

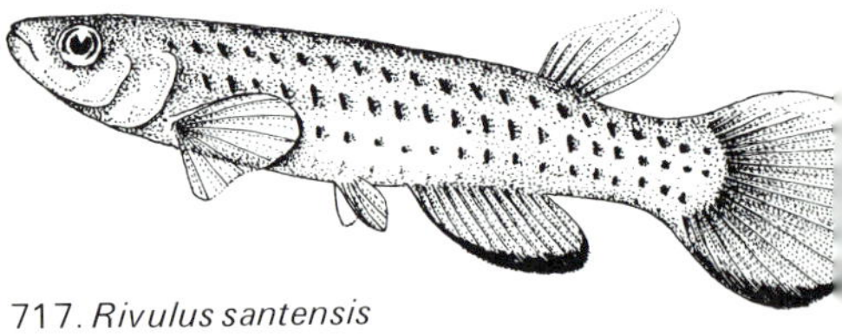

717. *Rivulus santensis*

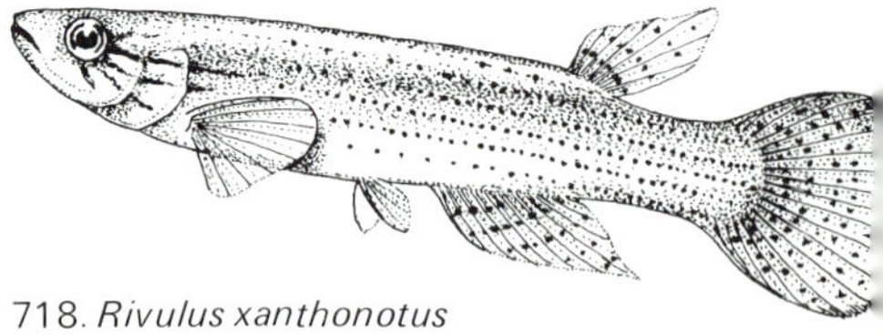

718. *Rivulus xanthonotus*

THE FAMILY CYPRINODONTIDAE

The genus Roloffia

The fish in the genus Roloffia are so closely related to those in the genus *Aphyosemion* that only specialists can distinguish between them. Indeed, until a few years ago, the two genera were considered as one, and all species were put in the genus *Aphyosemion,* under which they are still to be found in the works of older authorities, and it must be admitted that even today not all taxonomists are agreed on the distinctions between genera.

Suffice it to say that so far as the amateur aquarist is concerned, the species in the genus *Roloffia,* while in behavior identical to the *Aphyosemion,* tend to be somewhat larger than those species, and come in general from an area of West Africa just north of the region where the *Aphyosemion* are usually found.

The *Roloffia* and the *Aphyosemion* come from very similar habitats. Like the *Aphyosemion* the male *Roloffia* are extremely beautifully colored and marked. They tend to be aggressive fish and must be kept in species tanks. Their patterns of reproductive behavior, except as noted below, are also identical to those of the *Aphyosemion* species. Most of these fish are found, in the wild, in soft acid water.

ROLOFFIA BERTHOLDI

Family: *Cyprinodontidae*
Genus: *Roloffia*
English name: none
Origin: West Africa, eastern Sierra Leone
Size: Maximum 5 cm
Habitat: Found in small streams

SHAPE, COLORING AND MARKINGS: The body is elongated, torpedo-shaped and laterally scarcely compressed. The mouth is upper-positioned. The pectoral fins are relatively large: the ventral fins are small: the large dorsal and anal fins are set far back. The caudal fin is more or less rectangular, and rounded at the end. The basic coloration is greyish-brown with a steel blue sheen on the flanks, becoming darker towards the head. A large number of bright red marks lie on the body. The pectoral fins are more or less transparent, greyish-blue edged with white. The ventral, dorsal, anal and caudal fins are blue with an attractive pattern of red marks. The dorsal and anal fins have a horizontal red band edged on the outside by a greyish-blue border. The caudal fin has a beautiful pattern of bright red marks, a red band along the top and bottom, and a light blue edge.
Females are olive brown, darker on the back and lighter towards the flanks.
A number of dark grey marks form a narrow indistinct horizontal line across the middle of the body, which runs into the fins.
Males are as described above.

GENERAL CARE: *R.bertholdi* is best kept in a species tank: it will not survive long in a community tank. Only one male should be kept with two or three females. The tank should be of 10–15 liters capacity, with a 5 cm deep bottom of well-boiled and rinsed peat. The water should be fairly soft (6°DH) and slightly acid (pH 6–6.8): one gram of sea salt per liter of water should be added. Temperature 23°C. *R.bertholdi* dislikes the light, and the back and sides of the tank should be blacked out on the outside, with paint or paper. Floating plants should be added to reduce the overhead light. A piece of bogwood overgrown with Java moss *(Vesicularia dubyana)* should be put in one corner. About half the water must be changed once a week, because *R.bertholdi* is sensitive to water pollution. The diet should be live animal matter and particularly mosquito larvae: Enchytrae, which will encourage spawning, may be given in moderation. Tubifex is unsuitable.

BREEDING: If the species tank is arranged as described above, the fish will breed spontaneously in it, laying their eggs in the Java moss over a period of weeks. The moss should therefore be replaced with new moss each week, and the moss with eggs transferred to a separate tank kept in a dark place and filled with clean soft water with added salt. The eggs will hatch after 15–20 days: as soon as the fry are free swimming they should be fed on the finest pond infusoria and freshly hatched *Artemia nauplii.* About a tenth of the water must be changed daily, and the tank kept scrupulously clean: to ensure that all waste matter can be siphoned off easily, the tank should have no bed at all. A few fine-leaved plants, however, weighted with glass rods, can be put in to give the fry some shelter.

ROLOFFIA GERYI

Family: *Cyprinodontidae*
Genus: *Roloffia*
English name: none
Origin: West Africa, from Sierra Leone to Gambia
Size: Maximum 6 cm
Habitat: Found in small streams

SHAPE, COLORING AND MARKINGS: The body is elongated, torpedo-shaped and laterally scarcely compressed. The mouth is upper-positioned. The pectoral fins are relatively large: the ventral fins are small. The dorsal and anal fins are large and set far back. The caudal fin is rectangular, but rounded at the edges. The basic coloration is olive green. The flanks

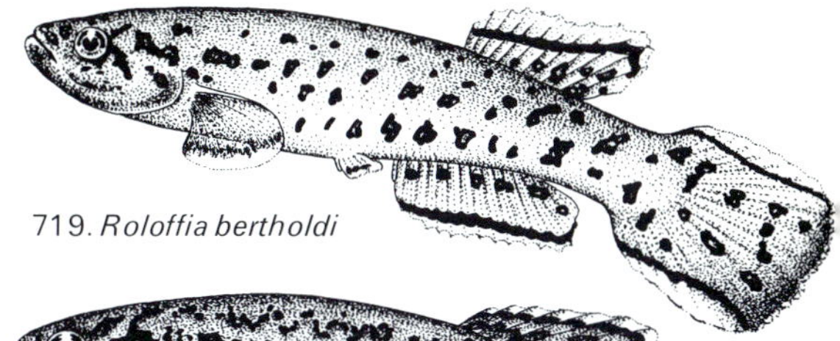

719. *Roloffia bertholdi*

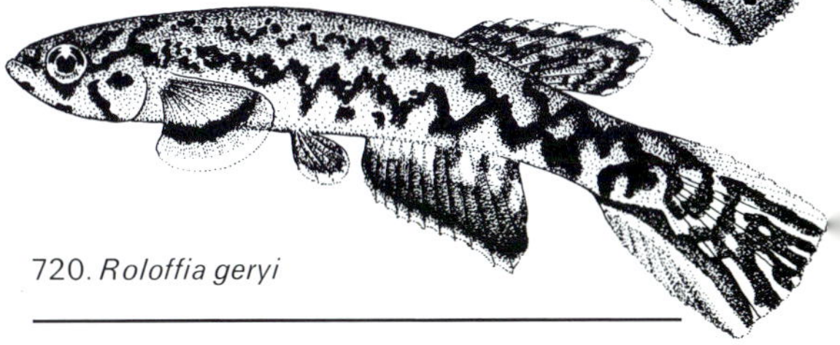

720. *Roloffia geryi*

have a beautiful, metallic bluish-green sheen. A large number of dots and marks lie on the body, and sometimes appear as a horizontal zig-zag line, especially on the caudal peduncle. The dorsal fin is bluish-green, with red marks and a red border within an outer blue border. The anal fin is bluish-green, with red marks and a red border. The center of the caudal fin is bluish-green with red marks and stripes: above and below lies a red line, bordered by an area of gold. The pectoral fins are orange with a wide blue edge. The color pattern can vary a great deal from specimen to specimen.
Females are olive brown to grey, dark on the back and lighter towards the belly. A dark, horizontal zig-zag line runs across the body and above and below it are a number of dark

721. *Roloffia geryi*

marks. The fins are colorless but with a pattern of dark markings.
Males are as described above.

General care: As for *R.bertholdi.*

Breeding: *R.geryi* will lay its eggs both on fine-leaved plants near the bed and in the bed itself. To encourage the production of as many eggs as possible in a short time, the sexes should be separated for a few days and generously fed with live animal matter. The male should then be put in the tank with two females. Many eggs will soon be laid. The breeding fish can be left in the tank for two weeks, and should then be transferred to another tank: if separated again for a few days, they will spawn again in the second tank. When in the breeding tanks the parent fish should be fed liberally, but Cyclops should be avoided. The eggs laid in the peat will hatch in two to three weeks. The fry are not difficult to raise and will be sexually mature after 6 months.

ROLOFFIA MONROVIAE

Family: *Cyprinodontidae*
Genus: *Roloffia*
English name: none
Origin: West Africa, Liberia, around Monrovia
Size: Maximum 10 cm
Habitat: Found in seasonal pools

Shape, coloring and markings: The body is elongated, torpedo-shaped and laterally scarcely compressed. The mouth is upper-positioned. The dorsal and anal fins are large and set far back. The caudal fin is almost rectangular. There is a blue and a red variety of *R.monroviae.* The basic coloration of the blue variety is greenish-blue: a large number of red dots are scattered over the body. On the gill covers just behind the eyes, red lines appear in the shape of a Y on its side. The dorsal fin is greenish-blue with a black mark at the front: the rays are red at the base: red marks are scattered near the edge, which has a narrow red line within a very narrow bluish-green line. The anal fin is bright blue, becoming greenish-blue towards the edge; the rays are red. The caudal fin is greenish-blue with red dots and stripes: a red line lies at the top and bottom, edged at the top with a narrow, greenish-blue border and at the bottom by a bright blue band. The small ventral fins are blue with red marks; the pectoral fins are transparent with a greenish-blue edge. The basic coloration of the red variety is a beautiful orangey-red which becomes yellowish-green with a metallic sheen on the front of the body: the back is dark becoming yellowish towards the belly. The pattern on the gill covers is the same in both varieties. The dorsal fin is orange-red, with a black mark in front, deep red marks, and is edged with a red border which in its turn has a greenish-blue outer edge. The center of the caudal fin has bright red marks, and is edged top and bottom with a wide red band. A narrow, greenish-yellow line appears along the top of the caudal fin and a wider band of the same color along the bottom. The anal fin is orangey-red at the base becoming bluish towards the tip which has a dark edge: the center of the fin has bright red marks.
Females are an olive or reddish-brown with fine red dots. The fins are colorless.
Males are as described above.

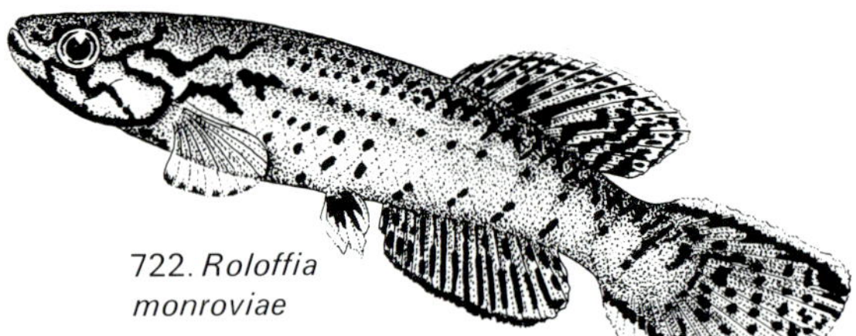
722. *Roloffia monroviae*

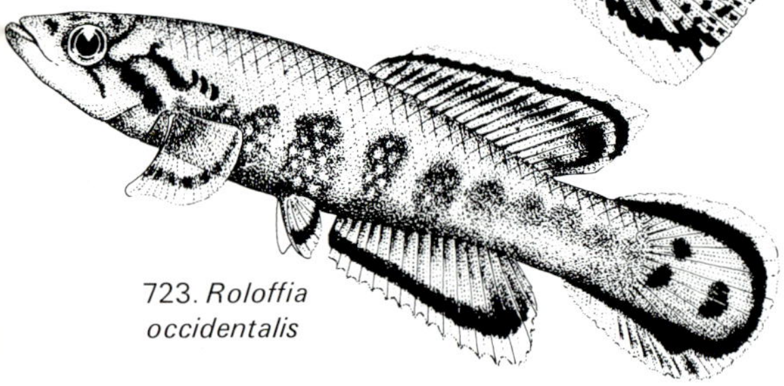
723. *Roloffia occidentalis*

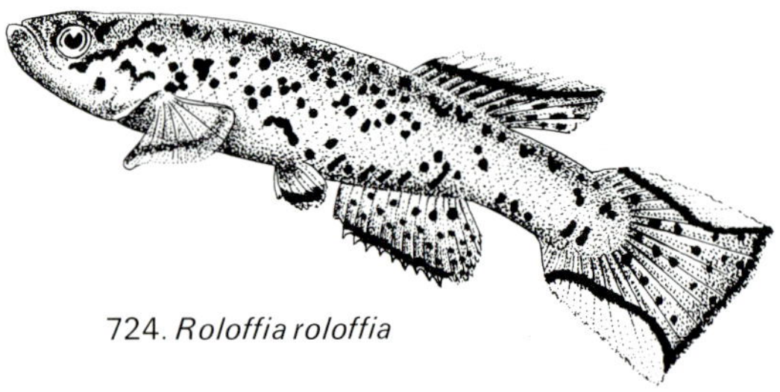
724. *Roloffia roloffia*

725. *Roloffia monroviae*

General care: *R.monroviae* is a seasonal fish. The species tank should be as for *R.bertholdi,* but with a large space left in the front where a bowl of peat may be placed when the fish spawn.

Breeding: *R.monroviae* may be allowed to spawn in the species tank, if a plastic bowl with a layer of 4 cm of well-boiled and rinsed peat is put in the tank. When the fish have laid their eggs in this peat, it should be treated in the same way as the peat bed in a breeding tank, if one is used. A breeding tank, if employed, should be of about 15 liters capacity. The back should be blacked out, the bed should be 4 cm of sterilized peat. The water should be as in the species tank: temperature 24°C. Some plants of the floating variety of Indian fern *(Ceratopteris thalictroides)* may be put in. The breeding fish should be fed well but not on red mosquito larvae or Tubifex. After two or three weeks the breeding fish should be transferred to another, identically fitted-out tank, and the peat bed drained, and stored at 23°C, in airtight plastic containers for two to three months. Soft water, at 25°C, should then be poured over the peat. The eggs will hatch almost immediately and the fry should be fed with *Artemia* or *Cyclops Nauplii.* They grow quickly and will be sexually mature in two months, but the water in the tank must be kept very clean and a proportion regularly changed.

ROLOFFIA OCCIDENTALIS

Family: *Cyprinodontidae*
Genus: *Roloffia*
English name: Red Aphyosemion
Origin: West Africa, Sierra Leone
Size: Maximum 12 cm
Habitat: Found in small streams

Shape, coloring and markings: *R.occidentalis* is the largest species in the genus. The body is elongated, slender, and laterally hard-

ly at all compressed. The mouth is upper-positioned. The pectoral fins are relatively large: the ventral fins are small. The dorsal and anal fins are very large and so positioned that the front rays of the two fins are opposite each other, about halfway along the body. The caudal fin is slightly curved and almost straight at the back. In some mature males the front rays of the dorsal fin and the back rays of the anal fin are longer than the membranes, giving the fins a fringe. The basic coloration is orangey-red. A wide, dark metallic blue horizontal line runs along the underside of the body, bordered above along the front of the body by a golden stripe which narrows beyond the gill covers. A number of irregular red marks are found on the gills and above the pectoral fins. The throat is dark blue. The dorsal fin is orangy-red with a bluish-green edge, separated from the center by a red line. The anal fin, crossed by a horizontal red line, is greyish-blue, and orange at the base. The caudal fin is greenish to greyish-blue, and orange at the base. The caudal fin is greenish to greyish-blue, with bright red marks in the center, bordered along the top and bottom by a wide unbroken red line, in turn edged with a fine blue border, except at the bottom where the border widens into a broad, bluish or greyish-green band.
Females are brownish to orangey-red, with colorless fins.
Males are as described above.

General care: As for *R.monroviae.*

Breeding: As for *R.monroviae,* but the eggs of *R.occidentalis* do not hatch for 6–12 months. During this rest period the stored peat containing the eggs must be checked regularly for mould. If no young fish hatch the first time water is poured over the peat, it should be put away in a dry place for another month, and if necessary, tested and stored again and again for a month at a time, until they finally do hatch.

Additional information: Sometimes called *R.occidentalis occidentalis* to distinguish it from *R.toddi* which was originally named *R.occidentalis todii.*

ROLOFFIA ROLOFFI

Family: *Cyprinodontidae*

Genus: *Roloffia*

English name: none

Origin: West Africa, Sierra Leone

Size: Maximum 5 cm

Habitat: Found in wooded streams

Shape, coloring and markings: The body is elongated, torpedo-shaped and laterally scarcely compressed. The mouth is upper-positioned. The pectoral fins are relatively large: the ventral fins are small. The dorsal and anal fins are large and set far back. The caudal fin is oblong and slightly rounded: the back is straight with elongated tips. The basic coloration is olive green with a pale bluish-green sheen. A large number of reddish-brown or bright red marks lie on the body, and sometimes merge to form an irregular pattern of stripes. The dorsal and anal fins are bluish-green with red marks: the former has a red band with a bluish-green edge: the latter has a red edge. The center of the caudal fin is bluish-green with red marks, and bordered by two dark red parallel lines: above and below are bright yellow bands which taper to a point.
Females are greyish-brown with red dots and stripes. A very prominent brownish-red mark lies on the caudal peduncle. The fins are brown with reddish-brown markings.
Males are as described above.

General care: As for *R.bertholdi.*

Breeding: As for *R.bertholdi.* The eggs hatch after 17–21 days. The young fish will be sexually mature after 6 months.

ROLOFFIA TODDI

Family: *Cyprinodontidae*

Genus: *Roloffia*

English name: none

Origin: West Africa, Sierra Leone, near Barmoi

Size: Maximum 11 cm

Habitat: Found only in some lakes in the above area

Shape, coloring and markings: The body is elongated and scarcely compressed laterally. The mouth is upper-positioned. The pectoral fins are relatively large and the ventral fins small. The large dorsal and anal fins are so positioned that the front rays of the two fins are opposite each other, a little further than half-way along the body. The caudal fin is rectangular and slightly rounded at the edges. The basic coloration is olive brown: the back and upper part of the body are a golden-yellow with a vivid blue or bluish-violet sheen. A wide band, of vertical dark marks runs across the flanks. The underside of the body is dark blue. The scales on the flanks have a red edge creating a net-like pattern. The dorsal and anal fins are blue with dark red marks, enclosed by a dark red horizontal line which in turn is edged with a fine blue border. The caudal fin is blue with dark red marks enclosed by a red band, which has a narrow blue edge along the top and bottom: the lower part of the caudal fin has a zone of greenish-yellow.
Females are smaller, brown with vertical dark marks. The fins are colorless.
Males are as described above.

General care: As for *R.occidentalis.*

Breeding: As for *R.occidentalis.*

Additional information: *R.toddi* was for long called *R.occidentalis toddi.*

THE FAMILY GOODEIDAE

An introductory description

Before turning to the characteristics of the family it is perhaps helpful to discuss generally this rather unusual group of families known to aquarists as livebearers.

There are six families of aquarium livebearing fish. The *Anablepidae,* or Four-eyes and the *Amblyopsidae* or North American cavefish. All, except the *Hemirhamphidae* which are distributed over Southeast Asia, are confined to the Americas. The exact physical characteristics vary from family to family, but in very general terms, all the livebearer males have a special copulatory organ which has developed out of, or is part of the anal fin. Fertilisation of the eggs takes place within the body of the female: except in the case of the *Goodeidae,* the female can store the milt for a considerable period of time, so that mating does not have to take place before each batch of eggs can be fertilised. Unless the female expels the young prematurely because of fright or other disturbance, the fertilised eggs are retained in the ovarian cavity for at least four to six weeks and the young are then expelled in fully developed form, and will be free swimming immediately.

Peculiarities of the individual families are dealt with below under the appropriate entry.

The *Goodeidae* are a small and very unusual family of livebearing fish, all of which are found only in Central Mexico. There are six genera, *Characodon, Goodea, Ilyodon, Lermichthys, Limnurgus* and *Neotoca.* Except for the genus *Goodea,* where there are four species, there are at present only one species in each of the genera.

The unusual feature of all these fish is their reproductive behavior, which is different from that of all other livebearers. The embryos do not, as with most livebearers, develop in the ovarian cavity within the female, but in a specially adapted part of the oviduct. Moreover, the embryos do not draw all their nourishment from their own yolk sacs, but some also directly from the mother, in a way similar to a human foetus. The *Goodeidae* are thus true viviparous fish. Moreover, the females cannot store fertile milt, so that for each brood the female must be fertilized anew by a male. The gonopodium in the *Goodeidae* is no more than the first few rays of the anal fin bunched closely together and separated from the rest of the fin by a notch: in the females the anal fin is well rounded.

All these fish are delicate and are by no means easy to keep or breed in the aquarium. This difficulty may be in part due to the unusual conditions in which they live in the wild. They are all found only in stony upland streams with very little vegetation which in the dry season almost dry up completely, but by contrast, in the rainy season are raging torrents.

The genus Goodea

There are four species in the genus *Goodea, Goodea atripinnis,* the Black Fin Goodea, *Goodea multipunctata,* the Piebald Goodea, *Goodea toweri* and *Goodea whitei.* Of these, only *Goodea atripinnis* is familiar to aquarists, and is described below.

The genus Neotaca

Only the Two-lined Neotoca, *Neotoca bilineata,* is to be found to date in this genus. A peaceful species, it is not very brightly colored but makes an attractive aquarium fish, although as noted below, care has to be taken because of its extreme sensitivity to water changes.

GOODEA ATRIPINNIS

Family: *Goodeidae*
Genus: *Goodea*
English name: Black Fin Goodea
Origin: Mexico
Size: Males to 8.5 cm; females to 13 cm
Habitat: Found in some streams and lakes

SHAPE, COLORING AND MARKINGS: The body is elongated and laterally somewhat compressed. The basic coloration is olive-green, tinged with pink and a slight bluish iridescence. The belly is a muddy yellow. The fins are the same color, with dark borders and flecks.

Females have a rounded anal fin and all the fins change color from yellow to black, according to the mood of the fish.

Males are as described above, with the gonopodium consisting of the first rays of the anal fin.

GENERAL CARE: *G.atripinnis* requires a large well-planted tank, with ample free swimming space. The composition of the water is not critical: temperature 18°–22° C. Both live and dried food should be given to provide a balanced diet. A very delicate fish which must be handled with care.

BREEDING: This is difficult. The period of gestation is six to eight weeks. Breeding temperature 20°–24° C. The female should be put in a special tank and the 20–40 young, which are about a cm. long when born, need careful attention and ought to be fed on the finest live and dried foods.

726. *Goodae atripinnis*

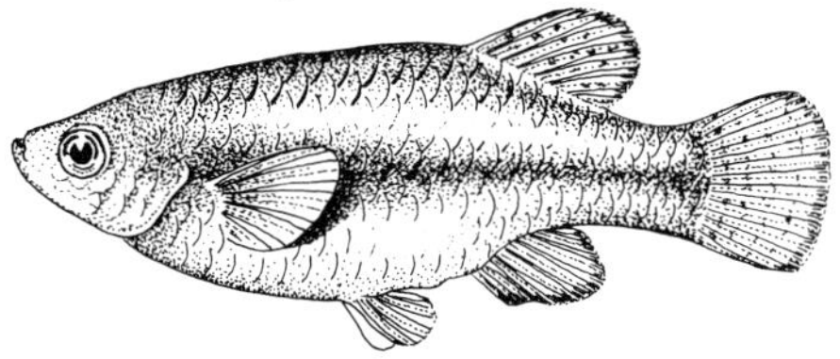

NEOTOCA BILINEATA

Family: *Goodeidae*
Genus: *Neotoca*
English name: Two-lined Neotoca
Origin: Central Mexico
Size: Males to 3.5 cm; females to 6 cm
Habitat: Found mainly in rivers in volcanic areas

SHAPE, COLORING AND MARKINGS: The body shape closely resembles that of the female Guppy *(Xiphophorus maculatus),* although the body is a little more elongated and laterally compressed. The dorsal fin begins exactly half way along the body. The anal fin shows the shape characteristic of the family. The basic coloration is a greyish greenish brown: the belly is yellowish grey. Above a narrow blue-green iridescent zone, a dark longitudinal line runs from the snout through the eye to the caudal peduncle, where it becomes a series of irregular transverse dark bars. The dorsal and anal fins are grey to black: the other fins are colorless, but the caudal fin has a dark spot at the base. There are no significant differences between the color patterns of males and females.

GENERAL CARE: *N.bilineata* needs a spacious but densely planted tank. The water should be as near to neutral (pH 7) as possible: temperature 22°–25° C. *N.bilineata* is very sensitive to changes in the composition of the water, and this must be carefully controlled if the fish are to thrive. Both live and dried food will be accepted.

727. *Neotoca bilineata*

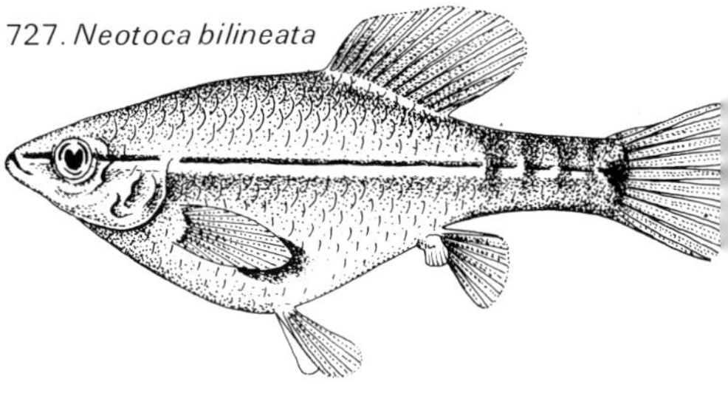

BREEDING: Breeding temperature 25°–26° C. The gestation period is six to eight weeks. The 5–40 young are born, relatively large and if well fed grow quickly.

728. *Belonesox belizanus*

THE FAMILY POECILIIDAE

An introductory description

The *Poeciliidae* family contains in all some 26 genera or subgenera and some 138 species but by no means all of these are generally accounted aquarium fish, although most have been kept in captivity by specialists at some time or another. In this encyclopaedia species are described from 12 genera, of which the majority are in the genera *Poecilia* and *Xiphophorus*.
The fish in this family come from a wide area of tropical America. The smaller species which are most suitable for the ordinary aquarium are hardy and extremely beautiful: many are classic aquarium fish, so much that many experienced amateurs, anxious for novelties, consider them too mundane to merit attention, which is a pity because they are an ornament to any collection.
In the fish of the *Poeciliidae* family the sexual organ of the male (the gonopodium) is formed from the third, fourth and fifth anal fin rays.

The genus Alfaro

Only two species, *Alfaro cultratus* and *Alfaro huberi* are found in this genus of livebearers from tropical America. The distinctive feature of the genus is the very sharp line to the under edge of the caudal peduncle, which has given rise to the name Knife Livebearers. These are rare fish and are hardly ever imported.

The genus Belonesox

There is only one species in this genus, *Belonesox belizanus* described below, so named because it was first found around Belize in British Honduras. Although classed in this family, *B.belizanus* is completely different in appearance from all the other species of *Poeciliidae*. A predatory fish, it is totally unsuitable for the normal community tank.

The genus Brachyrhaphis

There are seven species in this genus: *Brachyrhaphis cascajalensis, Brachyrhaphis episcopi, Brachyrhaphis hartwegi, Brachyrhaphis parismina, Brachyrhaphis rhabdophora* and *Brachyrhaphis terrabensis*, but of these only one species, *B.episcopi* has been kept in aquariums. More accommodating and peaceful than the species in related genera, it is nevertheless an extremely difficult fish to breed. It is however, a very attractive species and an ornament to any aquarium.

The genus Gambusia

There are some 35 species identified to date in the genus *Gambusia* and most of these are quite common in their natural habitats. Very few of these species however are ever imported or found in aquariums. No more than perhaps nine are seen even rarely in captivity.
The species in this genus, although very similar physically, have significant differences in behavior: some are suitable for community tanks, some are not. Some have been of inestimable benefit to man, for example one variety of *G.affinis*, the Mosquito fish has been the main instrument in controlling mosquitos and hence the incidence of malaria in Panama.

The genus Girardinus

The genus *Girardinus* contains eight species, all of which are found principally in Cuba. Two species, *Girardinus falcatus*, the Yellow Belly, and *Girardinus metallicus*, the Girardinus are quite well-known to aquarists.
Generally undemanding fish, these species are an interesting addition to the aquarium and being avid eaters of algae can, when suitable for a community tank, be very useful.

The genus Heterandria

There are only two species known in the the genus *Heterandria*: the very attractive and extemely small *Heterandria formosa*, or Mosquito fish, described below and *Heterandria bimaculata*, the Two-spotted Heterandria or Pseudo-Helleri. This latter fish is more than twice the size of *H.formosa*, comes from central Mexico and Guatemala and is extremely aggressive. It is totally unsuitable for a community tank, is very rarely

729. *Girardinus metallicus*

imported and is unlikely to be of interest to most amateurs. In all these respects it is quite different from *H.formosa*.
It shares with *H.formosa* however, a very unusual if not unique pattern of reproductive behavior. Whereas in most livebearers the eggs in the female are produced in batches and develop in batches, in the *Heterandria* species the female produces eggs which are fertilised in her body as they develop, so that at any time while she is fertile, embryos will be found in the ovary in all stages of individual development: consequently the young are produced over a relatively long period, which leads to complications in raising the fry, to which reference is made below under breeding instructions for *H.formosa*.

The Genus Phallichthys

The fish in this genus are confined to Central America and some to very restricted areas indeed. There are three species known to date, *Phallichthys amates*, *Phallichthys fairweatheri* and *Phallichthys tico*.
Phallichthys amates is fairly well known to aquarists. There are two sub-species, *P.amates amates*, the Merry Widow and *P.amates pittieri*, the Orange-dorsal livebearer. One sub-species is described below. Some authorities still refer to these two sub-species as separate species, *P.amates* and *P.pittieri*.

The genus Phalloceros

The genus *Phalloceros* is, at first sight, somewhat confusing. There is within it only one true species, *Phalloceros caudimaculatus*, the Caudo or Dusky Millions fish. There are however a number of very well-known varieties, which have become so established as to be thought of by many people as quite separate species: notable among these are *Phalloceros caudomaculatus auratus*, the Golden One-Spot, *Phalloceros caudomaculatus reticulatus*, the Spotted Livebearer and *Phalloceros caudomaculatus reticulatus auratus*, the Golden Spotted Livebearer.
To add to the confusion, the specific name *caudimaculatus* means of course, 'a spot on the caudal peduncle', but in fact none of the varieties has any such distinctive mark.

ALFARO CULTRATUS

Family: *Poeciliidae*
Genus: *Alfaro*
English names: Knife Livebearer, Alfaro's Livebearer
Origin: Brazil, Panama, Costa Rica
Size: The Brazilian variety, maximum 6 cm; others, maximum 10 cm
Habitat: Found in the deeper waters of clear streams

Shape, coloring and markings: The body is slender and laterally very compressed. Two rows of scales, set very close together on the lower edge of the caudal peduncle suggest a knife blade. The anal fin is set far forward. The basic coloration is a pale brown to olive: the flanks are greenish grey. The body is translucent and the backbone shows up as a black longitudinal stripe. The whole body, particularly the back, is covered with small black dots. The fins are a greenish yellow: the caudal fin has a narrow black border.
Females are less deeply colored.
Males are as described above.

General care: *A.cultratus* is a shy but somewhat aggressive fish which should be kept in a well-planted species tank, with adequate free swimming space and plenty of hiding places. A small amount of sea salt should be added to the water: temperature 25°–28°C. All kinds of live animal matter will be accepted as food.
Breeding: This has only rarely been achieved in the aquarium. Temperature 25°–28°C. The period of gestation is eight to ten weeks. The brood is small (no more than 30): the fry will be hunted by the parent and suitable precautions must be taken.

Additional information: A rare species which is seldom imported.

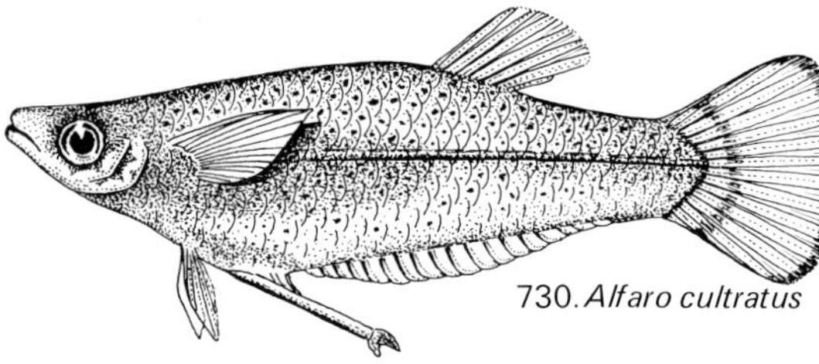
730. *Alfaro cultratus*

ALFARO HUBERI

Family: *Poeciliidae*
Genus: *Alfaro*
English name: none
Origin: Guatemala, Honduras, Nicaragua
Size: Maximum 10 cm
Habitat: Found in freshwater streams

Shape, coloring and markings: The body shape is identical to that of *A.cultratus* but the knife edge to the caudal peduncle is less prominent. The basic coloration is a pale brown to olive. All the scales have a black edge which show up as a dark network pattern, particularly on the back. The caudal fin is grey: the other fins are colorless but flecked with black.
Females are somewhat larger than males: they are less deeply colored.
Males are as described above.

General care: No reliable information is available on the care required by *A.huberi* in the aquarium. It would be reasonable experimentally to treat it as *A.cultratus* but being found only in fresh water, no salt should be added to the aquarium tank.

Breeding: Nothing is known of the reproductive behavior of this species.

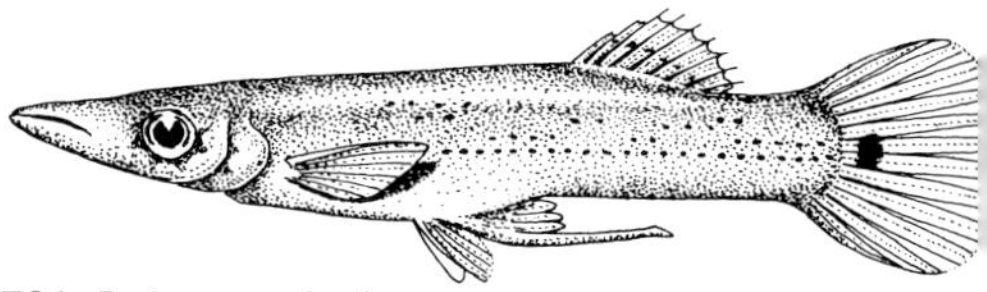
731. *Belonesox belizanus*

BELONESOX BELIZANUS

Family: *Poeciliidae*
Genus: *Belonesox*
English name: Pike Top Minnow
Origin: Central and South America, as far as Nicaragua
Size: Females to 18 cm; males to 10 cm
Habitat: Found in still or slow running waters

Shape, coloring and markings: The body is laterally slightly compressed. The head is long, flattened at the top like that of a pike. The lower jaw protrudes beyond the upper jaw: the teeth are sharp and pointed. The male gonopodium is clearly visible. The scales are small. The basic coloration is a bronze green. Four or five rows of dark dots lie along the flanks. A large dark mark is sometimes found at the base of the caudal fin. The fins are colorless, save for a tinge of yellow and a blue sheen to the lower edge of the caudal fin. The fins become black at night when the lower part of the body also grows darker. The large eyes are edged with gold.
Females have no blue sheen to the caudal fin.
Males are as described above.

General care: *B.belizanus* is an aggressive predatory fish which must be kept in a species tank, preferably as a solitary pair. The tank must be large, deep and well-planted to provide retreats. A small quantity of sea water should be added to the water: temperature 20°–30°C. All live animal matter, including small fish, will be eaten.

BREEDING: Breeding temperature 25°C. The gestation period is 30–50 days. The female should be kept on her own when due to produce the young, in a tank with large quantities of *Riccia fluitans,* which will protect the fry from the voracious appetite of the mother who will not eat during the last few days before the birth of the fry and will as a result be very hungry, when the 20–80 young are produced. The fry should be fed on Cyclops: they grow quickly and will be sexually mature in 6 months.

BRACHYRHAPHIS EPISCOPI

Family: *Poeciliidae*

Genus: *Brachyrhaphis*

English name: The Bishop

Origin: Panama

Size: Females to 5 cm; males to 3.5 cm

Habitat: Found in all kinds of still waters

SHAPE, COLORING AND MARKINGS: The body is elongated and laterally very compressed. The head is flat. The basic coloration is an olive green to yellow brown: the back is darker: the belly pinkish white. The scales have a dark border which shows up as a net-like pattern. Two narrow red lines divided by a green iridescent stripe run from the gill covers to the caudal peduncle and another similar line runs from the gill covers to the area of the belly. Six to ten prominent vertical bars lie on the flanks. The dorsal fin is yellow, flecked with black and carries two transverse brown bars: the black flecked caudal fin is orange yellow with one brown bar.
Females have a sickle-shaped carmine red anal fin with black flecks and a milk white front edge.
Males are as described above.

GENERAL CARE: *B.episcopi* is a peaceful fish suitable even for small tanks. A small amount of sea water can be added to the tank but that is not essential: temperature 25°–30°C. The diet should be a variety of live animal matter, with occasional dried food.

BREEDING: This is very difficult, although some authorities suggest that it is easier in well-planted tanks with slightly brackish water and a great deal of algae. The period of gestation and most appropriate breeding temperature are not known. Between 20 and 30 young will be produced and must be able to shelter from the parents. There are no reliable reports of these very delicate young fish being as yet reared to maturity.

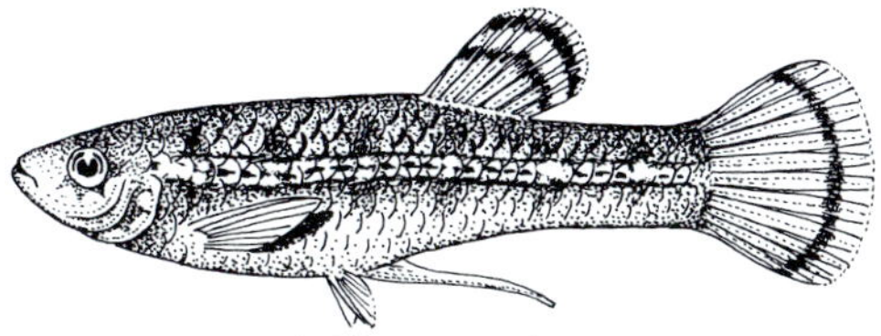

732. *Brachyrhaphis episcopi*

GAMBUSIA AFFINIS

Family: *Poeciliidae*

Genus: *Gambusia*

English names: Silver Gambusia, Spotted Gambusia and Western Mosquito Fish

Origin: Texas, the basins of the rivers San Antonio and Guadalupe

Size: Males to 4 cm; females to 6.5 cm

Habitat: Found in many different quiet waters

SHAPE, COLORING AND MARKINGS: The body is elongated and laterally only very slightly compressed. The head is large and flat on top. The females are almost cylindrical in the body.
The basic coloration is yellowish, becoming silvery white towards the belly. Irregular dark or black dots lie on the back and upper half of the body: a pattern of dark stripes appears below the eyes. The fins are predominantly colorless and transparent but the dorsal and caudal fins have dark marks.
Females are a light olive green with a few scattered dark marks. The fins are colorless.
Males are as described above.

GENERAL CARE: *G.affinis* can be kept in a large community tank but it can be very aggressive towards members of its own species as well as towards other species. A densely planted species tank with subdued lighting is therefore to be preferred. *G.affinis* is a shoal fish and requires a lot of free swimming space. The composition of the water is not critical but a small amount of salt (1 tablespoon for every 15 liters of water) should be added: temperature 20°–22°C. During the winter *G.affinis* will tolerate considerably lower temperatures, down to about 14°C. Aquatic insects and larvae are better than dried food as diet and these should be supplemented with lettuce or algae.

BREEDING: The gestation period is about 30 days. The best breeding temperature has not been determined. The 10–80 young fish should be separated from the parent. It is very important for the temperature of the tank containing the fry to be kept constant. The fry must be fed liberally, but even so will grow slowly and will only be sexually mature after about a year. Females which carry when they are too young often lose their offspring.

ADDITIONAL INFORMATION: There are a number of local varieties of *G.affinis,* and two recognised sub-species, *G.affinis affinis* and *G.affinis holbrooki.* Two other species (neither being usually an aquarium fish) *G.panuca* and *G.senilis* were formerly regarded as no more than varieties of *G.affinis.*

733. *Girardinus metallicus*

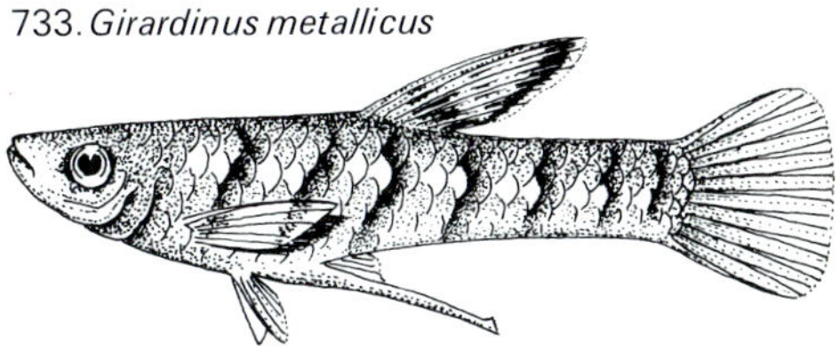

GIRARDINUS METALLICUS

Family: *Poeciliidae*

Genus: *Girardinus*

English name: Girardinus

Origin: Cuba, Costa Rica

Size: Males to 5 cm; females to 9 cm

Habitat: Found in small streams and ditches

SHAPE, COLORING AND MARKINGS: The body is fairly deep and laterally very compressed towards the tail. The head is broad and rather flat on top: the eyes and scales are large. The dorsal fin is very large, set almost exactly half way along the back. The basic coloration is a greenish brown to yellowish grey: the back is darker: the flanks have a light blue sheen: the belly is silvery white. A series of dark sickle-shaped bars lie across the body. The dorsal fin is a pale yellow, with dark flecks: the upper edge has a broad dark band with a narrow pale border. The other fins are colorless.
Females lack the sickle-shaped bars or at best carry them very indistinctly.
Males are as described above.

GENERAL CARE: *G.metallicus* is a peaceful fish, suitable for a well-planted community tank. It is relatively undemanding but does like pure clean water: a proportion of the water in the tank should be changed regularly. Temperature 22°–25°C. *G.metallicus* dislikes being moved to a completely new tank and if this is done, it must be done very carefully to accli-

734. *Heterandria formosa* (female)

matiese the fish to its new environment. All kinds of live and dried food will be eaten and algae will be voraciously devoured.

BREEDING: The breeding temperature should be 24°–26°C. The period of gestation is five to eight weeks, but much longer at lower temperatures. The 10–100 young are very small and should be reared apart from the parent in a well-lit tank.

HETERANDRIA FORMOSA

Family: *Poeciliidae*

Genus: *Heterandria*

English name: Mosquito Fish, Dwarf Top Minnow and Dwarf Livebearer

Origin: USA from North Carolina to Florida

Size: Males to 2 cm; females to 3.5 cm

Habitat: Found in all kinds of waters, from swift flowing mountain streams to stagnant pools

SHAPE, COLORING AND MARKINGS: The body is elongated and laterally only moderately compressed. *H.formosa* is the smallest of the livebearers and one of the smallest vertebrates in the animal kingdom. The basic coloration is a reddish brown with a pearly sheen that has at times a violet tinge. A broad irregular dark line runs from the snout to the root of the caudal fin: it is crossed by eight to twelve dark transverse bars. The fins are yellowish: large dark marks lie at the base of the anal and dorsal fins and the latter fin is bordered with orange.
Females have the same color pattern but a larger anal fin.
Males are as described above.

GENERAL CARE: *H.formosa* is suitable for a small species or community tank, with plenty of fine leaved plants either placed so as to receive the sun or provided with good artificial light. The composition of the water is not critical: temperature 20°–24°C, although temperatures as low as 16°–18°C will be tolerated. All kinds of live and dried food will be eaten.

BREEDING: The breeding temperature should be 22°–26°C. Unlike most livebearers which produce their young in batches, *H.formosa* produces the young singly or in twos and threes over a long period, because of the unusual way in which the young develop inside the females (see Introductory note on the genus). Thus up to 80 young may be produced over 10 or 11 weeks. The parents will eat the young if given the opportunity and it is best to transfer the female to a special small tank with ample quantities of *Nitella, Riccia* and *Vesicularia* to give the fry some shelter and also to remove the fry to a rearing tank whenever possible. Filamentous algae must not be allowed to remain in a tank with the fry because it will suffocate them.

PHALLICHTHYS AMATES AMATES

Family: *Poeciliidae*

Genus: *Phallichthys*

English name: Merry Widow

Origin: Principally Guatemala, but also Panama and Honduras

Size: Males to 4 cm; females to 7 cm

Habitat: Found in small, still or sluggish waters

SHAPE, COLORING AND MARKINGS: The body is rather deep and laterally very compressed towards the tail. The gonopodium is very long. The basic coloration is yellowish: the back is tinged with olive: the belly is yellowish white: the flanks have a metallic sheen. The gill covers and cheeks are an iridescent blue. A faint dark longitudinal line runs from the gill covers to the caudal peduncle. The fins are a dull yellow. The large dorsal fin has a black border within a white border: the caudal and anal fins have a less prominent dark border.
Females have an even less distinct longitudinal line.
Males are as described above.

GENERAL CARE: *P.amates amates* is a peaceful fish which can be kept in a community tank, although care must be taken to ensure that other quicker fish in the tank do not prevent its enjoying its fair share of food. A timid fish, *P.amates amates* needs to be given plenty of retreats among floating plants. The composition of the water is not critical: temperature 20°–25°C. All kinds of live and dried food will be eaten but algae should also always be given as a supplement.

BREEDING: The breeding temperature should be 22°–26°C. The period of gestation is four to six weeks. The female should be put in a small tank on her own and removed as soon as possible otherwise the fry will be hunted relentlessly. The 10–50 in the brood will grow slowly and are sexually mature after six months although the females will not be fully grown in much under a year.

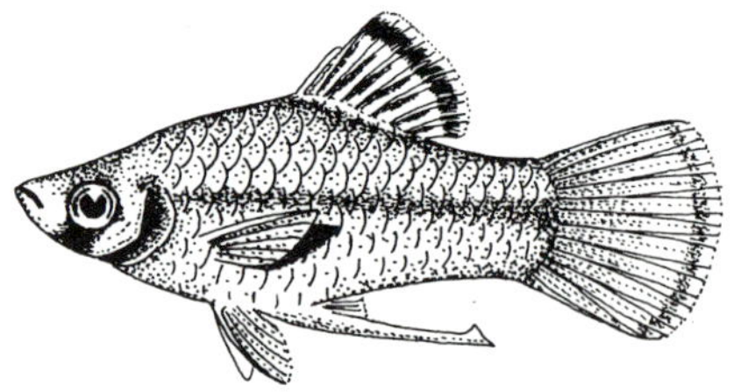

735. *Phallichthys amates amates*

736. *Phalloceros caudomaculatus*

PHALLOCEROS CAUDOMACULATUS

Family: *Poeciliidae*

Genus: *Phalloceros*

English names: The Caudo, The One-Spot Livebearer and The Dusky Millions fish

Origin: Argentina, Eastern Brazil, Paraguay, Uraguay

Size: Males to 3 cm; females to 5 cm

Habitat: Found in a variety of fresh and brackish waters

SHAPE, COLORING AND MARKINGS: The body is somewhat elongated and compressed laterally towards the tail: the snout is rather pointed, the back arched. The gonopodium is deeply forked. The basic coloration is an olive green: the back is darker. The scales have a dark edge which shows up as a network pattern over the whole body. Below the dorsal fin lies a black comma-shaped mark surrounded by an area of silver or gold. The fins are pale yellow, but the dorsal fin has a black border.
Females have a comma-shaped mark only when fully grown: the dorsal fin has no black border.
Males are as described above.

GENERAL CARE: *P.caudomaculatus* is a hardy peaceful undemanding fish, suitable for all sizes of properly stocked community tanks. The tank should contain some fine leaved plants. The composition of the water is not critical but the addition of a small amount of salt will be beneficial: temperature 20°–24°C. *P.caudomaculatus* is however very sensitive to water changes and no more than a third of the tank should be changed at a time. *P.caudomaculatus* will tolerate quite low temperatures however and can even be kept in an unheated aquarium. All kinds of live and dried food will be eaten.

BREEDING: Breeding temperature about 22°C. The period of gestation is five to six weeks. The 20–80 young will be preyed on by the parents and suitable precautions must be taken, including providing the breeding tank with some clumps of *Riccia* and *Vesicularia.*

THE FAMILY POECILIIDAE

The genus Poecilia

Until 1963 this genus contained only two species, including, under a synonym, *Poecilia sphenops* (see below): after a revision of the classification however, the number of species rose to 32 and now includes those species previously placed in the genera *Lebistes* and *Mollienisia*. To the amateur aquarist the genus *Poecilia* is particularly important because it includes both the fascinating Black Mollies and the ever popular Guppies. Both these groups of fish have been the subject of much cross-breeding and there are now available a bewildering number of varieties. The six most important true species in this genus are described below.

738. *Poecilia latipinna*

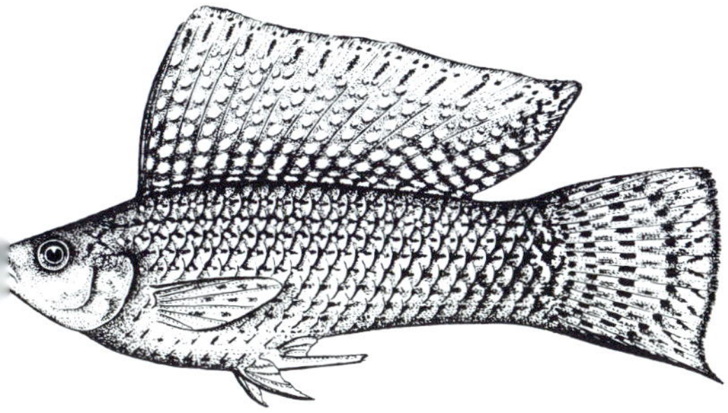

737. *Poecilia latipinna*

POECILIA LATIPINNA

Family: *Poeciliidae*

Genus: *Poecilia*

English name: Sailfin Molly

Origin: South and southeast USA, Mexico

Size: Males to 7 cm; females to 9 cm

Habitat: Common in both fresh and brackish waters

SHAPE, COLORING AND MARKINGS: The body is elongated and broad, laterally somewhat compressed. The dorsal fin is large and in males may be very high indeed. The basic coloration is brownish: the back is a dark olive green to brown: the flanks are light blue to salmon with a vivid pearly sheen and five or six horizontal lines of blue, green and red dots. The throat and belly are white: the latter may have dark transverse bands. The powerful dorsal fin is light blue with light and dark marks between the rays and a yellow border. The upper half of the caudal fin is orange, the center bluish and the lower half a vivid blue, with elongated sword shaped rays and a pattern of dots and marks.
Females are less vividly colored and have a smaller dorsal fin.
Males are as described above.

GENERAL CARE: *P.latipinna* needs a large tank with a dark bed, dense vegetation round the sides and plenty of free swimming space among floating plants. It is not a shoal fish but may be kept in pairs or in a small group, although the males may be aggressive towards each other. The composition of the water is not critical but it should be changed regularly: temperature 25°–28°C. *P.latipinna* will swim freely at all levels. All kinds of live and dried food will be accepted but that diet should be supplemented with lettuce unless there is a great deal of algae in the tank. Imported specimens should be kept in quarantine tanks with brackish water, one teaspoonful of common salt being added for every ten liters of water.

BREEDING: As with related species, breeding presents few problems, but successive generations bred from aquarium fish lose the brilliant colors and large dorsal fins of their ancestors. The period of gestation is eight to ten weeks: the 20–80 young should be reared in tanks with plenty of vegetation and at a temperature not above 24°C.

POECILIA HETERANDRIA

Family: *Poeciliidae*

Genus: *Poecilia*

English name: Dwarf Limia

Origin: Venezuela

Size: Males to 3 cm; females to 5 cm

Habitat: Found in sluggish waters

SHAPE, COLORING AND MARKINGS: The body is rather short and stout and laterally somewhat compressed. The head is broad and flat on top: the caudal peduncle is unusually wide and the caudal fin broad. The basic coloration is a yellowish olive green: the back is darker: the flanks silvery and the belly whitish. A dark longitudinal stripe runs from the eye to the caudal peduncle and three vertical marks lie on the flanks below the dorsal fin which has two black bands divided by a zone of orange.
Females have a less prominent longitudinal stripe, no vertical marks on the side and a round black spot on the dorsal fin instead of two bands.
Males are as described above.

GENERAL CARE: *P.heterandria* is an undemanding fish that should be kept in a fairly well planted tank positioned so as to catch the sun. The composition of the water is not critical: temperature 22°–26°C. All kinds of live and dried food will be accepted and a supplement of lettuce or algae should be given.

BREEDING: The period of gestation is four to six weeks: the 20–50 young are very small when born but grow rapidly. They should be reared under the same conditions as recommended above for the care of the species.

739. *Poecilia reticulata*

740. *Poecilia reticulata*

741. *Poecilia reticulata*

742. *Poecilia reticulata*

743. *Poecilia reticulata*

◁ 744. *Poecilia reticulata*

745. *Poecilia reticulata*

POECILIA PETENSIS

Family: *Poeciliidae*

Genus: *Poecilia*

English name: Spiketail Molly

Origin: Guatemala, Lake Petén

Size: Males to 12 cm; females to 10 cm

Habitat: Found only in fresh water

SHAPE, COLOR AND MARKINGS: The body shape closely resembles that of *P.latipinna* but is somewhat deeper. The dorsal fin is remarkably large and is seen to best advantage when the fish is excited. The basic coloration is brownish with a vivid blue or silvery sheen on the flanks: the back is darker, the belly a light or yellow brown. The scales each carry a decorative light or dark green iridescent spot which lie in rows and show up as horizontal lines across the body. The very large dorsal fin is brown at the base, becomes a vivid blue and has an orange border: light and dark marks lie between the rays. The caudal fin has a dark edge and the lower rays are elongated and sword-shaped. The pectoral fins are colorless.
Females are less vividly colored and have a smaller dorsal fin.
Males are as described above.

GENERAL CARE: As for *P.latipinna,* but the temperature must not drop below 25°C.

BREEDING: As for *P.latipinna.*

ADDITIONAL INFORMATION: *P.petensis* is rarely imported. Until recently it was known as *Mollienesia petensis.* It is also called *P.petenensis.*

POECILIA RETICULATA

Family: *Poeciliidae*

Genus: *Poecilia*

English names: Guppy and Millions Fish

Origin: South America, north of the Amazon; now also found elsewhere, having been introduced by man to control mosquitoes

Size: Males to 3.5 cm: females to 6 cm

Habitat: Found in both fresh and brackish waters, slow running streams and pools

SHAPE, COLORING AND MARKINGS: *P.reticulata* has been for so long one of the favorite aquarium fish and has received so much attention from breeders that it now appears in a bewildering variety of shapes and color patterns. The original basic body color is a brownish olive but with a wide variation in the color of the iridescent lateral scales. The cross-breeding of various strains has now produced guppies of almost every conceivable color pattern.

GENERAL CARE: *P.reticulata* is an undemanding species but should not because it is so tolerant be kept without regard to what is appropriate for so active and ebullient a fish. It should have a fairly large and well planted tank with plenty of free swimming space. The composition of the water is not critical and may even with advantage be slightly salty: temperature 20°–25°C. *P.reticulata* is however sensitive to sudden changes in temperature and water composition and any changes should be made gradually. All kinds of live and dried food will be eaten and should be supplemented with lettuce or algae.

BREEDING: This prolific fish is easy to breed. The period of gestation is four to six weeks. The 20–100 young grow quickly and reach maturity in about six months. Breeding temperature 23°–28°C. The young fish should be provided with good cover in dense vegetation. Although easy to breed, the responsible amateur should only breed those pairs that will preserve the particular color pattern and fin shape he observes in the parents, and this does involve an elementary knowledge of genetics and information about the pedigree of the parent fish. There are now many Guppy societies around the world and the interested amateur should not only study the literature but also establish contact with a society before breeding these fish otherwise he runs the risk of encouraging poor strains.

ADDITIONAL INFORMATION: *P.reticulata* until the recent revision of the genus *Poecilia* was known as *Lebistes reticulatus*.

POECILIA SPHENOPS

Family: *Poeciliidae*

Genus: *Poecilia*

English names: Pointed-mouth Molly and Short-finned Molly

Origin: North and South America, from Texas to Colombia

Size: Males to 8 cm; females to 12 cm

Habitat: Found in fresh and brackish waters

SHAPE, COLORING AND MARKINGS: The body

746. *Poecilia sphenops*

747. *Poecilia velifera* ▷

closely resembles that of related species but the dorsal fin is significantly smaller and the mouth slightly more pointed. There are many varieties of this fish known to aquarists including both a black spotted variety and the completely black variety called the Black Molly. Many of these varieties have a color pattern that is very different from that of the fish in the wild, where the upper half of the body is a greyish blue, the flanks are a vivid bluish green with rows of blue or green iridescent spots and the whole body has a violet sheen. The lower half of the body is a light pale blue to salmon. The dorsal fin is colorless but carries a profusion of dark dots: the caudal fin has a blue base, an orange band in the center and a black border.
Females are a dull blue, with rows of brownish red dots: the fins are colorless.
Males are as described above.

GENERAL CARE: As for *P.latipinna* but a small quantity of salt should always be added to the water: about a teaspoonful for every ten liters of water in the tank.

BREEDING: As for *P.latipinna*.

ADDITIONAL INFORMATION: One of the best known and most beautiful varieties of *P.sphenops* is the Liberty Molly from Yucatan, which is a deep iridescent black, although the females are often not as uniformly black as the males.

POECILIA VELIFERA

Family: *Poeciliidae*

Genus: *Poecilia*

English name: Sailfin Molly

Origin: Central America, Mexico

Size: Both males and females grow to about 12 cm

Habitat: Found in both fresh and brackish waters

SHAPE, COLORING AND MARKINGS: *P.velifera* although larger than *P.latipinna* closely resembles that latter species except that *P.velifera* has a fuller belly and the dorsal fin is set further forward. The basic coloration is a dark olive green to blue. The flanks are bluish green with innumerable light blue iridescent dots: the belly and throat are blue, green or orange with dark transverse bands across the belly. The dorsal fin is very large: larger than in related species, greyish with a bluish base and a pearly sheen, an orange border and many light and dark dots and flecks. The grey caudal fin has a bluish base, orange dots and marks and and black elongated sword shaped rays.
Females are less vividly colored.
Males are as described above.

GENERAL CARE: As for *P.sphenops*.

BREEDING: Not a very prolific species. The period of gestation is about eight weeks and the 30–50 young should be reared at first in a tank with no more than 9–15 cm of water, care being taken that all water added to the tank is at exactly the same temperature as that already in it.

ADDITIONAL INFORMATION: Formerly named *Mollienesia velifera*, *P.velifera* is unusual in being peculiarly sensitive to any disturbance of the biological balance in its environment. If the water is polluted or too full of bacteria or if the temperature is too low, the fish will tremble and twitch and remedial action must be taken immediately.

THE FAMILY POECILIIDAE

The genus Priapella

There are only three species known in this genus, *Priapella bonita, Priapella compressa* and *Priapella intermedia.* All three have been found to date only in Mexico and only *Priapella intermedia,* described below is generally regarded as an aquarium fish. Of *P.compressa,* first described in 1948, very little is known and *P.bonita,* a dark greenish grey fish with a very unusual flat back from the snout to the beginning of the dorsal fin, is hardly ever seen in the aquarium.

The genus Quintana

The only species at present classified in the genus *Quintana* is the beautiful but timid Black-barred Livebearer *Quintana atrizona,* described below. This very delicate fish which has become quite popular with aquarists, is still only to be found in Cuba in a very restricted area around Havana.

PRIAPELLA INTERMEDIA

Family: *Poeciliidae*
Genus: *Priapella*
English name: none
Origin: Mexico
Size: Males to 5 cm: females to 7 cm
Habitat: Found in clear fast-flowing waters

SHAPE, COLORING AND MARKINGS: *P.intermedia* in shape closely resembles the popular Swordtail, *Xiphophorus helleri,* described below. The basic coloration varies from yellow to olive green: the irises and gill covers are a luminescent bluish green. A prominent brown line runs along the body. The yellow fins are transparent: the dorsal and ventral fins have white leading edges and the caudal fin has a white edge all the way round.
There are no significant differences between the color patterns of males and females.

GENERAL CARE: *P.intermedia* should be kept in a small shoal in a fairly spacious tank: only when kept in a shoal will the fish develop their full color pattern. The water should be aerated to ensure a high oxygen level, but the composition of the water otherwise is not critical: temperature 24°–26° C. *P.intermedia* is a timid fish and sudden changes in lighting should be avoided. All kinds of live and dried food will be eaten.

BREEDING: The gestation period is four to six weeks. The 10–75 young are about 1 cm long when born but grow quickly. Breeding temperature 24°–26° C.

QUINTANA ATRIZONA

Family: *Poeciliidae*
Genus: *Quintana*
English name: Black-barred Livebearer
Origin: Cuba, around Havana
Size: Males to 2.5 cm: females to 5 cm
Habitat: Found in still and sluggish waters

SHAPE, COLORING AND MARKINGS: The body is rather broad and laterally very compressed: the male has an unusually deep body and the gonopodium which can be moved in all directions, is relatively long. The basic coloration is a yellowish olive, with in some lights, a bluish iridescence. Except for the silvery white belly, the body is translucent, and the swim bladder and backbone are clearly visible. Three to nine black transverse bars lie on the body and vary in intensity according to the mood of the fish. The dorsal fin has a dark border and a dark crescent-shaped mark: the yellowish caudal fin has a dark base.
Females have a pale blue outer edge to the ventral and anal fins.
Males are as described above.

GENERAL CARE: *Q.atrizona* requires a well-lit tank well stocked with fine leaved plants. The composition of the water is not critical: temperature 24°–28° C. These very timid fish are best kept in a species tank and must be handled very carefully. All kinds of live and dried food will be eaten and lettuce or algae should be given as a supplement.

BREEDING: The gestation period is five to eight weeks. The 10–30 young are no more than 0.7 cm long when born and are produced over a period of several days.

748. *Quintana atrizona*

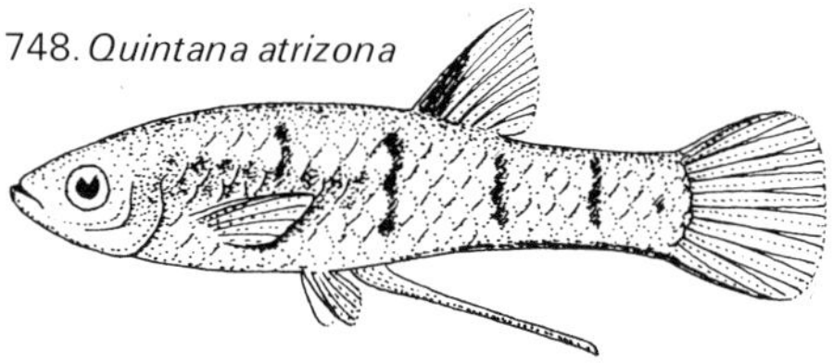

THE FAMILY POECILIIDAE

The genus Xiphophorus

The genus *Xiphophorus* which now includes the popular Swordtail and Platy species has had a confusing and complicated history. Originally there were two distinct genera, *Xiphophorus* and *Platypoecilus,* but although the species in these two genera do not look very much alike to the casual observer, taxonomists concluded that the real scientific differences were insufficient to justify retaining two separate genera. At first, after the two genera were combined, *Platypoecilus* was retained as the name of a sub-genus but this has now been discarded and all species are now within the one main genus *Xiphophorus.* Nevertheless, the species in this genus are recognised as belonging to three separate groups:

1. The Helleri group which includes *Xiphophorus clemenciae,* the Yellow Swordtail, *Xiphophorus helleri alvarezi, Xiphophorus helleri guentheri, Xiphophorus helleri helleri* and *Xiphophorus helleri strigatus.* These last four are sub-species and only *Xiphophorus helleri helleri.* The Swordtail is usually an aquarium fish but that species is one of the most popular fish and, as explained below has been the subject of a great deal of attention from breeders with the result that there are a multitude of different color varieties available.
2. The Montezumae group which contains four species or sub-species, *Xiphophorus milleri, Xiphophorus montezumae montezumae, Xiphophorus pygmaeus nigrensis* and *Xiphophorus pygmaeus pygmaeus.* There are also a very large number of hybrids in this group. Two of these species are common aquarium fish and are described below.
3. The Maculatus group which contains the following species and sub-species, *Xiphophorus couchianus couchianus, Xiphop-*

horus couchianus gordoni, Xiphophorus maculatus, Xiphophorus variatus evelynae, Xiphophorus variatus variatus and *Xiphophorus xiphidium.*

In addition to these 16 species and sub-species there are a large number of hybrid varieties because both the Swordtails and Platys have been found to be peculiarly responsive to cross-breeding and their popularity has encouraged breeders to develop unusually attractive forms. Thus the Swordtails and Platys purchased by an amateur may well not be from a pure strain although the average amateur will be less concerned about that than about the beauty and elegance of his particular fish.

749. *Xiphophorus maculatus*

XIPHOPHORUS CLEMENCIAE

Family: *Poeciliidae*

Genus: *Xiphophorus*

English name: Yellow Swordtail

Origin: Mexico

Size: Males to 3.5 cm: females to 4 cm

Habitat: Found only in the clear fast flowing waters of a tributary of the River Coatzacoalcos

SHAPE, COLORING AND MARKINGS: The body is slender and the gonopodium has a large and powerful claw. The sword of the caudal fin is long. The basic coloration is yellowish green. A prominent red stripe, bordered by one or two less distinct parallel red stripes, runs from the gill covers to the caudal peduncle. The sword is gold, with a black border. Three to six red or orange spots lie at the base of the caudal fin and irregular rows of black or red spots appear on the dorsal fin. There are no significant differences between the color patterns of males and females.

GENERAL CARE: Although a relatively small species, *X.clemenciae* requires a fair sized tank with some plants but also a great deal of free swimming space. The composition of the water is not critical but it must be filtered or aerated: the temperature must be 24°–26° C. *X.clemenciae* is omnivorous but should be given a varied diet including algae or a vegetable supplement.

BREEDING: Not difficult. The pregnant female should be transferred to a special densely planted tank. Temperature 26° C. The gestation period is four to six weeks. The brood may vary considerably in number. The young fish should be fed for the first week on *Artemia nauplii* and fine dried food and for the second week on Cyclops and microworms.

ADDITIONAL INFORMATION: There is some doubt as to whether *X.clemenciae* is a true species or nothing more than a local variety of *X.helleri.*

XIPHOPHORUS HELLERI HELLERI

Family: *Poeciliidae*

Genus: *Xiphophorus*

English name: Swordtail

Origin: Central America

Size: Males to 10 cm: females to 12 cm

Habitat: Found in a wide variety of waters

SHAPE, COLORING AND MARKINGS: The body is slender and laterally somewhat compressed. The gonopodium has well developed hooks and the sword is long. The dorsal and caudal fins are relatively large. The basic coloration of the common wild fish is a pale olive brown: the back is often a bright green: the belly is silver. Along the body runs a red stripe which turns black on the caudal peduncle and becomes the black edge to the sword which in the center may be green, yellow, orange or red. There is no significant difference between the color patterns of the males and the females. These natural colors are however quite different from those of many varieties found in the aquarium and briefly noted below.

GENERAL CARE: As for *X.clemenciae* but at least one part of the tank should be densely planted to give shelter to the more timid specimens if the swordtails are kept in a small group for some individuals can be rather overbearing. The composition of the water is not critical but temperature 22°–26° C. Diet as for *X.clemenciae.*

BREEDING: As for *X.clemenciae.*

750. *Xiphophorus helleri*

ADDITIONAL INFORMATION: There are only four scientifically recognised sub-species of *X.helleri,* as listed in the Introductory note to the genus, but a large number of varieties exist, of which the following are some of the most important.

X.helleri var. *jalapae,* the Jalapa Swordtail with an olive brown back, white belly and brown longitudinal stripes. The center of the sword is bright yellow.

X-helleri var. *rachovii,* the Twin-spot Swordtail which has a basic coloration almost identical to *X.helleri helleri* but in addition four to ten dark transverse bands on the body and two large round blue black spots at the base of the caudal fin: the fins are yellow with red flecks and the sword golden and blue green.

X.helleri var.*aurata,* The Golden Helleri, is pale yellow with a red longitudinal stripe, pale yellow fins and a yellow sword with a black edge only along the bottom.

The Blood Swordtail has a dark orange and dark red body, with a violet longitudinal line: the sword is bright green with a deep black border: the fins are almost colorless.

The Black Helleri has a deep blue-black body with green scales with black borders.

The Wagtail Helleri has a red or green body with black fins.

The Banded Helleri has a red-brown body with one or more darker red longitudinal stripes and to the rear of the pectoral fins, a series of black transverse bands.

There are many more intermediate variations on these patterns and some even more unusual ones offered for sale from time to time. It is often difficult to determine the origin of these individual varieties.

XIPHOPHORUS MACULATUS

Family: *Poeciliidae*

Genus: *Xiphophorus*

English name: Platy, Moonfish, Southern Platyfish

Origin: The Atlantic slopes of Central America

Size: Males to 3.5 cm: females to 6 cm

Habitat: Found mainly in ponds, swamps and pools but also in some sluggish waters

SHAPE, COLORING AND MARKINGS: The body is fairly deep and broad. There is no hook on the genopodium. There is no sword and the dorsal fin is rounded. The basic coloration is yellowish to olive brown, with one or two small spots on the caudal peduncle which, when developed form the basis for the various patterns discussed below. There are usually two to five indistinct transverse bars across the body. The pectoral ventral and caudal fins are colorless. The caudal fin has a blue or greenish border.
Females have no transverse bars across the body.
Males are as described above.

GENERAL CARE: *X.maculatus* needs a fairly spacious tank with some dense vegetation as well as adequate free swimming space. The water should be hard rather than soft: temperature 20°–25°C. *X.maculatus* is omnivorous but should always be given a vegetable supplement.

BREEDING: The period of gestation is usually four weeks but may be up to six. The 10–50 young are no more than 0.8 cm long when born. For the first week they should be fed on infusoria and *Artemia nauplii*: during the second week the diet should be fine dried food and microworms. The parents will not usually attack the young but the occasional female is cannibalistic.

ADDITIONAL INFORMATION: The Platys offered to aquarists are very rarely the pure wild strain. Much care in breeding has produced two distinctive features of interest to the connoisseur: these are the general color pattern of the fish and the pattern of marks on the base of the caudal fin.
There are seven different basic patterns for the caudal finand six incomplete variations. The general color patterns are legion. Some seven variations have been identified as occurring naturally: at least 33 others have been recognised as the production of specialised breeding. The amateur with a particular interest in these variations should consult the specialist literature but the following eight varieties are of more general interest.

1. Spotted Platy.
2. Black Platy.
3. Golden Platy.
4. Black-banded Platy.
5. Red Crescent Platy.
6. Golden Moon Platy.
7. Black Wagtail Platy.
8. Bleeding Heart Platy.

751. *Xiphophorus helleri*

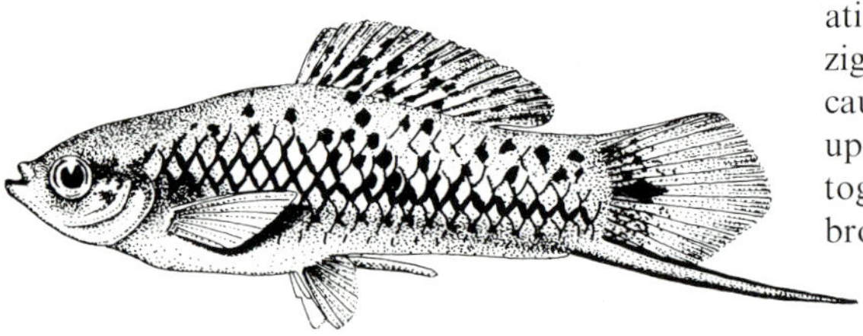

752. *Xiphophorus montezuma montezuma*

XIPHOPHORUS MONTEZUMA - MONTEZUMA

Family: *Poeciliidae*

Genus: *Xiphophorus*

English name: Montezuma Helleri

Origin: Southern Mexico

Size: Males to 5.5 cm: females to 6.5 cm

Habitat: Found in fairly fast flowing waters

SHAPE, COLORING AND MARKINGS: The general body shape is identical to that of *X.helleri helleri* but the dorsal fin is taller and the shorter sword curves upwards. The basic coloration is a dark greenish brown and a brown zig-zag stripe runs from the lower jaw to the caudal peduncle: this stripe is usually made up of small individual spots set closely together. In some specimens additional broken lines of the same color lie on the rear part of the body. The belly is silvery yellow. The sword has a sea green center and a dark border. The dorsal fin is greenish yellow flecked with black: the caudal fin is yellow.
Females have a smaller dorsal fin.
Males are as described above.

GENERAL CARE: *X.montezuma montezuma* is a timid fish and needs a well planted tank. Otherwise care as for *X.clemenciae* but temperature 20°–24°C.

BREEDING: As for *X.clemenciae*

ADDITIONAL INFORMATION: There is a closely related sub-species *X.montezuma cortezi* with a longer head and a bright orange yellow dorsal fin: the overall color pattern may be very varied. This sub-species is rarely seen in aquariums.

XIPHOPHORUS VARIATUS - VARIATUS

Family: *Poeciliidae*

Genus: *Xiphophorus*

English names: Variatus, Variegated Platy and Variable Platyfish

Origin: Mexico

Size: Males to 5.5 cm: females to 7 cm

Habitat: Found in quiet but cool backwaters in lowland regions

SHAPE, COLORING AND MARKINGS: The body shape closely resembles that of *X.helleri helleri*. The color patterns vary significantly (see below) but the basic coloration in the wild

is a yellowish green becoming olive green towards the tail. Irregular black marks lie along the flanks: some specimens carry six to eight dark but indistinct transverse bands. The dorsal fin is yellow, flecked with black: the caudal fin is yellowish red.
Females are paler in color.
Males are as described above.

GENERAL CARE: As for *X.clemenciae* but temperature 20°–24°C and the tank should be well-lit.

BREEDING: The period of gestation is four to six weeks. The 20–200 young are born over a period of some days and the female is best put alone in a special well-lit and well planted tank: temperature 22°–27°C. The young fish grow slowly and should be fed as recommended for *X.clemenciae*.

ADDITIONAL INFORMATION: A number of hybrids have been produced of *X.variatus variatus* including a number now very rarely seen but which the interested amateur can find recorded in the specialist literature. The Silver-headed Variatus, almost black with a silvery head and belly is however worthy of note. A similar hybrid is the Golden-headed Variatus. The Marigold Platy, predominantly red with a gold tinge on the pectoral fins is another interesting hybrid which is not uncommon. There is also a related subspecies, *X.variatus evelynae*, rarely imported, which has a duller color pattern than *X.variatus variatus*.

XIPHOPHORUS XIPHIDIUM

Family: *Poeciliidae*
Genus: *Xiphophorus*
English name: Swordtail Platy
Origin: Mexico
Size: Males to 4 cm: females to 5 cm
Habitat: Found in many of the smaller rivers

SHAPE, COLORING AND MARKINGS: The body profile resembles that of *X.maculatus*: the back is high and the lower lobe of the caudal fin in the male is slightly extended to form a very short sword. The basic coloration is an olive yellow: the belly is white to silvery. A somewhat indistinct zig-zag line runs along the body and this is crossed by irregular dark marks. The sword is colorless.
Females lack the irregular marks present on the flanks of the males.
Males are as described above.

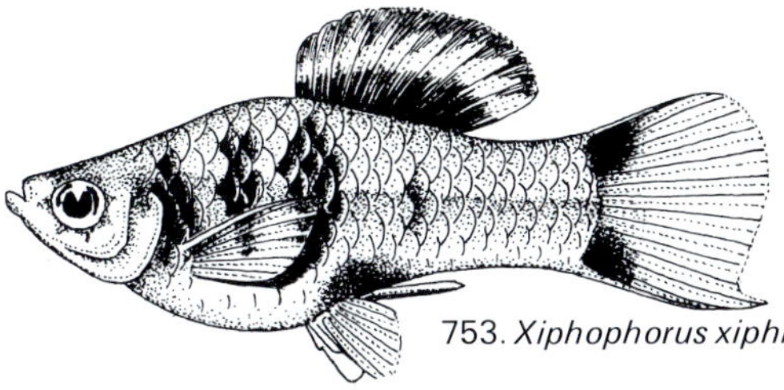

753. *Xiphophorus xiphidium*

GENERAL CARE: *X.xiphidium* is a very delicate fish. It should be treated in general as *X.clemenciae*, but is very sensitive to fluctuations in temperature.

BREEDING: Difficult. As for *X.clemenciae* but the young are very difficult to rear.

ADDITIONAL INFORMATION: *X.xiphidium* is considered by some authorities to be a subspecies of *X.variatus* and is often cited as *X.variatus xiphidium*.

◁ 754. *Xiphophorus variatus*

755. *Xiphophorus variatus*

756. *Xiphophorus variatus*

THE FAMILY HEMIRHAMPHIDAE

An introductory description

The *Hemirhamphidae* is a large family, containing four subfamilies and many genera, only one of which, the genus *Dermogenys* is however of practical interest to aquarists. Some genera in this family contain egg-laying species, and some, including the genera *Dermogenys* and *Hemirhamphodon*, contain livebearers. As livebearers they are unusual in coming from Southeast Asia, in contrast to all the other families of livebearers, which are restricted in origin to Central America.

The appearance of these fish is also both unusual and distinctive. In the livebearer groups the male sexual organ, as in the case of the *Goodeidae* species, has developed from the front rays of the anal fin, and the dorsal fin is set very far back on the body. Finally the peculiar mouth, with a very elongated lower jaw, is not only unmistakable but has also given rise to the popular name of 'Half beaks'.

The genus Dermogenys

The genus *Dermogenys* is the only genus in the family *Hemiramphidae* which contains species normally considered to be aquarium fish. There are three species, *Dermogenys pogonognathus*, the Red Halfbeak, *Dermogenys pusillus*, the Wrestling Halfbeak, and *Dermogenys sumatranus*, the Sumatra Half-

beak. Of these, only the last two are usually found in aquariums. *D.pogonognathus* is somewhat larger than *D.pusillus* and has a faint red tinge to the whole body: otherwise it closely resembles *D.pusillus,* and in the very unlikely event of an amateur aquiring a specimen, it should be given the same care as *D.pusillus. D.pogonognathus* was formerly called *Hemirhamphodon pogonognathus.*
All these species come from Southeast Asia, where they are much valued as a natural control of mosquitoes and other dangerous surface insects, for their unusual mouths are admirably suited to catching these insects which constitute their main diet.

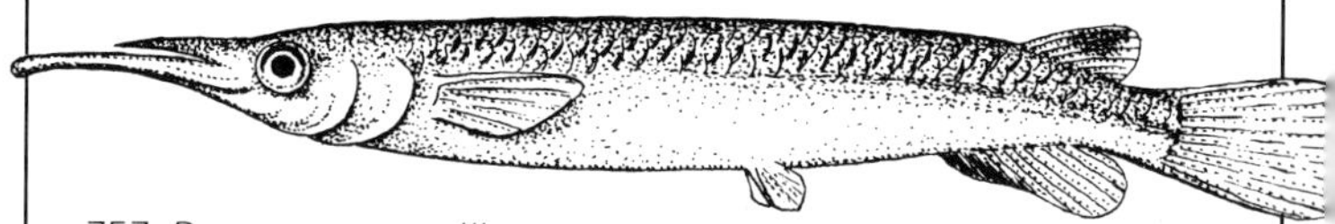
757. *Dermogenys pusillus*

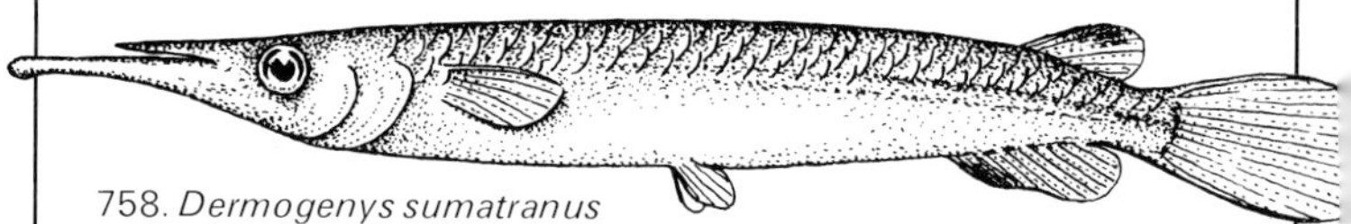
758. *Dermogenys sumatranus*

DERMOGENYS PUSILLUS

Family: *Hemirhamphidae*

Genus: *Dermogenys*

English name: Wrestling Halfbeak

Origin: Thailand, Malaysia, Singapore and the islands of the Sunda strait.

Size: Approximately 6 cm

Habitat: Found in both brackish and fresh waters

SHAPE, COLORING AND MARKINGS: The body is elongated, slender and laterally slightly compressed. The lower jaw is greatly elongated and beak-like. The basic coloration varies significantly according to the place of origin. Specimens from Java are predominantly silvery: the back is a pale brown tinged with green; the belly silvery white. Under bright light a bluish tinge becomes apparent. The elongated lower jaw usually has a decorative dark, sometimes red line running along its length. Some specimens have an indistinct shoulder mark on the dorsal fin. The front fin rays of the anal fin are usually black.
Females are slightly larger than males. There is no red mark on the dorsal fin.
Males are as described above, with on the anal fin, short front rays which form the sexual organ.

GENERAL CARE: *D.pusillus* is suitable for a large aquarium with plenty of floating plants. The composition of the water is not critical but a small amount of salt, about two or three teaspoons full for every 10 liters, should be added, particularly when caring for imported specimens. Temperature 18°–22°C. Males may be very aggressive towards each other, but are tolerant of all other species. *D.pusillus* keeps mainly to the top of the tank. Any live animal matter close to the surface will be snapped up. Winged surface insects are an essential part of the diet if the fish are being prepared for breeding: dried food will also be accepted for a change.

BREEDING: Not difficult. The reproductive behavior is unusual. The male swims under the female and pricks her belly with the point of his 'beak' for some time. If the female tolerates these advances, both fish jump out of the water quite unexpectedly and fertilization takes place. Depending on the temperature, the gestation period is four to six weeks. The brood of at most 20 are not difficult to raise with the usual food for fry. The 'beak' only starts to develop after about 6 weeks.
ADDITIONAL INFORMATION: D. pusillus is sometimes called *Hemirhamphus fluviatilis.* Although not common in aquariums it has been known to aquarists for a long time.

DERMOGENYS SUMATRANUS

Family: *Hemirhamphidae*

Genus: *Dermogenys*

English name: Sumatra Halfbeak

Origin: Singapore, Sumatra, Borneo

Size: Approximately 5 cm

Habitat: Found in both brackish and fresh waters

SHAPE, COLORING AND MARKINGS: The body shape and beak are almost identical to those of *D.pusillus* but in *D.sumatranus* the ventral fin lies nearer to the head than to the anal fin, which is not the case with *D.pusillus.* The basic coloration of *D.sumatranus* is more brownish than that of *D.pusillus,* and the former has no line on the jaw. The fins are yellowish or bright lemon: males have a red mark on the dorsal fin. The front rays of the anal fin are generally black, or very dark.
Females are slightly larger than males and have no mark on the dorsal fin.
Males are as described above. The anal fin is as in *D.pusillus.*

GENERAL CARE: As for *D.pusillus.*

BREEDING: *D.sumatranus* has not yet it seems been bred in captivity.

THE FAMILY CENTRARCHIDAE

An introductory description

The family *Centrarchidae* contains the Sunfishes and Basses. All these fish come from North America, generally from the central and eastern regions, and are found usually in clear waters, inland: usually fairly quiet waters with a sandy bottom and some vegetation. They are related to the Perch family and most species have the same rather stocky body profile. They also have another family characteristic, that of two nostrils on either side of the snout.

There are a number of genera in the family and quite a large number of species, but very few in fact have become popular or common aquarium fish. They are not of course really tropical fish at all and this is one reason probably why they have not acquired, or in the case of *Mesogonistius chaetodon* retained, popularity with aquarists. One species however, *Elassoma evergladei,* is well known and is described below.
The Sunfish are on the whole fairly robust, and many can be kept very successfully in outdoor ponds provided the winters are not too severe: however they are sensitive to sudden changes of temperature or water composition, and any change to the environment should be made carefully and gradually.
Some of the larger species are predatory, but Sunfish generally take great care of their young. The eggs are usually laid in carefully prepared hollows or quasi-nests, and when hatched are shepherded by the male.

THE FAMILY CENTRARCHIDAE

The genus Elassoma

There are only three species in this genus, *Elassoma okefenokee* (which is very rarely seen) *Elassoma zonatum*, the Banded Pigmy or Dwarf Sunfish, and *Elassoma evergladei*, the well-known Dwarf or Pigmy Sunfish. *E.zonatum*, which is found somewhat further south than *E.evergladei*, is distinguished, as its name would suggest, by the 11–12 prominent dark bands on the flanks. It requires the same care as *E.evergladei*.

ELASSOMA EVERGLADEI

Family: *Centrarchidae*

Genus: *Elassoma*

English names: Dwarf Sunfish, Pygmy Sunfish

Origin: USA, North Carolina to Florida

Size: Maximum 3.5 cm

Habitat: Found in the Everglades.

SHAPE, COLORING AND MARKINGS: The body is slightly elongated, relatively high and laterally only slightly compressed. The dorsal fin has a long base: the anal fin is slightly smaller. All the fins are rounded. The mouth is small and slightly upward pointing. The basic coloration is a greenish yellow to muddy brown, with irregular dark dots and stripes producing a marbling effect.
Females are a darker color during the spawning season and have more rounded bellies.
Males are as described above, but in the spawning season the body and fins become a deep bluish or velvety black with shiny, greenish-blue flecks.

GENERAL CARE: *E.evergladei* is a territorial fish best kept in a spacious species tank, well stocked round the edges with fine leaved plants. The water should be matured, and medium hard: temperatures 15°–22° C, and lower in winter. Only if kept at a low temperature during the winter will the fish be in good condition the following summer. The diet should consist of small live animal matter, Tubifex, Cyclops and mosquito larvae.

BREEDING: The fish will often spawn in the ordinary species tank. If a special breeding tank is used, it should have old hard water and a bottom of well-boiled peat fibres. *E.evergladei* wil develop its mating color pattern when the temperature rises to about 20° C. The small eggs are laid among the fineleaved plants: the parent fish should be removed after spawning. The fry (up to 40) are extremely small and stay among the pieces of peat on the bed for a few days, invisible even to the expert eye. The fry should be fed with the finest pond infusoria as soon as they begin to swim freely.

THE FAMILY CENTROPOMIDAE

An introductory description

The *Centropomidae* or Glassfish family is made up of a group of fish that are found over a wide area of East Africa and the Pacific. Most of them are however salt-water fish and it is only species in the genus, *Chanda* that is of interest to aquarists: it includes the popular Indian Glassfish, *Chanda ranga*. As their name suggests these fish are almost transparent: their delicately colored translucent bodies make them very delicate and attractive fish in an aquarium.
For a long time the family was named *Ambassidae*, and the genus *Chanda* was called *Ambassis*: amateurs will still find that nomenclature used in the older literature.

The genus Chanda

The genus *Chanda* (formerly *Ambassis*) contains a number of species of Glassfish. Two of these, *Chanda ranga*, the Indian Glassfish and *Chanda wolffi* are quite well known to aquarists and are described below. Other species are: *Chanda agassizi*, *Chanda buruensis*, *Chanda commersoni*, and *Chanda nama*.

CHANDA RANGA

Family: *Centropomidae*

Genus: *Chanda*

English name: Indian Glassfish

Origin: Eastern India, Pakistan, Burma, Western Thailand

Size: Maximum 6 cm

Habitat: Found mainly in coastal areas, in both fresh and brackish waters

SHAPE, COLORING AND MARKINGS: The body is rather stocky, relatively deep and laterally very compressed. The dorsal, anal and ventral fins are divided into two parts: the front part has only hard rays: the first ray of the second part is also hard, but the others are soft. The caudal fin is fairly deeply forked. The entire

759. *Chanda ranga* (male)

body is glassy and transparent, with irregular black flecks and, under bright light an iridescent bluish green, golden sheen. The fins are yellowish: the dorsal and anal fins have sky blue borders.
Females are less vividly colored.
Males are as described above.

GENERAL CARE: *C.ranga* is suitable for a community tank with other peaceful species. The tank should have dense clumps of fine leaved plants as well as plenty of free swimming space. The water should not be too soft and four grams of sea salt should be added for every ten liters: temperature 25°C. *C.ranga* is sensitive to environmental changes, which should only be made very gradually. The only suitable food is live animal matter, Daphnia, Cyclops and mosquito larvae.

BREEDING: The fry will only eat Cyclops *nauplii*. Unless plenty are available, these fish should not be bred because the fry will inevitably starve to death. For breeding, a small tank(of about 20 liters capacity) should be used with a bed of well-rinsed sand: some clumps of Myrophyllum should be put in. Fresh fairly hard water with one gram of sea salt for every liter of water should be used. Temperature 27°C. The tank should be put in a sunny position. When the breeding pair are introduced they will hide among the plants for the first few days but will soon become less timid, particularly if fed on Enchytrae. They will usually begin mating in the early morning. The eggs are laid among the plants, usually over a period of a few days. The parent fish should be removed when the fry are free swimming. The fry will not hunt for food. The water should therefore be no deeper than 10 cm and be slightly aerated so that the Cyclops *nauplii* circulate around the fry. Alternatively three sides of the tank can be darkened with black paper on the outside and then both the fry and the Cyclops *nauplii* will tend to congregate at the lightest point and the chances of the fry catching their food will be improved. Nests of 300 or more are not unusual. The water should be changed daily. The fry should be fed sparingly but frequently each day rather than given one substantial feeding. Once the fry have become accustomed to other kinds of food (after a week or so) the fish can be raised like other perch. At first they grow quickly but after about a month the rate of growth slows down: this is natural and is no cause for alarm.

760. *Chanda wolffi* (female)

CHANDA WOLFFI

Family: *Centropomidae*
Genus: *Chanda*
English name: none
Origin: Indonesia, Thailand
Size: Maximum 20 cm in the wild, but no more than 10 cm in captivity
Habitat: Found only in fresh waters

SHAPE, COLORING AND MARKINGS: The body shape and fin structure is identical to that of *C.ranga*. The glassy translucent body is a pale yellow, without the iridescence of *C.ranga*. No fin has a blue edge.
There are no known external sexual characteristics.

GENERAL CARE: As for *C.ranga* but no salt should be added to the water.

BREEDING: *C.wolffi* has not it seems, as yet been bred in captivity.

THE FAMILY CICHLIDAE

An introductory description

The perch-like *Cichlidae* family is part of the sub-order *Percoides*. The *Cichlidae* or cichlids, are found principally in Africa, Central America and tropical areas of South America: few species are found in southern Asia. They are distinguished by taxonomists from true perches by the structure of the pharynx and by having only one nostril on each side of the snout. The body is usually deep, or very deep, occasionally disc shaped and then it is laterally very compressed: few species have elongated bodies. The head is relatively large and in older males, in certain species, becomes disproportionately so through layers of fat that develop there. The snout is usually large and bulging. The front parts of the dorsal and anal fins have a number of quill-like rays. In males these fins are frequently elongated, often with some very extended rays. In a few species such as the Angelfish in the genus *Pterophyllum*, the fins are extended with thread-like rays. The caudal fin may be rounded or fairly square at the end. The lateral line is usually broken into two sections.

761. *Aequidens curviceps*

In the wild most cichlids live in still or slow moving waters (although a few are found in brackish waters) and where there are a lot of good hiding places to be found, along banks, among tree roots or submerged branches, in heaps of stones or in dense plant growth. Most species lay claim to a territory and will defend it against intruders, especially during the mating season. Most species are predatory, feeding on smaller fishes (including those in their own species) and insects. The *Geophagus* and *Tilapia* species are exceptions and feed mainly on vegetable matter.

Keeping cichlids can be very interesting but these fish (except for the Dwarf cichlids and Discus fish) have acquired a bad reputation among amateurs because they tend to dig up the bottom, damage plants and behave intolerantly towards their own and other species. This reputation is largely unmerited. Most aquarists now find that if the tank is suitably arranged for them, cichlids will behave well. Many traditional difficulties arose simply because these fish were kept in unsuitable aquariums. In the section on the Layout of the Aquarium full details are given on the best way to arrange a specialist tank for cichlids and it is well worth the trouble of doing that. Only in such a specialist tank will the larger species such as the *Aequidens, Cichlasoma, Geophagus, Hemichromis* and *Tilapia* be seen to advantage. A gravelly bottom, no submerged plants, plenty of hiding places among rocks and bogwood, with some tough floating vegetation will provide the perfect environment for these fish. Other species which do not dig so enthusiastically can be given some tough marsh plants, preferably put in pots submerged in the gravel. Of course, the species that in the wild like to hide among plants should be provided with some dense vegetation: details are given under the species descriptions in the genera *Apistogramma, Pelmatochromis, Pterophyllum* and *Symphysodon* below.

Cichlids are not fussy about food. All kinds of live food will be eaten greedily and some dried food should be given for variety. Many species will eat horseflesh, ox heart and liver. Vegetarians like the *Tilapia* and some of the *Cichlasoma* and *Geophagus* require fresh lettuce, boiled spinach, oatmeal and algae. Most cichlids have a voracious appetite and will, if allowed to, overeat. A modest amount of food is better for the fish and overfeeding is all too common.

The problems of breeding have not yet been solved for some of these species: many others however can be bred without too much difficulty in captivity. Details are given in the species descriptions below. Very often the main difficulty is in selecting a pair that will mate and where the male will overcome his aggressiveness. Young cichlids are usually very tolerant and frequently live in shoals: intolerance, greed and even cannibalistic tendencies develop as the fish mature. Adult cichlids are usually very aggressive: it is not uncommon for one dominant specimen to kill off all the other fish in the tank. Some of this aggressiveness can be curbed by providing the fish with a large tank with plenty of hiding places, but the need for caution always remains. Particular care must be taken when bringing a male and female together: the most likely pair to agree is a pair from the same nest. Natural pairing can sometimes be observed taking place at a very early age, when a couple move away from the shoal together: this kind of natural pairing may also happen when the fish are somewhat older and such spontaneous pairing is of course ideal. Otherwise a selected pair should be put in one tank but separated by a sheet of glass: after several days the glass can be removed for a few hours while the fish are kept under observation. It should always be replaced at night however until the daytime behavior of the male shows that the pair are happy together and are showing an inclination to mate. Even than however the male may suddenly change and attack the female.

Fortunately not all cichlids are so intolerant. The *Pterophyllum, Cichlasoma severum,* most *Tilapia* and *Aequidens* species and some of the *Haplochromis* are usually more tolerant of each other and mating therefore present fewer problems.

Mating generally follows very quickly after a harmonious pairing has been achieved, and most species are very prolific. However some of these fish, brooders, the *Symphysodon* and *Uaru* are difficult even for the experienced amateur to breed.

Many cichlids lay their eggs on stones, in hollows or on broad leaved plants. The site is first carefully cleaned and this may take several days. Other species, including the mouth brooders, excavate a flat bottomed depression before mating.

Females ready to spawn can usually be identified by their rounded bellies. In other species the sexes are easily distinguished by the genital papillae which appear shortly before mating. In the females the oviduct is almost always short and cone-shaped: its equivalent in the males is more pointed and considerably shorter.

Mating behavior differs according to the species: in some it is gentle and relaxed and in others it involves what seems like vicious biting.

The females usually lays the eggs in rows or heaps, three to eight on each occasion: the male follows immediately behind her with genital papillae erect, and fertilises the eggs. Many matings may well take place successively. The size of the clutch varies from species to species: mouth brooders and dwarf cichlids usually lay a smaller number of larger eggs than the bigger species. The eggs themselves are very adhesive. Both parents usually help to guard them, circulating the water around them by fanning with their pectoral fins. In the genus *Apistogramma* the male alone guards and fans the eggs. In some species, the parents chew the egg coverings to release the young. Most

eggs hatch two to four days after being laid. Mouth brooders however behave differently. The newly-laid eggs are moved to new hollows or on to broad leaved plants and then when hatched the fry are constantly moved about between such sites by the watchful parents. If the fry become contaminated with dirt, the parents will clean them in their mouths. As soon as the fry are able to swim freely they are taken about on exploratory tours by the parents and are made to keep in a strict tight shoal formation. Laggards are chased back into the pack and may even be brought back to it in the parent's mouth. The movement of the shoal is controlled by signals from the parents. Recent studies show that the fry react not only to the movements of the parents but also to sounds they emit.
The parents will often masticate food and then expel it for the fry to eat, but the breeder should still give the fry plenty of live animal food to train them in hunting. Young cichlids grow very quickly and the shoal pattern soon disintegrates. The parents' brood care instincts also then begin to weaken and at that point it is best to separate the parents from the fry, although this is not necessary in the case of *Pterophyllum eimeki* and *Pterophyllum scalare*.
Some of the most unusual fish are those mouth brooders that store the eggs, once they have been laid and fertilised, in their mouths. The eggs are kept in the throat sac and are moved about there to receive adequate oxygen. The young remain in the parent's mouth until they have fed off the yolk sac and may even afterwards retreat back into the mouth if in danger. It is usually the female that looks after the brood in this way but in the case of *Tilapia galilea* both parents are involved and in the case of *Pelmatochromis guentheri* they take it in turn. The parents do not take any food during the period of mouth brooding, which may extend over four or five weeks.
Many pairs eat the first clutch of eggs but pay more attention to subsequent clutches. However, if the breeding tank is disturbed or the fish become frightened they may always destroy the clutch or eat the fry.
Cichlids are not usually fussy about the composition of the water in the tank but are very sensitive to sudden changes in the composition of the water and to being moved from one environment to another.

The genus Aequidens

The genus *Aequidens* contains a group of very attractive cichlids all of which come from South America and most of which have found considerable favor with amateurs. Five species are described below, *A.curviceps,* the Flag cichlid, *A.maroni,* the Keyhole cichlid, *A.portalgrensis,* the Port or Black Acara *A.pulcher,* the Blue Acara, and *A.tetramerus,* the Saddle cichlid. There is another species, *A.thayeri* which seems never to have been imported, although specimens of *A.curviceps* are sometimes sold under that name. Some authorities also list another species *A.latifrons,* but this name is a synonym for *A.pulcher:* nevertheless amateurs will often find the Blue Acara listed in the literature as *Aequidens latifrons.* Most species of Aequidens are fairly tolerant and, as noted in the descriptions below, are not too difficult to keep, provided their basic needs are taken into account. This is a genus of special interest to aquarists who are beginning to take an interest in Cichlids for the first time: it contains species of different, but characteristic disposition. *A.curviceps,* although just too large technically to be considered a dwarf cichlid, closely resembles dwarf cichlids in behavior; *A.portelagrenis* is probably the easiest of all cichlids to breed; the shy *A.maroni* will introduce the aquarist to get other characteristicly cichlid patterns of behavior.

762. *Aequidens maronii*

AEQUIDENS CURVICEPS

Family: *Cichlidae*

Genus: *Aequidens*

English names: Flag Cichlid, Sheepshead Acara

Origin: South America, the Amazon basin

Size: Maximum 8 cm

Habitat: No details are available of its natural habitat

SHAPE, COLORING AND MARKINGS: The front of the body is very deep and laterally very compressed: the head is relatively large. The basic coloration is a silvery green: the back is a brownish to olive green: the flanks are silvery grey to greenish, sometimes yellow green or even dark blue: the belly silver, white or gold. Iridescent specks and stripes lie on the gill covers and cheeks. The scales on the upper half of the body have a dark border. Two prominent dark patches lie on the body, one immediately behind the gill covers, the other, rather smaller, level with the front rays of the anal fin: in some specimens a pale longitudinal stripe runs from the eye to these dark patches. The iris is gold, with red iridescence above. The base of the dorsal fin is blue-green, the center a gleaming gold, the border greenish to white, often with red tips. The caudal and anal fins are greenish, the ventral fins pale blue, the pectoral fins pale green. Pale blue iridescent spots appear in the soft rays of the dorsal, anal and caudal fins.
Females are less vividly colored and have shorter rays.
Males are as described above.

GENERAL CARE: *A.curviceps* is suitable for the conventional community tank except during the mating period: it does not attack plants.

It is tolerant towards members of its own and other species except when spawning. It occupies the lower and middle water levels. The composition of the water is not critical: temperature 18°–25°C. All kinds of live animal food will be accepted.

BREEDING: This is not difficult. The first clutch is usually eaten after a day or two but subsequent broods are tended very carefully. Breeding temperature 27°C: the water should be pH 7–7.2. The 150–250 eggs hatch in three days: the fry remain in the nest for three days and are free swimming on the seventh day. They should be fed then for a week on *Artemia nauolii*, and during the second week on microworms.

AEQUIDENS MARONII

Family: *Cichlidae*

Genus: *Aequidens*

English name: Keyhole Cichlid

Origin: The Guianas

Size: Maximum 10 cm

Habitat: No details are available of its natural habitat

SHAPE, COLORING AND MARKINGS: The body shape closely resembles that of *A.curviceps*, but the forehead is very high. The basic coloration varies, usually from yellow to pale brown, but sometimes it is even chocolate. 12–13 indistinct longitudinal stripes of dark stipples lie on the body and a deep black longitudinal stripe runs across the forehead, over the eye to the edge of the cheeks. A round black patch with a golden center lies on the back, and depending on the mood of the fish may extend to the belly, when it then resembles a keyhole. Rows of pale green iridescent flecks are found on the soft rays of the dorsal and anal fins, which usually have white tips.

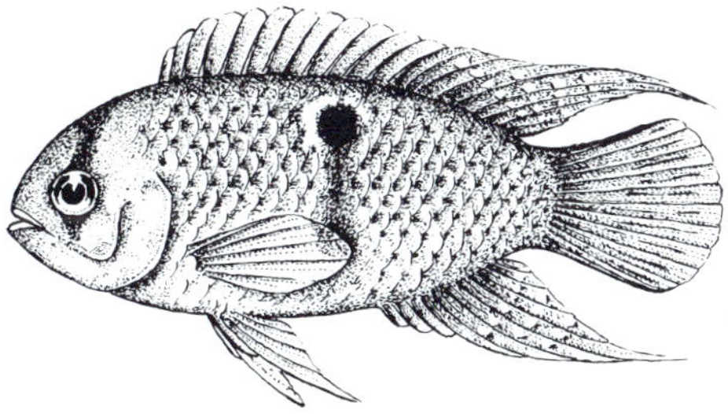

763. *Aequidens maroni*

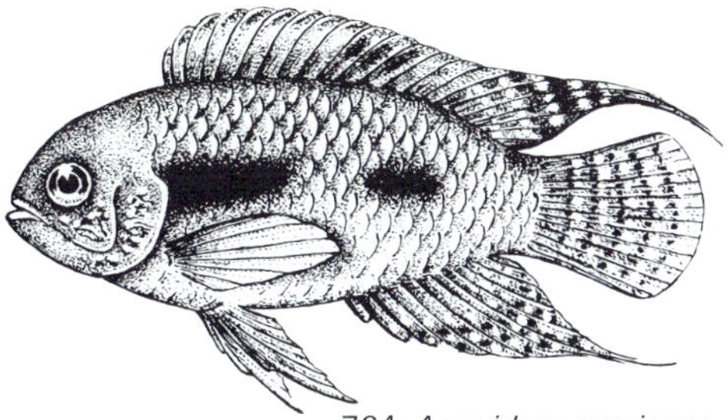

764. *Aequidens curviceps*

765. *Aequidens portelagrensis*

Females have less well developed dorsal and anal fins.
Males are as described above.

GENERAL CARE: As for *A.curviceps*, but *A.maronii* needs a relatively large tank.

BREEDING: Not difficult. As for *A.curviceps*, but there is no need to separate the father from the fry for about 6 months.

ADDITIONAL INFORMATION: One of the best species.

AEQUIDENS PORTELAGRENSIS

Family: *Cichlidae*

Genus: *Aequidens*

English name: Port or Black Acara

Origin: South Brazil, Bolivia

Size: Maximum 25 cm in the wild, but considerably smaller in captivity, when it is sexually mature at 10 cm

Habitat: No details are available of its natural habitat

SHAPE, COLORING AND MARKINGS: The body shape is identical to *A.curviceps*. The basic coloration varies significantly according to the age of the fish and its place of origin. Young specimens may be greenish, bluish or brownish with a blue, yellow or reddish sheen. The scales on the upper part of the body have dark borders. A prominent broad dark longitudinal stripe runs along the body and ends as a dark brown patch, bordered by a zone of pale green or gleaming yellow, on the caudal peduncle. When the fish is excited the whole body may become very dark or black. The caudal and anal fins are a pale to brownish green with a pale green iridescent stripe and patches. The dorsal fin is a bluish grey: the pectoral fins a pale wine red.
Females have browner fins.
Males are as described above.

GENERAL CARE: *A.portelagrensis* needs a large species tank, or an aquarium shared only with large species. It likes to grub about at the bottom and will dig up plants: a bottom of sand should therefore be provided, with bogwood for shelter. This species is fairly tolerant outside the mating season, and will be found in all water levels. The composition of the water is not critical but it should be changed regularly: temperature; winter, 16°–20°C, summer 20°–24°C. Diet as for *A.curviceps*.

BREEDING: Not difficult: as for *A.curviceps*, but *A.portelagrensis* will always dig the bed to make breeding cavities.

AEQUIDENS PULCHER

Family: *Cichlidae*

Genus: *Aequidens*

English name: Blue Acara

Origin: Columbia, Panama, Trinidad, Venezuela

Size: Maximum 17 cm in the wild, but usually remains much smaller in captivity

Habitat: Found in still and sluggish waters

SHAPE, COLORING AND MARKINGS: The body is egg-shaped, deep and laterally very compressed. The basic coloration is an olive to yellow green: the back is darker: the belly grey-green to bluish. On the flanks lie eight faint transverse bars, and a number of more prominent transverse lines, each separated by rows of gleaming gold or green scales. Dark patches lie under the eye and in the middle of the body: a crescent-shaped transverse band is found on the caudal peduncle. The gill covers and cheeks have green iridescent patches, and similar but smaller patches are found on the body. The dorsal and anal fins are an ochre yellow: the ventral and pectoral fins blue-green: the dorsal, anal and caudal fins have patterns of dark spots.
Females have usually darker bellies.

766. *Aequidens pulcher*

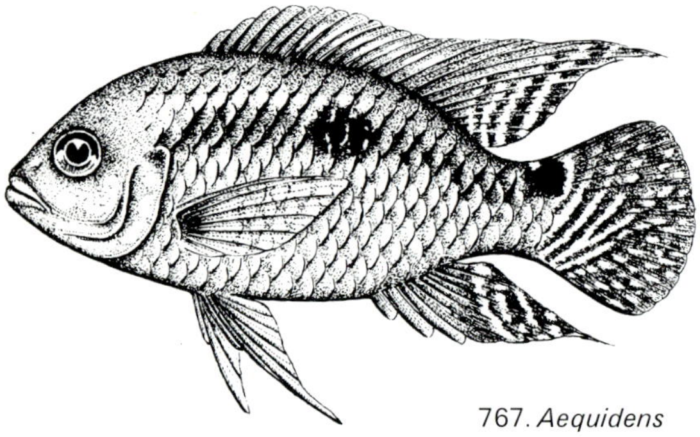

767. *Aequidens pulcher*

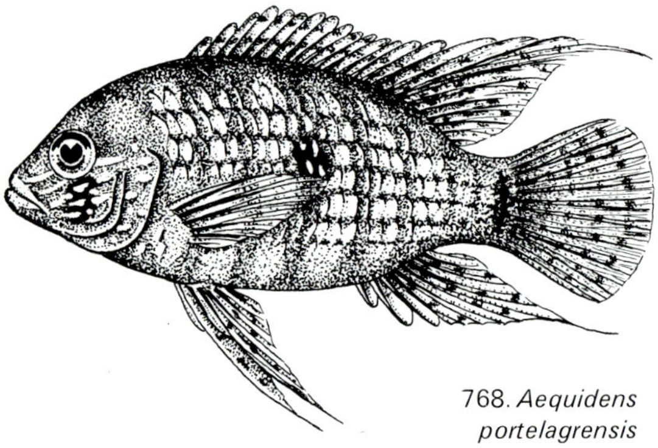

768. *Aequidens portelagrensis*

Males are as described above, with elongated rays to the anal and dorsal fins.

GENERAL CARE: As for *A.portelagrensis* but temperature 18°–25°C. *A.pulcher* will be very prone to diseases if the water becomes old: it must be changed frequently.

BREEDING: Not difficult. As for *A.curviceps*. *A.pulcher* is sexually mature at 7–8 cm, and will breed many times a year.

AEQUIDENS TETRAMERUS

Family: *Cichlidae*

Genus: *Aequidens*

English name: Saddle Cichlid

Origin: Northeast and Central South America

Size: Maximum 20 cm in the wild: no more than 15 cm in captivity

Habitat: Found in still and running waters

SHAPE, COLORING AND MARKINGS: The body is more slender than in related species. The basic coloration varies from greyish green to brownish, depending on the locality of origin. A dark line runs from the eye to a characteristic black patch ringed with gold on the caudal peduncle: a black mark lies within this dark band, halfway along the body, but varies in intensity according to the mood of the fish, as do a number of less distinct transverse bands. The head is an iridescent green with a pattern of luminescent blue marks.
Females are less vividly colored and are usually greyish brown. The dorsal and anal fins are more or less rounded.
Males are as described above. The rays of the dorsal and anal fins are elongated and taper to a point.

GENERAL CARE: As for *A.portelagrensis*. *A.tetramerus* can be very aggressive. The hardness of the water should not exceed 13°DH: temperature 21°–24°C, although lower temperatures will be tolerated for short periods.

BREEDING: As for *A.curviceps*. Because of its aggressive nature, *A.tetramerus* is best bred from natural pairs (see Family introduction). The young fish are a beautiful bluish green.

THE FAMILY CICHLIDAE

The genus Apistogramma

The *Apistogramma,* a genus of Dwarf Cichlids, are only found in South America, in slightly acid waters, where the vegetation is mostly floating plants or plants with floating leaves, and where there are dene clumps of roots along the banks which provide numerous shaded hiding places.

These fish need a carefully arranged aquarium as described in the section on Aquarium lay out. The water should be soft or mildly acid, preferably filtered through peat, and some must be regularly changed. The temperature should be 23°–25° C, although a few species such as *A.agassizi* can be kept at temperatures as low as 17°–19° C during the winter. A carefully chosen diet including Daphnia, Cyclops and mosquito larvae or worms is essential to health. Most species are highly sensitive to a wide range of aquarium diseases and chemical water pollution.

Those species which will breed in captivity can usually be bred with little difficulty in tanks with plenty of floating plants: eggs will usually be laid several times a year. The eggs will usually be laid in cavities with restricted entrances, for example inverted flower pots, or pieces of coconut shell, but may be laid on the underside of flat stones. The eggs are usually yellow to brownish red, oval, and adhesive.

The female looks after the brood. The amateur can tell when eggs have been laid by the change in coloration and behavior of the female: she takes on a very attractive patterning and starts to chase all other fish, including her mate, out of the area. It is best to remove the male after mating. The eggs usually hatch after 2–5 days although the fry are not free swimming for another four to six days, and meanwhile feed off the yolk sac. The female will move them about from one nesting place to another. Once the fry are free swimming the mother leads them through the tank in a group. It is interesting to observe how the different species react to danger signals from the parent: some drop swiftly to the bottom and become almost invisible, others cluster round her in a dense swarm.

The fry can be reared with little difficulty on *Artemia nauplii* and similar sieved food. The *Apistogramma* quite often eat the first clutch of eggs, but subsequent clutches are carefully tended: these will be produced at intervals of 4–6 weeks in many species. The female will remove unfertilized eggs and in many species will chew away the hard covering of the egg. It is not unusual for more males than females to be produced.

Many species in this genus are peculiarly liable to tuberculosis, and this condition may be confused with Ichthyosporidium disease (for which see the section on deseases).

APISTOGRAMMA AGASSIZI

Family: *Cichlidae*

Genus: *Apistogramma*

English name: Agassiz' Dwarf Cichlid

Origin: From the Amazon Basin to Bolivia

Size: Maximum 7.5 cm

Habitat: Found in shaded waters, particularly between submerged roots

SHAPE, COLORING AND MARKINGS: The body is elongated and laterally compressed. The basic coloration is orange with a green overtone: the back is brownish yellow to blue-green: the whole body is flecked with tiny iridescent blue-green specks. A distinct brown longitudinal stripe runs back from the snout to the caudal peduncle but avoids the eye: a darker stripe lies on the cheek. The gill covers have pale blue iridescent marks. The elongated dorsal fin is black at the base, blue-green at the front and greyish, with a pale red border and elongated rays at the back. The anal fin is yellow-green with a red edge, and elongated rays. The caudal fin is heart-shaped: the upper lobe is a marbled green-grey, the center an ivory yellow with bluish green marks, the lower lobe orange-red, becoming bluish-green towards the edge. The ventral fin is orange-red with black rays, the pectoral fin colorless and transparent.

Females are smaller, and predominantly lemon-yellow: the longitudinal line is indistinct and sometimes broken up into a number of patches. The dorsal and anal fins are more rounded, and the rays never elongated.

Males are as described above.

GENERAL CARE: *A.agassizi* needs a large tank with plenty of hiding places between stones, or bogwood or in flower pots or coconut shells. Scattered clumps of broad leaved plants should be put in the tank. The water should be soft, preferably filtered through peat and regularly topped up: temperature 23°–26° C in summer, 17°–19° C in winter. *A.agassizi* will usually swim in the lower reaches and is a tolerant species except during mating periods. The diet should be live food such as Daphnia, Cyclops, mosquito larvae and worms: dried foods will not be accepted at all.

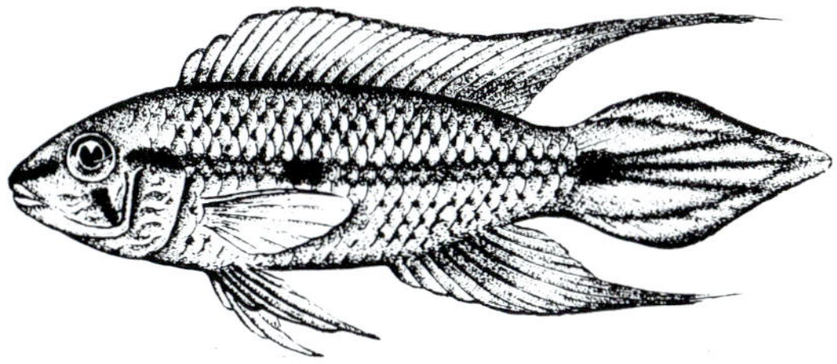

770. *Apistogramma agassizi*

BREEDING: See Introductory note. The temperature should be 26°–27° C, and the water in the breeding tank as above. There will be 80–150 eggs, probably laid in a flower pot, and they will hatch in about three days: the fry will be free-swimming in seven days and should be fed from the first week on *Artemia nauplii* and microworms.

769. *Apistogramma borellii*

APISTOGRAMMA BORELLII

Family: *Cichlidae*

Genus: *Apistogramma*

English name: Borelli's Dwarf Cichlid

Origin: Northern South America, the Matto Grosso, the Paraguay River, Argentina

Size: Maximum 7.5 cm

Habitat: Found in shaded waters

SHAPE, COLORING AND MARKINGS: The body is fairly deep and laterally compressed. The basic coloration is brownish with a blue overtone: the back a dark brown to brownish green: the throat and belly an ochre yellow.

A very dark line runs from the eye to the throat: other less prominent lines are found running from the eye to the gill covers and along the side to the caudal peduncle. The scales below this latter longitudinal stripe have dark edges which show up as a netlike pattern. The dorsal, anal and caudal fins are blue: the anal and caudal fins have pale blue iridescent flecks, and the latter a yellow gleam. Similarly colored flecks lie on the cheeks and gill covers.
Females are usually smaller, less vividly colored, and have no elongated fin rays.
Males are as described above, with elongated rays in the dorsal, anal and caudal fins.

GENERAL CARE: As for *A.agassizi* but temperature 23°–26° C, not below 22° C in winter.

BREEDING: Not too difficult: as for *A.agassizi.*

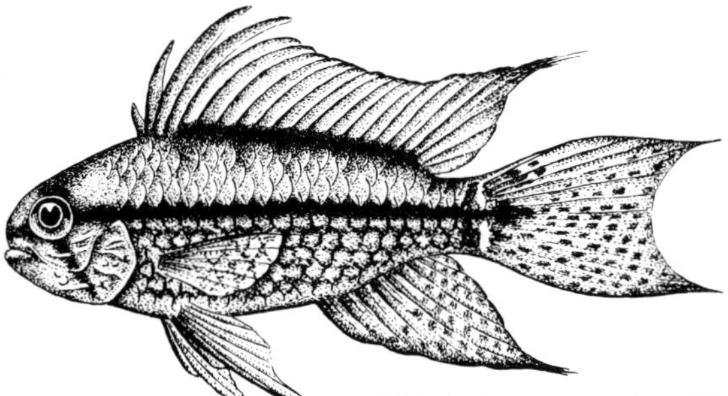

771. *Apistogramma borellii*

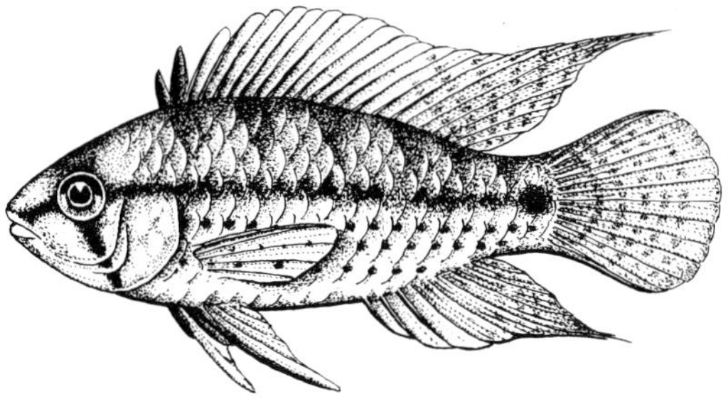

772. *Apistogramma commbrae*

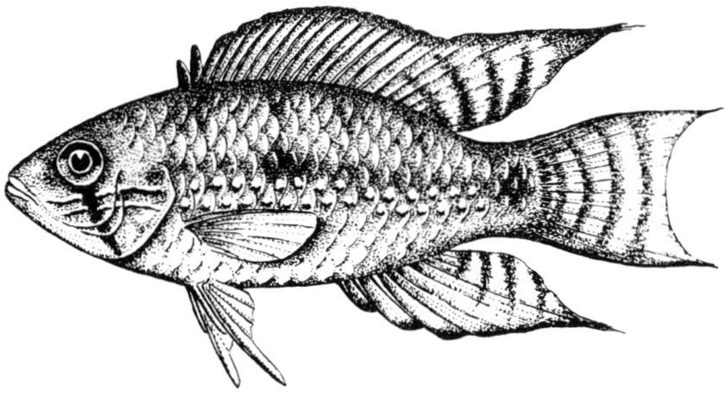

773. *Apistogramma ornatipinnis*

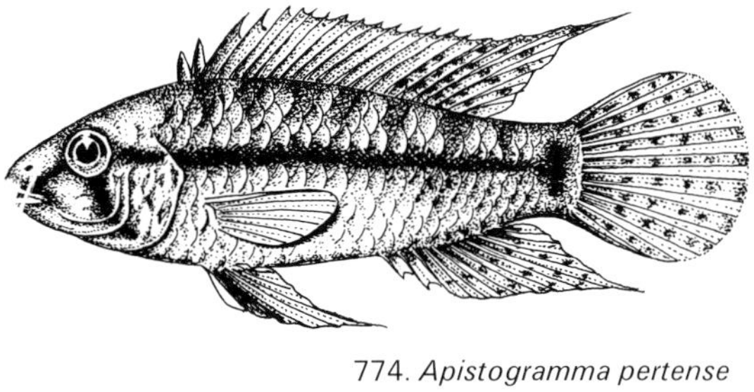

774. *Apistogramma pertense*

APISTOGRAMMA CACATUOIDES

Family: *Cichlidae*

Genus: *Apistogramma*

English names: Cockatoo Dwarf Cichlid, Crested Dwarf Cichlid

Origin: The Guianas

Size: Males to 5 cm: females somewhat smaller

Habitat: Found in shaded waters

SHAPE, COLORING AND MARKINGS: The body is fairly slender but more cylindrical than in related species. The basic coloration is a brownish yellow: the belly is lighter: the scales have a bluish sheen. A prominent dark band runs from the eye to the caudal peduncle, another runs down from the eye to the edge of the gill covers. A sometimes indistinct dark mark lies at the base of the dorsal fin. The rays of the ventral, anal and dorsal fins are elongated, the latter a bluish black. The caudal, dorsal and anal fins are whitish with a light blue pattern.
Females are less vividly colored, and the fin rays are shorter. When spawning the females are a canary yellow, with a deep black horizontal line on the head.
Males are as described above: during the spawning season the colors become more vivid.

GENERAL CARE: As for *A.agassizi,* but very soft, slightly acid water is needed. Temperature 25° C. One male should be kept with two females, or three males with a group of females.

BREEDING: As for *A.agassizi,* but the eggs are deposited on the roof of a cavity, and the female turns on her back to lay them. A male may mate with two females, and will then guard both nests. The fry need to be fed on infusoria for the first few days.

ADDITIONAL INFORMATION: It is likely that *Apistogramma* U_2, a name applied to a variety in the USA, is a synonym for *A.cacatuoides.*

APISTOGRAMMA COMMBRAE

Family: *Cichildae*

Genus: *Apistogramma*

English name: Corumba Dwarf Cichlid

Origin: Brazil, the basin of the Paraná river

Size: Maximum 5.5 cm

Habitat: Found in shaded waters

SHAPE, COLORING AND MARKINGS: The body is slender and laterally very compressed. The basic coloration varies according to the mood of the fish and its locality of origin, but is commonly yellow-brown to ochre: the back has a vivid green sheen: the belly is off-white. A prominent black longitudinal stripe runs across the eye, along the body and becomes a round patch on the caudal peduncle. A number of sometimes indistinct dark transverse bands lie on the upper part of the body, and dark specks appear on the underside. A distinctive curved stripe is found on the cheeks and gill covers, and may extend to the throat. All the fins are grey: the soft rays of the dorsal, anal and caudal fins have lines of dark stipples.
Females are smaller and have no elongated rays in the dorsal and anal fins.
Males are as described above, with elongated dorsal and anal fin rays.

GENERAL CARE: As for *A.borellii,* but winter temperature not lower than 19°C.

BREEDING: Not too difficult: as for *A.agassizi.* The female becomes very aggressive after spawning and it is best to remove her.

ADDITIONAL INFORMATION: This species was first described by Charles Tait Regan in 1906. It seems that he intended to give it a different name from *A.commbrae,* and in an article written in 1913 called it *A.corumbae,* but nevertheless the ungainly name *A.commbrae* is still used.

APISTOGRAMMA KLEEI

Family: *Cichlidae*

Genus: *Apistogramma*

English name: none

Origin: The Amazon basin

Size: Maximum 7 cm

Habitat: No details are available

SHAPE, COLORING AND MARKINGS: The body is elongated and laterally slightly compressed. The basic coloration is a greyish, yellowish brown. A black band runs from the eye to the caudal peduncle: another runs down from the eye to the edge of the gill cover. The dorsal fin rays are elongated, the front rays being black. Some of the outer rays of the caudal fin are elongated so that the fin tapers to two points. The middle rays of the anal fin, and the front rays of the ventral fins are also elongated. The fins are a soft violet blue: a yellow band lies at the base of the dorsal fin, and varies in intensity, according to mood. The caudal and anal fins have red marks and flecks.
Females are smaller. Usually a dull brown: in the spawning season and when excited they become yellow with deep black marks.
Males are as described above.

GENERAL CARE: As for *A.cacatuoides,* but temperature 26° C.

775. *Apistogramma kleei*

BREEDING: As for *A.cacatuoides*, but males do not mate with more than one female.

APISTOGRAMMA ORNATIPINNIS

Family: *Cichlidae*

Genus: *Apistogramma*

English name: none

Origin: The central Amazon region

Size: Maximum 7 cm

Habitat: Found in shaded waters

SHAPE, COLORING AND MARKINGS: The body is elongated and laterally very compressed. The basic coloration is fawn to ochre: the back is a rusty brown with irregular dark patches. A sometimes indistinct dark longitudinal line runs from the eye to the caudal peduncle: two prominent dark patches lie, one in the center of the body, and the other on the caudal peduncle, and a prominent dark stripe is found on the cheeks and gill covers which also bear two silvery wavy lines. Two lines of iridescent stipples lie on the underside of the body. The dorsal and anal fins are orange, with dark borders and very elongated rays: the front rays are black and an attractive stripe appears at the back. The upper and lower edges of the striped caudal fin are reddish, and an orange zone lies in the center. The ventral fins are grey, with deep black front rays.
Females are smaller with no extended rays.
Males are as described above.

GENERAL CARE: As for *A.borellii.*

BREEDING: As for *A.agassizi.*

APISTOGRAMMA ORTMANNI

Family: *Cichlidae*

Genus: *Apistogramma*

English name: Ortmann's Dwarf Cichlid

Origin: The central Amazon basin

Size: Maximum 7 cm

Habitat: Found in shaded waters

SHAPE, COLORING AND MARKINGS: The body is elongated and laterally very compressed. The basic coloration is a dull yellow with a greenish blue sheen. There are a number of transverse bands, and one horizontal band on the body: all vary in intensity according to the mood of the fish. The back rays of the dorsal fin are elongated, as are a number of rays in the caudal fin, which thus tapers to two points. A vertical, oval black mark lies on the caudal peduncle. The fins are grey to yellow: a pattern of dark marks appears on the back part of the dorsal, the caudal and the anal fins.
Females are smaller, and less vividly colored, without elongated fin rays. During the mating season their yellow color becomes very vivid and a black horizontal line and marks on the head are prominent.
Males are as described above.

GENERAL CARE: As for *A.cacatuoides,* but temperature not below 24° C.

BREEDING: As for *A.kleei.* The nests may be very large: 200 eggs are not unusual.

APISTOGRAMMA PERTENSE

Family: *Cichlidae*

Genus: *Apistogramma*

English name: Yellow Dwarf Cichlid

Origin: Found in the region where the Negro and Tapajos rivers join the Amazon

Size: Maximum 5 cm

Habitat: Found in shaded waters

SHAPE, COLORING AND MARKINGS: The body of this small cichlid is fairly elongated and laterally slightly compressed. The basic coloration is a yellowish grey with a greenish sheen. A dark but not at all times distinct horizontal line runs along the body. A number of transverse bands sometimes appear and then the metallic green sheen and the yellow of the belly become more vivid. The back rays of the dorsal fin are greatly elongated: the front rays are darker, but not elongated. The caudal fin is rounded.
Females are less vividly colored, but during the mating season they are a golden yellow with two dark dots, one on the caudal peduncle and one on the body.
Males are as described above.

GENERAL CARE: As for *A.cacatuoides,* but temperature not lower than 26° C.

BREEDING: As for *A.cacatuoides:* the eggs will hatch in two to five days, depending on the temperature.

APISTOGRAMMA RAMIREZI

Family: *Cichlidae*

Genus: *Apistogramma*

English name: Ramirez's Dwarf Cichlid

Origin: Possibly Venezuela but more likely Bolivia

Size: Maximum 5 cm

Habitat: No details are available of its natural habitat

SHAPE, COLORING AND MARKINGS: The body is deep, stocky and laterally very compressed. The basic coloration is a delicate crimson but this can be suffused with all the colors of the rainbow. Below the dorsal fin lies a prominent black mark ringed by iridescent greenish blue. The body is covered by sometimes indistinct lines. The ventral fins are blood red: the other fins are brownish violet with iridescent bluish green dots. The front rays of the dorsal fin, divided from the rest of the fin, are a deep black.
Females are smaller: the dorsal fin rays are shorter. During the spawning season the belly becomes a deep rich red.
Males are as described above with longe rays to the dorsal fin.

GENERAL CARE: As for *A.cacatuoides*. This is a relatively peaceful species.

BREEDING: The reproductive behavior of *A.ramirezi* differs significantly from that of all other *Apistogramma* species. The eggs are laid on flat stones or pieces of wood which the parents have thoroughly cleaned. Both the parents guard the eggs and fry as well as guarding the territory. Before they are free swimming the fry will hide in the shade and the breeder must ensure that they secure enough food.

ADDITIONAL INFORMATION: *A.ramirezi* is very prolific but successive generations bred in the aquarium lack the brilliant colors of the wild fish. The behavior and biology of this species is so different from other species in the genus that it has been suggested that this fish should be moved to a new genus, *Microgeophagus*.

777. *Apistogramma ramirezi* ▷

776. *Apistogramma reitzigi*

APISTOGRAMMA REITZIGI

Family: *Cichlidae*
Genus: *Apistogramma*
English name: Yellow Dwarf Cichlid
Origin: Paraguay
Size: Maximum 5 cm
Habitat: Found in shaded waters

SHAPE, COLORING AND MARKINGS: The body is stocky and laterally slightly compressed. The basic coloration is a greyish green: the flanks are lighter: the belly yellow. The whole body has a greenish blue metallic sheen and the yellow of the belly may be very deep and vivid. The back rays of the dorsal fin, the front rays of the ventral fins and some rays of the anal fin are all much extended. The back of the dorsal fin and the caudal and ventral fins are a pale yellow.
Females are smaller and usually darker but in the spawning season they become a bright yellow with prominent deep black marks on the head.
Males are as described above.

GENERAL CARE: As for *A.cacatuoides* but temperature 24°C.

BREEDING: As for *A.cacatuoides* but the female takes the initiative in courtship.

THE FAMILY CICHLIDAE

The genus Astronotus

Only one species, the Velvet Cichlid, *Astronotus ocellatus*, described below is found in this genus. Widely distributed in northern South America, it is quite frequently offered for sale and young specimens, with their attractive black and white colors, are often bought by inexperienced amateurs, who are quite unaware that this robust and hardy fish will, with its voracious appetite, very rapidly grow too large for all but the biggest aquariums. It can easily grow to 30 cm.
In other respects it can be an attractive fish, although some specimens are of uncertain temperament. If the aquarist with facilities for keeping them has the good fortune to acquire a pair of a peaceful disposition, they may become very tame and endearing and even enjoy being stroked by their keeper.

778. *Astronotus ocellatus*

ASTRONOTUS OCELLATUS

Family: *Cichlidae*

Genus: *Astronotus*

English name: Oscar, Velvet Cichlid and Peacock-Eye Cichlid

Origin: Northern South America

Size: Maximum 33 cm

Habitat: Found in a wide variety of waters

SHAPE, COLORING AND MARKINGS: The body is fairly slender and laterally compressed. The head is blunt: the mouth large with a protruding lower jaw. The basic coloration is variable, but usually a dark olive green to chocolate: on the flanks lie irregular, generally black bordered, ivory or reddish stripes. A large round dark mark, ringed with red, lies at the base of the caudal fin. The fins are olive green, flecked with black and gold. Females are as described above. Males often have two or three dark patches at the base of the dorsal fin.

GENERAL CARE: *A.ocellatus* requires a tank proportionate to its size, but may be kept with other large species of cichlids. Most specimens are relatively peaceful. The tank should be arranged as recommended for cichlids in the section on Aquarium layout. The composition of the water is not critical: temperature 20°–25°C. A voracious omnivorous fish, *A.ocellatus* will eat almost anything including minced beef heart, dried food and aquatic insects.

BREEDING: This is not difficult. The fish are sexually mature when 10–12 cm long. The eggs are laid on a stone or other surface previously cleaned by both parents, who share in the brood care. Three days after the eggs have been laid the parents will dig a trench in the gravelly bottom and transfer the fry there. The fry are free swimming after five or six days and grow very quickly when fed on Cyclops *nauplii* and and other fine animal food.

779. *Astronotus ocellatus (juv)*

THE FAMILY CICHLIDAE

The genus Aulonocara

This is a small genus, with only three species, of cichlids that come from Africa and belong to that curious group restricted in general to areas of Lakes Malawi and Tanganyika. These fish are unfamiliar to many amateurs but there has been a great increase in interest in them in recent years and many are now kept in aquariums. Only *Aulonocora nyassae* is normally seen in captivity, but two other species are known: *Aulonocora macrochir*, which closely resembles *A.nyassae* but has more prominent eyes and longer pectoral fins and *Aulonocara rostrata* which has six or seven transverse bands below the dorsal fin, instead of the nine or ten bands present in *A.nyassae*.

These are attractive fish and not at all aggressive, but as noted below, they do need a fairly large tank, arranged as suggested in the article on lay-out.

AULONOCARA NYASSAE

Family: *Cichlidae*

Genus: *Aulonocara*

English name: none

Origin: Africa, Lake Malawi

Size: Maximum 18 cm in the wild but rarely larger than 15 cm in captivity

Habitat: Found where the bed changes from rock to sand

SHAPE, COLORING AND MARKINGS: The body is fairly deep and laterally compressed. The basic coloration of young males and all females is brown, with a hint of blue round the mouth. Nine or ten dark transverse bands appear under the dorsal fin. The fins are transparent, with occasional blue marks. The front rays of the ventral fins are white and indistinct darker patches appear on the anal fin. When they grow to 7–9 cm the appearance of males changes radically. A white, later bright blue edge appears along the dorsal fin. The head turns blue and the body is tinged with blue. The transverse bands remain and the front of the body retains its reddish brown color. The dorsal, caudal and anal fins turn dark blue, the last with orangey yellow oval marks. The pectoral fins remain colorless but the ventral fins become reddish brown. A large number of indentations appear on the snout, cheeks and lower part of the head, forming a sensory organ analogous to the lateral line.

GENERAL CARE: *A.nyassae* is not aggressive: a number of males can be kept in a large species tank. The composition of the water is not critical: temperature about 26°C. It will often go short of food if kept with other more domineering species of African cichlids. In the wild *A.nyassae* eats insects but in the aquarium will usually accept all kinds of food.

BREEDING: *A.nyassae* is a mouth-brooder. It prefers to spawn on stones but the 50 or more eggs may also be laid in holes. The fry need to be fed on the finest of infusoria.

THE FAMILY CICHLIDAE

The genus Chalinochromis

This is another very small genus of African cichlids. The only species of interest to aquarists is the little-known *Chalinochromis brichardi* described below. Only very recently introduced to the aquarium world, not a great deal of experience can be drawn on to give guidance on its care and breeding. The genus however is very closely related to the better known genus *Julidochromis*, although the natural habitats differ somewhat: it can therefore be assumed with some degree of certainty that the general care of *C.brichardi* should be same as that accorded to members of the genus *Julidochromis*. Indeed, when first discovered, *C.brichardi* was wrongly named *Julidochromis brichardi*. Like the *Julidochromis* species, *C.brichardi* comes from Lake Tanganyika. No cichlids from this lake are as common in aquariums as the cichlids from Lake Malawi: they have received less attention because they are less easy to acquire rather then because they are more difficult to keep, in a suitable species tank.

CHALINOCHROMIS BRICHARDI

Family: *Cichlidae*

Genus: *Chalinochromis*

English name: none

Origin: Africa, northeast Lake Tanganyika

Size: Maximum 11 cm

Habitat: Found where there is a rocky bed and water depth of 8–9 m

SHAPE, COLORING AND MARKINGS: The body is elongated and only slightly compressed laterally. The lips are thick and bumpy. The basic coloration is olive grey: the belly is lighter. Three prominent black transverse bands lie across the forehead: one runs from the upper lip to the back of the eye: one runs over the forehead, through the eye to the center of the gill cover: the third runs over the head to the back of the eye. A black mark lies on the gill covers: a similar mark is found above the base of the pectoral fin. The fins are grey or dark grey. A black mark is found on the soft rays of the dorsal fin which has also a white edge with a black border. There is no significant difference between the color patterns of the sexes.

GENERAL CARE: See Introductory note on the genus. *C.brichardi* should be given a spacious tank laid out as suggested for cichlids. So far as is known the composition of the water is not critical: temperature about 26°C. A variety of foods including algae and lettuce should be offered.

BREEDING: Nothing is known about the reproductive behavior of this species.

THE FAMILY CICHLIDAE

The genus Cichlasoma

The genus *Cichlasoma* is the most important and largest genus of South American Cichlids. There are in all some 60 species, virtually all of which can be kept in captivity, although many species are very rarely kept by amateurs in aquariums, and some species grow so large as to be unmanageable for most aquarists.

As might be expected in so large a genus, various species are found in a wide variety of natural habitats: some live in fast-flowing waters, others in sluggish densely overgrown waters and some are even found in brackish as well as fresh waters.

Most of these fish are attractively colored. They are not on the whole difficult to keep provided they are given the kind of tank recommended for cichlids in the section on Aquarium lay out. In disposition however the species vary enormously: the genus includes not only some aggressive fish, such as the well-known Jack Dempsey, *Cichlasoma biocellatum* but also some unusually peaceful species such as the Festive Cichlid, *Cichlasoma festivum*. Many of these species are easy to breed, but some very rarely if ever breed in captivity.

Eight of the more interesting or popular species are described below and the amateur with a particular interest in the other less common species should consult the specialist literature. The less well-known species in this genus can be interesting and challenging fish for the amateur.

780. *Cichlasoma biocellatum*

CICHLASOMA ARNOLDI

Family: *Cichlidae*

Genus: *Cichlasoma*

English name: none

Origin: Brazil, the southern tributaries of the Amazon

Size: Maximum 13 cm

Habitat: Found only in fresh waters

SHAPE, COLORING AND MARKINGS: The body is elongated, rather deep and laterally very compressed. The basic coloration is a dark brown: the belly is lighter. Large numbers of irregularly shaped dark patches lie on the back below the dorsal fin and dark lines are found on the gill covers: a crescent shaped black patch lies at the base of the caudal fin. The fins are dark grey with blackish bands: the caudal fin has a black border. In some lights the gill covers have a green iridescence and yellow patches are seen on the back.
There are no known external sexual characteristics.

GENERAL CARE: See Introductory note to the genus and family. *C.arnoldi* may be kept in a community tank when young but adults should only be kept in large species tanks with a sandy bottom and plenty of hiding places between stones and pieces of bogwood. *C.arnoldi* is very intolerant of its own kind. It grubs up the bottom during the mating season. The composition of the water is not critical: temperature 22°–25°C. *C.arnoldi* requires a substantial and varied diet of both live animal matter and vegetable food, including lettuce

BREEDING: This species does not seem to have been bred as yet in captivity.

CICHLASOMA AUREUM

Family: *Cichlidae*

Genus: *Cichlasoma*

English name: Golden Cichlid

Origin: Guatemala, southern Mexico

Size: Maximum 16 cm

Habitat: Found in fresh, densely overgrown waters and also sometimes in brackish waters

SHAPE, COLORING AND MARKINGS: The body is elongated, rather deep and laterally very compressed. The basic coloration varies significantly according to the locality of origin. It is usually a greenish brown with a red or golden gleam on the flanks. Dark marks lie on the center of the body, on the caudal peduncle and on the lower part of the gill covers: when the fish is excited a dark longitudinal stripe and dark transverse bands also

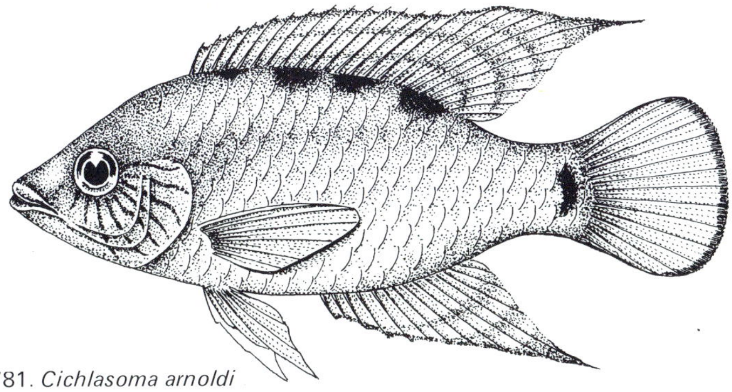

781. *Cichlasoma arnoldi*

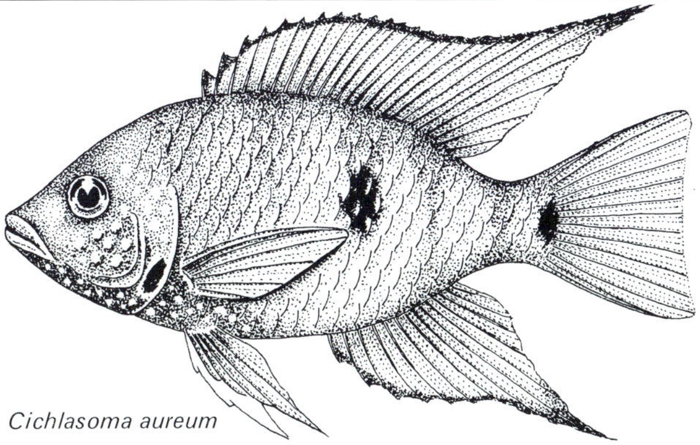

782. *Cichlasoma aureum*

appear on the body. The powerful dorsal and anal fins are elongated, brown at the base and with a yellow green to black border. The caudal fin is a yellow green and the pectoral fins blue at the tips.
Females are usually smaller and less vividly colored.
Males are as described above.

GENERAL CARE: As for *C.arnoldi.*

BREEDING: This species does not seem as yet to have been bred in captivity.

CICHLASOMA BIOCELLATUM

Family: *Cichlidae*
Genus: *Cichlasoma*
English name: Jack Dempsey
Origin: The central Amazon basin
Size: Maximum 20 cm in the wild but usually remains considerably smaller in captivity
Habitat: Found in a variety of waters

SHAPE, COLORING AND MARKINGS: The body is elongated, fairly deep and laterally compressed. The basic coloration varies from yellowish brown to a deep bluish black. The body and the dark dorsal, anal and caudal fins are flecked with innumerable shiny, metallic greenish blue dots. The dorsal fin has also a narrow red border. Young specimens also have a pattern of dark stripes on the body and two gold patches, one below the dorsal fin and the other on the caudal peduncle.
Females are slightly smaller, less vividly colored and with more rounded dorsal and anal fins.
Males are as described above with the dorsal and anal fins tapering to points.

GENERAL CARE: As for *C.arnoldi.*

BREEDING: The breeding pair should be at least a year old. The eggs are laid on stones or pieces of wood which have been thoroughly cleaned by both parents who share the guarding of the eggs and the fry. When free swimming the fry can be fed with sieved Cyclops and Daphnia. They will also be fed with coarser food by their parents who will give them pre-masticated Tubifex and Enchytrae. The parents usually tend the fry until they start a new nest, when it is better to transfer the fry to a separate tank. Nests of 800 are not uncommon and it is important to ensure that the water in the breeding tank is regularly changed.

ADDITIONAL INFORMATION: The generally accepted name is now *C.octofasciatum*

783. *Cichlasoma festivum (juv)*

CICHLASOMA FESTIVUM

Family: *Cichlidae*
Genus: *Cichlasoma*
English name: The Festive Cichlid
Origin: The central Amazon basin
Size: Maximum 15 cm in the wild but remains considerably smaller in captivity
Habitat: Found in sluggish or still waters

SHAPE, COLORING AND MARKINGS: The body is elongated and laterally very compressed. The dorsal and anal fins taper and give the fish an almost triangular profile. A broad deep black line runs from the mouth through the eye to the tip of the dorsal fin and accentuates this triangular shape. The basic coloration is brown to greenish yellow. The scales have a dark edge and this gives rise to a net-like pattern. On the back there is often a green marbling. A black patch edged with yellow lies on the caudal fin.

GENERAL CARE: *C.festivum* may be kept in a well-planted aquarium but it will dig during the mating season and only strong, fairly coarse leaved plants should be put in the spacious deep tank these fish require. Smooth stones and bogwood should be provided. *C.festivum* is peaceful and can be kept with other small species but it dislikes the company of livelier fish. Older specimens often find it difficult to settle down in a new environment. The water should not be too hard (not above 6° DH) and slightly acid (just below pH 7): temperature 25°–26° C. The diet should include both live animal matter and a vegetable supplement.

BREEDING: Not difficult. The breeders should be at least a year old. It is not advisable to transfer them to a special tank. The temperature in the ordinary tank should be raised to 28° C and feeding the fish on vitamin enriched Enchytrae may encourage the production of fertile eggs. Vitamin enriched Enchytrae can be produced by feeding the worms in the culture on a diet containing wheat germ oil. *C.festivum* lays its eggs on flat stones, bogwood or the leaves of sturdy plants. It does not usually dig very much into the bottom. As soon as they are free swimming the fry should be fed on Cyclops and *Artemia nauplii*.

CICHLASOMA MEEKI

Family: *Cichlidae*

Genus: *Cichlasoma*

English name: Fire-mouth Cichlid

Origin: Central America, Guatemala, Yucatan

Size: Maximum 15 cm in the wild but remains considerably smaller in captivity

Habitat: Found in shaded waters

SHAPE, COLORING AND MARKINGS: The body is elongated, fairly deep and laterally compressed. The basic coloration is a violet grey: the back is darker: the belly lighter: the throat and front of the belly are deep red. A number of dark vertical bands lie on the body and vary in intensity according to the mood of the fish. A prominent irregular deep black mark edged with gold lies on the gill covers and a smaller black mark lies just behind them. A black stripe runs from the gill covers to the caudal peduncle where it ends in a dark patch surrounded by a zone of gold. The fins are wine red with light green edges.
Females are usually smaller and less vividly colored, with less pointed dorsal and anal fins. During the spawning season the belly may become off-white.
Males are as described above.

GENERAL CARE: As for *C.festivum* but *C.meeki* is less timid than that species. The composition of the water is not critical: temperature about 24° C, but much lower temperatures will be tolerated for short periods.

BREEDING: As for *C.biocellatum* but *C.meeki* will not pre-masticate food for the fry whose feeding will be left entirely to the keeper. A very prolific species.

CICHLASOMA NIGROFASCIATUM

Family: *Cichlidae*

Genus: *Cichlasoma*

English names: Zebra Cichlid and Convict Cichlid

Origin: Central America, Guatemala

Size: Maximum 10 cm

Habitat: Found in large lakes and rivers

SHAPE, COLORING AND MARKINGS: The body is slightly elongated and laterally compressed. The basic coloration is a bluish grey: eight or nine black vertical bands run from the dorsal fin to the belly. The broad based dorsal and anal fins have greatly elongated rays at the back which make the fins taper to points. All the fins are bluish grey to green.
Females when young are indistinguishable from males: adult females have less pointed fins and during the spawning season have an orange mark on the flanks.
Males are as described above.

GENERAL CARE: As for *C.arnoldi*: *C.nigrofasciatum* is aggressive and needs a large tank. Temperature as for *C.meeki*.

BREEDING: As for *C.biocellatum*.

CICHLASOMA SEVERUM

Family: *Cichlidae*

Genus: *Cichlasoma*

English name: Banded Cichlid

Origin: The central Amazon basin, southern Central America

Size: Maximum 20 cm in the wild, but remains considerably smaller in captivity

Habitat: Found in a variety of large waters

785. *Cichlasoma severum*

◁ 784. *Cichlasoma meeki*

SHAPE, COLORING AND MARKINGS: The body is rather stocky and laterally compressed. The fish appears to be unusually sturdy because its body depth is greatest at the front. The basic coloration varies from yellowish brown to brownish black. The flanks bear reddish brown dots which sometimes merge into patches. Young specimens have a pattern of dark vertical stripes only two of which are found in adults: one of these runs from a black, yellow edged mark on the back of the dorsal fin to a similar mark on the back of the anal fin: the other lies beyond, on the caudal peduncle. The dorsal, anal and caudal fins are greenish: the ventral fins are reddish brown.

786. *Cichlasoma nigrofasciatum*

Females are less deeply colored with less pointed fins.
Males are as described above and have reddish brown marks on the head.

GENERAL CARE: As for *C.arnoldi* but temperature ideally 25°C and certainly not below 21°C.

BREEDING: As for *C.biocellatum* but not every pair of *C.severum* will mate. A natural pair (see Family Introduction) are most likely to breed successfully. The brood may be up to 700.

ADDITIONAL INFORMATION: *C.severum* is one of the most peaceful species in the genus, except during the mating season when, by contrast, it becomes one of the most aggressive, and must be kept on its own.

CICHLASOMA SPILURIUM

Family: *Cichlidae*
Genus: *Cichlasoma*
English name: none
Origin: Central America
Size: Maximum 10 cm
Habitat: Found in shaded waters

SHAPE, COLORING AND MARKINGS: The body is fairly deep and the line of the head rises sharply from the snout. The basic coloration is yellow brown to olive green. The scales are edged with dark blue and show up as a net-like pattern. The flanks have prominent, irregular, steel blue marks. The dorsal and anal fins taper to points at the back. The fins are a soft red with blue flecks.
Females are considerably smaller with less pointed fins. The basic coloration is a greyish blue with a deep blue throat, especially during the spawning season.
Males are as described above.

GENERAL CARE: As for *C.arnoldi* but temperature 24°C.

BREEDING: *C.spilurum* is often described in the literature as a 'hole breeder' but in fact these fish are not consistent in their behavior and are as likely to lay their eggs on stones or in flower pots. Not a very prolific species, nests of over 200 being exceptional. Care as for *C.biocellatum*.

787. *Cichlasoma spilurum* ♂

788. *Cichlasoma spilurum* ♀

THE FAMILY CICHLIDAE

The genus Crenicara

Only *Crenicara filamentosa,* the Chess board Cichlid, described below, is, in this genus, of interest to aquarists. Restricted to South America, it is both an attractively colored and pleasantly peaceful fish for an appropriately furnished community tank. Unfortunately, as noted below, it is acutely sensitive to water pollution, and even when given ideal conditions, does not always settle down happily in the aquarium.

789. *Crenicara filamentosa*

CRENICARA FILAMENTOSA

Family: *Cichlidae*

Genus: *Crenicara*

Enlgish name: Chess board Cichlid

Origin: The Middle Amazon basin

Size: Maximum (or Checker-) 10 cm

Habitat: Found in shaded waters, with overhanging vegetation

SHAPE, COLORING AND MARKINGS: The body is elongated and laterally somewhat compressed: that of the female is distinctly deeper. The fins of the male are elongated, the outer rays of the caudal fin being very long. In the female the anal fin is relatively large and rounded, and the dorsal fin quite high at the front. The basic coloration is a muddy yellow, with orange to red blotches. Two rows of large, almost square black marks lie along the body. The eye is a vivid red. The anal, dorsal and caudal fins are red, the latter with 10–12 rows of dark spots: the ventral fins are flecked with blue.

Females have a more blunt head and less vividly colored fins, without elongated rays. Males are as described above.

GENERAL CARE: *C.filamentosa* is a peaceful species that will establish a territory in the lower reaches of the tank. It can therefore be kept in a fairly large community tank, with retreats provided in bogwood and rocks. Some robust and firmly embedded or potted plants should be included. The water should be no harder than 10° DH, and slightly peaty: temperature 23°–25° C. *C.filamentosa* is very sensitive to water pollution, and appropriate precautions must be taken.

Both live animal matter and dried food will be accepted.

BREEDING: Not too difficult if the fish have settled down in the aquarium. The eggs will be laid on stones or in cavities among the rocks. Both parents will guard the nest and fry. The eggs will hatch in two to five days, and the fry will be free swimming after another four to six days, when they should be fed on sieved Cyclops and *Artemia nauplii.*

THE FAMILY CICHLIDAE

The genus Crenicichla

Members of the genus *Crenicichla* are found over a wide area of South America, in a variety of waters. There are some 25 species, and all are voracious predators. They attack the very fish which are most popular as aquarium pets, and therefore must never be introduced into community tanks.

They must be given a very large aquarium with numerous hiding places in arrangements of bogwood and dense vegetation. They are shy and display their color best in subdued light. The composition of the water is not critical, nor is the temperature, provided it is not allowed to drop below 20° C. The diet must be smaller fish, aquatic insects and larvae.

Breeding is not easy: it is difficult to match a pair: best results are achieved with two fish from the same nest. The eggs are laid in a shallow depression and usually guarded by the male, though the female can be left in the breeding tank after spawning. These species are usually prolific and the eggs extremely small. During brood care and the rearing of the young, a rich and varied diet is essential.

790. *Crenicichla lepidota*

The genus Cyphotilapia

There is one species in this genus, an unusually shaped fish *Cyphotilapia frontosa.* It has an extraordinary head, with a large bulging forehead. It is one of the few species of fish that show allometric growth – that is, different parts of the body grow at different rates, for this unusual bulging head is not present in juveniles, but as the fish matures, there is an acceleration in the growth rate of the back muscles above the eyes, which gives rise to this hump.

The genus Eretmodus

There is one species in this genus, *Eretmodus cyanostictus* only found in Lake Tanganyika. This rather squat cichlid is found in shallow rocky waters.

Its habits are very much akin to those of the Goby fish in the family *Eleotridae:* it is a bottom feeding fish, and hunts for insects and small crustaceae hiding in the rocks: it has spatulate shaped teeth that are admirably suited to extracting such small animals from their lairs. Moreover, both its ventral and pectoral fins have developed from the conventional cichlid shape into a shape which allows them to be used for resting on stones while watching for prey. In turn of course, this unusual shape of the fins means that *E.cyanostictus* is less swift a swimmer and less adept at maneuvering in the water than many cichlids. When threatened, it will rush for shelter among its native rocks.

The genus Etroplus

The genus *Etroplus* is the only group of fish in the cichlid family that originate in India and nearby places. To date, only two species are known: the Orange and the Green Chromide, *Etroplus maculatus* and *Etroplus suratensis*, described below. In the wild they live in both fresh and brackish waters near to coasts, and in captivity are more hardy if a small amount of salt is added to the tank. They are peaceful fish and are an interesting addition to the aquarium.

CRENICICHLA DORSOCELLATA

Family: *Cichlidae*
Genus: *Crenicichla*
English name: Two Spot Pike Cichlid
Origin: The Amazon Basin
Size: Maximum 20 cm
Habitat: Found in a variety of waters

SHAPE, COLORING AND MARKINGS: The body is elongated, and like that of a pike: laterally slightly compressed, and with a broad head. The basic coloration is a muddy greenish blue: the flanks are pale green: the underside a pale blue. Young specimens bear seven to nine narrow transverse bands, which in older specimens are visible only when the fish is excited. A number of blue-black patches lie on the gill covers and above the pectoral fins. A dark longitudinal line runs along the body, and may be broken into irregular patches. A prominent black patch edged with white and red lies on the dorsal fin, which is otherwise brownish or green. The caudal fin is reddish above, greenish below, with rusty brown specks and a black patch at the base. The anal fin is sometimes sky blue.
Females have rounded, or only slightly tapering dorsal and anal fins.
Males are as described above: the dorsal and anal fins taper to a point.

GENERAL CARE: See Introduction to the genus.

BREEDING: See Introduction to the genus.

ADDITIONAL INFORMATION: This is the least intolerant of the species currently imported.

CRENICICHLA LEPIDOTA

Family: *Cichlidae*
Genus: *Crenicichla*
English name: Pike Cichlid
Origin: The whole of Central America
Size: Maximum 20 cm in the wild but remains smaller in captivity
Habitat: Found in a wide variety of waters

SHAPE, COLORING AND MARKINGS: The body profile is identical to that of *C.dorsocellata*. The color pattern varies significantly according to the locality of origin and mood of the specimen. Usually the back is an olive green: the flanks greenish to a brown yellow, with a pearly iridescence. The underside may be brownish, silvery white, yellow or wine red. A number of short dark transverse bands are visible on young specimens. One or more black patches ringed with gold or silver lie behind the gill covers, and an identical patch appears at the base of the caudal fin. All the fins have a green and yellow shading.
Females have rounded dorsal and anal fins.
Males are as described above, with tapered dorsal and anal fins.

GENERAL CARE: See Introduction to the genus.

BREEDING: *C.lepidota* does not seem as yet to have been bred in captivity.

CYPHOTILAPIA FRONTOSA

Family: *Cichlidae*
Genus: *Cyphotilapia*
English name: none
Origin: Lake Tanganyika
Size: Maximum 33 cm in the wild but usually no more than 20 cm in captivity
Habitat: Found above a rocky bed, at depths between 6 m and 30 m, and normally at a depth of 19 m

SHAPE, COLORING AND MARKINGS: The body is fairly high and laterally compressed. The forehead has a bulging lump. The basic coloration is white and beige. Six wide black transverse bands lie across the body: the first runs through the eye: the last runs over the caudal peduncle. The upper lip and the top of the head are light blue. The pectoral fins are colorless: the ventral and anal fins are shot with light blue: the dorsal and caudal fins are greyish.
There are no known external sexual characteristics but the bulge on the forehead is less prominent in females than in males.

GENERAL CARE: *C.frontosa* is suitable only for a very large species tank with a sandy bed and plenty of cavities preferably in plant pots. It will accept any sort of food but in the wild is carnivorous, and it should have a varied diet.
The composition of the water is not critical: temperature 22°–25° C.

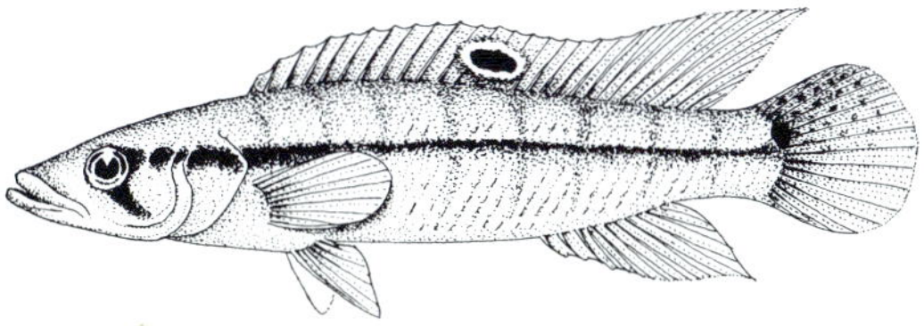

791. *Crenicichla dorsocellata*

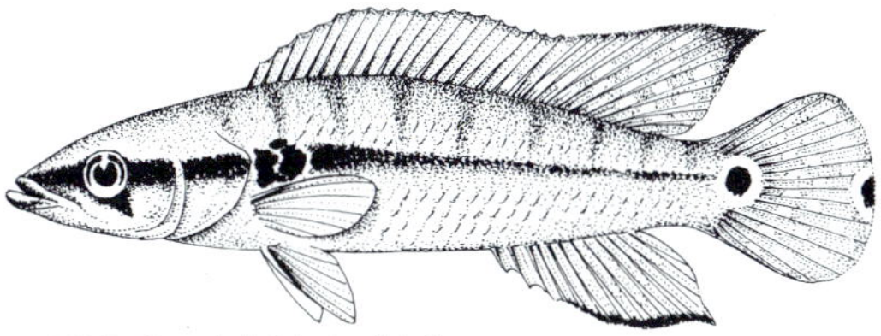

792. *Crenicichla lepidota*

793. *Cyphotilapia frontosa*

BREEDING: *C.frontosa* is a mouth brooder. The fish retreat to a cave to lay the eggs. The male stays behind the female while she lays a row of 2–4 eggs, and then swims in front of her, brushing the eggs with his belly and thus fertilizing them. In the meantime the female turns round and takes the eggs into her mouth. This pattern is repeated many times, but eggs are not laid every time. Females up to 13 cm long may lay 8–25 eggs: females 20 cm long may lay 36 eggs. The eggs are very large, from 0.6–0.8 cm in diameter and light yellow. The incubation period depends on the temperature, and can last up to 24 days at a temperature of 25°–27° C.

ERETMODUS CYANOSTICTUS

Family: *Cichlidae*
Genus: *Eretmodus*
English name: none
Origin: Lake Tanganyika
Size: Maximum 7.5 cm
Habitat: Found above rocky beds with stones, in shallow waters close to the shore

SHAPE, COLORING AND MARKINGS: The body is fairly deep and laterally very compressed. The snout is very long, the mouth under-positioned and the eyes prominent. The basic coloration is yellow. Nine or ten dark brown transverse bands and some patches of blue lie on the body: the lips, snout and throat are also shot with blue. Except for the colorless pectoral fin, the fins are greyish: the caudal and dorsal fins have a very narrow black edge: the ventral fins are black at the front.
Females are as described above.
Males have longer ventral fins.

GENERAL CARE: *E.cyanostictus* needs a spacious tank with plenty of stones and retreats. The composition of the water is not critical: temperature 22°–25°C. It will accept almost any food but prefers that which disintegrates easily in the water. It seems to have difficulty in assimilating animal fat, and foods containing that (such as beef heart) should be avoided: their consumption may lead to death from constipation.

BREEDING: Extremely difficult. A mouth brooder, but nearly always the eggs disappear within a few days, probably having been eaten by the female. The fish establish a territory which they both defend. The orange eggs are about 0.5 cm in diameter. The incubation period varies from 35–40 days. *E.cyanostictus* is not prolific, no more than 25 eggs are laid.

794. *Eretmodus cyanostictus*

795. *Etroplus maculatus*

ETROPLUS MACULATUS

Family: *Cichlidae*
Genus: *Etroplus*
English name: Orange Chromide
Origin: India and Sri Lanka
Size: Maximum 10 cm
Habitat: Found in fresh and brackish coastal waters

SHAPE, COLORING AND MARKINGS: Adult fish have very deep or disc shaped bodies and are laterally very compressed. The basic coloration is grey-blue: the back is darker: the flanks and belly golden yellow to light orange. Three almost round brown-black to blue-black patches lie on the upper half of the body: the middle one is the most prominent. Almost all the scales have an iridescent pattern which produces an overall impression of regular spotting. The dorsal fin is orange with a brownish pattern and a red border. The anal fin is yellow with a black border at the front: the yellow caudal fin has a red line at the base. The ventral fins are black with an extended bright blue ray. The iris is red, and pale blue iridescent scales appear beneath the eye. Outside the mating season the colors are more uniform and the fins have a greyish black tone.
Females are less vividly colored: only the dorsal and caudal fins have a reddish border.
Males are as described above.

GENERAL CARE: *E.maculatus* may be kept in a species tank or a large community tank. There should be plenty of plants and arrangements of bogwood to provide retreats and spawning mediums. Mature water is best: fresh water should be avoided and one tablespoon of rock salt added for each 10 liters of water: temperature 21°–26°C. *E.maculatus* swims at all levels and is tolerant. The diet should be varied, with both insect larvae and a vegetable supplement.

BREEDING: *E.maculatus* prefers to lay its eggs on flat stones or in cavities in wood. The eggs have threads. Both parents assist in brood care. The eggs hatch in about two days. The young attach themselves to the sides of their parents until they are free swimming, after four or five days. They should be fed on the finest fry foods.

ETROPLUS SURATENSIS

Family: *Cichlidae*
Genus: *Etroplus*
English name: Green Chromide
Origin: Sri Lanka
Size: Maximum 30 cm in the wild, but remains considerably smaller in captivity
Habitat: Found mainly in brackish waters

SHAPE, COLORING AND MARKINGS: The body is very deep, almost oval and laterally very compressed. The basic coloration is greyish blue to green, with a pearly iridescence and blue to green iridescent patches on the scales. Six to eight diagonal transverse bands lie on the upper half of the body: these become very distinct when the species is kept in the right conditions. The scales on the lower half of the body carry black marks which show up as a black patterning. The pectoral fins are yellowish, with a deep black patch at the base: the other fins are greyish green to blue. During the breeding season fishes kept in pure seawater take on an attractive purple-red tone and their transverse bands become much darker.
There are no known external sexual characteristics.

GENERAL CARE: *E.suratensis* needs a large species or community tank with brackish water and can only be kept in fresh water for brief periods: it feels quite at home in seawater. Temperature 23°–24°C. Diet as for *E.maculatus*.

BREEDING: Nothing is known about the reproductive behavior of this species.

THE FAMILY CICHLIDAE

The genus Geophagus

The *Geophagus* genus of South American cichlids contains seven species, all of which are kept from time to time by amateurs. Most of these fish display what might be described as the generally accepted behavior characteristics of cichlids: they are aggressive, territorial fish that nevertheless practice careful brood care and which can if given adequately large, appropriately furnished tanks be persuaded generally to moderate their apparently determined anti-social behavior. The taxonomy and nomenclature of species in this genus caused problems, but these have been solved through the re-classification of several species. Since 1975, the species known formerly as *Geophagus australe*, has been labelled *Gymnogeophagus australis*. *Geophagus cupido* has recently been changed to *Biodotoma cupido*, a different genus; *Geophagus gymnogenys* to *Gymnogeophagus gymnogenus*. In this encyclopedia the species remain classified under their former names.

796. *Geophagus acuticeps*

GEOPHAGUS ACUTICEPS

Family: *Cichlidae*
Genus: *Geophagus*
English name: none
Origin: The Amazon basin
Size: Approximately 25 cm
Habitat: No details are available of its natural habitat

SHAPE, COLOR AND MARKINGS: The body is elongated, fairly deep and laterally very compressed: the back is particularly high. The head is pointed and the mouth large. The basic coloration is olive-green: the flanks are a yellowish green, the underside of the body silvery. Seven to eight indistinct wedge-shaped transverse bands lie on the body: the second, fourth and sixth end on the flanks as prominent black patches, another of which lies on the caudal peduncle. The large scales have grassy green iridescent spots, particularly on the upper half of the body. Green iridescent flecks lie on the snout and gill covers. The unpaired fins are greenish, with a few darker rays: the anal and dorsal fins have brownish bands, the latter a dark border. The ventral fins are bluish at the base and have yellow elongated tips. The color patterns are more brilliant during the mating season and become paler with age.
Females have no elongated rays to the dorsal and anal fins.
Males are as described above.

GENERAL CARE: *G.acuticeps* is only suitable for a large species tank with a fine sandy bottom and plenty of hiding places among rocks and bogwood: the rocks are best built up high towards the back of the tank, but must of course be very securely fixed in place. *G.acuticeps* is intolerant both of its own kind and other species, if there is not sufficient room for it to establish a territory. It lives mainly in the middle reaches of the tank and tends to remain a great deal in one place. The composition of the water is not critical: temperature 22°–25°C. The diet should include ample quantities of both live animal and vegetable matter.

BREEDING: *G.acuticeps* likes to deposit its eggs on stones. Both parents share in brood care. The fry are not difficult to raise on the normal foods.

GEOPHAGUS AUSTRALE

Family: *Cichlidae*
Genus: *Geophagus*
English name: none
Origin: Argentina, around Buenos Aires.
Size: Maximum 18 cm
Habitat: No further details are available of its natural habitat

SHAPE, COLORING AND MARKINGS: The body shape and profile are identical to those of *G.acuticeps*. The basic coloration is brown to greyish green, with a strong pearly iridescence. The scales on the upper half of the body in particular are dark edged and most carry green iridescent specks. Six to nine indistinct transverse bands lie on the body: a dark patch lies on the flanks and a curved dark band runs from the neck through the eye into the throat. The gill covers have an alternating pattern of dark and green iridescent patches. The dorsal and anal fins are bluish green at the front with pearly patches in the soft rays: the dorsal fin has a bluish band running parallel to its edge. The caudal fin has dark specks at the base. The ventral fins are a vivid green.
There are no known external sexual characteristics.

GENERAL CARE: As for *G.acuticeps* but temperature 20°–23°C and as low as 12°–15°C will be tolerated in winter.

BREEDING: *G.australe* has not it seems as yet been bred in captivity.

GEOPHAGUS BRASILIENSIS

Family: *Cichlidae*
Genus: *Geophagus*
English name: Pearl Cichlid
Origin: Eastern Brazil
Size: Maximum 30 cm in the wild but remains considerably smaller in captivity
Habitat: Found in both fresh and brackish waters

SHAPE, COLORING AND MARKINGS: The body is elongated, very deep or disc shaped and laterally very compressed. Young specimens have a rather pointed snout: older specimens have a high forehead. The basic coloration is very variable and may be from a muddy

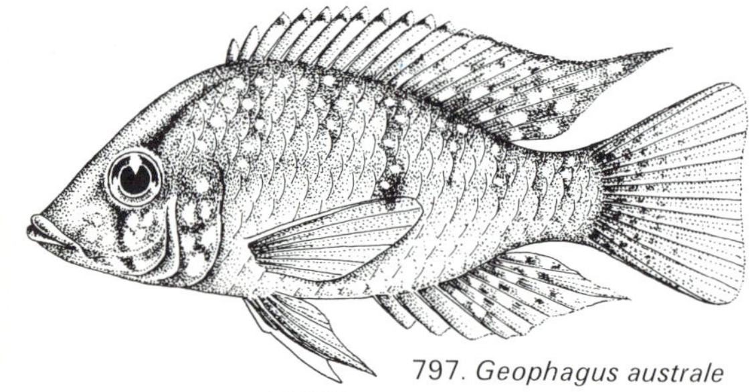

797. *Geophagus australe*

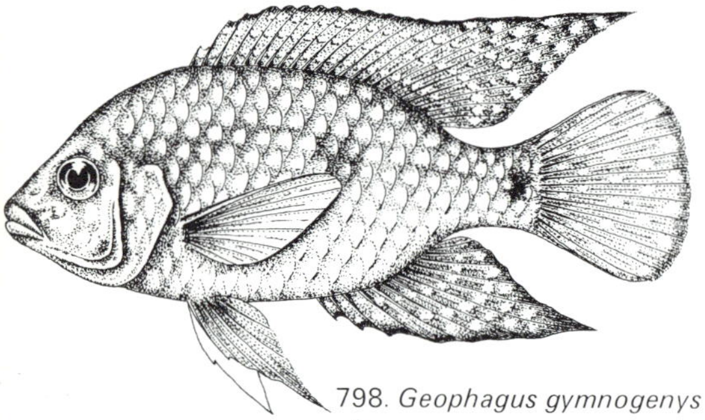

798. *Geophagus gymnogenys*

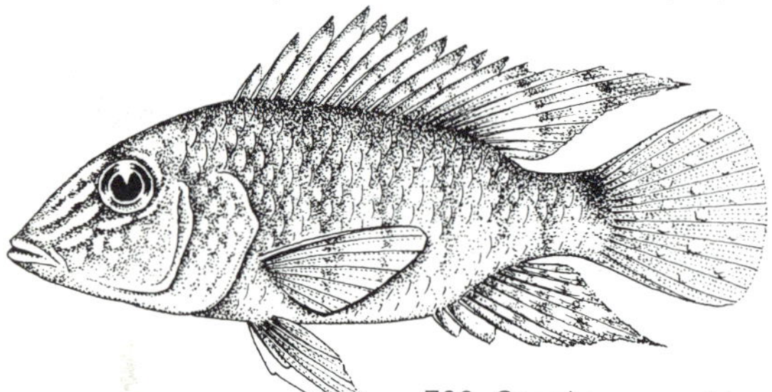

799. *Geophagus cupido*

yellow to ochre with a greenish overtone. The head bears pearly marks. The scales on the flanks are dark with pearly flecks. Young fish have five to seven fairly prominent transverse bands on the body: adult fish have a prominent dark patch below the dorsal fin. A dark line curves from the neck, across the eye into the throat. The anal, dorsal and caudal fins are yellow green to brown with wine red, yellow or silvery white patches.
Females have blunter genital papilae. during the spawning season.
Males are as described above.

General care: As for *G.acuticeps* but a teaspoonful of salt should be added to the tank for every ten liters of water.

Breeding: No details are available of the reproductive behavior of this species.

GEOPHAGUS CUPIDO

Family: *Cichlidae*

Genus: *Geophagus*

English name: none

Origin: Western Guyana and the central Amazon basin

Size: Maximum 13 cm

Habitat: No details are available of its natural habitat

Shape, coloring and markings: The body shape is identical to that of *G.acuticeps*. The basic coloration is a dark brown: the back is a chocolate brown, usually with a green iridescent overtone. The flanks are yellowish brown with gleaming blue green spots: the belly is lighter. Young fish have a number of transverse bands on the body. A large deep black patch surrounded by a pearly zone lies immediately below the dorsal fin. A black line curves from the neck to the throat across the eye. Blue iridescent flecks are found below the eye. The dorsal and anal fins are brownish or yellow brown with several bands in the soft rays: the caudal fin is yellow green, with a deep black edge tipped top and bottom with white. The pectoral and ventral fins are ochre. There are no known external sexual characteristics.

General care: As for *G.acuticeps*.

Breeding: *G.cupido* has not it seems as yet been bred in captivity but it is believed be a mouth brooder.

GEOPHAGUS GYMNOGENYS

Family: *Cichlidae*

Genus: *Geophagus*

English name: none

Origin: Southern Brazil

Size: Maximum 20 cm in the wild but usually remains smaller in captivity, when it is sexually mature at approximately 12 cm

Habitat: No details are available of its natural habitat

Shape, coloring and markings: The body shape is identical to that of *G.acuticeps*. The basic coloration is a dark greenish brown. The head is ochre, with light blue or greenish flecks, the front of the body a yellow-brown. The scales have pale blue iridescent spots, giving the fish a pearly gleam. An indistinct dark patch lies on the flank, in front of the anal fin: a similar but more prominent patch lies at the base of the caudal fin. The fins are usually brownish to brown-red, but can be greenish, with an iridescent sky blue patterning.
Females have less well developed fins.
Males are as described above.

General care: As for *G.acuticeps*, but winter temperature may be as low as 12°–14° C.

Breeding: As for *G.acuticeps*.

GEOPHAGUS JURUPARI

Family: *Cichlidae*

Genus: *Geophagus*

English name: none

Origin: Northern Brazil

Size: Maximum 25 cm in the wild, but usually remains smaller in captivity, when it is sexually mature at 12 cm

Habitat: No details are available of its natural habitat

Shape, coloring and markings: The body profile is identical to that of *G.acuticeps*. The

800. *Geophagus cupido*

basic coloration is a dark ochre: the flanks are yellowish, with a green overtone: the belly is lighter or pale yellow. Young specimens have many dark transverse bands on the body. Yellow or brown lines lie on the snout. The scales on the flanks have a pearly sheen. The fins are grey-brown with lighter patches. There are no known external sexual characteristics.

GENERAL CARE: As for *G.acuticeps* but *G.jurupari* is more usually tolerant of other fish.

801. *Geophagus brasiliensis*

However, it is of uncertain temperament and is best kept in a species tank. Temperature not lower than 22°C, or the fish becomes prone to fungus diseases. *G.jurupari* prefers live animal food.

BREEDING: *G.jurupari* is a mouth brooder. It lays its eggs on flat stones and covers them with a fine layer of sand. The fry are sheltered for about two weeks in the mother's mouth. The male should be removed from the breeding tank after the eggs have hatched. The fry are not difficult to raise with the normal fry foods.

THE FAMILY CICHLIDAE

The genus Haplochromis

The genus *Haplochromis* is the largest genus of African cichlids, and the authorities list some 145 or more species, only a very small number of which are both potentially aquarium fish and are imported. There is still a great deal of confusion over the nomenclature of these fish, and the amateur with a particular interest in them is advised to study the specialist literature. The species best known among aquarists, and one or two less common but of particular interest are described below.

Two species formerly of this genus no longer belong to it: *Haplochromis multicolor*, which was changed to *Pseudocrenilabris multicolor*, and *Haplochromis philander dispersus*, which has become *Pseudocrenilabris philander*. In this encyclopedia they remain classified under their former names.

A fairly large tank not too densely planted but only softly lit is best. Retreats between stones or bogwood are essential, and bogwood is particularly appropriate because it more closely simulates the natural environment of the fish. The bottom should be of well washed but not too fine river sand: gravel is not suitable. These fish live, in the wild, in such varied waters that in general the composition of the water in the aquarium is not critical.

All the species described below are mouth brooders. Breeding is not difficult. The eggs are deposited by the female in a shallow depression and may be fertilized by the male who follows her immediately. The fish circle round the depression, and the female very quickly gathers up the eggs (rarely more than 70–80) in her mouth. The eggs are so quickly gathered that the male may not have fertilized them. Males have on their anal fin, marks which resemble eggs, and females are seen sometimes to bite at these marks: it may be that this stimulates the male to discharge milt which then fertilizes the eggs already in the female's mouth, but which were gathered so quickly he could not fertilize them earlier.

The male takes little part in brood care and it is best to remove him immediately after mating. The female keeps the eggs in her throat sac for about 10 days. As soon as the fry have hatched they leave the mouth but are taken up into it again at night and when danger threatens: this will cease however after about a week and when the fry no longer react to danger in this way the female should be removed.

802. *Haplochromis burtoni*

HAPLOCHROMIS BURTONI

Family: *Cichlidae*

Genus: *Haplochromis*

English name: none

Origin: Lake Tanganyika, and the slow flowing rivers that drain into it

Size: Maximum 12 cm in the wild, but remains smaller in captivity

Habitat: Found in waters no deeper than 5 m

SHAPE, COLORING AND MARKINGS: The body is fairly high and laterally compressed. The basic coloration is greyish yellow: the flanks are shot with blue. Six or seven indistinct transverse bands run across the body: a black stripe runs from the lower edge of the eye to the corner of the mouth. Two black transverse bands lie across the snout: a black mark lies on the gill covers and an orangey red mark on the shoulders. The lips are blue. The front of the ventral fins is black: the pectoral fins are transparent. The blue tinged dorsal fin has a narrow red edge and rows of round red or orange marks: similar but more reddish marks lie on the caudal fin. The anal fin has a reddish tip and is light blue at the base, where three to seven oval marks are often found. There are two varieties: a blue and a yellow variety, depending on which color is dominant. The yellow variety is presumed to live in cloudy water.

Females are smaller and have no oval marks on the anal fin.

Males are as described above.

GENERAL CARE: *H.burtoni* needs a large species tank, with some dense vegetation round the sides but also some free swimming space. The bottom should be of fine sand. The composition of the water is not critical: temperature 20°–25°C. The preferred diet is live animal matter such as Tubifex, Daphnia and Cyclops, but dried food will be eaten.

BREEDING: See genus Introduction.

ADDITIONAL INFORMATION: In Lake Malawi is found *H. callipterus*, identical to *H. burtoni*, except that it lacks the latter's orange shoulder mark and black forehead bands. It requires the same care as *H. burtoni*. Its breeding habits are identical.

HAPLOCHROMIS COMPRESSICEPS

Family: *Cichlidae*
Genus: *Haplochromis*
English name: Malawi Eye-bitter
Origin: Lake Malawi
Size: Maximum 20 cm
Habitat: Found in areas where there are thick growths of *Vallisneria*.

SHAPE, COLORING AND MARKINGS: The body is slender and quite unusually compressed laterally. The snout is long, the lower jaw protrudes and the teeth are prominent. The basic coloration is greenish. The fins are colorless. There are no known external sexual characteristics.

GENERAL CARE: *H.compressiceps* is a predatory fish with the particularly unpleasing habit of biting out the eyes of other fish. It should on no account be kept with other fish, and is not really suitable for any kind of aquarium. If kept, it must be given a large tank laid out, in general, as for *H.burtoni*, but with plenty of dense vegetation amongst which it can lurk. It will accept insect food, but its principal diet is smaller fish which it eats tail first, unlike most piscivores that eat their prey head first.
BREEDING: Nothing is known about the reproductive behavior of this species.

803. *Haplochromis compressiceps*

804. *Haplochomis livingstonii*

HAPLOCHROMIS DESFONTAINESI

Family: *Cichlidae*
Genus: *Haplochromis*
English name: none
Origin: North Africa
Size: Approximately 15 cm
Habitat: Found in streams, oases and artesian wells

SHAPE, COLORING AND MARKINGS: The body is fairly deep and laterally compressed: the head and neck are relatively large. The basic coloration is a brown or olive green. The scales have a pearly or bluish iridescence. Some specimens have a number of fairly distinct transverse bands on the body: all specimens have a very dark diagonal band running between the eye and the corner of the mouth, and a black gold-edged patch on the gill covers. The caudal and dorsal fins have tiny orange or brown flecks, the latter also an orange border. The anal fin bears black-edged egg-shaped orange specks. The ventral fins are black. In the mating season the whole body is suffused with a steely blue tone and the fins become practically black, with orange-red patterning.
Females are smaller.
Males are as described above.

GENERAL CARE: As for *H.burtoni* but temperature 26°–28°C.

BREEDING: See Introduction to the genus. Males become aggressive towards smaller fish during the breeding season. The young can be raised without difficulty on the usual foods.

HAPLOCHROMIS LIVINGSTONII

Family: *Cichlidae*
Genus: *Haplochromis*
English name: none
Origin: Lake Malawi
Size: Maximum 20 cm
Habitat: Found in waters with a sandy bottom

SHAPE, COLORING AND MARKINGS: The body is somewhat elongated and laterally compressed. The mouth is upward pointing, and the teeth prominent. The basic coloration is a muddy white, with random darker blotches, and a slightly pearly iridescence. The fins are colorless.
There are no known external sexual characteristics.

GENERAL CARE: *H.livingstonii* is a predatory fish which should only be kept by specialists. It requires general care similar to *H.burtoni*, but its principal diet is smaller fish.

BREEDING: *H.livingstonii* is a mouth brooder, but nothing is known in detail about its reproductive behavior.

ADDITIONAL INFORMATION: *H.livingstonii* is a most unusual species in that in order to lure its prey it will sham death on the sandy bed in its natural habitat. Its unusual color pattern suggests a dead fish. When inquisitive small fish approach, the 'corpse' springs to life and catches them.

HAPLOCHROMIS MOORII

Family: *Cichlidae*

Genus: *Haplochromis*

English name: none

Origin: Lake Malawi

Size: Maximum 20 cm

Habitat: Found where the bed is sandy

SHAPE, COLORING AND MARKINGS: The body shape (particularly the bulging forehead) is identical to that of *Cyphotilapia frontosa* (see above), found in Lake Tanganyika. The dorsal fin has a very long base. The basic coloration is blue. The fins are tinged with blue, and the anal fin carries the spots characteristic of this genus.
There are no known external sexual characteristics.

GENERAL CARE: As for *H.burtoni*.

BREEDING: See introduction to the genus.

ADDITIONAL INFORMATION: *H.moorii* is, in the wild, a bottom feeder and is one of the four species that evinces behavior patterns of commensalism, that is, remaining close to fish of another species in order to benefit from what those fish do. In this case *H.moorii* is usually found associating with *Haplochromis rostratus*, or other bottom feeders who dig for food. As these fish dig they throw up a cloud of sand and in this cloud of sand *H.moorii* finds what it wants itself to eat.

HAPLOCHROMIS MULTICOLOR

Family: *Cichlidae*

Genus: *Haplochromis*

English name: Small or Egyptian Mouth Brooder

Origin: East Africa

Habitat: Approximately 8 cm

Habitat: Found in a wide variety of waters

SHAPE, COLORING AND MARKINGS: The body is fairly deep and laterally compressed, particularly towards the tail. The basic coloration is ochre to salmon: in certain lights the whole body has a golden iridescence overlaid here and there on the back with lustrous green or bluish green. The gill covers are a pale iridescent grassy green with a deep black patch. The rusty brown dorsal fin has green or bluish bands and a black border, green rays or green stipples and spots at the base. The anal fin has a similar color pattern but is a little darker. The caudal fin is yellowish green with darker flecks. The pectoral fins are yellowish with a blue green iridescent ray at the front.
Females are more yellowish.
Males are as described above.

GENERAL CARE: As for *H.burtoni* but temperature 22°–26° C. *H.multicolor* is a peaceful species and can be kept in a suitable community tank but may be aggressive during the mating season: it is then best transferred to a species tank.

BREEDING: See Introduction to the genus, and notes above.

806. *Haplochromis moorii*

807. *Haplochromis multicolor*

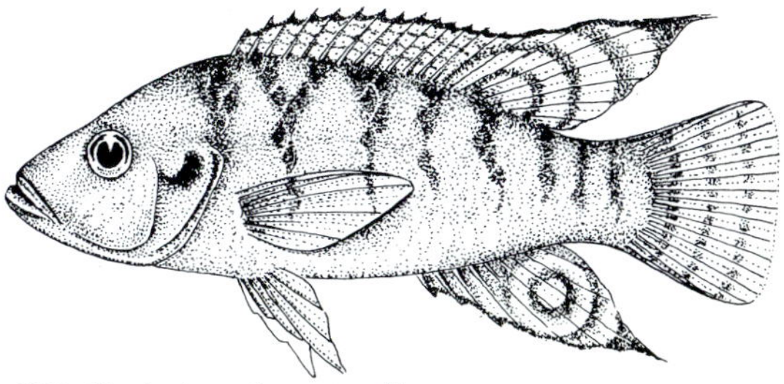

805. *Haplochromis pectoralis*

HAPLOCHROMIS PECTORALIS

Family: *Cichlidae*

Genus: *Haplochromis*

English name: none

Origin: East Africa, Lake Victoria and the area to the south

Size: Approximately 10 cm

Habitat: Found in a variety of waters

SHAPE, COLORING AND MARKINGS: The body is fairly deep and laterally compressed. The basic coloration is a dark brown-green: the flanks are reddish brown, the belly fawn or yellowish. In certain lights the whole body has a red iridescence. Fairly prominent but irregular transverse bands lie on the upper part of the body. The front parts of the dorsal and anal fins are yellow-green with paler spots: the anal fin has curved violet marks of varying intensity. The caudal fin is yellow-green with light and dark patches.
There are no known external sexual characteristics.

GENERAL CARE: As for *H.multicolor*, but behavior during the breeding season is unknown.

BREEDING: No information is available on the reproductive behavior of this species.

HAPLOCHROMIS PHILANDER DISPERSUS

Family: *Cichlidae*

Genus: *Haplochromis*

English name: none

Origin: Southwest Africa

Size: Approximately 11 cm

Habitat: Found in a wide variety of waters

SHAPE, COLORING AND MARKINGS: The body is fairly deep and laterally compressed. The basic coloration varies significantly according to the locality of origin: it is usually ochre to salmon. In some lights the whole body has a vivid golden gleam overlaid here and there with green, and, on the back and belly, with blue. Some specimens have prominent transverse bands on the flanks and a longitudinal line made up of individual patches. The caudal, dorsal and anal fins are red with blue iridescent specks: the latter fin occasionally becomes cobalt blue, and at the back reddish. The lower lip is bright blue. When the fish is excited the throat and belly become reddish. Females are less vividly colored. Males are as described above.

GENERAL CARE: As for *H.burtoni*, but temperature 22°–26° C.

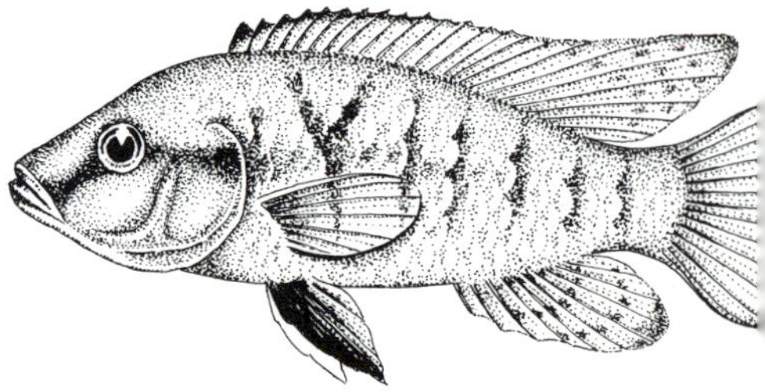

808. *Haplochromis philander dispersus*

BREEDING: See Introduction to the genus. The male should be removed immediately after spawning and the female as soon as the fry are hunting independently for food, which will be some six to nine days after the end of the 10 days of mouth brooding.

THE FAMILY CICHLIDAE

The genus Hemichromis

The genus *Hemichromis* contains three species of which *Hemichromis bimaculatus* and *Hemichromis fasciatus* are described below. These are African cichlids, but with a much wider distribution than many related species. They are somewhat aggressive fish that need relatively large tanks, and are really fish only for the experienced amateur. They have however been subject to an unusual amount of scientific observation, and more is known about their behavior patterns, especially those of *H.bimaculatus*, than is known about many fish. It is evident that *H.bimaculatus* is very intelligent and amateurs interested in this species' ability in problem solving should read the relevant chapter in the distinguished naturalist Konrad Lorenz's *King Solomon's Ring*. The third species is *H.elongatus*.

809. *Hemichromis bimaculatus*

HEMICHROMIS BIMACULATUS

Family: *Cichlidae*

Genus: *Hemichromis*

English names: Jewel Fish, Red Cichlid and Jewel Cichlid

Origin: Throughout tropical Africa

Size: Maximum 15 cm

Habitat: Found in still and flowing waters

SHAPE, COLORING AND MARKINGS: The body is elongated, fairly deep and laterally slightly compressed. The basic coloration is olive brown: the throat and belly are red. One black patch lies on the middle of the body, and another, edged with gold, on the gill covers. The body is flecked with glistening, bluish green spots. During the spawning season the body and all the fins (except the pectoral) in both sexes become a beautiful red and the iridescent spots turn into larger vivid bluish green marks. There are no external sexual characteristics.

GENERAL CARE: The aggressive *H.bimaculatus* is only suitable for a community tank if the aquarium is very spacious and provides other fish with ample retreats, in bogwood and robust plants. It insists on establishing a fairly large territory. The composition of the water is not critical: temperature 25° C. A varied diet of live animal matter should be provided.

BREEDING: Not difficult. The eggs are laid on a stone or wood previously cleaned, principally by the male. Both parents guard the eggs and fry. *H.bimaculatus* digs holes when breeding, but does less damage to sturdy plants than some other Cichlids. Raising the fry is straightforward but adequate food must be given to ensure that the large broods are adequately fed.

ADDITIONAL INFORMATION: H. bimaculatus is well known for its exceptional brood care.

HEMICHROMIS FASCIATUS

Family: *Cichlidae*

Genus: *Hemichromis*

English name: none

Origin: Throughout central West Africa

Size: Maximum 25 cm

Habitat: Found in running and still fresh waters, and some brackish coastal waters

SHAPE, COLORING AND MARKINGS: The body is elongated, relatively narrow and laterally compressed. The head is pointed, the line of the forehead slightly concave, and the mouth large. The fins (except the pectoral) are rounded. The basic coloration is a yellowish bronze: the back is darker or a yellowish green. Five black marks, distinct only in adults, lie on the body: in younger specimens these marks form a single dark horizontal line. Another black mark edged with gold lies on the gill covers. During the spawning season the throat and

belly in both sexes becomes bright red.
There are no known external sexual characteristics.

General care: *H.fasciatus* is an aggressive predator, only suitable for a very large species tank with a good sandy bed and plenty of retreats among rock and bogwood. Even when very young these fish tend to bite and are very intolerant, even towards their own species. The composition of the water is not critical: temperature 25° C. A very substantial diet of live animal matter including fish is needed.

Breeding: Because of their tendency to bite each other, it is difficult to identify a suitable pair. If found however, the pair should be transferred to a separate tank with a thick sandy bed and some smooth stones. The eggs are laid on a stone or on wood and both parents share in guarding the eggs and fry. Large nesting holes will be dug. The fry can be raised without difficulty on the usual fry foods.

810. *Hemichromis fasciatus*

THE FAMILY CICHLIDAE

The genus Julidochromis

In this small genus of five species only two, *J.marlieri* and the more attractively colored *J.ornatus*, are of general interest to aquarists: three other species, *J.dickfeldi*, *J.regani* and *J.transcriptus* are also very occasionally encountered by amateurs. These fish are cichlids restricted in the wild to Lake Tanganyika, and are less frequently seen in aquariums than similar fish from Lake Malawi, but this is because of the difficulties of importing them, not because in themselves they are less attractive than their more popular cousins.
Like so many species found in these unusual lakes, the *Julidochromis* show in their body form and habits a very exact adjustment to their natural environment. In these fish, the very slender elongated bodies are supremely well adapted to their life style, in which they are continuously slipping in and out of crevices in the rocks in search of food and indeed, breeding caves. These environmental preferences must be taken into account in the lay out of the tank if these somewhat shy fish are to feel at home in the aquarium.

JULIDOCHROMIS MARLIERI
Family: *Cichlidae*
Genus: *Julidochromis*
English name: none
Origin: Lake Tanganyika
Size: Maximum 8.5 cm
Habitat: Found only in the extreme southwest part of the lake.

Shape, coloring and markings: The body is very slender, elongated and laterally very compressed. The dorsal fin has a very long base and reaches very nearly to the upper lobe of the caudal fin, which is rounded at the end.
The basic color is an orange yellow. Four black horizontal stripes run across the flanks: the lowest stripe may be indistinct or even absent in some specimens. The two lower stripes run into the snout, the two upper ones onto the forehead, and eight or nine black vertical lines cross the horizontal stripes on the body. The pectoral fins are transparent: the dorsal fin is black with light beige flecks and a yellow border. The caudal fin is black, with light flecks towards the back. Many variations of this color pattern exist.
There are no known external sexual characteristics.

811. *Julidochromis marlieri*

General care: *J.marlieri* requires a fairly large tank with scattered clumps of dense vegetation, some free swimming space, and structures of stone to stimulate its natural environment of rocks and crevices. The composition of the water is not critical, but should be hard rather than soft: temperature 22°–25°C. All kinds of live animal matter, dried food and algae and lettuce should be offered.

Breeding: *J.marlieri* lays its eggs on the underside of stones, or the roof of a rock cavity. A pair may either spawn very frequently, producing each time a small nest or, only every six or so weeks, when a much larger nest will be produced, of 100–150 eggs. The parents practice brood care but are not as diligent as some other cichlids. The fry are not difficult to raise on the normal fry foods.

Additional information: In the southern part of Lake Tanganyika is found *J.ornatus*. The body shape is identical to that of *J.marlieri* but the color pattern is more vivid. The basic coloration is orange. The throat is lighter. Three black or dark brown horizontal stripes run from the snout to the caudal peduncle, where they become indistinct. A black mark lies on the base of the caudal fin, a blue mark on the gill covers. The dorsal, anal and caudal fins are brown with a narrow bluish, white stripe: the dorsal fin has also a black border across the top. The ventral fins are orange, the pectoral fins transparent. It requires care, and should be bred as *J.marlierli*. *J. dickfeldi*, a predominantly black and brown fish, is found in the southwest part of Lake Tanganyika, while the larger *J.regani*, a light brown fish, is more generally distributed.

812. *Julidochromis ornatus*

THE FAMILY CICHLIDAE

The genus Labeotropheus

There are only two species in the genus *Labeotropheus*: both are only found in Lake Malawi. They are distinctive because of their 'parrot-like' snout which has an enlarged, fleshy upper lip. This fleshy snout with a short lower jaw, and the adapted arrangement of the teeth allow these fish to scrape algae off rocks while lying on them. This snout is not always very prominent, and after a few generations aquarium bred specimens lose it. The *Labeotropheus* are a genus of Mbuna. They can be kept in the aquarium in the same way as other Mbunas, and although they feed mainly on algae in the wild, they will accept a more normal diet in captivity.

LABEOTROPHEUS FUELLEBORNI

Family: *Cichlidae*
Genus: *Labeotropheus*
English name: none
Origin: Lake Malawi
Size: Maximum 12 cm
Habitat: Found along rocky shores and near islands in the lake

SHAPE, COLORING AND MARKINGS: The body is fairly deep, two to three times as long as it is deep, and laterally only slightly compressed. The basic coloration of the female is usually greyish blue: the belly is lighter. Dark, sometimes indistinct transverse bands lie on the body, eight below the dorsal fin, and two on the snout: a dark mark is found at the back of the gill covers. The anal, dorsal and caudal fins are blue. The pectoral fins are transparent: the ventral fins are dark with a narrow, white margin. The male is a vivid blue with two to four orange oval marks on the anal fin.

GENERAL CARE: *L.fuelleborni* requires a fairly spacious species tank, with plenty of rocks and some very robust plants. The composition of the water is not critical: temperature 22°–25° C. A varied diet of live animal matter such as Cyclops, Tubifex and mosquito larvae should be given, with algae or lettuce.

BREEDING: *L.fuelleborni* is a mouth brooder. The fry are not difficult to raise on normal fry foods.

ADDITIONAL INFORMATION: A number of color varieties are known. There is a spotted variety where orange and black marks appear on a basic color of mottled white, and a speckled variety where the marks are similar in color but very small. These color varieties are usually restricted to females, but males also occasionally appear with these patterns.

813. *Labeotropheus trewavasae*

LABEOTROPHEUS TREWAVASAE

Family: *Cichlidae*
Genus: *Labeotropheus*
English name: none
Origin: Lake Malawi
Size: Maximum 11 cm
Habitat: Found along rocky shores and near islands in the lake

SHAPE, COLORING AND MARKINGS: The body is elongated and laterally only very slightly compressed. *L.trewavasae* is much more slender than *L.fuelleborni*, the body being three or three and a half times as long as its depth. The basic coloration varies significantly according to the locality of origin. Many specimens are bright blue with nine to eleven black transverse bands across the body. Three black bands lie across the forehead and snout and form a mask. The fins are blue. Other specimens (from the southern part of the lake) have orange or red tones in the fins. Fish from the southeastern part of the lake have reddish fins, and the upper half of the body is a reddish brown. Four or five orange, oval marks lie on the anal fin.
Females usually have the blue color pattern described above: spotted and speckled varieties occur, as with *L.fuelleborni*.
Males are as described above.

GENERAL CARE: As for *L.fuelleborni*.

BREEDING: As for *L.fuelleborni*.

THE FAMILY CICHLIDAE

The genus Labidochromis

The genus *Labidochromis,* a group of insect eating cichlids from Lake Malawi, is one of the most confused at the present time.
Two established species exist, *L.caeruleus* and *L.vellicans,* although even in respect of these there is not a great deal of authoritative information on their requirements in aquariums. In recent years a number of other species have been tentatively identified, but their nomenclature has not been settled. Among these are four species, *L.freibergi, L.fryeri* (also incorrectly named *L.joanjohnsonae*), *L.mathotho* and *L.textillis* occasionally encountered.
There are also a number of trade names used by various dealers, among them *L.davies, L.marineatus, L.minutus* and *L.samueli,* which have no scientific basis, but which amateurs may come across.

814. *Labidochromis caeruleus*

LABIDOCHROMIS CAERULEUS

Family: *Cichlidae*
Genus: *Labidochromis*
English name: none
Origin: Lake Malawi
Size: Maximum 10 cm
Habitat: Found near the surface, by rocky shores

SHAPE, COLORING AND MARKINGS: The body is somewhat elongated and laterally compressed. The basic coloration is a bright blue, sometimes light blue or almost white. The lighter the basic color the more prominent are the six transverse bands which run across the body below the dorsal fin. The dorsal fin is blue with a wide black band just below the edge. The ventral fins are black at the front: the anal fin is blue with a black border.
Females are as described above.
Males have a bright orange oval mark on the back of the anal fin.

GENERAL CARE: *L.caeruleus* does not seem as yet to have been imported but it can be presumed that it would require, in an aquarium, care similar to that recommended for *Labidochromis vellicans* below.

BREEDING: No information is available on the reproductive behavior of this species.

ADDITIONAL INFORMATION: An uncommon species *L.caeruleus 'likomae'* was once the name of *L.textilis.*

LABIDOCHROMIS VELLICANS

Family: *Cichlidae*
Genus: *Labidochromis*
English name: none
Origin: Lake Malawi
Size: Maximum 10 cm
Habitat: Found near the surface near rocky shores

SHAPE, COLORING AND MARKINGS: The body is elongated and laterally compressed. The back is not quite as deep as that of *L.caeruleus.* The basic coloration is yellow brown: the belly is considerably lighter. Some specimens have dark horizontal or transverse bands on the body which give it a checkered pattern. The flanks are shot with blue. The lips and throat are bright blue. The membranes of the dorsal, caudal and anal fins are dark blue: the rays are a contrasting light blue: the dorsal fin has an orange yellow border. The ventral fins are light blue at the front and black at the back.
Females are as described above.
Males have orange yellow oval marks on the anal fin.

GENERAL CARE: *L.vellicans* is an aggressive fish which should be kept in a fairly large species tank, with plenty of well-secured rock structures and only the most robust plants. The composition of the water is not critical: temperature 22°–25°C. A substantial and varied diet of Tubifex, Cyclops, mosquito larvae, dried food, algae and lettuce should be provided.

BREEDING: Little is known about the reproductive behavior of this species: it is reported that both parents share brood care and guard the fry.

THE FAMILY CICHLIDAE

The genus Lamprologus

Most species in the genus *Lamprologus* are found only in Lake Tanganyika but some are also found in neighboring rivers. The genus includes a large number of species but most of these are of no interest to aquarists. There are really three groups

815. *Lamprologus leleupi*

within the genus, divided according to size and feeding habits. The smallest species (on average 6 cm) are found in shallow waters above a sandy or muddy bed: they feed mainly on prawns, small shrimps and similar creatures. The second group (on average 12 cm) prefer waters over a rocky bed and feed on molluscs, shrimps, insects and young fish. The largest species (on average 24 cm) are found in a variety of waters and prey on other fish. All these fish lay their eggs in hollows or cavities: those that live above a sandy bed in the wild spawn in empty snail shells. Thus when furnishing an aquarium for these fish it is important to provide rock cavities. All species in this genus form pairs, except for *L.congolensis,* but the tie is not very strong. Three species of possible interest to aquarists are described below.

LAMPROLOGUS BRICHARDI

Family: *Cichlidae*
Genus: *Lamprologus*
English name: none
Origin: Lake Tanganyika
Size: Maximum 11 cm
Habitat: Found above a rocky bed in waters up to a depth of 10 m

SHAPE, COLORING AND MARKINGS: The body is fairly elongated and laterally compressed. The basic coloration is a light brownish grey. A cone-shaped black mark lies on the back of the gill covers and a short black line runs from the back of the eye to the middle of the gill cover: an indistinct black stripe runs from the lower edge of the eye to the corner of the mouth. All the fins except for the colorless pectoral fins, are brownish. The dorsal fin has a narrow white border: the anal fin has a bluish white border. The front rays of the ventral fins are white, as are the elongated rays at the top and bottom of the caudal fin. There are no known external sexual characteristics.

GENERAL CARE: *L.brichardi* needs a large tank with a gravelly bottom and well-secured structures of rock. It may be kept with other large surface fish or in a species tank. The composition of the water is not critical: temperature 23°–25°C. A varied diet of live animal matter should be provided.

BREEDING: Between 20 and 100 eggs are laid in a cavity. They hatch in six to eight days and the fry are free swimming after a further three to five days. Both parent fish guard the eggs and the fry. The eggs are often laid at intervals of three to five weeks and young fish from different nests live together.

ADDITIONAL INFORMATION: *L.brichardi* was long known as *L.savoryi elongatus.* In 1974 three sub-species of *L.savoryi,* of which this was one, were re-classified as separate species.

816. *Lamprologus brichardi*

LAMPROLOGUS FURCIFER

Family: *Cichlidae*
Genus: *Lamprologus*
English name: none
Origin: Lake Tanganyika
Size: Maximum 20 cm
Habitat: Found in shallow waters

SHAPE, COLORING AND MARKINGS: The body is extremely elongated and laterally hardly at all compressed. Mature specimens have a prominent lump on the top of the head. The basic coloration is brown. A large black mark runs from the eye to the cheek: four or five dark transverse bands lie across the body. The dorsal fin is brown with a black border above a narrow, light blue band. The ventral fins are orange: the caudal and anal fins are brown with black borders: the top and bottom rays of the caudal fin are elongated.
There are no known external sexual characteristics.

GENERAL CARE: As for *L.brichardi* but *L.furcifer* is very aggressive and best kept in a species tank.

BREEDING: The eggs are laid, for preference against the ceiling of a cavity and *L.furcifer* is very adept at swimming upside down. Brood care as for *L.brichardi.*

LAMPROLOGUS LELEUPI

Family: *Cichlidae*
Genus: *Lamprologus*
English name: none
Origin: Lake Tanganyika
Size: Maximum 9 cm
Habitat: Found in shallow waters over a rocky bed

SHAPE, COLORING AND MARKINGS: The body is very elongated and laterally only slightly compressed. When the fish is in good condi-

tion the whole body is an orange yellow: except for the white ventral fins, the fins are the same color. The iris is blue. When not in good condition the fish turns a plain rust brown.
There are no known external sexual characteristics.

GENERAL CARE: *L.leleupi* can be kept in a fairly small aquarium. It is quite tolerant both of its own kind and other species. Otherwise, as for *L.brichardi*.

BREEDING: As for *L.furcifer:* no more than 50 eggs are usually laid.

ADDITIONAL INFORMATION: *L.leleupi* must not be confused with *L.leloupi*, another smaller species. In 1962 a sub-species of *L.leleupi*, *L.leleupi melas* was described: it has an almost completely black body and rows of scales on the flanks whose green bases show up as horizontal lines.

THE FAMILY CICHLIDAE

The genus Lobochilotes

There is at present only one species in the genus *Lobochilotes*, the large *Lobochilotes labiatus* described below. As will be seen, its most distinctive feature is its very thick fleshy lips: it is the only fish of its kind found in Lake Tanganyika but, as so often with these strange African cichlids, there are other species of cichlids with similarly unusual lips (and similar food preferences) in both Lake Malawi and Lake Victoria.

817. *Lobochilotes labiatus*

LOBOCHILOTES LABIATUS
Family: *Cichlidae*
Genus: *Lobochilotes*
English name: none
Origin: Lake Tanganyika
Size: Maximum 36 cm in the wild but remains considerably smaller in captivity
Habitat: Found above a rocky bed

SHAPE, COLORING AND MARKINGS: The body is fairly deep and laterally compressed. The protuberant and very sensitive lips are very thick. The basic coloration is a yellowish green: eleven to twelve dark brown transverse bands lie across the body. A black stripe runs from the neck, through the eye to the corner of the mouth. The scales on the flanks have a dark dot at the center and these show up as narrow horizontal stripes. The fins are transparent. Black marks lie between the rays of the caudal fin and the soft rays of the dorsal fin: orange oval marks lie on the male anal fin. There are no known external sexual characteristics save the occasional marks on the anal fins of the males.

GENERAL CARE: *L.labiatus* is a relatively peaceful species that requires a large tank with a gravelly bottom and well-secured rock structures. It can be kept with other large species but is best kept in a species tank. The composition of the water is not critical: temperature 22°–25°C. In the wild, *L.labiatus* lives almost entirely on insects which it hunts with its sensitive lips: in the aquarium it will eat almost anything but live animal matter should form a large part of the diet.

BREEDING: *L.labiatus* is a mouth brooder but no information is available on its reproductive behavior.

THE FAMILY CICHLIDAE

The genus Limnochromis

These are at present some nine species in the genus *Limnochromis*, a group of cichlids restricted to Lake Tanganyika. It is likely that this genus will be revised by taxonomists, but hopefully the one species of interest to aquarists, *Limnochromis auritus*, described below, will remain within it. In the wild the species in this genus display some unusual characteristics: they are zooplankton eaters and accordingly tend to move in loose shoals and to live in deeper waters than most of the cichlids found in the lake. At night, as a result of complicated behavior patterns not yet fully understood, they move in-shore to shallower waters. The closed environment within which these fish live with other cichlids has encouraged biologists to study them and interested amateurs will find a great deal of fascinating information in the specialist literature.

818. *Limnochromis auritus*

LIMNOCHROMIS AURITUS
Family: *Cichlidae*
Genus: *Limnochromis*
English name: none
Origin: Lake Tanganyika
Size: Maximum 18 cm
Habitat: Found generally in waters as deep as 35 m

SHAPE, COLORING AND MARKINGS: The body is fairly deep and laterally compressed. The basic coloration is olive with a silvery sheen. A pale red tone, especially on the back is sometimes apparent. Four wide transverse bands cross the body: the first lies immediately behind the gill covers, the last lies on the caudal peduncle. A black mark is found on the gill covers which, with the cheeks, are shot with blue or green. Pearly marks appear on some of the scales. The ventral and pectoral fins are yellowish: the dorsal, caudal and anal fins are transparent. The iris is golden.
There are no known external sexual characteristics.

GENERAL CARE: *L.auritus* needs a large tank and keeps as a rule to the middle reaches. It will however dig in the bed and only robust plants in pots should be put in the aquarium. The composition of the water is not critical: temperature 22°–25° C.
The diet should be principally made up of live animal matter.

BREEDING: *L.auritus* is a mouth brooder. The eggs are laid in a dark cavity, after the breeders have engaged in a great deal of digging. Some reports suggest that so many eggs can be laid that the male as well as the female has to take some of them in his mouth. Both parents guard the fry which are not difficult to raise on the normal fry food.

THE FAMILY CICHLIDAE

The genus Melanochromis

The genus *Melanochromis* contains another group of Mbuna fish from lake Malawi. These fish are closely related to those in the genus *Pseudotropheus*, but have technical differences in dentition and also have somewhat more pointed snouts, which facilitate their finding the insects on which they principally feed.

This is another genus in which there has been a great deal of confusion over nomenclature. At present it would seem that there are some seven species: five are described below. It will be seen however that some of these resemble very closely indeed, species in other genera, and this no doubt has increased the confusion.
In addition, there are a number of names (notably *M.chipokae*, *M.interruptus* and *M.loriae*) used by some amateurs, which have no scientific justification. The same is true of a number of descriptive names in the trade, in particular *auratus*, *bentonii caelestris*, *chipokae*, *sestonii* and *sprengeri*.

MELANOCHROMIS BREVIS
Family: *Cichlidae*
Genus: *Melanochromis*
English name: none
Origin: Lake Malawi
Size: Maximum 12 cm
Habitat: Found in shallow waters

SHAPE, COLORING AND MARKINGS: The body is fairly slender but the back is higher than in related species described below. The basic coloration is a reddish brown: a dark mark lies on the gill covers. The fins are the same color as the body: the dorsal fin has an indistinct dark band at the top: the anal fin has large oval orange marks.
Females are a dull rust brown, without orange marks on the anal fin.
Males are as described above, with distinctive orange marks on the anal fin.

GENERAL CARE: *M.brevis* is a somewhat aggressive fish and should be kept in a large species tank, furnished with secure structures of rock and some floating plants. The composition of the water is not critical: temperature 23°–25° C. A varied diet of live animal matter, including Tubifex, Daphnia, Cyclops and mosquito larvae should be provided for these fish.

BREEDING: *M.brevis* has not it seems as yet been bred in captivity.

MELANOCHROMIS MELANOPTERUS
Family: *Cichlidae*
Genus: *Melanochromis*
English name: none
Origin: Lake Malawi
Size: Maximum 13 cm
Habitat: Found in shallow waters

SHAPE, COLORING AND MARKINGS: The body is slender and laterally compressed. The basic coloration is light black. The head is dark grey. Two greenish blue lines appear: one on the base of the dorsal fin, the other from the gill covers to the base of the caudal fin. The yellow brown dorsal fin and the black caudal fin have narrow yellow borders. The ventral and pectoral fins are colorless.
There are no known external sexual characteristics.
GENERAL CARE: As for *M.brevis*.
BREEDING: This species has not as yet it seems been bred in captivity.

MELANOCHROMIS PARALLELUS
Family: *Cichlidae*
Genus: *Melanochromis*
English name: none
Origin: Lake Malawi
Size: Approximately 10 cm
Habitat: Found in shallow waters

SHAPE, COLORING AND MARKINGS: The body is slender but deeper than in most related species: the snout is less pointed. The basic coloration is black, with a blue horizontal line across the body. The coloration is at first sight similar to that of *Pseudotropheus auratus*, described below. In *M.parallelus* however, the dark marks on the caudal fin are less numerous and less prominent. The fins themselves are colorless.
Females are predominantly yellowish.
Males are as described above.

GENERAL CARE: As for *M.brevis*.

BREEDING: No information is available on the reproductive behavior of this species.

ADDITIONAL INFORMATION: *M.parallelus* was only established as a species with this name in 1976. Before then it was often known to amateurs as a variety of *Pseudotropheus auratus*, under the name 'the white auratus'.

MELANOCHROMIS SIMULANS
Family: *Cichlidae*
Genus: *Melanochromis*
English name: none
Origin: Lake Malawi
Size: Approximately 10 cm
Habitat: Found in shallow waters

SHAPE, COLORING AND MARKINGS: The body

shape is almost identical to that of *M.melanopterus*. The color patterns are virtually indistinguishable from those of *Pseudotropheus auratus* described below and like *M.parallelus* above, the snout is less pointed. When specimens of *M.simulans* and *M.parallelus* are compared it will be seen that *M.simulans* has the blunter snout.
There are no known external sexual characteristics.

GENERAL CARE: As for *M.brevis*.

BREEDING: No information is available on the reproductive behavior of this species.

MELANOCHROMIS VERMIVORUS

Family: *Cichlidae*
Genus: *Melanochromis*
English name: none
Origin: Lake Malawi
Size: Approximately 10 cm
Habitat: Found in shallow waters

SHAPE, COLORING AND MARKINGS: The body shape is identical to that of *M.melanopterus*. The basic coloration is black. A bright blue horizontal line runs from the forehead through the eye to the base of the caudal fin: a second blue line runs from the neck to the top of the caudal fin. The bright blue dorsal fin has a black base and streaks of black in the membranes. The pectoral, anal and caudal fins are black: the pectoral and anal fins have a light blue vorder and the latter, orange oval marks: the caudal fin has blue rays.
Females are yellow brown with two black lines replacing the blue lines of the male.
Males are as described above.

GENERAL CARE: As for *M.brevis*.

BREEDING: *M.vermivorus* has not as yet it seems, been bred in captivity.

819. *Nannacara anomala*

THE FAMILY CICHLIDAE

The genus Nannacara

There are three species in this genus of which *Nannacara anomala* and *Nannacara taenia* are described below. These South American Dwarf cichlids have been known to and kept by aquarists for quite a long time and have endeared themselves to amateurs because of their unusually peaceful disposition. They are rewarding pets and strongly to be recommended to those beginning to take an interest in cichlids. The third species is called *N.bimaculata*.

NANNACARA ANOMALA

Family: *Cichlidae*
Genus: *Nannacara*
English name: Golden-eyed Dwarf Cichlid
Origin: The Guianas
Size: Approximately 8 cm
Habitat: No information is available

SHAPE, COLORING AND MARKINGS: The body is elongated but laterally only moderately compressed. The outlines of the back and the belly are almost identical. The basic coloration is very variable. It is generally an olive brown. The flanks are an olive or iridescent metallic green, with gold or coppery overtones. Each scale has a dark spot. Variable iridescent green, dark blue or black marks lie on the gill covers. The eye is orange to red. When the fish is excited two dark longitudinal stripes, and sometimes indistinct transverse bars, appear on the flanks. The dorsal fin is olive to rust brown or orange red, with a dark or deep black edge and a pale green iridescent stripe below. The caudal fin is reddish: the anal fin has an orange red border. The ventral fins are yellowish green.
Females are predominantly greenish yellow. The fins are a plain yellow.
Males are as described above.

GENERAL CARE: *N.anomala* is suitable for a large species or community tank with some vegetation and plenty of retreats provided among stones, bogwood, flowerpots or pieces of coconut shell. The water should be mature and some of it changed regularly: temperature 24°–25° C. *N.anomala* is tolerant except during the mating season. The diet should be live animal matter, especially mosquito larvae, Enchytrae and Tubifex.

BREEDING: *N.anomala* will breed quite readily in any tank that is not overpopulated. No special breeding tank is required. The eggs will be laid in cavities in the flowerpots or coconut shells. The female alone guards the nest: the male should be removed immediately after spawning. The fry hatch after two or three days and are transferred by the female to a hole or depression where she continues to guard them for about five days until they are free swimming. The fry can then be raised on the normal fry foods.

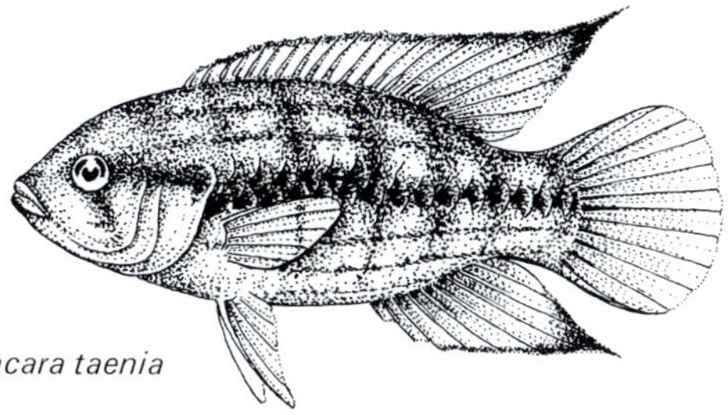

820. *Nannacara taenia*

NANNACARA TAENIA

Family: *Cichlidae*
Genus: *Nannacara*
English name: Lattice Dwarf Cichlid
Origin: The Amazon region
Size: Approximately 5 cm
Habitat: No details are available of

SHAPE, COLORING AND MARKINGS: The body shape and profile are identical to those of *N.anomala*. The basic coloration is variable: it is usually a dull yellow-brown, but may be yellowish or coppery. The throat is yellow to dark brown, but may be bluish or black in particularly well-colored specimens. A broad dark longitudinal band and other parallel but narrower bands run from the eye to the base of the caudal peduncle and may be crossed by transverse bands. The fins are colorless except for the bluish or violet dorsal and anal fins, which have a red border and black spots.
Females are predominantly a pale or greenish yellow.
Males are as described above.

GENERAL CARE: As for *N.anomala*.

BREEDING: No details are available on the reproductive behavior of this species.

THE FAMILY CICHLIDAE

The genus Nanochromis

821. *Nanochromis nudiceps*

There are at most three species in this small genus of African cichlids. The best known species and the only one normally kept by aquarists is *Nanochromis nudiceps* described below, a pleasing and usually unaggressive fish that can easily be kept in a community tank. *Nanochromis dimidiatus*, an almost entirely black fish with plain yellowish fins seems never to be imported and the third species, *Nanochromis squamiceps* was suspected to be no more than a variety of *N.dimidiatus*. This, however, has proved not to be the case.

NANOCHROMIS NUDICEPS

Family: *Cichlidae*
Genus: *Nanochromis*
English name: none
Origin: The Congo basin
Size: Males to 8 cm: females to 6 cm
Habitat: Found in a variety of waters

SHAPE, COLORING AND MARKINGS: The body is elongated and laterally very slightly compressed. The dorsal fin is low but with a very long base running from immediately behind the head to the caudal peduncle where it has a pointed tip. The caudal fin is rounded: the anal, pectoral and ventral fins taper to points. The basic coloration is bluish violet: the belly is a shiny green. The fins, except for the colorless pectoral fins are bluish or bluish grey. The dorsal fin has a yellowish or white border above a dark margin. Alternate patches of light and dark stipples appear in the upper lobe of the caudal fin.
Females are smaller, with more rounded bellies and a shorter base to the dorsal fin. Males are as described above.

GENERAL CARE: *N.nudiceps* is suitable for a well planted community tank, with retreats among rocks, flowerpots and coconut shells, and a sandy bottom. Its inclination to dig is moderated when given sufficient hiding places. The water should be fairly soft (6° DH) and slightly acid (pH 6.8): temperature 25° C. A varied diet of live animal matter, especially insects, should be given.

BREEDING: If a spawning pair can be identified and caught in the community tank they should be transferred to a fairly large breeding tank with soft, slightly acid water at 27°–28° C. A flower pot, with a broken edge (to allow access by the fish) should be filled with sand and left, covered with a flat stone, in the darkest corner of the tank. There should be plenty of plants and retreats to give cover to the fry and to allow the female to escape from the male if, at first, the breeders do not establish a friendly relationship. Both adults will clean the nesting cavity and up to 100 eggs will be laid on the underside of the roof of the pot. Only the female guards the eggs: the male merely guards the territory. Both fish will however guard the fry who should be fed liberally on *Artemia* and Cyclops *nauplii*. If a suitable breeding pair cannot be identified in the community tank, the fish can be allowed to spawn in that tank but the fry should be reared apart.

THE FAMILY CICHLIDAE

The genus Pelmatochromis

These dwarf African cichlids are very beautifully colored, relatively unaggressive fish and are not too difficult to keep. If put in a community tank however, the amateur must keep a careful watch on them when the spawning season begins: at that time when they begin to mate they may become very aggressive towards other fish, at best chasing them away relentlessly and, at worst, in a crowded small tank where the victims have no place to hide, killing them. Some species are quite determined diggers and plants should be protected in concealed pots. The nomenclature of this genus has been unsettled for some time. Recent publications indicate that the correct scientific name for *Pelmatochromis annectens* is *Thysia annectens*. *P.arnoldi* is now known as *Thysia ansorgei; P.guentheri* changed to *Chromidotilapia guntheri; P.kingsleyae* to *Chromidotilapia kingsleyae; P.Kribensis* to *Pelvicachromis kribensis; P.Pulcher* to *Pelvicachromis pulcher* and *P.Subocellatus* to *Pelvicachromis subocellatus*. In this encyclopedia these species remain classified under their former names.

PELMATOCHROMIS ANNECTENS

Family: *Cichlidae*
Genus: *Pelmatochromis*
English name: none
Origin: Tropical West Africa from Liberia to Nigeria
Size: Approximately 10 cm
Habitat: Found in fresh and brackish waters near the coast

SHAPE, COLORING AND MARKINGS: The body is elongated, fairly deep and laterally very compressed. The back has a rather more rounded profile than the belly. The basic coloration varies according to the condition and mood of the fish. It should be very dark to black, with a green iridescence on the flanks. The throat is pale blue to bright red. A number of indistinct irregular transverse bands and a longitudinal stripe lie on the body: four dark patches on the flanks and a large red-edged, blue-green patch on the gill covers are prominent. The dorsal and anal fins are yellow to greenish at the front and greenish with red patches at the back. The caudal fin has light and dark patterning. The vertical fins are blue black with elongated rays.
Females have less vivid colors. The dorsal and anal fins are less pointed: the ventral fins have no elongated rays. Sexually mature females have two white patches at the level of the vent. Males are as described above.

GENERAL CARE: *P.annectens* is suitable for a large aquarium with scattered plants and plenty of retreats in bogwood, pieces of coconut shell and similar structures. It is a peaceful species outside the mating season, and quite suitable for a community tank (see Introduction to the genus, above). Floating plants should be introduced for *P.annectens* dislikes strong light. The composition of the water is not critical, but fairly hard water is best and one tablespoonful of salt may be added to the tank for every ten liters of water. Temperature 22°–26°C. All live foods will be accepted eagerly: dried food may be given for a change.

BREEDING: This is not difficult. It is best to allow the fish to pair off naturally, rather than to select pairs. *P.annectens* prefers to lay its eggs in upturned flowerpots or pieces of coconut shell. The light brown eggs hatch in about three days. Both parents share in brood care. The fry can be fed with the usual fry foods.

PELMATOCHROMIS ARNOLDI

Family: *Cichlidae*

Genus: *Pelmatochromis*

English name: none

Origin: Topical West Africa from Liberia to Nigeria

Size: Approximately 10 cm

Habitat: Found in fresh and brackish waters near the coast

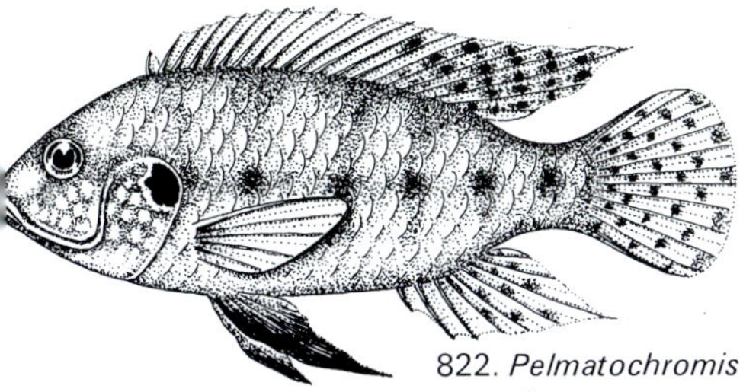

822. *Pelmatochromis annectens*

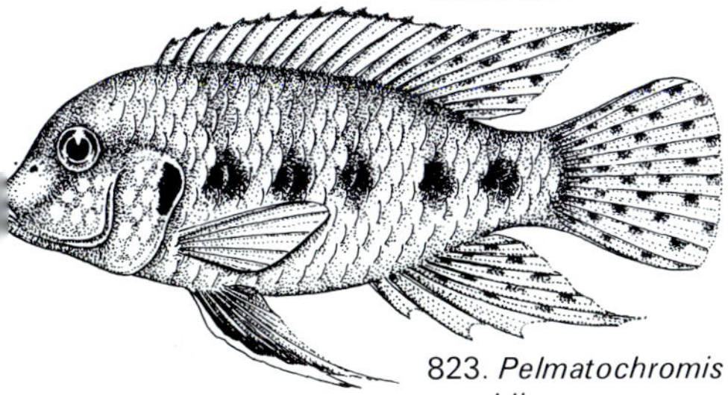

823. *Pelmatochromis arnoldi*

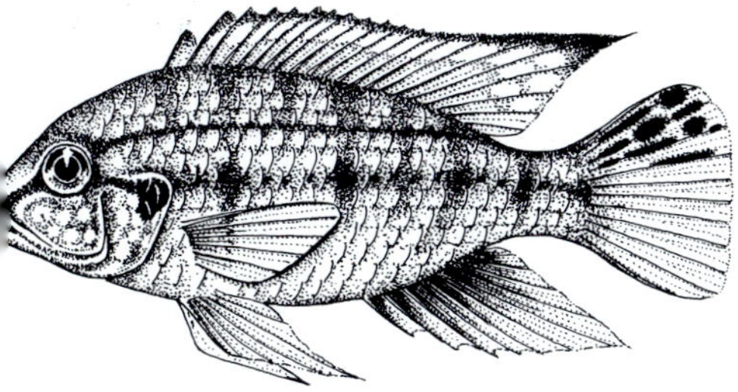

824. *Pelmatochromis guentheri*

SHAPE, COLORING AND MARKINGS: The body profile and shape are identical to those of *P.annectens*, but the head is somewhat more elongated. The basic coloration is ochre to grey, with a silvery overtone. Five dark patches lie on the flanks and a vivid iridescent area is found on the gill covers. The fins are pale green: the dorsal and anal fins have dark marks at the back. During the mating season the lower half of the body of the male has a deep terracotta to orange red color.
No further external sexual characteristics are known.

GENERAL CARE: As for *P.annectens*.

BREEDING: No information is available on the reproductive behavior of the species which is however likely to be similar to that of related species.

PELMATOCHROMIS GUENTHERI

Family: *Cichlidae*

Genus: *Pelmatochromis*

English name: none

Origin: West Africa, from Gabon to Ghana

Size: Approximately 16 cm in the wild but remains considerably smaller in captivity where it is sexually mature at 8 cm

Habitat: Found in both fresh and brackish waters

SHAPE, COLORING AND MARKINGS: The body shape and profile are identical to those of *P.annectens*, but the head is rather pointed. The basic coloration is an olive green with a bluish overtone. The back is much darker: the belly is a pale green to yellowish. A distinct but irregular longitudinal stripe runs from the snout, across the eye to the caudal peduncle, parallel to and below a narrow very regular dark line running from the eye to the caudal peduncle. A number of transverse bands, intersecting both these longitudinal stripes may also be present. A prominent iridescent blue green patch lies on the gill covers. The dorsal fin is yellowish, with a reddish border and pearly flecks in the center: the anal fin is bright red: the ventral fins are green or silvery. The iris is red.
Females when adult are more finely patterned. The anal, dorsal and caudal fins have dark borders: a line of black specks lies at the base of the dorsal fin.
Males are as described above.

GENERAL CARE: As for *P.annectens* but *P.guentheri* is somewhat intolerant even outside the mating season and therefore unsuitable for a community tank. This species is a voracious eater.

BREEDING: Not difficult. *P.guentheri* is a mouth brooder. Both parents share brood care.

PELMATOCHROMIS KINGSLEYAE

Family: *Cichlidae*

Genus: *Pelmatochromis*

English name: none

Origin: Nigeria

Size: Approximately 10 cm

Habitat: No details are available

SHAPE, COLORING AND MARKINGS: The body shape and profile closely resemble those of *P.annectens* but *P.kingsleyae* has a slightly deeper body, with a steep forehead, a pointed snout and fleshy lips. Outside the breeding season the coloration is not very striking: the basic coloration is a yellowish brown with a greenish overtone. Six dark transverse bands may be present on the body and may be crossed by a dark longitudinal line. The fins are

825. *Pelmatochromis kribensis*

a transparent ochre: the dorsal and anal fins have a dark border.
Females are usually larger and have red bellies with a number of dark patches.
Males are as described above.

GENERAL CARE: As for *P.guentheri* but the diet should include a vegetable supplement.

BREEDING: Not difficult. *P.kingsleyae* is a mouth brooder. The best breeding temperature is about 28°C.

ADDITIONAL INFORMATION: *P.kingsleyae* closely resembles *P.guentheri* of which it may indeed be no more than a sub-species.

PELMATOCHROMIS KRIBENSIS

Family: *Cichlidae*

Genus: *Pelmatochromis*

English name: none

Origin: Cameroon

Size: Males to 9 cm: females to 7 cm

Habitat: No details are available of its natural habitat

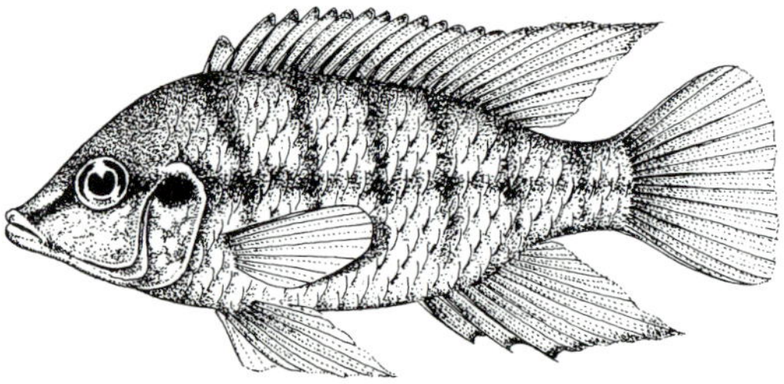

826. *Pelmatochromis kingsleyae*

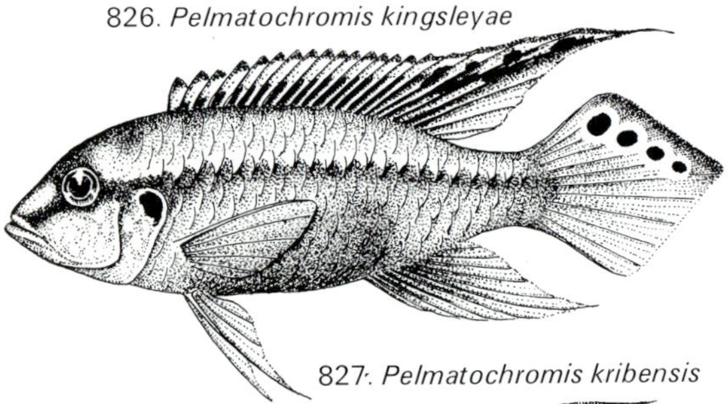

827. *Pelmatochromis kribensis*

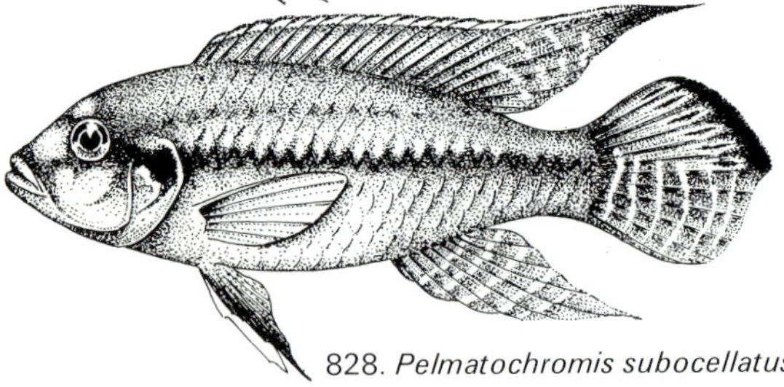

828. *Pelmatochromis subocellatus*

SHAPE, COLORING AND MARKINGS: The body shape and profile are identical to those of *P.annectens*. The basic coloration is variable but usually the upper half of the body is brown with a blue to violet overtone. The flanks and underside of the body are pale blue to violet, with greenish iridescent patches. A red patch appears on the belly and a brown patch with red above and blue below, on the gill covers. In young specimens a dark longitudinal stripe may be visible on the back and another running from the snout, across the eye to the base of the caudal fin. The fins are multicolored.
Females are usually more brightly patterned. The ventral fins are a deep wine red with a blue leading edge.
Males usually have a number of dark patches in the upper lobe of their yellow bordered caudal fin. The pectoral fins are violet with a blue leading edge.

GENERAL CARE: As for *P.annectens*.
BREEDING: As for *P.annectens*.

PELMATOCHROMIS PULCHER

Family: *Cichlidae*
Genus: *Pelmatochromis*
English name: none
Origin: Nigeria, the mouth of the Niger river
Size: Approximately 10 cm
Habitat: Found in both fresh and brackish waters

SHAPE, COLORING AND MARKINGS: The body shape and profile are identical to those of *P.annectens*. The basic coloration is a dark green, with a brownish overtone. The belly is reddish. Occasionally the flanks are also reddish but otherwise they are a delicate green with a blue overtone. The gill covers bear a number of bluish green iridescent lines and a large coppery to blue black iridescent patch. The dorsal fin is pale green, dark violet at the base, with red patches and a red border in the soft rays. The caudal fin is greenish with a black border along the upper edge and rust brown marks elsewhere. The anal fin is violet with a black border: the ventral fins are a very dark blue to black. Young specimens are predominantly yellow and may carry dark longitudinal stripes.
Females when sexually mature have a distinct red patch at the level of the pectoral fins.
Males are as described above.

GENERAL CARE: As for *P.annectens*.

BREEDING: *P.pulcher* has not as yet it seems been bred in captivity.

PELMATOCHROMIS SUBOCELLATUS

Family: *Cichlidae*
Genus: *Pelmatochromis*
English name: none
Origin: The central Congo region
Size: Approximately 10 cm
Habitat: Found in both fresh and brackish waters

SHAPE, COLORING AND MARKINGS: The body is elongated and only moderately compressed. The curve of the back is almost the same as that of the underside of the body. The basic coloration is variable. The back is usually grey green to green black: the underside is a pale red and the flanks are olive green to ochre with a strong brassy gleam. A prominent longitudinal stripe runs from the eye to the base of the caudal fin: a rather less prominent line may be present above it and transverse bands may also be visible. The fins are usually predominantly yellow to rust brown with shades of every color in the rainbow and countless pale blue specks and stripes.
Females during the mating season have a gold eye-like black spot on the dorsal fin.
The fish turns quite black for the duration of the spawning period except for a small area above the rear edge of the pectoral fins and the section of the dorsal fin above, which areas become white. At other times females are distinguished by their smaller ventral fins and rounded dorsal and anal fins.
Males are as described above.

829. *Pelmatochromis subocellatus*

GENERAL CARE: As for *P.annectens*.

BREEDING: This is not difficult if a suitable pair can be found: finding such a pair is not always simple. The eggs will be laid under a flat stone and *P.subocellatus* will energetically dig up the bed. The fry are easy to raise on the normal fry foods.

830. *Pelmatochromis pulcher*

THE FAMILY CICHLIDAE

The genus Pseudotropheus

The genus *Pseudotropheus* is far and away the largest group of Mbuna fish found in Lake Malawi. There are at least fifteen species, but it is a group in which there is great confusion over nomenclature, and some recently named species have not perhaps been as yet subjected to full critical scientific investigation. One or two species, such as *Pseudotropheus auratus* and *Pseudotropheus zebra* are quite well-known to aquarists, others are only known to a small group of specialists. Eleven species are discussed below, including one or two of uncertain status, but concerning which there has in recent years been considerable mention.

All these fish are found near rocky shores of the lake, in generally crowded communities. In the aquarium they tend to be aggressive, and should be kept in species tanks where their generally vivid colors and generally hardy nature make them very attractive pets. They are perhaps one of the genera that will be of most immediate interest to amateurs who are beginning to take an interest in cichlids for the first time. They are not as demanding as some of the more unusual cichlids and accordingly are particularly suitable for the less experienced amateur.

831. *Pseudotropheus auratus* ♂

832. *Pseudotropheus auratus* ♀

PSEUDOTROPHEUS AURATUS

Family: *Cichlidae*
Genus: *Pseudotropheus*
English name: none
Origin: Lake Malawi
Size: Maximum 12 cm
Habitat: Found near rocky shores

SHAPE, COLORING AND MARKINGS: The body is fairly deep and laterally somewhat compressed: the curve of the back is almost identical to that of the belly. The dorsal fin has a very long base: the edge of the caudal fin is rounded. The basic coloration is a deep black. Two bright blue horizontal lines run along the body: one runs from the eye to the caudal peduncle, the other lies above, just below the base of the dorsal fin. Two or three transverse bands lie on the forehead. The black anal fin is blue towards the edge and carries an oval orange spot. The dorsal fin is bright blue: the other fins are colorless, but the caudal fin may be shaded black.

Females are a bright golden yellow, with three black horizontal lines, two positioned as the blue lines in the males, and the third running along the top of the dorsal fin.

Males, when mature, are as described above: immature males, and mature males when alarmed, wear the colors of females.

GENERAL CARE: *P.auratus* is an aggressive territorial fish only suitable for a large species tank with well-secured large rock structures and very robust plants, to provide adequate retreats. The composition of the water is not critical: temperature 22°–25°C. *P.auratus* will usually remain in the lower middle reaches of the tank. A varied diet of live animal matter, dried food, algae and lettuce should be provided.

BREEDING: *P.auratus* is a mouth brooder. There are few detailed accounts of the reproductive behavior of this species, but it seems in general to be the same as that of the *Haplochromis* species.

ADDITIONAL INFORMATION: There is a variety of *P.auratus* from the neighborhood of the island of Likoma, in which the bright blue horizontal bands of the male are dark blue.

PSEUDOTROPHEUS ELONGATUS

Family: *Cichlidae*
Genus: *Pseudotropheus*
English name: none
Origin: Lake Malawi
Size: Maximum 12 cm
Habitat: Found near rocky shores

SHAPE, COLORING AND MARKINGS: The body is very much more slender than in related species. The basic coloration is a light brown. The body is crossed by a number of dark vertical bands which descend to the level of the pectoral fins. All the fins, and especially the anal, dorsal and caudal fins are almost black. There are no known external sexual characteristics.

GENERAL CARE: As for *P.auratus*.
BREEDING: As for *P.auratus*.

ADDITIONAL INFORMATION: A very similar fish has been named *P.modestus*

PSEUDOTROPHEUS FUSCUS

Family: *Cichlidae*
Genus: *Pseudotropheus*
English name: none
Origin: Lake Malawi
Size: Approximately 12 cm
Habitat: Found near rocky shores

SHAPE, COLORING AND MARKINGS: The body shape closely resembles that of *P.auratus*. The basic coloration is black. Two dark blue horizontal lines run across the body, one along the middle of the flanks, the other from the neck to the caudal peduncle.

Females are beige, with two black horizontal lines.
Males are as described above.

General care: As for *P. auratus*.

Breeding: As for *P.auratus*.

PSEUDOTROPHEUS LIVINGSTONII

Family: *Cichlidae*
Genus: *Pseudotropheus*
English name: none
Origin: Lake Malawi
Size: Approximately 12 cm
Habitat: Found near rocky shores but also in deeper water in the lake

Shape, coloring and markings: The body shape is identical to that of *P.auratus*. The basic coloration is a bright golden orange. Three indistinct dark vertical bars lie on the body. In some specimens the basic coloration may be more brown. The fins are white to bluish white: the dorsal fin has an orange border. The anal fin bears two oval orange spots.
Females are brownish, and the dorsal, anal and caudal fins are yellow.
Males are as described above.

General care: As for *P.auratus*.

Breeding: As for *P.auratus*.

833. *Pseudotropheus livingstonii*

PSEUDOTROPHEUS MICROSTOMA

Family: *Cichlidae*
Genus: *Pseudotropheus*
English name: none
Origin: Lake Malawi
Size: Approximately 12 cm
Habitat: Found near rocky shores

Shape, coloring and markings: The body shape is identical to that of *P.auratus*. The eyes are small. The basic coloration is a bright yellow: the flanks are an iridescent blue. The pectoral and ventral fins are colorless: the dorsal, caudal and anal fins are yellow, the last has a dark edge.
Females have no blue on the flanks.
Males are as described above.

General care: As for *P.auratus*.

Breeding: As for *P.auratus*.

834. *Pseudotropheus microstoma* ♂

835. *Pseudotropheus microstoma* ♀

PSEUDOTROPHEUS MINUTUS

Family: *Cichlidae*
Genus: *Pseudotropheus*
English name: none
Origin: Lake Malawi
Size: Approximately 10 cm
Habitat: Found very near to rocky shores

Shape, coloring and markings: The body shape is identical to that of *P.auratus*. The basic coloration is a bright blue. Across the body lie a number of indistinct transverse bands, five being below the dorsal fin. Two dark marks lie on the snout, and another on the gill covers. The pectral and ventral fins are colorless, the latter with a dark edge: the anal, caudal and dorsal fins are an orange brown.
Females are a brownish green, sometimes tinged with blue: the transverse bands are less distinct.
Males are as described above.

General care: As for *P.auratus*.

Breeding: As for *P.auratus*.

PSEUDOTROPHEUS NOVEMFASCIATUS

Family: *Cichlidae*
Genus: *Pseudotropheus*
English name: none
Origin: Lake Malawi
Size: Approximately 10 cm
Habitat: Found near rocky shores

Shape, coloring and markings: The body shape is very similar to that of *P.auratus* but is slightly deeper. The basic coloration is a reddish brown. Nine dark but indistinct transverse bands lie across the body and the caudal peduncle. The tip of the snout and the lower jaw are very dark or black, and dark patches are found on the gill covers and at the root of the tail. The fins are colorless, tinged with red, and the dorsal fin has a dark band near the top.
There are no known external sexual characteristics.

General care: As for *P.auratus*.

Breeding: As for *P.auratus*.

PSEUDOTROPHEUS TROPHEOPS

Family: *Cichlidae*
Genus: *Pseudotropheus*
English name: none
Origin: Lake Malawi
Size: Approximately 12 cm
Habitat: Found near rocky shores

SHAPE, COLORING AND MARKINGS: The body shape resembles that of *P.auratus*, but is somewhat deeper. The basic coloration is very dark, and in the spawning season, almost black, when each scale develops a brilliant blue spot. Darker transverse bands lie on the body, and are prominent or almost invisible, according to the mood of the fish. The fins

836. *Pseudotropheus novemfasciatus*

are dark, with lighter edges, and one orange oval patch lies on the anal fin.
Females are bright lemon, with a prominent dark stripe along the top of the dorsal fin. Males are as described above.

GENERAL CARE: As for *P.auratus*.

BREEDING: As for *P.auratus*.

ADDITIONAL INFORMATION: There is a subspecies, *P.tropheops gracilior*, with a more slender body.

PSEUDOTROPHEUS TURSIOPS

Family: *Cichlidae*
Genus: *Pseudotropheus*
English name: none
Origin: Lake Malawi
Size: Approximately 12 cm
Habitat: Found near rocky shores

SHAPE, COLORING AND MARKINGS: The basic shape is identical to that of *P.auratus*. The

837. *Pseudotropheus zebra*

838. *Pseudotropheus tropheops* ▷

basic coloration is brown: the back is tinged with blue, the underside with violet. An indistinct dark horizontal line runs along the center of the body, below another even less distinct line beneath the dorsal fin. A dark mark lies on the gill covers. The fins are dark, and an oval orange spot lies on the anal fin.
There are no known external sexual characteristics.

GENERAL CARE: As for *P.auratus*.

BREEDING: As for *P.auratus*.

PSEUDOTROPHEUS WILLIAMSI

Family: *Cichlidae*
Genus: *Pseudotropheus*
English name: none
Origin: Lake Malawi
Size: Approximately 12 cm
Habitat: Found near rocky shores

SHAPE, COLORING AND MARKINGS: The body shape is identical to that of *P.auratus*. The basic coloration is a dark brown. Three rows of dark marks lie on the body, one on the middle of the flanks, another on the lateral line, the third along the base of the dorsal fin. The fins are grey, and the dorsal and caudal fins have a wide dark edge.
There are no known external sexual characteristics.

GENERAL CARE: As for *P.auratus*.

BREEDING: As for *P.auratus*.

PSEUDOTROPHEUS ZEBRA

Family: *Cichlidae*
Genus: *Pseudotropheus*
English name: none
Origin: Lake Malawi
Size: Maximum 16 cm
Habitat: Found near rocky shores

SHAPE, COLORING AND MARKINGS: The body shape is identical to that of *P.auratus*. The color patterns can vary a great deal, but the basic coloration is grey. Six dark transverse bands lie across the body. A black sickle-shaped stripe runs across the forehead between the eyes and another transverse stripe runs across the neck. The ventral fins are very dark: the pectoral fins are colorless. The dorsal, caudal and anal fins are grey, the last with three round white spots. There are no known external sexual characteristics.

GENERAL CARE: As for *P.auratus*.

BREEDING: As for *P.auratus*.

THE FAMILY CICHLIDAE

The genus Pterophyllum

The genus *Pterophyllum* contains some of the best known and most popular of cichlids, or indeed of all aquarium fish. These Angelfish have always appealed to amateurs because of their majesty and beauty. They were formerly rare and expensive but in recent years have become much more readily available: their decrease in scarcity has not however affected their popularity.

It is not surprising that the interest in and demand for these fish has led to the selective breeding of varieties not known in the wild. In nature there are only three species: *Pterophyllum altum*, the Deep Angelfish, *Pterophyllum dumerilii* and the most common, *Pterophyllum scalare*, the Angelfish. Another species, *Pterophyllum eimekei* is often mentioned in the older literature but it is now accepted that this name is only a synonym for *P.scalare*.

PTEROPHYLLUM ALTUM

Family: *Cichlidae*

Genus: *Pterophyllum*

English name: Deep Angelfish

Origin: Venezuela, the basin of the Orinoco river

Size: Maximum 15 cm

Habitat: Found in overgrown, sluggish or still waters

SHAPE, COLORING AND MARKINGS: The body is flat and disc-shaped. In profile there is a sharp indentation in the head, just above the eye. The extremely long dorsal and anal fins and the oval body increase the impression of depth. The basic coloration is silvery with a slight bronze sheen. The back is darker, almost olive brown: the belly is a shiny silvery white. Four dark vertical or transverse bands lie across the body: the first runs down in an almost straight line from the eye: the second runs from the front of the dorsal fin to the base of the anal fin: the third runs from the tip of the dorsal fin to the tip of the anal fin: the fourth runs across the caudal peduncle. Between the first and second bands an indistinct vertical greyish stripe runs from the base of the dorsal fin through the edge of the gill cover to the base of the ventral fin. The fins are bluish grey.

There are no known external sexual characteristics.

GENERAL CARE: *P.altum* needs a deep spacious species tank with principally ribbon-leaved plants such as large varieties of *Echinodorus*, grouped to provide retreats and allow territories to be established. There must also be adequate free swimming space. A community tank is only suitable if the other denizens are very quiet peaceful fish. The water should be fairly soft (6°DH), and slightly acid (pH 6.8): temperature 25°–27°C. Because of its small mouth *P.altum* can only catch small animal matter such as mosquito larvae and Enchytrae but it will enthusiastically hunt Daphnia and Cyclops. It is not a predatory fish as that term is generally understood but it will eat small Tetras.

BREEDING: A breeding pair when identified by their behavior and tendency to pair off should be transferred to a special tank laid out as recommended above. Breeding temperature 26°C. The fish will spawn on a ribbon leaf or on any imitation leaf put in the tank after meticulously cleaning it. The 300–400 eggs should be removed while attached to the leaf and put in a small tank with 10 cm of peaty water with gentle aeration. The eggs hatch in three days and the fry will be free swimming after a week. They should be fed for the first week on infusoria and *Artemia nauplii*, and during the second week on the latter alone. Alternatively the eggs can be left in the care of the parents who will fan them until they hatch: they may chew the eggs to release the fry. The parents practice brood care and the fry are gathered into a tight ball every evening.

ADDITIONAL INFORMATION: *P.altum* is very delicate and very sensitive to chemicals customarily used to treat fish diseases. If the fish seem sickly they should, before being given drugs, be subject to heat treatment, where the temperature of the tank is raised to 32°–33°C for a short time. This is often effective.

Rival or courting males may emit loud croaks, caused by the movement of the jaws.

839. *Pterophyllum scalare*

PTEROPHYLLUM SCALARE

Family: *Cichlidae*

Genus: *Pterophyllum*

English name: Angelfish

Origin: The Amazon basin

Size: Maximum 15 cm

Habitat: Found in sluggish and still overgrown waters

SHAPE, COLORING AND MARKINGS: The body is slightly longer than it is deep, but still gives the impression of being very deep and almost disc-shaped: the snout is slightly protuberant and the forehead rises much more sharply than in *P.altum*. The basic coloration is greyish green with a silvery sheen: the back is olive green: the belly lighter. Four prominent and three less prominent dark bands lie on the flanks: the most prominent of all runs from the tip of the elongated dorsal fin to the tip of the elongated anal fin. The dorsal fin is bluish grey and white: the anal fin is darker: the ventral fins are yellowish green, tipped with orange. The caudal fin is bluish grey and is wider at the edge than in related species.

There are no known external sexual characteristics.

GENERAL CARE: As for *P.altum* but *P.scalare* is a more robust fish and while it will appreciate the same care as *P.altum* it will not be upset if these critical conditions are not strictly maintained, although it is best to do so.

BREEDING: As for *P.altum*.

ADDITIONAL INFORMATION: See *P.altum*.

THE FAMILY CICHLIDAE

The genus Steatocranus

Only one species, the unusual African Blockhead, *Steatocranus casuarius*, described below, is of interest to aquarists in this genus. A hardy, aggressive fish, it is not particularly attractively colored, and has not become very popular with amateurs. Nevertheless, its life style is a little unusual, and kept under the right conditions, it can be an interesting pet. In the wild, it is found in very fast flowing waters, but it confines itself to the bed and swims about little. In consequence, its swim bladder has degenerated, and it can no longer maneuver itself for any length of time at any other water level. As noted below however, unlike many bottom loving fish, *S.casuarius* will not as a rule, damage the plants on the bed.

840. *Steatocranus casuarius*

STEATOCRANUS CASUARIUS

Family: *Cichlidae*

Genus: *Steatocranus*

English name: African Blockhead

Origin: The lower reaches of the Congo

Size: Maximum 10 cm

Habitat: Found near rapids and waterfalls, living in cracks and crevasses among the rocks

SHAPE, COLORING AND MARKINGS: The body is elongated and laterally somewhat compressed. A large bump appears on the forehead. The dorsal fin has a very long base, and like the shorter anal fin, extends to the rounded caudal fin. The basic coloration is variable. It is usually a uniform brown or leaden grey, sometimes with a slight violet tinge. The edges of the scales are lighter, creating a distinct net like pattern. The fins are transparent.
Females are smaller and have a smaller bump on the forehead.
Males are as described above.

GENERAL CARE: *S.casuarius* needs a spacious aquarium with plenty of retreats among cavities, plant pots or coconut shells buried in the bed: these it will soon begin to inhabit. The composition of the water is not critical: temperature 25°C. It requires a substantial diet of live animal matter. It will usually leave plants alone, but is not suitable for an attractively planted aquarium and should only be kept with other species of large, surface loving fish as its companions.

BREEDING: *S.casuarius* can be very aggressive, even towards larger fish, during the spawning season, and is best bred in a special tank. Both parents will empty a plant pot they find in the bed, and lay the eggs there. They both practice brood care, and at first the fry live on food pre-masticated by the male. The eggs hatch after about three weeks. The fry are about 1 cm long, and can eat immediately Enchytrae, chopped up Tubifex, and Daphnia. At this stage, holes are dug near the nest where the young can retreat in times of danger. The young fish spend the night in the nest, guarded by the parents.

THE FAMILY CICHLIDAE

The genus Symphysodon

There are only four species known in this, one of the most beautiful genera of fresh water tropical fish. These discus or pompadour fish are as beautiful and majestic in their deportment as they are unusual in shape. There are few amateurs who do not aspire to keeping and breeding these lovely fish. They are however delicate and somewhat difficult to keep in good condition. Nevertheless they more than repay the care they both need and deserve. There are two distinct groups: *Symphysodon discus*, and *Symphysodon aequifasciata*, of which latter species there are three sub-species, *S.aequifasciata aequifasciata*, *S.aequifasciata axelrodi*, and *S.aequifasciata haraldi*.

SYMPHYSODON AEQUIFASCIATA AEQUIFASCIATA

Family: *Cichlidae*

Genus: *Symphysodon*

English name: Green Discus

Origin: The central and western Amazon basin

Size: Maximum 15 cm

Habitat: Found in still waters in the bends of rivers, where there are scattered rocks and overhanging vegetation

SHAPE, COLORING AND MARKINGS: The body is almost as deep as it is long, laterally very compressed, and almost round. The dorsal and anal fins are not very deep, but have very long based. The tapering ventral fins are elongated. The end-positioned mouth is small: the eyes are large. The basic coloration is brown with a slight greenish tinge. Nine dark, vertical stripes lie across the body: the first runs through the eyes, the last across the caudal peduncle. A pattern of luminescent blue stripes appears along the top and bottom of the body and on the head. The ventral fins are red, the front ray blue. The dorsal and anal fins are edged with red, black at the base and carry a pattern of blue stripes and dots.
There are no known external sexual characteristics.

GENERAL CARE: *S.aequifasciata aequifasciata* needs a large quiet species tank, with some clumps of ribbon-leaved plants arranged to give plenty of free swimming space as well as adequate retreats, provided also with bogwood. The water should be soft (not above 5°DH) and slightly acid (pH 6–6.5) and its composition checked regularly: temperature 28°–32°C. All sorts of small, live animal matter will be eaten, but only thoroughly clean, small quantities of Tubifex should be given. Shredded beef heart should also be included in a varied diet. Depending on the size of the tank, one or more pairs may be kept.

BREEDING: Discus fish must be allowed to pair naturally. Only those raised in soft water and fed properly will breed successfully. A spacious breeding tank with subdued lighting and plenty of retreats is needed. Some pieces of bogwood, anchored on the bed and reaching to the surface are essential: the fish will lay eggs on one of the pieces, roughly halfway up the tank. The water should be very soft (not above 3° DH) and slightly acid (approximately pH 6): temperature 30°C. The tank must be kept very quiet. Both fish will meticulously clean the chosen breeding spot before the yellowish eggs are laid: both guard the eggs. They will often eat them (especially with the first few nests), but this cannot be prevented. The eggs hatch after about two days, often helped by the parent fish. The fry hang by a thread for a few days. When the yolk sac is digested, the young fish begin to swim and attach themselves to the skin of one of the parent fish. The parents at this time, if well fed previously, secrete a white mucus on their skin, which is the only food the young fish can eat for the first few days. The fry feed as a group on each parent fish alternately. When it is time to change from one fish to the other, the parents move alongside each other, tails together and heads facing in opposite directions. The fins are moved, the body of the fish on which the young are feeding shudders violently, and the young fish swim to the other parent. After a time, the skin secretions decrease and the young fish become more independent. They can now be fed with larger sorts of food, such as Enchytrae, small mosquito larvae, finely seived water fleas, and extremely finely shredded beef heart. If the parents do not secrete sufficient mucus to continue feeding the fry, then young fish which have fed on their parents for at least four days can be raised artificially: they should be fed at least six times a day with freshly hatched *Artemia nauplii* and infusoria, but not with Cyclops *nauplii*, Because of the large amount of food in the breeding tank, it must be kept scrupulously clean, but otherwise rearing the fry is not difficult.

841. *Symphysodon discus*

SYMPHYSODON AEQUIFASCIATA AXELRODI

Family: *Cichlidae*

Genus: *Symphysodon*

English name: Brown Discus

Origin: The Amazon region

Size: Maximum 14 cm

Habitat: Found in still waters with overhead vegetation

SHAPE, COLORING AND MARKINGS: The body shape is identical to that of *S.aequifasciata aequifasciata*. The basic coloration is a light or dark brown: nine vertical dark stripes lie across the body, of which usually only the first and last, which run respectively through the eye and across the caudal peduncle, are clearly visible. The dorsal and anal fins are the same color, but turn reddish brown towards the tips. The ventral fins are red with a blue front ray. A beautiful pattern of iridescent greenish blue stripes and dots lies on the head, the neck and the dorsal and anal fins.
There are no known external sexual characteristics.

GENERAL CARE: As for *S.aequifasciata aequifasciata*.

BREEDING: As for *S.aequifasciata aequifasciata*.

ADDITIONAL INFORMATION: *S.aequifasciata axelrodi* is the most common species in aquariums. In the wild there is also a red variety of the species, with a red body.

SYMPHYSODON AEQUIFASCIATA HARALDI

Family: *Cichlidae*

Genus: *Symphysodon*

English name: Blue Discus

Origin: The Amazon region

Size: Maximum 12 cm

Habitat: Found in still waters with overhead vegetation

SHAPE, COLORING AND MARKINGS: The body shape is identical to that of *S.aequifasciata aequifasciata*. The basic coloration is dark yellowish-brown: the front of the body and the head are reddish-brown. Nine dark, vertical stripes lie across the body, but often only the one across the caudal peduncle is visible. The dorsal and anal fins are reddish-purple, becoming an orangey-yellow towards the back. A beautiful pattern of iridescent, greenish-blue horizontal lines lies over most of the body, and in some specimens over the entire body including the fins. The lines break up into dots towards the edges of the fins.

842. *Symphysodon aequifasciata haraldi*

There are no known external sexual characteristics.

GENERAL CARE: As for *S.aequifasciata aequifasciata.*

BREEDING: As for *S.aequifasciata aequifasciata.*

SYMPHYSODON DISCUS

Family: *Cichlidae*

Genus: *Symphysodon*

English name: Discus

Origin: The Amazon region

Size: Maximum 15 cm

Habitat: Found in still waters with overhanging vegetation

SHAPE, COLORING AND MARKINGS: The body shape is virtually identical to that of *S.aequifasciata aequifasciata,* but slightly longer. The basic coloration is reddish-brown. Nine dark, vertical transverse bands lie across the body and all are usually clearly visible. A pattern of bluish-green, iridescent horizontal lines is found on the head, the body and the fins. The red-edged dorsal fin and the anal fin are reddish-brown. The red ventral fins are elongated and taper to a point.
There are no known external sexual characteristics.

GENERAL CARE: As for *S.aequifasciata aequifasciata.*

BREEDING: As for *S.aequifasciata aequifasciata.*

THE FAMILY CICHLIDAE

The genus Tilapia

The genus *Tilapia* is the largest group of African cichlids and includes about 100 species although many of these are not accounted aquarium fish. Most of them are found exclusively in Africa: a few are also (or only) found in Jordan and Syria.
Extensive changes have been made in the nomenclature of the genus *Tilapia*. These changes affect the following species: *Tilapia dolloi* became *Sarotherodon nigripinnis; T.lepidura* changed to *Sarotherodon lepidurus; T.macrocephala* to *Sarotherodon melanoteron; T.nilotica* became *S.niloticus; T.vorax* changed to *S.mossambicus*, while the other species *T.galilea, T.guinasana* and *T.cillii* have kept their original names.
Nevertheless, the species of this genus appear in this encyclopedia under the traditional names by which they are commonly known.

All these fish really seek to establish territories and therefore must have a tank with plenty of space and a number of well-separated structures of rock or bogwood to provide individual retreats. Robust plants in pots may be included and there should be some floating plants to cut off some of the light. Many species are enthusiastic diggers and the bed should be of well-washed sand.
These fish are greedy. They will all accept a varied diet of live animal matter as well as dried food: a vegetable supplement is essential.
Breeding is not usually difficult. Most but not all species are mouth brooders. The fry are not difficult to rear but the tank should be kept very quiet and any parent not involved in brood care should be removed with as little disturbance to the tank as possible. The light should not be too bright and the parents involved in brood care must be given substantial amount of food.
One characteristic of this genus is that the young fish almost always have a significantly different color pattern from that of the adults, and these differences are noted in the descriptions below.

TILAPIA DOLLOI

Family: *Cichlidae*
Genus: *Tilapia*
English name: none
Origin: Cameroon
Size: Maximum 14 cm
Habitat: Found in brackish waters near the coast

SHAPE, COLORING AND MARKINGS: The body is quite deep and laterally very compressed. The basic coloration is a brown to olive green with a brassy gleam: the flanks are sea green with a pearly gleam. The scales have dark edges which show up as a network pattern over the whole body. The gill covers bear a black patch: the breast and throat are black or have black patches. The belly is light yellow to green. The dark shaded dorsal fin has a deep black border and a prominent round dark spot. The front rays of the anal fin are black, the rest brownish: the ventral fins are deep black. The caudal and pectoral fins are colorless or greyish. The eye has a yellow gleam.
Females are less robust and the breast and throat less deeply colored.
Males are as described above.

GENERAL CARE: *T.dolloi* needs a large species tank with a fine sandy bottom and plenty of retreats in rocks and bogwood. A peaceful species, *T.dolloi* will swim at all levels. The composition of the water is not critical: temperature 22°–24°C. A varied diet of live animal matter, with a vegetable supplement should be offered: dried food will be accepted.

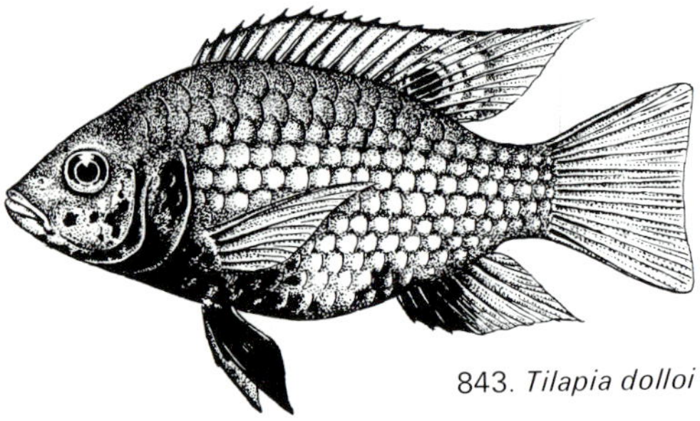
843. *Tilapia dolloi*

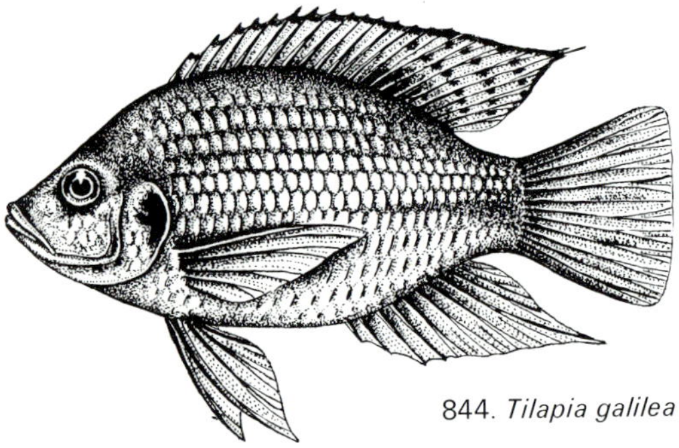
844. *Tilapia galilea*

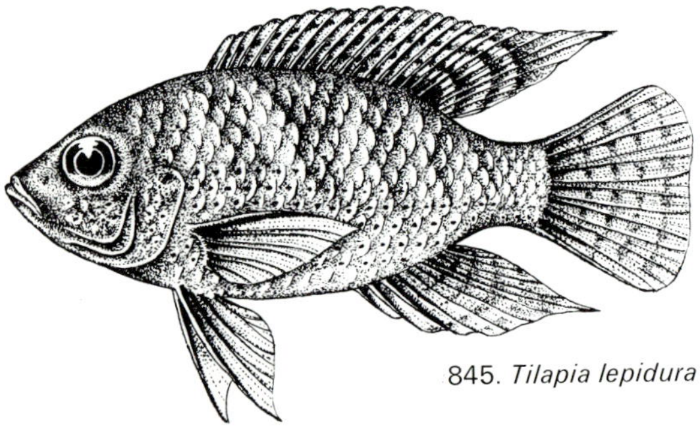
845. *Tilapia lepidura*

BREEDING: Not difficult: the fry hatch after about ten days and remain in the female's throat sac for another 10–14 days. See Introduction to the genus above.

ADDITIONAL INFORMATION: *T.dolloi* is the most peaceful species in the genus. Young specimens can be left in a community tank for a long time: they will not grub up the bottom or chew the plants if they are well fed with lettuce at regular intervals.

TILAPIA GALILEA

Family: *Cichlidae*
Genus: *Tilapia*
English name: Galilee Cichlid
Origin: Jordan, East and Central Africa
Size: Maximum 40 cm in the wild but remains considerably smaller in captivity

SHAPE, COLORING AND MARKINGS: The body is rather deep and laterally very compressed. The basic coloration is brown to olive green. The flanks are silvery with a bluish gleam: the belly is light yellow to silvery white. The gill covers are gold with an iridescent blue or black patch. The fins are pale pink. The dorsal fin usually has a dark margin and dark flecks. Young specimens bear dark transverse bands and a prominent black patch on the dorsal fin.
There are no known external sexual characteristics.

GENERAL CARE: As for *T.dolloi.*

BREEDING: No information is available on the breeding habits of this species in captivity.

ADDITIONAL INFORMATION: Curiously little is known about this species even though it has been imported since 1934. In the wild it seems that both the male and the female carry the fry in their throat sacs.

TILAPIA GUINASANA

Family: *Cichlidae*
Genus: *Tilapia*
English name: none
Origin: South West Africa, Lake Guinas
Size: Maximum 14 cm
Habitat: Found in the crystal clear waters of this lake, 1270 m above sea level

846. *Tilapia guinasana*

SHAPE, COLORING AND MARKINGS: The body is fairly deep and laterally very compressed: the curve of the back and of the underside are almost identical. The basic coloration varies. Two different color varieties have been imported, one pale and the the other dark. The pale variety is predominantly a dull blue with a cobalt blue gleam along the flanks. When the fish is excited, two dark longitudinal stripes (the upper shorter than the lower) and prominent transverse bands appear on the body. The dark variety is ochre, with a coppery gleam: the underside (including the ventral and anal fins) is predominantly black. The dorsal and caudal fins are bright yellow with rusty brown to dark orange lines and patches.
Females are more robust and have rounded dorsal and anal fins.
Males are as described above with extends rays to the dorsal and anal fins.

GENERAL CARE: As for *T.dolloi:* young fish may be kept in a community tank.

BREEDING: Not difficult. The eggs are laid on the underside of a stone and guarded usually by the female but both parents may share brood care. Many holes are dug near the eggs and the fry are subsequently moved from one to another of these.

ADDITIONAL INFORMATION: A very attractive species admirably suited to the aquarium. destroy any plants out in the tank.

TILAPIA LEPIDURA

Family: *Cichlidae*
Genus: *Tilapia*
English name: none
Origin: Angola
Size: Maximum 20 cm
Habitat: Found in brackish water

SHAPE, COLORING AND MARKINGS: The body shape and profile are identical to those of *T.guinasana.* The basic. Indistinct dark transverse bands may lie on the body. Most of the scales on the underside of the body have a bright red spot, which together form iridescent longitudinal lines. The fins are pale yellow to light green. The dorsal, caudal and anal fins have brownish bands.
Females are less vividly colored.

Males are as described above, with elongated rays in the dorsal and anal fins.

GENERAL CARE: As for *T.dolloi* but temperature 24°–28° C.

BREEDING: No information is available on the reproductive behavior of this species.

TILAPIA MACROCEPHALA

Family: *Cichlidae*
Genus: *Tilapia*
English name: none
Origin: West Africa
Size: Maximum 17 cm in the wild but remains considerably smaller in captivity
Habitat: Found widely in brackish waters

SHAPE, COLORING AND MARKINGS: The body shape and profile are similar to those of *T.guinasana* but the body is deeper. The basic coloration varies and a number of color varieties are known. The most common pattern is a pale green, with the back considerably darker and a belly a pale iridescent violet. The throat is black or speckled with black: the gill covers are a gleaming green, bordered with black. The dorsal, caudal and anal fins are brownish, becoming white or violet towards the edges: the dorsal and anal fins have rows of ochre to rusty brown spots. The ventral fins are dark brown to violet, with iridescent blue green rays at the front. Young specimens have dark transverse bands on the body. The eye is golden yellow.
Females are less vividly colored and the anal and dorsal fins are rounded.
Males are as described above with elongated rays to the anal and dorsal fins.

GENERAL CARE: As for *T.dolloi* but *T.macrocephala* is very intolerant. Newly imported specimens should be kept in a separate tank at first and salt added to the water which should then gradually be diluted to acclimatise the fish to fresh water.

BREEDING: No reliable information is available on the reproductive behavior of this species which is reputed to be a mouth brooder.

TILAPIA NILOTICA

Family: *Cichlidae*
Genus: *Tilapia*
English name: Nile Mouth Brooder
Origin: Syria, Egypt, East and West Africa
Size: Maximum 50 cm in the wild but remains considerably smaller in captivity.
Habitat: Found in a wide variety of waters

SHAPE, COLORING AND MARKINGS: The body is elongated, very deep and laterally very compressed. The basic coloration varies. Generally it is a silver grey with a violet overtone particularly prominent along the flanks: the belly is silvery white with a pale red gleam. Young specimens have prominent transverse bands. A prominent black patch lies on the gill covers. The dorsal, caudal and anal fins are pale brown to red, with elongated rays and red edges. Some specimens have dark flecks in the dorsal and caudal fins. During the mating season the throat, pectoral and usually the ventral fins become dark red.
Females are less vividly colored: the throat is a pale pink during the breeding season.
Males are as described above.

GENERAL CARE: As for *T.dolloi*.

BREEDING: This is not practical in the domestic aquarium for *T.nilotica* is not sexually mature until it has grown to 30 cm.

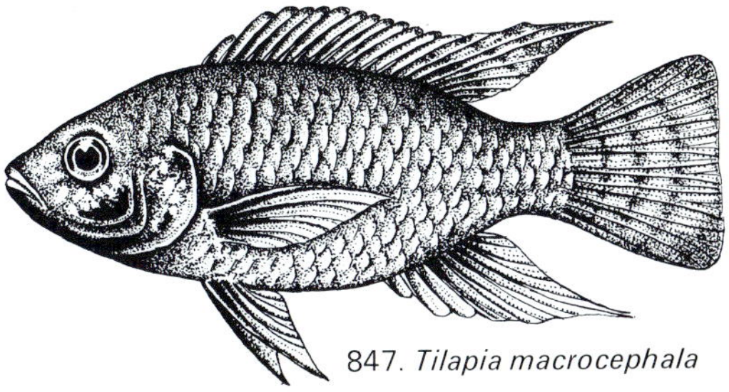

847. *Tilapia macrocephala*

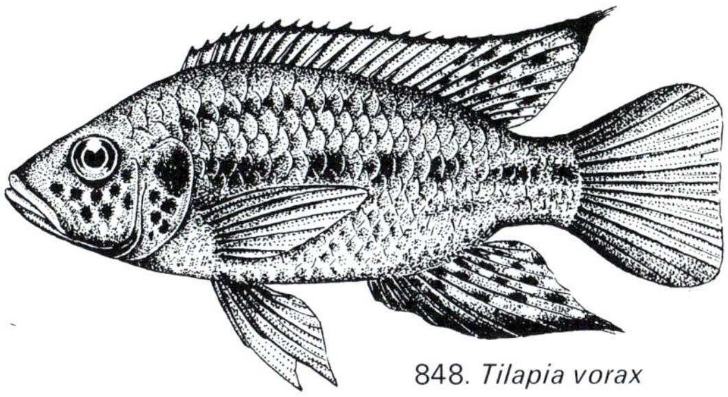

848. *Tilapia vorax*

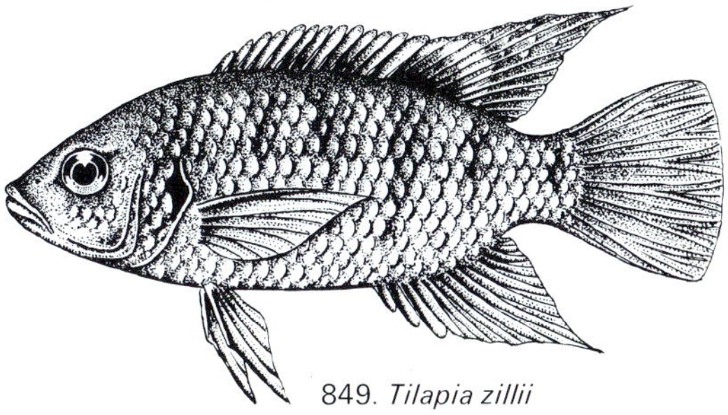

849. *Tilapia zillii*

TILAPIA VORAX

Family: *Cichlidae*
Genus: *Tilapia*
English name: none
Origin: East Africa
Size: Maximum 15 cm
Habitat: Found in a variety of waters from Lake Victoria to the Zambesi

SHAPE, COLORING AND MARKINGS: The body is elongated, fairly deep and laterally very compressed. The basic coloration is yellow to

850. *Tilapia nilotica*

851. *Tilapia nilotica*

blue green with a tinge of red. The back is a green brown: prominent brown patches lie on the flanks which have a pearly gleam. The belly is pale yellow to silver white. The dorsal and anal fins have a dark border and an alternately dark and light pattern in the soft rays. The caudal fin is terracotta. During the mating season the basic coloration is green: the upper part of the body ochre: the belly and throat deep black. The front part of the anal and the ventral fins are also black. The dorsal and caudal fins become red or have a red border. Pale blue stipples appear over the whole body. The lips become blue.
Females are smaller and less vividly colored.
Males are as described above with extended rays to the anal and dorsal fins.

General care: As for *T.dolloi* but *T.vorax* is both very intolerant and an enthusiastic digger.

Breeding: No information is available on the reproductive behavior of this species which is almost certainly a mouth brooder.

TILAPIA ZILLII

Family: *Cichlidae*

Genus: *Tilapia*

English name: none

Origin: Africa, north of the Equator, Jordan, Syria

Size: Maximum 30 cm in the wild but remains considerably smaller in captivity

Habitat: Found in a variety of waters

Shape, coloring and markings: The body is very deep and laterally very compressed. The basic coloration varies from silver grey to dark olive green, generally with a green, yellow or reddish overtone. When the fish is excited, irregular transverse bands appear on the body. A dark patch lies on the gill covers which, like the cheeks, are green to gold. The throat, breast and belly are dark. The fins are brownish. At the base of the dorsal fin lies a prominent black patch with a paler border. During the mating season the transverse bands become very prominent: the back becomes a gleaming olive green: the lower part of the body becomes a delicate red: the throat and breast blood red: the belly and head blue black with pale blue iridescent cheek marks.
Females have two prominent milk white patches at the base of the dorsal fin.
Males are as described above.

General care: As for *T.dolloi*. Specimens from North Africa can normally winter at 14°–16° C.

Breeding: As for *T.guinasana*.

852. *Tropheus duboisi*

THE FAMILY CICHLIDAE

The genus Tropheus

There are now three species in this small genus, of which *Tropheus duboisi* and *Tropheus moorei* are described below. They are rock scraping algae eaters and found only in Lake Tanganyika, where they play a part in the ecological balance identical to that played by the *Pseudotropheus* species found in Lake Malawi. These fish, in the wild, live in very large colonies, very near to rocky shores and there are significant variations in the color patterns of members of different geographically well-separated colonies.

TROPHEUS DUBOISI

Family: *Cichlidae*

Genus: *Tropheus*

English name: none

Origin: Lake Tanganyika

Size: Maximum 12 cm

Habitat: Found in large colonies close to rocky shores at depths up to 15 m

Shape, coloring and markings: The body is deep, and laterally scarcely compressed. The mouth is large: the forehead rises steeply from the snout. The body is black. A wide white transverse band runs down over the body from between the fourth and sixth rays of the dorsal fin. In young specimens this band is absent but the body and fins are covered with white dots arranged in eight or nine transverse rows and four or five horizontal rows. The fins are always the body color.
Females have shorter ventral fins.
Males are as described above.

General care: *T.duboisi* needs a spacious species tank with well secured rock structures. The composition of the water is not critical: temperature 25° C. A varied diet should be offered, and a vegetable supplement is essential.

Breeding: This is difficult. Rarely are more than ten fry produced. The eggs, some 0.7 cm in diameter, are hatched after four weeks at 27° C.

Additional information: There is a colored variety of *T.duboisi* in which the white band is replaced by a golden-yellow band.

TROPHEUS MOOREI

Family: *Cichlidae*

Genus: *Tropheus*

English name: none

Origin: Lake Tanganyika

Size: Maximum 12 cm

Habitat: Found near rocky shores at depths of no more than 4 m

Shape, coloring and markings: The body shape is identical to that of *T.duboisi*. There are at least 10 different color varieties of *T.moorei*, and each of these varies in color according to its mood. The most common variety in aquariums comes from the northern part of the lake. The whole body, including the fins, is black. When excited, a light triangular mark appears on the belly between the ventral and anal fins, and a similar mark slightly above, at an angle on the back, often continuing into the dorsal fin. When the fish becomes more excited, the whole body between these two marks changes color, giving rise to a very wide transverse band, the part closest to the belly being reddish, the part on the back yellow, and the part on the dorsal fin red. When the fish is frightened, the body in front of the base of the anal fin turns grey, sometimes tinged with a rust color: the back of the body stays black. There are often light marks on the anal fin.
There are no known external sexual characteristics.

General care: *T.moorei* is a difficult species

to keep, its general care should be as for *T.duboisi*, but *T.moorei* lives in a small group with a rigid hierarchy. Some 10–15 specimens need to be kept, but the hierarchy must emerge naturally. New specimens introduced into the tank are unlikely to be accepted.

BREEDING: The eggs are usually laid some distance above the bed and the female takes them into her mouth before they sink to the bottom. Ten eggs is an exceptional nest: usually only seven to nine eggs are laid. The 0.7 cm eggs hatch after about 30 days at a temperature of 27°C.

ADDITIONAL INFORMATION: Other varieties have a basic color that is brownish, with six to eight lighter transverse stripes.

853. *Tropheus moorei*

THE FAMILY CICHLIDAE

The genus Uaru

Only one species, *Uaru amphiacanthoides,* described below, is at present found in this genus. An attractive but very delicate fish, it is almost as demanding as the Discus, but not as unusual or striking in appearance. It has accordingly not attracted a great deal of attention from amateurs. Nevertheless, it is an interesting species, and one that the amateur with a specialist interest might well seek to acquire. In the wild *U.amphiacanthoides* is generally found living in association with Discus and Angel fish and like them is a species which much appreciates the warmth. It has not however been studied in detail and as noted below there are still some unsolved problems in keeping it in captivity in aquariums.

854. *Uaru amphiacanthoides*

UARU AMPHIACANTHOIDES

Family: *Cichlidae*

Genus: *Uaru*

English name: none

Origin: The central Amazon basin

Size: Maximum 30 cm in the wild, but remains much smaller in the aquarium

Habitat: Found in still waters with overhanging vegetation

SHAPE, COLORING AND MARKINGS: The body is elongated, relatively deep and laterally very compressed. The dorsal and anal fins are large and taper to a point, the last rays being elongated. The basic coloration is a yellowish-brown. The flanks bear a black cone-shaped mark which narrows towards the caudal fin: a second black mark lies on the caudal peduncle and a third on the gill covers behind the eyes. The iris is red. Young specimens (up to 5 cm) are blackish-brown: greenish dots subsequently spread over the body, and as the fish mature they gradually develop the color pattern described above.
There are no known external sexual characteristics.

GENERAL CARE: The sturdy appearance of *U.amphiacanthoides* belies the fact that it is very delicate. It requires a very spacious tank with plenty of retreats. The water should preferably be soft and slightly acid: temperature 27°C. The diet should include a vegetable supplement as well as substantial amounts of live animal matter. It will eat delicate plants. It is a peaceful fish and is easy to keep with other species provided that they are not too small.

BREEDING: The eggs are laid on stones or pieces of wood in dark corners or hollows. Both parents guard the eggs. As soon as the fry are free swimming, they should be fed on infusoria, and then *Artemia nauplii*. The water must be changed regularly and the breeding tank kept meticulously clean. Even so, sudden deaths amongst the fry are not unusual, which otherwise are easy to raise.

ADDITIONAL INFORMATION: *U.amphiacanthoides* is prone to disease, and often dies suddenly for no evident reason.

THE FAMILY MONODACTYLIDAE

An introductory description

This family includes five genera, each of which has a small number of species only very few of which are of interest to aquarists. These fish are found along the coasts of Africa, southern Asia, Indonesia and Australia, where they are very common in coastal waters and river estuaries: some species are also found in fresh waters, or spend part of their lives in them.

These fish resemble somewhat the *Pterophyllum* species or Moonfish. They have unusually deep bodies, but they lack the impressive fins of Moonfish. The dorsal and anal fins are in fact stunted, but the bases are scaly and powerfully developed. Indeed, the name *Monodactylidae* alludes to the almost finger-like shape of the bases of the fins (mono = single, dactylos = finger). The ventral fins consist of a single spine, or a small number of fin rays or sometimes are entirely absent. The *Monodactylidae* are omnivorous and in the wild are often found in large shoals near sewage outlets.

Two of the more interesting species are described below.

855. *Monodactylus sebae*

The genus Monodactylus

This is the only genus in the family containing species that are normally kept by amateurs. Two species, *M.argenteus* and the rather more unusually shaped *M.sebae*, described below, are not infrequently seen in specialist aquariums: another species, *M.falciformis*, has very occasionally been imported.

MONODACTYLUS ARGENTEUS

Family: *Monodactylidae*

Genus: *Monodactylus*

English name: Fingerfish

Origin: Malaysia, East Africa, the Red Sea

Size: Maximum 25 cm

Habitat: Found in brackish and fresh coastal waters

SHAPE, COLORING AND MARKINGS: The body is very deep, circular and laterally very compressed. The ventral fins are very small. The basic coloration is silvery white: the back is an iridescent yellowish-green. Two deep black transverse bands lie on the body: one runs in an arc through the eye, the other, less prominent, runs in an arc from the front of the dorsal fin to the front of the anal fin. The dorsal and anal fins are yellow to orange and almost completely edged with black. The other fins are pale yellow.

There are no known external sexual characteristics.

GENERAL CARE: *M.argenteus* needs to be kept in a small shoal in a large aquarium with plenty of free swimming space and only sparse vegetation. The water should be hard, with one teaspoonful of rock salt added for every ten liters of water: temperature 24°–28° C. *M.argenteus* is peaceful and swims at all levels. A varied diet of live animal matter and dried food should be given: if the diet is adequate the plants will not be eaten.

BREEDING: Nothing is known about the reproductive behavior of this fish.

GENERAL INFORMATION: In the wild, *M.argenteus* is found in both fresh and brackish waters, but it does not thrive in the aquarium if kept in fresh water.

MONODACTYLUS SEBAE

Family: *Monodactylidae*

Genus: *Monodactylus*

English name: none

Origin: West Africa

Size: Maximum 20 cm

Habitat: Found in the estuaries of the Congo and Senegal rivers

SHAPE, COLORING AND MARKINGS: The body is extremely deep and laterally very compressed. The ventral fins are very small. The basic coloration is silvery white: the back is yellowish-brown. Two to five dark transverse bands, three of which are very prominent, lie on the body: one runs in an arc through the eye to the edge of the gill covers, one runs straight across the body from the dorsal to the anal fin, one runs across the base of the caudal fin. These bands become fainter as the fish grows older. The dorsal and anal fins are pale yellow and almost completely edged with brown. The ventral, pectoral and caudal fins are colorless.

There are no known external sexual characteristics.

GENERAL CARE: As for *M.argenteus*.

BREEDING: Nothing is known about the reproductive behavior of this fish.

ADDITIONAL INFORMATION: *M.sebae*, like *M.argenteus*, will not thrive if kept in fresh water for long periods. Although it will tolerate freshwater for longer than *M.argenteus* and seems generally more hardy.

THE FAMILY NANDIDAE

An introductory description

Various species in the family *Nandidae* are found in South America, West Africa and Southern Asia. Almost all these fish are aggressive, greedy predators, and with the exception of *Badis badis* are totally unsuitable for a community tank: for most of them, their main diet (and they will eat their own body weight in food daily) is smaller fish. It is however usually possible to keep a number of individuals of the same species together in a species tank, provided they are all more or less of the same size.

Six genera are known in the family: *Afronandus, Badis, Monocirrhus, Nandus, Polycentropsis* and *Pristolepsis*. Species of all these genera have been kept in captivity, including the curious African Leaf Fish, *Polycentropsis abbreviata,* but generally these are fish only for the specialist.
A few of the less predatory and more amenable species are described below.

The genus Badis

Two species in this genus are of interest to amateurs, the well-known *Badis badis,* and the less common *Badis badis burmanicus,* or Red Badis. *B.badis* is probably the only species in the family that can with safety be kept in a suitably furnished community tank, and has accordingly become much better known among aquarists than any other *Nandidae* species.

BADIS BADIS

Family: *Nandidae*
Genus: *Badis*
English name: Badis
Origin: Southeast Asia
Size: Males to 8 cm. Females to 5–6 cm
Habitat: Found only in still fresh waters

SHAPE, COLORING AND MARKINGS: The body is elongated, relatively low and scarcely laterally compressed. The line of the neck makes it look very sturdy. The head and mouth are small. The base of the dorsal fin is very long, extending along some two thirds of the back: that of the anal fin is short. The color patterns are variable and subject to sudden dramatic changes. Commonly the fish is blue with a greenish sheen and some indistinct dark transverse bands across the body, but may suddenly change to a greyish-yellow or green, with darker marks on the flanks. During the spawning season it may become midnight blue or black.
Females are brownish-yellow or brown with dark or bluish dots on the flanks: they are smaller, with more rounded bellies.
Males are as described above. The belly is flat or even slightly concave.

GENERAL CARE: *B.badis* can be kept in a well planted community tank, arranged to provide plenty of retreats in rock and bogwood. The male will claim a retreat as his territory and spend much time there. Many aquarists consider *B.badis* a dull and inactive fish because of this habit, but if a number of pairs are kept, then the need to defend the territory leads to much (but not dangerous) activity. The composition of the water is not critical: temperature 25°C. A varied diet of live animal matter is required.

BREEDING: *B.badis* will breed in a community tank if it is not too crowded and there is a sheltered spot that receives little or no light. The male takes the initiative and cleans the chosen spot, removing all the sand from it. Once the hollow is ready and a spawning female approaches, part of the male's back becomes darker, and the pair will mate. Up to 200 eggs are laid in the hollow at random. The female will then be chased away: the male alone guards the eggs, which hatch after a few days. Once the yolk sacs have been digested, the fry appear outside the hollow with the male looking for food and should be given infusoria and Cyclops *nauplii.*
It is difficult however adequately to feed the fry if they have been hatched in a community tank and it is better to put a breeding pair in a special breeding tank with suitable dark corners. The female should be removed after spawning, and the male after the fry begin to swim freely. The fry grow slowly at first, and must be given frequent changes of water. A female in good condition may well breed again 14 days after spawning.

BADIS BADIS BURMANICUS

Family: *Nandidae*
Genus: *Badis*
English name: The Red Badis
Origin: Burma, Lake Inlé
Size: Maximum 8 cm
Habitat: Found only along the shores of the lake and in neighboring streams, where there is plenty of algae and vegetation

856. *Badis badis burmanicus*

SHAPE, COLORING AND MARKINGS: The body shape and profile are identical to that of *B.badis*. The basic coloration is variable. Usually it is a warm, reddish-brown. The back is very dark: the belly yellowish-brown. Eight rows of carmine dots run from the gill covers to the caudal peduncle. At the base of the dorsal fin lie eight iridescent green marks from which run irregular, iridescent green transverse bands: four other iridescent green marks lie behind these bands, below the back of the dorsal fin. A green band runs across the caudal peduncle, along the base of the caudal fin. Except for the colorless pectoral fins, the fins are blackish with a brown tinge. The top edge of the dorsal fin has a wide, cream colored border: the bottom of the anal fin has a narrow blue border. When upset *B.badis burmanicus* turns a dull, dirty yellow with some dark spots. In the breeding season or when defending its territory, it may become a deep purplish-brown with sparkling carmine spots: the green transverse bands disappear, but may reappear occasionally and replace these red spots.
Females are smaller than males, less vividly colored and have more rounded bellies.
Males are as described above.

GENERAL CARE: *B.badis burmanicus* is best kept as two or three pairs in a species tank in which it can also breed without disturbance. The tank should be 50 × 30 × 30 cm, furnished with fine-leaved plants, a few clumps of thread algae, a bed of well-boiled peat, and pieces of bogwood with Java fern. The water should not be too hard: temperature 22°C. Diet as for *B.badis*.

BREEDING: The male will hollow out a nest in a clump of thread algae. The mating is violent and the female's fins may be damaged. Thereafter the male guards the eggs and fry, which are best raised as recommended for *B.badis*.

THE FAMILY NANDIDAE

The genus Nandus

The species in this small genus come from India and Southeast Asia. They are more aggressive and predatory than the *Badis* species, and must, as noted below, be provided with large species tanks. Scientifically these fish, belonging to a primitive group, are of great interest, but they are only to be recommended to amateurs who have a special inclination towards such unusual fish.

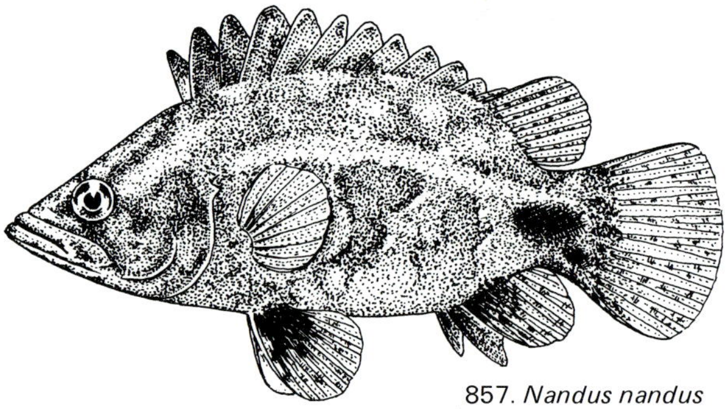

857. *Nandus nandus*

NANDUS NANDUS

Family: *Nandidae*
Genus: *Nandus*
English name: none
Origin: India, Burma, Thailand
Size: Maximum 20 cm in the wild but remains considerably smaller in captivity
Habitat: Found in jungle creeks, in coastal regions, in fresh or brackish water

SHAPE, COLORING AND MARKINGS: The body is elongated, deep and laterally compressed. The head is very large and scaly: the mouth is extremely large and protuberant. The basic coloration is dark brown with large, irregular, yellowish-green, olive and dark brown marks, alternating with and separated by lighter marks. The overall effect is very much like a number of overlapping autumn leaves. The fins vary from ochre to greenish and marks on the dorsal fin usually merge into similar marks on the upper half of the body. The other fins also have irregular marks but their pattern varies from specimen to specimen.
Females are slightly paler, with smaller fins.
Males are as described above.

GENERAL CARE: *N.nandus* is only suitable for a large species tank with plenty of retreats among bogwood and rocks and a dark bed.

858. *Nandus nebolosus*

Only sturdy bogplants can be introduced into the tank. *N.nandus* is very timid, but if kept in a dimly lit aquarium, it will learn to recognize its keeper. The composition of the water is not critical but a teaspoonful of rock salt should be added for every ten liters: temperature 20° C. In the wild its diet is solely other fish, but in captivity it will also accept shredded beef and horsemeat.

BREEDING: Little is known about the reproductive behavior of this fish, but it is certainly a cave breeder.

NANDUS NEBOLOSUS
Family: *Nandidae*
Genus: *Nandus*
English name: none
Origin: Malaya, Thailand
Size: Approximately 12 cm
Habitat: Found in jungle creeks in coastal regions in fresh and brackish waters

SHAPE, COLORING AND MARKINGS: The body shape is almost identical to that of *N.nandus*, but there are technical differences in the fin formula. The basic coloration is also identical to that of *N.nandus* but a dark band runs from the snout, through the eye which has a luminescent yellow border. The spines of the dorsal and anal fins are brown: the other fins are colorless and transparent.
There are no known external sexual characteristics.

GENERAL CARE: As for *N.nandus*.

BREEDING: As for *N.nandus*.

THE FAMILY SCATOPHAGIDAE

An introductory description

These fish are found in coastal areas of south and southeast Asia, in off-shore islands, around northern Australia and east Africa, in salt, brackish and fresh waters. It is believed that they breed in coral reefs. The young fish swim inland through brackish waters to fresh waters and return to the sea when mature. Known as dung eaters, they are often found near sewage outlets.
The body of these fish is disc-shaped and laterally very compressed. The head and mouth are relatively small: the scales are small and cover not only the head and body but also part of the soft rays of the dorsal and anal fins. The front part of these fins consists of a number of spines which can be a formidable weapon. These spines are almost completely separated from the soft rays and usually lie flat against the body while the latter stand upright.
Little is known about the reproductive behavior of the *Scatophagidae*, which have not as yet been bred in captivity. However, it is known that the fry undergo a larval stage, called 'Tholichthys', when the head is disproprotionately large and is covered with bony plates, which disappear as the fish mature.

The genus Scatophagus

There are only two true species in the genus *Scatophagus*: the very popular *Scatophagus argus*, or Argus Fish, and the less well-known African Scat, *Scatophagus tetracanthus*. Peaceful, attractive fish, these species are deservedly popular with amateurs, and it is regrettable that to date no success has been achieved in breeding these fish in captivity. This may well be because of their migratory reproductive patterns in the wild.
Reference is sometimes made to a species *S.rubifrons*, but this is not a true species, merely a color variety of *S.argus*.

859. *Scatophagus argus*

SCATOPHAGUS ARGUS
Family: *Scatophagidae*
Genus: *Scatophagus*
English name: Scat, Argus Fish
Origin: India, Indonesia, Thailand, Vietnam
Size: Maximum 30 cm in the wild but remains considerably smaller in captivity
Habitat: Found in coastal waters, river estuaries and fresh waters

SHAPE, COLORING AND MARKINGS: The body is disc-shaped and laterally very compressed: the head and mouth are relatively small. The basic coloration varies significantly according to the locality of origin. The most attractive color pattern is found in young fish about 6 cm long: the body is bluish-green with a pronounced silvery sheen, or coffee colored with an attractive bronze sheen on the back. Orange or red marks often appear on the back and may stretch across the body as irregular bands. Older specimens are usually greyish-green or shiny silver with large black marks. The base of the fins have yellowish brown or black marks.
There are no known external sexual characteristics.

GENERAL CARE: Young specimens can be kept as a pair, in a large or small community tank, with other small peaceful fish: plenty of free swimming space is needed. All plants will be at risk. The water should be hard and one teaspoonful of rock salt should be added for every ten liters: temperature 20°–28°C. The diet should be large amounts of live animal matter and a great deal of lettuce.

BREEDING: Little is known about the reproductive behavior of this species.

ADDITIONAL INFORMATION: Adult specimens look best in a salt water aquarium.

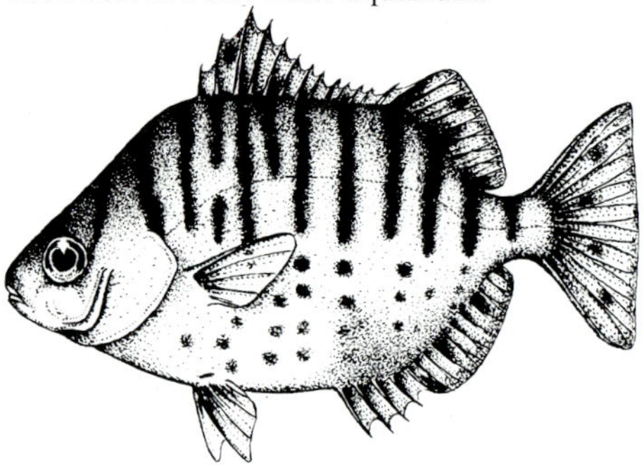

SCATOPHAGUS TETRACANTHUS

Family: *Scatophagidae*

Genus: *Scatophagus*

English name: The African Scat

Origin: North Australia, north New Guinea, East Africa

Size: Maximum 40 cm in the wild but remains considerably smaller in captivity

Habitat: Found in coastal waters, river estuaries and fresh waters

SHAPE, COLORING AND MARKINGS: The body shape is identical to that of *S.argus*. The basic coloration is yellowish to silvery blue. The body is crossed by brownish-black transverse bands, which can vary in number and individual width: their length decreases as the fish matures. The dorsal and anal fins are brownish-yellow. The base of the caudal fin is yellow: the ventral fins vary from dark brown to black.
There are no known external sexual characteristics.

860. *Scatophagus tetracanthus*

GENERAL CARE: As for *S.argus*.

BREEDING: Nothing is known about the reproductive behavior of this fish.

ADDITIONAL INFORMATION: Only young specimens are suitable for a freshwater aquarium: older specimens do best in an marine aquarium with coral; even more than *S.argus* most certainly needs salt water to thrive.

THE FAMILY TOXOTIDAE

An introductory description

The Archer fish in the *Toxotidae* family are found in the Philippines, Australia, Malayasia, Thailand, Southern China, Burma and India, generally in muddy brackish waters along the coasts, in mangrove swamps and river estuaries. It is thought that young fish move into inland fresh waters and that adults swim out to coral reefs to breed.
These unusual fish owe their popular name to the curious way in which they shoot down insects that live above the water. The fish swim to the surface and shoot out a powerful stream of water droplets at their prey: the victim, with sodden wings, can no longer fly, falls on the water surface and is snapped up by the fish. Adult Archer fish can shoot down insects moving on branches and leaves 1.5 m above the surface. If the fish misses the first time, it will shoot again up to seven times in succession. Young Archer fish soon develop this skill and when they are no more than 2–3 cm long are able to shoot a stream of water 10–20 cm in the air: at first their aim is not very accurate but it soon improves. In the wild, Archer fish obtain only some of their food in this way and they are unlikely to perform in the aquarium unless they are hungry and some suitable insect such as a cockroach or moth is above the surface. Both the tongue and roof of the mouth are an unusual shape and function together like the barrel of a gun. Force is provided by a sharp powerful contraction of the gill covers and the tip of the tongue is moved to adjust the direction of the jet. How the fish assesses distance and direction is not known.
Young Archer fish are characterised by the presence of 'light spots' on the body. These are iridescent yellow patches on the upper half of the body, between the dark transverse bands.

861. *Toxotes jaculatrix*

It is thought that these patches play a part in recognition and communication, while these young fishes are living in shoals in muddy waters: adult fish which tend to live more solitary lives in clear waters around coral reeds have no such marks.
The body shape of these fish is typical of species which live close to the surface: it is elongated, deep and laterally very compressed. The line of the back is almost straight from the snout to the dorsal fin: the mouth is large, deep and upward directed.
There is only one genus in the family: it contains six species, only two of which are regularly found in aquariums.
These fish are barely suitable for an ordinary tank. A more natural environment is a large paludarium.

The genus Toxotes

In this, the only genus of the family *Toxotidae*, there are six known living species, although fossils have been found in Indonesia of another, now extinct species, *Toxotes beauforti*. Of the six extant species, *T.blythi*, *T.chatereus*, *T.jaculatrix*, *T.lorentzi*, *T.microlepis* and *T.oligolepis*, only *T.chatereus* and *T.jaculator* are normally found in aquariums.

TOXOTES CHATEREUS

Family: *Toxotidae*

Genus: *Toxotes*

English name: none

Origin: India, Malaya, southern Thailand, the Philippines, Australia

Size: Maximum 27 cm

Habitat: Found mainly in the brackish waters of river estuaries

SHAPE, COLORING AND MARKINGS: The body is elongated, deep and laterally very compressed. There are five spines in the dorsal fins. The eyes are large. The basic coloration varies from greyish green to muddy yellow: the back is yellowish green or brown: the belly is off-white or silvery white. Dark marks lie above and below the eyes and on the upper half of the body, but rarely extend as far as the back: a few smaller spots may lie in between these latter marks. The dorsal fin is yellowish-green with a dark border along the soft rays, above a line of dark flecks. The caudal fin is ochre or greenish: the anal fin is silvery-white. The transparent pectoral and ventral fins are colorless or greyish.
There are no known external sexual characteristics.

GENERAL CARE: *T.chatereus* needs a large species tank with plenty of free swimming space and a large surface area without plants. It is best kept as a single pair or solely with other bottom-living fish: a paludarium is ideal. Young specimens can be acclimatised to an aquarium fairly quickly but older fish are often very susceptible to diseases. Three teaspoonfuls of sea salt should be added for every ten liters of fairly hard water in the tank: temperature 26°–28°C. The water should be regularly changed and fresh water avoided. Diet: water creatures, larvae flies, and moths.

BREEDING: Nothing is known about the reproductive behavior of this species, which has not yet been bred in captivity.

TOXOTES JACULATRIX

Family: *Toxotidae*

Genus: *Toxotes*

English name: Archer Fish

Origin: Australia, the Indian sub-continent, Thailand, the Philippines

Size: Maximum 24 cm

Habitat: Found mainly in the brackish waters of river estuaries

SHAPE, COLORING COLORING AND MARKINGS: The body shape and basic coloration are identical to those of *T.chatereus*, except that *T.jaculatrix* has four spines in the dorsal fin and the mouth is more pointed. The color patterns can vary according to the locality of origin. Young fish from Southeast Asia for example, are usually yellowish-brown on the upper half of the body with four to six prominent dark brown or black, transverse bands which run down to the belly. As the fish matures, these bands become shorter and in old specimens are visible only on the upper half of the body. In *T.jaculatrix* very few marks are found between these bands. The dorsal fin is yellowish-green with a dark border. The muddy green caudal fin and the silvery-white anal fin have black borders. The transparent pectoral and ventral fins are colorless or greyish.
There are no known external sexual characteristics.

GENERAL CARE: As for *T.chatereus* but three to five teaspoonfuls of salt should be added for every ten liters of water in the tank, rather more than for *T.chatereus*.

BREEDING: This species has not as yet been bred in captivity.

THE FAMILY GOBIIDAE

An introductory description

Gobiidae species are found all over the world, but all save a few species are tropical salt water fish. They are bottom loving fish and are characterised, as a family, by having the ventral fins joined to form a funnel-shaped sucker-like organ with which they can attach themselves to stones and rocks.

In many other respects they closely resemble the Sleeper Gobies in the family *Eleotridae* but these latter fish do not have the ventral fins fused in this way. All the *Gobiidae* also have two dorsal fins, one set behind the other and the anal fin usually positioned opposite the second, back dorsal fin.
The family includes the intriguing species in the sub-family *Periophthalminae* or Mudskippers, some of the few fish that have become true amphibians. These fish, interesting as they are, are in no way suitable for aquariums and are therefore not treated in detail in this encyclopaedia, but they are so curious as to merit a brief review in this introductory note. Mudskippers are found in coastal regions of Africa, southern Asia, Indonesia, the Philippines and Japan, where they are very common in coastal mangrove swamps and mudflats. They feed mainly on crustacea and mud worms which they hunt in the mud when the tide is out. They climb on to branches and rocks and survey their territory for prey with their large mobile eyes. They can move very quickly overland with the aid of their strong pectoral fins and they are also good jumpers. They are however poor swimmers, and have no swim bladder but it is necessary for them to enter the water (if only the mud pools left by the receeding tide) regularly, to keep their bodies moist. Very occasionally they are imported but cannot be kept properly in an aquarium: they need a large paludarium with salt water pools. No amateur without the right facilities should try and keep these very attractive and interesting fish. Rather the amateur should concentrate on the different but very interesting species in the genera *Brachygobius* and *Stigmatogobius*: many of these can be kept without undue difficulty

862. *Brachygobius doriae*

in an aquarium, although sometimes for no apparent reason these fish when in captivity will refuse to eat and will pine away. They need species tanks with very shallow water and, according to their particular natural habitats, some salt added to it: details are given in the species descriptions below.

The genus Brachygobius

One or another species in the genus *Brachygobius* is to be found somewhere in the Far East, in fresh, brackish or salt waters. Few will survive long in fresh water and although little is known in detail about the life style of these fish in the wild, it seems likely that they all spend much of their lives in salt water: the exception may be *Brachygobius doriae,* which experience shows can be kept in a freshwater aquarium.

All these fish have a cylindrical body and the fused ventral fins characteristic of the family. They will often, in aquariums, be seen to have attached themselves to the glass sides by means of their sucker.

They are extraordinarily difficult fish to identify because the basic color pattern of each species is very similar but the pattern may at the same time vary significantly in detail from one specimen to another. Various authorities have sought to devise elaborate guides to their identification, and those with a special interest should consult the specialist literature: a few helpful notes are included in the species descriptions which follow. It is an indication of the difficulty of identifying these fish that the four species most likely to be found in aquariums all have the same English name.

BRACHYGOBIUS AGGREGATUS

Family: *Gobiidae*

Genus: *Brachygobius*

English names: Golden Banded Goby, Bumblebee Fish

Origin: North Borneo, the Philippines

Size: Approximately 4.5 cm

Habitat: Found in salt, and fresh waters

Shape, coloring and markings: The body is almost cylindrical: only the base of the caudal fin is laterally slightly compressed. The relatively large head gives the fish a club-like profile. There is one spine and six soft rays in the anal fin. The basic coloration is bright yellow: the underside of the head and the belly are ochre to grey. A pattern of dark transverse bands lies over the body but may vary enormously. Often there are four bands: one lies behind the gill covers and merges with another below the front dorsal fin: a third runs below the back dorsal fin: the last runs across the base of the caudal fin. A cone-shaped mark lies on the caudal peduncle between the third and fourth bands: some dark spots appear on the throat and cheeks. The first dorsal fin is dark at the front and base, but the rest of the fins are colorless and transparent.

There are no known external sexual characteristics.

General care: *B.aggregatus* needs a small tank with a sandy bed and plenty of retreats under stones and rocks and a few plants. The water should be hard and two tablespoonfuls of rock salt should be added for every ten liters: temperature 20°–24°C. *B.aggregatus* is tolerant and can be kept with other small fish in a community tank but is best kept in a species tank with shallow water. A varied diet of live animal matter, particularly worm-like creatures should be given.

Breeding: Very little reliable information is available about the reproductive behavior of this species but probably, like related species, it lays its eggs under stones.

Additional information: *Brachygobius kalibiensis* may be a synonym for *B.aggregatus.*

BRACHYGOBIUS DORIAE

Family: *Gobiidae*

Genus: *Brachygobius*

English names: Golden Banded Goby, Bumblebee Fish

Origin: The Far East

Size: Maximum 4.5 cm

Habitat: Found in both brackish and fresh waters

Shape, coloring and markings: The body shape and basic coloration are identical to those of *B.aggregatus.* In *B.doriae* however the anal fin has one spine and seven soft rays. *B.doriae,* like *B.aggregatus* has four dark transverse bands but the first and second do not merge. The two dorsal fins are dark, but the first has a narrow light border and the second a small uncolored triangular patch at the front: a similar triangular patch appears on the anal fin. The ventral and pectoral fins have dark bases but otherwise, like the caudal fin, are colorless and transparent.

There are no known external sexual characteristics.

General care: As for *B.aggregatus,* but one tablespoonful of salt should be added for every ten liters of water. Temperature 20°–25°C.

Breeding: The amber eggs are laid under overhanging rocks or in other shady spots. They hatch after about four days. The fry soon display the color pattern of transverse bands and can be raised with the normal fry foods. They grow slowly.

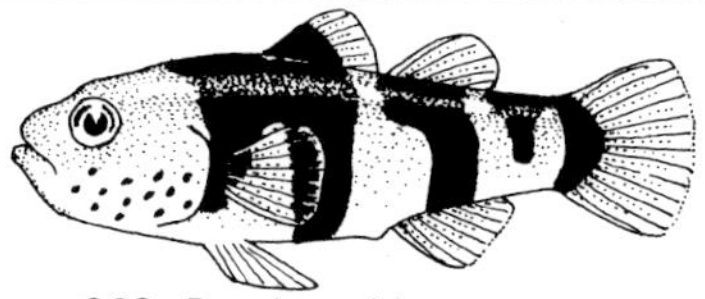

863. *Brachygobius aggregatus*

864. *Brachygobius xanthozona*

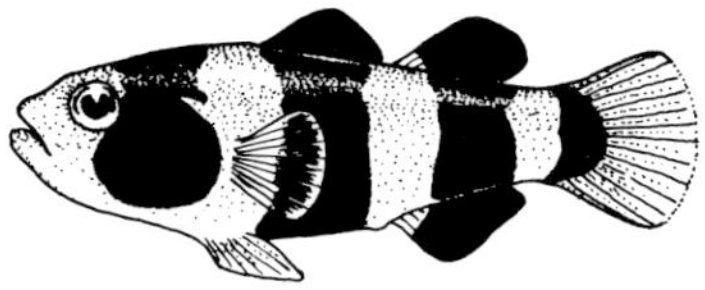

Additional information: *B.dories* is often known to amateurs as *B.nunus.*

BRACHYGOBIUS XANTHOZONA

Family: *Gobiidae*

Genus: *Brachygobius*

English names: Golden Banded Goby, Bumblebee Fish

Origin: Uncertain, but probably Borneo and Indonesia

Size: Approximately 4.5 cm

Habitat: Found in fresh and brackish waters

Shape, coloring and markings: The body shape and profile, the basic coloration and the pattern of dark transverse bands are all identical to those of *B.aggregatus* but *B.xanthozona* has one spine and eight or nine soft rays in the anal fin. The front dorsal fin is dark: the back dorsal fin and the anal fin are dark save for a small triangular light patch at the front of each. The other fins are colorless and transparent.

There are no known external sexual characteristics.

General care: As for *B.doriae.*

Breeding: Nothing is known about the reproductive behavior of this species.

THE FAMILY GOBIIDAE

The genus Gobius

Only two species in this genus, *Gobius guineensis* and *Gobius lyricus* are of interest to aquarists. Curiously these two species come from very different areas, one being an African, the other a South American fish. Another species, *Gobius vaimosa balteati,* from Sri Lanka has occasionally been seen in aquariums: it has an unusually shaped dorsal fin which resembles the horn of a rhinoceros and has given rise to the species' common name of Rhino-horn Goby: this small, predominantly yellow Goby, with two prominent black bars across the body and head remains however rare in aquariums.

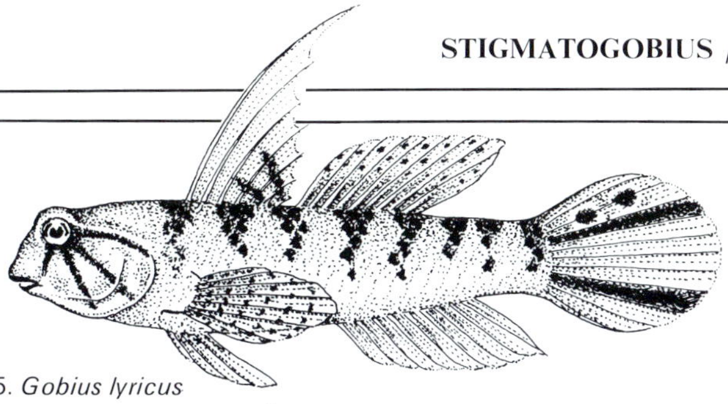

865. *Gobius lyricus*

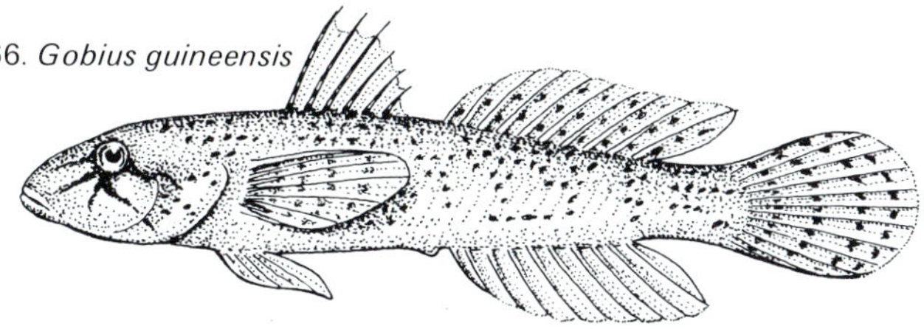

866. *Gobius guineensis*

GOBIUS GUINEENSIS

Family: *Gobiidae*
Genus: *Gobius*
English name: none
Origin: West Africa
Size: Approximately 15 cm
Habitat: Found in coastal streams

SHAPE, COLORING AND MARKINGS: The body is slim and cylindrical: and slightly compressed towards the tail: the snout is rather blunt. The basic coloration is ochre to greenish-yellow: the lower half of the body is reddish. Numerous small dark or reddish marks lie on the body, forming irregular transverse bands or an irregular horizontal line. Thin red lines appear below the eyes. The fins are colorless but the back dorsal fin and the caudal fin have dark spots.
Females have no spots on the dorsal and caudal fins.
Males are as described above.

GENERAL CARE: This species requires a large tank with a sandy bed and retreat. Fairly hard water is required, with one tablespoon of rock salt added for every ten liters of water. Temperature 23°–26° C. Diet should include Tubifex and mosquito larvae.

BREEDING: No information available.

GOBIUS LYRICUS

Family: *Gobiidae*
Genus: *Gobius*
English name: none
Origin: Central America, Cuba
Size: Approximately 10 cm
Habitat: Found in coastal streams

SHAPE, COLORING AND MARKINGS: The body shape is identical to that of *G.guineensis*. The basic coloration is brown to olive green: the back is darker and the lower half of the body varies from ochre to red. A number of cone-shaped marks lie on the upper half of the body. The head and gill covers are bright yellow: narrow lines lie below the eye. The lips are black. Two crescent-shaped dark bands lie on the otherwise colorless front dorsal fin: the back dorsal fin is usually colorless but sometimes is a light brown at the base. Two dark horizontal lines cross the caudal fin below dark oval marks. The anal fin is usually brown: the pectoral fins flecked
Females are less vividly colored: the front dorsal fin has no elongated rays.
Males are as described above: the rays of the front dorsal fin are greatly elongated.

GENERAL CARE: As for *G.guineensis,* but temperature 20°–22° C.

BREEDING: Nothing is known about the reproductive behavior of this species.

THE FAMILY GOBIIDAE

The genus Stigmatogobius

This is a small genus and within it only two species have attracted the attention of aquarists, *Stigmatogobius hoeveni* and *Stigmatogobius sadanundio,* described below. They are interesting, unusual fish which are relatively easy to keep and deserve perhaps more attention than they have hitherto received from amateurs.

Both species are indigenous to the Far East.
S.sadanundio normally lives in fresh water and is the most imported species of this family, with the possible exception of the Bumblebee Fish, *Brachygobius doriae*.

867. *Stigmatogobius sadanundio*

STIGMATOGOBIUS HOEVENI

Family: *Gobiidae*
Genus: *Stigmatogobius*
English name: none
Origin: The Far East
Size: Approximately 6 cm
Habitat: Found in salt, brackish and fresh waters

SHAPE, COLORING AND MARKINGS: The body is slim and cylindrical, but slightly compressed laterally towards the tail. The basic coloration is ochre: the upper half of the body is greenish: the flanks are often tinged with red: the lower half of the body is lighter or a muddy yellowish-white. All the scales have a dark edge. On the flanks lie a number of irregular marks which often merge into irregular transverse bands. Two or three prominent marks lie, one above the other, on the caudal peduncle. Both dorsal fins are deep blue or black in the center, lighter or even white towards the edge, with blue borders. The caudal fin has irregular dark marks.

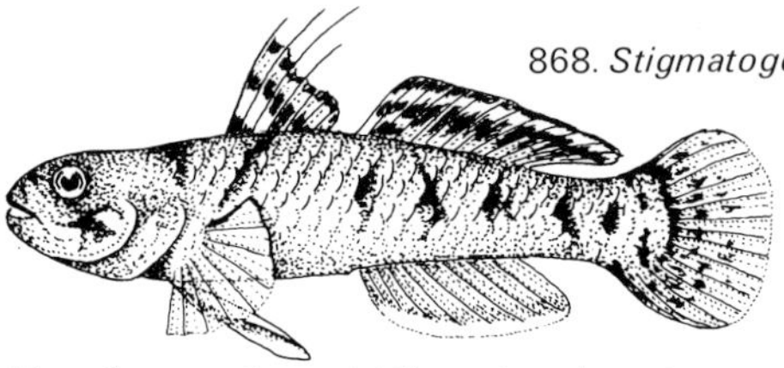

868. *Stigmatogobius hoeveni*

Females are less vividly colored and more sturdily built.
Males are as described above with elongated rays in the front dorsal fin.

GENERAL CARE: As for *Gobius guineensis* but temperature 21°–24°C.

BREEDING: No reliable information is available about the reproductive behavior of this species.

STIGMATOGOBIUS SADANUNDIO

Family: *Gobiidae*
Genus: *Stigmatogobius*
English name: none
Origin: Indonesia, the Philippines
Size: Approximately 8 cm
Habitat: Found mainly in fresh waters

SHAPE, COLORING AND MARKINGS: The body is stocky and cylindrical but slightly compressed laterally towards the tail. The basic coloration is pale blue or bluish-grey. A row of prominent dark dots lies across the flanks. The fins are light grey with alternating light and dark patches. The dorsal and anal fins have light border. Some specimens have a more yellowish tinge to the body.
Females are more yellowish and have less powerfully developed fins.
Males are as described above, with elongated rays to the dorsal fins.

GENERAL CARE: As for *Gobius guineensis* but temperature 22°–26°C.

BREEDING: Nothing is known about the reproductive behavior of this species, which has not yet been bred it seems in captivity by aquarists.

ADDITIONAL INFORMATION: *S.sadanundio* is quite frequently imported and is probably better known to aquarists than most species of *Gobiidae*.

THE FAMILY ELEOTRIDAE

An introductory description

Species of *Eleotridae* are found throughout the world. They are closely related to the *Gobiidae* but are clearly distinguishable because the ventral fins are not joined together as they are in the latter family.
The body is usually slim and quite often very elongated. The caudal peduncle may be slightly or greatly compressed, but the rest of the body is cylindrical. The two dorsal fins are clearly separated: the caudal fin is rounded and the anal fin is generally the same length at the base as the second, back dorsal fin. The lateral line is missing in most members of this family. The *Eleotridae* are most common in brackish waters along tropical coasts: some species are also found in fresh waters and a few even live exclusively in such waters. Most species however are poor swimmers in mid-water although they can move over the bed very rapidly and can stop very suddenly: then they blend perfectly with their surroundings because of the camouflage effect of their color patterns. Some species dig themselves partially into the bed to escape from predators. Most *Eleotridae* are themselves predators and feed on smaller fish and the fry of other species that live near the bottom: many are voracious and eat the equivalent of their own body weight in food every day.
Most species that come from fresh waters or brackish waters can be kept without difficulty in aquariums but even those species that come from fresh waters should have a tank with added salt and any other species of fish chosen to share the tank must be selected with care.

The genus Dormitator

This small genus of *Eleotridae* species contains some fish that grow very large indeed. Only two species, *Dormitator latifrons*, the Broad-headed Sleeper Goby and *Dormitator maculatus*, the Spotted Sleeper Goby, are normally kept in aquariums. These two South American Gobies are described below.

Breeding these species in an aquarium usually doesn't present many problems.

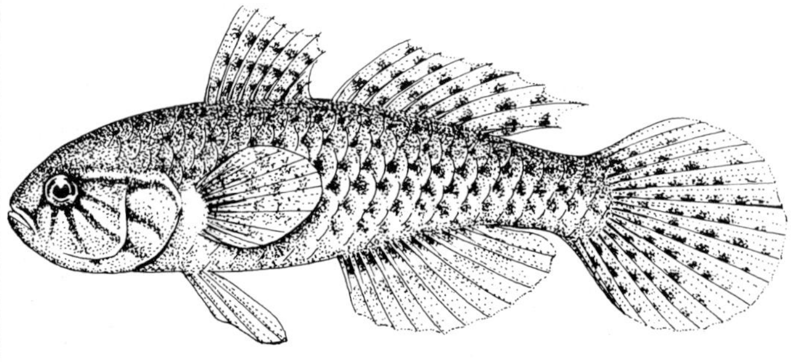

869. *Dormitator latifrons*

DORMITATOR LATIFRONS

Family: *Eleotridae*

Genus: *Dormitator*

English name: Broad-headed Sleeper Goby

Origin: Central America, Mexico

Size: Approximately 25 cm in the wild but remains much smaller in captivity and is sexually mature at about 10 cm

Habitat: Found only in brackish and salt waters along the west coast

Shape, coloring and markings: The body is very stocky and cylindrical: the snout is blunt. The basic coloration varies from brown to pale reddish-brown, often with a greenish tinge. The flanks are lighter with reddish-brown marks on the scales that form a pattern of stripes. The underside is yellowish to orange yellow. Thin reddish-brown marks run from the eyes over the gill covers. A light blue iridescent mark lies between the back edge of the gill covers and the base of the pectoral fins. Both dorsal fins have rows of reddish-brown marks against an almost colorless background. The anal fin is reddish at the base and has a light border. Young specimens have diagonal transverse bands against a reddish background.
Females are lighter, with less prominent marks on the gill covers and the scales.
Males are as described above.

General care: *D.latifrons* needs a tank with brackish water, a clean deep sandy bed and plenty of retreats among stones and bogwood. The water should be fairly hard and 50–100 gms of sea salt should be added for every ten liters of water: temperature 18°–22° C. *D.latifrons* is predatory and can only be kept with other larger species of fish. All sorts of live animal matter will be eaten and the diet should also include smaller fish but if this is not possible, it should be given raw fish and shredded beef heart.

Breeding: The large batch of eggs will be laid in rows under a flat stone, cleaned previously by both parents, who will fan the eggs. The parents should be removed from the tank as soon as the eggs hatch. The fry should be fed with infusoria and *Artemia nauplii*, and are not too difficult to raise.

DORMITATOR MACULATUS

Family: *Eleotridae*

Genus: *Dormitator*

English name: Spotted Sleeper Goby,

Origin: Central America

Size: Approximately 25 cm in the wild but remains much smaller in captivity and is sexually mature at about 10 cm

Habitat: Found in brackish and salt waters near the coast and rarely in fresh waters

Shape, coloring and markings: The body shape is identical to that of *D.latifrons*. The basic coloration varies from a dull to dark brown with a greenish tinge. On the flanks lie dark marks which may merge into a horizontal line. Thin reddish-brown lines run from the eyes over the gill covers. The caudal anal and dorsal fins have rows of dark marks, the anal fin has also light blue flecks.
Females are lighter with fever marks
Males are as described above.

General care: As for *D.latifrons*.

Breeding: As for *D.latifrons*.

870. *Eleotris lebretonis*

THE FAMILY ELEOTRIDAE

The genus Eleotris

The genus *Eleotris*, whose members are found principally but by no means exclusively in Africa, is the largest genus of *Eleotridae* fish. They are typical of the family in their life style but some are very predatory and these, as noted below, should not be kept with other species that would be at risk. A number of species have been kept in aquariums but perhaps *Eleotris lebretonis* is the most promising for the amateur.

ELEOTRIS AFRICANA

Family: *Eleotridae*

Genus: *Eleotris*

English name: none

Origin: Tropical West Africa, from Guinea to the Congo delta

Size: Approximately 10 cm

Habitat: Found usually in brackish waters but also occasionally in fresh waters

Shape, coloring and markings: The body is long and slim, cylindrical at the front but laterally very compressed towards the tail. The scales are very small. The basic coloration is a dull brown: the underside is yellowish to white. Young specimens have indistinct dark marks over the entire body: these may merge together to form transverse bands. Rows of dark marks lie on the dorsal fins: the caudal fin has irregular dark flecks and one large dark mark on the upper lobe: the lower lobe is an iridescent light blue. The anal fin and the tips of the ventral fins have a light blue border.
Females are less distinctly marked on the fins.
Males are as described above.

General care: *E.africana* needs a spacious tank with a deep sandy bed and plenty of retreats among stones and bogwood. The water should be hard or medium hard and 50–100 grams of sea salt should be added for every ten liters of water: temperature 20°–25° C. *E.africana* is predatory and can only be kept with larger species which remain in the middle and upper reaches of the tank. The diet should be live animal matter and if possible smaller fish: alternatively shredded beef heart and raw fish may be offered.

Breeding: Nothing is known about the reproductive behavior of this species.

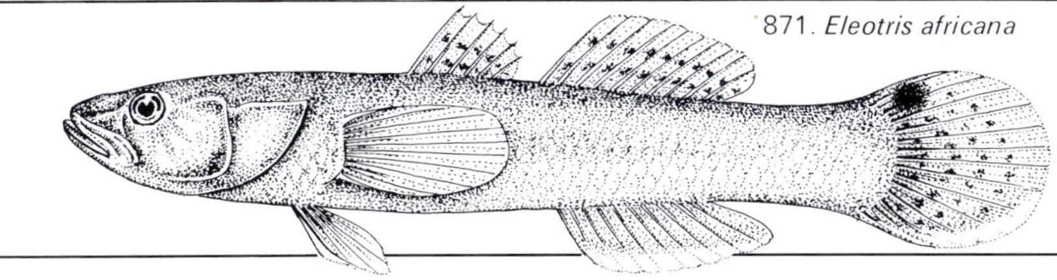

871. *Eleotris africana*

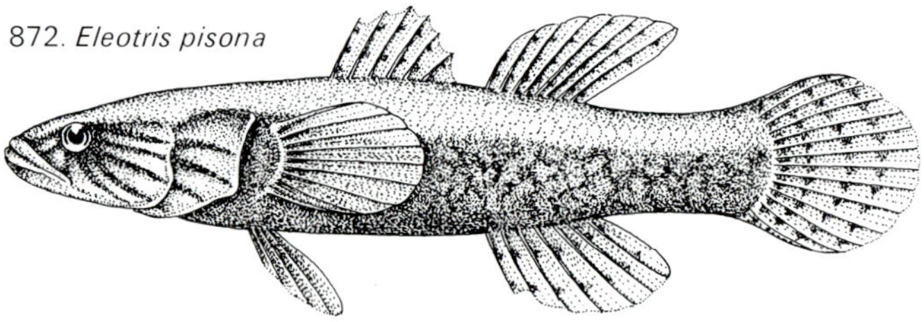

872. *Eleotris pisona*

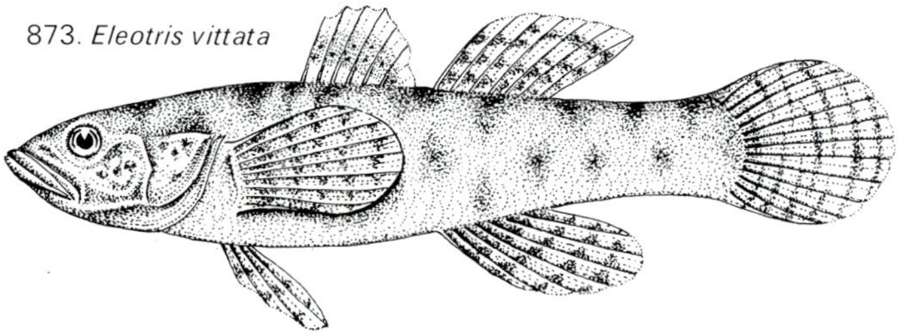

873. *Eleotris vittata*

ELEOTRIS LEBRETONIS

Family: *Eleotridae*

Genus: *Eleotris*

English name: none

Origin: West Africa, the Congo region

Size: Approximately 12 cm

Habitat: Found in coastal districts principally in fresh waters but also occasionally in brackish river estuaries

Shape, coloring and markings: The body shape is identical to that of *E.africana*: the upward pointing mouth is large. The basic coloration is a yellowish to greenish-brown: the back is darker: the underside is ochre to off-white. Dark red or brownish marks lie on the scales, most prominently on the flanks. The fins are white or grey, with dark marks. During the spawning season the colors become more vivid: the back turns an iridescent olive green, becoming red towards the caudal peduncle: the flanks become orange and luminescent: the belly turns vermilion and the marks on the fins become bluish-violet.
Females have rounded ventral fins.
Males are as described above. The back dorsal fin has elongated rays and the ventral fins taper.

General care: *E.lebretonis* requires a tank furnished as for *E.africana* and can share it only with larger species that remain in the upper and middle reaches of the tank. It benefits from having two teaspoonfuls of salt added for every ten liters of water but can survive in fresh water: temperature 20°–28°C. Diet as for *E.africana* but dried food will also be eaten.

Breeding: This is not difficult. The large batch of eggs will be laid among fine leaved plants. The fry are extremely small and should be fed on fine infusoria for the first few days after which they may be reared on the normal foods for fry.

ELEOTRIS PISONIS

Family: *Eleotridae*

Genus: *Eleotris*

English name: none

Origin: Central and South America, the West Indies

Size: Approximately 12 cm

Habitat: Found in salt, brackish and fresh waters

Shape, coloring and markings: The body is elongated and laterally compressed only towards the tail. The basic coloration is ochre to brown. The flanks and belly are dark brown, with irregular reddish-brown marks. Narrow black lines run from the eyes to the snout and over the gill covers. The fins are yellowish. The anal, caudal and dorsal fins have dark marks in rows which may become unbroken bands: the ventral fins are very dark.
There are no known external sexual characteristics.

General care: As for *E.africana* but temperature 20°–28°C. *E.pisonis* will accept dried food.

Breeding: Nothing is known about the reproductive behavior of this species.

ELEOTRIS VITTATA

Family: *Eleotridae*

Genus: *Eleotris*

English name: none

Origin: Tropical West Africa; the lower reaches of the Congo

Size: Approximately 22 cm

Habitat: Found mainly in fresh waters.

Shape, coloring and markings: The body is elongated and laterally compressed only towards the tail. The basic coloration is ochre to fawn: the back is fawn to reddish brown, with dark marks: the flanks are lighter. Young specimens have a dark horizontal line below a lighter band on the flanks. Golden and bluish silver iridescent marks lie on the gill covers. The underside of the head is usually dark, with light flecks. The anal, caudal and dorsal fins are yellowish with brown or rust colored marks. The front dorsal fin has a wide brown band and a white border.
Females are less vividly colored and the back dorsal fin is less powerfully developed.
Males are as described above.

General care: As for *E.lebretonis*.

Breeding: Nothing is known about the reproductive behavior of this species.

THE FAMILY ELEOTRIDAE

The genus Hypseleotris

This small genus is closely related to the larger species in the genus *Eleotris*, but the species in this genus are only found in Indonesia and neighboring areas. Although *H.bipartita*, from the Philippines has, it seems been imported, only the two species noted below are regularly seen in aquariums and indeed it may well be that *H.cyprinoides* is only a color variant of *H.modestus*, the more common of the two species. Neither species is usually bred in captivity.

874. *Hypseleotris cyprinoides*

HYPSELEOTRIS CYPRINOIDES

Family: *Eleotridae*
Genus: *Hypseleotris*
English name: none
Origin: Indonesia
Size: Approximately 7 cm
Habitat: Found in brackish and fresh waters

SHAPE, COLORING AND MARKINGS: The body is elongated and laterally slightly compressed. The basic coloration is ochre to a translucent yellowish-green. A dark horizontal band runs from the eye through the gill covers to the base of the caudal fin. Dark marks may lie above this band. The fins are transparent: the anal caudal and dorsal fins have a light blue border, sometimes edged with black: the dorsal fins have light blue flecks.
Females are ochre with iridescent marks above the dark horizontal band. The fins lack the light blue borders of those of the males but do have dark rays.
Males are as described above.

GENERAL CARE: *H.cyprinoides* needs a spacious tank with a deep sandy bed and retreats among stones and bogwood. It is tolerant and is best kept in a community tank with other related small species. The water should be fairly hard and one tablespoonful of salt should be added for every ten liters of water: temperature 20°–28°C. It should be offered all sorts of live animal matter and for a change, dried food.

BREEDING: It appears that this species has been bred in captivity but no detailed reports are available on its reproductive behavior.

ADDITIONAL INFORMATION: A beautiful, lively and tolerant species that keeps mainly to the middle reaches of the tank.

HYPSELEOTRIS MODESTUS

Family: *Eleotridae*
Genus: *Hypseleotris*
English name: none
Origin: Indonesia
Size: Approximately 7 cm
Habitat: Found in both brackish and fresh waters

SHAPE, COLORING AND MARKINGS: The body shape is identical to that of *H.cyprinoides*. The basic coloration is pale green: the whole body is translucent. The upper part of the body has a reddish hue: the underside is lighter. The fins are orangey yellow and transparent: sometimes they bear light blue marks, but the general absence of marks is a characteristic of this species. Only very exceptionally are there any marks on the pectoral fines.
There are no known external sexual characteristics.

GENERAL CARE: As for *H.cyprinoides*.

BREEDING: Nothing is known about the reproductive behavior of this species.

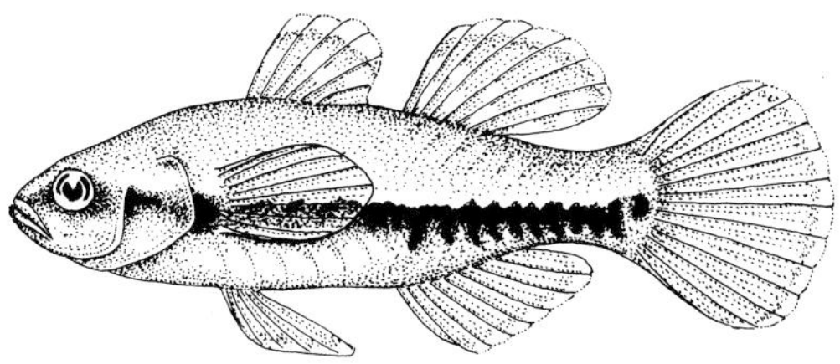

875. *Hypseleotris cyprinoides*

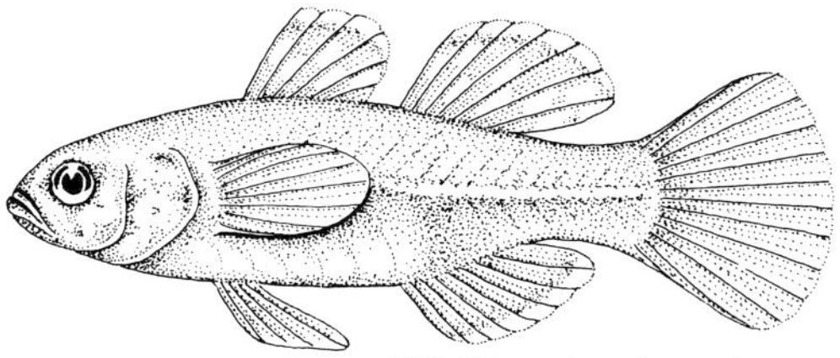

876. *Hypseleotris modestus*

THE FAMILY ANABANTIDAE

The *Anabantidae* are to be found over a very wide area of Asia and Africa. There are significant differences between the African and Asian groups and they are accordingly treated separately below. However the characteristic feature shared by all the *Anabantidae* or Labyrinth fish is the supplementary respiratory organ which lies behind the eyes and gives rise to their popular name. This is indeed a more appropriate name than that suggested by their latin name which can be translated as 'climbing bass' for although a few species will, in the wild, climb out of the water and move overland to another better environment, most species of *Anabantidae* do not behave in this way. The Labyrinth fish of Asia are much better known among aquarists than the related species from Africa which are less popular because they are usually predators.

The Asian Labyrinth fish
Most of these fish have a body that is elongated, quite deep and laterally very compressed: Biologically they are distinguished by the presence of the labyrinth, made up of countless very thin plates *(lamellae)* which seem to be scattered at random in the gill cavities and at first sight looks like a maze or labyrinth, hence its popular name. The labyrinth is used to extract oxygen from the air which, when breathed by the fish at the surface of the water, is forced through these plates. In most labyrinth fish the gills are used much less for breathing than they are in other types of fish and even when living in oxygen rich waters the labyrinth fish have to come to the surface to breathe through that organ. On the other hand of course, because they rely less on their gills, the labyrinth fish are less likely than other fish to suffocate in polluted waters with little oxygen, provided they can reach the surface to breathe. It is important to remember that when *Anabantidae* are transported, they may well suffocate if put into air-tight containers.
These fish usually have another feature in common: the pectoral fins have developed into thread-like tactile organs which are also used as organs of taste and smell: they can be moved independently of each other and are often seen to be moving in the tank, exploring the region around the fish. The anal fin is usually elongated at the back: in some species the dorsal fin is similarly shaped. Most species have a rounded caudal fin.
Various species are found in a wide cariety of natural habitats. In general, in the aquarium, the conditions for keeping them are not critical, but most species like a spacious tank with plenty of vegetation to provide them with adequate retreats. Except for those species that come from North China and Korea and need a lower temperature, most species are happy

at 23°–28° C. They are not as a rule fussy about their diet although some species must have a vegetable supplement to the more generally acceptable live animal matter and dried food.

Breeding most species is not difficult: details are given in the descriptions below. The male usually builds a bubble nest and alone looks after the eggs. The fry are not difficult to raise except that when the labyrinth organ begins to develop during the second and third weeks, the young fish are unusually vulnerable and care must be taken to maintain the breeding tank (and the air immediately above it) at the right temperature.

The African Labyrinth fish

There is only one genus of African labyrinth fish, *Ctenopoma* and the species in that genus bear little resemblance to the Asian labyrinth fish described above: they are much more akin, in appearance and behavior, to Cichlids. They are predatory and are much less attractive fish for the amateur without specialised interests. They have a labyrinth organ that is far less well developed than the Asian Labyrinth fish but they have the reputation of being unusually long lived.

The genus Anabas

Only one species in the genus Anabas, *Anabas testudineus,* the Climbing fish, described below is of interest to aquarists and even that species has, in recent years, become much less popular than it was formerly because despite its interesting habits it is more aggressive and more difficult to feed than most other labyrinth fish.

877. *Anabas testudineus*

The genus *Anabas* is very closely related to the genera *Ctenopoma* and *Helistoma* considered below. Indeed, the differences between the genera *Anabas* and *Ctenopoma* on the one hand and *Helostoma* on the other are restricted to differences in dentition and the number of soft rays in the dorsal and anal fins. These features are identical in the genera *Anabas* and *Ctenopoma* and between these two genera the only difference is that species in the genus *Ctenopoma* have a smooth edge to the gill covers whereas in the genus *Anabas,* the gill covers have a serrated edge.

ANABAS TESTUDINEUS

Family: *Anabantidae*

Genus: *Anabas*

English names Climbing Fish, Climbing Perch

Origin: Southeast Asia, from India to the Philippines

Size: Maximum 25 cm in the wild but remains considerably smaller in captivity

SHAPE, COLORING AND MARKINGS: The body is very elongated, fairly deep and laterally compressed: in profile the back and bally run almost parallel from the neck and throat to the caudal peduncle. The dorsal and anal fins are very long. The wide mouth is upward pointing. Spines are found on the gill covers and on the exceptionally powerful pectoral fins. The basic coloration is olive green to grey brown: younger specimens sometimes have vertical stripes with darker spots on the gill covers and the caudal peduncle. The fins are colorless or brownish, occasionally yellowish. Females have smaller dorsal and anal fins.

Males are as describe above: the anal fin tapers.

GENERAL CARE: *A.testudineus* retains its climbing propensity in captivity and the tank must be very securely covered. It needs a large well-planted species tank, being shy but aggressive. The composition of the water is not critical: temperature 15°–30° C, the higher temperatures being preferred. Until they are about 7 cm young specimens can be fed on a conventional diet of mixed live and dried food with a vegetable supplement but larger specimens will only accept live food, such as other fish.

BREEDING: A suitable pair should be transferred to a special breeding tank with a low water level but temperature at least 28° C. Up to 1000 eggs will be laid and will float to the surface. No form of brood care is practised by the parents, but they do not, it seems prey on the fry.

ADDITIONAL INFORMATION: *A.testudineus* is the only species in the family that actually crawls out of the water: it is also a very good jumper.

THE FAMILY ANABANTIDAE

The genus Belontia

There is only one species of interest to aquarists in the genus *Belontia, Belontia signata,* the Comb-tail Paradise fish described below. As its common name implies, it is closely related to the Paradise fish in the genus *Macropodus,* although its distribution is much more restricted. Among amateurs this attractive species has a bad name as an aggressive predatory fish. These unwelcome characteristics can however be greatly moderated by keeping *B.signata* in the proper environment.

878. *Belontia signata*

BELONTIA SIGNATA
Family: *Anabantidae*
Genus: *Belontia*
English name: Comb-tail Paradise Fish
Origin: Sri Lanka
Size: Maximum 13 cm
Habitat: Found in still, vegetated waters

SHAPE, COLORING AND MARKINGS: The body is elongated, relatively deep and laterally only moderately compressed. The large mouth is upward pointing. The long dorsal and anal fins, extend half the length of the body and taper with elongated rays at the back. The caudal fin is fan-shaped. The front rays of the elongated ventral fins and several rays of the caudal fin project beyond the body of the fin proper. The basic coloration varies considerably from specimen to specimen. The back may be olive green, the belly lighter, or the back may be an iridescent green with reddish brown indistinct transverse bands. The fins are yellowish to blue green: the rays red brown. The tips of the dorsal and anal fins have narrow cream edges. Older specimens have a dark patch at the back of the dorsal fin.
Females are less vividly colored with less tapered dorsal and anal fins.
Males are as described above.

GENERAL CARE: *B.signata* requires a large densely planted tank. The composition of the water is not critical: temperature 25° C. Any other fish present in the tank must be fairly large and agile. A substantial and varied diet of live animal matter must be provided.
BREEDING: A potential pair, although difficult to catch, should be transferred to a special tank at least 60×30×30 cm with a sandy bottom, some floating plants, and others in the tank to provide retreats. The water should be fresh: temperature 28° C. The male will construct a somewhat perfunctory bubble nest. Mating will take place beneath this nest. The eggs will float to the surface and will be gathered by the male and put in the nest. The first fry hatch in 48 hours and will be free swimming after about four days. The female will be driven away from the nest immediately after mating and is best then removed from the tank. The male will not injure the fry but is best removed when they are free swimming. The fry, which are quite large should be fed on *Artemia* and Cyclops *nauplii* immediately. The labyrinth organ will develop during the fourth week but does not usually cause any difficulties in rearing.

THE FAMILY ANABANTIDAE

The genus Betta

Nomenclature is the genus *Betta* is somewhat confused. There are twelve species at the present time, but many of these are thought by some authorities to be no more than varieties of the best known species, *Betta splendens*, the Siamese Fighting Fish. However, the problems of nomenclature are not of great concern to the amateur, for most *Betta* species are rarely if ever imported. Three species are described below. *B.fasciata*, and *B.pugnax* are uncommon, although more interest has been taken in them in recent years. The third species treated in this encyclopaedia is the ever popular *B.splendens*, although here it must be remembered that the flamboyant specimens so often seen and admired in aquariums are not the wild fish, but domesticated varieties produced by selective breeding. Despite its pugnacious character, it remains a favorite with many amateurs.

BETTA FASCIATA
Family: *Anabantidae*
Genus: *Betta*
English name: Striped Fighting Fish
Origin: Indonesia, Sumatra
Size: Maximum 10 cm
Habitat: Found in pools and other still waters

SHAPE, COLORING AND MARKINGS: The body is elongated, very slender and laterally only slightly compressed. The basic coloration is very dark, varying from a bluish black to a dark bluish green or reddish brown. Transverse bands, sometimes indistinct, lie on the flanks. The scales have greenish, iridescent marks, especially on the lower part of the body. The colorless or dark fins usually bear darker marks. The anal and caudal fins have greenish, iridescent flecks.
Females have less powerfully developed fins.
Males have elongated dorsal and anal fins.

GENERAL CARE: *B.fasciata* needs a large, well-planted tank with a dark bed and arrangements of rock and bogwood. The composition of the water is not critical: temperature 26°–28° C. *B.fasciata* is tolerant of other species, but hostile to males of its own kind. It swims freely throughout the tank if the water is at the right temperature. In community tanks where the temperature is usually lower, it keeps almost exclusively near the surface and does not thrive. Live animal matter and dried food will both be eaten.

BREEDING: Little is known in detail about the breeding habits of this species, but it certainly builds bubble nests.

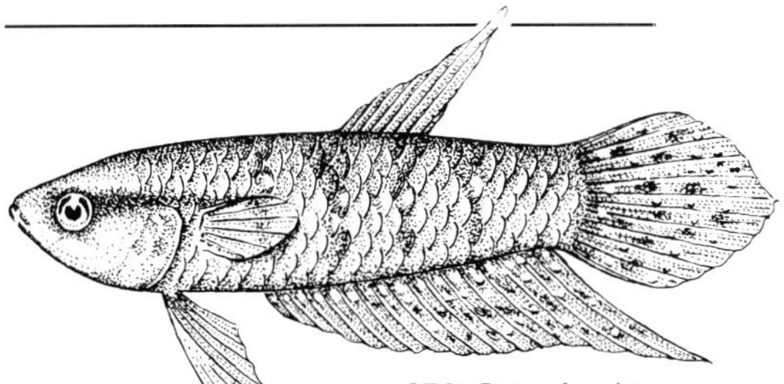
879. *Betta fasciata*

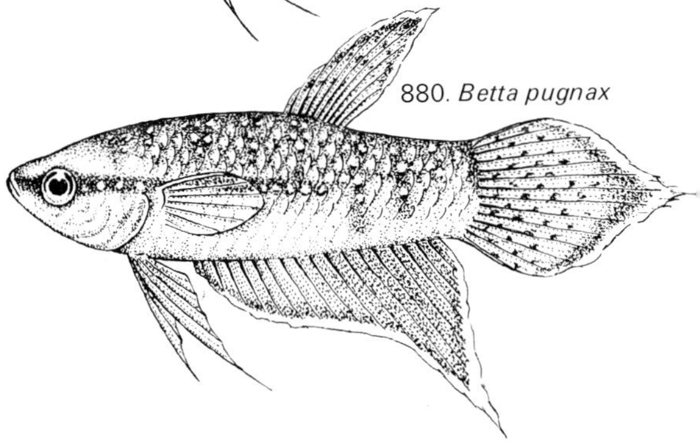
880. *Betta pugnax*

BETTA PUGNAX
Family: *Anabantidae*
Genus: *Betta*
English name: Penang Mouth-brooding Fighting Fish
Origin: Malaya
Size: Maximum 9 cm
Habitat: No details are available of its natural habitat

SHAPE, COLORING AND MARKINGS: The body is elongated, and laterally only slightly compressed. The basic coloration varies from a dull blue to rust: the upper half of the head is light brown. A number of sometimes indistinct transverse bands lie across the body: a prominent dark horizontal line runs from the snout to just behind the last rays of the dorsal fin, and in some specimens is bordered above and below by a light band. The fins are brownish with dark flecks, especially on the dorsal and caudal fins which, with the anal fin, have a light edge.

881. *Betta splendens*

Females are less vividly colored and have shorter fins.
Males have elongated dorsal and anal fins.

GENERAL CARE: As for *B.fasciata*.

BREEDING: Very little is known in detail about the breeding behavior of this fish: it is it appears a mouth brooder. Breeding temperature 26°–29°C.

BETTA SPLENDENS
Family: *Anabantidae*
Genus: *Betta*
English name: Siamese Fighting Fish
Origin: The Far East; Malaya and Thailand
Size: Approximately 6 cm
Habitat: Found in many different kinds of waters

SHAPE, COLORING AND MARKINGS: The body is elongated and laterally only slightly compressed. The coloring and markings vary according to the locality of origin. Some specimens are a beautiful reddish brown with a bluish green iridescent tinge: all the scales have a decorative, green, or sometimes blue or red, metallic shiny dot. The large dorsal fin is set quite far back, and is a reddish brown with green iridescent stripes and dark marks. The round caudal fin is the same basic color, with similar green stripes, and often has an orange edge. The long anal fin is bluish green with brown and red marks: the long ventral fins are orangey red with milky white tips.
Females are a yellowish brown, with barely visible transverse bands. The ventral fins are short.
Males are as described above.

GENERAL CARE: As for *B.fasciata*.

BREEDING: Not difficult: *B.splendens* builds a bubble nest. The male guards the eggs, and the female should be removed after spawning. The fry hatch in two or three days and are free swimming on the sixth day. The male should be removed when the fry are free swimming, and they should be fed on infusoria and later *Artemia nauplii*.

ADDITIONAL INFORMATION: *B.splendens* is hardly ever kept by aquarists in its natural form. The fish shown is a veiled variety bred in many colors, which is very popular.

THE FAMILY ANABANTIDAE

The genus Colisa

The genus *Colisa* contains only four species, but they are all well-known to aquarists and are popular aquarium fish. Two species, *C.labiosa,* the Thick-lipped Gourami and *C.lalia,* the Dwarf Gourami are long established favorites: *C.fasciata,* the Giant Gourami is a quite separate species but is very often confused with *C.labiosa.* The fourth species, *C.chuna,* the Honey Gourami has become popular in recent years.
These are not difficult species to keep or breed and their undemanding nature makes them unusually attractive Labyrinth fish for the novice as well as the advanced aquarist.

882. *Colisa fasciata*

COLISA CHUNA
Family: *Anabantidae*
Genus: *Colisa*
English name: Honey Gourami
Origin: The Indian sub-continent
Size: Maximum 5 cm
Habitat: Found in a variety of waters

SHAPE, COLORING AND MARKINGS: The body is elongated, fairly deep and laterally compressed. The long base of the dorsal fin runs from the neck to the caudal peduncle, to which also extends the base of the somewhat shorter anal fin. The ventral fins are thread-like. Outside the breeding season the basic coloration is ochre with a silvery gleam. The fins are yellowish to red. In the breeding season the body has an orange-red tone: the snout and throat become a velvety green-black. The anal and ventral fins are orange: the caudal fin becomes yellow green with orange rays: the upper part of the dorsal fin becomes canary yellow above a narrow band of blue, and orange below.
Females are less vividly colored during the breeding season, but carry a dark longitudinal stripe along the body.
Males are as described above.

883. *Colisa lalia*

GENERAL CARE: *C.chuna* requires a fairly large tank, densely planted in such a way as to allow each male to establish his own small territory. Some floating plants are desirable. If kept in a community tank only other very peaceful species should be included. The composition of the water is not critical: temperature 25° C. A varied diet of live and dried food should be given and mosquito larvae are an essential element.

BREEDING: The temperature in the tank should be raised to about 28° C. The male constructs an insubstantial bubble nest. The courtship involves the pair engaging in an unusual waltz which ends with both fish vertical below the nest, where they embrace and 10–20 eggs are released. Over 1–1½ hours several hundred eggs will be laid. The male will gather them into the nest. The eggs hatch in 24 hours and the fry are free swimming after four days, when they are best transferred to a special rearing tank and fed on infusoria with the water being changed frequently. During the second week the fry should be fed on infusoria and egg yolk: during the third week on infusoria and *Artemia nauplii.* The Labyrinth begins to develop during the fourth week and care must be taken to ensure that, with a good cover to the tank (and insulation if necessary) the air above the surface is at the same temperature as the water: the water level at this stage should not be more than 10 cm.

COLISA FASCIATA

Family: *Anabantidae*

Genus: *Colisa*

English names: Giant Gourami, Striped Gourami, Banded Gourami

Origin: The Indian sub-continent, Burma, Thailand, Malaya

Size: Maximum 10 cm

Habitat: Found in still, shaded waters

SHAPE, COLORING AND MARKINGS: The body shape and fin formation are identical to those of *C.chuna* but the caudal fin is more forked. The basic coloration is red brown. Transverse blue-green iridescent bands lie on the body. The iris is red. The ventral fins are reddish-orange: the tapering dorsal fin has a fine blue-green patterning and red-brown transverse bands. The anal fin is blue with an orange border: the caudal fin is transparent, red-brown with a pattern of dark spots.
Females are less vividly colored: the dorsal and anal fins are more rounded.
Males are as described above.

GENERAL CARE: As for *C.chuna* but each male requires a larger territory.

BREEDING: SEE *C.chuna*: 1000 eggs may be laid.

COLISA LABIOSA

Family: *Anabantidae*

Genus: *Colisa*

English name: Thick-lipped Gourami

Origin: Burma

Size: Maximum 8 cm

Habitat: Found in a variety of shaded waters

SHAPE, COLORING AND MARKINGS: The body shape is identical to that of *C.fasciata* but smaller: the skin thickens towards the mouth, making the lips rather thick. The basic coloration is greenish. Irregular red-brown transverse bands lie on the body: a white patterning is evident on the throat and belly. The fins are colorless, save for the brown caudal fin and the deep blue band on the anal fin, but the tips of the elongated rays are blood red as are the ventral fins.
Females are less vividly colored: the ventral fins are colorless.
Males are as described above.

GENERAL CARE: As for *C.fasciata.*

BREEDING: As for *C.chuna.*

ADDITIONAL INFORMATION: Some authorities maintain that *C.labiosa* is no more than a color variety of *C.fasciata.*

COLISA LALIA

Family: *Anabantidae*

Genus: *Colisa*

English name: Dwarf Gourami.

Origin: Eastern areas of the Indian sub-continent

Size: Maximum 5 cm

Habitat: Found in still, shaded waters

SHAPE, COLORING AND MARKINGS: The body shape closely resembles that of *C.chuna.* The basic coloration is a gleaming gold to deep red. The throat and belly are an iridescent dark blue. Several red irregular transverse stripes run across the flanks. The ventral fins are orange-red: the dorsal, anal and caudal fins are red with sky blue flecks.
Females are more golden with fewer blue flecks. The dorsal and anal fins are rounded. Males have tapered dorsal and anal fins.

GENERAL CARE: As for *C.chuna.*

BREEDING: As for *C.chuna* but *C.lalia* builds a very deep substantial bubble nest, reinforced with small pieces of vegetation.

884. *Colisa chuna*

THE FAMILY ANABANTIDAE

The genus Ctenopoma

Eleven species are known in this, the only important genus of African Labyrinth fish. They have not gained much popularity among amateurs and they are not commonly imported. They are singularly aggressive fish and moreover, not particularly colorful. However aquarists who have a special interest in these fish find them well worth keeping, in the proper conditions. They are hardy and long-lived and not difficult to breed although few amateurs seem to breed them. Three of the more frequently imported species are described below.

885. *Ctenopoma acutirostre*

CTENOPOMA ACUTIROSTRE

Family: *Anabantidae*

Genus: *Ctenopoma*

English name: Spotted Climbing Perch

Origin: The Congo Basin

Size: Maximum 12 cm

Habitat: Found in both still and running waters

SHAPE, COLORING AND MARKINGS: The body is fairly elongated, relatively deep and laterally very compressed. The head is long and pointed: the mouth is very large: the eyes are big. The long-based anal and dorsal fins have elongated rays at the front and back, where they touch the rounded caudal fin. The basic coloration is a muddy or ochre yellow. The whole of the body is covered with very dark brown spots. The anal, dorsal and ventral fins are colorless: the caudal fin is yellow, with a colorless edge beyond a dark brown band. There are no known external sexual characteristics.

GENERAL CARE: *C.acutirostre* requires a large well planted tank with plenty of retreats among the plants and bogwood. It dislikes strong light and floating plants should be included. The water should not be hard: temperature 25° C. Only live animal matter will be eaten and larger specimens have a voracious appetite that will only be satisfied with small fish. Only large fish may be kept with it in a community tank.

886. *Ctenopoma nanum*

BREEDING: No information is available on the reproductive behavior of this species.

CTENOPOMA ANSORGEI

Family: *Anabantidae*

Genus: *Ctenopoma*

English name: none

Origin: The Congo basin

Size: Maximum 7 cm

Habitat: Found in still and sluggish waters

SHAPE, COLORING AND MARKINGS: The body is very elongated and laterally compressed. The snout tapers. The long based tapering anal and dorsal fins have elongated rays at the front. The caudal fin is rounded. The basic coloration is reddish brown. Dark iridescent vertical bands lie on the body and run into the dorsal and anal fins. The tips of the elongated rays of these fins are a vivid white. The caudal fin is reddish-brown with darker rays. Females are less vividly colored and have rounded anal and dorsal fins.
Males are as described above.

GENERAL CARE: As for *C.acutiroste* but *C.ansorgei* is only aggressive during the breeding season. It can be persuaded to accept a diet of beef heart. A breeding tank tank at least 50×30×30 cm is required with plenty of retreats and floating plants. The water should be soft: temperature 28° C. The male builds a deep nest of fine bubbles while the female remains hidden. Mating usually takes place at night. The eggs are numerous, tiny, clear as glass and very difficult to see in the nest. Once they have been laid the female should be removed. The male guards the nest. When the fry have hatched the male should also be removed. The fry congregate in the darkest part of the tank and are difficult to find. They should be fed on the finest infusoria and later on *Artemia nauplii.* When the Labyrinth begins to develop in the third week the floating plants should be removed, the water level reduced to 10 cm and the air above kept at the same temperature as the water.

CTENOPOMA NANUM

Family: *Anabantidae*

Genus: *Ctenopoma*

English name: Dwarf Climbing Perch

Origin: Zaire

Size: Maximum 8 cm

Habitat: Found in shaded, still and sluggish waters

SHAPE, COLORING AND MARKINGS: The body shape and fin pattern closely resemble those of *C.ansorgei.* The basic coloration is olive brown. Broad dark transverse bands and paler spots lie on the body. The fins are grey-green or yellowish. Young specimens have a dark spot at the base of the caudal fin.
Females are less deeply colored and have rounded anal and dorsal fins.
Males are as described above with tapering anal and dorsal fins.

GENERAL CARE: As for *C.acutirostre* but *C.nanum* is very tolerant of all other fish except during the breeding season. A diet of live animal matter is needed but *C.nanum* will not eat other fish.

BREEDING: The eggs are laid in a substantial bubble nest which the male builds in the darkest corner of the tank. The nest and eggs should be transferred to a separate tank after 24 hours and the procedure suggested above for *C.ansorgei* then followed.

THE FAMILY ANABANTIDAE

The genus Helostoma

Only one species, *Helostoma temmincki,* the Kissing Gourami, is found in this genus. It is a species in many respects quite different from most of the *Anabantidae,* although it is a labyrinth fish. It is much larger than most of its near relatives, it does not build a bubble nest, and it has very thick protruding lips. It used to be a very popular fish with amateurs, but then became far less common in aquariums: recently it has become more popular again. It is not a very colorful species, but this drawback is compensated for by its peaceful, albeit somewhat timid nature.

887. *Helostoma temmincki*

HELOSTOMA TEMMINCKI

Family: *Anabantidae*
Genus: *Helostoma*
English name: Kissing Gourami
Origin: Thailand, Malaya
Size: Maximum 30 cm in the wild but remains considerably smaller in captivity
Habitat: Found in many different kinds of waters

SHAPE, COLORING AND MARKINGS: The body is deep and oval. The head is somewhat pointed: the lips are thick and protuberant. The basic coloration varies from a yellowish to a greenish silver: the upper half of the body is darker, or an olive green: the belly is almost white. A number of dark, horizontal stripes usually lie on the flanks. The fins are a greenish or dull yellow: the front rays of the dorsal and anal fins have a dark edge. When in good condition *H.temmincki* displays a pattern of dark crescent shaped bands at the back of the dorsal and anal fins, and on the base of the caudal fin. The eyes are yellowish brown. Some specimens offered for sale commercially are almost entirely silvery or flesh colored.
There are no known external sexual characteristics.

GENERAL CARE: *H.temmincki* requires a large tank with plenty of free swimming space but also sufficient plants to provide retreats: floating plants should also be included to reduce the light. The composition of the water is not critical: temperature 25° C. Tolerant of its own kind and other species, *H.temmincki* will swim freely throughout the tank provided the temperature and aquarium lay-out are suitable. It is rather timid and dislikes a brightly lit tank. It will hunt for live animal matter but requires a primarily vegetarian diet. The aquarium must be rich in algae, but boiled lettuce leaves should also be given. It will not normally damage aquarium plants.

BREEDING: There are no reliable reports of successful breeding.

ADDITIONAL INFORMATION: The Kissing Gourami owes its popular name to the way in which it feeds off the algae on plants and other objects in the aquarium with its thick, protuberant lips. Sometimes the fish seem to kiss; this is probably a threat display.

THE FAMILY ANABANTIDAE

The genus Macropodus

The small genus *Macropodus,* in which the well known Paradise Fish are classified, is one in which nomenclature is somewhat complicated, partly because of the attention these beautiful fish have received from breeders. There are usually held to be three species: *Macropodus chinensis,* the Roundtailed Paradise Fish, *Macropodus cupanus,* the Spiketailed Pardise Fish, and *Macropodus opercularis,* the Paradise Fish. The two most commonly species, *M.cupanus cupanus,* and *M.opercularis,* are described below: neither *M.chinensis,* nor *M.cupanus dayi* is frequently seen in aquariums, but when found, both require the same care as *M.opercularis.* These fish are not as popular as they used to be, but still merit the attention of amateurs.

MACROPODUS CUPANUS CUPANUS

Family: *Anabantidae*
Genus: *Macropodus*
English name: Spike-tailed, Paradise Fish
Origin: India, Sri Lanka
Size: Approximately 7 cm
Habitat: Found in many different kinds of waters, particularly around the coasts

SHAPE, COLORING AND MARKINGS: The body is elongated, and laterally compressed. The basic coloration varies from yellowish-brown to reddish or dark brown with a strong iridescent green tinge, specially prominent on the head and gill covers. The throat and belly are very dark or blackish. A number of green, horizontal stripes sometimes lie on the flanks, separated from each other by lighter bands: a dark mark may be found at the base of the caudal fin. The fins are bright yellow or bluish-grey: the dorsal, anal and caudal fins have reddish marks and are usually edged with blue. The ventral fins are orangey-red. The irises are bright red.
Females have no elongated rays in the dorsal and anal fins. During the mating season the basic coloration is very dark or even black. Males have dorsal and anal fins which taper, with elongated rays.

GENERAL CARE: *M.cupanus cupanus* needs a fairly large well-planted tank with adequate retreats, arrangements of wood or inverted flower pots and coconut shells. The composition of the water is not critical. Temperature 18°–23° C. *M.cupanus cupanus* is tolerant of its own species and other fish. All kinds of live animal matter will be eaten, and dried food should be given occasionally.

BREEDING: Depending on the conditions in the tank, *M.cupanus cupanus* will build a bubble nest on the water surface, on a leaf below it, or inside an upturned coconut shell. The eggs hatch after 48 hours and the fry are not difficult to raise with the usual foods but the water must be changed regularly. It is not however a very prolific species.

MACROPODUS OPERCULARIS

Family: *Anabantidae*

Genus: *Macropodus*

English name: Paradise Fish

Origin: Korea, Eastern China, South Vietnam

Size: Approximately 9 cm

Habitat: Found in many different kinds of waters

SHAPE, COLORING AND MARKINGS: The body is elongated, and laterally fairly compressed. The basic coloration varies from a brownish to a greenish-yellow grey. The upper half of the head and the neck are brownish-black with an olive green marbling. A large number of transverse bands lie on the flanks: they vary from bluish-green to carmine red and are irregularly spaced, sometimes merging together. A dark brown or bluish-black line runs from the eye to the gill cover, surrounded by an orangey-red or vivid red patch: in bright light this patch is a beautiful iridescent green. The fins are rust brown or bright red, with alternating light and dark patches. The dorsal and anal fins often have a light edge: the caudal fin is predominantly red: the ventral fins are orangey-red with white tips.
Females are lighter, with less powerfully developed fins. The transverse bands are usually a dull orange color.
Males are as described above, with very strongly developed fins.

GENERAL CARE: *M.opercularis* is aggressive, and unsuitable for a community tank. A pair should be kept in a species tank which needs no special furnishings. The composition of the water is not critical, nor is the temperature. *M.opercularis* can be kept in an unheated aquarium, and in the summer can even be kept in a pond out of doors. Diet as for *M.cupanus cupanus*.

BREEDING: Not difficult: at 20°–24°C, *M.opercularis* will often reproduce spontaneously.

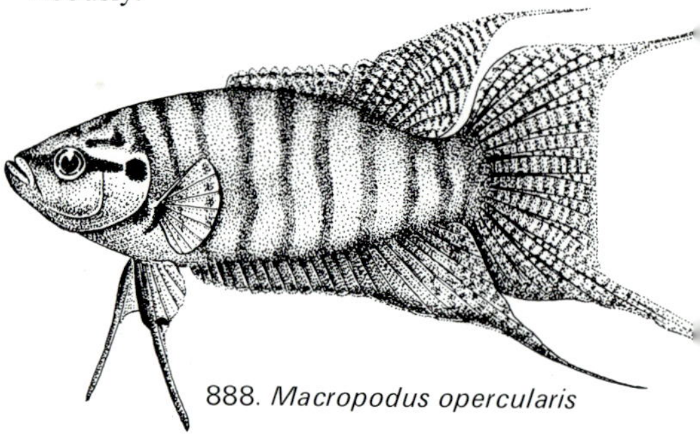

888. *Macropodus opercularis*

889. *Trichogaster trichopterus*

THE FAMILY ANABANTIDAE

The genus Trichogaster

The genus *Trichogaster* contains four popular species of Gourami, well-known to many amateurs: *Trichogaster leeri,* the Pearl Gourami, *Trichogaster microlepsis,* the Moonlight Gourami, *Trichogaster pectoralis,* the Snake-skinned Gourami, and *Trichogaster trichopterus,* the Three-spot Gourami. Of the last of these, *T.trichopterus,* there is a sub-species or variety, *T.trichopterus sumatranus* which may or may not occur naturally in the wild, but is very popular with aquarists, who because of its predominantly blue color, call this beautiful fish the Blue Gourami. The Blue Gourami is sometimes found with a blue-green basic coloration, and darker irregular patches on the back and flanks: this variety is sometimes described as *Trichogaster* 'Cosby', but is not a true species. All the species in this genus are easy to keep, and fully deserve their continuing popularity in aquarist circles.

TRICHOGASTER LEERI

Family: *Anabantidae*

Genus: *Trichogaster*

English names: Pearl Gourami, Mosaic Gourami

Origin: Malaya, Thailand, Borneo

Size: Maximum 10 cm

Habitat: Found in small streams

SHAPE, COLORING AND MARKINGS: The body is elongated and laterally strongly compressed. The snout is pointed: the mouth small. The rather narrow dorsal fin has long rays which give the leading edge a frilly appearance, and is set back on the body. The ventral fins are very long and thread-like. The anal fin has a very long base, and very extended rays at the back. The basic coloration is an olive brown: the flanks are paler, pearl grey with a greenish-blue overtone. The throat, belly, ventral fins and part of the anal fin are red. A narrow black zig-zag longitudinal stripe runs from the mouth across the eye to the root of the tail, where it ends in a black spot. The entire body except for the head, throat and belly is covered with tiny mother-of-pearl dots and flecks. The dorsal fin is a yellowish-brown.
Females have no red on the throat and belly and the fins are more rounded than in the males.
Males are as described above. The red on the throat and belly is less intense outside the mating season.

GENERAL CARE: *T.leeri* is eminently suitable for a large community tank with other fairly quiet species. Plenty of plants, including some floating plants, should be included, and the tank should have a dark bed. The water should not be hard: temperature 25°C. A varied diet of live and dried food should be given, but *T.leeri* has a small mouth.

BREEDING: A separate breeding tank is desirable, although *T.leeri* will spawn in a well maintained community tank. The breeding tank should be at least 50 × 30 × 30 cm, with a dark bed, plenty of vegetation including some floating plants and soft water: temperature 27°–28°C. The male will build a bubble nest: the female will not be allowed near, although *T.leeri* does not indulge in those dis-

890. *Trichogaster leeri*

plays of aggression typical of many other related species. The bubble nest is only a few centimeters deep, with a surface area of 15–20 sq. cm. A breeding pair in good condition may produce up to 1000 eggs. Once the eggs have been laid the female may be removed. The male tends the nest and often gathers sand from the bottom and spits it into the nest: this may be a way of encouraging unfertile eggs to sink to the bottom. The eggs hatch after two or three days and the fry are free swimming after about four days. The male may then be removed from the tank. The fry should be fed at first on pond infusoria, and then on fine fry foods. Great care must be taken, about the fourth week, to ensure that, as the labyrinth develops, the air above the tank is the same temperature as the water.

TRICHOGASTER TRICHOPTERUS

Family: *Anabantidae*

Genus: *Trichogaster*

English name: Three-spot Gourami

Origin: South Vietnam, Thailand, Malaya

Size: Maximum 15 cm in the wild but remains considerably smaller in captivity and is sexually mature at 8–10 cm

Habitat: Found in jungle streams

SHAPE, COLORING AND MARKINGS: The body is deep and laterally only slightly compressed. *T.trichopterus* closely resembles *T.leeri* but it is more powerfully built and has a deeper body. The basic coloration varies according to where the fish is found. The most common variety is a silvery blue, with a darker or bluish green back and an off-white or very shiny silvery belly. Two striking dark marks, sometimes with a light edge, lie on the flanks: the first is directly below the center of the dorsal fin, the second on the caudal peduncle. Some specimens have about 20 irregular transverse bands, but these are uncommon. The fins vary from green to grey: the anal, dorsal and caudal fins have white, yellowish or even orange patches and stripes.
Females have a short rounded dorsal fin.
Males are as described above. The dorsal fin is more pointed.

GENERAL CARE: As for *T.leeri* but temperature 23°–28°C. *T.trichopterus* keeps mainly to the middle reaches of the tank. It dislikes a change of environment and will often not settle down in a new tank.

BREEDING: Not difficult: as for *T.leeri.*

ADDITIONAL INFORMATION: *T.trichopterus* is well-known to aquarists as an admirable destroyer of pests of the genus *Hydra.* See introduction to the genus for notes on *T.trichopterus sumatranus.*

THE FAMILY ANABANTIDAE

The genus Trichopsis

This small genus of labyrinth fish has only three species, two of which have for long been well-known to amateurs. *Trichopsis pumilis,* the Dwarf Gourami, and *Trichopsis vittatus,* the Croaking Gourami, are well-established aquarium fish. *Trichopsis schalleri* is a recently discovered species, and not yet as well-known, but should soon acquire a popularity comparable to that enjoyed by its more frequently imported cousins. Biologically these fish are very closely related to the species in the genera *Betta* and *Ctenopoma.*

891. *Trichopsis vittatus*

TRICHOPSIS PUMILIS

Family: *Anabantidae*

Genus: *Trichopsis*

English name: Dwarf Gourami,

Origin: South Vietnam, Thailand, Indonesia

Size: Approximately 3.5 cm

Habitat: Found in densely vegetated jungle streams

SHAPE, COLORING AND MARKINGS: The body is slender and laterally very compressed. The basic coloration is ochre: the back is a dark olive green: the flanks are lighter: the belly and caudal peduncle are greenish or white. A number of irregular, bluish-black marks run from the snout to the base of the caudal fin, forming a broken horizontal line bordered above and below by luminescent turquoise or light blue flecks. The dorsal fin is pennant-shaped and pointed, green or yellowish, flecked with blue and red and edged with dark red. The caudal fin is rounded, the anal fin is long: in coloring and markings both are similar to the dorsal fin. The ventral fins are between a yellow and white, and the pectoral fins are colorless and transparent.
Females are duller, with a more rounded, shorter dorsal fin.
Males are as described above.

GENERAL CARE: *T.pumilis* is only suitable for a small, specially arranged tank with a dark bed of peat fibre. There should be a great variety of plants, and arrangements of bogwood. The water should preferably be acid and quite soft: temperature, 27°–28°C. This species is very tolerant, both towards members of its own kind and other species. It keeps mainly to the middle and bottom of the tank. The overhead light should be filtered through floating plants. All sorts of aquatic creatures can be given as food.

BREEDING: *T.pumilis* has been bred successfully, but the species is not very productive. During courtship these fish produce sounds audible outside the aquarium, like *Trichopsis vittatus.* The breeding is most likely to be successful if the water level is low. Quite often a bubble nest is built below the surface or even near the bed. The young hatch after about 36 hours at a temperature of about 28°C.

ADDITIONAL INFORMATION: This is a very attractive species which is easy to keep together with *Spaerichthys osphromenoides* (the Chocolate Gourami) and *Trichopsis vittatus* (the Croaking Gourami).

TRICHOPSIS VITTATUS

Family: *Anabantidae*

Genus: *Trichopsis*

English name: Croaking Gourami

Origin: South Vietnam, Thailand, Malaya, Indonesia

Size: Maximum 6.5 cm

Habitat: Found in jungle streams

SHAPE, COLORING AND MARKINGS: The body is slender and laterally very compressed. The basic coloration varies from ochre to brownish: the back is darker: the belly yellowish-white. In bright light the flanks appear to be tinged bluish white. Two distinct dark brown or black horizontal lines run from the eye to the base of the caudal fin: some specimens have in addition one or two other less distinct lines. All the fins are reddish, tinged with violet or blue, with numerous red, greenish or blue iridescent flecks and stripes. The eyes are striking: the outer part is a deep red, the inner bluish-green. The anal, dorsal and caudal fins are powerfully developed with some elongated rays.
Females are duller, with smaller anal fins. Males are as described above. The anal fin is very long and has a dark edge.

GENERAL CARE: As for *T.pumilis*, but *T.vittatus* can be kept in both large and small aquariums.

BREEDING: *T.vittatus* has been bred successfully in captivity, but it is not easy. The best results are obtained in the early spring in a densely planted aquarium at a temperature of about 30°C. The fish take great care over the building of the bubble nest. During the courtship both sexes make grunting noises which are clearly audible outside the aquarium. Care must be taken when the labyrinth develops.

THE FAMILY OPHICEPHALIDAE

An introductory description

Members of the *Ophicephalidae* family ('snake-head' fish) are found in many parts of Africa and Asia. They live in a variety of different environments, and a number of species are bred for food in artificial waters.
It is not difficult to breed these fish in captivity if they are healthy and well looked after. The male swims restlessly around the female, approaching her rather threateningly with the mouth wide open. After a few quasi-matings in which the fish wrap themselves round each other like labyrinth fish, the eggs are laid close to the surface. Altogether about 2,000 eggs are laid, and the male guards them so vigilantly that even the female is not allowed near. The eggs take three days to develop fully and during this period the male does not move from them or bother with food.
The eggs are sensitive to light or most of the light should be excluded from the tank after mating. When the eggs have hatched, the fry float to the surface and remain there for three or four days. Only after to large yolk bag has been digested can the fry swim normally. Then their consistent search for food, to satisfy an almost insatiable appetite, begins.
The male will gradually prey on to fry and must be removed.

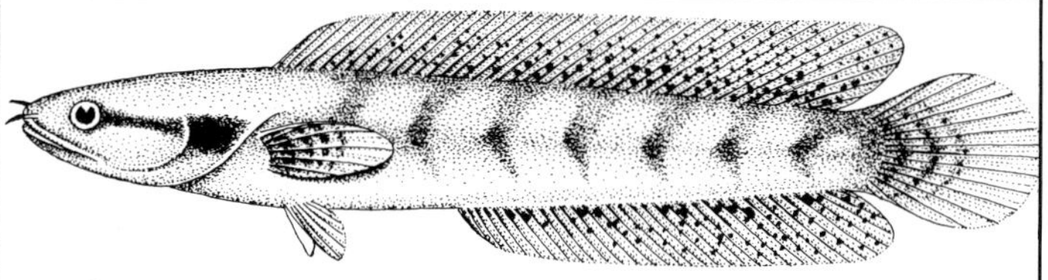

892. *Ophicephalus africanus*

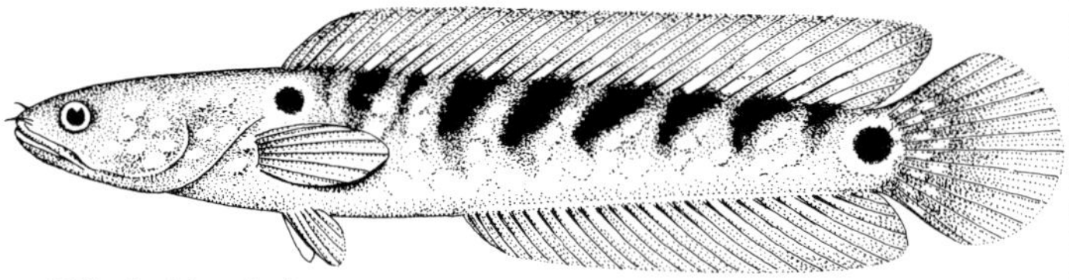

893. *Ophicephalus astratus*

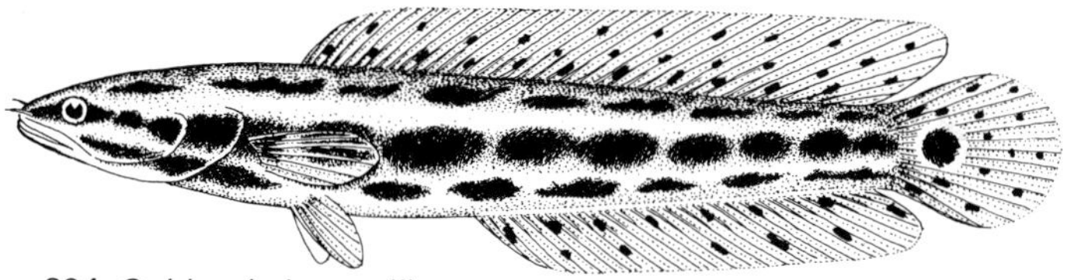

894. *Ophicephalus marilius*

The genus Ophicephalus

Of the three genera in the family *Ophicephalidae, (Channa, Ophicephalus* and *Parophiocephalus),* only some species in the genus *Ophicephalus* are usually accounted aquarium fish, and even these, are really for the specialist or experienced amateur with a particular interest in these curious fish. Two species of possible interest to aquarists are described below.

OPHICEPHALUS AFRICANUS

Family: *Ophicephalidae*

Genus: *Ophicephalus*

English name: African snake-head

Origin: West Africa, from Lagos to Cameroon

Size: Approximately 30 cm

Habitat: Found in many different waters

SHAPE, COLORING AND MARKINGS: The body is long and slender, cylindrical at the front, becoming laterally slightly compressed towards the tail. It has a large head, a deeply forked mouth, and the nostrils are tubular. The dorsal and anal fins have very long bases: the caudal fin is round: the ventral fins small. The basic coloration of adult specimens is something between ochre and yellowish grey. A large number of dark, wedge-shaped marks lie on the flanks: usually only the centers of these marks are distinct. The lower half of the body varies from light yellow to whitish. A large dark mark lies on the gill covers and a narrow dark stripe runs from the gill covers to the eye. The fins are a greyish green to brown, with dark marks. The basic coloration of young specimens is bright yellow with a prominent horizontal dark line.
There are no known external sexual characteristics.

GENERAL CARE: Only very young specimens are suitable for even a large home aquarium, and then only if kept with larger fish. A very predatory fish, *O.africanus* should have a tank with thick vegetation and irregular arrangements of bogwood. The composition of the water is not critical. Temperature 23°–28° C. *O.africanus* is very intelligent and easily learns to recognize its keeper. The demands of its almost insatiable appetite can only be met with live fish, and only young specimens are satisfied with large quantities of Enchytrae and earthworms. Adult or half-grown fish can be trained to eat lean pieces of beef or fresh fish, but only with great difficulty.

Breeding: Nothing is known about the breeding habits of *O.africanus*, but it is likely that they are similar to those of related species which have been bred successfully in captivity. Undoubtedly the fry will be at risk from the predatory parents, and the male will have to be removed from the tank before the fry are eaten. The brood will probably be reduced by natural selection but there is no way of preventing this.

OPHICEPHALUS OBSCURUS

Family: *Ophicephalidae*

Genus: *Ophicephalus*

English name: none

Origin: Africa

Size: Approximately 35 cm

Habitat: Found in large numbers over a very wide area in many different kinds of waters

Shape, coloring and markings: The body shape is identical to that of *O.africanus*. The basic coloration is ochre, fawn or dull grey. A horizontal line of dark irregular marks runs from the snout to the base of the caudal fin: additional dark marks appear on the back and flanks. The fins are yellowish-brown with darker flecks: elsewhere random dark marks appear varying according to the age of the fish.
There are no known external sexual characteristics.

895. *Ophicephalus obscurus*

General care: As for *O.africanus*.

Breeding: See *O.africanus*.

THE FAMILY ATHERINIDAE

An introductory description

The *Atherinidae* family containing the Sand Smelts, Silversides and Whitebaits, is a large family many of whose members are marine fish and most of whom are shoaling fish, found in shallow coastal waters in temperate and sub-tropical areas. Relatively few fish in this family are of interest to freshwater aquarium amateurs, but a few species, in the three genera *Bedotia*, *Melanotaenia* and *Telmatherina* are occasionally encountered in aquariums and are described below.
Scientifically the family is divided into two sub-families, the *Nannatherininae* and the *Atherininae*, the principal and most immediately evident distinction between the two groups being that the *Nannatherininae* fish have only one, long based dorsal fin whereas species in the sub-family *Atherininae* have two separate dorsal fins, set one behind the other.

The genera Bedotia, Melanotaenia and Telmatherina

Only one species, *Bedotia geayi* described below, a fairly recent import from Malagasy, is of interest to aquarists in tenus Bedotia.
Three species in the small genus *Melanotaenia* or Rainbow fish have been considered as suitable for aquariums. They are unusual in being native to Australasia. *Melanotaenia fluviatilis* is a relatively recent import but both *Melanotaenia macculochi* and *Melanotaenia nigrans* are quite well-known.
In the genus *Telmatherina*, to date only the Celebes Sailfish, *Telmatherina ladigesi*, has been accepted as an aquarium fish. It deserves to become more popular among amateurs.

896. *Bedotia geayi*

BEDOTIA GEAYI

Family: *Atherinidae*

Genus: *Bedotia*

English name: none

Origin: Malagasy

Size: Maximum 10 cm

Habitat: Found in a wide variety of waters

Shape, coloring and markings: The body is elongated, almost cylindrical and laterally only very slightly compressed. The mouth is upward directed: the eyes are relatively large. There are two clearly separated dorsal fins: the second, larger dorsal fin is set well back and runs as far back as the root of the tail. The pectoral fins are set high on the body and incline upwards. The anal fin has a very long base. The basic coloration is a glistening brassy yellow: the back is darker: the belly greyish. Two deep black longitudinal stripes run along the body- the upper one is the broader, running from the mouth, across the eye to the caudal peduncle. The lower stripe runs from the throat, following the line of the belly to the back of the anal fin. In some lights a large number of blue-green iridescent scales are visible, particularly on the broader band. The pectoral fins are colorless: the ventral fins

and the dorsal fin are yellowish. The back dorsal fin and the anal fin are orange yellow with a black border. The caudal fin may be orange yellow to white, with a black border surrounded with a whitish edge or alternatively it may carry a scarlet border at the extremity, with an iridescent black pattern across the rest of the fin. Specimens with red-edged caudal fins have more of a golden yellow to red pattern, sometimes with a black border, on the anal and back dorsal fins.
There are no known external sexual characteristics.

GENERAL CARE: *B.geayi* is best kept in a small group in a large community tank with plenty of free swimming space. They tend to keep to the upper reaches of the tank. The composition of the water is not critical: temperature 25°C. A varied diet of live and dried food should be given and the larvae of aquatic insects are an essential element.

BREEDING: A group of four to six specimens should be put in a tank 60×30×30 cm. A bed need not be provided: nylon breeding mops are the best spawning medium. The eggs will be laid over quite a long period of time. They should be gathered weekly from the breeding mops and put in special rearing tanks. The eggs hatch after eight to ten days. The fry can be fed immediately on *Artemia nauplii*. They will only feed at the surface and the tank must be aerated to direct the food to them. The water must be changed regularly.

897. *Melanotaenia macculochi*

MELANOTAENIA MACCULOCHI

Family: *Atherinidae*

Genus: *Melanotaenia*

English names: Dwarf Rainbowfish, Black-lined Rainbowfish

Origin: Northeastern Australia

Size: Maximum 7 cm

Habitat: Found in well-oxygenated running waters

SHAPE, COLORING AND MARKINGS: The body is elongated and laterally compressed; the second dorsal fin is very large. The basic coloration is silvery with a metallic gleam: the back is brown; the belly yellowish. Large numbers of reddish brown longitudinal stripes run across the body and in certain lights the areas between these stripes have a brassy gleam. The anal and second dorsal fins are greenish at the base, becoming brownish red and have a yellowish border. The caudal fin may be deep red.
Females are less vividly colored and have more rounded bellies.
Males are slimmer and more intensely colored.

GENERAL CARE: As for *Bedotia Geayi* but temperature 22°–25°C.

BREEDING: As for *Bedotia Geayi* but fine leaved plants should be put in the tank and and the fry left to hatch in it.

TELMATHERINA LADIGESI

Family: *Atherinidae*

Genus: *Telmatherina*

English names: Celebes Sailfish, Celebes Rainbowfish

Origin: Sulawesi (Celebes)

Size: Maximum 7 cm

Habitat: Found in freshwater lakes

SHAPE, COLORING AND MARKINGS: The body is elongated and laterally very compressed. The second dorsal fin and the anal fin are both large, with extended rays which incline backwards towards the tail. The caudal peduncle is translucent. The basic coloration is an olive yellow: the underside is yellow. A blue green iridescent stripe runs from the middle of the body (or as a narrow line from the gill covers) to the caudal peduncle. The first ray of the second dorsal fin is black, turns yellow and ends in a white spot: the second ray is shorter and entirely black: the other rays are lemon and, not being linked by membranes appear ragged. The anal fin has a similar appearance. The ventral fins are yellow: the pectoral fins are colorless and transparent, with a milky white dot. The caudal fin is rather deeply forked, dark at the base and yellowish towards the center: the top and bottom edges have a black border edged with yellow, with white dots.
Females are smaller, with less vividly colored fins: the second dorsal fin and the anal fin have no elongated rays: the pectoral fins lack the white spot of the males, the caudal fin has no border.
Males are as described above.

GENERAL CARE: As for *Aplocheilichthys macrophthalmus*, a suitable companion for *T.ladegesi*.

BREEDING: As for *Bedotia gayei* but initially the fry need fine infusoria.

THE FAMILY TETRAODONTIDAE

An introductory description

The *Tetraodontidae* or Pufferfish or Globe Fish family includes some species that live solely in brackish waters, some that live entirely in fresh waters and some that divide their time between the two kinds of waters. Little is known about their life styles in the wild; many are difficult to keep, as they find it difficult to accommodate to artificial waters.

The name *Tetraodontidae* refers to the four tooth plates which are also characteristic of this family and give these fish very powerful teeth which they use to eat snails by crushing the shells. Eating snails keeps these teeth in good condition and specimens kept in captivity and not fed sufficient snails will develop the kinds of tusks common in rodents that are not given a diet that allows them to gnaw.
Many pufferfish die in aquariums for this reason. Thus the bulk of the diet must consist of snails. However the common pond snail, *Limnoea aricularia,* as all aquarists know, can be a danger to aquarium fish because of the diseases carried by its parasites. Accordingly Pufferfish should be fed only with apple snails, *Ampullaria cuprina* or other snails that live in the aquarium bed.

THE FAMILY TETRAODONTIDAE

The genus Tetraodon

The genus *Tetraodon* is by far the largest genus in the family and contains species found over very wide areas, from Africa to Southeast Asia. Among these are some of the most common and popular aquarium Pufferfish: moreover some of these species have been bred successfully by amateurs. Three of these species are described below.

898. *Tetraodon palembangensis*

TETRAODON CUTCUTIA

Family: *Tetraodontidae*

Genus: *Tetraodon*

English name: Common Pufferfish

Origin: India, the Far East

Size: Approximately 15 cm

Habitat: Found in both fresh and brackish waters

SHAPE, COLORING AND MARKINGS: The body is cone-shaped: the skin is leathery and devoid of scales. Sometimes the nostrils are elongated and tubular, but they are unforked. The back is a dark or olive green: the flanks are yellowish or grey: the belly is off-white. A large, round black mark with a light edge lies on the back in front of the dorsal fin: a similar mark lies just behind the pectoral fins. The whole of the rest of the body including the head is covered with dark brown marbling, of a pattern which varies from specimen to specimen. The fins are yellowish to olive green. The caudal fin has a light green edge and the upper and lower rays are brownish or brick red.
Females are slightly smaller, with less vivid colors, being predominantly yellowish.
Males are as described above.

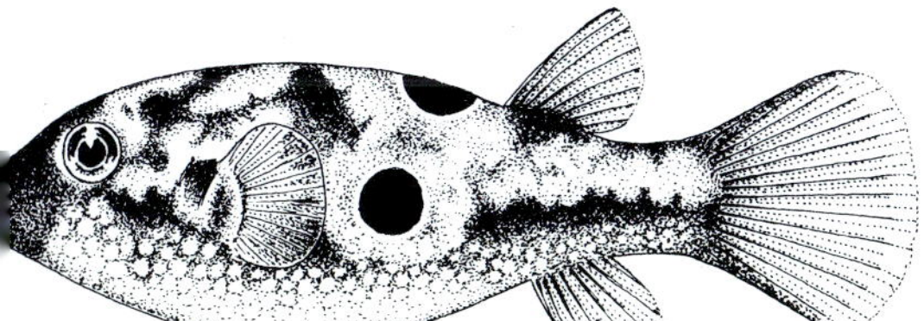

899. *Tetraodon cutcutia*

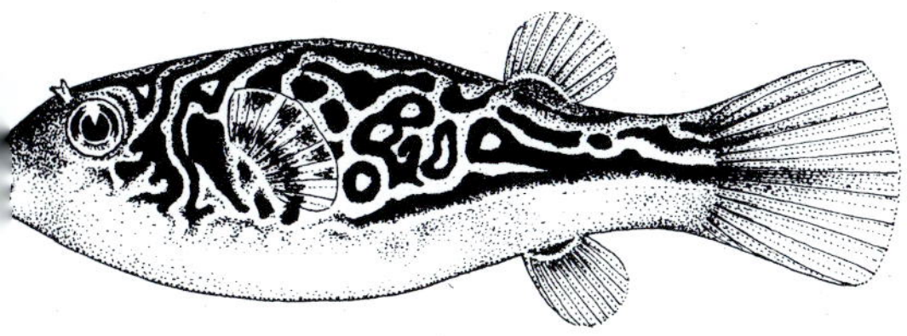

900. *Tetraodon mbu*

GENERAL CARE: *T.cutcutia* is very aggressive and attacks the fins of other fish. Accordingly it is unsuitable for the normal domestic community tank. In a species tank the composition of the water is not critical although soft water should be avoided: temperature 21°–27°C. Fresh tapwater may be used for the frequent changes of water that are necessary. Sturdy bog plants, rocks and bogwood may be put in the tank. The preferred diet is snails: all kinds of aquatic insects and larvae will also be eaten but *C.cutcutia* will eat Tubifex only with reluctance and dried food is unsuitable.

BREEDING: Temperature 28°C or thereabouts. *C.cutcutia* lays its eggs on flat shaded stones or in the cavities between stones and arrangements of rock. The mating pattern somewhat resembles that of some Cichlids. The female lays the eggs while calmly swimming and twisting from side to side and the male follows her immediately, fertilising the eggs. The 200–300 eggs are usually glassy but may be light brown. The male alone tends the eggs, guarding them by settling on top of them. Fresh water is fanned round them by his moving his pectoral fins. The eggs hatch in six to eight days. For the first few days after they have hatched and while they consume their large yolk sac, the fry are guarded by the male in a hollow he excavates in the bed. Breeders have found great difficulties in providing the right food for the fry. Some have succeeded by feeding them successively on pond infusoria, Cyclops and *Artemia nauplii* Daphnia and mosquito larvae: others have succeeded with snails' eggs: the breeder must make judicious experiments.

TETRAODON MBU

Family: *Tetraodontidae*

Genus: *Tetraodon*

English name: none

Origin: The Congo basin

Size: Approximately 75 cm in the wild but remains considerably smaller in captivity

Habitat: Found only in fresh waters

SHAPE, COLORING AND MARKINGS: The body is cone-shaped and slightly more slender than in related species. The skin is leathery, with small spines except on the snout and lower part of the caudal peduncle. The two nostrils on either side of the head are elongated, tubular and forked. The basic coloration is yellow or yellowish-orange, with prominent brownish or bluish-black wavy marks on the back and flanks which contrast sharply with the lighter background. The lower half of the body is a bright yellow. The translucent fins are pale yellow to orange. The caudal fin often bears dark marks running parallel to the fin rays. The coloring and markings of young specimens are very variable, but the body is always covered with irregular dark patches with one or more horizontal lines on the caudal peduncle.
There are no known external sexual characteristics.

GENERAL CARE: As for *T.cutcutia* but temperature 23°–28°C and no salt should be added to the water.

BREEDING: Nothing is known about the reproductive behavior of this species.

ADDITIONAL INFORMATION: Although first identified in 1899, *T.mbu* has remained almost unknown to aquarists, no doubt partly because of its size.

TETRAODON PALEMBANGENSIS

Family: *Tetraodontidae*

Genus: *Tetraodon*

English name: none

Origin: Southeast Asia

Size: Approximately 20 cm in the wild but remains considerably smaller in captivity.

Habitat: Found only in fresh waters

SHAPE, COLORING AND MARKINGS: The body is cone-shaped: the leathery skin is covered with small but prominent spines. The single nostril on either side of the head is elongated and tubular. The basic coloration varies from lemon yellow to an iridescent green, becoming a pale yellow or silvery white towards the belly. A number of wide dark brown or brownish-black bands on the head and back contrast sharply with the lighter background. Prominent wavy lines lie on the head and flanks the areas between showing up as almost circular patches, below the dorsal fin and on the caudal peduncle. No dark marks appear on the lower half of the body.

There are no known external sexual characteristics.

GENERAL CARE: As for *T.mbu,* but if given the opportunity to establish its own territory in a tank, *T.palembangensis* becomes less aggressive. It will, after a time, accept both Tubifex and lean beef if other foods are not available.

BREEDING: No information is available on the reproductive behavior of this species.

THE FAMILY MASTOCEMBELIDAE

An introductory description

These fish are found over large areas of South and Southeast Asia and tropical Africa. The family comprises only two genera: *Mastocembelus* and *Macrognathus* and all its members are commonly called Spiny eels. They are very intelligent fish and soon recognize their keeper and then lose a great deal of their shyness.

Very few species have been bred in captivity, but details of the observed behavior of *M.pancalus* are recorded below.

The Genus Mastocembelus

Almost all species of Spiny eels are found in the genus, which contains a wide variety of fish, some very slender and some relatively deep in the body. Experience shows that they will as a rule settle down happily in the aquarium provided their basic needs are met.

901. *Mastocembelus pancalus*

MASTOCEMBELUS ARGUS

Family: *Mastocembelidae*

Genus: *Mastocembelus*

English name: none

Origin: Thailand

Size: Approximately 25 cm

Habitat: Very rare but found in both brackish and fresh waters

SHAPE, COLORING AND MARKING: The body is slender and less deep and less compressed laterally than that of related species. The basic coloration varies from dark to yellowish-brown: the belly is lighter or whitish. Light stripes appear on the back: the rest of the body is covered with rows of light green or white, almost circular, marks which continue into the fins. The caudal, dorsal and anal fins are separate: there are no ventral fins. All the fins are opaque, brown and partly edged with yellow.

There are no known external sexual characteristics.

GENERAL CARE: *M.argus* needs a large tank with a sandy bottom and plenty of plants, rocks and bogwood to provide, with coconut shells and flowerpots, the retreats it will seek during the day. The composition of the water is not critical: temperature 22°–28° C. Part of the water must be changed regularly. Earthworms, Tubifex, Enchytrae and other wormlike creatures should form the staple diet. If well fed it is not predatory.

BREEDING: Nothing is known about the reproductive behavior of this species.

MASTOCEMBELUS ERYTHROTAENIA

Family: *Mastocembelidae*

Genus: *Mastocembelus*

English name: none

Origin: Thailand

Size: Approximately 100 cm in the wild but remains smaller in captivity

Habitat: Found in a variety of waters

SHAPE, COLORING AND MARKINGS: The body is slender, laterally very compressed and although less deep than in some related species, yet deeper than in others. The basic coloration is olive green to greenish-brown: the lower half of the body is lighter, or a pale green. A number of well-defined orangey red horizontal lines lie on the body: these may be a bright yellow in some specimens. The fins are dark brown with red marks. The anal, caudal and dorsal fins are linked.

There are no known external sexual characteristics.

GENERAL CARE: As for *M.argus.*

BREEDING: Not yet bred in captivity.

MASTOCEMBELUS PANCALUS

Family: *Mastocembelidae*

Genus: *Mastocembelus*

English name: none

Origin: India

Size: Approximately 20 cm

Habitat: Found in large rivers and coastal waters

SHAPE, COLORING AND MARKINGS: The body is slender and laterally very compressed. The basic coloration varies from brown to a dull yellowish grey. The back is olive green: the lower half of the body is yellowish-white to bright yellow. Numerous light marks appear on the body, especially on the back and between the dorsal and anal fins. A dark stripe runs from the snout, through the eye and over the gill covers: a narrow light stripe runs along the body parallel to the lateral line. Occasionally dark transverse bands are to be seen on the caudal peduncle.

The fins are yellowish with dark stripes.

Females are sturdier and the underside of the body is light grey or white.

Males are as described above.

GENERAL CARE: As for *M.argus.*

BREEDING: A few reports are recorded of this species having been bred in captivity. The glassy adhesive eggs. 0.13 cm in diameter have been laid in clumps of vegetation near the surface. Some eggs have hatched after being exposed to temperatures as low as 8° C. The fry it seems responded to being fed at first on infusoria and then on sieved Daphnia and Cyclops until, after about three weeks (when they were some 3 cm long) they took Tubifex.

INDEX OF FISHES

The numbers in italics refer to illustrations. The index of plants can be found on pages 83–85.

Explanatory note

Every fish which is described in the Encyclopaedia has been included in the Index. The English names and synonyms have also been included where they exist and a cross reference made to the name under which the fish is treated in the body of the work.
Page references in italics indicate illustrations. The abbreviations (g) and (f) after some entries indicate that these are genera or families.

A

B

C

Q

R

S

BIBLIOGRAPHY

Construction and maintenance of the aquarium

Frey, H., 1961. *Aquarienpraxis*. Radebeul.
Huckstedt, G., 1963. *Aquarienchemie*. Stuttgart.
Huckstedt, G., 1964. *Aquarientechnik*. Stuttgart.
Kübler, R., 1968. *Licht im Aquarium*. Stuttgart.
Kübler, R., 1971. *Aquariumgeräte-selbst gebaut*. Stuttgart.
Wagner, O., 1956. *Aquarienchemie*. Leipzig.
Wiegel, W., 1964. *Das Schmuck- und Schauaquarium*. Stuttgart.

Diseases of tropical freshwater fish

Allen, J.L. & Harman, P.D., 1970. *Progressive Fish Culturalist* (Washington) n° 32, 100.
Amlacher, E., 1961, 1972. *Taschenbuch der Fischkrankheiten*. Jena.
Amlacher, E., 1970. *Textbook of fish diseases*. Jersey City.
Amlacher, E., 1965. *Zeitschrift für Fischerei und deren Hilfswissenschaften* (Berlin) Neue Folge n° 13, 85–112.
Amlacher, E., 1968. *Zeitschrift für Fischerei und deren Hilfswissenschaften* (Berlin) Neues Folge n° 16, 1–30.
Blom, M.M., 1972. *Referaat Faculteit Diergeneeskunde*. Utrecht.
Bootsma, R. & Clerx, J.P.M., 1976. *Aquaculture* (Amsterdam) n° 7, 371–384.
Buza, L. & Szakolczai, J., 1968. *Zeitschrift für Fischerei und deren Hilfswissenschaften* (Berlin) Neue Folge n° 16, 209–219.
Bykhovskaya-Pavlovskaya, I.E. *et al.*, 1964. *Key to parasites of freshwater fish of the USSR*. Israel Program for Scientific Translations cat. n° 1136, Jerusalem.
Collins, M.T., Gratzek, J.B., Dawe, D.L. & Nemetz, T.G., 1976. *Journal of the Fisheries Research Board of Canada* (Ottawa) n° 33, 215–218.
Conroy, D.A., 1963. Microbiologia espanola (Madrid) n° 16, 47–54.
Cross, D.G. & Hursey, P.A., 1973. *Journal of Fish Biology* (London) n° 5, 798–798.
Davis, H.S., 1967. *Culture and diseases of game fishes*. Berkeley & Los Angeles.
Dorier, A. & Degrange, C., 1961–1962. *Travaux du Laboratoire d'Hydrobiologie et Pisciculture de l'Université de Grenoble* n° 51 & n° 52, 7–44.
van Duijn, C., 1973. *Diseases of fishes*. London.
EIFAC, 1970. *European Inland Fisheries Advisory Commission Technical Paper* (Rome) 11, 1–12.
Fijan, N.N. & Voorhees, P.R., 1969. *Veterinarski arhiv* (Zagreb) n° 39, 259–267.
Goldstein, R.J., 1971. *Diseases of aquarium fishes*. Neptune City.
Ghittino, P., 1967. Atti della Societa italiana delle scienze veterinaire. (Faenza) n° 21, 740–743.
Herkner, H., 1969. *Aquarien- und Terrarien-Zeitschrift* (Stuttgart) n° 22, 344–348.
Herkner, H., 1970. *Aquarien- und Terrarien-Zeitschrift* (Stuttgart) n° 23, 154–157.
Hines, R.S. & Spira, D.T., 1974. *Journal of Fish Biology* (London) n° 6, 189–196.
Hofer, B., 1893. *Allgemeine Fischerei-Zeitung* (München) n° 11.
Jacobs, D.L., 1946. *Transactions of the American Microscopical Society* (Lancaster, Pa.) n° 55, 1–17.
Jones, J.R.E., 1964. *Fish and river pollution*. London.
Krause, H., 1973. *Aquarien- und Terrarien-Zeitschrift* (Stuttgart) n° 26, 359–360.
Kulda, J. & Lom., J., 1964. *Parasitology* (London) n° 54, 753–762.
Leadbetter, E.R., 1974. Chapter on genus Flexibacter (pp. 105–107). In: Bergey's *Manual of determinative bacteriology*. (8th edition). Baltimore.
Lom, J. & Corliss, J.O., 1967. *Journal of Protozoology* (New York) n° 14, 141–152.
Mawdesley-Thomas, L.E., 1969. *Journal of Fish Biology* (London) n° 1, 19–23.
Mawdesley-Thomas, L.E. (ed.), 1972. Diseases of fish. *Symposia of the Zoological Society of London* (London) n° 30.
Poisson, C., 1971. *Les maladies des poissons d'aquarium*.
Redeke, H.C., 1948. In C. de Boer Jr. *Hydrobiologie van Nederland*. Amsterdam, 145–146.
Reichenbach-Klinke, H.H., 1970. *Zeitschrift* für Fischerei und deren Hilfswissenschaften (Berlin) Neue Folge n° 18, 289–297.
Reichenbach-Klinke, H.H., 1972. *Krankheiten der Aquarienfische*. Stuttgart.
Riedmüller, S., 1965. *Allgemeine Fischerei-Zeitung* (München) n° 19, 28–35.
Roberts, R.J. & Shepherd, C.J., 1974. *Handbook of trout and salmon diseases*. West Byfleet, Surrey.
Rucker, R.R., 1972. *Technical Paper Bureau of Sport Fisheries & Wildlife* (Washington) 58.
Russo, R.C., Smith, C.E. & Thurston, R.V., 1974. *Journal of the Fisheries Research Board of Canada* (Ottawa) n° 31, 1653–1655.
Schäperclaus, W., 1951. *Aquarien- und Terrarien-Zeitschrift* (Stuttgart) n° 4, 169–171.
Schäperclaus, W., 1953. *Aquarien- und Terrarien-Zeitschrift* (Stuttgart) n° 6, 177–182.
Schäperclaus, W., 1954. *Fischkrankheiten*. Berlin.
Schubert, G., 1964. *Krankheiten der Fische*. Stuttgart.
Schubert, G., *Ziekten van aquariumvissen*. Zutphen.
Smies, J.F. & Murris, H.H., 1962. *Water: in het aquarium en in de natuur*. Baarn.
Schmidt, G., 1975. *Nos poissons malades*. Elsevier Séquoia, Paris-Bruxelles.
Smith, C.E. & Russo, R.C., 1975. *Progressive Fish Culturist* (Washington) n° 37, 150–152.
Sprague, V., 1966. *Journal of Protozoology* (New York) n° 13, 356–358.
Trussell, R.P., 1972. *Journal of the Fisheries Research Board of Canada* (Ottawa) n° 29, 1505–1507.
Wagner, G., 1960, *Zeitschrift für Fischerei und deren Hilfswissenschaften* (Berlin) Neue Folge n° 9, 425–441.
Westin, D.T., 1974. *Progressive Fish Culturist* (Washington) n° 36, 86–89.
Wuhrmann, K. & Woker, H., 1949. *Schweizerische Zeitschrift für Hydrobiologie* (Basel) n° 11, 210–244.

General books on fishes

Arnoult, J. 1950. *Les poissons.*

Berg, L.S., 1932. Übersicht der Verbreitung der Süsswasserfische Europas. *Zoogeographia*, Jena, 1–107–208.

Berg, L.S., 1958. *System der rezenten und fossilen Fischartigen und Fische.* Deutscher Verlag der Wissenschaften. Berlin.

Boulenger, G.A., 1909–1916. *Catalogue of the freshwater fishes of Africa.* London. (1964 reprint Wheldon & Wesley, Codicote, Herts).

Burton, M. & Burton, R., 1975. *Encyclopedia of fish.* London.

Carli (de), F., 1976. *L'univers inconnu des poissons.* Elsevier Séquoia. Paris-Bruxelles.

Dottrens, E., 1970. *Les poissons d'eau douce.* Neuchâtel.

Eigenmann, C.H., 1910. Catalogue of the freshwater fishes, of tropical and south temperature America. *Report of the Princetown University Expedition of Patagonia* n° 3, part 4: 375–511.

Eigenmann, C.H., 1912. The freshwater fishes of British Guiana. *Memoirs of the Carnegie Museum* n° 5: 1–577.

Eigenmann, C., 1924. Fishes of northwestern South America. *Memoirs of the Carnegie Museum* n° 9, 1–346.

Eigenmann, C. & Allen, W.R., 1962. *Fishes of western South America.* Lexington, Kentucky.

Eigenmann, C. & Eigenmann, R.S., 1892. A catalogue of the freshwater fishes of South America. *Proceedings of the United States National Museum* n° 14, 1–81.

Frank, S., 1969. *Das grosse Bilderlexikon der Fische.* Gütersloh.

Frank, S., 1971. *The pictorial encyclopedia of Fishes.* London.

Greenwood, P.H., Rosen, D.E., Weitzman, S.H. & Meyers, G.D., 1966. Phyletic studies of teleostean fishes, with a provisional classification of living forms. *Bulletin of the American Museum of Natural History*, New York, n° 131, 339–456.

Herald, E.S., 1961. *Living fishes of the world.* London.

Herald, E.S., 1963. *Das Tierbuch in Farben-Fische.* Berlin-Darmstadt-Wien.

Jocher, W., 1965. *Futter für Vivarientiere.* Stuttgart.

Ladiges, W., 1951. *Der Fisch in der Landschaft.* (2nd ed.). Braunschweig.

Maitland, P.S., 1977. *Les poissons des lacs et rivières d'Europe.* Elsevier Séquoia, Paris-Bruxelles.

Marshall, N.B., 1965. *The life of fishes.* London.

Mayland, H.J., 1973. *Poissons d'eau chaude.* Elsevier Séquoia. Paris-Bruxelles.

Mayland, H.J., 1973. *Poissons d'eau froide.* Elsevier Séquoia, Paris-Bruxelles.

Norman, J.R. & Greenwood, P.H., 1976. *A history of fishes* (3rd ed.) London.

Norman, J.R., 1966. *Die Fische.* Hamburg-Berlin.

Ostermöller, W., 1970. *Fische züchten nach Rezept.* Stuttgart.

Remane, A., 1971. *Sozialleben der Tiere.* Stuttgart.

Rosen, D.E. & Bailey, R.M., 1963. The Poeciliid fishes (Cyprinodontiformes), their structure, zoogeography, and systematics. *Bulletin of the American Museum of Natural History* n° 126, 1–176.

Rosen, D.E., 1964. The relationships and taxonomic position of the halfbeaks, killifishes, silversides, and their relatives. *Bulletin of the American Museum of Natural History*, n° 127, 217–267.

Schröder, J.H., 1974. *Vererbungslehre für Aquarianer.* Stuttgart.

Smith, H.M., 1945. The fresh-water fishes of Siam, or Thailand. *Bulletin United States National Museum* n° 188, 1–622. (Reprint 1965, Smithsonian Institute).

Weber, M. & de Beaufort, L.F., 1957–1962. *The fishes of the Indo-Australian archipelago*, vols 1–11, Leiden.

Wheeler, A., 1975. *Fishes of the world: an illustrated dictionary.* New York.

Whitehead, P.J., 1976. *Ainsi vivent les poissons.* Elsevier Séquoia, Paris-Bruxelles.

Wickler, W., 1962. *Das Zuchten von Aquarienfischen.* Stuttgart.

Aquarium Plants

Brünner, G., 1953. *Wasserflanzen.* Braunschweig.

Brünner, G., 1966. *Aquarienflanzen.* (4th ed.). Stuttgart.

Brünner, G., 1971. *Pflanzen im Aquariumrichtig gepflegt.* Stuttgart.

Cook, C.D.K., 1974. *Water plants of the world.* Den Haag.

Eyles, D.E. & Robertson, J.L., 1944. Guide and key to the aquatic plants of the S.E. United States. *Public Health Bulletin*, Washington, n° 286.

François, M., 1970. *Décors exotiques et plantes d'aquariums.*

Friesen, G., 1953. *Botanik für Aquarianer.* Stuttgart.

Jahn, J., 1975. *Aquarienpflanzen.* Minden.

Jahn, J., 1975. *Les plantes aquatiques.* Elsevier Séquoia, Paris-Bruxelles.

Roe, C.D., 1964. *A manual of aquarium plants.* Monkspath.

Wendt, A., 1975. *Die Aquarienpflanzen in Wort und Bild.* Stuttgart.

Aquarium Fish

Anon., 1970. *The aquarist's guide to freshwater tropical fishes.* n.p.

Arnold, J.P. & Ahl, E., 1936. *Fremdländische Süsswasserfische.* Braunschweig.

Axelrod, H.R., 1974. *Freshwater fishes book 1.* Neptune City.

Axelrod, H.R. & Vorderwinkler, W., 1957. *Encyclopedia of tropical fishes.* Jersey City.

Braun, E. & Paysan, K., 1972. *Aquarienfische.* Stuttgart.

Favré, H., 1968. *Le guide Marabout de l'aquarium.* Verviers.

Favré, H., 1972. *Le grand livre de l'aquarium.* Elsevier Séquoia, Paris-Bruxelles.

Frey, H., 1965. *Das Süsswasseraquarium.* (13th ed.) Radebeul.

Frey, H., 1966. *Das Aquarium von A bis Z.* (7th ed.) Radebeul.

Hervey, G.F. & Hems, J., 1952. *Freshwater Tropical Aquarium fishes.* London.

Hervey, G.F. & Hems, J., 1975. *L'aquarium d'eau douce.* Elsevier Séquoia, Paris-Bruxelles.

Hoedeman, J.J., 1974. *Naturalists' guide to fresh-water aquarium fish.* New York.

Holly, M., Meinken, H. & Rachow, A., 1934–1940. *Die Aquarienfische in Wort und Bild.* Stuttgart.

Innes, W.T., 1951. *Exotic aquarium fishes.* (12th ed.) Philadelphia.

Langel-Kretchmar, L., 1961. *Aquariums d'eau douce et d'eau de mer.* Neufchâtel.

Madsen, J.M., 1975. *Aquarium fishes in colour.* Poole.

Mandahl-Barth, G., 1970. *Poissons d'aquarium.*

Mayland, H.J., 1972. *L'aquarium.* Elsevier Séquoia, Paris-Bruxelles.

Mayland, H.J., 1974. *L'élevage des poissons d'aquarium.* Elsevier Séquoia, Paris-Bruxelles.

Ostermöller, X., 1968. *Die Aquarienfibel.* Stuttgart.

Paysan, K., 1970. *Welcher Zierfisch ist das?* Stuttgart.

Paysan, K., 1975. *The Hamlyn guide to freshwater fishes.* London.

Pinter, H., 1966. *Handbuch der Aquarienfisch-Zucht.* Stuttgart.

Schiotz, A. & Dahlstrøm, P., 1972. *Collins Guide to Aquarium fishes and plants.* London.

Stein, K.H., 1966. *Basteln für Aquarienfreunde.* Stuttgart.

Sterba, G., 1954–56. *Aquarienkunde, 2 vols.* Leipzig.

Sterba, G., 1959. *Süsswasserfische aus aller Welt.* Leipzig.

Sterba, G., 1959–60. *Aquarienkunde* (2nd ed.). 2 vols. Leipzig.

Sterba, G., 1959. *Fresh water fishes of the world.* New York.

Sterba, G., 1966. *Freshwater fishes of the world.* London.

Vesco, V.O., Klausewitz, W., Peyronel, B. & Tortonese, E., 1975. *Life in the aquarium.* London.

Visser, C.H., 1969–1975. *Aquaristisch Kompas.* Roden.

Weiss, W., 1973. *Fische für Gesellschaftsbecken.* Stuttgart.

Families and species of tropical freshwater fish

Axelrod, H.R., 1970. *All about discus.* Neptune City.

Axelrod, H.R., 1973. *African cichlids of Lakes Malawi and Tanganyika.* Neptune City.

Dzwillo, M., 1961. *Lebendgebärende Zahnkarpfen.* Stuttgart.

Frey, H., 1971. *Zierfisch-Monographien. Bd 1, Salmer.* Radebeul.

Frey, H., 1973. *Zierfisch-Monographien. Bd 2, Karpfenfische.* Radebeul.

Frey, H., 1974. *Zierfisch-Monographien. Bd 3, Welse und andere Sonderling.* Radebeul.

Fryer, G. & Iles, T.D., 1972. *The cichlid fishes of the Great Lakes of Africa.* Edinburgh.

Goldstein, R.J., 1969. *Cichlids.* Neptune City.

Goldstein, R.J., 1971. *Anabantoids gouramis and related fishes.* Jersey City.

Goldstein, R.J., 1971. *Introduction to the cichlids.* Neptune City.

Goldstein, R.J., 1973. *Cichlids of the World.* Neptune City.

Goldstein, R.J., 1974. *Buntbarsche für Aquarium.* Stuttgart.

Gordon, M. & Axelrod, H.R., 1968. *Siamese fighting fish.* Jersey City.

Jackson, P.B.N. & Ribbinck, T., 1975. *Mbuna (rock-dwelling cichlids of Lake Malawi, Africa).* Neptune

Jacobs, K., 1969. *Die lebendgebärenden Fische der Süssergewässer.* Frankfurt-am-Main–Zürich.

Jacobs, K., 1971. *Livebearing Aquarium Fishes.* London.

Kahl, B., 1970. *Samler im Aquarium.* Stuttgart.

Keller, G., 1974. *Der Diskus.* Stuttgart.

Knaack, K., 1970. *Killifische im Aquarium.* Stuttgart.

Ladiges, W., 1962. *Barben.* Stuttgart.

Ladiges, W., 1962. *Bärblinge.* Stuttgart.

Mayland, H.J., 1975. *Les discus.* Elsevier Séquoia, Paris-Bruxelles.

Nieuwenhuizen, A. van den, 1961. *Labyrinthfische.* Stuttgart.

Nieuwenhuizen, A. van den, 1964. *Zwergbuntbarsche.* Stuttgart.

Petzold, H.G., 1967. *Der Guppy.* Wittenberg-Luth.

Pronek, N., 1972. *Oscars.* Neptune City.

Scheel, J., 1968. *Rivulins of the World.* Jersey City.

Staeck, W., 1973. *Cichliden-Verbreitung, Verhalten, Arten.* Wuppertal-Elberfeld.

Vogt, D., 1959. *Salmler, 1+2.* Stuttgart.

Vogt, D., 1962. *Buntbarsche.* Stuttgart.

Vogt, D., 1962. *Welse.* Stuttgart.

Walker, B., 1974. *Sharks and loaches.* Neptune City.

Willwock, W., 1962. *Eierlegende Zahnkarpfen.* Stuttgart.

Journals in the French language

Aquarama. Sopic, 3 rue St-Pierre-le-Jeune, Strasbourg.

Revue française d'aquariologie. Cercle Aquariophile de Nancy, 34 rue Ste. Catherine, Nancy.

L'Aquariophile Franco-Belge. 3/22, Avenue Guillaume Stasscart, 1070 Bruxelles.

Journals in the English language

The Aquarist and Pondkeeper. Buckley Press, The Butts, Half Acre, Brentford, Middlesex, England.

Tropical Fish Hobbyist. TFH Publications, Neptune City, USA.

Buntbarsche Bulletin, Journal of the American Cichlid Association, c/o J. & L. Pierce, 15019 N. 21st Pl. Phoenix, Arizona 85022.

Cichlidae, British Cichlid Association, 280 Northridge Way, Hemel Hempstead, Herts.

Journals in the German language

Die Aquarien- und Terrarien-Zeitschrift. (DATZ) Alfred Kernen Verlag, Stuttgart.

Aquarien-Magazin. Franckische Verlagshandlung. Kosmos-Verlag, Stuttgart.

Aquarien und Terrarien. Urania-Verlag. Otto Nuschkerstr. 28, Berlin 108.

Der Aquarien-Freund. H.O. Berkenkamp, D-294 Wilhelmshaven.

Deutsche Cichliden-Gesellschaft EV. Anograben 72, 5303 Bornheim-Walberberg.